Eleventh Edition

CompTIA A+

Guide to IT Technical Support

Jean Andrews, Ph.D.
Joy Dark Shelton
Nicholas Pierce

IT Tech Support

 Cengage

Australia • Brazil • Canada • Mexico • Singapore • United Kingdom • United States

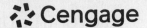

CompTIA A+ Guide To IT Technical Support,
11th edition

**Jean Andrews, Joy Dark Shelton, Nicholas
Pierce**

SVP, Product: Erin Joyner

VP, Product: Thais Alencar

Product Director: Mark Santee

Product Manager: Natalie Onderdonk

Product Assistant: Ethan Wheel

Learning Designer: Carolyn Mako

Senior Content Manager: Brooke Greenhouse

Digital Delivery Quality Partner: Jim Vaughey

Technical Editor: Danielle Shaw

Developmental Editor: Mary Pat Shaffer

VP, Product Marketing: Jason Sakos

Director, Product Marketing: Danaë April

Product Marketing Manager: Mackenzie Paine

IP Analyst: Ann Hoffman

IP Project Manager: Lumina Datamatics

Production Service: Straive

Senior Designer: Erin Griffin

Cover Image Source: Vik Y/Shutterstock.com.

For product information and technology assistance, contact us at
Cengage Customer & Sales Support, 1-800-354-9706
or support.cengage.com.

For permission to use material from this text or product, submit all
requests online at **www.copyright.com.**

Library of Congress Control Number: 2022905147

ISBN: 978-0-357-67416-1

Cengage
200 Pier 4 Boulevard
Boston, MA 02210
USA

Cengage is a leading provider of customized learning solutions with
employees residing in nearly 40 different countries and sales in more than
125 countries around the world. Find your local representative at
www.cengage.com.

To learn more about Cengage platforms and services, register or access
your online learning solution, or purchase materials for your course,
visit **www.cengage.com.**

Notice to the Reader

Publisher does not warrant or guarantee any of the products described herein or perform any independent analysis in connection
with any of the product information contained herein. Publisher does not assume, and expressly disclaims, any obligation to obtain
and include information other than that provided to it by the manufacturer. The reader is expressly warned to consider and adopt
all safety precautions that might be indicated by the activities described herein and to avoid all potential hazards. By following
the instructions contained herein, the reader willingly assumes all risks in connection with such instructions. The publisher makes
no representations or warranties of any kind, including but not limited to, the warranties of fitness for particular purpose or
merchantability, nor are any such representations implied with respect to the material set forth herein, and the publisher takes no
responsibility with respect to such material. The publisher shall not be liable for any special, consequential, or exemplary damages
resulting, in whole or part, from the readers' use of, or reliance upon, this material.

Printed in the United States of America
Print Number: 01   Print Year: 2022

Contents

Module 3

Supporting Processors and Upgrading Memory   115

Module 4

Power Supplies and Troubleshooting Computer Problems   159

Module 5

Supporting Hard Drives and Other Storage Devices   211

Module 6

Supporting I/O Devices   261

Module 7

Networking Fundamentals   309

Module 8

Network Infrastructure and Cloud Computing   363

Module 9

Supporting Mobile Devices   417

Module 10

Supporting Printers   459

Part 2

CompTIA A+ Core 2 (220-1102)   511

Module 11

The Complex World of IT Professionals   513

Module 12

Installing Windows   557

Module 13

Maintaining Windows   621

Module 14

Troubleshooting Windows After Startup   669

Module 15

Troubleshooting Windows Startup   719

Module 16

Security Strategies   767

Module 17

Securing and Sharing Windows Resources   809

Module 18

Mobile Device Security   869

Module 19

Network Security and Troubleshooting   899

Module 20

Supporting macOS   965

Module 21

Linux and Scripting   1005

Appendix A

Safety Procedures and Environmental Concerns   1057

Appendix B

Entry Points for Windows Startup Processes   1077

Appendix C

CompTIA Acronyms   1079

Glossary   1087

Index   1139

CompTIA A+ Core 1 (220-1101) and A+ Core 2 (220-1102) Exam Objectives Mapped to Modules

CompTIA A+ Guide to IT Technical Support, Eleventh Edition fully meets all of the CompTIA's A+ Core 1 (220-1101) and A+ Core 2 (220-1102) Exam Objectives.

CompTIA A+ Core 1 (220-1101)

1.0 Mobile Devices

1.1 Given a scenario, install and configure laptop hardware and components.

Objectives	Primary Module
• Hardware/device replacement	Supporting Processors and Upgrading Memory
▪ Battery	Taking a Computer Apart and Putting It Back Together
▪ Keyboard/keys	Supporting I/O Devices
▪ Random-access memory (RAM)	Supporting Processors and Upgrading Memory
▪ Hard disk drive (HDD)/solid-state drive (SSD) migration	Hard Drives and Other Storage Devices
▪ HDD/SSD replacement	Hard Drives and Other Storage Devices
▪ Wireless cards	Supporting I/O Devices
• Physical privacy and security components	Supporting Mobile Devices
▪ Biometrics	Supporting Mobile Devices
▪ Near-field scanner features	Supporting Mobile Devices

1.2 Compare and contrast the display components of mobile devices.

Objectives	Primary Module
• Types	Supporting I/O Devices
▪ Liquid crystal display (LCD)	Supporting I/O Devices
• In-plane switching (IPS)	Supporting I/O Devices
• Twisted nematic (TN)	Supporting I/O Devices
• Vertical alignment (VA)	Supporting I/O Devices
▪ Organic light-emitting diode (OLED)	Supporting I/O Devices
• Mobile display components	Supporting I/O Devices
• WiFi antenna connector/placement	Supporting I/O Devices
• Camera/webcam	Supporting I/O Devices
• Microphone	Supporting I/O Devices
• Touch screen/digitizer	Supporting I/O Devices
• Inverter	Supporting I/O Devices

1.3   Given a scenario, set up and configure accessories and ports of mobile devices.

Objectives	Primary Module
• Connection methods	Supporting Mobile Devices
▪ Universal Serial Bus (USB)/USB-C/microUSB/miniUSB	Supporting Mobile Devices
▪ Lightning	Supporting Mobile Devices
▪ Serial interfaces	Supporting Mobile Devices
▪ Near-field communication (NFC)	Supporting Mobile Devices
▪ Bluetooth	Supporting Mobile Devices
▪ Hotspot	Supporting Mobile Devices
• Accessories	Supporting Mobile Devices
▪ Touch pens	Supporting Mobile Devices
▪ Headsets	Supporting Mobile Devices
▪ Speakers	Supporting Mobile Devices
▪ Webcam	Supporting Mobile Devices
• Docking station	Taking a Computer Apart and Putting It Back Together
• Port replicator	Taking a Computer Apart and Putting It Back Together
• Trackpad/drawing pad	Taking a Computer Apart and Putting It Back Together

1.4   Given a scenario, configure basic mobile-device network connectivity and application support.

Objectives	Primary Module
• Wireless/cellular data network (enable/disable)	Supporting Mobile Devices
▪ 2G/3G/4G/5G	Supporting Mobile Devices
▪ Hotspot	Supporting Mobile Devices
▪ Global System for Mobile Communications (GSM) vs. code-division multiple access (CDMA)	Supporting Mobile Devices
▪ Preferred Roaming List (PRL) updates	Supporting Mobile Devices
• Bluetooth	Supporting Mobile Devices
▪ Enable Bluetooth	Supporting Mobile Devices
▪ Enable pairing	Supporting Mobile Devices
▪ Find a device for pairing	Supporting Mobile Devices
▪ Enter the appropriate PIN code	Supporting Mobile Devices
▪ Test connectivity	Supporting Mobile Devices
• Location services	Supporting Mobile Devices
▪ Global Positioning System (GPS) services	Supporting Mobile Devices
▪ Cellular location services	Supporting Mobile Devices
• Mobile device management (MDM)/mobile application management (MAM)	Supporting Mobile Devices
▪ Corporate email configuration	Supporting Mobile Devices
▪ Two-factor authentication	Supporting Mobile Devices
▪ Corporate applications	Supporting Mobile Devices

Objectives	Primary Module
• Mobile device synchronization	Supporting Mobile Devices
▪ Account setup	Supporting Mobile Devices
• Microsoft 365	Supporting Mobile Devices
• Google Workspace	Supporting Mobile Devices
• iCloud	Supporting Mobile Devices
▪ Data to synchronize	Supporting Mobile Devices
• Mail	Supporting Mobile Devices
• Photos	Supporting Mobile Devices
• Calendar	Supporting Mobile Devices
• Contacts	Supporting Mobile Devices
• Recognizing data caps	Supporting Mobile Devices

2.0 Networking

2.1 Compare and contrast Transmission Control Protocol (TCP) and User Datagram Protocol (UDP) ports, protocols, and their purposes.

Objectives	Primary Module
• Ports and protocols	Networking Fundamentals
▪ 20/21 – File Transfer Protocol (FTP)	Networking Fundamentals
▪ 22 – Secure Shell (SSH)	Networking Fundamentals
▪ 23 – Telnet	Networking Fundamentals
▪ 25 – Simple Mail Transfer Protocol (SMTP)	Networking Fundamentals
▪ 53 – Domain Name System (DNS)	Networking Fundamentals
▪ 67/68 – Dynamic Host Configuration Protocol (DHCP)	Networking Fundamentals
▪ 80 – Hypertext Transfer Protocol (HTTP)	Networking Fundamentals
▪ 110 – Post Office Protocol 3 (POP3)	Networking Fundamentals
▪ 137/139 – Network Basic Input/Output System (NetBIOS)/ NetBIOS over TCP/IP (NetBT)	Networking Fundamentals
▪ 143 – Internet Mail Access Protocol (IMAP)	Networking Fundamentals
▪ 161/162 – Simple Network Management Protocol (SNMP)	Networking Fundamentals
▪ 389 – Lightweight Directory Access Protocol (LDAP)	Networking Fundamentals
▪ 443 – Hypertext Transfer Protocol Secure (HTTPS)	Networking Fundamentals
▪ 445 – Server Message Block (SMB)/Common Internet File System (CIFS)	Networking Fundamentals
▪ 3389 – Remote Desktop Protocol (RDP)	Networking Fundamentals
• TCP vs. UDP	Networking Fundamentals
▪ Connectionless	Networking Fundamentals
• DHCP	Networking Fundamentals
• Trivia File Transfer Protocol (TFTP)	Networking Fundamentals
▪ Connection-oriented	Networking Fundamentals
• HTTPS	Networking Fundamentals
• SSH	Networking Fundamentals

2.2   Compare and contrast common networking hardware.

Objectives	Primary Module
• Routers	Networking Fundamentals
• Switches	Networking Fundamentals
▪ Managed	Network Infrastructure and Cloud Computing
▪ Unmanaged	Network Infrastructure and Cloud Computing
• Access points	Network Infrastructure and Cloud Computing
• Patch panel	Network Infrastructure and Cloud Computing
• Firewall	Network Infrastructure and Cloud Computing
• Power over Ethernet (PoE)	Network Infrastructure and Cloud Computing
▪ Injectors	Network Infrastructure and Cloud Computing
▪ Switch	Network Infrastructure and Cloud Computing
▪ PoE standards	Network Infrastructure and Cloud Computing
• Hub	Networking Fundamentals
• Cable modem	Networking Fundamentals
• Digital subscriber line (DSL)	Network Infrastructure and Cloud Computing
• Optical network terminal (ONT)	Network Infrastructure and Cloud Computing
• Network interface card (NIC)	Networking Fundamentals
• Software-defined networking (SDN)	Network Infrastructure and Cloud Computing

2.3   Compare and contrast protocols for wireless networking.

Objectives	Primary Module
• Frequencies	Network Infrastructure and Cloud Computing
▪ 2.4GHz	Network Infrastructure and Cloud Computing
▪ 5GHz	Network Infrastructure and Cloud Computing
• Channels	Network Infrastructure and Cloud Computing
▪ Regulations	Network Infrastructure and Cloud Computing
▪ 2.4GHz vs. 5GHz	Network Infrastructure and Cloud Computing
• Bluetooth	Supporting Mobile Devices
• 802.11	Network Infrastructure and Cloud Computing
▪ a	Network Infrastructure and Cloud Computing
▪ b	Network Infrastructure and Cloud Computing
▪ g	Network Infrastructure and Cloud Computing
▪ n	Network Infrastructure and Cloud Computing
▪ ac (WiFi 5)	Network Infrastructure and Cloud Computing
▪ ax (WiFi 6)	Network Infrastructure and Cloud Computing
• Long-range fixed wireless	Network Infrastructure and Cloud Computing
▪ Licensed	Network Infrastructure and Cloud Computing
▪ Unlicensed	Network Infrastructure and Cloud Computing

Objectives	Primary Module
▪ Power	Network Infrastructure and Cloud Computing
▪ Regulatory requirements for wireless power	Network Infrastructure and Cloud Computing
• NFC	Supporting Mobile Devices
• Radio-frequency identification (RFID)	Supporting Mobile Devices

2.4 Summarize services provided by networked hosts.

Objectives	Primary Module
• Server roles	Networking Fundamentals
▪ DNS	Networking Fundamentals
▪ DHCP	Networking Fundamentals
▪ Fileshare	Networking Fundamentals
▪ Print servers	Networking Fundamentals
▪ Mail servers	Networking Fundamentals
▪ Syslog	Networking Fundamentals
▪ Web servers	Networking Fundamentals
▪ Authentication, authorization, and accounting (AAA)	Networking Fundamentals
• Internet appliances	Network Infrastructure and Cloud Computing
▪ Spam gateways	Network Infrastructure and Cloud Computing
▪ Unified threat management (UTM)	Network Infrastructure and Cloud Computing
▪ Load balancers	Network Infrastructure and Cloud Computing
▪ Proxy servers	Networking Fundamentals
• Legacy/embedded systems	Network Infrastructure and Cloud Computing
▪ Supervisory control and data acquisition (SCADA)	Network Infrastructure and Cloud Computing
• Internet of Things (IoT) devices	Network Infrastructure and Cloud Computing

2.5 Given a scenario, install and configure basic wired/wireless small office/home office (SOHO) networks.

Objectives	Primary Module
• Internet Protocol (IP) addressing	Networking Fundamentals
▪ IPv4	Networking Fundamentals
• Private addresses	Networking Fundamentals
• Public addresses	Networking Fundamentals
▪ IPv6	Networking Fundamentals
▪ Automatic Private IP Addressing (APIPA)	Networking Fundamentals
▪ Static	Networking Fundamentals
▪ Dynamic	Networking Fundamentals
▪ Gateway	Networking Fundamentals

2.6   Compare and contrast common network configuration concepts.

Objectives	Primary Module
• DNS	Networking Fundamentals
▪ Address (A)	Networking Fundamentals
▪ Address (AAAA)	Networking Fundamentals
▪ Mail exchanger (MX)	Networking Fundamentals
▪ Text (TXT)	Networking Fundamentals
• Spam management	Networking Fundamentals
(i) DomainKeys Identified Mail (DKIM)	Networking Fundamentals
(ii) Sender Policy Framework (SPF)	Networking Fundamentals
(iii) Domain-based Message Authentication, Reporting, and Conformance (DMARC)	Networking Fundamentals
• DHCP	Networking Fundamentals
▪ Leases	Networking Fundamentals
▪ Reservations	Networking Fundamentals
▪ Scope	Networking Fundamentals
• Virtual LAN (VLAN)	Network Infrastructure and Cloud Computing
• Virtual private network (VPN)	Network Infrastructure and Cloud Computing

2.7   Compare and contrast Internet connection types, network types, and their features.

Objectives	Primary Module
• Internet connection types	Network Infrastructure and Cloud Computing
▪ Satellite	Network Infrastructure and Cloud Computing
▪ Fiber	Network Infrastructure and Cloud Computing
▪ Cable	Network Infrastructure and Cloud Computing
▪ DSL	Network Infrastructure and Cloud Computing
▪ Cellular	Network Infrastructure and Cloud Computing
▪ Wireless Internet service provider (WISP)	Network Infrastructure and Cloud Computing
• Network types	Network Infrastructure and Cloud Computing
▪ Local area network (LAN)	Network Infrastructure and Cloud Computing
▪ Wide area network (WAN)	Network Infrastructure and Cloud Computing
▪ Personal area network (PAN)	Network Infrastructure and Cloud Computing
▪ Metropolitan area network (MAN)	Network Infrastructure and Cloud Computing
▪ Storage area network (SAN)	Network Infrastructure and Cloud Computing
▪ Wireless local area network (WLAN)	Network Infrastructure and Cloud Computing

2.8 Given a scenario, use networking tools.

Objectives	Primary Module
• Crimper	Network Infrastructure and Cloud Computing
• Cable stripper	Network Infrastructure and Cloud Computing

Objectives	Primary Module
• WiFi analyzer	Network Infrastructure and Cloud Computing
• Toner probe	Network Infrastructure and Cloud Computing
• Punchdown tool	Network Infrastructure and Cloud Computing
• Cable tester	Network Infrastructure and Cloud Computing
• Loopback plug	Network Infrastructure and Cloud Computing
• Network tap	Network Infrastructure and Cloud Computing

3.0 Hardware

3.1 Explain basic cable types and their connectors, features, and purposes.

Objectives	Primary Module
• Network cables	Network Infrastructure and Cloud Computing
▪ Copper	Network Infrastructure and Cloud Computing
• Cat 5	Network Infrastructure and Cloud Computing
• Cat 5e	Network Infrastructure and Cloud Computing
• Cat 6	Network Infrastructure and Cloud Computing
• Cat 6a	Network Infrastructure and Cloud Computing
• Coaxial	Network Infrastructure and Cloud Computing
• Shielded twisted pair	Network Infrastructure and Cloud Computing
(i) Direct burial	Network Infrastructure and Cloud Computing
• Unshielded twisted pair	Network Infrastructure and Cloud Computing
▪ Plenum	Network Infrastructure and Cloud Computing
▪ Optical	Network Infrastructure and Cloud Computing
• Fiber	Network Infrastructure and Cloud Computing
▪ T568A/T568B	Network Infrastructure and Cloud Computing
• Peripheral cables	Supporting I/O Devices
▪ USB 2.0	Supporting I/O Devices
▪ USB 3.0	Supporting I/O Devices
▪ Serial	Supporting I/O Devices
▪ Thunderbolt	Supporting I/O Devices
• Video cables	Supporting I/O Devices
▪ High-Definition Multimedia Interface (HDMI)	Supporting I/O Devices
▪ DisplayPort	Supporting I/O Devices
▪ Digital Visual Interface (DVI)	Supporting I/O Devices
▪ Video Graphics Array (VGA)	Supporting I/O Devices
• Hard drive cables	Hard Drives and Other Storage Devices
▪ Serial Advanced Technology Attachment (SATA)	Hard Drives and Other Storage Devices
▪ Small Computer System Interface (SCSI)	Hard Drives and Other Storage Devices
▪ External SATA (eSATA)	Hard Drives and Other Storage Devices
▪ Integrated Drive Electronics (IDE)	Hard Drives and Other Storage Devices

Objectives	Primary Module
• Adapters	Supporting I/O Devices
• Connector types	
▪ RJ11	Network Infrastructure and Cloud Computing
▪ RJ45	Network Infrastructure and Cloud Computing
▪ F type	Network Infrastructure and Cloud Computing
▪ Straight tip (ST)	Network Infrastructure and Cloud Computing
▪ Subscriber connector (SC)	Network Infrastructure and Cloud Computing
▪ Lucent connector (LC)	Network Infrastructure and Cloud Computing
▪ Punchdown block	Network Infrastructure and Cloud Computing
▪ microUSB	Supporting I/O Devices
▪ miniUSB	Supporting I/O Devices
▪ USB-C	Supporting I/O Devices
▪ Molex	All About Motherboards
▪ Lightning port	Supporting I/O Devices
▪ DB9	Supporting I/O Devices

3.2   Given a scenario, install the appropriate RAM.

Objectives	Primary Module
• RAM types	Supporting Processors and Upgrading Memory
▪ Virtual RAM	Supporting Processors and Upgrading Memory
▪ Small outline dual inline memory module (SODIMM)	Supporting Processors and Upgrading Memory
▪ Double Data Rate 3 (DDR3)	Supporting Processors and Upgrading Memory
▪ Double Data Rate 4 (DDR4)	Supporting Processors and Upgrading Memory
▪ Double Data Rate 5 (DDR5)	Supporting Processors and Upgrading Memory
▪ Error correction code (ECC) RAM	Supporting Processors and Upgrading Memory
• Single-channel	Supporting Processors and Upgrading Memory
• Dual-channel	Supporting Processors and Upgrading Memory
• Triple-channel	Supporting Processors and Upgrading Memory
• Quad-channel	Supporting Processors and Upgrading Memory

3.3   Given a scenario, select and install storage devices.

Objectives	Primary Module
• Hard drives	Hard Drives and Other Storage Devices
▪ Speeds	Hard Drives and Other Storage Devices
• 5,400rpm	Hard Drives and Other Storage Devices
• 7,200rpm	Hard Drives and Other Storage Devices
• 10,000rpm	Hard Drives and Other Storage Devices
• 15,000rpm	Hard Drives and Other Storage Devices

Objectives	Primary Module
▪ Form factor	Hard Drives and Other Storage Devices
• 2.5	Hard Drives and Other Storage Devices
• 3.5	Hard Drives and Other Storage Devices
• SSDs	Hard Drives and Other Storage Devices
▪ Communications interfaces	Hard Drives and Other Storage Devices
• Non-volatile Memory Express (NVMe)	Hard Drives and Other Storage Devices
• SATA	Hard Drives and Other Storage Devices
• Peripheral Component Interconnect Express (PCIe)	Hard Drives and Other Storage Devices
▪ Form factors	Hard Drives and Other Storage Devices
• M.2	Hard Drives and Other Storage Devices
• mSATA	Hard Drives and Other Storage Devices
• Drive configurations	Hard Drives and Other Storage Devices
▪ Redundant Array of Independent (or Inexpensive) Disks (RAID) 0, 1, 5, 10	Hard Drives and Other Storage Devices
• Removable storage	Hard Drives and Other Storage Devices
▪ Flash drives	Hard Drives and Other Storage Devices
▪ Memory cards	Hard Drives and Other Storage Devices
▪ Optical drives	Hard Drives and Other Storage Devices

3.4 Given a scenario, install and configure motherboards, central processing units (CPUs), and add-on cards.

Objectives	Primary Module
• Motherboard form factor	All About Motherboards
▪ Advanced Technology eXtended (ATX)	All About Motherboards
▪ Information Technology eXtended (ITX)	All About Motherboards
• Motherboard connector types	All About Motherboards
▪ Peripheral Component Interconnect (PCI)	All About Motherboards
▪ PCI Express (PCIe)	All About Motherboards
▪ Power connectors	All About Motherboards
▪ SATA	All About Motherboards
▪ eSATA	All About Motherboards
▪ Headers	All About Motherboards
▪ M.2	All About Motherboards
• Motherboard compatibility	Supporting Processors and Upgrading Memory
▪ CPU sockets	Supporting Processors and Upgrading Memory
• Advanced Micro Devices, Inc. (AMD)	Supporting Processors and Upgrading Memory
• Intel	Supporting Processors and Upgrading Memory

Objectives	Primary Module
▪ Server	Supporting Processors and Upgrading Memory
▪ Multisocket	Supporting Processors and Upgrading Memory
▪ Desktop	All About Motherboards
▪ Mobile	All About Motherboards
• Basic Input/Output System (BIOS)/Unified Extensible Firmware Interface (UEFI) settings	All About Motherboards
▪ Boot options	All About Motherboards
▪ USB permissions	All About Motherboards
▪ Trusted Platform Module (TPM) security features	All About Motherboards
▪ Fan considerations	All About Motherboards
▪ Secure Boot	All About Motherboards
▪ Boot password	All About Motherboards
• Encryption	All About Motherboards
▪ TPM	All About Motherboards
▪ Hardware security module (HSM)	All About Motherboards
• CPU architecture	Supporting Processors and Upgrading Memory
▪ x64/x86	Supporting Processors and Upgrading Memory
▪ Advanced RISC Machine (ARM)	Supporting Processors and Upgrading Memory
▪ Single-core	Supporting Processors and Upgrading Memory
▪ Multicore	Supporting Processors and Upgrading Memory
▪ Multithreading	Supporting Processors and Upgrading Memory
▪ Virtualization support	Supporting Processors and Upgrading Memory
• Expansion cards	Supporting I/O Devices
▪ Sound card	Supporting I/O Devices
▪ Video card	Supporting I/O Devices
▪ Capture card	Supporting I/O Devices
▪ NIC	Supporting I/O Devices
• Cooling	Power Supplies and Troubleshooting Computer Problems
▪ Fans	Power Supplies and Troubleshooting Computer Problems
▪ Heat sink	Power Supplies and Troubleshooting Computer Problems
▪ Thermal paste/pads	Power Supplies and Troubleshooting Computer Problems
▪ Liquid	Power Supplies and Troubleshooting Computer Problems

3.5   Given a scenario, install or replace the appropriate power supply.

Objectives	Primary Module
• Input 110–120 VAC vs. 220–240 VAC	Power Supplies and Troubleshooting Computer Problems
• Output 3.3V vs. 5V vs. 12V	Power Supplies and Troubleshooting Computer Problems
• 20-pin to 24-pin motherboard adapter	Power Supplies and Troubleshooting Computer Problems

Objectives	Primary Module
• Redundant power supply	Power Supplies and Troubleshooting Computer Problems
• Modular power supply	Power Supplies and Troubleshooting Computer Problems
• Wattage rating	Power Supplies and Troubleshooting Computer Problems

3.6   Given a scenario, deploy and configure multifunction devices/printers and settings.

Objectives	Primary Module
• Properly unboxing a device – setup location considerations	Supporting Printers
• Use appropriate drivers for a given OS	Supporting Printers
▪ Printer Control Language (PCL) vs. PostScript	Supporting Printers
• Device connectivity	Supporting Printers
▪ USB	Supporting Printers
▪ Ethernet	Supporting Printers
▪ Wireless	Supporting Printers
• Public/shared devices	Supporting Printers
▪ Printer share	Supporting Printers
▪ Print server	Supporting Printers
• Configuration settings	Supporting Printers
▪ Duplex	Supporting Printers
▪ Orientation	Supporting Printers
▪ Tray settings	Supporting Printers
▪ Quality	Supporting Printers
• Security	Supporting Printers
▪ User authentication	Supporting Printers
▪ Badging	Supporting Printers
▪ Audit logs	Supporting Printers
▪ Secured prints	Supporting Printers
• Network scan services	Supporting Printers
▪ Email	Supporting Printers
▪ SMB	Supporting Printers
▪ Cloud services	Supporting Printers
• Automatic document feeder (ADF)/flatbed scanner	Supporting Printers

3.7   Given a scenario, install and replace printer consumables.

Objectives	Primary Module
• Laser	Supporting Printers
▪ Imaging drum, fuser assembly, transfer belt, transfer roller, pickup rollers, separation pads, duplexing assembly	Supporting Printers
▪ Imaging process: processing, charging, exposing, developing, transferring, fusing, and cleaning	Supporting Printers
▪ Maintenance: Replace toner, apply maintenance kit, calibrate, clean	Supporting Printers
• Inkjet	Supporting Printers
▪ Ink cartridge, print head, roller, feeder, duplexing assembly, carriage belt	Supporting Printers
▪ Calibration	Supporting Printers
▪ Maintenance: Clean heads, replace cartridges, calibrate, clear jams	Supporting Printers
• Thermal	Supporting Printers
▪ Feed assembly, heating element	Supporting Printers
▪ Special thermal paper	Supporting Printers
▪ Maintenance: Replace paper, clean heating element, remove debris	Supporting Printers
▪ Heat sensitivity of paper	Supporting Printers
• Impact	Supporting Printers
▪ Print head, ribbon, tractor feed	Supporting Printers
▪ Impact paper	Supporting Printers
▪ Maintenance: Replace ribbon, replace print head, replace paper	Supporting Printers
• 3-D printer	Supporting Printers
▪ Filament	Supporting Printers
▪ Resin	Supporting Printers
▪ Print bed	Supporting Printers

4.0 Virtualization and Cloud Computing

4.1   Summarize cloud-computing concepts.

Objectives	Primary Module
• Common cloud models	Network Infrastructure and Cloud Computing
▪ Private cloud	Network Infrastructure and Cloud Computing
▪ Public cloud	Network Infrastructure and Cloud Computing
▪ Hybrid cloud	Network Infrastructure and Cloud Computing
▪ Community cloud	Network Infrastructure and Cloud Computing
▪ Infrastructure as a service (IaaS)	Network Infrastructure and Cloud Computing
▪ Software as a service (SaaS)	Network Infrastructure and Cloud Computing
▪ Platform as a service (PaaS)	Network Infrastructure and Cloud Computing
• Cloud characteristics	Network Infrastructure and Cloud Computing
▪ Shared resources	Network Infrastructure and Cloud Computing
▪ Metered utilization	Network Infrastructure and Cloud Computing

Objectives	Primary Module
▪ Rapid elasticity	Network Infrastructure and Cloud Computing
▪ High availability	Network Infrastructure and Cloud Computing
▪ File synchronization	Network Infrastructure and Cloud Computing
• Desktop virtualization	Network Infrastructure and Cloud Computing
▪ Virtual desktop infrastructure (VDI) on premises	Network Infrastructure and Cloud Computing
▪ VDI in the cloud	Network Infrastructure and Cloud Computing

4.2 Summarize aspects of client-side virtualization.

Objectives	Primary Module
• Purpose of virtual machines	Network Infrastructure and Cloud Computing
▪ Sandbox	Network Infrastructure and Cloud Computing
▪ Test development	Network Infrastructure and Cloud Computing
▪ Application virtualization	Network Infrastructure and Cloud Computing
• Legacy software/OS	Network Infrastructure and Cloud Computing
• Cross-platform virtualization	Network Infrastructure and Cloud Computing
• Resource requirements	Network Infrastructure and Cloud Computing
• Security requirements	Network Infrastructure and Cloud Computing

5.0 Hardware and Network Troubleshooting

5.1 Given a scenario, apply the best practice methodology to resolve problems.

Objectives	Primary Module
• Always consider corporate policies, procedures, and impacts before implementing changes	Power Supplies and Troubleshooting Computer Problems
1. Identify the problem	Power Supplies and Troubleshooting Computer Problems
• Gather information from the user, identify user changes, and, if applicable, perform backups before making changes	Power Supplies and Troubleshooting Computer Problems
• Inquire regarding environmental or infrastructure changes	Power Supplies and Troubleshooting Computer Problems
2. Establish a theory of probable cause (question the obvious)	Power Supplies and Troubleshooting Computer Problems
• If necessary, conduct external or internal research based on symptoms	Power Supplies and Troubleshooting Computer Problems
3. Test the theory to determine the cause	Power Supplies and Troubleshooting Computer Problems
• Once the theory is confirmed, determine the next steps to resolve the problem	Power Supplies and Troubleshooting Computer Problems
• If the theory is not confirmed, re-establish a new theory or escalate	Power Supplies and Troubleshooting Computer Problems

Objectives	Primary Module
4. Establish a plan of action to resolve the problem and implement the solution	Power Supplies and Troubleshooting Computer Problems
• Refer to the vendor's instructions for guidance	Power Supplies and Troubleshooting Computer Problems
5. Verify full system functionality and, if applicable, implement preventive measures	Power Supplies and Troubleshooting Computer Problems
6. Document the findings, actions, and outcomes	Power Supplies and Troubleshooting Computer Problems

5.2   Given a scenario, troubleshoot problems related to motherboards, RAM, CPU, and power.

Objectives	Primary Module
• Common symptoms	Power Supplies and Troubleshooting Computer Problems
▪ Power-on self-test (POST) beeps	Power Supplies and Troubleshooting Computer Problems
▪ Proprietary crash screens (blue screen of death [BSOD]/pinwheel)	Power Supplies and Troubleshooting Computer Problems
▪ Black screen	Power Supplies and Troubleshooting Computer Problems
▪ No power	Power Supplies and Troubleshooting Computer Problems
▪ Sluggish performance	Power Supplies and Troubleshooting Computer Problems
▪ Overheating	Power Supplies and Troubleshooting Computer Problems
▪ Burning smell	Power Supplies and Troubleshooting Computer Problems
▪ Intermittent shutdown	Power Supplies and Troubleshooting Computer Problems
▪ Application crashes	Power Supplies and Troubleshooting Computer Problems
▪ Grinding noise	Power Supplies and Troubleshooting Computer Problems
▪ Capacitor swelling	Power Supplies and Troubleshooting Computer Problems
▪ Inaccurate system date/time	Power Supplies and Troubleshooting Computer Problems

5.3 Given a scenario, troubleshoot and diagnose problems with storage drives and RAID arrays.

Objectives	Primary Module
• Common symptoms	Hard Drives and Other Storage Devices
▪ Light-emitting diode (LED) status indicators	Hard Drives and Other Storage Devices
▪ Grinding noises	Hard Drives and Other Storage Devices
▪ Clicking sounds	Hard Drives and Other Storage Devices
▪ Bootable device not found	Hard Drives and Other Storage Devices
▪ Data loss/corruption	Hard Drives and Other Storage Devices
▪ RAID failure	Hard Drives and Other Storage Devices
▪ Self-monitoring, Analysis, and Reporting Technology (S.M.A.R.T.) failure	Hard Drives and Other Storage Devices
▪ Extended read/write times	Hard Drives and Other Storage Devices
▪ Input/output operations per second (IOPS)	Hard Drives and Other Storage Devices
▪ Missing drives in OS	Hard Drives and Other Storage Devices

5.4 Given a scenario, troubleshoot video, projector, and display issues.

Objectives	Primary Module
• Common symptoms	Supporting I/O Devices
▪ Incorrect data source	Supporting I/O Devices
▪ Physical cabling issues	Supporting I/O Devices
▪ Burned-out bulb	Supporting I/O Devices
▪ Fuzzy image	Supporting I/O Devices
▪ Display burn-in	Supporting I/O Devices
▪ Dead pixels	Supporting I/O Devices
▪ Flashing screen	Supporting I/O Devices
▪ Incorrect color display	Supporting I/O Devices
▪ Audio issues	Supporting I/O Devices
▪ Dim image	Supporting I/O Devices
▪ Intermittent projector shutdown	Supporting I/O Devices

5.5 Given a scenario, troubleshoot common issues with mobile devices.

Objectives	Primary Module
• Common symptoms	Supporting Mobile Devices
▪ Poor battery health	Supporting Mobile Devices
▪ Swollen battery	Supporting Mobile Devices
▪ Broken screen	Supporting Mobile Devices
▪ Improper charging	Supporting Mobile Devices
▪ Poor/no connectivity	Supporting Mobile Devices
▪ Liquid damage	Supporting Mobile Devices
▪ Overheating	Supporting Mobile Devices
▪ Digitizer issues	Supporting Mobile Devices
▪ Physically damaged ports	Supporting Mobile Devices
▪ Malware	Supporting Mobile Devices
▪ Cursor drift/touch calibration	Supporting Mobile Devices

5.6 Given a scenario, troubleshoot and resolve printer issues.

Objectives	Primary Module
• Common symptoms	Supporting Printers
▪ Lines down the printed pages	Supporting Printers
▪ Garbled print	Supporting Printers
▪ Toner not fusing to paper	Supporting Printers
▪ Paper jams	Supporting Printers
▪ Faded print	Supporting Printers
▪ Incorrect paper size	Supporting Printers
▪ Paper not feeding	Supporting Printers

Objectives	Primary Module
▪ Multipage misfeed	Supporting Printers
▪ Multiple prints pending in queue	Supporting Printers
▪ Speckling on printed pages	Supporting Printers
▪ Double/echo images on the print	Supporting Printers
▪ Incorrect color display	Supporting Printers
▪ Grinding noise	Supporting Printers
▪ Finishing issues	Supporting Printers
• Staple jams	Supporting Printers
• Hole punch	Supporting Printers
▪ Incorrect page orientation	Supporting Printers

5.7   Given a scenario, troubleshoot problems with wired and wireless networks.

Objectives	Primary Module
• Common symptoms	Network Infrastructure and Cloud Computing
▪ Intermittent wireless connectivity	Network Infrastructure and Cloud Computing
▪ Slow network speeds	Network Infrastructure and Cloud Computing
▪ Limited connectivity	Network Infrastructure and Cloud Computing
▪ Jitter	Network Infrastructure and Cloud Computing
▪ Poor Voice over Internet Protocol (VoIP) quality	Network Infrastructure and Cloud Computing
▪ Port flapping	Network Infrastructure and Cloud Computing
▪ High latency	Network Infrastructure and Cloud Computing
▪ External interference	Network Infrastructure and Cloud Computing

CompTIA A+ Core 2 (220-1102)

1.0 Operating System

1.1   Identify basic features of Microsoft Windows editions.

Objectives	Primary Module
• Windows 10 editions	Installing Windows
▪ Home	Installing Windows
▪ Pro	Installing Windows
▪ Pro for Workstations	Installing Windows
▪ Enterprise	Installing Windows
• Feature differences	Installing Windows
▪ Domain access vs. workgroup	Installing Windows
▪ Desktop styles/user interface	Installing Windows

Objectives	Primary Module
• Availability of Remote Desktop Protocol (RDP)	Installing Windows
• Random-access memory (RAM) support limitations	Installing Windows
• BitLocker	Installing Windows
• gpedit.msc	Installing Windows
• Upgrade paths	The Complex World of IT Professionals
• In-place upgrade	The Complex World of IT Professionals

1.2   Given a scenario, use the appropriate Microsoft command-line tool.

Objectives	Primary Module
• Navigation	Maintaining Windows
• cd	Maintaining Windows
• dir	Maintaining Windows
• md	Maintaining Windows
• rmdir	Maintaining Windows
• Drive navigation inputs:	Maintaining Windows
• C:\ or D:\ or x:\	Maintaining Windows
• Command-line tools	
• ipconfig	Network Security and Troubleshooting
• ping	Network Security and Troubleshooting
• hostname	Network Security and Troubleshooting
• netstat	Network Security and Troubleshooting
• nslookup	Network Security and Troubleshooting
• chkdsk	Maintaining Windows
• net user	Network Security and Troubleshooting
• net use	Network Security and Troubleshooting
• tracert	Network Security and Troubleshooting
• format	Maintaining Windows
• xcopy	Maintaining Windows
• copy	Maintaining Windows
• robocopy	Maintaining Windows
• gpupdate	Securing and Sharing Windows Resources
• gpresult	Securing and Sharing Windows Resources
• shutdown	Maintaining Windows
• sfc	Troubleshooting Windows After Startup
• [command name] /?	Maintaining Windows
• diskpart	Maintaining Windows
• pathping	Network Security and Troubleshooting
• winver	Maintaining Windows

1.3   Given a scenario, use features and tools of the Microsoft Windows 10 operating system (OS).

Objectives	Primary Module
• Task Manager	Troubleshooting Windows After Startup
▪ Services	Troubleshooting Windows After Startup
▪ Startup	Troubleshooting Windows After Startup
▪ Performance	Troubleshooting Windows After Startup
▪ Processes	Troubleshooting Windows After Startup
▪ Users	Troubleshooting Windows After Startup
• Microsoft Management Console (MMC) snap-in	
▪ Event Viewer (eventvwr.msc)	Troubleshooting Windows After Startup
▪ Disk Management (diskmgmt.msc)	Maintaining Windows
▪ Task Scheduler (taskschd.msc)	Troubleshooting Windows After Startup
▪ Device Manager (devmgmt.msc)	Installing Windows
▪ Certificate Manager (certmgr.msc)	Security Strategies
▪ Local Users and Groups (lusrmgr.msc)	Securing and Sharing Windows Resources
▪ Performance Monitor (perfmon.msc)	Troubleshooting Windows After Startup
▪ Group Policy Editor (gpedit.msc)	Securing and Sharing Windows Resources
• Additional tools	
▪ System Information (msinfo32. exe)	Installing Windows
▪ Resource Monitor (resmon.exe)	Troubleshooting Windows After Startup
▪ System Configuration (msconfig. exe)	Troubleshooting Windows After Startup
▪ Disk Cleanup (cleanmgr.exe)	Maintaining Windows
▪ Disk Defragment (dfrgui.exe)	Maintaining Windows
▪ Registry Editor (regedit.exe)	Troubleshooting Windows After Startup

1.4   Given a scenario, use the appropriate Microsoft Windows 10 Control Panel utility.

Objectives	Primary Module
• Internet Options	Network Security and Troubleshooting
• Devices and Printers	Securing and Sharing Windows Resources
• Programs and Features	Installing Windows
• Network and Sharing Center	Network Security and Troubleshooting
• System	Maintaining Windows
• Windows Defender Firewall	Network Security and Troubleshooting
• Mail	Maintaining Windows
• Sound	Maintaining Windows
• User Accounts	Securing and Sharing Windows Resources
• Device Manager	Installing Windows
• Indexing Options	Maintaining Windows
• Administrative Tools	Troubleshooting Windows After Startup

Objectives	Primary Module
• File Explorer Options	Maintaining Windows
▪ Show hidden files	Maintaining Windows
▪ Hide extensions	Maintaining Windows
▪ General options	Maintaining Windows
▪ View options	Maintaining Windows
• Power Options	Maintaining Windows
▪ Hibernate	Maintaining Windows
▪ Power plans	Maintaining Windows
▪ Sleep/suspend	Maintaining Windows
▪ Standby	Maintaining Windows
▪ Choose what closing the lid does	Maintaining Windows
▪ Turn on fast startup	Maintaining Windows
▪ Universal Serial Bus (USB) selective suspend	Maintaining Windows
• Ease of Access	Installing Windows

1.5   Given a scenario, use the appropriate Windows settings.

Objectives	Primary Module
• Time and Language	Maintaining Windows
• Update and Security	Installing Windows
• Personalization	Maintaining Windows
• Apps	Installing Windows
• Privacy	Maintaining Windows
• System	Maintaining Windows
• Devices	Maintaining Windows
• Network and Internet	Maintaining Windows
• Gaming	Maintaining Windows
• Accounts	Maintaining Windows

1.6   Given a scenario, configure Microsoft Windows networking features on a client/desktop.

Objectives	Primary Module
• Workgroup vs. domain setup	
▪ Shared resources	Securing and Sharing Windows Resources
▪ Printers	Securing and Sharing Windows Resources
▪ File servers	Securing and Sharing Windows Resources
▪ Mapped drives	Securing and Sharing Windows Resources
• Local OS firewall settings	Network Security and Troubleshooting
▪ Application restrictions and exceptions	Network Security and Troubleshooting
▪ Configuration	Network Security and Troubleshooting

Objectives	Primary Module
• Client network configuration	Installing Windows
▪ Internet Protocol (IP) addressing scheme	Installing Windows
▪ Domain Name System (DNS) settings	Installing Windows
▪ Subnet mask	Installing Windows
▪ Gateway	Installing Windows
▪ Static vs. dynamic	Installing Windows
• Establish network connections	
▪ Virtual private network (VPN)	Network Security and Troubleshooting
▪ Wireless	Installing Windows
▪ Wired	Installing Windows
▪ Wireless wide area network (WWAN)	Network Security and Troubleshooting
• Proxy settings	Network Security and Troubleshooting
• Public network vs. private network	Installing Windows
• File Explorer navigation – network paths	Securing and Sharing Windows Resources
• Metered connections and limitations	Network Security and Troubleshooting

1.7   Given a scenario, apply application installation and configuration concepts.

Objectives	Primary Module
• System requirements for applications	Installing Windows
▪ 32-bit vs. 64-bit dependent application requirements	Installing Windows
▪ Dedicated graphics card vs. integrated	Installing Windows
▪ Video Random-access memory (VRAM) requirements	Installing Windows
▪ RAM requirements	Installing Windows
▪ Central processing unit (CPU) requirements	Installing Windows
▪ External hardware tokens	Installing Windows
▪ Storage requirements	Installing Windows
• OS requirements for applications	Installing Windows
▪ Application to OS compatibility	Installing Windows
▪ 32-bit vs. 64-bit OS	Installing Windows
• Distribution methods	Installing Windows
▪ Physical media vs. downloadable	Installing Windows
▪ ISO mountable	Installing Windows
• Other considerations for new applications	Installing Windows
▪ Impact to device	Installing Windows
▪ Impact to network	Installing Windows
▪ Impact to operation	Installing Windows
▪ Impact to business	Installing Windows

1.8   Explain common OS types and their purposes.

Objectives	Primary Module
• Workstation OSs	The Complex World of IT Professionals
▪ Windows	The Complex World of IT Professionals
▪ Linux	The Complex World of IT Professionals
▪ macOS	The Complex World of IT Professionals
▪ Chrome OS	The Complex World of IT Professionals
• Cell phone/tablet OSs	Mobile Device Security
▪ iPadOS	Mobile Device Security
▪ iOS	Mobile Device Security
▪ Android	Mobile Device Security
• Various filesystem types	
▪ New Technology File System (NTFS)	The Complex World of IT Professionals
▪ File Allocation Table 32 (FAT32)	The Complex World of IT Professionals
▪ Third extended filesystem (ext3)	The Complex World of IT Professionals
▪ Fourth extended filesystem (ext4)	Linux and Scripting
▪ Apple File System (APFS)	Supporting macOS
▪ Extensible File Allocation Table (exFAT)	Maintaining Windows
• Vendor life-cycle limitations	The Complex World of IT Professionals
▪ End-of-life (EOL)	The Complex World of IT Professionals
▪ Update limitations	The Complex World of IT Professionals
• Compatibility concerns between OSs	The Complex World of IT Professionals

1.9   Given a scenario, perform OS installations and upgrades in a diverse OS environment.

Objectives	Primary Module
• Boot methods	The Complex World of IT Professionals
▪ USB	The Complex World of IT Professionals
▪ Optical media	The Complex World of IT Professionals
▪ Network	The Complex World of IT Professionals
▪ Solid-state/flash drives	The Complex World of IT Professionals
▪ Internet-based	The Complex World of IT Professionals
▪ External/hot-swappable drive	The Complex World of IT Professionals
▪ Internal hard drive (partition)	The Complex World of IT Professionals
• Types of installations	The Complex World of IT Professionals
▪ Upgrade	Installing Windows
▪ Recovery partition	Troubleshooting Windows Startup
▪ Clean install	Installing Windows
▪ Image deployment	Installing Windows
▪ Repair installation	Troubleshooting Windows Startup
▪ Remote network installation	Installing Windows

Objectives	Primary Module
▪ Other considerations	Installing Windows
• Third-party drivers	The Complex World of IT Professionals
• Partitioning	The Complex World of IT Professionals
▪ GUID [globally unique identifier] Partition Table (GPT)	The Complex World of IT Professionals
▪ Master boot record (MBR)	The Complex World of IT Professionals
• Drive format	The Complex World of IT Professionals
• Upgrade considerations	Installing Windows
▪ Backup files and user preferences	Installing Windows
▪ Application and driver support/backward compatibility	Installing Windows
▪ Hardware compatibility	Installing Windows
• Feature updates	The Complex World of IT Professionals
▪ Product life cycle	The Complex World of IT Professionals

1.10   Identify common features and tools of the macOS/desktop OS.

Objectives	Primary Module
• Installation and uninstallation of applications	Supporting macOS
▪ File types	Supporting macOS
• .dmg	Supporting macOS
• .pkg	Supporting macOS
• .app	Supporting macOS
▪ App Store	Supporting macOS
▪ Uninstallation process	Supporting macOS
• Apple ID and corporate restrictions	Supporting macOS
• Best practices	Supporting macOS
▪ Backups	Supporting macOS
▪ Antivirus	Supporting macOS
▪ Updates/patches	Supporting macOS
• System Preferences	Supporting macOS
▪ Displays	Supporting macOS
▪ Networks	Supporting macOS
▪ Printers	Supporting macOS
▪ Scanners	Supporting macOS
▪ Privacy	Supporting macOS
▪ Accessibility	Supporting macOS
▪ Time Machine	Supporting macOS
• Features	Supporting macOS
▪ Multiple desktops	Supporting macOS
▪ Mission Control	Supporting macOS

Objectives	Primary Module
▪ Keychain	Supporting macOS
▪ Spotlight	Supporting macOS
▪ iCloud	Supporting macOS
▪ Gestures	Supporting macOS
▪ Finder	Supporting macOS
▪ Remote Disc	Supporting macOS
▪ Dock	Supporting macOS
• Disk Utility	Supporting macOS
• FileVault	Supporting macOS
• Terminal	Supporting macOS
• Force Quit	Supporting macOS

1.11   Identify common features and tools of the Linux client/desktop OS.

Objectives	Primary Module
• Common commands	Linux and Scripting
▪ ls	Linux and Scripting
▪ pwd	Linux and Scripting
▪ mv	Linux and Scripting
▪ cp	Linux and Scripting
▪ rm	Linux and Scripting
▪ chmod	Linux and Scripting
▪ chown	Linux and Scripting
▪ su/sudo	Linux and Scripting
▪ apt-get	Linux and Scripting
▪ yum	Linux and Scripting
▪ ip	Linux and Scripting
▪ df	Linux and Scripting
▪ grep	Linux and Scripting
▪ ps	Linux and Scripting
▪ man	Linux and Scripting
▪ top	Linux and Scripting
▪ find	Linux and Scripting
▪ dig	Linux and Scripting
▪ cat	Linux and Scripting
▪ nano	Linux and Scripting
• Best practices	Linux and Scripting
▪ Backups	Linux and Scripting
▪ Antivirus	Linux and Scripting
▪ Updates/patches	Linux and Scripting

Objectives	Primary Module
• Tools	Linux and Scripting
▪ Shell/terminal	Linux and Scripting
▪ Samba	Linux and Scripting

2.0 Security

2.1   Summarize various security measures and their purposes.

Objectives	Primary Module
• Physical security	Security Strategies
▪ Access control vestibule	Security Strategies
▪ Badge reader	Security Strategies
▪ Video surveillance	Security Strategies
▪ Alarm systems	Security Strategies
▪ Motion sensors	Security Strategies
▪ Door locks	Security Strategies
▪ Equipment locks	Security Strategies
▪ Guards	Security Strategies
▪ Bollards	Security Strategies
▪ Fences	Security Strategies
• Physical security for staff	Security Strategies
▪ Key fobs	Security Strategies
▪ Smart cards	Security Strategies
▪ Keys	Security Strategies
▪ Biometrics	Security Strategies
• Retina scanner	Security Strategies
• Fingerprint scanner	Security Strategies
• Palmprint scanner	Security Strategies
▪ Lighting	Security Strategies
▪ Magnetometers	Security Strategies
• Logical security	Security Strategies
▪ Principle of least privilege	Security Strategies
▪ Access control lists (ACLs)	Security Strategies
▪ Multifactor authentication (MFA)	Security Strategies
▪ Email	Security Strategies
▪ Hard token	Security Strategies
▪ Soft token	Security Strategies
▪ Short message service (SMS)	Security Strategies
▪ Voice call	Security Strategies
▪ Authenticator application	Security Strategies

Objectives	Primary Module
• Mobile device management (MDM)	Mobile Device Security
• Active Directory	Securing and Sharing Windows Resources
▪ Login script	Securing and Sharing Windows Resources
▪ Domain	Securing and Sharing Windows Resources
▪ Group Policy/updates	Securing and Sharing Windows Resources
▪ Organizational units	Securing and Sharing Windows Resources
▪ Home folder	Securing and Sharing Windows Resources
▪ Folder redirection	Securing and Sharing Windows Resources
▪ Security groups	Securing and Sharing Windows Resources

2.2   Compare and contrast wireless security protocols and authentication methods.

Objectives	Primary Module
• Protocols and encryption	Network Security and Troubleshooting
▪ WiFi Protected Access 2 (WPA2)	Network Security and Troubleshooting
▪ WPA3	Network Security and Troubleshooting
▪ Temporal Key Integrity Protocol (TKIP)	Network Security and Troubleshooting
▪ Advanced Encryption Standard (AES)	Network Security and Troubleshooting
• Authentication	Network Security and Troubleshooting
▪ Remote Authentication Dial-In User Service (RADIUS)	Network Security and Troubleshooting
▪ Terminal Access Controller Access-Control System (TACACS+)	Network Security and Troubleshooting
▪ Kerberos	Network Security and Troubleshooting
▪ Multifactor	Security Strategies

2.3   Given a scenario, detect, remove, and prevent malware using the appropriate tools and methods.

Objectives	Primary Module
• Malware	Security Strategies
▪ Trojan	Security Strategies
▪ Rootkit	Security Strategies
▪ Virus	Security Strategies
▪ Spyware	Security Strategies
▪ Ransomware	Security Strategies
▪ Keylogger	Security Strategies
▪ Boot sector virus	Security Strategies
▪ Cryptominers	Security Strategies
• Tools and methods	Security Strategies
▪ Recovery console	Security Strategies
▪ Antivirus	Security Strategies
▪ Anti-malware	Security Strategies

Objectives	Primary Module
▪ Software firewalls	Security Strategies
▪ Anti-phishing training	Security Strategies
▪ User education regarding common threats	Security Strategies
▪ OS reinstallation	Security Strategies

2.4   Explain common social-engineering attacks, threats, and vulnerabilities.

Objectives	Primary Module
• Social engineering	Security Strategies
▪ Phishing	Security Strategies
▪ Vishing	Security Strategies
▪ Shoulder surfing	Security Strategies
▪ Whaling	Security Strategies
▪ Tailgating	Security Strategies
▪ Impersonation	Security Strategies
▪ Dumpster diving	Security Strategies
▪ Evil twin	Security Strategies
• Threats	Security Strategies
▪ Distributed denial of service (DDoS)	Security Strategies
▪ Denial of service (DoS)	Security Strategies
▪ Zero-day attack	Security Strategies
▪ Spoofing	Security Strategies
▪ On-path attack	Security Strategies
▪ Brute-force attack	Security Strategies
▪ Dictionary attack	Security Strategies
▪ Insider threat	Security Strategies
▪ Structured Query Language (SQL) injection	Security Strategies
▪ Cross-site scripting (XSS)	Security Strategies
• Vulnerabilities	Security Strategies
▪ Non-compliant systems	Security Strategies
▪ Unpatched systems	Security Strategies
▪ Unprotected systems (missing antivirus/missing firewall)	Security Strategies
▪ EOL OSs	Security Strategies
▪ Bring your own device (BYOD)	Security Strategies

2.5   Given a scenario, manage and configure basic security settings in the Microsoft Windows OS.

Objectives	Primary Module
• Defender Antivirus	Security Strategies
▪ Activate/deactivate	Security Strategies
▪ Updated definitions	Security Strategies

Objectives	Primary Module
• Firewall	Network Security and Troubleshooting
▪ Activate/deactivate	Network Security and Troubleshooting
▪ Port security	Network Security and Troubleshooting
▪ Application security	Network Security and Troubleshooting
• Users and groups	Securing and Sharing Windows Resources
▪ Local vs. Microsoft account	Installing Windows
▪ Standard account	Installing Windows
▪ Administrator	Installing Windows
▪ Guest user	Securing and Sharing Windows Resources
▪ Power user	Securing and Sharing Windows Resources
• Login OS options	Securing and Sharing Windows Resources
▪ Username and password	Securing and Sharing Windows Resources
▪ Personal identification number (PIN)	Securing and Sharing Windows Resources
▪ Fingerprint	Securing and Sharing Windows Resources
▪ Facial recognition	Securing and Sharing Windows Resources
▪ Single sign-on (SSO)	Installing Windows
• NTFS vs. share permissions	Securing and Sharing Windows Resources
▪ File and folder attributes	Securing and Sharing Windows Resources
▪ Inheritance	Securing and Sharing Windows Resources
• Run as administrator vs. standard user	Installing Windows
▪ User Account Control (UAC)	Installing Windows
• BitLocker	Securing and Sharing Windows Resources
• BitLocker To Go	Securing and Sharing Windows Resources
• Encrypting File System (EFS)	Securing and Sharing Windows Resources

2.6   Given a scenario, configure a workstation to meet best practices for security.

Objectives	Primary Module
• Data-at-rest encryption	Securing and Sharing Windows Resources
• Password best practices	Securing and Sharing Windows Resources
▪ Complexity requirements	Securing and Sharing Windows Resources
• Length	Securing and Sharing Windows Resources
• Character types	Securing and Sharing Windows Resources
▪ Expiration requirements	Securing and Sharing Windows Resources
▪ Basic input/output system (BIOS)/Unified Extensible Firmware Interface (UEFI) passwords	Securing and Sharing Windows Resources
• End-user best practices	Security Strategies
▪ Use screensaver locks	Security Strategies
▪ Log off when not in use	Security Strategies
▪ Secure/protect critical hardware (e.g., laptops)	Security Strategies
▪ Secure personally identifiable information (PII) and passwords	Security Strategies

Objectives	Primary Module
• Account management	Securing and Sharing Windows Resources
▪ Restrict user permissions	Securing and Sharing Windows Resources
▪ Restrict login times	Securing and Sharing Windows Resources
▪ Disable guest account	Securing and Sharing Windows Resources
▪ Use failed attempts lockout	Securing and Sharing Windows Resources
▪ Use timeout/screen lock	Securing and Sharing Windows Resources
• Change default administrator's user account/password	Securing and Sharing Windows Resources
• Disable AutoRun	Securing and Sharing Windows Resources
• Disable AutoPlay	Securing and Sharing Windows Resources

2.7   Explain common methods for securing mobile and embedded devices.

Objectives	Primary Module
• Screen locks	Mobile Device Security
▪ Facial recognition	Mobile Device Security
▪ PIN codes	Mobile Device Security
▪ Fingerprint	Mobile Device Security
▪ Pattern	Mobile Device Security
▪ Swipe	Mobile Device Security
• Remote wipes	Mobile Device Security
• Locator applications	Mobile Device Security
• OS updates	Mobile Device Security
• Device encryption	Mobile Device Security
• Remote backup applications	Mobile Device Security
• Failed login attempts restrictions	Mobile Device Security
• Antivirus/anti-malware	Mobile Device Security
• Firewalls	Mobile Device Security
• Policies and procedures	Mobile Device Security
▪ BYOD vs. corporate owned	Mobile Device Security
▪ Profile security requirements	Mobile Device Security
• Internet of Things (IoT)	Network Security and Troubleshooting

2.8   Given a scenario, use common data destruction and disposal methods.

Objectives	Primary Module
• Physical destruction	Security Strategies
▪ Drilling	Security Strategies
▪ Shredding	Security Strategies
▪ Degaussing	Security Strategies
▪ Incinerating	Security Strategies

Objectives	Primary Module
• Recycling or repurposing best practices	Security Strategies
▪ Erasing/wiping	Security Strategies
▪ Low-level formatting	Security Strategies
▪ Standard formatting	Security Strategies
• Outsourcing concepts	Security Strategies
▪ Third-party vendor	Security Strategies
▪ Certification of destruction/recycling	Security Strategies

2.9 Given a scenario, configure appropriate security settings on small office/home office (SOHO) wireless and wired networks.

Objectives	Primary Module
• Home router settings	Network Security and Troubleshooting
▪ Change default passwords	Network Security and Troubleshooting
▪ IP filtering	Network Security and Troubleshooting
▪ Firmware updates	Network Security and Troubleshooting
▪ Content filtering	Network Security and Troubleshooting
▪ Physical placement/secure locations	Network Security and Troubleshooting
▪ Dynamic Host Configuration Protocol (DHCP) reservations	Network Security and Troubleshooting
▪ Static wide-area network (WAN) IP	Network Security and Troubleshooting
▪ Universal Plug and Play (UPnP)	Network Security and Troubleshooting
▪ Screened subnet	Network Security and Troubleshooting
• Wireless specific	Network Security and Troubleshooting
▪ Changing the service set identifier (SSID)	Network Security and Troubleshooting
▪ Disabling SSID broadcast	Network Security and Troubleshooting
▪ Encryption settings	Network Security and Troubleshooting
▪ Disabling guest access	Network Security and Troubleshooting
▪ Changing channels	Network Security and Troubleshooting
• Firewall settings	Network Security and Troubleshooting
▪ Disabling unused ports	Network Security and Troubleshooting
▪ Port forwarding/mapping	Network Security and Troubleshooting

2.10 Given a scenario, install and configure browsers and relevant security settings.

Objectives	Primary Module
• Browser download/installation	Network Security and Troubleshooting
▪ Trusted sources	Network Security and Troubleshooting
• Hashing	Network Security and Troubleshooting
▪ Untrusted sources	Network Security and Troubleshooting
• Extensions and plug-ins	Network Security and Troubleshooting
▪ Trusted sources	Network Security and Troubleshooting
▪ Untrusted sources	Network Security and Troubleshooting

Objectives	Primary Module
• Password managers	Network Security and Troubleshooting
• Secure connections/sites – valid certificates	Network Security and Troubleshooting
• Settings	Network Security and Troubleshooting
▪ Pop-up blocker	Network Security and Troubleshooting
▪ Clearing browsing data	Network Security and Troubleshooting
▪ Clearing cache	Network Security and Troubleshooting
▪ Private-browsing mode	Network Security and Troubleshooting
▪ Sign-in/browser data synchronization	Network Security and Troubleshooting
▪ Ad blockers	Network Security and Troubleshooting

3.0 Software Troubleshooting

3.1   Given a scenario, troubleshoot common Windows OS problems.

Objectives	Primary Module
• Common symptoms	
▪ Blue screen of death (BSOD)	Troubleshooting Windows Startup
▪ Sluggish performance	Troubleshooting Windows After Startup
▪ Boot problems	Troubleshooting Windows Startup
▪ Frequent shutdowns	Troubleshooting Windows Startup
▪ Services not starting	Troubleshooting Windows After Startup
▪ Applications crashing	Troubleshooting Windows After Startup
▪ Low memory warnings	Troubleshooting Windows After Startup
▪ USB controller resource warnings	Troubleshooting Windows After Startup
▪ System instability	Troubleshooting Windows After Startup
▪ No OS found	Troubleshooting Windows Startup
▪ Slow profile load	Troubleshooting Windows Startup
▪ Time drift	Troubleshooting Windows After Startup
• Common troubleshooting steps	
▪ Reboot	Troubleshooting Windows After Startup
▪ Restart services	Troubleshooting Windows After Startup
▪ Uninstall/reinstall/update applications	Troubleshooting Windows After Startup
▪ Add resources	Troubleshooting Windows After Startup
▪ Verify requirements	Troubleshooting Windows After Startup
▪ System file check	Troubleshooting Windows After Startup
▪ Repair Windows	Troubleshooting Windows After Startup
▪ Restore	Troubleshooting Windows After Startup
▪ Reimage	Troubleshooting Windows Startup
▪ Roll back updates	Troubleshooting Windows After Startup
▪ Rebuild Windows profiles	Troubleshooting Windows Startup

3.2   Given a scenario, troubleshoot common personal computer (PC) security issues.

Objectives	Primary Module
• Common symptoms	Security Strategies
▪ Unable to access the network	Security Strategies
▪ Desktop alerts	Security Strategies
▪ False alerts regarding antivirus protection	Security Strategies
▪ Altered system or personal files	Security Strategies
• Missing/renamed files	Security Strategies
▪ Unwanted notifications within the OS	Security Strategies
▪ OS update failures	Security Strategies
• Browser-related symptoms	Security Strategies
▪ Random/frequent pop-ups	Security Strategies
▪ Certificate warnings	Security Strategies
▪ Redirection	Security Strategies

3.3   Given a scenario, use best practice procedures for malware removal.

Objectives	Primary Module
1. Investigate and verify malware symptoms	Security Strategies
2. Quarantine infected systems	Security Strategies
3. Disable System Restore in Windows	Security Strategies
4. Remediate infected systems	Security Strategies
a. Update anti-malware software	Security Strategies
b. Scanning and removal techniques (e.g., safe mode, preinstallation environment)	Security Strategies
5. Schedule scans and run updates	Security Strategies
6. Enable System Restore and create a restore point in Windows	Security Strategies
7. Educate the end user	Security Strategies

3.4   Given a scenario, troubleshoot common mobile OS and application issues.

Objectives	Primary Module
• Common symptoms	Mobile Device Security
▪ Application fails to launch	Mobile Device Security
▪ Application fails to close/crashes	Mobile Device Security
▪ Application fails to update	Mobile Device Security
▪ Slow to respond	Mobile Device Security
▪ OS fails to update	Mobile Device Security
▪ Battery life issues	Mobile Device Security
▪ Randomly reboots	Mobile Device Security

Objectives	Primary Module
▪ Connectivity issues	Mobile Device Security
• Bluetooth	Mobile Device Security
• WiFi	Mobile Device Security
• Near-field communication (NFC)	Mobile Device Security
• AirDrop	Mobile Device Security
▪ Screen does not autorotate	Mobile Device Security

3.5   Given a scenario, troubleshoot common mobile OS and application security issues.

Objectives	Primary Module
• Security concerns	Mobile Device Security
▪ Android package (APK) source	Mobile Device Security
▪ Developer mode	Mobile Device Security
▪ Root access/jailbreak	Mobile Device Security
▪ Bootleg/malicious application	Mobile Device Security
• Application spoofing	Mobile Device Security
• Common symptoms	Mobile Device Security
▪ High network traffic	Mobile Device Security
▪ Sluggish response time	Mobile Device Security
▪ Data-usage limit notification	Mobile Device Security
▪ Limited Internet connectivity	Mobile Device Security
▪ No Internet connectivity	Mobile Device Security
▪ High number of ads	Mobile Device Security
▪ Fake security warnings	Mobile Device Security
▪ Unexpected application behavior	Mobile Device Security
▪ Leaked personal files/data	Mobile Device Security

4.0 Operational Procedures

4.1   Given a scenario, implement best practices associated with documentation and support systems information management.

Objectives	Primary Module
• Ticketing systems	The Complex World of IT Professionals
▪ User information	The Complex World of IT Professionals
▪ Device information	The Complex World of IT Professionals
▪ Description of problems	The Complex World of IT Professionals
▪ Categories	The Complex World of IT Professionals
▪ Severity	The Complex World of IT Professionals
▪ Escalation levels	The Complex World of IT Professionals
▪ Clear, concise written communication	The Complex World of IT Professionals
• Problem description	The Complex World of IT Professionals

Objectives	Primary Module
• Progress notes	The Complex World of IT Professionals
• Problem resolution	The Complex World of IT Professionals
• Asset management	The Complex World of IT Professionals
▪ Inventory lists	The Complex World of IT Professionals
▪ Database system	The Complex World of IT Professionals
▪ Asset tags and IDs	The Complex World of IT Professionals
▪ Procurement life cycle	The Complex World of IT Professionals
▪ Warranty and licensing	The Complex World of IT Professionals
▪ Assigned users	The Complex World of IT Professionals
• Types of documents	The Complex World of IT Professionals
▪ Acceptable use policy (AUP)	The Complex World of IT Professionals
▪ Network topology diagram	The Complex World of IT Professionals
▪ Regulatory compliance requirements	The Complex World of IT Professionals
• Splash screens	The Complex World of IT Professionals
▪ Incident reports	Security Strategies
▪ Standard operating procedures	The Complex World of IT Professionals
• Procedures for custom installation of software package	The Complex World of IT Professionals
▪ New-user setup checklist	The Complex World of IT Professionals
▪ End-user termination checklist	The Complex World of IT Professionals
• Knowledge base/articles	The Complex World of IT Professionals

4.2 Explain basic change-management best practices.

Objectives	Primary Module
• Documented business processes	The Complex World of IT Professionals
▪ Rollback plan	The Complex World of IT Professionals
▪ Sandbox testing	The Complex World of IT Professionals
▪ Responsible staff member	The Complex World of IT Professionals
• Change management	The Complex World of IT Professionals
▪ Request forms	The Complex World of IT Professionals
▪ Purpose of the change	The Complex World of IT Professionals
▪ Scope of the change	The Complex World of IT Professionals
▪ Date and time of the change	The Complex World of IT Professionals
▪ Affected systems/impact	The Complex World of IT Professionals
▪ Risk analysis	The Complex World of IT Professionals
• Risk level	The Complex World of IT Professionals
▪ Change board approvals	The Complex World of IT Professionals
▪ End-user acceptance	The Complex World of IT Professionals

4.3   Given a scenario, implement workstation backup and recovery methods.

Objectives	Primary Module
• Backup and recovery	Maintaining Windows
▪ Full	Maintaining Windows
▪ Incremental	Maintaining Windows
▪ Differential	Maintaining Windows
▪ Synthetic	Maintaining Windows
• Backup testing	Maintaining Windows
▪ Frequency	Maintaining Windows
• Backup rotation schemes	Maintaining Windows
▪ On site vs. off site	Maintaining Windows
▪ Grandfather-father-son (GFS)	Maintaining Windows
▪ 3-2-1 backup rule	Maintaining Windows

4.4   Given a scenario, use common safety procedures.

Objectives	Primary Module
• Electrostatic discharge (ESD) straps	Safety Procedures and Environmental Concerns
• ESD mats	Safety Procedures and Environmental Concerns
• Equipment grounding	Safety Procedures and Environmental Concerns
• Proper power handling	Safety Procedures and Environmental Concerns
• Proper component handling and storage	Safety Procedures and Environmental Concerns
• Antistatic bags	Safety Procedures and Environmental Concerns
• Compliance with government regulations	Safety Procedures and Environmental Concerns
• Personal safety	Safety Procedures and Environmental Concerns
▪ Disconnect power before repairing PC	Safety Procedures and Environmental Concerns
▪ Lifting techniques	Safety Procedures and Environmental Concerns
▪ Electrical fire safety	Safety Procedures and Environmental Concerns
▪ Safety goggles	Safety Procedures and Environmental Concerns
▪ Air filtration mask	Safety Procedures and Environmental Concerns

4.5   Summarize environmental impacts and local environmental controls.

Objectives	Primary Module
• Material safety data sheet (MSDS)/documentation for handling and disposal	Safety Procedures and Environmental Concerns
▪ Proper battery disposal	Safety Procedures and Environmental Concerns
▪ Proper toner disposal	Safety Procedures and Environmental Concerns
▪ Proper disposal of other devices and assets	Safety Procedures and Environmental Concerns
• Temperature, humidity-level awareness, and proper ventilation	Safety Procedures and Environmental Concerns
▪ Location/equipment placement	Safety Procedures and Environmental Concerns
▪ Dust cleanup	Safety Procedures and Environmental Concerns
▪ Compressed air/vacuums	Safety Procedures and Environmental Concerns

Objectives	Primary Module
• Power surges, under-voltage events, and power failures	Safety Procedures and Environmental Concerns
▪ Battery backup	Safety Procedures and Environmental Concerns
▪ Surge suppressor	Safety Procedures and Environmental Concerns

4.6   Explain the importance of prohibited content/activity and privacy, licensing, and policy concepts.

Objectives	Primary Module
• Incident response	Security Strategies
▪ Chain of custody	Security Strategies
▪ Inform management/law enforcement as necessary	Security Strategies
▪ Copy of drive (data integrity and preservation)	Security Strategies
▪ Documentation of incident	Security Strategies
• Licensing/digital rights management (DRM)/end-user license agreement (EULA)	Security Strategies
▪ Valid licenses	Security Strategies
▪ Non-expired licenses	Security Strategies
▪ Personal use license vs. corporate use license	Security Strategies
▪ Open source license	Security Strategies
• Regulated data	Security Strategies
▪ Credit card transactions	Security Strategies
▪ Personal government-issued information	Security Strategies
▪ PII	Security Strategies
▪ Healthcare data	Security Strategies
▪ Data retention requirements	Security Strategies

4.7   Given a scenario, use proper communication techniques and professionalism.

Objectives	Primary Module
• Professional appearance and attire	The Complex World of IT Professionals
▪ Match the required attire of the given environment	The Complex World of IT Professionals
• Formal	The Complex World of IT Professionals
• Business casual	The Complex World of IT Professionals
• Use proper language and avoid jargon, acronyms, and slang, when applicable	The Complex World of IT Professionals
• Maintain a positive attitude/project confidence	The Complex World of IT Professionals
• Actively listen, take notes, and avoid interrupting the customer	The Complex World of IT Professionals
• Be culturally sensitive	The Complex World of IT Professionals
▪ Use appropriate professional titles, when applicable	The Complex World of IT Professionals
• Be on time (if late, contact the customer)	The Complex World of IT Professionals
• Avoid distractions	The Complex World of IT Professionals
▪ Personal calls	The Complex World of IT Professionals
▪ Texting/social media sites	The Complex World of IT Professionals
▪ Personal interruptions	The Complex World of IT Professionals

Objectives	Primary Module
• Dealing with difficult customers or situations	The Complex World of IT Professionals
▪ Do not argue with customers or be defensive	The Complex World of IT Professionals
▪ Avoid dismissing customer problems	The Complex World of IT Professionals
▪ Avoid being judgmental	The Complex World of IT Professionals
▪ Clarify customer statements (ask open-ended questions to narrow the scope of the problem, restate the issue, or question to verify understanding)	The Complex World of IT Professionals
▪ Do not disclose experience via social media outlets	The Complex World of IT Professionals
• Set and meet expectations/time line and communicate status with the customer	The Complex World of IT Professionals
▪ Offer repair/replacement options, as needed	The Complex World of IT Professionals
▪ Provide proper documentation on the services provided	The Complex World of IT Professionals
▪ Follow up with customer/user at a later date to verify satisfaction	The Complex World of IT Professionals
• Deal appropriately with customers' confidential and private materials	The Complex World of IT Professionals
▪ Located on a computer, desktop, printer, etc.	The Complex World of IT Professionals

4.8   Identify the basics of scripting.

Objectives	Primary Module
• Script file types	Linux and Scripting
▪ .bat	Linux and Scripting
▪ .ps1	Linux and Scripting
▪ .vbs	Linux and Scripting
▪ .sh	Linux and Scripting
▪ .js	Linux and Scripting
▪ .py	Linux and Scripting
• Use cases for scripting	Linux and Scripting
▪ Basic automation	Linux and Scripting
▪ Restarting machines	Linux and Scripting
▪ Remapping network drives	Linux and Scripting
▪ Installation of applications	Linux and Scripting
▪ Automated backups	Linux and Scripting
▪ Gathering of information/data	Linux and Scripting
▪ Initiating updates	Linux and Scripting
• Other considerations when using scripts	Linux and Scripting
▪ Unintentionally introducing malware	Linux and Scripting
▪ Inadvertently changing system settings	Linux and Scripting
▪ Browser or system crashes due to mishandling of resources	Linux and Scripting

4.9 Given a scenario, use remote access technologies.

Objectives	Primary Module
• Methods/tools	Network Security and Troubleshooting
▪ RDP	Network Security and Troubleshooting
▪ VPN	Network Security and Troubleshooting
▪ Virtual network computer (VNC)	Network Security and Troubleshooting
▪ Secure Shell (SSH)	Linux and Scripting
▪ Remote monitoring and management (RMM)	Network Security and Troubleshooting
▪ Microsoft Remote Assistance (MSRA)	Network Security and Troubleshooting
▪ Third-party tools	Network Security and Troubleshooting
• Screen-sharing software	Network Security and Troubleshooting
• Video-conferencing software	Network Security and Troubleshooting
• File transfer software	Network Security and Troubleshooting
• Desktop management software	Network Security and Troubleshooting
• Security considerations of each access method	Network Security and Troubleshooting

Introduction: CompTIA A+ Guide to IT Technical Support

CompTIA A+ Guide to IT Technical Support, Eleventh Edition was written to be the very best tool on the market today to prepare you to support users and their resources on networks, desktops, laptops, mobile devices, virtual machines, and in the cloud. This edition has been updated to include the most current hardware and software technologies; this text takes you from the just-a-user level to the I-can-fix-this level for hardware, software, networks, and virtual computing infrastructures. It achieves its goals with an unusually effective combination of tools that powerfully reinforce both concepts and hands-on, real-world experiences. It also provides thorough preparation for the content on the new CompTIA A+ Core 1 and Core 2 Certification exams. Competency in using a computer is a prerequisite to using this text. No background knowledge of electronics or networking is assumed. An appropriate prerequisite course for this text would be a general course in computer applications.

This text includes:

- **Several in-depth, hands-on projects** at the end of each module that invite you to immediately apply and reinforce critical thinking and troubleshooting skills and are designed to make certain that you not only understand the material but also execute procedures and make decisions on your own.
- **Comprehensive review and practice end-of-module material**, including a module summary, key terms list, critical thinking questions that focus on the type of scenarios you might expect on A+ exam questions, and real-world problems to solve.
- **Step-by-step instructions** on installation, maintenance, optimization of system performance, and troubleshooting.
- **A wide array of photos, drawings, and screenshots** support the text, displaying in detail the exact software and hardware features you will need to understand to set up, maintain, and troubleshoot physical and virtual computers and small networks.

In addition, the carefully structured, clearly written text is accompanied by graphics that provide the visual input essential to learning and to help students master difficult subject matter. For instructors using the text in a classroom, instructor resources are available online.

Coverage is balanced—while focusing on new technologies and software, including virtualization, cloud computing, the Internet of Things, and Windows 10/11, the text also covers the real world of an IT support technician, where some older technologies remain in widespread use and still need support. For example, the text covers M.2 motherboard slots and NVMe, the latest drive interface standard for solid-state devices (SSDs), but also addresses how to install SSDs and magnetic hard drives using the older Serial Advanced Technology Attachment (SATA) interfaces. The text focuses on Windows 10, the most popular operating system for desktops and laptops, but also covers

Windows 11, macOS, Linux, and Chrome OS for desktops and Android and iOS for mobile devices. Other covered content that is new with the latest A+ Core 1 and Core 2 exams includes enhanced coverage for Domain Name Service (DNS), security and backup techniques, software troubleshooting, macOS, Linux, and scripting.

This text provides thorough preparation for CompTIA's A+ Core 1 and Core 2 Certification examinations. This certification credential's popularity among employers is growing exponentially, and obtaining certification increases your ability to gain employment and improve your salary. To get more information on CompTIA's A+ certification and its sponsoring organization, the Computing Technology Industry Association, see their website at *www.comptia.org*.

Features

To ensure a successful learning experience, this text includes the following pedagogical features:

- **A Clean Split Between Core 1 and Core 2.** The first 10 modules focus on content on the A+ Core 1 exam, while the remaining 11 modules and an appendix focus on the A+ Core 2 exam. The appendix "Safety Procedures and Environmental Concerns," covered on the Core 2 exam, is set apart from Core 2 modules as an appendix to make it easier for students studying modules about hardware to find this content, which is so important to protecting yourself, the hardware, and the environment.
- **Learning Objectives.** Every module opens with lists of learning objectives and A+ certification objectives that set the stage for you to absorb the lessons of the text.
- **Comprehensive Step-by-Step Troubleshooting Guidance.** Troubleshooting guidelines are included in almost every module. In addition, the Core 1 module "Power Supplies and Troubleshooting Computer Problems" gives insights into general approaches to troubleshooting that help apply the specifics detailed in each module for different hardware and software problems. Several Core 2 modules focus on troubleshooting networks, applications, and Windows.
- **Step-by-Step Procedures.** The text is chock-full of step-by-step procedures covering subjects from hardware and operating system installations and maintenance to troubleshooting the boot process or a failed network connection and optimizing system performance.
- **Visual Learning.** Numerous visually detailed photographs, three-dimensional art, and screenshots support the text, displaying hardware and software features exactly as you will see them in your work.
- **CompTIA A+ Objectives Mapped to Modules.** This table lists the module that provides the primary content for each certification objective on the A+ exams. This is a valuable tool for quick reference.
- **Applying Concepts.** These sections offer real-life, practical applications for the material being discussed. Whether outlining a task, developing a scenario, or providing pointers, the Applying Concepts sections give you a chance to apply what you've learned to a typical computer or network problem, so you can understand how you will use the material in your professional life.
- **Page edge colors distinguish Core 1 modules from Core 2 modules.** To help you keep track of which exam is covered by each module, the pages of modules with Core 1 content are edged in teal while the Core 2 modules are edged in orange. Although not essential, it is suggested that you cover the Core 1 modules before you complete the Core 2 modules. This suggestion especially applies to the modules on networking.

`Core 1 Objective`

`Core 2 Objective`

`Notes ◐`

`Exam Tip ✔`

`Caution ❗`

`Core to Core ⇆`

- **Exam Objectives.** The relevant exam objective numbers are included for all content that relates to CompTIA's A+ Core 1 and A+ Core 2 Certification exams. This unique feature highlights the relevant content at a glance, so that you can pay extra attention to the material.
- **Notes.** Numbered Note boxes highlight additional helpful information related to the subject being discussed.
- **Exam Tip Boxes.** These boxes highlight additional insights and tips to remember if you are planning to take the CompTIA A+ exams.
- **Caution Boxes.** These icons highlight critical safety information. Follow these instructions carefully to protect the computer and its data and to ensure your own safety.
- **Core to Core.** These boxes point you to content in other modules that might be helpful in understanding the topic being discussed and reference content that you may find on both the Core 1 and Core 2 exams.

- **End-of-Module Material.** Each module closes with the following features, which reinforce the material covered in the module and provide real-world, hands-on testing:
  - **Module Summary:** This bulleted list of concise statements summarizes all major points of the module.
  - **Key Terms:** The content of each module is further reinforced by an end-of-module key term list. The definitions of all terms are included with this text in a full-length glossary.
  - **Thinking Critically Questions:** You can test your understanding of each module with a comprehensive set of "Thinking Critically" questions to help you synthesize and apply what you've learned in scenarios that test your skills at the same depth as the A+ exams.
  - **Hands-On Projects:** These sections give you practice using the skills you have just studied so that you can learn by doing and know you have mastered a skill.
  - **Real Problems, Real Solutions:** Each comprehensive problem allows you to find out if you can apply what you've learned in the module to a real-life situation.
- **Student Companion Site.** Additional content included on the companion website includes information on electricity and multimeters as well as FAT details. Other helpful online references include Frequently Asked Questions, sample reports, a "Computer Inventory and Maintenance" form, and troubleshooting flowcharts.

What's New in the Eleventh Edition

Here's a summary of what's new in the Eleventh Edition:

- Content maps to all of the latest CompTIA's A+ Core 1 and Core 2 exams.
- There is a clean split between Core 1 and Core 2 modules. No module contains overlapping content.
- The modules focus on Windows 10 with some content about Windows 11, which is the same approach taken on the A+ Core 2 exam.
- New content is added (all new content was also new to the A+ Core 1 and Core 2 exams).
  - Windows 11 is added. Operating systems covered now include Windows 10 and Windows 11. Windows 8 and Windows 7 are no longer covered. New content on Linux, macOS, and mobile operating systems (Android, iOS, and iPadOS) is added.
  - Enhanced content on DNS, security, backups, call tracking, and troubleshooting is included in various modules.
  - Because we no longer have modules that contain a mix of Core 1 and Core 2 content, the new Core 2 module "Network Security and Troubleshooting" has been added, with enhanced coverage of these topics. Before studying this module, it is suggested you complete the Core 1 modules "Networking Fundamentals" and "Network Infrastructure and Cloud Computing."
  - To address new content on mobile devices, we have two modules on this topic: the Core 1 module "Supporting Mobile Devices" and the Core 2 module "Mobile Device Security."
  - New content on the macOS has been added, and this topic now has its own Core 2 module, "Supporting macOS."
  - New content on Linux and understanding and writing scripts is covered in the module "Linux and Scripting."
  - Hands-On Projects in several modules use virtual machines so that you get plenty of practice using this essential cloud technology.

Features of the New Edition

Module Objectives appear at the beginning of each module, so you know exactly what topics and skills are covered.

A+ **Exam Tips** include key points pertinent to the A+ exams. The icons identify the sections that cover information you will need to know for the A+ certification exams.

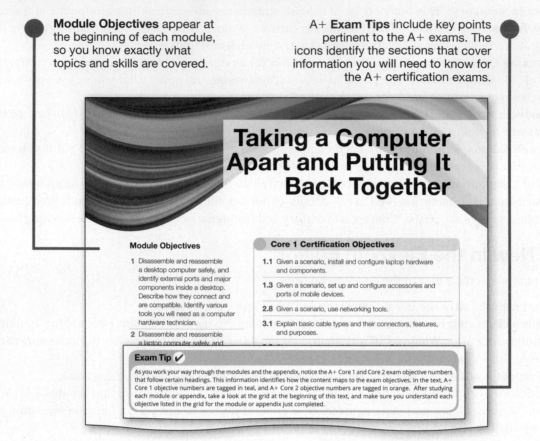

Taking a Computer Apart and Putting It Back Together

Module Objectives

1 Disassemble and reassemble a desktop computer safely, and identify external ports and major components inside a desktop. Describe how they connect and are compatible. Identify various tools you will need as a computer hardware technician.

2 Disassemble and reassemble a laptop computer safely, and

Core 1 Certification Objectives

1.1 Given a scenario, install and configure laptop hardware and components.

1.3 Given a scenario, set up and configure accessories and ports of mobile devices.

2.8 Given a scenario, use networking tools.

3.1 Explain basic cable types and their connectors, features, and purposes.

Exam Tip ✔

As you work your way through the modules and the appendix, notice the A+ Core 1 and Core 2 exam objective numbers that follow certain headings. This information identifies how the content maps to the exam objectives. In the text, A+ Core 1 objective numbers are tagged in teal, and A+ Core 2 objective numbers are tagged in orange. After studying each module or appendix, take a look at the grid at the beginning of this text, and make sure you understand each objective listed in the grid for the module or appendix just completed.

Caution ❗

When you power down a computer and even turn off the power switch on the rear of the computer case, residual power is still on. Some motherboards have a small light inside the case to remind you of this fact and to warn you that power is still getting to the system. Therefore, be sure to always unplug the power cord before opening a case.

Cautions identify critical safety information.

Visual full-color graphics, photos, and screenshots accurately depict computer hardware and software components.

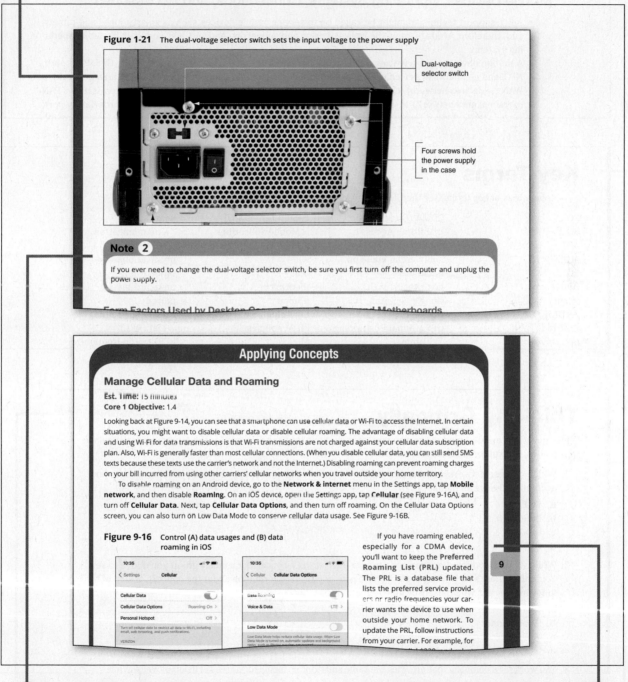

Figure 1-21   The dual-voltage selector switch sets the input voltage to the power supply

Dual-voltage selector switch

Four screws hold the power supply in the case

Note 2

If you ever need to change the dual-voltage selector switch, be sure you first turn off the computer and unplug the power supply.

Form Factors Used by Desktop Cases, Power Supplies, and Motherboards

Applying Concepts

Manage Cellular Data and Roaming

Est. Time: 15 minutes
Core 1 Objective: 1.4

Looking back at Figure 9-14, you can see that a smartphone can use cellular data or Wi-Fi to access the Internet. In certain situations, you might want to disable cellular data or disable cellular roaming. The advantage of disabling cellular data and using Wi-Fi for data transmissions is that Wi-Fi transmissions are not charged against your cellular data subscription plan. Also, Wi-Fi is generally faster than most cellular connections. (When you disable cellular data, you can still send SMS texts because these texts use the carrier's network and not the Internet.) Disabling roaming can prevent roaming charges on your bill incurred from using other carriers' cellular networks when you travel outside your home territory.

To disable roaming on an Android device, go to the **Network & internet** menu in the Settings app, tap **Mobile network**, and then disable **Roaming**. On an iOS device, open the Settings app, tap **Cellular** (see Figure 9-16A), and turn off **Cellular Data**. Next, tap **Cellular Data Options**, and then turn off roaming. On the Cellular Data Options screen, you can also turn on Low Data Mode to conserve cellular data usage. See Figure 9-16B.

Figure 9-16   Control (A) data usages and (B) data roaming in iOS

If you have roaming enabled, especially for a CDMA device, you'll want to keep the **Preferred Roaming List (PRL)** updated. The PRL is a database file that lists the preferred service providers or radio frequencies your carrier wants the device to use when outside your home network. To update the PRL, follow instructions from your carrier. For example, for

9

Notes indicate additional content that might be of student interest or information about how best to study.

Applying Concepts sections provide practical advice or pointers by illustrating basic principles, identifying common problems, providing steps to practice skills, and encouraging solutions.

Module Summary bulleted lists of concise statements summarize
all major points of the module, organized by primary headings.

Module Summary

9

Mobile Devices, Operating Systems, Connections, and Accessories

- An IT support technician might be called on to service mobile devices such as smartphones and tablets, and, therefore, needs to know the basics of using and supporting Android, iOS, and iPadOS mobile operating systems.
- A mobile device might have several antennas for wireless connections—primarily Wi-Fi, GPS, Bluetooth, NFC, and cellular. The device uses a Wi-Fi or cellular antenna to connect to a LAN (local area network), a WAN (wide area network), or to create its own hotspot, and it uses Bluetooth or NFC to connect to a PAN (personal area network). A wired connection might use a microUSB, miniUSB, USB-C, or proprietary port,

Key Terms

For explanations of key terms, see the Glossary for this text.

2G	CDMA (Code Division	IMSI (International	near-field
3G	Multiple Access)	Mobile Subscriber	communication
4G	cellular data	Identity)	(NFC)
4G LTE	commercial mail app	iOS	notifications
5G	dock	iPad	off-boarding
ActiveSync	favorites tray	iPadOS	on-boarding
agent	Google account	iPhone	paired
AirDrop	Google Play	Lightning port	Preferred Roaming
Android	GPS (Global Positioning	MDM policies	List (PRL)
app drawer	System)	Microsoft 365	RFID (radio-frequency

Thinking Critically

These questions are designed to prepare you for the critical thinking required for the A+ exams and may use information from other modules and the web.

1. Which of these network connections would allow your smartphone to sync your photos to your online account? (Choose all that apply.)
   a. Wi-Fi
   b. Bluetooth
   c. GPS
   d. Cellular

2. While visiting a coffee shop, you see a poster advertising a concert for a music group you'd love to see. You notice there's an NFC tag at the bottom with additional information about the concert. Which of the following devices would likely be able to read the NFC tag?
   a. GPS
   b. Smartphone
   c. eReader
   d. Laptop

3. You work for a company that provides the same smartphone model for dozens of its employees. While

Key Terms are defined as they are introduced and listed at the end of each module. Definitions can be found in the Glossary.

Thinking Critically sections require you to analyze and apply what you've learned.

Hands-On Project 1-4

1

Closing the Case

Est. Time: 15 minutes
Core 1 Objective: 3.4

The case cover to your desktop computer is off from doing the previous exercises. Before you close your case, it's always a good idea to quickly clean it first. Using a can of compressed air, blow the dust away from fans and other components inside the case. Be careful not to touch components unless you are properly grounded. When you're done, close the case cover.

Real Problems, Real Solutions

Real Problem 1-1

Planning Your Computer Repair Toolkit

Est. Time: 30 minutes
Core 1 Objectives: 2.8, 3.4

Do research online to find the following tools for sale: ESD strap, set of flathead and Phillips-head screwdrivers, can of compressed air, monitor-cleaning wipes, multimeter, power supply tester, cable ties, flashlight, loopback plug to test an Ethernet port, POST diagnostic card, and toolbox.

(continues)

Real Problems, Real Solutions allow you to apply what you've learned in the module to a real-life situation.

Hands-On Projects provide practical exercises at the end of each module so that you can practice the skills as they are learned.

What's New with CompTIA® A+ Certification

The CompTIA A+ certification includes two exams, and you must pass both to become CompTIA A+ certified. The two exams are Core 1 (220-1101) and Core 2 (220-1102).

Here is a breakdown of the domain content covered on the two A+ exams.

CompTIA A+ 220-1101 Exam	
Domain	Percentage of Examination
1.0 Mobile Devices	15%
2.0 Networking	20%
3.0 Hardware	25%
4.0 Virtualization and Cloud Computing	11%
5.0 Hardware and Network Troubleshooting	29%
Total	**100%**

CompTIA A+ 220-1102 Exam	
Domain	Percentage of Examination
1.0 Operating Systems	31%
2.0 Security	25%
3.0 Software Troubleshooting	22%
4.0 Operational Procedures	22%
Total	**100%**

Instructor's Materials

Please visit *cengage.com* and log in to access instructor-specific resources, which include the Instructor's Manual, Solutions Manual, test-creation tools, PowerPoint Presentation, and Syllabus.

Instructor's Manual: The Instructor's Manual that accompanies this textbook includes additional instructional material to assist in class preparation, including suggestions for classroom activities, discussion topics, and additional projects.

Solutions: Answers or solution guidance to the end-of-module material are provided. These include the answers to the Thinking Critically questions and solution guidance to the Hands-On Projects and Real Problems, Real Solutions exercises, as well as Lab Manual Solutions.

Cengage Learning Testing Powered by Cognero: This flexible, online system allows you to do the following:

- Author, edit, and manage test bank content from multiple Cengage Learning solutions.
- Create multiple test versions in an instant.
- Deliver tests from your LMS, your classroom, or wherever you want.

PowerPoint Presentations: This text comes with Microsoft PowerPoint slides for each module. These are included as a teaching aid for classroom presentation, to make available to students on the network for module review, or to be printed for classroom distribution. Instructors, please feel free to add your own slides for additional topics you introduce to the class.

Total Solutions for CompTIA A+

MindTap for A+ Guide to IT Technical Support, Eleventh Edition

MindTap is an online learning solution designed to help students master the skills they need in today's workforce. Research shows employers need critical thinkers, troubleshooters, and creative problem-solvers to stay relevant in our fast-paced, technology-driven world. MindTap helps you achieve this with assignments and activities that provide hands-on practice, real-life relevance, mastery of difficult concepts, and certification test prep. Students are guided through assignments that progress from basic knowledge and understanding before moving on to more challenging problems. MindTap features include the following:

- Live Virtual Machine labs allow you to practice, explore, and try different solutions in a safe sandbox environment.
- The Adaptive Test Prep (ATP) app is designed to help you quickly review and assess your understanding of key IT concepts. Test yourself multiple times to track your progress and improvement by filtering results by correct answer, by all questions answered, or by only incorrect answers to show where additional study help is needed.
- IT for Life assignments encourage you to stay current with what's happening in the IT field.
- Pre- and Post-Quizzes assess your understanding of key concepts at the beginning and end of the course.
- All new Reflection activities encourage classroom and online discussion of key issues covered in the modules.

MindTap is designed around learning objectives and provides the analytics and reporting so the instructor can easily see where the class stands in terms of progress, engagement, and completion rates. Use the content and learning path as is, or pick and choose how our materials will wrap around the course as it is taught. The instructor controls what the students see and when they see it. Learn more at *cengage.com/mindtap*.

- Instant Access Code: ISBN: 9780357674185
- Printed Access Code: ISBN: 9780357674185

Lab Manual for A+ Guide to IT Technical Support, Eleventh Edition

The Lab Manual, both in print and as part of your MindTap course, contains over 110 labs to provide students with additional hands-on experience and to help prepare for the A+ exam. The Lab Manual includes lab activities, objectives, materials lists, step-by-step procedures, illustrations, and review questions.

- Lab Manual ISBN: 9780357674567

Acknowledgments

Thank you to the wonderful people at Cengage who continue to give their best and go the extra mile to make the books what they are: Mark Santee, Natalie Onderdonk, and Brooke Greenhouse. We're grateful for all you've done. Thank you, Mary Pat Shaffer, our Developmental Editor extraordinaire, for upholding us with your unwavering, calm demeanor in the face of impossible schedules and inboxes, and to Elizabeth Kelly, our excellent copyeditor/proofreader. Thank you, Danielle Shaw, for your careful attention to the technical accuracy of the book.

Thank you to all the people who took the time to voluntarily send encouragement and suggestions for improvements to the previous editions. Your input and help are very much appreciated. The reviewers of this edition provided invaluable insights and showed a genuine interest in the book's success. Thank you to:

Luis Alfonso Lopez Lerma – Southwest University at El Paso

Kimberly Perez – Tidewater Community College

Gregg Tennefoss – Tidewater Community College

To the instructors and learners who use this book, we invite and encourage you to send suggestions or corrections for future editions. Please write to the author team at *jean.andrews@cengage.com*. We never ignore a good idea! And to instructors, if you have ideas for how to make a class in A+ Preparation a success, please share your ideas with other instructors!

Thank you to our families and friends who have supported and encouraged us through the writing process.

This book is dedicated to the covenant of God with man on earth.

Jean Andrews, Ph.D.
Joy Dark Shelton
Nicholas Pierce

About the Authors

Jean Andrews has more than 30 years of experience in the computer industry, including more than 13 years in the college classroom. She has worked in a variety of businesses and corporations designing, writing, and supporting application software; managing a help desk for computer support technicians; and troubleshooting wide area networks. Jean has written numerous books on software, hardware, and the Internet, including the best-selling *CompTIA A+ Core 1 Exam Guide to Computing Infrastructure, Tenth Edition*, and *CompTIA A+ Core 2 Exam Guide to Operating Systems and Security, Tenth Edition*. She lives in northern Georgia.

Joy Dark Shelton has worked in the IT field as a help-desk technician providing first-level support for a company with presence in 29 states, a second-tier technician in healthcare IT, and an operations specialist designing support protocols and structures. As a teacher, Joy has taught online courses in IT and has taught English as a Second Language in the United States and South America. She has helped write several technical textbooks with Jean Andrews. She also creates many photographs used in educational content. Joy and her husband, Jason, live in northwest Georgia with their two daughters and Brittany dog.

Nicholas Pierce is an information systems and cybersecurity instructor with a background in radio frequency and network troubleshooting. Nicholas delivers courses to high schools, community colleges, and universities, as well as in the private sector as a contractor with the Department of Defense. Nicholas lives in Virginia Beach, Virginia.

Read This Before You Begin

The following hardware, software, and other equipment are needed to do the Hands-On Projects in each module:

- You need a working desktop computer and laptop that can be taken apart and reassembled. You also need a working computer on which you can install an operating system. These computers can be the same or different computers.
- Troubleshooting skills can better be practiced with an assortment of nonworking expansion cards that can be used to simulate problems.
- Windows 10 Pro is needed for most modules. In addition, Windows 11 is needed for the module "Installing Windows," and macOS is used in the module "Supporting macOS."
- Internet access is needed for most modules.
- Equipment required to work on hardware includes an electrostatic discharge strap and flathead and Phillips-head screwdrivers. In addition, a power supply tester, cable tester, and can of compressed air are useful. Network wiring tools needed for the module "Network Infrastructure and Cloud Computing" include a wire cutter, wire stripper, and crimper.
- An iOS or Android smartphone or tablet is needed for the modules "Supporting Mobile Devices" and "Mobile Device Security."
- A small-office-home-office (SOHO) router that includes a wireless access point is needed for the modules "Networking Fundamentals" and "Network Security and Troubleshooting."

Caution !

Before undertaking any of the lab exercises, starting with the module "Taking a Computer Apart and Putting It Back Together," please review the safety guidelines in the appendix "Safety Procedures and Environmental Concerns."

CompTIA.

Your Next Move Starts Here!

Get CompTIA certified to help achieve your career goals and gain a powerful, vendor-neutral credential that is trusted by employers.

Why get CompTIA certified?

Increase your confidence
91% of certification earners show increased confidence.*

Earn more money
77% of IT pros got a raise within six months of earning their certification.*

Stand out to employers
64% of IT decision makers say certified employers add additional value.**

Join a global community
92% of IT professionals hold at least one certification.**

Get ready for exam day.

- **Download the exam objectives:** Visit CompTIA.org to find the exam objectives for your IT certification and print them out. This is your roadmap!

- **Create your study plan:** Decide how many hours each week you are going to dedicate to studying, choose your preferred study tools and get to work. Studying is a unique experience. Download a study plan worksheet on CompTIA.org.

- **Get certified:** If you haven't already, use the coupon on this page when you purchase your exam voucher and schedule your exam. CompTIA offers flexible testing options to fit your busy life.

Choose your testing option.

Online testing
Earn a CompTIA certification online, from your home – or any quiet, distraction-free, secure location – at a time that's convenient for you.

In-person testing
Test at any of the Pearson VUE test centers around the world, where you can use their equipment under the supervision of a proctor.

To purchase your exam voucher and learn how to prepare for exam day, visit CompTIA.org.

*Pearson VUE 2021 Value of IT Certifications
**2021 Global Knowledge IT Skills and Salary Report

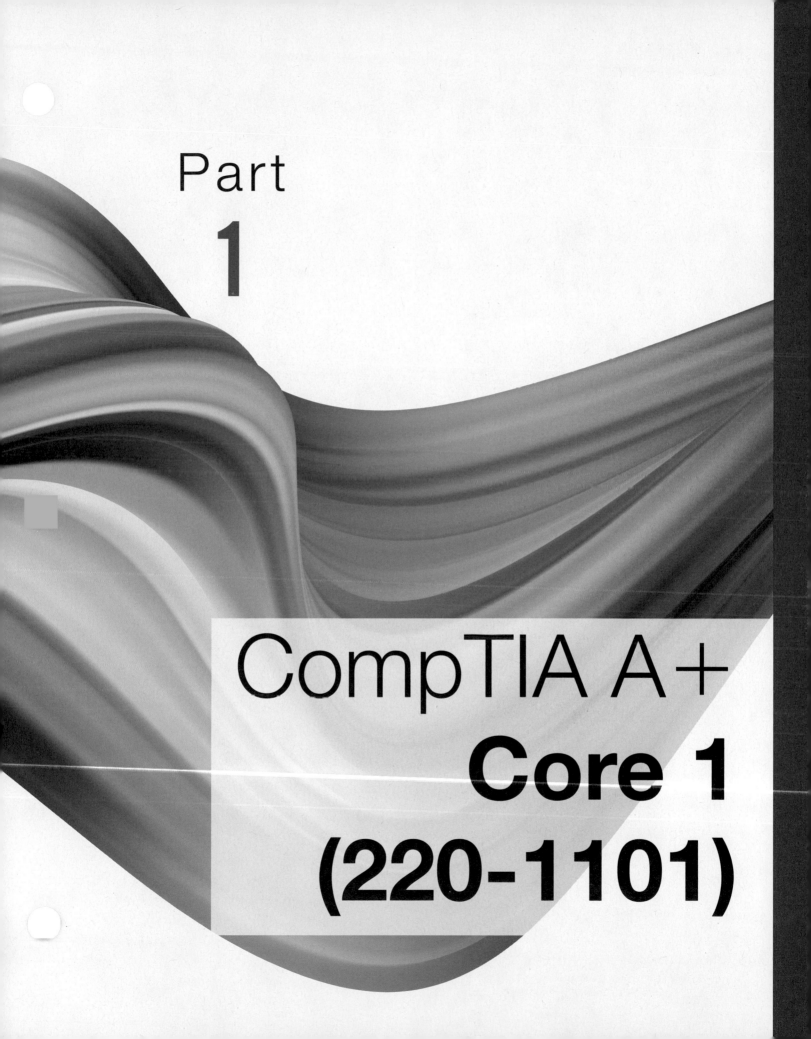

Part

1

CompTIA A+
Core 1
(220-1101)

Module
1

Taking a Computer Apart and Putting It Back Together

Module Objectives

1 Disassemble and reassemble a desktop computer safely, and identify external ports and major components inside a desktop. Describe how they connect and are compatible. Identify various tools you will need as a computer hardware technician.

2 Disassemble and reassemble a laptop computer safely, and identify external ports and slots and major internal components. Understand special concerns when supporting and maintaining laptops.

Core 1 Certification Objectives

1.1 Given a scenario, install and configure laptop hardware and components.

1.3 Given a scenario, set up and configure accessories and ports of mobile devices.

2.8 Given a scenario, use networking tools.

3.1 Explain basic cable types and their connectors, features, and purposes.

3.2 Given a scenario, install the appropriate RAM.

3.3 Given a scenario, select and install storage devices.

3.4 Given a scenario, install and configure motherboards, central processing units (CPUs), and add-on cards.

3.5 Given a scenario, install or replace the appropriate power supply.

Introduction

Like many other computer users, you have probably used your personal computer to play games, check your email, write papers, or build Excel worksheets. This text takes you from being an end user of your computer to becoming an information technology (IT) support technician able to support all types of personal computers. The only assumption made here is that you are a computer user—that is, you can turn on your machine, load a software package, and use that software to accomplish a task. No experience in electronics is assumed.

As an IT support technician, you'll want to become A+ certified, which is the industry standard certification for IT support technicians. This text prepares you to pass the A+ 220-1101 Core 1 and 220-1102 Core 2 exams by CompTIA (*comptia.org*). The exams are required by CompTIA for A+ certification.

In this module, you take apart and reassemble a desktop computer and laptop while discovering the various hardware components inside the cases. You also learn about the tools you need to work inside the case.

> **Exam Tip** ✔
>
> As you work your way through the modules and the appendix, notice the A+ Core 1 and Core 2 exam objective numbers that follow certain headings. This information identifies how the content maps to the exam objectives. In the text, A+ Core 1 objective numbers are tagged in teal, and A+ Core 2 objective numbers are tagged in orange. After studying each module or appendix, take a look at the grid at the beginning of this text, and make sure you understand each objective listed in the grid for the module or appendix just completed.

Taking apart and servicing a computer are tasks that every A+ certified technician needs to know how to do. As part of your preparation to become A+ certified, try to find old desktop and laptop computers you can take apart. If you can locate the service manual for a laptop, you should be able to take it apart, repair it (assuming the parts are still available and don't cost more than the computer is worth), and get it up and running again. Have fun with this module, and enjoy tinkering with these computers!

Exploring a Desktop Computer

 Core 1 Objectives 1.1, 2.8, 3.1, 3.2, 3.3, 3.4, 3.5

In this section of the module, you learn how to take apart a desktop computer and put it back together. This skill is needed in this module and others as you learn to add or replace computer parts inside the case and perhaps even build a system from scratch. As you read the following steps, you might want to refer to the Hands-On Projects at the end of the module, which allow you to follow along by taking a computer apart. As you do so, be sure to follow all the safety precautions found in the appendix "Safety Procedures and Environmental Concerns." In the steps that follow, each major computer component is identified and described. You learn much more about each component later in the text. Take your time—don't rush—as you take apart a computer for the first time. It can be a great learning experience or an expensive disaster! As you work, pay attention to the details and work with care.

Protecting Yourself and the Equipment

 Core 1 Objectives 1.1, 3.4

Protecting yourself and the equipment is essential for having a positive experience working inside a computer. When you follow the safety guidelines, you will be more likely to successfully complete your task and enjoy yourself while doing it. Remember to always ask your instructor for help if you have any questions about safety.

Follow these guidelines to protect yourself:

- Remove loose jewelry that might get caught in cables and components as you work.
- As you work, watch out for sharp edges on computer cases that can cut you.

- Consider the monitor and the power supply to be "black boxes." Never remove the cover or put your hands inside this equipment unless you know about the hazards of charged capacitors and have been trained to deal with them. The power supply and monitor contain enough power to kill you, even when they are unplugged.
- Power down the system and unplug it.
- For a computer, press and hold down the power button for three seconds to completely drain any residual power in the power supply.
- Never, ever touch the inside of a computer that is turned on. The one exception to this rule is when you're using a multimeter to measure voltage output.

Follow these guidelines to protect the equipment:

- Always wear an **ESD strap** (also called a ground bracelet, antistatic wrist strap, or ESD bracelet), which protects against electrostatic discharge when working inside the computer case. **Electrostatic discharge (ESD)** is another name for static electricity, which can damage chips and destroy motherboards, even though it might not be felt or seen with the naked eye. When you use the strap to connect or ground your hand to the case, as shown in Figure 1-1, any static electricity between you and the case is dissipated.

Figure 1-1   An ESD strap, which protects computer components from ESD, can clip to the side of the computer case and eliminate ESD between you and the case

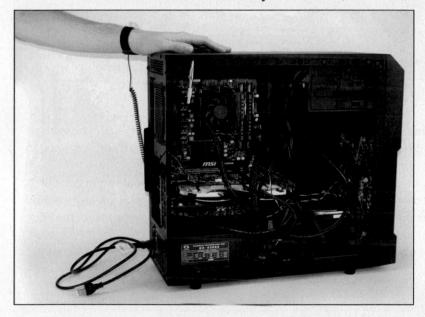

- If an ESD strap is unavailable or won't work, use a **ground mat**, also called an **ESD mat**, to dissipate ESD (see Figure 1-2). While the equipment is resting on the ground mat, it is protected from ESD; however, if you lift the equipment off the mat, it is no longer protected, unless you are wearing an ESD strap.

Figure 1-2   An ESD mat dissipates ESD and should be connected to the ground

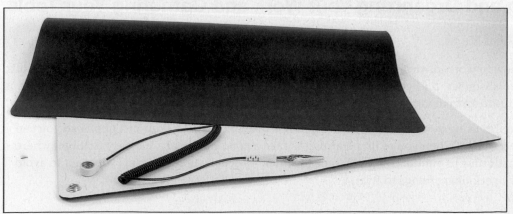

- Place equipment in a static shielding bag, also called an **antistatic bag**. These bags act as a type of Faraday cage, named after Michael Faraday, who built the first cage in 1836. A Faraday cage is any device that protects against an electromagnetic field. Save antistatic bags as you find them, and use them whenever you take a piece of equipment out of a computer. Remember that a device that is set on top of an antistatic bag is not protected; it is only protected when it is placed inside the bag (see Figure 1-3).

Figure 1-3   An antistatic bag helps protect components from ESD

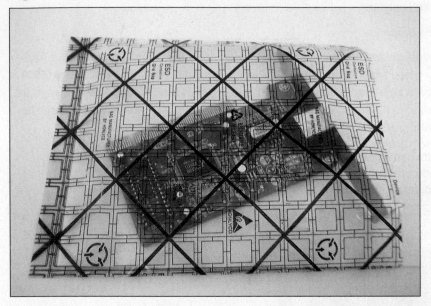

- Don't stack boards on top of each other. You could accidentally dislodge a chip this way. When you remove a circuit board or drive from a computer, carefully lay it on an antistatic mat or set it in an antistatic bag in a place where it won't get bumped.
- When handling motherboards, cards, or drives, don't touch the chips on the device. Hold expansion cards by the edges. Don't touch any soldered components on a card, and don't touch the edge connectors unless it's absolutely necessary. All this helps prevent damage from static electricity. Also, fingerprints on the edge connectors can cause later corrosion.
- To prevent damage to a microchip, don't touch it with a magnetized screwdriver.

Core to Core

It's important to know how to stay safe when working inside computers. Before opening a computer case and using the tools described in this section, be sure to read the appendix "Safety Procedures and Environmental Concerns." As you work inside a computer, follow all the safety guidelines discussed in that appendix.

Step 1: Planning and Organizing Your Work and Gathering Your Tools

Core 1 Objectives 2.8, 3.4

When you begin to learn how to work inside a computer case, make it a point to practice good organizational skills. If you keep your notes, tools, screws, and computer parts well organized, your work goes more smoothly and is more fun. Here are some tips to keep in mind:

- As you work, make notes using pencil and paper, and perhaps take photos with your cell phone so you can backtrack later if necessary. (When you're first learning to take a computer apart, it's easy to forget where everything fits when it's time to put the computer back together. Also, in troubleshooting, you want to avoid repeating actions or overlooking things to try.)

- To stay organized and avoid losing small parts, keep screws and spacers orderly and in one place, such as a cup or tray.
- In a classroom environment, after you have reassembled everything, have your instructor check your work before you put the cover back on and power up.

Tools Used by a Computer Hardware Technician

Every IT support technician who plans to repair desktop or laptop computers or mobile devices needs a handy toolbox with a few essential tools. Several hardware and software tools can help you maintain a computer and diagnose and repair computer problems. The tools you choose depend on the amount of money you can spend and the level of hardware support you expect to provide.

Essential tools for computer hardware troubleshooting are listed here, and several of them are shown in Figure 1-4. You can purchase some of these tools in a computer toolkit, although most toolkits contain items you really can do without.

Figure 1-4   Tools used by IT support technicians when maintaining, repairing, or upgrading computers

Here is a list of essential tools:

- An ESD strap (also called a ground bracelet)
- Flathead screwdriver
- Phillips-head or crosshead screwdriver
- Torx screwdriver set, particularly size T15
- Tweezers, preferably insulated ones, for picking pieces of paper out of printers or dropped screws out of tight places
- Software, including recovery DVDs or USB recovery drives for any operating system (OS) you might work on (you might need several, depending on the OSs you support), antivirus software on bootable DVDs or USB flash drives, and diagnostic software

The following tools might not be essential, but they are very convenient to have on hand:

- Cans of compressed air (see Figure 1-5), small portable compressor, or antistatic vacuum cleaner to clean dust from inside a computer case
- Cleaning solutions and pads such as contact cleaner, monitor wipes, and cleaning solutions for CDs and DVDs
- Multimeter to check cables and the power supply output
- Power supply tester
- POST diagnostic cards
- Needle-nose pliers for removing jumpers and for holding objects in place while you screw them in (especially handy for those pesky nuts on cable connectors)

Figure 1-5   A can of compressed air is handy to blow dust from a computer case

- Cable ties to keep cables out of the way inside a computer case
- Flashlight to see inside the computer case
- AC outlet ground tester
- Network cable tester
- Loopback plugs to test ports
- Small cups or bags to help keep screws organized as you work
- Antistatic bags to store unused parts
- Pen and paper for taking notes

Keep your tools in a toolbox designated for hardware troubleshooting. If you put discs and hardware tools in the same box, be sure to keep the discs inside a hard plastic case to protect them from scratches and dents. In addition, make sure the diagnostic and utility software you use is recommended for the hardware and software you are troubleshooting.

Now that you've prepared your work area and tools, put on your ESD strap—let's get started with opening the computer case.

Step 2: Opening the Case

Core 1 Objectives 2.8, 3.1, 3.2, 3.3, 3.4, 3.5

Before we discuss the parts inside a desktop case, let's take a quick look at the outside of the case and the ports and switches on it.

What's on the Outside of a Desktop Case

Figure 1-6   This slimline tower case supports a microATX motherboard

© Courtesy of IN WIN Development, Inc.

A computer case for any type of computer is sometimes called the **chassis**, and it houses the power supply, motherboard, processor, memory modules, expansion cards, hard drive, optical drive, and other drives. A computer case can be a tower case, a desktop case that lies flat on a desk, an all-in-one case used with an all-in-one computer, or a mobile case used with laptops and tablets. A **tower case** (see Figure 1-6) sits upright; it can be as high as two feet and has room for several drives. Often used for servers, this type of case is also good for desktop computer users who anticipate upgrading because tower cases provide maximum space for working inside a computer and moving components around. A **desktop case** lies flat and sometimes serves double-duty as a monitor stand. Later in this module, you learn how to work inside a tower case, desktop case, laptop case, and all-in-one case.

Note 1

Don't lay a tower case on its side when the computer is in use because the CD or DVD drive might not work properly. For the same reason, if a desktop case is designed to lie flat, don't set it on its end when the computer is in use.

Table 1-1 lists ports you might find on a desktop or mobile computer. Consider this table your introduction to these ports so you can recognize them when you see them. Later in the text, you learn more about the details of each port.

Exam Tip ✔

The A+ Core 1 exam expects you to know how to identify the ports shown in Table 1-1.

Table 1-1   Ports used with desktop and laptop computers

Port	Description
	A **VGA (Video Graphics Array) port**—also called a DB-15 port, **DB15 port**, **HD15 port**, or **DE15 port**—is a 15-pin, D-shaped, female port that transmits analog video. (**Analog** means a continuous signal with infinite variations as compared with **digital**, which is a series of binary values—1s and 0s.) All older monitors use VGA ports. (By the way, the HD15 [high-definition 15-pin] name for the port is an older name that distinguishes it from the early 9-pin VGA ports.)
	A **DVI (Digital Video Interface) port** transmits digital or analog video. You learn about the three types of DVI ports in the module "Supporting I/O Devices."
	An **HDMI (High-Definition Multimedia Interface) port** transmits digital video and audio (not analog transmissions) and is often used to connect to home theater equipment.
	A **DisplayPort** transmits digital video and audio (not analog transmissions) and is slowly replacing VGA and DVI ports on personal computers.
Source: Wikimedia Commons	A **Thunderbolt 3 port** transmits video, data, and power on the same port and cable and is popular with Apple computers. The port is shaped the same as the USB-C port and is compatible with USB-C devices. Up to six peripherals (for example, monitors and external hard drives daisy-chained together) can use the same Thunderbolt port.
	A system usually has three or more round **audio ports**, also called sound ports, for a microphone, audio in, audio out, and stereo audio out. These types of audio ports can transmit analog or digital data. If you have one audio cable to connect to a speaker or earbuds, plug it into the lime green sound port in the middle of the three ports. The microphone uses the pink port.

(continues)

Table 1-1   Ports used with desktop and laptop computers (Continued)

Port	Description
	An **SPDIF (Sony-Philips Digital Interface) sound port** connects to an external home theater audio system, providing digital audio output and the best signal quality. SPDIF ports always carry digital audio and can work with electrical or optical cable. When connected to a fiber-optic cable, the port is called an **optical connector**.
	A **USB (Universal Serial Bus) port** is a multipurpose I/O port that comes in several sizes and is used by many different devices, including printers, mice, keyboards, scanners, external hard drives, and flash drives. Some USB ports are faster than others. There are several USB standards, with speeds consistently improving with each new release.
	An **external SATA (eSATA) port** is used by an external hard drive or other device using the eSATA interface.
	A **PS/2 port**, also called a mini-DIN port, is a round 6-pin port used by a keyboard or mouse. The ports look alike but are not interchangeable. On a desktop, the purple port is for the keyboard, and the green port is for the mouse. Most newer computers use USB ports for the keyboard and mouse rather than the older PS/2 ports.
	An older **serial port**, sometimes called a **DB9 port**, is a 9-pin male port used on older computers. It has been mostly replaced by USB ports. Occasionally, you see a serial port on a router, where the port is used to connect the router to a device a technician can use to monitor and manage the router.
	A **modem port**, also called an **RJ-11 port**, is used to connect dial-up phone lines to computers. A modem port looks like a network port but is not as wide. In the photo, the right port is a modem port, and the left port is a network port shown for comparison.
	A **network port**, also called an **Ethernet port** or an **RJ-45 port**, is used by a network cable to connect to the wired network. Fast Ethernet ports run at 100 Mbps (megabits per second), and Gigabit Ethernet runs at 1000 Mbps or 1 Gbps (gigabits per second). A megabit is one million bits, and a gigabit is one billion bits. A bit is a binary value of 1 or 0.

Loopback Plugs

A **loopback plug** is used to test a network port in a computer or other device to make sure the port is working. It might also test the throughput or speed of the port. Figure 1-7 shows a loopback plug testing a network port on a laptop. You know both the port and the network cable are good because the lights on either side of the port are lit. You can also buy a USB loopback plug to test USB ports.

Figure 1-7   A loopback plug testing a network port and network cable

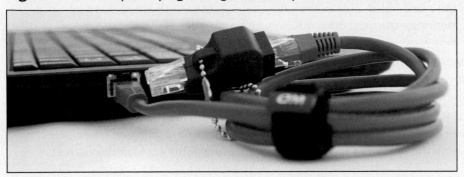

What's Inside a Desktop Case

Now that you're familiar with the outside of the case, let's open the case to see what is inside. Here are the steps to open a computer case:

1. **Back up important data.** If you are starting with a working computer, make sure important data is backed up first. Copy the data to an external storage device such as a flash drive or external hard drive. If something goes wrong while you're working inside the computer, at least your data will be safe.

2. **Power down the system and unplug it.** Remove discs from the optical drive. Then power down the system, and unplug the power, monitor, mouse, and keyboard cables and any other peripherals or cables attached. Then move these cables out of your way.

> **Caution** ⚠️
>
> When you power down a computer and even turn off the power switch on the rear of the computer case, residual power is still on. Some motherboards have a small light inside the case to remind you of this fact and to warn you that power is still getting to the system. Therefore, be sure to always unplug the power cord before opening a case.

3. **Press and hold down the power button for a moment.** After you unplug the computer, press the power button for about three seconds to completely drain the power supply (see Figure 1-8). Sometimes when you do so, you'll hear the fans quickly start and go off as residual power is drained. Only then is it safe to work inside the case.

Figure 1-8   Press the power button after the computer is unplugged

4. **Have a plastic bag or cup handy to hold screws.** When you reassemble the computer, you will need to insert the same screws in the same holes. This is especially important with the hard drive because screws that are too long can puncture the hard drive housing, so be careful to label those screws clearly.

5. **Open the case cover.** Sometimes, figuring out how to open a computer case is the most difficult part of disassembling a computer. If you need help figuring it out, check the user manual or website of the case manufacturer. To remove the computer case cover, do the following:

   - Some cases require you to start by laying the case on its side and removing the faceplate on the front of the case first. Other cases require you to remove a side panel first, and much older cases require you to first remove all the sides and top as a single unit. Study your case for the correct approach.

   - Most cases have panels on each side that can be removed. It is usually necessary to remove only one panel to expose the top of the motherboard. To know which panel to remove, look at the port locations on the rear of the case. For example, in Figure 1-9, the ports on the motherboard are on the left side of the case, indicating the bottom of the motherboard is on the left. Therefore, you will want to remove the right panel to expose the top of the motherboard. Lay the case down to its left so the ports and the motherboard are on the bottom. Later, depending on how drives are installed, it might become necessary to remove the other side panel in order to remove the screws that hold the drives in place.

Figure 1-9   Decide which side panel to remove

Motherboard is mounted to this side of the case

   - Locate the screws or clips that hold the side panel in place. Be careful not to unscrew any screws besides these. The other screws probably are holding the power supply, fan, and other components in place (see Figure 1-10). Place the screws in the cup or bag used for that purpose. Some cases use clips on a side panel in addition to or instead of screws (see Figure 1-11).

Figure 1-10   Locate the screws that hold the side panel in place

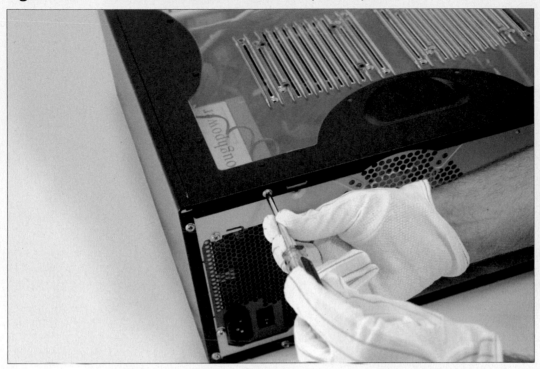

Figure 1-11   On this system, clips hold the side panel in place

- After the screws are removed, slide the panel toward the rear, and then lift it off the case (see Figure 1-12).

Figure 1-12   Slide the panel to the rear of the case

6. **Clip your ESD strap to the side of the computer case.** To dissipate any charge between you and the computer, put on your ESD strap if you have not already done so. Then clip the alligator clip on the strap cable to the side of the computer case (see Figure 1-13).

Figure 1-13   Attach the alligator clip of your ground bracelet to the side of the computer case

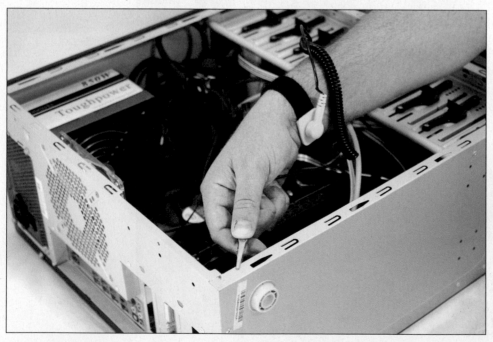

After you open a computer case, as shown in Figure 1-14, the main components you see inside are the power supply, motherboard, expansion card, and drives installed in drive bays. You also see a lot of cables and wires connecting various components. These cables are power cables from the power supply to various components, or cables carrying data and instructions between components. The best way to know the purpose of a cable is to follow it from its source to its destination.

Figure 1-14   Inside the computer case

Here is a quick explanation of the main components installed in the case, which are called **internal components**:

- **The motherboard, processor, and cooler.** The **motherboard**—also called the **main board**, the **system board**, or the techie jargon term, the mobo—is the largest and most important circuit board in the computer. The motherboard contains a socket to hold the processor or CPU. The **central processing unit (CPU)**, also called the **processor** or **microprocessor**, does most of the processing of data and instructions for the entire system. Because the CPU generates heat, a fan and heat sink might be installed on top to keep it cool. A **heat sink** consists of metal fins that draw heat away from a component. The fan and heat sink together are called the processor cooler. Figure 1-15 shows the top view of a motherboard, and Figure 1-16 shows the ports on the side of a motherboard.

Figure 1-15   All hardware components are either located on the motherboard or directly or indirectly connected to it because they must all communicate with the CPU

Figure 1-16   Ports provided by a motherboard

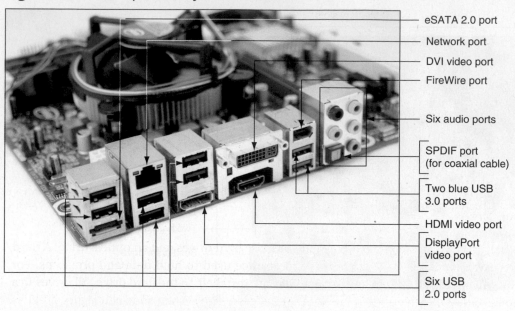

- eSATA 2.0 port
- Network port
- DVI video port
- FireWire port
- Six audio ports
- SPDIF port (for coaxial cable)
- Two blue USB 3.0 ports
- HDMI video port
- DisplayPort video port
- Six USB 2.0 ports

- **Expansion cards.** A motherboard has expansion slots to be used by expansion cards. An **expansion card**, also called an adapter card, is a circuit board that provides more ports than those provided by the motherboard. Figure 1-17 shows a video card that provides three video ports. Notice the cooling fan and heat sink on the card, which help to keep the card from overheating. The trend today is for most ports in a system to be provided by the motherboard (called onboard ports), with decreased use of expansion cards.

Figure 1-17   The easiest way to identify this video card is to look at the ports on the end of the card

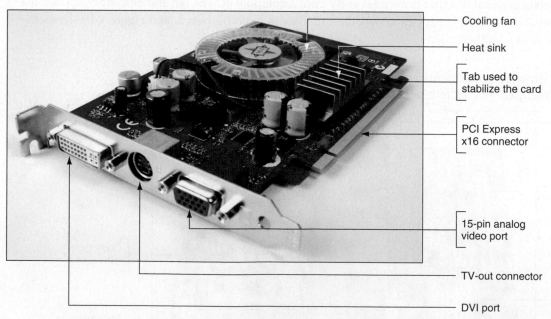

- Cooling fan
- Heat sink
- Tab used to stabilize the card
- PCI Express x16 connector
- 15-pin analog video port
- TV-out connector
- DVI port

- **Memory modules.** A desktop motherboard has memory slots, called **DIMM (dual inline memory module)** slots, to hold memory modules. Figure 1-18 shows a memory module installed in one DIMM slot along with three empty DIMM slots. Memory, also called **RAM (random access memory)**, is temporary storage for data and instructions as they are being processed by the CPU. The memory module shown in Figure 1-18 contains several RAM chips. Video cards also contain some embedded RAM chips for **video memory**.

Figure 1-18   A DIMM holds RAM and is mounted directly on a motherboard

One installed
DIMM

Three empty
DIMM slots

- **Hard drives and other drives.** A system might have one or more hard drives and an optical drive. A **hard drive**, also called a **hard disk drive (HDD)**, is permanent storage used to hold data and programs. For example, the Windows 10 operating system and applications are installed on the hard drive. All drives in a system are installed in a stack of drive bays at the front of the case. The system shown in Figure 1-14 has two hard drives and one optical drive installed. These three drives are also shown in Figure 1-19. The larger hard drive is a magnetic drive, and the smaller hard drive is a solid-state drive (SSD). Each drive has two connections for cables: The power cable connects to the power supply, and another cable, used for data and instructions, connects to the motherboard.

Figure 1-19   Two types of hard drives (a larger magnetic drive and a smaller
solid-state drive) and a DVD drive

3.5" hard drive   2.5" hard drive   DVD drive

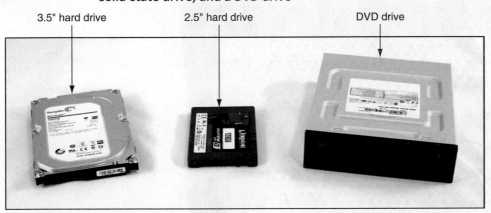

- **The power supply.** A computer **power supply**, also known as a **power supply unit (PSU)**, is a box installed in a corner of the computer case (see Figure 1-20) that receives and converts the house current so components inside the case can use it. Most power supplies have a **dual-voltage selector switch** on the back of the computer case where you can switch the input voltage to the power supply if necessary—115 V is used in the United States, and 220 V is used in other countries. See Figure 1-21. The power cables can connect to and supply power to the motherboard, expansion cards, and drives.

Figure 1-20   A power supply with attached power cables

Power cables

Power supply unit

Figure 1-21   The dual-voltage selector switch sets the input voltage to the power supply

Dual-voltage
selector switch

Four screws hold
the power supply
in the case

Note ②

If you ever need to change the dual-voltage selector switch, be sure you first turn off the computer and unplug the
power supply.

Form Factors Used by Desktop Cases, Power Supplies, and Motherboards

The desktop computer case, power supply, and motherboard must all be compatible and fit together as an inter-
connecting system. The standards that describe the size, shape, screw hole positions, and major features of these
interconnected components are called **form factors**. Using a matching form factor for the motherboard, power
supply, and case assures you that

- The motherboard fits in the case.
- The power supply cords to the motherboard provide the correct voltage, and the connectors match the connections on the board.
- The holes in the motherboard align with the holes in the case so you can anchor the board to the case. The holes in the case align with ports coming off the motherboard.
- For some form factors, wires for switches and lights on the front of the case match up with connections on the motherboard.
- The holes in the power supply align with holes in the case for anchoring the power supply to the case.

The two form factors used by most desktop and tower computer cases and power supplies are the ATX and microATX form factors. Motherboards use these and other form factors that are compatible with ATX or microATX power supplies and cases. You learn about other motherboard form factors in the module "All About Motherboards." Following are important details about ATX and microATX:

- **ATX (Advanced Technology Extended)** is the most commonly used form factor today. It is an open, non-proprietary industry specification originally developed by Intel. An ATX power supply has a variety of power connectors (see Figure 1-22). The power connectors are listed in Table 1-2, and several of them are described next.

Figure 1-22   An ATX power supply with connectors

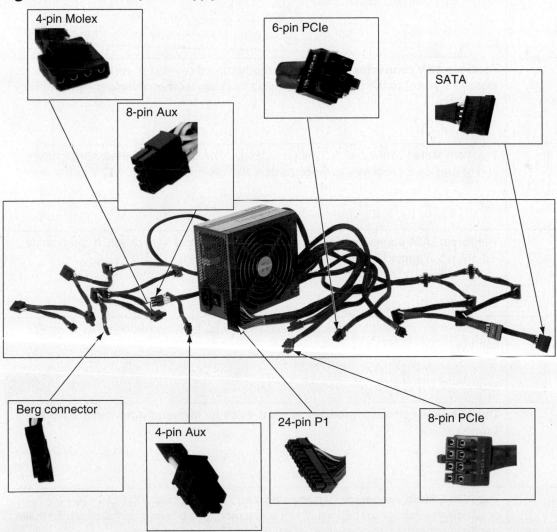

Table 1-2   Power supply connector

Connector	Description
	The **20-pin P1 connector** is the main motherboard power connector used in the early ATX systems.
	The **24-pin P1 connector**, also called the 20+4-pin connector, is the main motherboard power connector used today.
	The 20+4-pin P1 connector has four pins removed so the connector can fit into a 20-pin P1 motherboard connector.
	The **4-pin 12 V connector** is an auxiliary motherboard connector, which is used for extra 12 V power to the processor.
	The **8-pin 12 V connector** is an auxiliary motherboard connector, which is used for extra 12 V power to the processor, providing more power than the older 4-pin auxiliary connector.
	The 4-pin **Molex connector** is used for older IDE drives and some newer SATA drives, and to provide extra power to video cards. It can provide +5 V and +12 V to the device.
	The 15-pin **SATA power connector** is used for SATA (Serial ATA) drives. It can provide +3.3 V, +5 V, and +12 V, although +3.3 V is seldom used.
	The PCIe 6-pin connector provides an extra +12 V for high-end video cards using PCI Express.
	The PCIe 8-pin connector provides an extra +12 V for high-end video cards using PCI Express.
	The **PCIe 6/8-pin connector** is used by high-end video cards using PCIe ×16 slots to provide extra voltage to the card; it can accommodate a 6-hole or 8-hole port. To make the 8-pin connector, combine both the 6-pin and 2-pin connectors.

Power connectors have evolved because components that use new technologies require more power. As you read about the following types of power connectors and why each came to be, you'll also learn about the evolving expansion slots and expansion cards that drove the need for more power:

- **4-pin and 8-pin auxiliary connectors.** When processors began to require more power, the ATX Version 2.1 specifications added a 4-pin auxiliary connector near the processor socket to provide an additional 12 V of power (see Figure 1-23). A power supply that provides this 4-pin 12 V power cord is called an **ATX12V power supply**. Later boards replaced the 4-pin 12 V power connector with an 8-pin motherboard auxiliary connector that provided more amps for the processor. See Figure 1-24.

Figure 1-23   The 4-pin 12 V auxiliary power connector on a motherboard with a power cord connected

Figure 1-24   An 8-pin, 12 V auxiliary power connector for extra power to the processor

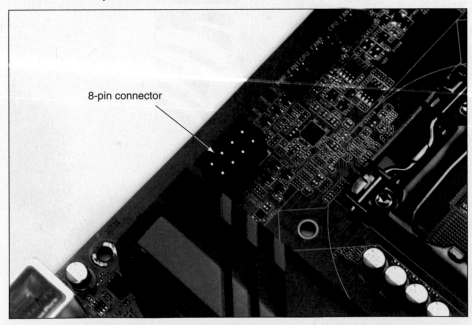

8-pin connector

- **24-pin or 20+4-pin P1 connector.** The original P1 connector had 20 pins. Later, when faster **PCI Express (PCIe)** slots were added to motherboards, more power was required and a new ATX specification (ATX Version 2.2) allowed for a 24-pin P1 connector, also called the 20+4 power connector.

  All motherboards today use a 24-pin P1 connector. The extra four pins on the 24-pin P1 connector provide +12 volts, +5 volts, and +3.3 volts. Figure 1-25 shows a 24-pin P1 power cord from the power supply and a 24-pin P1 connector on a motherboard. Figure 1-26 shows the pinouts for the 24-pin power cord connector, which is color-coded to wires from the power supply.

Figure 1-25   A 24-pin power cord ready to be plugged into a 24-pin P1 connector on an ATX motherboard

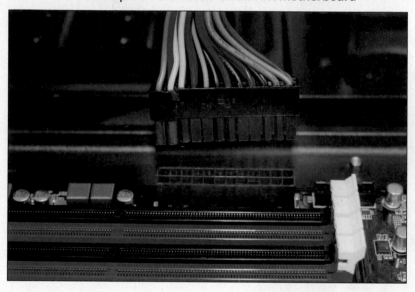

Figure 1-26   A P1 24-pin power connector follows ATX Version 2.2 and higher standards

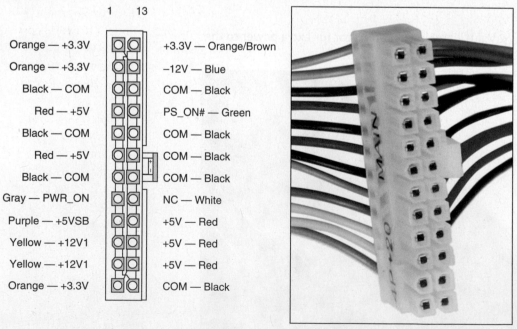

	1	13	
Orange — +3.3V			+3.3V — Orange/Brown
Orange — +3.3V			−12V — Blue
Black — COM			COM — Black
Red — +5V			PS_ON# — Green
Black — COM			COM — Black
Red — +5V			COM — Black
Black — COM			COM — Black
Gray — PWR_ON			NC — White
Purple — +5VSB			+5V — Red
Yellow — +12V1			+5V — Red
Yellow — +12V1			+5V — Red
Orange — +3.3V			COM — Black

- **6-pin and 8-pin PCIe connectors.** Video cards draw the most power in a system, and ATX Version 2.2 provides for power cables to connect directly to a video card and provide it more power than what comes through the PCIe slot on the motherboard. The PCIe power connector might have six or eight pins. Figure 1-27 shows a PCIe ×16 video card. The edge connector has a break that fits the break in the slot. The tab at the end of the edge connector fits into a retention mechanism at the end of the slot, which helps to stabilize a heavy video card. The video card has a 6-pin connector on the end of the card. A PCIe 6-pin power cord from the power supply plugs into the connector. The power supply connector is shown earlier in Table 1-2.

Figure 1-27   This PCIe ×16 video card has a 6-pin PCIe power connector to receive extra power from the power supply

PCIe 6-pin power connector on the end of the video card

Edge connector

Figure 1-28   This microATX motherboard by ASUS is designed to support an AMD processor

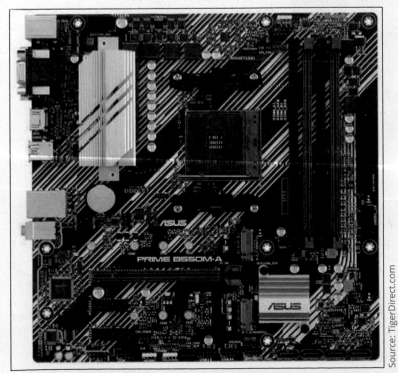

Source: TigerDirect.com

- The **microATX (mATX)** form factor is a major variation of ATX and addresses some technologies that have emerged since the original development of ATX. MicroATX reduces the total cost of a system by reducing the number of expansion slots on the motherboard, which in turn reduces the power supplied to the board and allows for a smaller case size. A microATX motherboard (see Figure 1-28) will fit into a case that follows the ATX 2.1 or higher standard. A microATX power supply uses a 24-pin P1 connector and is not likely to have as many extra wires and connectors as those on an ATX power supply.

Now let's learn about the expansion cards you might find installed inside a system.

Step 3: Removing Expansion Cards

Core 1 Objective 3.4

If you plan to remove several components, draw a diagram of all cable connections to the motherboard, expansion cards, and drives. You might need this cable connection diagram to help you reassemble. Note where each cable begins and ends, and pay particular attention to the small wires and connectors that connect the lights, switches, and ports on the front of the case to the motherboard front panel connectors. It's important to be careful about diagramming these because it is easy to connect them in the wrong position later when you reassemble. You can use a felt-tip marker to make a mark across components, which can indicate a cable connection, board placement, motherboard orientation, speaker connection, brackets, and so on. Then you can simply line up the marks when you reassemble. This method, however, probably won't work for the front case wires because they are so small. For these, consider writing down the colors of the wires and their positions on the pins or taking a photo of the wires in their positions with your cell phone (see Figure 1-29).

Figure 1-29   Diagram the pin locations of the color-coded wires that connect to the front of the case

Note ③

A header is a connector on a motherboard that consists of pins that stick up from the board. For example, the group of pins shown in Figure 1-29 is called the **front panel header**.

Computer systems vary in so many ways that it's impossible to list the exact order to disassemble one. Most likely, however, you need to remove the expansion cards first. Do the following to remove the expansion cards:

1. Remove any wire or cable connected to the card.
2. Remove the screw holding the card to the case (see Figure 1-30).

Figure 1-30   Remove the screw holding the expansion card to the case

3. Grasp the card with both hands, and remove it by lifting straight up. If you have trouble removing it from the expansion slot, you can very slightly rock the card from end to end (not side to side). Rocking the card from side to side might spread the slot opening and weaken the connection.

4. As you remove the card, don't put your fingers on the edge connectors or touch a chip, and don't stack the cards on top of one another. Lay each card aside on a flat surface, preferably in an antistatic bag.

Note 4

Cards installed in PCI Express × 16 slots use a latch that helps to hold the card securely in the slot. To remove these cards, use one finger to hold the latch back from the slot, as shown in Figure 1-31, as you pull the card up and out of the slot.

Figure 1-31   Hold the retention mechanism back as you remove a video card from its expansion slot

Step 4: Removing the Motherboard

Core 1 Objective 3.4

Depending on the system, you might need to remove the motherboard or the drives next. My choice is to first remove the motherboard. It and the processor are the most expensive and most easily damaged parts of the system. I like to get them out of harm's way before working with the drives. However, in some cases, you must remove the drives or the power supply before you can get to the motherboard. Study your situation and decide which to do first. To remove the motherboard, do the following:

1. Unplug the power supply lines to the motherboard.
2. Unplug SATA cables connected to the motherboard.
3. Disconnect the wires leading from the front or top of the computer case to the motherboard; these wires are called the **front panel connectors**. If you don't have the motherboard manual handy, be very careful to diagram how these wires connect because they are rarely labeled well on a motherboard. Make a careful diagram, and then disconnect the wires. Figure 1-32 shows five leads and the pins on the motherboard front panel header that receive these leads. The pins are color-coded and cryptically labeled on the board.

Figure 1-32   Five leads from the front panel connect to two rows of pins on the motherboard front panel header

4. Disconnect any other cables or wires connected to the motherboard. A case fan might be getting power by a small wire connected to the motherboard. In addition, USB ports on the front of the computer case might be connected by a cable to the motherboard.
5. You're now ready to remove the screws that hold the motherboard to the case. A motherboard is installed so that the bottom of the board does not touch the case. If the fine traces or lines on the bottom of the board were to touch the case, a short would result when the system runs again. To keep the board from touching the case, screw holes are elevated using **spacers**, also called **standoffs**, which are round plastic or metal pegs that separate the board from the case. Carefully pop off these spacers and/or remove the screws (up to nine) that hold the board to the case (see Figure 1-33) and then remove the board. Set it aside in a safe place.

Figure 1-33   Remove up to nine screws that hold the motherboard to the case

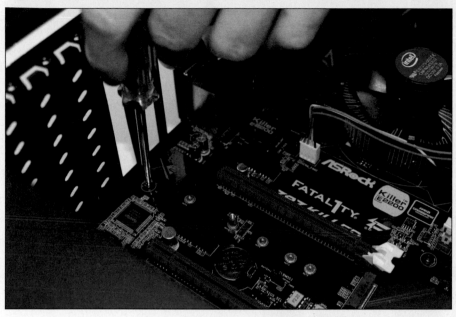

Figure 1-34 shows a motherboard sitting to the side of these spacers. Two spacers are in place, and the other is lying beside its case hole. In the figure, also notice the holes in the motherboard where screws are used to connect the board to the spacers.

Figure 1-34   This motherboard connects to a case using screws and spacers that keep the board from touching the case

Holes in motherboard

Spacers

Note 5

When you're replacing a motherboard that is not the same size as the original board in a case, you can use needle-nose pliers to unplug a standoff so you can move it to a new hole.

6. The motherboard should now be free, and you can carefully remove it from the case, as shown in Figure 1-35. Lift the board by its edges, as shown in the figure.

Figure 1-35   Remove the motherboard from the case

Caution

Never lift a motherboard by the cooler because doing so might create an air gap between the cooler and the processor, which can cause the processor to overheat later.

Caution

Some processors have heavy or bulky cooling assemblies installed on top of them. For these systems, it is best to remove the cooler before you take the motherboard out of the case because the motherboard is not designed to support the heavy cooler when the motherboard is not securely seated in the case. Removal of the cooler is covered in the module "Supporting Processors and Upgrading Memory."

POST Diagnostic Cards

When supporting a motherboard, a **POST diagnostic card**, also called a **POST card** or motherboard test card, can be of great help in discovering and reporting computer errors and conflicts that occur after you first turn on a computer but before the operating system (such as Windows 10) is launched. To understand what a POST card does, you need to know about the **firmware**—the programs and data stored on the motherboard.

Firmware consists of the older **BIOS (basic input/output system)** firmware and the newer **UEFI (Unified Extensible Firmware Interface)** firmware and is usually referred to as BIOS or UEFI. Figure 1-36 shows an embedded firmware chip on a motherboard that contains the BIOS/UEFI programs. BIOS/UEFI is responsible for managing essential devices (for example, keyboard, mouse, hard drive, and monitor) before the OS is launched, starting the computer, and managing motherboard settings. A feature of the newer UEFI is that it can manage a secure boot, assuring that no rogue malware or operating system hijacks the system during the boot.

Figure 1-36   This firmware chip contains BIOS/UEFI, flash ROM, and CMOS RAM; CMOS RAM is powered by the coin battery located near the chip

Coin battery

Firmware chip

A POST card is not essential, but it can be quite useful. The **POST (power-on self-test)** is a series of tests performed by the startup BIOS/UEFI when you first turn on a computer. These tests determine if the startup BIOS/UEFI can communicate correctly with essential hardware components required for a successful boot. If you have a problem that prevents the computer from booting and that you suspect is related to hardware, you can install the POST card in an expansion slot on the motherboard. For laptops, some cards install in a USB port. You can then attempt to boot. The card monitors the boot process and reports errors, usually as coded numbers on a small LED panel on the card. You then look up the number online or in the documentation that accompanies the card to get more information about the error and its source. Figure 1-37 shows a POST diagnostic card, the Post Code Master card by Microsystems Developments, Inc.

Figure 1-37   The Post Code Master diagnostic card by Microsystems Developments, Inc., installs in
a PCI slot

Before purchasing this or any other diagnostic tools or software, read the documentation about what they can and cannot do, and read some online product reviews. Try using *google.com* and searching on "computer diagnostic card reviews."

Note 6

Some Dell computers have lights on the case that blink in patterns to indicate a problem early in the boot before the OS loads. These blinking lights give information similar to that given by POST cards.

Step 5: Removing the Power Supply

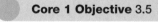   **Core 1 Objective** 3.5

To remove the power supply from the case, look for screws that attach the power supply to the computer case, as shown in Figure 1-38. Be careful not to remove any screws that hold the power supply housing together. You do not want to take the housing apart. After you have removed the screws, the power supply still might not be free. Sometimes, it is attached to the underside of the case by recessed slots. Turn the case over, and look on the bottom for these slots. If they are present, determine in which direction you need to slide the power supply to free it from the case.

Figure 1-38   Remove the power supply mounting screws

Power Supply Tester

A **power supply tester** is used to measure the output of each connector coming from the power supply. You can test the power supply when it is outside or inside the case. As you saw earlier in Figure 1-20, the power supply provides several cables and connectors that power various components inside the computer case. A power supply tester has plugs for each type of cable. Connect a power cable to the tester, plug up the power supply, and turn on the tester. An LCD panel reports the output of each lead (see Figure 1-39).

Figure 1-39   Use a power supply tester to test the output of each power connector on a power supply

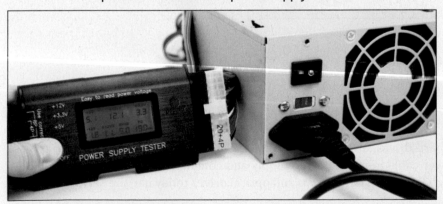

Multimeter

A **multimeter** (see Figure 1-40) is a more general-purpose tool that can measure several characteristics of electricity in a variety of devices. Some multimeters can measure voltage, current, resistance, and continuity. (Continuity determines that two ends of a cable or fuse are connected without interruption.) When set to measure voltage, you can use it to measure output of each pin on a power supply connector. When set to measure continuity, a multimeter is useful to test fuses, to determine if a cable is good, or to match pins on one end of a cable to pins on the other end.

Figure 1-40   This digital multimeter can be set to measure voltage, resistance, or continuity

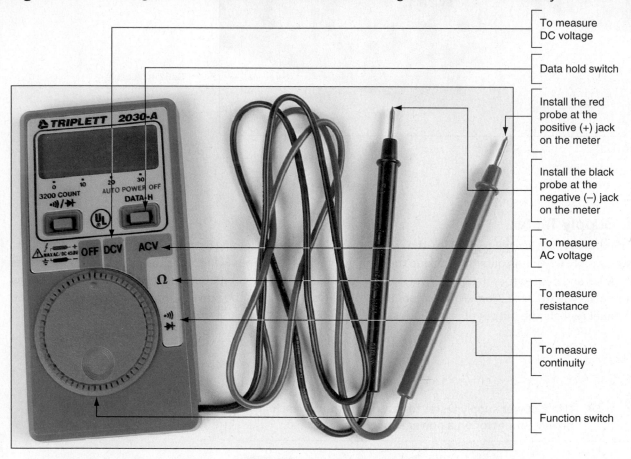

- To measure DC voltage
- Data hold switch
- Install the red probe at the positive (+) jack on the meter
- Install the black probe at the negative (−) jack on the meter
- To measure AC voltage
- To measure resistance
- To measure continuity
- Function switch

Step 6: Removing the Drives

Core 1 Objective 3.3

A computer might have one or more hard drives, an optical drive (CD, DVD, or Blu-ray), or some other type of drive. A drive receives power by a power cable from the power supply and communicates instructions and data through a cable attached to the motherboard. Most hard drives and optical drives today use the **serial ATA (SATA)** standard.

Figure 1-41 shows a SATA cable connecting a hard drive and motherboard. SATA cables can only connect to a SATA connector on the motherboard in one direction (see Figure 1-42). SATA drives get their power from a power cable that connects to the drive using a SATA power connector (refer back to the photo in Table 1-2).

Figure 1-41   A hard drive subsystem using the SATA data cable

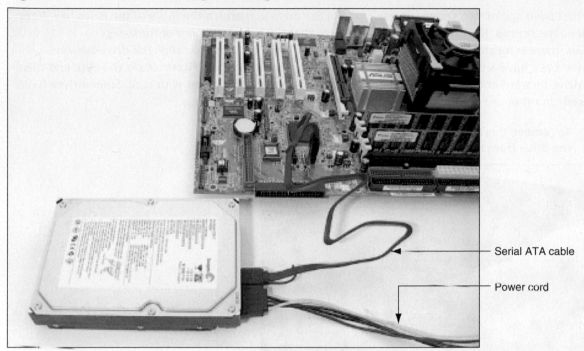

Serial ATA cable

Power cord

Figure 1-42   A SATA cable connects to a SATA connector in only one direction; for this system, use red connectors on the motherboard first

Remove each drive next, handling them with care. Here are some tips:

- Some drives have one or two screws on each side of the drive that attach the drive to the drive bay. After you remove the screws, the drive slides to the front or to the rear and then out of the case.
- Sometimes, there is a catch underneath the drive that you must lift up as you slide the drive forward.
- Some drive bays have a clipping mechanism to hold the drive in the bay. First release the clip, and then pull the drive forward and out of the bay (see Figure 1-43). Handle the drives with care. Some drives have an exposed circuit board on the bottom of the drive. Don't touch this board.

Figure 1-43   To remove this optical drive, first release the clip to release
                    the drive from the bay

- Some drives must be removed through the front of the case, especially optical drives. After removing all screws or releasing the clipping mechanism, you might need to remove the front panel of the case to remove the drive. See Figure 1-44.

Figure 1-44   Some cases require you to remove the front panel before
                    removing the optical drive

- Some cases have a removable bay for smaller hard drives (see Figure 1-45). The bay is removed first, and then the drives are removed from the bay. To remove the bay, first remove the screws or release the clip holding the bay in place, and then slide the bay out of the case. The drives are usually installed in the bay with two screws on each side of each drive. Remove the screws and then the drives (see Figure 1-46).

Figure 1-45   Push down on the clip, and then slide the removable bay forward and out of the case

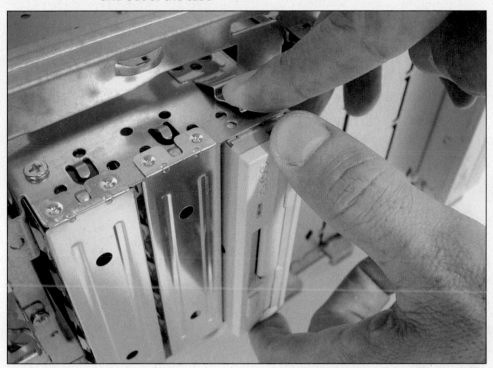

Figure 1-46   Drives in this removable bay are held in place with screws on each side of the bay and drive

Steps to Put a Computer Back Together

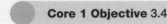
Core 1 Objective 3.4

To reassemble a computer, reverse the process of disassembling. Here is where your diagrams will be especially useful; having the screws and cables organized will also help. In the directions that follow, we're also considering the possibility that you are installing a replacement part as you reassemble the system. Do the following:

1. Install components in the case in this order: power supply, drives, motherboard, and cards. When installing drives, know that for some systems, it's easier to connect data cables to the drives and then slide the drives into the bay. If the drive is anchored to the bay with screws or latches, be careful to align the front of the drive flush with the front of the case before installing screws or pushing in the latches (see Figure 1-47).

Figure 1-47   Align the front of the drive flush with the case front, and then anchor with a screw

2. Place the motherboard inside the case. Make sure the ports stick out of the I/O shield at the rear of the case and the screw holes line up with screw holes on the bottom of the case. Figure 1-48 shows how you must align the screw holes on the motherboard with those in the case. There should be at least six screw sets, and there might be as many as nine. Use as many screws as there are holes in the motherboard.

Figure 1-48   Align screw holes in the case with those on the motherboard

3. Connect the power cords from the power supply to the motherboard. A system will always need the main P1 power connector and most likely will need the 4-pin auxiliary connector for the processor. Other power connectors might be needed depending on the devices you later install in the system. Here are the details:

- Connect the P1 power connector from the power supply to the motherboard (refer back to Figure 1-25).
- Connect the 4-pin or 8-pin auxiliary power cord from the power supply to the motherboard, as shown in Figure 1-49. This cord supplies the supplemental power required for the processor.

Figure 1-49   The auxiliary 4-pin power cord provides power to the processor

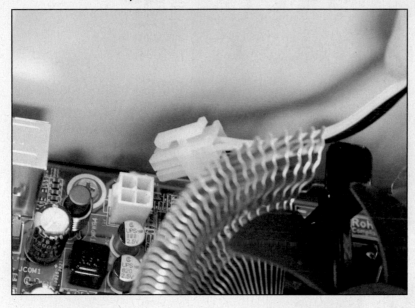

- To power the case fan, connect the power cord from the fan to pins on the motherboard labeled Fan Header. Alternately, some case fans use a 4-pin Molex connector that connects to a power cable coming directly from the power supply.
- If a CPU and cooler are already installed on the motherboard, connect the power cord from the CPU fan to the pins on the motherboard labeled CPU Fan Header.

4. Connect the wire leads from the front panel of the case to the front panel header on the motherboard. These are the wires for the switches, lights, and ports on the front or top of the computer. Because your case and your motherboard might not have been made by the same manufacturer, you need to pay close attention to the source of the wires to determine where they connect on the motherboard. For example, Figure 1-50 shows a computer case that has seven connectors from the front panel that connect to the motherboard. Figure 1-51 shows the front panel header on the motherboard for these lights and switches. If you look closely at the board in Figure 1-51, you can see labels identifying the pins.

The five smaller connectors on the right side of Figure 1-50 are labeled from right to left as follows:

- **Power SW.** Controls power to the motherboard; must be connected for the PC to power up
- **HDD LED.** Controls the drive activity light on the front panel that lights up when any SATA or IDE device is in use (HDD stands for hard disk drive and LED stands for light-emitting diode; an LED is a light on the front panel.)
- **Power LED+.** Controls the power light and indicates that power is on
- **Power LED−.** Controls the power light; the two positive and negative leads indicate that power is on
- **Reset SW.** Switch used to reboot the computer

Figure 1-50   Seven connectors from the front panel connect to the motherboard

Triangle used to orient connector on pins

Figure 1-51   The front panel header uses color-coded pins and labels

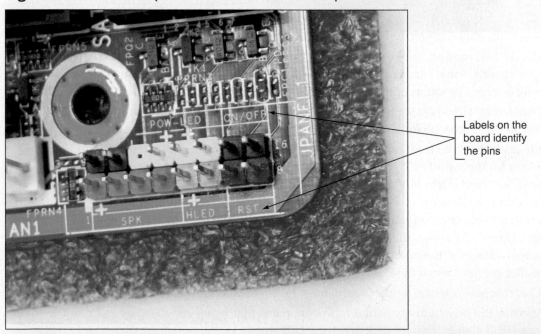

Labels on the board identify the pins

Note 7

Positive wires connecting the front panel to the motherboard are usually a solid color, and negative wires are usually white or striped.

To help orient the larger connectors on the motherboard pins, look for a small triangle embedded on the connector that marks one of the outside wires as pin 1 (see Figure 1-50). Look for pin 1 to be labeled on the motherboard as a small 1 embedded to either the right or left of the group of pins. If the labels on the board are not clear, turn IT technical motherboard user guide for help. The diagram in Figure 1-52 shows what you can expect from one motherboard user guide. Notice pin 1 is identified as a square pin in the diagram, rather than round like the other pins.

Figure 1-52   Documentation for front panel header connections

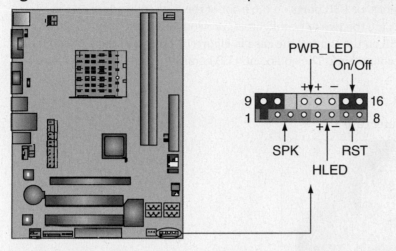

Pin	Assignment	Function	Pin	Assignment	Function
1	+5 V		9	N/A	N/A
2	N/A	Speaker	10	N/A	
3	N/A	connector	11	N/A	N/A
4	Speaker		12	Power LED (+)	
5	HDD LED (+)	Hard drive	13	Power LED (+)	Power LED
6	HDD LED (−)	LED	14	Power LED (−)	
7	Ground	Reset button	15	Power button	Power-on button
8	Reset control		16	Ground	

Sometimes the motherboard documentation is not clear, but guessing is okay when connecting a wire to a front panel header connection. If it doesn't work, no harm is done. Figure 1-53 shows all front panel wires in place and the little speaker also connected to the front panel header pins.

Note 8

If the user guide is not handy, you can download it from the motherboard manufacturer's website. Search on the brand and model number of the board, which is imprinted somewhere on the board.

Figure 1-53   A front panel header with all connectors in place

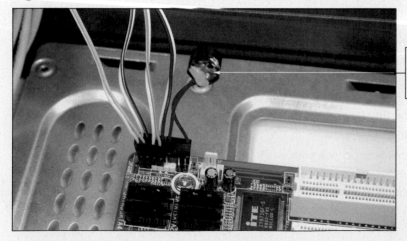

Speaker connected to front panel header

5. Connect wires to ports on the front panel of the case. Depending on your motherboard and case, there might be cables to connect audio ports or USB ports on the front of the case to headers on the motherboard. Audio and USB connectors are the two left connectors, previously shown in Figure 1-50. You can see these ports for audio and USB on the front of the case in Figure 1-54. Look in the motherboard documentation for the location of these connectors. The audio and USB connectors are labeled for one board in Figures 1-55A and 1-55B.

Figure 1-54   Ports on the front of the computer case

Audio-out and microphone ports

USB ports

Figure 1-55   Connectors for front panel ports

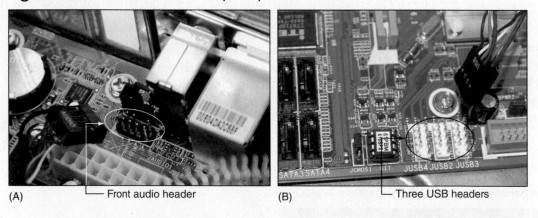

(A)   └─ Front audio header   (B)   └─ Three USB headers

6. Install the video card and any other expansion cards. Push the card straight down into the slot, being careful not to rock it side to side, and install the screw to secure the card to the case.

7. Take a few minutes to double-check each connection and make sure it is correct and snug. Verify that all required power cords are connected correctly and that the video card is seated solidly in its slot. Also verify that no wires or cables are obstructing fans. You can use cable ties to keep wires out of the way.

8. Plug in the keyboard, monitor, and mouse.

9. In a classroom environment, have the instructor check your work before you close the case and power up.

10. Turn on the power, and check that the PC is working properly. If the PC does not work, the problem is most likely a loose connection. Just turn off the power, and recheck each cable connection and each expansion card. You probably have not solidly seated a card in the slot. After you have double-checked, try again.

Now step back and congratulate yourself on a job well done! By taking a computer apart and putting it back together, you've learned how computer parts interconnect and work.

Now let's turn our attention to how to disassemble and reassemble a laptop.

First Look at Laptop Components

Core 1 Objectives 1.1, 1.3

A **laptop**, also called a **notebook**, is designed for portability (see Figures 1-56A and 1-56B) and can be just as powerful as a desktop computer. Nearly 75 percent of personal computers purchased today are laptops, and that percentage is growing. Laptops use the same technology as desktops, but with modifications to use less power, take up less space, and operate on the move.

Laptops come in several varieties, including some with a touch screen that allows you to handwrite on it with a stylus and some with a rotating or removable screen that allows you to use the laptop as a tablet (see Figure 1-57). Another variation of a laptop is a **netbook** (Figure 1-56B), which is smaller and less expensive than a laptop and has fewer features. An **all-in-one computer** (Figure 1-56C) has the monitor and computer case built together and uses components that are common to both a laptop and desktop. Because all-in-one computers use many laptop components and are serviced in similar ways, we include them in this part of the module.

Figure 1-56   A laptop, netbook, and all-in-one computer

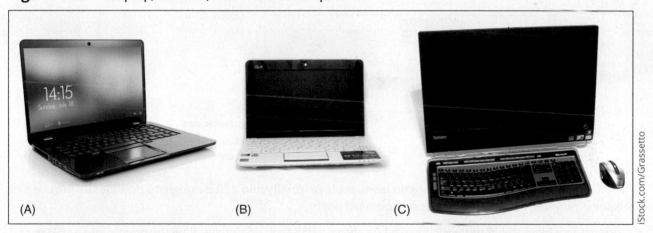

(A)   (B)   (C)

iStock.com/Grassetto

Figure 1-57   A laptop with a rotating screen can do double duty as a tablet computer

iStock.com/Rasslava

A laptop provides ports on its sides, back, or front for connecting peripherals (see Figure 1-58). Ports common to laptops as well as desktop systems include USB, network, and audio ports (for a microphone, headset, or external speakers). Video ports might include one or more VGA, DisplayPort, Thunderbolt (on Apple laptops), or HDMI ports to connect to a projector, second monitor, or television. On the side or back of the laptop, you'll see a DC jack to receive power from the AC adapter. A laptop may also have an optical drive, but netbooks usually don't have them.

Notice the two slots in Figure 1-58 used for flash memory cards: a MagicGate slot and an SD card slot. Each can support several types of flash memory cards, which you learn about later in the text.

Figure 1-58 Ports and slots on a laptop computer

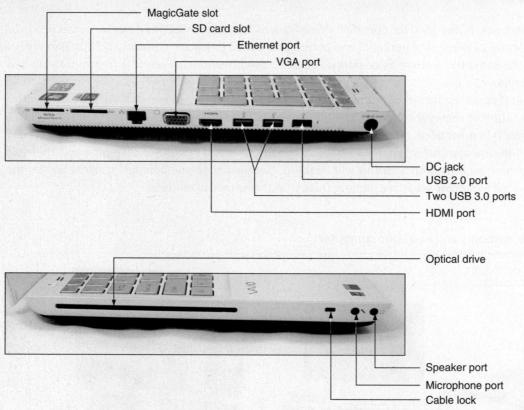

When a laptop is missing a port or slot you need, you can usually find a USB dongle to provide the port or slot. Here are some possible solutions for a missing or failed port:

- **Connect to a local wired network.** Figure 1-59 shows a **USB to RJ-45 dongle**. Plug the dongle into a USB port, and plug a network cable into the RJ-45 port the dongle provides to connect the laptop to a wired network.

Figure 1-59 A USB to RJ-45 dongle provides a network port to connect to a wired network

Kensington Technology Group

Figure 1-60   This USB to Wi-Fi adapter plugs into a USB port to connect to a local wireless network

- **Connect to a local wireless network.** Figure 1-60 shows a **USB to Wi-Fi dongle**, which allows you to connect a laptop that doesn't have wireless capability to a wireless network or when the laptop's wireless component has failed. **Wi-Fi (Wireless Fidelity)** is the common name for standards for a local wireless network.
- **Connect to a cellular network.** Some laptops have embedded capability to connect to a cellular network. Figure 1-61 shows a USB cellular modem that can be used for a laptop that doesn't have the embedded technology. A **cellular network** consists of geographic areas of coverage called cells, each controlled by a tower called a **base station**. Cell phones are so named because they use a cellular network.

Figure 1-61   This USB device by Sierra Wireless provides a wireless connection to a cellular network

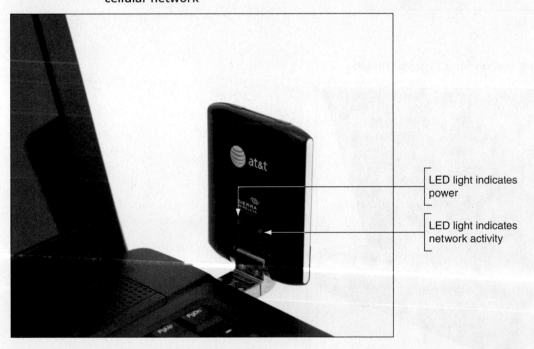

LED light indicates power

LED light indicates network activity

- **Connect to a Bluetooth device.** When a laptop doesn't have Bluetooth capability, you can use a **USB to Bluetooth adapter** to connect to a Bluetooth wireless device such as a Bluetooth printer, headphones, or smartphone. **Bluetooth** is a short-range wireless technology to connect two devices in a small personal network.
- **Use an external optical drive.** When a laptop or netbook doesn't have an optical drive, you can use a **USB optical drive**. Plug the USB optical drive into a USB port so you can use CDs and DVDs with the laptop or netbook.

Docking Stations and Port Replicators

 Core 1 Objective 1.3

The bottom or sides of some laptops have a proprietary connector, called a **docking port** (see Figure 1-62), that connects to a docking station. A **docking station** provides ports to allow a laptop to easily connect to a full-sized monitor, keyboard, AC power adapter, and other peripheral devices. See Figure 1-63. Laptop manufacturers usually offer a docking station as an additional option on most business laptops and a few consumer laptops as well. A disadvantage of a docking station is that when you upgrade your laptop, you typically must purchase a new compatible docking station.

Figure 1-62   The docking port and sheet battery connector on the bottom of a laptop

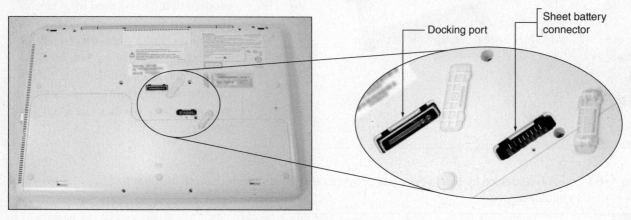

Figure 1-63   A docking station for a Lenovo ThinkPad

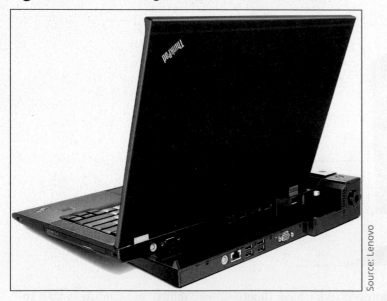

Source: Lenovo

A **port replicator**, sometimes called a universal docking station, is a device that provides ports to allow a laptop to easily connect to peripheral devices, such as an external monitor, network, printer, keyboard and mouse, or speakers. See Figure 1-64. Some port replicators also supply power to the laptop to charge the battery. The difference between a port replicator and a docking station is that a port replicator isn't proprietary to a single brand or model of laptop because it typically connects to a laptop using a single USB port.

Figure 1-64   This port replicator provides USB 3.0, USB 2.0, HDMI, DVI, and network ports

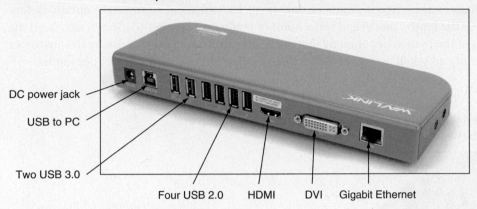

DC power jack

USB to PC

Two USB 3.0

Four USB 2.0   HDMI   DVI   Gigabit Ethernet

To use a docking station or port replicator, plug all the peripherals into the docking station or port replicator. Then connect your laptop to the station. No software needs to be installed. When you need to travel with your laptop, you don't have to unplug all the peripherals; all you have to do is disconnect the laptop from the docking station or port replicator.

Special Considerations When Supporting Laptops

 Core 1 Objectives 1.1, 1.3

Laptops and their replacement parts cost more than desktop computers with similar features because laptop components are designed to be more compact and stand up to movement. Laptops use compact hard drives, small memory modules, and CPUs that require less power than regular components. Whereas a desktop computer is often assembled from parts made by a variety of manufacturers, laptop computers are almost always sold by a vendor that either manufactured the laptop or had it manufactured as a consolidated system. Notable factors that generally apply more to laptop than desktop computers include the following:

- The original equipment manufacturer's warranty
- The service manuals and diagnostic software provided by the manufacturer
- The customized installation of the OS that is unique to laptops
- The need to order replacement parts directly from the laptop manufacturer or other source authorized by the manufacturer

In many situations, the tasks of maintaining, upgrading, and troubleshooting a laptop require the same skills, knowledge, and procedures as when servicing a desktop computer. However, you should take some special considerations into account when supporting, upgrading, and troubleshooting laptops. The same concerns apply to netbooks and all-in-one computers. Let's begin with warranty concerns.

Warranty Concerns

Most laptop manufacturers or retailers offer at least a one-year warranty and the option to purchase an extended warranty. If problems arise while the laptop is under warranty, you only have to deal with a single manufacturer or retailer to get support or parts. After the laptop is out of warranty, this manufacturer or retailer can still be your one-stop shop for support and parts.

Caution (!)

The warranty often applies to all components in the system, but it can be voided if someone other than an authorized service center representative services the laptop. Therefore, you as a service technician must be very careful not to void a warranty that the customer has purchased. Warranties can be voided by opening the case, removing part labels, installing other-vendor parts, upgrading the OS, or disassembling the system unless directly instructed to do so by authorized service center personnel.

Before you begin servicing a laptop, avoid potential problems with a warranty by always asking the customer, "Is the laptop under warranty?" If the laptop is under warranty, look at the documentation to find out how to get technical support. Options are online chat sessions, phone numbers, and email. Use the most appropriate option. Before you contact technical support, have the laptop model and serial number ready (see Figure 1-65). You'll also need the name, phone number, and address of the person or company that made the purchase. Consider asking the customer for a copy of the receipt and warranty so you'll have the information you need to talk with support personnel.

Figure 1-65   The model and serial number stamped on the bottom of a laptop are used to identify the laptop to service desk personnel

Based on the type of warranty purchased by the laptop's owner, the manufacturer might send an on-site service technician, ask you to ship or take the laptop to an authorized service center, or help you solve the problem by an online chat session or over the phone. Table 1-3 lists some popular manufacturers of laptops, netbooks, and all-in-ones. Manufacturers of laptops typically also produce all-in-ones because of the features they have in common.

Table 1-3   Laptop, Netbook, and All-in-One Manufacturers

Manufacturer	Website
Acer	*acer.com* and *us.acer.com/support*
Apple Computer	*apple.com* and *support.apple.com*
ASUS	*asus.com* and *asus.com/us/support*
Dell Computer	*dell.com* and *dell.com/support*
Hewlett Packard (HP)	*hp.com* and *support.hp.com*
Lenovo	*lenovo.com* and *support.lenovo.com*
Microsoft	*microsoft.com* and *support.microsoft.com*
Razer	*razer.com* and *support.razer.com*
Samsung	*samsung.com* and *samsung.com/support*
VAIO	*us.vaio.com* and *support.us.vaio.com*
Toshiba	*toshiba.com* and *support.dynabook.com*

Service Manuals and Other Sources of Information

Desktop computer cases tend to be similar to one another, and components in desktop systems are usually inter-changeable among manufacturers. Not so with laptops. Laptop manufacturers typically take great liberty in creating their own unique computer cases, buses, cables, connectors, drives, circuit boards, fans, and even screws, all of which are likely to be proprietary in design.

Every laptop model has a unique case. Components are installed in unique ways, and opening the case for each laptop model is done differently. Because of these differences, servicing laptops can be very complicated, tedious, and time consuming. For example, a hard drive on one laptop is accessed by popping open a side panel and sliding the drive out of its bay. However, to access the hard drive on another model of laptop, you must remove the keyboard. If you are not familiar with a particular laptop model, you can damage the case frame or plastics as you pry and push while trying to open it. Using trial and error is likely to damage a case. Even though you might successfully replace a broken component, the damaged case will result in an unhappy customer.

Fortunately, a laptop service manual can save you considerable time and effort—if you can locate one online (see Figure 1-66). Most laptop manufacturers closely guard these service manuals and release them only to authorized service centers. Two laptop manufacturers, Lenovo and Dell, provide their service manuals online free of charge. ASUS and HP also do an excellent job of offering online support.

Figure 1-66   Download the laptop service manual to learn how to use diagnostic tools, troubleshoot a laptop, and replace components

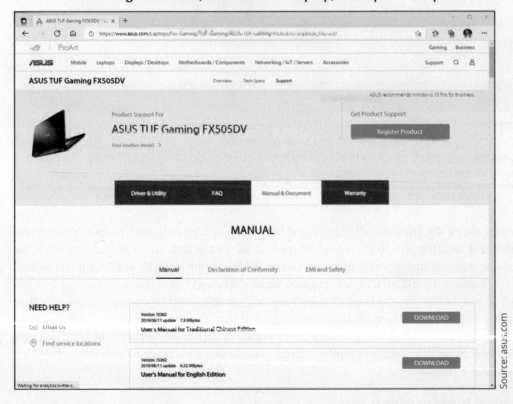

Source: asus.com

For example, Figure 1-67 shows a screenshot from a video that walks through the steps to replace the top cover on an HP laptop. I applaud Lenovo, Dell, and HP for their generous documentation about how their laptops are disassembled and for the options they provide for purchasing proprietary parts without first being an authorized service center.

Figure 1-67 The HP website (*support.hp.com*) provides detailed instructions and videos for troubleshooting and replacing components

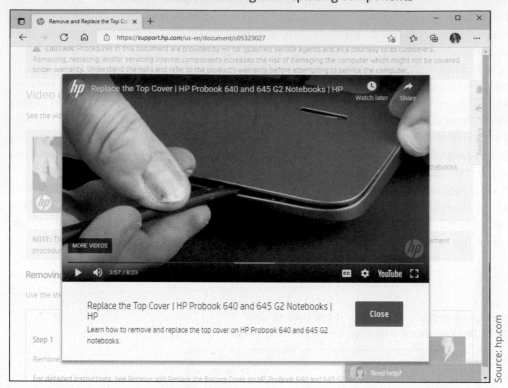

Source: hp.com

Note **9**

The wiki-type website *ifixit.com* does an excellent job of providing its own teardown and reassembly instructions for many brands and models of laptops. You can also buy parts and tools on the site.

Videos at *youtube.com* can also help teach you how to disassemble a specific model of laptop. However, be aware that not all videos posted on YouTube follow recommended best practices.

For all laptop manufacturers, check the Support or FAQ pages of their websites for help with tasks such as opening a case without damaging it and locating and replacing a component. Be aware that some manufacturers offer almost no help at all. Sometimes, you can find service manuals online. To find your manual, search on the laptop model—for example, search on "Lenovo ThinkPad L15 Gen 2 laptop service manual."

Don't forget about the user manuals. They might contain directions for upgrading and replacing components that do not require disassembling the case, such as how to upgrade memory or install a new hard drive. User manuals also include troubleshooting tips and procedures and possibly descriptions of BIOS/UEFI settings. In addition, you can use a web search engine to search on the computer model, component, or error message, which might give you information about the problem and solution.

Diagnostic Tools Provided by Manufacturers

Most laptop manufacturers provide diagnostic software that can help you test components to determine which component needs replacing. As one of the first steps when servicing a laptop, check the user manual, service manual, or manufacturer's website to determine if diagnostic software exists and how to use it. Use the software to pinpoint the problem component, which can then be replaced.

Check the manufacturer's website for diagnostics software that can be downloaded for a specific model of laptop or stored on the hard drive or on CDs bundled with the laptop. Figure 1-68 shows a window provided by the diagnostics program installed on the hard drive of one laptop.

Figure 1-68   Use diagnostics software provided by a laptop manufacturer to troubleshoot hardware problems

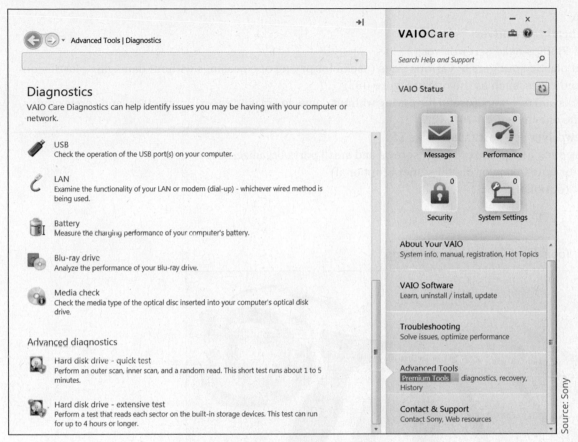

Source: Sony

Note 10

> When you purchase a replacement part for a laptop from the laptop's manufacturer, most often the manufacturer also sends detailed instructions for exchanging the part and/or phone support to talk you through the process.

One example of diagnostic software is PC-Doctor (*pc-doctor.com*), which is recommended by some manufacturers. The diagnostic software is stored on the hard drive or on CD. If stored on CD, you can boot from the CD to run the tests. If the software is stored on the hard drive, you can run it from the Windows Start menu or by pressing a function key at startup before Windows loads. Either way, PC-Doctor can run tests on the keyboard, video, speakers, touch pad, optical drive, wireless LAN, motherboard, processor, ports, hard drive, and memory. To learn how to use the software, see the laptop's service manual or user manual. You can find a standalone version of PC-Doctor for DOS and PC-Doctor for Windows at *pc-doctor.com*. You can purchase it at this site; it's expensive but might be worth it if you plan to service many laptops.

Working Inside a Laptop Computer

Core 1 Objective 1.1

Sometimes it is necessary to open a laptop case so you can upgrade memory, exchange a hard drive, or replace a failed component such as the keyboard, Mini PCIe card, or wireless card. Most laptops sold today are designed so that you can easily purchase and exchange memory modules or hard drives. However, replacing a failing processor or motherboard can be a complex process, taking several hours. Most often, you will choose to replace the entire laptop rather than doing these labor-intensive and costly repairs.

Screws and nuts on a laptop are smaller than those on a desktop system, requiring smaller tools. Figure 1-69 shows several tools used to disassemble a laptop, although you can get by without several of them. Here's the list:

- ESD strap
- Small flathead screwdriver
- Number 1 Phillips-head screwdriver
- Metal and plastic **spudgers** in various sizes (useful for prying open casings without damaging plastic connectors and cases, such as the one in Figure 1-67)
- Dental picks and tweezers (useful for prying without damaging plastic cases, connectors, and screw covers, such as the one in Figure 1-70)
- Torx screwdriver set, particularly size T5
- Something such as a pillbox to keep screws and small parts organized
- Notepad for note-taking or digital camera (optional)
- Flashlight (optional)

Figure 1-69   Tools for disassembling a laptop

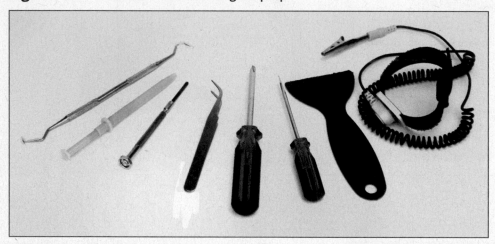

Figure 1-70   Use a small screwdriver or dental pick to pry up
the plastic cover hiding a screw

Working on laptops requires extra patience. As with desktop systems, before opening the case of a laptop or touching sensitive components, you should always wear an ESD strap to protect the system against ESD. You can attach the alligator clip end of the strap to an unpainted metallic surface on the laptop. This surface could be, for instance, a port on the back of the laptop (see Figure 1-71). If a ground strap is not available, first dissipate any ESD between you and the laptop by touching a metallic, unpainted part of it, such as a port on the back, before you touch a component inside the case.

Figure 1-71 To protect the system against ESD, attach the alligator clip of a ground strap to an I/O port on the back of the laptop

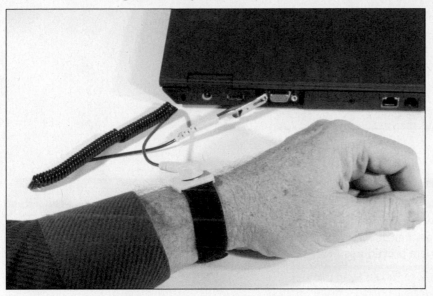

Figure 1-72 Using a notepad can help you organize screws so you know which screw goes where when reassembling

Laptops contain many small screws of various sizes and lengths. When reassembling the system, put screws back where they came from so you won't use screws that are too long and that can protrude into a sensitive component and damage it. As you remove a screw, store or label it so you know where it goes when reassembling. One method is to place screws in a pillbox with each compartment labeled. Another way is to place screws on a soft, padded work surface and use white labeling tape to label each set of screws. A third way to organize screws is to put them on notebook paper and write beside them where the screw belongs (see Figure 1-72). My favorite method of keeping up with all these screws is to tape each one beside the manufacturer documentation that I'm following to disassemble the laptop (see Figure 1-73). Whatever method you use, work methodically to keep screws and components organized so you know what goes where when reassembling.

Figure 1-73   Tape screws beside the step in the manufacturer documentation that told you to remove the screw

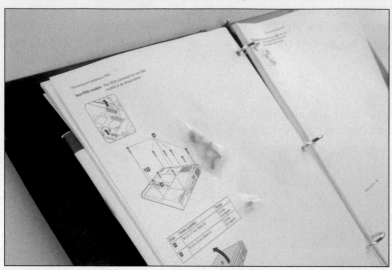

Exam Tip ✔

The A+ Core 1 exam expects you to know the importance of keeping parts organized when disassembling a laptop as well as the importance of having manufacturer documentation to know the steps for disassembly. Given a scenario, you should be able to adhere to appropriate procedures.

If you disassemble a computer and are not following directions from a service manual, keep notes as you work to help you reassemble later. Draw diagrams and label things carefully. Include cable orientations and screw locations in your drawings. You might consider using a digital camera. Photos taken at each step in the disassembly process will be a great help when it's time to put the laptop back together.

When disassembling a laptop, consider the following tips:

- Make your best effort to find the hardware service manual for the particular laptop model you are servicing. The manual should include all the detailed steps to disassemble the laptop and a parts list of components that can be ordered from the laptop manufacturer. If you don't have this manual, your chances of successfully replacing an internal component are greatly reduced! Another helpful resource is searching the Internet for video tutorials for the teardown of the model you are using. If you don't have much experience disassembling a laptop, it isn't wise to attempt to do so without the service manual.
- Consider the warranty that might still apply to the laptop. Remember that opening the case of a laptop under warranty most likely will void the warranty.
- Make certain that any component you have purchased to replace an internal component will work in the model of laptop you are servicing.
- Take your time. Patience is needed to keep from scratching or marring plastic screw covers, hinges, and the case.
- As you work, don't force anything. If you do, you're likely to break it.
- Always wear an ESD strap or use other protection against ESD.
- When removing cables, know that some ribbon cable connectors are **ZIF connectors**, which stands for zero insertion force. To disconnect a cable from a ZIF connector, first lift up the connector's lever and then easily remove the cable, as shown in Figure 1-74. Figure 1-75 shows a laptop that uses three ZIF connectors to hold the three keyboard cables in place. For some ribbon cables, you simply pull the cable out of the connector. For these cables, it's best to use two tweezers, one on each side of the connector, to remove the cable.

Figure 1-74   To disconnect a ZIF connector, first lift up on the lever or locking bar to release the latch, and then remove the cable using the pull tab, which is blue on this laptop

Figure 1-75   Three ZIF connectors hold the three keyboard cables in place

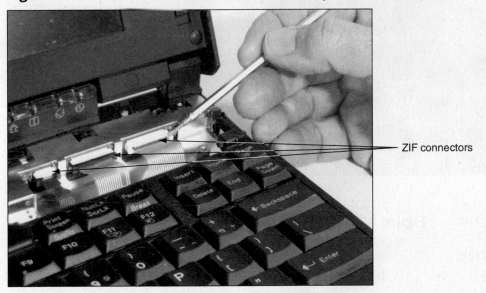

ZIF connectors

- Again, use a spudger, dental pick, or very small screwdriver to pry up a plastic cover hiding a screw.
- Some laptops use plastic screws that are intended to be used only once. The service manual will tell you to be careful not to overtighten these screws and to always use new screws when reassembling a laptop.
- Disassemble the laptop by removing each field replaceable unit (FRU) in the order given by the laptop's service manual.
- At some point in the disassembly process after all appropriate covers and screws have been removed, you must crack the case, which means you separate the top and bottom parts of the case. The parts might be tightly sealed together. To separate them, use a plastic or metal spudger to slide along the seal and pry open the case, as shown earlier in Figure 1-67.

When reassembling a laptop, consider these general tips:

- Reassemble the laptop in the reverse order you disassembled it. Follow each step carefully.
- Be sure to tighten, but not overtighten, all screws. Loose screws or metal fragments in a laptop can be dangerous; they might cause a short as they shift about inside the laptop.

- Before you install the battery or AC adapter, verify that there are no loose parts inside the laptop. Pick it up and gently shake it. If you hear anything loose, open the case, find the loose component, screw, spring, or metal flake, and fix the problem.

Exploring Laptop Internal Components

Core 1 Objective 1.1

Here is a list of important components you are likely to be instructed to remove when disassembling a laptop and the typical order you remove them. However, know that the components and the order of disassembly vary from one laptop to another:

1. **Remove or disable the battery pack.** To start the disassembly, disconnect all peripherals, remove discs from the optical drive, and shut down the system. Then, disconnect the AC adapter and remove the battery. Removing the battery (see Figure 1-76) assures you that no power is getting to the system, which keeps the laptop and you safe as you work. Some laptops and netbooks have built-in batteries. For these devices, follow the manufacturer instructions to disable the battery (often called Ship Mode), which prevents it from providing power to any component.

Figure 1-76   Remove the battery pack before opening a laptop case

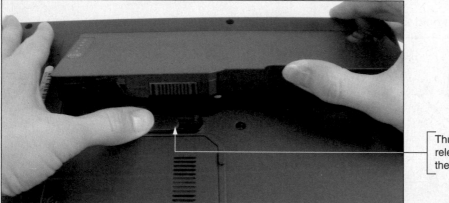

Thumb latch releases the battery

2. **Remove the hard drive.** For some laptops, the hard drive is accessed by removing the hard drive compartment cover from the bottom of the laptop. For example, Figure 1-77 shows the hard drive is secured in its bay with screws. When you remove the screws and disconnect the ribbon cable, you can lift the drive from its bay. For other hard drives, you unplug the drive from its drive socket rather than disconnecting a ribbon cable from the drive.

Figure 1-77   Remove all screws that secure the hard drive in its bay

3. **Remove memory.** Laptops use smaller memory modules than the DIMMs used in desktop computers. Figure 1-78 shows a DIMM and a **SO-DIMM (small outline DIMM)** for size comparison. For one laptop, you first remove the memory/Mini PCI Express Card compartment cover to access the memory modules. Release two latches on both edges of the socket at the same time to remove the memory modules, as shown in Figure 1-79.

Figure 1-78   A DIMM used in desktops compared with a SO-DIMM used in laptops

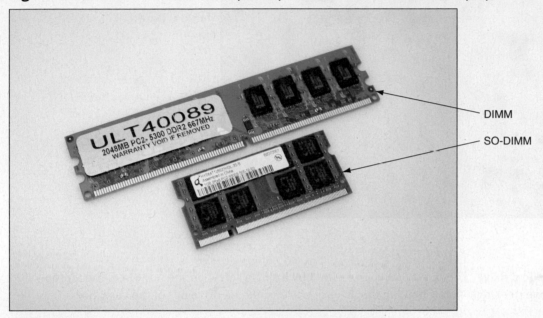

Figure 1-79   Release the latches on both edges of the socket to remove the memory modules

4. **Remove the wireless card.** For the laptop in Figure 1-79, the Mini PCI Express wireless card is installed in the same compartment as the memory modules. Disconnect the two wires leading to the wireless antennas, which are located in the laptop lid. Next, remove the screw securing the wireless card, then pull the card directly away from the socket, as shown in Figure 1-80.

Figure 1-80   Pull the wireless card directly away from the socket to
prevent damage to the card and socket

5. **Remove the optical drive.** The optical drive is secured by a single screw on the bottom of the laptop. After you remove the single screw holding the drive in place, slide the drive out of the case. See Figure 1-81.

Figure 1-81   Slide the optical drive out of the case after removing the
screw securing the optical drive to the laptop

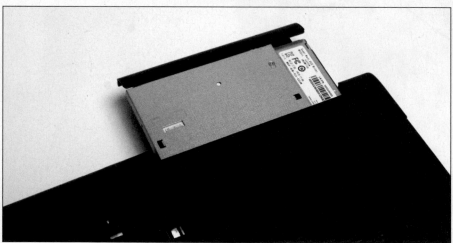

6. **Crack the case.** After removing compartment covers and the components accessible inside these compartments (for example, memory, optical drive, and hard drive), you are ready to remove any other screws as directed in the service manual, and then you can crack the case. Use a spudger to slide along the seal between the case top and bottom, and pry open the plastic casing on the side, as shown in Figure 1-82.

Figure 1-82   Using a spudger helps prevent harming the casing
when prying it open

7. **Remove the keyboard bezel.** The keyboard bezel is the keyboard casing surrounding the keyboard of a laptop. For some laptops, such as the one shown in Figure 1-83, the keyboard bezel is the top of the case. For other laptops, you remove the case top and then remove the keyboard. Once you remove screws and disconnect the cables from the motherboard, the keyboard bezel should easily lift away from the laptop, as shown in Figure 1-83. You might need a spudger to help.

Figure 1-83   Disconnect both the touch pad board cable and the
keyboard cable to remove the keyboard

Other hardware components you are likely to find in a laptop case include the system board, CPU, heat sink, fan, and the LCD panel and components in the laptop lid.

Exploring Inside an All-in-One Computer

Core 1 Objective 1.1

An all-in-one computer uses a mix of components sized for a desktop computer and a laptop. Let's get the general idea of what's inside the case of an all-in-one by looking inside the Lenovo ThinkCentre all-in-one, which was shown earlier in Figure 1-56. Figure 1-84 shows the computer with the case cover removed. Notice that, in the figure, the hard drive is a 3.5-inch drive appropriate for a desktop system, and the memory modules are SO-DIMMs appropriate for a laptop. So goes the hybrid nature of an all-in-one. The fan and heat sink look more like that of a laptop computer, but the processor socket on the motherboard is a desktop processor socket, another hybrid design.

Figure 1-84 Components inside an all-in-one computer

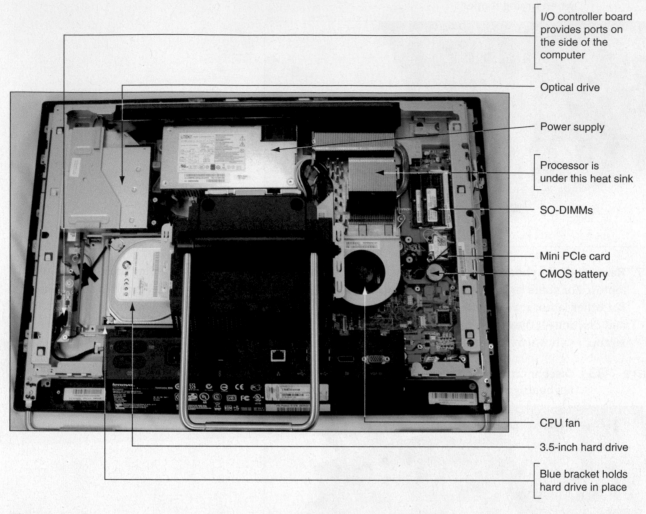

I/O controller board provides ports on the side of the computer

Optical drive

Power supply

Processor is under this heat sink

SO-DIMMs

Mini PCIe card

CMOS battery

CPU fan

3.5-inch hard drive

Blue bracket holds hard drive in place

Figure 1-85 A CMOS battery and Mini PCIe wireless card

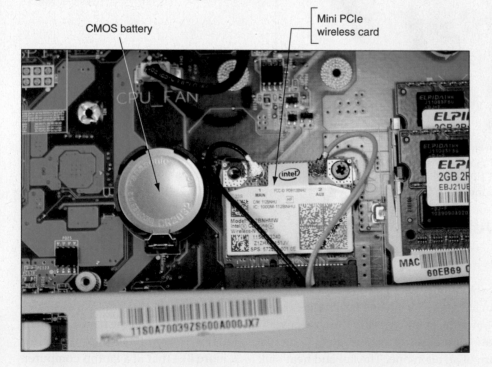

CMOS battery

Mini PCIe wireless card

Several components are easy to exchange in this all-in-one without further disassembly. For example, the Mini PCIe card for wireless connectivity is easy to get to, as are the SO-DIMMs you can partially see on the right side of Figure 1-85.

To work inside an all-in-one, you'll need the service manual to know how to open the case and replace internal components. Replacements for some components, such as the motherboard and power supply, must be purchased from the all-in-one manufacturer because they are likely to be proprietary, as with many laptop components. For specific directions about replacing parts in an all-in-one, see the service manual.

Now that you are familiar with some major components of a laptop, let's learn some special considerations when maintaining laptops.

Maintaining Laptops

 Core 1 Objectives 1.1, 1.3

Laptops and mobile devices tend not to last as long as desktop computers because they are portable and therefore subject to more wear and tear. A device's user manual gives specific instructions on how to care for the device. Those instructions follow these general guidelines:

- LCD panels on devices are fragile and can be damaged fairly easily. Take precautions against damaging a laptop or other device's LCD panel. Don't touch it with sharp objects like ballpoint pens.
- Don't pick up or hold a laptop by the lid. Pick it up and hold it by the bottom. Keep the lid closed when the laptop is not in use.
- Only use battery packs and AC adapters recommended by the laptop manufacturer. Keep the battery pack away from moisture or heat, and don't attempt to take the pack apart. When it no longer works, dispose of it correctly. For laptops, you might consider buying an extra battery pack to use when the first one discharges. You can also buy battery chargers so that you can charge one while the other is in use.
- Don't tightly pack a laptop or tablet in a suitcase because the LCD panel might get damaged. Use a good-quality carrying case, and make a habit of always transporting the laptop in the carrying case. Don't place heavy objects on top of the laptop case.
- Don't move the laptop while the hard drive is being accessed (when the drive indicator light is on). Wait until the light goes off.
- Don't put the laptop close to an appliance such as a TV, large audio speakers, or refrigerator that generates a strong magnetic field, and don't place your cell phone on a laptop while the phone is in use.
- Always use passwords to protect access to your laptop so you are better protected when connected to a public network or if the device is stolen or used by an unauthorized person.
- Keep your laptop or device at room temperature. For example, never leave it in a car overnight during cold weather, and don't leave it in a car during the day in hot weather. Don't expose your laptop or device to direct sunlight for an extended time.
- Don't leave the laptop or device in a dusty or smoke-filled area. Don't use it in a wet area such as near a swimming pool or in the bathtub. Don't use it at the beach where sand can get in it.
- Don't power it up and down unnecessarily.
- Protect the laptop from overheating by not running it when it's still inside the carrying case, not resting it on a pillow, and not partially covering it with a blanket or anything else that would prevent proper air circulation around it.
- If a laptop has just been brought indoors from the cold, don't turn it on until it reaches room temperature. In some cases, condensation can cause problems. Some manufacturers recommend that when you receive a new laptop shipped to you during the winter, you should leave it in its shipping carton for several hours before you open the carton to prevent subjecting the laptop to a temperature shock.
- Protect a laptop against static electricity. If you have just come in from the cold on a low-humidity day when there is the possibility that you are carrying static electricity, don't touch the laptop until you have grounded yourself.
- Before placing a laptop in a carrying case for travel, remove any CDs, DVDs, or USB flash drives, and put them in protective covers. Verify that the system is powered down and not in sleep mode, which will drain the battery.

- If a laptop gets wet, you can partially disassemble it to allow internal components to dry. Give the laptop several days to dry before attempting to turn it on. Don't use heat to speed up the drying time.
- Keep current backups of important data on a laptop or device in case it fails or is stolen.

A well-used laptop, especially one that is used in dusty or dirty areas, needs cleaning occasionally. Here are some cleaning tips:

1. Clean the LCD panel with a soft, dry cloth. If the panel is very dirty, you can use monitor wipes or lightly dampened cloths to clean it. Some manufacturers recommend using a mixture of isopropyl alcohol and water to clean an LCD panel. Be sure the LCD panel is dry before you close the lid.

2. Use a can of compressed air meant for use on computer equipment to blow dust and small particles out of the keyboard, trackball, and touch pad. Turn the laptop at an angle and direct the air into the sides of the keyboard. Then use a soft, damp cloth to clean the key caps and touch pad.

3. Use compressed air to blow out all air vents on the laptop to make sure they are clean and unobstructed.

4. If a laptop is overheating, the CPU fan might be clogged with dust. The overheating problem might be solved by disassembling the laptop and blowing out the fan with compressed air.

5. If keys are sticking, remove the keyboard so you can better spray under the keys with compressed air. If you can remove the key cap, remove it and clean the key contact area with contact cleaner. One example of a contact cleaner you can use for this purpose is Stabilant 22 (*stabilant.com*). Reinstall the keyboard and test it. If the key still sticks, replace the keyboard.

6. Remove the battery and clean the battery connections with a contact cleaner.

Exam Tip ✔

The A+ Core 1 exam expects you to know how to solve the problem of sticking keys on a laptop, given a scenario.

Module Summary

Exploring a Desktop Computer

- When hardware support technicians disassemble or reassemble a computer, they need to stay organized, keep careful notes, and follow all the safety procedures to protect the computer equipment and themselves.
- Before opening a computer case, shut down the system, unplug it, disconnect all cables, and press the power button to drain residual power.
- Common tools for a computer hardware technician include an ESD strap, screwdrivers, tweezers, flashlight, compressed air, and cleaning solutions and pads.
- Special tools a hardware technician might need include a POST diagnostic card, power supply tester, multimeter, and loopback plugs.
- A computer's video ports might include the VGA, DVI, DisplayPort, and HDMI ports. Other ports include RJ-45, audio, SPDIF, USB, eSATA, PS/2, serial, and RJ-11 ports. A Thunderbolt port can transmit video, data, and power.
- Internal computer components include the motherboard, processor, expansion cards, DIMM memory modules, hard drive, optical drive, and power supply.
- Cases, power supplies, and motherboards use ATX and microATX form factors. The form factor determines how the case, power supply, and motherboard fit together and the cable connectors and other standards used by each.

- Power connectors used by the ATX and microATX form factors include the older 20-pin P1, current 24-pin P1, 4-pin and 8-pin CPU auxiliary motherboard, 4-pin Molex, 15-pin SATA, and 6/8-pin PCIe connectors.
- An expansion card fits in a slot on the motherboard and is anchored to the case by a single screw or clip.
- Firmware consists of the older BIOS (basic input/output system) firmware and the newer UEFI (Unified Extensible Firmware Interface) firmware. This BIOS/UEFI firmware is responsible for managing essential devices (for example, keyboard, mouse, hard drive, and monitor) before the OS is launched, starting the computer, and managing motherboard settings.
- Most hard drives and optical drives today use the serial ATA (SATA) standards for the drive to interface with the motherboard and power supply.

First Look at Laptop Components

- Laptop computers are designed for travel. They use the same technology as desktop computers, with modifications for space, portability, and power conservation. A laptop generally costs more than a desktop with comparable power and features.
- A laptop docking station or port replicator can make it easy to connect and disconnect peripheral devices.
- You can use the USB ports for expansion—for example, you can add a USB to RJ-45 dongle, a USB to Wi-Fi dongle, Bluetooth capability, or a USB optical drive.
- The laptop manufacturer documentation—including the service manual, diagnostic software, and recovery media—is useful when disassembling, troubleshooting, and repairing a laptop.
- Field replaceable units (FRUs) in a laptop can include the memory modules, hard drive, keyboard, Mini PCIe card, and wireless card.
- When an internal component needs replacing, consider the possibility of disabling the component and using an external peripheral device in its place. Don't jeopardize the warranty on a laptop by opening the case or using components not authorized by the manufacturer.
- Replacing the laptop might be more cost effective than performing labor-intensive repairs, such as replacing the system board.
- When disassembling a laptop, the manufacturer's service manual is essential.
- When upgrading components on a laptop, including memory, use components that are the same brand as the laptop, or use only components recommended by the laptop's manufacturer.
- Follow the directions in a service manual to disassemble a laptop. Keep small screws organized as you disassemble a laptop because they come in a variety of sizes and lengths. Some manufacturers use plastic screws and recommend you use new screws rather than reuse the old ones.
- Special concerns when supporting a laptop also apply to supporting a netbook or all-in-one computer.
- When replacing an FRU, you might need to remove internal laptop components such as the keyboard, hard drive, memory, wireless card, and battery pack.
- An all-in-one computer uses a combination of components designed for desktop computers and laptops.

Key Terms

For explanations of key terms, see the Glossary for this text.

4-pin 12 V connector	ATX12V power supply	chassis	docking port
8-pin 12 V connector	audio ports	DB9 port	docking station
20-pin P1 connector	base station	DB15 port	dual-voltage selector
24-pin P1 connector	BIOS (basic input/output system)	DE15 port	switch
all-in-one computer		desktop case	DVI (Digital Video Interface) port
analog	Bluetooth	digital	electrostatic discharge (ESD)
antistatic bag	cellular network	DIMM (dual inline memory module)	
ATX (Advanced Technology Extended)	central processing unit (CPU)	DisplayPort	ESD mat

ESD strap

loopback plug

power supply

standoff

Ethernet port

main board

power supply tester

system board

expansion card

microATX (mATX)

power supply unit (PSU)

Thunderbolt 3 port

external SATA (eSATA)
   port

microprocessor

processor

tower case

firmware

modem port

PS/2 port

UEFI (Unified Extensible

Molex connector

RAM (random access
   memory)

   Firmware Interface)

form factor

motherboard

USB (Universal Serial

front panel connectors

multimeter

RJ-11 port

   Bus) port

front panel header

netbook

RJ-45 port

USB optical drive

ground mat

network port

SATA power connector

USB to Bluetooth

hard disk drive (HDD)

notebook

serial ATA (SATA)

   adapter

hard drive

optical connector

serial port

USB to RJ-45 dongle

HD15 port

PCI Express (PCIe)

SO-DIMM (small outline

USB to Wi-Fi dongle

HDMI (High-Definition
   Multimedia Interface)
   port

PCIe 6/8-pin connector

port replicator

POST card

   DIMM)

spacer

SPDIF (Sony-Philips
   Digital Interface)

VGA (Video Graphics
   Array) port

video memory

heat sink

POST diagnostic card

   sound port

Wi-Fi (Wireless Fidelity)

internal component

POST (power-on

spudger

ZIF connector

laptop

   self-test)

Thinking Critically

These questions are designed to prepare you for the critical thinking required for the A+ exams and may use information from other modules and the web.

1. You purchase a new desktop computer that does not have wireless capability, and then you decide that you want to use a wireless connection to the Internet. What are the two least expensive ways to upgrade your system to wireless? (Choose two.)

   a. Trade in the computer for another computer that has wireless installed.
   b. Purchase a second computer that has wireless capability.
   c. Purchase a wireless expansion card, and install it in your system.
   d. Purchase a USB wireless adapter, and connect it to the computer by way of a USB port.

2. What type of computer is likely to use SO-DIMMs, have an internal power supply, and use a desktop processor socket?

3. When troubleshooting a computer hardware problem, which tool might help with each of the following problems?

   a. You suspect the network port on a computer is not functioning.
   b. The system fails at the beginning of the boot, and nothing appears on the screen.
   c. A hard drive is not working, and you suspect the Molex power connector from the power supply might be the source of the problem.

4. You disassemble and reassemble a desktop computer. When you first turn it on, you see no lights and hear no sounds. Nothing appears on the monitor screen. What is the most likely cause of the problem? Explain your answer.

   a. A memory module is not seated properly in a memory slot.
   b. You forgot to plug in the monitor's external power cord.
   c. A wire in the case is obstructing a fan.
   d. Power cords to the motherboard are not connected.

5. You are looking to buy a laptop on a budget that requires you to service and repair the laptop yourself, and you want to save money by not purchasing an extended service agreement beyond the first year. To limit

your search, what should you consider when choosing manufacturers? Which manufacturers would you choose and why?

6. A four-year-old laptop will not boot and presents error messages on-screen. You have verified with the laptop technical support that these error messages indicate the wireless card has failed and needs replacing. What is the first step you should take to prepare for the repair?

   a. Ask yourself if replacing the wireless card will cost more than purchasing a new laptop.
   b. Find a replacement wireless card.
   c. Find the service manual to show you how to replace the wireless card.
   d. Ask if the laptop is still under warranty.

7. Why are laptops usually more expensive than desktop computers with comparable power and features?

8. When a laptop internal device fails, what three options can you use to deal with the problem?

9. A friend was just promoted to a new job that requires part-time travel, and they have been promised a new laptop after their first month with the company. They need an easy way to disconnect and reconnect all their peripheral devices to their new laptop. Devices include two external monitors (one HDMI, one DVI), a USB wireless mouse, USB wireless keyboard, Ethernet network, USB printer, headphones, and microphone. The budget is $100. What kind of device would best suit your friend's needs? Why? Research online to find a recommendation for a device that will work best. What is your recommendation and why?

10. Your laptop LCD panel is blank when you boot up. You can hear the laptop turn on, and the keyboard backlight is on. You have checked the brightness using the function keys, and that is not the problem. What is an easy next step to determine if the LCD panel has failed? Describe how that next step can also allow you to continue to use your laptop if the LCD panel has failed, but the replacement components won't arrive for a week.

11. A foreign exchange student brought a desktop computer from home (Europe) to the United States. The student brought a power adapter so that the power cord would plug into the power outlet and tried turning on their computer, but it wouldn't power on. What is likely the problem? What warning should you give when the student returns home at the end of the year?

12. You're building a new desktop computer from parts you picked out and purchased. You invested a good deal of money in this computer and want to be sure to protect your investment while you assemble it. What precautions should you take to protect your computer from damage and electrostatic discharge?

13. Your friend asks for your help because their laptop's Wi-Fi connection keeps dropping. What are some options you could offer your friend to fix the problem?

14. Your boss asks you to upgrade a desktop computer to add an extra DVI port for a second monitor. How would you recommend completing this request?

15. After troubleshooting a problem, you decide that the wireless card has failed in a laptop. What do you do first before you disassemble the laptop?

Hands-On Projects

Hands-On Project 1-1

Opening a Computer Case

Est. Time: 30 minutes
Core 1 Objectives: 2.8, 3.1, 3.2, 3.3, 3.4, 3.5

Using a desktop or tower computer, identify all the ports on the front or rear of the case. If you need help, see Table 1-1. Look at the rear of the case. On which side is the motherboard? Examine the case and determine how to open it. Shut down the system, and unplug the power cable. Disconnect all other cables. Press the power button

(continues)

Hands-On-Project Contined

on the front of the case to discharge residual power. Carefully open the case. Remember not to touch anything inside the case unless you are using an ESD strap or antistatic gloves to protect components against ESD.

Draw a diagram of the inside of the case, and label all drives, the motherboard, the cooler, DIMM memory modules, the power supply, and any expansion cards installed. Then do the following:

1. Write down how many power cables are coming from the power supply. How many of these cables are connected to the motherboard? To other devices inside the computer? Identify each type of power cable the system is using.

2. For the motherboard, list the number and type of expansion slots on the board. Does the board have a 20-pin or 24-pin P1 connector? What other power connectors are on the board? How many memory slots does the board have? Locate the screws that attach the motherboard to the case. How many screws are used? Do you see screw holes in the motherboard that are not being used? As a general rule of thumb, up to nine screws can be used to attach a motherboard to a case.

3. For expansion cards, examine the ports on the back of the card. Can you determine the purpose of the card by looking at its ports? What type of slot does the card use?

Leave the case open so you'll be ready for Hands-On Project 1-2 next.

Hands-On Project 1-2

Identifying Connectors Used on an Installed Motherboard

Est. Time: 15 minutes
Core 1 Objective: 3.4

If necessary, remove the case cover to your desktop computer. Next, remove the expansion cards from your system. With the expansion cards out of the way, you can more clearly see the power cables and other cables and cords connected to the motherboard. Diagrams and notes are extremely useful when disassembling and reassembling a system. To practice this skill, draw a large rectangle that represents the motherboard. On the rectangle, label every header or connector that is used on the board. Note on the label the type of cable that is used and where the other end of the cable connects.

Hands-On Project 1-3

Identifying Drives and Their Connectors

Est. Time: 15 minutes
Core 1 Objectives: 3.1, 3.3, 3.4

If your instructor has provided a display of drives, identify the purpose of each drive (for example, a hard drive or optical drive) and the type of power connector each drive uses (for example, SATA or Molex). If you have access to a computer with the case cover removed, complete the following:

1. List the drives installed, the purpose of each drive, and the type of interface and power connector it uses.

2. How many connectors does the motherboard have for drives? Identify each type of connector.

Hands-On Project 1-4

Closing the Case

Est. Time: 15 minutes
Core 1 Objective: 3.4

The case cover to your desktop computer is off from doing the previous exercises. Before you close your case, it's always a good idea to quickly clean it first. Using a can of compressed air, blow the dust away from fans and other components inside the case. Be careful not to touch components unless you are properly grounded. When you're done, close the case cover.

Hands-On Project 1-5

Observing Laptop Features

Est. Time: 30 minutes
Core 1 Objective: 1.1

Do the following to find a service manual for a laptop you have available, such as one that belongs to you or a friend:

1. What are the brand, model, and serial number of the laptop?
2. What is the website of the laptop manufacturer? Print or save a webpage on that site that shows the documentation and/or drivers available for this laptop.
3. If the website provides a service manual for disassembling the laptop, download the manual. Print two or three pages from the manual showing the title page and table of contents for the manual.
4. If the website does not provide a service manual, search the Internet for the manual. If you find it, download it, and print the title page and table of contents.

After examining a laptop, its documentation, and the manufacturer's website, complete the following:

1. What ports are on the laptop?
2. What type of memory slots does the laptop have?
3. List the steps you would take to upgrade memory.
4. What is the cost of a new battery pack?

Real Problems, Real Solutions

Real Problem 1-1

Planning Your Computer Repair Toolkit

Est. Time: 30 minutes
Core 1 Objectives: 2.8, 3.4

Do research online to find the following tools for sale: ESD strap, set of flathead and Phillips-head screwdrivers, can of compressed air, monitor-cleaning wipes, multimeter, power supply tester, cable ties, flashlight, loopback plug to test an Ethernet port, POST diagnostic card, and toolbox.

(continues)

Real Problem Continued ————————————————————————————————

Print or save the webpages that show each tool and its price. What is the total cost of this set of tools? If you were building your own computer repair toolkit, which tools would you purchase first if you could not afford the entire set of tools? Which tools not listed would you add to your toolbox?

Real Problem 1-2

Setting Up a Service Center for Laptops

Est. Time: 30 minutes
Core 1 Objective: 1.1

If you intend to set up your own computer repair shop, you might want to consider becoming a service center for a few brands of the more popular laptops. Reasons to become an authorized service center include having access to service manuals, parts lists, and wholesale parts for laptops. Do the following to research becoming an authorized service center:

1. Select a brand of laptops that you think you would like to service.
2. Research the website of this manufacturer, and answer these questions:
   a. Where is the closest authorized service center for this brand of laptops?
   b. What are the requirements to become an authorized service center? Print or save the webpage showing the requirements.
   c. Is A+ certification one of those requirements?
   d. Some laptop manufacturers offer a program that falls short of becoming an authorized service center but does provide support for IT professionals so that repair technicians can order laptop parts. Does the manufacturer offer this service? If so, what must you do to qualify?

If you try one brand of laptop and can't find the information you need, try another brand. Sometimes this information can only be obtained by contacting the manufacturer directly. And one more hint: To use *google.com* to search a particular site, begin the search string with **site:hostname.com**, for example, **site:microsoft.com**.

Real Problem 1-3

Taking Apart a Laptop

Est. Time: 1 hour
Core 1 Objective: 1.1

If you enjoy putting together thousand-piece jigsaw puzzles, you'll probably enjoy working on laptop computers. With desktop systems, replacing a component is not a time-consuming task, but with laptops, the job could take half a day. If you take the time to carefully examine the laptop's case before attempting to open it, you will probably find markings provided by the manufacturer to assist you in locating components that are commonly upgraded. If you have a service manual, your work will be much easier than without one.

The best way to learn how to disassemble a laptop is to practice on an old one that you can afford to break. Find an old Dell, Lenovo, or IBM ThinkPad for which you can download the service manual from the appropriate website. Carefully and patiently follow the disassembly instructions and then reassemble the laptop. Write down the challenges you faced while disassembling and reassembling the laptop. What might you do to overcome these challenges next time? When done, you can congratulate yourself and move on to newer laptops.

Module
2

All About Motherboards

Module Objectives

1 Describe and contrast various types and features of motherboards

2 Configure a motherboard using BIOS/UEFI firmware

3 Maintain a motherboard by updating drivers and firmware, using jumpers to clear BIOS/UEFI settings, and replacing the CMOS battery

4 Select, install, and replace a desktop motherboard

Core 1 Certification Objectives

3.1 Explain basic cable types and their connectors, features, and purposes.

3.4 Given a scenario, install and configure motherboards, central processing units (CPUs), and add-on cards.

Introduction

In the module "Taking a Computer Apart and Putting It Back Together," you learned how to work inside a desktop or laptop computer and began the process of learning about each major component or subsystem in a computer case. In this module, you build on that knowledge to learn about motherboards, which techies sometimes call the mobo. You'll learn about motherboard sizes (called form factors), connectors, expansion slots, sockets, onboard ports, and chipsets. Then you'll learn how to support a motherboard, which includes configuring, maintaining, installing, and replacing it.

A motherboard is considered a field replaceable unit, so it's important to know how to replace one, but the good news is you don't need to know how to repair one that is broken. Troubleshooting a motherboard works hand in hand with troubleshooting the processor and other components that must work to boot up a computer, so we'll leave troubleshooting the motherboard until later modules.

Motherboard Types and Features

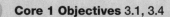

Core 1 Objectives 3.1, 3.4

A motherboard is the most complicated component in a computer. When you put together a computer from parts, generally you start by deciding which processor and motherboard you will use considering the purpose of the computer. Everything else follows these two decisions. Take a look at the details of Figure 2-1, which shows a

Figure 2-1   The ASUS Prime Z590-Plus motherboard uses the microATX form
            factor and LGA1200 11th and 10th generation processor socket

Source: asus.com

2

microATX motherboard, the ASUS Prime Z590-Plus, that can hold various Intel Core, Pentium, and Celeron processors in the LGA1200 11th and 10th generation processor socket. When selecting a motherboard, generally you need to pay attention to the form factor, processor socket, chipset, expansion slots, and other connectors, slots, and ports. In this section of the module, we look at the details of each of these features so you can read a technical motherboard ad with the knowledge of a pro and know how to select the right motherboard when replacing an existing one or building a new system.

Motherboard Form Factors

Core 1 Objective 3.4

The motherboard form factor determines the size of the board and its features that make it compatible with power supplies and cases. The most popular motherboard form factors are ATX, microATX (a smaller version of ATX, sometimes called the mATX), **Extended ATX (E-ATX)** (a larger version of ATX), and **Mini-ITX**, also called **mITX** (a smaller version of microATX). Figure 2-2 shows an ATX board. You saw a microATX motherboard in Figure 2-1. A Mini-ITX board is shown in Figure 2-3. The Mini-ITX board is also commonly referred to as an **ITX** board.

Figure 2-2   The ASUS Prime Z590-A motherboard uses the ATX form factor

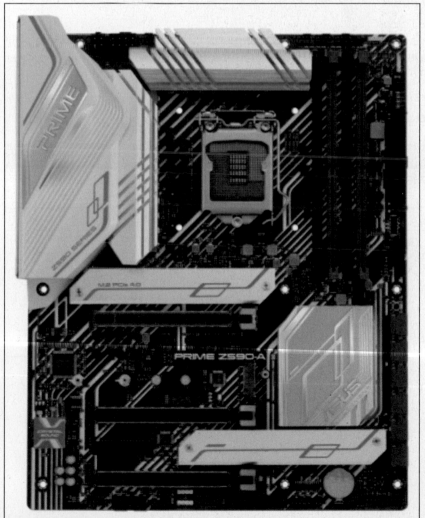

Source: asus.com

Figure 2-3   A Mini-ITX motherboard

Source: Courtesy of ASUSTeK Computer, Inc.

Table 2-1 lists form factor sizes and descriptions, and Figure 2-4 shows a comparison of the sizes and hole positions of three ATX boards. Each of those three boards can fit into an ATX computer case and use an ATX power supply.

Table 2-1   Five motherboard form factors

Form Factor	Motherboard Size	Description
ATX, full size	Up to 12″ × 9.6″ (305 mm × 244 mm)	A popular form factor that has had many revisions and variations
MicroATX (mATX)	Up to 9.6″ × 9.6″ (244 mm × 244 mm)	A smaller version of ATX
Extended ATX (E-ATX)	Up to 12″ × 13″ (305 mm × 330 mm)	A larger version of ATX
ITX (Mini-ITX and mITX)	Up to 6.7″ × 6.7″ (170 mm × 170 mm)	A **small form factor (SFF)** board used in low-end computers and home theater systems; the boards are often used with an Intel Celeron or Atom processor and are sometimes purchased as a motherboard-processor combo unit

Figure 2-4   Sizes and hole positions for the ATX, microATX, and Mini-ITX motherboards

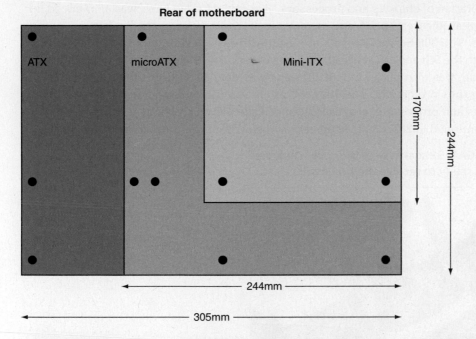

Exam Tip ✔

The A+ Core 1 exam expects you to know how to match up an ATX or ITX motherboard with the appropriate case and power supply that support the same form factor.

Intel and AMD Chipsets and Processor Sockets

Core 1 Objective 3.4

A **chipset** is a set of chips on the motherboard that works closely with the processor to collectively control the memory, buses on the motherboard, and some peripherals. The chipset must be compatible with the processor it serves. A **socket** is rectangular with pins or pads to connect the processor to the motherboard and a mechanism to hold the processor in place. This chipset and socket determine which processors a board can support.

The two major chipset and processor manufacturers are Intel (*intel.com*) and AMD (*amd.com*). Intel dominates the chipset market for several reasons. It knows more about its own Intel processors than other manufacturers do, and it produces the chipsets most compatible with the Intel family of processors. However, AMD's market share is currently about 20 percent and growing.

Intel Chipsets

Intel makes desktop, mobile, and server chipsets and processors. To see a complete comparison chart of all Intel chipsets and processors, start at the Intel webpage *ark.intel.com*. Intel groups its chipsets and processors in generations, and each generation has a code name. Here is the list of generations from the past several years:

- **600 Series Desktop Chipsets.** The latest Intel chipsets are the 600 Series Chipsets, used with the LGA1700 socket, also called Socket V. The 600 Series Chipsets are compatible with the 12th generation (formally called Alder Lake) desktop processors. Thus far, the only chipset in this family is the Z690 chipset, which was released at the end of 2021. The current 12th generation processors include the Core i5, Core i7, and Core i9 processors; these processors can have up to 10 cores.
- **400 and 500 Series Desktop Chipsets.** The 400 and 500 Series Chipsets are used with the LGA1200 socket and are compatible with the 10th and 11th generation desktop processors. Some motherboards based on the 400 Series Chipset may need a BIOS/UEFI update to support the 11th generation of processors, also called Rocket Lake, which were released in March 2021. The 11th generation started a new development

cycle based on the new Cypress Cove microarchitecture. The 11th generation offers increased performance in speed, memory, and graphics in an attempt to win back some of the market from AMD, specifically in the gaming market. The 10th generation of chipsets and processors, also called Comet Lake, was announced in 2019. The 10th generation increased cores, speed, and memory support over earlier generations.

- **300 Series Desktop Chipsets.** The 300 Series Chipsets are used with the altered pinout of the LGA1151 socket and are compatible with the 9th and 8th generation of processors. The 9th generation of processors, also called Coffee Lake Refresh, was introduced in late 2018 and was defined by adjusting the integrated heat spreader and increasing the core counts. The 9th generation was discontinued at the end of 2021. The 8th generation of chipsets and processors, also called Coffee Lake, began shipping at the end of 2017. The 8th generation was discontinued in 2021. A close-up of this open socket is shown in Figure 2-5.

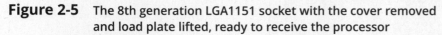

Figure 2-5 The 8th generation LGA1151 socket with the cover removed and load plate lifted, ready to receive the processor

- **200 Series Desktop Chipsets.** The 200 Series Chipsets are used with the original version of the LGA1151 socket and are compatible with the 7th and 6th generation desktop processors. The 7th generation processors, also called Kaby Lake, began shipping in 2016, and mobile processors were launched in 2017. The 7th generation was discontinued in 2020. The 6th generation processors, also called Skylake, were launched in 2015. Even though the 6th generation processors and chipsets were discontinued in 2020, they are the base architecture that the next several generations optimize.

Since the release of the 2nd generation Intel Core family of processors, you can identify which generation a processor fits in by the four or five digits in the model number. The first of the four digits is the generation. For example, the Core i5-9600K processor is a 9th generation processor, and the Core i5-11500 processor is an 11th generation processor.

Sockets for Intel Processors

The Intel name for a socket includes the number of pins the socket has. Intel uses a **land grid array (LGA)** for all its current sockets. These sockets have blunt pins that project up to connect with lands on the bottom of the processor. You can see these lands when you look closely at Figure 2-5.

Here are the current Intel sockets for desktop computers:

- The **LGA1700** socket (also called Socket V) was released in 2021 and is compatible with 12th generation (Alder Lake) processors. Because this socket is larger than previous sockets, heat sinks and coolers that worked with previous sockets won't work with the LGA1700 socket.
- The **LGA1200** socket was released in 2020. This socket is compatible with Intel's 10th and 11th generation processors and chipsets and is shown in Figure 2-6. This socket design offers improved power delivery and support for I/O features.

Figure 2-6   The LGA1200 socket is compatible with the 11th
and 10th generation Intel processors

- The **LGA1151** socket was first released in 2015. The first release of the socket works with Intel's 6th and 7th generation processors and chipsets and is shown in Figure 2-7. The second release works with Intel 8th and 9th generation processors and chipsets.

Figure 2-7   The 6th and 7th generation LGA1151 open socket
and the bottom of an Intel processor

Here are the Intel sockets used in servers and high-performance workstations:

- The LGA2066 socket is used with 8th through 6th generation processors and chipsets. It was introduced with Skylake-X high-end 6th generation processors in 2017.
- LGA2011 is used with 5th through 2nd generation processors and chipsets and has several variations for different generations, including LGA2011-0, LGA2011-1, and LGA2011-v3.

> **Caution** ⚠️
>
> When a processor is installed in a socket, extreme care must be taken to protect the socket and the processor against ESD and from damage caused by bending the pins or scratching the processor pads during the installation. Take care not to touch the bottom of the processor or the pins of the socket. Doing so can leave finger oil on the gold plating of the contact surfaces. This oil can later cause tarnishing and lead to a poor contact.

To ensure that even force is applied when inserting the processor in the socket, sockets have one or two levers on the sides. These sockets are called **zero insertion force (ZIF) sockets**, and the levers are used to lift the processor up and out of the socket. When you push the levers down, the processor moves into its pin connectors with equal force over the entire housing. Because the socket and processor are delicate, processors generally should not be removed or replaced repeatedly.

AMD Chipsets and Sockets

Currently, AMD has four chipset and socket categories for personal computers:

- Figure 2-8 shows the **sTRX4 socket**, a land grid array (LGA) socket that supports 3rd generation Threadripper processors and uses the TRX40 chipset. The sTRX4 socket was released in 2019. The Threadripper processors are part of the AMD Ryzen series of high-end processors.

Figure 2-8 The sTRX4 socket supports the 3rd generation Threadripper processors and the TRX40 chipset

Source: asrock.com

- The **TR4 (Threadripper 4) socket**, released in 2017, is an LGA socket that supports Threadripper processors and uses the AMD X399 chipset.
- The **AM4** chipset family and AM4 socket are used with AMD Ryzen and Athlon processors. While the AM4 socket was launched in 2016, it is still a highly popular socket. AMD chipsets in the AM4 family include A300, B300, and X300. The processors and chipsets support mainstream desktop systems. The socket has 1331 pins in a **pin grid array (PGA)**, which means the socket has 1331 holes and the AMD processor has 1331 pins that fit into those socket holes. AMD has announced that in 2022, the Ryzen processors will use a new socket and chipset to replace the popular AM4 socket and chipset.
- The **AM3+** and AM3 are PGA sockets used with AMD Piledriver and Bulldozer processors and the 9 series chipsets, including 970, 980G, and 990X. The processors and chipsets are used in high-end gaming systems. AM3+ and AM3 processors can fit in either socket. Figure 2-9 shows the AM3+ socket and the bottom of the AMD FX processor.

Figure 2-9   The AMD AM3+ open socket; notice the holes in the socket and pins on the bottom of the processor

- The FM2+ is an older PGA socket used with AMD Athlon, Steamroller, and Excavator processors and A-series chipsets such as the A58 and A68H.

Match a Processor to the Socket and Motherboard

For both Intel and AMD, the processor families (for example, Intel Core i3, Intel Core i5, AMD Athlon, or AMD Ryzen) are used with various chipset generations and sockets. Therefore, you must pay close attention to the actual model number of the processor to know which socket it requires and which motherboards can support it. If you install a processor on a motherboard that can fit the socket but has the wrong chipset for the processor, you can damage both the motherboard and the processor. Sometimes, you can install a newer processor on an older motherboard by first updating the firmware on the motherboard, which you learn to do later in this module. To match a processor to a motherboard and socket:

- Look at the motherboard manufacturer's website or user guide for a list of processors the motherboard supports. If a motherboard requires a firmware update to use a newer processor, the motherboard manufacturer's website will alert you and provide the downloaded firmware update. Updating chipset firmware is covered later in this module. If an update is required, you must update the firmware before you install the new processor.
- You can also search the Intel (*ark.intel.com*) or AMD (*amd.com*) website for the exact processor to make sure the socket it uses is the same as the socket on the motherboard. You can also use the website to find other information about the processor.

Exam Tip ✔

The A+ Core 1 exam does not expect you to be familiar with the processor sockets used by laptop computers. It is generally more cost effective to replace a laptop that has a damaged processor than to replace the processor. If you are called on to replace a laptop processor, however, always use a processor the laptop manufacturer recommends for the particular laptop model and system board CPU socket.

Buses and Expansion Slots

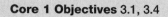

Core 1 Objectives 3.1, 3.4

When you look carefully at a motherboard, you may see many fine lines on both the top and the bottom of the board's surface (see Figure 2-10). These lines, sometimes called **traces**, are circuits or paths that enable data, instructions, timing signals, and power to move from component to component on the board. This system of pathways used for communication and the protocol and methods used for transmission are collectively called a **bus**. (A **protocol** is a set of rules and standards that any two entities use for communication.)

Figure 2-10   On the bottom of the motherboard, you can see bus lines terminating at the processor socket

The specifications of a motherboard always include the expansion slots on the board. Take a look at a motherboard ad that shows detailed specifications, and identify the types of expansion slots on the board. Table 2-2 lists the various expansion slots found on today's motherboards.

Table 2-2   Expansion slots and internal connectors listed by throughput

Expansion Slot or Internal Connector	Performance	Year Introduced
Each revision of PCI Express basically doubles the throughput of the previous revision.		
PCI Express Version 6.0	Up to 126 GB/sec for 16 lanes	Expected in 2022
PCI Express Version 5.0	Up to 63 GB/sec for 16 lanes	2019
PCI Express Version 4.0	Up to 32 GB/sec for 16 lanes	2017
PCI Express Version 3.0	Up to 16 GB/sec for 16 lanes	2010
Conventional **PCI (Peripheral Component Interconnect)** slots transfer data at about 500 MB/sec and have gone through several variations, but only the latest variation is seen on today's motherboards. A notch in the slot prevents the wrong type of PCI card from being installed. The PCI standard has been replaced by PCI Express.		
SATA (Serial Advanced Technology Attachment or Serial ATA) connectors on a motherboard are mostly used by storage devices, such as hard drives or optical drives.		
SATA Revision 3.x (Revisions 3.1 through 3.5) aka SATA 6Gb/s	6 Gb/sec or 600 MB/sec	SATA Revision 3.x was released in 2009. The latest revision (SATA 3.5) was released in 2020.
SATA Revision 2.x aka SATA 3Gb/s	**3 Gb/sec or 300 MB/sec**	**2004**
USB (Universal Serial Bus) might have internal connectors and external ports, which are used by a variety of USB devices.		
USB 4	Up to 40 Gb/sec	2019
USB 3.2	Up to 20 Gb/sec	2017
USB 3.1	Up to 10 Gb/sec	2014
USB 3.0	Up to 5 Gb/sec	2011–2017
USB 2.0	Up to 480 Mb/sec	2001

Exam Tip ✔

The A+ Core 1 exam expects you to know about the various PCI, PCIe, and SATA slots and how to select add-on cards to use them. You also need to know how to install external USB devices and how to use the internal USB headers on a motherboard.

Now let's look at the details of the PCIe and PCI expansion slots used in desktops.

PCI Express

PCI Express (PCIe) currently comes in four different slot sizes called PCI Express ×1 (pronounced "by one"), ×4, ×8, and ×16. Figure 2-11 shows three of these slots. Notice in the figure the sizes of the slots and the positions of the notches in the slots, which prevent a card from being inserted in the wrong direction or in the wrong slot.

Figure 2-11   Three types of expansion slots: PCIe ×1, PCIe ×16, and conventional PCI

A PCIe ×1 slot contains a single lane for data. PCIe ×4 has four lanes, PCIe ×8 has eight lanes, and PCIe ×16 has 16. The more lanes an add-on card uses, the more data is transmitted in a given time. Data is transferred over one, four, eight, or 16 lanes, which means that a 16-lane slot is faster than a shorter slot when the add-on card in the slot is using all 16 lanes. If you install a short card in a long slot, the card uses only the lanes it connects to. PCIe is used by a variety of add-on cards. The PCIe ×16 slot is used by graphics cards that require large throughput.

Less expensive motherboards may not have a full PCIe ×16 bus and yet provide PCIe ×16 slots. The longer cards can fit in the ×16 slot but only use four lanes for data transfers. The version of PCIe also matters; the latest currently available is Version 5, which is the fastest. (Version 6 is expected to be released in 2022.) Learn to read motherboard ads carefully. For example, look at the ad snippet shown in Figure 2-12. One of the longer PCIe ×16 slots operates in ×4 mode, only using four lanes, and uses the PCIe Version 2 standard. If you were to install a graphics card in one of these two PCIe ×16 slots, you would want to be sure you install it in the faster of the two ×16 slots.

Figure 2-12   PCIe documentation for one motherboard

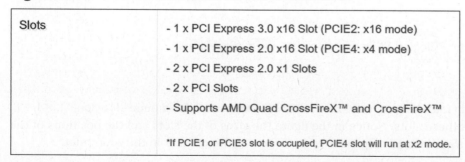

Slots	- 1 x PCI Express 3.0 x16 Slot (PCIE2: x16 mode)
	- 1 x PCI Express 2.0 x16 Slot (PCIE4: x4 mode)
	- 2 x PCI Express 2.0 x1 Slots
	- 2 x PCI Slots
	- Supports AMD Quad CrossFireX™ and CrossFireX™
	*If PCIE1 or PCIE3 slot is occupied, PCIE4 slot will run at x2 mode.

A graphics card that uses a PCIe ×16 slot may require as much as 450 watts. A typical PCIe ×16 slot provides 75 watts to a card installed in it. To provide the extra wattage for the card, a motherboard may have power connectors near the ×16 slot, and the graphics card may have one, two, or even three connectors to connect the card to the extra power (see Figure 2-13). Possibilities for these connectors are a 6-pin PCIe (which provides 75 watts)

Figure 2-13   The graphics card has a PCIe 8-pin power connector on top

and/or an 8-pin PCIe connector (which provides 150 watts), a 4-pin Molex connector, or a SATA-style connector. Connect power cords from the power supply to the power connector type you find on the graphics card. Alternately, some motherboards provide Molex or SATA power connectors on the board to power PCIe graphics cards. See Figure 2-14. When installing a graphics card, always follow the manufacturer's directions for connecting auxiliary power for the card. If the card requires extra wattage, the package will include power cords you need for the installation.

Figure 2-14   Auxiliary power connectors to support PCIe

SATA-style power connector

Molex-style power connector

Core to Core ⇆

To learn more about wattage, refer to the appendix "Safety Procedures and Environmental Concerns."

PCI

Conventional PCI slots and buses are slower than those of PCI Express. The slots are slightly taller than PCIe slots (look carefully at the two PCI slots labeled in Figure 2-11); they are positioned slightly closer to the rear of the computer case, and the notch in the slot is near the front of the slot. The PCI bus transports 32 data bits in parallel and operates at about 500 Mbps. The PCI slots are used for all types of add-on cards, such as Ethernet network cards, wireless cards, and sound cards. Although most graphics cards use PCIe, you can buy PCI video cards to use if your PCIe slots are not working.

Onboard Ports and Connectors

In addition to expansion slots, a motherboard might also have several ports and internal connectors. Ports coming directly off the motherboard are called **onboard ports** or integrated components. For external ports, the motherboard provides an I/O panel of ports that stick out the rear of the case. These ports may include multiple USB ports, PS/2 mouse and keyboard ports, video ports (HDMI, DVI-D, DVI-I, or DisplayPort), sound ports, a LAN RJ-45 port (to connect to the network), and an eSATA port (for external SATA drives). Figure 2-15 shows ports on an entry-level desktop motherboard.

Figure 2-15 A motherboard provides ports for common I/O devices

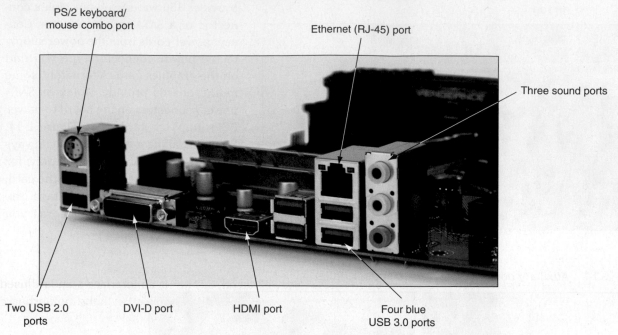

PS/2 keyboard/
mouse combo port

Ethernet (RJ-45) port

Three sound ports

Two USB 2.0
ports

DVI-D port

HDMI port

Four blue
USB 3.0 ports

When you purchase a motherboard, the package includes an **I/O shield**, which is the plate you install in the computer case that provides holes for the I/O ports. The I/O shield is the size designed for the case's form factor, and the holes in the shield are positioned for the motherboard ports (see Figure 2-16).

Figure 2-16 The I/O shield fits the motherboard ports to the computer case

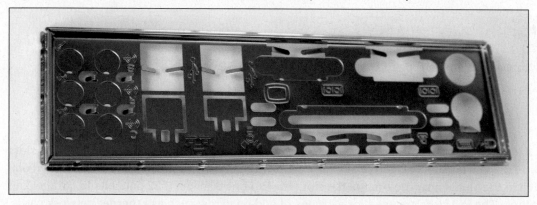

A motherboard might have several internal connectors, including USB, M.2, SATA, and PCIe connectors. When you purchase a motherboard, look in the package for the motherboard manual, which is either printed or on DVD; you can also find the manual online at the manufacturer's website. The manual will show a diagram of the board with a description of each connector. For example, the connectors for the motherboard in Figure 2-17 are labeled as the manual describes them. If a connector is a group of pins sticking up on the board, the connector is called a **header**. You will learn to use most of these connectors in later modules.

Figure 2-17   Internal connectors on a motherboard for front panel ports

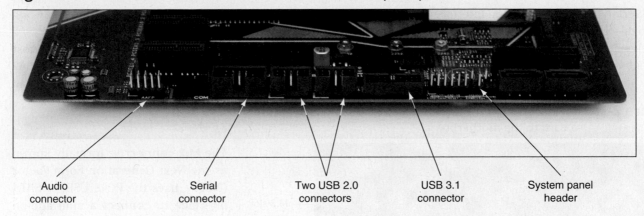

Audio connector   Serial connector   Two USB 2.0 connectors   USB 3.1 connector   System panel header

Next is a rundown of the internal connectors you need to know about.

SATA

SATA (Serial Advanced Technology Attachment or Serial ATA), pronounced "*say*-ta," is an interface standard used mostly by storage devices. To attach a SATA drive to a motherboard, you need a data connection to the motherboard and a power connection to the power supply. Figure 2-18 shows a motherboard with seven SATA connectors. Six use the SATA Revision 3 standard, and one is a shorter SATA Express connector.

Figure 2-18   Seven SATA connectors on a motherboard

The following are currently used versions of SATA:

- SATA Express (SATAe) combines SATA and PCIe to provide a faster bus than SATA Revision 3, although the standard is seldom used.
- SATA Revision 3.x (third generation) is commonly known by its throughput as SATA 6Gb/s.
- SATA Revision 2.x (second generation) is commonly known by its throughput as SATA 3Gb/s.

SAS

SAS (Serial Attached SCSI) is an interface standard used mostly by storage devices—typically in servers and workstations—and the successor of SCSI. SAS is significantly more expensive, more durable, and faster than SATA. SAS is well suited for a server setting where many users will be accessing the data at the same time. SAS-4 is the most current version of SAS, completed in 2017, and has speeds up to 22.5 Gb/s. If a motherboard does not have any SAS ports or needs more, you can use an expansion card with SAS ports.

Figure 2-19 An M.2 slot and three possible screw positions to secure a card to the motherboard

M.2 slot

M.2

The **M.2 connector**, formally known as the Next Generation Form Factor (NGFF), uses the PCIe, USB, or SATA interface to connect a mini add-on card. The card fits flat against the motherboard and is secured with a single screw. Figure 2-19 shows the slot and three screws for M.2 cards. The three screws allow for the installation of cards of three different lengths.

The M.2 connector or slot was first used on laptops and is now common on desktop motherboards. It is commonly used by wireless cards and solid-state drives (SSDs). When the PCIe interface is used, the slot is faster than all the SATA standards normally used by hard drives; therefore, the M.2 slot is often the choice to support the SSD that will hold the Windows installation. However, before installing Windows on an M.2 drive, make sure the motherboard BIOS/UEFI firmware will boot from an M.2 device. (Look for the option in the boot priority order in BIOS/UEFI setup, which is discussed later in this module.) Some motherboards have a cover over an M.2 slot. Figure 2-20 shows documentation in the motherboard's user manual with instructions on how to remove this cover to install the M.2 card.

Be aware there are multiple M.2 standards and M.2 slots. An M.2 slot is keyed for certain M.2 cards by matching keys on the slot with notches on the card. Figure 2-21 shows three popular options, although other options exist. Before purchasing an M.2 card, make sure the card matches the M.2 slot and uses an interface standard the slot supports. For example, for one motherboard, the M.2 slot uses either the PCIe or SATA interface. When a card that uses the SATA interface is installed in the slot, the motherboard uses SATA for the M.2 interface and disables one of the SATA connectors. When a PCIe M.2 card is installed, the motherboard uses the PCIe interface for the slot.

Figure 2-20 A motherboard user manual gives instructions on how to install an M.2 card on a slot with a cover

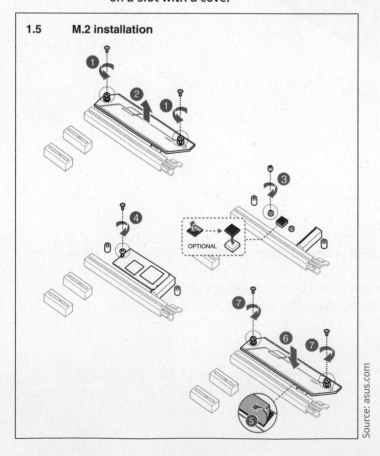

1.5   M.2 installation

OPTIONAL

Source: asus.com

Figure 2-21   An M.2 slot is keyed with a notch to hold an M.2 card with an B key
or M key edge connector

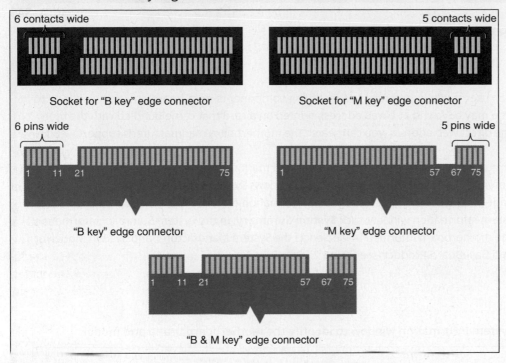

6 contacts wide   5 contacts wide

Socket for "B key" edge connector   Socket for "M key" edge connector

6 pins wide   5 pins wide

1   11   21   75   1   57   67   75

"B key" edge connector   "M key" edge connector

1   11   21   57   67   75

"B & M key" edge connector

Exam Tip ✔

The A+ Core 1 exam expects you to be able to recognize SATA, M.2, and USB internal motherboard connectors and decide which connector to use in a given scenario.

USB

A motherboard may have USB headers or USB connectors. (Recall that a header is a connector with pins sticking up.) The USB header is used to connect a cable from the motherboard to USB ports on the front of the computer case (see Figure 2-22).

Figure 2-22   USB headers are used to connect the motherboard
to USB ports on the front of the computer case

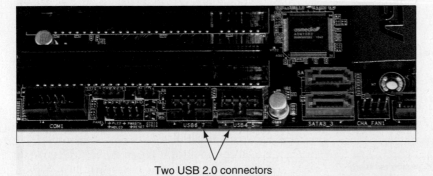

Two USB 2.0 connectors

Applying Concepts

Finding the Motherboard Documentation

Est. Time: 15 minutes
Core 1 Objective: 3.4

The motherboard manual or user guide is essential to identifying components on a board and knowing how to support the board. This guide may be found at a web address printed on a card that came bundled with the motherboard. If you don't have the direct web address, you can search the motherboard manufacturer's support website for the user guide.

To find the correct user guide online, you need to know the board manufacturer and model. If a motherboard is already installed in a computer, you can use BIOS/UEFI setup or the Windows System Information utility (msinfo32.exe) to report the brand and model of the board. To access System Information for Windows, enter `msinfo32.exe` in the search box. In the System Information window, click **System Summary**. In the System Summary information in the right pane, look for the motherboard information labeled as the System Manufacturer and System Model or BaseBoard Manufacturer and BaseBoard Product (see Figure 2-23).

Figure 2-23   Use the System Information window to identify the motherboard brand and model

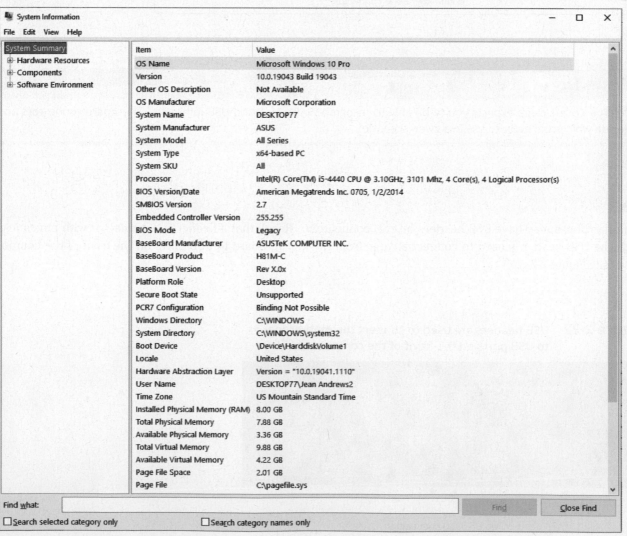

If the motherboard is not installed or the system is not working, look for the brand and model imprinted somewhere on the motherboard (see Figure 2-24). Next, go to the website of the motherboard manufacturer and download the user guide. Websites for several motherboard manufacturers are listed in Table 2-3. The diagrams, pictures, charts, and explanations of settings and components in the user guide will be invaluable to you when supporting this board.

Figure 2-24   The motherboard brand and model are imprinted somewhere on the board

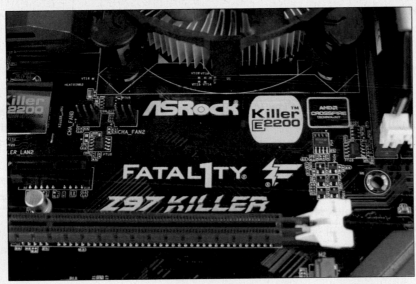

Table 2-3   Major Manufacturers of Motherboards

Manufacturer	Web Address
ASRock	asrock.com
ASUS	asus.com
BIOSTAR	biostar-usa.com
EVGA	evga.com
Gigabyte Technology Co., Ltd.	gigabyte.com
Intel Corporation	intel.com
Micro-Star International (MSI)	us.msi.com
NZXT	nzxt.com

Now that you know what to expect when examining or selecting a motherboard, let's see how to configure a board.

Using BIOS/UEFI Setup to Configure a Motherboard

 Core 1 Objective 3.4

Firmware on the motherboard is used to enable or disable a connector, port, or component; control the frequency and other features of the CPU; manage security features; control what happens when the computer first boots; and monitor and log various activities of the board.

Motherboards made after 2012 use BIOS/UEFI firmware; prior to 2012, all motherboards used BIOS firmware. UEFI (Unified Extensible Firmware Interface) improves on BIOS but includes BIOS for backward compatibility with older devices. UEFI is managed by several manufacturers and developers under the UEFI Forum (see *uefi.org*).

Facts you need to know about UEFI include the following:

- Microsoft requires UEFI in order for a system to be certified for Windows 10.
- UEFI is required for hard drives larger than 2 TB. (One terabyte, or TB, equals 1000 gigabytes, or GB.) A hard drive uses one of two methods for partitioning the drive: The **Master Boot Record (MBR)** method is older, allows for four partitions, and is limited to 2 TB drives. The **GUID Partition Table (GPT)** method is newer, allows for any size of hard drive, and, for Windows, can have up to 128 partitions on the drive. GPT is required for drives larger than 2 TB or for systems that boot using UEFI firmware.
- UEFI offers **Secure Boot**, which prevents a system from booting up with drivers or an OS not digitally signed and trusted by the motherboard or computer manufacturer. For Secure Boot to work, the OS must support UEFI. Microsoft requires Secure Boot be enabled for a system to install Windows 11.
- For backward compatibility, UEFI can boot from an MBR hard drive and provide a BIOS boot through its **Compatibility Support Module (CSM)** feature. CSM is backward compatible with devices and drivers that use BIOS.

The motherboard settings don't normally need to be changed except, for example, when you are first setting up the system, when there is a problem with hardware or the OS, or when a power-saving feature or security feature (such as a power-on password) needs to be disabled or enabled.

Exam Tip ✔

The A+ Core 1 exam expects you to know about BIOS/UEFI settings for boot options, firmware updates, security settings, and interface configurations. Security settings include passwords, drive encryption, the TPM chip, HSM, and Secure Boot. All these settings and features are covered in this section of the module. In a given scenario, you need to know which BIOS/UEFI setting to use to solve a problem, install a new component or feature, or secure a system.

Accessing the BIOS/UEFI Setup Program

 Core 1 Objective 3.4

You access the BIOS/UEFI setup program by pressing a key or combination of keys during the boot process; for some laptops, you press a button on the side of the laptop. For most motherboards, you press F12, F2, or Del during the boot. Sometimes, a message such as *Press F12 or Del to enter UEFI BIOS Setup* appears near the beginning of the boot, or a boot menu with the option to access BIOS setup appears after you have pressed a special button. See the motherboard documentation to know for sure which key or button to press.

When you press the appropriate key or button, a setup screen appears with menus and Help features that are often very user-friendly. Although the exact menus depend on the BIOS/UEFI maker, the sample screens shown in the following section will help you become familiar with the general contents of BIOS/UEFI setup screens.

Note

BIOS firmware uses only the keyboard for input, whereas UEFI firmware can use the keyboard and mouse. Some manufacturers use BIOS firmware with integrated UEFI functionality, and the setup screens are controlled only by the keyboard.

Viewing and Monitoring Information

Core 1 Objective 3.4

The first screen you see in the firmware utility usually gives you information about the system, including the BIOS/UEFI version and information about the CPU, memory, hard drive, optical drive, date, and time. BIOS/UEFI menus and screens differ, so you might need to browse through the screens to find what you're looking for. For example, Figure 2-25 shows information on the Configuration screen about installed hard drives and optical drives. This system has five internal SATA and eSATA ports and one external eSATA port. As you can see, a 120 GB hard drive is installed on SATA port 0, and another 1000 GB hard drive is installed on SATA port 1. Both ports are internal SATA connectors on the motherboard. Notice the optical drive is installed on SATA port 3, which is also an internal connector on the motherboard.

Figure 2-25   A BIOS/UEFI setup screen showing a list of drives installed on the system

```
                              System Setup
   Main    Configuration    Performance   Security   Power   Boot    Exit

   SATA Drives                                          Enables of disables the
                                                        Chipset SATA Controller.
   Chipset SATA Controller Configuration                The Chipset SATA
     Chipset SATA              <Enable>                 controller supports the 2
     Chipset SATA Mode         <AHCI>                   blue internal SATA ports
     S.M.A.R.T.                <Enable>                 (up to 6Gb/s supported per
     SATA Port 0               KINGSTON SUP20(120.0GB-6.0Gb/s)  port) and the 2 black and
     SATA Port 1               ST1000DM003-9Y(1000.2GB-6.0Gb/s) 2 red internal and
     SATA Port 2               [Not Installed]          external SATA ports (up to
     SATA Port 3               TSSTcorp CDDVD(1.5GB/s)  3Gb/s supported per port).

   eSATA Ports                 <Enable>
     Internal eSATA Port 4     [Not Installed]
     External eSATA Port 5     [Not Installed]

   Hard Disk Pre-Delay         <No>                     → ←: Select Screen
                                                        ↑ ↓: Select Item
                                                        Enter:Select
                                                        +/-: Change Opt.
                                                        F9: Load Defaults
                                                        F10:Save ESC:Exit
```
Source: Intel

Figure 2-26 shows the BIOS/UEFI screen for another system with a graphical BIOS/UEFI interface. Notice information about the BIOS version, CPU type, total memory installed, current temperature and voltage of the CPU, how the two memory slots on the motherboard are used (one is populated and one is empty), and RPMs of CPU fans.

When you click **Advanced Mode**, you see the SATA configuration. For example, Figure 2-27 shows a 1000 GB hard drive using the first SATA6G yellow port and a DVD device using the second SATA3G brown port. The other SATA ports are disabled. Also notice in the figure that S.M.A.R.T. is enabled. **S.M.A.R.T. (Self-Monitoring Analysis and Reporting Technology)** monitors statistics reported by a hard drive and can predict when the drive is likely to fail. It displays a warning when it suspects a failure is about to happen.

Figure 2-26   Information about the system is reported when you first access BIOS/UEFI setup

Source: American Megatrends, Inc.

Figure 2-27   SATA configuration displayed by the ASUS BIOS/UEFI utility shows the status of four SATA connectors on the motherboard

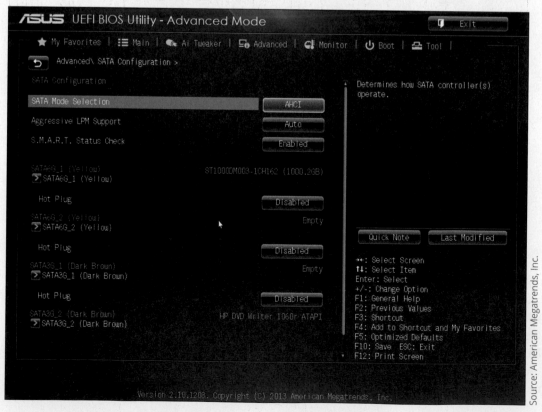

Source: American Megatrends, Inc.

Changing Boot Options

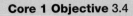 **Core 1 Objective** 3.4

Figure 2-28 shows an example of a boot menu in BIOS/UEFI setup. Here, you can set the order in which the system tries to boot from certain devices (called the boot priority order or boot sequence).

Figure 2-28   Set the boot priority order in BIOS setup

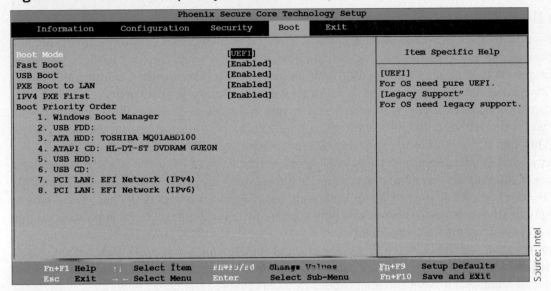

Source: Intel

Boot Priority Order

Here are some examples of when you might want to change the boot priority order:

- Some distributions of the Linux operating system (OS) can be installed on a USB flash drive; you can boot the OS from this drive when you put the USB device first in the boot priority order.

> **Caution** !
>
> Booting the system directly from a USB flash drive causes the system to ignore any OS that might be installed on the hard drive, which can be a security issue because data stored on the hard drive might be vulnerable. To help close this security hole, set the boot priority order to first boot from the hard drive, and password-protect access to BIOS/UEFI setup so others cannot change the boot order. Other ways to protect the OS and data on the hard drive are addressed later in this text.

> **Note** 2
>
> Some computers with multiple USB ports limit the capability to boot to only a single USB port.

- When you first install an OS on the hard drive, you might want BIOS/UEFI to first boot from a DVD so you can install Windows from the Windows setup DVD.
- If you are installing the OS from a server on the network, put the *PCI LAN: EFI Network* option at the top of the boot priority order, and enable *PXE Boot to LAN*. This causes the computer to boot to the firmware program called the **Preboot eXecution Environment or Pre-Execution Environment (PXE)**, which then searches the network for an OS it receives from a deployment server. Notice in Figure 2-28 that when booting to access a deployment server on the network, you must choose whether your network is using IPv4 or IPv6 for IP addressing. You learn more about these concepts later in the text.

- When Windows is installed on the hard drive but refuses to start, you can boot from the Windows setup DVD to troubleshoot and repair the installation.

After the OS is installed, you can prevent accidental or malicious boots from a DVD or other removable media by changing the boot priority order to boot first from the hard drive. Also, BIOS/UEFI screens might give you options regarding built-in diagnostics that occur at the boot. You can configure some motherboards to perform a fast boot and bypass the extensive POST. When troubleshooting a boot problem, be sure to set BIOS/UEFI to perform the full POST.

Manage Secure Boot

You also need to know how to manage Secure Boot, which was invented to help prevent malware from launching before the OS and anti-malware software are launched. Secure Boot works only when the boot mode is UEFI (and not CSM) and the OS supports it. Windows 10 and several distributions of Linux (for example, Ubuntu and Red Hat) support Secure Boot to ensure that programs loaded by firmware during the boot are trustworthy.

Secure Boot holds digital signatures, encryption keys, and drivers in databases stored in flash memory on the motherboard and/or on the hard drive. Initially, the motherboard manufacturer stores the data on the motherboard before it is shipped. This data is provided by OS and hardware manufacturers.

After the OS is installed, UEFI databases are stored in a system partition named efi on the hard drive. Database names are db (approved digital signatures), dbx (blacklist of signatures), and KEK (signatures maintained by the OS manufacturer). After an OS is installed on the hard drive, updates to the OS include updates to the KEK. The **Platform Key (PK)** is a digital signature that belongs to the motherboard or computer manufacturer. The PK authorizes turning Secure Boot on or off and updating the KEK database.

When Secure Boot is enabled, it checks each driver, the OS, and applications before UEFI launches these programs during the early stages of the boot to verify it is signed and identified in the Secure Boot databases. After the OS is launched, it can load additional drivers and applications that UEFI Secure Boot does not verify.

For normal operation, you would not be required to change Secure Boot settings unless you want to install hardware or an OS (for example, Kali Linux) that is not certified by the computer manufacturer. In this situation, you could disable Secure Boot. Before you make any changes to the Secure Boot screen, be sure to use the option to save Secure Boot keys if that option is available. Doing so saves all the databases to a USB flash drive so you can backtrack your changes later if needed.

Take a look at Figure 2-29, which shows the Security screen for one laptop where Secure Boot can be enabled or disabled. Also notice the option highlighted to Restore Factory Keys. This option may be helpful if BIOS/UEFI refuses to allow a fresh installation of an OS or hardware device. On this system, before you can enable Secure Boot, you must go to the Boot screen and select UEFI as the Boot Mode.

Figure 2-29   Manage Secure Boot on the Security screen of BIOS/UEFI setup

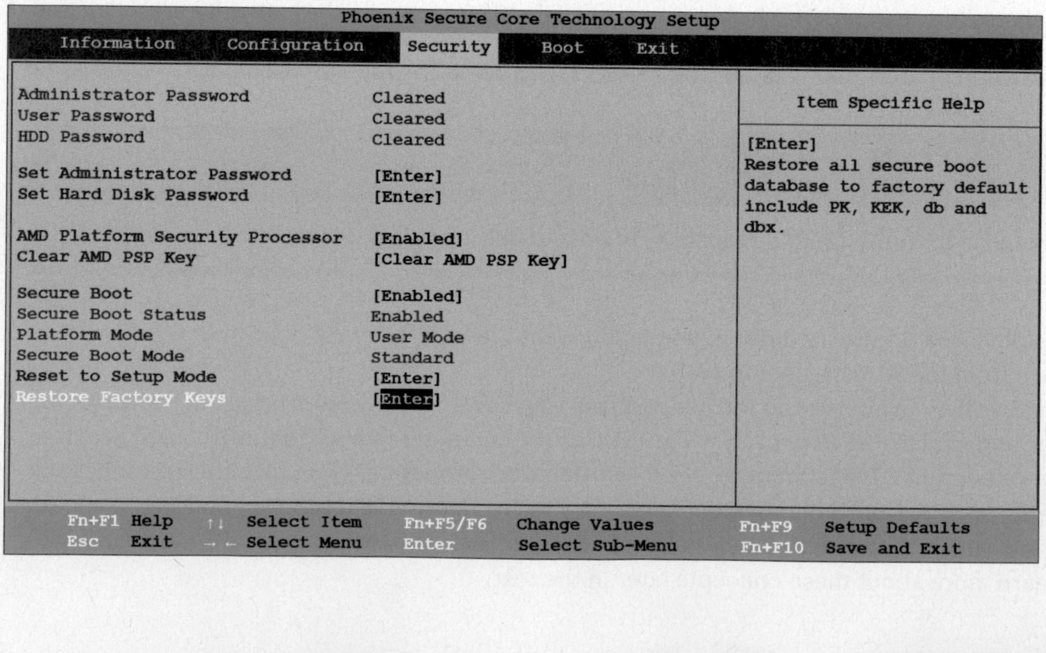

Manage CSM and UEFI Boot

The Boot screen allows you to select UEFI mode or CSM (also called Legacy Support) mode. UEFI mode is required for Secure Boot to be enabled. For example, in Figure 2-30, you first must disable Fast Boot, and then you can select either CSM (Compatibility Support Module) or Secure Boot. When you select Secure Boot, UEFI mode is enabled. Use CSM for backward compatibility with older BIOS devices and drivers and MBR hard drives.

Figure 2-30   Use CSM to boot a legacy BIOS system or disable it to implement UEFI Secure Boot

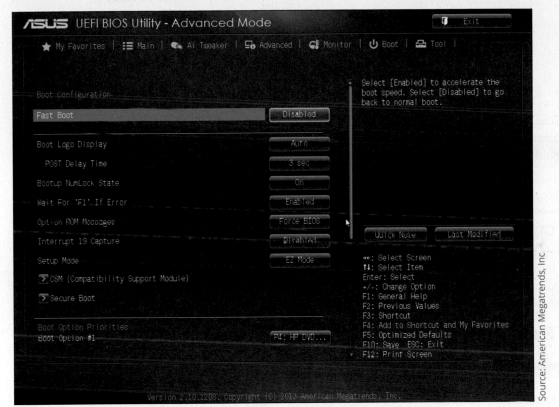

Source: American Megatrends, Inc

Configuring Onboard Devices

Core 1 Objective 3.4

You can enable or disable some onboard devices (for example, a wireless LAN, a network port, USB ports, or video ports) using BIOS/UEFI setup. For one system, the Configuration screen shown in Figure 2-31 does the job. On this screen, you can enable or disable a port or group of ports; you can configure the Front Panel Audio ports for Auto, High Definition audio, and Legacy audio; or you can disable these audio ports. What you can configure on your system depends on the onboard devices the motherboard offers.

In BIOS/UEFI you might encounter a couple of options for the USB ports. One possible setting you can change is **USB power share**, which enables you to charge a USB device even when the computer is turned off. Another setting is **USB wake support**, which allows a USB device to wake a computer on action.

Figure 2-31   Enable and disable onboard devices

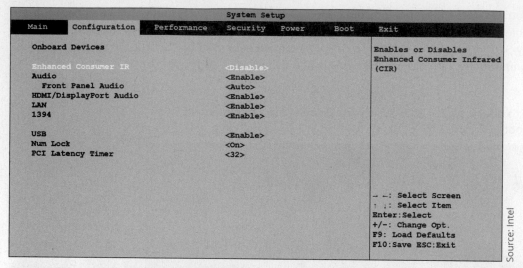

Note 3

You don't have to replace an entire motherboard if one port fails. For example, if the network port fails, use BIOS/UEFI setup to disable the port. Then use an expansion card for the port instead.

Processor and Clock Speeds

Overclocking is running a processor, memory, motherboard, or video card at a higher speed than the manufacturer recommends. Some motherboards and processors allow overclocking, but it is not a recommended best practice. If you decide to overclock a system, pay careful attention to the temperature of the processor so it does not overheat; overheating can damage the processor.

Configuring Security Features

Core 1 Objective 3.4

Other security features besides Secure Boot are power-on passwords, drive password protection, the TPM chip, HSMs, and drive encryption. All are discussed next.

Power-On Passwords

Power-on passwords are assigned in BIOS/UEFI setup to prevent unauthorized access to the computer and/or the BIOS/UEFI setup utility. For one motherboard, this security screen looks like the one shown in Figure 2-32, where

Figure 2-32   Set supervisor and user passwords in BIOS/UEFI setup to help lock down a computer

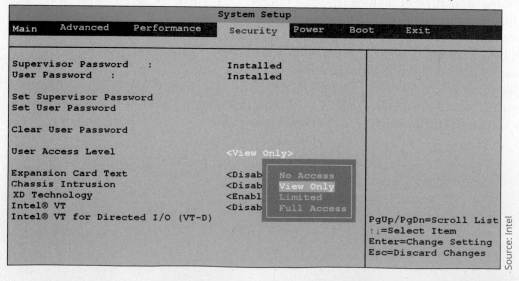

you can set a supervisor password and a user password. In addition, you can configure how the user password works.

The choices under User Access Level are No Access (the user cannot access the BIOS/UEFI setup utility), View Only (the user can access BIOS/UEFI setup but cannot make changes), Limited (the user can access BIOS/UEFI setup and make a few changes, such as date and time), and Full Access (the user can access the BIOS/UEFI setup utility and make any changes). When supervisor and user passwords are both set and you boot the system, a box to enter a password is displayed. The access you have depends on which password you enter. Also, if both passwords are set, you must enter a valid password to boot the system. By setting both passwords, you can totally lock down the computer from unauthorized access.

Exam Tip ✔

The A+ Core 1 exam expects you to know how to use BIOS/UEFI setup to secure a workstation from unauthorized use.

Caution ❗

In the event that passwords are forgotten, supervisor and user passwords to the computer can be reset by setting a jumper (group of pins) on the motherboard to clear all BIOS/UEFI customized settings and return BIOS/UEFI setup to its default settings. To keep someone from using this technique to access the computer, you can use a computer case with a lockable side panel and install a lock on the case. Using jumpers is covered later in this module.

Also, the BIOS/UEFI utility might have an intrusion detection alert feature that requires a cable to be connected to a switch on the case. When the case is opened, the action is logged in BIOS/UEFI and a message appears at the beginning of the boot that an intrusion has been detected. This security feature is easily bypassed by hackers and is therefore not considered a best practice.

Drive Password Protection

Some laptop BIOS/UEFI utilities offer the option to set a hard drive password. For example, look back at Figure 2-29 and the option Set Hard Disk Password. Using this option, you can set Master and User passwords for all hard drives installed in the system. When you first turn on the computer, you must enter a power-on password to boot the computer and a hard drive password to access the hard drive.

Using a hard drive password encrypts only a few organizational sectors—not all the data on the drive. Therefore, a hacker can move the drive to another computer and use software that can read sectors where data is kept without having to read the organizational sectors. Password-protected drives are therefore not as secure as drive encryption, which is discussed next.

The TPM Chip, HSMs, and Hard Drive Encryption

Many motherboards contain a chip called the **TPM (Trusted Platform Module) chip**. The **BitLocker Encryption** tool in Windows is designed to work with this chip, which holds the BitLocker encryption key (also called the startup key). The TPM chip can also be used with encryption software other than BitLocker that may be installed on the hard drive. If the hard drive is stolen from the computer and installed in another computer, the data will be safe because BitLocker has encrypted all contents on the drive and will not allow access without the startup key stored on the TPM chip. Therefore, this method assures that the drive cannot be used in another computer. However, if the motherboard fails and is replaced, you'll need a backup copy of the startup key to access data on the hard drive.

Exam Tip ✔

The A+ Core 1 exam expects you to know about drive encryption, the TPM chip, and how to use both to secure a workstation or laptop.

When you use Windows to install BitLocker Encryption, the initialization process also initializes the TPM chip. Initializing the TPM chip configures it and turns it on. After BitLocker is installed, you can temporarily turn it off, which also turns off the TPM chip. For example, you might want to turn off BitLocker to test the BitLocker recovery process. Normally, BitLocker will manage the TPM chip for you, and there is no need for you to manually change TPM chip settings. However, if you are having problems installing BitLocker, one thing you can do is clear the TPM chip. Be careful! If the TPM chip is being used to hold an encryption key to protect data on the hard drive and you clear the chip, the encryption key will be lost. That means all the data will be lost, too. Therefore, don't clear the TPM chip unless you are certain it is not being used to encrypt data.

Figure 2-33 An HSM expansion card offers drive encryption when the TPM chip isn't available

Source: entrust.com

Drive encryption might still be needed when the system does not have a TPM chip or the chip is not working. In this situation, you can install in the system an encryption device called a **hardware security module (HSM)**. An HSM can be installed on a workstation or server computer using an expansion card, as in Figure 2-33, as a small external USB device connected to a single computer, or as a larger appliance that connects to the network to service applications and devices on the network.

Note **4**

Drive encryption might be too secure at times. I know of a situation where an encrypted hard drive became corrupted. Normally, you might be able to move the drive to another computer and recover some data. However, this drive asked for the encryption password but then could not confirm it. Therefore, the entire drive, including all the data, was inaccessible.

BIOS Support for Virtualization

 Core 1 Objective 3.4

Virtualization in computing is when one physical computer uses software to create multiple virtual computers, and each virtual computer or **virtual machine (VM)** simulates the hardware of a physical computer. Each VM running on a computer works like a physical computer and is assigned virtual devices such as a virtual motherboard and virtual hard drive. Examples of VM software are Microsoft Hyper-V and Oracle VirtualBox. For most VM software to work, virtualization must be enabled in BIOS/UEFI setup. Looking back at Figure 2-32, you can see the option to enable Intel VT, the name Intel gives to its virtualization technology.

Exiting the BIOS/UEFI Setup Menus

Core 1 Objective 3.4

When you finish with BIOS/UEFI setup, an Exit screen such as the one shown in Figure 2-34 gives you various options, such as saving your changes and exiting or discarding your changes and exiting. Notice in the figure that you also have the option to Load Optimized Defaults. This option can sometimes solve a problem if a user has made several inappropriate changes to the BIOS/UEFI settings or if you are attempting to recover from an error created while updating the firmware.

Figure 2-34   The BIOS/UEFI Utility Exit screen

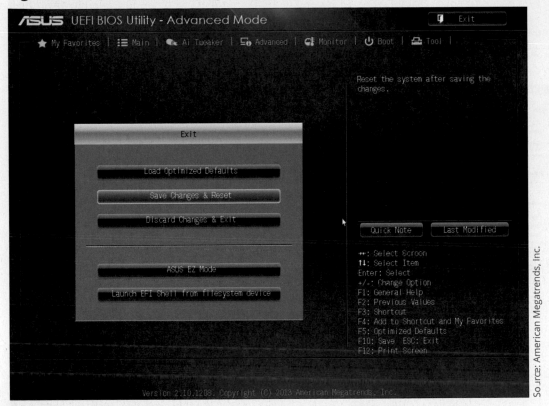

Source: American Megatrends, Inc.

Applying Concepts

Managing the TPM Chip

Est. Time: 15 minutes
Core 1 Objective: 3.4

To manage the TPM chip, follow these steps:

1. In BIOS/UEFI, verify that the TPM chip is enabled.

2. Sign in to Windows using an administrator account.

3. In the Windows search box, enter the `tpm.msc` command. If necessary, respond to the UAC box. The TPM Management console opens.

4. If no TPM chip is present or it's not enabled in BIOS/UEFI setup, the console reports that. If your system has a TPM chip that is not yet initialized, the Status pane in the console reports TPM is not ready for use (see Figure 2-35). To initialize the TPM, click **Prepare the TPM** in the Actions pane. After Windows initializes the TPM and you close the dialog box, the console will report that the TPM is ready for use (also shown in Figure 2-35).

(continues)

Applying Concepts Continued

Figure 2-35   Use the TPM Management console to manage the TPM chip in Windows

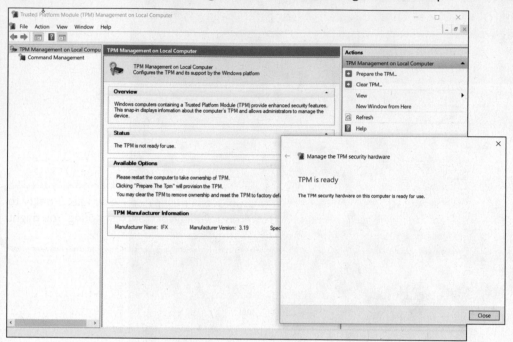

5. Using the console, you can change the TPM owner password, turn TPM on or off in Windows, reset the TPM when it has locked access to the hard drive, and clear the TPM, which resets it to factory defaults. After you have made changes to the TPM chip, you will most likely be asked to restart the computer for the changes to take effect.

Updating Motherboard Drivers and BIOS/UEFI

Core 1 Objective 3.4

When a motherboard is first installed or causing problems or you want to use a new OS or hardware device, you might need to install or update the motherboard drivers or update the BIOS/UEFI firmware. Both skills are covered in this section of the module.

Exam Tip

The A+ Core 1 exam expects you to know how to update drivers and firmware and replace the CMOS battery. Given the symptom of a problem, you must first determine if the source of the problem is a device, motherboard firmware, or the CMOS battery, and then decide what to do to resolve the problem.

Installing or Updating Motherboard Drivers

Core 1 Objective 3.4

Device drivers are small programs stored on the hard drive that an operating system such as Windows or Linux uses to communicate with a specific hardware device—for example, a printer, network port on the motherboard, or video card. The CD or DVD that comes bundled with the motherboard contains a user guide and drivers for its onboard components (for example, chipset, graphics, audio, network, and USB drivers), and these drivers need to be installed in the OS. After installing a motherboard, you can install the drivers from CD or DVD and later update them by downloading updates from the motherboard manufacturer's website. Updates to motherboard drivers are sometimes included in updates to Windows.

> **Note 5**
>
> The motherboard CD or DVD or the manufacturer's website might contain useful utilities—for example, a utility to monitor the CPU temperature and alert you if overheating occurs or a diagnostics utility for troubleshooting. You might also find a utility that works in Windows or Linux to update the BIOS/UEFI firmware.

If you don't have the CD or DVD that came with the motherboard or you want to update the drivers already installed on the system, go to the motherboard manufacturer website to find the downloads you need. Figure 2-36 shows the download page for the ASUS Prime B460M-A motherboard. On this page, you can download manuals, drivers, utility tools, and BIOS/UEFI updates for the board. You can also access a list of CPUs and memory modules the board can use. Be sure to get the correct drivers for the OS edition and type (for example, Windows 10 64-bit) you are using with the board.

Figure 2-36   Download drivers, utilities, BIOS/UEFI updates, documentation, and other help software from the motherboard manufacturer's website

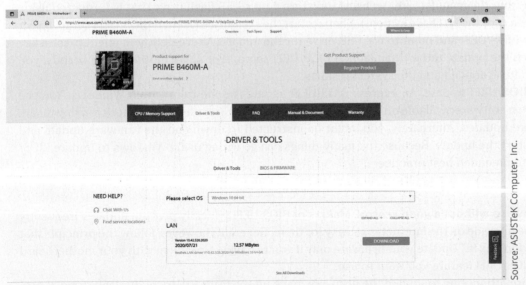

Source: ASUSTeK Computer, Inc.

> **Note 6**
>
> To know what edition and type of Windows you are using, use the System Information utility (msinfo32.exe).

Updating Firmware

 Core 1 Objective 3.4

The process of upgrading or refreshing the programming and data stored on the firmware chip is called updating firmware, **flashing BIOS/UEFI**, or **flashing BIOS**. Here are some good reasons to flash the BIOS/UEFI:

- The system hangs at odd times or during the boot.
- Some motherboard functions have stopped working or are causing problems. For example, the onboard video port is not working.
- You get errors when trying to install a new OS or hardware device.
- You want to incorporate some new features or a new component on the board. For example, a BIOS upgrade might be required before you upgrade the processor.

> **Caution** (!)
>
> It's extremely important that you use the correct motherboard brand and model when selecting the BIOS/UEFI update on the manufacturer's website. Trying to use the wrong update can cause problems. Also, get your updates directly from the manufacturer website rather than third-party sites.

To flash BIOS/UEFI, always follow the directions that you can find in the user guide for your motherboard. Motherboards can use one or more of these methods:

- **Download and update from within BIOS/UEFI setup.** Some motherboards allow you to enter BIOS/UEFI setup and select the option for BIOS/UEFI to connect to the Internet, check for updates, download the update, and apply it.
- **Update from a USB flash drive using BIOS/UEFI setup.** Download the latest firmware update file for your BIOS/UEFI version from the manufacturer website and store it on a USB flash drive that is formatted using the FAT32 file system (not the NTFS file system). Then restart the system and launch BIOS/UEFI setup. Select the option to flash BIOS/UEFI and point to the USB drive for the update. Alternately, you might press a key at startup to launch the update rather than launch BIOS/UEFI setup. (For some motherboard brands, you press F7.) The update is applied and the system restarts.
- **Run an express BIOS/UEFI update.** An express BIOS/UEFI update is done from within Windows. You use Windows application software available on the motherboard manufacturer website to check for, download, and install firmware updates. Alternately, you might be instructed to download the firmware update and double-click it to start the update. Because too many things can go wrong using Windows to update BIOS/UEFI, it is not a recommended best practice.

Be aware of these cautions when updating BIOS/UEFI firmware:

- **Don't update firmware without a good reason.** Makers of BIOS/UEFI typically provide updates frequently because putting the upgrade on the Internet is so easy for them. Generally, however, follow the principle that "if it's not broken, don't fix it." Update your firmware only if you're having a problem with your motherboard or there's a new BIOS/UEFI feature you want to use.
- **Back up first.** Before attempting to update the firmware, back up the firmware to a USB flash drive, if possible. See the motherboard user manual to find out how.
- **Select the correct update file.** Always use an update version that is more recent than the BIOS/UEFI version already installed, and carefully follow manufacturer directions. Upgrading with the wrong file could make your BIOS/UEFI useless. If you're not sure that you're using the correct upgrade, <u>don't guess</u>. Check with the technical support for your BIOS/UEFI before moving forward. Before you call technical support, have the information available that identifies your BIOS/UEFI and motherboard.

Note 7

To identify the BIOS/UEFI version installed, look for the BIOS version number displayed on the main menu of BIOS/UEFI setup. Alternately, you can use the System Information utility (msinfo32.exe) in Windows to display the BIOS version.

- **Don't interrupt the update.** Be sure not to turn off your computer while the update is in progress. For laptops, make sure the AC adapter is plugged in and powering the system.

If the BIOS update is interrupted or the update creates errors, you are in an unfortunate situation. Search the motherboard manufacturer website for help. Here are some options:

- **Back flash.** You might be able to revert to the earlier version, which is called a **back flash**. To do this, generally you download the recovery file from the website and copy the file to a USB flash drive. Then set the jumper on the motherboard to recover from a failed BIOS update. When you reboot the system, the BIOS automatically reads from the device and performs the recovery. Then reset the jumper to the normal setting and boot the system.
- **Bootable media and restore defaults.** You might be instructed to make a bootable CD or DVD using support tools from the motherboard manufacturer. Boot the system from the CD or DVD and enter commands to attempt the update again from the file stored on the USB flash drive. Then enter BIOS/UEFI setup and restore defaults.

Note 8

If a BIOS/UEFI update fails to complete, BIOS/UEFI may reboot and try again up to three times. After the third attempt, the update will be discarded, and the firmware will roll back a partial update.

Using Jumpers to Clear BIOS/UEFI Settings

Core 1 Objective 3.4

A motherboard may have jumpers that you can use to clear BIOS/UEFI settings, which returns the BIOS/UEFI setup to factory default settings. You might want to clear settings if flashing BIOS/UEFI didn't work or failed to complete correctly, or if a power-on password is forgotten and you cannot boot the system.

Note 9

A laptop or other mobile device likely won't have this option available for better security of the device.

A **jumper** is two small posts or metal pins that stick up on the motherboard; it's used to hold configuration information. An open jumper has no cover, and a closed jumper has a cover on the two pins (see Figure 2-37). Look at the jumper cover in Figure 2-37(B) that is "parked," meaning it is hanging on a single pin for safekeeping but is not being used to turn on a jumper setting.

Figure 2-37   A 6-pin jumper group on a circuit board: (A) has no jumpers set to on, (B) has a cover parked on one pin, and (C) is configured with one jumper setting turned on

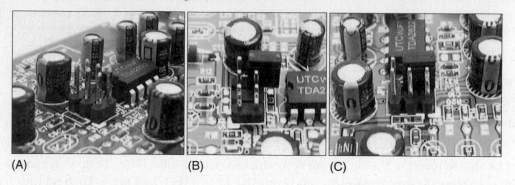

(A)   (B)   (C)

Figure 2-38 shows one example of a group of three jumpers. (The yellow jumper cap is positioned on the first two jumper pins on the left side of the group.) Figure 2-39 shows the motherboard documentation for how to use these jumpers. When jumpers 1 and 2 are closed, which they are in the figure, normal booting happens. When jumpers 2 and 3 are closed, passwords to BIOS/UEFI setup can be cleared on the next boot. When no jumpers are closed, the

Figure 2-38   This group of three jumpers controls the BIOS configuration

BIOS jumper group

Figure 2-39   BIOS configuration jumper settings

Jumper Position	Mode	Description
1 ▢ / ● / ○ 3	Normal (default)	The current BIOS configuration is used for booting.
1 ▢ / ● / ● 3	Configure	After POST, the BIOS displays a menu in BIOS setup that can be used to clear the user and supervisor power-on passwords.
1 ▢ / ○ / ○ 3	Recovery	Recovery is used to recover from a failed BIOS update. Details can be found in the motherboard manual.

BIOS/UEFI will recover itself on the next boot from a failed update. Once set for normal booting, the jumpers should be changed only if you are trying to recover when a power-up password is lost or flashing BIOS/UEFI has failed. To learn how to set jumpers, see the motherboard documentation.

Now let's see what other tasks you might need to do when you are installing or replacing a motherboard.

Installing or Replacing a Motherboard

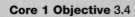 Core 1 Objective 3.4

A motherboard is considered a field replaceable unit, so you need to know how to replace one when it goes bad. In this part of the module, you learn how to select a motherboard and then how to install or replace one in a desktop or laptop computer.

How to Select a Desktop Motherboard

Core 1 Objective 3.4

Because the motherboard determines so many of your computer's features, selecting the motherboard is often your most important decision when you purchase a desktop computer or assemble one from parts. Depending on which applications and peripheral devices you plan to use with the computer, you can take one of three approaches to selecting a motherboard. The first approach is to select the board that provides the most room for expansion, so you can upgrade and exchange components and add devices easily. A second approach is to select the board that best suits the needs of the computer's current configuration, knowing that when you need to upgrade, you will likely switch to new technology and a new motherboard. The third approach is to select a motherboard that meets your present needs with moderate room for expansion.

Ask the following questions when selecting a motherboard:

1. How is the motherboard going to be used? (For example, it might be used for light business and personal use, as a gaming system, for a server, or for a high-powered workstation.) Knowing how the board will be used helps you decide about the most important features and overall power of the board. For example, a motherboard to be used in a server might need support for RAID (an array of multiple hard drives to improve performance and fault tolerance). In another example, a motherboard used in a gaming system will not need RAID support but might need a chipset that supports two high-end graphics adapters.

2. What form factor does the motherboard use?

3. Which brand (Intel or AMD) and model processors does the board support? Which chipset does it use? Which processors does it support?

    Most motherboard manufacturers offer a motherboard model in two versions: one version with an Intel chipset and a second version with an AMD chipset. Here are the criteria to decide which brand of chipset to use:

    - If price is a concern, consider a board with an AMD chipset, which generally costs less than comparable boards with Intel chipsets.
    - AMD is popular in the hobbyist and gaming market, and many of its chipsets and processors are designed with high-end graphics in mind. AMD puts graphics first and processing power second. For the hobbyist, many AMD processors can be overclocked.
    - Intel offers the most options in processor models and chipset and processor features. Intel typically targets the consumer, business, and server markets, and generally is strong in power conservation, processing power, and graphics.
    - Intel dominates the laptop, pre-built desktop, consumer, and server markets.

4. Which type and speed of memory does the board support?

5. What are the embedded expansion slots, internal and external connectors, and devices on the board? (For example, the board might provide multiple PCIe ×16 v4 slots, SATA3 connectors, a network port, a wireless component, multiple USB ports, an M.2 slot, HDMI port, DVI-D port, and so forth.)

6. Does the board fit the case you plan to use?

7. What is the price of the board? Does the board get good reviews?

8. How extensive and user-friendly is the documentation, and how helpful is the manufacturer website?

9. What warranty and how much support does the manufacturer supply for the board?

Sometimes a motherboard contains an onboard component more commonly offered as a separate device. One example is support for video. The video port might be on the motherboard, or it might require a video card. A motherboard with embedded video is less expensive than a motherboard and a graphics card you plan to install in a PCIe ×16 slot, but the latter plan gives higher-quality video.

Note 10

If you have an embedded component, make sure you can disable it so you can use another external component if needed. Components are disabled in BIOS/UEFI setup.

Table 2-3, shown earlier in the module, lists some manufacturers of motherboards and their web addresses. For motherboard reviews, do a general search of the web.

Note 11

Get very familiar with the manufacturer's website of the motherboard you plan to purchase. It tells you which processors and memory modules the board can support. Make sure the processor and memory you plan to use with the board are on these lists.

How to Install or Replace a Motherboard

Core 1 Objective 3.4

When you purchase a motherboard, the package comes with the board, I/O shield, documentation, drivers, and various screws, cables, and connectors. When you replace a motherboard, you pretty much have to disassemble an entire computer, install the new motherboard, and reassemble the system, which you learned to do in the module "Taking a Computer Apart and Putting It Back Together." The following steps are meant to be a general overview of the process and are not meant to include the details of all possible installation scenarios, which can vary according to the components and case you are using. The best place to go for detailed installation instructions is the motherboard user guide.

Caution !

As with any installation, remember the importance of using an ESD strap to ground yourself when working inside a computer case to protect components against ESD. Other precautions to protect the hardware and you are covered in the appendix "Safety Procedures and Environmental Concerns."

The general process for replacing a motherboard is as follows:

1. **Verify that you have selected the right motherboard to install in the system.** The new motherboard should have the same form factor as the case, support the RAM modules and processor you want to install on it, and have other internal and external connectors you need for your system.

2. **Get familiar with the motherboard documentation, features, and settings.** Especially important are any connectors and jumpers on the motherboard. It's a great idea to read the motherboard user guide from cover to cover. At the least, get familiar with what it has to offer, and study the diagrams in it that label all the components on the board. Learn how each connector and jumper is used. You can also check the manufacturer's website for answers to any questions you might have.

3. **Remove components so you can reach the old motherboard.** Use an ESD strap. Turn off the system, and disconnect all cables and cords. Press the power button to dissipate the power. Open the case cover, and remove all expansion cards. Disconnect all internal cables and cords connected to the old motherboard. To safely remove the old motherboard, you might have to remove drives. If the processor cooler is heavy and bulky, you might remove it from the old motherboard before you remove the motherboard from the case.

4. **Install the I/O shield.** The I/O shield is a metal plate that comes with the motherboard and fits over the ports to create a well-fitting enclosure for them. A case might come with a standard I/O shield already in place. Hold the motherboard up to the shield, and make sure the ports on the board will fit the holes in the shield (see Figure 2-40). If the holes in the shield don't match up with the ports on the board, punch out the shield, and replace it with the one that came bundled with the motherboard.

Figure 2-40   Make sure the holes in the I/O shield match up with the ports on the motherboard

I/O shield installed
on the back
of the case

5. **Install the motherboard.** Place the motherboard into the case and, using spacers or screws, securely fasten the board to the case. Because coolers are heavy, most processor instructions say to install the motherboard before installing the processor and cooler to better protect the board or processor from being damaged. On the other hand, some motherboard manufacturers say to install the processor and cooler and then install the motherboard. Follow the order given in the motherboard user guide. The easiest approach is to install the processor, cooler, and memory modules on the board and then place the board in the case (see Figure 2-41).

Figure 2-41   A motherboard with processor, cooler, and memory modules installed is ready to go in the case

6. **Install the processor and processor cooler.** The processor comes already installed on some motherboards, in which case you just need to install the cooler. The steps for installing a processor and cooler are covered in the module "Supporting Processors and Upgrading Memory."

7. **Install RAM into the appropriate slots on the motherboard.** You learn how to install RAM in the module "Supporting Processors and Upgrading Memory."

8. **Attach the wires and cables.** Attach the wire leads from the front panel of the case to the front panel connector or header on the motherboard, as you learned to do in the module "Taking a Computer Apart and Putting It Back Together." You'll also need to attach the P1 power connector, fan connectors, processor auxiliary power connector, and SATA cables to the internal drives. If the case has ports on the front, such as USB or sound ports, connect cables from the ports to the appropriate headers on the motherboard. Position and tie cables neatly together to make sure they don't obstruct the fans and the airflow.

9. **Install the video card on the motherboard.** If the motherboard does not have onboard video, install the video card now. It should go into the primary PCI Express ✕16 slot. If the motherboard has onboard video, use the video port, and check out how the system functions until you know everything else is working. Then go back and install an optional video card. If you plan to install two video cards, verify that one is working before installing the second one.

10. **Plug the computer into a power source, and attach the monitor, keyboard, and mouse.** Initially install only the devices you absolutely need.

11. **Boot the system and enter BIOS/UEFI setup.** Make sure the settings are set to the defaults. If the motherboard comes new from the manufacturer, it will already be at default settings. If you are salvaging a motherboard from another system, you might need to reset settings to the defaults. You will need to do the following while you are in BIOS/UEFI setup:
    - Check the time and date.
    - Make sure Fast Boot (also called abbreviated POST) is disabled. While you're installing a motherboard, you generally want it to do as many diagnostic tests as possible. After you know the system is working, you can choose Fast Boot.
    - Set the boot order to the hard drive, and then the USB drive, if you will be booting the OS from the hard drive.
    - Leave everything else at their defaults unless you know that particular settings should be otherwise.
    - Save and exit.

12. **Observe POST and verify that no errors occur.**

13. **Verify that Windows starts with no errors.** If Windows is already installed on the hard drive, boot to the Windows desktop. Use Device Manager to verify that the OS recognizes all devices and that no conflicts are reported.

14. **Install the motherboard drivers.** If your motherboard comes with a CD or DVD that contains some motherboard drivers, install them now. You will probably need Internet access so the setup process can download the latest drivers from the motherboard manufacturer's website. Reboot the system one more time, checking for errors.

15. **Install any other expansion cards and drivers.** Install each device and its drivers, one device at a time, rebooting and checking for conflicts after each installation.

16. **Verify that everything is operating properly, and make any final OS and BIOS/UEFI adjustments, such as setting power-on passwords.**

Note 12

Whenever you install or uninstall software or hardware, keep a notebook with details about the components you are working on, configuration settings, manufacturer specifications, and other relevant information. This helps if you need to backtrack later and can also help you document and troubleshoot your computer system. Keep all hardware documentation for this system together with the notebook in an envelope in a safe place.

Module Summary

Motherboard Types and Features

- The motherboard is the most complicated of all components inside the computer. It contains the processor socket and accompanying chipset, firmware holding the BIOS/UEFI, memory slots, expansion slots, jumpers, ports, and power supply connections. Sometimes, the processor is embedded on the board. The motherboard you select determines both the capabilities and limitations of your system.
- The most popular motherboard form factors are ATX, microATX, Extended ATX, and ITX. The form factor determines the size of the board and the case and power supply the board can use.
- The chipset embedded on the motherboard determines what kind of processor and memory the board can support.
- Typically, a motherboard will have one or more Intel sockets for an Intel processor or one or more AMD sockets for an AMD processor.
- Major advancements in past Intel chipsets and processors are labeled as generations and include 12th generation (Alder Lake), 11th generation (Rocket Lake), 10th generation (Comet Lake), 9th generation (Coffee Lake Refresh), 8th generation (Coffee Lake), 7th generation (Kaby Lake), and 6th generation (Skylake).
- Current Intel desktop processors use the LGA1700, LGA1200 or LGA1151 socket. Server processors use the LGA2066 or LGA2011 socket.
- Current AMD processors use the sTRX4, TR4, AM4, AM3+, AM3, or FM2+ socket. These sockets are used to identify the current AMD generations of chipsets and processors.
- When matching a motherboard to a processor, use only processors the motherboard manufacturer recommends for the board. Even though a processor might fit the processor socket on a board, using a match not recommended by the manufacturer can damage both the board and the processor.
- For laptops, it's usually more cost effective to replace the laptop than to replace a failed system board.
- Current buses and expansion slots used on motherboards include PCI Express ×1, ×4, ×8, and ×16, Versions 3, 4, 5, and 6; conventional PCI; SATAe; SATA Revision 3.x; SATA Revision 2.x; SAS; M.2; and USB.
- Components that are built into the motherboard are called onboard components. Other components can be attached to the system in some other way, such as on an expansion card, internal connector, or external port.

Using BIOS/UEFI Setup to Configure a Motherboard

- The firmware that controls current motherboards is a combination of the older BIOS and the newer UEFI. Microsoft requires UEFI firmware in order for a system to be certified for Windows 10.
- UEFI supports the GPT partitioning system for hard drives, which supports hard drives larger than 2 TB. The older MBR partitioning system is limited to drives smaller than 2 TB.
- Booting using UEFI mode is required to use Windows Secure Boot, which protects a system against malware launching before Windows or anti-malware software is started. For legacy hardware and operating systems, a UEFI system can be booted in CSM or legacy mode, which is a BIOS boot.
- Motherboard settings that can be configured using BIOS/UEFI setup include changing the boot priority order, managing Secure Boot options, selecting UEFI mode or CSM mode, enabling or disabling onboard devices, overclocking the CPU, and managing power-on passwords, the TPM chip, and support for virtualization. You can also view information about the installed processor, memory, storage devices, CPU and chassis temperatures, fan speeds, and voltages.
- Secure Boot uses databases to verify that hardware drivers are digitally signed by their manufacturers. These databases are stored in firmware on the motherboard before the board ships and later on the Windows hard drive. Updating firmware can update databases in firmware, and you can restore these databases to their factory state. In addition, Microsoft may include updates to its Secure Boot databases kept on the hard drive in normal Windows updates. Secure Boot must be enabled before Windows 11 will install.

Updating Motherboard Drivers and BIOS/UEFI

- Device drivers for motherboard components are installed in the operating system when you first install a motherboard. These drivers might need updating to fix a problem with a board component or to use a new feature provided by the motherboard manufacturer. Drivers come bundled on CD or DVD with the motherboard and can be downloaded from the motherboard manufacturer website.
- Update motherboard firmware when a component on the board is causing problems or you want to incorporate a new feature or component on the board.
- To update BIOS/UEFI, you can use BIOS/UEFI setup to check online for updates and apply them, or you can apply updates previously downloaded to a USB flash drive. Alternately, you might be able to install an app in Windows that can check for BIOS/UEFI updates and apply them; however, this option is not recommended.
- When flashing BIOS/UEFI, don't update firmware without a good reason, back up the firmware before you update it, be certain to select the correct update file, and make sure the update process is not interrupted.
- Jumpers on the motherboard may be used to clear BIOS/UEFI settings, restoring them to factory defaults.

Installing or Replacing a Motherboard

- When selecting a motherboard, pay attention to the form factor, chipset, expansion slots and memory slots used, and the processors supported in reference to the purpose of the computer. Also notice the internal and external connectors and ports the board provides.
- When installing a motherboard, first study the motherboard and its manual, and set jumpers on the board. Sometimes it is best to install the processor and cooler before installing the motherboard in the case. When the cooling assembly is heavy and bulky, you should install it after the motherboard is securely seated in the case. Finally, install the latest drivers from the manufacturer's website.

Key Terms

For explanations of key terms, see the Glossary for this text.

AM3+
AM4
back flash
BitLocker Encryption
bus
chipset
Compatibility Support Module (CSM)
device driver
Extended ATX (E-ATX)
flashing BIOS
flashing BIOS/UEFI
GUID Partition Table (GPT)
hardware security module (HSM)
header

I/O shield
ITX
jumper
land grid array (LGA)
LGA1151
LGA1200
LGA1700
M.2 connector
Master Boot Record (MBR)
Mini-ITX
mITX
onboard port
overclocking
PCI (Peripheral Component Interconnect)

pin grid array (PGA)
Platform Key (PK)
Preboot eXecution Environment or Pre-Execution Environment (PXE)
protocol
SAS (Serial Attached SCSI)
Secure Boot
small form factor (SFF)
S.M.A.R.T. (Self-Monitoring Analysis and Reporting Technology)
socket
sTRX4 socket

TPM (Trusted Platform Module) chip
TR4 (Threadripper 4) socket
trace
USB (Universal Serial Bus)
USB power share
USB wake support
virtualization
virtual machine (VM)
zero insertion force (ZIF) socket

Thinking Critically

These questions are designed to prepare you for the critical thinking required for the A+ Core 1 exam and may use information from other modules or the web.

1. After trying multiple times, a coworker is unable to fit a motherboard in a computer case and is having difficulty aligning screw holes in the motherboard to standoffs on the bottom of the case. Which is most likely the source of the problem?

   a. The coworker is trying to use too many screws to secure the board; only four screws are required.
   b. The form factors of the case and the motherboard don't match.
   c. The form factors of the motherboard and the power supply don't match.
   d. The board is not oriented correctly in the case. Rotate the board.

2. Which type of boot authentication is more secure?

   a. Power-on password or supervisor password
   b. Drive password
   c. Full disk encryption
   d. Windows password

3. You are replacing a processor on an older motherboard and see that the board has the LGA1200 socket. You have three processors on hand: Intel Core i3-10105, Intel Core i5-8400, and Intel Core i5-6500. Which of these three processors will most likely fit the board? Why?

4. You are looking at a motherboard that contains Z490 in the motherboard model name, and the socket appears to be an Intel LGA socket. Which socket is this board most likely using?

   a. LGA1200, 10th generation
   b. LGA1151, 7th generation
   c. LGA1151, 8th generation
   d. LGA1151, all generations

5. Windows is displaying an error about incompatible hardware. You enter BIOS/UEFI setup to change the boot priority order so you can boot from the Windows setup DVD to troubleshoot the system. However, when you get to the Boot screen, you find that the options to change the boot priority order are grayed out and not available. What is most likely the problem?

   a. You signed in to BIOS/UEFI with the user power-on password rather than the supervisor power-on password.
   b. A corrupted Windows installation is not allowing you to make changes in BIOS/UEFI setup.
   c. Motherboard components are malfunctioning and will not allow you to change BIOS/UEFI options.
   d. The keyboard and mouse are not working.

6. Your supervisor has asked you to set up a RAID hard drive array in a tower system, which has a motherboard that uses the B360 chipset. You have installed the required three matching hard drives to hold the array. When you enter BIOS/UEFI to configure the RAID, you cannot find the menus for the RAID configuration. What is most likely the problem?

   a. A RAID array requires at least four matching hard drives.
   b. RAID arrays are not configured in BIOS/UEFI.
   c. Your supervisor did not give you the necessary access to BIOS/UEFI to configure RAID.
   d. The B360 chipset does not support RAID.

7. A customer asks you over the phone how much it will cost to upgrade memory on their desktop system to 16 GB. The customer is a capable Windows user and able to access BIOS/UEFI setup using the user power-on password you set up for them. Which actions can you ask the customer to perform as you direct them over the phone to get the information you need to develop an estimate of the upgrade's cost?

   a. Use BIOS/UEFI to view how much memory is installed and how much memory the system can hold.
   b. Enter info32.exe to determine how much memory is currently installed.
   c. Use BIOS/UEFI to show which memory slots are used and how much memory is installed in each slot.
   d. View the System Information window to determine how much memory is currently installed.

8. The GeForce GTX 1060 graphics card requires 120 W of power. You plan to install it in a PCIe 3.0 ×16 slot. Will you need to also install extra power to the card? If so, how can you do that?

   a. Yes. The PCIe 3.0 ×16 slot provides 75 W, and you need to connect the card using a PCIe 8-pin connector to gain additional power.
   b. No. The PCIe 3.0 ×16 slot provides all the necessary power, and no extra power connection is required.
   c. Yes. The PCIe 3.0 ×16 slot provides 75 W, and you need to connect the card using a PCIe 6-pin connector to gain additional power.
   d. Yes. The PCIe 3.0 ×16 slot provides 100 W, and you need to connect the card using a Molex connector to gain an additional 20 W.

9. While building a high-end gaming system, you are attempting to install the EVGA GeForce GTX 1080 graphics card, and you discover there is not enough clearance above the motherboard for the card. What is your best solution?

   a. Use a different case that allows for the height of the expansion card.
   b. Use a smaller form factor motherboard to make more room in the case.
   c. Use an onboard component rather than the graphics card.
   d. Use a conventional PCI graphics card that fits the motherboard and case.

10. Your manager has purchased a new laptop for business use and has asked you to make sure the data they plan to store on the laptop is secure. Which of the following security measures is the most important to implement to keep the data secure? Which is second in importance?

    a. Use BitLocker Encryption with the TPM chip.
    b. Enable Secure Boot.
    c. Set a supervisor password to BIOS/UEFI.
    d. Disable booting from the optical drive.

11. Which of the following might cause you to flash BIOS/UEFI?

    a. Windows displays error messages on the screen at startup and fails to start.
    b. You are installing an upgraded processor.
    c. You are installing a new graphics card to replace onboard video.
    d. Windows continually shows the wrong date and time.

12. Which of the following must be done before you can install the Intel Core i7-7700 processor on the Gigabyte GA-H110M-S2 motherboard?

    a. Flash BIOS/UEFI.
    b. Install motherboard drivers.
    c. Clear CMOS RAM.
    d. Exchange the LGA1151 socket for one that can hold the new processor.

13. Decide which of these statements about SATA and SAS data storage interfaces are true. (Choose all that are true.)

    a. SAS interfaces are expected to replace SATA interfaces for home use.
    b. The SATA interface is better suited than the SAS interface for use in servers where many users will be using the data at the same time.
    c. The SAS interface is more than three times faster than the SATA interface.
    d. Because SATA drives are less expensive, higher-volume drives are more common in small offices.

14. Which partitioning method must be used for partitioning a 4 TB hard drive?

15. If a USB port on the motherboard is failing, what can you do that might fix the problem?

16. What is the purpose of installing standoffs or spacers between the motherboard and the case?

17. When installing a motherboard, suppose you forget to connect the wires from the case to the front panel header. Will you be able to power up the system? Why or why not?

18. When building a computer to use for home theater, which form factor would you most likely use?

19. When troubleshooting a desktop motherboard, you discover the network port no longer works. What is the best and least expensive solution to this problem? If this solution does not work, which solution should you try next? (Choose all that apply.)

    a. Replace the motherboard.
    b. Disable the network port and install a network card in an expansion slot.
    c. Use a wireless network device in a USB port to connect to a wireless network.
    d. Return the motherboard to the factory for repair.
    e. Update the motherboard drivers.

20. A computer freezes at odd times. At first, you suspected the power supply of overheating, but you have eliminated overheating and replaced the power supply without solving the problem. What do you do next?

    a. Replace the processor.
    b. Replace the motherboard.
    c. Reinstall Windows.
    d. Replace the memory modules.
    e. Flash BIOS/UEFI.

Hands-On Projects

Hands-On Project 2-1

Examining a Motherboard in Detail

Est. Time: 30 minutes
Core 1 Objective: 3.4

1. Look at the back of a desktop computer. Without opening the case, list the ports that you believe come directly from the motherboard.

2. Remove the cover of the case, as you learned to do in the module "Taking a Computer Apart and Putting It Back Together." List the different expansion cards in the expansion slots. Was your guess about which ports come from the motherboard correct?

3. To expose the motherboard so you can identify its parts, remove all the expansion cards.

4. Draw a diagram of the motherboard and label these parts:

    a. Processor socket
    b. Chipset
    c. RAM (each DIMM slot)
    d. CMOS battery
    e. Expansion slots (Identify the slots as PCI, PCIe ×1, PCIe ×4, or PCIe ×16.)
    f. Each port coming directly from the motherboard
    g. Power supply connections
    h. SATA drive connectors

(continues)

Hands-On Project Continued

5. What is the brand and model of the motherboard?

6. Locate the manufacturer's website. If you can find the motherboard manual on the site, download it. Find the diagram of the motherboard in the manual and compare it with your diagram. Did you label components correctly?

7. Reassemble the computer, as you learned to do in the module "Taking a Computer Apart and Putting It Back Together."

Hands-On Project 2-2

Examining Motherboard Documentation

Est. Time: 15 minutes
Core 1 Objective: 3.4

Using the motherboard brand and model installed in your computer or another motherboard brand and model assigned by your instructor, download the user guide from the motherboard manufacturer website and answer these questions:

1. List up to 10 processors the board supports.

2. What type of RAM does the board support?

3. What is the maximum RAM the board can hold?

4. Which versions of PCIe does the board use?

5. What chipset does the board use?

6. On the motherboard diagram, locate the jumper group on the board that returns BIOS/UEFI setup to default settings. It is often found near the CMOS battery. Some boards might have more than one, and some have none. Label the jumper group on your own diagram.

Hands-On Project 2-3

Matching a Processor to a Motherboard and Socket

Est. Time: 15 minutes
Core 1 Objective: 3.4

You are designing a desktop system, and your friend has offered to sell you their unused Core i5-10600K processor at a reduced price. Research the processor and possible motherboards that will support it and answer the following questions:

1. What is the best online price you can find for the processor?

2. What socket does the processor use?

3. What is one ASUS motherboard that supports this processor? Which chipset does the board use? Does the board require a firmware (BIOS) update to use this processor?

4. What is one GIGABYTE (*gigabyte.com*) motherboard that supports this processor? Which chipset does the board use? Which firmware (BIOS/UEFI) version is necessary to use this processor?

Hands-On Project 2-4

Identifying the Intel Chipset and Processor on Your Computer

Est. Time: 30 minutes
Core 1 Objective: 3.4

Intel offers two utilities you can download and run to identify an installed Intel processor or chipset. Do the following to use the utilities:

- If you are using a computer with an Intel processor, download and run the Intel® Processor Identification Utility available at *downloadcenter.intel.com/download/7838*.
- If you are using a computer with an Intel processor, download and run the Intel® Chipset Identification Utility available at *downloadcenter.intel.com/product/2715/Intel-Chipset-Identification-Utility*.

Websites change often, so if these links don't work, try searching the Intel website for each utility. What information does each utility provide about your processor and chipset?

Hands-On Project 2-5

Researching the Intel ARK Database

Est. Time: 15 minutes
Core 1 Objective: 3.4

Intel provides an extensive database of all its processors, chipsets, motherboards, and other products at *ark.intel.com*. Research the database and answer these questions:

1. List three 9th generation Core i7 processors. For each processor, list the processor number (model), the maximum memory it supports, the PCI Express version it supports (Version 3.0, 4.0 or 5.0), and the socket it uses.
2. List three Intel motherboards for desktops: an ATX board, a microATX board, and a Mini-ITX board. For each motherboard, list the processor socket it provides, the chipset it uses, the maximum memory it supports, and the number of PCIe slots it has.
3. The Z490 chipset is designed for gaming computers. What is the launch date for the Z490 chipsets? What Intel generation is the chipset? How many displays does the chipset support?

Hands-On Project 2-6

Examining BIOS/UEFI Settings

Est. Time: 30 minutes
Core 1 Objective: 3.4

Access the BIOS/UEFI setup program on your computer, and answer the following questions:

1. What key(s) did you press to access BIOS/UEFI setup?
2. What brand and version of BIOS/UEFI are you using?
3. What is the frequency of your processor?

(continues)

Hands-On Project Continued

4. What is the boot sequence order of devices?

5. Do you have an optical drive installed? What are the details of the installed drive?

6. What are the details of the installed hard drive(s)?

7. Does the BIOS/UEFI offer the option to set a supervisor or power-on password? What is the name of the screen where these passwords are set?

8. Does the BIOS/UEFI offer the option to overclock the processor? If so, list the settings that apply to overclocking.

9. Can you disable the onboard ports on the computer? If so, which ports can you disable, and what is the name of the screen(s) where this is done?

10. List up to three BIOS/UEFI settings that control how power is managed on the computer.

Hands-On Project 2-7

Inserting and Removing Motherboards

Est. Time: 15 minutes
Core 1 Objective: 3.4

Using old or defective expansion cards and motherboards, practice inserting and removing expansion cards and motherboards. In a lab or classroom setting, the instructor can provide extra cards and motherboards for exchange.

Real Problems, Real Solutions

Real Problem 2-1

Labeling the Motherboard

Est. Time: 15 minutes
Core 1 Objective: 3.4

Figure 2-42 shows a diagram of an ATX motherboard. Label as many of the 22 components as you can. If you would like to print the diagram, look for "Figure 2-42" in the student companion site that accompanies this text at *cengage.com.*

2

Figure 2-42   Label the 22 components on the motherboard

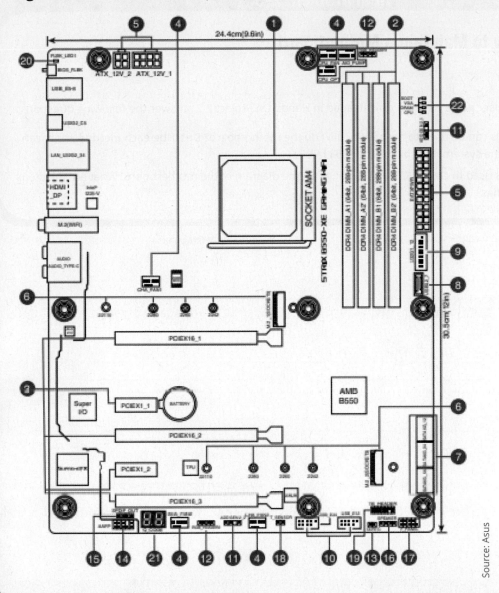

Source: Asus

Real Problem 2-2

Selecting a Replacement Motherboard

Est. Time: 30 minutes
Core 1 Objective: 3.4

When a motherboard fails, you can select and buy a new board to replace it. Suppose the motherboard in your computer has failed, and you want to buy a replacement and keep your repair costs to a minimum. Try to find a replacement motherboard on the web that can use the same case, power supply, processor, memory, and expansion cards as your current system. If you cannot find a good match, what other components might have to be replaced (for example, the processor or memory)? What is the total cost of the replacement parts? Save or print webpages that show what you need to purchase.

Real Problem 2-3

Researching How to Maintain a Motherboard

Est. Time: 30 minutes
Core 1 Objective: 3.4

Using the motherboard user guide that you downloaded in Hands-On Project 2-2, answer the following questions:

1. How many methods can be used to flash BIOS/UEFI on the motherboard? Describe each method. What can you do to recover the system if flashing BIOS/UEFI fails?

2. Locate the jumpers used to clear BIOS/UEFI settings on the diagram of the motherboard. What are the steps to clear these settings?

Module

3

Supporting Processors and Upgrading Memory

Module Objectives

1 Compare characteristics and features of processors used for personal computers

2 Select, install, and upgrade a processor

3 Compare the different kinds of physical memory and how they work

4 Upgrade memory

Core 1 Certification Objectives

1.1 Given a scenario, install and configure laptop hardware and components.

3.2 Given a scenario, install the appropriate RAM.

3.4 Given a scenario, install and configure motherboards, central processing units (CPUs), and add-on cards.

Introduction

Previously, you learned about motherboards. In this module, you learn about the two most important components on the motherboard: the processor and memory. You learn how a processor works, about different types and brands of processors, and how to match a processor to the motherboard.

Memory technologies have evolved over the years. When you support an assortment of desktop and laptop computers, you'll be amazed at all the variations of memory modules used not only in newer computers, but also in older computers still in use. A simple problem of replacing a bad memory module can become a complex research project if you don't have a good grasp of current and legacy memory technologies.

The processor and memory modules are considered field replaceable units (FRUs), so you'll learn how to install and upgrade a processor and memory modules. Upgrading the processor or adding more memory to a system can sometimes greatly improve performance. You will learn how to troubleshoot problems with the processor or memory in the module "Power Supplies and Troubleshooting Computer Problems."

Types and Characteristics of Processors

 Core 1 Objective 3.4

The processor installed on a motherboard is the primary component that determines the computing power of the system (see Figure 3-1). Recall that the two major manufacturers of processors are Intel (*intel.com*) and AMD (*amd.com*).

Figure 3-1   An AMD Ryzen Threadripper processor installed in an sTRX4 socket with the cooler not yet installed

Source: Advanced Micro Devices, Inc. – AMD

Here are the features of a processor that affect performance and compatibility with motherboards:

- **Feature 1: Processor speed.** The **processor frequency** is the speed at which the processor operates internally and is measured in gigahertz, such as 3.3 GHz. Current Intel and AMD processors run from about 2.0 GHz up to more than 5.3 GHz.
- **Feature 2: Lithography.** The lithography is the average space between transistors printed on the surface of the silicon chip. The measurement is in nanometers (nm); 1 nm is 1 billionth of a meter. Current processor lithography ranges from 7 nm to 14 nm. The lower the measurement, the better and faster the processor performs.
- **Feature 3: Socket and chipset the processor can use.** Recall that current Intel sockets for desktop and server systems are LGA1700, LGA1200, LGA1151, LGA2066, and LGA2011. AMD's current desktop sockets are sTRX4, TR4, AM4, AM3+, AM3, and FM2+.

- **Feature 4: Multiprocessing abilities.** The ability of a system to do more than one task at a time is accomplished by several means:
  - **Multiprocessing.** Using two processing units (called arithmetic logic units or ALUs) installed within a single processor is called **multiprocessing**. With multiprocessing, the processor, also called the core, can execute two instructions at the same time.
  - **Multithreading.** Each processor or core processes two threads at the same time. When Windows hands off a task to the CPU, it is called a **thread** and might involve several instructions. To handle two threads, the processor requires extra registers, or holding areas, within the processor housing that it uses to switch between threads. In effect, you have two logical processors for each physical processor or core. Intel calls this technology **Hyper-Threading** and AMD calls it **HyperTransport**. The feature must be enabled in BIOS/UEFI setup, and the operating system (OS) must support the technology.
  - **Multicore processing.** A single processor in the processor package is called **single-core processing**, and using multiple processors installed in the same processor housing is called **multicore processing**. Multicore processing might contain up to 32 cores (dual-core, triple-core, quad-core, and so forth). In Figure 3-2, the quad-core processor contains four cores or CPUs. Using multithreading, each core can handle two threads. Therefore, the processor appears to have up to eight logical processors, as it can handle eight threads from the operating system.
  - **Dual processors.** A server motherboard might have two processor sockets, called **multisocket**, **dual processors**, or a **multiprocessor platform** (see Figure 3-3). A processor (for example, the Xeon processor for servers) must support this feature.

- **Feature 5: Memory cache, which is the amount of memory included within the processor package.** Today's processors all have some memory on the processor chip (called a die). Memory on the processor die is called **Level 1 cache (L1 cache)**. Today's processors might have 8 MB to 64 MB of L1 cache. In addition to L1 cache, a processor may

Figure 3-2   This quad-core processor has four cores, and each core can handle two threads

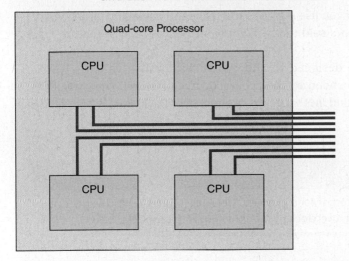

Figure 3-3   This Intel Server Board S2600ST has two Xeon processor sockets and 16 slots for DDR4 memory

Source: intel.

have some **Level 2 cache (L2 cache)**, which is memory in the processor package but not on the processor die. Some processors use a third cache farther from the processor's core, but still in the processor package, which is called **Level 3 cache (L3 cache)**.

Note 1

Memory used in a memory cache is **static RAM** (**SRAM**; pronounced "S-Ram"). Memory used on the motherboard loses data rapidly and must be refreshed often. It is therefore called **dynamic RAM** (**DRAM**; pronounced "D-Ram"). SRAM is faster than DRAM because it doesn't need refreshing. Both SRAM and DRAM are called volatile memory because they can only hold data as long as power is available.

- **Feature 6: The memory features on the motherboard that the processor can support.** DRAM memory modules used on a motherboard that a processor might support include DDR3, DDR4, or DDR5. Besides the type of memory, a processor can support certain amounts of memory, memory speeds, and a number of memory channels (single, dual, triple, or quad channels). All these characteristics of memory are discussed later in the module.
- **Feature 7: Support for virtualization.** A computer can use software to create and manage multiple virtual machines and their virtual devices. Most processors sold today support virtualization. The feature must be enabled in BIOS/UEFI setup.
- **Feature 8: Overclocking.** Some processors are designed to allow for overclocking, which is to run the processor at a higher frequency than recommended by the processor manufacturer. As you learned in the module "All About Motherboards," if a CPU and motherboard support overclocking, it is managed in BIOS/UEFI.

Exam Tip ✔

The A+ Core 1 exam expects you to be able to select a processor for a given motherboard, considering these processor features: Hyper-Threading, number of cores, virtualization, overclocking, and the motherboard CPU socket.

Older processors could process 32 bits at a time and were known as x86 processors because Intel used the number 86 in their model number. Today's processor architectures fall into two categories:

- **Hybrid processors can process 32 bits or 64 bits.** All of today's processors for desktop systems can process either 32 bits or 64 bits. These hybrid processors are known as **x86-64 bit processors**. An operating system, such as Windows or Linux, is installed as a 32-bit OS or a 64-bit OS. For most situations, when the OS installation gives you the option, you should choose to install it as a 64-bit OS to get the best performance. Applications are created as 32-bit apps or 64-bit apps, and both can be installed in a 64-bit OS. However, you cannot install a 64-bit app in a 32-bit installation of an OS.
- **64-bit processors.** Intel makes several 64-bit processors for workstations or servers that use fully implemented 64-bit processing, including the Itanium and Xeon processors. Intel calls the technology IA64, but they are also called x64 processors. They require a 64-bit operating system and can handle 32-bit applications only by simulating 32-bit processing.

Note 2

To know which type of operating system is installed (32-bit or 64-bit) and other information about the Windows installation, open the **About** window. Open the **Settings** app and click **System**. Click **About** in the left panel of the System page to view system information. Figure 3-4 shows the About page.

Figure 3-4 The System window displays the type of operating system installed

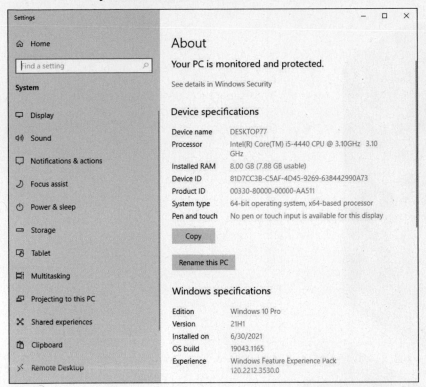

Intel Processors

Core 1 Objective 3.4

As you learned in the module "All About Motherboards," Intel groups its processors in generations. (Recall that the 12th generation, also called Alder Lake, and the 11th generation, Rocket Lake, were released in 2021.) Intel also groups its processors in families that can span several generations. To find details about any Intel processor, search the Intel ARK database at *ark.intel.com*. Current families of processors for desktops and laptops include the following:

- The Intel Core processors, first introduced in the 2nd generation, target the mid- to high-end consumer market and are currently Intel's most popular processor family:
  - Core X-series are made for the most powerful high-end desktops with graphics-heavy usage in mind. These processors are ideal for gaming, animation, photo and video editing, creation, and development.
  - Core i9 and Core i7 are made for high-end desktops and laptops. The latest Core i9 processor has up to 16 cores, 5.3 GHz, and a 16 MB cache.
  - Core i5 is well suited for mainstream desktops and laptops (see Figure 3-5).
  - Core i3 is an entry-level processor for desktops and laptops.
- Pentium processors are designed for entry-level desktops and laptops.
- Atom is made for low-end desktops, netbooks, and laptops, and the Celeron is made for low-end netbooks and laptops.

Intel dominates the processor and chipset market for servers with highly stable and powerful processors. Some models of the Core i9, Core i7, Core i5, and Core i3 processors are designed for server use, and some of the Atom processors target energy-efficient servers. For high-end servers, Intel offers the Xeon and Xeon Scalable processors. Processors designed for servers are more expensive because they are more stable and error-free than comparable desktop processors.

Note

Notice the processor in Figure 3-5 is advertised as unlocked, which means it can be overclocked.

Figure 3-5   The Intel Core i5-8600K 14 nm, 3.60 GHz, 9 MB cache
processor installs in the 8th generation LGA1151 socket

AMD Processors

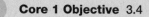
Core 1 Objective 3.4

Processors by Advanced Micro Devices, Inc., or AMD (*amd.com*), are popular in the game and hobbyist markets and are generally less expensive than comparable Intel processors. Recall that AMD processors use different sockets than Intel processors, so the motherboard must be designed for one manufacturer's processor or the other, but not both. Many motherboard manufacturers offer two comparable motherboards—one for an Intel processor and one for an AMD processor.

The current AMD processor families include the following:

- For desktops, the Ryzen, Ryzen Threadripper, Ryzen with Graphics, Athlon with Graphics, Ryzen Pro, and Athlon Pro. The Threadripper can have up to 64 cores. A Threadripper processor by AMD was shown earlier in Figure 3-1.
- For laptops, the Ryzen, Athlon, and Chromebook.
- For servers, the EPYC can have up to 64 cores.

ARM Processors

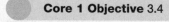
Core 1 Objective 3.4

ARM (Advanced RISC Machine) is a processor architecture designed to simplify the instruction set used for computing. Arm Limited, the company behind the ARM technology, is not a manufacturer; rather, the company licenses its designs to other companies that use them in their products. Because ARM processors are low cost, low power, and low heat, they are typically found embedded in mobile devices, such as smartphones, laptops, and tablets. Companies that use ARM processors include Samsung, Intel, Nvidia, Qualcomm, and Apple (see Figure 3-6). ARM processors can also be found in desktops and servers. One ARM processor claim to fame is that it is used in the world's fastest supercomputer.

Figure 3-6   The M1 processor with ARM-based architecture was introduced for Apple's Mac in 2020

iStock.com/Nature

In the next section of the module, you learn the detailed steps to select and install a processor in several of the popular Intel and AMD sockets used by desktops.

Selecting and Installing a Processor

Core 1 Objective 3.4

A hardware technician is sometimes called on to assemble a desktop computer from parts, exchange a processor that is faulty, add a second processor to a dual-processor system, or upgrade an existing processor to improve performance. In each situation, it is necessary to know how to match a processor for the system in which it is installed. You also need to know how to install the processor on the motherboard for each of the current Intel and AMD sockets used for desktop and laptop systems.

Selecting a Processor to Match System Needs

Core 1 Objective 3.4

When selecting the motherboard and processor, recall you must choose between the AMD and Intel chipset and processor. How to make this decision between the two brands was covered earlier in the text. When selecting a processor to match a motherboard you already have, the first requirement is to select one that the motherboard is designed to support. Among the processors the board supports, you need to select the one that best meets the general requirements of the system and the user's needs. Here are some processor features to consider:

- To get the best performance, use the highest-performing processor the board supports. Performance can be measured by clock speed, the number of tasks a CPU can run per clock cycle, and the size of the processor cache.

- Understand the processor's ability to multitask, considering the number of cores and multithreading abilities. Know, however, that applications must be able to take advantage of multiple cores. If not, some cores will sit idly while others do all the work. If the system will only be used for browsing the web, a single-core processor will do the job. However, Adobe Premier Pro, AutoCAD, The Isle, and Excel are examples of applications that take full advantage of multiple CPU cores.
- Balance the performance and power of the CPU with that of the entire system. For example, if the system has a high-performing graphics adapter, don't install a low-performing processor or hard drive to save on cost. One bottleneck can slow down the entire system.
- Be sure to read reviews of the processors you are considering and look for reviews that include comparison benchmarks of several processors. Also, know that you sometimes need to sacrifice performance and power for cost.

Applying Concepts

Selecting a Processor

Est. Time: 30 minutes
Core 1 Objective: 3.4

Your friend, Alice, is working toward her A+ certification. She has decided that the best way to get the experience she needs before she sits for the exam is to build a system from scratch. She has purchased an ASUS motherboard and asked you for some help selecting the right processor. She tells you that the system will later be used for light business needs and she wants to install a processor that is moderately priced to fit her budget. She doesn't want to install the most expensive processor the motherboard can support, nor does she want to sacrifice too much performance or power.

The documentation on the ASUS website (*asus.com/us/support*) for the ASUS Prime Z490-A motherboard provides this information:

- The ATX board contains the Z490 chipset and 10th generation LGA1200 socket and uses up to 128 GB of DDR4 memory.
- CPUs supported include a long list of 10th generation, 14 nm CPU Core, Pentium, and Celeron processors. Here are five processors found in this list:
  - Intel Core i7-10700K, 3.8 GHz, 125 W, 16 MB L3 cache, eight cores
  - Intel Core i5-10400T, 2.0 GHz, 35 W, 12 MB L3 cache, six cores
  - Intel Core i3-10300, 3.7 GHz, 65 W, 8 MB L3 cache, four cores
  - Intel Core i3-10100, 3.6 GHz, 65 W, 6 MB L3 cache, four cores
  - Intel Pentium Gold G6400T, 3.4 GHz, 35 W, 4 MB L3 cache, two cores

Based on what Alice has said, you decide to eliminate the most expensive processors (the Core i7 and i5) and the worst-performing processor (the Pentium Gold). That decision narrows your choices down to a Core i3. Before you select one of these processors, you need to check the list on the ASUS site to make sure the specific Core i3 processor is included. Look for the exact processor number—for example, the Core i3-10300.

You will also need a cooler assembly. If your processor doesn't come boxed with a cooler, select a cooler that fits the processor socket and gets good reviews. You'll also need some thermal compound if it is not included with the cooler.

The cooler is bracketed to the motherboard using a wire or plastic clip. A creamlike **thermal compound** is placed between the bottom of the cooler heat sink and the top of the processor. This compound eliminates air pockets, helping to draw heat off the processor. The thermal compound transmits heat better than air and makes an airtight connection between the fan and the processor. When processors and coolers are boxed together, the cooler heat sink might have thermal compound already applied to the bottom (see Figure 3-7).

Figure 3-7   Thermal compound is already applied to the bottom of this cooler that was purchased boxed with the processor

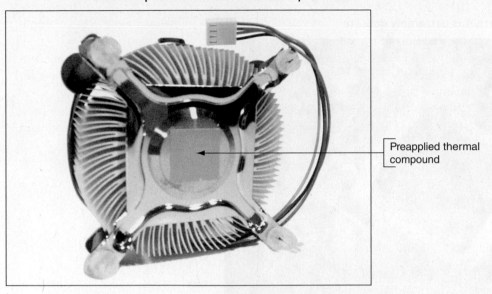

Preapplied thermal compound

Installing a Processor and Cooler Assembly

Core 1 Objective 3.4

Now let's look at the details of installing Intel and AMD processors and the cooler assembly.

Exam Tip ✔

The A+ Core 1 exam expects you to know how to install Intel and AMD processors.

Install an Intel Processor

If you are building a new system and the motherboard is not already installed in the case, follow the directions of the motherboard manufacturer to install the motherboard and then the processor, or follow the directions to install the processor and then the motherboard. The order of installation varies among manufacturers. Also, a cooler assembly might have nuts, bolts, screws, and plates that must be installed on the motherboard before you install the motherboard in the case. Here is the general procedure for installations, but always read and follow the specific directions for your motherboard and cooler assembly during your installation:

Figure 3-8   The Intel LGA1151 socket with a protective cover in place

1. Use an ESD strap or antistatic gloves to protect the processor, motherboard, and other components against ESD.

2. When replacing a processor in an existing system, power down the system, unplug the power cord, press the power button to drain the system of power, and open the case.

3. For a new motherboard, look for a protective cover over the processor socket (see Figure 3-8). Remove this socket cover and keep it in a safe place. If you ever remove the processor, put the cover back on the socket to protect it.

4. While the socket is exposed, as in Figure 3-9, be *very careful* not to touch the pins in the socket. Open the socket by pushing down on the socket lever and gently pushing it away from the socket to lift the lever.

Figure 3-9   The exposed socket is extremely delicate

Lever

5. As you lift the lever, the socket load plate is raised, as shown in Figure 3-10. Notice the two posts (labeled in Figure 3-11) on either side of the socket next to the hinge. These posts help orient the processor in the socket.

Figure 3-10   Lift the socket load plate to expose the processor
            socket

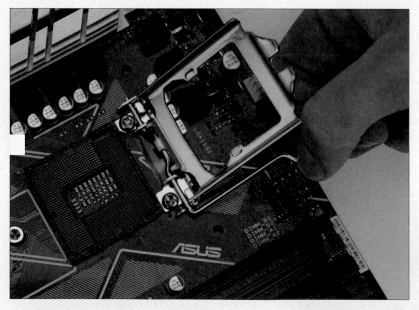

6. Open the clear plastic protective cover around the processor, and locate the two notches and one gold triangle that help you orient the processor in the socket. Figure 3-11 shows the posts on the socket that are used with the notches on the processor to orient the processor in the socket. You can then carefully remove the plastic cover. While the processor contacts are exposed, take extreme care not to touch the bottom of the processor. Hold it only at its edges. (It's best to use antistatic gloves as you work, but the gloves make it difficult to handle the processor.) Put the processor cover in a safe place, and use it to protect the processor if you ever remove the processor from the socket.

3

Figure 3-11   Two posts near the socket hinges help you orient the processor in the socket

Two posts match up
with two notches on
processor package

7. Hold the processor with your index finger and thumb, and orient the processor so that the two notches on its edge line up with the posts embedded on the socket. Gently lower the processor straight down into the socket. See Figure 3-12. Don't allow the processor to tilt, slide, or shift as you put it in the socket. To protect the pads, the processor needs to go straight down into the socket.

Figure 3-12   Align the processor in the socket using the gold triangle and the right-angle mark

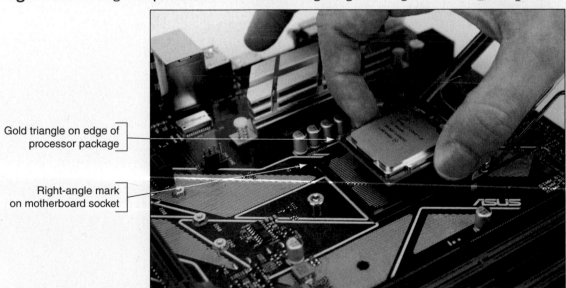

Gold triangle on edge of
processor package

Right-angle mark
on motherboard socket

8. Check carefully to make sure the processor is aligned correctly in the socket. Closing the socket without the processor fully seated can destroy the socket. Figure 3-13 shows the processor fully seated in the socket. Close the socket load plate so it catches under the screw head at the front of the socket.

9. Push down on the lever, and gently return it to its locked position.

Figure 3-13 Verify that the processor is seated in the socket with notches aligned to socket posts

Notches on processor align with posts on socket

Install the Cooler Assembly

You are now ready to install the cooler. Some coolers are lightweight with heat sinks and a fan on top. Some are heavier with heat sinks, fins, and a fan on the side, and they require a plate installed on the bottom of the motherboard to strengthen the board for the heavy cooler (see Figure 3-14).

Figure 3-14 A heavy-duty cooler may have a strengthening plate, heat sink, fins, fan, and several screws, nuts, and bolts

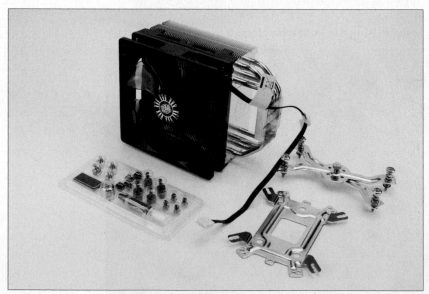

Before installing a cooler, read the directions carefully, and make sure you understand them. The cooler may be designed for either an Intel or AMD socket and may have to be installed differently depending on the socket type, so be sure you're following the correct directions.

Note **4**

For complicated cooler assemblies such as the Cooler Master Hyper 212 EVO shown in Figure 3-14, look for helpful YouTube videos that show how to install the assembly.

Here are the general steps for installing a cooler assembly:

1. Motherboards with Intel sockets have four holes to anchor the cooler (for example, see Figure 3-15). Examine the cooler posts that fit over these holes and the clips, nuts, bolts, screws, or plates that will hold the cooler firmly in place. Make sure you understand how this mechanism works because it may be difficult to install.

Figure 3-15   If the cooler does not have preapplied thermal compound, apply it on top of the processor

Four holes in motherboard to attach cooler assembly

Thermal compound applied

2. If the cooler has thermal compound preapplied, remove the plastic from the compound. If the cooler does not have thermal compound applied, put a small dot of compound (about the size of a small pea) in the center of the processor, as shown in Figure 3-15. When the cooler is attached and the processor is running, the compound spreads over the surface. Don't use too much—apply just enough that will later create a thin layer. If you use too much compound, it can slide off the housing and damage the processor or circuits on the motherboard. To get just the right amount, you can buy individual packets that each contain a single application of thermal compound.

Note **5**

When removing and reinstalling a processor, use a soft, dry cloth to carefully remove all the old thermal compound from both the processor and the cooler. Don't try to reuse the compound.

3. Some heavy coolers provide a plate that fits underneath the motherboard, with nuts, bolts, and screws to secure it to the board. The plate strengthens the board to help protect it from bending when the heavy cooler is installed. Install the plate, such as the one shown in Figure 3-16. The bolts on top of the board are now ready to receive the cooler.

Figure 3-16   A cooler assembly plate on the bottom of the motherboard
prevents a heavy cooler from bending the board

4. After the plate is installed, install the cooler on top of the processor. Be very careful to place the cooler straight down on the processor without shifting it so you don't smear the thermal compound off the top of the processor. Work very slowly and deliberately. To help keep the cooler balanced and in position, partly secure screws in two opposite bolts and then into the other two bolts. Rotate among the screws to partially tighten each one several times and keep the cooler in balance. See Figure 3-17. You can then clip the fan to the side of the cooler fins.

Figure 3-17   To keep the cooler balanced, rotate among the four
screws as you partially tighten each screw in turn

5. For lighter coolers with locking pins, verify that the locking pins are turned as far as they will go in a counterclockwise direction. (Make sure the pins don't protrude into the hollow plastic posts that go down into the motherboard holes.) Align the cooler over the processor so all four posts fit into the four holes on the motherboard and the fan power cord can reach the fan header on the motherboard. Then

push down on each locking pin until you hear it pop into the hole. To help keep the cooler balanced and in position, push down two opposite pins, and then push the remaining two pins in place. Using a flathead screwdriver, turn each locking pin clockwise to secure it. Figure 3-18 shows a cooler with locking pins secured. (Later, if you need to remove the cooler, turn each locking pin counterclockwise to release it from the hole.)

Figure 3-18   The pins are turned clockwise to secure the cooler to the motherboard

Fan header

> **Note 6**
>
> If you later notice the CPU fan is running far too often, you might need to tighten the connection between the cooler and the processor.

6. The fan on a cooler receives its power from a 4-pin CPU fan header on the motherboard. Connect the power cord from the cooler fan to this 4-pin header, which you should find on the board near the processor (see Figure 3-19).

Figure 3-19   Connect the cooler fan power cord to the motherboard 4-pin CPU fan header

After the processor and cooler are installed and the motherboard is installed in the case, make sure cables and cords don't obstruct fans or airflow, especially airflow around the processor and video card. Use cable ties to tie cords and cables up and out of the way.

Make one last check to verify that all power connectors are in place and that other cords and cables are connected to the motherboard correctly. You are now ready to plug the system back in, turn it on, and verify all is working. If the power comes on (you hear the fan spinning and see lights) but the system fails to work, the processor is most likely not seated solidly in the socket, or some power cord has not yet been connected or is not solidly connected. Turn everything off, unplug the power cord, press the power button to drain power, open the case, and recheck your installation.

If the system comes up and begins the boot process but suddenly turns off before the boot is complete, the processor is most likely overheating because the cooler is not installed correctly. Turn everything off, unplug the power cord, press the power button to drain power, open the case, and verify that the cooler is securely seated and connected.

After the system is up and running, you can check BIOS/UEFI setup to verify the system recognized the processor correctly. The setup screen for one processor is shown in Figure 3-20. Also, check the CPU and motherboard temperatures in BIOS/UEFI setup to verify that CPU is not overheating. In the BIOS/ UEFI utility shown in Figure 3-20, you can see the temperatures and fan RPMs.

Figure 3-20   Verify the CPU is recognized correctly by BIOS/UEFI and that CPU and motherboard temperatures are within acceptable range

Source: American Megatrends, Inc.

The maximum processor temperature varies by processor; to know the maximum, download the datasheet specifications for the processor from the Intel website (*ark.intel.com*). For example, the Intel Core i5-8600K 6-core processor shown earlier in this module will stop execution if the temperature rises above 100 degrees. If you see the temperature rising this high, open the case cover and verify the processor fan is running. Perhaps a wire is in the way and preventing the fan from turning or the fan power wire is not connected. Other troubleshooting tips for processors are covered in the module "Power Supplies and Troubleshooting Computer Problems."

Install an AMD Processor and Cooler Assembly

When installing an AMD Ryzen or Athlon processor, do the following:

1. Open the socket lever. If there's a protective cover over the socket, remove it.
2. Holding the processor very carefully so you don't touch the bottom, orient the four empty pin positions on the bottom with the four filled hole positions in the socket (see Figure 3-21). For some AMD sockets, a gold triangle on one corner of the processor matches up with a small triangle on a corner of the socket. Carefully lower the processor straight down into the socket. Don't allow it to tilt or slide as it goes into the socket. The pins on the bottom of the processor are very delicate, so take care as you work.

Figure 3-21   Orient the four alignment positions on the bottom of the processor
                  with those in the socket

3. Check carefully to make sure the pins in the processor are sitting slightly in the holes. Make sure the pins are not offset from the holes. If you try to use the lever to put pressure on these pins and they are not aligned correctly, you can destroy the processor. You can feel the pins settle into place when you're lowering the processor into the socket correctly.

4. Press the lever down and gently into position (see Figure 3-22).

Figure 3-22   Lower the lever into place, which puts pressure on the
                  processor

5. You are now ready to apply the thermal compound and install the cooler assembly. For most AMD sockets, the black retention mechanism for the cooler is already installed on the motherboard (see Figure 3-23). Set the cooler on top of the processor, aligning it inside the retention mechanism.

Figure 3-23 Align the cooler over the retention mechanism

Black retention
mechanism is
preattached

6. Next, clip the clipping mechanism into place on one side of the cooler. Then push down firmly on the clip on the opposite side of the cooler assembly; the clip will snap into place. Figure 3-24 shows the clip on one side in place for a system that has a yellow retention mechanism and a black cooler clip. Later, if you need to remove the cooler, use a Phillips screwdriver to remove the screws holding the retention mechanism in place. Then remove the retention mechanism along with the entire cooler assembly.

7. Connect the power cord from the fan to the 4-pin CPU fan header on the motherboard next to the processor.

Figure 3-24 The clips on the cooler attach the cooler to the retention mechanism on the motherboard

Cooler clip

Retention mechanism

Note 7

AMD changed the installation process with Ryzen Threadripper's TR4 socket. To watch a video describing how to install a Ryzen Threadripper processor into a TR4 socket, go to *amd.com/en/support/kb/faq/cpu-install-tr*.

Note 8

You will learn how to troubleshoot problems with the processor, motherboard, and RAM in the module "Power Supplies and Troubleshooting Computer Problems."

Now let's turn our attention to the various memory technologies used in personal computers and learn how to upgrade memory.

Memory Technologies

 Core 1 Objectives 1.1, 3.2

Recall that random access memory (RAM) temporarily holds data and instructions as the CPU processes them and that the memory modules used on a motherboard are made of dynamic RAM or DRAM. DRAM loses its data rapidly, and the memory controller must refresh it several thousand times a second. RAM is stored on memory modules, which are installed in memory slots on the motherboard (see Figure 3-25).

Figure 3-25   RAM on motherboards today is stored in DIMMs

One populated black slot and one empty black slot

Two empty blue slots

Exam Tip ✔

The A+ Core 1 exam expects you to know the purposes and characteristics of DDR3, DDR4, DDR5, and SO-DIMM memory technologies and how to match memory for an upgrade to memory already installed in a system.

Several variations of DRAM have evolved over the years. Here are the two major categories of memory modules:

- All current motherboards for desktops use a type of memory module called a DIMM (dual inline memory module).
- Laptops use a smaller version of a DIMM called a SO-DIMM (small outline DIMM, pronounced "sew-dim").

DIMMs have seen several evolutions, and you need to know about the latest, which are shown in Table 3-1. Notice the notches on the edge connector of each module, which prevent the wrong type of module from being inserted into a memory slot on the motherboard.

Table 3-1   Types of memory modules

Description of Module	Example
A 288-pin DDR5 DIMM is currently the fastest memory with lower voltage requirements. It can support quad or dual channels or function as single DIMMs. It has one notch near the center of the edge connector.	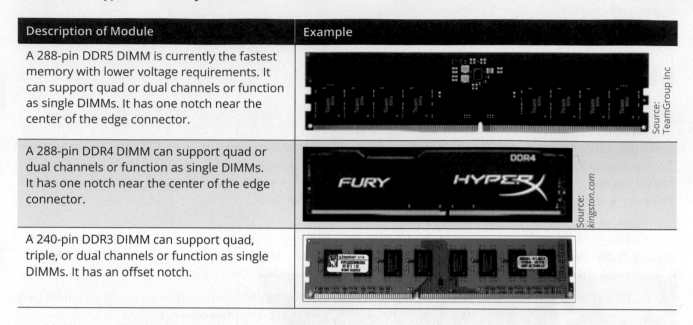 *Source: TeamGroup Inc*
A 288-pin DDR4 DIMM can support quad or dual channels or function as single DIMMs. It has one notch near the center of the edge connector.	*Source: kingston.com*
A 240-pin DDR3 DIMM can support quad, triple, or dual channels or function as single DIMMs. It has an offset notch.	

Note 9

JEDEC (*jedec.org*) is the organization responsible for standards used by solid-state devices, including RAM technologies.

Many DIMM technologies exist because they have evolved to improve capacity, speed, and performance without greatly increasing the cost. A quick Google search for buying RAM turns up details such as those shown in Figure 3-26. In this section of the module, you learn about these technologies so you can make the best selections of memory for a particular motherboard and customer needs.

We'll now look at each of the types of DIMM and SO-DIMM modules and the technologies they use.

Figure 3-26   Evolving memory technologies result in many details and options

Source: Google.com

DIMM and SO-DIMM Technologies

Core 1 Objective 3.2

To understand the details of a memory ad, let's start with a few important acronyms:

- The "D" in DIMM stands for "dual," named for the independent pins on both sides of the module's edge connector. All DIMMs have a 64-bit data path.
- A **DDR (Double Data Rate)** DIMM gets its name from the fact that it ran twice as fast as earlier DIMMs when it was invented. It was able to double the effective data rate because a DDR DIMM processes data at the rise and fall of the motherboard clock beat, rather than at each clock beat.
- **DDR3** uses 240 pins. DDR3 DIMMs are not compatible with other DIMM types because their notches are not in the same position.
- **DDR4** is faster and uses less power than DDR3. A DDR4 module offers up to 16 Gb DRAM, uses 288 pins, and has a single notch in the edge connector.
- **DDR5** is faster and uses less power than DDR4. A DDR5 module offers up to 64 Gb DRAM and also uses 288 pins. While the DDR5 has a single notch in the edge connector similar to the DDR4, the DDR5 is not compatible with DDR4 memory slots because the notch is closer to the center.

Factors that affect the capacity, features, and performance of DIMMs include the number of channels they use, how much RAM is on one DIMM, the speed, error-checking abilities, and buffering. All these factors are discussed next.

Single, Dual, Triple, and Quad Channels

Early DIMMs only used a **single channel**, which means the memory controller can access only one DIMM at a time. To improve overall memory performance, **dual channels** allow the memory controller to communicate with two DIMMs at the same time, effectively doubling the speed of memory access. A motherboard that supports **triple channels** can access three DIMMs at the same time, and a **quad channel** motherboard can access four DIMMs at the same time. DDR3, DDR4, and DDR5 DIMMs can use dual channels. DDR3 DIMMs can also use triple channels. DDR3, DDR4, and DDR5 DIMMs can use quad channels. For dual, triple, or quad channels to work, the motherboard and the DIMM must support the technology.

Motherboard manufacturers typically color-code DIMM slots to show you how to configure dual, triple, or quad channeling. For example, Figure 3-27 shows how dual channeling works on a board with two black DIMM slots and two gray slots. The board has two memory channels, channel 1 and channel 2. With dual channeling, two DIMMs installed in the two gray slots are each using a different channel and, therefore, can be addressed at the same time. If two more DIMMs are installed in the two black slots, they can be accessed at the same time.

Figure 3-27   Using dual channels, the memory controller can read from two DIMMs at the same time

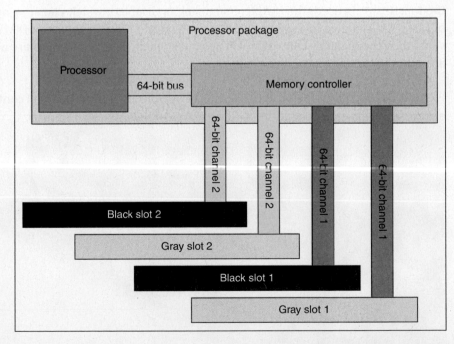

When setting up dual channeling, know that the pair of DIMMs to be addressed at the same time must be equally matched in size, speed, and features, and it is recommended they come from the same manufacturer. (Two matching DIMMs are often sold as a DIMM kit.) A motherboard that supports dual channels was shown earlier in Figure 3-25. To use dual channeling, this motherboard requires matching DIMMs to be installed in the black slots and another matching pair in the blue slots, as shown in Figure 3-28. Know that the second pair of DIMMs does not have to match the first pair of DIMMs because the blue slots run independently of the black slots. If the two DIMM slots of the same color are not populated with matching pairs of DIMMs, the motherboard will revert to single channeling.

Figure 3-28   Matching pairs of DIMMs installed in four DIMM slots that support dual channeling

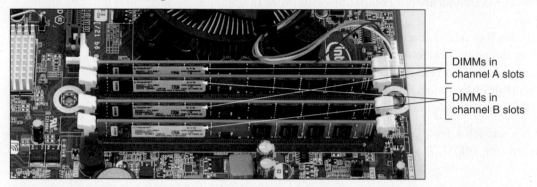

DIMMs in channel A slots

DIMMs in channel B slots

Exam Tip ✔

The A+ Core 1 exam expects you to be able to distinguish among single-channel, dual-channel, triple-channel, and quad-channel memory installations and to configure these installations for best performance.

For a triple-channel installation, three DIMM slots must be populated with three matching DDR3 DIMMs (see Figure 3-29). The three DIMMs are installed in the three blue slots on the board. The motherboard in the figure has a fourth black DIMM slot. You can barely see this black slot behind the three populated slots in the photo. If the fourth slot is used, then triple channeling is disabled, which can slow down performance. If a matching pair of DIMMs is installed in the first two slots and another matching pair of DIMMs is installed in the third and fourth slots, then the memory controller will use dual channels. Dual channels are not as fast as triple channels, but they are certainly better than single channels.

Figure 3-29   Three identical DDR3 DIMMs installed in a triple-channel configuration

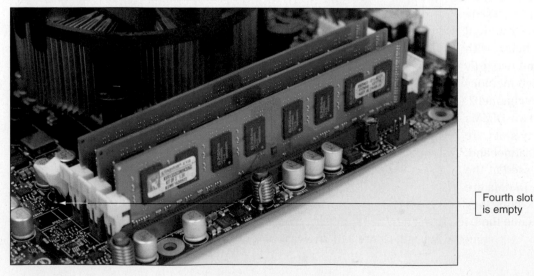

Fourth slot is empty

Expect a motherboard that uses quad channeling to have eight memory slots. For example, the Gigabyte AMD X399 Gaming motherboard has four DIMM slots on each side of the AMD TR4 processor socket (see Figure 3-30). The eight DIMM slots support four channels; each channel has two slots. The processor can address four slots or four channels at the same time. To know which of the eight slots to populate for optimum performance, see the motherboard user manual; in the figure, the manufacturer did not color-code the slots.

Figure 3-30   The Gigabyte AMD X399 Gaming motherboard has eight DIMM DDR4 slots and supports quad channeling

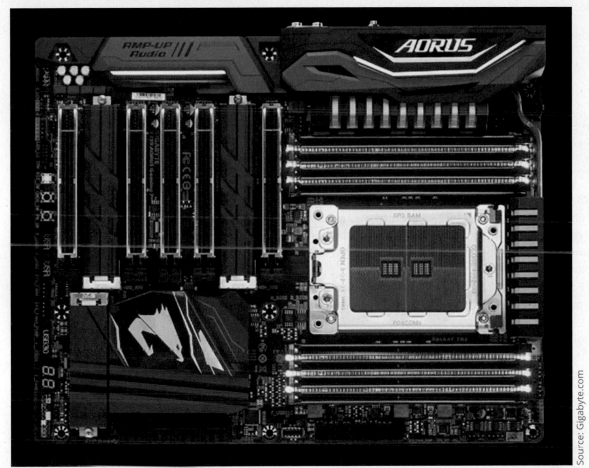

Source: Gigabyte.com

DIMM Speeds

DIMM speeds are measured either in MHz (such as 3000 MHz or 1600 MHz) or PC rating (such as PC4 24000 or PC3 12800). A PC rating is a measure of the total bandwidth (in MB/second) of data moving between the module and the CPU. To calculate the PC rating for a DDR4 DIMM, multiply the speed by 8 bytes because a DIMM has an 8-byte or 64-bit data path. For example, a DDR4 DIMM that runs at 3000 MHz has a bandwidth or transfer rate of 3000 × 8 or 24,000 MB/second, which is expressed as a PC rating of PC4 24000. (A DDR4 PC rating is labeled PC4.)

A second example calculates the PC rating for a DDR3 DIMM running at 1600 MHz: PC rating = 1600 × 8 = 12,800, which is written as PC3 12800.

Error Checking

Because DIMMs intended to be used in servers must be extremely reliable, error-checking technology called **ECC (error-correcting code)** is sometimes used. Figure 3-31 shows four modules with ECC designed for server use.

Figure 3-31   Server memory uses ECC for fault tolerance

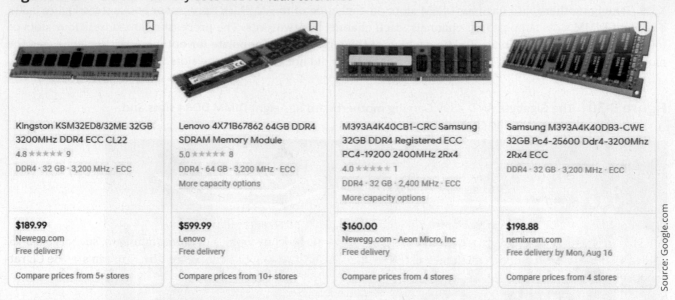

Kingston KSM32ED8/32ME 32GB
3200MHz DDR4 ECC CL22
4.8 ★★★★★ 9
DDR4 · 32 GB · 3,200 MHz · ECC

$189.99
Newegg.com
Free delivery

Compare prices from 5+ stores

Lenovo 4X71B67862 64GB DDR4
SDRAM Memory Module
5.0 ★★★★★ 8
DDR4 · 64 GB · 3,200 MHz · ECC
More capacity options

$599.99
Lenovo
Free delivery

Compare prices from 10+ stores

M393A4K40CB1-CRC Samsung
32GB DDR4 Registered ECC
PC4-19200 2400MHz 2Rx4
4.0 ★★★★★ 1
DDR4 · 32 GB · 2,400 MHz · ECC
More capacity options

$160.00
Newegg.com - Aeon Micro, Inc
Free delivery

Compare prices from 4 stores

Samsung M393A4K40DB3-CWE
32GB Pc4-25600 Ddr4-3200Mhz
2Rx4 ECC
DDR4 · 32 GB · 3,200 MHz · ECC

$198.88
nemixram.com
Free delivery by Mon, Aug 16

Compare prices from 4 stores

Source: Google.com

Some DDR3, DDR4, and DDR5 memory modules support ECC. A DIMM that supports ECC will have an extra chip, the ECC chip. ECC compares bits written to the module to what is later read from the module, and it can detect and correct an error in a single bit of the byte. If there are errors in 2 bits of a byte, ECC can detect the error but cannot correct it. The data path width for DIMMs is normally 64 bits, but with ECC, the data path is 72 bits. The extra 8 bits are used for error checking. ECC memory costs more than non-ECC memory, but it is more reliable. For ECC to work, the motherboard and all installed modules must support it. Also, it's important to know that you cannot install a mix of ECC and non-ECC memory on the motherboard—the resulting system will not work.

As with most other memory technologies discussed in this module, when adding memory to a motherboard, match the type of memory to the type the board supports. To see if your motherboard supports ECC memory, look for the ability to enable or disable the feature in BIOS/UEFI setup, or check the motherboard documentation.

Exam Tip ✔

The A+ Core 1 exam expects you to be familiar with ECC and non-ECC memory technologies and to know when the technology is recommended or required in a given scenario.

Note 10

RAM chips on DIMMs can cause errors if they become undependable and cannot hold data reliably. Sometimes this happens when chips overheat or power falters.

Buffered and Registered DIMMs

Buffers and registers hold data and amplify a signal just before the data is written to the module, and they can increase memory performance in servers. (Buffers are an older technology than registers.) Some DIMMs use buffers, some use registers, and some use neither. If a DIMM doesn't support registers or buffers, it's referred to as an unbuffered DIMM or UDIMM. When looking at advertisements for DIMMs, you might see registered memory written as RDIMM.

Note 11

In memory ads, CAS Latency is sometimes written as CL.

Note 12

When selecting memory, use the memory type that the motherboard manufacturer recommends.

CAS Latency

Another memory feature is **CAS Latency** (CAS stands for "column access strobe"), which is a way of measuring access timing. The feature refers to the number of clock cycles it takes to write or read a column of data off a memory module. Lower values are better than higher ones. For example, CL8 is a little faster than CL9.

Ads for memory modules might give the CAS Latency value within a series of timing numbers, such as 5-5-5-15. The first value is CAS Latency, which means the module is CL5. Looking back at Figure 3-31, you can see the CL rating for the first module is CL22.

Types of Memory Used in Laptops

Today's laptops use DDR4, DDR3L, or DDR3 SO-DIMM memory. Table 3-2 lists current SO-DIMMs. All these memory modules are smaller than regular DIMMs and use the same technologies as DIMMs.

Table 3-2 Memory modules used in laptop computers

Memory Module Description	Sample Memory Module
A 2.74" 260-pin SO-DIMM contains DDR4 memory. The one notch on the module is offset from the center of the module.	Source: crucial.com
A 2.66" 204-pin SO-DIMM contains DDR3 memory. The one notch on the module is offset from the center of the module. A **DDR3L** SO-DIMM uses less power than a regular DDR3 SO-DIMM.	Courtesy of Kingston Technology Corporation

Exam Tip ✔

The A+ Core 1 exam expects you to know that DDR4 and DDR3 memory can be found on SO-DIMMs and to know when to use each type of memory in a given scenario.

Note 13

At the time of this writing, DDR5 SO-DIMM has been announced, but no timeline has been released for when it will be available.

As with memory modules used in desktop computers, you can only use the type of memory the laptop is designed to support. The number of pins and the position of the notches on a SO-DIMM keep you from inserting the wrong module in a memory slot.

Virtual RAM

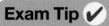

Core 1 Objective 3.2

Virtual RAM, or **virtual memory**, is the way Windows uses space on the hard drive to enhance the amount of RAM in a system. Windows normally stores virtual memory in pagefile.sys, a hidden file stored in the root directory of drive C:. Windows automatically manages the size of the file, and not having enough free space on drive C: can cause pagefile.sys to be too small, resulting in a low memory warning. Pagefile .sys should be able to be at least three times the size of installed RAM.

Exam Tip ✔

The A+ Core 1 exam expects you to know how to configure virtual memory for optimal performance.

Applying Concepts

Verifying Virtual Memory Settings

Est. Time: 15 minutes
Core 1 Objective: 3.4

Do the following to check and adjust virtual memory settings:

1. Open the **About** window in the Settings app, and then click **Advanced system settings**. The System Properties dialog box appears with the Advanced tab selected (see Figure 3-32).

Figure 3-32   Manage virtual memory using the System Properties dialog box

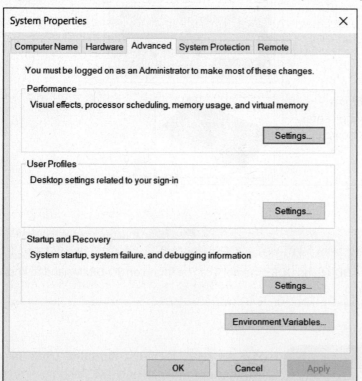

2. In the Performance section, click **Settings**. In the Performance Options dialog box, select the **Advanced** tab and click **Change**. The Virtual Memory dialog box appears. See the right side of Figure 3-33.

Figure 3-33   Move pagefile.sys to a different drive

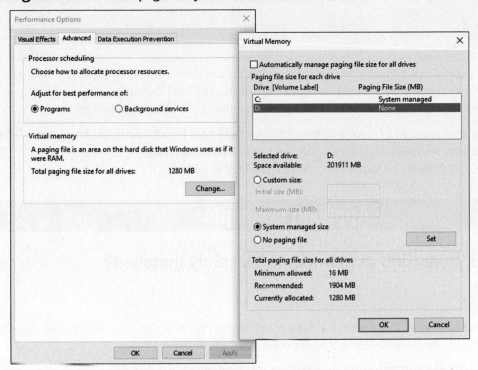

3. Generally, you should allow Windows to manage pagefile.sys without your help. To do that, select **Automatically manage paging file size for all drives**. However, if there is not enough free space on drive C: for pagefile.sys, you can move the file to another volume. To move the file, uncheck **Automatically manage paging file size for all drives**, and select the drive where you want to move the paging file, as shown in Figure 3-33.

4. Click **OK**. Windows informs you that you must restart the system for the change to take effect. Click **OK** to close the warning box.

5. Click **Apply** and close all dialog boxes. Then restart the system.

How to Upgrade Memory

 Core 1 Objectives 1.1, 3.2

To upgrade memory means to add more RAM to a computer. Adding more RAM might solve a problem with slow performance, applications refusing to load, or an unstable system. When Windows does not have adequate memory to perform an operation, it displays an "Insufficient memory" error, or it slows down to a painful crawl.

When first purchased, many computers have empty slots on the motherboard, allowing you to add DIMMs or SO-DIMMs to increase the amount of RAM. Sometimes a memory module goes bad and must be replaced.

When you add more memory to your computer, you need answers to these questions:

- How much RAM do I need, and how much is currently installed?
- What type of memory is currently installed?
- How many and what kind of modules can I fit on my motherboard?
- How do I select and purchase the right modules for my upgrade?
- How do I physically install the new modules?

All these questions are answered in the following sections.

How Much Memory Do I Need, and How Much Is Currently Installed?

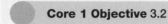

Core 1 Objective 3.2

With the demands that today's software places on memory, the answer is probably, "All you can get." When deciding how much memory the system can support, consider the limitations of the motherboard, processor, and operating system. For the motherboard, research the motherboard user manual or manufacturer website. For the processor, see the Intel or AMD website. Here are the limitations when considering the operating system:

- Windows requires a minimum of 1 GB for a 32-bit installation and 2 GB for a 64-bit installation, but more is better.
- For 64-bit installations, Windows 10 Pro can support up to 2 TB of memory.
- A 32-bit Windows installation can support no more than 4 GB of memory.

Applying Concepts

How Much and What Kind of Memory Is Currently Installed?

Est. Time: 15 minutes
Core 1 Objective: 3.2

When you execute **msinfo32.exe** in Windows, the System Information window shown in Figure 3-34 reports the amount of installed physical memory. Notice in the window that 8 GB is installed.

Figure 3-34 The System Information window reports installed physical memory

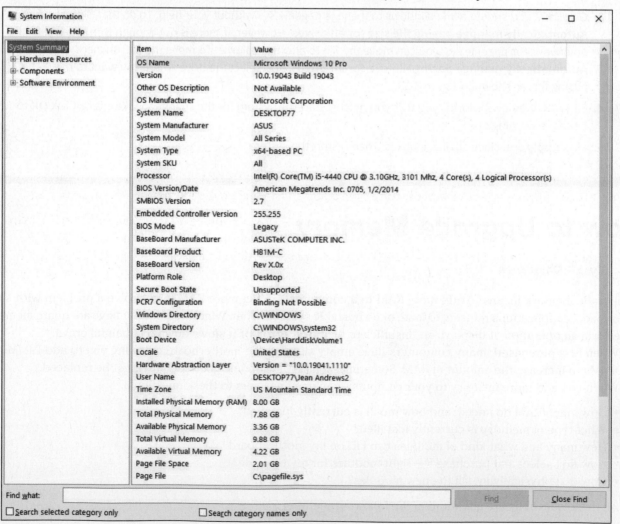

The BIOS/UEFI setup screen shows more information about installed memory than Windows does. Reboot the computer and access BIOS/UEFI setup, as you learned in the module "All About Motherboards." The BIOS/UEFI setup main menu for one system is shown in Figure 3-35. This screen shows that there are four memory slots and that each contains a 4 GB DIMM. You can also see that the memory speed is 1333 MHz and the board supports dual channeling.

Because all the slots are populated, you know you must replace existing 4 GB DIMMs with larger-capacity DIMMs, which will increase the price of the upgrade.

On other BIOS/UEFI screens, you should be able to identify the motherboard brand and model. For the BIOS/UEFI in Figure 3-35, select **System Identification Information**; you see that the motherboard is the Intel DH67GD.

Figure 3-35   BIOS/UEFI setup reports the memory configuration and amount

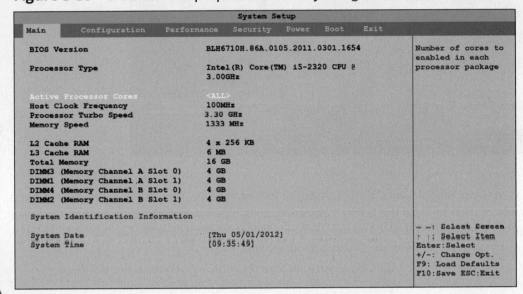

What Type of Memory Is Already Installed?

> **Core 1 Objective** 3.2

If the board already has memory installed, you want to do your best to match the new modules with the existing modules. To learn what type of memory modules are already installed, do the following:

1. Open the case and look at the memory slots. How many slots do you have? How many are filled? Remove each module from its slot, and examine it for the imprinted type, size, and speed. In Figure 3-36, the module is 4 GB PC4-17000 CL 15-15-15-36, and the brand of RAM is GEIL.

Figure 3-36   Use the label on this DIMM to identify its features

Source: Intel

2. If you have not already identified the motherboard, examine it for the imprinted manufacturer and model (see Figure 3-37).

Figure 3-37   Look for the manufacturer and model of a motherboard imprinted somewhere on the board

Model

Manufacturer

3. Find the motherboard documentation online, and read it to find the type of memory the board supports. Look in the documentation to see if the board supports dual channels, triple channels, or quad channels. If the board supports multiple channels and modules are already installed, verify that matching DIMMs are installed in each channel, as recommended in the documentation.

4. If you still have not identified the module type, you can take the motherboard and the old memory modules to a good computer store; the staff there should be able to match it for you.

How Many and What Kind of Modules Can Fit on My Motherboard?

 Core 1 Objective 3.2

Now that you know what memory modules are already installed, you're ready to decide how much memory and what kind of modules you can add to the board. Keep in mind that if all memory slots are full, you can sometimes take out small-capacity modules and replace them with larger-capacity modules, but you can only use the type, size, and speed of modules that the board can support. Also, if you must discard existing modules, the price of the upgrade increases.

To know how much memory your motherboard can physically hold, read the documentation that comes with the board. You can always install DIMMs as single modules, but you might not get the best performance by doing so. For best performance, install matching DIMMs in each channel (two, three, or four slots). Now let's look at two examples, one using dual channels and another using triple channels.

Motherboard Using DDR4 Dual-Channel DIMMs

The ASUS Prime Z370-P motherboard, shown earlier in Figure 3-37, has four 288-pin DDR4 DIMM slots. It supports 2 GB, 4 GB, 8 GB, and 16 GB unbuffered, non-ECC DDR4 DIMMs with dual channeling. DIMM voltage cannot exceed 1.35 V, and DIMMs with the same CAS Latency must be installed. The user manual recommends installing memory from the same manufacturer and same product line. It also says the maximum speed of the DIMMs supported varies by the processor. The processor shown in Figure 3-37 is the Intel Core i5-8600K; a quick check at *ark.intel.com* tells us that the maximum memory speed supported by this processor is 2666 MHz. The information imprinted on the two DIMMs currently installed (see Figure 3-38) is DDR4 3000 MHz 15-17-17-35 1.35 V Vengeance by Corsair.

Figure 3-38   Look for imprinted information about a DIMM

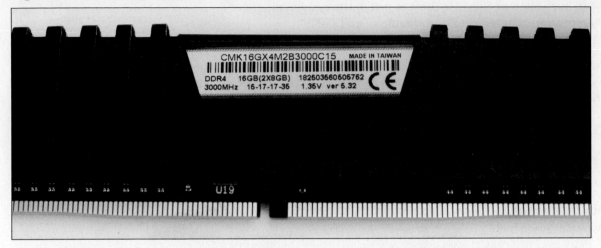

You want to upgrade memory from the current 16 GB to 32 GB. To get the full benefit of dual channeling, based on your research, you need to purchase two matching DIMMs using these specifications:

- Corsair Vengeance DDR4 DIMM
- CAS Latency 15, unbuffered, non-ECC
- Minimum speed of 2666 MHz

To support dual channeling, the two existing DIMMs are installed in the two gray slots on the board; you plan to install the two new DIMMs in the two black slots.

Motherboard Using DDR3 Triple-Channel DIMMs

The Intel motherboard shown earlier in Figure 3-29 has four DDR3 memory slots that can be configured for single, dual, or triple channeling. The four empty slots are shown in Figure 3-39. If triple channeling is used, three matching DIMMs are used in the three blue slots. If the fourth slot is populated, the board reverts to single channeling. For dual channeling, install two matching DIMMs in the two blue slots farthest from the processor and leave the other two slots empty. If only one DIMM is installed, it goes in the blue slot in the farthest position from the processor.

Figure 3-39   Four DDR3 slots on a motherboard

The motherboard documentation says that these types of DIMMs can be used:

- DIMM voltage rating no higher than 1.6 V
- Non-ECC DDR3 memory
- Serial Presence Detect (SPD) memory only

- Gold-plated contacts (some modules use tin-plated contacts)
- 1333 MHz, 1066 MHz, or 800 MHz (best to match the system bus speed)
- Unbuffered, nonregistered single- or double-sided DIMMs
- Up to 16 GB total installed RAM

The third item in the list needs an explanation. SPD is a DIMM technology that declares the module's size, speed, voltage, and data path width to system BIOS/UEFI at startup. If the DIMM does not support SPD, the system might not boot or boot with errors. Today's memory always supports SPD.

How Do I Select and Purchase the Right Memory Modules?

 Core 1 Objective 3.2

You're now ready to make a purchase. As you select your memory, it might be difficult to find an exact match to DIMMs already installed on the board. Compromises might be necessary, but understand that there are some you can make and some you cannot:

- Mixing unbuffered memory with buffered or registered memory won't work.
- When matching memory, you should also match the module manufacturer for best results. But in a pinch, you can try using memory from two different manufacturers.
- If you mix memory speeds, know that all modules will perform at the slowest speed.

Now let's look at how to use a website or computer ad to search for the right memory.

Use a Website to Research Your Purchase

When purchasing memory from a website, such as Crucial Technology's site (*crucial.com*) or Kingston Technology's site (*kingston.com*), look for a search utility that will match memory modules to your motherboard. These utilities are easy to use and help you confirm you have made the right decisions about type, size, and speed to buy. They can also help if motherboard documentation is inadequate and you're not exactly sure what memory to buy.

Let's look at one example on the Crucial site. We are looking to install memory in the ASUS Prime Z370-P motherboard discussed earlier in the module. After selecting the manufacturer, product, and model (see Figure 3-40), click **Compatible RAM**.

Figure 3-40   Use the Crucial upgrade utility to find the correct memory for an upgrade

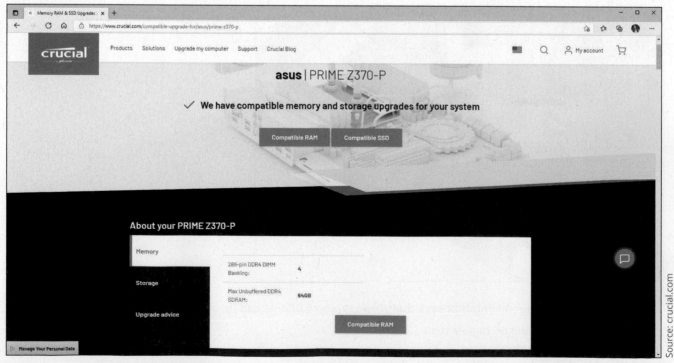

Source: crucial.com

The search results include the DIMMs shown in Figure 3-41. You can see all our criteria are met (unbuffered, CAS Latency 15, Non-ECC, 3000 MHz, and 1.35 V) except the brand. These criteria validate what we have already determined based on our research, and we can now search for the matching brand on other memory sites. If we can't find the matching brand, this hit will certainly work for our upgrade.

Note 14

RAM modules may have heat spreaders, which are fins or heat sinks on the side of the module to keep it from overheating. Some modules have cool lights for visual appeal in see-through cases.

Figure 3-41   Selecting memory off the Crucial website

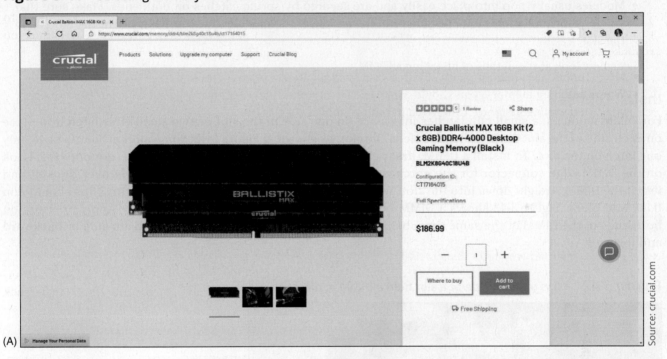

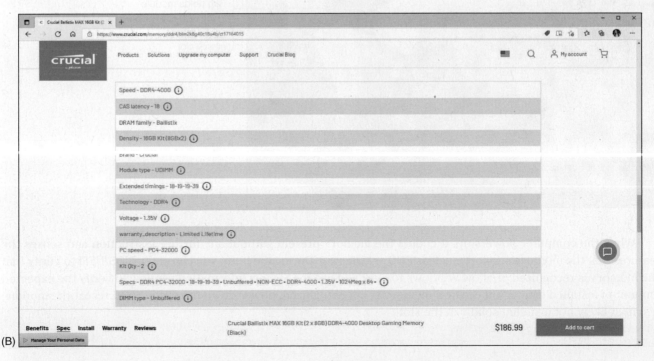

Source: crucial.com

How Do I Install the New Modules?

 Core 1 Objective 3.2

When installing RAM modules, be careful to protect the chips against static electricity, as you learned in the module "Taking a Computer Apart and Putting It Back Together." Follow these precautions:

- Always use an ESD strap as you work.
- Turn off the power, unplug the power cord, press the power button, and remove the case cover.
- Handle memory modules with care.
- Don't touch the edge connectors on the memory module or on the memory slot.
- Don't stack cards or modules because this can loosen a chip.
- Modules usually pop into place easily and are secured by spring catches on both ends. Make sure that you look for the notches on one side or in the middle of the module; these notches orient the module in the slot.

Let's now look at the details of installing a DIMM.

Install DIMMs

For DIMM modules, a small clip latches into place on one side of the slot or two small clips latch into place on each side of the slot to hold the module in the slot, as shown in Figure 3-42. Some motherboards have only one latch on the slot. To install a DIMM, first pull the supporting arms on the sides of the slot outward. Look on the DIMM edge connector for the notches, which help you orient the DIMM correctly over the slot and insert the DIMM straight down into the slot. When the DIMM is fully inserted, the supporting clips should pop back into place. Figure 3-43 shows a DIMM being inserted into a slot on a motherboard. Apply pressure on both ends of the DIMM at the same time, being careful not to rock the module from side to side or backward and forward.

Figure 3-42   Clips on each side of a slot hold a DIMM in place

Clip holds module in place

Open clip on empty slot

When the computer powers up, it counts the memory present without any further instruction and senses the features that the modules support, such as ECC or buffering. During the boot, you can enter BIOS/UEFI to verify that the memory is recognized or allow Windows to start and use the System Information window to verify the expected amount of installed memory. If the new memory is not recognized, power down the system and reseat the module. It's most likely not installed solidly in the slot.

Figure 3-43   Insert the DIMM into the slot by pressing down until the support
clips lock into position

How to Upgrade Memory on a Laptop

> **Core 1 Objective** 1.1

Before upgrading memory on a laptop, make sure you are not voiding the laptop's warranty. Search for the best buy, but make sure you use memory modules made by or authorized by your laptop's manufacturer and designed for the exact model of your laptop. Installing generic memory might save money but might also void the laptop's warranty.

Upgrading memory on a laptop works about the same way as upgrading memory on a desktop: Decide how much memory you can upgrade and what type of memory you need, purchase the memory, and install it. As with a desktop computer, be sure to match the type of memory to the type the laptop supports.

Applying Concepts

Upgrading Memory on a Laptop

Est. Time: 30 minutes
Core 1 Objective: 1.1

Most laptops are designed to allow easy access to memory. Follow these steps to exchange or upgrade memory for a typical laptop:

1. Back up data and shut down the system. Remove peripherals, including the AC adapter. Remove the battery. Be sure to use an ESD strap as you work.

2. Many laptops have a RAM compartment on the bottom. For some laptops, this compartment is in the battery cavity. Turn the laptop over, and loosen the screws on the RAM compartment cover. (It is not necessary to remove the screws.)

(continues)

Applying Concepts Continued

3. Raise the cover (see Figure 3-44), and remove it from its hinges. The two memory slots are exposed.

Figure 3-44   Raise the DIMM door on the bottom of the notebook

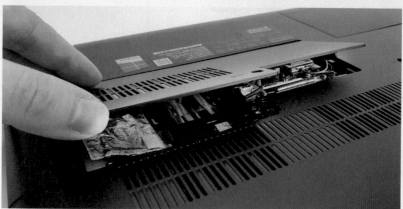

4. Notice in Figure 3-45 that the SO-DIMM slots are stacked on top of each other. When you remove one SO-DIMM from the laptop, you can see the slot under it that holds a second SO-DIMM. Also notice in the figure that when you remove the RAM door, the wireless card is exposed. This easy access to the wireless card makes exchanging it very easy. To remove a SO-DIMM, pull the clips on the side of the memory slot apart slightly (see Figure 3-45). The SO-DIMM will pop up and out of the slot and can then be removed. If it does not pop up, you can hold the clips apart as you pull the module up and out of the slot.

Figure 3-45   Pull apart the clips on the memory slot to release
the SO-DIMM

5. To install a new SO-DIMM, insert the module at an angle into the slot (see Figure 3-46), and gently push it down until it snaps into the clips (see Figure 3-47). Replace the RAM door.

Figure 3-46   Insert a new SO-DIMM into a memory slot

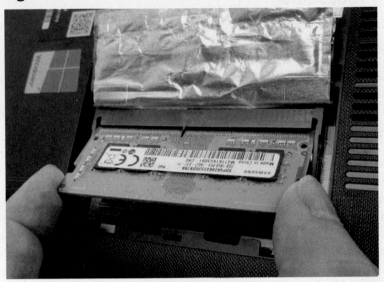

Figure 3-47   Push down on the SO-DIMM until it pops into the clips

6. Replace the battery, plug in the power adapter, and power up the laptop.

Module Summary

Types and Characteristics of Processors

- The most important component on the motherboard is the processor, or central processing unit. The two major manufacturers of processors are Intel and AMD.
- Processors are rated by their processor speed, lithography, the socket and chipset they can use, multiprocessing features (multithreading, multicore rating, and dual processors), memory cache, memory features supported, virtualization, overclocking, and processor architecture (32-bit or 64-bit).
- A processor's memory cache inside the processor housing can be an L1 cache (contained on the processor die), L2 cache (off the die), and L3 cache (farther from the core than L2 cache).
- The core of a processor has two arithmetic logic units (ALUs). Multicore processors have two, three, or more cores (called dual core, triple core, quad core, and so forth). Each core can process two threads at once if the feature is enabled in BIOS/UEFI setup.
- The current families of Intel processors for desktops include Core, Pentium, Atom, and Celeron. Several different processors and generations are within each family.
- The current AMD desktop and laptop processor families are Ryzen, Ryzen Threadripper, Ryzen with Graphics, Athlon with Graphics, Ryzen Pro, Athlon Pro, Athlon, and Chromebook. In addition, the Ryzen Threadripper and Ryzen are the latest processors for desktops. Several processors exist within each family.
- ARM processors are commonly used in mobile devices.

Selecting and Installing a Processor

- Select a processor that the motherboard supports. A board is likely to support several processors that vary in performance and price.
- When installing a processor, always follow the directions in the motherboard user guide, and be careful to protect the board and processor against ESD. Current Intel sockets use a socket lever and socket load plate. When opening these sockets, lift the socket lever and then the socket load plate, install the processor, and then close the socket. Many AMD sockets have a socket lever but not a socket load plate.
- Always apply thermal compound between the processor and cooler assembly to help draw heat from the processor.

Memory Technologies

- DRAM is stored on DIMMs for desktop computers and SO-DIMMs for laptops.
- Types of current DIMMs are DDR5 and DDR4, which have 288 pins, and DDR3 DIMMs, which have 240 pins.
- Matching DIMMs can work together in dual channels, triple channels, and quad channels so the memory controller can access more than one DIMM at a time to improve performance. In a channel, all DIMMs must match in size, speed, and features. DDR3 DIMMs can use dual, triple, or quad channeling. DDR 5 DIMMs and DDR4 DIMMs can use dual or quad channels.
- DIMM speeds are measured in MHz (for example, 3000 MHz) or PC rating (for example, PC4 24000).
- The memory controller can check memory for errors and possibly correct them using ECC (error-correcting code).
- Buffers and registers are used to hold data and amplify a data signal. A DIMM is rated as a buffered, registered (RDIMM), or unbuffered DIMM (UDIMM).
- CAS Latency (CL) measures access time to memory. Lower values are faster than higher values.
- Today's laptops use DDR4, DDR3L, or DDR3 SO-DIMMs.
- Virtual RAM is the way Windows uses space on the hard drive to enhance the amount of RAM in a system. Windows normally stores virtual memory in pagefile.sys.

How to Upgrade Memory

- When upgrading memory, use the type, size, and speed the motherboard supports, and match new modules to those already installed. Features to match include DDR5, DDR4, DDR3, size in MB or GB, speed (MHz or PC rating), buffered, registered, unbuffered, CL rating, tin or gold connectors, support for dual, triple, or quad channeling, ECC, and non-ECC. Using memory made by the same manufacturer is recommended.
- When upgrading components on a laptop, including memory, use components that are the same brand as the laptop, or use only components recommended by the laptop's manufacturer.

Key Terms

For explanations of key terms, see the Glossary for this text.

CAS Latency	dynamic RAM (DRAM)	msinfo32.exe	single-core processing
DDR (Double Data Rate)	ECC (error-correcting	multicore processing	static RAM (SRAM)
DDR3	code)	multiprocessing	thermal compound
DDR3L	Hyper-Threading	multiprocessor platform	thread
DDR4	HyperTransport	multisockct	triple channels
DDR5	Level 1 cache (L1 cache)	processor frequency	virtual RAM
dual channels	Level 2 cache (L2 cache)	quad channel	virtual memory
dual processors	Level 3 cache (L3 cache)	single channel	x86-64 bit processor

Thinking Critically

These questions are designed to prepare you for the critical thinking required for the A+ exams and may use information from other modules and the web. As always, remember Google is your friend!

1. An experienced user has installed Oracle VM VirtualBox on their workstation and is attempting to use it to create a virtual machine (VM). The software is causing error messages while attempting to create the VM. What is the most likely problem?

   a. The user does not know how to use the software.
   b. Virtualization is not enabled in BIOS/UEFI.
   c. The version of Windows they are using is not rated for installations of Oracle software.
   d. The processor is not rated to support VirtualBox and VMs.

2. A friend has asked you to help them find out if their computer is capable of overclocking. How can you direct them? (Choose all that apply.)

   a. Show them how to find System Summary data in the System Information utility in Windows and then do online research.
   b. Show them how to access BIOS/UEFI setup and browse through the screens.
   c. Explain to your friend that overclocking is not a recommended best practice.
   d. Show them how to open the computer case, read the brand and model of their motherboard, and then do online research.

3. A customer has a system with a Gigabyte B450 Aorus Pro motherboard. They want to upgrade the processor from the AMD Athlon X4 950 to the AMD Ryzen 7 2700X. Which of the following accurately describes this upgrade?

   a. The upgrade is possible and will yield a significant increase in performance.
   b. The upgrade is not possible because the new processor is not supported by this motherboard.
   c. The upgrade is possible, but it will not yield a significant increase in performance.
   d. The upgrade is not possible because this motherboard has an embedded processor that cannot be exchanged.

4. What new parts will you need to replace a failing processor? (Choose all that apply.)

   a. Power cable
   b. Processor
   c. Cooling assembly
   d. Thermal compound

5. How many threads can a quad-core processor handle at once?

6. A motherboard has four DIMM slots; three slots are gray and the fourth is black. What type of memory is this board designed to use?

   a. DDR4
   b. DDR3
   c. DDR5
   d. All the options listed.

7. What prevents a DDR3 DIMM from being installed in a DDR4 DIMM slot on a motherboard?

8. In memory ads for DIMMs, you notice DDR 2400 CL15 in one ad and PC4 21300 CL9 in another. Which ad is advertising the faster memory?

9. When planning a memory upgrade, you discover that Windows reports 4 GB of memory installed. In BIOS/UEFI, you see that two of four slots are populated. You install two 2 GB DIMMs in the two empty DIMM slots. When you boot the system, Windows still reports 4 GB of memory. Order the four steps you should take to troubleshoot the problem of missing memory.

   a. Open the case and verify that the DIMM modules are securely seated.
   b. Go into BIOS/UEFI and verify it recognized 8 GB of installed memory.
   c. Open the System Information window to verify the edition or version of Windows installed.
   d. Inspect the DIMMs you installed to verify they match the existing DIMMs and those the motherboard can support.

10. If 2 bits of a byte are in error when the byte is read from ECC memory, can ECC detect the error? Can it fix the error?

11. A DIMM memory ad displays 5-5-5-15. What is the CAS Latency value of this DIMM?

12. What is the speed in MHz of a DIMM rated at PC4 24000?

13. A motherboard uses dual channeling, but you have four DIMMs available that differ in size. The motherboard supports all four sizes. Can you install these DIMMs on the board? Will dual channeling be enabled?

14. Which is faster, CL3 memory or CL5 memory?

15. If your motherboard supports ECC DDR3 memory, can you substitute non-ECC DDR3 memory?

16. You have just upgraded memory on a computer from 4 GB to 8 GB by adding one DIMM. When you first turn on the PC, the memory count shows only 4 GB. Which of the following is most likely the source of the problem? What can you do to fix it?

   a. Windows is displaying an error because it likely became corrupted while the computer was disassembled.
   b. The new DIMM you installed is faulty.
   c. The new DIMM is not properly seated.
   d. The DIMM is installed in the wrong slot.

17. Your motherboard supports dual channeling, and you currently have two slots populated with DIMMs; each module holds 2 GB. You want to install an additional 4 GB of RAM. Will your system run faster if you install two 2 GB DIMMs or one 4 GB DIMM? Explain your answer.

Hands-On Projects

Hands-On Project 3-1

Researching a Processor Upgrade or Replacement

Est. Time: 45 minutes
Core 1 Objective: 3.4

To identify your motherboard and find out what processor and processor socket a motherboard is currently using, you can use BIOS/UEFI setup, Windows utilities, or third-party software such as Speccy at *ccleaner.com/speccy*. To research which processors a board can support, you can use the motherboard user guide, the website of the motherboard manufacturer, and, for Intel processors, the Intel site at *ark.intel.com*. Research the current processor and processor socket of your computer's motherboard, research which processors your board can support, and answer the following questions:

1. What is the brand and model of your motherboard? What processor socket does it use? How did you find your information?

2. Identify the currently installed processor, including its brand, model, speed, and other important characteristics. How did you find your information?

3. List three or more processors the board supports, according to the motherboard documentation or website.

4. Search the web for three or more processors that would match this board. Save or print three webpages that show the details and prices of a high-performing, moderate-performing, and low-performing processor the board supports.

5. If your current processor fails, which processor would you recommend for this system? Explain your recommendation.

   Now assume the processor is Core i5-11500, and it has gone bad. The motherboard in which it is installed is the ASUS Prime Z590-PLUS desktop board. The owner of the motherboard has requested that you keep the replacement cost as low as possible without sacrificing too much performance. What processor would you recommend for the replacement? Save or print a webpage that shows the processor and its cost.

Hands-On Project 3-2

Removing and Inserting a Processor

Est. Time: 15 minutes
Core 1 Objective: 3.4

In this project, you remove and install a processor. As you work, be very careful not to bend pins on the processor or socket, and protect the processor and motherboard against ESD. Do the following:

1. Verify that the computer is working. Turn off the system, unplug it, press the power button, and open the computer case. Put on your ESD strap. Remove the cooler assembly, remove all the thermal compound from the cooler and processor, and then remove the processor.

2. Reinstall the processor and thermal compound. Have your instructor check the thermal compound. Install the cooler.

3. Replace the case cover, power up the system, and verify that everything is working.

Hands-On Project 3-3

Examining BIOS/UEFI Settings

Est. Time: 15 minutes
Core 1 Objective: 3.4

On your home or lab computer, use BIOS/UEFI setup to answer these questions:

1. Which processor is installed? What is the processor frequency?
2. What are the BIOS/UEFI settings that apply to the processor, and how is the processor configured?
3. What information does BIOS/UEFI report about total memory installed and how each memory slot is populated? Does the board support dual, triple, or quad channeling? How do you know?

Hands-On Project 3-4

Planning and Pricing a Memory Upgrade

Est. Time: 30 minutes
Core 1 Objective: 3.2

Research your own computer or a lab computer to determine how much and what type of memory is currently installed and how much the system can support. Then research on the web to determine the total cost of a memory upgrade so you can max out the total memory on your system. Consider the maximum memory your motherboard, processor, and operating system can support. You can keep the cost down by using the modules you already have, but don't forget to match important features of the modules already installed. Save or print webpages from two retail sites that show modules you would purchase. Answer the following questions:

1. How much memory is currently installed? After the upgrade, how much memory would be installed?
2. Which component—the motherboard, processor, or OS—dictated the maximum memory that could be installed in your system?
3. Describe the details of the currently installed memory. Describe the details of the new memory you would purchase for the upgrade.
4. How much will the upgrade cost?

Hands-On Project 3-5

Explaining Triple and Quad Channeling

Est. Time: 45 minutes
Core 1 Objective: 3.2

You have volunteered to help tutor some learners who are preparing to take the A+ Core 1 exam, and they have asked you to explain triple channeling and quad channeling. Draw a diagram similar to the dual-channeling diagram in Figure 3-27 to explain triple channeling, and then draw another diagram to explain quad channeling. Compare your diagrams with those of others in your class, and make any necessary changes.

3

Hands-On Project 3-6

Upgrading Memory

Est. Time: 30 minutes
Core 1 Objective: 3.2

To practice installing additional memory in a computer in a classroom environment, remove the DIMMs from one computer, and place them in another computer. Boot the second computer, and check that it counts the additional memory. When finished, return the borrowed modules to the original computer.

Hands-On Project 3-7

Upgrading Laptop Memory

Est. Time: 30 minutes
Core 1 Objective: 1.1

A friend, Tangela, is looking for ways to improve the performance of her Windows Lenovo laptop and has turned to you for advice. She has cleaned up the hard drive and is now considering the possibility of upgrading memory. In a phone conversation, Tangela reported the following:

1. When she opened the System Information window, she saw 8.0 GB as Installed Physical Memory.
2. When she looked on the bottom of the laptop, she saw the model "IdeaPad 310-15ABR."
3. When she opened a cavity cover on the bottom of the case, she discovered one SO-DIMM slot filled with a SO-DIMM that has "4GB PC4-2400T" imprinted on it.

Tangela is now puzzled why Windows reports 8 GB of memory, but the one SO-DIMM contains only 4 GB. With this information in hand, research the possible upgrade and answer the following:

1. Explain why Windows reports 8 GB of memory even though the one SO-DIMM contains 4 GB of memory.
2. Can the laptop receive a memory upgrade? Save or print a webpage showing a SO-DIMM that can fit the system. How much will the upgrade cost?

Real Problems, Real Solutions

Real Problem 3-1

Using Memory Scanning Software

Est. Time: 45 minutes
Core 1 Objective: 3.2

A great shortcut to research a memory upgrade is an online memory scanner. Follow these directions to use three free products to scan your system and report information about it. (As you work, be careful not to download extra software advertised on these sites.)

1. Go to *crucial.com/systemscanner* by Crucial and then download and run the Crucial System Scanner.
2. Go to *cpuid.com/softwares/cpu-z.html* and then download and run the CPU-Z scanner.

(continues)

Real Problem Continued

3. Go to *ccleaner.com/speccy* and then download and run the Speccy scanner.

4. Using any of these scanners, answer these questions:

   a. Which motherboard do you have installed?

   b. How much memory is installed?

   c. How many memory slots does the board have?

   d. How many are populated?

   e. What is the CAS Latency of memory?

   f. How many cores does your processor have?

   g. What is the maximum memory the board supports?

   h. What type of memory does the board support?

   i. What would be the total cost of the memory upgrade if you were to max out the total memory on the board?

   j. Which scanner did you use to answer these questions? Why did you select this particular scanner?

Real Problem 3-2

Troubleshooting Memory

Est. Time: 15 minutes
Core 1 Objective: 3.2

Follow the rules outlined earlier in the text to protect the computer against ESD as you work. Remove the memory module in the first memory slot on a motherboard, and boot the PC. Did you get an error? Why or why not?

Real Problem 3-3

Playing the Memory Research Game

Est. Time: 30 minutes
Core 1 Objective: 3.2

Play the Memory Research game. You will need a group with three other players, Internet access, and a fifth person who is the scorekeeper. The scorekeeper asks a question and then gives players one minute to find the best answer. Five points are awarded to the player who has the best answer at the end of each one-minute play. The scorekeepers can use the following questions or make up their own. If you use these questions, mix up the order:

1. What is the fastest DDR5 DIMM sold today?

2. What is the largest DDR4 DIMM sold today?

3. What is the largest fully buffered ECC 240-pin DDR3 DIMM sold today?

4. What is the lowest price for an 8 GB 240-pin ECC DDR3 DIMM?

Module

4

Power Supplies and Troubleshooting Computer Problems

Module Objectives

1. Describe the methods and devices for keeping a system cool

2. Select a power supply to meet the power needs of a system

3. Demonstrate an organized approach to solving any computer problem, especially hardware problems occurring during the boot

4. Troubleshoot problems with the electrical system

5. Troubleshoot problems with the motherboard, processor, and RAM

Core 1 Certification Objectives

1.1 Given a scenario, install and configure laptop hardware and components.

3.4 Given a scenario, install and configure motherboards, central processing units (CPUs), and add-on cards.

3.5 Given a scenario, install or replace the appropriate power supply.

5.1 Given a scenario, apply the best-practice methodology to resolve problems.

5.2 Given a scenario, troubleshoot problems related to motherboards, RAM, CPU, and power.

Introduction

In the first modules of this text, you learned about the motherboard, processor, and RAM. This module focuses on how to keep these heat-producing components cool by using fans, heat sinks, and other cooling devices and methods. You also learn about one more essential component of a computer system, the power supply, including how to select a power supply to meet the wattage needs of a system.

Then we focus on troubleshooting these various hardware subsystems and components. You study the troubleshooting techniques and procedures to get the full picture of what it's like to have the tools and knowledge in hand to solve any computer-related problem. Then you learn to practically apply these skills to troubleshooting the electrical system, motherboard, processor, and memory. By the end of this module, you should feel confident that you can face a problem with hardware and understand how to zero in on the source of the problem and its solution.

Cooling Methods and Devices

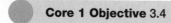

Core 1 Objective 3.4

The processor, motherboard, memory modules, expansion cards, and other components in the case produce heat. If they get overheated, the system can become unstable, and components can fail or be damaged. As a hardware technician, you need to know how to keep a system cool. Devices that are used to keep a system cool include CPU fans, case fans, coolers, heat sinks, and liquid cooling systems.

In this section of the module, you learn about several methods to keep the system cool, beginning with these general rules to cool the inside of a computer case:

- **Keep the case closed.** This may seem counterintuitive, as you might think an open case allows for better airflow, but consider the dust that will clog your fans and how fans are designed to draw hot air out of a closed case. If airflow is disrupted, an open case is a temporary fix to an overheating computer and should not be used long term.
- **Clean the inside of the computer.** Dust and debris clog your computer. Dirt and dust cake on the equipment and essentially insulate the heat-sensitive components. Use a can of compressed air to blow clean the inside of the case and its components.
- **Move the computer.** If the computer is in a fairly dusty or warm space, the computer might overheat. If overheating is a problem, try moving the computer to a new area that is cleaner and cooler.

Processor Coolers, Fans, and Heat Sinks

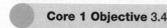

Core 1 Objective 3.4

Because a processor generates so much heat, computer systems use a cooling assembly designed for a specific processor to keep temperatures below the processor maximum temperature. If a processor reaches its maximum temperature, it automatically shuts down. Good processor coolers maintain a temperature of 90–110 degrees Fahrenheit (32–43 degrees Celsius). The **cooler** (see Figure 4-1) sits on top of the processor and consists of a fan and

Figure 4-1   A cooler sits on top of a processor to help keep it cool

Figure 4-2   The Thermaltake V1 copper cooler is a multisocket cooler that fits several Intel and AMD sockets

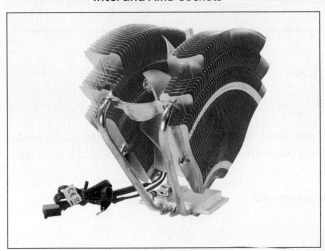

a heat sink, which is made of metal and draws the heat away from the processor into the fins. The fan can then blow the heat away. You learned to install a cooler in the module "Supporting Processors and Upgrading Memory."

A cooler is made of aluminum, copper, or a combination of both. Copper is more expensive but does a better job of conducting heat. For example, the Thermaltake (*thermaltakeusa.com*) multisocket cooler shown in Figure 4-2 is made of copper and has an adjustable fan control.

To get its power, the cooler fan power cord connects to a 4-pin fan header on the motherboard (see Figure 4-3). The fan connector will have three or four holes. A three-hole connector can fit onto a 4-pin header; just ignore the last pin. A 4-pin header on the motherboard supports pulse width modulation (PWM), which controls fan speed in order to reduce the overall noise in a system. If you use a cooler fan power cord with three pins, know that the fan will always operate at the same speed.

Figure 4-3   A cooler fan gets its power from a 4-pin PWM header on the motherboard

— 3-pin CPU fan power cord

— 4-pin CPU fan header

Thermal Compound and Thermal Pads

Core 1 Objective 3.4

Recall that the cooler is bracketed to the motherboard using a wire or plastic clip, and thermal compound is placed between the bottom of the cooler heat sink and the top of the processor. Thermal compound, also called **thermal paste** or thermal grease, is essential to effectively transfer heat by completely filling the gap between the processor and the cooling device. There are microscopic ridges on the surface of the contact plate on each component. The gel-like paste spreads in a thin layer to fill the gaps created by those ridges, removing air pockets that are inefficient at conducting heat.

An alternative to thermal paste is a thermal pad. A **thermal pad** is thicker than thermal paste and therefore fills larger gaps better. However, because thermal pads are less malleable, they still allow for air gaps. Thermal pads are more easily applied and are sized for the contact plate. Never use thermal pads and thermal compound at the same time, and never stack thermal pads together. Reusing thermal pads is not recommended.

Case Fans, Other Fans, and Heat Sinks

Core 1 Objective 3.4

To prevent overheating, you can also install additional case fans. Most cases have one or more positions to hold a **case fan** to help draw air out of the case. Figure 4-4 shows holes on the rear of a case designed to hold a case fan.

Figure 4-4   Install a case fan on the rear of this case to help keep the system cool

— Install case fan here

— Install power supply here

Figure 4-5   A PCI fan card by Vantec can be used next to a high-end graphics card to help keep it cool

Source: Courtesy of Vantec Thermal Technologies

A computer case might need as many as seven or eight fans mounted inside the case; however, the trend is to use fewer and larger fans. Generally, large fans tend to perform better and run more quietly than small fans.

Processors and video cards, also called graphics cards, are the two greatest heat producers in a system. Some graphics cards come with a fan on the side of the card. You can also purchase heat sinks and fans to mount on an expansion card to keep it cool. Another solution is to use a fan card mounted next to the graphics card. Figure 4-5 shows a PCI fan card. Be sure you select a fan card that fits the expansion slot you plan to use, and make sure there's enough clearance beside the graphics card for the fan card to fit and for airflow.

For additional cooling, consider a RAM cooler such as the one shown in Figure 4-6. It clips over a DIMM. A fan might be powered by a SATA power connector or 4-pin Molex power connector. The fan shown in Figure 4-6 uses a Molex connector. If you need a different or extra power connector that isn't available on a power supply, you can use an adapter to change an unused SATA or Molex connector into the connector you need.

When selecting any fan or cooler, take into consideration the added noise level and the ease of installation. Some coolers and fans can use a temperature sensor that controls the fan. Also consider the guarantee made by the cooler or fan manufacturer.

Figure 4-6   A RAM cooler keeps memory modules cool

4-pin power connector

DIMM cover

Liquid Cooling Systems

Core 1 Objective 3.4

In addition to using fans, heat sinks, and thermal compound to keep a processor cool, a liquid cooling system can be used. For the most part, these systems are used by hobbyists attempting to overclock to the max a processor in a gaming computer because those types of high-powered systems tend to run hot. Liquid cooling systems tend to run more quietly than other cooling methods. They might include a PCIe card that has a power supply, temperature sensor, and processor to control the cooler.

In a liquid cooling system, a small pump sits inside the computer case, and tubes move liquid around components and then away from them to a place where fans can cool the liquid, similarly to how a car radiator works. Figure 4-7 shows one liquid cooling system where the liquid is cooled by fans sitting inside a large case. Sometimes, however, the liquid is pumped outside the case, where it is cooled.

Now let's turn our attention to the power supply.

Figure 4-7   A liquid cooling system pumps liquid outside and away from components where fans can then cool the liquid

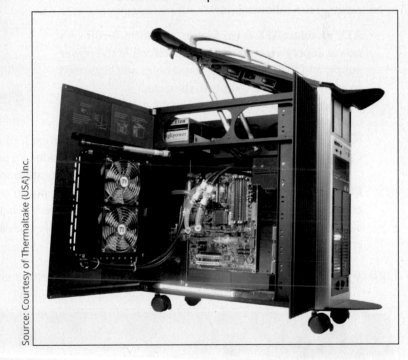

Source: Courtesy of Thermaltake (USA) Inc.

Selecting a Power Supply

 Core 1 Objective 3.5

In the module "Taking a Computer Apart and Putting It Back Together," you learned about the different types of power connectors and how to uninstall and install a power supply unit (PSU). You might need to replace a power supply when it fails or if the power supply in an existing system is not adequate. When building a new system, you can purchase a computer case with the power supply already installed (see Figure 4-8), or you can purchase a power supply separate from the case.

Types and Characteristics of Power Supplies

 Core 1 Objective 3.5

As you select the right power supply for a system, you need to be aware of the following power supply features:

- **ATX or microATX form factor.** The form factor of a power supply determines the dimensions of the power supply and the placement of screw holes and slots used to anchor the power supply to the case.
- **Wattage ratings.** A power supply has a wattage rating for total output maximum load (for example, 500 W, 850 W, or 1000 W) and individual wattage ratings for each of the voltage output circuits. These wattage capacities are listed in the documentation and on the side of a power supply, as shown in Figure 4-9.

Figure 4-8   This case comes with a power supply, power cord, and bag of screws

When selecting a power supply, pay particular attention to the capacity for the +12 V rail. (A "rail" is the term used to describe each circuit provided by the power supply.) The +12 V rail is the one most used, especially in high-end gaming systems. Notice in Figure 4-9 that the +12 V rail gets 360 W of the maximum 525 W load. Sometimes you need to use a power supply with a higher-than-needed overall wattage to get enough wattage on this one rail.

Figure 4-9   Consider the number and type of power connectors and the wattage ratings of a power supply

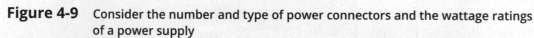

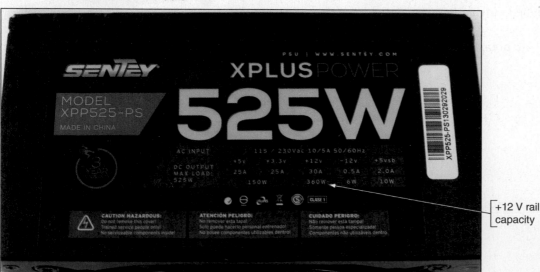

+12 V rail capacity

4

Note 2

To calculate wattage, know that the power in watts (W) is equal to the current in amps (A) times the voltage in volts (V): $W = A \times V$.

- **Number and type of connectors.** Consider the number and type of power cables and connectors the unit provides. Connector types are shown in Table 1-2 in the module "Taking a Computer Apart and Putting It Back Together." Table 4-1 lists some common connectors and the voltages they supply. A **modular power supply** includes detached power cables, sometimes called modular cable systems, that you can plug into connectors on the side of the unit. By using only the power cables you need, you eliminate unnecessary power cables, which can obstruct airflow inside the computer case.

Table 4-1 Power supply connectors and voltages

Connector	Voltages	Description
SATA	+3.3 V, +5 V, +12 V	Power to SATA drives, 15-pin
Molex	+5 V, +12 V	Power to older IDE drives and used with some older SATA drives, 4-pin
24-pin P1	+3.3 V, +5 V, ±12 V	Newer main power connector to motherboard

Exam Tip ✔

The A+ Core 1 exam expects you to know the voltage output of the power connectors listed in Table 4-1. Consider memorizing the table.

Note 3

If a power supply doesn't have the connector you need, you can probably buy an adapter to convert one connector to another. For example, Figure 4-10 shows an adapter that converts an older 20-pin connector to the newer 24-pin motherboard connector. Without this adapter, the motherboard would likely fry if you plugged a 20-pin cable into a 24-pin motherboard connector when the motherboard is drawing the full power of a 24-pin cable.

- **Fans inside the PSU.** Every power supply has a fan inside its case; some have two fans. The fan may be mounted on the back or top of the PSU. Fans range in size from 80 mm to 150 mm wide. The larger the fan, the better it is at cooling, and the quieter it runs. Some PSUs can automatically adjust the fan speed based on the internal temperature of the system.

Figure 4-10 This adapter converts a 20-pin connector to a 24-pin motherboard connector

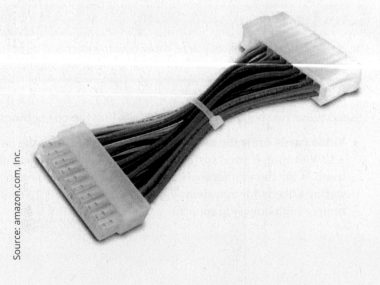

Source: amazon.com, Inc.

Note 4

Some power supplies are designed without fans so they can be used in home theater systems or other areas where quiet operation is a requirement.

- **Dual voltage options.** Expect a power supply to have a dual-voltage selector switch on the back where you can switch input voltage in the range 110 to 120 V AC for the United States or in the range 220 to 240 V AC for other countries.
- **Extra features.** Consider the warranty of the power supply, the overall quality, and extra features based on the needs of the user:
  - Some power supplies are designed to support two video cards used in a gaming computer. Two technologies used for multiple video cards are SLI by NVIDIA and Crossfire by AMD. If you plan to use multiple video cards, use a PSU that supports SLI or Crossfire.
  - Know that more expensive power supplies are quieter, last longer, and don't put off as much heat as less expensive ones. Also, expect a good power supply to protect the system against overvoltage.
  - A power supply rated with Active PFC (power factor correction) runs more efficiently and uses less electricity than other power supplies.

Figure 4-11 A redundant power supply uses two identical power supply units

Source: amazon.com, Inc.

Commonly used with equipment found in server racks—and sometimes in high-end computers—a redundant power supply ensures there is no interruption in power. A **redundant power supply (RPS)** uses two identical power supplies, as shown in Figure 4-11. Only one of the power supplies is used at a time, and both are capable of supplying the full power requirements of the equipment. In the event that one power supply fails, the transition to the other is seamless to prevent any disruption to power to essential devices.

How to Calculate Wattage Capacity

Core 1 Objective 3.5

When deciding what wattage capacity you need for the power supply, consider the total wattage requirements of all components inside the case as well as USB devices that get their power from ports connected to the motherboard.

Exam Tip ✔

The A+ Core 1 exam expects you to know how to select and install a power supply. You need to know how to decide on the wattage, connectors, and form factor of the power supply.

Keep these two points in mind when selecting the correct wattage capacity for a power supply:

- **Video cards draw the most power.** Video cards draw the most power in a system, and they draw from the +12 V output. If your system has a video card, pay particular attention to the +12 V rating. The current trend is for the motherboard to provide the video components and video port, thus reducing the overall wattage needs for a system. Video cards are primarily used in gaming computers or other systems that require high-quality graphics.

- **The power supply should be rated about 30% higher than expected needs.** Power supplies that run at less than peak performance last longer and don't overheat. In addition, a power supply loses some of its capacity over time. Also, don't worry about a higher-rated power supply using too much electricity. Components only draw what they need. For example, a power supply rated at 1000 W and running at a 500 W draw will last longer and give off less heat than a power supply rated at 750 W and running at a 500 W draw.

To know what size of power supply you need, add up the wattage requirements of all components, and then add 30%. Technical documentation for these components should give you the information you need. Table 4-2 lists appropriate wattage ratings for common devices. Alternately, you can use a wattage calculator provided on the website of many manufacturers and vendors. Using the calculator, you enter the components in your system, and then the calculator will recommend the wattage you need for your power supply.

Table 4-3 lists a few case and power supply manufacturers.

> **Caution** ⓘ
>
> Some older Dell motherboards and power supplies do not use the standard P1 pinouts for ATX, although the power connectors look the same. For this reason, never use a Dell power supply with a non-Dell motherboard or a Dell motherboard with a non-Dell power supply without first verifying that the power connector pinouts match; otherwise, you might destroy the power supply, the motherboard, or both.

Table 4-2   To calculate the power supply rating you need, add up total wattage

Devices	Approximate Wattage
Motherboard, processor, memory, keyboard, and mouse	200–300 W
Fan	5 W
SATA hard drive	15–30 W
BD/DVD/CD drive	20–30 W
PCI video card	50 W
PCI card (network card or other PCI card)	20 W
PCIe ×16 video card	150–300 W
PCIe ×16 card other than a video card	100 W

Table 4-3   Manufacturers of cases and power supplies for personal computers

Manufacturer	Website
Antec	antec.com
Cooler Master	coolermaster.com
Corsair	corsair.com
EVGA	evga.com
PC Power & Cooling	pcpowerandcooling.com
Rosewill	rosewill.com
Seasonic	seasonic.com
Sentey	sentey.com
Silverstone	silverstonetek.com
Thermaltake	thermaltakeusa.com
Zalman	zalman.com

So far in the text, you have learned about motherboards, processors, RAM, and the electrical system, which are the principal hardware components of a computer. With this hardware foundation in place, you're ready to learn about computer troubleshooting. Let's start with an overview of how to approach any hardware problem, and then we'll turn our attention to the details of troubleshooting the electrical system, motherboard, RAM, and CPU.

Strategies to Troubleshoot Any Computer Problem

Core 1 Objective 5.1

When a computer doesn't work and you're responsible for fixing it, you should generally approach the problem first as an investigator and discoverer, always being careful not to compound the problem through your actions. If the problem seems difficult, see it as an opportunity to learn something new. Ask questions until you understand the source of the problem. Once you understand it, you're almost done because the solution most likely will be evident. If you take the attitude that you can understand the problem and solve it, no matter how deeply you must dig, you probably will solve it.

One systematic method used by most expert troubleshooters to solve a problem comprises the six steps diagrammed in Figure 4-12, which can apply to both software and hardware problems. As an IT technician, expect that you will develop your own style and steps for troubleshooting based on your own experiences over time.

Exam Tip ✔

The A+ Core 1 exam expects you to know about all the aspects of troubleshooting theory and strategy and how to apply the troubleshooting procedures and techniques described in this section. Read A+ Core 1 Objective 5.1, and compare it with Figure 4-12. You'll find the objectives with this text.

Here are the steps:

1. Interview the user and back up data before you make any changes to the system.
2. Examine the system, analyze the problem, and make an initial determination of the source of the problem.
3. Test your theory. If the theory is not confirmed, form another theory or document what you've discovered so far. If you have run out of ideas, escalate the problem to someone higher in your organization with more experience or resources.
4. After you know the source of the problem, plan what to do to fix the problem, and then fix it.
5. Verify that the problem is fixed and that the system works. Take any preventive measures to make sure the problem doesn't happen again.
6. Document activities, outcomes, and what you learned.

Over time, a good IT support technician builds a strong network of resources they can count on when solving computer problems. Here are some resources to help you get started with your own list of reliable and time-tested sources of assistance:

- **The web.** Do a web search on an error message, a short description of the problem, or the model and manufacturer of a device to get help. Check out the website of the product manufacturer or search a support forum. It's likely that other technicians have encountered the same problem and posted the question and

Figure 4-12 A general approach to problem solving

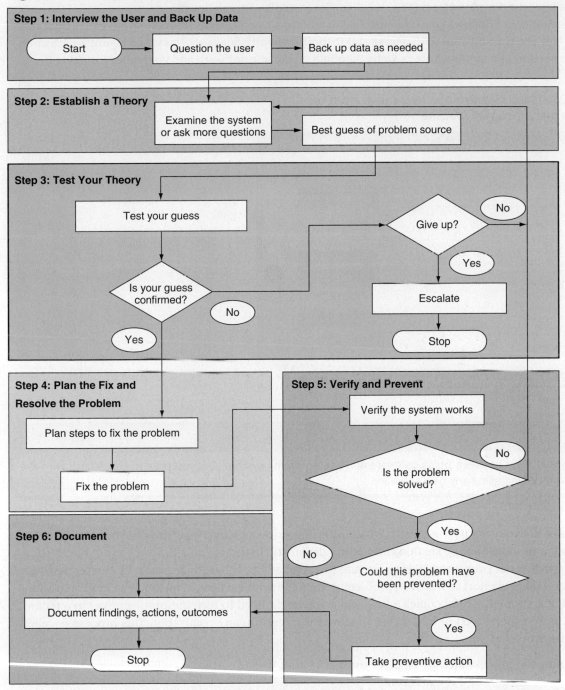

answer. If you search and cannot find your answer, you can post a new question. *Youtube.com* videos might help. Many technicians enjoy sharing online what they know, but be careful—not all technical advice found online is correct or well intentioned.

- **Chat, forums, or email technical support.** Support from hardware and software manufacturers can help you interpret an error message or provide general support in diagnosing a problem. Most technical support is available during working hours by way of an online chat session. Support from the manufacturer is considered the highest authority for the correct fix to a problem.

- **Manufacturer's diagnostic software.** Many hardware device manufacturers provide diagnostic software, which is available for download from their websites. For example, you can download Seagate Toolkit (to back up data), SeaTools for Windows (must be installed in Windows), or SeaTools Bootable (to create a bootable USB drive) and use the software to diagnose and fix problems with Seagate drives. See Figure 4-13. Search the support section of a manufacturer's website to find diagnostic software and guidelines for using it.

Figure 4-13   Download diagnostic software tools from a manufacturer's website

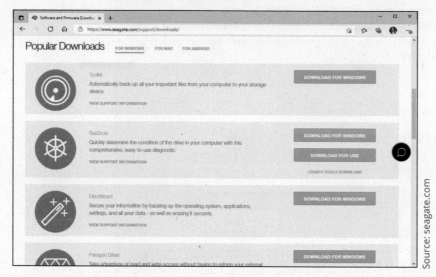

Source: seagate.com

Note 5

Always check compatibility between utility software and the operating system (OS) you plan to use. Check with the computer owner before installing any new software.

- **User manuals.** Refer to the user manuals, which often list error messages and their meanings. They also might contain a troubleshooting section and list any diagnostic tools available.
- **Technical associates in your organization.** Be sure to ask for advice when you're stuck. Also, after making a reasonable and diligent effort to resolve a problem, getting the problem fixed could become more important than resolving it yourself. There comes a time when you might need to turn the problem over to a technician who is more experienced or has access to more resources. (In an organization, this process is called escalating the problem.)

Now let's examine the process step by step. As you learn about these six steps, you'll also learn about 13 rules useful when troubleshooting. Here's the first rule.

Rule 1: Approach the Problem Systematically

When trying to solve the problem, start at the beginning and walk through the situation in a thorough, careful way. This rule is invaluable. Remember it and apply it every time. If you don't find the explanation to the problem after one systematic walk-through, then repeat the entire process. Check and double-check to find the step you overlooked the first time. Most problems with computers are simple, such as a loose cable or incorrect Windows setting. Computers are logical through and through. Whatever the problem is, it's also very logical. Also, if you are faced with more than one problem on the same computer, work on only one problem at a time. Trying to solve multiple problems at the same time can get too confusing.

Step 1: Interviewing the User and Backing Up Data

Core 1 Objective 5.1

Every troubleshooting situation begins with interviewing the user if possible. If you have the opportunity to speak with the user, ask questions to help you identify the problem, how to reproduce it, and possible sources of the problem. Also ask about any data on the hard drive that is not backed up.

Exam Tip ✔

The A+ Core 1 exam expects you to know how to interact with a user and know what questions to ask in a troubleshooting scenario without accusing or disrespecting the user.

Here are some questions that can help you learn as much as you can about the problem and its root cause:

1. Please describe the problem. What error messages, unusual displays, or failures did you see? (Possible answer: I see this blue screen with a funny-looking message on it that makes no sense to me.)
2. When did the problem start? Does the computer have a history of similar problems? (Possible answer: When I first booted after loading this neat screen saver I downloaded from the web.)
3. What was the situation when the problem occurred? (Possible answers: I was trying to start up my laptop. I was opening a document in Microsoft Word. I was using the web to research a project.)
4. What programs or software were you using? (Possible answer: I was using Microsoft Edge.)
5. What changes have recently been made to the system? For example, did you recently install new hardware or software or move your computer system? (Possible answer: Well, yes. Yesterday I moved the computer case across the room.)
6. Has there been a recent thunderstorm or electrical problem? (Possible answer: Yes, last night. Then when I tried to turn on my computer this morning, nothing happened.)
7. Have you made any hardware, software, or configuration changes? Have there been any infrastructure changes? (Possible answer: No, but I think my sister might have.)
8. Has someone else used your computer recently? (Possible answer: Sure, my son uses it all the time.)
9. Is there some valuable data on your system that is not backed up that I should know about before I start working on the problem? (Possible answer: Yes! Yes! My term paper! It's not backed up! You have to save that!)
10. Can you show me how to reproduce the problem? (Possible answer: Yes, let me show you what to do.)

Based on the answers you receive, ask more penetrating questions until you feel the user has given you all the information that might help you solve the problem. As you talk with the user, keep in mind rules 2, 3, and 4.

Rule 2: Establish Your Priorities

This rule can help make for a satisfied customer. Decide what your first priority is. For example, it might be to recover lost data or to get the computer back up and running as soon as possible. When practical, ask the user or customer for help deciding on priorities. For most users, data is the first priority unless they have a recent backup.

Rule 3: Beware of User Error

Remember that many problems stem from user error. If you suspect this is the case, ask the user to show you the problem and carefully watch what the user is doing. Be careful to handle a user error delicately because some people don't like to hear that they made a mistake.

Rule 4: Keep Your Cool and Don't Rush

In some situations, you might be tempted to act too quickly and to be drawn into the user's sense of emergency. But keep your cool and don't rush. For example, if a computer stops working and unsaved data is still in memory or if data on the hard drive has not been backed up, look and think carefully before you leap! A wrong move can be costly. The best advice is refrain from hurrying. Carefully plan your moves. Research the problem using documentation or the web if you're not sure what to do, and don't hesitate to ask for help. Don't simply try something, hoping it will work, unless you've run out of more intelligent alternatives!

After you have talked with the user, be sure to back up any important data that is not currently backed up before you begin work on the computer. Here are three options:

- **Use Explorer to copy the data to another system.** If the computer is working well enough to boot to the Windows desktop, you can use Windows File Explorer to copy data to a flash drive, another computer on the network, or other storage media.
- **Move the hard drive to another system.** If the computer is not healthy enough to use Explorer, don't do anything to jeopardize the data. If you must take a risk with the data, let it be the user's decision to do so, not yours. When a system won't boot from the hard drive, consider removing the drive and installing it as a second drive in a working system. If the file system on the problem drive is intact, you might be able to copy data from the drive to the primary drive in the working system.

To move the hard drive to a working computer, you don't need to physically install the drive in the drive bay. Open the computer case. Carefully lay the drive on the case and connect a power cord and data cable (see Figure 4-14). Then turn on the computer. While you have the computer turned on, be <u>very careful</u> not to touch the drive or touch inside the case. Also, while a tower case is lying on its side like the one in Figure 4-14, don't use the optical drive.

Figure 4-14   Move a hard drive to a working computer to recover data on the drive

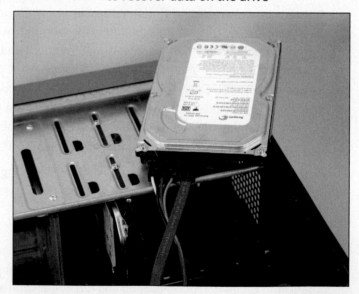

Start the computer and sign in to Windows using an Administrator account. (If you don't sign in with an Administrator account, you must provide the password to an Administrator account before you can access the files on the newly connected hard drive.) When Windows finds the new drive, it assigns a drive letter. Use Explorer or third-party software to copy files from this drive to the primary hard drive in this system or to other storage media. Then return the drive to the original system and turn your attention to solving the original problem.

Note 6

An easier way to temporarily install a hard drive in a system is to use a USB port. Figure 4-15 shows a USB-to-SATA converter kit. The SATA connector can be used for desktop or laptop hard drives because a SATA connector is the same for both. A USB-to-SATA converter is handy when recovering data and troubleshooting problems with hard drives that refuse to boot.

Figure 4-15   Use a USB-to-SATA converter to recover data from a drive that has a SATA connector

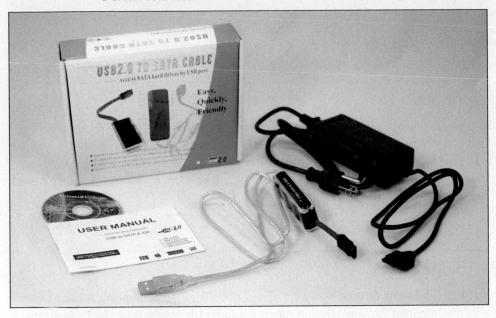

- **Hire a professional file recovery service.** If your data is extremely valuable and other methods have failed, you might want to consider a professional data recovery service. They're expensive but may be worth it if getting the data back is a high priority. To find a service, do a web search on "data recovery." Before selecting a service, be sure to read reviews, understand the warranty and guarantees, and perhaps get a recommendation from a satisfied customer.

Exam Tip ✔

The A+ Core 1 exam expects you to know the importance of making backups before you make changes to a system.

If possible, have the user verify that all important data is safely backed up before you continue to the next troubleshooting step.

Caution ❗

Don't take chances with a user's important data. If the user tells you the data has already been backed up, ask them to verify that they can recover the data from the backup website or media before you assume the data is safely backed up.

If you're new to troubleshooting and don't want the user looking over your shoulder while you work, you might want to let them know you'd prefer to work alone. You can say something like, "Okay, I think I have everything I need to get started. I'll let you know if I have another question."

Step 2: Examining the System and Making Your Best Guess

Core 1 Objective 5.1

You're now ready to start solving the problem. Rules 5 and 6 can help.

Rule 5: Make No Assumptions

This rule is the hardest to follow because there is a tendency to trust anything in writing and assume that people are telling you exactly what happened. But documentation is sometimes wrong, and people don't always describe events as they occurred, so do your own investigating. For example, if the user tells you that the system boots up with no error messages but that the software still doesn't work, boot for yourself. You never know what the user might have overlooked.

Rule 6: Try the Simple Things First

The solutions to most problems are so simple and obvious that we overlook them because we expect the problem to be difficult. Don't let the complexity of computers fool you. Most problems are easy to fix. Really, they are! To save time, check the simple things first, such as whether a power switch is not turned on or a cable is loose. Generally, it's easy to check for a hardware problem before you check for a software problem. For example, if a USB drive is not working, verify that the drive works on another port or another computer before verifying the drivers are installed correctly.

Follow this process to form your best guess (best theory) and test it:

1. **Reproduce the problem and observe for yourself what the user has described.** For example, if the user tells you the system is totally dead, find out for yourself. Plug in the power and turn on the system. Listen for fans and look for lights and error messages. Suppose the user tells you that Microsoft Edge will not open. Try opening it yourself to see what error messages might appear. As you investigate the system, refrain from making changes until you've come up with your theory for the source of the problem. Can you duplicate the problem? Intermittent problems are generally more difficult to solve than problems that occur consistently.

2. **Decide if the problem is hardware or software related.** Sometimes you might not be sure, but make your best guess. For example, if the system fails before Windows starts to load, chances are the problem is a hardware problem. If the user tells you the system has not worked since the lightning storm the night before, chances are the problem is electrical. If the problem is that Explorer will not open even though the Windows desktop loads, you can assume the problem is software related. In another example, suppose a user complains that their Word documents are getting corrupted. Possible sources of the problem might be that the user does not know how to save documents properly, the application or the OS might be corrupted, the computer might have a virus, or the hard drive might be intermittently failing. Investigate for yourself, and then decide if the problem is caused by software, hardware, or the user.

3. **Make your best guess as to the source of the problem, and don't forget to question the obvious.** Here are some practical examples of questioning the obvious and checking the simple things first:

   - The video doesn't work. Your best guess is the monitor cables are loose or the monitor is not turned on.
   - Excel worksheets are getting corrupted. Your best guess is the user is not saving the workbook files correctly.
   - The DVD drive is not reading a DVD. Your best guess is the DVD is scratched.
   - The system refuses to boot and displays the error that the hard drive is not found. Your best guess is internal cables to the drive are loose.

Rule 7: Become a Researcher

Following this rule is the most fun. When a computer problem arises that you can't easily solve, be as tenacious as a bulldog. Search the web, ask questions, read more, make some phone calls, and ask more questions. Take advantage of every available resource, including online help, documentation, technical support, and books such as this one. Learn to perform advanced searches using a good search engine on the web, such as *google.com*. What you learn will be yours to take to the next problem. This is the real joy of computer troubleshooting. If you're good at it, you're always learning something new.

If you're having trouble deciding what might be the source of the problem, keep rule 7 in mind, and try searching these resources for ideas and tips:

1. The specific application, operating system, or hardware you support must be available to you to test, observe, and study and to use to recreate a customer's problem whenever possible.

2. Verify any system or application changes by referring to the system or application event logs. Windows keeps comprehensive logs about the system, hardware, applications, and user activities; these logs can be viewed using Windows **Event Viewer**. Many applications keep logs of events or changes to the system or application. Some applications might pop up error messages, such as a low-disk-space error. Open the application log to evaluate the error more closely and to see if any more details are provided in the log.

3. Use a search engine to search the web for help. In your search string, include an error message, symptom, hardware device, or description of the problem. The chances are always good that someone else has had the same problem and has written about it online, and that someone else has presented a step-by-step solution. All you have to do is find it! As you practice this type of web research, you'll get better and better at knowing how to form a search string and knowing which websites are trustworthy and present the best information. If your first five minutes of searching doesn't turn up a solution, please don't give up! It might take patience and searching for 20 minutes or more to find the solution you need. As you search, you'll most likely learn more and more about the problem, and you'll slowly zero in on a solution.

Note 7

To limit your search to a particular site when using *google.com*, use the site: parameter in the search box. For example, to search only the Microsoft site for information about the defrag command, enter this search string:

```
defrag site:microsoft.com
```

4. Some companies offer an expert system for troubleshooting. An **expert system** is software that is designed and written to help solve problems. It uses databases of known facts and rules to simulate human experts' reasoning and decision making. Expert systems for IT technicians work by posing questions about a problem to be answered by the technician or the customer. The response to each question triggers another question from the software until the expert system arrives at a possible solution or solutions. Many expert systems are "intelligent," meaning the system will record your input and use it in subsequent sessions to select more questions to ask and approaches to try. Therefore, future troubleshooting sessions on the same type of problem tend to zero in more quickly toward a solution.

Step 3: Testing Your Theory

 Core 1 Objective 5.1

As you test your theories, keep in mind rules 8–11.

Rule 8: Divide and Conquer

This rule is the most powerful. Isolate the problem. In the overall system, remove one hardware or software component after another until the problem is isolated to a small part of the whole system. As you divide a large problem into smaller components, you can analyze each component separately. You can use one or more of the following to help you divide and conquer:

- In Windows, perform a clean boot to eliminate all nonessential startup programs and services as a possible source of the problem.
- Boot from a bootable DVD or flash drive to eliminate the Windows installation and the hard drive as the problem.
- Remove any unnecessary hardware devices, such as a second video card, optical drive, or even the hard drive. You don't need to physically remove the optical drive or hard drive from the bays inside the case. Simply disconnect the data cable and the power cable.

Rule 9: Write Things Down

Keep good notes as you're working. Notes will help you think more clearly. Draw diagrams. Make lists. Clearly and precisely write down what you're learning. If you need to leave the problem and return to it later, it's difficult to remember what you have observed and already tried. When the problem gets cold like this, your notes will be invaluable.

Rule 10: Don't Assume the Worst

When it's an emergency and your only copy of data is on a hard drive that is not working, don't assume that the data is lost. Much can be done to recover data. If you want to recover lost data on a hard drive, don't write anything to the drive; you might write on top of lost data, eliminating chances of recovery.

Rule 11: Reboot and Start Over

This is an important rule. Fresh starts are good, and they uncover events or steps that might have been overlooked. Take a break! Get away from the problem. Begin again.

Most computer problems are simple and can be simply solved, but you do need a game plan. That's how Figure 4-16 can help. The flowchart focuses on problems that affect the boot. As you work your way through it, you're eliminating one major computer subsystem after another until you zero in on the problem. After you've discovered the problem, the solution is often obvious.

As Figure 4-16 indicates, troubleshooting a computer problem is divided into problems that occur during the boot and those that occur after the Windows Start screen or desktop has successfully loaded. Problems that occur during the boot might happen before Windows starts to load or during Windows startup. Read the flowchart in Figure 4-16 very carefully to get an idea of the symptoms that would cause you to suspect each subsystem.

Figure 4-16   Use this flowchart when first facing a computer problem

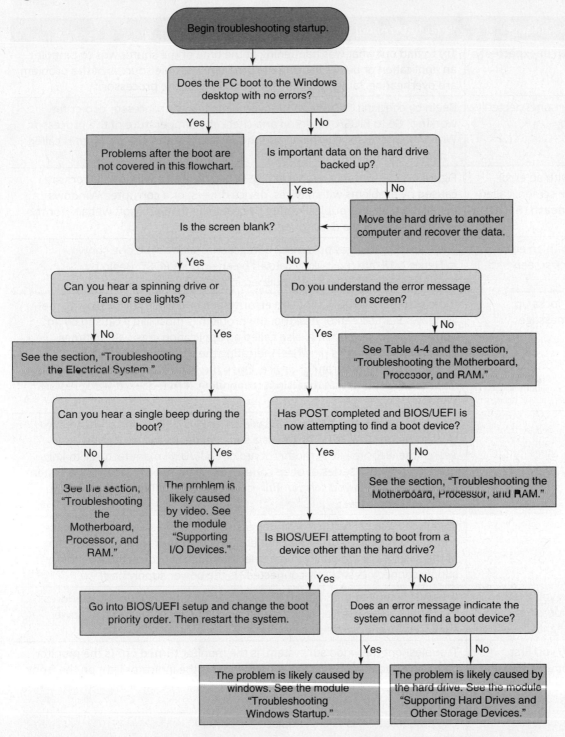

Also, Table 4-4 provides general troubleshooting guidelines related to common symptoms and error messages, the likely sources of each type of problem, and tips for solving the problem.

Exam Tip ✔

The A+ Core 1 exam might give you a symptom and expect you to select a probable source of a problem from a list of sources. These examples of what can go wrong can help you connect problem sources to symptoms.

Table 4-4   Symptoms or error messages caused by hardware problems and what to do about them

Symptom or Error Message	What to Do About the Problem
System shuts down unexpectedly	Try to find out what was happening at the time of the shutdowns to pinpoint an application or device causing the problem. Possible sources of the problem are overheating, faulty RAM, the motherboard, or the processor.
System shuts down unexpectedly and starts back up	Begin by checking the system for overheating. Is the processor cooler fan working? Go to BIOS/UEFI setup and check the temperature of the processor. When the processor overheats and the system restarts, the problem is called a **processor thermal trip error**.
System locks up with an error message on a blue screen, called a **blue screen of death (BSOD)**	Figure 4-17 shows an example of a BSOD error. These Windows errors are caused by problems with devices, device drivers, or a corrupted Windows installation. Begin troubleshooting by searching the Microsoft website for the error message and a description of the problem.
System locks up with an error message on a black screen	These error messages on a black background, such as the one shown in Figure 4-18, are most likely caused by an error at POST. Begin by troubleshooting the device mentioned in the error message.
System freezes or locks up without an error message	If the system locks up without an error screen and while still displaying the Windows Start screen or desktop, the problem is most likely caused by an application not responding, also called an application crash. Sometimes you'll see the Windows pinwheel indicating the system is waiting for a response from a program or device. Open the Windows Task Manager utility and end any application that is not responding. If that doesn't work, restart Windows.
POST code beeps	One or no beep indicates that all is well after POST. However, startup BIOS/UEFI communicates POST errors as a series of beeps before it tests video. Search the website of the motherboard or BIOS/UEFI manufacturer to know how to interpret a series of beep codes. You might need to restart the system more than once so you can carefully count the beeps. Table 4-5 lists some common beep codes.
No power	If you see no lights on the computer case and hear no spinning fans, make sure the surge protector or wall outlet has power. Is the switch on the rear of the case on? Is the dual-voltage selector switch set correctly? Are power supply connectors securely connected? Is the power supply bad?
Blank screen when you first power up the computer, and no noise or indicator lights	Is power getting to the system? If power is getting to the computer, address the problem as electrical. Make sure the power supply is good and power supply connectors are securely connected.
Blank screen when you first power up the computer, and you can hear the fans spinning and see indicator lights	Troubleshoot the video subsystem. Is the monitor turned on? Is the monitor data cable securely connected at both ends? Is the indicator light on the front of the monitor on?
BIOS/UEFI loses its time and date settings "CMOS battery low" error message appears during the boot	The CMOS battery is failing. Replace the battery.
System reports less memory than you know is installed	A memory module is not seated correctly or has failed. Begin troubleshooting memory.
System attempts to boot to the wrong boot device	Go into BIOS/UEFI setup and change the boot device priority order.

(continues)

Table 4-4   Symptoms or error messages caused by hardware problems and what to do about them (Continued)

Symptom or Error Message	What to Do About the Problem
Fans spin, but no power to other devices	Begin by checking the power supply. Are connectors securely connected? Use a power supply tester to check for correct voltage outputs.
Smoke or burning smell	Consider this a serious electrical problem. Immediately unplug the computer.
Loud whining noise	Most likely the noise is made by the power supply or a failing hard drive. There might be a short. The power supply might be going bad or is underrated for the system.
Grinding noise	Most likely the noise is made by the ball bearings of a fan. Using compressed air to clean all the fans might fix the problem, but you might have to replace a failing fan.
Clicking noise	A clicking noise likely indicates the magnetic hard drive is failing. Replace the drive as soon as possible.
Intermittent device failures	Failures that come and go might be caused by overheating or failing RAM, the motherboard, the processor, or the hard drive. Begin by checking the processor temperature for overheating. Then check RAM for errors and run diagnostics on the hard drive.
Distended capacitors	Failed capacitors on the motherboard or other circuit board are sometimes distended and discolored on the top of the capacitor. Replace the motherboard.
Possible error messages: "No boot device available" "Hard drive not found" "Fixed disk error" "Invalid boot disk" "Inaccessible boot device or drive" "Invalid drive specification"	Startup BIOS/UEFI did not find a device to use to load the operating system. Make sure the boot device priority order is correct in BIOS/UEFI setup. Try booting from a bootable USB flash drive or DVD. If this works, begin troubleshooting the hard drive, which is covered in the module "Hard Drives and Other Storage Devices."
Possible error messages: "Missing operating system" "Error loading operating system"	Windows startup programs are missing or corrupted. How to troubleshoot Windows startup is covered in the module "Troubleshooting Windows Startup."

Figure 4-17   Search the Microsoft website for information about a BSOD error

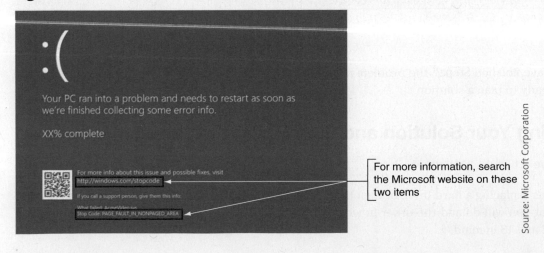

Source: Microsoft Corporation

Figure 4-18   A POST error message on a black screen shown early in the boot

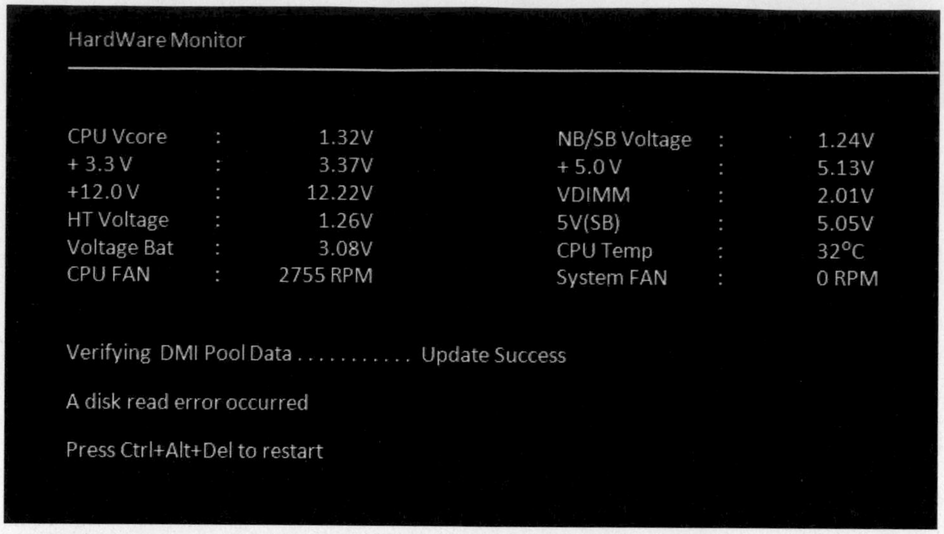

```
HardWare Monitor


CPU Vcore        :        1.32V        NB/SB Voltage    :        1.24V
+ 3.3 V          :        3.37V        + 5.0 V          :        5.13V
+12.0 V          :        12.22V       VDIMM            :        2.01V
HT Voltage       :        1.26V        5V(SB)           :        5.05V
Voltage Bat      :        3.08V        CPU Temp         :        32°C
CPU FAN          :        2755 RPM     System FAN       :        0 RPM


Verifying  DMI Pool Data . . . . . . . . . . .  Update Success

A disk read error occurred

Press Ctrl+Alt+Del to restart
```

Source: Intel

Table 4-5   Common beep codes and their meanings for Intel and Award BIOS

Beeps During POST	Description
1 short beep or no beep	The computer passed all POST tests
1 long and 2 short beeps	Award BIOS: A video problem, no video card, bad video memory
	Intel BIOS: A video problem
Continuous short beeps	Award BIOS: A memory error
	Intel BIOS: A loose card or short
1 long and 1 short beep	Intel BIOS: Motherboard problem
1 long and 3 short beeps	Intel BIOS: A video problem
3 long beeps	Intel BIOS: A keyboard controller problem
Continuous 2 short beeps and then a pause	Intel BIOS: A video card problem
Continuous 3 short beeps and then a pause	Intel BIOS: A memory error
8 beeps followed by a system shutdown	Intel BIOS: The system has overheated
Continuous high and low beeps	Intel BIOS: CPU problem

By the time you have finished Step 3, the problem might already be solved or you will know the source of the problem and will be ready to plan a solution.

Step 4: Planning Your Solution and then Fixing the Problem

Core 1 Objective 5.1

Some solutions, such as replacing a hard drive or a motherboard, are expensive and time consuming. You need to carefully consider what you will do and the order in which you will do it. When planning and implementing your solution, keep rules 12 and 13 in mind.

Rule 12: Use the Least Invasive Solution First

As you solve computer problems, always keep in mind that you don't want to make things worse, so you should use the least invasive solution. You want to fix the problem in such a way that the system is returned to normal working condition with the least amount of effort and fewest changes. For example, don't format the hard drive until you've first tried to fix the problem without having to erase everything on the drive. As another example, don't reinstall Microsoft 365 until you have tried applying patches to the existing installation.

Rule 13: Know Your Starting Point

Find out what works and doesn't work before you take anything apart or try a possible fix. Suppose you decide to install a new anti-malware program. After the installation, you discover Microsoft 365 gives errors and you cannot print to the network printer. You don't know if the anti-malware program is causing problems or the problems existed before you began work. As often as possible, find out what works or what doesn't work before you attempt a fix.

Do the following to plan your solution and fix the problem:

1. Consider different solutions and select the least invasive one. When appropriate, talk with the user or owner about the best solution.
2. Before applying your solution, do your best to determine what works and doesn't work in the system so you know your starting point.
3. Fix the problem. This might be as simple as switching to a new monitor, or it might be as difficult as reinstalling Windows and applications software and restoring data from backups.

Hardware and software products generally have **technical documentation** available. If you don't find it on hand, know that you are likely to find user manuals and technical support manuals as .pdf files that can be downloaded from the product manufacturers' websites. These sites might offer troubleshooting and support pages, help forums, chat sessions, email support, and links to submit a troubleshooting ticket to the manufacturer (see Figure 4-19). For Windows problems, the best websites to search are *docs.microsoft.com* and *support.microsoft.com*.

Figure 4-19   Search manufacturer websites for help with a hardware or software product

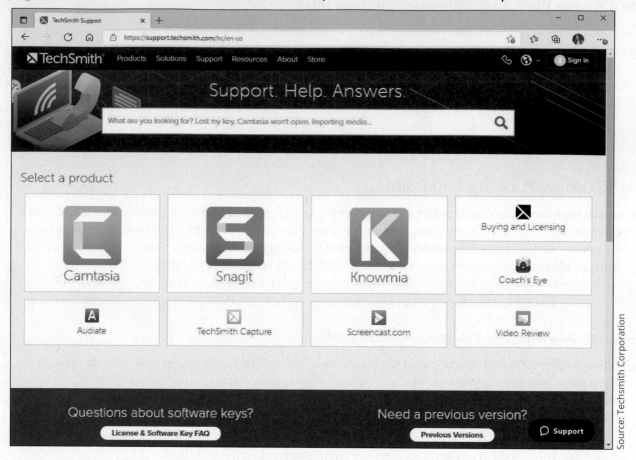

Source: Techsmith Corporation

Step 5: Verifying the Fix and Taking Preventive Action

Core 1 Objective 5.1

After you have fixed the problem, reboot the system and verify that all is well. Can you reach the Internet, use the printer, or use Excel in Microsoft 365? If possible, have the user check everything and verify that the job is done satisfactorily. If either of you finds a problem, return to Step 2 in the troubleshooting process to examine the system and form a new theory as to the cause of the problem.

After you and the user have verified all is working, ask yourself the question, "Could this problem have been prevented?" If so, go the extra mile to instruct the user, set Windows to automatically install updates, or do whatever else is appropriate to prevent future problems.

Step 6: Documenting What Happened

Core 1 Objective 5.1

Good documentation helps you take what you learned into the next troubleshooting situation, train others, develop effective preventive maintenance plans, and satisfy any audits or customer or employer queries about your work. Most companies use call-tracking software for this purpose. Be sure to include initial symptoms, the source of the problem, your troubleshooting steps, and what you did to ultimately fix it. Make the notes detailed enough so that you or someone else can use them later, when solving similar problems.

For on-site support, a customer expects documentation about your services. Include in the documentation sufficient details broken down by cost of individual parts, hours worked, and cost per hour. Give the documentation to the customer at the end of the service, and keep a copy for yourself. For phone support, the documentation stays in-house.

Now you're ready to look at how to troubleshoot each subsystem that is critical to booting up the computer. We begin with the electrical system.

Applying Concepts

Taking Good Notes

Est. Time: 30 minutes
Core 1 Objective: 5.1

Darnell had not been a good notetaker in school, and his ineffectiveness in this area was affecting his work. His manager, Jonathan, had been reviewing Darnell's notes in the ticketing system at the help desk and was not happy with what he saw. Jonathan had pointed out to Darnell more than once that his cryptic, incomplete notes with sketchy information would one day cause major problems.

On Monday morning, calls were hammering the help desk because a server had gone down over the weekend, and many internal customers were not able to get to their data. Darnell escalated one call from a customer named Andre to a tier-two help desk. Later that day, Asia, a tier-two technician, received the escalated ticket, and to her dismay, the phone number of the customer was missing. She called Darnell. "How am I to call this customer? You only have his first name, and these notes about the problem don't even make sense!" Darnell apologized to Asia, but the damage was done.

Two days later, an angry Andre calls the manager of the help desk to complain that his problem is still not solved. Jonathan listens to Andre vent and apologizes for the problem his help desk has caused. It's a little embarrassing to Jonathan to have to ask Andre for his callback information and to repeat the details of the problem. He gives the information to Asia, and the problem gets a quick resolution.

Discuss this situation in a small group, and answer the following questions:

1. If you were Darnell, what could you do to improve note-taking in the ticketing system?
2. After Asia called, do you think Darnell should have told Jonathan about the problem? Why or why not?
3. If you were Jonathan, how would you handle the situation with Darnell?

Have two students play the roles of Darnell and Jonathan when Jonathan calls Darnell into his office to discuss the call he just received from Andre. The other students in the group can watch and make suggestions as to how to improve the conversation.

Troubleshooting the Electrical System

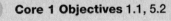
Core 1 Objectives 1.1, 5.2

Electrical problems can occur before or after the boot and can be consistent or intermittent. Repair technicians often don't recognize the cause of a problem to be electrical because of the intermittent nature of some electrical problems. In these situations, the hard drive, memory, the OS, or even user error might be suspected as the source of the problem and then systematically eliminated before the electrical system is suspected. This section will help you to be aware of symptoms of electrical problems so you can zero in on the source of an electrical problem as quickly as possible.

Applying Concepts

Exploring a Computer Problem

Est. Time: 5 minutes
Core 1 Objective: 5.2

Your friend Sharon calls to ask for your help with a computer problem. Her system has been working fine for more than a year, but now strange things are happening. Sometimes the system powers down for no apparent reason while she is working, and sometimes Windows locks up. As you read this section, look for clues as to what the problem might be. Also, think of questions to ask your friend that will help you diagnose the problem.

The following are possible symptoms of a problem with the electrical system:

- The computer appears "dead"—no indicator lights and no spinning drive or fan.
- The computer sometimes locks up during booting. After several tries, it boots successfully. Error codes or beeps occur during booting, but they come and go.
- You smell burnt parts or odors. (Definitely not a good sign!)
- The computer powers down at unexpected times.
- The computer appears dead, but you hear a whine coming from the power supply.

The following list contains some questions you can ask and things you can do to solve a problem with the electrical system without opening the computer case. The rule of thumb is "Try the simple things first." Most computer problems have simple solutions.

- If you smell any burnt parts or odors, don't try to turn the system on. Identify the component that is fried, and replace it.
- If you hear a whine coming from the power supply when you first plug up power to a system, the power supply might be inadequate for the system, or there might be a short. Don't press the power button to start up the system. Unplug the power cord so the power supply will not be damaged. The next step is to open the case and search for a short. If you don't find a short, consider upgrading the power supply.
- Is the power cord plugged in? If it is plugged into a power strip or surge suppressor, is the device turned on and plugged in?
- Is the power outlet controlled by a wall switch? If so, is the switch turned on?
- Are any cable connections loose?
- Is the circuit breaker blown? Is the house circuit overloaded?
- Are all switches on the system turned on? Computer? Monitor? Surge suppressor or UPS (uninterruptible power supply)?
- Is there a possibility the system has overheated? If so, wait a while and try turning on the computer again. If the system comes on but later turns itself off, you might need additional cooling fans inside the unit. How to solve problems with overheating is covered later in this module.
- Older computers might be affected by electromagnetic interference (EMI). Check for sources of electrical or magnetic interference such as fluorescent lighting or an electric fan or copier sitting near the computer case.

> **Caution**
>
> Before opening the case of a brand-name computer, such as an HP or Dell, consider the warranty. If the system is still under warranty, sometimes the warranty is voided if the case is opened. If the warranty prevents you from opening the case, you might need to return the system to a manufacturer's service center for repairs.

If the problem is still not solved, it's time to look inside the case. First, turn off the computer, unplug it, press the power button to drain residual power, and then open the case. Next, do the following:

- Check all power connections from the power supply to the motherboard and drives. Also, some cases require the front panel to be in place before the power-on button will work. Are all cards securely seated?
- If you smell burnt parts, carefully search for shorts and for frayed and burnt wires. Also look for cracked chips, chips with a burnt hole on top, or fine black dust around a chip. Disassemble the parts until you find the one that is damaged.
- If you suspect the power supply is bad, test it with a power supply tester.

Problems That Come and Go

Core 1 Objective 5.2

If a system boots successfully to the Windows Start screen or desktop, you still might have a power system problem. Some problems are intermittent; that is, they come and go. Generally, intermittent problems are more difficult to solve than a dead system. There can be many causes of intermittent problems, such as an inadequate power supply, overheating, and devices and components damaged by ESD. Here are some symptoms that might indicate an intermittent problem with the electrical system after the boot:

- The computer stops or hangs for no reason. Sometimes it might even reboot itself.
- Memory errors appear intermittently.
- Data is written incorrectly to the hard drive or files are corrupted.
- The keyboard stops working at odd times.
- The motherboard fails or is damaged.
- The power supply overheats and becomes hot to the touch.
- The power supply fan whines and becomes very noisy or stops.

Here is what to do to eliminate the electrical system as the source of an intermittent problem:

1. **Consider the power supply may be inadequate.** If the power supply is grossly inadequate, it will whine when you first plug up the power. If you have just installed new devices that are drawing additional power, verify that the wattage rating of the power supply is adequate for the system.

    You can also test the system to make sure you don't have power problems by making all the devices in your system work at the same time. For instance, you can make two hard drives and the DVD drive work at the same time by copying files from one hard drive to the other while playing a movie on the DVD. If the drives and the other devices each work independently, but data errors occur when all work at the same time, suspect a shortage of electrical power.

2. **Suspect the power supply is faulty.** You can test it using either a power supply tester (the easier method) or a multimeter (the more tedious method). However, know that a power supply that gives correct voltages when you measure it might still be the source of problems because power problems can be intermittent. Also be aware that an ATX power supply monitors the range of voltages provided to the motherboard and halts the motherboard if voltages are inadequate. Therefore, if the power supply appears "dead," your best action is to replace it.

3. **The power supply fan might not work.** Don't operate the computer if the fan does not work; computers without cooling fans can quickly overheat. Usually just before a fan stops working, it hums or grinds, especially when the computer is first turned on. If this has just happened, replace the power supply. If the new fan does not work after you replace the power supply, you have to dig deeper to find the source of the problem. You can now assume the problem wasn't the original fan. A short drawing too much power somewhere else in the system might cause the problem. To troubleshoot a nonfunctional fan, which might be a symptom of another problem and not of the fan itself, follow these steps:

    a. Turn off the power and remove all power cord connections to all components except the motherboard. Turn the power back on. If the fan works, the problem is with one of the systems you disconnected, not with the power supply, the fan, or the motherboard.

    b. Turn off the power and reconnect one card or drive at a time until you identify the device with the short.

    c. If the fan does not work when all devices except the motherboard are disconnected, the problem is the motherboard or the power supply. Because you have already replaced the power supply, you can assume that the motherboard needs to be replaced.

Power Problems with the Motherboard

Core 1 Objective 5.2

A short might occur if some component on the motherboard makes improper contact with the chassis. This short can seriously damage the motherboard. For some cases, check for missing standoffs (small plastic or metal spacers that hold the motherboard a short distance away from the bottom of the case). A missing standoff most often causes these improper connections. Also check for loose standoffs or screws under the board that might be touching a wire on the bottom of the board and causing a short. Shake the case gently, and listen for loose screws or any other small pieces of a component.

Shorts in the circuits on the motherboard might also cause problems. Look for damage on the bottom of the motherboard. These circuits are coated with plastic, and quite often damage is difficult to spot. Also look for burned-out capacitors that are spotted brown or corroded. You'll see examples of burned-out capacitors later in the module.

> **Caution**
>
> Never replace a damaged motherboard with a good one without first testing or replacing the power supply. You don't want to subject another good board to possible damage.

Applying Concepts

Investigating a Computer Problem

Est. Time: 15 minutes
Core 1 Objective: 5.2

Let's return to Sharon's computer problem. Here are some questions that will help you identify the source of the problem:

- Have you added new devices to your system? (These new devices might be drawing too much power from an overworked power supply.)
- Have you moved your computer recently? (It might be sitting beside a heat vent or electrical equipment.) Does the system power down or hang after you have been working for some time? (This symptom might have more than one cause, such as overheating or a power supply, processor, memory, or motherboard about to fail.)
- Has the computer case been opened recently? (Someone working inside the case might not have used a ground bracelet, and components are now failing because of ESD damage.)
- Are case vents free so air can flow? (The case might be close to a curtain covering the vents.)

Intermittent problems like the one Sharon described are often heat related. If the system only hangs but does not power off, the problem might be caused by faulty memory or bad software, but because it actually powers down, you can assume the problem is related to power or heat.

If Sharon tells you that the system powers down after she's been working for several hours, you can probably assume overheating. Check that first. If that's not the problem, the next thing to do is replace the power supply.

Problems with Overheating

Core 1 Objective 5.2

As a repair technician, you're sure to eventually face problems with computers overheating. Overheating can happen as soon as you turn on the computer or after it has been working a while. Overheating can cause intermittent errors, the system to hang, or components to fail or not last as long as they normally would. (Overheating can significantly shorten the life span of the CPU and memory.) Overheating happens for many reasons, including improper installation of the CPU cooler or fans, overclocking, poor airflow inside the case, an underrated power supply, a component going bad, or the computer's environment (for example, heat or dust).

Here are some symptoms that a system is overheating:

- The system hangs or freezes at odd times or freezes just a few moments after the boot starts.
- A Windows BSOD error occurs during the boot.
- You cannot hear a fan running, or the fan makes a grinding sound.
- You cannot feel air being pulled into or out of the case.

If you suspect overheating, go into BIOS/UEFI setup and view the temperature monitors for the system. To protect the expensive processor and other components, you can also purchase a temperature sensor. The sensor plugs into a power connection coming from the power supply and mounts on the side of the case or in a drive bay. The sensor sounds an alarm when the inside of the case becomes too hot. To decide which temperature sensor to buy, use one recommended by the case manufacturer. You can also install utility software that can monitor system temperatures. For example, SpeedFan by Alfredo Comparetti is freeware that can monitor fan speeds and temperatures (see Figure 4-20). A good website to download the freeware is *filehippo.com/download_speedfan*. Be careful not to download other freeware available on the site.

Here are some simple things you can do to solve an overheating problem:

Figure 4-20   SpeedFan monitors fan speeds and system temperatures

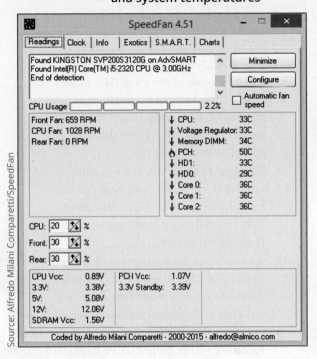

Source: Alfredo Milani Comparetti/SpeedFan

1. If the system refuses to boot or hangs after a period of activity, suspect overheating. Immediately after the system hangs, go into BIOS/UEFI setup and find the screen that reports the CPU temperature. The temperature should not exceed that recommended by the CPU manufacturer.

2. Excessive dust insulates components and causes components to overheat. Use compressed air, a blower, or an antistatic vacuum to remove dust from the power supply, the vents over the entire computer, and the processor cooler fan (see Figure 4-21). To protect the fan, don't allow it to spin as you blow air into it. Overspinning might damage a fan.

Figure 4-21   Dust in this cooler fan can cause the fan to fail and the processor to overheat

Note 8

When working in a customer's office or home, be sure you clean up any mess you create from blowing dust out of a computer case.

3. Check airflow inside the case. Are all fans running? You might need to replace a fan. Is there an empty fan slot on the rear of the case? If so, install a case fan in the slot (see Figure 4-22). Orient the fan so it blows air out of the case. The power cord to the fan can connect to a fan header on the motherboard or to a power connector coming directly from the power supply.

4. If there are other fan slots on the side or front of the case, you can also install fans in these slots. However, don't install more fans than the case is designed to use.

5. A case is generally designed for optimal airflow when slot openings on the front and rear of the case are covered and when the case cover is securely in place. To improve airflow, replace missing faceplates over empty drive bays, and replace missing slot covers over empty expansion slots. See Figure 4-23.

6. Are cables in the way of airflow? Use cable ties to secure cables and cords so they don't block airflow across the processor or get in the way of fans turning. Figure 4-24 shows the inside of a case where cables are tied up and neatly out of the way of airflow from the front to the rear of the case.

7. A case needs some room to breathe. Place it so there are at least a few inches of space on both sides and the top of the case. If the case is sitting on carpet, put it on a computer stand so air can circulate under the case and to reduce carpet dust inside the case. Many cases have a vent on the bottom front, and carpet can obstruct airflow into this vent (see Figure 4-25). Make sure drapes are not hanging too close to fan openings.

8. Verify that the cooler is connected properly to the processor. If it doesn't fit well, the system might not boot, and the processor will overheat. If the cooler is not tightly connected to the motherboard and processor or the cooler fan is not working, the processor will quickly overheat as soon as the computer is turned on. Has thermal compound been installed between the cooler and processor?

9. After you close the case, leave your system off for at least 30 minutes. When you power up the computer again, let it run for 10 minutes, go into BIOS/UEFI setup, check the temperature readings, and reboot.

Figure 4-22   Install one exhaust fan on the rear of the case to help pull air through the case

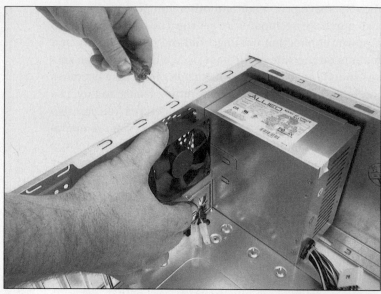

Figure 4-23   For optimum airflow, don't leave empty expansion slots and bays uncovered

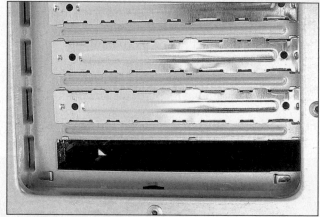

Figure 4-24   Use cable ties to hold cables out of the way of fans and airflow

Figure 4-25   Keep a tower case off carpet to allow air to flow into
the bottom air vent

Next, let your system run until it shuts down. Power it up again and check the temperature in BIOS/ UEFI setup again. A significant difference between this reading and the first one you took after running the computer for 10 minutes indicates an overheating problem.

10. Check BIOS/UEFI setup to see if the processor is being overclocked. Overclocking can cause a system to overheat. Try restoring the processor and system bus frequencies to default values.

11. Have too many peripherals been installed inside the case? Is the case too small for all these peripherals? Larger tower cases are better designed for good airflow than smaller slimline cases. Also, when installing expansion cards, try to leave an empty slot between each card for better airflow. The same goes for drives. Try not to install a group of drives in adjacent drive bays. For better airflow, leave empty bays between drives. Take a close look at Figure 4-24, where you can see space between each drive installed in the system.

12. Flash BIOS/UEFI to update the firmware on the motherboard. How to flash BIOS/UEFI is covered in the module "All About Motherboards."

13. Thermal compound should last for years, but it will eventually harden and need replacing. If the system is several years old, replace the thermal compound.

Exam Tip ✔

The A+ Core 1 exam expects you to recognize that a given symptom is possibly power related or heat related.

If you try the preceding list of things to do and still have an overheating problem, it's time to move on to more drastic solutions. Consider whether the case design allows for good airflow; the problem might be caused by poor air circulation inside the case. The power supply fan in ATX cases blows air out of the case, pulling outside air from the vents in the front of the case across the processor to help keep it cool. Another exhaust fan is usually installed on the back of the case to help the power supply fan pull air through the case. In addition, most processors require a cooler with a fan installed on top of the processor. Figure 4-26 shows a good arrangement of vents and fans for proper airflow and a poor arrangement.

For better ventilation, use a power supply that has vents on the bottom and front, as shown in Figure 4-27. Compare that with the power supply in Figure 4-22, which has vents only on the front and not on the bottom.

Figure 4-26   Vents and fans need to be arranged for best airflow

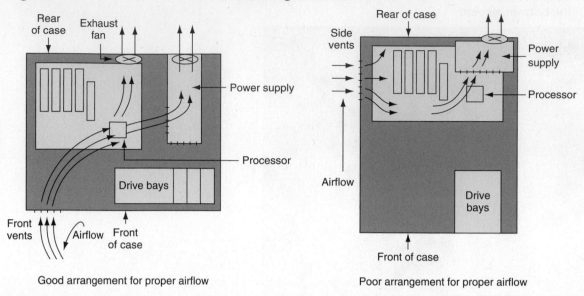

Good arrangement for proper airflow

Poor arrangement for proper airflow

Figure 4-27   This power supply has vents on the bottom to provide better airflow inside the case

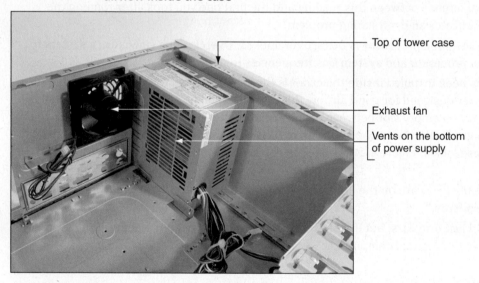

An intake fan on the front of the case might help pull air into the case. Intel recommends you use a front intake fan for high-end systems, but AMD says a front fan for ATX systems is not necessary. Check with the processor and case manufacturers for specific instructions as to the placement of fans and what type of fan and heat sink to use.

Be careful when trying to solve an overheating problem. Excessive heat can damage the CPU and the motherboard. Never operate a system if the case fan, power-supply fan, or cooler fan is not working.

Problems With Laptop Power Systems

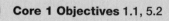 **Core 1 Objectives** 1.1, 5.2

A laptop can be powered by an **AC adapter** (which uses regular house current to power the laptop) or an installed battery pack. Battery packs today use **lithium ion** technology. Most AC adapters today are capable of **auto-switching** from 110 V to 220 V AC power. Figure 4-28 shows an AC adapter that has a green light indicating the adapter is receiving power.

Figure 4-28   This AC adapter for a laptop uses a green light to indicate power

Some mobile users like to keep an extra battery on hand in case the first one uses up its charge. When the laptop signals that power is low, shut down the system, remove the old battery, and replace it with a charged one. To remove a battery, you usually must release a latch first.

> **Note 9**
>
> If you're using the AC adapter to power your laptop when the power goes out, the installed battery serves as a built-in UPS. The battery immediately takes over as your uninterruptible power supply (UPS). Also, a laptop has an internal surge protector. However, for extra protection, you might want to use a power strip that provides surge protection.

Here are some problems you might encounter with laptop power systems and their solutions:

- If power is not getting to the system or the battery indicator light is lit when the AC adapter should be supplying power, verify that the AC adapter is plugged into a live electrical outlet. Is the light on the AC adapter lit? Check if the AC adapter's plug is secure in the electrical outlet. Check the connections on both sides of the AC adapter transformer. Check the connection at the DC jack on the laptop. Try exchanging the AC adapter for one you know is good.
- If the battery is not charging when the AC adapter is plugged in, the problem might be with the battery or the motherboard. A hot battery might not charge until it cools down. If the battery is hot, remove it from the computer, and allow it to cool to room temperature. Check the battery for physical damage. If the battery is swollen or warped, replace it. If it shows no physical signs of damage, try to recharge it. If it does not recharge, replace the battery pack. If a known good battery does not recharge, you have three options: (1) Involve the manufacturer for repair under warranty, (2) replace the laptop, or (3) use the laptop only when it's connected to power using the AC adapter.

Applying Concepts

Testing an AC Adapter

Est. Time: 15 minutes
Core 1 Objective: 5.2

If the system fails only when the AC adapter is connected, it might be defective. Try a new AC adapter, or, if you have a multimeter, use it to verify the voltage output of the adapter. Do the following for an adapter with a single centerpin connector:

1. Unplug the AC adapter from the computer, but leave it plugged into the electrical outlet.
2. Most laptops run on 19 V DC, but a few run on 45 V DC. To be on the safe side, set the multimeter to measure voltage in the range of 1–200 V DC. Place the red probe of the multimeter in the center of the DC connector that would normally plug into the DC outlet on the laptop. Place the black probe on the outside cylinder of the DC connector (see Figure 4-29).

(continues)

Applying Concepts Continued

Figure 4-29   To use a multimeter to test this AC adapter, place the red probe in the center of the connector and the black probe on the outside

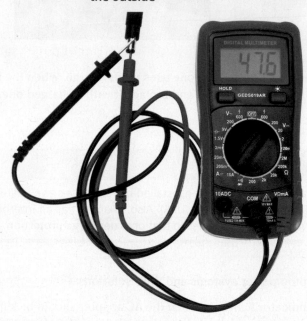

3. The voltage range should be plus or minus 5% of the accepted voltage. For example, if a laptop is designed to use 16 V, the voltage should measure somewhere between 15.2 and 16.8 V DC.

Troubleshooting the Motherboard, Processor, and RAM

Core 1 Objective 5.2

The field replaceable units (FRUs) on a motherboard are the processor, the processor cooler assembly, RAM, and the CMOS battery. Also, the motherboard itself is an FRU. As you troubleshoot the motherboard and discover that some component, such as a network port, is not working, you might be able to disable that component in BIOS/UEFI setup and install a card to take its place.

Exam Tip

The A+ Core 1 exam expects you to know how to troubleshoot problems with motherboards, processors, and RAM.

When you suspect a bad component, a good troubleshooting technique is to substitute a known good component for the one you suspect is bad. Be cautious here. A friend once had a computer that wouldn't boot. They replaced the hard drive, with no change. They replaced the motherboard next. The computer booted up with no problem; they were delighted, until it failed again. Later they discovered that a faulty power supply had damaged the original motherboard. When they traded the bad one for a good one, the new motherboard also got zapped! If you suspect problems with the power supply, check the voltage coming from the power supply before putting in a new motherboard.

The following symptoms can indicate that a motherboard, processor, or memory module is failing:

- The system begins to boot but then powers down.
- An error message is displayed during the boot. Investigate this message.
- The system reports less memory than you know is installed.
- The system becomes sluggish, unstable, hangs, or freezes at odd times. (This symptom can have multiple causes, including a failing power supply, RAM, hard drive, motherboard, or processor, Windows errors, and overheating.)
- Intermittent Windows or hard drive errors occur.
- Components on the motherboard or devices connected to it don't work.

Remember the troubleshooting principle to check the simple things first. The motherboard and processor are expensive and time consuming to replace. Unless you're certain the problem is one of these two components, don't replace either until you first eliminate other components as the source of the problem.

If you can boot the system, follow these steps to eliminate Windows, software, RAM, BIOS/UEFI settings, and other software and hardware components as the source of the problem:

1. If an error message appears, google the error message. Pay particular attention to search results about the motherboard or processor manufacturer or Microsoft websites. Search forums for information about the error.

2. The problem might be a virus. If you can boot the system, run a current version of antivirus software to check for viruses.

3. A memory module might be failing. In Windows use the **Memory Diagnostic Tool** to test memory. Even if Windows is not installed, you can still run the tool by booting the system from the Windows setup flash drive or DVD. How to use the Memory Diagnostic Tool is coming up later in this module.

Note 10

Besides the Windows Memory Diagnostic Tool, you can use the Memtest86+ utility to test installed memory modules. Check the site *memtest86.com* to download this program.

4. Suspect the problem is caused by an application or by Windows. In Windows, Device Manager is the best tool to check for potential hardware problems.

5. In Windows, check Event Viewer logs for a record about a hardware or application problem. You learn to use Event Viewer in a project at the end of this module.

6. In Windows, download and install any Windows updates or patches. These updates might solve a hardware or application problem.

7. Ask yourself what has changed since the problem began. If the problem began immediately after installing a new device or application, uninstall it.

8. A system that does not have enough RAM can sometimes appear to be unstable. Using the Windows About window, find out how much RAM is installed, and compare that with the recommended amounts. Consider upgrading RAM.

9. The BIOS/UEFI might be corrupted or have wrong settings. Check BIOS/UEFI setup. Have settings been tampered with? Is the CPU speed set incorrectly, or is it overclocked? Reset BIOS/UEFI setup to restore default settings.

10. Disable any quick booting features in BIOS/UEFI so you get a thorough report of POST. Then look for errors reported on the screen during the boot.

11. Flash BIOS/UEFI to update the firmware on the board.

12. Check the motherboard manufacturer's website for diagnostic software that might identify a problem with the motherboard.

13. Update all drivers of motherboard components that are not working. For example, if the USB ports are not working, try updating the USB drivers with those downloaded from the motherboard manufacturer's website. This process can also update the chipset drivers.

14. If an onboard port or device isn't working, but the motherboard is stable, follow these steps:

    a. Verify that the problem is not with the device using the port. Try moving the device to another port on the same computer or move the device to another computer. If it works there, return it to this port. The problem might have been a bad connection.

    b. Go into BIOS/UEFI setup and verify that the port is enabled.

    c. Check Device Manager and verify that Windows recognizes the device or port with no errors. For example, Device Manager shown in Figure 4-30 reports the onboard Bluetooth device is disabled. Try to enable the device.

Figure 4-30   Device Manager reports a problem with an onboard device

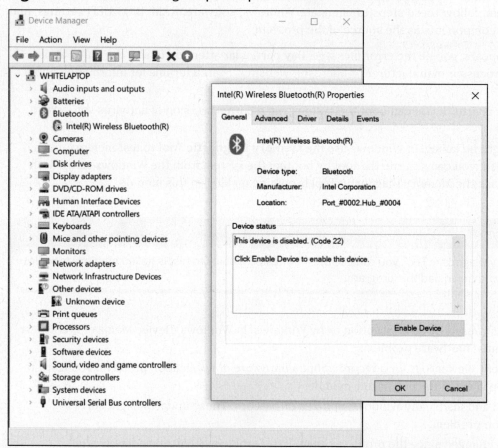

    d. Next try updating the motherboard drivers for this device from the motherboard manufacturer's website.

    e. If you have a loopback plug, use it to test the port.

    f. If the problem is still not solved, disable the port in BIOS/UEFI setup and install an expansion card to provide the same type of port or connector.

15. Suspect the problem is caused by a failing hard drive. How to troubleshoot a failing drive is covered in the module "Hard Drives and Other Storage Devices."

16. Suspect the problem is caused by overheating. How to check for overheating is covered earlier in this module.

17. Verify that the installed processor is supported by the motherboard. Perhaps someone has installed the wrong processor.

Applying Concepts

Using the Windows Memory Diagnostic Tool

Est. Time: 30 minutes
Core 1 Objective: 5.2

Errors with memory are often difficult to diagnose because they can appear intermittently and might be mistaken as sluggish performance, application errors, user errors, or other hardware component errors. Sometimes these errors cause the system to hang, a blue screen error might occur, or the system continues to function with applications giving errors or data getting corrupted. You can quickly identify a problem with memory or eliminate memory as the source of a problem by using the Windows Memory Diagnostic tool. Use one of these two methods to start the utility:

- **Use the mdsched.exe command in Windows.** To open a command prompt window from the Windows desktop, enter the **cmd** command in the Windows search box. In the command prompt window, enter **mdsched.exe** and press **Enter**. A dialog box appears (see Figure 4-31) and asks if you want to restart and run the test now or run the test on the next restart.

Figure 4-31   Use the mdsched.exe command to test memory

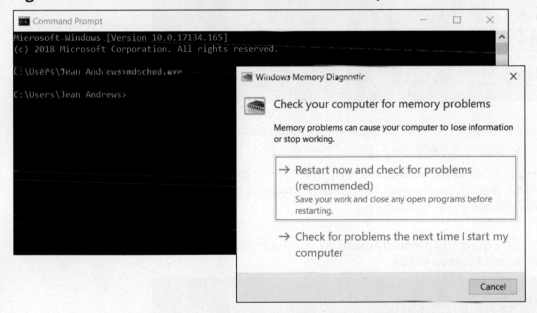

- **Boot from the Windows setup DVD.** If Windows is not the installed operating system or you cannot boot from the hard drive, boot the computer from the Windows setup USB drive or DVD to test memory for errors. Follow these steps:
  1. If necessary, change the boot priority order in BIOS/UEFI setup to boot first from the optical drive or USB drive. Boot from the Windows setup DVD or USB drive.
  2. On the opening screen for Windows, select your language and click **Next**. On the next screen (see Figure 4-32), click **Repair your computer**. Next choose **Troubleshoot**. The Advanced options screen appears.

(continues)

Applying Concepts Continued

Figure 4-32   The opening menu when you boot from Windows 10 setup media

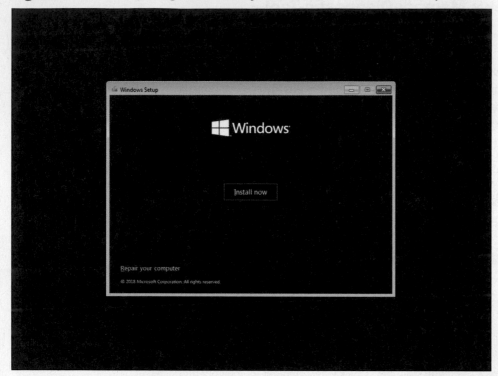

3. On the Advanced options screen (see Figure 4-33), choose **Command Prompt**. In the command prompt window, enter the **mdsched.exe** command.

To find the results, open **Event Viewer** and search for "MemoryDiagnostics-Results," and click **Find Next**. These event logs report memory errors or no memory errors detected. If the tool reports memory errors, replace all memory modules installed on the motherboard.

Figure 4-33   The Windows 10 Advanced options screen launched from Windows 10 setup media

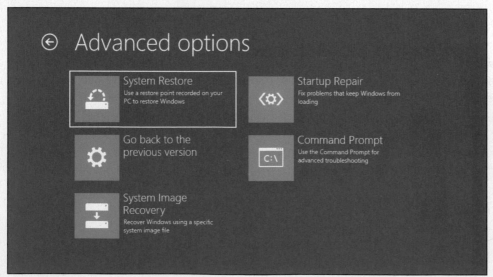

Note 11

You learn to use Event Viewer in a project at the end of this module.

Applying Concepts

Using Device Manager to Delete the Driver Store

Est. Time: 15 minutes
Core 1 Objective: 5.2

One thing you can do to solve a problem with a device is to uninstall and reinstall the device. When you first install a device, Windows stores a copy of the driver package in a **driver store**. When you uninstall the device, you can also tell Windows to delete the driver store. If you don't delete the driver store, Windows uses it when you install the device again. That's why the second time you install the same device, Windows does not ask you for the location of the drivers. Windows might also use the driver store to automatically install the device on the next reboot without your involvement.

All this is convenient unless there is a problem with the driver store. To get a true fresh start with an installation, you need to delete the driver store. First sign in to Windows using an account with administrative privileges and then follow these steps:

1. To open Device Manager from the Windows desktop, right-click **Start** and click **Device Manager**. Device Manager opens. Alternately, you can enter devmgmt.msc in the Windows search box or in a command prompt window.

2. Right-click the device and click **Properties** in the shortcut menu. Click the **Driver** tab and click **Uninstall Device**. In the Uninstall Device box, check **Delete the driver software for this device**, and click **Uninstall**. See Figure 4-34. The installed drivers and the driver store are both deleted. When you reinstall the device, you'll need the drivers on CD or downloaded from the web.

Figure 4-34   Use Device Manager to uninstall the drivers and delete the driver store for a device

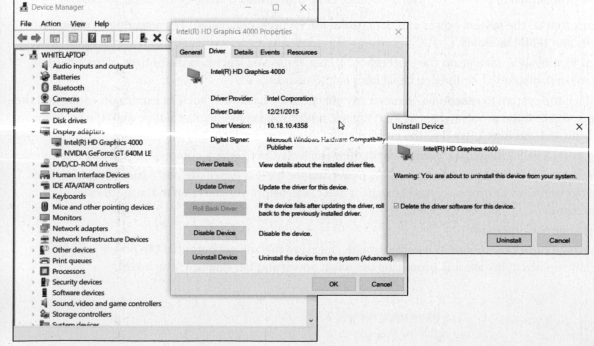

(continues)

Applying Concepts Continued

Also know that if the check box is missing in the Uninstall Device dialog box, the drivers are embedded in Windows, and you cannot delete the driver store for these devices. Examples of these devices are an optical drive, a hard drive, and a generic keyboard, which all have embedded Windows drivers.

We're working our way through what to do when the system locks up, gives errors, or generally appears unstable. Another problem that can occur at the boot is continuous reboots, which can be caused by overheating, a failing processor, motherboard, or RAM, or a corrupted Windows installation.

Windows Startup Repair

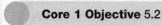
Core 1 Objective 5.2

Many continuous restart errors can be solved by performing a Startup Repair process. The **Startup Repair** utility restores many of the Windows files needed for a successful boot. After several restarts, Windows will try to automatically run the Startup Repair process. If Startup Repair does not automatically start or does not fix the problem, try running it from Windows setup media.

Follow these steps to run Startup Repair from the Windows setup USB drive or DVD:

1. If necessary, change the boot priority order in BIOS/UEFI setup to boot first from the USB drive or optical drive. Boot from the Windows setup USB drive or DVD.
2. On the opening screen, select your language and click **Next**. On the next screen, click **Repair your computer**. Next, choose **Troubleshoot**. The Advanced options screen appears (refer back to Figure 4-33). On the Advanced options screen, choose **Startup Repair**, and select your operating system. Windows will attempt to repair the system and restart to the Windows desktop.

If you have tried to repair Windows, checked BIOS/UEFI settings, searched the web for help, and still have not identified the source of the problem, it's time to open the case and check inside. Be sure to use an ESD strap and follow other procedures to protect the system against ESD. With the case open, follow these steps:

1. Check that all the system power and data cables are securely connected. Try reseating all expansion cards and DIMM modules.
2. Look for physical damage on the motherboard. Look for frayed traces on the bottom of the board or discolored, distended, or bulging capacitors on the board.
3. Reduce the system to essentials. Remove any unnecessary hardware, such as expansion cards, and then watch to see if the problem goes away. If it does, replace one component at a time until the problem returns and you have identified the component causing the trouble.
4. Try using a POST diagnostic card. It might offer you a clue as to which component is giving a problem.
5. Suspect the problem is caused by a failing power supply. It's less expensive and easier to replace than the motherboard or processor, so eliminate it as a cause before you move on to the motherboard or processor.
6. Exchange the processor.
7. Exchange the motherboard, but before you do, measure the voltage output of the power supply or simply replace it, in case it is producing too much power and has damaged the board.

Applying Concepts

Discolored Capacitors

Est. Time: 15 minutes
Core 1 Objective: 5.2

Benafsha complained to DeShaun, her IT support technician, that Windows was occasionally giving errors, data would get corrupted, or an application would not work as it should. At first, DeShaun suspected Benafsha might need a little more training on how to open and close an application or save a file, but he discovered user error was not the problem. He tried reinstalling the application software Benafsha most often used and even reinstalled Windows, but the problems persisted.

Note 12

Catastrophic errors (errors that cause the system not to boot or a device not to work) are much easier to resolve than intermittent errors (errors that come and go).

DeShaun began to suspect a hardware problem. Carefully examining the motherboard revealed the source of the problem: failing capacitors. Look carefully at Figure 4-35 and you can see five bad **discolored capacitors** with bulging heads. (Know that sometimes a leaking capacitor can also show crusty corrosion at its base.) When DeShaun replaced the motherboard, the problems went away.

Figure 4-35   These five bad capacitors have bulging and discolored heads

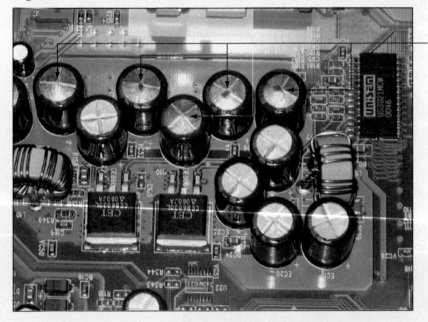

Bad capacitors

Applying Concepts

Lessons Learned

Est. Time: 15 minutes
Core 1 Objective: 5.2

Kiara is putting together a computer from parts for the first time. She has decided to keep costs low and is installing an AMD processor on a microATX motherboard, using all low-cost parts. She installed the hard drive, optical drive, and power supply in the computer case. Then she installed the motherboard in the case, followed by the processor, cooler, and memory. Before powering up the system, she checked all connections to make sure they were solid and read through the motherboard documentation to make sure she did not forget anything important. Next, she plugs in the monitor to the onboard video port and then plugs in the keyboard and power cord. She takes a deep breath and turns on the power switch on the back of the computer. Immediately, she hears a faint whine, but she's not sure what is making the noise. When she presses the power button on the front of the case, nothing happens. No fans, no lights. Here are the steps Kiara takes to troubleshoot the problem:

1. She turns off the power switch and unplugs the power cord. She remembers to put on her ground bracelet and carefully checks all power connections. Everything looks okay.

2. She plugs in the system and presses the power button again. Still all she hears is the faint whine.

3. She presses the power button a second and third time. Suddenly, a loud pop followed by smoke comes from the power supply, and the strong smell of electronics fills the room! Kiara jumps back in dismay.

4. She removes a known good power supply from another computer, disconnects the blown power supply, and connects the good one to the computer. When she turns on the power switch, she hears that same faint whine. She quickly turns off the switch and unplugs the power cord. She does not want to lose another power supply!

5. Next, Kiara calls technical support of the company that sold her the computer parts. A very helpful technician listens carefully to the details and tells Kiara that the problem sounds like a short in the system. He explains that a power supply might whine if too much power is being drawn. As Kiara hangs up the phone, she begins to think that the problem might be with the motherboard installation.

6. She removes the motherboard from the case, and the source of the problem is evident: She forgot to install spacers between the board and the case. The board was sitting directly on the bottom of the case, which had caused the short.

7. Kiara installs the spacers and reinstalls the motherboard. Using the good power supply, she turns on the system. The whine is gone, but the system is dead.

8. Kiara purchases a new power supply and motherboard and this time carefully uses spacers in every hole used by the motherboard screws. Figure 4-36 shows one installed spacer and one ready to be installed. The system comes up without a problem.

Figure 4-36   Spacers installed in case holes keep the motherboard from causing a short

In evaluating her experience with her first computer build, Kiara declares the project a success. She was grateful she had decided to use low-cost parts for her first build. She learned much from the experience and will never, ever forget to use spacers. She told a friend, "I made a serious mistake, but I learned from it. I feel confident I know how to put a system together now, and I'm ready to tackle another build." When you make mistakes and get past them, your confidence level grows because you learn you can face a serious problem and solve it.

Module Summary

Cooling Methods and Devices

- Devices that are used to keep a processor and system cool include CPU coolers and fans, thermal compound, case fans, heat sinks, and liquid cooling systems.
- Liquid cooling systems use liquids pumped through the system to keep it cool and are sometimes used by hobbyists when overclocking a system.

Selecting a Power Supply

- Important features of a power supply to consider before purchase are its form factor, wattage capacity, number and type of connectors it provides, and warranty.
- To decide on the wattage capacity of a power supply, add up the wattage requirements for all components in a system and then increase that total by about 30%. The wattage provided by the +12 V rail is also important.

Strategies to Troubleshoot Any Computer Problem

- The six steps in the troubleshooting process are (1) interview the user and back up data, (2) examine the system and form a theory of probable cause (your best guess), (3) test your theory, (4) plan a solution and implement it, (5) verify that everything works and take appropriate preventive measures, and (6) document what you did and the final outcome.
- If possible, always begin troubleshooting a computer problem by interviewing the user. Find out when the problem started and what happened about the time it started. You also need to know if important data on the computer is not backed up. When troubleshooting, set your priorities based on user needs.
- Sources that can help with hardware troubleshooting are the web, online technical support and forums, diagnostic software, user manuals, and your network of technical associates.
- When troubleshooting, check the simple things first. For example, you can scan for viruses, test RAM, and run diagnostic software before you begin the process of replacing expensive components.
- Decide if a computer problem occurs before or after a successful boot and if it is caused by hardware or software. After you have fixed the problem, verify the fix and document the outcome.
- When troubleshooting laptops, consider the warranty and that replacing a component might cost more than replacing the device. If possible, substitute an external component for an internal one.

Troubleshooting the Electrical System

- To determine if a system is getting power, listen for spinning fans or drives and look for indicator lights.
- Use a power supply tester to test the power supply.
- Intermittent problems that come and go are the most difficult to solve and can be caused by hardware or software. The power supply, motherboard, RAM, processor, hard drive, and overheating can cause intermittent problems.

- Removing dust from a system, providing for proper ventilation, and installing extra fans can help keep a system from overheating.
- A laptop battery is considered a field replaceable unit (FRU) that pertains to the power system.
- Use a multimeter to check the voltage output of a laptop AC adapter.

Troubleshooting the Motherboard, Processor, and RAM

- BIOS/UEFI gives beep codes when a POST error occurs during the boot before it tests video.
- Error messages on a black screen during the boot are usually put there by startup BIOS/UEFI during POST.
- Error messages on a blue screen during or after the boot are put there by Windows and are called the blue screen of death (BSOD).
- The motherboard, processor, RAM, processor cooler assembly, and CMOS battery are field replaceable units.
- An unstable system that freezes or hangs at odd times can be caused by a faulty power supply, RAM, hard drive, motherboard, or processor, a Windows error, or overheating.
- A POST diagnostic card can troubleshoot problems with the motherboard.

Key Terms

For explanations of key terms, see the Glossary for this text.

AC adapter	discolored capacitor	modular power supply	technical documentation
auto-switching	driver store	processor thermal trip	thermal pad
blue screen of death	Event Viewer	error	thermal paste
(BSOD)	expert system	redundant power	
case fan	lithium ion	supply (RPS)	
cooler	Memory Diagnostic Tool	Startup Repair	

Thinking Critically

These questions are designed to prepare you for the critical thinking required for the A+ exams and may use information from other modules and the web.

1. How much power is consumed by a load drawing 5 A with 120 V across it?

2. What is a reasonable wattage capacity for a power supply to be used with a system that contains a DVD drive, three hard drives, and a high-end video card?
   a. 250 W
   b. 1000 W
   c. 700 W
   d. 150 W

3. You upgrade a faulty PCIe video card to a recently released higher-performing card. Now the user complains that Windows hangs a lot and gives errors. Which is the most likely source of the problem? Which is the least likely source?
   a. A component of the computer is overheating.
   b. Windows does not support the new card.
   c. The drivers for the card need updating.
   d. Memory is faulty.

4. What should you immediately do if you turn on a computer and smell smoke or a burning odor?

   a. Unplug the computer.
   b. Dial 911.
   c. Find a fire extinguisher.
   d. Press a key on the keyboard to enter BIOS setup.

5. When you boot up a computer and hear a single beep, but the screen is blank, what can you assume is the source of the problem?

   a. The video card or onboard video
   b. The monitor or monitor cable
   c. Windows startup
   d. The processor

6. You suspect that a power supply is faulty, but you use a power supply tester to measure its voltage output and find it to be acceptable. Why is it still possible that the power supply may be faulty?

7. Someone asks you for help with a computer that hangs at odd times. You turn it on and work for about 15 minutes, and then the computer freezes and powers down. What do you do first?

   a. Replace the surge protector.
   b. Replace the power supply.
   c. Wait about 30 minutes for the system to cool down and try again.
   d. Install an additional fan.

8. You own a small computer repair company, and a customer comes to you with a laptop that will not boot. After investigating, you discover the hard drive has crashed. What should you do first?

   a. Install a hard drive that's the same capacity and speed as the original.
   b. Ask the customer's advice about the capacity of the drive to install, but select a drive that's the same speed as the original drive.
   c. Ask the customer's advice about the capacity and speed of the new drive to install.
   d. If the customer looks like they can afford it, install the largest capacity and fastest drive the system can support.

9. You have replaced a power supply in a client's computer. However, while you were working, you tripped on the power cord and bent the prongs on the plug so that it now is difficult to plug in an outlet. The customer receives the computer, notices the bent prongs, and begins shouting at you. What do you do first? Second?

   a. Explain to the customer you are sorry but that it was an accident.
   b. Listen carefully to the customer and don't get defensive.
   c. Apologize and offer to replace the power cord.
   d. Tell the customer not to speak to you like that.

10. As a help desk technician, list four good detective questions to ask if a user calls to say, "My computer won't turn on."

11. If the power connector from the CPU fan has only three pins, it can still connect to the 4-pin header, but what functionality is lost?

12. How do you determine the wattage capacity needed by a power supply?

13. You've decided to build a new gaming computer, and you are researching which power supply to buy. Which component in a high-end gaming computer is likely to draw the most power? What factor in a power supply do you need to consider to ensure this component has enough wattage?

14. Your friend Alexus calls to ask for help with her computer. She says when she first turns on the computer, she doesn't hear a spinning drive or fan or see indicator lights, and the monitor is blank. Is the problem hardware related or software related?

15. Which two components in a system might make a loud whining noise when there is a problem? Why?

16. Your manager assigns you a trouble ticket that says a computer is randomly shutting off after about 15 minutes of use. You have a theory that the computer is overheating. What utility program can you use to read system temperatures?

17. What are two reasons to tie cables up and out of the way inside a computer case?

18. You suspect a component in a computer is fried. You remove any unnecessary hardware devices one by one to narrow down where the problem exists. Which step in the troubleshooting process is this?

Hands-On Projects

Hands-On Project 4-1

Calculating Wattage Capacity for Your System

Est. Time: 15 minutes
Core 1 Objective: 3.5

Do the following to compare the wattage capacity of the power supply installed in your computer with the recommended value:

1. Search the web for a power supply wattage calculator. Be sure the one you use is provided by a reliable website. For example, the ones at *newegg.com* and *outervision.com* are reliable. (At *newegg.com*, click **Components** and then under Shopping Tools, click **Power Supply Wattage Calculator**. At *outervision.com*, click **Outervision Power Supply Calculator**.)

2. Enter the information about your computer system. Print or save the webpage showing the resulting calculations.

3. What is the recommended wattage capacity for a power supply for your system?

4. Look on the printed label on the power supply currently installed in your computer. What is its wattage capacity?

5. If you had to replace the power supply in your system, what wattage capacity would you select?

Hands-On Project 4-2

Researching Beep Codes

Est. Time: 15 minutes
Core 1 Objective: 5.2

Identify the motherboard and BIOS/UEFI version installed in your computer. Locate the motherboard user guide on the web, and find the list of beep codes that the BIOS/UEFI might give at POST. If the manual doesn't give this information, search the support section on the website of the motherboard manufacturer or search the website of the BIOS/UEFI manufacturer. List the beep codes and their meanings for your motherboard.

Hands-On Project 4-3

Identifying Airflow Through a Case

Est. Time: 15 minutes
Core 1 Objective: 3.4

Turn on a computer and feel the front and side vents to determine where air is flowing into and out of the case. Identify where you believe fans are working to produce the airflow. Power down the computer, unplug it, and press the power button to completely drain the power. Then open the computer case. Are fans located where you expected? Which fans were producing the strongest airflow through the case when the system was running? In which direction is each case fan drawing air: into the case or out of the case?

Hands-On Project 4-4

Blowing Dust Out of a Case

Est. Time: 15 minutes
Core 1 Objective: 3.4

If necessary, open the case cover to your desktop computer. Using a can of compressed air, blow the dust away from all fans and other components inside the case. Be careful not to touch components unless you are properly grounded. When you're done, close the case cover.

Hands-On Project 4-5

Troubleshooting Memory

Est. Time: 45 minutes
Core 1 Objective: 5.2

Do the following to troubleshoot memory:

1. Open the **Windows System Information** window, and record the amount of memory in your system.
2. Follow the rules to protect a computer against ESD as you work. Remove the memory module in the first memory slot on the motherboard, and boot the computer. Did you get an error? Why or why not? Replace the module, verify that the system starts with no errors, and verify that the full amount of memory is recognized by Windows.
3. Use the Windows Memory Diagnostic Tool to test memory. About how long did the test take? Were any errors reported?

Hands-On Project 4-6

Sabotaging and Repairing a Computer

Est. Time: 45 minutes
Core 1 Objective: 5.1

Open the computer case, and create a hardware problem with your computer that prevents it from booting without damaging a component. For example, you can disconnect a data cable or power cable or loosen a DIMM in a memory slot. Close the computer case, and restart the system. Describe the problem as if you were a user who does not know much about computer hardware. Power down the system, and fix the problem. Boot up the system, and verify that all is well.

Hands-On Project 4-7

Documenting an Intermittent Problem

Est. Time: 15 minutes
Core 1 Objective: 5.1

Intermittent problems can make troubleshooting challenging. The trick in diagnosing problems that come and go is to look for patterns or clues as to when the problems occur. If you or the user can't reproduce the problem at will, ask the user to keep a log of when the problems occur and exactly what messages appear. Tell the user that intermittent problems are the hardest to solve and might take some time, but you won't give up. Show the user how to take a screenshot of the error messages when they appear. It might also be appropriate to ask the user to email the screenshot to you. Do the following:

1. Use the Windows Snipping Tool to take a snip of your Windows desktop showing the Explorer window open. If you need help using the Snipping Tool, see Windows Help and Support, or search the web.
2. Save the snip and email it to your instructor.

Hands-On Project 4-8

Researching IT Support Sites

Est. Time: 45 minutes
Core 1 Objective: 5.1

The web is an excellent resource to use when problem-solving, and it's helpful to know which websites are trustworthy and useful. Access each of the websites listed in Table 4-6, and print one webpage from each site that shows information that might be useful for a support technician. If the site offers a free email newsletter, consider subscribing to it. Answer the following questions about these sites:

1. Which site can help you find out what type of RAM you can use on your computer?
2. Which site explains Moore's Law? What is Moore's Law?
3. Which site has a store with tools to repair computers?

4. Which site gives a review about registry cleaning software?

5. Which two sites allow you to post a question about computer repair to a forum?

6. Which site offers a tutorial to learn C programming?

7. Which site offers free antivirus software published by the site owners?

Table 4-6   Technical information websites

Organization	Website
CNET, Inc.	*cnet.com*
Experts Exchange (subscription site)	*go.experts-exchange.com*
F-Secure Corp.	*f-secure.com*
How Stuff Works	*howstuffworks.com*
How-To Geek	*howtogeek.com*
IFixit	*ifixit.com*
Kingston Technology (information about memory)	*kingston.com*
Microsoft Technical Resources	*support.microsoft.com* *answers.microsoft.com* *docs.microsoft.com*
PCWorld	*pcworld.com*
TechRepublic	*techrepublic.com*

List some other websites you found when answering these questions. Would you consider these websites authoritative and why?

Real Problems, Real Solutions

Real Problem 4-1

Replacing a Power Supply

Est. Time: 30 minutes
Core 1 Objective: 3.5

Suppose you turn on a system and everything is dead—no lights, nothing on the monitor screen, and no spinning fan or hard drive. You verify that the power to the system works, all power connections and power cords are securely connected, and all pertinent switches are turned on. You can assume the power supply has gone bad. It's time to replace it. To prepare for this situation in a real work environment, exchange power supplies with another student in your lab who is using a computer that has a power supply rated at about the same wattage as yours. Then verify that your system starts up and works.

Real Problem 4-2

Using Event Viewer to Troubleshoot a Hardware Problem

Est. Time: 15 minutes
Core 1 Objective: 5.1

Just about anything that happens in Windows is recorded in Event Viewer (eventvwr.msc). You can find information about events such as a hardware or network failure, OS error messages, or a device that has failed to start. When you first encounter a Windows, hardware, application, or security problem, get in the habit of checking Event Viewer as one of your first steps toward investigating the problem. To save time, first check the Administrative Events log because it filters out all events except Warning and Error events, which are the most useful for troubleshooting. Then start looking in the other logs if you can't find an event you know happened. Do the following to practice using Event Viewer:

1. Enter **eventvwr.msc** in the Windows search box or in a command prompt window. Event Viewer opens. Drill down into the **Custom Views** list in the left pane, and click **Administrative Events**. Scroll through the list of Error or Warning events, and list any that indicate a possible hardware problem. Make note of the first event in the list.

2. Disconnect the network cable.

3. In the Event Viewer menu bar, click **Action** and **Refresh** to refresh the list of events. How many new events do you see? Click each new event to see its details below the list of events until you find the event that tells you the network cable was unplugged. Figure 4-37 shows Event Viewer's Administrative Events view. Describe the details of the event about the network cable.

Figure 4-37   Use Event Viewer to find logs that can help you troubleshoot hardware problems

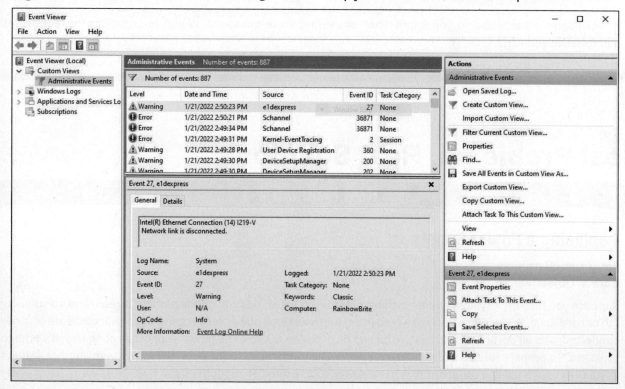

4. Tinker around with other hardware on your computer. What actions did you take that triggered a Warning or Error event in Event Viewer?

Real Problem 4-3

Troubleshooting a Hung System

Est. Time: 30 minutes
Core 1 Objective: 5.2

A user complains to you that the system hangs for no known reason. After asking them a few questions, you identify these symptoms:

- The system hangs after about 15–20 minutes of operation.
- When the system hangs, it doesn't matter which application is open or how many applications are open.
- When the system hangs, it appears as though power is turned off: There are no lights, spinning drives, or other evidence of power.

You suspect overheating might be the problem. To test your theory, you decide to do the following:

1. You want to verify that the user has not overclocked the system. How do you do that?
2. You decide to check for overheating by examining the temperature of the system immediately after the system is powered up and then again immediately after the system hangs. Describe the steps you take to do this.
3. After doing the first two steps, you decide overheating is the cause of the problem. What are four things you can do to fix the problem?

Module
5

Supporting Hard Drives and Other Storage Devices

Module Objectives

1 Describe and contrast technologies used inside a hard drive and how a computer communicates with a hard drive

2 Select and install a hard drive

3 Troubleshoot hard drives

4 Support optical drives, solid-state storage, and flash memory devices

Core 1 Certification Objectives

1.1 Given a scenario, install and configure laptop hardware and components.

3.1 Explain basic cable types and their connectors, features, and purposes.

3.3 Given a scenario, select and install storage devices.

5.3 Given a scenario, troubleshoot and diagnose problems with storage drives and RAID arrays.

Introduction

The hard drive is the most important permanent storage device in a computer, and supporting hard drives is one of the more important tasks of a computer support technician. This module introduces the different kinds of hard drive technologies and the ways a computer interfaces with a hard drive. You learn how to select and install the different types of hard drives and how to troubleshoot hard drive problems. You also learn how to select and install optical drives in desktops. This module also covers solid-state storage, including flash drives and memory cards, and which type to buy for a particular need.

Hard Drive Technologies and Interface Standards

> **Core 1 Objectives** 1.1, 3.1, 3.3

Note 1

In technical documentation, you might see a hard drive abbreviated as HDD (hard disk drive). However, this module uses the term "hard drive".

A hard disk drive (HDD), most often called a hard drive, is rated by its physical size, capacity, speed, technologies used inside the drive, and interface standards. First, we look at the features of a hard drive, and then we turn to how the drive interfaces with the computer.

Technologies and Form Factors of Hard Drives

> **Core 1 Objectives** 1.1, 3.1, 3.3

The two types of hardware technologies used inside the drive are magnetic and solid-state. Each hard drive technology uses several form factors, all discussed in this section of the module.

Magnetic Hard Drives

A **magnetic hard drive** has one, two, or more platters, or disks, that stack together and spin in unison inside a sealed metal housing that contains firmware to control reading and writing data to the drive and to communicate with the motherboard. The top and bottom of each disk have a **read/write head** that moves across the disk surface as all the disks rotate on a spindle (see Figure 5-1). All the read/write heads are controlled by an actuator, which moves the read/write heads across the disk surfaces in unison. The disk surfaces are covered with a magnetic medium that can hold data as magnetized spots. The spindle rotates at 5400, 7200, 10,000, or 15,000 RPM (revolutions per minute). The faster the spindle, the better the drive performs. Most consumer hard drives are rated at 5400 or 7200 RPM.

Figure 5-1   Inside a magnetic hard drive

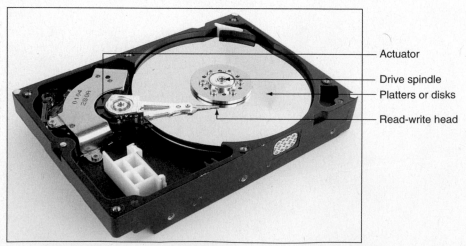

Data is organized on a magnetic hard drive in concentric circles called tracks (see Figure 5-2). Each track is divided into segments called sectors (also called records). Older hard drives used sectors that contained 512 bytes. Most current hard drives use 4096-byte sectors.

Figure 5-2 A hard drive is divided into tracks and sectors

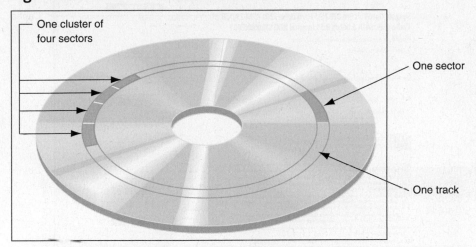

Form factors for internal magnetic hard drives are 3.5" for desktops and 2.5" for laptop computers. See Figure 5-3.

Figure 5-3 A magnetic hard drive for a desktop is larger than that used in laptops

Note **2**

Magnetic drives have a solid-state cache to improve performance, as seen referenced in the advertisement in Figure 5-4.

Figure 5-4   An advertisement for a hard drive

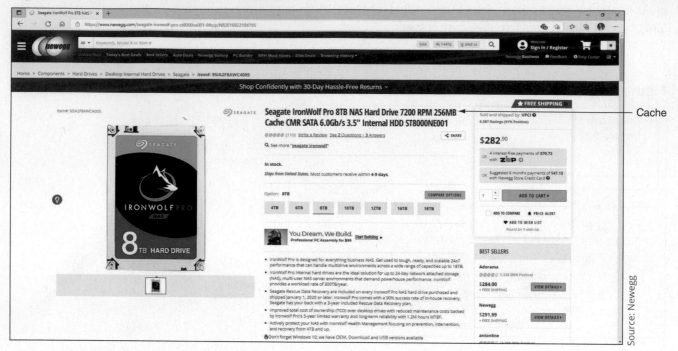

Source: Newegg

Solid-State Drives

A **solid-state drive (SSD)**, also called a **solid-state device**, is so named because it has no moving parts. The drives are built using nonvolatile memory, which is similar to that used for USB flash drives and memory cards. Recall that this type of memory does not lose its data even after the power is turned off.

In an SSD, flash memory is stored on chips on a circuit board inside the drive housing (see Figure 5-5). The chips contain grids of rows and columns with two transistors at each intersection that hold a 0 or 1 bit. One of these transistors is called a floating gate and accepts the 0 or 1 state according to a logic test called NAND (stands for "Not AND"). Therefore, the memory in an SSD is called **NAND flash memory**.

Transistors are limited to the number of times they can be reprogrammed. Therefore, the life span of an SSD is based on the number of write operations to the drive, and it can be expressed as TBW (terabytes written) or DWPD (drive writes per day) over its expected life. (The number of read operations does not affect the life span.) For example, one SSD manufacturer guarantees its SSDs for 70 TBW, which means 70 TB or 70,000 GB write operations for the duration of the drive. Another manufacturer might rate the drive as DWPD—for example, 70 GB write operations per day for five years. For normal use, a drive would not be used that much and would last much longer. However, the drive warranty is only for five years.

Figure 5-5   A circuit board with NAND memory inside an SSD

Source: istock.com/AlexLMX

Because flash memory is expensive, solid-state drives are much more expensive than magnetic hard drives of the same capacity, but they are faster and more reliable, last longer, and use less power than magnetic drives.

You need to be aware of four popular form factors used by SSDs:

- **2.5" SSD.** The 2.5" SSD (see the left side of Figure 5-6) is used in desktops and laptops and can mount in the same bays and use the same cable connectors as those used by 2.5" magnetic drives.
- **M.2 SSD card.** The M.2 SSD form factor (see the right side of Figure 5-6) is a small M.2 card that uses the motherboard M.2 slot you learned about in the module "All About Motherboards."

Figure 5-6   Solid-state drives in two form factors: 2.5" SSD and two lengths of M.2 SSD cards

2.5" SSD

M.2 SSDs

5

- **mSATA SSD.** The mSATA, or miniSATA, uses SATA Revision 3.x and is a smaller, thinner version of a full-sized SATA SSD without a casing (see Figure 5-7). The mSATA and mini PCIe slots share the same form factor, but not all hosts or motherboards support both in the same slot. Always refer to your motherboard documentation to find out if the slot will support an mSATA SSD.
- **PCI Express SSD expansion card.** An SSD can be embedded on a PCIe expansion card (see Figure 5-8). These drives generally have a faster interface with the CPU than 2.5" SSDs and may also be faster than an M.2 SSD, depending on how the M.2 slot interfaces with the CPU. A PCIe SSD uses the NVMe interface discussed later in the module.

Figure 5-7   An mSATA card

Source: kingscor.com

Hard Drive Performance

There are three primary measurements for hard drive performance in both magnetic hard drives and SSDs. You can use these measurements to decide which hard drive best meets the needs of the computer or to diagnose a problem with the hard drive performance. The measurements are as follows:

- **Throughput** is typically measured in MB/sec, and it describes the amount of data that flows through a point in the data path over one second's time. A higher throughput means better performance. This measurement is important for streaming large files, such as videos.

Figure 5-8   This SSD by Plextor is embedded on a PCIe ×4 version 3.0 expansion card and uses the NVMe interface standard

Source: Plextor

- **IOPS (input/output operations per second)** measures the amount of read or write operations performed in one second. A higher IOPS means better performance.
- **Latency** measures the time required to process a data request or transaction. A lower latency time means better performance.

Logical Block Addressing and Capacity

Before a magnetic drive leaves the factory, sector markings are written to it in a process called **low-level formatting**. (This formatting is different from the high-level formatting that Windows does after a drive is installed in a computer.) The hard drive firmware, BIOS/UEFI on the motherboard, and the OS use a simple sequential numbering system called logical block addressing (LBA) to address all the sectors on the drive. SSDs are marked into blocks, which are communicated to the motherboard and OS; they read/write to the drive in blocks, just as with magnetic drives. SSDs are also low-level formatted before they leave the factory.

The size of each block and the total number of blocks on the drive determine the drive capacity. Today's drive capacities are usually measured in GB (gigabytes) or TB (terabytes, each of which is 1024 gigabytes). Magnetic drives are generally much larger in capacity at a lower cost than SSDs.

Note 3

Many solid-state drive manufacturers reserve blocks on the drive that are used when other blocks begin to prove they are no longer reliable. Also, a technique called **wear leveling** assures that the logical block addressing does not always address the same physical blocks in order to distribute write operations more evenly across the device.

S.M.A.R.T.

You need to be aware of one more technology supported by both SSD and magnetic hard drives: S.M.A.R.T. (self-monitoring, analysis, and reporting technology), which is used to predict when a drive is likely to fail. System BIOS/UEFI uses S.M.A.R.T. to monitor drive performance, temperature, and other factors. For magnetic drives, it monitors disk spin-up time, distance between the head and the disk, and other mechanical activities of the drive. Many SSDs report to the BIOS/UEFI the number of write operations, which is the best measurement of when the drive might fail. If S.M.A.R.T. suspects a drive failure is about to happen, it displays a warning message. S.M.A.R.T. can be enabled and disabled in BIOS/UEFI setup.

Now let's look at how the drive's firmware or controller communicates with the motherboard and processor.

Note 4

Malware has been known to give false S.M.A.R.T. alerts.

Interface Standards Used by Hard Drives

Core 1 Objectives 3.1, 3.3

Four interface standards used by hard drives include IDE (outdated), SCSI (also outdated), SATA (the most popular current standard), and NVMe (the latest and fastest standard.)

Exam Tip ✔

The A+ Core 1 exam expects you to recognize the cables and connectors for the IDE, SCSI, SATA, eSATA, and NVMe interfaces. Given a scenario, you may be expected to decide which interface to use (PCIe, SATA, or NVMe) and be able to install and configure devices that use these interfaces.

IDE

Years ago, hard drives used the Parallel ATA (PATA) standards, also called the **IDE (Integrated Drive Electronics)** standards, to connect to a motherboard. PATA allowed for one or two IDE connectors on a motherboard, each using a 40-pin data cable. Two drives could connect to one cable (see Figure 5-9).

Two types of IDE cables are the older cable with a 40-pin connector and 40 wires and a newer cable with the same 40-pin connector and 80 thinner wires (see Figure 5-10). The additional 40 wires reduce crosstalk (interference that can lead to corrupted communication) on the cable. The later IDE standards required the 80-wire cable. The maximum recommended length of an IDE cable is 18". The IDE standard is seldom used today.

Figure 5-9   A computer's hard drive subsystem using an IDE interface to the motherboard

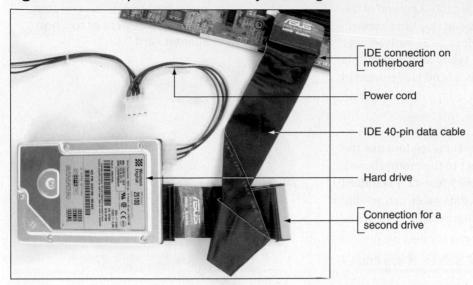

- IDE connection on motherboard
- Power cord
- IDE 40-pin data cable
- Hard drive
- Connection for a second drive

5

Figure 5-10   In comparing the 80-conductor cable with the 40-conductor cable, note they are about the same width, but the 80-conductor cable has twice as many fine wires

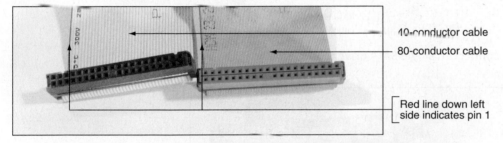

- 40-conductor cable
- 80-conductor cable
- Red line down left side indicates pin 1

SCSI

In the distant past, a few personal computer hard drives designed for high-end workstations used the **SCSI (Small Computer System Interface)** standard. SCSI (pronounced "scuzzy") can support up to seven or 15 SCSI-compliant devices in a system. Most often, a SCSI expansion card (see Figure 5-11), called the SCSI host adapter, used a PCIe slot and provided one external connector for an external SCSI device, such as a SCSI printer, and one internal connector

Figure 5-11   This Adaptec SCSI card uses a PCIe ×1 slot and supports up to 15 devices in a SCSI chain

Source: Courtesy of PMC-Sierra, Inc.

for internal SCSI devices, such as hard drives and optical drives. Figure 5-12 shows a long SCSI cable. One end of the cable connects to the host adapter, and the other connectors are used for external SCSI devices. SCSI evolved over the years with various connector types and cables. It is now sometimes found on servers but is no longer used in personal computers.

SATA

Most hard drives in today's personal computers use the SATA interface standards to connect to the motherboard. The serial ATA or SATA (pronounced "say-ta") standard uses a serial data path, and a SATA data cable can accommodate a single SATA drive (see Figure 5-13). The three SATA standards are as follows:

- SATA Revision 3.x, rated at 6 Gb/sec, is sometimes called SATA 6 Gb/s.
- SATA Revision 2.x, rated at 3 Gb/sec, is sometimes called SATA 3 Gb/s.
- SATA Revision 1.x, rated at 1.5 Gb/sec, is seldom seen today.

Figure 5-12   This 50-pin external SCSI-2 cable can connect several SCSI peripheral devices or to a host adapter card

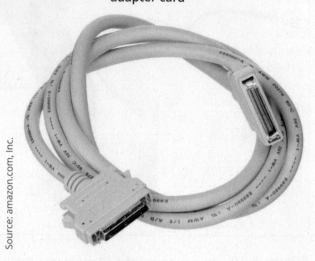

Source: amazon.com, Inc.

Figure 5-13   A SATA cable connects a single SATA drive to a motherboard SATA connector

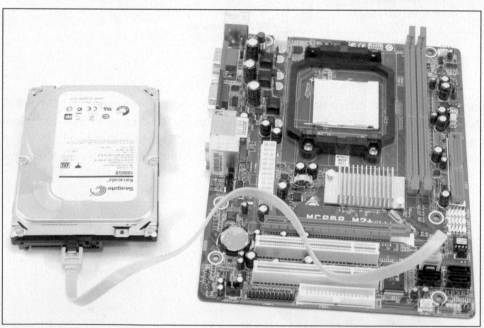

Note 5

Interface standards for drives define data speeds and transfer methods between the drive controller, the BIOS/UEFI, the chipset on the motherboard, and the OS. The standards also define the type of cables and connectors used by the drive and the motherboard or expansion cards. SATA cables work for all three SATA standards.

SATA interfaces are used by all types of drives, including hard drives, CD, DVD, and Blu-ray. SATA supports hot-swapping, also called hot-plugging. With **hot-swapping**, you can connect and disconnect a drive while the system is running. Hard drives that can be hot-swapped cost significantly more than regular hard drives and are generally used in servers or other network storage devices.

A SATA drive connects to one internal SATA connector on the motherboard by way of a 7-pin SATA data cable and uses a 15-pin SATA power connector (see Figure 5-14). An internal SATA data cable can be up to 1 meter in length. A motherboard might have two or more SATA connectors; use the connectors in the order recommended in the motherboard user guide. For example, for the four connectors shown in Figure 5-15, the motherboard user guide recommends using the red ones before the black ones.

Figure 5-14   A SATA data cable and SATA power cable

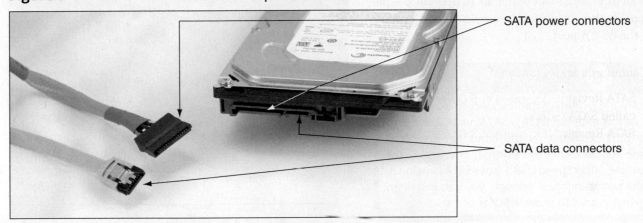

SATA power connectors

SATA data connectors

Figure 5-15   This motherboard has two black and two red SATA II ports

The SATA 3.2 revision allows for PCIe and SATA to work together in a technology called **SATA Express**, which uses a new SATA connector. The speed of SATA Express is about three times that of SATA 3.0. However, because SATA Express is not as fast as NVMe, hard drive manufacturers have been slow to invest in SATA Express drives, and only a few motherboards have SATA Express slots. Figure 5-16 shows a

Figure 5-16   One SATA Express port is grouped with two normal SATA ports

SATA Express connector

Two SATA connectors grouped with the SATA Express connector

board with seven SATA ports. When the one SATA Express port is used, the two normal SATA ports grouped with it are disabled.

In addition to internal SATA connectors, the motherboard or an expansion card can provide external SATA (eSATA) ports for external drives (see Figure 5-17). External SATA drives use a special external shielded SATA cable up to 2 meters long. Seven-pin eSATA ports run at the same speed as the internal ports using SATA Revision 1.x, 2.x, or 3.x standards. The eSATA port is shaped differently from an internal SATA connector to prevent people from using the unshielded internal SATA data cables with the eSATA port.

Figure 5-17   Two eSATA ports on a motherboard

> **Note 6**
>
> External hard drives can connect to a computer by way of external SATA (eSATA) or USB. Be sure the port provided by the computer uses the same standard that the external drive uses—for example, SuperSpeed USB 3.0 or eSATA Revision 3. If the port is not fast enough, you can install an expansion card to provide faster ports.

When purchasing a SATA hard drive, keep in mind that the SATA standards for the drive and the motherboard need to match. If either the drive or the motherboard uses a slower SATA standard than the other device, the system will run at the slower speed.

NVMe

Whereas the SATA interface is used by both magnetic and solid-state drives, the newer **NVMe (Non-Volatile Memory Express or NVM Express)** interface standard is used only by SSDs. Magnetic hard drives are slow enough that a SATA interface is adequate, but SSDs are so fast that the SATA interface becomes a performance bottleneck. NVMe uses the faster PCI Express ×4 interface to communicate with the processor. Here are the comparisons:

- The most common SATA standard, SATA Revision 3.x, transfers data at 6 Gb/sec.
- NVMe uses one of two common PCIe standards, PCIe 4.0 or PCIe 3.0, which transfers data at 2 GB/sec per lane and 1 GB/sec per lane, respectively. Converted from gigabyte to gigabit, PCIe 3.0 transfers data at 8 Gb/sec per lane. NVMe uses four lanes (PCIe ×4), yielding a transfer rate of 8 Gb/sec x 4 = 32 Gb/sec. Therefore, the NVMe transfer rate of 32 Gb/sec is more than five times faster than SATA Revision 3.x's transfer rate of 6 Gb/sec. PCIe 4.0 is twice as fast as PCIe 3.0.

The PCIe NVMe interface might be used in three ways:

- **PCIe expansion card.** The NVMe interface is used by SSDs embedded on PCIe expansion cards. Refer back to Figure 5-8.
- **U.2 or U.3 slot.** A 2.5" SSD can support the NVMe interface using a U.2 or U.3 connector on the drive and a U.2 or U.3 port on the motherboard. A U.3 drive is compatible with a U.2 or U.3 port on a motherboard, but a U.2 drive is only compatible with a U.2 port on a motherboard. See Figure 5-18. These drives might be advertised as a PCIe drive, U.2/U.3 drive, or NVMe solid-state drive.

- **M.2 port.** An M.2 SSD card might use the NVMe or SATA standard. Recall that an M.2 slot on a motherboard might interface with the processor using the USB, SATA, or PCIe bus. If the slot uses the PCIe bus and the M.2 SSD card uses the NVMe interface, the 32 Gb/sec transfer rate can be attained. If your motherboard does not have an M.2 port, you can use a PCIe adapter card (also called a carrier card) to provide M.2 ports for M.2 SSDs (see Figure 5-19).

Most motherboards today have PCIe expansion slots, and M.2 slots are more common on motherboards than U.2 ports. For M.2 slots, check the motherboard documentation to find out which bus the M.2 slot uses and whether you can boot the system from the SSD card installed in the slot. Some motherboards, such as the ASUS Prime Z370P, provide two M.2 slots, which can be configured in a RAID array. For this board, you can purchase the ASUS Hyper M.2 ×16 card (see Figure 5-20) to install in the first PCIe ×16 slot and install up to four M.2 SSDs on the card. These four drives can be configured in a RAID array, and you can use BIOS/UEFI to enable the card so you can boot the system from this RAID array of SSDs.

You learn more about RAID later in this module.

Now that you know about the various hard drive technologies and interfaces, let's see how to select and install a hard drive.

Figure 5-18 A U.2 2.5" SSD uses the NVMe and PCIe interface standards and connects to a U.2 port on the motherboard

Source: Micron Technology, Inc

Figure 5-19 A PCIe ×4 adapter card provides one M.2 slot for an M.2 SSD

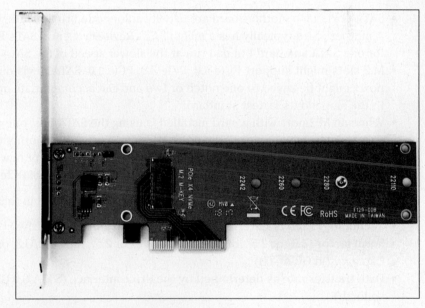

Figure 5-20 Install up to four M.2 SSDs in a bootable RAID array on this adapter card by ASUS

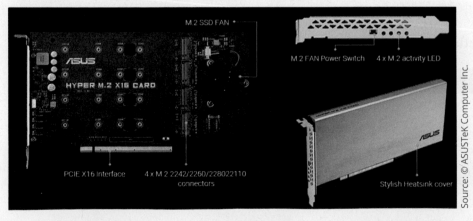

Source: © ASUSTeK Computer Inc.

How to Select and Install Hard Drives

 Core 1 Objectives 1.1, 3.1, 3.3

In this section of the module, you learn how to select a hard drive for your system. Then you learn the details of installing a SATA drive. Next, you learn how to deal with using removable bays, the problem of installing a hard drive in a bay that is too wide for it, and special considerations for installing a hard drive in a laptop. You also learn how to set up a RAID system.

Selecting a Hard Drive

 Core 1 Objective 3.3

When selecting a hard drive, keep in mind that to get the best performance from the system, the motherboard and drive must support the same interface standard. If they don't support the same standard, they revert to the slower standard that both can use, or the drive will not work at all. There's no point in buying an expensive hard drive with features that your system cannot support.

Therefore, when making purchasing decisions, you need to know the standards for the motherboard slot or port and perhaps for the expansion card that might provide the drive interface. Find out by reading the motherboard manual. Here are some options for compatibility:

- SATA ports on a motherboard are usually color-coded to indicate which SATA standard the port supports. A motherboard typically has a mix of SATA Revision 3.x and SATA Revision 2.x ports. A SATA drive is rated for one SATA standard but can run at the slower speed of the SATA port.
- M.2 slots might support PCIe 4.0, PCIe 3.0, PCIe 2.0, SATA Revision 2.x, SATA Revision 3.x, or USB 3.0. M.2 ports might be keyed to one notch or two and can accommodate up to three sizes of cards. Match the card to the slot and its fastest standard.
- When an M.2 port with a card installed is using the SATA bus, one of the SATA ports might be disabled. Be sure to know which one so you don't attempt to use it for another device.
- NVMe expansion cards most likely use a PCIe ×4 version 3.0 or newer slot. A motherboard might have multiple PCIe ×4 slots. Use one that supports the latest version of PCIe.

Besides compatibility, consider the features already discussed in this module when purchasing a hard drive:

- Technology (SSD is faster and lasts longer than a magnetic drive)
- Form factor (3.5" or 2.5" for magnetic drives or 2.5", M.2, U.2/U.3, or PCIe card for SSDs)
- Capacity (in GB or TB)
- Data transfer rate as determined by the drive interface (SATA 6.0 Gb/s, SATA 3.0 Gb/s, PCIe ×4 32 Gb/s, and so forth)
- For magnetic drives, the spindle speed (5400, 7200, 10,000, or 15,000 RPM), which affects performance

Some hard drive manufacturers are listed in Table 5-1. Most manufacturers of memory also make solid-state drives.

Table 5-1 Hard drive manufacturers

Manufacturer	Website
Kingston Technology (SSD only)	kingston.com
Samsung (SSD only)	samsung.com
Seagate Technology (magnetic and SSD)	seagate.com
Western Digital (magnetic and SSD)	westerndigital.com
Toshiba (magnetic and SSD)	toshiba.com

Now let's turn our attention to the step-by-step process of installing a SATA drive.

Steps to Install a Sata Drive

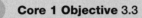 Core 1 Objective 3.3

In Figure 5-21, you can see the back of a SATA hard drive. A SATA drive might have jumpers used to set features such as the ability to power up from standby mode. Most likely, if jumpers are present on a SATA drive, the factory has set them as they should be and advises you not to change them.

Figure 5-21   The rear of a SATA drive

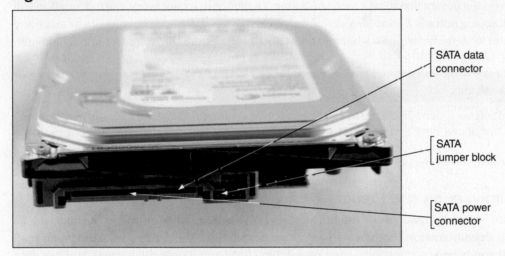

- SATA data connector
- SATA jumper block
- SATA power connector

Exam Tip ✔

The A+ Core 1 exam expects you to know how to configure SATA devices in a system. What you learn In this module about installing a SATA hard drive in a system also applies to installing a SATA optical drive. Hard drives and optical drives use a SATA data connector and a power connector.

Some SATA drives have two power connectors, as does the one in Figure 5-22. Choose between the SATA power connector (which is preferred) and the legacy 4-pin Molex connector, but never install two power cords to the drive at the same time because it could damage the drive.

Figure 5-22   The rear of a SATA drive with two power connectors

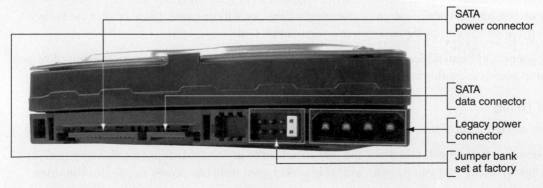

- SATA power connector
- SATA data connector
- Legacy power connector
- Jumper bank set at factory

Step 1: As Best You Can, Protect the User's Data

Recall from the module "Power Supplies and Troubleshooting Computer Problems" that before you work on solving any computer problem, you need to establish your priorities. Your first priority might be the user's data. If the user tells you there is important data on the current hard drive and you can boot from it, back up the data to other media and verify that you can access the data on that media. If the current hard drive will not boot, recall you can move it to another computer and transfer data to other media. Make every effort possible to protect the user's data before you move on to the next step.

Step 2: Know Your Starting Point

As with replacing or installing any other devices, make sure you know your starting point before you begin installing a hard drive. Answer these questions: How is your system configured? Is everything working properly? Verify which of your system's devices are working before installing a new one. Later, if a device does not work, the information will help you isolate the problem. Keeping notes is a good idea whenever you install new hardware or software or make any other changes to your computer system. Write down what you know about the system that might be important later.

> **Note 7**
>
> When installing hardware and software, don't install too many things at once. If something goes wrong, you won't know what's causing the problem. Install one device, start the system, and confirm that the new device is working before installing another.

Step 3: Read the Documentation and Prepare Your Work Area

Before you take anything apart, carefully read all the documentation for the drive and controller card, as well as the part of your motherboard documentation that covers hard drive installation. Make sure you can visualize all the steps in the installation. If you have any questions, keep researching until you locate the answer. You can do a Google search, have a chat session with technical support, or ask a knowledgeable friend for help. As you get your questions answered, you might discover that what you are installing will not work on your computer, but that is better than coping with hours of frustration and a disabled computer. You cannot always anticipate every problem, but at least you can know that you made your best effort to understand everything in advance. What you learn with thorough preparation pays off every time!

You're now ready to set out your tools, documentation, new hardware, and notebook. Remember the basic rules concerning static electricity. Be sure to protect against electrostatic discharge (ESD) by wearing an ESD strap during the installation. You also should avoid working on carpet in the winter when there's a lot of static electricity.

Some added precautions for working with a hard drive are as follows:

- Handle the drive carefully.
- Do not touch any exposed circuitry or chips.
- Prevent other people from touching exposed microchips on the drive.
- When you first take the drive out of the static-protective package, touch the package containing the drive to a screw holding an expansion card or cover, or to a metal part of the computer case, for at least two seconds. This drains the static electricity from the package and from your body.
- If you must set down the drive outside the static-protective package, place it component-side-up on a flat surface.
- Do not place the drive on the computer case cover or on a metal table.

If you're assembling a new system, it's usually best to install drives before you install the motherboard so you do not accidentally bump sensitive motherboard components with the drives.

Step 4: Install the Drive

Now you're ready to get started. Follow these steps to install the drive in the case:

1. Shut down the computer, unplug it, and press the power button to drain residual power. Remove the computer case cover. Check that you have an available power cord from the power supply for the drive.

Note 8

If there are not enough power cords from a power supply, you can purchase a Y connector that can add another power cord.

2. For 2.5" or 3.5" drives, decide which bay will hold the drive by examining the locations of the drive bays and the length of the data cables and power cords. Bays designed for hard drives do not have access to the outside of the case, unlike bays for optical drives. Also, some bays are wider than others to accommodate wide drives such as a DVD drive. Will the data cable reach the drives and the motherboard connector? If not, rearrange your plan for locating the drive in a bay, or purchase a custom-length data cable. Some bays are stationary, meaning the drive is installed inside the bay because it stays in the case. Other bays are removable; you remove the bay, install the drive in it, and then return the bay to the case.

3. For a stationary bay, slide the drive in the bay, and then use a screwdriver to secure one side of the drive with one or two short screws (see Figure 5-23). It's best to use two screws so the drive will not move in the bay, but sometimes a bay only provides a place for a single screw on each side. Some drive bays provide one or two tabs that you pull out before you slide the drive in the bay and then push in to secure the drive. Another option is a sliding tab (see Figure 5-24) that is used to secure the drive. Pull the tab back, slide in the drive, and push the tab forward to secure the drive.

Figure 5-23   Secure one side of the drive with one or two screws

Figure 5-24   This drive bay uses tabs to secure the drive

Caution ❗

Be sure the screws are not too long. If they are, you can screw too far into the drive housing, which will damage the drive itself.

4. When using screws to secure the drive, carefully turn the case over without disturbing the drive, and put one or two screws on the other side of the drive (see Figure 5-25). To best secure the drive in the case, use two screws on each side of the drive.

Figure 5-25   Secure the other side of the drive with one or two screws

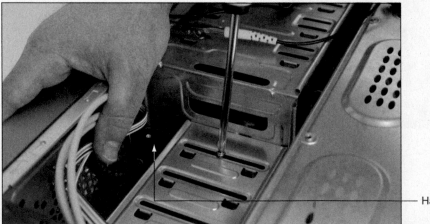

Hard drive

Note 9

Do not allow torque to stress the drive. In other words, don't force a drive into a space that is too small for it. Also keep in mind that placing two screws in diagonal positions across the drive can place pressure diagonally on the drive.

5. Check the motherboard documentation to find out which SATA connectors on the board to use first. For example, five SATA connectors are shown in Figure 5-26. The documentation says the two blue SATA connectors support 6.0 Gb/sec and slower speeds, and the two black and one red SATA connectors support 3.0 Gb/sec and slower speeds. On this board, be sure to connect your fastest hard drive to a blue connector. For some boards, the hard drive that has the bootable OS installed must be connected to the first SATA connector, which is usually labeled SATA 0. For both the drive and the motherboard, you can only plug the cable into the connector in one direction. A SATA cable might provide a clip on the connector to secure it (see Figure 5-27).

Figure 5-26   Five SATA connectors support different SATA standards

Figure 5-27   A clip on a SATA connector secures the connection

6. Connect a 15-pin SATA power connector or 4-pin Molex power connector from the power supply to the drive (see Figure 5-28).

Figure 5-28   Connect the SATA power cord to the drive

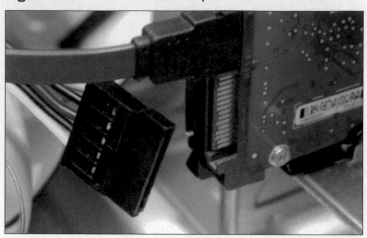

7. Check all your connections and power up the system.

8. To verify that the drive was recognized correctly, enter BIOS/UEFI setup and look for the drive. Figure 5-29 shows a BIOS/UEFI setup screen on one system that has four SATA connectors. A hard drive is installed on one of the faster yellow SATA connectors, and a DVD drive is installed on one of the slower brown SATA connectors.

Figure 5-29   A BIOS/UEFI setup screen showing a SATA hard drive and DVD drive installed

Source: American Megatrends, Inc.

Note 10

If the drive light on the front panel of the computer case does not work after you install a new drive, try reversing the LED wire on the front panel header on the motherboard.

You are now ready to prepare the hard drive for first use. If you are installing a new hard drive in a system that will be used for a new Windows installation, boot from the Windows setup DVD or USB drive, and follow the directions on the screen to install Windows on the new drive. If you are installing a second hard drive in a system that already has Windows installed on the first hard drive, use the Disk Management utility in Windows to prepare the drive for first use (called partitioning and formatting the drive).

Installing a Drive in a Removable Bay

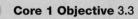

Core 1 Objective 3.3

Now let's see how a drive installation goes when you are dealing with a removable bay. Figure 5-30 shows a computer case with a removable bay that has a fan at the front of the bay to help keep the drives cool. (The case manufacturer calls the bay a fan cage.) The bay is anchored to the case with three black locking pins. The third locking pin from the bottom of the case is disconnected in the photo.

Figure 5-30   The removable bay has a fan in front and is anchored to the
case with locking pins

> Three locking pins
> used to hold the
> bay in the case

Unplug the cage fan from its power source. Turn the handle on each locking pin counterclockwise to remove it. Then slide the bay to the front and out of the case. Insert the hard drive in the bay, and use two screws on each side to anchor the drive in the bay (see Figure 5-31). Slide the bay back into the case, and reinstall the locking pins. Plug in the cage fan power cord.

Figure 5-31   Install the hard drive in the bay using two screws on
each side of the drive

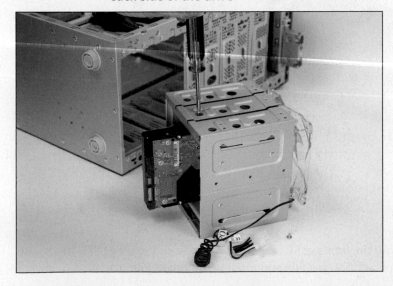

Installing a Small Drive in a Wide Bay

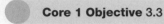 Core 1 Objective 3.3

Because 2.5" drives are smaller than the bays designed for 3.5" drives, you'll need a universal bay kit to fit these drives into most desktop computer cases. These inexpensive kits should create a tailor-made fit. In Figure 5-32, you can see how the universal bay kit adapter works. The adapter spans the distance between the sides of the drive and the bay. Figure 5-33 shows a SATA SSD with the brackets connected.

Figure 5-32   Use the universal bay kit to make the drive fit the bay

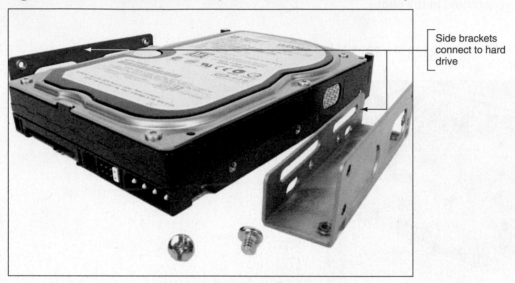

Side brackets connect to hard drive

Figure 5-33   An SSD with a bay kit connected

Installing An M.2 SSD Card

 Core 1 Objective 3.3

As always, read the motherboard manual to find out the types of M.2 cards the board supports. For SSD cards, the manual or motherboard website is likely to list specific SSD brands and models the board can use. Also be aware

that if the M.2 slot is used and the SSD card uses the SATA interface standard, it might disable a SATA Express or SATA connector on the board. Do the following to install the card:

1. Measure the length of the card, and decide which screw hole for the M.2 slot the card requires. Install a standoff in the hole.

2. Slide the card straight into the slot but not from an upward angle because you might bend open the slot and prevent a good connection. Make sure the card is installed securely in the slot. In Figure 5-34, you can see the card has two notches and can be used in either a B-key M.2 slot (the key on the left of the slot) or an M-key M.2 slot (the key on the right of the slot). This motherboard has an M-key slot. Also notice in the figure that the standoff is installed, ready to secure the card to the board.

Figure 5-34   Slide an SSD card straight into an M.2 slot

Standoff

3. Install the one screw in the standoff to secure the card to the motherboard. Don't overtighten the screw because you might damage the card.

4. Start the system, go into BIOS/UEFI setup, and make sure the M.2 card is recognized by the system. If it will be the boot device, make the appropriate changes in BIOS/UEFI.

Installing a Hard Drive in a Laptop

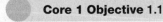 **Core 1 Objective 1.1**

When purchasing and installing an internal hard drive or optical drive in a laptop, see the laptop manufacturer's documentation about specific capacities, form factors, and connectors that will fit the laptop. Before deciding to replace a hard drive, consider these issues:

• Be aware of voiding a warranty if you don't follow the laptop manufacturer's directions.
• If the old drive has crashed, you'll need the recovery media to reinstall Windows and the drivers. Make sure you have the recovery media before you start.
• If you are upgrading from a lower-capacity drive to a higher-capacity drive, you need to consider how you will transfer data from the old drive to the new one. One way is to use a USB-to-SATA converter. Using this converter, both drives can be up and working on the laptop at the same time, so you can copy files.

Here is what you need to know when shopping for a laptop hard drive:

- Purchase a hard drive recommended by the laptop manufacturer. The drive might be magnetic or SSD, and you'll need a 2.5" drive. Some high-end laptops use an M.2 SSD.
- For a 2.5" drive, expect it to use the SATA interface. SATA data and power connectors on a laptop hard drive look the same as those in a desktop installation.

Older laptop computers required that you disassemble the laptop to replace a hard drive. With newer laptops, you should be able to easily replace a drive. For the laptop shown in Figure 5-35, first power down the system; remove peripherals, including the AC adapter; and remove the battery pack. On the bottom of the laptop, remove a screw that holds the drive cover in place (see Figure 5-35).

Figure 5-35 This one screw holds the hard drive cover in position

Caution ❗

To protect sensitive components, never open a laptop case without first unplugging the AC adapter and removing the battery pack.

Remove the plastic cover, revealing the drive. Lift and remove the hard drive from the case and bay, and insert the new drive (see Figure 5-36). Next, replace the cover and the screw, then power up the system.

When the system boots up, BIOS/UEFI should recognize the new drive and search for an operating system. If the drive is new, boot from the Windows setup or recovery DVD or USB flash drive, and install the OS.

Figure 5-36 Lift the drive out of the case and then the bay

Note 11

It is possible to give general directions on desktop computer repair that apply to all kinds of brands, models, and systems. Not so with laptops. Learning to repair laptops involves learning unique ways to assemble, disassemble, and repair components for specific brands and models of laptops.

Setting Up Hardware RAID

Core 1 Objective 3.3

For most personal computers, a single hard drive works independently of any other installed drives. A technology that configures two or more hard drives to work together as an array of drives is called **RAID (redundant array of inexpensive disks** or **redundant array of independent disks)**. Here are two reasons you might consider using RAID:

- To improve performance by writing data to two or more hard drives so that a single drive is not excessively used.

- To improve **fault tolerance**, which is a computer's ability to respond to a fault or catastrophe, such as a hardware failure or power outage, so data is not lost. If data is important enough to justify the cost, you can protect the data by continuously writing two copies of it, each to a different hard drive. This method is most often used on high-end, expensive file servers, but it is occasionally appropriate for a single-user workstation.

Types of RAID

Several types of RAID exist; the four most commonly used are RAID 0, RAID 1, RAID 5, and RAID 10. The following is a brief description of each, including another method of two disks working together called spanning. Four methods are diagrammed in Figure 5-37.

Figure 5-37   Ways that hard drives can work together

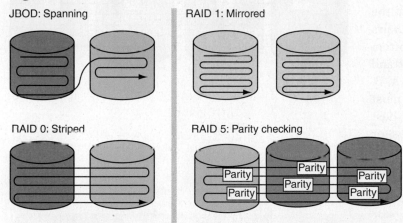

JBOD: Spanning

RAID 1: Mirrored

RAID 0: Striped

RAID 5: Parity checking

- **Spanning**, sometimes called JBOD (just a bunch of disks), uses two hard drives to hold a single Windows volume, such as drive E:. Data is written to the first drive, and when it is full, the data continues to be written to the second. The purpose of spanning is to increase the disk space available for a single volume.

Note 12

A Windows volume is a logical hard drive that is assigned a drive letter like C: or E:. The volume can be part or all of a physical hard drive or can span multiple physical hard drives. Earlier in the module, you learned about the ASUS Prime Z370-P motherboard, which has two M.2 slots. When you install matching M.2 SSD cards in these slots, you can use BIOS/UEFI setup to configure these two cards in a RAID 0 array, which creates a superfast single logical hard drive or Windows volume.

- **RAID 0** also uses two or more physical disks to increase the disk space available for a single volume. RAID 0 writes to the physical disks evenly across both disks so that neither receives all the activity; this improves performance. Windows calls RAID 0 a **striped volume**. To understand that term, think of data striped—or written—across several hard drives. RAID 0 is preferred to spanning.
- **RAID 1** is a type of mirroring that duplicates data on one drive to another drive and is used for fault tolerance. Each drive has its own volume, and the two volumes are called mirrors. If one drive fails, the other continues to operate, and data is not lost. Hot-swapping is allowed in RAID 1. Windows calls RAID 1 a **mirrored volume**.

- **RAID 5** stripes data and parity information across three or more drives and uses parity checking, so if one drive fails, the other drives can recreate the data stored on the failed drive by using the parity information. Data is not duplicated; therefore, RAID 5 makes better use of volume capacity. RAID 5 drives increase performance and provide fault tolerance. Hot-swapping is allowed in RAID 5. Windows calls these drives **RAID 5 volumes**.

- **RAID 10**, also called **RAID 1+0** and pronounced "RAID one zero" (not "RAID ten"), is a combination of RAID 1 and RAID 0. It takes at least four disks for RAID 10. Data is mirrored across pairs of disks, as shown at the top of Figure 5-38. In addition, the two pairs of disks are striped, as shown at the bottom of Figure 5-38. To help you better understand RAID 10, notice the data labeled as A, A, B, B across the first stripe. RAID 10 is the most expensive solution that provides the best redundancy and performance and allows for hot-swapping.

Figure 5-38   RAID 1 and RAID 10

RAID 1: Two pairs of mirrored disks

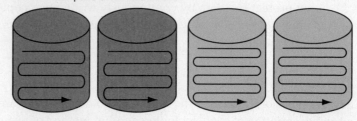

RAID 10: Mirrored and striped

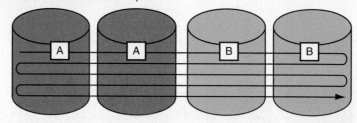

Exam Tip ✔

The A+ Core 1 exam may give you a scenario and expect you to select the appropriate RAID 0, RAID 1, RAID 5, or RAID 10 configuration. You are also expected to be able to install and configure a RAID system.

All RAID configurations can be accomplished at the hardware level (called hardware RAID) or at the operating system level (called software RAID). In Windows, you can use the Disk Management utility to group hard drives in a RAID array. Windows also offers the Storage Spaces utility to implement software RAID. However, software RAID is considered an unstable solution and is not recommended by Microsoft. Configuring RAID at the hardware level is considered best practice because if Windows gets corrupted, the hardware might still be able to protect the data. Also, hardware RAID is generally faster than software RAID.

How to Implement Hardware RAID

Hardware RAID can be set up by using a RAID-enabled motherboard that is managed in BIOS/UEFI setup or by using a RAID controller card. When using a RAID controller card, run the software that comes with the card to set up your RAID array.

For best performance in any RAID system, all hard drives in an array should be identical in brand, size, speed, and other features. If you use different hard drives, the RAID system treats all hard drives the same as the slowest and smallest hard drive. Also, if Windows will be installed on a hard drive that is part of a RAID array, RAID must be implemented before Windows is installed because all data on the drives will be lost when you configure RAID. As with installing any hardware, first read the documentation that comes with the motherboard or RAID controller and follow those specific directions rather than the general guidelines given here. Make sure you understand which RAID configurations the board or card supports.

Exam Tip ✔

The A+ Core 1 exam expects you to be able to set up hardware RAID given a scenario.

For one motherboard that has six SATA connectors that support RAID 0, 1, 5, and 10, here are the general directions to install three hard drives in a RAID 5 array:

1. Install the three SATA drives in the computer case, and connect each drive to a SATA connector on the motherboard (see Figure 5-39). To help keep the drives cool, install them with an empty bay between each drive.

2. Boot the system and enter BIOS/ UEFI setup. On the Advanced setup screen, verify that the three drives are recognized. Select the option to configure SATA Mode Selection, and then select RAID from the menu (see Figure 5-40). Press the **F10** key to save your changes and reset.

Figure 5-39 Install three matching hard drives in a system

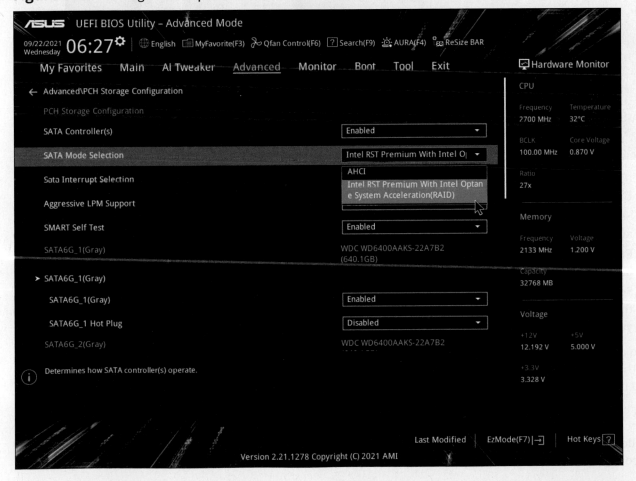

Three hard drives

Figure 5-40 Configure SATA ports on the motherboard to enable RAID

3. When the system reboots, enter BIOS/UEFI again. On the Advanced page, select **Intel(R) Rapid Storage Technology**. Notice that in the information area, the three drives are recognized, and their current status is Non-RAID Disk.

4. Select **Create RAID Volume**. On the next screen, shown in Figure 5-41, enter a RAID volume name (FileServer1 in our example).

Figure 5-41   Use a BIOS/UEFI utility to create a RAID array

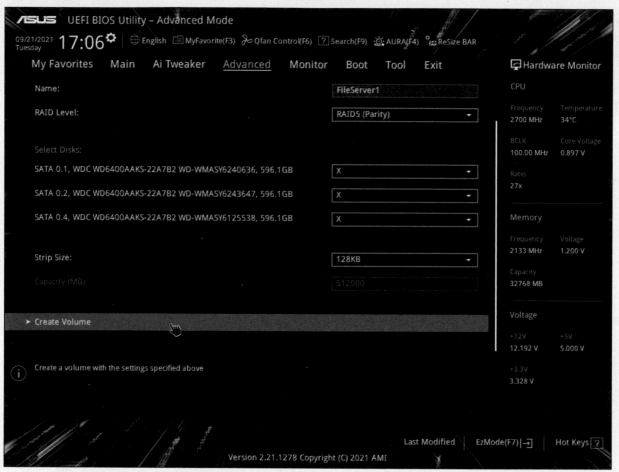

5. Under RAID Level, select **RAID5 (Parity)**. Select disks to use in the RAID configuration.

6. Select the value for the Strip Size. (This is the amount of space devoted to one strip across the striped array. Choices are 32 KB, 64 KB, or 128 KB.)

7. Enter the size of the volume. You don't have to use all the available space. The space you don't use can later be configured as another array.

8. Select **Create Volume** to complete the RAID configuration. Be warned that if you proceed, all data on all three hard drives will be lost. The array is created and the system reboots. If you go back into BIOS/UEFI, you can see the RAID 5 volume is set up; see Figure 5-42.

You are now ready to install Windows. Windows has built-in hardware RAID drivers and therefore automatically "sees" the RAID array as a single 500 GB hard drive. After Windows is installed on this one logical drive, Windows will call it volume C:.

Figure 5-42   Verify the RAID array is created

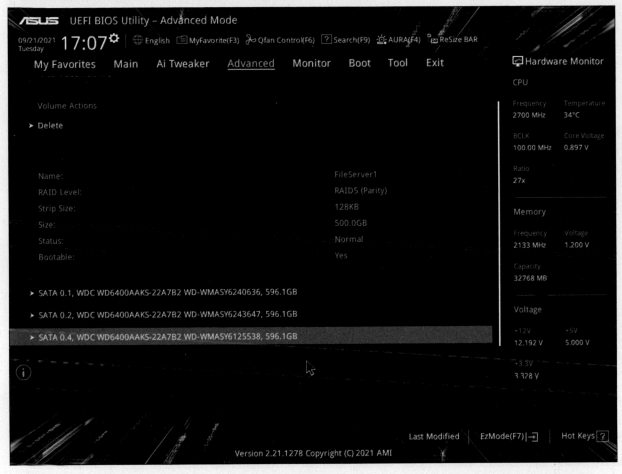

Applying Concepts

Troubleshooting Hard Drive Installations

Est. Time: 15 minutes
Core 1 Objective: 5.3

Sometimes trouble crops up during an installation. Keeping a cool head, thinking things through carefully several times, and using all available resources will most likely get you out of any mess.

Installing a hard drive is not difficult unless you have an unusually complex situation. For example, your first hard drive installation should not involve the extra complexity of installing a RAID array. If a complicated installation is necessary and you have never installed a hard drive, ask for expert help.

The following list describes errors that cropped up during a few hard drive installations; the list also includes the causes of the errors and what was done about them. Everyone learns something new when making mistakes, and you probably will, too. You can then add your own experiences to this list:

- When first turning on a previously working computer, Temuulen received the following error message: "Hard drive not found." She turned off the machine, checked all cables, and discovered that the data cable from the motherboard to the drive was loose. She reseated the cable and rebooted. POST found the drive.

(continues)

Applying Concepts Continued

- Lucia physically installed a new hard drive, replaced the cover on the computer case, and booted the computer with a Windows setup DVD in the drive. POST beeped three times and stopped. Recall that diagnostics during POST are often communicated by beeps if the tests take place before POST has checked video and made it available to display the messages. Three beeps on some computers signal a memory error. Lucia turned off the computer and checked the memory modules on the motherboard. A module positioned at the edge of the motherboard next to the cover had been bumped as she replaced the cover. She reseated the module and booted again, this time with the cover still off. The error disappeared.

- Jason physically installed a new hard drive and turned on the computer. He received the following error: "No boot device available." He had forgotten to insert a Windows setup DVD. He put the disc in the drive and rebooted the machine successfully.

- The hard drive did not physically fit into the bay. The screw holes did not line up. Juan got a bay kit, but it just didn't seem to work. He took a break, went to lunch, and came back to make a fresh start. Juan asked others to help him view the brackets, holes, and screws from a fresh perspective. It didn't take long to discover that he had overlooked the correct position for the brackets in the bay.

> **Caution**
>
> When things are not going well, you can tense up and make mistakes more easily. Be certain to turn off the machine before doing anything inside! Not doing so can be a costly error. For example, a friend had been trying and retrying to boot for some time and got frustrated and careless. They plugged the power cord into the drive without turning the computer off. The machine began to put off an electrical odor, and everything went dead. The next thing they learned was how to replace a power supply!

Troubleshooting Hard Drives

 Core 1 Objectives 1.1, 5.3

In this section of the module, you learn how to troubleshoot problems with hard drives. Hard drive problems during the boot can be caused by the hard drive subsystem, the file system on the drive, or files required by Windows when it begins to load. The LED status indicator on a hard drive is the start to identifying whether a hard drive is failing. To understand the color coding or blinking patterns, refer to the hard drive or laptop manufacturer documentation. Generally speaking, a green light means the hard drive is functioning correctly, and an amber light means the hard drive has failed and needs replacing. When trying to solve a problem with the boot, you need to decide if the problem is caused by hardware or software. All the problems discussed in this section are caused by hardware.

Slow Performance

Core 1 Objectives 1.1, 5.3

One of the most common complaints about a computer is that it is running slowly. In general, the overall performance of a system depends on the individual performances of the processor, motherboard, memory, and hard drive; often, the hard drive (for example, a 5400 RPM magnetic drive) or the hard drive interface (SATA Revision 2.x, for example) is the bottleneck.

If not managed well, hard drives can run slower over time, and full hard drives run slower than others. For best performance, don't allow an SSD to exceed 70% capacity and a magnetic drive to exceed 80% capacity.

You can use Windows tools or tools provided by the hard drive manufacturer to optimize a drive. To diagnose an issue with hard drive performance, such as extended or slow read/write times, use a hard drive speed test utility program that includes IOPS measurements. Microsoft recommends using DISKSPD. You can download and install DISKSPD to test your hard drive performance at this website: *https://github.com/Microsoft/diskspd*.

Windows Automatically Optimizes a Drive

First, let's understand why performance might slow down for magnetic drives and SSDs:

- **Magnetic drives.** When a magnetic drive is new, files are physically written in contiguous sectors (one following another without a break). Over time, as more files are written and deleted, files are stored in disconnected fragments on the drive, and slow performance can result. To improve performance, every week Windows automatically defragments a magnetic drive, rearranging fragments—or parts of files—in contiguous clusters.
- **SSDs.** For SSDs, data is organized in blocks, and each block contains many pages. A file can spread over several pages in various blocks. Each time a new page is written to the drive, the entire block to which it belongs must be read into a buffer, erased, and then rewritten with the new page included. When a file is deleted, information about the file is deleted, but the actual data in the file is not erased. This can slow down SSD performance because the unused data must still be read and rewritten in its block. To improve performance, Windows sends the trim command to an SSD to erase a block that no longer contains useful data so that a write operation does not have to manage the data. Once a week, Windows also sends a retrim command to the SSD to erase all blocks that are filled with unused data.

You can use the Windows **Defrag and Optimization tool (dfrgui.exe)** to verify that Windows is defragmenting a magnetic drive and trimming an SSD. Run the `dfrgui` command in Windows to open the Optimize Drives window, which reports the status of each drive installed in the system (see Figure 5-43). To verify the settings, click **Change settings**. If a drive has not been recently optimized, select the drive, and then click **Optimize**.

Figure 5-43   Windows reports volume C: is trimmed and volume D: is not fragmented

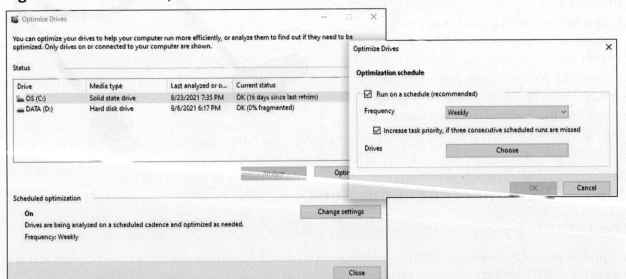

Note 13

To run a command in Windows, enter the command (for example, `dfrgui`) in the Windows search box.

Drive Manufacturer Utilities

Most magnetic drive and SSD manufacturers offer free utilities you can download and use to update drive firmware and optimize and troubleshoot a drive. For example, Intel offers the Intel Memory and Storage Tool for its SSDs, Seagate has SeaTools for its magnetic drives and SSDs, and Kingston offers SSD Manager for its drives. Search the manufacturer website to find and download the tools and get other hard drive support.

Migrating Data to a New SSD in a Laptop

You can migrate data to a new SSD if you need more storage space, to improve performance, or if you suspect a failing hard drive due to data loss or corruption. When you upgrade to a new SSD from a magnetic hard drive, you can migrate data from an old hard drive to the new SSD without reinstalling Windows, copying all your data files, or losing your system configuration. Recreating the system configuration onto the new hard drive is called **disk cloning**. When looking to purchase an SSD for a laptop to use in a data migration, consider the following:

- The SSD needs to be just as large or larger as the old hard drive.
- The SSD type needs to be compatible with the system board connector. Many laptops with a standard hard drive have a 2.5 inch SATA drive, which should be replaced with a 2.5 inch SATA SSD.
- The quality of the SSD needs to be considered for the performance and activity of the laptop. Read several reviews and tests of SSDs to find an appropriate drive.
- Purchase a SATA-to-USB data transfer cable; see Figure 5-44.
- Access cloning software to perform the migration. Your new SSD or SATA-to-USB cable might include a free download to cloning software. If neither does, then you can find several free disk-cloning programs online.

To perform the migration, complete the following steps:

1. Install the cloning software on your laptop.
2. Attach the SATA-to-USB data transfer cable to a USB port on your laptop. The USB 3.x ports offer the best transfer speeds.
3. Attach the new SSD to the SATA-to-USB data transfer cable.
4. Follow the on-screen instructions in the cloning software to complete the data migration.
5. Remove the old hard drive, and install the new SSD into the laptop.
6. Install the drive management software from the SSD manufacturer to keep the SSD drive firmware up to date.

Figure 5-44   Use a SATA-to-USB adapter to migrate data

Source: Amazon.com, Inc.

Hard Drive Problems During the Boot

Core 1 Objective 5.3

Hardware problems usually show up at POST unless there is physical damage to an area of the hard drive that is not accessed during POST. Hardware problems often make the hard drive totally inaccessible. If BIOS/UEFI cannot find a hard drive at POST, it displays an error message similar to one of the following. Most likely, the error message is in white text on a black background.

```
No boot device available
Hard drive not found
OS not found
Read/write failure
```

```
Fixed disk error
Invalid boot disk
Inaccessible boot device
Drive not recognized
RAID not found
RAID stops working
Numeric error codes in the 1700s or 10400s
S.M.A.R.T. errors during the boot
```

If BIOS/UEFI cannot access the drive, the cause might be the drive, the data cable, the electrical system, the motherboard, or a loose connection. Here is a list of things to do and check before you open the case:

1. If BIOS/UEFI displays numeric error codes or cryptic messages during POST, check the website of the motherboard manufacturer for explanations of these codes or messages, or do a general Google search.

2. Check BIOS/UEFI setup for errors in the hard drive configuration. If you suspect an error, set BIOS/ UEFI to default settings, make sure autodetection is turned on, and reboot the system.

3. Try booting from other bootable media such as the Windows setup DVD or a USB flash drive or CD with the Linux OS and diagnostics software installed. You learn more about this in a project at the end of this module. If you can boot using other media, you have proven that the problem is isolated to the hard drive subsystem. You can also use the bootable media to access the hard drive, run diagnostics on the drive, and possibly recover its data.

4. For a RAID array, use the firmware utility to check the status of each disk in the array and to check for errors. Press a key at startup to access the RAID BIOS/UEFI utility. This utility lists each disk in the array and its status. You can search the website of the motherboard or RAID controller manufacturer for an interpretation of the messages on this screen and what to do about them. If one of the disks in the array has gone bad, it might take some time (as long as two days for large-capacity drives) for the array to rebuild using data on the other disks. In this situation, the status for the array is likely to show as Caution.

After the array has rebuilt, your data should be available. However, if one of the hard drives in the array has gone bad, you need to replace the hard drive. After you have replaced the failed drive, you must add it back to the RAID array. This process is called rebuilding a RAID volume. How to do this depends on the RAID hardware you are using. For some motherboards or RAID controller cards, you use the RAID firmware. For others, you use the RAID management software that came bundled with the motherboard or controller. You install this software in Windows and use the software to rebuild the RAID volume using the new hard drive.

If the problem is still not solved, open the case and check the following things. Be sure to protect the system against ESD as you work:

1. Remove and reattach all drive cables.

2. If you're using a RAID or SATA controller card, remove and reseat it or place it in a different slot. Check the documentation for the card, looking for directions for troubleshooting.

3. Inspect the drive for damage, such as bent pins on the cable or drive connection.

4. Determine if a magnetic hard drive is spinning by listening to it or lightly touching the metal drive (with the power on).

5. Check the cable for frayed edges or other damage.

6. Check the installation manual for things you might have overlooked. Look for a section about system setup, and carefully follow all directions that apply.

7. S.M.A.R.T. errors that display during the boot result from BIOS/UEFI reporting that the drive has met a threshold point of failure. Back up the data, and replace the drive as soon as possible.

8. When Windows is installed on a hard drive but cannot launch, it might present a blue screen with error messages, called a blue screen of death (BSOD), or it might hang and display a never-ending, spinning Windows pinwheel or wait icon. Windows includes several tools for checking a hard drive for errors and repairing a corrupted Windows installation, as you learn in the module "Troubleshooting Windows Startup." Without getting into the details of supporting Windows, here are a few simple things you can try:

a. **Use Windows Startup Repair.** In the module "Power Supplies and Troubleshooting Computer Problems," you learned that the Startup Repair utility restores many of the Windows files needed for a successful boot. Following directions given in that module, boot from the Windows setup DVD or flash drive, select the option to **Repair your computer**, and perform a **Startup Repair**.

b. **Use the chkdsk command.** To make sure the hard drive does not have bad sectors that can corrupt the file system, you can use the **chkdsk** command. The command works from Windows, but if you cannot start Windows from the hard drive, you can use the command after booting the system from Windows setup media and selecting the option to **Repair your computer**. Then go to the **Advanced options** screen (see Figure 5-45). Next, select **Command Prompt**. At the command prompt that appears, run this chkdsk command to search for bad sectors on drive C: and recover data:

```
chkdsk C: /r
```

Figure 5-45   Select Command Prompt, where you can execute the chkdsk command

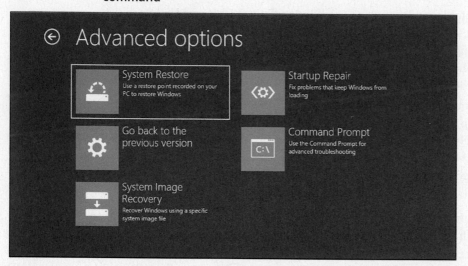

Note 14

Early in the boot, BIOS/UEFI error messages usually display in white text on a black screen. Windows BSOD boot error messages display on a blue screen. As an IT help desk technician, you might find yourself talking on the phone with a customer about their boot problem. To help you decide if the problem is happening during POST or as Windows is loading, ask the customer to tell you the color of the screen that shows the error message.

9. Before Windows can format and install a file system on a drive, it first separates the drive into one or more partitions using the older Master Boot Record (MBR) or newer GPT (GUID [Globally Unique Identifier] Partition Table) partitioning system. Here are steps you can take to repair an MBR hard drive:

a. **Repair the BCD.** The **BCD (Boot Configuration Data)** is a small database that holds parameters Windows needs for a successful boot. At a command prompt, enter this **bootrec** command to rebuild the BCD:

```
bootrec /RebuildBCD
```

b. **Repair the boot sector.** The first sector of a hard drive is called the boot sector and holds the MBR partition table, which maps the locations of partitions on the drive. To repair a corrupted boot sector, run this command:

```
bootrec /FixBoot
```

c. **Repair the MBR.** The bootrec command can be used to fix problems with the MBR program in the boot sector that is needed to start Windows. Enter this command:

```
bootrec /FixMBR
```

10. Check the drive manufacturer's website for diagnostic software such as SeaTools, which is used to diagnose problems with Seagate drives. Sometimes these types of software, including SeaTools, can be run from a bootable USB flash drive or CD. Run the software to test the drive for errors.

11. If it is not convenient to create a bootable USB flash drive or DVD with hard drive diagnostic software installed, you can move the drive to a working computer and install it as a second drive in the system. Then you can use the diagnostic software installed on the primary hard drive to test the problem drive. While you have the drive installed in a working computer, be sure to find out if you can copy data from it to the good drive so that you can recover any data not backed up (if the hard drive is encrypted, you'll need the recovery password to access the data). Remember that you set the drive on the open computer case (see Figure 5-46) or use a SATA-to-USB converter to connect the drive to a USB port. If you have the case open with the computer turned on, be <u>very careful</u> not to put your hands inside the case.

12. After you have tried to recover the file system and data on the drive and before you decide to replace the hard drive, try these things to clean the drive and get a fresh start:

  a. Format a hard drive volume. If you decide the hard drive volume is corrupted and you want to start over, boot the system from Windows setup media and open a Windows command prompt. Then run the format command to erase everything on the volume. In this example, D: is the drive letter for the volume:

Figure 5-46 Temporarily connect a faulty hard drive to another system to diagnose the problem and try to recover data

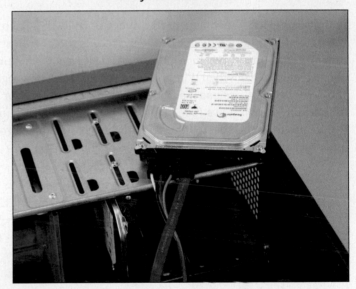

```
format D:
```

  b. Use diskpart to start over with a fresh file system. If formatting the volume doesn't work, you can erase the hard drive partitions using the **diskpart** command. When you enter diskpart at a command prompt, the DISKPART> prompt appears. Then run the following commands to wipe everything off the hard drive. In the example, you are erasing partition 1 on disk 0.

```
list disk
select disk 0
list partition
select partition 1
clean
```

Enter the **exit** command to exit the diskpart utility. You can then reinstall Windows, which partitions the hard drive again. If Windows cannot recognize the drive, it's probably time to replace hardware in the hard drive subsystem.

13. If the drive still does not boot, exchange the three field replaceable units—the data cable, the storage card (if the drive is connected to one), and the hard drive itself—for a hard drive subsystem. Do the following, in order, and test the hard drive after each step:

  a. Try connecting the drive data cable to a different SATA connector on the motherboard. A SATA connector might be disabled when the system is using an M.2 slot.

  b. Reconnect or swap the drive data cable.

  c. Reseat or exchange the drive controller card, if one is present.

  d. Exchange the hard drive for a known good drive.

14. Sometimes older drives refuse to spin at POST or a failing drive can make a loud clicking or grinding noise. Drives that have trouble spinning often whine at startup for several months before they finally refuse to spin altogether. If your drive whines loudly when you first turn on the computer, <u>do not</u> turn off the computer; immediately back up the data. Then replace the drive. One of the worst things you can do for a drive that has difficulty starting is to leave the computer turned off for an extended period of time. Some drives, like old cars, refuse to start if they are unused for a long time. A drive making a loud clicking or grinding noise most likely is not accessible and must be replaced.

15. A bad power supply or a bad motherboard also might cause a disk boot failure.

If the problem is solved by exchanging the hard drive, take the extra time to reinstall the old hard drive and verify that the problem was not caused by a bad connection.

Now let's move on to other types of storage devices, including optical drives and flash cards.

Supporting Other Types of Storage Devices

 Core 1 Objective 3.3

Before we explore the details of several other types of storage devices—including optical discs, USB flash drives, and memory cards—let's start with the file systems they might use.

File Systems Used by Storage Devices

 Core 1 Objective 3.3

A storage device—such as a hard drive, CD, DVD, USB flash drive, or memory card—uses a file system to manage the data stored on the device. A **file system** is the overall structure the operating system uses to name, store, and organize files on a drive. In Windows, each storage device or group of devices, such as a RAID array, is treated as a single logical drive. When Windows first recognizes a new logical drive in the system, it determines which file system the drive is using, assigns it a drive letter (for example, C: or D:), and calls it a **volume**. Use Explorer to see volumes and devices in Windows (see Figure 5-47). To see information about the volume or device, right-click it and select Properties from the shortcut menu. The device or volume Properties dialog box appears, which shows its file system and storage capacity (see the right side of Figure 5-47).

Figure 5-47   This 16 GB USB flash drive is using the FAT32 file system

Using Windows to install a new file system on a device or logical drive is called **formatting**, a process that erases all data on the device or drive. One way to format a device is to right-click it and select **Format** from the shortcut menu. In the dialog box that appears, you can select the file system that works for this device (see Figure 5-48). If you have problems with a device, make sure it's using a file system appropriate for your situation:

Figure 5-48 A storage device can be formatted using File Explorer

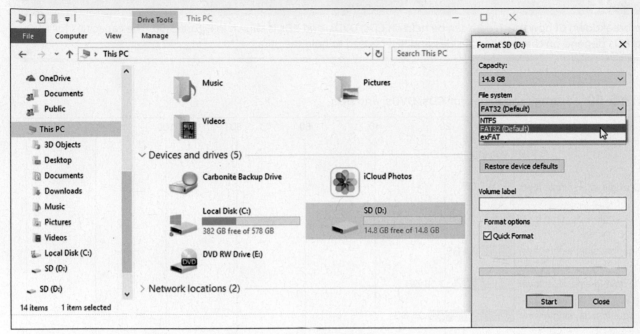

- NTFS (New Technology file system) is primarily used by hard drives.
- The exFAT file system is used by large-capacity removable storage devices, including some USB flash drives, memory cards, and external hard drives.
- FAT32 and FAT file systems are used by smaller-capacity devices.
- **CDFS (Compact Disc File System)** or the **UDF (Universal Disk Format)** file system is used by CDs.
- A newer version of the UDF file system is used by DVDs and BDs (Blu-ray discs).

Now let's look at the types of optical drives you might be called on to support.

Standards Used by Optical Discs and Drives

> **Core 1 Objective** 3.3

CDs (compact discs), DVDs (digital versatile discs or digital video discs), and BDs (Blu-ray discs) use similar laser technologies. Tiny lands and pits on the surface of a disc represent bits, which a laser beam can read. This is why they are called optical storage technologies.

Optical Discs

Data is written to only one side of a CD, but it can be written to one or both sides of a DVD or Blu-ray disc. Also, a DVD or Blu-ray disc can hold data in two or more layers on each side. For example, a dual-layer, double-sided DVD can hold a total of four layers on one disc (see Figure 5-49).

Figure 5-49 A DVD can hold data in double layers on both the top and bottom of the disc, yielding a maximum capacity of 17 GB

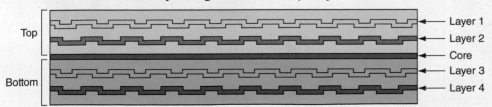

Note 15

The breakdown of how much data can be held on CDs, DVDs, and BDs is shown in Figure 5-50. The capacities for DVDs and BDs depend on the number of sides and layers used to hold the data.

Figure 5-50   Storage capacities for CDs, DVDs, and BDs

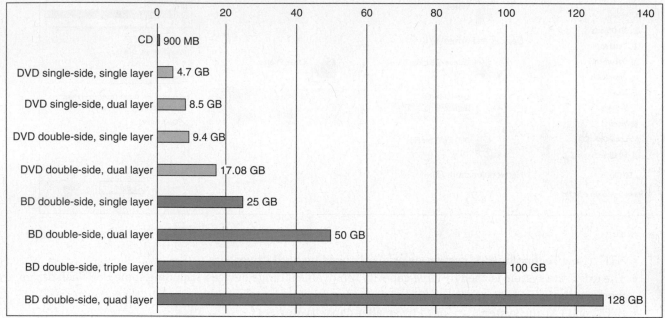

CD	900 MB
DVD single-side, single layer	4.7 GB
DVD single-side, dual layer	8.5 GB
DVD double-side, single layer	9.4 GB
DVD double-side, dual layer	17.08 GB
BD double-side, single layer	25 GB
BD double-side, dual layer	50 GB
BD double-side, triple layer	100 GB
BD double-side, quad layer	128 GB

Optical Drives and Burners

Blu-ray drives are backward compatible with DVD and CD technologies, and DVD drives are backward compatible with CD technologies. Depending on the drive features, an optical drive might be able to read and write to BDs, DVDs, and CDs. A drive that can write to discs is commonly called a burner. Today's internal optical drives interface with the motherboard by way of a SATA connection. An external drive might use an eSATA or USB port. Figure 5-51 shows an internal DVD drive, and Figure 5-52 shows an external DVD drive.

Figure 5-51   This internal DVD drive uses a SATA connection

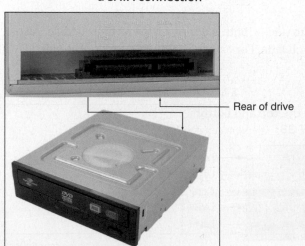

Rear of drive

Figure 5-52   The PX-610U external DVD±RW drive by Plextor uses a USB 2.0 port

When shopping for an optical drive or burner, you might see ads like those shown in Figure 5-53. Table 5-2 can help you sort out the mix of disc standards. The table lists the popular CD, DVD, and Blu-ray disc and drive standards.

Figure 5-53   Ads for external DVD and Blu-ray burners offer many options

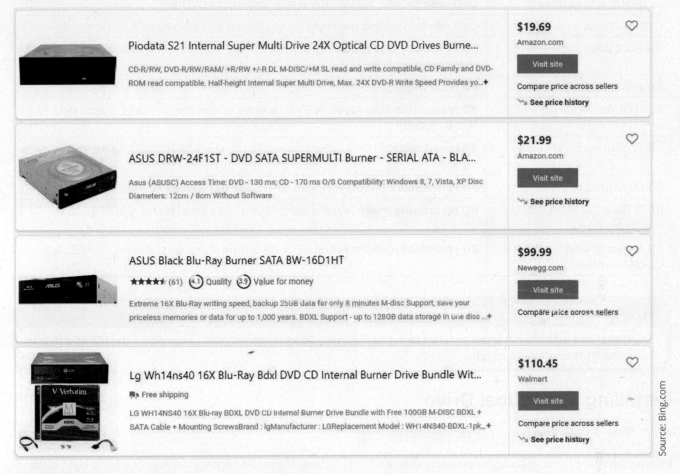

Piodata S21 Internal Super Multi Drive 24X Optical CD DVD Drives Burne...

CD-R/RW, DVD-R/RW/RAM/ +R/RW +/-R DL M-DISC/+M SL read and write compatible, CD Family and DVD-ROM read compatible. Half-height Internal Super Multi Drive, Max. 24X DVD-R Write Speed Provides yo...+

$19.69
Amazon.com
Visit site
Compare price across sellers
See price history

ASUS DRW-24F1ST - DVD SATA SUPERMULTI Burner - SERIAL ATA - BLA...

Asus (ASUSC) Access Time: DVD - 130 ms; CD - 170 ms O/S Compatibility: Windows 8, 7, Vista, XP Disc Diameters: 12cm / 8cm Without Software

$21.99
Amazon.com
Visit site
See price history

ASUS Black Blu-Ray Burner SATA BW-16D1HT

★★★★☆ (61) (4.1) Quality (3.9) Value for money

Extreme 16X Blu-Ray writing speed, backup 25GB data for only 8 minutes M-disc Support, save your priceless memories or data for up to 1,000 years. BDXL Support - up to 128GB data storage in one disc ...+

$99.99
Newegg.com
Visit site
Compare price across sellers

Lg Wh14ns40 16X Blu-Ray Bdxl DVD CD Internal Burner Drive Bundle Wit...

🚚 Free shipping

LG WH14NS40 16X Blu-ray BDXL DVD CD Internal Burner Drive Bundle with Free 100GB M-DISC BDXL + SATA Cable + Mounting ScrewsBrand : IgManufacturer : LGReplacement Model : WH14NS340-BDXL-1pk...+

$110.45
Walmart
Visit site
Compare price across sellers
See price history

Source: Bing.com

Table 5-2   Optical disc and drive standards

Standard	Description
CD-ROM disc or drive	**CD read-only memory.** A CD-ROM disc burned at the factory can hold music, software, or other data.
CD-R disc	**CD recordable.** A CD-R disc is a write-once CD.
CD-RW disc or drive	**CD rewriteable.** A CD-RW disc can be written to many times.
DVD-ROM drive	**DVD read-only memory**.
DVD-R disc	**DVD recordable, single layer.** A DVD-R disc can hold up to 4.7 GB of data.
DVD-R DL disc	**DVD recordable in dual layers.** A DVD-R DL disc doubles storage to 8.5 GB of data on two layers.
DVD-RW disc or drive	**DVD rewriteable.** A DVD-RW disc is also known as an erasable, recordable disc or a write-many disc.
DVD-RW DL disc or drive, aka DL DVD drive	**DVD rewriteable, dual layers.** A DVD-RW DL disc has a storage capacity of 8.5 GB.
DVD+R disc or drive	**DVD recordable.** Similar to DVD-R but faster, a DVD+R disc holds about 4.7 GB of data.

(continues)

Table 5-2   Optical disc and drive standards (Continued)

Standard	Description
DVD+R DL disc or drive	**DVD recordable, dual layers.** A DVD+R DL disc has 8.5 GB of storage.
DVD+RW disc or drive	**DVD rewriteable.** A DVD+RW disc is faster than DVD-RW.
DVD-RAM disc or drive	**DVD random access memory.** A DVD-RAM disc is rewriteable and erasable.
BD-ROM drive	**BD or Blu-ray disc read-only memory.** A BD-ROM drive can also read DVDs, and some can read CDs.
BD-R disc or drive	**BD recordable.** The drive reads/writes only one layer of data, for a capacity of 25 GB.
BD-R DL disc or drive	**BD recordable dual-layer.** A BD-R DL drive or disc handles dual layers, yielding a 50 GB capacity.
BD-RE disc or drive	**BD rewriteable.** A BD-RE drive may read/write single layers, yielding a 25 GB capacity.
BD-RE DL disc or drive	**BD rewriteable dual-layer.** A BD-RE DL disc has a capacity of 50 GB.
BD-R TL disc or drive BD-R XL TL disc or drive	**BD recordable triple-layer.** A BD-R TL disc uses three layers, yielding 100 GB capacity.
BD-R QL disc or drive BD-R XL QL disc or drive	**BD recordable quad-layer.** BD-R QL discs have four layers, yielding 128 GB capacity.

Note 16

CDs, DVDs, and BDs are expected to hold their data for many years; however, you can prolong the life of a disc by protecting it from exposure to light.

Installing An Optical Drive

Core 1 Objective 3.3

Internal optical drives on today's computers use a SATA interface. Figure 5-54 shows the rear of a SATA optical drive. An optical drive is usually installed in the drive bay at the top of a desktop case (see Figure 5-55). After the drive is installed in the bay, connect the data and power cables.

Figure 5-54   The rear of a SATA optical drive

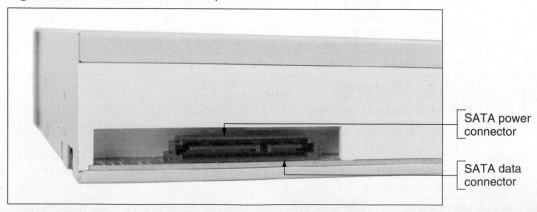

SATA power connector

SATA data connector

Exam Tip ✔

The A+ Core 1 exam expects you to know how to select and install a CD, DVD, or Blu-ray drive.

Figure 5-55   Slide the drive into the bay flush with the front panel

Windows supports optical drives using its own embedded drivers without add-on drivers. Therefore, when Windows first starts up after the drive is installed, it recognizes the drive and installs drivers. Use Device Manager to verify that the drive is installed with no errors and is ready to use.

Solid-State Storage

  Core 1 Objective 3.3

Types of solid-state storage include SSDs, USB flash drives, and memory cards. Current USB flash drives range in size from 256 MB to 2 TB and go by many names, including a flash pen drive, jump drive, thumb drive, and key drive. Several USB flash drives are shown in Figure 5-56. Flash drives might work at USB 2.0 or USB 3.x speed and use the FAT (for small-capacity drives) or exFAT file system (for large-capacity drives). Windows has embedded drivers to support flash drives. To use one, simply insert the device in a USB port. It then appears in Explorer as a drive with an assigned letter.

Figure 5-56   USB flash drives come in a variety of styles and sizes

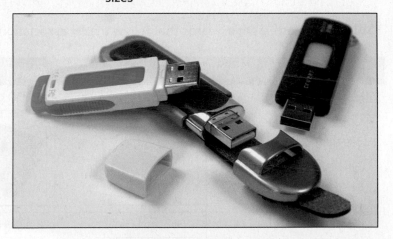

Note 17

To make sure that data written to a flash drive is properly saved, right-click the drive in Explorer, and select **Eject** from the shortcut menu. It is then safe to remove the drive.

Memory cards might be used in digital cameras, tablets, smartphones, MP3 players, digital camcorders, and other portable devices, and most laptops have memory card slots provided by a built-in smart card reader. If there is not a memory card slot in the device, you can add an external smart card reader/writer that uses a USB connection. For a desktop, you can install a universal smart card reader/writer in a drive bay. For a laptop or desktop, you can use an external USB memory card reader. For example, both devices shown in Figure 5-57 read and write to several types of smart cards. The first device plugs into an external USB 3.0 port. The second device installs in a desktop

Figure 5-57   A. This seven-slot USB 2.0 Internal Memory Card Reader and Writer by Sabrent supports multiple types of smart cards   B. This USB 3.0 external memory card reader and writer supports SD and MicroSD cards

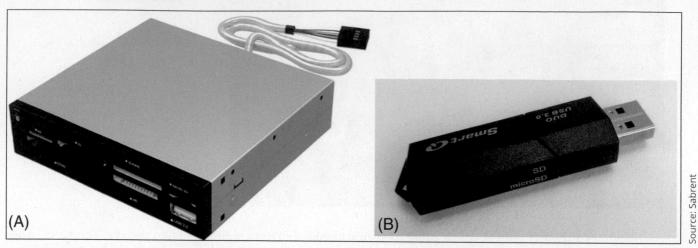

(A)   (B)

Source: Sabrent

drive bay and connects to the motherboard by way of a 9-pin USB cable. For this device, plug the cable into an empty 9-pin USB 2.0 header on the motherboard.

The most popular memory cards are **Secure Digital (SD) cards**, which follow the standards of the SD Association (*sdcard.org*) and are listed in Table 5-3. The four standards for capacity used by SD cards are 1.x (regular SD), 2.x (SD High Capacity or SDHC), 3.x (SD eXtended Capacity or SDXC), and 7.x (SD Ultra Capacity or SDUC). Besides capacity, SD cards come in three physical sizes (full-size, MiniSD, and MicroSD) and are rated for speed in classes.

Table 5-3   Flash memory cards that follow the SD association standards

	Full-size SD	MiniSD	MicroSD
SD SD 1.x Holds up to 2 GB	SD card	MiniSD card	MicroSD card
SD High Capacity SD 2.x Holds 2 GB to 32 GB	SDHC card	MiniSDHC card	MicroSDHC card
SD eXtended Capacity SD 3.x Holds 32 GB to 2 TB	SDXC card	N/A	MicroSDXC card

Source: Courtesy of SanDisk

Note 18

The SDUC card technology was developed and announced by the SD Association in 2018; however, demand for production hasn't met the market yet, so SDUC cards are absent from retail supply. The SDUC card can theoretically hold 2 TB up to 128 TB of memory.

Figure 5-58 shows several flash SD memory cards together so you can get an idea of their relative sizes. Sometimes a memory card is bundled with one or more adapters so that a smaller card will fit a larger card slot.

Figure 5-58   Flash memory cards

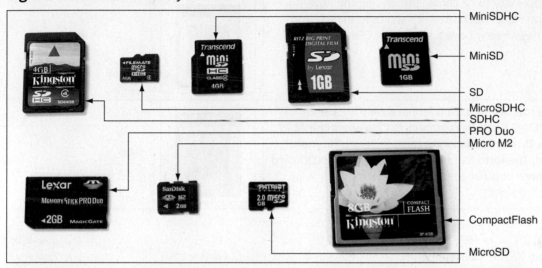

- MiniSDHC
- MiniSD
- SD
- MicroSDHC
- SDHC
- PRO Duo
- Micro M2
- CompactFlash
- MicroSD

Exam Tip ✔

The A+ Core 1 exam expects you to know about memory cards. Given a scenario, you need to know which type of flash storage device is appropriate for the situation.

Popular classes for rating speeds, from slowest to fastest, are Speed Class C2, C4, C6, and C10; Ultra High Speed Class 1 (U1) and U3; Video Speed Class 6 (V6), V10, V30, V60, and V90. For digital cameras, class 4 or 6 should be fast enough. For high-resolution video recording, use class 10 or higher. To know the class rating, look for a symbol (see Figure 5-59) on the card. Generally, the higher the speed, the more expensive the card becomes. For SD cards rated in UHS or Video Speed classes, the device must also be rated for UHS or Video Speed, respectively, to get the higher speeds.

Figure 5-59   Look for one of these symbols on an SD card to indicate class rating speed

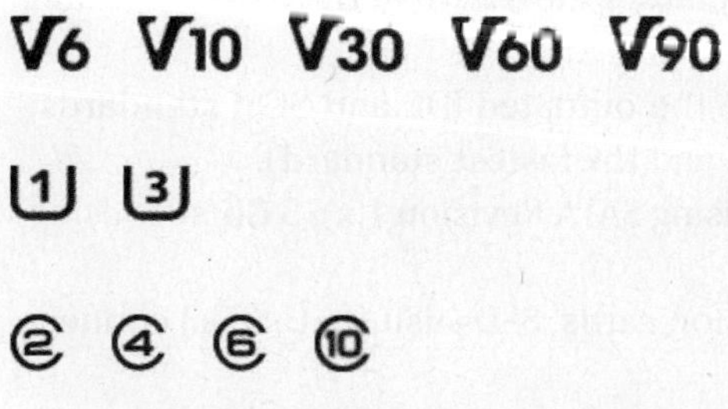

V6 V10 V30 V60 V90

U1 U3

C2 C4 C6 C10

Source: SD Association.

SD slots are backward compatible with earlier standards for SD cards. However, you cannot use an SDHC card in an SD slot, and you cannot use an SDXC card in an SDHC slot or SD slot. Only use SDUC cards in SDUC slots.

SD and SDHC cards use the FAT file system, whereas SDXC and SDUC cards use the exFAT file system. Windows supports both file systems, so you should be able to install an SD, SDHC, SDXC, or SDUC card in an SD slot on a Windows laptop with no problems (assuming the slot supports the SDHC, SDXC, or SDUC card you are using).

Memory cards other than SD cards are shown in Table 5-4. Some of the cards in the table are seldom used today.

Table 5-4   Flash memory cards

Flash Memory Device	Example
CompactFlash (CF) cards were popular among early memory cards but are quickly being replaced by faster cards with higher capacities. CF cards come in two types: Type I and Type II. Type II cards are slightly thicker. The CF standard allows for sizes up to 512 GB.	
XQD cards are the successor to CF cards, introducing the PCIe 2.0 standard as the interface. XQD cards are still used in high-end cameras today, but they already have a successor: CFexpress.	 Source: amazon.com/ Sony-Professional- 120GB-Memory- QD-G120F/dp/ B07HFT541Y
CFexpress cards offer faster data transfer because they are designed using the PCIe 3.0 interface standard. CFexpress comes in three form factors: A, B, and C. The larger form factors offer more PCIe lanes to be used. The form factor B is compatible with XQD card slots, making it the more popular successor. The form factor A is compatible with SD card slots.	 Source: amazon. com/SanDisk- Extreme-PRO- CFexpress-Type-B/ dp/B08927HG8B

Module Summary

Hard Drive Technologies and Interface Standards

- A hard disk drive (HDD) can be a magnetic drive or a solid-state drive. A magnetic drive comes in two sizes: 3.5" for desktop computers and 2.5" for laptops.
- A solid-state drive contains NAND flash memory and is more expensive, faster, more reliable, and uses less power than a magnetic drive. Form factors used by SSDs include 2.5", mSATA, M.2, and PCIe cards.
- Hard drive performance is measured by throughput, IOPS, and latency.
- S.M.A.R.T. is a self-monitoring technology whereby the BIOS/UEFI monitors the health of the hard drive and warns of an impending failure.
- Interface standards used by hard drives and optical drives include the outdated IDE and SCSI standards, SATA (the most popular standard), and NVMe (applies only to SSDs and the fastest standard).
- The three SATA standards provide data transfer rates of 1.5 Gb/sec (using SATA Revision 1.x), 3 Gb/sec (using SATA Revision 2.x), and 6 Gb/sec (using SATA Revision 3.x).
- The NVMe standard can be used by SSDs embedded on PCIe expansion cards, SSDs using a U.2/U.3 connector, and SSD M.2 cards using an M.2 slot.

How to Select and Install Hard Drives

- When selecting a hard drive, consider the interface standards, storage capacity, technology (solid-state or magnetic), form factor, spindle speed (for magnetic drives), and interface standard.
- SATA drives require no configuration and are installed using a power cord and a single SATA data cable.

- Laptop hard drives plug directly into a SATA connection on the system board.
- RAID technology uses an array of hard drives to provide fault tolerance and/or improved performance. The following are choices for RAID:
  - RAID 0 (striping using two drives and improves performance)
  - RAID 1 (mirroring using two drives and provides fault tolerance)
  - RAID 5 (parity checking using three drives; provides fault tolerance and improves performance)
  - RAID 10 (striping and mirroring combined using four drives; provides optimum fault tolerance and performance)
- Hardware RAID is implemented using the motherboard BIOS/UEFI or a RAID controller card. Software RAID is implemented in Windows. The best practice is to use hardware RAID rather than software RAID.

Troubleshooting Hard Drives

- Defragmenting a magnetic hard drive can sometimes improve slow performance of the drive. Trimming an SSD improves performance.
- Hard drive problems during the boot can be caused by the hard drive subsystem, the file system on the drive, or the files required by Windows when it begins to load. After the boot, bad sectors on a drive can cause problems with corrupted files.
- To determine if the hard drive is the problem when booting, try to boot from other media, such as the Windows setup DVD or a bootable USB flash drive.
- For problems with a RAID volume, use the RAID controller firmware (on the motherboard or on the RAID controller card) or RAID management software installed in Windows to report the status of the array and to rebuild the RAID volume.
- To determine if a drive has bad sectors, use the chkdsk command. You can run the command after booting the system using Windows setup media.
- Use the format command to erase everything on a Windows volume.
- Use commands within the diskpart utility to completely erase a partition on a hard drive.
- Field replaceable units in the hard drive subsystem are the data cable, optional storage card, and hard drive.

Supporting Other Types of Storage Devices

- File systems a storage device might use in Windows include NTFS, exFAT, FAT32, FAT, CDFS (used by CDs), and UDF (used by CDs, DVDs, and BDs).
- CDs, DVDs, and BDs are optical discs with data physically embedded into the surface of the disc. Laser beams are used to read data off the disc by measuring light reflection.
- Optical discs can be recordable (such as a CD-R disc) or rewriteable (such as a DVD-RW disc). A BD-R QL (Blu-ray disc quad-layer) can hold 128 GB.
- Flash memory cards are a type of solid-state storage. Types of flash memory card standards by the SD Association include SD, MiniSD, MicroSD, SDHC, MiniSDHC, MicroSDHC, SDXC, MicroSDXC, SDUC, and microSDUC. Other memory cards include CompactFlash, XQD, and CFexpress.

Key Terms

For explanations of key terms, see the Glossary for this text.

BCD (Boot Configuration Data)	CD (compact disc)	chkdsk	disk cloning
BD (Blu-ray disc)	CDFS (Compact Disc File System)	CompactFlash (CF) card	diskpart
bootrec	CFexpress card	Defrag and Optimization tool (dfrgui.exe)	DVD (digital versatile disc or digital video disc)

fault tolerance	magnetic hard drive	RAID 1	SSD (solid-state
file system	mirrored volume	RAID 5	drive or solid-state
formatting	NAND flash memory	RAID 5 volume	device)
hot-swapping	NVMe (Non-Volatile	RAID 10 or RAID 1+0	striped volume
IDE (Integrated Drive	Memory Express or	read/write head	throughput
Electronics)	NVM Express)	SATA Express	UDF (Universal Disk
IOPS (input/output	RAID (redundant array	SCSI (Small Computer	Format)
operations per	of inexpensive disks	System Interface)	volume
second)	or redundant array of	SD (Secure Digital)	wear leveling
latency	independent disks)	card	XQD card
low-level formatting	RAID 0	spanning	

Thinking Critically

These questions are designed to prepare you for the critical thinking required for the A+ exams and may use information from other modules and the web.

1. Your friend has an ASUS TUF505DU laptop, and the magnetic hard drive has failed. Their uncle has offered to give them a working hard drive he no longer needs, the Toshiba MK8009GAH 80 GB 4200RPM drive. Will this drive fit this laptop? Why or why not?

   a. Yes, the drive form factor and interface connectors match.
   b. No, the drive form factor matches, but the interface does not match.
   c. Yes, the drive form factor, spindle speed, and interface all match.
   d. No, the drive form factor and interface do not match.

2. You have four hard drives on hand and need a replacement drive for a desktop system. The documentation for the motherboard installed in the system says the board has six SATA 3 Gb/s connectors and one IDE connector. Which of the four hard drives will work in the system and yield the best performance?

   a. Ultralock IDE ATA 4500-RPM 3.5" HDD
   b. WD 3.5" 7200-RPM SATA Revision 3.0 HDD
   c. Seagate IDE ATA 4500-RPM 3.5" HDD
   d. WD 2.5" 4500-RPM SATA 6 Gb/s HDD

3. You are setting up a RAID system in a server designed for optimum fault tolerance, accuracy, and minimal downtime. Which hard drive is best for this system, assuming the motherboard supports it?

   a. Hot-swap 2.5" SATA Revision 2.0 SSD
   b. Hot-swap 3.5" SATA Revision 3.0 10,000 RPM drive
   c. 3.5" SATA Revision 3.0 15,000 RPM drive
   d. 2.5" SATA 6 Gb/s SSD

4. You have two matching hard drives in a system, which you plan to configure as a RAID array to improve performance. Which RAID configuration should you use?

   a. RAID 0
   b. RAID 1
   c. RAID 5
   d. RAID 10

5. Which RAID level stripes data across multiple drives to improve performance and provides fault tolerance?

6. Which of the following situations allows for data not to be lost in a RAID array?

   a. RAID 0 and one hard drive fails
   b. RAID 1 and one hard drive fails
   c. RAID 5 and two hard drives fail
   d. RAID 10 and three hard drives fail

7. A laptop has an SD card slot that no longer reads cards inserted in the slot. Which is the first and best solution to try? Second?

   a. Download and install the latest drivers from the laptop manufacturer for the card slot.
   b. Purchase a USB memory card adapter to replace the SD card slot.
   c. Replace the card reader on the system board, being careful to only use parts sold or recommended by the laptop manufacturer.
   d. Update Windows on the laptop.
   e. Reinstall Windows on the laptop.

8. Explain how a DVD manufacturer can advertise that a DVD can hold 4.7 GB, but Explorer reports the DVD capacity as 4,706,074,624 bytes, or 4.38 GB.

   a. Manufacturers are allowed to over-advertise their products.
   b. The manufacturer measures capacity in decimal, and the OS measures capacity in binary.
   c. The actual capacity is 4.7 GB, but the OS requires overhead to manage the DVD, and the overhead is not included in the reported DVD capacity.
   d. The DVD was formatted to have a capacity of 4.38 GB, but it could have been formatted to have a capacity of 4.7 GB.

9. You discover Event Viewer has been reporting hard drive errors for about a month. What is the first solution you should try to fix the problem?

   a. Use the chkdsk command to repair the drive.
   b. Use Explorer to reformat the drive.
   c. Replace the drive with a known good one.
   d. Download and install firmware updates to the drive from the hard drive manufacturer.

10. You install a SATA hard drive and then turn on the computer for the first time. You access BIOS/UEFI setup and see that the drive is not recognized. Which of the following do you do next?

    a. Turn off the computer, open the case, and verify that memory modules on the motherboard have not become loose.
    b. Turn off the computer, open the case, and verify that the data cable and power cable are connected correctly.
    c. Update BIOS/UEFI firmware to make sure it can recognize the new drive.
    d. Reboot the computer and enter BIOS/UEFI setup again to see if it now recognizes the drive.

11. You want to install an SSD in your desktop computer, but the drive is far too narrow to fit snugly into the bays of your computer case. Which of the following do you do?

    a. Install the SSD in a laptop computer.
    b. Buy a bay adapter that will allow you to install the narrow drive in a desktop case bay.
    c. This SSD is designed for a laptop. Flash BIOS/UEFI so your system will support a laptop hard drive.
    d. Use a special SATA controller card that will support the narrow hard drive.

12. Mark each statement as true or false:

    a. PATA hard drives are older and slower than SATA hard drives.
    b. SATA Revision 1.x is about 10 times faster than SATA Revision 3.x.
    c. RAID 0 can be implemented using only a single hard drive.
    d. RAID 5 requires five hard drives working together at the same speed and capacity.
    e. You can use an internal SATA data cable with an eSATA port.
    f. A SATA internal data cable has seven pins.

13. Why do hard drives tend to slow down over time?

    a. Drives can reach full capacity, which hinders where data can be written to the drive.
    b. SSDs must erase a block before a block can be written.
    c. Magnetic drives take longer when having to read data from noncontiguous locations on the drive.
    d. All of the answers are correct.

14. Of the following hard drives, which one is fastest?

   a. SATA 6 Gb/s SSD
   b. SATA 6 Gb/s 10,000 RPM drive
   c. M.2 SSD using a SATA Revision 3.0 interface
   d. PCIe NVMe SSD card

15. You install an M.2 SSD card in an M.2 slot on a motherboard. When you boot up the system, you discover the DVD drive no longer works. What are likely causes of this problem? (Choose two.)

   a. The DVD drive SATA connector is disabled.
   b. The DVD drive cable is loose or disconnected.
   c. The installation corrupted the DVD drivers.
   d. The DVD drive has failed and must be replaced.

Hands-On Projects

Hands-On Project 5-1

Examining BIOS/UEFI Settings for a Hard Drive

Est. Time: 15 minutes
Core 1 Objective: 3.3

Following the directions given in the module "All About Motherboards," view the BIOS/UEFI setup information on your computer, and write down all the BIOS/UEFI settings that apply to your hard drive. Explain each setting that you can. The web and motherboard documentation can help. What is the size of the installed drive? Does your system support S.M.A.R.T.? If so, is it enabled?

Hands-On Project 5-2

Selecting a Replacement Hard Drive

Est. Time: 15 minutes
Core 1 Objective: 3.3

Suppose one of the 1 TB Western Digital hard drives installed in the RAID array shown in Figure 5-39 has failed. Search the Internet and find a replacement drive as close to this drive as possible. Save or print three webpages showing the sizes, features, and prices of three possible replacements. Which drive would you recommend as the replacement drive and why?

Hands-On Project 5-3

Preparing for Hard Drive Hardware Problems

Est. Time: 30 minutes
Core 1 Objectives: 3.3, 5.3

1. Boot your computer and make certain that it works properly. Turn off your computer, remove the computer case, and disconnect the data cable to your hard drive. Turn on the computer again. Write down the message that appears.

2. Turn off the computer and reconnect the data cable. Reboot and make sure the system is working again.

3. Turn off the computer and disconnect the power supply cord to the hard drive. Turn on the computer. Write down the error message that appears.

4. Turn off the computer, reconnect the power supply, and reboot the system. Verify that the system is working again.

Hands-On Project 5-4

Installing a Hard Drive

Est. Time: 30 minutes
Core 1 Objective: 3.3

In a lab that has one hard drive per computer, you can practice installing a hard drive by removing it from one computer and installing it as a second drive in another computer. When you boot up the computer with two drives, verify that both drives are accessible in Explorer. Then remove the second hard drive and return it to its original computer. Verify that both computers and drives are working.

Hands-On Project 5-5

Shopping for Storage Media

Est. Time: 30 minutes
Core 1 Objective: 3.3

Shop online and then print or save webpages showing the following devices. One way to shop online is to do a general Google search, and then click **Shopping**. Select ads to answer these questions.

1. DVD+R DL discs are usually sold in packs. What is the storage capacity of each disc? How many discs are in the pack? What is the price per disc?

2. DVD+RW discs are usually sold as singles or in packs. What is the price per disc? How many more times expensive is a DVD+RW disc than a DVD+R disc?

3. BD-R 100 GB discs are sold as singles or in packs. What is the price per disc?

4. What is the largest-capacity USB flash drive you can find? What is its capacity and price?

5. The eight types of SD memory cards are shown in Table 5-3. What is the storage capacity and price of each card? Which type of SD card gives you the most storage per dollar?

Hands-On Project 5-6

Using Speccy to Inspect Your System

Est. Time: 15 minutes
Core 1 Objectives: 3.3, 5.3

In a project at the end of the module "Supporting Processors and Upgrading Memory," you downloaded and installed Speccy at *ccleaner.com/speccy*. If Speccy is not still installed, install it now. Run it to inspect your system, and answer the following questions:

1. What is the manufacturer and product family of your primary hard drive? What is the capacity of the drive? Is the drive magnetic or SSD?

2. Looking at the S.M.A.R.T. data reported by Speccy, how many read errors has S.M.A.R.T. reported? Of the many drive attributes that S.M.A.R.T. monitors, has it reported a status other than good? If so, which attributes have led to problems?

3. Which SATA type is your hard drive using?

4. For your optical drive, which read capabilities does the drive support? Which write capabilities does the drive support?

5. List three ways Speccy might be able to help you when troubleshooting hard drive problems.

Real Problems, Real Solutions

Real Problem 5-1

Recovering Data

Est. Time: 15 minutes
Core 1 Objective: 5.3

Your friend has a Windows 10 desktop system that contains important data. They frantically call you to say that when they turn on the computer, the lights on the front panel light up, they can hear the fan spin for a moment, and then all goes dead. The most urgent problem is the data on the hard drive, which is not backed up. The data is located in several folders on the drive. What is the quickest and easiest way to solve the most urgent problem, recovering the data? List the major steps in that process.

Real Problem 5-2

Using Hardware RAID

Est. Time: 30 minutes
Core 1 Objective: 3.3

You work as an IT support technician for a manager who believes you are really bright and can solve just about any problem that is thrown at you. Folks in the company have complained one time too many that the file server downtime is just killing them, so your manager asks you to solve this problem. Your task is to figure out what hardware is needed to implement hardware RAID for fault tolerance.

You check the file server's configuration and discover it has a single hard drive using a SATA connection with Windows Server 2019 installed. There are four empty bays in the computer case and four extra SATA power cords. You also discover an empty PCIe ×4 slot on the motherboard. BIOS/UEFI setup does not offer the option to configure RAID, but you think the slot might accommodate a RAID controller.

Complete the investigation and do the following

1. Decide what hardware you must purchase, and save or print webpages showing the products and their cost.

2. What levels of RAID does the RAID controller card support? Which RAID level is best to use? Cite any important information in the RAID controller documentation that supports your decisions.

3. What is the total hardware cost of implementing RAID? Estimate how much time you think it will take for you to install the devices and test the setup.

5

Real Problem 5-3

Creating a Bootable Ubuntu USB Drive

Est. Time: 45 minutes
Core 1 Objective: 3.3

Every IT technician who works on personal computers needs a bootable USB flash drive or DVD in their toolkit to use when they cannot boot from the hard drive. If you can boot from other media, you have proven the problem is not the motherboard, processor, or memory, and you can turn your attention to the hard drive subsystem and Windows. In this project, you create an Ubuntu bootable USB flash drive, called a Live USB. (A live Ubuntu flash drive or disc can boot and launch Ubuntu from the drive without changing anything on the hard drive.) You'll need at least 4 GB of free space (more is recommended) on a USB flash drive that has been formatted with the FAT32 file system. Follow these steps to create and test the drive:

1. Go to *ubuntu.com/tutorials/create-a-usb-stick-on-windows* and follow the directions to download the latest Ubuntu desktop OS to your USB flash drive.

2. Your Live USB can have persistent storage, which means that you can write files to the Ubuntu flash drive, and the files will still be there next time you launch Ubuntu from the drive. Note: If you want to use persistent storage, consider using a much larger-capacity (at least 32 GB) USB drive to have room for any application or files you want to store on the USB drive. Research how to create a live Ubuntu USB drive with persistent storage. What benefits does persistent storage have for you as an IT technician?

3. You can boot from the flash drive on this or another computer to launch Ubuntu. First, make sure the BIOS/UEFI boot priority is set to boot first from the USB drive. Then shut down the system and restart it. Ubuntu Desktop loads. Hold on to your Live USB drive for another project in the module "Linux and Scripting."

4. Some systems don't give the option to boot to a USB drive. For these systems, you'll need a bootable DVD. Search the web for directions to create a live Ubuntu bootable DVD. Ubuntu calls this a Live DVD. Which site gives the best directions?

Module

6

Supporting I/O Devices

Module Objectives

1. Describe the general approach technicians use to install and support I/O devices

2. Install and configure several I/O devices, such as mice, keyboards, webcams, microphones, touch screens, and display devices

3. Install and configure adapter cards

4. Support the video subsystem, including selecting a monitor and video card and supporting dual monitors

5. Troubleshoot common problems with I/O devices

Core 1 Certification Objectives

1.1 Given a scenario, install and configure laptop hardware and components.

1.2 Compare and contrast the display components of mobile devices.

3.1 Explain basic cable types and their connectors, features, and purposes.

3.4 Given a scenario, install and configure motherboards, central processing units (CPUs), and add-on cards.

5.4 Given a scenario, troubleshoot video, projector, and display issues.

Introduction

This module is packed full of details about the many I/O (input/output) devices an IT support technician must be familiar with and must know how to install and support. Most of us learn about new technologies when we need to use a device or when a client or customer requests our help making a purchasing decision or solving a problem with a device. Good technicians soon become skilled at searching the web for explanations, reviews, and ads about a device and can quickly turn to support websites for how to install, configure, or troubleshoot a device. This module can serve as your jump start for learning about some of the different computer parts and devices used to enhance a system. It contains enough information to get you started on the path toward becoming an expert with computer devices.

We begin with the basic skills common to supporting any device, including how to use Device Manager and how to select the right port for a new peripheral device. Then you learn to install I/O devices and adapter cards and to support the video subsystem. Finally, you learn how to troubleshoot problems with I/O devices.

Basic Principles for Supporting I/O Devices

 Core 1 Objective 3.1

An I/O or storage device can be either internal (installed inside the computer case) or external (installed outside the case and called a peripheral device). These basic principles apply to supporting both internal and external devices:

- **Every device is controlled by software.** When you install a new device, such as a webcam, you must install both the device and the device drivers to control it. These device drivers must be written for the OS (operating system) you are using. Recall from earlier modules that the exceptions to this principle are some simple devices, such as the keyboard, which are controlled by the system BIOS/UEFI. Also, Windows has embedded device drivers for many devices. For example, when you install a video card, Windows can use its embedded drivers to communicate with the card, but to use all the features of the card, you can install the drivers that came bundled with it or download the drivers from the manufacturer's website.
- **When it comes to installing or supporting a device, the manufacturer knows best.** In this module, you learn a lot of principles and procedures for installing and supporting a device, but when you're on the job installing a device or fixing a broken one, read the manufacturer's documentation, and follow those guidelines first. For example, for most installations, you install the device before you install the device drivers. However, for some devices, such as a wireless keyboard, you might need to install the device drivers first. Check the device documentation to know which to do first.
- **Some devices need application software to use the device.** For example, after you install a capture card and its device drivers, you might also need to install the Wondershare Demo Creator software to use the capture card.
- **A device is no faster than the port or slot it is designed to use.** When buying a new external device, pay attention to the type of port for which it is rated. For example, an external hard drive designed to use a USB 2.0 port will work using a USB 3.0 port, but it will work at the USB 2.0 speed even when it's connected to the faster USB 3.0 port. As another example, a video card in a PCI slot will not work as fast as a video card in a PCI Express slot because of the different speeds of the slots.
- **Use an administrator account in Windows.** When installing hardware devices under Windows, you need to be signed in to the system with a user account that has the highest level of privileges to change the system. This type of account is called an administrator account.
- **Problems with a device can sometimes be solved by updating the device drivers.** Device manufacturers often release updates to device drivers. Update the drivers to solve problems with the device or to add new features. You can use Device Manager in Windows to manage devices and their drivers.
- **Install only one device at a time.** If you have several devices to install, install one and restart the system. Make sure that device is working and that all is well with the system before you move on to install another device.

Recall that **Device Manager** (its program file is named devmgmt.msc) is your primary Windows tool for managing hardware. It lists almost all installed hardware devices and the drivers they use. (Printers and many USB devices are not listed in Device Manager.) Using Device Manager, you can disable or enable a device, update its drivers, uninstall a device, and undo a driver update (called a driver rollback).

Before we move on to installing devices, you need to be familiar with the ports on a computer. When selecting a new device, you can get the best performance by selecting one that uses the fastest wired or wireless connection standard available on your computer.

Wired and Wireless Connection Standards Used by Peripheral Devices

 Core 1 Objective 3.1

When deciding which connection standard to use for a new device, the speed of the transmission standard is often a tiebreaker. Table 6-1 shows the speeds of various wired and wireless standards, from fastest to slowest. This table can help you decide whether speed should affect your purchasing decisions—for example, when you are deciding between a USB 2.0 printer connection and a Bluetooth wireless connection. Standards for video transmissions are not included in this table.

> **Exam Tip** ✔
>
> The A+ Core 1 exam expects you to be able to decide the best connection type given a scenario. Some of the facts you need to know are found in Table 6-1.

Table 6-1   Data transmission speeds for various wired and wireless connections

Port or Wireless Type	Maximum Speed	Maximum Cable Length or Wireless Range
Thunderbolt 4	40 Gbps	Copper cables up to 2 meters; compatible with a USB-C connector
USB4	40 Gbps	Cable lengths up to 1 meter
Thunderbolt 3	40 Gbps	Copper cables up to 2 meters; compatible with a USB-C connector
Thunderbolt 2	20 Gbps	Copper cables up to 100 meters
SuperSpeed+ USB (USB 3.2)	20 Gbps	For maximum speed, cable length up to 1 meter; requires USB-C connector
SuperSpeed+ USB (USB 3.1)	10 Gbps	Cable lengths up to 3 meters
Wi-Fi 802.11ax (WiFi 6) RF (radio frequency) of 2.4 GHz or 5.0 GHz	9.6 Gbps	Undetermined
eSATA Version 3 (eSATA-600)	6.0 Gbps	Cable lengths up to 2 meters
SuperSpeed USB (USB 3.0)	5.0 Gbps	Cable lengths up to 3 meters
eSATA Version 2 (eSATA 300)	3.0 Gbps	Cable lengths up to 2 meters
eSATA Version 1 (eSATA-150)	1.5 Gbps or 1500 Mbps (megabits per second)	Cable lengths up to 2 meters
Wi-Fi 802.11ac (WiFi 5) RF of 5.0 GHz	3.5 Gbps	Range up to 50 meters
Wi-Fi 802.11n RF of 2.4 GHz or 5.0 GHz	Up to 600 Mbps	Range up to 70 meters
Lightning	480 Mbps	Cable lengths up to 2 meters
Hi-Speed USB (USB 2.0)	480 Mbps	Cable lengths up to 5 meters
Wi-Fi 802.11g RF of 2.4 GHz	Up to 54 Mbps	Range up to 100 meters

(continues)

Table 6-1   Data transmission speeds for various wired and wireless connections (Continued)

Port or Wireless Type	Maximum Speed	Maximum Cable Length or Wireless Range
Wi-Fi 802.11a RF of 5.0 GHz	Up to 54 Mbps	Range up to 50 meters
Wi-Fi 802.11b RF of 2.4 GHz	Up to 11 Mbps	Range up to 100 meters
Bluetooth wireless RF of 2.45 GHz	Up to 3 Mbps	Range up to 10 meters
Near Field Communication (NFC) RF of 13.56 MHz	Up to 424 kbps	Range up to 4 centimeters

Connectors and Ports Used by Peripheral Devices

Core 1 Objective 3.1

Take a look at the back of a computer, and you're likely to see a group of ports, several of which you saw in Table 1-1 in the module "Taking a Computer Apart and Putting It Back Together." In this section of the module, we survey ports used by a variety of I/O devices and ports used for video, TV, and other specific uses. We begin our survey with USB.

USB Connections and Ports

Here is a summary of important facts you need to know about USB connections:

- The USB Implementers Forum, Inc. (*usb.org*), the organization responsible for developing USB, uses the symbols shown in Figure 6-1 to indicate **USB4**, SuperSpeed+ USB (USB 3.2 and USB 3.1), SuperSpeed USB (**USB 3.0**), Hi-Speed USB (**USB 2.0**), or Original USB (USB 1.1).

Figure 6-1   USB4, SuperSpeed+, SuperSpeed, Hi-Speed, and Original USB logos appear on products certified by the USB Forum

Source: USB Forum

- As many as 127 USB devices can be daisy-chained together using USB cables. In a daisy chain, one device provides a USB port for the next device.
- USB uses serial transmissions, and USB devices are **hot-swappable**, meaning that you can plug in or unplug one without first powering down the system.
- A USB cable has four wires, two for power and two for communication. The two power wires (one is hot and the other is ground) allow the host controller to provide power to a device. Four general categories of USB ports and connectors are USB-C, regular USB, micro USB, and mini USB. **Mini USB** connectors are smaller and more durable than **micro USB**, which are smaller than regular USB connectors. USB4 only uses USB-C connectors. Table 6-2 shows the different USB connectors on USB cables.

Note 1

Sometimes a mouse that uses USB 2.0 gives problems when plugged into a USB 3.0 port. If a mouse refuses to work or is unstable, try moving it to a USB 2.0 port.

Table 6-2   USB connectors

Cable and Connectors	Description
A-Male to B-Male cable	The A-Male connector on the left is flat and wide and connects to an A-Male USB port on a computer or USB hub.
	The B-Male connector on the right is square and connects to a USB 1.x or 2.0 device such as a printer.
Mini-B to A-Male cable	The Mini-B connector has five pins and is often used to connect small electronic devices to a computer.
A-Male to Micro-B cable	The Micro-B connector has five pins and has a smaller height than the Mini-B connector. It's used on tablets, cell phones, and other small electronic devices.
A-Male to Micro-A cable	The Micro-A connector has five pins and is smaller than the Mini-B connector. It's used on cell phones and other small electronic devices.
USB 3.0 A-Male to USB 3.0 B-Male cable	This USB 3.0 B-Male connector is used by SuperSpeed USB 3.0 devices such as printers or scanners. Devices that have this connection can also use regular B-Male connectors, but this USB 3.0 B-Male connector will not fit the connection on a USB 1.1 or 2.0 device. USB 3.0 A-Male and B-Male connectors and ports are blue.
USB 3.0 A-Male to USB 3.0 Micro-B cable	The USB 3.0 Micro-B connector is used by SuperSpeed USB 3.0 devices. The connectors are not compatible with regular Micro-B connectors.
USB 3.1 A-Male to USB-C 3.1 cable	The **USB-C** connector (also called the USB Type-C connector) on the right is flat with rounded sides and connects to a USB-C port on a computer or device, such as the latest smartphones or a graphics tablet. USB-C connectors do not have a specific orientation and are backward compatible with USB 2.0 and USB 3.0. The connector is required to attain maximum speeds with USB 3.2 devices.

6

> ### Note 2
>
> A USB 3.0 A-Male connector or port has additional pins compared with USB 1.1 or 2.0 ports and connectors, but it is still backward compatible with USB 1.1 and 2.0 devices. A USB 3.0 A-Male or B-Male connector or port is usually blue. Take a close look at the blue and black USB ports shown in Figure 1-16 in the module "Taking a Computer Apart and Putting It Back Together."

Video Connectors and Ports

Video ports are provided by a video card or the motherboard. Video cards (see Figure 6-2) are sometimes called graphics adapters, graphics cards, or display cards. Most motherboards sold today have one or more video ports integrated into the motherboard and are called onboard ports. If you are buying a motherboard with a video port, make sure that you can disable the video port on the motherboard if it gives you trouble. You can then install a video card and use its video port rather than the port on the motherboard. Recall that a video card can use a PCI or PCI Express slot on the motherboard. The fastest slot to use is a PCIe ×16 slot.

Figure 6-2   The PCX 5750 graphics card by MSI Computer Corporation uses the PCI Express ×16 local bus

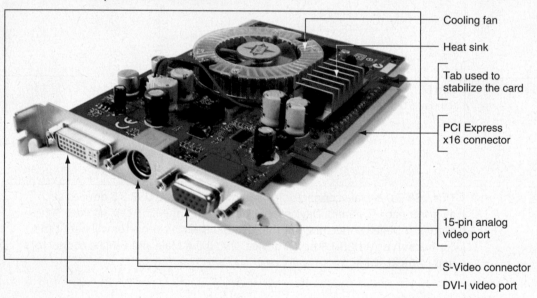

Cooling fan

Heat sink

Tab used to stabilize the card

PCI Express x16 connector

15-pin analog video port

S-Video connector

DVI-I video port

Recall that types of video ports include VGA, DVI, DisplayPort, and HDMI connectors. In addition to these ports, you also need to know about DVI-I and DVI-D ports. These ports are described here:

- **VGA.** The 15-pin VGA port is the standard analog video port and transmits three signals of red, green, and blue (RGB). A VGA port is sometimes called a DB-15 port.
- **DVI ports.** DVI ports were designed to replace VGA, and variations of DVI can transmit analog and/or digital data. The DVI standards specify the maximum length for DVI cables as 5 meters, although some video cards produce a strong enough signal to allow for longer DVI cables.

  Here are the variations of DVI:

  - **DVI-D.** The **DVI-D** port only transmits digital data. Using an adapter to convert a VGA cable to the port won't work. You can see a DVI-D port in Figure 6-3A.
  - **DVI-I.** The **DVI-I** port (see Figure 6-3B) supports both analog and digital signals. Analog data is transmitted using the extra four holes on the right side of the connector. If a computer has this type of port, you can use a digital-to-analog adapter to connect an older analog monitor to the port using a VGA cable (see Figure 6-4). If a video card has a DVI port, it most likely will be the DVI-I port (the one with the four extra holes) so you can use an adapter to convert the port to a VGA port.

Figure 6-3 Two types of DVI ports: (A) DVI-D and (B) DVI-I

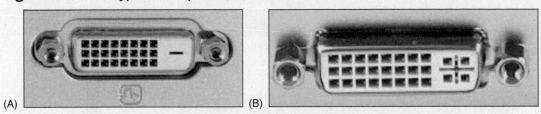

(A)   (B)

Figure 6-4 A digital-to-analog video port converter using a DVI-I connector with four extra pins

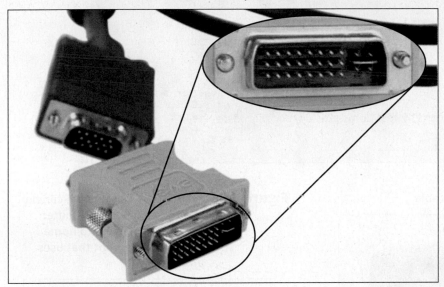

- **DisplayPort.** DisplayPort was designed to replace DVI and can transmit digital video and audio data. It uses data packet transmissions similar to those of Ethernet, USB, and PCI Express and is expected to ultimately replace VGA, DVI, and HDMI on desktop and laptop computers. Besides the regular DisplayPort used on video cards and desktop computers, laptops might use the smaller **Mini DisplayPort**. Figure 6-5 shows a DisplayPort to Mini DisplayPort cable. The maximum length for DisplayPort cables is 15 meters.

  BIOS/UEFI setup can be used to manage onboard DisplayPort and HDMI ports. For example, Figure 6-6 shows the BIOS screen where you can enable or disable the audio transmissions of DisplayPort and HDMI ports and still use these ports for video.

- **HDMI connectors.** HDMI transmits both digital video and audio, and it was designed to be used by home theater equipment. The HDMI standards allow for several types of HDMI connectors. The best known, which is used on most computers and televisions, is the Type A 19-pin **HDMI connector**. Figure 6-7 shows a cable with HDMI and mini HDMI connectors, which is useful when connecting devices like a smartphone to a computer. Figure 6-8 shows an HDMI to DVI-D cable. The maximum length of an HDMI cable depends on the quality of the cable; no maximum length has been specified.

Figure 6-5 A DisplayPort to Mini DisplayPort cable

6

Figure 6-6   Use BIOS/UEFI setup to enable or disable onboard ports

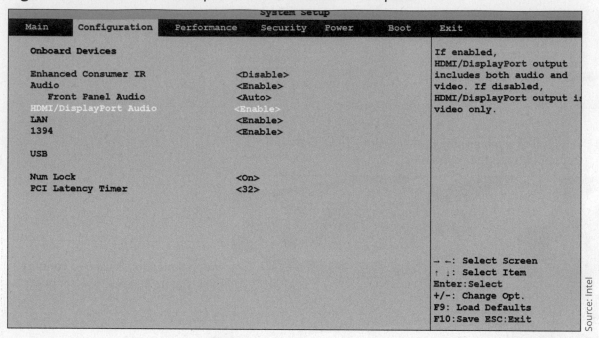

```
                              System Setup

  Main     Configuration    Performance   Security   Power   Boot    Exit

  Onboard Devices                                              If enabled,
                                                               HDMI/DisplayPort output
  Enhanced Consumer IR          <Disable>                      includes both audio and
  Audio                         <Enable>                       video. If disabled,
     Front Panel Audio          <Auto>                         HDMI/DisplayPort output i:
  HDMI/DisplayPort Audio        <Enable>                       video only.
  LAN                           <Enable>
  1394                          <Enable>

  USB

  Num Lock                      <On>
  PCI Latency Timer             <32>




                                                               → ←: Select Screen
                                                               ↑ ↓: Select Item
                                                               Enter:Select
                                                               +/-: Change Opt.
                                                               F9: Load Defaults
                                                               F10:Save ESC:Exit
```

Source: Intel

Figure 6-7   An HDMI to mini-HDMI cable

Figure 6-8   An HDMI-to-DVI-D cable can be used to connect a computer that has a DVI port to home theater equipment that uses an HDMI port

Source: Courtesy of Belkin Corporation

Exam Tip ✔

The A+ Core 1 exam expects you to know about these video connector types: HDMI, DisplayPort, DVI, and VGA. You must also be able to choose which connector type is the right solution given a scenario.

Additional Connectors and Ports

Besides USB and video, here are a few other ports and connectors you need to know about:

- **Thunderbolt.** Thunderbolt is a multipurpose connector used to connect high-end displays and external storage devices and to provide power for smartphones and laptops (see Figure 6-9). Earlier versions of

Thunderbolt were limited to Apple products and used the DisplayPort base connection. The latest two versions, Thunderbolt 4 and Thunderbolt 3, use the USB-C connection (marked with a lightning bolt symbol), which opens the compatibility of Thunderbolt connections to non-Apple products. The USB-C Thunderbolt 4 and 3 ports can support data transfer rates up to 40 Gbps.

- **eSATA.** The eSATA port is used for connecting external storage devices to a computer (see Figure 6-10).
- **Lightning.** The **Lightning** connector is an Apple-specific connector for its mobile devices (see Figure 6-11). It is used to charge mobile devices, to transfer data, and to connect peripheral devices, such as a credit card payment device or headphone jack, to the Apple mobile device. The connector is reversible.
- **RS-232.** USB or other connectors have replaced the serial **RS-232** connectors once used with mice, keyboards, dial-up modems, and peripheral connections. However, you might see a serial RS-232 connector on a rack server to set up a terminal to access the server. An earlier version of RS-232 had a 25-pin connector, but all RS-232 connectors today use nine pins and are often called DB-9 connectors (see Figure 6-12).

Now that you know about the connection standards, ports, and connectors for external devices, let's see how to install them.

Figure 6-9 The Thunderbolt 3 cable uses the USB-C connector

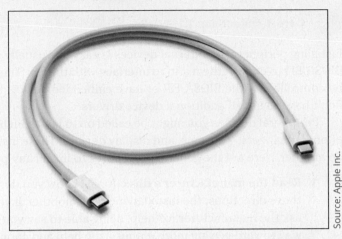

Source: Apple Inc.

Figure 6-10 An eSATA connection is used to connect external storage devices to a computer

Source: Amazon.com, Inc.

Figure 6-11 This Lightning-to-USB-C cable connects an Apple mobile device to a USB-C port

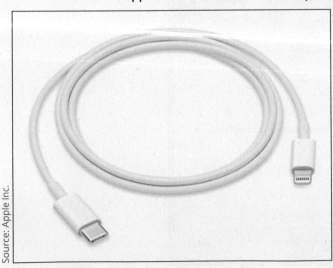

Source: Apple Inc.

Figure 6-12 The serial DB-9 connector may be used to connect a terminal to a server installed in a rack

Source: Cablestogo.com

Identifying and Installing I/O Peripheral Devices

 Core 1 Objectives 1.1, 1.2, 3.4

Installing peripheral or external devices is easy and usually goes without a hitch. All devices need device drivers or BIOS/UEFI to control them and to interface with the OS. Simple input devices, such as the mouse and keyboard, can be controlled by the BIOS/UEFI or have embedded device drivers built into the OS. For these devices, you usually don't have to install additional device drivers.

Peripheral devices you might be called on to install include keyboards, mice, touch pads, touch screens, microphones, digitizers, webcams, and display devices. These installations are similar, so learning to do one will help you do another. Here are the general procedures to install any peripheral device:

1. **Read the manufacturer's directions.** I know you don't want to hear that again, but when you follow these directions, the installation goes smoother. If you later have a problem with the installation and you ask the manufacturer for help, being able to say you followed the directions exactly as stated goes a long way toward getting more enthusiastic help and cooperation.

2. **Make sure the drivers provided with the device are written for the OS you are using.** Recall that 64-bit drivers are required for a 64-bit OS, and 32-bit drivers are required for a 32-bit OS. You can sometimes use drivers written for older Windows versions in newer Windows versions, but for best results, use drivers written for the OS installed. You can download the drivers you need from the manufacturer's website.

3. **Make sure the motherboard port you are using is enabled.** It is most likely enabled, but if the device is not recognized when you plug it in, go into BIOS/UEFI setup and make sure the port is enabled. In addition, BIOS/UEFI setup might offer the option to configure a USB port to use USB4, SuperSpeed+ (USB or 3.2 or 3.1), SuperSpeed (USB 3.0), Hi-Speed USB (USB 2.0), or original USB (USB 1.1). Refer back to Figure 6-6, which shows the BIOS setup screen for one system where you can enable or disable onboard devices. In addition, if you are having problems with a motherboard port, don't forget to update the motherboard drivers that control the port.

4. **Install drivers or plug in the device.** Some devices, such as a USB printer, require that you plug in the device before installing the drivers, and some devices require you to install the drivers before plugging in the device. For some devices, it doesn't matter which is installed first. Carefully read and follow the device documentation. For example, the documentation for one scanner says that if you install the scanner before installing the drivers, the drivers will not install properly.

   If you plug in the device first, Device Setup launches and steps you through the installation of drivers (see Figure 6-13). As Device Setup works, an icon appears in the taskbar. To see the Device Setup dialog box, as shown in the figure, click the icon.

Figure 6-13   Device Setup begins installing a new device

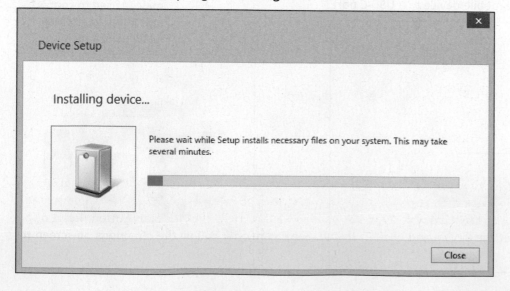

If you need to install the drivers first, run the setup program on CD or DVD. If you downloaded drivers from the web, double-click the driver file and follow the directions on-screen. It might be necessary to restart the system after the installation. After the drivers are installed, plug the device into the port. The device should immediately be recognized by Windows. If you have problems using the device, turn to Device Manager for help.

5. **Install the application software to use the device.** For example, a USB camcorder is likely to come bundled with video-editing software. Run the software to use the device.

Now let's look at some key features and any specific installation concerns for several peripheral devices.

Mouse or Keyboard

 Core 1 Objective 1.1

When you plug a mouse or keyboard into a USB port, Windows should immediately recognize it and install generic drivers. (Older computers used PS/2 ports for the mouse and keyboard. Because these ports were not hot-pluggable, you had to restart Windows after plugging in a mouse or keyboard.) For keyboards with special features such as the one shown in Figure 6-14, you need to install the drivers that came with the keyboard before you can use these features.

Figure 6-14   The mouse and keyboard require drivers to use the extra buttons and zoom bar

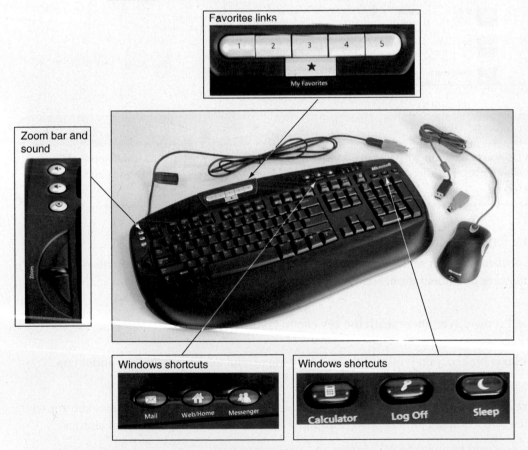

You can use Device Manager to uninstall, disable, or enable most devices. However, USB devices are managed differently. To uninstall a USB device such as a USB graphing tablet, use the Programs and Features window or the Apps & features window. To open the Windows 10 Apps & features window, right-click the **Start** button, select **Apps and Features**, and then select the device and click **Uninstall**. See Figure 6-15. Follow the directions on-screen to uninstall the device.

Figure 6-15   USB devices are listed as installed programs

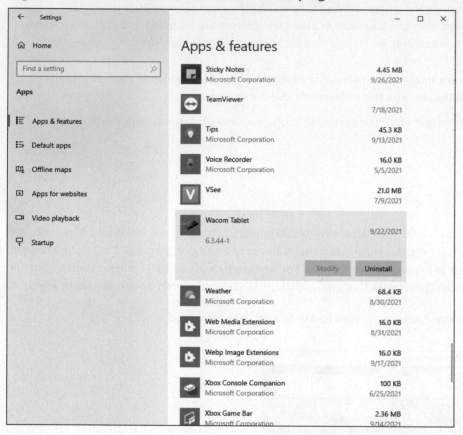

Note 3

The A+ Core 1 exam expects you to use Control Panel in Classic view, which presents a list of individual items. If Control Panel is in Category view, which presents items in groups, you can get Classic view by clicking **Category** and then clicking **Small icons** or **Large icons**.

Replace a Key or the Keyboard and Touch Pad in a Laptop

When individual keys are broken, you can replace just the key fairly easily. Before you begin any disassembly of a laptop, refer to the manufacturer documentation. Follow these standard steps that are similar for many models of laptops:

1. Slide a small flathead screwdriver underneath the key cap to hold down the key retainer clip, and then pull up on the key cap.
2. If the key retainer clip is broken, pop it off and replace it, being careful to not pull on the rubber cup.
3. Pop a new key cap on the key retainer clip.

Replacing the whole keyboard is pretty easy, too. Always follow the steps provided by the manufacturer when disassembling a laptop. Here are the steps for a Lenovo laptop that are similar for many models of laptops:

1. Power down the laptop, and remove the AC adapter and the battery pack.
2. Remove two or more screws on the bottom of the laptop. (Only the manufacturer documentation can tell you which ones because there are probably several used to hold various components in place.)
3. Remove the lid on the bottom of the laptop to expose the keyboard ribbon cable attached underneath the board. Use a screwdriver, spudger, or tweezers to lift the cable connector up and out of its socket (see Figure 6-16).

Figure 6-16   Disconnect the keyboard cable from the motherboard

4. Turn the laptop over and open the lid. Use a spudger to gently pry the keyboard bezel away from the case (see Figure 6-17).

Figure 6-17   Use a spudger to pry up the keyboard bezel

5. Lift the keyboard bezel from the case (see Figure 6-18).

Figure 6-18   Lift the keyboard from the case

6. Replace the keyboard following the steps in reverse order.

Sometimes the touch pad and keyboard are one complete field replaceable unit (FRU). If the touch pad is a separate component, it might be part of the keyboard bezel, also called the palm rest. This bezel is the flat cover that surrounds the keyboard. You most likely have to remove the keyboard before you can remove the keyboard bezel.

Webcams

Core 1 Objective 1.2

A webcam (web camera) is embedded in most laptops and can also be installed as a peripheral device using a USB port or some other port. For example, the webcam shown in Figure 6-19 works well for personal chat sessions and videoconferencing and has a built-in microphone. First, install the software, and then plug in the webcam to a USB port.

Figure 6-19   This personal web camera clips to the top of your laptop and has a built-in microphone

A webcam comes with a built-in microphone. You can use this microphone or the microphone port on the computer. Most software for using a webcam and microphone allows you to select these input devices. For example, Figure 6-20 shows the input options for VCam by XSplit (*xsplit.com*).

Figure 6-20   The VCam application by XSplit allows you to change the input devices used for video and sound

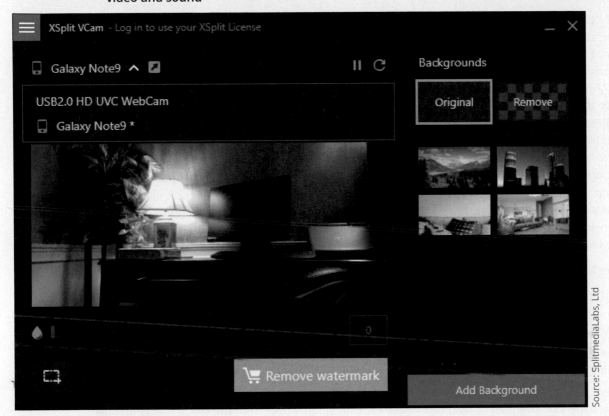

Graphics Tablets

Core 1 Objective 1.2

Another input device is a **graphics tablet**, also called a **digitizing tablet** or **digitizer**, which is used to hand draw. It is likely to connect using a USB port (see Figure 6-21). It comes with a **stylus** that works like a pencil on the tablet and controls the pointer on the screen. The graphics tablet and stylus can be a replacement for a mouse or touch pad on a laptop, and some graphics tablets come with a mouse. Graphics tablets are popular with graphic artists and other content creators who use desktop publishing applications.

Install the graphics tablet the same way you do other USB devices. Additional software might be bundled with the device to enhance its functions, such as inputting handwritten signatures into Microsoft Word documents.

Figure 6-21   A graphics tablet and stylus are used to digitize a hand drawing

Installing and Configuring Adapter Cards

Core 1 Objectives 1.1, 1.2, 3.4

In this section of the module, you learn to install and configure adapter cards. These types of cards include video cards, sound cards, network interface cards (NIC), capture cards, and USB expansion cards. The purpose of adding an adapter card to a system is to add external ports or internal connectors the card provides.

Regardless of the type of card you are installing, be sure to verify and do the following when preparing to install one:

- **Verify that the card fits an empty expansion slot.** Recall that there are several PCI and PCI Express standards; therefore, make sure the card will fit the slot. To help with airflow, try to leave an empty slot between cards. Especially try to leave an empty slot beside the video card, which puts off a lot of heat. PCIe slots on a motherboard might support different PCIe standards. The motherboard manual tells you which slot is rated for which PCIe standard.

- **Verify that the device drivers for your OS are available.** Check the card documentation, and make sure you have the drivers for your OS. For example, you need to install 64-bit Windows 10 device drivers in a 64-bit installation of Windows 10. You might find drivers to download for your OS from the website of the card manufacturer.

- **Back up important data that is not already backed up.** Before you open the computer case, be sure to back up important data on the hard drive.

- **Know your starting point.** Know what works and what doesn't work on the system. Can you connect to the network and the Internet, print, and use other installed adapter cards without errors? After installing a new card, verify your starting point again before installing another card.

Here are the general directions to install an adapter card. They apply to any type of card.

1. Read the documentation that came with the card. For most cards, you install the card first and then the drivers, but some installations might not work this way.

2. If you are installing a card to replace an onboard port, access BIOS/UEFI setup and disable the port.

3. Wear an ESD strap as you work to protect the card and the system against ESD. Shut down the system, unplug power cords and cables, and press the power button to drain the power. Remove the computer case cover.

4. Locate the slot you plan to use, and remove the faceplate cover from the slot if one is installed. Sometimes a faceplate punches or snaps out, and sometimes you have to remove a faceplate screw to remove the faceplate. Remove the screw in the top of the expansion slot or raise the clip on the top of the slot. Save the screw; you'll need it later.

5. Remove the card from its antistatic bag, and insert it into the expansion slot. Be careful to push the card straight down into the slot without rocking the card from side to side. Rocking the card can widen the expansion slot, making it difficult to keep a good contact. If you have a problem getting the card into the slot, resist the temptation to push the front or rear of the card into the slot first. You should feel a slight snap as the card drops into the slot.

   Recall that PCIe ×16 slots use a retention mechanism in the slot to help stabilize a heavy card (see Figure 6-22). For these slots, you might have to use one finger to push the stabilizer to the side as you push the card into the slot. Alternately, the card might snap into the slot, and then the retention mechanism snaps into position. Figure 6-23 shows a PCIe video card installed in a PCIe ×16 slot.

Figure 6-22   A white retention mechanism on a PCIe ×16 slot pops into place to help stabilize a heavy video card

Figure 6-23   A PCIe video card installed in a PCIe ×16 slot

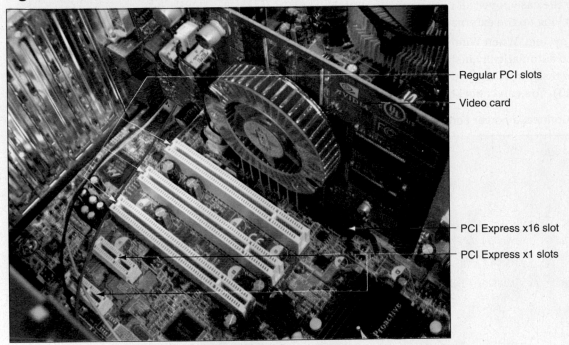

— Regular PCI slots

— Video card

— PCI Express x16 slot

— PCI Express x1 slots

6. Insert the screw that anchors the card to the top of the slot (see Figure 6-24). Be sure to use this screw. If it's not present, the card can creep out of the slot over time, causing a loose connection.

Figure 6-24   Secure the card to the case with a single screw

7. Connect any power cords or data cables the card might use. For example, a video card might have a 6-pin or 8-pin PCIe power connector for a power cord from the power supply to the card, as shown in Figure 6-25.

Note 4

If the power supply does not have the right connector, you can buy an inexpensive adapter to convert a 4-pin Molex connector to a PCIe connector.

8. Make a quick check of all connections and cables, and then replace the case cover. (If you want, you can leave the case cover off until you've tested the card, in case it doesn't work and you need to reseat it.) Plug up the external power cable and essential peripherals.

9. Start the system. When Windows starts, it should detect that a new hardware device is present and attempt to automatically install the drivers. As the drivers are installed, a message might appear above the taskbar. When you click the message, the Device Setup dialog box appears (refer back to Figure 6-13). You can cancel the wizard and manually install the drivers.

Figure 6-25   Connect a power cord to the PCIe power connector on the card

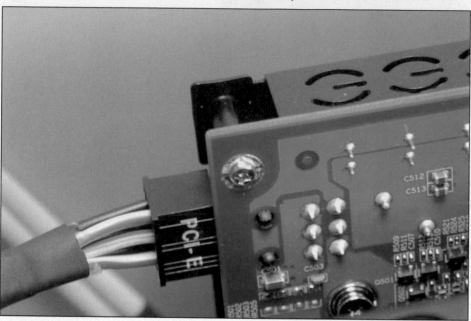

10. Download the drivers from the manufacturer website, or insert the CD that came bundled with the card and launch the setup program. The card documentation will tell you the name of the program (examples are Setup.exe and Autorun.exe). Figure 6-26 shows the opening menu for one setup program for a video card. Follow the on-screen instructions to install the drivers.

Figure 6-26   An opening menu to install video drivers

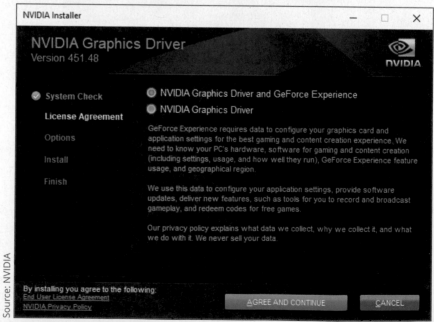

Source: NVIDIA

Note 5

All 64-bit drivers must be certified by Microsoft to work in Windows. However, some 32-bit drivers might not be certified. During the driver installation, if you see a message that 32-bit drivers have not been certified, go ahead and give permission to install the drivers if you obtained them from the manufacturer or another reliable source.

11. After the drivers are installed, you might be asked to restart the system. Then you can configure the card or use it with application software. If you have problems with the installation, turn to Device Manager and look for errors reported about the device. The card might not be properly seated in the slot.

Now let's turn our attention to types of cards you might be called on to install. As with any adapter card you install, be sure to become familiar with the user guide before you start the installation so you know the card's hardware and software requirements and what peripheral devices it supports.

Sound Cards and Onboard Sound

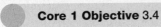
Core 1 Objective 3.4

A **sound card** (an expansion card with sound ports) or onboard sound (sound ports embedded on a motherboard) can play and record sound and save it in a file. Figure 6-27 shows a sound card by Creative (*creative.com*). This Sound Blaster card uses a PCIe ×1 slot and supports up to eight surround sound speakers. The color-coded speaker ports are for these speakers: front left and right, front center, rear left and right, subwoofer, and two additional rear speakers. The two SPDIF (Sony-Philips Digital InterFace) ports are used to connect to external sound equipment such as a Blu-ray disc player.

Figure 6-27   The Sound Blaster X-Fi Titanium sound card by Creative uses a PCIe ×1 slot

Source: Creative Technology Ltd.

Note 6

If you are using a single speaker or two speakers with a single sound cable, connect the cable to the lime-green sound port on the motherboard, which is usually the middle port.

Capture Cards

Core 1 Objective 3.4

A **capture card** is a peripheral device or an expansion card used to record and stream content from an external device, such as a gaming console or webcam. Capture cards are primarily used by video game streamers. Some capture cards use a PCIe port on the motherboard. Figure 6-28 shows a capture card by AVerMedia (*avermedia.com*).

Figure 6-28   This capture card by AVerMedia uses a PCIe slot to connect to the computer

Source: Amazon.com, Inc.

Another type of capture card is a peripheral device that connects to the computer using a USB, USB-C, or Thunderbolt port. Capture cards have a passthrough between the source of content (e.g., a gaming console or camera) and the display, typically using HDMI in/out connections. The data is sent via the passthrough to the computer to record and stream (see Figure 6-29). Some capture cards also offer ports for input from a microphone and output to a headset.

Figure 6-29   Connections on a capture card

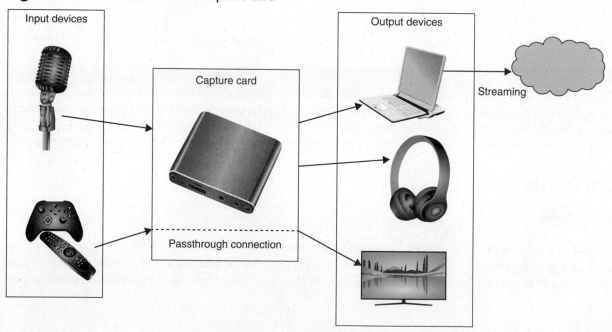

After installing a capture card, you can download and use the proprietary software that comes with the card, or you can choose third-party software. Third-party software is usually more robust than proprietary software offered by the manufacturer. Windows 10 offers Xbox Game Bar for recording (see Figure 6-30). To open Microsoft Xbox Game Bar, press the **Windows key+G**.

Figure 6-30   Windows Game Bar can be used for recording

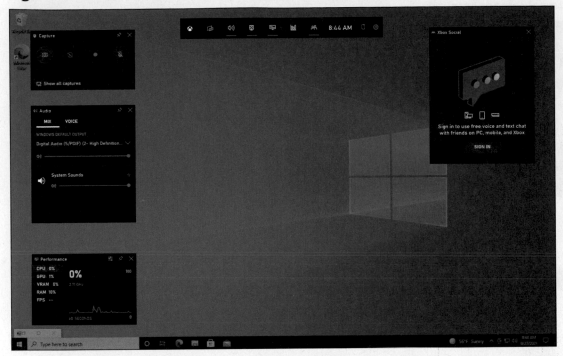

Replacing Expansion Cards in a Laptop

Core 1 Objective 1.1

A laptop does not contain the normal PCI Express or PCI slots found in desktop systems. Many laptops provide **Mini PCI Express** slots (also called **Mini PCIe** slots) that use the PCI Express standards applied to laptops. Mini PCI Express slots use 52 pins on the edge connector. These slots can be used by many kinds of Mini PCIe cards. These cards are often used to enhance communications options for a laptop, including Wi-Fi wireless, video, and Bluetooth Mini PCIe cards. Figure 6-31 shows a Mini PCI Express card by Sierra Wireless that provides mobile broadband Internet.

For many laptops, you can remove a cover on the bottom to expose expansion cards so that you can exchange them without an extensive disassembly. For example, to remove the cover on the bottom of one Lenovo laptop, first remove several screws, and then lift the laptop cover up and out. Several internal components are exposed, as shown in Figure 6-32.

The half-size Mini PCIe wireless Wi-Fi card shown in Figure 6-33 has two antennas. To remove the card, first disconnect the black and the gray antenna wires, and remove the one screw shown in the photo. Note the black and white triangles labeled with a 1 and a 2 on the label of the card so you know which wire goes on which connector when replacing the card. Typically, the black antenna wire goes to the black triangle, and the gray antenna wire goes with the white triangle. Then slide the card forward and out of the slot. You can then install a new card.

Figure 6-31   The MC8775 Mini PCI Express card by Sierra Wireless used for voice and data transmissions on cellular networks

Source: Sierra Wireless

Figure 6-32   Removing the cover from the bottom of a laptop exposes several internal components

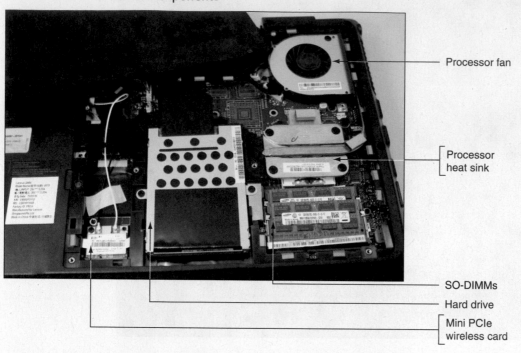

Processor fan

Processor heat sink

SO-DIMMs

Hard drive

Mini PCIe wireless card

Figure 6-33   This half-size Mini PCIe wireless card is anchored in the expansion slot with one screw

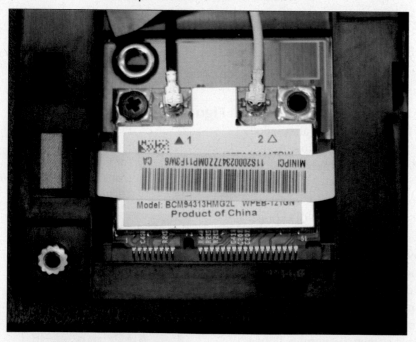

Figure 6-34 shows another Mini PCIe card installed in a laptop. First remove the one screw at the top of the card and disconnect the two antenna wires, and then pull the card forward and out of the slot.

After you have installed a Mini PCIe card that is a Bluetooth or other wireless adapter, try to connect the laptop to the wireless network. If you have problems making a connection, verify that Device Manager reports the device is working properly and that Event Viewer has not reported error events about the device.

Figure 6-34   How to remove a Mini PCI Express card

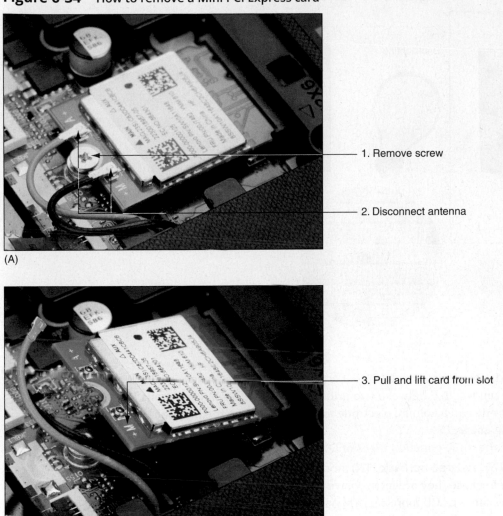

1. Remove screw

2. Disconnect antenna

(A)

3. Pull and lift card from slot

(B)

Supporting the Video Subsystem

 Core 1 Objectives 1.2, 3.1, 3.4

The primary output device of a computer is the monitor. The two necessary components for video output are the monitor and the video card (also called the video adapter and graphics card) or a video port on the motherboard. In this section of the module, you learn about monitors and how to support the video subsystem.

Monitor Technologies and Features

 Core 1 Objectives 1.2, 3.1

The most popular type of monitor for laptop and desktop systems is an LCD flat-screen monitor (see Figure 6-35), but you have other choices as well. Here is a list and description of each type of display:

- **LCD monitor.** The **LCD (liquid crystal display) monitor**, also called a **flat-panel monitor**, was first used in laptops. The monitor produces an image using a liquid crystal material made of large, easily polarized molecules. Figure 6-36 shows the layers of the LCD panel that together create the image. At the center of

Figure 6-35   An LCD monitor   **Figure 6-36**   Layers of an LCD panel

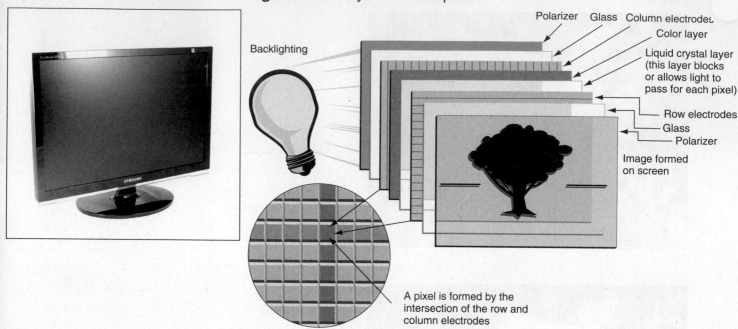

A pixel is formed by the intersection of the row and column electrodes

the layers is the liquid crystal material. Next to it is the layer responsible for providing color to the image. These two layers are sandwiched between two grids of electrodes forming columns and rows. Each intersection of a row electrode and a column electrode forms one **pixel** on the LCD panel. Software can address each pixel to create an image.

The following are the three common types of LCD monitors:

- **Twisted nematic (TN). Twisted nematic (TN)** monitors are the oldest type of LCD monitor and are still widely popular because they are inexpensive and easy to produce. They have lowest latency and highest refresh rates among LCD monitors. The viewing angles and color range of TN monitors are lacking.

- **In-plane switching (IPS). In-plane switching (IPS)** monitors improved on TN monitors in terms of viewing angles and color range. In addition, IPS monitors provide the most accurate color and the best LED (light-emitting diode) backlighting for viewing photography; however, these types of monitors also have an "IPS glow" at extreme viewing angles. IPS monitors, which are quickly closing the gap with TN monitors in latency and refresh rates, are the most expensive option.

- **Vertical alignment (VA). Vertical alignment (VA)** monitors are a compromise between TN and IPS monitors. VA monitors are ideal for general use and in TVs. They offer the best contrast ratio and picture depth. VA monitors offer better color range than TN monitors, and they do not have the IPS glow. They have poor latency, which creates motion blur or ghosting on fast-moving pictures, making them unpopular among competitive gamers.

- **OLED monitor.** An **OLED (organic light-emitting diode)** monitor uses a thin LED (light-emitting diode) layer or film between two grids of electrodes and does not use backlighting. It does not emit as much light as an LCD monitor and, therefore, can produce deeper blacks, provide better contrast, work in darker rooms, and use less power than an LCD monitor. On the other hand, LCD monitors give less glare than OLED monitors. OLED screens are primarily used by mobile devices and other portable electronic devices. OLED monitors are available for desktop systems but are significantly more expensive than LCD monitors.

- **Projector.** A digital **projector** (see Figure 6-37) shines a light that projects a transparent image onto a large screen and is often used in classrooms or with other large groups. Several types of technologies are used by projectors, including LCD. A projector is often installed as a dual monitor on a computer, which you learn how to do later in the module.

Figure 6-37   A portable XGA projector by Panasonic

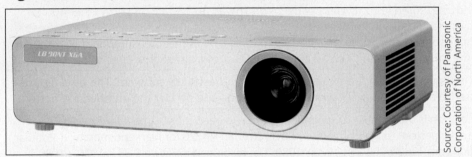

Source: Courtesy of Panasonic Corporation of North America

6

Exam Tip ✔

The A+ Core 1 exam expects you to compare LCD and OLED monitor types and choose which one is the best fit for a given scenario.

Although a laptop display almost always uses LCD technology, laptops that use an OLED display are available. Some laptop LCD panels use LED backlighting to improve display quality and conserve power. For desktops, LCD is by far the most popular monitor type. Figure 6-38 shows an ad for one best-selling LCD monitor. Table 6-3 explains the features mentioned in the ad.

Exam Tip ✔

The A+ Core 1 exam expects you to know about the components within the display of a laptop, including the components used in LCD and OLED displays. You also need to know about backlighting and the function of an inverter.

Figure 6-38   An ad for a monitor lists the monitor's features

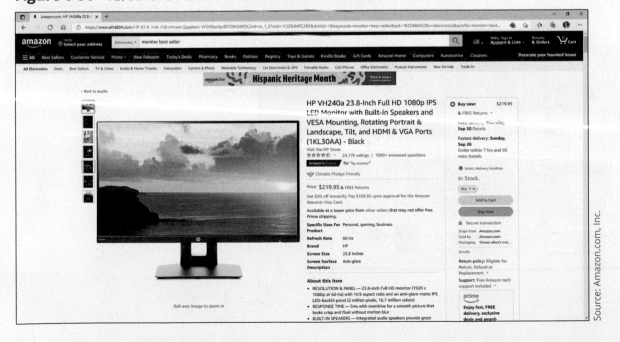

Source: Amazon.com, Inc.

Table 6-3   Important features of a monitor

Monitor Characteristic	Description
Screen size	The screen size is the diagonal length of the screen surface in inches.
Refresh rate	The refresh rate is the number of times a monitor screen is built or refreshed in 1 second, measured in Hz (cycles per second). The ad in Figure 6-38 shows the monitor refresh rate as 60 Hz (60 frames per second)—the higher, the better. Related to refresh rate, the response time is the time it takes to build one frame, measured in milliseconds (ms)—the lower, the better. The ad in Figure 6-38 shows a response time of 5 ms.
Pixel pitch	A pixel is a spot or dot on the screen that can be addressed by software. The pixel pitch is the distance between adjacent pixels on the screen—the smaller the number, the better.
Resolution	The resolution is the number of spots or pixels on a screen that can be addressed by software. Values can range from 640 × 480 up to 7680 × 4320 for high-end monitors. Popular resolutions are 1280 × 720 and 1920 × 1080. The resolution in Figure 6-38 is 1920 × 1080.
Contrast ratio	Contrast ratio is the contrast between true black and true white on the screen—the higher the contrast ratio, the better. 1000:1 is better than 700:1. An advertised dynamic contrast ratio is much higher than the contrast ratio, but it is not a true measurement of contrast. Dynamic contrast adjusts the backlighting to give the effect of an overall brighter or darker image. For example, if the contrast ratio is 1000:1, the dynamic ratio is 20,000,000:1. When comparing quality of monitors, pay more attention to the contrast ratio than the dynamic ratio.
Viewing angle	The viewing angle is the angle at which a monitor becomes difficult to see from the side. A viewing angle of 170 degrees is better than 140 degrees.
Backlighting or brightness	Brightness is measured in cd/m² (candela per square meter), which is the same as lumens/m² (lumens per square meter).
Connectors	Popular options for connectors are VGA, DVI-I, DVI-D, HDMI, DisplayPort, and Thunderbolt. Some monitors offer more than one connector (see Figure 6-39).
Other features	LCD monitors can also provide a privacy or antiglare surface, tilt screens, microphone input, speakers, USB ports, adjustable stands, and perhaps even an input for your smartphone. Some monitors are also touch screens, so they can be used with a stylus or finger touch.

Figure 6-39   The rear of this LCD monitor shows digital and analog video ports to accommodate a video cable with either a 15-pin analog VGA connector or a digital DVI connector

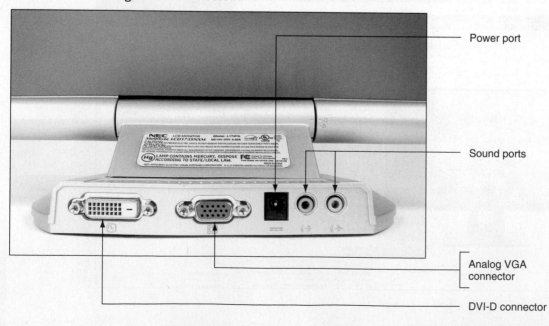

Power port

Sound ports

Analog VGA connector

DVI-D connector

Exam Tip ✔

The A+ Core 1 exam expects you to know about monitor features such as refresh rate, resolution, brightness in lumens, and connectors used.

Caution

If you spend many hours in front of a computer, you may strain your eyes. To protect your eyes from strain, look away from the monitor into the distance every few minutes. Use a good monitor with a high refresh rate or low response time. The lower refresh rates that cause monitor flicker can tire and damage your eyes. When you first install a monitor, set the refresh rate at the highest value the monitor can support.

6

Now let's see how to configure a monitor or dual monitors connected to a Windows computer.

Changing Monitor Settings

Core 1 Objective 1.2

Settings that apply to the monitor can be managed by using the monitor buttons, function keys on a keyboard, and Windows utilities. Using the monitor buttons, you can adjust the horizontal and vertical position of the screen on the monitor surface and change the brightness and contrast settings. Adjust these settings to correct a distorted image. For laptops, the brightness and contrast settings can be changed using function keys on the laptop.

Applying Concepts

Installing Dual Monitors

Est. Time: 30 minutes
Core 1 Objective: 1.2

To increase the size of your Windows desktop, you can install more than one monitor for a single computer. To install dual monitors, you need two video ports on your system, which can come from motherboard video ports, a video card that provides two video ports, or two video cards.

To install a second monitor in a dual-monitor setup using two video cards, follow these steps:

1. Verify that the original video card works properly, and decide whether it will be the primary monitor.

2. Boot the computer and enter BIOS/UEFI setup. If BIOS/UEFI setup has the option to select the order in which video cards are initialized, verify that the currently installed card is configured to initialize first. For example, for the BIOS/UEFI system in Figure 6-40, the video adapter in the PCIe slot initializes first before other video adapters. If it does not initialize first and you install the second card, video might not work at all when you first boot with two cards.

(continues)

Applying Concepts Continued

Figure 6-40   In BIOS/UEFI setup, verify that the currently installed video adapter is set to initialize first

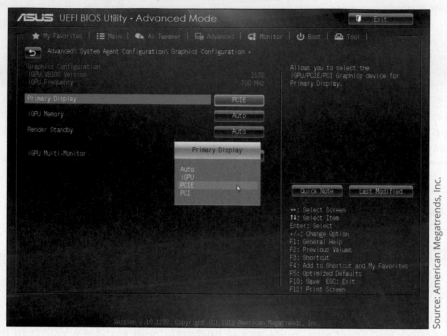

Source: American Megatrends, Inc.

3. Install a second video card in an empty slot. A computer might have a second PCIe slot or an unused PCI slot you can use. Attach the second monitor.

4. Boot the system. Windows recognizes the new hardware and launches Device Setup. You can use the utility to install the video card drivers or cancel the utility and install them manually, as you learned to do earlier in the module.

Here are the steps to configure dual monitors:

1. Connect two monitors to your system. In Windows 10, open the **Settings** app, and click the **System** group. The display settings appear, as shown in Figure 6-41.

Figure 6-41   Configure each monitor in a dual-monitor configuration

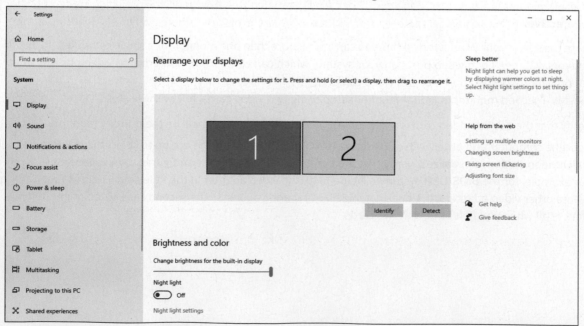

6

2. Notice the two numbered boxes that represent your two monitors. When you click one of these boxes, the settings shown apply to the selected monitor, and the screen resolution and orientation (Landscape, Portrait, Landscape flipped, or Portrait flipped) follow the selected monitor. This lets you customize the settings for each monitor separately. If necessary, use drag-and-drop to arrange the boxes so they represent the physical arrangement of your monitors.

Note 7

If you see both numbered displays in the same box, the Multiple displays setting is set to Duplicate these displays. To separate the displays, change the Multiple displays setting to **Extend these displays**. Then click **Keep changes**.

Note 8

In Figure 6-41, if you arrange the two boxes side by side, your extended desktop will extend left or right. If you arrange the two boxes one on top of the other, your extended desktop will extend up and down.

---

3. Adjust the screen resolution according to your preferences. The highest resolution is most often the best resolution for the monitor.

4. The Multiple displays setting allows you to select how to handle multiple displays. You can extend your desktop onto the second monitor, duplicate displays, or disable the display on either monitor. To save the settings, click **Keep changes**. The second monitor should initialize and show the extended or duplicated desktop.

5. Close the **Settings** app. For an extended desktop, open an application and verify that you can use the second monitor by dragging the application window over to the second monitor's desktop.

After you add a second monitor to your system, you can move from one monitor to another simply by moving your mouse over the extended desktop. Switching from one monitor to the other does not require any special keystroke or menu option.

Most laptop computers are designed to be used with projectors and provide a VGA, DisplayPort, or HDMI port for this purpose. To use a projector, plug it in to the extra port, and then turn it on. For a laptop computer, use a function key to activate the video port and toggle between extending the desktop to the projector, using only the projector, duplicating the screen on the projector, or not using the projector. When giving a presentation, most people prefer to see it duplicated on the LCD screen and the projector.

Note 9

For group presentations that require a projector, the most common software used is Microsoft PowerPoint. If you configure your projector as a dual monitor, you can use PowerPoint to display a presentation to your audience on the projector at the same time you are using your LCD display to manage your PowerPoint slides. To do so, select the **Slide Show** tab in PowerPoint. In the Set Up group, click **Set Up Slide Show**. In the Set Up Show box under Multiple monitors, check **Use Presenter View** and click **OK**.

Troubleshooting I/O Devices

 Core 1 Objectives 1.2, 3.4, 5.4

A computer usually has so many types of peripheral devices that you'll probably troubleshoot at least one of each at some point in your technical career. When this happens, always try the least invasive and least expensive solutions first. For example, try updating drivers of a graphics tablet before replacing it. Now let's learn how to handle some of the errors or problems you might encounter.

Numlock Indicator Light

 Core 1 Objective 5.4

If a user complains they cannot sign in to Windows even when they are certain they are entering the correct password, ask them to make sure the NumLock key is set correctly. Laptops use this key to toggle between the keys interpreted as letters and numbers. Most laptops have a NumLock indicator light near the keyboard.

Device Manager

 Core 1 Objectives 3.4, 5.4

Device Manager is usually a good place to start troubleshooting. A Device Manager window is shown on the left side of Figure 6-42. Click a white arrow to expand the view of an item and click a black arrow to collapse the view. Notice the yellow triangle beside the SM Bus Controller, which indicates a problem with this motherboard component. To see a device's properties dialog box, right-click the device and click **Properties**.

First try updating the drivers. Click **Update Driver** on the General tab or the Driver tab. If a driver update creates a problem, you can roll back (undo) the update if the previous drivers were working. (Windows does not save drivers that were not working before the driver update.) If you are still having a problem with a device, try uninstalling it and installing it again. To uninstall the device, click **Uninstall** on the Driver tab. Then reboot and reinstall the device, looking for problems during the installation that point to the source of the problem. Sometimes reinstalling a device is all that's needed to solve the problem.

Figure 6-42   Use Device Manager to solve problems with hardware devices

If Windows is not able to locate new drivers for a device, locate and download the latest driver files from the manufacturer's website to your hard drive. For the SB Bus Controller, you would download the chipset drivers from the motherbaord manufacturer's website. Be sure to use 64-bit drivers for a 64-bit OS and 32-bit drivers for a 32-bit OS. If possible, use Windows 10 drivers for Windows 10, and Windows 11 drivers for Windows 11. You can double-click the downloaded driver files to launch the installation.

Update Port or Slot Drivers on a Laptop

If you ever have a problem with a port or slot on a laptop, first turn to Device Manager to see if errors are reported and to update the drivers for the port or slot. The laptop manufacturer has probably stored backups of the drivers on the hard drive under support tools and on the recovery media if available. You can also download the latest drivers from the manufacturer's website. If the problem is still not solved after updating the drivers, try using Device Manager to uninstall the port or slot drivers, and then use the support tools to reinstall the drivers.

> **Note 10**
>
> If a port or slot on a desktop or laptop fails even after updating the drivers, you can install an external device to replace the port or slot. For example, if the network port fails, you can purchase a USB to Ethernet adapter dongle to connect an Ethernet cable to the system using a USB port.

Audio Issues

Core 1 Objective 5.4

You're trying to play a video or listen to music, and you know sound should be coming out of the speakers, but they are quiet. When you're having audio issues, there are a few things you can try:

1. Make sure volume is turned up.
2. Check all audio cables, plugs, jacks, speakers, and headphone connections.
3. Update audio drivers.

> **Note 11**
>
> If you continue to struggle getting audio to play, the issue might not be with hardware. Microsoft offers some guidance to troubleshoot audio issues using Windows 10 tools here: *support.microsoft.com/en-us/windows/fix-sound-problems-in-windows-10-73025246-b61c-40fb-671a-2535c7cd56c8.*

Troubleshooting Video, Monitors, and Projectors

Core 1 Objective 5.4

For monitor and video problems, as with other devices, try doing the easy things first. For instance, try to make simple hardware and software adjustments. Many monitor problems are caused by poor cable connections or bad contrast/brightness adjustments. Typical monitor and video problems and how to troubleshoot them are described next. Then, you learn how to troubleshoot video problems on laptop computers.

> **Note 12**
>
> A user very much appreciates a support technician who takes a little extra time to clean a system being serviced. When servicing a monitor, take the time to clean the screen with a soft, dry cloth or monitor wipe.

Blurry Image

A fuzzy or blurry image on the screen can be quite frustrating and can strain your eyes if you stare at the screen for hours. Try these three steps when dealing with a blurry screen:

1. Clean the screen with an electronics-safe cleaning wipe or cloth.
2. Set your monitor resolution to its native or recommended resolution.
3. Check your cable connections. If you are using a VGA cable with an LCD monitor, it might create a blurry image. Upgrade to a digital connection using DVI, HDMI, or DisplayPort to optimize the video connection.

Problems with Video Card Installations

When you install a video card, here is a list of things that can go wrong and what to do about them:

- **When you first power up the system, you hear a whining sound.** This is caused by the card not getting enough power. Make sure a 6-pin or 8-pin power cord is connected to the card if it has this connector. The power supply might be inadequate.
- **When you first start up the system, you see nothing but a black screen.** This is most likely caused by the onboard video port not being disabled in BIOS/UEFI setup. Disable the port.
- **When you first start up the system, you hear a series of beeps.** BIOS/UEFI cannot detect a video card. Make sure the card is securely seated. The video slot or video card might be bad.
- **Error messages about video appear when Windows starts.** This can be caused by a conflict between onboard video and the video card. Try disabling onboard video in Device Manager.
- **Games crash or lock up.** Try updating drivers for the motherboard, the video card, and the sound card. Also install the latest version of DirectX. Then try uninstalling the game and installing it again. Then download all patches for the game.

Monitor Indicator Light Is Not On; No Image on Screen

If you hear one or no beep during the boot and you see a blank screen, then BIOS/UEFI has successfully completed POST, which includes a test of the video card or onboard video. You can then assume the problem must be with the monitor or the monitor cable. Ask these questions and try these things:

1. Is the monitor power cable plugged in?
2. Is the monitor turned on? Try pushing the power button on the front of the monitor. An indicator light on the front of the monitor should turn on, indicating it has power.
3. Is the monitor cable plugged into the video port at the back of the computer and the connector on the rear of the monitor?
4. Try a different monitor and a different monitor cable that you know are working.

> **Note 13**
>
> When you turn on your computer, the first thing you see on the screen is the firmware on the video card identifying itself. You can use this information to search the web, especially the manufacturer's website, for troubleshooting information about the card.

Monitor Indicator Light Is On; No Image on Screen

For this problem, try the following:

1. Make sure the video cable is securely connected at the computer and the monitor. The problem is most likely a bad cable connection.
2. Confirm that the video input source is set to the connector that you have the cable plugged into.

3. If the monitor displays POST but goes blank when Windows starts to load, the problem is Windows and not the monitor or video. Boot from the Windows setup DVD, and perform a Startup Repair, which you learned to do in the module "Power Supplies and Troubleshooting Computer Problems." If this works, update the video drivers and verify the display resolution. Other tools for troubleshooting Windows are covered later in the text.

4. The monitor might have a switch on the back for choosing between 110 volts and 220 volts. Check that the switch is in the correct position.

5. The problem might be with the video card. If you have just installed the card and the motherboard has onboard video, go into BIOS/UEFI setup, and disable the video port on the motherboard.

6. Verify that the video cable is connected to the video port on the video card and not to a disabled onboard video port.

7. Using buttons on the front of the monitor, check the contrast adjustment. If there's no change, leave it at a middle setting.

8. Check the brightness or backlight adjustment. If there's no change, leave it at a middle setting.

9. If the monitor-to-computer cable detaches from the monitor, exchange it for a cable you know is good, or check the cable for continuity. If this solves the problem, reattach the old cable to verify that the problem was not simply a bad connection.

10. As a test, use a monitor you know is good on the computer you suspect to be bad. If you think the monitor is bad, make sure that it also fails to work on a good computer.

11. Open the computer case and reseat the video card. If possible, move the card to a different expansion slot. Clean the card's edge connectors using a contact cleaner purchased from a computer supply store.

12. If there are socketed chips on the video card, remove the card from the expansion slot, and then use a screwdriver to press down firmly on each corner of each socketed chip on the card. Chips sometimes loosen because of temperature changes; this condition is called chip creep.

13. Trade a good video card for the video card you suspect is bad. Test the video card you think is bad on a computer that works. Test a video card you know is good on the computer that you suspect is bad. Whenever possible, do both.

14. Test the RAM on the motherboard with memory diagnostic software.

15. For a motherboard that is using a PCI Express video card, try using a PCI video card in a PCI slot or a PCIe ×1 video card in a PCIe ×1 slot. A good repair technician keeps an extra PCI video card around for this purpose.

16. Trade the motherboard for one you know is good. Sometimes, though rarely, a peripheral chip on the motherboard can cause the problem.

Screen Goes Blank 30 Seconds or One Minute after the Keyboard Is Left Untouched

A "green" motherboard (one that follows energy-saving standards) used with an Energy Saver monitor or projector can be configured to go into standby or sleep mode after a period of inactivity. Using this feature can also help prevent burn-in. **Burn-in** is when a static image stays on a monitor for many hours, leaving a permanent impression of that image on the monitor. An alternate method to avoid burn-in is to use a screen saver that has a moving image or a rotation of varying images. To wake up the computer, press any key on the keyboard, or press the power button. Use the Power Options applet in Control Panel to configure the sleep settings on a computer.

Note 14

Problems might occur if the motherboard power-saving features or the Windows screen saver is turning off the monitor. If the system hangs when you try to get the monitor going again, try disabling one or the other. If this doesn't work, disable both.

Poor Display

In general, you can solve problems with poor display by using controls on the monitor and using Windows settings. Do the following:

- **LCD monitor controls.** Use buttons on the front of an LCD monitor to adjust color, brightness, contrast, focus, and horizontal and vertical positions.
- **Windows display settings.** Use Windows settings to adjust font size, refresh rate, screen resolution, brightness, color, and ClearType text. To adjust display settings in Windows 10, right-click the desktop, and click **Display settings**. Here are a few settings:
  - **Resolution.** The resolution is the number of horizontal and vertical pixels used to build one screen. In the Resolution drop-down menu, select the highest resolution. If the monitor shows **distorted geometry** where images are stretched inappropriately, make sure the resolution is set to its highest value. Also, a low resolution can cause oversized images or icons.
  - **Refresh rate.** The refresh rate is the number of times the monitor refreshes the screen in 1 second. To adjust the refresh rate, click **Display adapter properties**. On the Monitor tab, select the highest screen refresh rate available (see Figure 6-43).

Figure 6-43   Use the highest refresh rate the system supports

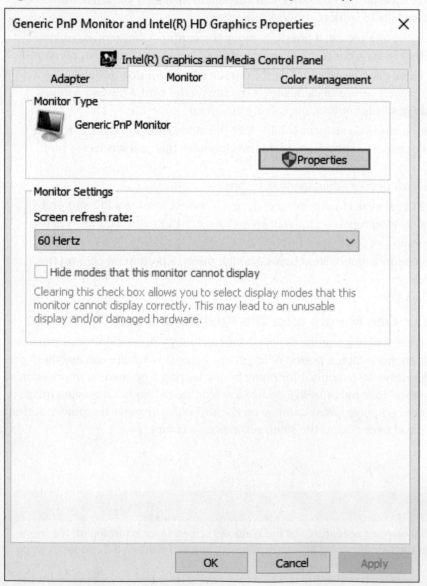

- **ClearType.** In Windows 10, open the **Settings** app, and open the **System** group to find display settings. To open the ClearType Text Tuner, search on **ClearType** in the search box of the Settings app, select **Adjust ClearType text**, and check **Turn on ClearType** (see Figure 6-44). Then follow the steps in the wizard to improve the quality of text displayed on the screen.

Figure 6-44   ClearType in Windows improves the display of text on the screen

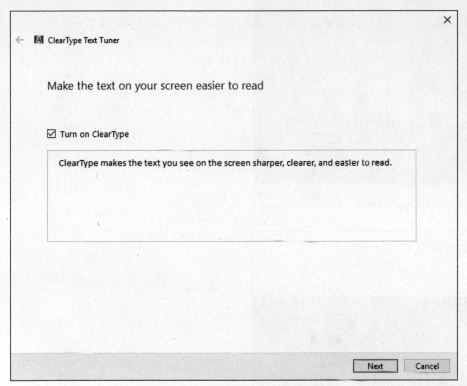

- **Color calibration.** If you have an incorrect color display, calibrate colors in Windows. First open the Settings app, search on **calibrate display color**, and follow the directions on-screen. As you do so, color patterns appear (see Figure 6-45). Use these screens to adjust the gamma settings, which define the relationships among red, green, and blue, as well as other settings that affect the display.

Figure 6-45 Two screens in the Windows 10 color calibration wizard

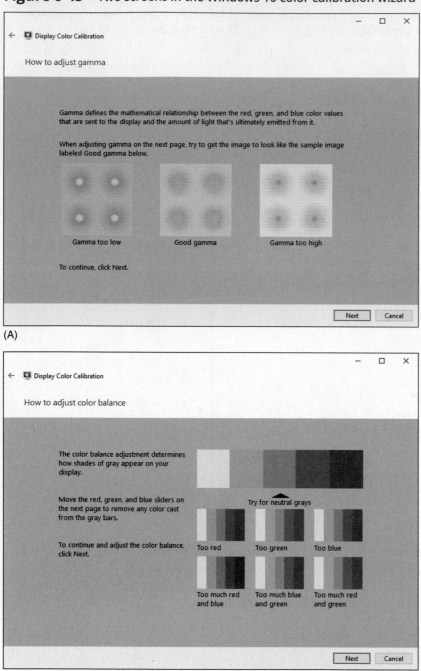

(A)

(B)

- **Update the video drivers.** The latest video drivers can often solve various problems with the video subsystem, including poor display.

Note 15

If adjusting the resolution doesn't correct distorted geometry or oversized images or icons, try updating the video drivers.

Here are a few other display problems and their solutions:

- **Dead pixels.** An LCD monitor might have pixels that are not working. These **dead pixels** can appear as small white, black, or colored spots on your screen. A black or white pixel is likely to be a broken transistor, which cannot be fixed. Having a few dead pixels on an LCD monitor screen is considered acceptable and usually is not covered under the manufacturer's warranty.

Note 16

A problematic pixel might not be a dead pixel (a hardware problem), but only a stuck pixel (a software problem). You might be able to use software to fix stuck pixels. For example, run the online software at *jscreenfix.com* to fix stuck pixels. The software works by rapidly changing all the pixels on the screen. (Be aware the screen flashes rapidly during the fix.)

- **Dim image.** A laptop computer dims the LCD screen when the computer is running on battery power to conserve the charge. You can brighten the screen by using the Windows display settings. In Windows 10, open the **Settings** app, click **System**, and then adjust the brightness slide bar (see Figure 6-41). To check whether settings to conserve power are affecting screen brightness, open **Control Panel** in Classic view, and click **Power Options**. Note the power plan that is selected. Click **Change plan settings** for this power plan. On the next screen, you can adjust when or if the screen will dim (see Figure 6-46). If the problem is still not resolved, it might be a hardware problem. How to troubleshoot hardware in laptops is covered later in this module.

  A dim image in a desktop monitor might be caused by a faulty video card or a faulty monitor. To find out which is the problem, connect a different monitor. If the LCD monitor is the problem, most likely the backlighting is faulty and the monitor needs replacing.

Figure 6-46   Change power plan options to affect how or if the screen dims

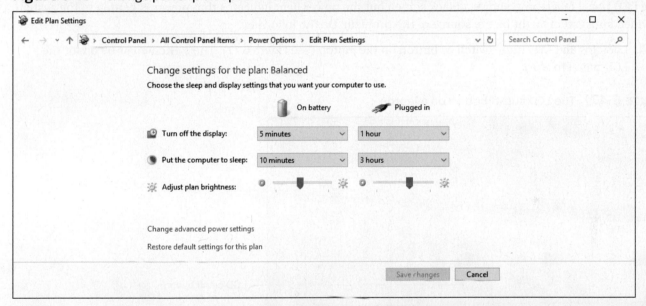

Note 17

In this text, we've given several options for various freeware utilities. It's a good idea to know about your options for several reasons: Each freeware utility has different options, owners of freeware might not update their utilities in a timely manner, and websites might decide to include adware with their downloads.

In general, you can improve video quality by upgrading the video card and/or monitor. Poor display might be caused by inadequate video RAM. Your video card might allow you to install additional video RAM. See the card's documentation.

Cannot Connect to External Monitor or Projector

If the connection to the external monitor or projector fails when you're setting up dual monitors for a desktop, using a projector for a presentation, or connecting a monitor to a laptop to troubleshoot video problems with the laptop, try the following solutions:

1. Make sure the monitor or projector is getting power. Is the power cord securely connected? Is the electrical outlet working?

2. Check the connection at both ends of the video cable.

3. Is the monitor or projector turned on? For some projectors, a remote control is used to turn on the projector or wake it from sleep mode. The remote control batteries might be dead and need replacing.

4. Use the Function keys on a laptop to toggle between the laptop display and the external monitor or projector. (Alternately, you can press Windows key+P to toggle between displays.)

5. Try using a different video cable.

6. Try using a different video connection if the laptop and monitor have another option available.

7. If the projector shuts off unexpectedly, it might have entered sleep mode because of inactivity. Press the power button to wake the projector. If you can't wake it, the problem might be **overheat shutdown**. Allow the projector lamp to cool down. Make sure the air vents are not obstructed and the room temperature is not too hot. The air filters inside the projector might be clogged with dust and need replacing.

Video System in a Laptop

 Core 1 Objectives 1.2, 5.4

If the LCD panel in a laptop shows a black screen but the power light indicates that power is getting to the system, the video subsystem might be the source of the problem. Do the following:

1. Look for an LCD cutoff switch or button on the laptop (see Figure 6-47). The switch must be on for the LCD panel to work.

Figure 6-47   The LCD cutoff button on a laptop

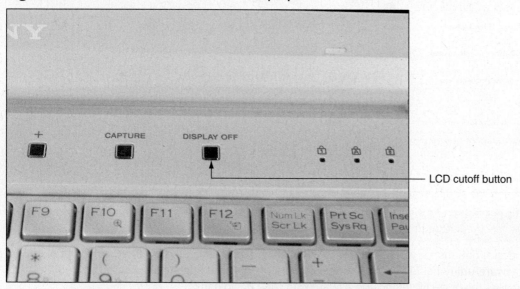

2. Try to use an onboard video port to connect an external monitor. After you connect the monitor, use a function key to toggle between the LCD panel, the external monitor, and both the panel and monitor. If the external monitor works but the LCD panel does not, use the external monitor to check Device Manager for warnings about the video controller and to update the video drivers.

3. If you still can't get the LCD panel to work but the external monitor does work, you have proven the problem is with the LCD panel assembly. In a laptop, a dim screen or no display can be caused by a bad inverter. Steps to replace the inverter board in a laptop are covered later in the module.

Flickering, Dim, or Otherwise Poor Video

Use these tips to solve problems with bad video:

- Verify Windows display settings. Try using the highest resolution for the LCD panel. This resolution will be the best available unless the wrong video drivers are installed.
- Try adjusting the brightness, which is a function of the backlight component of the LCD panel.
- Try updating the video drivers. Download the latest drivers from the laptop manufacturer's website. Bad drivers can cause an occasional ghost cursor on-screen. A **ghost cursor** is a trail left behind when you move the mouse.
- If the cursor drifts on the screen when the mouse or touch pad isn't being used, try using a different port on the computer or replacing the batteries in the mouse.
- A flickering or flashing screen can be caused by bad video drivers, a low refresh rate, a bad inverter, or loose connections inside the laptop. After setting the refresh rate to its highest setting, updating the video drivers, and checking for loose connections, try replacing the inverter.

Applying Concepts

Replace the Inverter Board in a Laptop

Est. Time: 1 hour
Core 1 Objective: 1.2

Because the LCD panel is so fragile, it is one component that is likely to be broken when a laptop is not handled properly. For a laptop that uses fluorescent backlighting, the problem might be the inverter if the screen is dim but some display is still present. The inverter board converts DC to the AC used to power the backlighting of the LCD panel (see Figure 6-48).

Figure 6-48   A ThinkPad inverter board

An LCD assembly might include a microphone, webcam, and speakers that are embedded in the laptop lid. For other laptops, the microphone and speakers are inside the case. In addition, a Wi-Fi antenna might be in the lid of the laptop, which is why you should raise the lid if you need a better Wi-Fi signal. To replace the inverter board, you will likely have to take apart the LCD assembly, as seen in Figure 6-49.

Before you begin any disassembly of a laptop, refer to the manufacturer documentation. The following are some general directions to replace an inverter board:

1. Remove the AC adapter and the battery pack.
2. Remove the upper keyboard bezel, which is the band around the keyboard that holds it in place. You might also need to remove the keyboard.
3. Remove the screws holding the hinge in place, and remove the hinge cover. Figure 6-50 shows a laptop with a metal hinge cover, but some laptops use plastic covers that can easily break as you remove them. Be careful with the plastic ones.
4. Remove the screws holding the LCD panel to the laptop.
5. You're now ready to remove the LCD panel from the laptop. Be aware there might be wires running through the hinge assembly, cables, or a pin connector. Cables might be connected to the motherboard using ZIF connectors. As you remove the LCD top cover, be careful to notice how the panel is connected. Don't pull on wires or cables as you remove the cover, but first carefully disconnect them.

(continues)

Applying Concepts Continued

6. Next, remove screws that hold the top cover and LCD panel together. Sometimes, these screws are covered with plastic or rubber circles or pads that match the color of the case. First use a dental pick or small screwdriver to pick off these covers. You should then be able to remove the front bezel and separate the rear cover from the LCD panel. A spudger can help separate the bezel from the case. For one LCD panel, you can see the inverter board when you separate the LCD assembly from the lid cover. Figure 6-51 shows the inverter being compared with the new one to make sure they match. The match is not identical but should work.

7. Disconnect the old inverter, and install the new one. When disconnecting the ribbon cable from the old inverter, notice you must first lift up on the lock holding the ZIF connector in place, as shown in Figure 6-52.

8. Install the new inverter. Reassemble the LCD panel assembly. Make sure the assembly is put together with a tight fit so all screws line up well.

9. Reattach the LCD panel assembly to the laptop.

Figure 6-49   **Components in an LCD assembly**

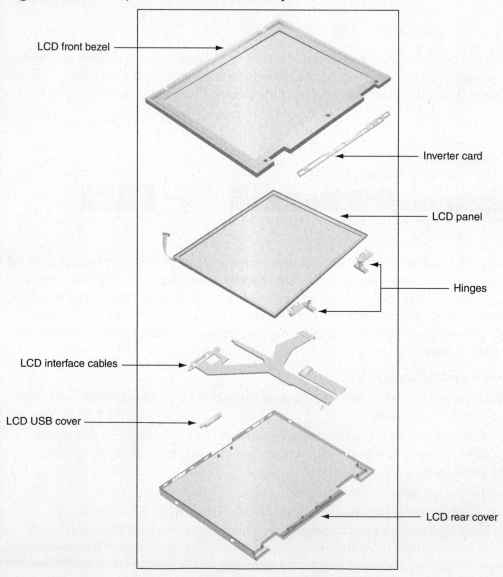

LCD front bezel

Inverter card

LCD panel

Hinges

LCD interface cables

LCD USB cover

LCD rear cover

Figure 6-50   Remove the hinge cover from the laptop hinge

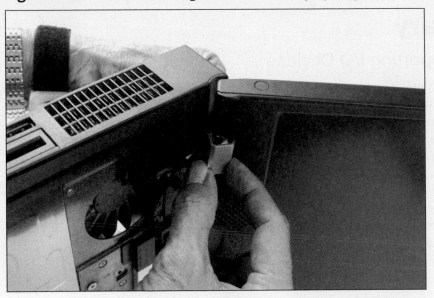

Figure 6-51   The inverter is exposed and is compared with the new one

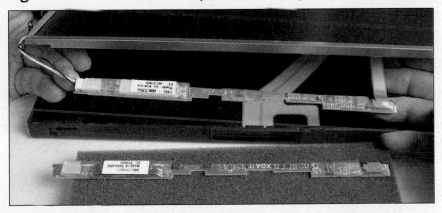

Figure 6-52   Lift up on the ZIF connector locking mechanism before removing the ribbon cable

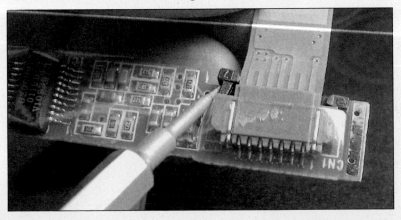

6

Module Summary

Basic Principles for Supporting I/O Devices

- Adding new devices to a computer requires installing hardware and software. Even if you generally know how to install an I/O device, always follow the specific instructions of the product manufacturer.
- Use Device Manager in Windows to manage hardware devices and to solve problems with them.
- Wired data transmission types include USB, eSATA, Thunderbolt, and Lightning. Wireless data transmission types include Wi-Fi, Bluetooth, and NFC.
- USB connectors include the A-Male, Micro-A, B-Male, Mini-B, Micro-B, and USB-C.
- Popular I/O ports on a desktop or laptop motherboard include eSATA and USB. Older computers sometimes used serial RS-232 ports.
- Video ports that a video card or motherboard might provide are VGA, DVI-I, DVI-D, DisplayPort, HDMI, HDMI mini, and multipurpose Thunderbolt ports.
- Other peripheral connectors and ports include eSATA, Lightning, and RS-232.

Identifying and Installing I/O Peripheral Devices

- Peripheral devices you might be called on to install include keyboards, mice, touch pads, microphones, digitizers, webcams, and display devices.
- When installing devices, use 32-bit drivers for a 32-bit OS and 64-bit drivers for a 64-bit OS.

Installing and Configuring Adapter Cards

- Generally, when an adapter card is physically installed in a system and Windows starts up, it detects the card, and then you install the drivers using the Windows wizard. However, always follow specific instructions from the device manufacturer when installing an adapter card because the order of installing the card and drivers might be different.
- A sound card allows you to input audio and use multispeaker systems.
- A capture card allows you to record and stream content from an external device.

Supporting the Video Subsystem

- Types of monitors include LCD and OLED.
- Technologies and features of LCD monitors include screen size, refresh rate, pixel pitch, resolution, contrast ratio, viewing angle, backlighting, and connectors that a monitor uses.
- Use the Windows 10 Settings app to configure monitor resolution and to configure dual monitors.

Troubleshooting I/O Devices

- Remember to try simple things first when troubleshooting I/O devices.
- Use Device Manager to update drivers on I/O devices giving trouble.
- Video problems can be caused by the monitor, video cable, video card, onboard video, video drivers, or Windows display settings.
- A few dead pixels on an LCD monitor screen are considered acceptable by the manufacturer.

Key Terms

For explanations of key terms, see the Glossary for this text.

burn-in	ghost cursor	Mini PCI Express	stylus
capture card	graphics tablet	Mini PCIe	Thunderbolt
dead pixel	HDMI connector	mini USB	twisted nematic (TN)
Device Manager	hot-swappable	OLED (organic light-	USB 2.0
digitizer	in-plane switching (IPS)	emitting diode)	USB 3.0
digitizing tablet	LCD (liquid crystal	overheat shutdown	USB4
distorted geometry	display) monitor	pixel	USB-C
DVI-D	Lightning	projector	vertical alignment
DVI-I	micro USB	RS-232	
flat-panel monitor	Mini DisplayPort	sound card	

Thinking Critically

These questions are designed to prepare you for the critical thinking required for the A+ exams and may use information from other modules and the web.

1. You want to connect an external hard drive for backups. Which is the fastest connection used by current external hard drives? What is the speed?

2. You're working on a server in a server room and need to connect a keyboard. The port available has 9 pins. What type of port is this?

3. You have a contactless magnetic stripe and chip reader by Square. What type of wireless transmission does the device use to receive encrypted data?

4. Your manager bought a new printer with a USB 3.0 port, and it came with a USB 3.0 cable. Your manager asks you if the printer will work if they connect the printer's USB cable into a USB 2.0 port on their computer. What is your answer?

   a. No, the printer can only use a USB 3.0 port.
   b. Yes, it will work, but at the USB 2.0 speed.
   c. Yes, it will work at the USB 3.0 speed.
   d. Yes, it will work, but at the USB 1.1 speed.

5. What is the easiest way to tell if a USB port on a laptop computer is using the USB 3.0 standard?

6. Your friend Jin calls you asking for help with her new LCD monitor. She says the monitor isn't showing the whole picture. What is the display resolution you should recommend for her to use?

7. Your manager has asked you what type of monitor they should use in their new office, which has a wall of windows. They are concerned there will be considerable glare. Which gives less glare, an LCD monitor or an OLED monitor?

8. Which Windows utility is most likely the best one to use when uninstalling an expansion card?

9. Would you expect all the devices listed in BIOS/UEFI setup to also be listed in Device Manager? Would you expect all devices listed in Device Manager to also be listed in BIOS/UEFI setup?

10. Why is it best to leave a slot empty between two expansion cards?

11. You're connecting a single speaker to your computer. Which speaker port should you use?

12. What can you do if a port on the motherboard is faulty and a device requires this type of port?

13. Which type of drivers must always be certified in order to be installed in Windows?

14. Your desktop computer has DVI and HDMI video ports. If a DVI monitor does not work on your system but you know the monitor is good, what is the best solution?

    a. Use a DVI to HDMI adapter to use the current DVI monitor and cable.
    b. Buy a new HDMI monitor to use with the HDMI port.
    c. Install a video card in your computer with a DVI port.
    d. Replace the motherboard with another motherboard that has a DVI port.

15. You plug a new scanner into a USB port on your Windows system. When you first turn on the scanner, what should you expect to see?

    a. A message is displayed by the scanner software telling you to reboot your system.
    b. Windows Device Setup launches to install drivers.
    c. Your system automatically reboots.
    d. An error message from the USB controller is displayed.

16. You turn on your Windows computer and see the system display POST messages. Then the screen goes blank with no text. Which of the following items could be the source of the problem?

    a. The video card
    b. The monitor
    c. Windows
    d. Microsoft Word software installed on the system

17. You have just installed a new sound card in your system, and Windows says the card installed with no errors. When you plug in the speakers and try to play music, you hear no sound. What is the first thing you should do? The second thing?

    a. Check Device Manager to see if the sound card is recognized and has no errors.
    b. Reinstall Windows.
    c. Use Device Manager to uninstall the sound card.
    d. Identify your sound card by opening the case and looking on the card for the manufacturer and model.
    e. Check the volume controls on the speaker amplifier and in Windows.
    f. Use Device Manager to update the sound card drivers.

18. You have just installed a new DVD drive and its drivers in Windows. The drive will read a CD but not a DVD. You decide to reinstall the device drivers. What is the first thing you do?

    a. Open the Settings app and click the System group.
    b. Open Device Manager and choose Update Driver.
    c. Remove the data cable from the DVD drive so Windows will no longer recognize the drive and allow you to reinstall the drivers.
    d. Open Device Manager and uninstall the drive.

19. Match the following ports to the diagrams in Figure 6-53: Dual Link DVI-I, USB Type A, USB Type B, VGA, DisplayPort, Mini DisplayPort, HDMI, and serial RS-232. (Note that some port diagrams are not used.)

Figure 6-53   Identify ports

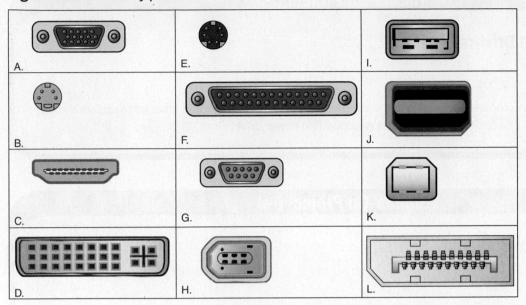

Hands-On Projects

Hands-On Project 6-1

Installing a Device

Est. Time: 30 minutes
Core 1 Objective: 1.2

Install a device on a computer. If you are working in a classroom environment, you can simulate an installation by moving a device from one computer to another. Devices that you might consider installing are a video card, webcam, or fingerprint reader.

Hands-On Project 6-2

Researching Connection Adapters

Est. Time: 15 minutes
Core 1 Objective: 3.1

Research the web and find devices that can be used as solutions to the following problems. Print or save the webpage showing the device and price:

1. Find an adapter that allows you to connect a HDMI port on a computer to an DVI monitor using a DVI cable.
2. Find an adapter that allows you to connect an Ethernet cable to a USB port on your laptop.
3. Find an adapter that allows you to use a VGA cable to connect a DVI-I port on your desktop to a VGA monitor.

Hands-On Project 6-3

Updating Device Drivers

Est. Time: 15 minutes
Core 1 Objectives: 1.1, 1.2, 3.4

Using your home or lab computer connected to the Internet, go to Device Manager and attempt to update the drivers on all your installed devices. Which devices did Windows find newer drivers for?

Hands-On Project 6-4

Adjusting Windows Display Settings

Est. Time: 30 minutes
Core 1 Objective: 1.2

To practice changing display settings, do the following:

1. Using the Settings app, open the Color Calibration window, and calibrate the color displayed on your monitor screen. Using the Settings app, verify that ClearType text is enabled.

2. Try different screen resolutions supported by your monitor. Then verify that the monitor is set to use the highest refresh rate it supports.

Hands-On Project 6-5

Recording Your Screen

Est. Time: 30 minutes
Core 1 Objective: 3.4

Practice recording your screen for a teaching video using the Windows Game Bar. Do the following:

1. Open the Windows Game Bar.
2. Start recording.
3. Open a browser and search for free streaming software.
4. If you have a microphone on your computer, add a recording of your voice explaining what you're doing on the screen.
5. Stop recording.
6. View your recording in your saved clips.

Note 18

If your Windows Game Bar won't record video of the screen, the option is likely disabled in the Settings app. To enable recording for Windows Desktop, open the **Settings** app, go to **Gaming**, and make sure the Game Bar is enabled. Then click **Captures** in the left pane. Make sure options to record are turned on.

Real Problems, Real Solutions

Real Problem 6-1

Helping with Upgrade Decisions

Est. Time: 45 minutes
Core 1 Objectives: 3.1, 3.4

Upgrading an existing system can sometimes be a wise thing to do, but sometimes the upgrade costs more than the system is worth. Also, if existing components are old, they might not be compatible with components you want to use for the upgrade. A friend, Renata, asks your advice about several upgrades she is considering. Answer these questions:

1. Renata has a six-year-old desktop computer that has a Core2 Duo processor and 2 GB of memory. It does not have an eSATA port. She wants to use an external hard drive that has an eSATA interface to her computer to back up and store her entertainment media. How would she perform the upgrade, and what is the cost? Save or print webpages to support your answers.

2. Her computer has one USB port, but she wants to use her USB printer at the same time she uses her USB scanner. How can she do this, and how much will it cost? Save or print webpages to support your answers.

3. Renata also uses her computer for gaming and wants to get a better gaming experience. The computer is using onboard video and has an empty PCI Express video slot. What is the fastest and best graphics card she can buy? How much does it cost? Save or print webpages to support your answer.

4. What is the total cost of all the upgrades Renata wants? Do you think it is wise for her to make these upgrades, or would it be wiser to purchase a new system? How would you explain your recommendation to her?

Real Problem 6-2

Using Mouse without Borders

Est. Time: 30 minutes
Core 1 Objectives: 1.1, 3.1

Mouse without Borders is software that lets you use one keyboard and mouse to control two or more computers that are networked together. You can download the free software from *microsoft.com/en-us/download/details.aspx?id=35460*. To use the software, you need to know the host name of each computer that will share the keyboard and mouse. To find out the host name, right-click **Start** and select **System**. The host name is listed as the Device name.

Working with a partner, download and install Mouse without Borders, and configure it so you and your partner are using the same keyboard and mouse for your computers.

Real Problem 6-3

Researching a Computer Ad

Est. Time: 1 hour
Core 1 Objectives: 1.1, 1.2

Pick a current website or magazine ad for a complete, working desktop computer system, including computer, monitor, keyboard, and software, together with extra devices such as a mouse or printer. Research the details of the ad, and write a one- to two-page report describing and explaining these details. This project provides a good opportunity to learn about the latest offerings on the market as well as current pricing.

Real Problem 6-4

Working with a Monitor

Est. Time: 1 hour
Core 1 Objective: 5.4

Do the following to practice changing monitor settings and troubleshooting monitor problems:

1. Practice changing the display settings, including the wallpaper, screen saver, and appearance. If you are not using your own computer, be sure to restore each setting after making changes.

2. Change the monitor resolution. Try several resolutions. Make a change and then make the change permanent. You can go back and adjust it later if you want.

3. Work with a partner who is using a different computer. Unplug the monitor in the computer lab or classroom, loosen or disconnect the computer monitor cable, or turn the contrast and brightness all the way down while your partner does something similar to the other computer. Trade computers and troubleshoot the problems.

4. Wear an ESD strap. Turn off the computer, press the power button, remove the case cover, and loosen the video card. Turn on the computer and write down the problem as a user would describe it. Turn off the computer, reseat the card, and verify that everything works.

5. Turn off your system. Insert into the system a defective video card provided by your instructor. Turn on the system. Describe the resulting problem in writing, as a user would.

Module
7

Networking Fundamentals

Module Objectives

1 Explain the TCP/IP protocols and standards an operating system uses for networking

2 Compare and contrast common networking hardware, including network interface cards (NICs), switches, hubs, cable modems, and routers

3 Configure routers, switches, and computers in a local network

Core 1 Certification Objectives

2.1 Compare and contrast Transmission Control Protocol (TCP) and User Datagram Protocol (UDP) ports, protocols, and their purposes.

2.2 Compare and contrast common networking hardware.

2.4 Summarize services provided by networked hosts.

2.5 Given a scenario, install and configure basic wired/wireless small office/home office (SOHO) networks.

2.6 Compare and contrast common network configuration concepts.

Introduction

An A+ support technician needs to prepare to assume total responsibility for supporting both wired and wireless networks in a small office/home office (SOHO) environment. The first step is to understand how computers, printers, and other devices communicate in a network. Communication happens in layers and involves applications, operating systems, device drivers, firmware, hardware, and cabling. In this module, you learn about these layers of communication. You also learn how to set up a simple network and connect it to the Internet.

Understanding TCP/IP and Windows Networking

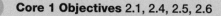 **Core 1 Objectives** 2.1, 2.4, 2.5, 2.6

This section of the module focuses on how a network works. Network communication begins when one application on one computer tries to find another application on another computer on a local or remote network. Most applications used on the Internet or a local network are **client/server applications**. Client applications—such as Microsoft Edge, Google Chrome, or Outlook—usually initiate communication with server applications such as a web server or email server.

For example, in Figure 7-1, someone uses a web browser (the client) to request a webpage from a **web server**. To handle this request, the client computer looks for the web server, the protocols (or rules for communication) are established, and then the request is made and answered. The application, the OS and hardware on both computers, and the network are all involved in this process.

Figure 7-1 A web browser (client software) requests a webpage from a web server (server software); the web server returns the requested data to the client

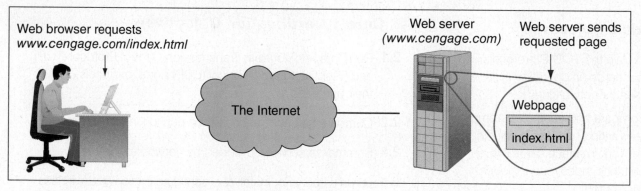

Both computers are called hosts or nodes on the network:

- A **host** is a computer that can be either the client or the server using client/server applications.
- A **node** is any computer, printer, smart thermostat, or other networked device that can be addressed on the network. Every host is a node, but not every node is a host.

Let's see how computers and networking devices can be addressed on a network.

Addresses Used on a Network

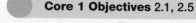 **Core 1 Objectives** 2.1, 2.5

The following three types of numeric addresses are used for communication on a network:

- **Port address identifies an application.** Each client or server application running on a computer is identified by a **port address**, also called a port or a port number. For example, a web server receives communication from a browser at port 80 using the HTTP protocol for unsecured communication and at port 443 using the HTTPS protocol for secured communication.

- **IP address identifies a node and its network connection.** An **IP address** is assigned to a node when the device first connects to the network, and it identifies the network connection. The following are two types of IP addresses:
  - A 32-bit string, written as four decimal numbers called octets and separated by periods, such as 192.168.100.4
  - A 128-bit string, written as eight hexadecimal numbers separated by colons, such as 2001:0000:B80:0000:0000:D3:9C5A:CC

  Most networks use 32-bit IP addresses, which are defined by **IPv4 (Internet Protocol version 4)**. Some networks use both 32-bit addresses and 128-bit addresses, which are defined by **IPv6 (Internet Protocol version 6)**.

- **MAC address identifies a network adapter.** Every wired or wireless network adapter, also called a network interface card (NIC), has a 48-bit (6-byte) identification number—called the **MAC address**, physical address, or network adapter address—hard-coded on the card by its manufacturer. Part of the MAC address identifies the manufacturer, who is responsible for making sure that no two network adapters have the same MAC address. Every device on a network (for example, computers, printers, smart thermostats, refrigerators, and smartphones) connects to the network by way of its NIC and its MAC address. An example of a MAC address, written in hexadecimal or hex, is 00-0C-6E-4E-AB-A5. Most likely, the MAC address is printed on the device (see Figure 7-2). Later in the module, you learn to use the ipconfig command to find out the MAC address of your installed NIC.

Figure 7-2   This Gigabit Ethernet adapter by Intel uses a PCIe ×1 slot

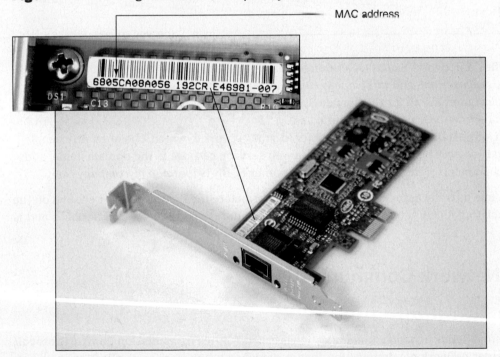

Although IP addresses can always be used to identify hosts on a network or the Internet, they are difficult for humans to remember. Therefore, character-based addresses are preferred:

- A **host name** or computer name identifies a host and can be used in place of its IP address on the local network. The name can have up to 63 characters, including letters, numbers, and special characters. Examples of computer names are www, ftp, JeanAndrews, TestBox3, and RedLaptop. You can assign a computer name while installing Windows. In addition, you can change the computer name at any time using the About window in the Settings app. See Figure 7-3.

Figure 7-3 Use the About window to change the computer name

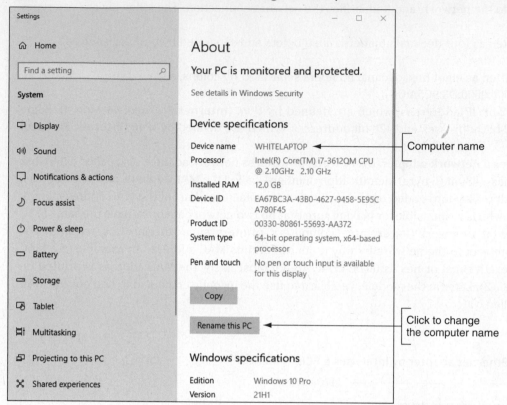

- A **domain name** identifies a network. Examples of domain names are the names that appear before the period in *microsoft.com*, *cengage.com*, and *mycompany.com*. The letters after the period are called the top-level domain and tell you something about the domain. Examples are .com (commercial), .org (nonprofit), .gov (government), .edu (education), and .info (general use).
- A **fully qualified domain name (FQDN)** identifies a computer and the network to which it belongs. An example of an FQDN is *www.cengage.com*. The host name is *www* (a web server), *cengage* is the domain name, and *com* is the top-level domain name of the Cengage network. Another FQDN is *joesmith.mycompany.com*.

A fully qualified domain name must be associated with an IP address before the computer can be found on the Internet. The process of associating a character-based name with an IP address is done via DNS services and is covered later in this module.

TCP/IP Model for Network Communication

Core 1 Objective 2.1

The suite of protocols or rules that define network communication is called **TCP/IP (Transmission Control Protocol/ Internet Protocol)**. Let's consider network communication that starts when a browser (an application) requests a webpage from a web server (another application). As you follow the blue arrows through the diagram, shown in Figure 7-4, you can see the layers of communication. The browser app passes the request to the OS, which passes the request to the network card, which passes the request on to the network. When the request reaches the network card on the server, the network card passes the request on to the OS, and then the OS passes it on to the web server application.

When studying networking theory, a simple model used to divide network communication into four layers is the **TCP/IP model**. In this model, protocols used by hardware function at the Link layer, and protocols used by the OS are divided into three layers (Internet, Transport, and Application layers). These four layers are shown on the left and right sides of Figure 7-4 and listed in Table 7-1.

Figure 7-4   Network communication happens in layers

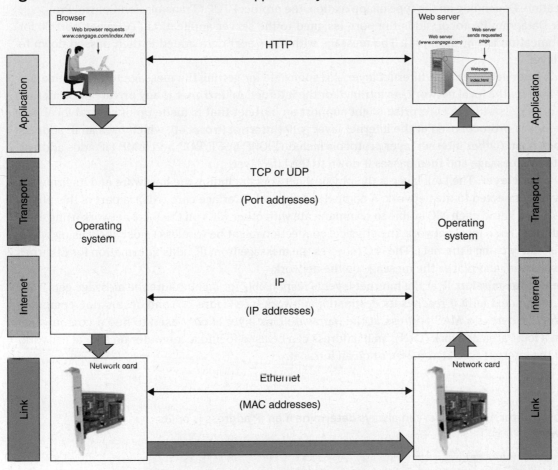

Table 7-1   TCP/IP model has four layers of communication

Layer	Addressing	Description
Layer 4: Application layer		Application-to-application communication is managed by the OS, using protocols specific to the application (HTTP, Telnet, FTP, and so forth). This layer of communication happens after the OSs have made a connection at the Transport layer.
Layer 3: Transport layer	Port addresses	Host-to-host communication, managed by the OS, primarily using TCP and UDP protocols.
Layer 2: Internet layer	IP addresses	Host-to-host on the local network or network-to-network communication, managed by the OS and network devices.
Layer 1: Link layer	MAC addresses	Device-to-device on the local network, managed by firmware on NICs. Layer 1 is also called the Network interface layer or Network access layer.

Let's follow a message from browser to web server, paying attention to each layer of communication:

- **Source Step 1: Application layer.** Recall that most applications that use a network are client/server applications. When a browser client makes a request to a web server, the browser passes the request to the OS. The OS formats the message using the appropriate application protocol (for example, HTTP, FTP, Telnet, DNS, and SSH). In our example, an HTTP message is created and passed down in the TCP/IP stack of protocols to the Transport layer.

- **Source Step 2: Transport layer.** The Transport layer adds information to the message to address the correct server application. Depending on the type of application, the protocol TCP (Transmission Control Protocol) or UDP (User Datagram Protocol) adds the port assigned to the server application (TCP uses port 80 for HTTP communication in our example). The message with Transport data added is then passed down to the Internet layer.

- **Source Step 3: Internet layer.** The Internet layer is responsible for getting the message to the destination computer or host on the local network, an intranet, or the Internet. An **intranet** is any private network that uses TCP/IP protocols. A large enterprise might support an intranet that is made up of several local networks. The primary protocol used at the Internet layer is **IP (Internet Protocol)**, which uses an IP address to identify each host. (Other Internet layer protocols include EIGRP, OSPF, BGP, and ICMP.) IP adds address information to the message and then passes it down to the Link layer.

- **Source Step 4: Link layer.** The Link layer is the physical network, including the hardware and its firmware for every device connected to the network. A computer's network interface card (NIC) is part of this physical network. As you know, each NIC is able to communicate with other NICs on the local network using each NIC's MAC address. For a local network, the physical connection might be wireless (most likely using Wi-Fi) or wired (most likely using Ethernet). The NIC receives the message from IP, adds information for Ethernet or Wi-Fi transmission, and places the message on the network.

- **Step 5: Network transmission.** IP at the Internet layer is responsible for making sure the message gets from one network to the next until it reaches its destination network (see Figure 7-5) and destination computer on that network. Whereas a MAC address at the hardware Link layer is only used to find a computer or other host on a local area network (LAN), an IP address can be used to find a computer on a local network, anywhere on the Internet (see Figure 7-6), or on an intranet.

Figure 7-5   A host (router, in this case) can always determine if an IP address is on its network

Figure 7-6   Computers on the same LAN can use MAC addresses to communicate, but computers on different LANs use IP addresses to communicate over the Internet

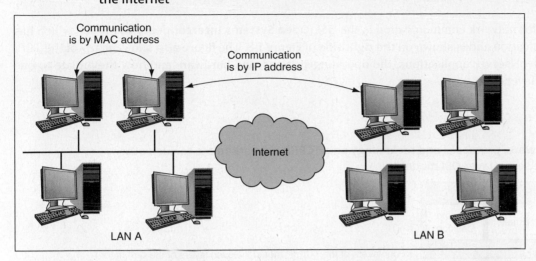

- **Step 6: Destination.** On the destination computer, its NIC receives the message, strips off Ethernet or Wi-Fi information at the Link layer, and passes the message up to the Internet layer. The Internet layer strips off IP address information and passes the message up to the Transport layer. The Transport layer strips off TCP or UDP information and passes the message to the correct port (see Figure 7-7) and on to the Application layer. The Application layer passes the message to the web server application.

Figure 7-7   Each server running on a computer is addressed by a unique port number

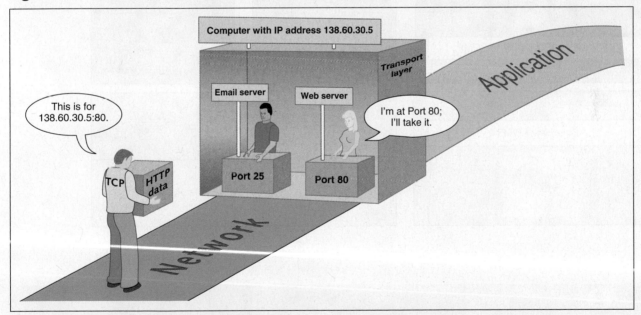

Note 1

Messages on a TCP/IP network might have different names depending on which layer's protocols have added information to the message, either at the beginning of the message (called a header) or at the end (called a trailer). For example, messages with IP address header information added are called packets. Messages with source and destination MAC addresses are called frames. In general, all of these messages can be referred to with the more technical term **protocol data unit (PDU)**.

The OSI Model for Network Communication

Core 1 Objective 2.1

A more detailed model for network communication is the **OSI (Open Systems Interconnection) model**, which has seven layers of communication and is shown on the right side of Figure 7-8. The figure also shows many of the TCP/IP protocols used by client/server applications, the operating systems, and hardware and how they relate to one another at the different layers.

Figure 7-8 How software, protocols, and technology on a TCP/IP network relate to each other using the seven-layer OSI model

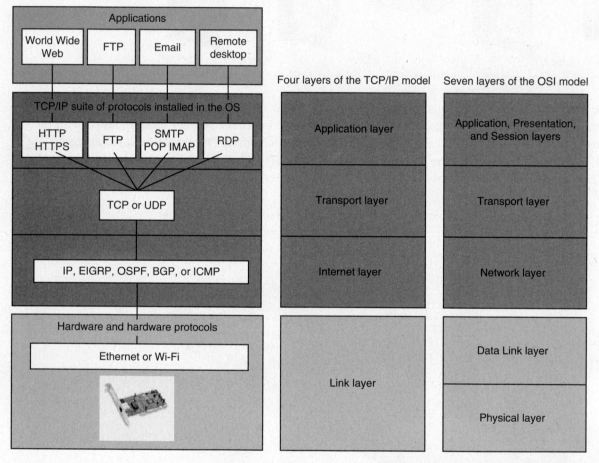

> ## Note 2
>
> In the following sections, the more significant application and operating system protocols are introduced. However, you should know that the TCP/IP protocol suite includes many more protocols than just those mentioned in this module; only some of them are shown in Figure 7-8.

As you continue reading the module, Figure 7-8 can serve as your road map to the different protocols. Let's begin with the higher-layer application protocols used by server applications.

Server Applications, Their Protocols and Ports

 Core 1 Objectives 2.1, 2.4

Recall that a client computer contacts a server in order to request information or perform a task, such as when a web browser connects with a web server and requests a webpage. Many other types of server resources exist on a typical network. A server application might be installed on a computer as a stand-alone application or embedded as firmware in other network devices such as a router. (A **router** is a device that manages traffic between two or more networks and can help find the best path for traffic to get from one network to another. You learn more about routers later in this module.)

Exam Tip ✔

The A+ Core 1 exam expects you to know the port addresses used by many server applications. As you read the list that follows, pay close attention and even memorize the port addresses used by each server application.

Ports are usually assigned to a client or server app when the app is first installed or configured later after the installation. For example, Figure 7-9 shows a settings window where the port for an FTP server is set to 21.

Figure 7-9   Configure an FTP server to use the default port 21 or any port between 1 and 65535

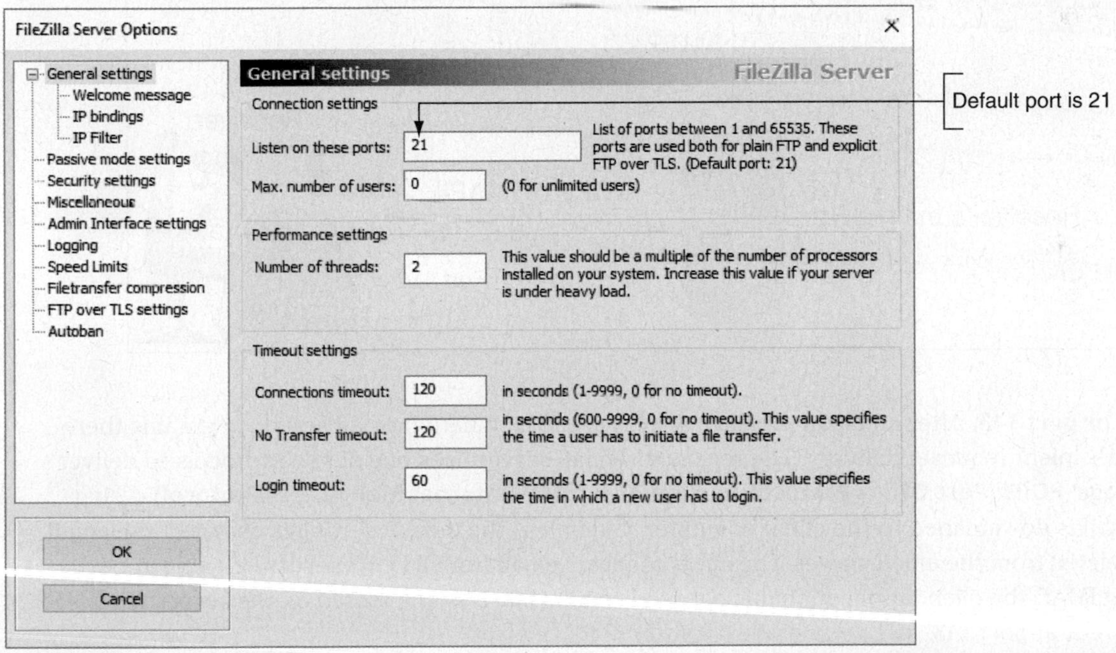

FileZilla Server Options

General settings — Connection settings — Listen on these ports: 21 — List of ports between 1 and 65535. These ports are used both for plain FTP and explicit FTP over TLS. (Default port: 21)   Default port is 21

Max. number of users: 0 (0 for unlimited users)

Performance settings — Number of threads: 2

Timeout settings — Connections timeout: 120 — No Transfer timeout: 120 — Login timeout: 60

Here's a brief list of several popular client/server resources used on networks and the Internet along with the protocols and ports they use:

- **Web server.** A web server serves up webpages to clients. Many corporations have their own web servers, which are available privately on the corporate network. Other web servers are public, accessible from anywhere on the Internet. The most popular web server applications are Apache (see *apache.org*) and Nginx (*nginx.org*). The most popular OSs for running a web server are UNIX and Linux. A web server uses the following ports and protocols:
  - **Port 80. HTTP (Hypertext Transfer Protocol)** is used by a browser and web server for unsecured communication. You can see when a browser is using this protocol by looking for "http" at the beginning of a URL in the address bar, such as *http://www.microsoft.com*. The web server listens at port 80.

- **Port 443. HTTPS (HTTP secure)** refers to the HTTP protocol working with a security protocol such as Secure Sockets Layer (SSL) or Transport Layer Security (TLS) to create a secured socket. (TLS is better than SSL.) A socket is a connection between a browser and web server. HTTPS is used by web browsers and servers to secure the socket by encrypting the data before it is sent and then decrypting it on the receiving end before the data is processed. To know a secured protocol is being used, look for "https" in the URL, as in *https://www.wellsfargo.com*. Most websites today use secure protocols.
- **Mail server.** Email is a client/server application that involves two mail servers, one to send the mail and another to deliver an email message to a client app. A mail server uses the following ports and protocols:
  - **Port 25. SMTP (Simple Mail Transfer Protocol)** is used to send an email message to its destination (see Figure 7-10). The email server that takes care of sending email messages (using the SMTP protocol) is often referred to as the SMTP server. The SMTP server listens at port 25.

Figure 7-10   The SMTP protocol is used to send email to a recipient's mail server, and the POP3 or IMAP4 protocol is used by the client to receive email

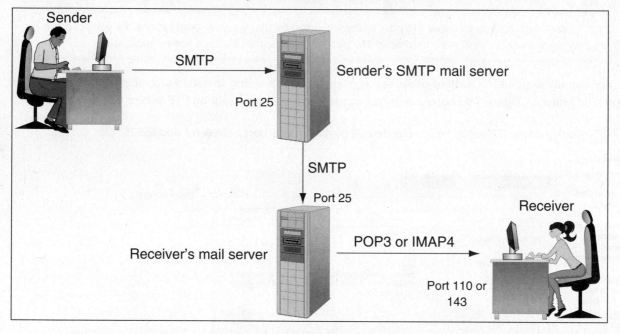

- **Port 110 or port 143.** After an email message arrives at the destination email server, it remains there until the recipient requests delivery. The recipient's email server uses one of two protocols to deliver the message: **POP3 (Post Office Protocol, version 3)** or **IMAP (Internet Mail Access Protocol)**. Using POP3, email is downloaded to the client computer, and unless the default setting is changed, the email is then deleted from the email server. The client requests email from a POP3 server listening at port 110. Using IMAP, the client application manages the email while it is still stored on the server. An IMAP server listens at port 143.
- **File server.** A **file server**, also called a file share server, stores files and makes them available to other computers. Windows uses the **Server Message Block (SMB)** protocol to share files and printers on a network. The current release of the SMB protocol is SMB 3; older versions include SMB 2 and a spin-off protocol called **CIFS (Common Internet File System)**. SMB might use the following ports:
  - **Ports 137 and 139.** SMB originally worked with **NetBIOS (Network Basic Input/Output System)**, an older protocol used by Windows for network communication. To support legacy NetBIOS applications on a TCP/IP network, Windows offered **NetBT (NetBIOS over TCP/IP)**. Earlier versions of SMB require NetBT to be enabled and use these ports:
    - SMB over UDP uses ports 137 and 138.
    - SMB over TCP uses ports 137 and 139.
  - **Port 445.** Current versions of SMB and CIFS don't require NetBT and use port 445.

Core to Core ⟷

You learn how to manage a file server in the A+ Core 2 module "Securing and Sharing Windows Resources."

- **Print server.** A **print server** manages network printers and makes them available to computers throughout the network. You learn more about print servers in the module "Supporting Printers."
- **DHCP server.** When a device first connects to a network, its IP address can have already been manually assigned; this type of IP address is called a **static IP address**. Alternately, the device can request an IP address from a **DHCP (Dynamic Host Configuration Protocol) server** that assigns the address from a pool of addresses it maintains; this type of IP address is called a **dynamic IP address**. A device that requests an IP address and other information from a DHCP server is called a **DHCP client**. It is said that the client is leasing an IP address. A DHCP server that serves up IPv6 addresses is often called a **DHCPv6 server**. Later in this module, you learn how to configure a DHCP server embedded in a SOHO router. DHCP uses the following ports:
  - **Port 67.** A DHCP server listens at port 67.
  - **Port 68.** A DHCP client receives messages on port 68.
- **DNS server. DNS servers** are part of a client/server system that associates FQDNs such as *www.cengage.com* with IP addresses. The process is called **name resolution**, and it begins when a DNS client, such as a laptop or workstation, makes a query to its DNS server. The server might turn to other DNS servers to find the IP address of a given domain name. A DNS server listens at port 53.
- **Proxy server.** A **proxy server** is a computer that intercepts requests that a client, such as a browser, makes of another server, such as a web server. The proxy server substitutes its own IP address for the request. It might also store, or cache, data that is used frequently by its clients. An example of using a proxy server is when an ISP caches webpages to speed up requests for the same pages. After it caches a page and another browser requests the same content, the proxy server can provide the content that it has cached. In addition, a proxy server sometimes acts as a router to the Internet, a firewall to protect the network, a filter for email, and to restrict Internet access by employees to prevent them from violating company policies. When functioning in these ways to give easy access to the Internet, a proxy server is known as an Internet appliance.
- **Authentication, authorization, and accounting (AAA) server.** An **authentication, authorization, and accounting (AAA) server** (pronounced a "triple-A server") is used to secure and control access to the network and its resources. Active Directory, which is a directory service included in Windows Server, is often used for these purposes on a Windows domain. AAA servers perform the following tasks:
  - Authenticate users or computers to the network so they can access network resources and stores user or device credentials, such as user names and passwords.
  - Authorize what a user or computer can do after they have access, including the resources they can access and what they can do with these resources.
  - Account for what a user or computer did with the resources and the time they took. These logs can be useful when users and computers are billed for services they used.

  One protocol a AAA server can use for communication is LDAP. The **Lightweight Directory Access Protocol** (**LDAP**, often pronounced "l-dap") uses port 389. LDAPS is the secure version of LDAP, and it listens at port 636.

Core to Core ⟷

You learn about other protocols a AAA server can use in the Core 2 module "Network Security and Troubleshooting."

- **Syslog server. Syslog** is a protocol that gathers event information about various network devices, such as errors, failures, maintenance tasks, and users logging in or out. The messages about these events are sent to a central location called a **syslog server**, which collects the events into a database. Some syslog servers can generate alerts or notifications to inform network administrators of problems that might need attention.

Exam Tip ✔

The A+ Core 1 exam expects you to be able to summarize services provided by several server applications, including AAA, DNS, DHCP, file share, mail, print, syslog, and web servers.

- **FTP server.** An **FTP (File Transfer Protocol)** server and the FTP protocol is used to transfer files between two computers on a network or the Internet. Web browsers can use the protocol, as can File Explorer in Windows. Also, third-party FTP client software, such as CuteFTP by GlobalSCAPE (*globalscape.com/cuteftp*) or open-source FileZilla (*filezilla-project.org*), offer additional features. By default, FTP transmissions are not secure. Two protocols that encrypt FTP transmissions are FTPS (FTP Secure), which uses SSL encryption, and SFTP (SSH FTP), which uses SSH encryption. FTP uses the following ports:
  - **Port 20.** The FTP client receives data on port 20 from the FTP server.
  - **Port 21.** The FTP server listens at port 21 for commands from an FTP client.

Exam Tip ✔

FTP has been largely replaced by other technologies, such as the BitTorrent and Streaming Sync protocols, for file transfers. However, the A+ Core 1 exam still expects you to be familiar with FTP.

- **Telnet server. Telnet** server and protocol can be used by an administrator or other user to control a computer remotely. Telnet is not considered secure because transmissions in Telnet are not encrypted. The Telnet server listens at port 23.
- **SSH server.** An SSH server and **Secure Shell (SSH)** protocol encrypt communications so hackers can't read the data if they intercept a transmission. The SSH protocol is used in various situations for encryption, such as when remotely controlling a computer or when communicating with a web server. SSH is commonly used in Linux to pass sign-in information to a remote computer and control that computer over a network. Because it's secure, SSH is preferred over Telnet. SSH uses port 22.
- **Remote Desktop and Remote Assistance. Remote Desktop Protocol (RDP)** is used by the Windows Remote Desktop and Remote Assistance utilities to connect to and control a remote computer. These two RDP servers both listen at port 3389.

Core to Core

You learn more about remotely controlling a computer, including how to use Remote Desktop and Remote Assistance, in the Core 2 module "Network Security and Troubleshooting."

- **SNMP server and agent. Simple Network Management Protocol (SNMP)** is a versatile service and protocol used to monitor network traffic and manage network devices. The SNMP server is called the manager, and a small application called an agent is installed on devices being managed by SNMP. The service can help create logs for monitoring device and network performance, make some automatic changes to devices being monitored, and alert network technicians when a bottleneck or other performance issues are causing problems on the network. SNMP uses the following ports:
  - **Port 161.** The SNMP agent on the monitored device listens at port 161.
  - **Port 162.** The SNMP server or manager listens at port 162.

In summary, Table 7-2 lists all the ports you are expected to have memorized in preparation for the A+ Core 1 exam. You need to know the app that uses each port, the purpose of the app, and whether the app uses TCP or UDP at the Transport layer. TCP and UDP are discussed next.

Exam Tip ✔

In preparation for the A+ Core 1 exam, memorize the details in Table 7-2. Questions at the end of this module will help you.

Table 7-2 Common TCP/IP port assignments for client/server applications

Port	Protocol and Role	TCP, UDP or Both	Description
20	FTP client	TCP	The FTP client receives data on port 20 from the FTP server.
21	FTP server	TCP	The FTP server listens at port 21 for commands from an FTP client.
22	SSH server	TCP	A server using the SSH protocol listens at port 22.
23	Telnet server	TCP	A Telnet server listens at port 23.
25	SMTP email server	TCP	An email server listens at port 25 to receive email from an email client.
53	DNS server	TCP/UDP	A DNS server listens at port 53.
67	DHCP server	UDP	A DHCP server listens at port 67.
68	DHCP client	UDP	A DHCP client receives messages on port 68.
80	HTTP	TCP	A web server listens at port 80 when receiving HTTP requests.
110	POP3 email server	TCP	An email client requests email from a POP3 server listening at port 110.
143	IMAP email server	TCP	An email client requests email from an IMAP server listening at port 143.
161	SNMP agent	UDP	An SNMP agent listens at port 161.
162	SNMP manager	UDP	An SNMP manager listens at port 162.
137 and 139	SMB with NetBT	TCP/UDP	SMB with NetBT uses ports 137 and 139 (for TCP traffic).
389	LDAP	TCP/UDP	AAA servers using LDAP listen at port 389.
443	HTTPS	TCP	A web server listens at port 443 when receiving HTTPS transmissions.
445	SMB and CIFS	TCP/UDP	SMB and CIFS use port 445 for both TCP and UDP traffic.
3389	RDP	TCP/UDP	Remote Desktop and Remote Assistance services listen at port 3389.

TCP and UDP Delivery Methods

Core 1 Objective 2.1

Looking back at Figure 7-8, you can see three layers of protocols working at the Application, Transport, and Internet layers. These three layers make up the heart of TCP/IP communication. As illustrated in the figure, TCP or UDP manages communication with the applications protocols in the layers above as well as those in the lower layers, which control communication on the network. TCP and UDP at the Transport layer are both charged with delivering an application's message to the destination host (refer back to Figure 7-5), but they do their jobs differently. Let's discuss next a few key differences between TCP and UDP that determine which of these two protocols is most appropriate for each situation.

> **Exam Tip** ✔
>
> The A+ Core 1 exam expects you to be able to contrast the TCP and UDP protocols.

TCP Guarantees Delivery

Remember that all communication on a network happens by way of messages delivered from one location on a network to another. **TCP (Transmission Control Protocol)** guarantees message delivery. TCP uses IP addresses to make a connection between a sending and destination host, sends the data, checks whether the data is received, and resends it if it is not. TCP is therefore called a **connection-oriented protocol**. TCP is used by applications such as web browsers (using HTTP and HTTPS protocols), email (using SMTP, POP3, and IMAP protocols), FTP file transfer apps (using FTP protocol), and SSH apps used to make secure connections to a server (using SSH protocol). Guaranteed delivery takes longer and is used when it is important to know that the data reached its destination. When a TCP message reaches its destination, an acknowledgment is sent back to the source (see Figure 7-11).

If the source TCP does not receive the acknowledgment, it resends the data or passes an error message back to the higher-level application protocol.

Figure 7-11   TCP guarantees delivery by requesting an acknowledgment

UDP Provides Fast Transmissions

On the other hand, **UDP (User Datagram Protocol)** does not guarantee delivery by first establishing a connection or by checking whether data is received; thus, UDP is called a **connectionless protocol** or **best-effort protocol** and is used where guaranteed delivery is not as important as fast transmission. Here are some example uses of UDP:

- **Broadcasting, such as streaming live video or sound over the web.** (TCP, however, is preferred for video on demand where quality is an issue.)
- **Monitoring network traffic.** Notice in Table 7-2 the SNMP agent and manager use UDP.
- **Completing simple file transfers. Trivial FTP (TFTP)** is a small, simple app often used to transfer BIOS updates to firmware on routers and smartphones. It's also used to transfer a lean pre-execution environment (PXE) operating system from a server to BIOS/UEFI on a computer to boot the computer when it does not have a working OS. TFTP over UDP is preferred in these situations because the program is small enough to store on firmware, and it is simple to implement and use.

- **Communicating between DHCP clients and servers.** DHCP uses UDP rather than TCP primarily because DHCP clients and servers use broadcasting to communicate on a local network; UDP supports broadcasting, but TCP does not.

TCP and UDP are responsible for delivering an application's message, and the IP protocol is responsible for finding the right destination host. Let's see how that's done.

How Computers Find Each Other

Core 1 Objective 2.5

To learn how computers use the IP protocol to find each other on a local network or the Internet, let's first discuss how IPv4 addresses are constructed and used. A 32-bit IPv4 address is organized into four groups of 8 bits each, which are presented as four decimal numbers separated by periods, such as 72.56.105.12. The largest possible 8-bit number is 11111111, which is equal to 255 in decimal, so the largest possible IPv4 address in decimal is 255.255.255.255, which in binary is 11111111.11111111.11111111.11111111. Each of the four numbers separated by periods is called an **octet** (for 8 bits) and can be any decimal value from 0 to 255, making a total of about 4.3 billion possible IPv4 addresses (256 × 256 × 256 × 256). Some IP addresses are reserved, so these numbers are approximations. IP addresses that are reserved for special use by TCP/IP and should not be assigned to a device on a network are listed in Table 7-3.

Table 7-3   Reserved IP addresses

IP Address	How It Is Used
127.0.0.1	Indicates your own computer and is called the **loopback address**.
0.0.0.0	Currently unassigned IP address.
255.255.255.255	Used for **broadcast messages** by TCP/IP background processes to communicate with all devices on a network at the same time or without needing specific recipient information, such as when a device broadcasts a message on the local network looking for a DHCP server from which it can lease an IP address. Broadcasting can cause a lot of network chatter; to reduce the chatter, **subnets** are created to subdivide a network into smaller networks so fewer devices receive and respond to broadcast messages.

To communicate on a network or the Internet, a host needs this TCP/IP information:

- Its own IP address—for example, 192.168.100.4. The first part of an IP address identifies the network, and the last part identifies the host.
- A **subnet mask**, which is four decimal numbers separated by periods—for example, 255.255.255.0. When a computer wants to send a message to a destination computer, it uses its subnet mask to decide whether the destination computer is on its own network or another network.
- The IP address of a **default gateway**. Computers can communicate directly with each other on the same network. However, when a computer sends a message to a computer on a different network, it sends the message to its default gateway, which is connected to the local network and at least one other network. The gateway sends the message on its way to other networks. For small businesses and homes, the default gateway is a router.
- The IP addresses of one or more DNS servers. It queries a DNS server to find out the IP address of the destination host when it knows only the domain name of the host.

Applying Concepts

Viewing TCP/IP Settings

Est. Time: 15 minutes
Core 1 Objective: 2.5

The IP address, subnet mask, default gateway, and DNS server addresses can be manually assigned to a computer's network connection, or this information can be requested from a DHCP server on the network when a computer first connects to the network. Follow these steps to view the current TCP/IP settings on a Windows 10 computer:

1. Right-click **Start** and click **Network Connections**. In the Status window, click **Change adapter options**.

2. In the Network Connections window, you can see all your connections. Right-click your current connection, and click **Properties** (see Figure 7-12).

Figure 7-12   View the TCP/IP settings for the current network connection

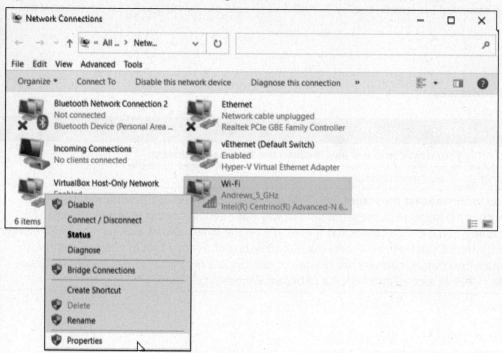

3. In the Properties dialog box, select **Internet Protocol Version 4 (TCP/IPv4)** and click **Properties**. In Figure 7-13, you can see the host is configured to request its IP address, subnet mask, default gateway and DNS server addresses from a DHCP server on the network.

Figure 7-13   This network connection is configured for dynamic IP addressing

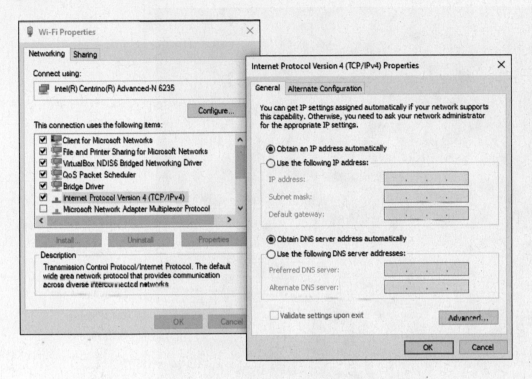

4. To find out what values have been assigned to this computer, enter **cmd** in the Windows search box. The Command Prompt window opens. In the window, enter the following:

```
ipconfig /all
```

5. Scroll through the results to locate information similar to that shown in Figure 7-14. Is your current network connection a wired or wireless connection? What is its MAC address (physical address)? IPv4 address? Subnet mask? Default gateway? DHCP server? DNS server?

6. Close all open windows.

(continues)

Applying Concepts Continued

Figure 7-14   Use the ipconfig /all command to show the MAC address and other information about the current network connections

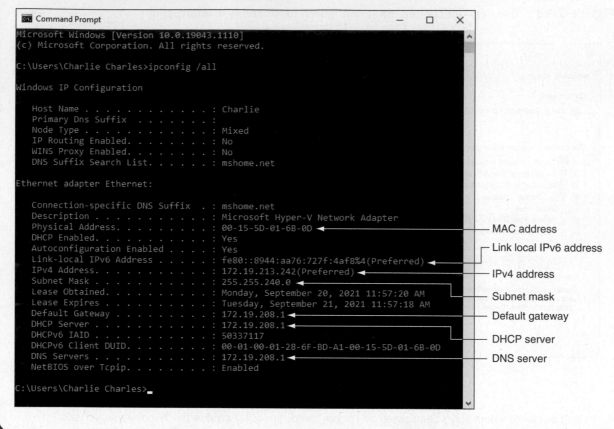

When TCP/IP receives a message to send to a destination computer, it first looks at the beginning or left part of its own IP address that identifies the network (called the **network ID**) and compares it to the network ID of the destination IP address. On the left side of Figure 7-15, the network ID of the host (192.168.1) matches the network ID of the destination (192.168.1); therefore, the two computers are on the same network. On the right side of Figure 7-15, the network ID (192.168.1) of the host does not match the network ID of the destination (9.125.18); therefore, the host sends the message to its default gateway, which sends the message to a different network.

The network ID of the destination IP address is used to locate the destination host's local network. After the message arrives at the local network, the host portion of the IP address is used to identify the one computer on the network that will receive the message.

Figure 7-15   A computer uses network IDs to determine whether a destination computer is on the same network

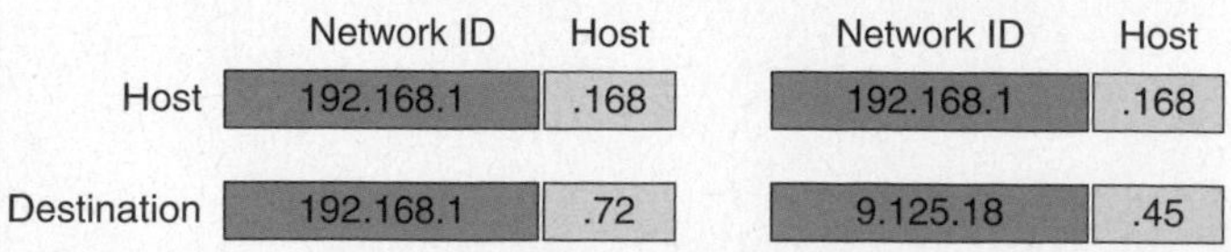

	Network ID	Host	Network ID	Host
Host	192.168.1	.168	192.168.1	.168
Destination	192.168.1	.72	9.125.18	.45

Subnet Masks

How does a computer or other network device know what part of an IP address identifies the network and what part identifies the host? It relies on a subnet mask for this information. All the IP addresses assigned to a local network or subnet have matching bits in the leftmost part of the IP address; these bits that identify the network are called the network ID. For example, the range of IP addresses assigned to a local network might be 192.168.80.1–100. The first three octets (192.168.80) identify the network and the last octet (1 through 100) identifies each host. The last bits in each IP address that identify the host must be unique for each IP address on the network.

A subnet mask has 32 bits and is a string of 1s followed by a string of 0s—for example, 11111111.11111 111.11110000.00000000. The 1s in a subnet mask say, "On our network, this part of an IP address identifies our network," and the group of 0s says, "On our network, this part of an IP address identifies each host." Usually, a subnet mask is displayed in decimal—for example, the subnet mask of 11111111.11111111.00000000.00000000 is 255.255.0.0 in decimal.

Figure 7-16 shows how a subnet mask serves as a type of filter to decide whether a destination IP address is on the local network or a remote network. In the figure, you can see that the subnet mask has 24 ones. Therefore, the computer compares the first 24 bits of the destination IP address to its own first 24 bits. If they match, it directs the message to the computer on its local network. If they don't match, it sends the message to its default gateway.

Figure 7-16   The subnet mask serves as a filter to decide whether a destination IP address is on its own network or another network

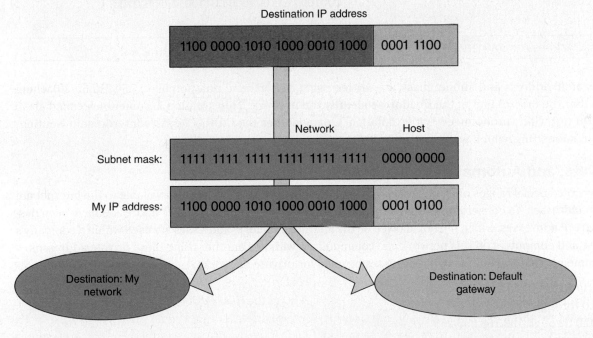

In another example, suppose the IP address of a computer is 201.18.20.160 and the subnet mask is 255.255.0.0, which is 11111111.11111111.00000000.00000000 in binary. The subnet mask tells Windows that the first 16 bits, or two octets (201.18), of the IP address is the network ID. Therefore, when Windows is deciding how to communicate with a computer that has an IP address of 201.18.20.208, it knows the computer is on its own network, but a computer with an IP address of 201.19.23.160 is on a different network.

Let's look at one more example. Suppose the IP address of a computer is 19.200.60.6 and its subnet mask is 255.255.240.0. Is a computer with the IP address 19.200.51.100 on its network? Table 7-4 shows the logic to find out:

Table 7-4   Logic of a subnet mask

Question	Answer
1. What is my IP address in binary?	19.200.60.6 in binary is 00010011.11001000.00111100.00000110.
2. What is my subnet mask in binary?	255.255.240.0 in binary is 11111111.11111111.11110000.00000000.
3. How many bits in my IP address identify my network?	There are 20 ones in the subnet mask. Therefore, 20 bits identify the network.
4. What is the other IP address in binary?	19.200.51.100 in binary is 00010011.11001000.00110011.01100100.
5. Do the first 20 bits in my IP address match the first 20 bits in the other IP address?	Compare the 20 red bits in the two IP addresses 00010011.11001000.00111100.00000110 00010011.11001000.00110011.01100100. Yes, they match.
6. Is the other IP address on my network?	Yes.

Sometimes an IP address and subnet mask are written using a shorthand notation like 15.50.212.59/20, where the /20 means that the first 20 bits in the IP address identify the network. This notation is sometimes called slash notation or **CIDR notation** (pronounced "cider notation"), named after the CIDR (Classless Interdomain Routing) standards about subnetting, which were written in 1993.

Public, Private, and Automatic Private IP Addresses

There are a few more special ranges of IP addresses you need to know about. IP addresses available to the Internet are called **public IP addresses**. To conserve the number of public IP addresses, some blocks of IP addresses have been designated as **private IP addresses**, which are not allowed on the Internet. Private IP addresses are used within a company's private network, and computers on this network can communicate with one another using these private addresses.

IEEE recommends that the following IP addresses be used for private networks:

- 10.0.0.0 through 10.255.255.255
- 172.16.0.0 through 172.31.255.255
- 192.168.0.0 through 192.168.255.255

Note 3

IEEE, a nonprofit organization, is responsible for many Internet standards. Standards are proposed to the networking community in the form of an RFC (Request for Comment). RFC 1918 outlines recommendations for private IP addresses. To view an RFC, visit the website *rfc-editor.org*.

Exam Tip ✔

The A+ Core 1 exam expects you to have memorized the private network IP address ranges and automatic private IP address range.

There's also a special type of private IP address range. If a computer first connects to a network that is using dynamic IP addressing and is unable to lease an IP address from the DHCP server, it generates its own **Automatic Private IP Address (APIPA)** in the address range 169.254.*x.y*.

Core to Core ⇄

If you are running a web server on the Internet, you will need a public IP address for your router and either a static or reserved private IP address for the web server. For this situation, you can lease a public IP address from your ISP at an additional cost. You will also need to enable port forwarding to the server, which is discussed in the Core 2 module "Network Security and Troubleshooting".

NAT (Network Address Translation) is a technique designed to conserve the number of public IP addresses needed by a network. A router stands between a private network and the Internet. It substitutes the private IP addresses used by computers on the private network with its own public IP address when these computers need access to the Internet. See Figure 7-17. Besides conserving public IP addresses, another advantage of NAT is security; the router hides the entire private network behind this one address. For a small office/home office (SOHO) router, expect that NAT is enabled by default.

Figure 7-17   NAT allows computers with private IP addresses to access the Internet

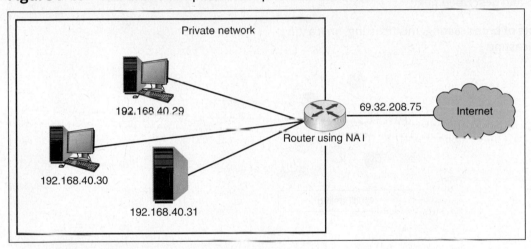

How IPv6 Addresses Are Used

Core 1 Objective 2.5

When the Internet and TCP/IP were first invented, it seemed that 32 bits were more than enough to satisfy any needs we might have for IP addresses because IPv4 created about four billion potential IP addresses. Today we need many more than four billion IP addresses over the world. Partly because of a shortage of 32-bit IP addresses, IPv6 was designed to use an IP address with 128 bits. Currently, the Internet uses a mix of 32-bit and 128-bit IP addresses. The Internet Assigned Numbers Authority (IANA at *iana.org*) is responsible for keeping track of assigned IP addresses and has already released all of its available 32-bit IPv4 addresses. IPv6 addresses leased from IANA today are all 128-bit addresses.

With the IPv6 standards, more has changed than just the number of bits in an IP address. To improve routing capabilities and speed of communication, IPv6 changed the way IP addresses are used to find computers on the Internet. Let's begin our discussion of IPv6 by looking at how IPv6 addresses are written and displayed:

- An IPv6 address has 128 bits that are written as eight blocks of hexadecimal numbers separated by colons, like this: 2001:0000:0B80:0000:0000:00D3:9C5A:00CC.
- Each block is 16 bits. For example, the first block in the preceding address is 2001 in hex, which can be written as 0010 0000 0000 0001 in binary.
- Leading zeroes in a four-character hex block can be eliminated. For example, the preceding IP address can be written as 2001:0000:B80:0000:0000:D3:9C5A:CC, where leading zeroes have been removed from three of the hex blocks.

- If blocks contain all zeroes, they can be written as double colons (::). The preceding IP address can be written two ways:
  - 2001::B80:0000:0000:D3:9C5A:CC
  - 2001:0000:B80::D3:9C5A:CC

To avoid confusion, only one set of double colons is used in an IPv6 address. In this example, the preferred method is the second one: 2001:0000:B80::D3:9C5A:CC because the address is written with the fewest zeroes.

The way computers communicate using IPv6 has changed the terminology used to describe TCP/IP communication. Here are a few terms used in the IPv6 standards:

- A **link** is a local area network (LAN) or wide area network (WAN).
- The last 64 bits or four blocks of an IPv6 address identify the interface and are called the **interface ID** or interface identifier. These 64 bits uniquely identify an interface on the local network.
- **Neighbors** are nodes on the same local network.

Recall that with IPv4 broadcasting, messages are sent to every node on a local network. However, IPv6 doesn't use broadcasting, thereby reducing network traffic. Instead, IPv6 uses multicasting, anycasting, and unicasting, as illustrated in Figure 7-18 and described next:

Figure 7-18   Concepts of broadcasting, multicasting, anycasting, and unicasting

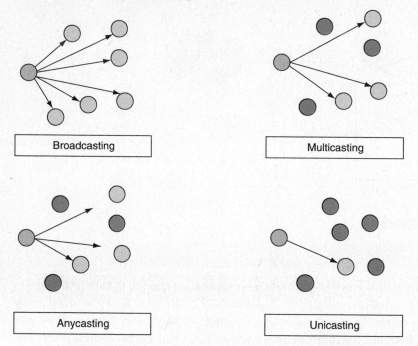

- A **multicast address** is used to deliver messages to all nodes in a targeted, multicast group, such as when video is streaming from a server to multiple nodes on a network.
- An **anycast address** is used by routers and can identify multiple destinations; a message is delivered only to the closest destination.
- A **unicast address** is used to send messages to a single node on a network. Three types of unicast addresses are link local addresses, unique local addresses, and global addresses. A single interface might have more than one unicast address assigned to it at any given time:
  - A **link local address**, also called a link local unicast address or local address, can be used for limited communication with neighboring nodes in the same link (the local network). These local addresses are similar to IPv4 APIPA addresses in that they are assigned to the computer by itself, as opposed to coming from a DHCPv6 server, and are not guaranteed to be unique on the network. Most link local addresses begin with FE80::/64. This prefix notation means the address begins with FE80 followed by enough zeroes to make 64 bits, as shown in Figure 7-19. Link local addresses are not allowed on the Internet or allowed to travel outside private networks.

Figure 7-19   Three types of IPv6 addresses: A link local address has a 64-bit prefix
followed by 64 bits to identify the host

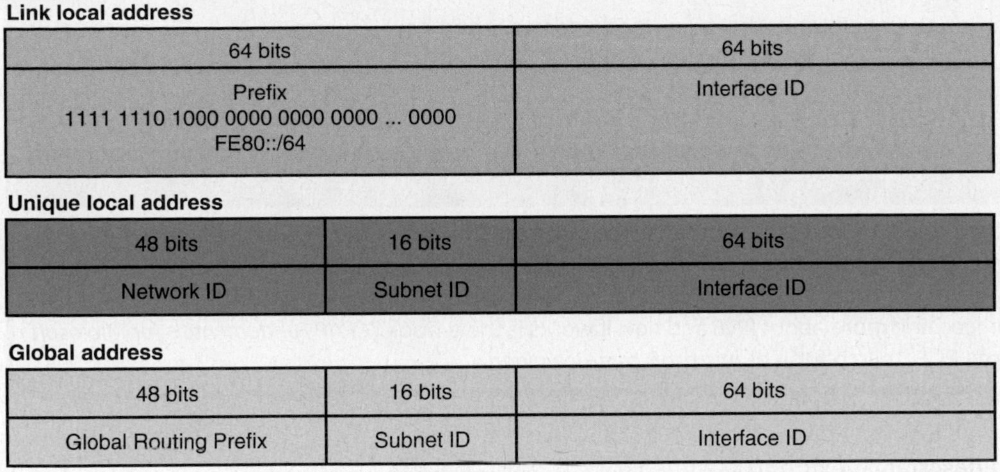

Link local address

64 bits	64 bits
Prefix 1111 1110 1000 0000 0000 0000 ... 0000 FE80::/64	Interface ID

Unique local address

48 bits	16 bits	64 bits
Network ID	Subnet ID	Interface ID

Global address

48 bits	16 bits	64 bits
Global Routing Prefix	Subnet ID	Interface ID

- Look back at Figure 7-14 to see an example of a link local address where the wired interface has the IPv6 address of fe80::8944:aa76:727f:4af8%4. The first 64 bits are fe80::, and the interface ID is 8944:aa76:727f:4af8. IPv6 addresses are followed by a % sign and a number; for example, %4 follows this sample IP address. This number is called the zone ID or scope ID and is used to identify the interface in a list of interfaces for this computer.
- A **unique local address** is a private address assigned by a DHCPv6 server that can communicate across subnets within the private network. They're used by network administrators when subnetting a large network. A unique local address always begins with FC or FD and is usually assigned to an interface in addition to its self-assigned link local address.
- A **global address**, also called a global unicast address, can be routed on the Internet. These addresses are similar to IPv4 public IP addresses. The first 48 bits of the address is the Global Routing Prefix. When an ISP assigns a global address to a customer, it's these 48 bits that are assigned. An organization that leases one Global Routing Prefix from its ISP can use it to generate many IPv6 global addresses.

Table 7-5 lists the currently used address prefixes for these types of IPv6 addresses. In the future, we can expect more prefixes to be assigned as they are needed.

Table 7-5   Address prefixes for types of IPv6 addresses

IP Address Type	Address Prefix
Multicast	FF00::/8 (The first 8 bits are always 1111 1111)
Link local address	FE80::/64 (The first 64 bits are always 1111 1110 1000 0000 ...)
Unique local address	FC00::/7 (The first 7 bits are always 1111 110; today's local networks assign 1 for the eighth bit, so the prefix typically shows as FD00::/8)
Global address	2000::/3 (The first three bits are always 001)
Unassigned address	0::0 (All zeroes)
Loopback address	0::1, also written as ::1 (127 zeroes followed by 1)

Note 4

IPv6 uses subnetting but doesn't need a subnet mask because the **subnet ID** is part of the IPv6 address. The subnet ID is the 16 bits following the first 48 bits of the address. When a large IPv6 network is subnetted, a DHCPv6 server assigns a node in a subnet a global address or unique local address that contains the correct subnet ID for the node's subnet.

An excellent resource for learning more about IPv6 and how it works is the e-book *TCP/IP Fundamentals for Microsoft Windows*. To download the free PDF, search for it at *microsoft.com/download*.

Now that you have an understanding of TCP/IP and Windows networking, let's turn our attention to the hardware used for local networks.

Network Hardware

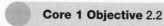

Core 1 Objective 2.2

In this section of the module, you learn about the hardware devices used to create local networks in homes and small businesses, including network adapters, switches, hubs, cable modems, and SOHO routers.

Network Adapters

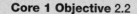

Core 1 Objective 2.2

A computer makes a wired or wireless connection to a local network by way of a network adapter, which might be a network port embedded on the motherboard or a **network interface card (NIC)** installed in an expansion slot on the motherboard. In addition, the adapter might be an external device plugged into a USB port (see Figure 7-20). A network adapter is often called a network interface card or NIC even when it's not really a card but rather a USB device or a device embedded on the motherboard. It might also be called a network controller or network adapter.

Figure 7-20   USB devices provide wired and wireless network connections

Here are a network adapter's features you need to be aware of:

- **NIC drivers.** A NIC usually comes bundled with drivers on CD or the drivers can be downloaded from the web. Windows has several embedded NIC drivers. After you install a NIC, you install its drivers. For best functionality and security, always use the latest drivers. Problems with the network adapter can sometimes be solved by using Device Manager to update the drivers or uninstall the drivers and then reinstall them.

- **Ethernet speeds.** A NIC supports wired Ethernet transmissions or wireless Wi-Fi transmissions. For wired networks, the four speeds for Ethernet are 10 Mbps, 100 Mbps (Fast Ethernet), 1 Gbps (Gigabit Ethernet), and 10 Gbps (10-gigabit Ethernet). Most network adapters sold today for local networks use Gigabit Ethernet and support the two slower speeds. To see the speeds a NIC supports, open its **Properties** dialog box in **Device Manager**. Select the **Advanced** tab. In the list of properties, select **Speed & Duplex**. You can then see available speeds in the Value drop-down list (see the right side of Figure 7-21). If the adapter connects with slower network devices on the network, the adapter works at the slower speed. Select **Auto Negotiation** for Windows to use the best possible speed for a particular connection.

Figure 7-21   Set the speed and duplex for the network adapter

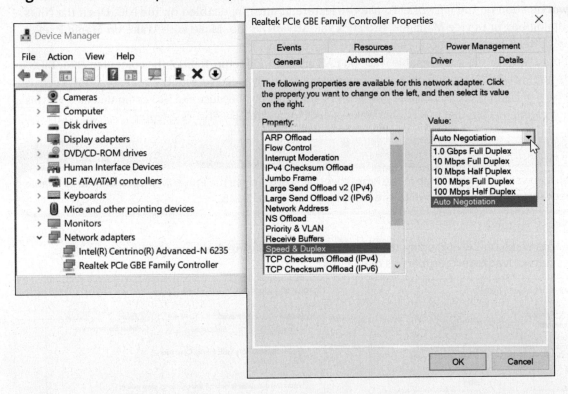

Note 5

The speed of a network depends on the speed of each device on the network and how well a router or switch manages that traffic. SOHO network devices typically offer three speeds: Gigabit Ethernet (1000 Mbps or 1 Gbps), Fast Ethernet (100 Mbps), or Ethernet (10 Mbps). If you want your entire network to run at the fastest speed, make sure all your devices are rated for Gigabit Ethernet.

- **RJ-45 port and status indicator lights.** A network port is called an **RJ-45** port, and it looks like a large phone jack. The RJ-45 Ethernet connector is similar to but larger than the RJ-11 phone connector (see Figure 7-22). A wired network adapter might provide indicator lights on the side of the network port that indicate connectivity and activity (see Figure 7-23). When you first discover you have a problem with a computer not connecting to a network, be sure to check the status indicator lights to verify you have connectivity and

Figure 7-22   RJ-45 and RJ-11 connectors

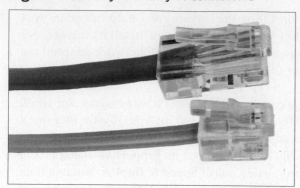

Figure 7-23   Status indicator lights for the onboard network port

activity. If not, then the problem is related to hardware. Next, check the cable connections to make sure they are solid.

- **Wake-on-LAN.** A NIC might support **Wake-on-LAN**, which allows it to wake up the computer when it receives certain communication on the network. To use the feature, it must be enabled on the NIC. Open the NIC's **Properties** dialog box in Device Manager, and click the **Advanced** tab. Make sure **Wake on Magic Packet** and **Wake on pattern match** are both enabled (see Figure 7-24A).
  - For an onboard NIC, you must also enable Wake-on-LAN in BIOS/UEFI setup. Reboot the computer, enter BIOS/UEFI setup, and look for the option on a power-management or advanced screen. For some systems, such as the one shown in Figure 7-25, you enable power-on by the PCI-E bus because the NIC communicates via this bus. It is not recommended that you enable Wake-on-LAN for a wireless network adapter.

Note 6

Some NICs provide a Power Management tab in the Properties dialog box. To use the Power Management tab to enable Wake-on-LAN, check **Allow this device to wake the computer** (see Figure 7-24B).

Figure 7-24   Enable Wake-on-LAN (A) using the Advanced tab, or (B) using the Power Management tab of the network adapter's Properties dialog box

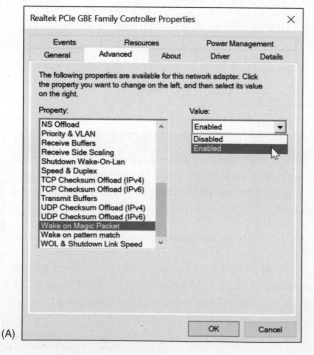

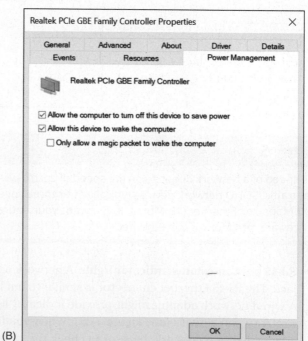

Figure 7-25   For this system, use the Advanced screen in the BIOS/UEFI setup to enable Wake-on-LAN by enabling power-on by the PCIe bus

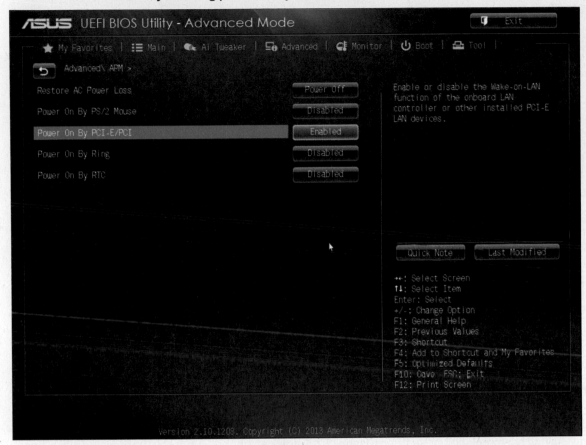

- **Quality of Service (QoS).** Another feature of a network adapter is **Quality of Service (QoS)**, the ability to control which applications' traffic have priority on the network. The feature must be enabled and configured on the router, enabled on the network adapters, and configured in Windows for every computer on the network that uses the high-priority applications. In the Core 2 module "Network Security and Troubleshooting," you learn how to configure a router to use QoS. To enable QoS on a Windows computer's NIC, open the network adapter **Properties** dialog box in Device Manager. On the **Advanced** tab, make sure **Priority Enabled** or **Priority & VLAN Enabled** is selected, as shown in Figure 7-26. If the option is not listed, the adapter does not support QoS.

Figure 7-26   Select Priority Enabled to allow the network adapter to support QoS on the network

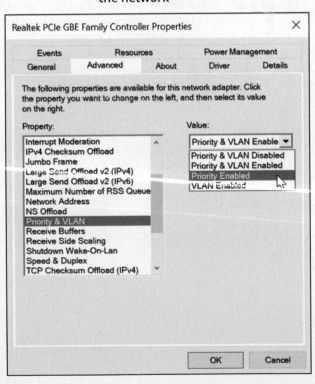

> **Note 7**
>
> A VLAN is a virtual LAN, and QoS is sometimes implemented using VLAN technology. You'll learn more about VLANs when you study virtualization.

Switches and Hubs

Core 1 Objective 2.2

Today's Ethernet networks use a design called a star bus topology, which means that nodes are connected to one or more centralized devices, which are connected to each other (see Figure 7-27). The three centralized devices shown in the figure are called switches.

Figure 7-27   A star bus network is formed by nodes connected to multiple switches

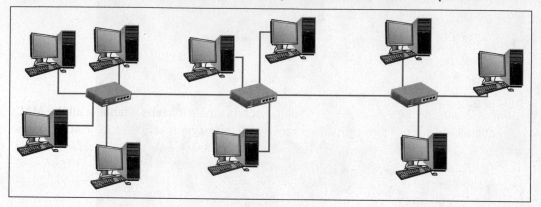

Here are the differences between a hub and a switch:

- An Ethernet **hub** sends a message to every device except the device that sent the message, as shown in Figure 7-28A. A hub is just a passthrough and distribution point for every device connected to it, without regard for what kind of data is passing through and where the data might be going. Hubs are outdated technology, having been replaced by switches. Figure 7-29 shows a hub that supports 10 Mbps and 100 Mbps Ethernet speeds. (You can't find hubs these days to support faster networks.)

Figure 7-28   (A) A hub is a simple pass-through device to connect nodes on a network, and (B) a switch sends a message to the destination node based on its MAC address

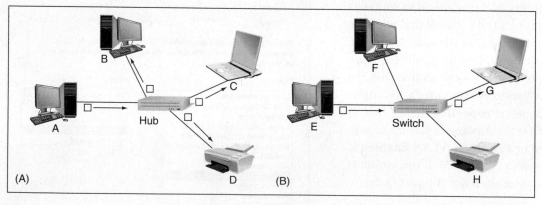

Figure 7-29   This hub supports 10 Mbps and 100 Mbps Ethernet speeds

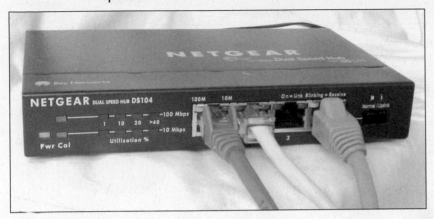

- A **switch** (see Figure 7-30) is smarter and more efficient than a hub because it keeps a table of all the MAC addresses for devices connected to it. When the switch receives a message, it searches its MAC address table for the destination MAC address of the message and sends the message only to the interface for the device using this MAC address (see Figure 7-28B). At first, a switch does not know the MAC addresses of every device connected to it. It learns this information as it receives messages and records each source MAC address in its MAC address table. When it receives a message destined to a MAC address not in its table, the switch acts like a hub and sends the message to all devices except the one that sent it. In the module "Network Infrastructure and Cloud Computing," you learn more about how switches manage network traffic.

Figure 7-30   This Gigabit Ethernet switch by NETGEAR has eight Ethernet ports

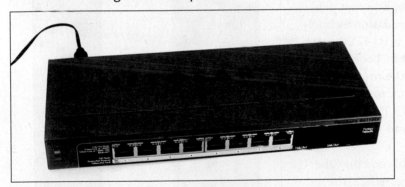

Cable Modem

Core 1 Objective 2.2

To connect to the Internet, a device or a network first connects to an **Internet service provider (ISP)**, such as Xfinity or Spectrum. The most common types of connections for SOHO networks are cable, fiber optic, and DSL. See Figure 7-31.

Figure 7-31   A modem stands between the ISP and the local network to convert signals to Ethernet used on the LAN

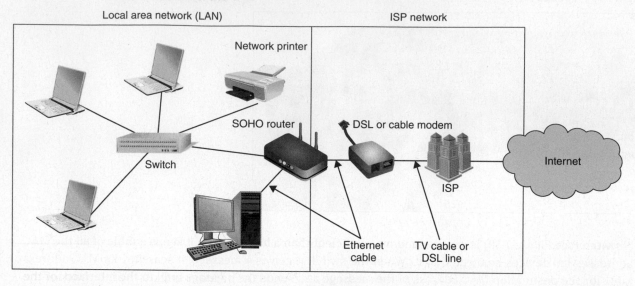

A device is needed to convert cable, DSL, or fiber optic transmissions to Ethernet transmissions used on a local network. For cable, this device is called a **cable modem** (see Figure 7-32). DSL uses a DSL modem, and fiber optic uses an optical network terminal (ONT). Cable modems and DSL modems usually sit beside the SOHO router inside an office or data closet. An ONT is usually mounted on the outside of the building where fiber optic cable terminates, and the ONT connects to an Ethernet cable that enters the building. Regardless of the transmission technology or converting device used, each provides an RJ-45 Ethernet port for a SOHO router or computer to connect to. Looking back at Figure 7-31, note that the LAN begins with the router, which is also considered part of the ISP network. (A router stands between and is part of two or more networks.) The ISP is normally responsible only for its system up to and including the modem or ONT.

To set up a modem, plug in the TV coax cable and the Ethernet cable, and turn on the modem. Notice in Figure 7-32, the red Reset button, which you can use to reset a modem to its factory default settings. When troubleshooting a modem, try rebooting it first, and only use the reset button as a last resort.

Figure 7-32   Use a cable modem to connect the ISP's coaxial cable to the LAN's Ethernet cable

Multifunction SOHO Router

Core 1 Objective 2.2

Routers can range from small ones designed to manage a SOHO network that connects to an ISP (costing around $50 to $300) to those that manage multiple networks and extensive traffic (costing several thousand dollars). On a small office or home network, a router stands between the ISP network and the local network (refer back to Figure 7-31), and the router is the local network's gateway to the Internet.

An example of a multifunction router is the Nighthawk AC1900 by NETGEAR, shown in Figures 7-33 and 7-34. It has one Internet port (also called the WAN or wide-area-network port) to connect to the ISP by way of a modem or ONT and four ports for devices on the network. The USB port can be used to plug in a USB external hard drive for file sharing on the network. The router is also a wireless access point with multiple antennas to increase speed and range.

Computer, printers, smartphones and other devices can connect to this router using wired or wireless connections. This is because a SOHO router often serves different functions in a single device. A typical SOHO router usually combines these functions:

- As a router, it stands between two networks—the ISP network and the local network—and routes traffic between the two networks.
- As a switch, it manages several network ports that can be connected to wired devices on the local network or to a dedicated switch that provides even more ports for locally networked computers. Looking back at Figure 7-31, one LAN port connects to a switch, and another LAN port connects to a desktop computer.
- As a DHCP server, it can provide IP addresses to computers and other devices on the local network.
- As a **wireless access point (WAP)**, it enables wireless devices to connect to the network. These wireless connections can be secured using wireless security features, which you learn about in the Core 2 module "Network Security and Troubleshooting."
- As a **firewall**, it blocks unwanted traffic from the Internet and can restrict Internet access for local devices behind the firewall. Restrictions on local devices can apply to days of the week, time of day, keywords used, certain websites, and specific applications.
- If an external storage device, such as a USB flash drive or external hard drive, connects to the router via the USB port, the router can be used to share files with network users.

Figure 7-33   The NETGEAR Nighthawk AC1900 dual band Wi-Fi Gigabit router

Source: Amazon.com, Inc.

Figure 7-34   Connections and ports at the back of the NETGEAR router

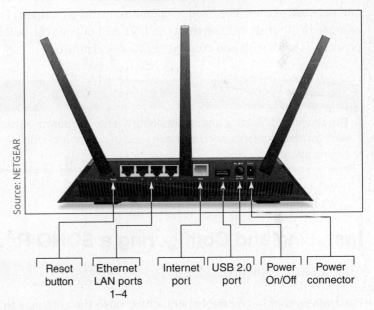

Source: NETGEAR

Reset button | Ethernet LAN ports 1–4 | Internet port | USB 2.0 port | Power On/Off | Power connector

Exam Tip

The A+ Core 1 and + Core 2 exams may require you to evaluate the needs of a business or residence in a given scenario and to install, configure, and secure a SOHO wired and wireless router based on those needs. You learn more about configuring routers in the Core 2 module "Network Security and Troubleshooting," including how to secure the local wired and wireless network using features on the router.

Now that you know about TCP/IP, Windows networking and networking hardware, let's see how to set up and configure a new network from scratch.

Local Network Setup and Configuration

Core 1 Objectives 2.5, 2.6

Suppose you are called on to help a small bookkeeping company with three employees set up its network in a single office space. You have purchased a SOHO router, switch, several patch cables, three laptops, a desktop computer, and network printer. The local telecommunications company has already installed the fiber optic cable to the office along with Ethernet cabling from the ONT unit outside the building to a wall jack in the office. Let's step through the process of setting up and configuring the local network.

Note 8

The process of building and maintaining a large, corporate network is outside the scope of this text. However, working with smaller networks, such as those used in homes and small businesses, helps prepare you to work in larger network environments.

We begin our setup with configuring the router.

Installing and Configuring a SOHO Router

Core 1 Objectives 2.5, 2.6

For routers that have external antennas, raise the antennas to vertical positions. Connect the network cable from the ISP modem or other device or wall jack to the WAN port on the router. Plug in and turn on the router. Indicator lights should indicate network activity on the WAN.

To configure a router for the first time, always follow the directions of the manufacturer. For most SOHO routers, you have some options:

- **For wireless connections.** Download the router manufacturer's app to your smartphone or laptop. Then to connect to the router's wireless network, for a smartphone, open the Settings app, go the Wi-Fi setup and select the name of the router's wireless network, which is called the **Service Set Identifier (SSID)**. It should be printed on the bottom of the router. Open the router app, which should step you through the router setup.
- **For wired connections.** Use a network cable to connect a laptop or desktop computer to a LAN port on the router. Open a browser window. The browser should automatically connect to the webpage of the router (see Figure 7-35). If it does not connect, look in the router documentation for the URL of the router's webpage (for example, *router.asus.com*) or the IP address of the router (for example, 192.168.1.1.).

Figure 7-35   Starting page for the router's quick Internet setup routine

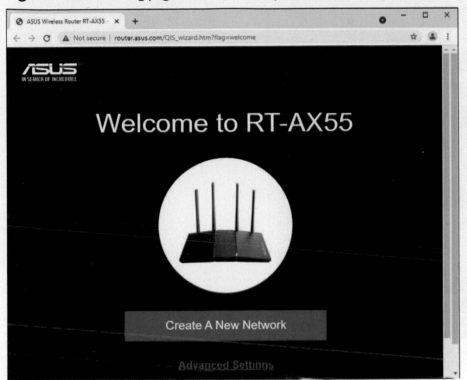

Regardless of how you connect to the router, the initial setup should:

- Provide a username and password if needed to connect to your ISP
- Assign a new SSID and password (security key) to the wireless network
- Update the router firmware
- Change the password for the router firmware
- Configure the DHCP server embedded in the router firmware

Core to Core ⬌

There's more you can do to configure a router to secure a local wired or wireless network, which you learn about in the Core 2 module "Network Security and Troubleshooting."

The setup screens for each router might be different. For the ASUS RT-AX55, on the router home page shown in Figure 7-35, click **Create A New Network**. On the screens that follow, you are given the chance to enter the optional username and password to the ISP, assign a new SSID and password to the wireless network (see Figure 7-36), update the router firmware, and assign a username and password to sign in to the router firmware (see Figure 7-37).

Caution ⓘ

Changing the router firmware login name and password is especially important if the router is a wireless router. Unless you have disabled or secured the wireless network, anyone within its range—even outside your building—can use your wireless network. If someone guesses the default login in name and password to the router, they can change the password to hijack your router and access your wireless network, potentially using it for criminal activity.

Figure 7-36   Set the SSID and password to the wireless network

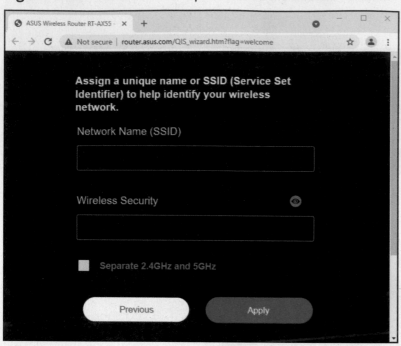

Figure 7-37   Change the router login name and password to the router firmware

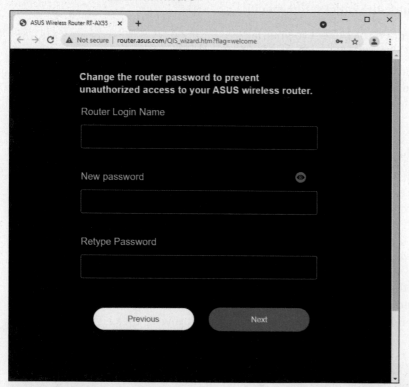

After the initial setup, you should be able to browse the web. If you ever need to further configure the router, using any computer on your local network, open a browser and point to your router's URL, such as *router.asus.com*, or its IP address.

Configure the DHCP Server

A DHCP server on a SOHO router is usually configured for dynamic IP addressing by default. To verify and change the DHCP settings, do the following:

1. Go to the router firmware home page (*router.asus.com*, for example) and sign in with your router account username and password that you set up earlier. The main menu for the router appears. Figure 7-38 shows the main menu for the ASUS RT-AX55, but yours might look different. To configure the DHCP server, click **LAN** in the left pane. The LAN submenu tabs appear.

Figure 7-38   Main menu for a router with LAN submenus shown

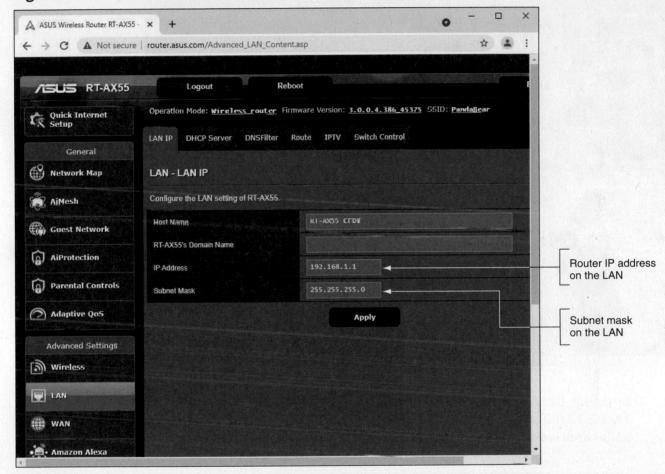

2. Notice in Figure 7-38 the IP address of the router on the LAN is 192.168.1.1 and the subnet mask for the LAN is 255.255.255.0. Click the **DHCP Server** tab to see options for configuring the DHCP server (see Figure 7-39).

Figure 7-39 Configure the DHCP server

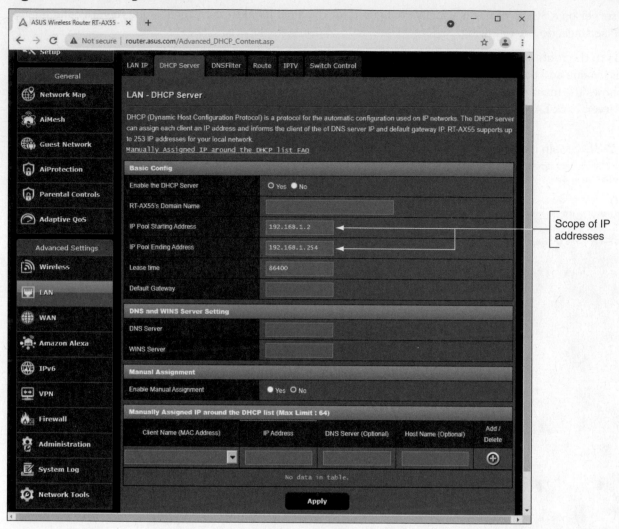

3. By default, DHCP is enabled and the scope of IP addresses that DHCP can lease to DHCP client devices is 192.168.1.2 through 192.168.1.254. Because the default gateway does not have a value, it is assumed the router itself is the gateway. After making changes on this page, click **Apply** to save your changes.

> **Note 9**
>
> As you advance in your networking skills, you'll learn how to choose subnet masks and ranges of IP addresses to divide a large network into more manageable subnets. For now, know that if your range of IP addresses varies only in the last octet, the subnet mask is 255.255.255.0. If the range of IP addresses varies in the last two octets, the subnet mask is 255.255.0.0. You'll learn more about subnets in the module "Network Infrastructure and Cloud Computing."

Reserve IP Addresses

A network device such as a printer needs a consistent IP address at all times, so computers that access the printer don't need to be told its new IP address each time it reconnects to the network. In addition, a computer that is running a service, such as a web server, needs a consistent IP address so other computers can consistently find the web server. You could assign the printer and web server IP addresses by configuring the device or computer for static IP addressing. Alternately, you can assign the same IP address to a device or computer by creating an **address**

reservation on the DHCP server so the DHCP client receives or leases the same IP address each time it connects to the network. Do the following to reserve an IP address:

1. To identify the computer or printer, you'll need its MAC address. When the client is connected to the network, the router can report its MAC address. Look for a Network Map page. If the router doesn't report the MAC address, look for a label near the network port of the printer or in its documentation.

2. To assign a reserved IP address to the client, go to the LAN-DHCP Server page shown earlier in Figure 7-39. For Enable Manual Assignment, select **Yes**. Enter the MAC address and reserved IP address for the client (see Figure 7-40). Be sure to use an IP address in the range of IP addresses assigned by the DHCP server. Click the + sign to the left of the entries, and then click **Apply**. In Figure 7-40, a Canon network printer is set to receive the IP address 192.168.1.100 each time it connects to the network. It's helpful to network users to write this IP address on a label taped in plain sight on the printer or web server.

Figure 7-40   Manually assign a reserved IP address to a printer or other device that needs a static IP address

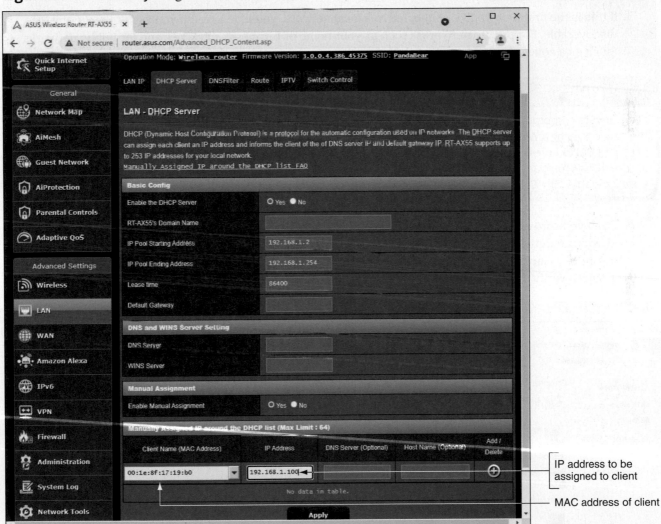

Now that you have set up and configured the router and verified the Internet connection, you can connect other computers to the network.

Connecting a Computer to a Local Network

 Core 1 Objectives 2.5, 2.6

Connecting a laptop or desktop computer to a network is quick and easy in most situations. To connect a computer to a network using an Ethernet wired or Wi-Fi wireless connection, follow these steps:

1. In general, before you connect to any network, the network adapter and its drivers must be installed, and Device Manager should report no errors.

2. Do one of the following to connect to the network:
   - For a wired network, plug in the network cable to a wall jack or switch, or directly to a SOHO router. Plug the other end into the computer's Ethernet port. Indicator lights near the network port should light up to indicate connectivity and activity. For Ethernet, Windows should automatically configure the connection.
   - For a wireless network, click the **Network** icon in the taskbar on the desktop, and select a wireless network. Click **Connect**. If the network is secured, you must enter the security key to the wireless network to connect.

3. If this is the first time you've connected to a local network, you'll be asked if you want to make the PC discoverable. For private networks (such as your home or business), click **Yes**, and for public networks (such as a coffee shop hotspot), click **No**.

> **Note 10**
>
> For a private corporate or enterprise network, Windows Server or Microsoft Azure is likely used to manage access to the network using a Windows domain. You must sign in to the Windows domain with a user name and password. Press Ctrl+Alt+Del to access the sign-on screen. The username might be text such as Jane Smith or an email address such as JSmith@mycompany.com. You learn more about private networks, public networks, and Windows domains in the Core 2 module "The Complex World of IT Professionals."

4. Open your browser and make sure you can access the web. For wireless connections, some hotspots provide an initial page called a captive portal, where you must enter a code or agree to the terms of use before you can use the network. On a private network, open **Explorer** and drill down into the Network group to verify that network resources are available (see Figure 7-41).

Figure 7-41   File Explorer shows resources on the network

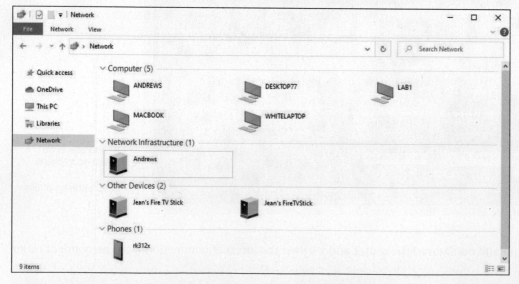

To view and change network security settings, in the Settings app, click **Network & Internet**. In the Status window (see Figure 7-42A), under *Network status*, click **Properties**. Under *Network profile*, select either **Public** or **Private**. See Figure 7-42B.

Figure 7-42   Configure the network connection for a public or private network

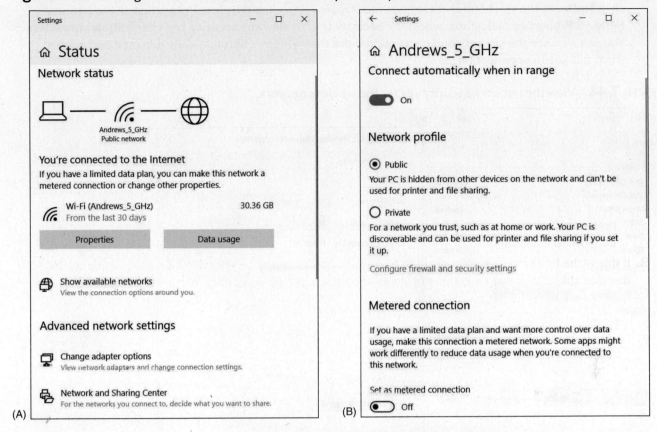

(A)   (B)

Although the Settings app provides several tools to manage network connections, you have more detailed control when using the Network and Sharing Center. For example, to view the security key used for a wireless connection, do the following:

1. Open **Control Panel** and open the **Network and Sharing Center**. Alternately, right-click **Start**, click **Network Connections**, and click **Network and Sharing Center**. In the Network and Sharing Center (see Figure 7-43), click **Change adapter settings**, or in the Network & Internet window, click **Change adapter options**.

Figure 7-43   The Network and Sharing Center reports a healthy wireless network connection

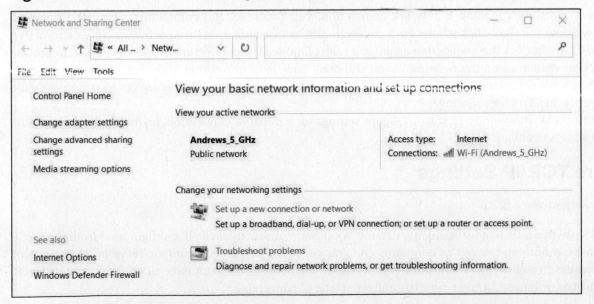

2. In the Network Connections window, right-click the **Wi-Fi** connection (refer back to Figure 7-12), and click **Status**. In the Wi-Fi Status dialog box (see Figure 7-44), click **Wireless Properties**. In the Wireless Network Properties dialog box, select the **Security** tab. To view the security key, check **Show characters**. You can also see the security and encryption types that Windows automatically detected and applied when it made the connection.

Figure 7-44   View the network security key for the wireless network

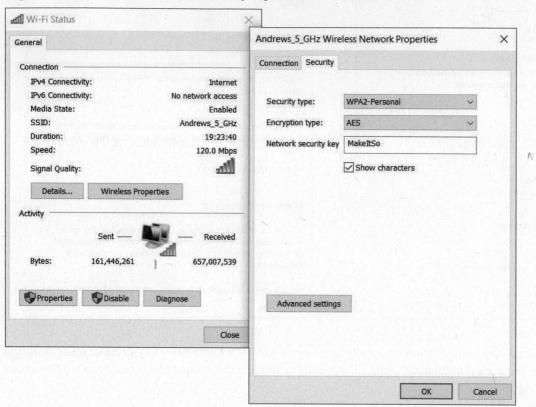

Core to Core

You learn more about wireless network security in the Core 2 module "Network Security and Troubleshooting."

If you have a problem making a network connection, you can reset the connection. Open the **Network Connections** window and right-click the network connection. Select **Disable** from the shortcut menu, as shown earlier in Figure 7-12. Right-click the connection again, and select **Enable**. The connection is reset. Try again to browse the web or access resources on the network. If you still don't have local or Internet access, it's time to dig a little deeper into the source of the problem. More network troubleshooting tools and solutions are covered in the module "Network Security and Troubleshooting."

Now let's turn our attention to how to configure settings for a network connection, including dynamic, static, and alternate address configurations.

Configure TCP/IP Settings

Core 1 Objectives 2.5, 2.6

Most networks use dynamic IP addressing. By default, Windows requests dynamic IP configuration from the DHCP server, and there is nothing for you to configure. (As you know, the DHCP server might serve up a dynamic or reserved IP address to a client.) In some situations, however, the network does not have a DHCP server, so as an IT support technician, you need to know how to configure static IP addressing.

Exam Tip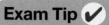

The A+ Core 1 exam expects you to know how to configure dynamic, reserved, and static IP addresses on a router or computer. You also need to recognize whether an IP address is an automatic private IP address.

Follow these steps to configure static IP addressing:

1. Open the **Network Connections** window. Right-click the network connection, and click **Properties**. In the Properties dialog box on the **Networking** tab (as shown in the middle box of Figure 7-45), select **Internet Protocol Version 4 (TCP/IPv4)**, and click **Properties**. The TCP/IPv4 Properties dialog box appears (see the right side of Figure 7-45).

2. As you saw in Figure 7-13, the default is dynamic IP addressing, which uses the *Obtain an IP address automatically* and *Obtain DNS server address automatically* settings. In Figure 7-45, static IP addressing is used. To change the settings to static IP addressing, select **Use the following IP address**. Then enter the IP address, subnet mask, and default gateway.

Figure 7-45   Configure TCP/IPv4 for static IP addressing

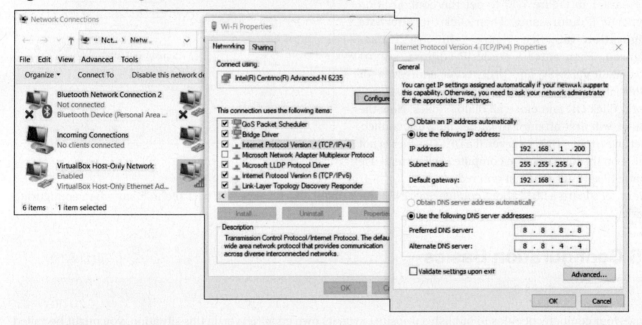

3. If your network administrator has given you the IP addresses of DNS servers, select **Use the following DNS server addresses**, and enter up to two IP addresses. If you have additional DNS IP addresses, click **Advanced** and enter them on the **DNS** tab of the Advanced TCP/IP Settings box.

Note 11

As an IT support technician, it's unlikely you'll ever be called on to configure static IPv6 addressing. However, to do so, use the Properties dialog box shown in the middle of Figure 7-45. Select Internet Protocol Version 6 (TCP/IPv6), and click Properties.

You can also uncheck Internet Protocol Version 6 (TCP/IPv6) to disable it. For most situations, you need to leave it enabled.

Alternate IP Address Configuration

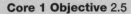

Core 1 Objective 2.5

Suppose an employee with a laptop often travels, and the work network uses static IP addressing, even though most public networks use dynamic IP addressing. How do you configure the employee's computer's network connection settings? For travel, you would configure the computer to use dynamic IP addressing in order to connect to public networks. However, using that configuration means that when the computer attempts to connect to the corporate network, it won't be able to find a DHCP server. Recall that, in this situation, the computer generates an Automatic private IP address (APIPA) in the address range 169.254.x.y. However, you can assign a static IP address by using an alternate configuration.

To create an alternate configuration, first use the General tab of the TCP/IPv4 Properties dialog box shown earlier in Figure 7-13 to set the configuration for dynamic IP addressing. Then click the **Alternate Configuration** tab. See Figure 7-46. Select **User configured**. Then enter a static IP address, subnet mask, default gateway, and DNS server addresses for the alternate configuration to be used on the company network. Click **OK** and close all dialog boxes. Now the computer will first attempt to gather network connection settings from a DHCP server. If a DHCP server is not available on the network, the computer will instead use the static IP settings you just entered.

Figure 7-46 Create an alternate static IP address configuration

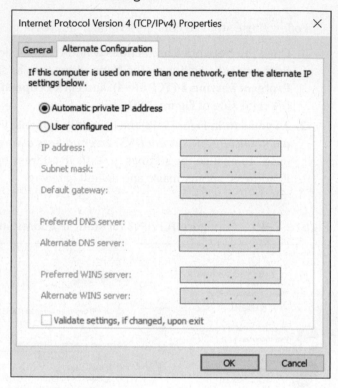

Next, let's learn a little about configuring DNS, which might also be expected of IT technicians when configuring networks.

DNS Configuration Basics

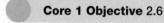

Core 1 Objective 2.6

Suppose your company decides to publish a website or run its own email server. In this situation, you might be called on to make entries in the DNS namespace so that the world will know how to reach your website or email server. The DNS **namespace** is the entire collection of DNS databases stored on DNS servers (also called name servers) around the globe. In these databases, an individual entry, such as one that associates a host name with a given IP address, is called a **resource record (RR)**. Resource records are collected into zone files. Often, one **zone file** holds all the records for a single domain, such as *cengage.com*. Each resource record can have up to six parts:

- Name of the resource (host name)
- Record type
- Class code (always IN, which means the record is allowed on the Internet)
- TTL (time-to-live)—the time a server can hold the record in its cache; the default is one hour
- Length of data
- Data

There are about 30 types of DNS records. Here are the most common types of records you might be called on to edit:

- **A record.** An **A record (address record)** points a host name to its IP address. A website requires an A record such as this one:

  ```
  www.mycompany.com A IN 14400 89.210.18.45
  ```

  Explanation:
  - The resource name is the host *www.mycompany.com*.
  - The record type is A.
  - The class is IN.
  - TTL is 14,400 seconds.
  - Data is the IP address mapped to the host.

- **AAAA record.** A **AAAA record** (pronounced "quad-A record") is an address record for IPv6 addresses. Here is an example:

  ```
  www.mycompany.com AAAA IN 2001:07b8:8ba3:0000:0000:6a22:0323:7223
  ```

- **CNAME record.** A **CNAME (Canonical Name) record** redirects from one host name to another, for example:

  ```
  www.mycompany.com CNAME IN newcompany.com
  ```

- **MX record.** The **MX (Mail Exchanger) record** points an email server domain name to an IP address:

  ```
  email.mycompany.com MX IN 95.165.13.45
  ```

- **TXT record.** A **TXT (Text) record** is a general-purpose record used to insert text into the DNS namespace. One clever way TXT records are used is when a company, such as PayPal, sends TXT records to an email provider, such as Yahoo!, to alert the email provider of potential fraudulent email, thereby preventing spoofing (email pretending to be from PayPal). Here are three ways TXT records are used for this purpose:

  - **DKIM (DomainKeys Identified Mail) records** authenticate that an email message came from a trusted source by attaching a domain name identifier to the message. For more info, see *dkim.org*.
  - **SPF (Sender Policy Framework) records** combat email spoofing by informing a recipient's mail server which email servers can send email from your domain.
  - **DMARC (Domain-based Message Authentication, Reporting, and Conformance) records** tell a recipient's mail server what to do when it receives a fraudulent email message and is designed to work with DKIM and SPF. Figure 7-47 shows how the process works. For more info, see *dmarc.org/overview*.

Figure 7-47   DKIM, SPF, and DMARC work together to reduce fraudulent email

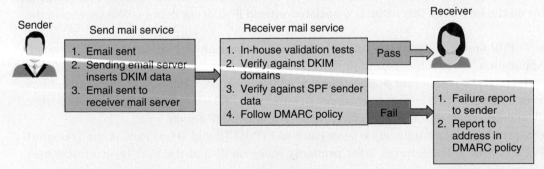

Applying Concepts

Viewing and Clearing the DNS Cache

Est. Time: 15 minutes
Core 1 Objective: 2.6

When Windows is trying to resolve a computer name to an IP address, it first looks in the DNS cache it holds in memory. If the computer name is not found in the cache, Windows then turns to a DNS server if it has the IP address of the server.

Suppose a user is unable to reach a website on their computer but you can access it from your help desk computer. One good step to use when troubleshooting name resolution problems is to clear the DNS cache. Open a command prompt window, and run the `ipconfig /displaydns` command to view the DNS cache on your computer. Then run the `ipconfig /flushdns` command to clear the DNS cache. Windows will rebuild its cache by collecting up-to-date DNS information from the DNS servers you've configured Windows to use.

> **Note 12**
>
> A telltale sign that the network's DNS server is malfunctioning is when you can reach a website by its IP address, but not by its FQDN.

Module Summary

Understanding TCP/IP and Windows Networking

- In networking, an application is identified by a port address. A device on the network—and its network connection—are identified by an IP address. A network adapter is identified by a MAC address.
- A computer can be assigned a computer name, and a network can be assigned a domain name. A fully qualified domain name (FQDN) includes the computer name and the domain name. An FQDN can be used to find a computer on the Internet if this name is associated with an IP address kept by DNS servers in the DNS namespace.
- According to the TCP/IP model, networking communication must happen at four layers: Link, Internet, Transport, and Application.
- The Internet primarily uses client/server applications for communication. Common server applications include a web server, mail server, file server, print server, DHCP server, DNS server, proxy server, AAA server, syslog server, FTP server, Telnet server, SSH server, RDP server, and SNMP server.
- TCP/IP uses several protocols at the Application layer (such as FTP, HTTP, and Telnet) and at the Transport layer (such as TCP and UDP). The Internet layer primarily relies on IP, and the Link layer mostly uses Ethernet and Wi-Fi protocols.
- At the Transport layer, TCP is a connection-oriented protocol, and UDP is a connectionless protocol.
- At the Internet layer, the OS identifies a network connection by an IP address. At the Transport layer, a port address identifies an application.
- At the Link layer, a network adapter has a MAC address that uniquely identifies it on the network.
- IP addresses can be dynamic or static. A dynamic IP address is assigned by a DHCP server when the computer first connects to a network. A static IP address is manually assigned.

- A host needs an IP address, a subnet mask, a default gateway, and IP addresses for DNS servers to communicate with other hosts on the local or remote networks.
- An IPv4 address has 32 bits, and an IPv6 address has 128 bits. Some IP addresses are private and can only be used on a local network.
- Using IPv4, the string of 1s in a subnet mask determines the number of leftmost bits in an IP address that identify the local network. The string of 0s determines the number of rightmost bits in the IP address that identify the host.
- Using IPv6, three types of IP addresses are a multicast address (used for one-to-many transmissions), anycast address (used by routers), and unicast address (used to address a single node on a network).

Network Hardware

- Network adapters, commonly called NICs, are rated by speed, and each has a MAC address. Some NICs have status indicator lights and wake-on-LAN and QoS features.
- A hub is an outdated networking distribution device that broadcasts messages. A switch is more efficient because it works to send a message only to the device to which the message is addressed.
- A cable modem stands between an ISP and a local network to convert signals from each network so the other network can understand it.
- A multifunction router for a small office/home office network might serve several functions, including router, switch, DHCP server, wireless access point, firewall, and FTP server.

Local Network Setup and Configuration

- It's extremely important to change the administrative password on a router as soon as you install it, especially if the router also serves as a wireless access point.
- A DHCP server is configured to lease a scope or range of IP addresses to DHCP clients on the network and can reserve certain IP addresses to be used as static IP addresses on the network.
- When connecting a computer to the local network, static or dynamic IP addressing can be used, and the computer recognizes the network as a public or private network.
- Four common types of DNS records include address records (A and AAAA), CNAME, MX records, and TXT records.

Key Terms

For explanations of key terms, see the Glossary for this text.

A record (address record)
AAAA record
address reservation
anycast address
authentication,
   authorization, and
   accounting (AAA)
   server
Automatic Private IP
   Address (APIPA)
best-effort protocol
broadcast message
cable modem
CIDR notation
CIFS (Common Internet
   File System)
client/server application

CNAME (Canonical
   Name) record
connectionless protocol
connection-oriented
   protocol
default gateway
DHCP (Dynamic
   Host Configuration
   Protocol) server
DHCP client
DHCPv6 server
DKIM (DomainKeys
   Identified Mail) record
DMARC (Domain-based
   Message Authentication,
   Reporting, and
   Conformance) record

DNS server
domain name
dynamic IP address
file server
firewall
FTP (File Transfer
   Protocol)
fully qualified domain
   name (FQDN)
global address
host
host name
HTTP (Hypertext
   Transfer
   Protocol)
HTTPS (HTTP secure)
hub

IMAP (Internet Mail
   Access Protocol)
interface ID
Internet service
   provider (ISP)
intranet
IP (Internet Protocol)
IP address
IPv4 (Internet Protocol
   version 4)
IPv6 (Internet Protocol
   version 6)
Lightweight Directory
   Access Protocol (LDAP)
link
link local address
loopback address

MAC address	OSI (Open Systems	Server Message Block	TCP (Transmission
multicast address	Interconnection)	(SMB)	Control Protocol)
MX (Mail Exchanger)	model	Service Set Identifier	TCP/IP (Transmission
record	POP3 (Post Office	(SSID)	Control Protocol/
name resolution	Protocol, version 3)	Simple Network	Internet Protocol)
namespace	port address	Management Protocol	TCP/IP model
NAT (Network Address	print server	(SNMP)	Telnet
Translation)	private IP address	SMTP (Simple Mail	Trivial FTP (TFTP)
neighbors	protocol data unit (PDU)	Transfer Protocol)	TXT (Text) record
NetBIOS (Network Basic	proxy server	SPF (Sender Policy	UDP (User Datagram
Input/Output System)	public IP address	Framework) record	Protocol)
NetBT (NetBIOS over	Quality of Service (QoS)	static IP address	unicast address
TCP/IP)	Remote Desktop	subnet ID	unique local address
network ID	Protocol (RDP)	subnet mask	wake-on-LAN
network interface	resource record (RR)	subnet	web server
card (NIC)	RJ-45	switch	wireless access
node	router	syslog	point (WAP)
octet	Secure Shell (SSH)	syslog server	zone file

Thinking Critically

These questions are designed to prepare you for the critical thinking required for the A+ exams and may use information from other modules and the web.

1. You just finished installing a network adapter, and after booting up the system, you installed the drivers. You open Explorer on a remote computer and don't see the computer on which you installed the new NIC. What is the first thing you check? What is the second thing?

   a. Has IPv6 addressing been enabled?
   b. Can the computer on which you installed the NIC access the network?
   c. Do the lights on the adapter indicate it's functioning correctly?
   d. Has the computer been assigned a computer name?

2. Your manager has asked you to configure a DHCP reservation on the network for a Windows computer that is used to configure other devices on a network. To do this, you need the computer's MAC address. What command can you enter at the command line to access this information?

3. The DHCP server in a SOHO router is using the IP scope of 192.168.50.2 to 192.168.50.254. The subnet mask is 255.255.255.0. The technician has configured one computer with the static IP address of 192.168.1.100 and subnet mask of 255.255.255.0. This computer cannot communicate with other computers on the local network. What is the problem and a workable solution?

   a. The computer is not in the same subnet as others on the network. Change the static IP address to 192.168.100.1.
   b. The subnet mask on the router is not correct. Change it to 255.255.255.255.
   c. The computer is not in the same subnet as others on the network. Change the static IP address to 192.168.50.100.
   d. The subnet needs to be enlarged to include more IP addresses. Change the subnet mask on the router to 255.255.0.0.

4. A computer on a LAN is not able to connect to the Internet even though other computers on the LAN are able to connect. You use the ipconfig command to discover the IP address of the computer is 169.254.18.45. What can you conclude from this information?

    a. The ISP connection is down, and you need to reboot the router.
    b. The computer did not connect to the router to receive a dynamic IP address.
    c. The computer's NIC is not functioning correctly, or a port on the router is bad.
    d. The router's DHCP server is not configured correctly.

5. Why does a DHCP server and client use UDP rather than TCP for transmissions? (Choose all that apply.)

    a. UDP is required for all client/server applications.
    b. A DHCP client broadcasts over the local network looking for a DHCP server when it first connects to the network.
    c. UDP relies on MAC addresses for communication and TCP does not.
    d. TCP works only on the Internet and not on the local network.

6. Your new company is setting up its first website with a public IP address it has leased from its ISP. Your manager has asked you to set up the necessary DNS records so the website can be found on the web. Which type of DNS record will you create?

    a. A record
    b. AAAA record
    c. MX record
    d. CNAME record

7. Which statements are true about TCP and UDP? (Choose all that apply.)

    a. TCP is generally faster than UPD.
    b. TCP guarantees delivery and UDP does not.
    c. UDP is used on the local network but not on the Internet; TCP works on both the local network and the Internet.
    d. TCP establishes a session between source and destination before it sends data, and UDP sends data without first establishing a session.

8. Which ports might you use when configuring email client/server applications? (Choose all that apply.)

    a. Ports 25, 110, and 143
    b. Ports 21, 22, and 23
    c. Ports 22, 110, and 143
    d. Ports 67, 68, 80, and 110

9. What does a web server use port 80 for, and what does it use port 443 for?

    a. For secured transmissions; for unsecured transmissions
    b. For sending data; for receiving data
    c. For unsecured transmissions; for secured transmissions
    d. For communication with browsers; for communication with smartphones

10. Which port is used by either TCP or UDP when Windows shares files across a local network?

    a. Port 443
    b. Port 445
    c. Port 3389
    d. Port 53

11. Computer A has an IP address of 10.200.45.60 and a subnet mask of 255.255.0.0. Which of the following statements are true? (Choose all that apply.)

    a. Computer B, with IP address of 10.200.200.200, is on the same local network as Computer A.
    b. Computer B, with IP address of 10.250.10.12, is on the same local network as Computer A.
    c. Computer B, with IP address of 10.200.45.200, is on the same local network as Computer A.
    d. Computer B, with IP address of 192.168.1.1, is on the same local network as Computer A.

7

12. Which of the following IP addresses are recommended for private networks? (Choose all that apply.)

    a. IP addresses that begin with 10 as their first octet

    b. IP addresses that begin with 172 as their first octet

    c. IP addresses that begin with 192.168 as their first two octets

    d. IP addresses that begin with 192 as their first octet

13. Which of the following IPv6 addresses are global addresses allowed on the Internet? (Choose all that apply.)

    a. 128-bit IP addresses that begin with 2001

    b. 128-bit IP addresses that begin with 2000

    c. 32-bit IP addresses that begin with 9 in the first octet

    d. 128-bit IP addresses that begin with 8888

14. When connecting a wireless device to a Wi-Fi network, the network is identified by which of the following?

    a. Service Set Identifier

    b. IP address

    c. Domain name

    d. MAC address

15. Which DNS record type is used to provide information intended to help filter email to allow only trusted sources?

    a. A records

    b. CNAME records

    c. AAAA records

    d. TXT records

Hands-On Projects

Hands-On Project 7-1

Using Subnet Masks

Est. Time: 30 minutes

Core 1 Objective: 2.5

To practice your skills using subnet masks, fill in Table 7-6. First, convert decimal values to binary, and then record your decisions in the last column.

Table 7-6   Practice using subnet masks

Local IP Address	Subnet Mask	Other IP Address	On the Same Network? (Yes or No)
15.50.212.59 Binary: _____	255.255.240.0 Binary: _____	15.50.235.80 Binary: _____	
192.168.24.1 Binary: _____	255.255.248.0 Binary: _____	192.168.31.198 Binary: _____	
192.168.0.1 Binary: _____	255.255.255.192 Binary: _____	192.168.0.63 Binary: _____	
192.168.0.10 Binary: _____	255.255.255.128 Binary: _____	192.168.0.120 Binary: _____	

Hands-On Project 7-2

Investigating Network Connection Settings

Est. Time: 15 minutes
Core 1 Objective: 2.5

Using a computer connected to a network, answer these questions:

1. What is the hardware device used to make this connection (network card, onboard port, wireless)? List the device's name as Windows sees it in the Device Manager window.
2. What is the MAC address of the wired or wireless network adapter? What command or window did you use to get your answer?
3. For a wireless connection, is the network secured? How do you know?
4. What is the IPv4 address of the network connection?
5. Are your TCP/IP version 4 settings using static or dynamic IP addressing?
6. What is the IPv6 address of your network connection?
7. Disable and enable your network connection. Now what is your IPv4 address?

Hands-On Project 7-3

Viewing and Clearing the DNS Cache

Est. Time: 15 minutes
Core 1 Objective: 2.4

Open a command prompt window, and run the **`ipconfig /displaydns`** command to view the DNS cache on your computer. Then run the **`ipconfig /flushdns`** command to clear the DNS cache.

Hands-On Project 7-4

Practicing TCP/IP Configuration

Est. Time: 30 minutes
Core 1 Objective: 2.6

Working with two networked computers that are using dynamic IP addressing, do the following to create a TCP/IP configuration error and then correct the error:

Open **Explorer** and verify that Computer A and Computer B can see each other in the Network area of their respective Explorer windows. By examining the IP addresses and subnet masks assigned to both computers, what do you think is the scope of IP addresses leased by the DHCP server on the network?

1. On Computer A, change the TCP/IP configuration so this computer is using static IP addressing. Set the static IP address outside the scope of IP addresses used by the DHCP server on the local network. What is the static IP address and subnet mask of Computer A?

(continues)

Hands-On Project Continued

2. Verify that Computer A and Computer B cannot see each other in the Network area of the Explorer window.

3. Correct the configuration area by assigning Computer A static IP address and subnet mask that is within the subnet of IP addresses leased by the DHCP server. Verify Computer A and Computer B can see each other in the Network area of the Explorer window.

4. Set Computer A back to dynamic IP addressing. Verify Computer A and Computer B can see each other in the Network area of the Explorer window.

Real Problems, Real Solutions

Real Problem 7-1

Setting Up a Small Network

Est. Time: 15 minutes
Core 1 Objective: 2.5

The simplest possible wired network is two computers connected together using a crossover cable. In a crossover cable, the send and receive wires are crossed so one computer can send and the other computer can receive on the same wire. At first glance, a crossover cable looks just like a regular network cable (also called a patch cable) except for the labeling, as shown in Figure 7-48. (In the module "Network Infrastructure and Cloud Computing," you learn how to distinguish between the cables by examining their connectors.)

Do the following to set up and test a small network:

Figure 7-48   A patch cable and crossover cable look the same but are labeled differently

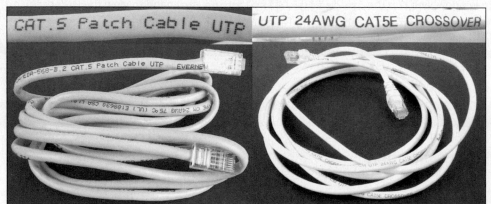

1. Connect two computers using a crossover cable. Using the Network and Sharing Center, verify that your network is up. Using ipconfig, determine each computer's IP address. What is the IPv4 address of Computer A? Of Computer B?

2. On each computer, open a command prompt window and use the ping command to test for connectivity. For example, to test connectivity to the computer with IP address 10.20.30.1, enter the `ping 10.20.30.1` command. Does it work? Why or why not? What specific output do you get?

3. Convert the TCP/IP configuration to static IP addressing. Assign 192.168.10.4 to one computer and 192.168.10.5 to the other computer. The subnet mask for both computers is 255.255.255.0.

4. Ping each computer from the other computer. Does it work? Why or why not?

5. Without changing the subnet masks, change the IP address of one computer to 192.168.90.1. Can you still ping each computer? What specific output do you get?

6. Return the computers to the same subnet and IP addresses you used in step 3. Verify that each computer can ping the other.

Real Problem 7-2

Installing and Using Packet Tracer

Est. Time: 1 hour
Core 1 Objective: 2.5

If you plan to pursue networking or security as your area of specialty in IT, you might consider earning a few Cisco networking certifications after you complete your CompTIA A+, Network+, and Security+ certifications. The Cisco Networking Academy website provides many useful tools for advancing your networking education. One of those tools is a network simulator called Packet Tracer. In this project, you download and install Packet Tracer and create a very basic network using simulated devices in Packet Tracer. This version of Packet Tracer is free to the public, and your school does not have to be a member of Cisco's Networking Academy for you to download and use it.

To get the Packet Tracer download, you must first sign up for the free Introduction to Packet Tracer online course on the Cisco Networking Academy website. Complete the following steps to create your account:

1. In your browser, navigate to **netacad.com/courses/packet-tracer**. Enroll in the Introduction to Packet Tracer course.

2. Open the confirmation email, and confirm your email address. Configure your account and save this information in a safe place. You will need this information again.

3. Click **Courses** and select **Packet Tracer**.

Now you are ready to download and install Packet Tracer. If you need help with the download and installation process, launch the course and navigate to Chapter 1, Section 1.1, Topic 1.1.2 for additional guidance. Complete the following steps:

1. Inside the course, click **Student Support and Resources**, and then click **Download and install the latest version of Packet Tracer**. Download the latest version for your computer, and then install Packet Tracer. When the installation is complete, run **Cisco Packet Tracer**.

2. When Packet Tracer opens, sign in with your Networking Academy account that you created earlier. If you see a Windows Security Alert, allow access through your firewall. Cisco Packet Tracer opens. The interface window is shown in Figure 7-49.

The Introduction to Packet Tracer course presents an excellent introduction to Packet Tracer and provides lab activities. We'll revisit the Packet Tracer course in later modules. In the meantime, let's build a very simple network in Packet Tracer so you can begin to get familiar with the user interface.

(continues)

Real Problem Continued

Figure 7-49   Explore the Packet Tracer window

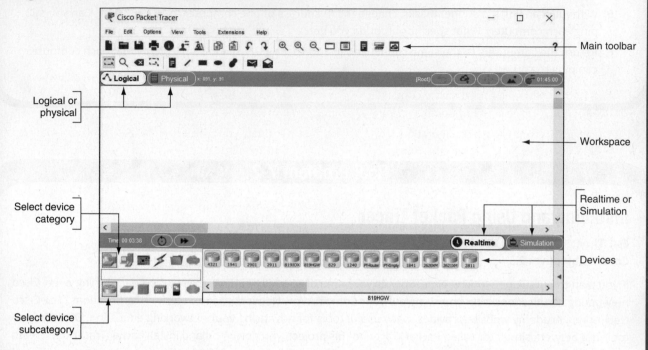

3. First, you need a router. In Packet Tracer (and in most network diagrams), routers look like a hockey puck with four arrows on top. In the Devices pane, make sure the **Network Devices** group is selected and the **Routers** subgroup is selected. Drag a **2901** router from the selection pane into the workspace.

4. Next, add a switch. In network diagrams, switches look like rectangular boxes with four arrows on top. Click to select the **Switches** subgroup, then drag a **2960-24TT** switch to the workspace.

5. Now you're ready to add a couple of computers. Select the **End Devices** group. Drag a **PC** and **Laptop** to the workspace. Arrange all the devices as shown in Figure 7-50.

Figure 7-50   Arrange the devices on your network diagram

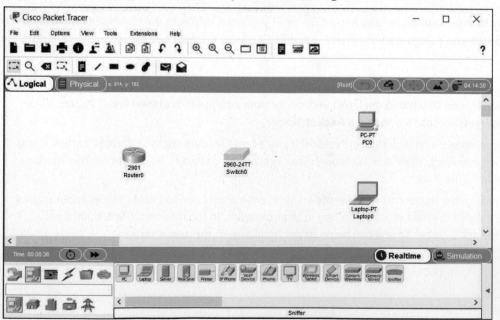

7

6. Now you're ready to connect the devices with Ethernet cables. Click the orange lightning icon to select the **Connections** group. Use the lightning icon from the selection pane to automatically select the correct connection type for each connection you make. (In the module "Network Infrastructure and Cloud Computing," you'll learn more about different types of cables so you can make those decisions yourself.) After you click the **Automatically Choose Connection Type** lightning icon, click **PC0** to start the connection, then click **Switch0** to complete the connection. The link starts as orange, and as the connection is negotiated between the PC and the switch, the link turns to green on both ends.

7. Create an automatic connection from **Laptop0** to **Switch0** and another automatic connection from **Switch0** to **Router0**. The laptop-to-switch connection will come up automatically. The switch-to-router connection will remain red because it requires additional configuration before it will work.

8. Click **Router0** to see its configuration window. On the Physical tab, you can see a picture of the device itself, both front and back. Explore this window to see what information is available to you, but don't change anything. When you're ready, click the **Config** tab.

   In Packet Tracer, you can perform all the configurations at the CLI (command line interface) or through a GUI (graphic user interface). In this project, you'll use the GUI options, and watch the *Equivalent IOS Commands* pane at the bottom of the window to see what commands you're executing.

9. To activate the router's interface, click the **GigabitEthernet0/0** interface in the left pane. Position the configuration window off to the side of the workspace so you can see Router0 and monitor any changes to the connection. Change the Port Status to **On**. What happens to the connection in the workspace?

10. Let's add IP configuration information. Give the connection the IP Address of **192.168.43.1** and a Subnet Mask of **255.255.255.0**. Then close Router0's configuration window.

11. Next, add IP address configuration information to the endpoint devices. Click **PC0** to open its configuration window. Here, you could use the Config tab or tools from the Desktop tab. Click **Desktop**, and then click **IP Configuration**. You have two options: DHCP or Static. For now, you'll have to use Static. Why?

12. Make sure **Static** is selected, then give the PC the following IP configuration:
    - IP Address: **192.168.43.100**
    - Subnet Mask: **255.255.255.0**
    - Default Gateway: **192.168.43.1**

    With this configuration, what device will the PC use as its default gateway?

13. Close PC0's configuration window, then use the same steps to give Laptop0 the following IP configuration:
    - IP Address: **192.168.43.200**
    - Subnet Mask: **255.255.255.0**
    - Default Gateway: **192.168.43.1**

14. On Laptop0, close the IP Configuration pane. On the Desktop tab, click **Command Prompt**. Ping PC0 from Laptop0. What command did you use? Did it work?

15. You can use Simulation mode to watch the ping messages travel over the network. Close Laptop0's configuration window, then click the **Simulation** button in the bottom right of the Packet Tracer window (refer back to Figure 7-49). Open Laptop0's **Command Prompt** window again, and position this window off to the side of the workspace so you can see the devices. Ping the router. What command did you use? Repeatedly tap the play button in the Simulation Panel to see each step in the process. (See Figure 7-51.) Did it work?

16. This network is not connected to a simulated WAN connection, although it could be. Which device in this network would you connect to the modem for the ISP's network?

(continues)

Real Problem Continued

Figure 7-51   Simulation mode shows packets stepping through the network

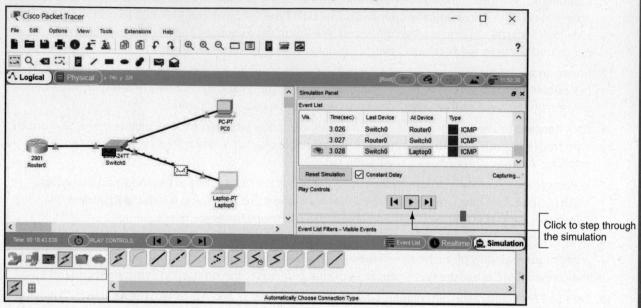

17. Packet Tracer gives you a safe and fun environment to explore networking concepts. Take a few minutes to look around the Packet Tracer menus and options, and perhaps add more devices to your network. When you're ready, close all open windows. You do not need to save your Packet Tracer file unless you want to.

Module

8

Network Infrastructure and Cloud Computing

Module Objectives

1 Identify, compare, and contrast network types

2 Identify, compare, and contrast various network hardware and infrastructure

3 Configure network infrastructure

4 Troubleshoot common network issues

5 Summarize client-side virtualization

6 Support cloud computing services on a network

Core 1 Certification Objectives

2.2 Compare and contrast common networking hardware.

2.3 Compare and contrast protocols for wireless networking.

2.4 Summarize services provided by networked hosts.

2.6 Compare and contrast common network configuration concepts.

2.7 Compare and contrast Internet connection types, network types, and their features.

2.8 Given a scenario, use networking tools.

3.1 Explain basic cable types and their connectors, features, and purposes.

4.1 Summarize cloud-computing concepts.

4.2 Summarize aspects of client-side virtualization.

5.7 Given a scenario, troubleshoot problems with wired and wireless networks.

Introduction

You've already learned how to connect a computer to a network and how to set up a wired and wireless router for a small network. This module takes you a step further in supporting networks. You learn about the hardware devices, cables, and connectors used to construct a network. Next, you learn about various specialized network systems and how networking tools are used to terminate network cables. You also learn how to troubleshoot problems with network hardware and software. Finally, after our exploration of network infrastructure, you are introduced to virtualization and cloud computing. Let's start by discussing the different types of networks you may be asked to set up or manage.

Types of Networks and Network Connections

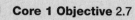 **Core 1 Objective** 2.7

A computer network is created when two or more computers can communicate with each other. Networks can be categorized by several methods, including the technology used and the size of the network. When networks are categorized by their size, or the physical area they cover, these are the categories used, listed from smallest to largest:

- **PAN.** A **PAN (personal area network)** consists of personal devices such as cell phones and laptop computers communicating at close range. PANs can use wired connections (such as USB or Lightning) or wireless connections (such as Bluetooth or near-field communications).
- **LAN.** A **LAN (local area network)** covers a small local area, such as a home, office, or a small group of buildings. LANs can use wired (most likely Ethernet) or wireless technologies (most likely Wi-Fi). A LAN allows workstations, servers, printers, and other devices to communicate and share resources.
- **SAN.** A **SAN (storage area network)** is a specialized, high-speed network for storing and sharing files. These storage locations can be accessed by network clients, as if they were directly connected to the local client machine.
- **WLAN.** A **WLAN (wireless local area network)** is a wireless-capable network that covers a small local area, just like a LAN.
- **MAN.** A **MAN (metropolitan area network)** covers multiple buildings in a large campus or a portion of a city, such as a downtown area. It's usually the result of a cooperative effort to improve service to its users. Network technologies used can be wireless (most likely LTE) and/or wired (for example, Ethernet with fiber-optic cabling).
- **WAN.** A **WAN (wide area network)** covers a large geographical area and is made up of many smaller networks. The best-known WAN is the Internet, or the World Wide Web. Some technologies that connect a single computer or LAN to the Internet include DSL, cable Internet, satellite, cellular WAN, and fiber optic.

Exam Tip ✔

The A+ Core 1 exam expects you to be able to compare PAN, LAN, SAN, WLAN, MAN, and WAN networks.

Now let's look at network technologies used for Internet connections.

Internet Connection Technologies

Core 1 Objectives 2.2, 2.3, 2.7

To connect to the Internet, a device or network first connects to an Internet service provider (ISP), such as Verizon or Spectrum. The common types of connections for SOHO networks are DSL and cable Internet. See Figure 8-1. When connecting to an ISP, know that upload speeds are generally slower than download speeds. These rates differ because users typically download more data than they upload. Therefore, an ISP devotes more of the available bandwidth to downloading and less of it to uploading.

Figure 8-1   The ISP stands between a LAN and the Internet

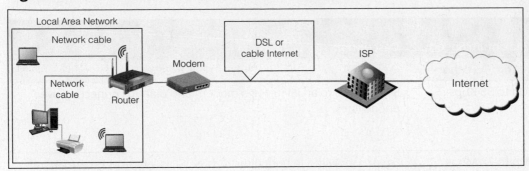

Networks are built using one or more technologies that provide varying degrees of bandwidth. **Bandwidth** is the theoretical maximum number of bits that can be transmitted over a network connection at one time, similar to the number of lanes on a highway. The networking industry refers to bandwidth as a measure of the maximum rate of data transmission in bits per second (bps), thousands of bits per second (Kbps), millions of bits per second (Mbps), or billions of bits per second (Gbps). Bandwidth is the theoretical or potential speed of a network, whereas data throughput is the average of the actual speed. In practice, network transmissions experience delays, called latency, that result in slower network performance. For example, wired signals traveling across long cables or wireless signals crossing long distances through the air can cause signal strength degradation, resulting in latency. Latency is measured by the round-trip time (RTT) it takes for a message to travel from source to destination and back to source.

Table 8-1 lists network technologies used by local networks to connect to the Internet. The table is more or less ordered from slowest to fastest maximum bandwidth within each category, although latency can affect the actual bandwidth of any network. We explore many of these technologies in more depth throughout this module.

Table 8-1   Networking technologies

Technology (Wireless or Wired)	Maximum Speed	Description
Wireless Internet Connection: Satellite and WiMAX		
Satellite	Up to 1000 Mbps	Requires an antenna to send to and receive from a satellite, which is in a relative fixed position above the Earth.
WiMAX	Up to 1 Gbps	Requires a transmitter to send to and receive from a WiMAX tower up to 30 miles away. WiMAX was once popular in rural areas for wireless Internet connections, but it has lost this market space to cellular solutions such as LTE.
Wireless Internet Connection: Cellular		
3G cellular (third-generation cellular)	At least 200 Kbps, but can be up to 21 Mbps	Improved over earlier technologies and allows for transmitting data and video. Uses either CDMA or GSM mobile phone services. Speeds vary widely according to the revision standards used.
4G cellular (fourth-generation cellular)	100 Mbps to 1 Gbps	Higher speeds are achieved when the mobile device stays in a fixed position. A 4G network typically uses LTE (Long Term Evolution) technology.
5G cellular (fifth-generation cellular)	Up to 10 Gbps and beyond	5G services are now widespread across many major metropolitan areas; coverage will continue to increase as providers implement more coverage antenna.

(continues)

Table 8-1   Networking technologies (Continued)

Technology (Wireless or Wired)	Maximum Speed	Description
Wired Internet Connection: Telephone		
Dial-up or regular telephone (POTS, for plain old telephone service)	Up to 56 Kbps	Slow access to an ISP using a modem and dial-up connection over phone lines.
SDSL (symmetric digital subscriber line)	Up to 22 Mbps	Equal bandwidth in both directions. SDSL is a type of broadband technology. (**Broadband** refers to a networking technology that carries more than one type of signal on the same cabling infrastructure, such as DSL and telephone or cable Internet and TV.) DSL uses regular phone lines and is an always-up or always-on connection that does not require a dial-up.
ADSL (Asymmetric DSL)	640 Kbps upstream and up to 24 Mbps downstream	Most bandwidth is allocated for data coming from the ISP to the user. ISP customers pay according to a bandwidth scale.
VDSL (very-high-bit-rate DSL)	Up to 70 Mbps	A type of asymmetric DSL that works only over a short distance.
Other Wired Internet Connections		
Cable Internet	Up to 160 Mbps, depending on the type of cable	Connects a home or small business to an ISP, usually comes with a cable television subscription, and shares cable TV lines. If available, fiber-optic cable gives highest speeds.
Dedicated line using fiber optic	Up to 10 Gbps	Dedicated fiber-optic line from ISP to business or home. Speeds vary widely with price.
Wired Local Network: Ethernet		
Fast Ethernet (100BaseT)	100 Mbps	Used for local networks.
Gigabit Ethernet (1000BaseT)	1000 Mbps or 1 Gbps	Fastest Ethernet standard for small, local networks.
10-Gigabit Ethernet (10GBaseT)	10 Gbps	Typically requires fiber media, is mostly used on the backbone of larger enterprise networks, and can also be used on WAN connections.
Wireless Local Network: Wi-Fi IEEE 802.11		
802.11a	Up to 54 Mbps	No longer used. Uses 5 GHz frequency.
802.11b	Up to 11 Mbps	Experiences interference from cordless phones and microwaves. Uses 2.4 GHz frequency.
802.11g	Up to 54 Mbps	Compatible with and has replaced 802.11b. Uses 2.4 GHz frequency.
802.11n (Wi-Fi 4)	Up to 600 Mbps	Uses multiple input/multiple output (MIMO), which means an access point can have up to four antennas to improve performance. Uses both 2.4 and 5 GHz frequencies.
802.11ac (Wi-Fi 5)	Theoretically up to 7 Gbps, but currently limited to 1.3 Gbps	Supports up to eight antennas and supports **beamforming**, which detects the locations of connected devices and increases signal strength in those directions. Uses 5 GHz frequency only.
802.11ax (Wi-Fi 6)	10 Gbps	This throughput is possible when using the 160 MHz channel spacing and the eight spatial streams. Uses both 2.4 and 5 GHz frequencies.
Bluetooth	Up to 25 Mbps for version 4.0	Originally defined under IEEE 802.15, but now maintained by the Bluetooth Special Interest Group (SIG).

Cable Internet and DSL are two options to make an Internet connection for a home network. Let's first quickly compare these two technologies and then look at fiber-optic dedicated lines, satellite, cellular WAN, wireless Internet service providers, and long-range fixed wireless connections that may be found in commercial applications.

Exam Tip ✔

The A+ Core 1 exam expects you to be able to compare these network types used for Internet connections: cable, DSL, dial-up, fiber, satellite, ISDN, and cellular (tethering and mobile hotspot).

Figure 8-2   When DSL is used in your home, filters are needed on every phone jack except the one used by the DSL modem

Cable Internet

Cable Internet is a broadband technology that uses cable TV lines and is always connected (always up). With cable Internet, the TV signal to your television and the data signals to your computer or LAN share the same **coaxial (coax) cable**, an older cable form that is still used today in local area networks. The cable modem converts the computer's digital signals to analog when sending them and converts incoming analog data to digital.

DSL Broadband

DSL (digital subscriber line) is a group of broadband technologies that covers a wide range of speeds. DSL uses ordinary copper phone lines and a range of frequencies on the copper wire that are not used by voice, making it possible for you to use the same phone line for voice and DSL at the same time. When you make a regular phone call, you dial in as usual. However, the DSL part of the line is always connected (always up) for most DSL services.

With DSL, static over phone lines in your house can be a problem. The DSL company normally provides filters to install at each phone jack (see Figure 8-2), but the problem still might not be fully solved. Figure 8-3 shows a **DSL modem** that can connect directly to a computer or to a router on your network.

Both cable and DSL connections typically require a modem device at the entry to your SOHO network. Although you might be able to find the modem's default login instructions online, you'll likely never have to change any settings on the modem itself. Configuring a DSL or cable modem consists of plugging the correct cables into the correct ports. For example, Figure 8-4 shows a cable modem with the ISP coax cable connected on the right. The yellow Ethernet cable connects to the local network, and a phone line is plugged into the Voice-over-IP (VoIP) phone service provided by the ISP over the Internet. Also notice the Reset button in the figure, which you can use to reset a modem to its factory default settings. When troubleshooting a modem, try rebooting it first, and only use the reset as a last resort.

Figure 8-3   This DSL modem connects to a phone jack and a computer or router to provide broadband connection to an ISP

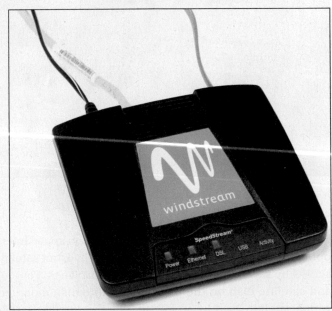

Figure 8-4 Use a cable modem to connect the ISP's coaxial cable to the LAN's Ethernet cable

Voice-over-IP phone line

Internal Ethernet network

Cable connection to ISP

Reset button

Dedicated Line Using Fiber Optic

Another broadband technology used for Internet access is **fiber optic**. This technology connects a dedicated line from your ISP to your place of business or residence. This dedicated line is called a point-to-point (PTP) connection because no other business or residence shares the line with you. Television, Internet data, and voice communication all share the broadband **fiber-optic cable**, which reaches all the way from the ISP to your home. This line then connects to an **optical network terminal (ONT)**. The ONT serves as a modem for the fiber connection (see Figure 8-5). Alternatively, the provider might install fiber-optic cabling up to your neighborhood and then run coaxial cable (like that used in cable Internet connections) for the last leg of the connection to your business or residence. Upstream and downstream speeds and prices vary.

Figure 8-5 AN ONT connects the ISP's fiber cable on the left and coverts it to a data-connection cable that is connected into your home

Wikimedia Commons

Satellite

People who live in remote areas and want high-speed Internet connections often have limited choices. DSL and cable options might not be available where they live, but satellite access is available from pretty much anywhere. Internet access by **satellite** is available even on airplanes. Passengers can connect to the Internet using a wireless hotspot and satellite dish on the plane. A satellite dish mounted on top of your house or office building communicates with a satellite used by an ISP offering the satellite service (see Figure 8-6). One disadvantage of satellite is that it requires line-of-sight wireless connectivity without obstruction from mountains, trees, and tall buildings. Another

Figure 8-6   Communications by satellite can include television and Internet access

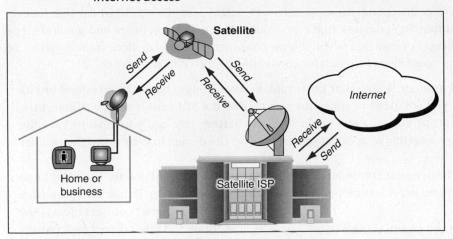

disadvantage is that it experiences higher delays in transmission (latency), especially when uploading, and is therefore not a good solution for an Internet connection that will be used for videoconferencing or voice over Internet.

Cellular WAN

A cellular network, also called a cellular WAN because it consists of cells, is provided by companies such as Verizon and AT&T. Each cell is controlled by a base station (see Figure 8-7), which might include more than one transceiver and antenna on the same tower to support various technologies for both voice and data transmission.

Cellular devices require a **SIM (subscriber identity module) card** to be installed in the device; the card contains the information that identifies your device to the carrier (see Figure 8-8).

Figure 8-7   A cellular network is made up of many cells that provide coverage over a wide area

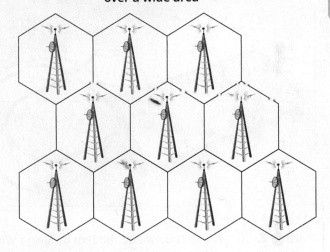

Figure 8-8   A SIM card contains information about the cellular networks it is authorized to connect to

Installed SIM card

Most smartphones are linked by the manufacturer to a specific cellular provider and will need to be validated on that provider's network to connect to it. To connect a computer using mobile broadband to a cellular network, you need the hardware and software to connect and, for most networks, a SIM card. The bulleted list that follows includes the options for software and hardware devices that can connect to a cellular network and general steps for how to create each connection. Keep in mind that when you purchase any of these devices from a carrier or manufacturer, detailed instructions are most likely included for connecting to the cellular network.

- **Embedded mobile broadband modem.** A laptop or other mobile device might have an embedded broadband modem. In this situation, you still need to subscribe to a carrier. If a SIM card is required, insert the card in the device. For some laptops, the card slot might be in the battery bay, and you must remove the battery to find the slot. Then use a setting or application installed on the device to connect to the cellular network.

- **Cell phone tethering.** You can tether your computer or another device to your cell phone. The cell phone connects to the cellular network and provides communication to the tethered device. To use your phone for tethering, your carrier contract must allow it. The phone and other device can connect by way of a USB cable (see Figure 8-9), a proprietary cable provided by your cell phone manufacturer, or a Bluetooth or Wi-Fi wireless connection. Your carrier is likely to provide you software to make the connection, or the setting might be embedded in the phone's OS.

Figure 8-9   Tethering a laptop to a cell phone using a USB cable

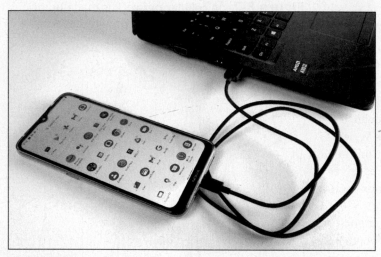

- **USB broadband modem.** For any computer, you can use a USB broadband modem (sometimes called an air card), such as the one shown in Figure 8-10. The device requires a contract with a cellular carrier. If needed when using a USB broadband modem, insert the SIM card in the modem (see Figure 8-11). When you insert the modem into a USB port, Windows finds the device, and the software stored on the device automatically installs and runs. A window provided by the software then appears and allows you to connect to the cellular network.

Figure 8-10   A USB broadband modem by Sierra Wireless

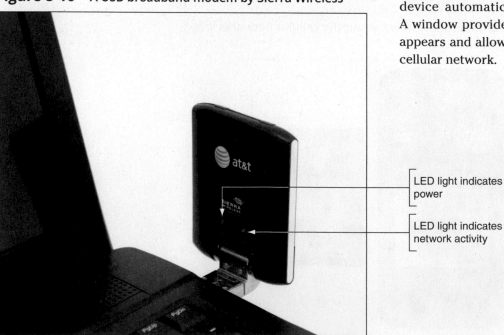

LED light indicates power

LED light indicates network activity

Figure 8-11   A SIM card with subscription information on it may be required to use a cellular network for data

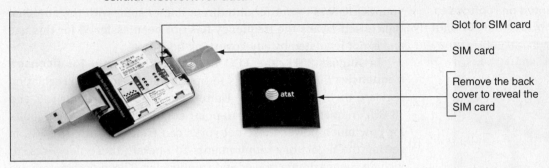

Slot for SIM card

SIM card

Remove the back cover to reveal the SIM card

- **LTE home Internet.** Some cellular companies offer home Internet service through their cellular WAN infrastructure. Verizon calls its service LTE Home Internet, and AT&T calls its service FWI (Fixed Wireless Internet). The ISP installs an LTE router at the home, possibly with an external antenna, which then connects wirelessly to the ISP's cellular network. The router provides a Wi-Fi hotspot as well as a few Ethernet ports for wired devices. Typically, the router can't be moved to other locations like a smartphone can—it's designed to be used only at the location where the subscription is established. Data usage caps also may apply.
- **Mobile hotspot.** Some mobile devices can create a **mobile hotspot**, which allows computers and other mobile devices to connect by Wi-Fi to the device and, through that connection, to the Internet. Some cellular ISPs, such as AT&T, also offer devices dedicated to this purpose.

Wireless Internet Service Providers

A **wireless Internet service provider (WISP)** provides wireless network coverage to a certain location using wireless broadband. These providers used to be found only in rural areas where conventional networking technologies such as cable or DSL were not available. Now, however, they can be found in metropolitan areas as well. Consisting of wireless transmitters and customer premise antennae, as shown in Figure 8-12, these networks can expand Internet coverage across the globe. Another example of a WISP was seen in the WiFi101 network project that ran from 2008 to 2015 in East Palo Alto, California. As part of that project, Google provided completely free wireless coverage to the entire community.

Long-Range Fixed Wireless

Long-range fixed wireless (LRFW) networks are used to provide low-cost, point-to-point connections. These networks are typically unregulated and provide an alternative to either cellular or satellite Internet access. These systems use highly directional antennas, which transmit at high power, to transmit the wireless signal across large distances, sometimes more than 100 miles. A LRFW antenna is shown in Figure 8-13.

Figure 8-12   WISP access point in Tyler, Texas

Wikipedia

Figure 8-13 Long-range fixed wireless antennas are mounted on rooftops to ensure clear line of sight

Wikimedia Commons

Currently, LRFW networks outside the United States use **unlicensed frequencies** within the 2.4 and 5 GHz spectrum—like your SOHO Wi-Fi—but require direct line of sight with the antenna. Unlicensed means the frequency has not been assigned for this use and is not regulated by any governing body.

In August 2011, the FCC began making room for **licensed frequencies** for these systems to operate and also began regulating regulate their use within the United States. By licensing the 7 and 13 GHz frequencies for point-to-point connections and setting limits for how much power these networks can transmit with, the FCC is setting the regulatory requirements to operate these networks, to include the maximum power and frequencies. These parameters are also intended to ensure that these networks do not interfere with other communication networks.

Now that you understand some basics about the different types of networks and methods of connecting those networks to the Internet, you're ready to learn about different devices used to connect computers to local networks.

Identifying Network Hardware and Infrastructure

Core 1 Objectives 2.2, 2.3, 2.4, 2.6, 3.1

In this section of the module, you learn about the hardware devices that create and connect to networks. We discuss desktop and laptop devices, switches, bridges, and other network devices, along with the cables and connectors these devices use.

Switches and Virtual LANs

Core 1 Objectives 2.2, 2.6

Recall that a switch is a device that connects other devices on a network. Two types of switches are managed and unmanaged switches. An **unmanaged switch** requires no setup or configuration other than connecting network cables to its ports. It does not require an IP address and is appropriate for SOHO networks. A **managed switch**, seen in Figure 8-14, has firmware that can be configured to monitor and manage network traffic. It's appropriate for larger networks and can be used to manage QoS for prioritizing network traffic and to control speeds for specific ports. The firmware on a managed switch is accessed through a browser using the switch's IP address, which is similar to how you access the firmware on a router. A switch requires an IP address only for the purpose of accessing its firmware to configure the switch.

Figure 8-14 The Gigabit Ethernet switch has eight ports for device connections

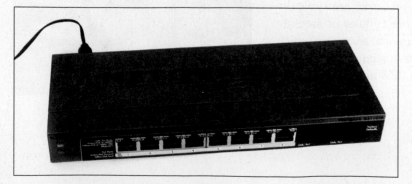

You can also use a managed switch to break up a large LAN into smaller networks called **virtual LANs (VLANs)**, which can reduce network traffic. VLANs are created by assigning a group of physical ports on the switch to a different VLAN. In Figure 8-15, the one physical LAN is broken up into two virtual LANs. With network segmentation, broadcast traffic is reduced because it is limited to each VLAN.

Figure 8-15   Ports on a managed switch can be assigned to a VLAN to logically break up a network

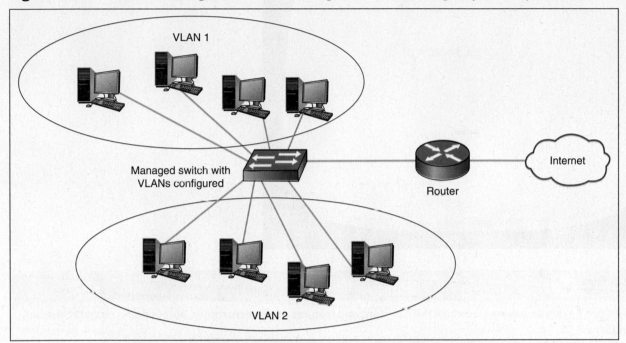

You can also break up a large network by subnetting, which involves using a DHCP server and assigning different IP address ranges and subnet masks to each smaller network. Subnetting also helps reduce broadcast traffic on the network and can optimize the network for faster service.

Here are reasons you might add switches to your network:

- **To add network connections.** A SOHO router usually has four to eight ports in a built-in switch. When you need more connections, add a switch in a location where you have multiple workstations or printers that need to connect to the network. In practice, a small network might begin as one switch and three or four computers. As the need for more computers grows, new switches are added to provide these extra connections.
- **To regenerate the network signal.** An Ethernet cable should not exceed 100 meters (about 328 feet) in length. If you need to reach distances greater than that, you can add a switch in the line, which regenerates the signal. An alternative to using a switch for this purpose would be to simply use a **repeater** device that amplifies the signal onto the new extended cable run.
- **To manage network traffic.** Managed switches can be installed in strategic places on the network to subnet the network and manage network traffic to improve performance.

Wireless Access Points

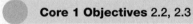

Core 1 Objectives 2.2, 2.3

You've already learned that a SOHO router can also be a wireless access point. In addition, a wireless access point can be a dedicated device. The wireless access point can also serve as a bridge, as shown in Figure 8-16. A **bridge** is a device that stands between two segments of a network and manages network traffic between them. For example, one network segment might be a wireless network and the other segment might be a wired network; the wireless access point (WAP) connects these two segments. Another use of a bridge can be found when a server is placed between two networks, as in the case of a proxy server. The server would have two network interface cards to connect to each network segment.

Figure 8-16   A wireless access point by TP-Link

Exam Tip ✔

The A+ Core 1 exam expects you to know the functions and features of a switch, router, access point, repeater, firewall, and modem.

Ethernet Cables and Connectors

 Core 1 Objective 3.1

Several variations of Ethernet cables and connectors have evolved over the years. They are primarily identified by their speeds and the types of connectors used to wire the networks. Table 8-2 compares cable types and Ethernet versions.

Table 8-2   Variations of Ethernet and Ethernet cabling

Cable System	Speed	Cables and Connectors	Example of Connectors	Maximum Cable Length
10BaseT, 100BaseT (Fast Ethernet), 1000BaseT (Gigabit Ethernet), and 10GBaseT (10-Gigabit Ethernet)	10 Mbps, 100 Mbps, 1 Gbps, or 10 Gbps	Twisted-pair (UTP or STP) uses an RJ-45 connector.	*Courtesy of Tyco Electronics*	100 meters or 328 feet
100BaseFL, 100BaseFX, 1000BaseFX, or 1000BaseX (fiber optic)	100 Mbps, 1 Gbps	Fiber-optic cable uses ST, SC, or LC connectors (ST and SC shown to the right)	*Courtesy of Black Box Corporation*	Up to 2 kilometers (6562 feet)
10GBase ER, 10GBase SR, 10GBase SW, 10GBase SX	10Gbps	Fiber-optic cable using SC or LC connectors (LC shown to the right)		Up to 550 meters

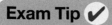

Exam Tip ✔

The A+ Core 1 exam expects you to know the details listed in Table 8-2. Given a scenario, you need to recognize that when a cable exceeds its recommended maximum length, limited connectivity problems can result.

Ethernet Standards and Cables

Ethernet can run at four speeds. Each version of Ethernet can use more than one cabling method. Here is a brief description of the transmission speeds and the cabling methods they use:

- **100 Mbps Ethernet or Fast Ethernet. Fast Ethernet** operates at 100 Mbps and typically uses copper cabling rated CAT-5 or higher. Fast Ethernet networks can support slower speeds of 10 Mbps, used by the original Ethernet standard, so devices that run at either 10 Mbps or 100 Mbps can coexist on the same LAN.
- **1000 Mbps Ethernet or Gigabit Ethernet.** This version of Ethernet operates at 1000 Mbps (1 Gbps) and uses twisted-pair cable and fiber-optic cable. **Gigabit Ethernet** is becoming the most popular choice for LAN technology. Because it can use the same cabling and connectors as Fast Ethernet, a company can upgrade from Fast Ethernet to Gigabit without rewiring the network.
- **10 Gbps Ethernet.** This version of Ethernet operates at 10 billion bits per second (10 Gbps) and typically uses fiber-optic cable. It can be used on LANs, MANs, and WANs and is also a good choice for network backbones. (A network backbone is a channel whereby local networks can connect to wide area networks or to each other.)

Twisted-Pair Cable

As you can see from Table 8-2, the two main types of cabling used by Ethernet are twisted pair and fiber optic. **Twisted-pair cabling** uses pairs of wires twisted together to reduce crosstalk, which is interference that degrades a signal on the wire. It's the most popular cabling method for local networks and uses an RJ-45 connector. The cable comes in two varieties: **unshielded twisted-pair (UTP) cable** and **shielded twisted-pair (STP) cable**. UTP cable is less expensive than STP and is commonly used on LANs. STP cable uses a covering or shield around each pair of wires inside the cable that protects it from electromagnetic interference caused by electrical motors, transmitters, or high-tension lines. Additional coatings can also shield the cable from the elements outside and allow the cable to be buried in the ground. This is known as **direct burial** cable. STP cable costs more than unshielded cable, so it's used only when the situation demands it. Twisted-pair cable is rated by category (CAT), as listed in Table 8-3. A rating indicates how well a cable can handle alien crosstalk (crosstalk between cables in a bundle) and near-end crosstalk (NEXT), which is crosstalk between pairs of twisted wires within a cable where the wires terminate at the end of the cable.

Table 8-3   Twisted-Pair Categories

Twisted-Pair Category	Cable System	Frequency	Shielded or Unshielded	Comment
CAT-5	10/100 Base T	Up to 100 MHz	Either	Has two wire pairs and is seldom used today
CAT-5e (Enhanced)	10/100 Base T, Gigabit Ethernet	Up to 350 MHz	Either	Has four twisted pairs and a heavy-duty sheath to help reduce crosstalk
CAT-6	10/100 Base T, Gigabit Ethernet, 10 Gigabit Ethernet at shorter distances	Up to 250 MHz	Either	Less alien crosstalk because it has a plastic core that keeps the twisted pairs separated
CAT-6A	10 G Base T	Up to 500 MHz	Either	Higher standards to reduce alien and near-end crosstalk

8

Note 1

At the time of this writing, CAT-7 and CAT-8 cables are starting to be used; however, the specifications have not been fully approved by the TIA/EIA. These cables offer increased speeds at higher frequencies. CAT-7 is rated up to 10 Gbps at 600 or 1000 MHz, and CAT-8 is rated up to 40 Gbps at 2 GHz. It should be noted that these cables are not for generic wiring within a building and will only be used in data centers for short runs between equipment such as switches and routers.

Figure 8-17 shows unshielded twisted-pair cables. Twisted-pair cable has four pairs of twisted wires for a total of eight wires. You learn more about how the eight wires are arranged later in this module.

Figure 8-17   Unshielded twisted-pair cables showing the twisted pairs. One cable has the RJ-45 connector attached. Note the core isolator in the CAT-6 cable.

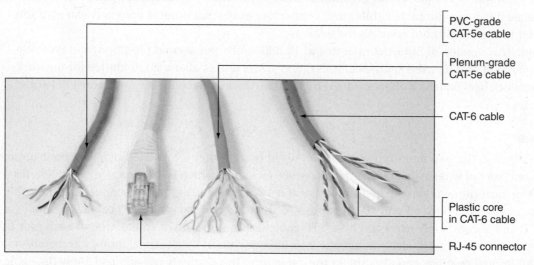

- PVC-grade CAT-5e cable
- Plenum-grade CAT-5e cable
- CAT-6 cable
- Plastic core in CAT-6 cable
- RJ-45 connector

Note 2

Normally, the plastic covering of a cable is made of **PVC (polyvinyl chloride)**, which is not safe when used inside the **plenum** (airspaces between the floors of buildings). In these situations, plenum cable covered with Teflon is used because it does not give off toxic fumes when burned. Plenum cable is two or three times more expensive than PVC cable. Because they can look essentially the same, check for labels printed on the cable to determine whether it's PVC or plenum rated.

Fiber Optic

Fiber-optic cables transmit signals as pulses of light over glass or plastic strands inside protective tubing, as illustrated in Figure 8-18. Fiber-optic cable comes in two types: single-mode (thin, difficult to connect, expensive, and best performing) and multimode (most popular). A single-mode cable uses a single path for light to travel through it and multimode cable uses multiple paths for light. Both single-mode and multimode fiber-optic cables can be constructed as loose-tube cables for outdoor use or tight-buffered cables for indoor or outdoor use.

Figure 8-18   Fiber-optic cables contain a glass or plastic core for transmitting light

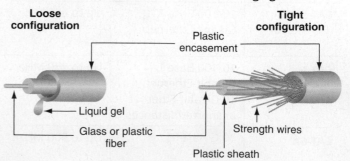

Loose configuration

Tight configuration

Plastic encasement

Liquid gel

Glass or plastic fiber

Strength wires

Plastic sheath

Figure 8-19 An ST (straight tip) fiber connector

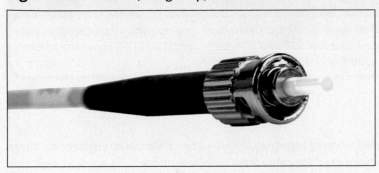

Loose-tube cables are filled with gel to prevent water from soaking into the cable, and tight-buffered cables are filled with synthetic or glass yarn, called strength wires, to protect the fiber-optic strands, as shown in Figure 8-18.

Fiber optic cables use a variety of connectors but the most common ones in networking are the **ST (straight tip) connector** shown in Figure 8-19, **LC (Lucent connector)** shown in Figure 8-20, and the **SC (subscriber connector)** shown in Figure 8-21. Depending on the hardware, the choice of connector should match the port you are connecting the cable to.

Figure 8-20 An LC (Lucent connector) fiber connector has a locking clip that locks the cable into the port, similar to an RJ-45 connector

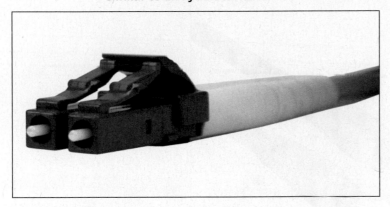

Figure 8-21 An SC (subscriber connector) fiber connector

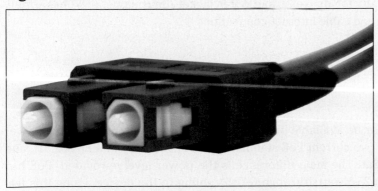

8

Coaxial

Coaxial cable, or coax, is a single conductor cable used to carry high-frequency electrical signals to customers. These cables have been around for many years and have been used for cable television, telephone, and Internet services. Coaxial cable was used for early implementations of Ethernet, but it is no longer used for that purpose. Today, the most common uses are for cable modem connections between a customer and Internet service provider. Common connectors using coaxial cable are the **BNC** and **F-Type**. BNC is normally found in industrial environments. Both are shown in Figure 8-22.

Figure 8-22   Coaxial cable normally uses the BNC (left) or the F-type connector (right)

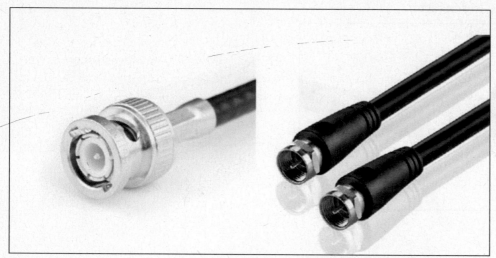

Coaxial cable is categorized by its inner conductor diameter and outer jacket dimensions. RG-6 has widely replaced older RG-59 cables to support television and cable Internet connections.

Power over Ethernet (PoE)

Core 1 Objective 2.2

Power over Ethernet (PoE) is a feature that might be available on high-end **PoE-rated switches** to allow power to be transmitted over Ethernet cable. There are two current PoE standards: **PoE** is specified in IEEE 802.3af, and **Power over Ethernet plus (PoE+)** is under 802.3at. The main difference is the power levels provided. PoE has a maximum of 15.4 watts, and PoE+ sends up to 25.5 watts through CAT-5 cabling to the device. Using this feature, you can place a wireless access point, webcam, IP phone, or other device that needs power in a position in a building where you don't have an electrical outlet. The Ethernet cable to the device provides both power and data transmissions. If your switch doesn't offer PoE, you can attach a **PoE injector** (see Figure 8-23), which adds power to an Ethernet cable.

Figure 8-23   A PoE injector introduces power onto the Ethernet cable

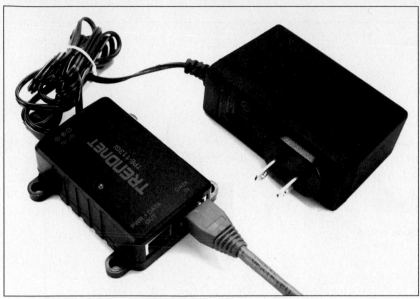

Some devices, such as a webcam, are designed to receive both power and data from the Ethernet cable. For other devices, you must use a splitter that splits the data and power transmissions before connecting to the non-PoE device. Figure 8-24 shows a PoE switch, as well as a splitter used to provide power to a non-PoE access point. When setting up a device to receive power by PoE, make sure the device sending the power, the splitter, and the device receiving the power are all compatible. Pay special attention to the voltage and wattage requirements and the type of power connector of the receiving device.

Figure 8-24   Use a PoE splitter if the receiving device is not PoE compatible

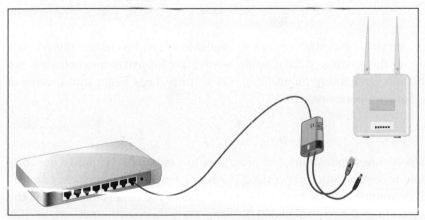

Internet of Things (IoT)

Core 1 Objective 2.4

The **Internet of Things (IoT)** is a term that is used to describe physical devices that are connected directly to a network and communicate directly to the Internet. Examples of IoT devices include cameras, doorbells, baby monitors, health and fitness wearable technology, and even refrigerators and other appliances. A smart home network using a variety of devices and wireless technologies (such as Bluetooth, Wi-Fi, and Zigbee) might look something like the one shown in Figure 8-25. These devices are all directly or indirectly connected to the Internet and allow for remote monitoring of your home or appliances from anywhere in the world.

Figure 8-25 IoT devices connected to a smart home network may use a variety of wireless technologies

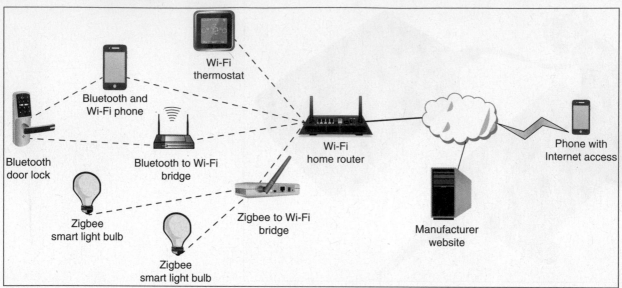

IoT devices are normally centered around increasing quality of life and convenience; however, they do bring questions of privacy and security because they can be accessed remotely. Imagine someone being able to connect to your cameras or baby monitor from across the globe and spy on you. If you decide these devices should be a part of your smart home, be sure to implement IoT security features that you learn about in the module "Network Security and Troubleshooting."

Devices and Software to Enhance Networking

Core 1 Objectives 2.4, 2.6

The best networks are those that make data, services, and other resources available to employees, customers, and others in the most efficient and reliable way. In this section of the module, we explore infrastructure software and hardware designed to improve network efficiency, reliability, monitoring, and security. Let's begin with looking at software designed to monitor and improve network performance.

Software-Defined Networking

Software-defined networking (SDN) uses software applications and programs to essentially virtualize networking. SDN applications replicate how a switch, router, or other networking hardware functions, all while constantly monitoring the status of each device. An SDN architecture separates the movement of the data (referred to as the data plane) from the hardware device (referred to as the control plane). By separating these two functions, an SDN can make smarter decisions about the path data should take across the network, configuring priorities for certain data or automating connections. This high-level view and the monitoring of the entire network are different from traditional hardware networks because the network can be configured remotely in the SDN application without having to configure individual networking devices.

Note 3

To view a short video about how a SDN works, go to *youtube.com/watch?v=XFXdWg1p5to*.

SCADA Systems

Supervisory control and data acquisition (SCADA) systems are embedded computer systems designed to monitor and control machinery from a single location. For example, a manufacturing plant can use SCADA to supervise an assembly line, or a nuclear power plant can use SCADA to control power production. SCADA systems can be used in commercial buildings to monitor heating, ventilation, and air conditioning (HVAC) and water supply systems. Because these systems control and operate important and critical systems, they should be protected from regular network access using a VLAN or dedicated subnet. Remote access to these systems should also be minimized or eliminated if possible. A SCADA system control room is shown in Figure 8-26.

Figure 8-26 A SCADA control station can visually show the systems it monitors for easy visual identification

Wikimedia Commons

Unified Threat Management (UTM) Appliance

Recall that a router stands between the Internet and a private network to route traffic between the two networks. It can also serve as a firewall to protect the network. A next-generation firewall (NGFW) combines basic firewall functions with antivirus/anti-malware functions and perhaps other functions as well. NGFW components might be installed on a dedicated appliance, router, server, or even in the cloud. In addition, an NGFW device can offer comprehensive **unified threat management (UTM)** services. A UTM appliance, also called a security appliance, stands between the Internet and a private network, as does a router, and it protects the network (see Figure 8-27). Figure 8-28 shows a UTM appliance by FortiNet.

Figure 8-27 A UTM appliance is considered a next-generation firewall that can protect a private network

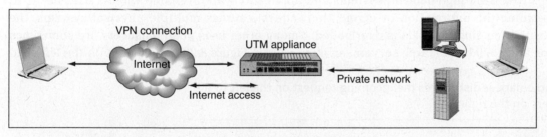

Figure 8-28 A FortiNet FortiGate Rugged 60D UTM appliance

A UTM appliance might offer these types of protections and services:

- **Firewall.** The firewall filters incoming and outgoing network traffic according to IP addresses, ports, the type of messages the traffic contains, and how the message was initiated.

- **Antivirus and anti-malware software.** This software is usually much more advanced than what might be installed on a server or workstation.
- **Spam gateway.** Spam gateways are used to control spam content and emails from entering a network. This helps to reduce the amount of content being sent into the network.
- **Identity-based access control lists.** These lists control access of users or user groups and can log and report activity of these users and groups to reveal misuse, data leaks, or unauthorized access to resources. The company can use this feature to satisfy legal auditing requirements for detecting and controlling data leaks.
- **Intrusion detection system.** An **intrusion detection system (IDS)** monitors all network traffic and creates alerts when suspicious activity happens. IDS software can run on a UTM appliance, router, server, or workstation.
- **Intrusion prevention system.** An **intrusion prevention system (IPS)** not only monitors and logs suspicious activity like the IDS, but it can also prevent the network traffic from entering the network, based on a set of rules programmed into it.
- **Endpoint management server.** An endpoint management server provides monitoring of various endpoint devices on the network, from computers and laptops to mobile devices like smartphones, tablets, or even barcode readers. The service can ensure that endpoints are kept up to date with current anti-malware requirements, operating system patches, and application updates. The system will restrict the device's access to the network until that device meets the security requirements, which gives an additional layer of protection to other network resources.
- **VPN.** The appliance can provide a **virtual private network (VPN)** to remote users of the network, as shown in Figure 8-27. This allows for secure remote access of your private network. You learn how to set up a VPN in the Core 2 module "Networking Security and Troubleshooting."

Exam Tip ✔

The A+ Core 1 exam expects you to be able to summarize the purposes of services provided by a UTM appliance, including an IDS, IPS, endpoint management server, and VPN provider.

Load Balancer

A **load balancer** helps to ensure high-demand systems and applications are available when a user needs to access them. By spreading the information or connection requests across multiple physical systems, the load balancer ensures that no single system is overloaded. Among other uses, load balancers are sometimes deployed on shopping and social media web servers. As illustrated in Figure 8-29, the devices on the left send

Figure 8-29   A load balancer distributes the incoming request on the left to the servers on the right

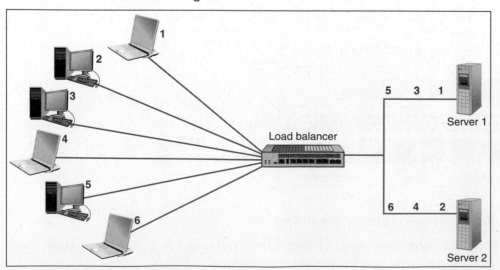

requests (marked by the numbers) that are spread across the two servers on the right. This ensures the two servers do not get overloaded. Load balancers, sometimes called elastic load balancers, are used frequently within cloud computing to spread the incoming requests across virtual servers in the cloud. The load balancer can also create new copies of the virtual server as the demand increases or shut down these systems as the demand decreases.

Configuring Network Infrastructure

 Core 1 Objectives 2.2, 2.3, 2.8, 3.1

In the module "Networking Fundamentals," you learned to configure a workstation and SOHO router to create a small network and connect it to a device (for example, a DSL or cable modem) that provides Internet access. If your network is not strictly a wireless network, you also need cabling and perhaps one or more switches to create a wired network. This section covers what you need to know to set up and troubleshoot both a wired and wireless network.

Designing a Wired Network

 Core 1 Objective 2.3

Begin your network design by deciding where to place your router. If the router is also your wireless access point, take care in where you place it. Place the wireless access point near the center of the area where you want your wireless hotspot to maximize its range for users and minimize your Wi-Fi network's exposure to unauthorized users outside your building. The router also needs to have access to your modem, and the modem needs access to the cable TV or phone jack where it receives service. For a business, the router, modem, and servers are often placed in an electrical closet that can be locked, with additional wireless access points placed where additional coverage is needed. Next, consider where the wired workstations will be placed. Position switches in strategic locations to provide extra network drops to multiple workstations.

Some network cables might be wired inside walls of your building with wall jacks that use RJ-45 ports. These cables might converge in an electrical closet or server room to connect to switches. If network cables are lying on the floor, be sure to install them against the wall so they won't be a trip hazard. To get the best performance from your network, follow these tips:

- Make sure cables don't exceed the recommended length (100 meters for twisted pair).
- Use twisted-pair cables rated at CAT-5e or higher. (CAT-6 gives better performance than CAT-5e for Gigabit Ethernet, but it's harder to wire and more expensive.)
- Use switches rated at the same speed as your router and network adapters.
- For Gigabit speed on the entire network, use all Gigabit switches, network adapters, and routers. However, if some devices run at slower speeds, a switch or router can likely still support the higher speeds for other devices on the network.

Figure 8-30 shows a possible inexpensive wiring job where two switches and a router are used to wire two rooms for five workstations and a network printer. The only inside-wall wiring required is two back-to-back RJ-45 wall jacks on either side of the wall between the two rooms. The plan allows for all five desktop computers and a network printer to be wired with cabling neatly attached to the baseboards of the office without being a trip hazard.

Figure 8-30   Plan of the physical configuration of a small office

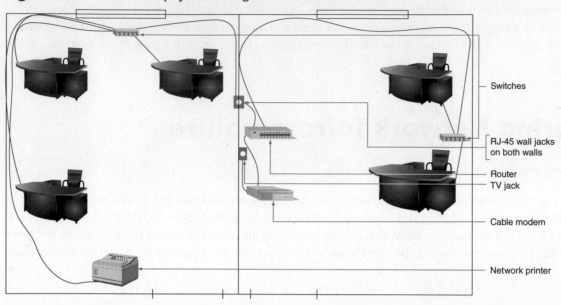

Switches

RJ-45 wall jacks
on both walls

Router
TV jack

Cable modem

Network printer

Now let's look at the tools you need to solve problems with network cabling, the details of how a network cable is wired, and how you can create your own network cables by installing RJ-45 connectors on twisted-pair cables.

Tools Used by Network Technicians

Core 1 Objective 2.8

Here's a list of tools a network technician might want in their toolbox:

- **Loopback plug.** A loopback plug can be used to test a network cable or port. To test a port, insert the loopback plug into the port. To test a cable, connect one end of the cable to a network port on a computer or other device, and connect the loopback plug to the other end of the cable (see Figure 8-31). If the LED lights on the network port light up, the cable and port are good. Another way to use a loopback plug is to find out which port on a switch in an electrical closet matches up with a wall jack. Plug the loopback plug into the wall jack. The connecting port on the switch in the closet lights up.

Figure 8-31   A loopback plug verifies that the cable and network port are good

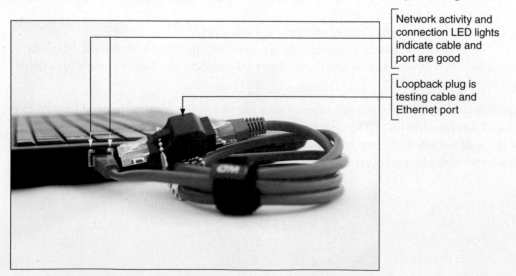

Network activity and
connection LED lights
indicate cable and
port are good

Loopback plug is
testing cable and
Ethernet port

- **Cable tester.** A **cable tester**, or cable certifier, is used to determine if a cable is good or to find out what type it is if the cable is not labeled. You can also use a cable tester to locate the ends of a network cable in a building. A cable tester has two components, the remote and the base (see Figure 8-32).

Figure 8-32   Use a cable tester pair to determine the type of cable and/or if the cable is good

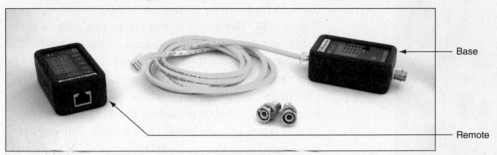

Base

Remote

To test a cable, connect each component to the ends of the cable, and turn on the tester. Lights on the tester will show you if the cable is good and what type of cable you have. You'll need to read the user manual that comes with the cable tester to know how to interpret the lights.

You can also use the cable tester to find the two ends of a network cable installed in a building. Suppose you see several network jacks on walls in a building, but you don't know which jacks connect back to the switch. Install a short cable in each of the two jacks or a jack and a port in a patch panel. A **patch panel** (see Figure 8-33) provides multiple network ports for cables that converge in one location such as an electrical closet or server room. Each port is numbered on the front of the panel. Use the cable tester base and remote to test the continuity between remote wall jacks and ports in the patch panel, as shown in Figure 8-34. Whereas a loopback plug works with live cables and ports, a cable tester works on cables that are not live. You might damage a cable tester if you connect it to a live circuit, so before you start connecting the cable tester to wall jacks, be sure that you turn off all devices on the network.

- **Wi-Fi analyzer.** A **Wi-Fi analyzer** is software that can find Wi-Fi networks, determine signal strengths, help optimize Wi-Fi signal settings, and help identify Wi-Fi security threats. For example, you can use

Figure 8-33   A patch panel provides Ethernet ports for cables converging in an electrical closet

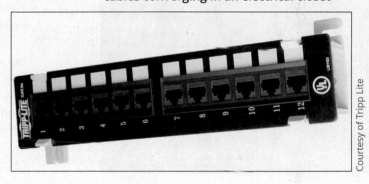

Courtesy of Tripp Lite

Figure 8-34   Use cable testers to find the two ends of a network cable in a building

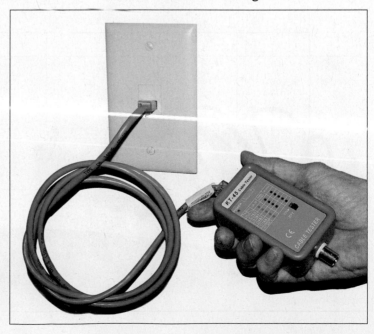

Figure 8-35   This Wi-Fi analyzer app detected three wireless networks

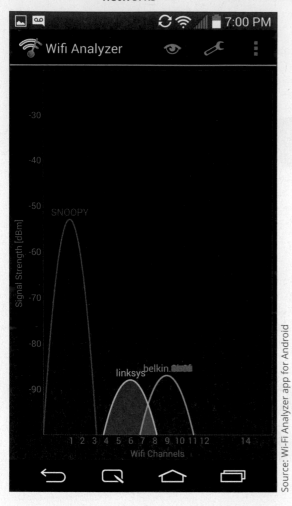

Source: Wi-Fi Analyzer app for Android

a Wi-Fi analyzer to find out which Wi-Fi channels are being used before you pick your channels. You can turn your smartphone into a Wi-Fi analyzer by installing a free or inexpensive app through your phone's app store (see Figure 8-35).

- **Toner probe.** A **tone generator and probe**, sometimes called a **toner probe**, is a two-part kit that is used to find cables in the walls of a building. See Figure 8-36. The toner connects to one end of the cable and puts out a continuous or pulsating tone on the cable. While the toner is putting out the tone, you use the probe to search the walls for the tone. The probe amplifies the audible tone, so you hear it as a continuous or pulsating beep. The beeps get louder when you are close to the cable and weaker when you move the probe away from the cable. With a little patience, you can trace the cable through the walls. Some toners can put out tones up to 10 miles on a cable and offer a variety of ways to connect to the cable, such as clips and RJ-45 and RJ-11 connectors.

- **Cable stripper.** A **cable stripper** is used to build your own network cable or repair a cable. Use the cable stripper to cut away the plastic jacket or coating around the wires inside a twisted-pair cable so you can install a connector on the end of the cable. How to use cable strippers is covered later in the module.

- **Crimper.** A **crimper** is used to attach a terminator or connector to the end of a cable. It applies force to pinch the connector to the wires in the cable to

Figure 8-36   A toner and probe kit by Fluke Corporation

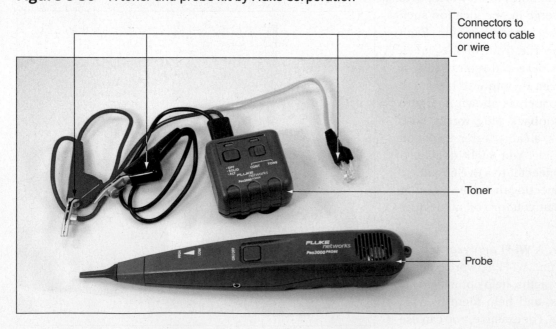

Connectors to connect to cable or wire

Toner

Probe

securely make a solid connection. Figure 8-37 shows a multifunctional crimper that can crimp an RJ-45 or RJ-11 connector. It also serves double duty as a wire cutter and wire stripper.

Figure 8-37   This crimper can crimp RJ-45 and RJ-11 connectors

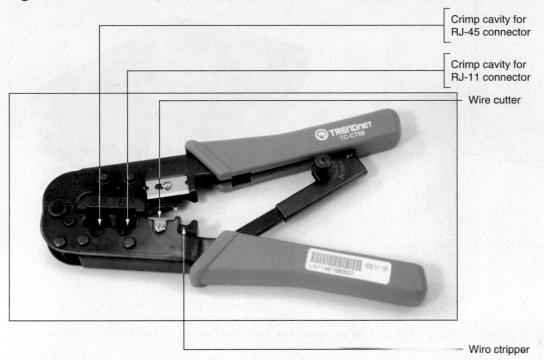

- Crimp cavity for RJ-45 connector
- Crimp cavity for RJ-11 connector
- Wire cutter
- Wire stripper

- **Punchdown tool.** A **punchdown tool** (see Figure 8-38) is used to punch individual wires in a network cable into their slots in a keystone RJ-45 jack, which is used in an RJ-45 wall jack. It can also be used to connect the cable to a patch panel or **punchdown block**, shown in Figure 8-39. In a project at the end of this module, you practice using a punchdown tool with a keystone jack.

Figure 8-38   A punchdown tool forces a wire into a slot and cuts off the extra wire

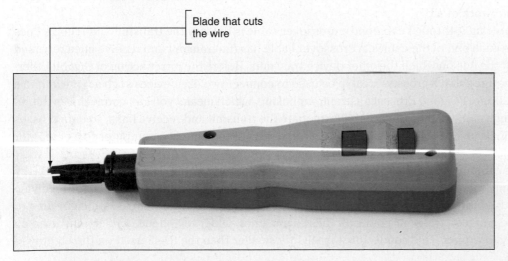

- Blade that cuts the wire

- **Network Tap.** A **network tap** is used to provide a connection point for monitoring devices such as an IDS or IPS system and allows the device to be "inline" with the communications on the network. The device can then copy or monitor the traffic without affecting the data flow. A network tap is shown in Figure 8-40.

Figure 8-39 A punchdown block allows for multiple cables to be connected to a circuit

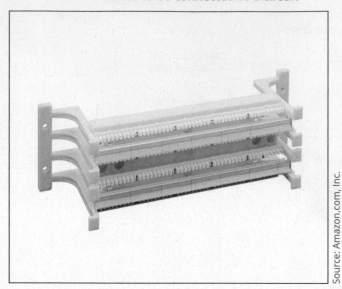

Source: Amazon.com, Inc.

Figure 8-40 A network tap is used to connect to a network inline with the traffic for monitoring

Source: Amazon.com, Inc.

Now that you know about the tools you need to wire networks, let's see how the cables and connectors are wired.

How Twisted-Pair Cables and Connectors Are Wired

 Core 1 Objectives 2.8, 3.1

Two types of network cables can be used when building a network: a straight-through cable and a crossover cable. A **straight-through cable** (also called a **patch cable**) is used to connect a computer to a switch or other network device. A **crossover cable** is used to connect two like devices such as a switch to a switch or a computer to a computer (to make the simplest network of all).

The difference between a straight-through cable and a crossover cable is the way the transmit and receive lines are wired in the connectors at each end of the cables. A crossover cable has the transmit and receive lines reversed so that one device receives off the line on which the other device transmits. Before the introduction of Gigabit Ethernet, 10BaseT and 100BaseT required that a crossover cable be used to connect two like devices such as a switch to a switch. Today's devices that support Gigabit Ethernet use auto-uplinking, which means you can connect a switch to a switch using a straight-through cable and the devices will negotiate the transmit and receive links, so data crosses the connection successfully. Crossover cables are seldom used today except to connect a computer to a computer to create a simple two-node network.

Twisted-pair copper wire cabling uses an RJ-45 connector that has eight pins, as shown in Figure 8-41. 10BaseT and 100BaseT Ethernet use only four of these pins: pins 1 and 2 for transmitting data and pins 3 and 6 for receiving data. The other pins can be used for phone lines or for power (using PoE). Gigabit Ethernet uses all eight pins to transmit and receive data and can also transmit power on these same lines. Older telephone connections used an RJ-11 connector that had only four pins. This connector was slightly smaller than the RJ-45 used on the eight wire Ethernet cables today.

Figure 8-41   Pinouts for an RJ-45 connector

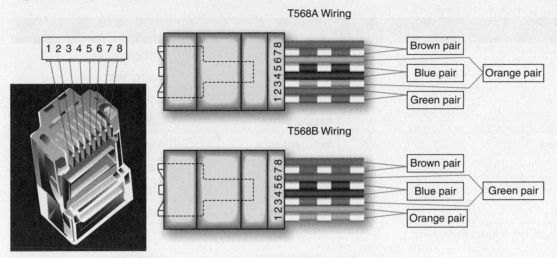

Twisted-pair cabling used with RJ-45 connectors is color-coded in four pairs: blue, orange, green, and brown, as shown in Figure 8-42. Each pair has one solid wire and one striped wire. Two standards have been established in the industry for wiring twisted-pair cabling and RJ-45 connectors: T568A and T568B. Both are diagrammed in Table 8-4. The **T568A** standard has the green pair connected to pins 1 and 2 and the orange pair connected to pins 3 and 6. The **T568B** standard has the orange pair using pins 1 and 2 and the green pair using pins 3 and 6, as shown in the diagram and the table. For both standards, the blue pair uses pins 4 and 5, and the brown pair uses pins 7 and 8.

Figure 8-42   Two crossed pairs in a crossover cable are compatible with 10BaseT or 100BaseT Ethernet; four crossed pairs in a crossover cable is compatible with gigabit Ethernet

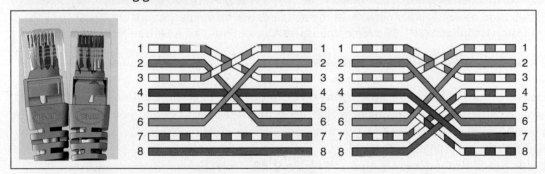

Table 8-4   The T568A and T568B Ethernet standards for wiring RJ-45 connectors

Pin	100BaseT Purpose	T568A Wiring	T568B Wiring
1	Transmit+	White/green	White/orange
2	Transmit-	Green	Orange
3	Receive+	White/orange	White/green
4	(Used only on Gigabit Ethernet)	Blue	Blue
5	(Used only on Gigabit Ethernet)	White/blue	White/blue
6	Receive-	Orange	Green
7	(Used only on Gigabit Ethernet)	White/brown	White/brown
8	(Used only on Gigabit Ethernet)	Brown	Brown

Note 4

The T568A and T568B standards, as well as other network wiring standards and recommendations are overseen by the Telecommunications Industry Association (TIA), Electronics Industries Alliance (EIA), and American National Standards Institute (ANSI).

If the wiring on one end of the cable matches the wiring on the other end, be it the T568A or T568B standard, you have a straight-through cable. If you're working on a 10BaseT or 100BaseT network and you use T568A wiring on one end of the cable and T568B on the other end, you have a crossover cable (see the diagram on the left side of Figure 8-42). For Gigabit Ethernet (1000BaseT) that transmits data on all four pairs, you must cross the green and orange pairs as well as the blue and brown pairs to make a crossover cable (see the diagram on the right side of Figure 8-42). Recall, however, that crossover cables are seldom used on Gigabit Ethernet. When you buy a crossover cable, it is most likely wired only for 10BaseT or 100BaseT networks. If you ever find yourself needing to make a crossover cable, be sure to cross all four pairs so the cable will work on 10BaseT, 100BaseT, and 1000BaseT networks. You can also buy an adapter to convert a straight-through cable to a crossover cable, but the adapter most likely will only cross two pairs and work only for 10BaseT or 100BaseT networks, such as the adapter shown in Figure 8-43.

Figure 8-43   A crossover adapter converts a patch cable to a crossover cable for a 10BaseT or 100BaseT network

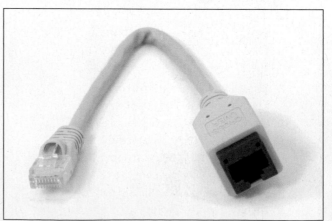

Although it's possible to mix standards on the same network, you should always <u>be consistent with which standard you use</u>. When you are wiring a network in a building that already has network wiring, be sure to find out if the wiring is using T568A or T568B, and then be sure you always use that standard. If you don't know which to use, use T568B because it's the most common.

Applying Concepts

Making a Straight-Through Cable Using T568B Wiring

Est. Time: 15 minutes
Core 1 Objective: 3.1

It takes a little practice to make a good network straight-through cable, but you'll get the hang of it after doing only a couple of cables. Figure 8-44 shows the materials and tools you'll need to make a network cable.

Figure 8-44   Tools and materials to make a network cable

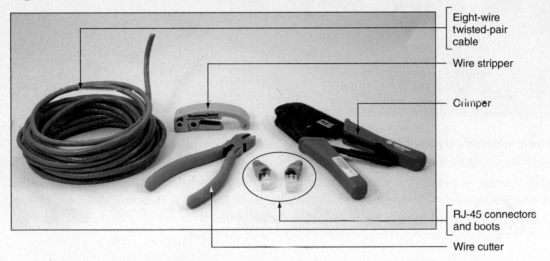

- Eight-wire twisted-pair cable
- Wire stripper
- Crimper
- RJ-45 connectors and boots
- Wire cutter

Here are the steps to make a straight-through cable using the T568B standard:

1. Use wire cutters to cut the twisted-pair cable the correct length plus a few extra inches.

2. If your RJ-45 connectors include boots, slide two boots onto the cable. Be sure they're each facing the correct direction.

3. Use wire strippers to strip off about two inches of the plastic jacket from the end of the wire. To do that, put the wire in the stripper and rotate the stripper around the wire to score the jacket (see Figure 8-45). You can then pull off the jacket.

Figure 8-45   Rotate a wire stripper around the jacket to score it so you can slide it off the wire

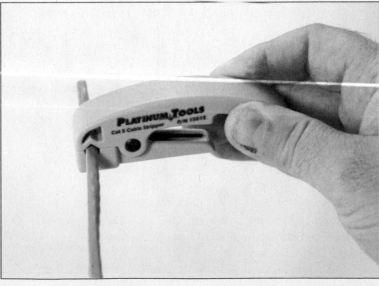

(continues)

Applying Concepts Continued

4. Use wire cutters to start a cut into the jacket, and then use the rip cord to pull the jacket back a couple of inches (see Figure 8-46). Next, cut off the rip cord and the jacket. You take the extra precaution of removing the jacket because you might have nicked the wires with the wire strippers.

Figure 8-46   Rip back the jacket, and then cut off the extra jacket and rip cord

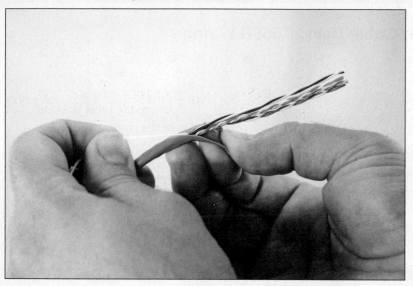

5. Untwist each pair of wires so you have eight separate wires. Smooth each wire to straighten out the kinks. Line up the wires in the T568B configuration (refer to Table 8-4).

6. Holding the tightly lined-up wires between your fingers, use wire cutters to cut the wires off evenly, leaving a little over an inch of wire. See Figure 8-47. To know how short to cut the wires, hold the RJ-45 connector up to the wires. The wires must go all the way to the front of the connector. The jacket must go far enough into the connector so that the crimp at the back of the connector will be able to solidly pinch the jacket.

Figure 8-47   Evenly cut off wires measured to fit in the RJ-45 connector with the jacket protruding into the connector

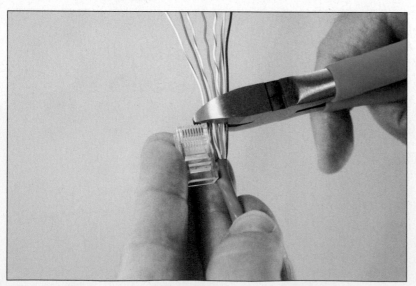

Note 5

You'll find several YouTube videos on network wiring. An excellent video by Ferrules Direct for making a straight-through cable is posted at *youtube.com/watch?v=WvP0D0jiyLg*.

7. Be sure you have pin 1 of the connector lined up with the orange-and-white wire. Then insert the eight wires in the RJ-45 connector. Guide the wires into the connector, making sure they reach all the way to the front. (It helps to push up a bit as you push the wires into the connector.) You can jam the jacket firmly into the connector. Look through the clear plastic connector to make sure the wires are lined up correctly, that they all reach the front, and that the jacket goes past the crimp.

8. Insert the connector into the crimper tool. Use one hand to push the connector firmly into the crimper as you use the other hand to crimp the connector. See Figure 8-48. Use plenty of force to crimp. The eight blades at the front of the connector must pierce through to each copper wire to complete each of the eight connections, and the crimp at the back of the connector must solidly crimp the cable jacket to secure the cable to the connector (see Figure 8-49). Remove the connector from the crimper, and make sure you can't pull the connector off the wire.

Figure 8-48   Use the crimper to crimp the connector to the cable

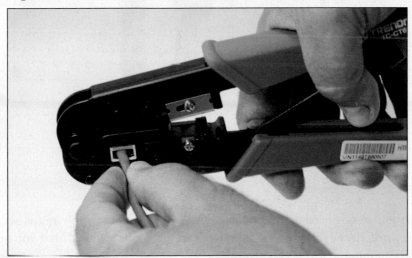

Figure 8-49   The crimper crimps the cable and cable jacket, and eight blades pierce the jacket of each individual copper wire

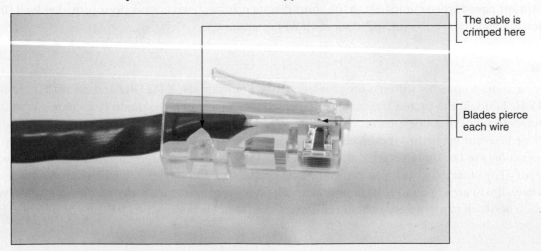

The cable is crimped here

Blades pierce each wire

(continues)

Applying Concepts Continued

9. Slide the boot into place over the connector. Now you're ready to terminate the other end of the cable. Configure it to also use the T568B wiring arrangement. Figure 8-50 shows the straight-through cable with only one boot in place.

10. Use a cable tester to make sure the cable is good.

Figure 8-50   A finished patch cable with one boot in place

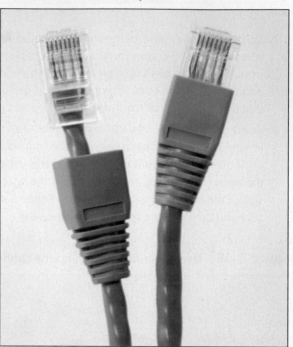

Note 6

According to networking standards for wiring a keystone RJ-45 jack and a straight-through cable, you can avoid crosstalk by removing the cable jacket to expose no more than three inches of twisted-pair wires, and you should untwist exposed twisted-pair wires no more than a half inch.

Wi-Fi Networking

Core 1 Objective 2.3

Wi-Fi, or wireless fidelity, networking uses radio frequencies to transmit and receive data between the wireless access point and the device connected to the network. Recall from the module "Networking Fundamentals" that you need the wireless network name, called the SSID, to join the wireless network.

As shown in Table 8-1 at the beginning of this module, each 802.11 standard can transmit on different frequencies: 2.4 GHz or 5 GHz (gigahertz). By using these radio frequencies, we can transmit data between devices easily because these frequencies are reserved for this special purpose. The 2.4 GHz frequency provides a longer transmit distance but has a slower speed when compared to the short distance, high-speed connections provided by 5 GHz. Refer to Table 8-1 for the maximum transmit speed for each Wi-Fi standard.

Wi-Fi Channels

A **channel** is a specific radio frequency within a broader frequency. For example, 2.412 GHz and 2.437 GHz are two channels in the 2.4 GHz band. In the United States, the FCC, which regulates Wi-Fi, has made 11 channels available for wireless communication in the 2.4 GHz band. To avoid channel overlap, however, devices in the 2.4 GHz band select channels 1, 6, or 11, resulting in three nonoverlapping channels available for use. The 5 GHz band offers up to 24 nonoverlapping channels in the United States, although some of those channels are restricted in certain areas, such as near an airport. For most networks, you can allow auto channel selection so the device scans for the least busy channel. However, if you are trying to solve a problem with interference from a nearby wireless network, you can manually set each network to a different channel and make the channels far apart to reduce interference. For example, in the 2.4 GHz band, set the network on one WAP to channel 1, and set a nearby WAP's network to channel 11. For one router, the Wi-Fi Settings page provides a dropdown menu to select a specific channel or to allow the router to automatically select the least busy channel (see Figure 8-51).

Figure 8-51   Wi-Fi channel selection can be set to auto or manually select a specific channel

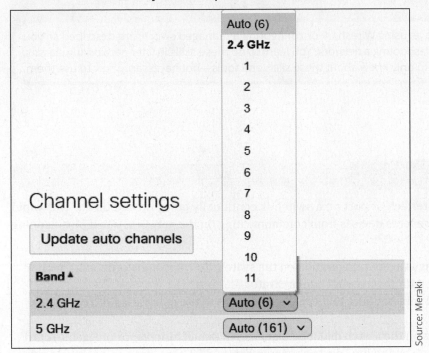

Source: Meraki

Troubleshooting Network Connections

Core 1 Objective 5.7

Troubleshooting networks is one of the primary tasks a help desk associate will be assigned in the course of their job. You may be asked to resolve issues caused by a simple loss of power or connectivity or those resulting from a broken network adapter or cable. Being able to quickly and thoroughly troubleshoot issues so employees and clients can continue their own work is important. In this section of the module, you learn to troubleshoot several network issues.

Limited or Slow Wired Connectivity

Core 1 Objective 5.7

Limited or slow wired connectivity to the network can be caused by many factors. When trying to resolve these types of network connectivity issues, check the following:

- Hardware configuration errors, such as speed or duplex settings on the network interface card.
- Switch port settings, which should be verified with network administrator.

- High usage by other network clients or users. Network monitoring software such as Wireshark (*wireshark. org*) or other software applications can be used to capture and analyze traffic.
- Configuration issues with a router or modem. Solving this type of issue may require calling your ISP for assistance.

Exam Tip ✔

Some skills mentioned in this section, such as using Wireshark or configuring a managed switch, are described so you have an idea of what to expect when troubleshooting a network. You learn to do these skills in later networking classes. For the A+ Core 1 exam, you are expected to only know about these skills and tools—not necessarily how to use them.

Port Flapping

  Core 1 Objective 5.7

Port flapping occurs when a particular interface or port on a switch is continually going up and down. This rapid switching between statuses, or flapping, prevents devices from communicating on the network. When port flapping occurs, check the following:

- The most likely cause of port flapping is a misconfiguration on the switch. To correct the problem, a technician should verify the configuration with the network administrator.
- Another cause of port flapping is bad cables. Check that cable connections to the port are solid. Try exchanging the cables.
- The SFP card that provides SFP ports on the switch might be bad. An SFP (small form-factor pluggable) card provides various SFP card ports, such as the four ports shown in Figure 8-52. One slot has a card already installed in it. Verify cable connections are solid, and try exchanging cables or exchanging the SFP card with a known good one.

Figure 8-52   A fiber-optic SFP port with an LC fiber cable attached

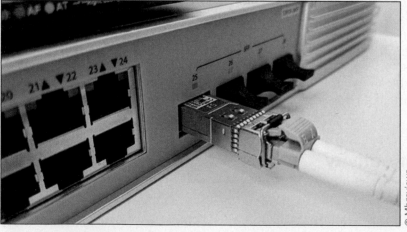

© Mbreviews

- Check for updates to the switch firmware. Sometimes outdated firmware can cause problems.

Network Jitter and High Latency

Core 1 Objective 5.7

Network jitter, or fluctuations in latency on your network, can cause network communication disruptions. Recall that latency is the measurement of time between when a packet is sent and when it is finally received by the end device. **High latency** situations can occur because of high network use or because of the technology your network uses for Internet connectivity. Satellite and wireless networks tend to have higher latency than a wired network. If the network is experiencing jitter, try the following:

- Check network cable connections at both the local workstation and at the wall jack and from the wall jack to the patch panel.
- Check for connectivity and activity lights on physical interfaces (the network ports on the computer, the switch, or the SOHO router). For wireless connectivity, check for signal strength on the connected network.
- Check connectivity between network infrastructure, such as connections between a switch and a router on the network. For a managed switch, verify with the network administrator how ports, including SFP interfaces, are configured.
- To check for connectivity, use the ping command. You can ping another computer on the network or on the Internet. For example, to check for connectivity on the Internet, ping a Google DNS server using its IP address:

```
ping 8.8.8.8
```

VoIP Call Quality

Core 1 Objective 5.7

VoIP (voice over IP) phones require high throughput in order to ensure high quality of service (QoS)—which, in turn, ensures that your phone calls are loud and clear, without echoing, delay, or static. Low QoS issues may be caused by the following:

- Other services being prioritized over the phone call
- Lack of bandwidth
- Misconfiguration of the phone system

To troubleshoot VoIP issues, check to make sure the VoIP phone system is correctly configured. You may want to isolate the phones to their own VLAN or subnet. You can also configure QoS settings on your network to prioritize the VoIP applications and devices over other applications and devices using the network. Recall that to implement QoS, priorities must be set on every device using the network, including the SOHO router and each network adapter and OS on the network.

Intermittent Wireless and External Interference

Core 1 Objective 5.7

Because wireless networks are susceptible to interference from a variety of sources—including neighboring wireless networks, other RF devices such as cordless phones or radios, microwaves, or walls—these types of issues can cause even experienced technicians to scratch their heads. The use of a wireless network analyzer—such as inSSIDer, shown in Figure 8-53—or an RF spectrum analyzer device, such as the one shown in Figure 8-54—can help identify the source of interference.

Figure 8-53 Wi-Fi analyzer software, such as inSSIDer, can be used to see details of nearby wireless networks

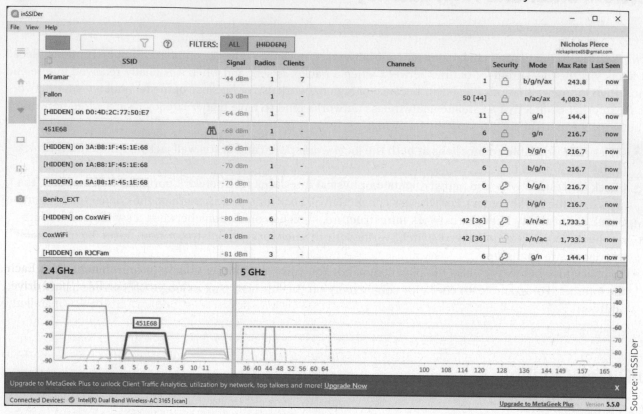

Source: inSSIDer

Figure 8-54 An RF spectrum analyzer can help
identify the source of interference

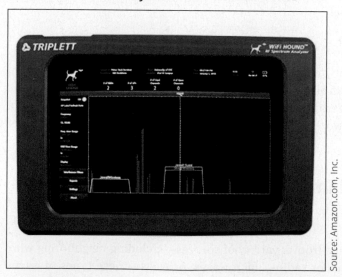

Source: Amazon.com, Inc.

Now that you have learned some basics of fixing problems with a network, let's look at how technology has evolved to allow for two or more systems to use the same physical hardware with virtualization.

Client-Side Virtualization

Core 1 Objectives 4.1, 4.2

Virtualization in computing is when one physical machine hosts multiple activities that are normally done on multiple machines. Desktop virtualization, also called **virtual desktop infrastructure (VDI)**, is when one computer provides multiple desktops for users. Each **virtual desktop**, or instance, is contained in its own virtual machine.

Note 7

When a user ends a session with a VDI virtual desktop, the user can request that changes they made to the virtual machine be saved until the next session. When changes are saved, the virtual desktop is said to be persistent and working in a persistent environment. If each time the user starts a new session, the virtual desktop resets to its default configuration and settings, the virtual desktop is said to be nonpersistent.

With desktop virtualization, software called a **hypervisor** creates and manages the virtual machines (VMs). Each VM that is managed by a hypervisor has its own virtual hardware (virtual motherboard, processor, RAM, hard drive, NIC, and so forth) and acts like a physical computer. After an OS is installed in a VM, applications can be installed.

Figure 8-55 shows a Windows 10 Professional desktop with two virtual machines running that were created by Oracle VirtualBox, which is hypervisor software. One VM is running Windows 10 and the other VM is running Ubuntu Desktop, which is a Linux OS. You'll learn about Linux in the Core 2 module "Linux and Scripting." In the Core 2 module "Installing Windows," you will complete an activity that involves installing Windows in a VM.

Figure 8-55   Two virtual machines running on a Windows 10 host, each with its own virtual hardware and OS (Windows 10 and Ubuntu Linux)

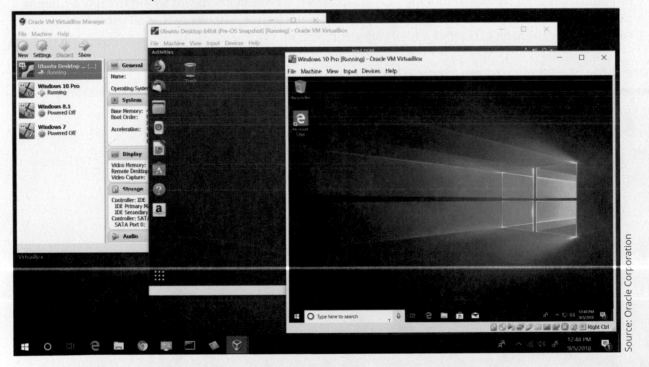

Source: Oracle Corporation

Virtualization can be used for many purposes, including the following:

- **Cross-platform virtualization.** With **cross-platform virtualization**, you install a different operating system in a VM than the one installed on your host machine supporting the VM. One reason to use cross-platform virtualization is when you install Linux in a VM on your Windows 10 laptop so that you can learn to use this OS.

- **Application virtualization.** You can run an application in a VM that is not meant for your normal operating system or platform, a practice referred to as **application virtualization**. For example, if you need to run an old application compiled for Windows 95, you can install Windows 95 in a VM on your Windows 10 desktop and run the **legacy software** in the Windows 95 VM. In another example, you can create a VM on your Windows 10 desktop, install Linux in the VM, and install Apache HTTP Server (a web server) in Linux.

- **Sandboxing.** A **sandbox** is an isolated environment where users and developers can learn and experiment safely without affecting the live environment. VMs are a popular sandboxing method for researching, experimenting, and testing. Researching computer security issues such as examining the latest malware within a virtual machine can help isolate the malware from the rest of your network and system. Software and app developers may use sandboxing in a VM for **test development** before publicly publishing it.

Setting Up Client-Side Virtualization

 Core 1 Objective 4.2

Desktop virtualization can be implemented in the cloud or on premises. On premises, an IT support technician might be called on to set up client-side virtualization on a workstation to host multiple VMs. The first step is to make sure the workstation can support the hypervisor and VMs.

Customize a Virtualization Workstation

Here are the requirements for a workstation that will host multiple virtual machines:

- **Maximum CPU cores.** Each VM has its own virtual processor, so it's important that the host's processor is a multicore processor. All dual-core or higher processors sold today support hardware-assisted virtualization (HAV), which is a technology that enhances the processor support for virtual machines. For Intel processors, this feature is called Intel VT. For AMD processors, the technology is called AMD-V.

- **The motherboard BIOS/UEFI.** Most of today's motherboards support HAV, and it must be enabled in the BIOS/UEFI setup. Figure 8-56 shows the UEFI setup screen for one motherboard where the HAV feature is called Intel Virtualization Technology. When you enable the feature, also verify that all subcategories are enabled under the main category for hardware virtualization.

Figure 8-56   A UEFI setup screen to enable hardware virtualization

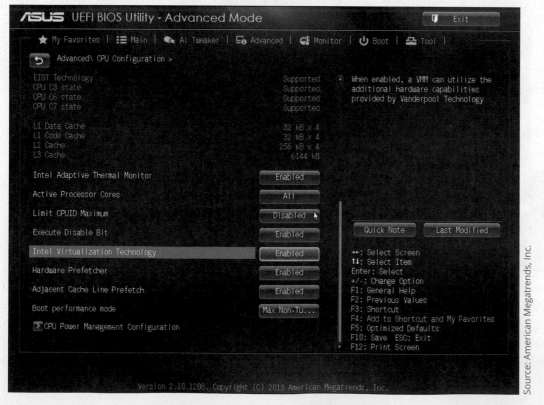

Source: American Megatrends, Inc.

- **Maximum RAM.** Some hypervisors are designed so that each VM that is running ties up all the RAM assigned to it. Therefore, you need large amounts of RAM when a computer is running several VMs.
- **Lots of storage space.** Each VM has its own virtual hard drive (VHD), which is a file stored on the physical hard drive that acts like an independent hard drive, complete with its own boot sector and file systems. You can configure this VHD to be a fixed size or dynamically expanding. The fixed size takes up hard drive space whether the VM uses the space or not. A dynamically allocated VHD increases in capacity as the VM uses the space. Each VM must have an operating system installed, which takes about 20 GB for a Windows 10 installation. In addition, each application installed in a VM requires storage space. Make sure you have adequate storage space for all the VMs the customer plans to create. See the requirements provided by the hypervisor manufacturer for additional recommendations.
- **Network requirements.** If multiple VMs on the workstation will be running at the same time, you'll need a fast network connection; make sure the NIC supports Gigabit Ethernet. Later, when you set up the workstation, it might require a static IP address so others on the network can reach the VMs. Also consider using two NICs in the workstation: The hypervisor can run all the VMs through one NIC that has the static IP address assignment, and the other NIC is used for other network activity on the host workstation. Some network administrators may also choose to set up the VMs in their own VLAN. When deciding how to use the overall budget for a virtualization workstation, prioritize the number of CPU cores and the amount of installed RAM.

Install and Configure a Hypervisor

A hypervisor offers a way to configure each VM, including which virtual hardware is installed. For example, when you launch **Oracle VirtualBox**, the VirtualBox Manager window shown on the left side of Figure 8-57 appears. To create a new VM, click **New** in the upper-left corner, and follow the directions on-screen. To change the configuration of a VM, select the VM in the left pane and click **Settings**. In the Settings dialog box, click **Storage**, as shown on the right side of Figure 8-57, to install and uninstall virtual hard drives and optical drives in the VM.

Figure 8-57   Emulated (virtual) hard drives and an optical drive are installed in a VM on VirtualBox

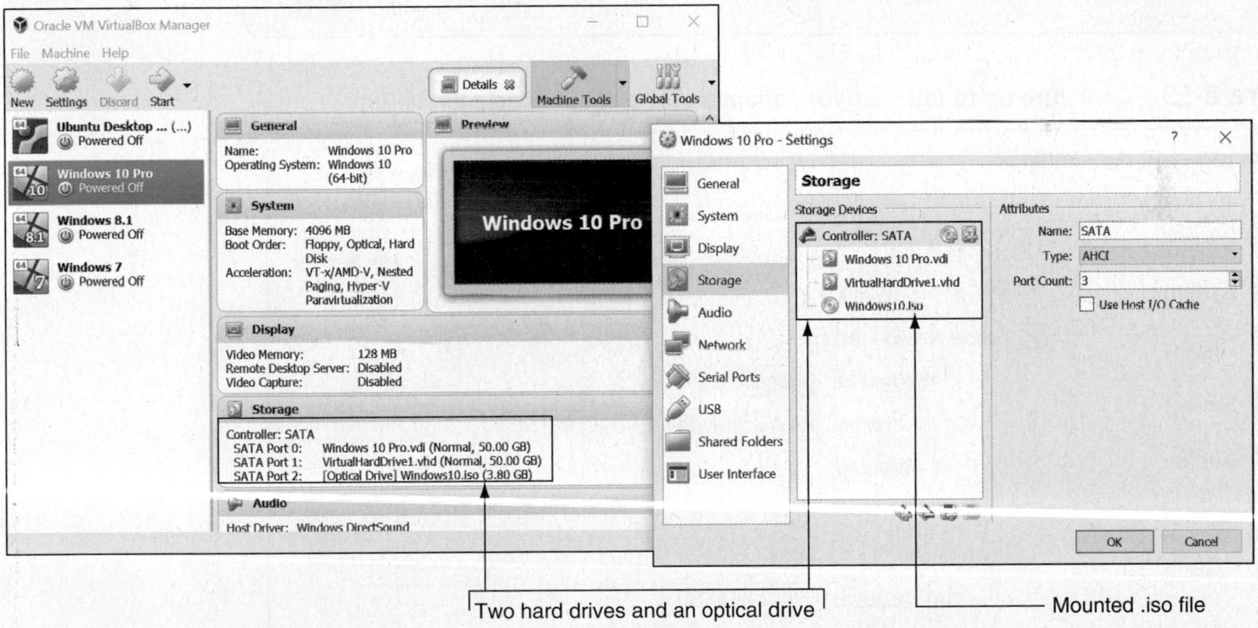

Two hard drives and an optical drive

Mounted .iso file

Source: Oracle Corporation

Notice in the Settings dialog box in Figure 8-57 that the VM, which does not yet have an OS installed, has two hard drives and an optical drive. The virtual hard drive named *Windows 10 Pro.vdi* is connected to SATA port 0 and will contain the Windows 10 installation. *VirtualHardDrive1.vhd*, a backup hard drive for this VM, is the same size (50 GB) and is connected through SATA port 1. The virtual optical drive is connected to SATA port 2 and holds the Windows 10 ISO file, ready for installation on the VM. An ISO file holds the image of a CD or DVD and can be used to provide Windows installation files. When you mount this file to the VM, you can install Windows in the VM from this virtual DVD; many hypervisor programs will perform this step for you during setup of a new VM.

In the Settings dialog box, click **System** to configure motherboard settings, such as boot order and memory (see Figure 8-58). Also consider network requirements for the VM. A VM can have one or more virtual network adapters, called a **virtual NIC**. Click **Network** (see Figure 8-59) to change adapter settings.

Figure 8-58 Configure motherboard settings in the VM to change the boot order

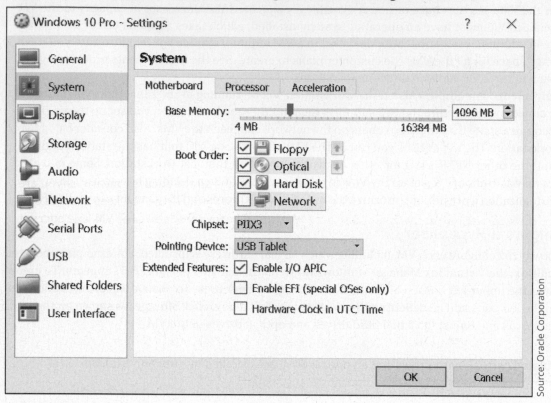

Source: Oracle Corporation

Figure 8-59 Configure up to four network adapters for a VM in Oracle VirtualBox

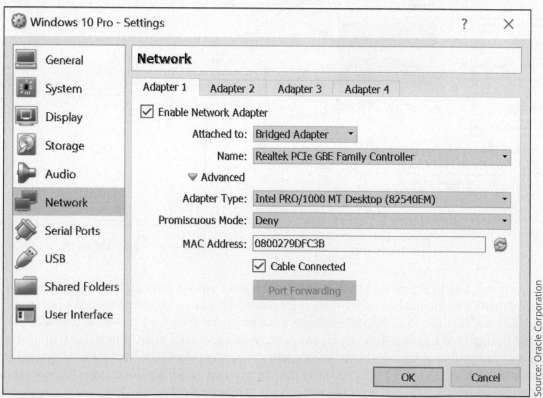

Source: Oracle Corporation

A VM can connect to a local network in the same way as other computers using the host computer's network interface, and it can share and use shared resources on the network. Alternatively, you can keep the VM isolated from the physical network while connected to other VMs on the host computer, or you can keep it completely isolated from all physical and virtual networks. In the Network pane of the Settings dialog box, you can control the number and type of installed network adapters—up to four adapters for this hypervisor, as shown in Figure 8-59.

To boot up a VM, select it in the left pane, and click **Start** in the menu. The VM boots up and works the same way as a physical computer.

Securing a Virtual Machine

> **Core 1 Objective** 4.2

Just like a physical machine, a virtual machine is susceptible to hackers and malware. When supporting a VM that holds sensitive data and has network and Internet connectivity or is in a public area, keep these points in mind for securing VM resources:

- **Secure the VM within the VM.** Using the OS installed in the VM, follow all the security measures you are learning throughout this text. For example, be sure to configure the OS firewall in the VM, keep updates current, install and run anti-malware software, require passwords for all user accounts in the VM, and encrypt data folders.
- **VMs should be isolated for best security.** One major advantage of using VMs on a workstation is that a VM on one workstation is better isolated from a VM on another because the workstations provide an extra layer of protection. Also, the host workstation for VMs should not be used for web surfing or other activities that might compromise its VMs. If a workstation has more than one NIC, a VM that should be kept especially secure can be isolated by dedicating a NIC solely to this VM and putting this NIC on its own subnet.
- **Secure the files that hold a VM.** You can move a VM from one computer to another by moving the files that contain the VM. Be sure these files that hold the VM are secured with permissions that allow access only to specific local or network users and apply file encryption to the files.
- **Secure the host computer.** Protect your VMs by applying security measures to protect the host computer that holds the VMs. For example, run anti-malware, keep Windows updated, require password authentication to sign in to the host computer, harden the host computer's firewall, and isolate it on the network in a protected subnet.

> **Exam Tip** ✔
>
> The A+ Core 1 exam might give you a scenario that requires you to secure a virtual machine installed on a host computer.

Just as virtualization can be set up on your own hardware, let's look how virtualization can be expanded across the Internet using a third party's hardware for your own computing needs. To the cloud we go!

Cloud Computing

> **Core 1 Objective** 4.1

In the module "Networking Fundamentals," you learn about server resources available on a network, and in this module, you learn some ways to virtualize network resources. Not all a network's resources reside on the local network. **Cloud computing** is when a vendor or corporation makes computing resources available over the Internet.

For example, Google Drive, iCloud Drive, Dropbox, and OneDrive are cloud file storage services that allow you to store your files in the cloud. These services work with synchronization apps on mobile devices and computers to sync data and settings under a user account—such as a Google, Apple, or Microsoft account—between the cloud and devices using the account. Cloud computing can also provide many other types of services and resources, including applications, network services, websites, database servers, specialized developer applications, and virtual desktops in VMs.

The current trend for both small and large businesses is to use cloud computing rather than local computing resources to expand current and future computing needs. As an IT technician, you need to understand how cloud computing works and how to support it.

Deployment Models for Cloud Computing

 Core 1 Objective 4.1

Cloud computing services are delivered by a variety of deployment models, depending on who manages the cloud and who has access to it. The main deployment models you are likely to encounter are as follows:

- **Public cloud.** In a **public cloud**, services are provided over the Internet to the general public. Google or Yahoo! email services are examples of public cloud deployment.
- **Private cloud.** In a **private cloud**, services are established on an organization's own servers or established virtually for a single organization's private use. For example, an insurance company might have a centralized data center that provides private cloud services to its branch offices throughout the United States.
- **Community cloud.** In a **community cloud**, services are shared among multiple organizations with a common interest, but the services are not available publicly. For example, a medical database might be shared among all hospitals in a geographic area, or government agencies might share regulatory requirements. In these cases, the community cloud could be hosted internally by one or more of the organizations involved or hosted externally by a third-party provider.
- **Hybrid cloud.** A **hybrid cloud** is a combination of public, private, and community clouds used by the same organization. For example, a company might store inventory databases in a private cloud but use a public cloud email service.

Characteristics of Cloud Computing

 Core 1 Objective 4.1

Regardless of the service provided, all cloud computing service models incorporate the following elements:

- **Elastic services and storage. Rapid elasticity** refers to the service's ability to be scaled up or down as the need level changes for a particular customer without requiring hardware changes that could be costly for the customer. Layers of services—such as applications, storage space, or number of users—can be added or removed when requested. Services can also be adjusted automatically, depending on the options made available by the service vendor.
- **Metered utilization.** Resources offered by a cloud computing vendor—such as storage, applications, bandwidth, and other services—are measured, or **metered**, for billing purposes and/or for the purpose of limiting any customer's use of that resource according to the service agreement.
- **Shared resources.** By enabling multiple customers to share the use and cost of cloud resources, a cloud service provider assists in reducing the cost of ownership for themselves and their customers.
- **High availability.** Cloud resources are considered highly available because they can be configured and turned on at a moment's notice. These services can be replicated, or copied, to data centers around the globe to ensure they are available even if one data center suffers an outage.
- **File synchronization.** Just as the services within the cloud are highly available, data files can be synchronized across the network to ensure all systems and users are working with the same versions of the same files.

Cloud Computing Service Models

Core 1 Objectives 2.2, 4.1

Cloud computing service models are categorized by the types of services they provide. The National Institute of Standards and Technology (NIST) has developed a standard definition for each category, which varies by the division of labor implemented. For example, as shown on the left side of Figure 8-60, an organization is traditionally responsible for its entire network, top to bottom. In this arrangement, the organization has its own network infrastructure devices, manages its own network services and data storage, and purchases licenses for its own operating systems and applications. The three cloud computing service models illustrated on the right side of Figure 8-60 incrementally increase the amount of management responsibilities outsourced to cloud computing vendors.

Figure 8-60   At each progressive level, the vendor takes over more computing responsibility for the customer

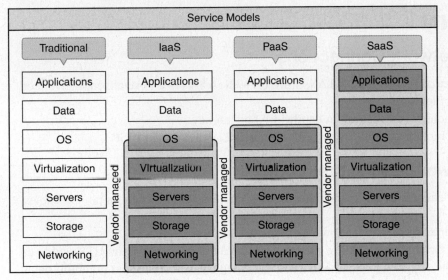

The following list describes these service models:

- **IaaS.** With **IaaS (Infrastructure as a Service)**, the customer rents hardware—including servers, storage, and networking—and can use these hardware services virtually. Customers are responsible for their own application installations, data management, and backup. In most situations, customers are also responsible for their own operating systems. For example, customers might rent several VMs and use them for servers by installing an OS in each VM and hosting applications such as web servers, email servers, DNS servers, or DHCP services, or by hosting productivity software such as Microsoft Office for employees. IaaS is ideal for fast-changing applications, to test software, or for startup businesses looking to save money by not having to invest in hardware. Examples of IaaS providers are Amazon Web Services (*aws.amazon.com*), Windows Azure (*azure.microsoft.com*), and Google Compute Engine (*cloud.google.com*).
- **PaaS.** With **PaaS (Platform as a Service)**, a customer rents hardware, operating systems, and some applications that might support other applications the customer may install. PaaS is popular with software developers who require access to multiple platforms during the development process. A developer can build and test an application on a PaaS virtual machine made available over the web, and then throw out the machine and start over with a new one with a few clicks in their browser window. Applications that a PaaS vendor might provide to a developer are tailored to the specific needs of the project, such as an application to manage a database of test data. Examples of PaaS services include Google Cloud Platform and Microsoft Azure.
- **SaaS.** With **SaaS (Software as a Service)**, customers use applications hosted on the service provider's hardware and operating systems, and typically access the applications through a web browser. Applications are provided through an online user interface and are compatible with a multitude of devices and operating systems. Online email services, such as Gmail and Yahoo!, are good examples of SaaS. Google offers an entire suite

of virtual software applications through Google Cloud and its other embedded products. Except for the interface itself (the device and whatever browser software is required to access the website), the vendor provides every level of support from network infrastructure through data storage and application implementation.

- **XaaS.** In the **XaaS (Anything as a Service** or **Everything as a Service)** model, the "X" represents an unknown, just as it does in algebra. Here, the cloud can provide any combination of functions, depending on a customer's exact needs. The XaaS model is not shown in Figure 8-60.

As you have seen in this module, networks can be small and housed within a single building or extend around the globe, like the Internet. You can use various types of hardware and cables to set up, manage, and expand your network to meet your changing requirements. Expanding your software systems using virtualization and the cloud can also help you meet those changing needs.

Module Summary

Types of Networks and Network Connections

- Networks are categorized by size as a PAN, LAN, WLAN, MAN, or WAN. A SAN is a specialized, high-speed network for storing and sharing files.
- Performance of a network technology is measured in bandwidth and latency.
- Ways to connect to the Internet include satellite, fiber optic, cable, DSL, cellular, and WISP.

Identifying Network Hardware and Infrastructure

- Networking hardware used on local networks can include switches, routers, wireless access points, cables, and connectors.
- Switches can be unmanaged or managed, which allows for configuration.
- Most wired local networks use twisted-pair cabling that can be unshielded twisted-pair (UTP) cable or shielded twisted-pair (STP) cable. Twisted-pair cable is rated by category, with the most common being CAT-5, CAT-5e, CAT-6, and CAT-6A.
- Fiber-optic cables can use one of the following connectors: ST, LC, or SC. Connectors should be selected to match the equipment being connected.
- Power over Ethernet (PoE) sends power over Ethernet cables for supported devices.
- IoT devices increase quality of life and convenience by connecting home and appliances to the Internet.
- SDN, SCADA systems, UTM technologies, and load balancers all can be integrated into a network to expand its functionality, increase security monitoring, and optimize the availability of the network.

Configuring Network Infrastructure

- Tools used to manage and troubleshoot network wiring and connectors include a loopback plug, cable tester, Wi-Fi analyzer, toner probe, cable stripper, crimper, punchdown tool, and network tap.
- The RJ-45 connector has eight pins. Four pins (pins 1, 2, 3, and 6) are used to transmit and receive data using the 10BaseT and 100BaseT speeds. Using 1000BaseT speed, all eight pins are used for transmitting and receiving data.
- Two standards used to wire network cables are T568A and T568B. The difference between the two standards is that the orange twisted-pair wires are reversed in the RJ-45 connector from the green twisted-pair wires.
- Either T568A or T568B can be used to wire a network. To avoid confusion, don't mix the two standards in a building.
- Use wire strippers, wire cutters, and a crimper to make network cables. A punchdown tool is used to terminate cables in a patch panel or keystone RJ-45 jack. Be sure to use a cable tester to test or certify a cable you have just made.
- Wi-Fi, or wireless fidelity, networking uses radio frequencies to transmit and receive data between the wireless access point and the device connected to the network.

Troubleshooting Network Connections

- Common issues of networks include limited or slow connectivity, port flapping, jitter or latency issues, quality of service issues for VoIP connections, and interference issues for wireless networks.
- Troubleshooting steps should include checking hardware and software configurations, allocation of bandwidth for high QoS services such as VoIP, and monitoring for interference from other networks or devices that are nearby.

Client-Side Virtualization

- Client-side virtualization is done by creating multiple virtual machines, each with its own virtual desktop, on a physical machine using a hypervisor.
- Virtualization can be used to allow for cross-platform virtualization, for application virtualization for support, or even to set up a sandbox environment to experiment with different operating systems or develop software.
- Considerations for virtualized systems include ensuring enough physical hardware resources are allocated for each virtual machine and ensuring the environment is maintained securely.

Cloud Computing

- Cloud computing is providing computing resources over the Internet to customers.
- A public cloud service is available to the public, and a private cloud service is kept on an organization's own servers or made available by a vendor only for a single organization's private use. A community cloud is shared between multiple organizations, and a hybrid cloud is any combination of these deployment models.
- All cloud computing service models incorporate rapid elasticity, metered utilization, resource sharing, high availability, and file synchronization.
- Cloud computing service models—including IaaS, PaaS, SaaS, and XaaS—are categorized by the types of services they provide and the degree that a third-party service or vendor is responsible for the resources.

Key Terms

For explanations of key terms, see the Glossary for this text.

802.11a	CAT-6a	hybrid cloud	managed switch
802.11ac (Wi-Fi 5)	channel	hypervisor	meter
802.11ax (Wi-Fi 6)	cloud computing	IaaS (Infrastructure as	mobile hotspot
802.11b	coaxial (coax) cable	a Service)	network jitter
802.11g	community cloud	Internet of Things (IoT)	network tap
802.11n (Wi-Fi 4)	crimper	intrusion detection	optical network terminal
application	crossover cable	system (IDS)	(ONT)
virtualization	cross-platform	intrusion protect	PaaS (Platform as
bandwidth	virtualization	system (IPS)	a Service)
beamforming	direct burial	LAN (local area	PAN (personal area
BNC	DSL (digital subscriber	network)	network)
bridge	line)	LC (Lucent connector)	patch cable
broadband	DSL modem	legacy software	patch panel
cable Internet	Fast Ethernet	licensed frequency	plenum
cable stripper	fiber optic	load balancer	PoE injector
cable tester	fiber-optic cable	long-range fixed wireless	PoE-rated switch
CAT-5	F-Type	(LRFW)	port flapping
CAT-5e	Gigabit Ethernet	MAN (metropolitan area	power over Ethernet
CAT-6	high latency	network)	(PoE)

8

power over Ethernet plus (PoE+)

private cloud

public cloud

punchdown block

punchdown tool

PVC (polyvinyl chloride)

rapid elasticity

repeater

SaaS (Software as a Service)

SAN (storage area network)

sandbox

satellite

SC (subscriber connector)

shielded twisted-pair (STP) cable

SIM (subscriber identity module) card

software-defined networking (SDN)

ST (straight tip) connector

straight-through cable

supervisory control and data acquisition (SCADA)

T568A

T568B

test development

tone generator and probe

toner probe

twisted-pair cabling

unified threat management (UTM)

unlicensed frequency

unmanaged switch

unshielded twisted-pair (UTP) cable

virtual desktop

virtual desktop infrastructure (VDI)

virtual LAN (VLAN)

virtual NIC

virtual private network (VPN)

WAN (wide area network)

Wi-Fi analyzer

wireless Internet service provider (WISP)

WLAN (wireless local area network)

XaaS (Anything/ Everything as a Service)

Thinking Critically

These questions are designed to prepare you for the critical thinking required for the A+ exams and may use information from other modules and the web.

1. Your customer, Miranda, recently installed a new router in her dance studio, as shown in the diagram in Figure 8-61. She then ran Ethernet cables through the drop ceiling to computers in various offices. Without any further testing, which computers do you suspect are experiencing connection problems? (Choose all that apply.)

   a. Computer A

   b. Computer B

   c. Computer C

   d. None of the answers are correct

Figure 8-61 A diagram of a dance studio

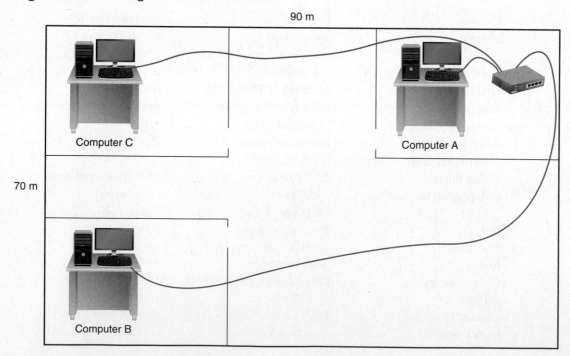

2. Which of the following tools can be used to determine if a network cable is good? (Choose all that apply.)

   a. Cable tester
   b. Crimper
   c. Loopback plug
   d. Patch panel

3. You've been hired to help with installing cable at a new office building for the local college. You're wiring a connection into the first room on your list. List the colors of the wires in the order you should place them into the connector, starting with pin 1.

4. You're setting up some VMs to test an application you're considering making available to employees of the small company you work for. You need to test the app in a variety of OSs, and you don't expect to need these VMs after testing is complete. You'd like setup to be as simple and straightforward as possible without needing to make any changes to the servers on your network. Which of these hypervisors will best serve your needs?

   a. XenServer
   b. Client Hyper-V
   c. Hyper-V
   d. ESXi

5. You have three VMs running on a Windows 10 computer. Two of the VMs—machines A and B—can communicate with the Internet and other network resources, as is the host Windows 10 machine. However, one VM, machine C, cannot access websites on the Internet. What is the first component you check? The second component?

   a. The host machine's network adapter
   b. The switch connected to the host machine
   c. VM C's virtual NIC
   d. The host machine's hypervisor settings

6. You're installing VirtualBox on a Windows 10 Home computer, and you get the following error message:

   ```
   VT-x is disabled in the BIOS for all CPU modes
   ```

   a. What is the problem?
   b. How do you fix it?

7. Which component in a thin client might need a higher rating than other components?

   a. The CPU, because most of the processing is done on the thin client
   b. RAM, because the system must have enough to hold a virtual desktop
   c. The hard drive, because a VM takes up a large amount of hard drive space
   d. The NIC, because most of the processing is done on the server

8. Your manager has instructed you to set up a virtualization workstation that will provide help desk users with access to Windows 10 Pro and Home, Ubuntu Desktop, Linux Mint, and Android Oreo and Pie. They also want you to use Client Hyper-V as the hypervisor. In what order should you install the operating systems and hypervisor?

   a. Ubuntu Desktop, Client Hyper-V, remaining OSs in VMs
   b. Client Hyper-V, Windows 10 Pro, remaining OSs in VMs
   c. Client Hyper-V, OSs in VMs
   d. Windows 10 Pro, Client Hyper-V, remaining OSs in VMs

9. You work for a small startup company that just hired five new employees, doubling its number of team members. In preparation for the new employees' first day in the office, you add five new user accounts to your CRM (customer relationship management) software subscription, a service that is hosted in the cloud. What aspect of cloud computing has worked to your advantage?

   a. High availability
   b. Rapid elasticity
   c. Metered service
   d. Resource pooling

10. Doctors at a regional hospital access an online database of patient records that is being developed and tested by a conglomerate of health insurance agencies. The database contains records of hundreds of thousands of patients and is regulated by HIPAA restrictions on protected health information (PHI). What kind of cloud deployment is this database?

11. Office 365 is an example of what type of cloud computing service model?

    a. IaaS
    b. Application streaming
    c. PaaS
    d. SaaS

12. Which of the following resources are shared between the host computer and a VM? (Choose all that apply.)

    a. NIC
    b. Operating system
    c. Hard drive
    d. Applications

13. A friend of yours is having trouble getting good Internet service. They say their house is too remote for cable TV, and they don't even have a telephone line to their house. They have been very frustrated with satellite service because storms and even cloudy skies can disrupt the signal. They use Verizon for their cell phone, which gets good signal at the house. What Internet service would you recommend they look into getting for their home network?

    a. Dial-up
    b. LTE installed Internet
    c. DSL
    d. Cable Internet

14. You recently installed a SOHO router in a customer's home, and the owner has called to say their child is complaining that Internet gaming is too slow on their wireless laptop. Which possibilities should you consider to speed up the gaming experience? (Choose all that apply.)

    a. Verify that the wireless connection is using the fastest wireless standard the router supports.
    b. Disable encryption on the wireless network to speed up transmissions.
    c. Suggest they use a wired Gigabit Ethernet connection to the network for gaming.
    d. Enable IPv6 for the laptop.

15. Which of the following tools can be used to monitor network traffic by a monitoring system such as an IDS or IPS?

    a. Crimper
    b. Tone generator and probe
    c. Cable tester
    d. Network tap

16. A power-over-Ethernet (PoE) switch provides power to end devices. What is the maximum voltage provided by a PoE+ switch port to the device?

    a. 25.5 watts
    b. 17 watts
    c. 34 watts
    d. 15.4 watts

17. Cable and fiber-optic modems are increasing in popularity with ISPs across the United States. While these are great for stationary connections to the Internet, travelers need another option for connectivity. Which of the following can provide a cost-effective solution for connectivity?

    a. Satellite
    b. Long-range fixed wireless
    c. Cellular WAN
    d. DSL

18. Alicía is having trouble browsing the Internet on the wireless network from the employee lunchroom on her lunch break. You check her connection, and it appears that the connection works for a few minutes but then disconnects. The NIC settings show the correct IP address and Wi-Fi settings, but you continue to see the up/down on the connection. Which of the following could best explain why Alicía is having problems?

    a. The wireless NIC is broken.

    b. The WAP is configured wrong.

    c. The microwave in the lunchroom is causing interference.

    d. The computer OS needs upgrades.

Hands-On Projects

Hands-On Project 8-1

Researching a Network Upgrade

Est. Time: 30 minutes
Core 1 Objectives: 2.2, 2.3, 2.7, 3.1

An IT support technician is often called on to research equipment to maintain or improve a computer or network and make recommendations for purchase. Suppose you are asked to upgrade a small network that consists of one switch and four computers from 100BaseT to Gigabit Ethernet. The switch connects to a router that already supports Gigabit Ethernet. Do the following to price the hardware needed for this upgrade:

1. Find three switches by different manufacturers that support Gigabit Ethernet and have at least five ports. Save or print the webpages describing each switch.

2. Compare the features and prices of the three switches. What additional information might you want to know before you make your recommendation for a small business network?

3. Find three network adapters by different manufacturers to install in the desktop computers to support Gigabit Ethernet. Save or print webpages for each NIC.

4. Compare features of the three network adapters. What additional information do you need to know before you make your recommendation?

5. Make your recommendations based on the moderate (middle-of-the-road) choices. What is the total price of the upgrade, including one switch and four network adapters?

6. What is one more question you need to have answered about other equipment before you can complete the price of the upgrade? Explain how you would find the answer to your question.

Hands-On Project 8-2

Wiring a Keystone Jack

Est. Time: 15 minutes
Core 1 Objectives: 2.8, 3.1

A keystone RJ-45 jack is used in a network wall jack. To practice wiring a keystone jack, you'll need a wire stripper, wire cutter, twisted-pair cabling, keystone jack, and punchdown tool. Here are the instructions to wire a keystone jack:

1. Using a wire stripper and wire cutter, strip and trim back the jacket from the twisted-pair wire, leaving about two inches of wire exposed. Untwist the wires only so far as necessary so each wire can be inserted in the color-coded slot in the jack. The untwisted wire should be no longer than a half inch. Why are twists so important when wiring connectors and jacks?

(continues)

Hands-On Project Continued

2. Insert each wire into the appropriate slots for either the T568A or the T568B standard, depending on the network where you might use this keystone jack. Figure 8-62 shows the wires in position for T568B wiring. Notice how the cable jacket goes into the keystone jack. Which wiring standard did you use? How did you choose that standard?

Figure 8-62   Eight wires are in position in a keystone jack for T568B wiring

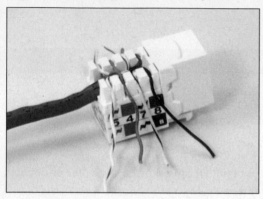
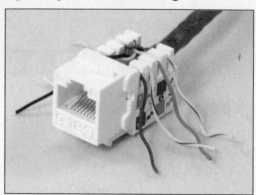

3. Using the punchdown tool, make sure the blade side of the tool is on the outside of the jack. (The punchdown tool has "Cut" embedded on the blade side of the tool.) Push down with force to punch each wire into its slot and cut off the wire on the outside edge of the slot. It might take a couple of punches to do the job. See the left side of Figure 8-63. Place the jack cover over the jack, as shown on the right side of Figure 8-63.

Figure 8-63   Use a punchdown tool to punch the wires into the keystone jack, and then place the cover in position

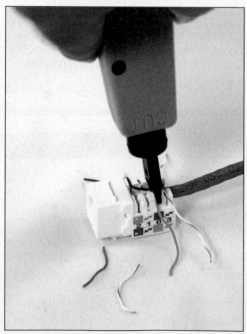

4. The jack can now be inserted into the back side of a wall faceplate (see Figure 8-64). Make sure the wires in the jack are at the top of the jack. If you look closely at the faceplate, you can see the arrow pointing up. It's important that the wires in the jack be at the top so dust doesn't settle on these wires over time. Use screws to secure the faceplate to the wall receptacle. Be sure to use a cable tester to check the network cable from its jack to the other end to make sure the wiring is good. When wiring a building, testing the cable and its two connections is called certifying the cable. Use a loopback plug or cable tester with cable to verify your jack works. Is it certified?

Figure 8-64   Insert the jack in the faceplate, making sure the wire connectors are at the top of the jack

Note 8

To see a video by DIY Telecom of using a punchdown tool to make an RJ-45 keystone jack, see *youtube.com/watch?v=Xkbz-uywLJs*.

Hands-On Project 8-3

Making Network Cables

Est. Time: 15 minutes
Core 1 Objectives: 2.8, 3.1

Using the tools and skills you learned about in this module, practice making a straight-through cable and a crossover cable. Use a cable tester to test both cables.

Answer the following questions:

1. Which wiring standard did you use for the straight-through cable? List the pinouts (pin number and wire color) for each of the eight pins on each connector.

2. Will your crossover cable work on a Gigabit Ethernet network? List the pinouts (pin number and wire color) for each of the eight pins on each connector.

Hands-On Project 8-4

Using Google Cloud

Est. Time: 45 minutes
Core 1 Objective: 4.1

Google Cloud Platform is an example of a PaaS. To use the service, do the following:

1. Go to *cloud.google.com* and click **Get Started for Free**. You will need to sign in using a Google account. If you don't have an account, you can create one with any valid email address. When you first set up an account, you must enter payment information, which Google promises not to use during your free trial period. Create an individual account type, enter your information, and click **START MY FREE TRIAL**.

2. You begin on the Getting started page for your first project, aptly named "My First Project." Click **COMPUTER ENGINE**, and, if necessary, click the **ENABLE button**. When the system is ready, click **CREATE INSTANCE** in the VM instances box to create a VM. Use the default settings, except the following:
    a. Change the name of the VM to dcserver.
    b. Change the Boot disk to **Windows Server 2019 Datacenter**.

3. Click **Select**, and then click **Create**. Wait for Google to create the instance.

Note 9

The Microsoft Windows OS selections are not part of the free tier of the Google Cloud Platform. If you want to complete this activity without incurring any associated cost, choose one of the Linux distributions, such as Ubuntu, from the list instead of a Windows OS. All other instructions will still apply. Additional information on costs associated with the Google Cloud Platform can be found at *https://cloud.google.com/free/docs/gcp-free-tier/#compute*.

4. In the VM instances list, click the **dcserver** instance, which takes you to the VM instance details page. Click **Set Windows password**, and assign a user name to your VM instance. Note the user name, and click **SET**. Google Cloud assigns a password, which displays on-screen. Copy the password, save it somewhere safe, and then click **CLOSE**.

5. Note the External IP assigned to the VM instance under the Network Interfaces section, shown near the center of Figure 8-65.

Figure 8-65 Google Cloud Platform serves up a VM that has Windows Server 2019 installed

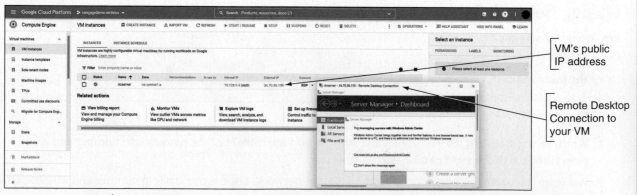

VM's public IP address

Remote Desktop Connection to your VM

6. On your computer, you can use Remote Desktop with screen and file sharing to access your VM. Follow these steps:

   a. Enter the `mstsc` command in the Windows 10 search box. In the Remote Desktop Connection dialog box, enter the External IP address of your VM, which is its public IP address available on the Internet. Click **Connect**.

   b. In the *Enter your credentials* box, your Windows user name appears. If your VM's user name is not the same as your Windows user name, click **More choices** and then click **Use a different account**. You can then enter the VM's user name and password. Click **OK** to connect.

   The bottom window in Figure 8-65 shows the VM in a Remote Desktop Connection window. This Windows Server setup screen is the first screen that appears immediately after the first restart when you've installed Windows Server 2019. Take a few minutes to explore your Windows Server VM.

7. To avoid accumulating any charges against your free quota, shut down the server VM in the Remote Desktop Connection window. You learn more about Remote Desktop in the module "Network Security and Troubleshooting."

> **Note 10**
>
> You will use the Google Cloud Platform service for other projects in the modules "Securing and Sharing Windows Resources" and "Linux and Scripting." Do not disable your Google Cloud Platform account until after you have completed these projects.

Real Problems, Real Solutions

Real Problem 8-1

Preparing a Quote for Network Solutions

Est. Time: 30 minutes
Core 1 Objectives: 2.2, 2.3, 3.1

As a computer and networking consultant to small businesses, you are frequently asked to find solutions to increasing demands for network and Internet access at a business. One business rents offices in a historical building that has strict rules for wiring. They have come to you asking for a solution for providing Wi-Fi access to their guests in the lobby of the building. Research options for a solution and answer the following questions:

1. Print or save webpages showing two options for a Wi-Fi wireless access point (WAP) that can mount on the wall or ceiling. For one option, select a device that can receive its power by PoE from the network cable run to the device. For the other option, select a device that requires an electrical cable as well as a network cable to the device.

2. Print or save two webpages for a splitter that can be mounted near the second wireless access point and that splits the power from data on the network cable. Make sure the power connectors for the splitter and the access point can work together.

(continues)

Real Problem Continued

3. To provide PoE on the network cable from the electrical closet to the wireless access point, you can use an injector that injects power into a network cable. Print or save the webpage for such an injector, making sure the voltage and wattage output for the injector are compatible with the needs of both wireless access points.

4. The distance for network cabling from the switch to the wireless access point is about 200 feet (61 meters). What is the cost of 200 feet of PVC CAT-6a cabling? For 200 feet of plenum CAT-6a cabling?

5. Of the options you researched, which do you recommend? Using this option, what is the total cost of the Wi-Fi hotspot?

Real Problem 8-2

Exploring Packet Tracer

Est. Time: 45 minutes
Core 1 Objective: 2.8

In the module "Networking Fundamentals," you installed Packet Tracer and created a very basic network. In this project, you work through three modules of the Packet Tracer Introduction course to take a brief tour of the simulator interface and create a more complex network in Packet Tracer. Notice in the Packet Tracer course that the activities refer to the OSI model instead of the TCP/IP model. Review the section titled "The OSI Model for Network Communication" in the module "Networking Fundamentals" for a brief refresher. Then complete the following steps to access your course:

1. Return to the Networking Academy website (*netacad.com*), sign in, and click **Launch Course**. You've already downloaded Packet Tracer, so you can skip chapter 1.

2. Complete chapters 2, 3, and 4, including the videos and labs, and complete the Packet Tracer Basics Quiz at the end of chapter 4. The other remaining chapters provide excellent information on Packet Tracer but are not required for this project. Answer the following questions along the way:
   a. What is a simple PDU in Packet Tracer?
   b. What is a .pka file?
   c. Which Packet Tracer feature do you think will be most helpful for you in learning how to manage a network?

Module
9

Supporting Mobile Devices

Module Objectives

1 Identify and use various types of mobile devices, mobile operating systems, wireless and wired connections, and accessories

2 Configure email and synchronize content on mobile devices for business use

3 Troubleshoot common problems with mobile devices

Core 1 Certification Objectives

1.1 Given a scenario, install and configure laptop hardware components.

1.3 Given a scenario, set up and configure accessories and ports of mobile devices.

1.4 Given a scenario, configure basic mobile-device network connectivity and application support.

2.3 Compare and contrast protocols for wireless networking.

4.1 Summarize cloud-computing concepts.

5.5 Given a scenario, troubleshoot common issues with mobile devices.

Introduction

Previous modules have focused on supporting personal computers. This module moves on to discuss supporting mobile devices such as smartphones and tablets. Most cell phones are also smartphones, which are often used to surf the web, access email, and manage apps and data. This module is intended to show you how to support a variety of mobile devices, including those you might not own or use. Technicians are often expected to do such things! As an IT support technician, you need to know about the hardware used with mobile devices and how to help a user configure and troubleshoot these devices.

Many employees expect to be able to use their mobile devices to access, synchronize, and edit data on the corporate network. Therefore, to protect this data, corporations require that employee mobile devices be secured and that data, settings, and apps be synchronized to other storage locations. In this module, you learn how you can synchronize content on mobile devices to a personal computer or to storage in the cloud (on the Internet). Finally, in this module, you learn about tools and resources available for troubleshooting mobile devices. In the Core 2 module "Mobile Device Security," you learn how to support mobile operating systems (iOS, iPadOS, and Android) and apps and how to secure mobile devices.

> **Exam Tip ✔**
>
> This module covers supporting mobile device hardware covered on the A+ Core 1 220-1001 exam. Content about mobile device operating systems and apps on the A+ Core 2 220-1102 exam is covered in the module "Mobile Device Security." Both modules contain content on troubleshooting mobile devices.

Mobile Devices, Operating Systems, Connections, and Accessories

Core 1 Objectives 1.1, 1.3, 1.4, 2.3

Mobile devices vary considerably by size, functionality, available connection types, and primary purpose(s), not to mention cost. A **smartphone** is primarily a cell phone that also can send text messages with photos, videos, or other multimedia content attached; surf the web; manage email; play games; take photos and videos; and download and use small apps. Most smartphones use touch screens for input (see Figure 9-1) and allow for voice input.

A **tablet** is a computing device with a touch screen that is larger than a smartphone and has functions similar to a smartphone. As you can see in Figure 9-2, a tablet might come with a detachable keyboard or a stylus. All tablets can connect to Wi-Fi networks and use Bluetooth or NFC (near-field communication), which you learn about later in this module, to wirelessly connect to nearby devices. Some tablets have the ability to use a cellular network for data transmissions and phone calls. Installed apps can be used to make voice phone calls, send text messages, and make video calls using data transmissions. When a tablet can be used to make a phone call, the distinction between a smartphone and a tablet is almost nonexistent, except for size.

Figure 9-1 Most smartphones don't have a physical keyboard and use a touch screen with an on-screen keyboard for input

iStock.com/Hocus-focus

Figure 9-2   Tablets are larger than smartphones and smaller than laptops, and can use touch or touch pen input

iStock.com/Orientfootage

Mobile Device Operating Systems

Core 1 Objective 1.3

The operating system for a mobile device is installed at the factory. **Android** OS by Google (*google.com* and *android.com*) is based on Linux and holds about 72% of the global mobile OS market. **iOS** for iPhones and **iPadOS** for iPads by Apple (*apple.com*) are based on macOS, and together hold about 27% of the global mobile OS market. Combined, Android, iOS, and iPadOS command about 99% of market share. Let's get familiar with each OS.

Get to Know an Android Device

Core 1 Objective 1.3

In the past, releases of Android were named after desserts. The last dessert release was Android Pie (version 9.0) in 2018. Now releases are merely numbered for the public. The current release is Android 11.0, and Android 12.0 has been released to a few devices. When a new release publishes, device manufacturers gradually release it. Not all Android devices can support a new release; it's up to the manufacturer to decide if a particular model can handle a new release and when that model gets the release.

Most current Android mobile devices have power and volume control buttons on the right side, and some have a third Google Assistant button to enable voice input on the left side. Earlier versions of Android used three soft buttons at the bottom of the screen, but Android 11 uses swipes or gestures rather than buttons to navigate the OS. Some of these gestures are described in Figure 9-3.

Figure 9-3 Android 11 home screen and user interface

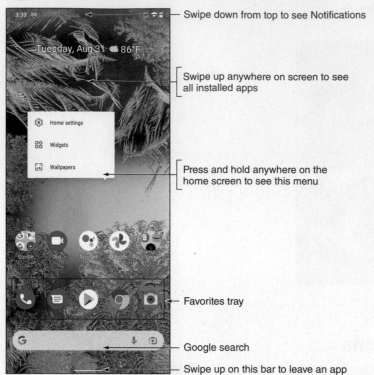

Swipe down from top to see Notifications

Swipe up anywhere on screen to see all installed apps

Press and hold anywhere on the home screen to see this menu

Favorites tray

Google search

Swipe up on this bar to leave an app

Note 1

You can use the Settings menu to configure Android to use the three legacy soft buttons at the bottom of the screen. In the Settings menu, tap **System**, **Gestures**, and **System navigation** and select **3-button navigation** (see Figure 9-4A). Figure 9-4B shows the home screen with the three buttons enabled.

Figure 9-4 (A) Choose gesture navigation or 3-button navigation, and (B) Android 11 home screen with 3-button navigation

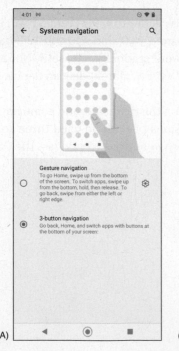

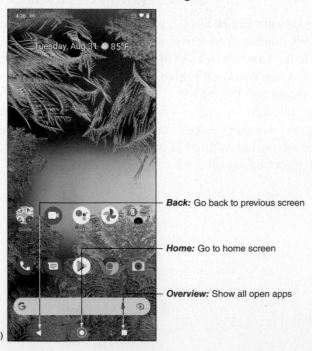

Back: Go back to previous screen

Home: Go to home screen

Overview: Show all open apps

(A)

(B)

> **Note 2**
>
> Android is installed by various device manufacturers before the device leaves the factory, and these manufacturers can customize the OS and how it works. Therefore, specific step-by-step directions will vary from device to device, even when the devices all use the same Android release. Remember that you don't need to memorize the steps—just learn general procedures for supporting a variety of mobile devices.

On Android phones, up to five apps or groups of apps can be pinned to the **favorites tray** just above the Google search box. Apps in the favorites tray stay put as you move from screen to screen by swiping left or right. Some other useful tools include the following:

- **App drawer.** Swipe up anywhere on the screen to access the **app drawer**, which lists and manages all apps installed on the phone. Press and hold an app in the app drawer to add it to an existing home screen or to add more home screens.
- **Notifications.** Swipe down the notifications shade from the top of the screen to see **notifications** that provide alerts and related information about apps and social media and quick settings to Wi-Fi, Bluetooth, and auto-rotate. See Figure 9-5A. Swipe down again to see more settings, including the cog icon to access the Settings app. See Figure 9-5B.

Figure 9-5   (A) The notifications shade includes quick access to a few settings; (B) swipe down again to access even more settings

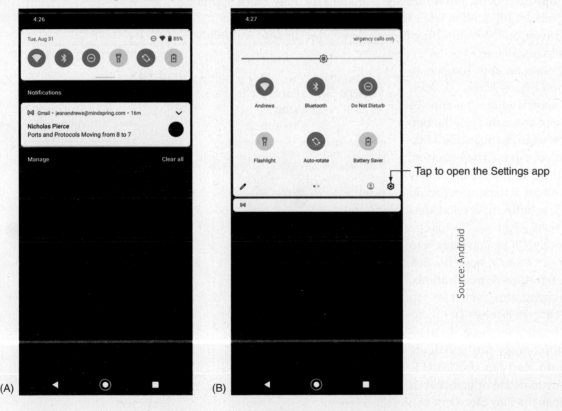

Tap to open the Settings app

Source: Android

(A)   (B)

- **Settings app.** To open Settings, tap the cog icon in the second notifications area, or open the app drawer and tap **Settings**. Most of the settings you need to use to support a mobile device are contained in the Settings app (see Figure 9-6). You can open the Settings app and search through its menus and submenus until you find what you need. If you get stuck, do a quick web search or check the user guide for the device.

Figure 9-6   The Android Settings app

Source: Android, Source: Apple Inc.

> **Note 3**
>
> One step in troubleshooting an OS is to update it. To update Android, in Settings, tap **About phone, Android version**, and **Google Play system update**. Know that a device might not be able to update to the latest version of Android.

Manage Android Apps

Android apps are sold or freely distributed by any source or vendor. For example, you can open the Chrome browser and download an app from a website, such as the Amazon Appstore for Android at *amazon.com* or directly from the website of a developer. However, the official source for apps is **Google Play** at *play.google.com*. A **Google account** is required to download content from Google Play and can be associated with any valid email address. Here's how to handle apps:

- **Install an app.** To get an app from Play Store, tap the **Play Store** app on the home screen. (If you don't see the app icon on the home screen, tap the **app drawer** and then tap **Play Store**.) Search for an app, and follow directions to install one.

- **Open and close an app.** To open an app, tap it on a home screen, or open the app drawer and tap the app. To leave the app, swipe up from the bottom of the screen or, when using 3-button navigation, tap the **Home** button. To close the app, swipe up slowly from the bottom of the screen (or tap the **Overview** button). All open apps appear in small windows. To close an app, swipe it up. If an app refuses to close, you can force it: open the **Settings** app, tap **Apps & notifications**, tap the running app, and then tap **FORCE STOP** (see Figure 9-7).

- **Delete or uninstall an app.** To uninstall an app, press the app icon, tap **App info**, and tap **UNINSTALL**. Another way to delete or uninstall an app is to open the **Play Store** app, tap your Google account profile icon (your photo), tap **Manage apps & devices**, tap **Manage**, tap the app, and then tap **Uninstall** (see Figure 9-8). Sometimes an Update option is also available on this screen. Also note that some embedded apps, such as the Phone app, can't be uninstalled.

Figure 9-7   Force stop an app

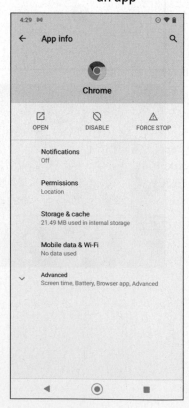

Figure 9-8   Use the Play Store app to uninstall an app

Get to Know iOS and iPadOS by Apple

Core 1 Objective 1.3

Apple Inc. (*apple.com*) develops, manufactures, and sells the Apple **iPhone** (a smartphone) and **iPad** (a handheld tablet). The latest releases for both OSs are versions 15. Apple maintains strict standards on its products, which means iOS and iPadOS are exceptionally stable and bug free; they are also very easy and intuitive operating systems to use.

iPhones have volume control buttons on the left side of the device and a physical side button on the upper-right side of the device. iPads have a top button on the top right side and volume buttons on the right side. Older devices also have a home button on the front of the device. The user interface is shown in Figure 9-9 for an iPad; an iPhone interface looks and works the same. Apps can be pinned to the **dock** at the bottom of the screen.

Figure 9-9   Access the dock on an iPad by swiping up from the bottom of the screen

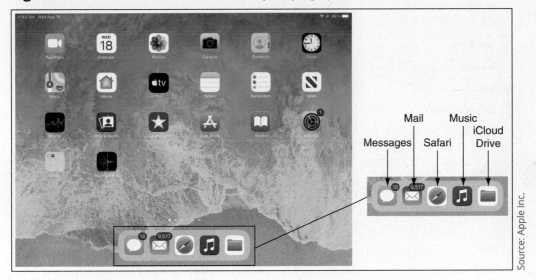

Source: Apple Inc.

Other useful tools include the following:

- **Control Center.** Swipe down from the upper-right corner to view the Control Center, where you can change basic settings such as brightness, volume, Wi-Fi, and Bluetooth. Use the Settings app to adjust which settings are available in the control center.
- **Settings app.** To open the Settings app, tap the **Settings** icon on the home screen. Just as with Android, the Settings app is the go-to place to manage the device, apps, and the OS. See Figure 9-10. For example, to manage iOS updates, in the Settings app, tap **General** and **Software Update**. You can set the device to automatically download and install updates or to download updates but not install them until you allow it.

9

Figure 9-10 Manage most iOS settings in the Settings app

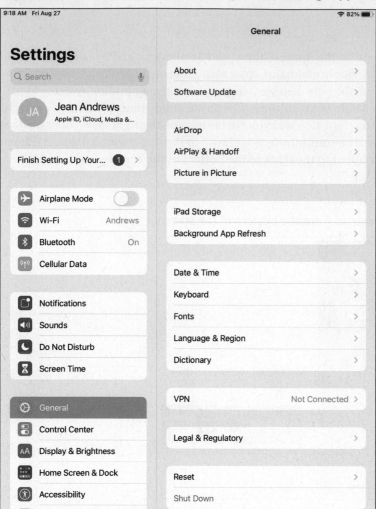

Manage iOS and iPadOS Apps

You can get Android apps from many sources, but the only place to go for an iOS/iPadOS app is Apple, which is the sole distributor of iOS apps at its App Store. (Also, entertainment, including movies and music, is available at the Apple iTunes Store.) Other developers can write apps for the iPhone or iPad, but these apps must be sent to Apple for close scrutiny. If they pass muster, they are distributed by Apple on its website. Apple offers app development tools, including the iOS SDK (software development kit), at *developer.apple.com*.

When you first purchase an iPad or iPhone, you activate it by signing in to the device with an **Apple ID**, or user account; using a valid email address and password; and associating the account with a credit card number. You need an Apple ID to download an app from the App Store. Here's how to manage apps:

- **Open and close apps.** Tap an app icon to open it. To leave the app, swipe up from the bottom of the screen. (For older devices with a Home button, press the Home button.) To close an app, swipe up slowly from the bottom of the screen. All open apps appear in small windows. Swipe up to close each app. (For older devices with a Home button, double-press the Home button to view all open apps. Swipe up to close each app.)
- **Install and uninstall apps.** Open the App Store app to search for and install an app. To delete or uninstall an app, press and hold the app icon, and tap **Remove App** or **Delete App**. Alternately, hold down the app until all icons start to jiggle. As the icons jiggle, press the dash beside an app icon to delete it. See Figure 9-11. To stop the jiggling, tap **Done** in the top-right corner of the screen.

Figure 9-11   To delete multiple apps, as app icons jiggle, tap the dash beside the icon

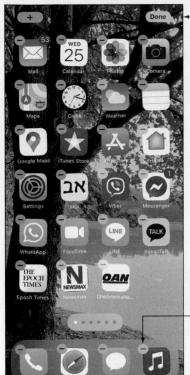

← Tap Done when finished

Press the dash beside an app icon to delete it

Source: Apple Inc.

Wireless Connections for Mobile Devices

Core 1 Objectives 1.3, 1.4

A mobile device might have several antennas—primarily cellular, Wi-Fi, GPS, Bluetooth, and NFC. The device uses a Wi-Fi or cellular antenna to connect to a LAN (local area network) or WAN (wide area network) and uses Bluetooth or NFC to connect to a PAN (personal area network). Settings on the device allow you to enable or disable each antenna. Network connections are configured using the Settings app. Let's look at each type of LAN, WAN, and PAN connection.

Two examples of LAN connections on a mobile device are when Wi-Fi is used to connect to a local network and when a device creates its own mobile Wi-Fi hotspot.

Wi-Fi Connections to a LAN

Core 1 Objectives 1.3, 1.4

Most mobile devices have Wi-Fi capability. On the Wi-Fi settings screen, you can add a Wi-Fi connection, manage existing networks, view available Wi-Fi hotspots, see which Wi-Fi network you are connected to, turn Wi-Fi off and on, and decide whether the device should ask the user before joining a Wi-Fi network. When the device is within range of Wi-Fi networks, it displays the list of networks. Select one to connect. If the Wi-Fi network is secured, enter the security key to complete the connection. To change to a different Wi-Fi hotspot, tap the name of the network, and select a new one from the list of available networks (see Figure 9-12). Searching for a Wi-Fi network can drain battery power. To make a battery charge last longer, disable Wi-Fi when you're not using it.

Mobile Hotspots and Tethering

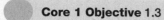

When a mobile device is connected to the Internet by way of its cellular WAN connection, you can allow other computers and devices to use this same connection. For example, in Figure 9-13, the smartphone is tethered by USB to a laptop so that the laptop can use the cellular network to connect to the Internet. If the smartphone has Wi-Fi capabilities, it can create its own Wi-Fi hotspot for other computers and devices to connect to wirelessly. An app on the smartphone controls these connections. To use your phone for tethering and for providing mobile hotspots, your carrier subscription must allow it. Also, know the extra burden on the phone can cause the battery to drain quicker and perhaps even overheat.

Cellular WAN Connections

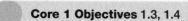

Smartphones—and some laptops, tablets, and wearable mobile devices—can connect to a cellular WAN if they have cellular capability and a subscription to the cellular network carrier. Recall from the module "Network Infrastructure and Cloud Computing" that a cellular network provided by a wireless carrier (for example, AT&T or Verizon) is used for voice, text, and data communication. As shown in Figure 9-14, cellular voice and SMS (Short Message Service) text messages transmit over the carrier's cellular network, and **cellular data** is sent from the carrier's cellular network to the Internet for distribution.

The following are two older radio bands a carrier might use on its cellular network for voice and SMS text communication:

- **CDMA. CDMA (Code Division Multiple Access)** communication is more popular in the USA than other nations and does not require a SIM card.
- **GSM. GSM (Global System for Mobiles)** communication is a global standard used in many nations and requires a SIM card installed in the device.

Older cell phones were built to support GSM or CDMA, but not both. Newer cell phones

Figure 9-12   Select a new Wi-Fi hotspot, or see details about the current connection

Source: Apple Inc.

Figure 9-13   Tether your smartphone to your laptop using a USB cable

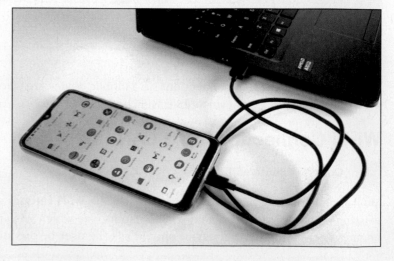

Figure 9-14   A smartphone can communicate on the Internet via a cellular network or Wi-Fi

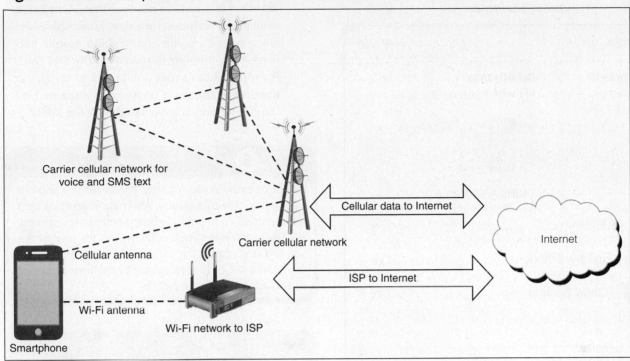

can support either technology. Both GSM and CDMA are being replaced by newer technologies, although they are still used as backups for voice calls in locations where more modern coverage is weak. Most carriers have announced they will stop supporting GSM and CDMA by the end of 2022.

Whereas GSM and CDMA are used only for voice and SMS texting, these standards can transmit cellular data (voice, text, video and graphics) to the Internet:

- **2G.** The **2G** standard was first used with GSM to transmit secured voice, text messages, and limited data. It was soon followed by a CDMA version of 2G that was slightly faster.
- **3G.** The **3G** standard was faster than 2G and used with CDMA and GSM. 3G can achieve download speeds up to 21 Mbps.
- **4G and 4G LTE.** The **4G** standard was faster than 3G but was soon replaced by an even faster standard: **4G LTE.** 4G and 4G LTE don't require the help of CDMA or GSM, which is why those older standards are being phased out. 4G LTE can achieve up to 1 Gbps speeds and requires a SIM card to function. 4G was the first standard that allowed a device to support a mobile hotspot.
- **5G.** The **5G** standard is the up-and-coming standard, and it currently has an average speed of 150 Mbps, with peak speeds up to 10 Gbps.

As noted, although CDMA does not require a SIM card, 4G LTE does—which is why all cell phones in the United States now use SIM cards. To make a cellular data connection, you must have a subscription with your carrier that includes a SIM card and cellular data plan. Here is information that might be used when a connection is first made to the carrier's WAN or when troubleshooting that connection:

- The **IMEI (International Mobile Equipment Identity)** is a unique number that identifies each mobile phone or tablet device worldwide. It's usually reported within the About menu in the OS (see Figure 9-15), and it might also be printed on a sticker on the device, such as behind the battery.

Note 5

If your phone gets stolen and you notify your carrier, the carrier can block its use based on the IMEI and alert other carriers to the stolen IMEI. Also, before buying a used phone, check its IMEI against blacklists of stolen phones by doing a Google search on **imei blacklist check.**

Figure 9-15 The IMEI value identifies a mobile device worldwide

• The **IMSI (International Mobile Subscriber Identity)** is a unique number that identifies a cellular subscription for a device or subscriber, along with its home country and mobile network. This number is stored on the SIM card. For older phones that don't use SIM cards, the number is kept in a database maintained by the carrier and is associated with the IMEI.

Note 6

SIM cards come in various sizes and install in a pop-out tray on the side of a phone. Alternately, an eSIM card is embedded on the motherboard and never removed. For SIM cards, when you switch carriers for your device you exchange cards. For eSIM cards, to switch carriers, you scan a QR code sent to you by the new carrier or use an app to make the switch.

Exam Tip ✔

The A+ Core 1 exam expects you to identify and distinguish between GSM and CDMA technologies, and might give you a scenario that requires you to know which communication technology a device is using.

Applying Concepts

Manage Cellular Data and Roaming

Est. Time: 15 minutes
Core 1 Objective: 1.4

Looking back at Figure 9-14, you can see that a smartphone can use cellular data or Wi-Fi to access the Internet. In certain situations, you might want to disable cellular data or disable cellular roaming. The advantage of disabling cellular data and using Wi-Fi for data transmissions is that Wi-Fi transmissions are not charged against your cellular data subscription plan. Also, Wi-Fi is generally faster than most cellular connections. (When you disable cellular data, you can still send SMS texts because these texts use the carrier's network and not the Internet.) Disabling roaming can prevent roaming charges on your bill incurred from using other carriers' cellular networks when you travel outside your home territory.

To disable roaming on an Android device, go to the **Network & internet** menu in the Settings app, tap **Mobile network**, and then disable **Roaming**. On an iOS device, open the Settings app, tap **Cellular** (see Figure 9-16A), and turn off **Cellular Data**. Next, tap **Cellular Data Options**, and then turn off roaming. On the Cellular Data Options screen, you can also turn on Low Data Mode to conserve cellular data usage. See Figure 9-16B.

Figure 9-16   Control (A) data usages and (B) data roaming in iOS

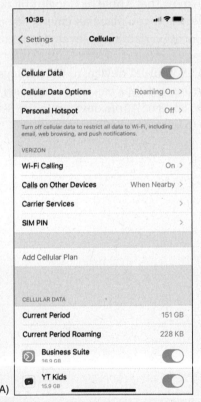

(A)

(B)

If you have roaming enabled, especially for a CDMA device, you'll want to keep the **Preferred Roaming List (PRL)** updated. The PRL is a database file that lists the preferred service providers or radio frequencies your carrier wants the device to use when outside your home network. To update the PRL, follow instructions from your carrier. For example, for Verizon, you dial *228, and select 2 to update your PRL. When the update completes, a message appears on your phone. For an Android phone, you then need to power down the device and turn it back on.

Note ⑦

Like desktop computers, a mobile device can be configured to communicate information securely over a virtual private network (VPN) connection. To create a VPN connection, in the Android Settings app, tap **Connections**, **More connection settings**, and **VPN**. In iOS Settings, tap **General**, **VPN**. To set up the VPN, you'll need to know the type of encryption protocol used (IKEv2, IPsec, or L2TP), the IP address or domain name of the VPN server, and the user name and password to the corporate network. Figure 9-17 shows the configuration options on an iOS smartphone. Also, Google offers a VPN connection for Android devices using the Google One mobile app when you subscribe to Google cloud storage.

Figure 9-17 Configure a VPN connection in iOS

Location Services

Core 1 Objective 1.4

Many mobile apps, such as Google Maps, require a location service to work. The following are two services a mobile device might use:

- **GPS.** A **GPS (Global Positioning System)** feature is embedded in smartphones, smart watches, tablets, some automobiles, and even some medical devices, making it possible to identify the device's location in relation to multiple satellites in orbit around the Earth. GPS data is never sent to these satellites; the device receives the data to determine its location. However, the device might send GPS location data to Apple or Google.
- **Cellular location service.** A mobile device can also determine its location from Bluetooth, crowd-sourced Wi-Fi, and cellular databases. These databases are built from geotagged locations of Wi-Fi hotspots and cell towers using anonymous and encrypted data sent from devices.

Location services are managed by Apple for iOS and iPadOS and by Google for Android. Using the Settings app, you can turn off location services and decide how apps can use the service. However, know that Apple or Google still has the right to locate your device—for example, when you place an emergency phone call or to enhance their crowd-sourced location database—even if location services is turned off.

To manage the location services on an Android device, in the Settings app, tap **Location**. See Figure 9-18A. To change the way apps can use location services, tap **App access to location** (see Figure 9-18B). For Apple devices, in the Settings app, tap **Privacy** and **Location Services** to turn the service on or off.

Figure 9-18 (A) Manage location services in the Settings app, and (B) fine-tune which apps can use Location services

(A)

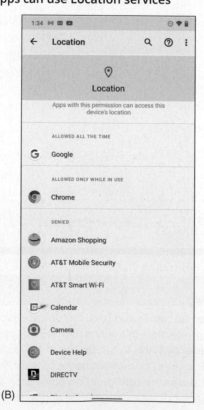

(B)

PAN Connections

Core 1 Objectives 1.1, 1.3, 1.4, 2.3

Mobile devices typically have the capability to connect to other nearby wireless devices and accessories using a Bluetooth or NFC wireless connection:

- **Bluetooth.** Bluetooth is a short-range (about 30 feet or 10 meters) wireless technology used to connect two devices in a small PAN. To create a Bluetooth connection, the two devices must be **paired**, a process you'll learn more about later in this module. Figure 9-19 shows a smartphone connected to a Bluetooth speaker.
- **NFC. Near-field communication (NFC)** is a wireless technology that establishes a communication link between two NFC devices that are within 10 centimeters (about 4 inches) of each other. For example, an NFC tag (see Figure 9-20) contains a small microchip that can be embedded in just about anything, including a key chain tag, printed flyer, or billboard. The NFC tag dispenses information to any NFC-enabled smartphone or other device that comes within 4 inches of the tag.

Figure 9-19   Smartphone connects to speaker via Bluetooth

iStock.com/Magnetic-Mcc

Figure 9-20   These programmable NFC tags have sticky backs for attaching to a flat surface such as a wall, desk, or car dashboard

NFC is a form of RFID; they both operate near the 13.56 MHz radio frequency. **RFID (radio-frequency identification)** is traditionally used in small tags that attach to and identify clothing inventory, car keys, bags, luggage, pets, cattle, hospital patients, and much more. An RFID tag contains a microchip and antenna and can be a passive or active tag. Active RFID tags have built-in batteries and transmitters to respond to commands or requests for information. Passive RFID tags, which cost much less, are essentially electronic barcodes that can be read from a few feet away without requiring line-of-sight access.

NFC operates at a slightly higher frequency than RFID, and its range is shorter, which makes it more secure. For example, two iPhones must be very close to each other for NFC to work. Although NFC can read RFID tags, a mobile device does not communicate peer-to-peer with RFID devices.

Contactless Payments

Credit card transactions processed using Apple Pay or Google Pay use NFC when the device comes close to a point-of-sale terminal. The transaction uses **two-factor authentication (2FA)**, which means two actions are needed to authenticate the payer. **Biometric authentication** can include a fingerprint or facial recognition. For example, when your iPhone comes near a point-of-sale terminal (see Figure 9-21), and you enter a passcode or PIN to access your phone, Apple Pay displays the payment amount on your phone for you to accept. You can then use FaceID or Touch ID to authenticate your face or fingerprint to complete the transaction.

Figure 9-21   Use NFC wireless with an iPhone to create a contactless payment

Prykhodov/Dreamstime.com

Near-Field Privacy

Wi-Fi, Bluetooth, and NFC technologies can be used to share data between two devices when they are in close range. To protect your privacy and secure the data on your device, you can manage this near-field scanner feature as follows:

- **Android Nearby Share.** On an Android device, in the Settings app, tap **Google**, **Devices & sharing**, and **Nearby Share** (see Figure 9-22). To control which contacts can be shared, tap **Device visibility**. You can share or hide all contacts or share just a few. When notifications are turned on, you will be notified when another device is scanning for a near-field connection.
- **iOS and iPadOS AirDrop. AirDrop** is an Apple wireless standard that uses both Bluetooth and Wi-Fi to provide near-field (within 30 feet) data transfers between iPhones, iPads, Macs, and other Apple devices. (AirDrop won't share with an Android device.) To manage AirDrop, swipe down from the upper-right corner of the screen to open the **Control Center** (see Figure 9-23A), press and hold the top-left group of controls, and tap the **AirDrop** icon (see Figure 9-23B). Then you can decide to turn AirDrop on or off and decide to share an item only with your contacts or with everyone. (You can also control AirDrop settings in the Settings app under General.) To share a selected item, tap the **Share** icon, and then tap **AirDrop** in the list of ways to share the item.

Figure 9-22 Manage what can be shared with near-field scanning on an Android device

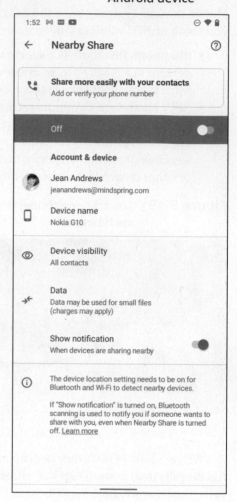

Figure 9-23 Press and hold the upper-left group of icons in the iOS Control Center to see two more icons in this group, including AirDrop

(A)   (B)

Exam Tip ✔

The A+ Core 1 exam expects you to be able to contrast and compare Bluetooth, NFC, and RFID. You also need to know how to make a Bluetooth connection and understand what two-factor authentication is.

Applying Concepts

Pairing Bluetooth Devices

Est. Time: 15 minutes
Core 1 Objective: 1.3

To configure a Bluetooth connection, complete the following steps:

1. Turn on the Bluetooth device—such as a speaker, headset, webcam, or keyboard—to which you want to connect your mobile device.

2. Enable Bluetooth on the device and enable pairing mode. Sometimes just turning on Bluetooth enables pairing automatically for a limited period of time. The device might have a pairing button or combination of buttons to enable pairing and a light that blinks to indicate the device is ready to receive a Bluetooth connection. This makes the device discoverable, which means it's transmitting a signal to identify itself to nearby Bluetooth devices.

3. On your mobile device, turn on Bluetooth. The mobile device searches for Bluetooth devices. If it discovers the Bluetooth device (see Figure 9-24), tap it to connect. The two Bluetooth devices now begin the pairing process. Some Bluetooth devices might require a code to connect. For example, when an iPad and Bluetooth keyboard are pairing, the iPad displays a four-digit code that must be entered on the keyboard.

4. Test the connection. For an audio device, play a video or audio recording on the mobile device, and for a keyboard, type into a notes application or text box.

Figure 9-24 Tap to connect the iPhone to the Sylvania Bluetooth speaker it has detected

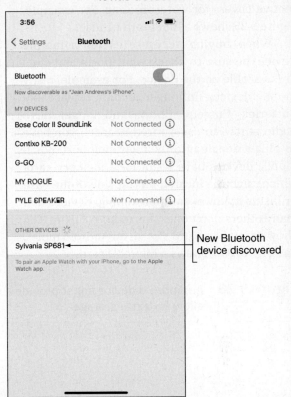

New Bluetooth device discovered

Exam Tip ✔

The A+ Core 1 exam might give you a scenario that requires you to pair Bluetooth devices and then test connectivity after the connection is established.

Note 8

You can automatically disable a mobile device antenna that transmits signals by enabling airplane mode so that the device can neither transmit nor receive the signals. Many newer devices do not disable the GPS or NFC antennas; GPS only receives and never transmits, and NFC signals don't reach very far. While airplane mode is on, you can manually enable some wireless connections, such as Bluetooth or Wi-Fi.

Mobile Device Ports and Accessories

Core 1 Objective 1.3

You can buy all kinds of mobile device accessories, such as wireless keyboards, touch pens, speakers, webcams, earbuds, headsets, game pads, docking stations, printers, extra battery packs and chargers, USB adapters, memory cards (usually the microSD form factor) to expand storage space, credit card readers for accepting payments by credit card, and protective covers for waterproofing. For example, Figure 9-25 shows a Bluetooth headset.

When buying accessories for a mobile device, be sure to check what ports and slots are available on the device. For example, many mobile devices no longer include replaceable batteries. Current iPhones no longer have audio ports—to use a wired headset, you have to plug a dongle into the Lightning port. Some mobile devices have a slot for a memory card, which might be located on the side of the case or inside it; however, Apple mobile devices and many others don't offer this feature. Figure 9-26 shows a memory card slot on an Android tablet, and Figure 9-27 shows a MicroSD card.

Figure 9-25   Bluetooth over-the-ear headset designed to connect with a smartphone

Source: Amazon.com, Inc.

Figure 9-26   An Android device might provide a memory card slot to allow for extra storage

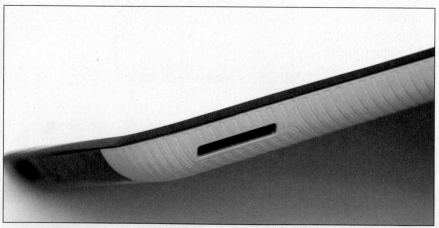

Figure 9-27   A mobile device might use a microSD card to add extra flash memory storage to the device

Wired Connections for Accessories

Smartphones, tablets, and wearable devices can make a wired connection to a computer. This connection can be used to charge the device, download software updates, upload data to the computer, back up data, and restore software or data. The device's port used for power and communication may be a type of USB (Universal Serial Bus) port or a proprietary, vendor-specific port. Some USB connectors used for this purpose include microUSB (see Figure 9-28A), the smaller miniUSB (see Figure 9-28B), and the newer USB-C (see Figure 9-28C). USB-C is the first USB connector that can plug into a port in either orientation. Apple iPhones, iPods, and iPads use the proprietary **Lightning port** and connector for power and communication (see Figure 9-29). Some newer iPads use the USB-C connector.

Figure 9-28   Some mobile devices may connect to a computer's USB port by way of a (A) microUSB, (B) miniUSB, or (C) USB-C cable

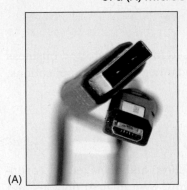

(A)

(B)

(C)

Figure 9-29   A Lightning cable by Apple Inc. has a USB connector for the computer end and a Lightning connector for an iPhone or iPad

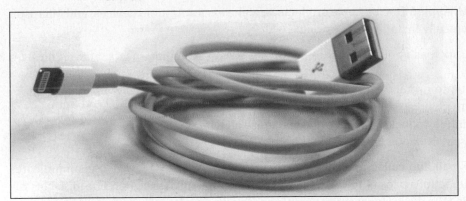

9

Also know that you can use USB adapter cables to work with the port your device has. For example, you can purchase a Lightning-to-USB-C adapter cable or a miniUSB-to-Ethernet adapter cable. You can even buy a USB to serial port adapter cables when you need to connect your tablet to a Linux server in a server room. (A server is likely to provide a serial port for that purpose.) See Figure 9-30.

Figure 9-30   A serial-to-USB adapter

Source: Amazon.com, Inc.

Exam Tip ✔

The A+ Core 1 exam expects you to know about USB-C, microUSB, miniUSB, Lightning, and serial wired connections.

Mobile Apps for Business Use

 Core 1 Objectives 1.4, 4.1

In this section of the module, you learn how to support mobile devices that are used for corporate and business needs, including configuring corporate email and synchronizing devices for email and other corporate applications.

Mobile Devices Managed by Corporate Policies

 Core 1 Objective 1.4

Corporations and schools might provide corporate-owned devices, which are secured and managed by corporate policies and procedures, and/or the organization might have **BYOD (bring your own device)** policies and procedures. With BYOD, an employee or student is allowed to connect their own device to the organization's network. For security purposes, an organization configures the person's device before allowing it to connect to the network.

Large corporations use **mobile device management (MDM)** software that provides tools for securing and tracking mobile devices—even when they're turned off—and managing the data on those devices. Examples of MDM software suites include Verizon MDM, Apple MDM for Apple products, Scalefusion for Android devices, and Microsoft Endpoint Manager. **MDM policies** typically include the following:

- Security policy enforcement, such as applying patches, enforcing password requirements, and requiring two-factor authentication
- Data encryption requirements, to protect data on the mobile device if it falls into the wrong hands, and synchronization of that data to cloud storage for backups
- Remote lock-and-wipe capabilities, to lock down a device and erase all data on it
- Restrictions on the use of unsecured apps

To do all this, MDM installs a small app called an **agent** on a managed mobile device, which communicates through various Wi-Fi or cellular connections back to the MDM server in the company data center. The initial installing of the agent and the agent checking the device for security compliance is called **on-boarding**. The reverse process when the mobile device is removed from the MDM fleet is called **off-boarding**.

When a corporation needs to keep financial, regulated, or other sensitive data on an employee's personal device, it might choose to enhance MDM with software that specifically targets protecting corporate apps and their data. **Mobile application management (MAM)** software serves that purpose by the following processes:

- Separating corporate data and apps from personal data and apps on a device, which is called sandboxing these corporate assets.
- Assuring that corporate data is only transmitted over a secure and encrypted connection, called a VPN (Virtual Private Network). The data is encrypted when it is at rest on the device and in transit.
- Managing and updating corporate applications remotely.

When MAM is protecting corporate data and apps, the user normally has more freedom to install their own personal apps and data on their device. MAM software is sometimes a part of MDM software, and it can also be a standalone product that works in addition to MDM software.

Configure Mobile Device Email

 Core 1 Objective 1.4

Android has its Gmail app, and iOS has its Mail app; either app can work with any email provider. Rather than using OS embedded mail apps, you can install your own. For example, Blue Mail or Spark are free open-source mail apps, and Polymail (*polymail.io*) and Microsoft Outlook (*Microsoft.com*) are paid-for **commercial mail apps**.

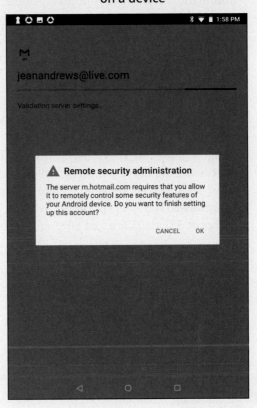

Note 9

When configuring corporate email addresses, messages such as that shown in Figure 9-31 might appear asking for permission to apply extra security to the device.

To configure email in iOS, use the Settings app. In Settings, tap **Mail**, **Accounts**, and **Add Account**. A list of popular email providers appears (see Figure 9-32). If your provider is not in the list, tap **Other** and enter the requested information to set up email, contacts, and calendars. For Android, tap the **Gmail** app, and then tap **Add an email address**.

Here is the information you'll need to configure an email app on a mobile device:

- **Your email address and password.** For iOS, iPadOS, and Android, if your email account is with Google, Microsoft Exchange, Outlook, Yahoo!, or AOL (iPhone and iPad only), your email address and password are all you need because the OS can automatically set up these accounts. If you are setting up a work account that uses Microsoft 365 for business, don't use the Outlook option, but rather check with your administrator for server settings.

Note 10

Microsoft Exchange is a private enterprise email service that is hosted on corporation or ISP servers to provide company email addresses and includes email, calendars, and contacts services. It can integrate with MDM software suites to enforce MDM policies on mobile devices.

If your email account is with any other provider, you'll also need the following information:

- **Names of your incoming and outgoing email servers.** To find this information, check the support page of your email provider's website. For example, the server you use for incoming mail might be *imap.mycompany.com*, and the server you use for outgoing mail might be *smtp.mycompany.com*. The two servers might have the same name.
- **Type of protocol your incoming server uses.** The incoming server uses IMAP4 or POP3. With IMAP4, you are managing your email on the server. For example, you can move a message from one folder to another on your device, which causes that change to happen on the remote server. Using POP3, the messages are downloaded to your device, where you manage them locally. Most POP3 mail servers give you the option to leave the messages on the server or delete them after they are downloaded.

Figure 9-32 When setting up email in iOS, select an email provider

9

- **Security used.** Most likely, if email is encrypted during transmission, the configuration will happen automatically, without your involvement. However, if you have problems, you need to be aware of these possible settings for the incoming server:
  - An IMAP server uses port 143 unless it is secured and using SSL/TLS, which uses port 993.
  - A POP3 server uses port 110 unless it is secured and using SSL/TLS, which uses port 995 (see Figure 9-33).
- **Outgoing server.** Previously, outgoing email was sent using the SMTP protocol, which uses port 25. Now, most SMTP servers support secure SMTP, which uses TLS encryption for sending messages and port 587 or 2525 as an alternative port.

Figure 9-33   A POP3 email server might use SSL/TLS encryption and port 995

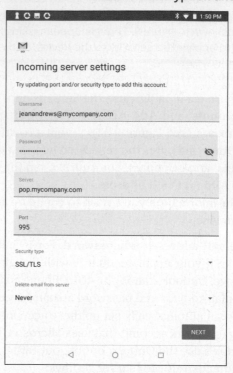

Exam Tip ✔

The A+ Core 1 exam expects you to know about POP3, IMAP, SMTP, and the ports they use, and it might require you to use this information in configuring email on a mobile device. Before you sit for the exam, memorize the protocols and ports discussed in this section, and understand how this information is used to configure email on a mobile device. A project at the end of this module will give you practice with this process.

When setting up corporate email that uses Microsoft Exchange, know that the Exchange server can control how the email service works on a mobile device based on MDM policies. These policies can include how email, calendars, contacts, and tasks are synced between the server and the device. Within Exchange, **ActiveSync** is responsible for syncing data between the server and device. If ActiveSync is disabled at the server end, no Exchange data is synced, which means no data is kept on the device, and, therefore, it is not available to the user when the mobile device is offline (not connected to the Internet). In addition, ActiveSync can perform remote wipes and enforce password policies and data encryption.

Exam Tip ✔

The A+ Core 1 exam expects you to describe the functions of ActiveSync in Microsoft Exchange.

Mobile Device Synchronization

Core 1 Objectives 1.4, 4.1

In this section of the module, you learn to use a Google or Apple account to sync or mirror data among your devices and the cloud. For example, a photo taken, new contact added, or calendar event created on one device is available in the cloud and on all other devices. As another example, when you sync email, the email app on your phone shows the same email messages as the browser or email client on your desktop computer.

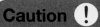

Caution ❗

It's not safe to store passwords in your browser. It's much more secure to use a password manager app, such as KeePass (*keepass.info*) or LastPass (*lastpass.com*). KeePass stores passwords only on the local computer, which is more secure but less convenient. LastPass can store passwords in the cloud and sync passwords across devices, which is more convenient but less secure.

Google Syncing

All data that Google keeps under your account at *google.com* can be synced with your Android devices. In the Google cloud, the first 15 GB of cloud storage is free. With Android devices, to manage what is synced, open the **Settings** app, tap **Google** and **Backup** (see Figure 9-34A). Then tap **Google Account data**. On the Account sync screen (see Figure 9-34B), turn on or off syncing for each type of Google account data. To sync now, tap the three-dot icon in the upper-right corner of the screen, and tap **Sync now**.

Figure 9-34   (A) Manage Google Backup and (B) manage Google account data syncing

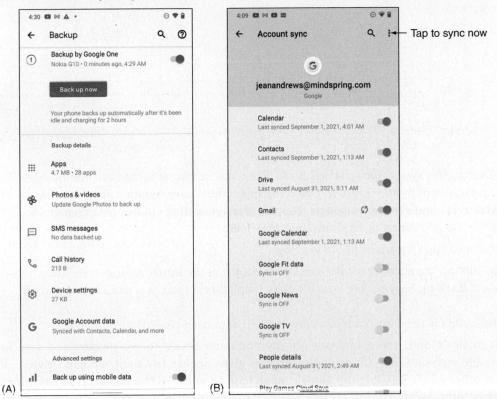

You can choose whether to sync only over Wi-Fi so that syncing doesn't use up your cellular data caps. On the Backup screen, shown in Figure 9-34A, turn on or off *Back up using mobile data*.

You can also control additional sync settings in the Settings app and in individual apps:

- **Contacts syncing.** Use the Settings app to sync Contacts:
    1. Open the **Settings** app, tap **Google**, **Settings for Google apps**, and **Google Contacts sync**. Notice in Figure 9-35A that Google contacts are syncing. To change this setting, tap **Manage settings** under Status. On the next screen, you can turn syncing off and on (see Figure 9-35B).

Figure 9-35   (A) Manage Google contact syncing and (B) turn on
syncing of non-Google contacts

(A)   (B)

2. Notice in Figure 9-35A that *Also sync device contacts* is off. When this setting is turned on, non-Google contacts—such as contacts kept by the Covve (*covve.com*) app, a third-party contact app—can be imported as Google contacts and synced by Google. Tapping **Manage settings** in this area changes the way Google handles non-Google contacts, as shown in Figure 9-35B.

- **Photo syncing.** Use the Photo app to manage photo syncing:

  1. Open the **Photo** app, and tap the account profile icon (your photo) in the upper-right corner. Then tap **Photos settings** and **Back up & sync** (see Figure 9-36A). Using this screen, you can turn on and off photo syncing.

  2. To manage how cellular data is used for photo syncing, tap Cell data usage (see Figure 9-36B).

To access your content in the cloud, use a browser on any computer to go to *google.com* and sign in to your Google account. A single sign-on (SSO) for multiple services gives access to Gmail, Google Drive, Calendar, Contacts, Photos, and other content. Click the **Google apps** icon to select different apps, as shown in Figure 9-37. When you select an app, such as Contacts or Calendar, the content in that app displays. You can also go directly to the Google content using direct links, such as *contacts.google.com*, *photos.google.com*, and *calendar.google.com*.

For a monthly fee, you can subscribe to Google Workspace Individual, which offers enhanced versions of Google Meet (a video conferencing tool), Google Calendar, and Gmail. Google Workspace for an organization is managed via an Admin console where you can add new users, migrate user content, and manage cloud storage and file sharing. To set up a user account on a mobile device for Google Workspace Individual or Google Workspace for an organization, follow the directions at *support.google.com/a/answer/3035792*.

Figure 9-36 (A) Turn on and off photo syncing and (B) manage data usage for photo syncing

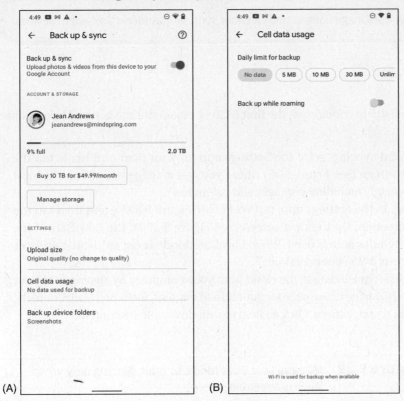

(A)

(B)

Figure 9-37 Access Google content on the web at *google.com*

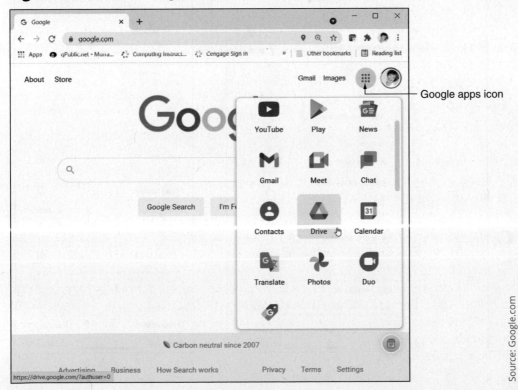

Google apps icon

Source: Google.com

9

Exam Tip ✔

The A+ Core 1 exam expects you to know how to manage contact and calendar syncing in Android and Apple devices.

Apple Syncing

iOS and iPadOS sync content to the Apple website at *icloud.com*; the first 5 GB of cloud storage is free. Here is what you need to know about Apple syncing:

- **Manage what is synced.** To set up iCloud syncing, go to the **Settings** app on your iPad or iPhone, tap the user name, and tap **iCloud** to go to the screen (see Figure 9-38) where you can manage your iCloud storage and decide which apps and data get synced (including contacts and calendars).
- **Manage cellular data used for syncing.** In the Settings app, tap **Wi-Fi** (see Figure 9-39A), and then tap the Info icon beside the current Wi-Fi connection. On the next screen (see Figure 9-39B), the Low Data Mode can be turned on or off to control how cellular data is used. When Low Data Mode is on, automatic updates and data syncing is paused unless there is a Wi-Fi connection.
- **Manage content in iCloud.** You can access synced data in the cloud from your computer by signing in to your Apple account at *icloud.com*. Figure 9-40 shows the home page for your iCloud content, including Mail, Contacts, Calendar, iCloud Drive, and location data, among others. Click an item to drill down into its content.

Figure 9-38 Manage iCloud syncing and storage on an iPhone

Figure 9-39 Manage Low Data Mode to limit syncing only when Wi-Fi is available

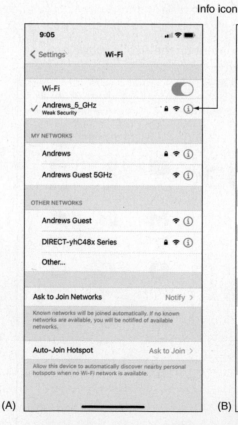

(A)

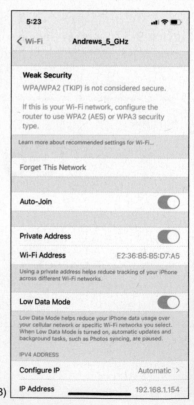

(B)

Figure 9-40   Access iOS content at *icloud.com*

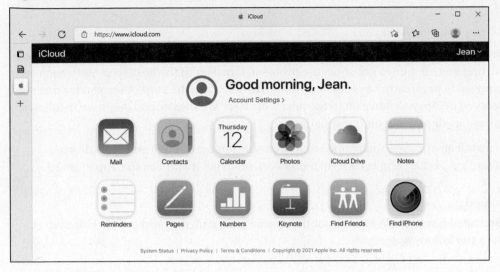

Microsoft 365, OneDrive, and SharePoint

Third-party apps and services can also be used to sync data. One example is **Microsoft 365**, previously called Office 365, which is a suite of productivity apps, including Word, Excel, PowerPoint, Outlook, and Visio. A subscription to Microsoft 365 includes 1 TB of OneDrive cloud storage (*onedrive.live.com*). Microsoft 365 installs on desktops, laptops, tablets, and smartphones and syncs data to OneDrive on multiple devices and in the cloud. When setting up a Microsoft 365 account for business, ask your administrator for the correct server settings for the account. Teams can collaborate with documents stored in OneDrive, or an individual user can share a document on OneDrive with anyone with a Microsoft account. OneDrive works well for syncing data for an individual or a few team members. SharePoint also provides cloud storage that integrates with Microsoft 365 but goes further than OneDrive as powerful content collaboration and management software in an enterprise.

> **Exam Tip** ✔️
>
> The A+ Core 1 exam expects you to know about mobile device synchronization with Microsoft 365.

Troubleshooting Mobile Devices

> **Core 1 Objective** 5.5

As an IT support technician for mobile devices, know that they contain few field replaceable units (FRU), or hardware that can be replaced by field technicians. The cost of repairing the device—including parts, special tools, and labor—generally exceeds the value of replacing the device. Although it is possible to replace the screens in some mobile devices, a support technician is generally not expected to take the time to do so.

There are, however, many problems with a device that you can troubleshoot using tools within the OS. When learning to troubleshoot any OS or device, remember the web is a great source of information. Depend on the *support.google.com/android* and *support.apple.com* websites to give you troubleshooting tips and procedures for their respective operating systems and mobile devices. For Android devices, also look for help on the device manufacturer website. Let's start with exploring the tools you need to troubleshoot mobile devices.

Troubleshooting Techniques

 Core 1 Objective 5.5

The following steps are ordered to solve a problem while making the least changes to the system (i.e., try the least invasive solution first). Try the first step; if it does not solve the problem, move on to the next step. With each step, first make sure the device is plugged in or already has sufficient charge to complete the step. After you try one step, check to see if the problem is solved before you move on to the next step. Here are the general steps we're following, although some might not be possible, depending on the situation:

1. Close, uninstall, and reinstall an app. Too many open apps can shorten battery life and slow down device performance. If you suspect an app is causing a problem, uninstall it and use the app store to reinstall it.

2. Use the Settings app to update the OS.

3. Restart the device (also called a soft boot) and reboot the device (also called a hard boot). This step is covered in more depth in the following section.

Restart or Reboot the Device

A restart powers down the device and restarts it, which is similar to a Windows restart. A reboot, also called a hard boot, is similar to a Windows shutdown and performs a full clean boot. First try a restart, and if that doesn't fix the problem, try a hard boot:

1. **Restart the device, also called a soft boot.** To restart an Android device, press and hold the power button, and select **Restart** (see Figure 9-41). To restart an iPhone or iPad, press and hold the side or top button, and slide the power-off message to the right. To turn the device back on, press and hold the Android power button or the iPhone or iPad side or top button. Power cycling a smartphone every few days is a good idea to keep the phone functioning at peak efficiency.

2. **Reboot the device using a hard boot.** When the menus in a device don't work or the device freezes entirely, a full clean boot might help. For most Android devices, hold down the power button to see the menu shown in Figure 9-41, and tap **Power off** twice. If that doesn't work, try holding down the power button and the volume-down button at the same time. (Check Android device manufacturers for details.) To reboot an iPhone or iPad, hold down the side or top button and the volume-down button at the same time until the Apple logo appears. (For older iPhones and iPads, press and hold the side or top button and the Home button.)

If the device has a removable battery and it refuses to hard boot, you can open the back of the device and then remove and reinstall the battery as a last resort (unless the device is under warranty).

In the module "Mobile Device Security," you learn more troubleshooting techniques to solve mobile device problems, including how to repair and reinstall the OS, perform a factory reset, and recover the system.

Figure 9-41 Restart an Android device

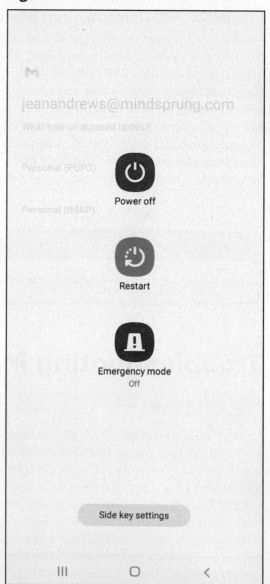

Common Mobile Device Malware Symptoms

Core 1 Objective 5.5

Android mobile devices are more susceptible to malware than iPhones and iPads because apps can be downloaded from sites other than Google. With iOS and iPadOS, apps can be obtained only from the Apple App Store and are therefore more strictly vetted. However, for any mobile device, malware can be introduced by a Trojan that a user accepts (for example, as an email attachment) or by macros embedded in shared documents.

Here are some symptoms that indicate malware might be at work on an Android, iOS, or iPadOS device:

- **Power drain, sluggish response time, slow data speeds, high network traffic, high number of ads, data-usage limit notification, limited or no Internet connectivity.** All these symptoms can indicate that apps are running in the background—draining resources and leaking your data to online servers. For example, when the XAgent malware app installs on an Apple device with iOS version 7 or older, the app icon is hidden, and the app runs in the background. When you close the app, it restarts. The malware not only uses resources; it also steals personal data and makes screenshots, which it sends to a remote command-and-control (C&C) server.
- **Fake security warnings, unexpected app behavior, and strange text messages.** A C&C server might send coded text messages back to the phone. If you receive strange text messages, suspect malware. Fake security warnings can bait you into installing an app, which is actually more malware, to clean the system
- **Dropped phone calls or weak signal.** Dropped phone calls can be caused by a weak signal, which can be resolved by moving to a place where cellular coverage is stronger. However, dropped phone calls can also happen when malware is interfering and trying to eavesdrop on your conversations or is performing other background activities.
- **Unintended Wi-Fi and Bluetooth connections.** Malicious Wi-Fi hotspots and Bluetooth devices can hijack a device or inject it with malware. When a mobile device connects to a malicious Wi-Fi hotspot, the device can receive a malicious script that repeatedly reboots the device, which makes it unusable. To prevent this type of attack, avoid free Wi-Fi hotspots or use a VPN connection. To prevent a device from pairing with a malicious Bluetooth device, turn off Bluetooth when it's not in use.
- **Unauthorized account access or leaked personal files or data.** A malicious app can steal passwords and data from other apps and can pretend to be a different app to get access to online accounts. If you suspect an online account has been hacked, consider malware might be on the mobile device that uses this account.
- **Unauthorized use of camera or microphone.** Unauthorized surveillance is a sure sign of malware. Stalker spyware apps have been known to take photos and send them to a C&C server; send a text alert to a hacker and then add the hacker to a live call; use the microphone to record live conversations and then send the recording to a C&C server; report Facebook, and iMessage activity, including passwords and location data; and upload all photos, videos, and text messages to a C&C server.

Note 11

When is spyware legal? Parents can legally install spyware (politely called monitoring software) on a minor child's phone, tablet, or computer, and employers can monitor employee devices when they are company owned. One example of a spyware app is FlexiSPY (*flexispy.com*), an app that runs in the background to monitor text, email, Facebook and other visited websites, apps, photos, videos, contacts, bookmarks, location tracking, and phone calls. It can also record calls and surrounding sounds. It comes with a mobile viewer app installed on the parent's or employer's smartphone.

Mobile Device Malware Removal

 Core 1 Objective 5.5

Here are general steps for removing malware from a mobile device, listed from least to most invasive:

- **Uninstall the offending app.** If you can identify the malware app, close the app and uninstall it. If the app won't uninstall, force stop the app or any background processes that belong to the app. Then try again to uninstall the app.
- **Update the OS.** Check to see if any updates are available for the device.
- **Perform a factory reset.** The most surefire way to remove malware is to back up data and other content, reset the device to its factory default state, and then restore the content from backup. How to perform a factory reset is covered in the module "Mobile Device Security."

After you have removed malware on a mobile device, you will want to keep it clean. Here are a few tips:

- Keep OS updates current.
- Educate users about the importance of privacy settings (for example, disable cookies, and turn off Bluetooth when it's not in use). Also, users should not open email attachments or download shared files from untrusted sources.
- Consider installing an anti-malware app. Search online reviews, and consider the features offered before deciding on an anti-malware app. An anti-malware app, such as Avast shown in Figure 9-42, can scan apps and files for malware, scan for unauthorized surveillance, monitor security and privacy settings, find the device when it's lost, lock and remote wipe it, and maintain automatic updates. It might even include a firewall or a VPN feature.

Figure 9-42   Avast performs regular scans once a day on an Android device

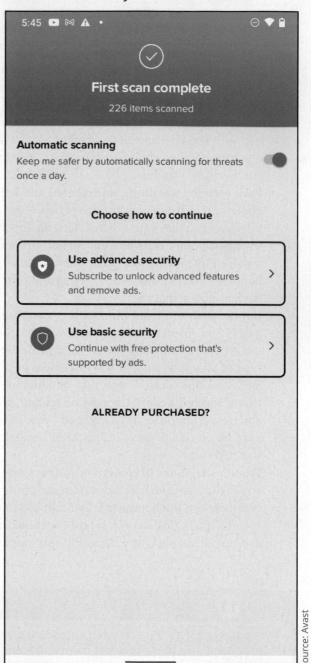

Source: Avast

Other Common Problems and Solutions

 Core 1 Objective 5.5

Several common problems with mobile devices can be addressed with a little understanding of what may have gone wrong behind the scenes. Here's a description of how to handle some common problems:

Display and Touchscreen Issues

Problems with the display and touchscreen might include the following:

- **Malfunctioning touch response.** Most smartphones today never need touch screen calibration, which is realigning the screen to touch. However, for Android, you can download and install the free Touchscreen Calibration app. There is no such app for an iPhone or iPad. If you think calibration is needed on these devices, Apple recommends you first try rebooting the device. If that doesn't work, go to Settings, and reset all settings. The next step is to take the phone to an Apple service center for repair.

  Here are some general tips to try when a touch screen is giving you problems:
  - Clean the screen with a soft, lint-free cloth.
  - Don't use the touch screen when your hands are wet or you are wearing gloves.
  - Restart the device.
  - Remove any plastic sheet or film protecting the touch screen. Some screen protectors are too thick and interfere with the touch screen interface. Bubbles and debris under the screen protector can also cause problems. Use a screen protector that is approved for your device, and carefully follow instructions for installing it. Turn on the screen protector's touch sensitivity setting if available.
  - If you recently installed a third-party app when the touch screen became unresponsive, try uninstalling the app.
  - Sometimes touch response and displays are affected by settings on the accessibility menu in the Settings app (for Android, see Figure 9-43).

- **Digitizer issues.** A mobile device screen contains three layers: a thin layer of glass, a digitizer, and the LCD screen that displays the graphical interface. The digitizer, also called a touch screen, is an electrical sheet just under the glass that turns a tap or swipe into digital data transmitted to the OS. The digitizer is often fused to the LCD component. When the digitizer stops working, touch does not work, and it's time to replace the digitizer. When you repair a device's screen, in most situations, you replace the entire screen—including the glass, digitizer, and LCD—as one component.

- **Broken screen.** If you can still use the device, first transfer all the data and settings to your computer or the cloud. How to do that is covered in the module "Mobile Device Security." If the device is under warranty, follow the warranty holder's directions for repairs or replacement. Alternately, you can take the device to a repair center or replace the screen yourself. For most mobile devices, you can find teardown instructions, videos, tools, and replacement parts for purchase online at various websites, such as *ifixit. com* (see Figure 9-44).

Figure 9-43 Accessibility settings can make a mobile device act in unexpected ways

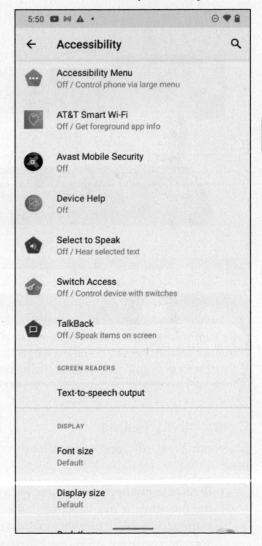

Figure 9-44 At *ifixit.com,* you can find instructions and purchase tools or parts to replace an iPhone screen

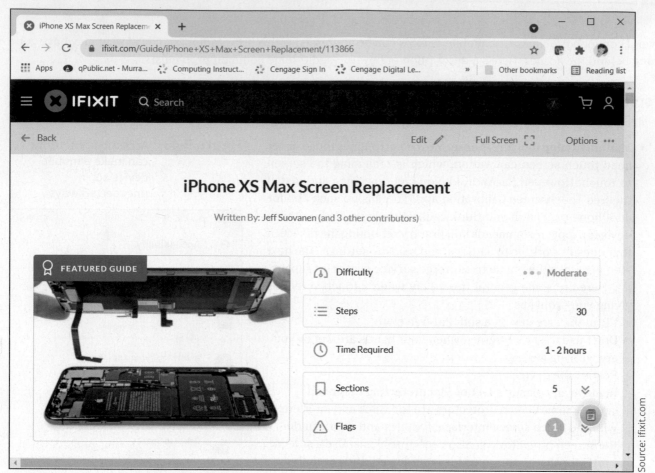

Source: ifixit.com

> **Caution** (!)
>
> Be sure to check out a cell phone repair (CPR) shop before you trust it with your device. Although there are many trustworthy businesses, some have been known to trade expensive parts inside a phone for cheap plastic ones while they perform a repair. In addition, the quality of the replacement components contributes to the success of the repair.

Connectivity Issues

Bluetooth, Wi-Fi, NFC, and Apple AirDrop connections may experience connectivity issues, such as those described here:

- **Bluetooth connectivity issues.** Turn the Bluetooth radio off and then back on again. Devices typically limit the time they're available for pairing, so reactivating Bluetooth restarts the pairing process. In Bluetooth settings, you might be able to adjust the visibility timeout so devices have more time to discover each other. You can also delete all known Bluetooth devices in the Settings app to try the pairing process from the beginning. Sometimes an OS update will cause issues with Wi-Fi network connectivity or Bluetooth pairings. In this case, reset network settings in the Settings app. This restores network settings to factory defaults, and then you can attempt pairing again.
- **Wi-Fi connectivity problems.** Intermittent connectivity problems or no wireless connectivity might be caused by problems with the signal that is being broadcast from the router or access point. First make sure the access point and router are working correctly, that they're positioned closely enough to each other and the device, that the Wi-Fi network you want to connect to is visible to the device (not hidden), and that

you're using the correct security key. For Wi-Fi issues on the device side, first start with Wi-Fi settings in the Settings app for the network to which you're trying to connect. Try renewing the IP address, and if that doesn't work, tell the device to forget the network (see Figure 9-45), and then retry connecting to the network. Finally, try resetting the network settings. By default, many mobile devices stop attempting to reconnect to a weak Wi-Fi signal to conserve battery power, but you can sometimes change this setting so the device will attempt to maintain a connection even with a weak signal.

- **Near-field communication (NFC) issues.** NFC range between devices should be less than eight inches. Verify the battery has at least a 75% charge and the OS is up to date. Try removing the device cover, which might be hindering a good wireless connection. With Android, to resolve NFC issues, try updating the Google Pay app. If you are trying to pay using a manufacturer's pay app, such as Samsung Pay, try updating the app, erasing data in the app, forcing the app to close, and then reopening the app. If NFC issues began immediately after an OS update, try a hard boot, which usually fixes an NFC issue after an OS update. If problems persist, consider a factory reset and restore from backup.

- **AirDrop connectivity issues.** AirDrop uses Bluetooth to find other Apple devices to connect with and then uses a peer-to-peer Wi-Fi connection to transmit files. Because of Bluetooth limits, the devices must be within a 30-foot range. For AirDrop to work, both Bluetooth and Wi-Fi radios must be turned on. To make the initial contact, both devices must be awake and AirDrop turned on and discoverable. To allow a Mac computer to be discovered by AirDrop, in the Finder window, select **AirDrop** in the left pane, and select an option in the right pane (see Figure 9-46). If you still have difficulty connecting, try turning AirDrop off and back on. To use the connection, select items to share, and then tap the share icon (see Figure 9-47).

Figure 9-45   Forget the Wi-Fi network and try to connect again

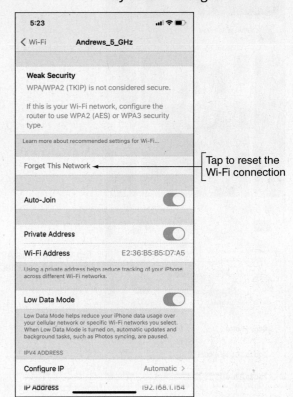

Figure 9-46   Allow the Mac computer to be discovered by other AirDrop devices

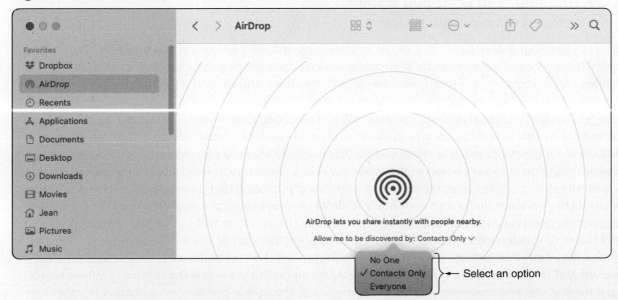

Figure 9-47 Share selected items over AirDrop

Tap to select the AirDrop device to receive the selected items

Damaged Ports and Liquid Damage

Physical damage to ports can include the following:

- **Physically damaged port.** Android devices might use a microUSB or USB-C port, and Apple devices use a Lightning port. Their connectors are shown earlier, in Figures 9-28 and 9-29. If a port is not working, try blowing out the port with compressed air. Dust or lint may be stuck in the port. Using a toothpick or needle to clean out a port is not recommended.

- **Water or other liquid damage.** When you connect a cable to an iPhone or iPad Lightning port and the device detects liquid in the port, it displays a Liquid Detected alert. Charging is not available, and accessories using the port won't connect. For any mobile device, don't use the port until it's completely dry. Tap your phone gently to shake out excess liquid. Put it in a dry place, in front of a cool fan. Wait at least 30 minutes before trying the port again. Don't use heat or compressed air to dry your device. For Android devices that are not under warranty, remove the battery to speed up drying.

Note 12

In an emergency, you might need to use or charge your phone even if it's wet. In this situation, Apple recommends you dismiss the Liquid Detected alert and try charging your phone anyway or use a wireless charger. Although recommended on many websites, Apple says not to put your device in a bag of rice to dry it out.

Battery, Overheating, and Charging Issues

Problems with the battery can include the following:

- **Improper charging.** A device charging slowly or not charging at all might be caused by a loose connection between the device and charging cable or electrical outlet, a damaged port the charger is used, or the electrical outlet. Do the simple things first: check the cable connections, and verify the electrical outlet is working. Try cleaning the port and exchanging the charging cable. Make sure the device is not overheating; when a device gets too hot, charging will stop. Try restarting and rebooting your device. Can you replace the battery?

- **Poor battery health.** Too many apps or malware running in the background will drain the battery quickly, as will Wi-Fi, Bluetooth, or other wireless technologies. Disable wireless connections and close apps when you're not using them to save battery juice. Consider that malware might be at work. If the battery charge still lasts an extremely short time, try exchanging the charging cable. If that doesn't work, exchange the battery unless the device is under warranty. Many Android devices have replaceable batteries, so if a battery is performing poorly, consider replacing it. Try searching the *ifixit.com* website on the device brand and model to see how complicated it is to replace the battery and the cost of a new battery.

- **Overheating or swollen battery.** For a true overheating problem where the device is too hot to touch safely, power off and replace the device. However, all devices can get fairly warm if the display is left on for too long, if the surrounding environment is particularly hot, if the device is sitting on a blanket or other soft surface, if the case is not properly vented, if the battery is going bad, or if the device remains plugged in to a power source for a long period of time. Don't use a mobile device for too long in direct sunlight, turn off the display when you're not using it, and close apps that you're not using. This will also help conserve battery power. Also, using the device as a mobile hotspot can stress the battery and cause it to overheat.

If you know where the battery is located inside a mobile device, check for heat originating from that area of the device. If the area is hot, replacing the battery might be your solution. First check if the phone is under warranty. If the phone is not under warranty, open the case, and examine the battery for damage. Is it swollen or warped? If so, replace the battery. If the phone is under warranty, do not open it. Instead, see if you can tell if the battery is swollen or warped by laying the phone on a flat surface. If the phone itself appears warped, take it in for repair.

> **Note 13**
>
> Some Android smartphones provide information about the device when you enter *#*#4636#*#* in the phone's dialer keypad. In the screen that appears, select Battery Information. If the Battery Health screen reports "unknown," suspect a bad battery. The screen also reports the temperature of the battery, which should be less than 40°C.

Module Summary

Mobile Devices, Operating Systems, Connections, and Accessories

- An IT support technician might be called on to service mobile devices such as smartphones and tablets, and, therefore, needs to know the basics of using and supporting Android, iOS, and iPadOS mobile operating systems.
- A mobile device might have several antennas for wireless connections—primarily Wi-Fi, GPS, Bluetooth, NFC, and cellular. The device uses a Wi-Fi or cellular antenna to connect to a LAN (local area network), a WAN (wide area network), or to create its own hotspot, and it uses Bluetooth or NFC to connect to a PAN (personal area network). A wired connection might use a microUSB, miniUSB, USB-C, or proprietary port, such as the Lightning port by Apple, for syncing with a computer or tethering to provide the computer with cellular WAN access.

Mobile Apps for Business Use

- Large corporations use mobile device management (MDM) software on mobile devices to secure and back up their content on the device. Mobile application management (MAM) software enhances MDM by providing additional protection for corporate apps and data.
- Email can be accessed on a mobile device through an email client embedded in the mobile OS or through third-party commercial mail apps. Microsoft Exchange is a private enterprise email service that is hosted on corporation or ISP servers.
- Syncing mirrors app data and other content among your devices and the cloud. Apple and Google both offer syncing that is linked to your Apple or Google account. In addition, Microsoft offers Microsoft 365 and OneDrive or SharePoint syncing as do other software and cloud providers.

Troubleshooting Mobile Devices

- To troubleshoot a mobile device using tools in the OS, you can close running apps, uninstall and reinstall an app, update the OS, and restart and reboot the device.
- Common problems a technician might face when supporting mobile devices include malware, malfunctioning touch response, digitizer issues, a broken screen, connectivity issues, damaged ports, liquid damage, improper charging, poor battery health, overheating, and a swollen battery.

Key Terms

For explanations of key terms, see the Glossary for this text.

2G	CDMA (Code Division	IMSI (International	near-field
3G	Multiple Access)	Mobile Subscriber	communication
4G	cellular data	Identity)	(NFC)
4G LTE	commercial mail app	iOS	notifications
5G	dock	iPad	off-boarding
ActiveSync	favorites tray	iPadOS	on-boarding
agent	Google account	iPhone	paired
AirDrop	Google Play	Lightning port	Preferred Roaming
Android	GPS (Global Positioning	MDM policies	List (PRL)
app drawer	System)	Microsoft 365	RFID (radio-frequency
Apple ID	GSM (Global System for	Microsoft Exchange	identification)
biometric	Mobiles)	mobile application	smartphone
authentication	IMEI (International	management (MAM)	tablet
BYOD (bring your own	Mobile Equipment	mobile device	two-factor
device)	Identity)	management (MDM)	authentication (2FA)

Thinking Critically

These questions are designed to prepare you for the critical thinking required for the A+ exams and may use information from other modules and the web.

1. Which of these network connections would allow your smartphone to sync your photos to your online account? (Choose all that apply.)

   a. Wi-Fi

   b. Bluetooth

   c. GPS

   d. Cellular

2. While visiting a coffee shop, you see a poster advertising a concert for a music group you'd love to see. You notice there's an NFC tag at the bottom with additional information about the concert. Which of the following devices would likely be able to read the NFC tag?

   a. GPS

   b. Smartphone

   c. eReader

   d. Laptop

3. You work for a company that provides the same smartphone model for dozens of its employees. While troubleshooting one smartphone that won't connect to the cellular network, you call the provider's tech support number for some assistance. The technician asks for the device's IMEI. What is she trying to determine?

   a. The OS version on the phone

   b. The specific device you're calling about

   c. The SIM card installed in the device

   d. The IP address of the phone on the cellular provider's data network

4. You're at the store to buy a car charger for your dad's iPhone. There are several options, with many different types of connectors. Which of these connectors should you choose?

   a. USB-C

   b. microUSB

   c. Lightning

   d. VGA

5. Place the following information in the correct fields in Figure 9-48 to add an email account to a smartphone using port 143 for the incoming mail server and port 25 for the outgoing mail server (not all information will be used):

   - imap-mail.sample.com
   - p@ssw0rd
   - pop-mail.sample.com
   - mjones@sample.com
   - smtp-mail.sample.com
   - Mary Jones

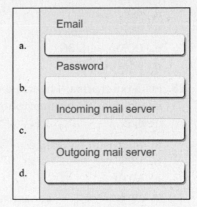

Figure 9-48 Configure email for a smartphone

6. Congratulations! You just bought a new-to-you car, and it comes with a media system that can sync with your iPhone. You're concerned about data usage on your cell phone, so before you go pick up your car, you decide to download the necessary app at home while you're connected to Wi-Fi. What app do you need to download?

7. You're traveling across the country for a much-anticipated vacation. When you get there, your smartphone seems to be having trouble connecting to the local cellular network. You call the provider, and the technician suggests you update the PRL. Why might this help? Where would you find this option on your Android smartphone to perform the update?

8. You're trying to cast a video presentation from your tablet to a projector for a training session with some new hires. Although you tested it successfully yesterday, today the connection is not cooperating. You've closed apps you're not using, and you've checked that the projector and the tablet are working otherwise. Of the following troubleshooting steps, which should you try first? Second?

   a. Restart the projector.
   b. Restart the tablet.
   c. Reinstall the presentation app.
   d. Verify that you have Internet access on the tablet.

9. Suppose you and your friend want to exchange lecture notes taken during class. She has an iPhone, and you have an iPad. What is the easiest way to do the exchange?

   a. Copy the files to an SD card and move the SD card to each device.
   b. Drop the files in OneDrive and share notebooks with each other.
   c. Send a text to each other with the files attached.
   d. Transfer the files through an AirDrop connection.

10. Jorge has asked you to explain to him how a touch pen can work with his Android tablet. Which of the following are true statements about touch pens? (Choose all that apply.)

    a. A touch pen might use a Bluetooth connection to write on a tablet.
    b. A touch pen is made of material that can touch the screen without damaging it.
    c. A touch pen might need charging.
    d. A touch pen does not use a Wi-Fi connection.

11. Android and iOS both offer a quick swipe to get to some basic settings such as those that allow you to turn on Bluetooth and adjust brightness. What are these tools called?

    a. Android Notifications and iOS Control Center
    b. Android Settings app and iOS Notifications
    c. Android Control Center and iOS Notifications
    d. Android Notifications and iOS Notifications

12. You are asked to help change some settings on an older smartphone. When you examine the phone, you find it doesn't have a slot for a SIM card. What type of technology can you confidently say this phone is not using? (Choose all that apply.)

    a. 4G
    b. 5G
    c. CDMA with 3G
    d. GSM with 3G

13. In an enterprise, when an employee is allowed to use their smartphone for business, which software is used to verify the smartphone satisfies the security requirements needs to protect enterprise data on the device?

    a. Microsoft Exchange
    b. VPN
    c. MDM
    d. ActiveSync

14. Dyane asks for your help to understand why her corporate email is not working as she expects on her tablet. The tablet has no cellular capability, but she connects to Wi-Fi when at work and at home. When she's at a customer site and needs to find a particular email about the customer, she finds that email is not available. What can you tell Dyane about the situation?

    a. Most likely, the email app is corrupted, and she needs to uninstall and install it again.
    b. Corporate policies don't allow email to be stored on her device.
    c. ActiveSync is enabled.
    d. She needs to download all her email while she's connected to Wi-Fi.

15. A friend calls to tell you they have just dropped their iPhone in water. They ask you what to do. What advice can you give your friend? (Choose all that apply.)

    a. Take the phone out of the case and dry off the surface.
    b. Place the phone in a bag of rice so the rice can absorb the moisture.
    c. Use a hair dryer set to medium heat to dry the phone.
    d. Set the phone in front of a cool fan.

Hands-On Projects

Hands-On Project 9-1

Selecting a Mobile Device

Est. Time: 15 minutes
Core 1 Objective: 1.3

Shop for a new smartphone or tablet. Be sure to read some reviews about a device you are considering. Select two devices that you might consider buying, and answer the following questions:

1. What is the device brand, model, and price?

2. What is the OS and version? Amount of storage space? Screen size? Types of network connections? Battery life? Camera pixels?

3. What do you like about each device? Which would you choose and why?

Hands-On Project 9-2

Exploring ifixit.com for Cost of Repair

Est. Time: 15 minutes
Core 1 Objective: 5.5

A friend just dropped their iPhone 11 Pro and broke the screen. They have asked you to help them decide how much they should pay for the repair and if you are willing to do it. Do the following:

1. Search the *ifixit.com* website, which is a wiki-based site with tons of guides for tearing down, repairing, and reassembling all kinds of products, including smartphones, tablets, and laptops. Locate the directions for an iPhone 11 Pro screen replacement. and browse through the instructions.

2. How much would the parts for the repair cost if they are purchased at *ifixit.com*?

3. How much would the tools to do the repair cost if they are purchased at *ifixit.com*?

4. What is the cost of a refurbished iPhone 11 Pro sold on other sites?

5. What advice should you give your friend? Is it better to buy a replacement phone or have the broken phone repaired? If you were willing to do the repair, how much would you charge for the labor?

Hands-On Project 9-3

Syncing to the Cloud

Est. Time: 15 minutes
Core 1 Objective: 1.4

Using an Android smartphone or tablet, do the following to manage data syncing on an Android device:

1. On your computer, go to *google.com* and sign in using your Google account. Browse through photos, contacts, and your calendar. Which of this content Is currently syncing with your Android device?

2. To manage what is synced, on your Android device, open the **Settings** app, tap **Google**, and tap **Settings for Google apps**. Set Google contacts for syncing.

3. Open your **Calendar** app, and verify calendars are syncing.

4. Make an entry in your calendar for a meeting tomorrow.

5. On your computer, go to Google Calendar. Did the meeting sync to your Google calendar?

6. Make an entry in the calendar.

7. On your Android device, verify the event showed up on your Android Calendar.

For an Apple device, do the following:

1. On your computer, go to *icloud.com*, and sign in using your Apple account. Browse through your mail, contacts, photos, notes, and iCloud Drive. What content is currently syncing with your Apple device?

2. To manage what syncs to iCloud, on your iPhone or iPad, open the **Settings** app, tap your account name, and tap **iCloud**. Turn on the items you want to sync. Make sure Notes is syncing.

3. On your device, type an entry into Notes.

4. On your computer, go to *icloud.com*. Did your entry in Notes sync to the cloud?

5. Make an entry in Notes.

6. Return to your Apple device. Did the entry show up in your Notes app?

Hands-On Project 9-4

Syncing Android Files to Google Drive

Est. Time: 15 minutes
Core 1 Objective: 1.4

Sometimes an Android user might want to sync data files between an Android device and Google Drive. To set up a two-way sync, you can use the Autosync for Google Drive third-party app. You'll need an Android device to do this project:

1. If you don't already have a Google account, go to *google.com* and create one. It's free and comes with 15 GB free storage. Create a folder in Google Drive to sync with your Android device. What did you name the folder?

2. If the Autosync for Google Drive app is not already installed on your Android device, download and install it.

3. Open the **Autosync** app where you set up the folder pair to sync. Set the app to sync your Pictures folder with the folder you created on Google Drive. Enable two-way syncing. Take a photo on your device.

4. Sign in to Google Drive. Did the photo appear on your Google Drive? Copy a photo from your computer to the Google Drive folder.

5. Check your Android device. Is the file on your device? The sync might take a few moments. If you don't want to wait, open the **Autosync** app, go to **SYNCED FOLDERS**, tap the three-dots menu beside the synced folder, and tap **Sync now**.

Real Problems, Real Solutions

Real Problem 9-1

Configuring Email on a Mobile Device

Est. Time: 15 minutes
Core 1 Objective: 1.4

For this project, use an Android device and an email account that you have not already set up on the device. If you don't already have an email account you can use, you can create a free one using *mail.google.com*, *outlook.live.com*, or *mail.yahoo.com*.

Follow these steps to manually configure the email client on an Android device:

1. Open the **Gmail** app. If an email address is already set up, tap the account profile photo, and tap **Add another account**. If this is the first email setup, tap **Add an email address**. Gmail can automatically configure email from many providers. Because it's essential that you know how to manually configure email on a mobile device, tap **Other**.

2. Add your email address and tap **MANUAL SETUP**. Check with your email provider to determine whether to use POP3 or IMAP. What is the main difference between these two protocols? What are the ports for these two protocols? What are the secure ports for these protocols?

3. Enter the password and click **NEXT**. On the Incoming server settings screen, verify the incoming server name, and, for POP3, decide when you want to delete mail on the server, and click **NEXT**. If the OS needs more direction for security settings, you might need to tell it which security protocol the email provider uses. Options are STARTTLS, SSL/TLS, and None.

4. Verify the outgoing server name and security settings, and tap **NEXT**.

5. Set your account options as desired, then tap **NEXT**.

6. If you were successful, you'll get a notice confirming your account is set up. Set the account name and your name as desired; then tap **NEXT**. If you weren't successful, backtrack and troubleshoot to solve the problem.

7. When you're finished, send an email to a classmate, and check an email sent from someone else to confirm your email account is working on your smartphone.

8. You need to know how to change the settings on an account. What steps are required to change the server settings for the account you just added?

9. You should also know how to remove an email account from a mobile device. What steps are required to remove the email account you just added?

Real Problem 9-2

Exporting and Importing Contacts

Est. Time: 30 minutes
Core 1 Objective: 1.4
Note: This problem works well as a group problem where at least one person in the group has an Apple device and another person in the group has an Android device. If you or a group member doesn't have access to an iPhone or iPad, Apple account, Android device, and Google account, list the basic steps to take rather than actually doing the work.

Jamal has just purchased a new Android phone and has asked for your help to import his contacts from his old iPhone to his new Android. If necessary, research how to help Jamal, and then do the following:

1. Export three contacts on your iPhone or iPad, using a single export operation.

2. Import these contacts to an Android device.

   Answer the following questions:

1. What is the file extension of your exported file? What does the three-character file extension stand for?

2. Use Notepad to examine the contents of the export file. In the file, what marks the beginning and end of the data for one contact?

3. List the steps you took to export and import the contacts.

   Conversely, suppose someone asks how to export contacts from an Android to an Apple device. Answer the following questions:

1. Which file types can Google use to export contacts?

2. Which file type would you use if you were exporting to an Apple device?

Module
10

Supporting Printers

Module Objectives

1 Discuss printer types and features

2 Install and share printers, and manage printer features, add-on devices, and the printer queue

3 Perform routine maintenance tasks necessary to support printers

4 Troubleshoot printer problems

Core 1 Certification Objectives

3.6 Given a scenario, deploy and configure multifunction devices/ printers and settings.

3.7 Given a scenario, install and replace printer consumables.

5.6 Given a scenario, troubleshoot and resolve printer issues.

Introduction

This module explores in depth the most popular types of printers and how to support them. As you work through the module, you learn about printer types and features, how to install a local or network printer, and how to share a printer with others on a network. You learn how to manage printer features, add-on devices, shared printers, and print jobs. Finally, you learn about maintaining and troubleshooting printers.

Printer Types and Features

 Core 1 Objectives 3.6, 3.7

Printers come in many different types with varying features and are chosen by the production needs of users. Printers are capable of printing anything from a simple document to an entire building. Commonly, IT technicians support printers that print documents, receipts, photos, and even 3D objects. Many of these printers are multifunctional and not only print but also scan and fax documents or photos.

On the output side of this process, the major categories of printer types include laser, inkjet (ink dispersion), impact, thermal, and 3D printers. In the following sections, we look at the different types of printers for desktop computing. Table 10-1 lists some popular printer manufacturers.

Table 10-1 Printer manufacturers

Printer Manufacturer	Website
Brother	*brother-usa.com*
Canon	*usa.canon.com*
Epson	*epson.com*
Hewlett-Packard	*hp.com*
Konica Minolta	*kmbs.konicaminolta.us*
Lexmark	*lexmark.com*
Oki Data	*okidata.com*
Xerox	*xerox.com*
Zebra Technologies	*zebra.com*

Scanners

As an output device, a printer converts digital data to hard copy on paper. Some printers are also multifunction input devices that can work as a scanner to scan printed paper and print additional hard copies of that information or create a digital file from it. The file can then be saved on a computer or sent out over a phone or network connection. A scanner can also be a dedicated device with no printing, copying, or faxing capability. Scanners, whether dedicated devices or integrated in a printer, come in two primary types:

- **Flatbed scanners** must be fed one page at a time, with each page being lined up on a glass surface.
- **ADF (automatic document feeder) scanners** can automatically process a stack of papers, cards, or envelopes, pulling each page individually into a roller system for scanning and then spitting it out into a separate tray.

Note

For heavy business use, sometimes it's best to purchase a dedicated machine for each purpose instead of bundling many functions into a single machine. For example, if you need a scanner and a printer, purchase a good printer and a good scanner rather than a combo machine. Routine maintenance and troubleshooting are easier and less expensive on single-purpose machines, although the initial cost is higher. On the other hand, for home or small office use, a combo device can save money and counter space.

Exam Tip ✔

The A+ Core 1 exam might give you a scenario that requires you to perform installation or maintenance steps on these types of printers: laser, inkjet, impact, thermal, and 3D printers.

Laser Printers

Core 1 Objective 3.7

A **laser printer** is a type of electro-photographic printer that can range from a small personal desktop model to a large network printer capable of handling and printing large volumes continuously. Figure 10-1 shows an example of a typical laser printer for a small office.

Figure 10-1   A Samsung Xpress color multifunction laser printer

10

Laser printers require the interaction of mechanical, electrical, and optical technologies. They work by placing toner on an electrically charged rotating drum called the **imaging drum**, transferring the toner onto paper as the paper moves through the system, and then fusing the toner to the paper. Figure 10-2 shows the seven steps of laser printing.

Note that Figure 10-2 shows only a cross-section of the drum, mechanisms, and paper. Remember that the drum is as wide as a sheet of paper. The mirror, blades, and rollers in the drawing are also as wide as paper. Also know that toner responds to a charge and moves from one surface to another if the second surface has a more positive charge than the first.

Figure 10-2 The seven progressive steps of laser printing

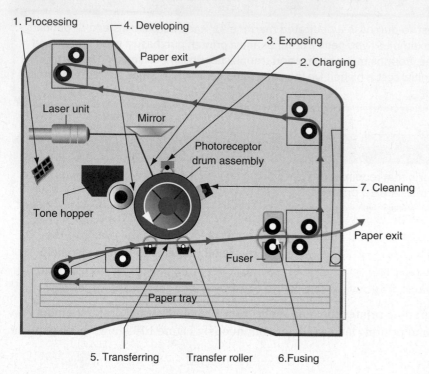

Laser Printing Steps

The seven steps of laser printing are described next:

1. **Processing the image.** A laser printer processes and prints an entire page at one time. The page data comes to the printer encoded in a **page description language (PDL)**, which describes the appearance of the printed page that the printer understands. The firmware inside the printer processes the incoming data to produce a bitmap (a bunch of bits in rows and columns) of the final page, which is stored in the printer's memory. One bitmap image is produced for monochrome images. For color images, one bitmap is produced for each of four colors. (The colors are blue, red, yellow, and black—better known as cyan, magenta, yellow, and black, and sometimes written as CMYK.)

2. **Charging or conditioning.** During **charging**, the drum is conditioned by a roller that places a high, uniform electrical charge of –600 V to –1000 V on the surface of the drum. The roller is called the primary charging roller or primary corona, and it is charged by a high-voltage power supply assembly. For some printers, a corona wire is used instead of the charging roller to charge the drum.

3. **Exposing or writing.** A laser beam controlled by motors and a mirror scans across the drum until it completes the correct number of passes. The laser beam is turned on and off continually as it makes a single pass down the length of the drum, once for each raster line, so that dots are exposed only where toner should go to print the image. A raster line, or scan line, is the horizontal line of dots across the page or image. For example, for a 1200 dots-per-inch (dpi) printer, the beam makes 1200 passes for every inch of the drum circumference. This means that 1200 dots are exposed or not exposed along the drum for every inch of linear pass. The 1200 dots per inch down this single pass, combined with 1200 passes

per inch of drum circumference, accomplish the resolution of 1200 × 1200 dots per square inch of many laser printers. For each exposed dot, the laser beam applies a charge of –100 V, which is significantly more positive than for the unexposed dots on the drum. The charge on this image area will be used in the developing stage to transmit toner to the drum surface.

4. **Developing.** The developing cylinder applies toner to the surface of the drum. The toner is charged between –200 V and –500 V, and it sticks to the developing cylinder because of a magnet inside it.

   A control blade prevents too much toner from sticking to the cylinder surface. As the cylinder rotates very close to the drum, the toner is attracted to the parts of the drum surface that have a –100 V charge, and it is repelled from the more negatively charged parts of the drum surface. The result is that toner sticks to the drum where the laser beam has hit, and it is repelled from the areas where the laser beam has not hit.

5. **Transferring.** During transfer, a strong electrical charge draws the toner off the drum onto the paper. This is the first step that takes place outside the cartridge and the first step that involves the paper. The soft, black **transfer roller** puts a positive charge on the paper to pull the toner from the drum onto the paper. Then the static charge eliminator weakens the charges on both the paper and the drum, so the paper does not stick to the drum. The stiffness of the paper and the small radius of the drum also help the paper move away from the drum and toward the fusing assembly. Very thin paper can wrap around the drum, which is why printer manuals usually instruct you to use only paper designated for laser printers.

6. **Fusing.** The **fuser assembly** uses heat and pressure to fuse the toner to the paper. Up to this point, the toner is merely sitting on the paper. The fusing rollers apply heat to the paper, which causes the toner to melt, and the rollers apply pressure to bond the melted toner into the paper. The temperature of the rollers is monitored by the printer. If the temperature exceeds an allowed maximum value (for example, 410°F), the printer shuts down.

7. **Cleaning.** A sweeping blade cleans the drum of any residual toner. The charge left on the drum is then neutralized. Some printers use erase lamps in the top cover of the printer for this purpose. The lamps use red light so they won't damage the photosensitive drum.

For color laser printers, the writing process repeats four times, one for each toner color of cyan, magenta, yellow, and black. Each color might require a separate image drum, although many color printers can use the same drum for all four colors. Then the paper passes to the fusing stage, where the fuser bonds all toner to the paper and aids in blending the four tones to form specific colors.

Exam Tip ✔

The A+ Core 1 exam expects you to know these laser printer terms: imaging drum, fuser assembly, transfer belt, transfer roller, pickup roller, separate pads, and duplexing assembly.

Note 2

Watching a video of the laser printing process can be helpful when trying to remember how it all works. A quick search on YouTube returns several good videos about the laser printing process. Watching a short video is worth the time.

Cartridges and Other Replaceable Parts

The charging, exposing, developing, and cleaning steps use the printer components that undergo the most wear. To make the printer last longer, some or all of these steps are done inside a removable cartridge that can be replaced as a single unit. For older printers, all four steps are done inside one cartridge. For newer printers, the charging, exposing, and cleaning steps are done inside the image drum cartridge. The developing cylinder is located inside the toner cartridge. The transferring is done using a **transfer belt** that can be replaced on some printers, and the fusing is done inside a fuser cartridge, which also might be replaceable.

By using these multiple cartridges inside laser printers, the cost of maintaining a printer is reduced. You can replace one cartridge without having to replace them all. The toner cartridge needs replacing the most often, followed by the image drum, the fuser cartridge, and the transfer assembly, in that order.

Other printer parts that might need replacing include the **pickup roller**, which pushes a sheet of paper forward from the paper tray, and the **separation pad** (also called a **separate pad**), which keeps more than one sheet of paper from moving forward. If the pickup roller is worn, paper may misfeed into the printer. If the separation pad is worn, multiple sheets of paper may be drawn into the printer. Sometimes you can clean a pickup roller or separation pad to prolong its life before it needs replacing.

Note 3

Before replacing expensive parts in a printer, consider whether purchasing a new printer might be more cost-effective than repairing the old one.

Duplexing Assembly

A printer that is able to print on both sides of the paper is called a **duplex printer** or a double-sided printer. Many laser printers and a few inkjet printers offer this feature. After the front of the paper is printed, a **duplexing assembly**, which contains several rollers, turns the paper around and draws it back through the print process to print on the back of the paper. Alternatively, some high-end printers have two print engines so both sides of the paper are printed at the same time.

Inkjet Printers

Core 1 Objective 3.7

An **inkjet printer** (see Figure 10-3) uses a type of ink-dispersion printing and doesn't normally provide the high-quality resolution of laser printers. Inkjet printers are popular because they are small and can print color inexpensively. Most inkjet printers today can print high-quality photos, especially when used with photo-quality paper.

Figure 10-3 An example of an inkjet printer with feeder trays open

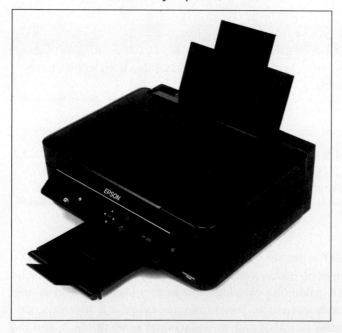

An inkjet printer uses a **print head** that moves across the paper, creating one line of the image with each pass. The printer puts ink on the paper using a matrix of small dots. Different types of inkjet printers form their droplets of ink in different ways. Printer manufacturers use several technologies, one of which is the bubble-jet. Bubble-jet printers use tubes of ink that have tiny resistors near the end of each tube. These resistors heat up and cause the ink to boil. Then a tiny air bubble of ionized ink (ink with an electrical charge) is ejected onto the paper. A typical bubble-jet print head has 64 or 128 tiny nozzles, all of which can fire a droplet simultaneously. (High-end printers can have as many as 3000 nozzles.) Plates carrying a magnetic charge direct the path of ink onto the paper to form shapes.

Inkjet printers include one or more **ink cartridges** to hold the different colors of ink for the printer. Figure 10-4 shows four ink cartridges. A black cartridge is on the left, and the three color cartridges are cyan, yellow, and magenta. For this printer, a print head is built into each ink cartridge.

Figure 10-4   The ink cartridges of an inkjet printer

A stepper motor moves the print head and ink cartridges across the paper using a carriage and belt to move the assembly and stabilizing bars to control the movement (see Figure 10-5). A paper tray can hold a stack of paper, and a paper feeder on the back of the printer can hold a few sheets of paper. The sheets stand up in the feeder and are dispensed one at a time. Rollers pull a single sheet into the printer from the paper tray or paper feeder. A motor powers these rollers and times the sheet going through the printer in the increments needed to print the image. When the printer is not in use, the assemblage sits in the far-right position, which is called the home position or parked position. This position helps protect the ink in the cartridges from drying out. Figure 10-5 shows the assemblage positioned so that the ink cartridges are accessible for replacement.

Figure 10-5   The belt and stabilizing bars used to move the print head across the page

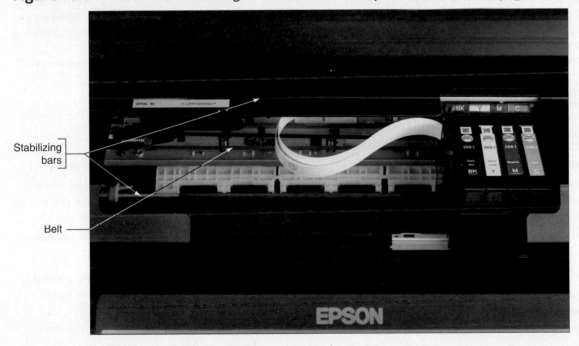

Some inkjet printers offer duplex printing. These printers are larger than normal inkjet printers because of the added space required for the duplexing assembly. For duplex printing, be sure to use heavy paper (rated at 24-pound paper or higher) so the ink doesn't bleed through.

Even with single-sided printing, inkjet printers tend to smudge on inexpensive paper, and they are slower than laser printers. If a printed page later becomes damp, the ink can run and get quite messy. The quality of the paper used with inkjet printers significantly affects the quality of printed output. You should use only paper that is designed for an inkjet printer, and you should use a high-grade paper to get the best results.

Note 4

Weight and brightness are the two primary ways of measuring paper quality. The rated weight of paper (for example, 20–32 pounds) determines the thickness of the paper. Brightness is measured on a scale of 92 to 100.

Note 5

Photos printed on an inkjet printer tend to fade over time, more so than photos produced professionally. To make your photos last longer, use high-quality photo paper (rated at high gloss or studio gloss) and use fade-resistant ink (such as Vivera ink by HP). Then protect these photos from exposure to light, heat, humidity, and polluted air. To best protect photos made by an inkjet printer, keep them in a photo album rather than displayed and exposed to light.

When purchasing an inkjet printer, look for the kind that uses two or four separate cartridges. One cartridge is used for black ink. Three cartridges, one for each color, give better-quality color than one cartridge that holds all three colors. Some low-end inkjet printers use a single three-color cartridge and don't have a black ink cartridge. These printers must combine all colors of ink to produce a dull black. Having a separate cartridge for black ink means that it prints true black and, more important, does not use the more expensive colored ink for black print. To save money, you should be able to replace an empty cartridge without having to replace all cartridges.

Note 6

It's possible to refill an ink cartridge, and many companies will sell you the tools and ink you need as well as show you how to do it. You can also purchase refilled cartridges at reduced prices. When you purchase ink cartridges, make sure you know if they are new or refilled. Also, for best results, don't refill a cartridge more than three times. Many manufacturers and retail shops will accept empty cartridges for recycling.

Impact Printers

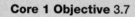 **Core 1 Objective** 3.7

An **impact printer** creates a printed page by using some mechanism that touches or hits the paper, similar to a typewriter. The best-known impact printer is a dot matrix printer, which prints only text that it receives as raw data. It has a print head that moves across the width of the paper, using pins to print a matrix of dots on the page. The pins shoot against a cloth ribbon, which hits the paper, depositing the ink. The ribbon provides both the ink for printing and the lubrication for the pinheads. The quality of the print on an impact printer is poor compared with other printer types. However, you still see impact printers in use for three reasons:

- They use continuous **tractor feeds** and fanfold paper (also called computer paper) rather than individual sheets of paper, making them useful for logging ongoing events or data.
- They can use carbon paper to print multiple copies at the same time.
- They are extremely durable, give little trouble, and seem to last forever.

Exam Tip ✔

The A+ Core 1 exam might give you a scenario that requires you to install or maintain an impact printer's print head, ribbon, and tractor feed, or to work with the impact paper used in the printer.

Maintaining a dot matrix impact printer is easy. The **impact paper** used by these printers comes as a box of fanfold paper or in rolls (used with receipt printers). When the paper is nearing the end of the stack or roll, a color on the edge alerts you to replace the paper. Occasionally, you should replace the ribbon of a dot matrix printer. If the print head fails, check on the cost of replacing the head versus the cost of buying a new printer. Sometimes, the cost of the head is so high that it's best to just buy a new printer. Overheating can damage a print head (see Figure 10-6), so keep it as cool as possible to make it last longer. Keep the printer in a cool, well-ventilated area, and don't use it to print more than 50–75 pages without allowing the head to cool down.

Figure 10-6   Keep the print head of a dot matrix printer as cool as possible so it will last longer

Print head

Thermal Printers

Core 1 Objective 3.7

Thermal printers use heat to create an image. Two types of thermal printers are a direct thermal printer and a thermal transfer printer. The older **direct thermal printer** burns dots onto specially coated paper called **thermal paper**; this process was used by older fax machines. The process requires no ink and does not use a ribbon. Direct thermal printers are often used as receipt printers that use rolls of thermal paper (see Figure 10-7). You know it's time to replace the paper roll on this type of thermal printer when it shows a color strip down one edge. The printed image can fade over time or if it interacts with another heat source or ultraviolet light.

Figure 10-7   The TM-T88V direct thermal printer by EPSON

Courtesy of EPSON America, Inc.

10

A **thermal transfer printer** uses a ribbon that contains wax-based ink. The heating element melts the ribbon (also called foil) onto special thermal paper so it stays glued to the paper as the feed assembly moves it through the printer. Thermal transfer printers are used to print receipts, barcode labels, clothing labels, or container labels. Figure 10-8 shows a thermal transfer printer used to make barcodes and other labels.

Figure 10-8   The GC420 printer by Zebra is both a thermal transfer printer and a direct thermal printer

Courtesy of Zebra Technologies

Thermal printers are reliable and easy to maintain. It's important to regularly clean the print head on a thermal printer because buildup can harden over time and permanently damage the head. Follow the printer manufacturer's directions to clean the print head. Some thermal printer ribbons have a print head cleaning stripe at the end, and it's a good idea to clean the head each time you replace the ribbon. Additionally, some manufacturers suggest cleaning the head with isopropyl alcohol wipes.

When cleaning, remove any dust and debris that get down in the print head assembly. As you work, ground yourself to protect the sensitive heating element against static electricity. Don't touch the heating element with your fingers. You might need to clean it with a lint-free cotton swab dabbed in isopropyl alcohol. Also, to prolong the life of the print head, use the lowest heat setting for the heating element that still gives good printing results.

Exam Tip ✔

The A+ Core 1 exam might give you a scenario that requires you to install or maintain the feed assembly or heating element used in thermal printers, or you might need to work with the special thermal paper used in the older direct thermal printers.

3D Printers

Core 1 Objective 3.7

While impact printers and thermal printers have been around for a very long time, a newer type of printer is the 3D printer. **3D printers** use a plastic filament or a resin to build a 3D model of a digital image. In Figure 10-9, notice the coil of **filament**, a thermoplastic strand, on the left that is fed into the 3D printer, which heats the plastic and deposits thin layer upon layer onto the print bed to build a three-dimensional object. A **print bed** on a 3D printer is where the filament is deposited to build the objects. Some print beds are fixed whereas others move, depending on the technology used in the printer. Filament 3D printers are better able to create hollow objects, and filament is less expensive than resin.

Figure 10-9   A 3D printer heats a plastic filament and layers the plastic to build three-dimensional objects

iStock.com/ zusek

A resin 3D printer uses **resin**, a liquid photopolymer, which is held in a resin tank with a transparent bottom. A resin 3D printer projects UV light up through the bottom of the resin tank to cure layer under layer to build three-dimensional objects. A 3D object printed using resin is printed upside down because it raises up out of the resin tank layer by layer (see Figure 10-10). Resin 3D printers produce objects that are stronger and smoother than filament 3D printers, but resin is more expensive than filament. When using a resin printer, always be sure to wear gloves because the resin is a toxin to your body. To fully harden an object printed using a resin 3D printer, you need a UV light-curing station. Both the resin tank and the print bed are considered consumable parts of a 3D printer.

Figure 10-10   A resin printer prints objects upside down

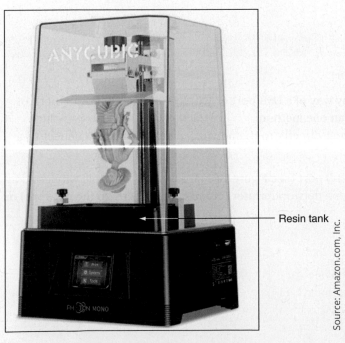

Resin tank

Source: Amazon.com, Inc.

When setting up a 3D printer, make sure the printer is level. The most common file type for a 3D image file is an STL file (.stl), which stands for stereolithography. You can buy premade images online from sites such as *thingiverse.com*. If you want to design your own images, you'll need a 3D modeling program. Some, such as Sketchup (*sketchup.com*) and Tinkercad (*tinkercad.com*), are free and easy to learn. Others have a much steeper learning curve and a higher price in exchange for more features. Any computer used for 3D imaging and design will perform more quickly and gracefully with more RAM and CPU power. Before you start printing, do some research online for tips on getting a cleaner finished product. YouTube has several informative videos by 3D Printing Nerd (*the3dprintingnerd.com*), Matter Hackers (*matterhackers.com*), Thomas Sanladerer (*toms3d.org*), and others.

Now let's turn our attention to using Windows to install, share, and manage printers.

Using Windows to Install, Share, and Manage Printers

 Core 1 Objectives 3.6, 3.7

In this section of the module, you learn to install local and network printers, share an installed printer, secure a shared printer, and remotely use a shared printer. You also learn about how to configure printer add-ons and features. We begin with how to unbox a printer and then move on to installing local and network printers.

To properly unbox a printer, consider the following guidelines:

- Remove the printer from the box, keeping it upright, and remove protective packing foam pieces.
- Place the printer on a flat, hard surface near an outlet. The printer needs room for air movement around it.
- Remove any protective tapes or film from the printer, including the control screen.
- Plug the power cord into the printer and the outlet.
- Press the power button on the printer, and allow it to turn on fully.
- Add paper to the paper tray. If needed, remove protective tape from ink cartridges.
- Configure settings for intended use.

Local or Network Printer

 Core 1 Objectives 3.6, 3.7

A printer connects to a single computer or to the network:

- A **local printer** connects directly to a computer by way of a USB port or wireless connection (Bluetooth or Wi-Fi). Most printers these days support more than one method.
- A **network printer** has an Ethernet port to connect directly to the network or uses Wi-Fi to connect to a wireless access point.

Some printers have both an Ethernet port and a USB-B port (see Figure 10-11), as well as multiple wireless connection options. These printers can be installed as either a network printer (connecting directly to the network) or a local printer (connecting directly to a computer).

Figure 10-11   This printer has an Ethernet port and a USB-B port

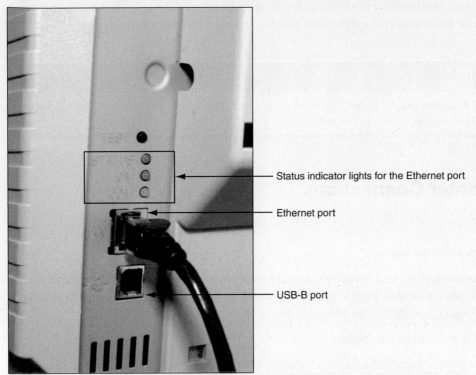

Status indicator lights for the Ethernet port

Ethernet port

USB-B port

Two ways to install a printer and make it available on a network are as follows:

- **Shared local printer.** Connect a local printer to a computer on the network, and then share the printer through the computer's network connection. See the local printer and computer A in Figure 10-12. Keep in mind the following two requirements when sharing a local printer:
  - For a shared local printer to be available to other computers on the network, the host computer must be turned on and not in sleep or standby mode.
  - For another computer on the network to use the shared printer, the appropriate printer drivers for the computer's OS must be installed on the remote computer.

Figure 10-12   A shared local printer and a network printer

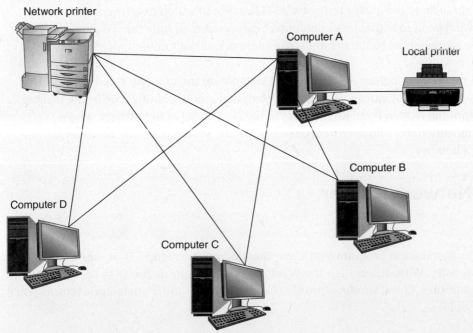

Network printer

Computer A

Local printer

Computer B

Computer D

Computer C

- **Network printer.** A network printer can connect directly to a network with its own NIC (see the network printer in Figure 10-12), and it is identified on the network by its IP address or host name. To use the printer, any computer on the network can install this printer and print to it; this is called **remote printing**.

Note 7

A computer can have several printers installed. Of these, Windows designates one printer to be the **default printer**, which is the one Windows prints to unless another is selected.

Wired or Wireless Printer Connections

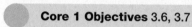
Core 1 Objectives 3.6, 3.7

Connecting a wired printer (USB or Ethernet) is easy:

- **USB.** Plug the USB cable into the printer and computer, and Windows installs the printer automatically.
- **Ethernet.** Plug the Ethernet cable into the printer and network wall jack, switch, or router, and install the printer as a network printer on any computer on the network.

Connecting a wireless printer is a little more complex:

- **Bluetooth.** For a Bluetooth printer installed as a local printer, turn on Bluetooth in Windows, move the printer within range of the computer, and watch as the two Bluetooth devices pair up. While you might need to navigate some of the Bluetooth settings on the printer's display to enable pairing, the process works like most other Bluetooth connections.
- **Wi-Fi infrastructure mode.** In **infrastructure mode**, Wi-Fi devices connect to a Wi-Fi access point, such as a SOHO router. Put the Wi-Fi printer within range of the access point and use controls on the printer to select the Wi-Fi network using the highest IEEE standard (802.11x) supported by both the access point and the printer. Enter the security key to the network if one is required. All Wi-Fi printers support infrastructure connections, and some Wi-Fi printers can handle ad hoc connections, which are discussed next.
- **Wi-Fi ad hoc mode.** Some Wi-Fi printers can connect directly to a nearby computer in a Wi-Fi **ad hoc mode** network to be installed as a local printer. This is accomplished in different ways depending on the technology available in the printer and the computer:
  - Many modern Wi-Fi printers include the ability to host a Wi-Fi hotspot to which nearby computers can connect. The main disadvantage here is that most computers can connect to only one Wi-Fi network at a time, so if a computer is connected to the printer's Wi-Fi network, it can't communicate with the Internet or other network resources.
  - The reverse arrangement might work better: Set up a mobile hotspot on the computer and connect the printer to the computer's hotspot. In Windows 10, click the computer's notifications icon in the taskbar, and click the **Mobile hotspot** tile to turn it on. Right-click the tile, and click **Go to Settings**, where you'll find the hotspot's network name and network password. On the printer, use that information to connect to the computer's hotspot.

Installing a Local or Network Printer

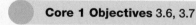
Core 1 Objectives 3.6, 3.7

With some printers, you launch the installation program that came bundled on the setup CD or was downloaded from the printer manufacturer's website. With others, use the Windows Settings app or the Devices and Printers window in Control Panel to install a printer. These windows are also used to manage and uninstall printers, as you'll see throughout the rest of this module.

Choosing a Driver

Core 1 Objective 3.6

When you install a printer, printer drivers are required that are compatible with the installed operating system. Be sure to use 32-bit drivers for a 32-bit OS and 64-bit drivers for a 64-bit OS. Windows has many printer drivers built in. The drivers might also come on a CD bundled with the printer or you can download them from the printer manufacturer's website. Using the drivers downloaded from the manufacturer's website ensures you have the most up-to-date version of the full drivers, with support for all of a printer's features.

Some printer manufacturers give you a choice of drivers based on the PDL included. The most common PDLs are PCL and Postscript. Hewlett-Packard developed **Printer Control Language (PCL)**, which is used by many different printer manufacturers and supported by many different OSs, providing you the flexibility to work in different environments. PCL depends on the drivers in the printer hardware for creating print data, which results in a higher print-processing speed compared to Postscript (described next). Consistency in printer outputs can vary between printers with PCL because hardware varies, which also means the final print quality depends on the quality of the printer.

The alternative, Adobe's **Postscript (PS)**, is also used by many different printer manufacturers but supported by fewer OSs compared to PCL because it is mostly focused for use with Macintosh devices. Postscript does not rely on the printer to create the print data; this creates consistency in print quality between different Postscript printers. In Postscript, graphics are more detailed and have larger file sizes. Postscript is favored by graphics-intense users, especially those who need to produce high-volume output. A designer can test their design with a sample on their printer and then outsource the volume print job to a print shop that uses Postscript to ensure consistent quality. When a printer offers a choice of drivers between PCL or Postscript, choose PCL for general applications and speed, and choose Postscript for graphic-intense applications printing.

Exam Tip ✔

The A+ Core 1 exam might give you a scenario that requires you need to know which type of driver to choose—PCL or Postscript.

Applying Concepts

Installing a Printer

Est. Time: 30 minutes
Core 1 Objectives: 3.6, 3.7

Installing a network printer is sometimes called mapping a printer. Windows has many preinstalled printer drivers that make printer installation particularly easy and straightforward. However, some manufacturers recommend that you install their drivers before connecting the printer to your computer or the network. This provides additional printer configuration and management tools that are not included in the Windows drivers. Follow these steps to install a wired or Wi-Fi network printer or Bluetooth printer using the Windows drivers, or follow more specific instructions from the printer's manufacturer:

1. Make sure the printer is connected to the network or the computer. In Windows, open the **Settings** app, click **Devices**, and then click **Printers & scanners**. Click **Add a printer or scanner**. (For Windows 11, in the Settings app, select **Bluetooth & devices, Printers & scanners**, and **Add device**.) Windows searches for available printers and lists them (see Figure 10-13).

(continues)

Applying Concepts Continued

Figure 10-13   Use the Printers & scanners window to install a printer

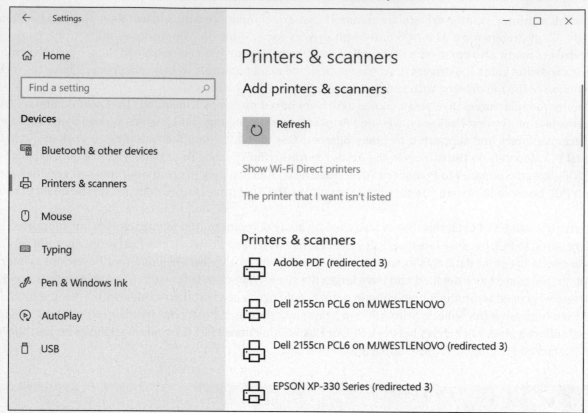

2. Select the printer, and click **Add printer**. Follow the on-screen instructions to add the printer.

3. If your printer isn't listed, open **Devices and Printers** in the Control Panel to add the printer. Click **Add a printer**, and then click **The printer that I want isn't listed**. Choose one of the following options:

   • **My printer is a little older** searches for older printer drivers.

   • **Select a shared printer by name** allows you to enter a network location for the printer.

   • **Add a printer using a TCP/IP address or hostname** allows you to address the printer by IP address or host name.

   • **Add a Bluetooth, wireless or network discoverable printer** searches again for printers connected through Bluetooth or the network.

   • **Add a local printer or network printer with manual settings** gives you the option to make more granular changes to the printer's installation, use a setup CD or downloaded drivers provided by the manufacturer, or select an appropriate driver from a list of available Windows printer drivers. In the next box, choose the port where the printer is connected, and click **Next**. Then you can select the brand and printer model to use drivers provided by Windows (see the left side of Figure 10-14), or you can use drivers stored on CD or previously downloaded from the web by clicking **Have Disk**. The Install From Disk box appears (see the right side of Figure 10-14). Click **Browse** to locate the drivers; Windows is looking for an .inf file. Be sure to select 32-bit or 64-bit drivers, depending on which type of OS you are using; then click **OK**.

Note 8

Use the About window to find out if a 32-bit or 64-bit OS is installed. To open the About window in Windows 10/11, press **Win+X**, and then click **System**.

Figure 10-14   Locate printer drivers on CD or downloaded from the web

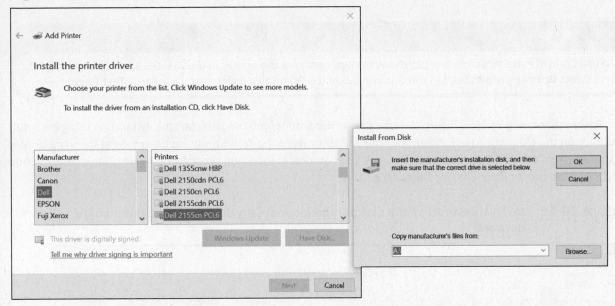

4. Continue to follow the wizard to install the printer. Dialog boxes give you the opportunity to change the name of the printer and designate it as the default printer. You can also test the printer. It's always a good idea to print a test page when you install a printer to verify that the installation works.

You can send a test page to the printer at any time. Click the printer in the Printers & scanners window, click **Manage**, and then click **Print a test page** (see Figure 10-15). This screen is also where you find printer properties and printing preferences.

Figure 10-15   Send a test page to the printer to test connectivity to the printer, the printer, and the printer installation

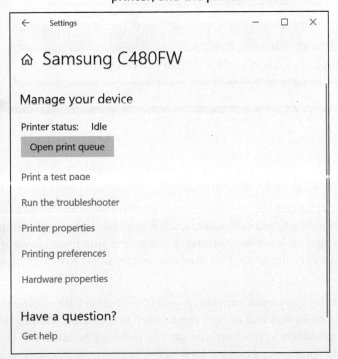

(continues)

Applying Concepts Continued

Note 9

To use Control Panel to print a test page in Windows, right-click the printer in the Devices and Printers window, and select **Printer properties**. On the General tab of the Properties dialog box, click **Print Test Page**.

Rather than using Windows tools to start a printer installation, you can also start the installation using the setup program on the CD that came bundled with the printer or using the setup program downloaded from the printer manufacturer's website. Figure 10-16 shows one such window in the setup process for an HP printer. This method might provide more customized installation options.

Figure 10-16   Installation process of a new printer automatically discovers the printer on the network.

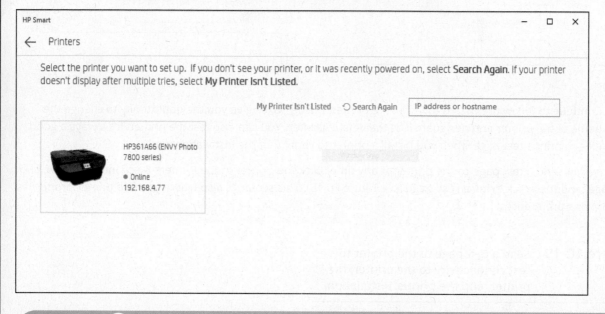

Exam Tip ✔

The A+ Core 1 exam might give you a scenario that requires you to install a local or network printer.

Sharing a Printer on a Network

Core 1 Objective 3.6

Recall from the module "Networking Fundamentals" that a print server manages network printers and makes them available to computers and other devices on the network. Any time a computer sends a print job to a printer through the network, whether that printer is a shared local printer or a network printer, print server functions play a role. However, the device that provides the print server can vary depending on how the printer is set up. Let's look at the available options:

- **Integrated print server.** Most printers today include network capability—you can connect them directly to a router or switch, and devices on the network can find and access the printer. In this case, the printer is providing its own **integrated print server** embedded in the firmware on the printer's hardware. Some integrated printers allow you to manage print protocols, start or stop jobs in the print queue, reorder jobs in the queue, cancel specific jobs coming from a particular computer on the network, monitor printer maintenance tasks, and set up your email address so the printer alerts you by email when it has a problem.

- **Computer as a print server.** When a computer shares its local printer with other computers on the network, the computer is considered to be a print server. If a network has several print servers, you might find it convenient as an IT support technician to use the Print Management console on your workstation to manage these print servers. Using Print Management, you can stop, start, and clear print jobs on any print server on the network and troubleshoot other printer problems from your workstation. Print Management is available under Windows 10 Administrative Tools or Windows 11 Windows Tools in the Control Panel.
- **Other network hardware.** Print server software might be embedded in other network devices, such as a router or firewall. Connect the printer to the network device, and use its configuration interface to manage the printer.

Applying Concepts

Configuring and Using a Shared Printer

Est. Time: 15 minutes
Core 1 Objective: 3.6

To share an installed local or network printer with others on the network, follow these steps:

1. In the printer Properties dialog box, which you access through the Settings app or Control Panel, click the **Sharing** tab. Check **Share this printer** (see the middle box in Figure 10-17).

Figure 10-17 Share the printer and decide how printer sharing is handled

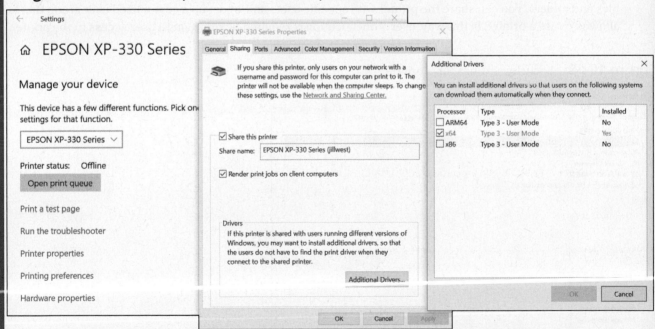

2. You can then change the share name of the printer. Notice in Figure 10-17 the option to control where print jobs are rendered. A print job can be prepared (rendered) on the remote computer (client computer) or this computer (print server). Your choice depends on which computer you think can best handle the computing burden. You can test several print jobs on remote computers with rendering at either location to see which method best uses computing resources on the network.

3. If you want to make drivers for the printer available to remote users who are using an operating system other than the OS on this computer, click **Additional Drivers**.

(continues)

Applying Concepts Continued

4. The Additional Drivers box opens (see the right side of Figure 10-17). For 32-bit operating systems, select **x86**. For 64-bit operating systems, select **x64**. Click **OK** to close the box. You might be asked for the Windows setup DVD or other access to the installation files.

5. Click **OK** to close the Properties dialog box. A shared printer shows a two-friends icon under it or in the status bar in the Devices and Printers window. The printer is listed in the Network group in File Explorer on other network computers.

   For the printer share to be successful, the following requirements must be met:

- The computer sharing the printer and the computer using the shared printer must both be connected to the same network.
- The shared printer and the computer sharing it must be turned on.
- Both computers must allow file and printer sharing.

Secure a Shared Printer

Consider the following features, which can be used to ensure the security of your shared printer and the privacy of data embedded in documents to be printed:

- **User authentication.** In the printer's Properties dialog box (refer back to Figure 10-17), click the **Security** tab to manage who has access to the printer and permissions allowed. Notice in Figure 10-18 that the Everyone group can print, but it is not allowed to manage the printer or documents sent to it. Just as with shared files and folders, you can share the printer with specific users and/or set up a customized user group that is allowed to use a printer. In this way, user authentication is required before giving a user access to the printer.

Figure 10-18   Security settings for a printer

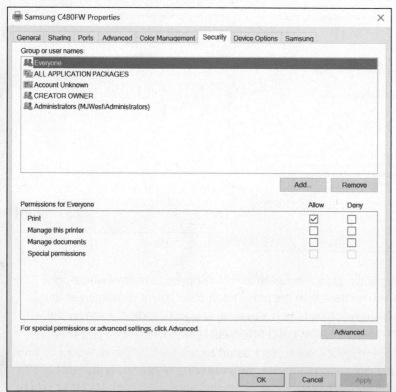

- **Secured printing.** Some larger network printers—such as those manufactured by Canon, Ricoh, and Xerox—offer features to help secure print jobs. **Secured printing** is a security feature that allows documents to print confidentially, only when the user knows the printing passcode and is ready at the printer to oversee the document as it prints. When secure print is enabled, the user enters a passcode in the Printing Preferences or the printer's Properties dialog box before printing. The print job does not start until the user goes to the printer and enters the passcode on the printer. The steps to enable secure printing vary based on the manufacturer. Refer to the printer's owner's manual to find the steps needed to use secure print. To enable secured printing, do the following:
  - On a Canon printer, change the profile to Secured Print.
  - On a Ricoh printer, change the output to Locked Print.
  - On a Xerox printer, change the job type to Secure Print.
- **Audit logs.** Windows is capable of maintaining a log of print jobs accessed in Event Viewer. These logs record when, by whom, and the type of print job processed.
- **Badging.** Special printers, such as a 3D printer at a university or public library, sometimes need to have restricted access. An organization can use badging to limit who is able to use the printer. Badging is a process of certifying users to use special printers. The badging process can include the following:
  - Attending an instructional class in person or online
  - Passing an assessment on content covered in the class
  - Signing an agreement about how the printer is to be used
  - Using a reservation system
  - Adding a badge to your credentials to access the equipment

Applying Concepts

Enable Printer Logging

Est. Time: 15 minutes
Core 1 Objective: 3.6

To enable printer logging in Event Viewer, follow these steps:

1. Open **Event Viewer**. Navigate to **Applications and Services Logs** > **Microsoft** > **Windows** > **PrintService**.
2. Right-click **Operational** in the left pane, and select **Properties**. The Log Properties – Operational dialog box opens.
3. Check **Enable logging**, and click **OK**.
4. Print a test page or print to a PDF to create an event in the printer logs.
5. Click **Action** in the Event Viewer menu bar, and select **Refresh**.
6. Review the printer logs that were recorded, and explore what information you find in the logs you just created.

10

Use a Shared Printer

To install a shared printer on a remote computer, you can (1) use the Settings app, (2) use the Devices and Printers window, or (3) use File Explorer. Here are the general steps for all three methods:

- **Settings app.** On a Windows 10 remote computer, open the **Printers & scanners** window, and click **Add a printer or scanner**. (For Windows 11, in the Settings app, open **Bluetooth & devices**, click **Printers & scanners**, and click **Add device**.) Click **The printer that I want isn't listed** to tell the computer where to find the printer. Choose **Select a shared printer by name** to locate the printer by name, such as \\MJWEST\ EPSON XP-330 Series (jillwest), or click **Browse** to find the printer on the network. You'll need to enter sign-in credentials for the computer sharing the printer. For the user name to work, the printer must be shared with this specific user or user group, and the password must match the password of this user on the remote computer. Then select the printer and click **Select** (see Figure 10-19). Click **Next**. Once the printer is selected, Windows attempts to use printer drivers found on the host computer. If it doesn't find the drivers, you will be given the opportunity to provide them on CD or other media.

Figure 10-19 Locate a shared printer on the network

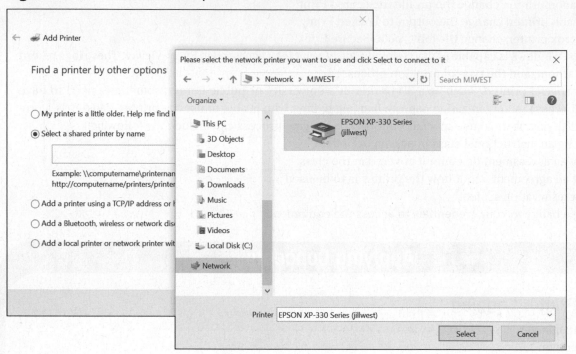

If you don't see a shared printer in the list of printers to add, the user account might not be authorized to access resources on the remote computer. In this situation, use the Explorer method discussed later in this list, which allows the user to authenticate to the remote computer.

- **Devices and Printers window.** On a remote computer, open the **Devices and Printers** window, click **Add a printer**, and follow the directions on-screen to add a network printer. Select the shared printer, which shows the sharing computer's host name and the printer name in the printer address column, or click **The printer I want isn't listed** and browse the network to find the printer. Windows attempts to use printer drivers found on the host computer. If it doesn't find the drivers, you will be given the opportunity to provide them on CD or other media.
- **File Explorer.** In the Explorer window, drill down into the computer that is sharing the printer. If required, authenticate to the remote computer with a valid user account and password on the remote computer. For the user name to work, the printer must be shared with this specific user or user group and the password must match the password of this user on the remote computer. After authentication, you can see the shared printer. Right-click the printer, and select **Connect** (see Figure 10-20). In the warning box that appears, click **Install driver**, and follow the directions on-screen.

Figure 10-20   Use File Explorer to connect to a shared printer

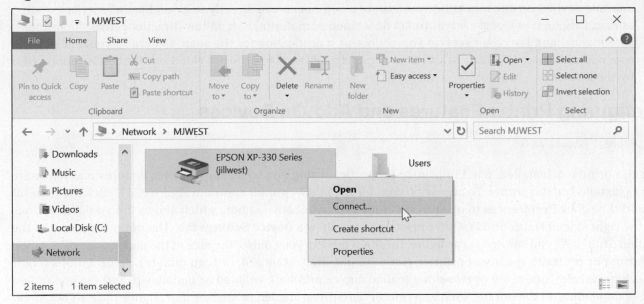

After the printer is installed, be sure to send a test page to the printer to verify that the installation is successful.

Network Scan Services

Multifunction and scanner devices typically offer a few convenient features for sending a scanned file to your desired location. The scanner might offer local destinations, such as printing a paper copy or sending a scan file to a USB flash drive connected directly to the scanner, but the scanner might also offer a few other destinations. The following scan destinations are common options on network printers/scanners:

- **Scan-to-email.** An email destination is fairly straightforward in its setup, but it can vary slightly from device to device. On the scanner, select **email** as the scan destination, and enter a valid email address. Some scanners will require an email verification before completing the email configuration. Usually this means the scanner will send a confirmation email to the email address provided with a PIN or code to verify the email address is valid. You can also choose to keep the address in a locally stored contact list for frequently used emails.

- **Scan-to-SMB.** Scan-to-SMB is a convenient way to scan files to a file server. Recall from the module "Networking Fundamentals" that SMB is a protocol used by file servers on the network. To set up scan-to-SMB, follow the specific steps from the printer's user manual. Generally, this is the information you'll need to set up scan-to-SMB:
  - Host IP address
  - File path to the SMB server or shared folder
  - User name and password for the SMB server or shared folder (Create a unique user name and password for the share folder ownership to limit access to another user's credentials.)

Core to Core

You learn more about creating and sharing a file server in the Core 2 module "Securing and Sharing Windows Resources."

- **Scan-to-cloud.** The cloud scan destination is convenient for making a scanned document available to multiple devices on different networks. Scan-to-cloud can upload directly to cloud hosting services, such as Box, Dropbox, or Google Drive. To set up a cloud scan destination, follow directions from the printer user manual and the cloud service you choose as a destination for the scan. Generally, you'll need the user name and password for the cloud service, and you'll need to choose a cloud service that is supported by the printer.

Configuring Printer Features and Add-On Devices

Core 1 Objective 3.6

After the printer is installed, use the printer Properties dialog box to manage printer features and hardware devices installed on the printer. To access settings for the EPSON printer shown in Figure 10-21, click the **General** tab, and then click **Preferences** to open the Printing Preferences dialog box, which shows the available options (see the right side of Figure 10-21). Other printers might show a **Device Settings** tab. The options depend on the installed printer. As you can see in the figure, the **Main** tab lets you control the size of the paper, page orientation (landscape or portrait), quality of printing (for example, draft, standard, or high quality), color options (color or black/grayscale), one-sided or two-sided (called duplex printing), collated or uncollated, and various add-on devices depending on the printer, such as a printer hard drive, stapler, or stacker unit. Figure 10-22 shows an HP Printing Preferences dialog box where you can choose the paper source, which determines which paper tray is used to print.

Figure 10-21   The Printing Preferences dialog box for an EPSON printer

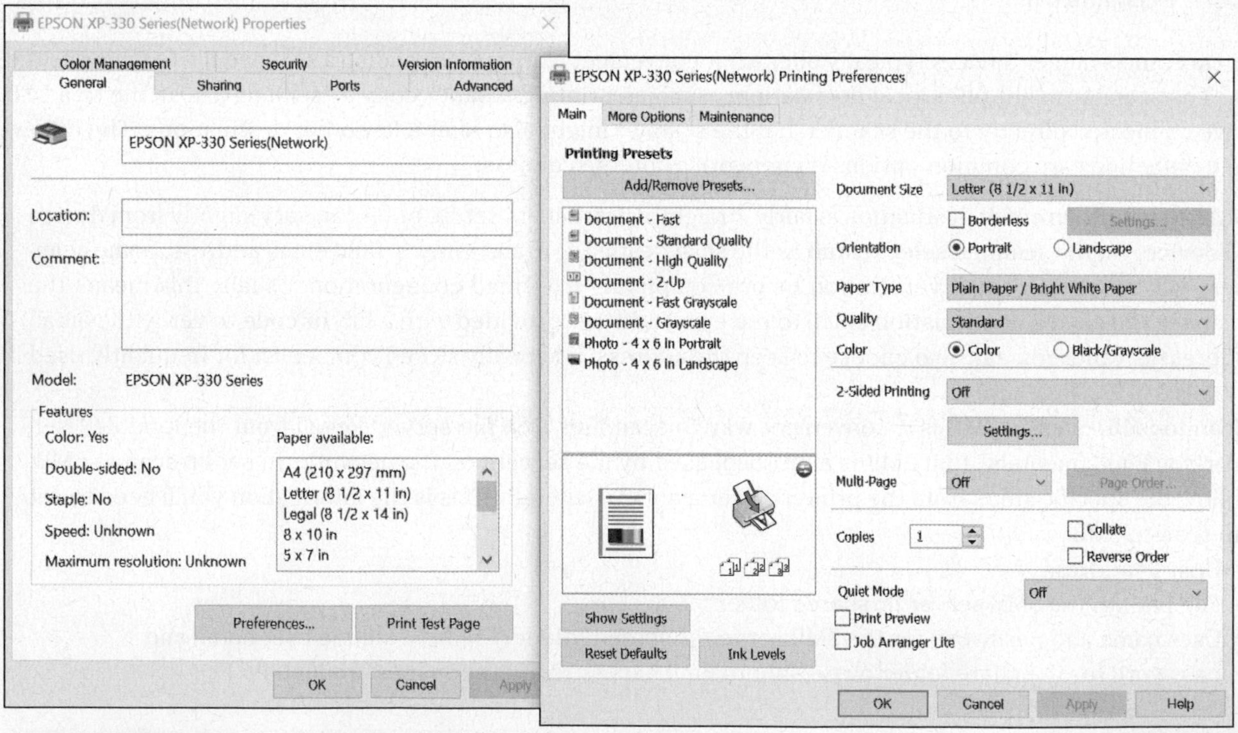

Figure 10-22   Select the paper source in Printer Preferences

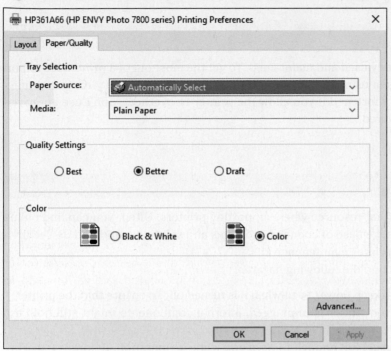

You can also manage many printer settings and features through the printer's own utility, which might be installed as an application on your computer or might be a firmware utility in the printer that is accessed through your browser. For example, for one Oki Data printer, enter the IP address of the printer in a browser, and then enter the administrative password to the printer firmware. The firmware utility (see Figure 10-23) allows you to manage printer settings and features.

Figure 10-23   The user interface for a network printer accessed through a network computer's browser

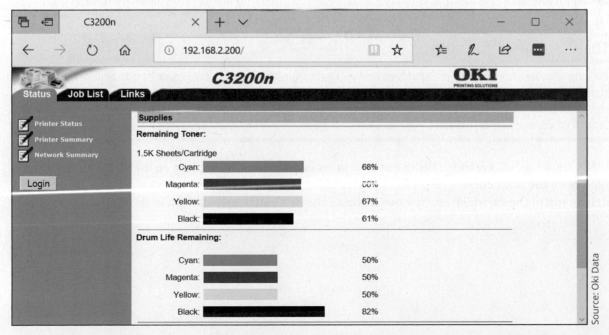

Source: Oki Data

Now let's turn our attention to tasks you might be called on to do when maintaining and upgrading a printer.

Printer Maintenance

 Core 1 Objective 3.7

Printers generally last for years if they are properly used and maintained. To get the most out of a printer, it's important to follow the manufacturer's directions when using the device and to perform the necessary routine maintenance. For example, the life of a printer can be shortened if you allow the printer to overheat, don't use approved paper, or don't perform maintenance when required.

Online Support for Printers

 Core 1 Objective 3.7

The printer manufacturer's website is an important resource when supporting printers. Often, you can find online documentation, warranty information, a knowledge base of common problems and solutions, updated device drivers, replacement parts available for order, and printer maintenance kits.

When working on printers, always keep in mind the following hazards:

- **Dangerous electricity.** A printer might still keep power even when it is turned off. To ensure that the printer has no power, unplug it. Even when a laser printer is unplugged, internal components might still hold a dangerous electrical charge for some time.
- **Hot to touch.** Some laser printer parts can get hot enough to burn you while in operation. Before you work inside a laser printer, turn it off, unplug it, and wait about 30 minutes for it to cool down.
- **Laser beam.** For your protection, the laser beam in a laser printer is always enclosed inside a protective case. Therefore, when servicing a laser printer, you should never have to look at the laser beam, which can damage your eyes.
- **Static electricity.** To protect sensitive memory modules and hard drives inside printers, be sure to use an ESD strap when installing them. You don't need to wear an ESD strap when exchanging consumables such as toner cartridges, fuser assembles, or image drums.
- **Working inside high-voltage equipment when no one is around.** Here's one more tip to stay safe, although we don't want it to frighten you: When you work inside high-voltage equipment such as a laser printer, don't do it when no one else is around. If you have an emergency, someone needs to be close by to help you.

> **Note 10**
>
> If you're working with laser printer toner cartridges and you get toner dust on your clothes or hands while exchanging the cartridge, don't use hot water to clean it up. Remember that heat sets the toner. Go outdoors, and use a can of compressed air to blow off the toner. Then use cold water to clean your hands and clothes. It's a good idea to wear a smock or apron when working on printers.

Figure 10-24 shows an ink cartridge being installed in an inkjet printer. To replace an inkjet cartridge, turn on the printer and open the front cover. The printer releases the cartridges from their parked positions. You can then open the latch on top of the cartridge and remove it. Install the new cartridge as shown in the figure.

Figure 10-24   Installing an ink cartridge in an inkjet printer

Cleaning a Printer

> Core 1 Objective 3.7

A printer gets dirty inside and outside as stray toner, ink, dust, and bits of paper accumulate. As part of routine printer maintenance, you need to regularly clean the printer. How often depends on how much the printer is used and the environment in which it is used. Some manufacturers suggest that a heavily used printer be cleaned weekly, and others suggest you clean it whenever you exchange the toner, ink cartridges, or ribbon.

Clean the outside of the printer with a damp cloth. Don't use ammonia-based cleaners. Clean the inside of the printer with a dry cloth and remove dust, bits of paper, and stray toner. Picking up stray toner can be a problem. Don't try to blow it out with compressed air because you don't want the toner in the air. Also, don't use an anti-static vacuum cleaner. You can, however, use a specialized vacuum cleaner designed to pick up toner, called a **toner vacuum**. This type of vacuum does not allow the toner that it picks up to touch any conductive surface.

Some printer manufacturers also suggest you use an **extension magnet brush**. The long-handled brush is made of nylon fibers that are charged with static electricity and easily attract the toner like a magnet. For a laser printer, wipe the rollers from side to side with a dry cloth to remove loose dirt and toner. Don't touch the soft, black roller (the transfer roller), or you might affect the print quality. You can find specific instructions for cleaning a printer on the printer manufacturer's website.

Calibrating a Printer

> Core 1 Objective 3.7

An inkjet printer might require **calibration** to align and/or clean the inkjet nozzles, which can solve a problem when colors appear streaked or out of alignment. To calibrate the printer, you might use the menu on the printer's control panel or use software that came bundled with the printer. How to access these tools differs from one printer to another. See the printer manual to learn how to perform the calibration. For some printers, a Services tab is added to the printer Properties window. Other printer installations might put utility programs in the Start menu. The first time you turn on a printer after installing ink cartridges, it's a good idea to calibrate the printer.

If an inkjet printer still does not print after calibrating it, you can try to manually clean the cartridge nozzles. Check the printer manufacturer's website for directions. For most inkjet printers, you are directed to use clean, distilled water and cotton swabs to clean the face of the ink cartridge, being careful not to touch the nozzle plate.

To prevent the inkjet nozzles from drying out, don't leave the ink cartridges out of their cradle for longer than 30 minutes. Here are some general directions:

1. Following the manufacturer's directions, remove the inkjet cartridges from the printer, and lay them on their sides on a paper towel.
2. Dip a cotton swab in distilled water (not tap water), and squeeze out any excess water.
3. Hold an ink cartridge so that the nozzle plate faces up, and use the swab to clean the area around the nozzle plate, as shown in Figure 10-25. Do not clean the plate itself.

Figure 10-25   Clean the area around the nozzle plate with a damp cotton swab

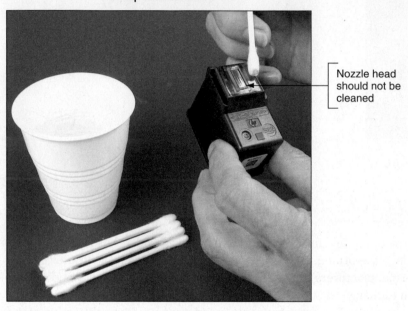

Nozzle head should not be cleaned

4. Hold the cartridge up to the light and make sure that no dust, dirt, ink, or cotton fibers are left around the face of the nozzle plate. Make sure the area is clean.
5. Clean all the ink cartridges the same way, and replace the cartridges in the printer.
6. Print a test page. If print quality is still poor, try calibrating the printer again.
7. If you still have problems, you need to replace the ink cartridges.

Laser printers automatically calibrate themselves periodically. You can instruct a laser printer to calibrate at any time by using the controls on the front of the printer or the browser-based utility program that is included in the firmware of a network printer. To access the utility, enter the IP address of the printer in the browser address box, and sign in.

Printer Maintenance Kits

 Core 1 Objective 3.7

Manufacturers of high-end printers provide **printer maintenance kits**, which include specific printer components, step-by-step instructions for performing maintenance, tips for how often maintenance should be done, and information on any special tools or equipment you need to do maintenance. For example, the maintenance plan for the HP Color LaserJet 4600 printer says to replace the transfer roller assembly after printing 120,000 pages and to replace the fusing assembly after 150,000 pages. The plan also says the black ink cartridge should last for about 9000 pages and the color ink cartridge should last about 8000 pages. HP sells the image transfer kit, the image fuser kit, and the ink cartridges designed for this printer.

To find out how many pages a printer has printed to determine if you need to do the maintenance, have the printer give you the page count since the last maintenance. You can tell the printer to display the information or print a status report by using buttons on the front of the printer (see Figure 10-26), or you can use utility software using a computer connected to the printer. See the printer documentation to know how to get this report. For network printers that offer a browser-based utility, enter the IP address of the printer in your browser, and use the utility to find the counters. (Figure 10-27 shows such a utility for an Oki Data network printer.)

Figure 10-26   Use buttons on the front of the printer to display information, including the page count

Figure 10-27   Use the web-based printer utility to read the printer counters

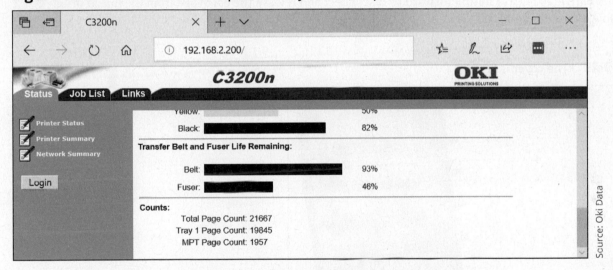

Source: Oki Data

After you have performed the maintenance, be sure to reset the page count so it will be accurate when you need to do the next routine maintenance. Keep a written record of the maintenance and other service done.

As examples of replacing printer consumables, let's look at how to replace a toner cartridge, image drum, and fuser for an Oki Data color laser printer.

Exam Tip ✔

The A+ Core 1 exam might give you a scenario that requires you to replace a toner cartridge or apply a maintenance kit for a laser printer.

A toner cartridge for this Oki Data printer generally lasts for about 1500 pages. Here are the steps to replace a color toner cartridge:

1. Turn off and unplug the printer. Press the cover release button on the upper-left corner of the printer, and open the printer cover (see Figure 10-28).

Figure 10-28   Open the printer cover

Source: Oki Data

2. Figure 10-29 shows the cover up. Notice the four erase lamps on the inside of the cover. Look inside the printer for the four toner cartridges and the fuser assembly labeled in Figure 10-30. Push or pull the blue toner cartridge release button forward to disconnect and release the cartridge from the image drum below it (see Figure 10-31).

Figure 10-29   The cover is lifted

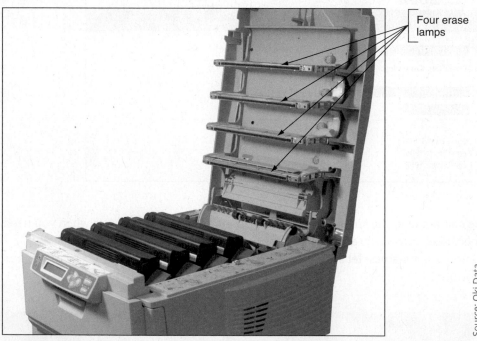

Four erase lamps

Source: Oki Data

Figure 10-30 Inside the Oki Data printer

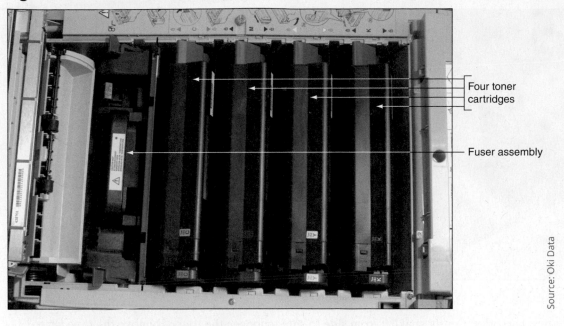

Four toner
cartridges

Fuser assembly

Source: Oki Data

Figure 10-31 Push the blue lever forward to release the toner
cartridge

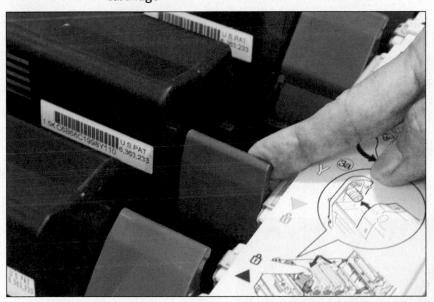

3. Lift the cartridge out of the printer, lifting up on the right side first and then removing the left side
(see Figure 10-32). Be careful not to spill loose toner.

Figure 10-32   Remove the toner cartridge

4. Unpack the new cartridge. Gently shake it from side to side to loosen the toner. Remove the tape from underneath the cartridge, and place the cartridge in the printer by inserting the left side first and then the right side. Push the cartridge lever back into position to lock the cartridge in place. Close the printer cover.

This printer has four image drums, one for each color. The drums are expected to last for about 15,000 pages. When you purchase a new drum, the kit comes with a new color toner cartridge. Follow these steps to replace the cartridge and image drum. In these steps, we are using the yellow drum and cartridge:

1. Turn off and unplug the printer. Wait about 30 minutes for it to cool down, then open the printer cover. The toner cartridge is connected to the image drum. Lift the drum together with the toner cartridge out of the printer (see Figure 10-33). Be sure to dispose of the drum and cartridge according to local regulations.

Figure 10-33   Remove the image drum and toner cartridge as one
unit

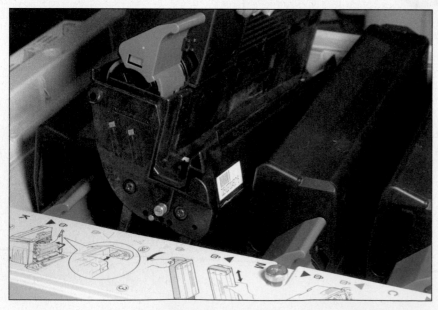

2. Unpack the new image drum. Peel the tape off the drum and remove the plastic film around it. As you work, be careful to keep the drum upright so as not to spill the toner. Because the drum is sensitive to light, don't allow it to be exposed to bright light or direct sunlight. Don't expose it to normal room lighting for longer than five minutes.

3. Place the drum in the printer. Install the new toner cartridge in the printer. Close the printer cover.

The fuser should last for about 45,000 pages. To replace the fuser, follow these steps:

1. Turn off and unplug the printer. Allow the printer to cool, and open the cover.

2. Pull the two blue fuser levers forward to unlock the fuser (see Figure 10-34).

Figure 10-34   Pull the two fuser levers forward to release the fuser

3. Lift the fuser out of the printer using the handle on the fuser, as shown in Figure 10-35.

Figure 10-35   Remove the fuser

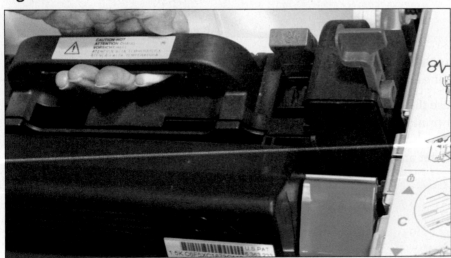

4. Unpack the new fuser, and place it in the printer. Push the two blue levers toward the back of the printer to lock the fuser in place.

As a last step whenever you service the inside of this printer, always carefully clean the LED erase lamps on the inside of the top cover (see Figure 10-36). The printer maintenance kits you've just learned to use all include a wipe to clean these strips.

Figure 10-36   Clean the LED strips on the inside top cover

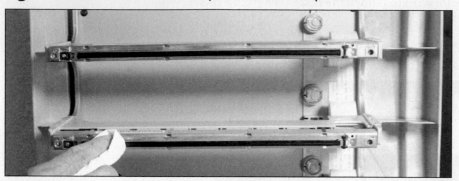

Troubleshooting Printers

 Core 1 Objectives 3.7, 5.6

In this part of the module, you learn some general and specific printer troubleshooting tips. As with all computer problems, begin troubleshooting by interviewing the user, finding out what works and doesn't work, and making an initial determination of the problem. When you think the problem is solved, ask the user to check things out to make sure they are satisfied with your work. After the problem is solved, be sure to document the symptoms of the problem and what you did to solve it.

Printer Does Not Print

 Core 1 Objectives 3.7, 5.6

When a printer does not print, the problem can be caused by any number of things. As you can see in Figure 10-37, the problem can be isolated to one of the following areas:

- The application attempting to use the printer
- Windows, Windows settings, or printer drivers
- The printer itself
- Connectivity between the computer and its local printer or a network printer

Figure 10-37   How to isolate a printer problem

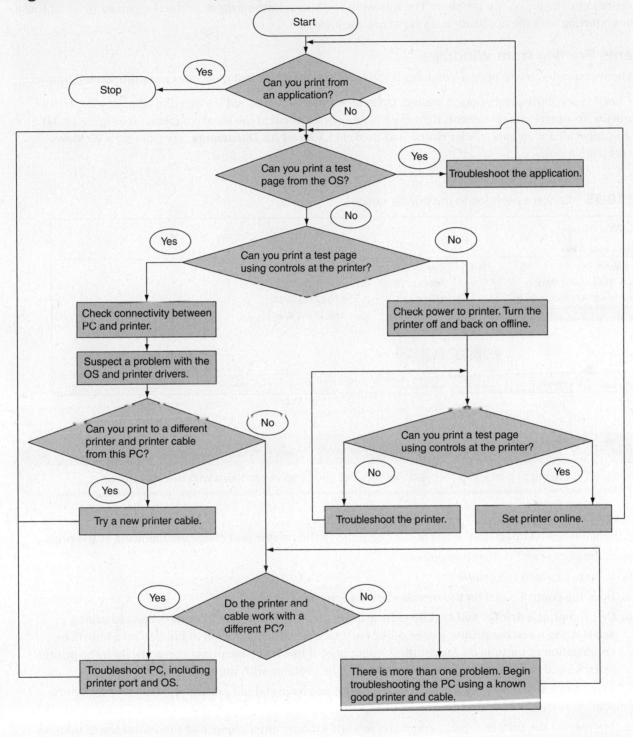

In addition, if this is the first time you have tried to use the printer after installing it, the printer drivers or the printer installation might be the problem. The following sections address printer problems caused by all of these categories, starting with the application trying to use the printer.

Problems Printing from Windows

On the client computer, try to print a Windows test page. If the Windows test page does not print, do the following:

1. Check to see if the print spool is stalled. Open the printer's queue, and try deleting all print jobs in the queue. To cancel one document, right-click it, and click **Cancel** in the shortcut menu (see Figure 10-38). To cancel all documents, click **Printer**, and then click **Cancel All Documents**. Try printing a Windows test page again.

Figure 10-38 Cancel a print job in the printer queue

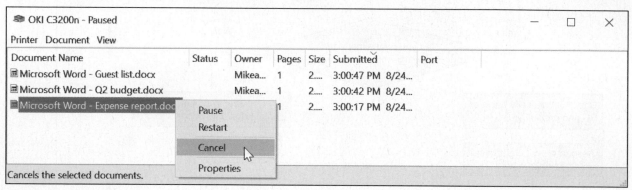

Exam Tip ✔

The A+ Core 1 exam might give you a scenario that requires you to solve problems with the print queue.

2. If the Windows test page also stalls in the queue, go to the printer, and check the following at the printer:
   a. Is the printer on? Is it getting power?
   b. Is there paper in the printer?
   c. Does the control panel on the printer show an error code?
   d. Can you print a **printer self-test page** by using controls at the printer? For directions to print a self-test page, see the printer's user guide. For example, you might need to hold down a button or combination of buttons on the printer's front panel. If this test page prints correctly, then the printer is working. If the test page does not print, solve the problem with the printer itself.

3. If the printer is working, do a quick check to be sure you have communication with the printer before you continue troubleshooting. Do the following:
   a. Try pinging the printer. Open a command prompt window, enter **ping**, and then enter the IP address of your printer. In Figure 10-39, the address is **192.168.2.200**. If the printer replies (see Figure 10-39), the problem is not network connectivity.

Figure 10-39   Use the ping command to determine if you have network connectivity with the printer

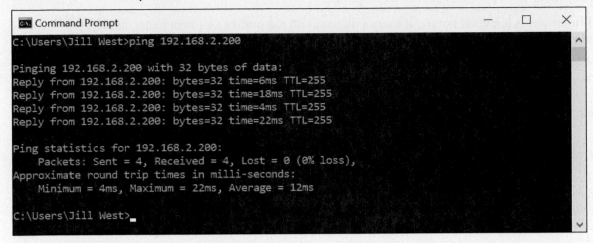

```
C:\Users\Jill West>ping 192.168.2.200

Pinging 192.168.2.200 with 32 bytes of data:
Reply from 192.168.2.200: bytes=32 time=6ms TTL=255
Reply from 192.168.2.200: bytes=32 time=18ms TTL=255
Reply from 192.168.2.200: bytes=32 time=4ms TTL=255
Reply from 192.168.2.200: bytes=32 time=22ms TTL=255

Ping statistics for 192.168.2.200:
    Packets: Sent = 4, Received = 4, Lost = 0 (0% loss),
Approximate round trip times in milli-seconds:
    Minimum = 4ms, Maximum = 22ms, Average = 12ms

C:\Users\Jill West>_
```

    b. If the ping does not work, move on to steps covered in the section, "Problems with Connectivity for a Network Printer or Shared Printer."

    c. For a USB printer, check the cable connection between the computer and the local printer.

  4. If you have concluded you have connectivity with the printer, stop and restart the Windows Print Spooler service. Windows uses the **Services console** to stop, start, and manage background services used by Windows and applications. Do the following:

    a. Enter `services.msc` in the Windows Run box. In the Services console, select **Print Spooler** (see Figure 10-40). Click **Stop** to stop the service.

Figure 10-40   Use the Services console to stop and start the print spooler

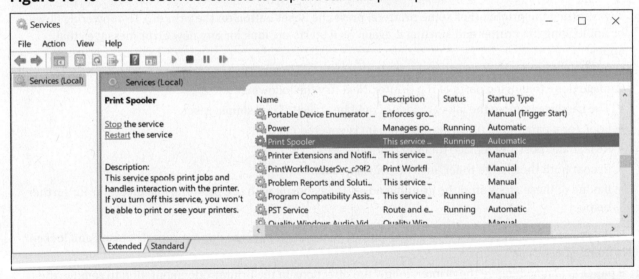

    b. To delete any print jobs left in the queue, open **Explorer**, and delete all files in the C:\Windows\System32\spool\PRINTERS folder.

    c. Restart the print spooler. Return to the Services console, make sure Print Spooler is selected, and click **Start**. Close the Services console window.

  5. If you still cannot print, reboot the computer. Try deleting the printer and then reinstalling it.

  6. Check the printer manufacturer's website for an updated printer driver. Download and install the correct driver.

10

Problems with the Printer Itself

To eliminate the printer as the problem, check these things:

1. Is the printer on? Is it getting power? If there's no image on the printer's control panel display, the printer is not getting power or it is turned off.
2. Does the printer have paper?
3. Look for an error message or error code in the control panel on the front of the printer. If the control panel reports "Ready" or "Online," then you can assume a network printer is communicating with the network.

Note 11

If you see an error code you don't understand, search the printer documentation or website to find out its meaning. Follow the directions on the printer manufacturer's website to address the error code.

4. Can you print a printer self-test page, as described earlier? If this test page prints correctly, then the printer is working.

Note 12

A printer self-test page might tell you the printer resolution and how much memory is installed. If this information is not correct, try upgrading firmware on the printer.

5. Try resetting the printer. (For some printers, press the Reset button on the printer.) Try powering down or unplugging the printer and starting it again. As it starts up, look for any new error messages that appear.
6. Is there a grinding noise? Typically a grinding noise means there is a problem with a gear, so look for damage done to moving parts of the printer. Next, try the following:
   - The carriage holding the ink cartridges could be stalled. Try a simple reset.
   - Look for a paper jam. (Clearing a paper jam is covered next.)
   - Reseat and possibly replace toner cartridges.
   - Reseat both the charge roller and the transfer roller.
   - If none of these steps stop the grinding noise, then consult with the printer's manufacturer for further help.
7. Is the paper installed correctly? Are the printer cover and rear access doors properly closed and locked? Is there a paper jam?
8. If paper is jammed inside the printer, follow the directions in the printer documentation to remove the paper. Don't jerk the paper from the printer mechanism, but pull evenly on the paper, with care. You don't want to leave pieces of paper behind. Check for jammed paper from both the input tray and the output bin. Check both sides. Laser and inkjet printers likely have a door in the back that you can open to gently clear the jammed paper, as shown in Figure 10-41.

Figure 10-41 Open the door on the back of an inkjet printer to remove jammed paper

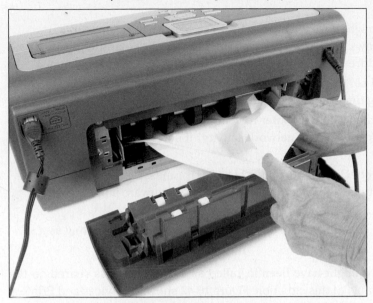

9. Is the paper not feeding? Remove the paper tray and check the metal plate at the bottom of the tray. Can it move up and down freely? If not, replace the tray. When you insert the tray in the printer, does the printer lift the plate as the tray is inserted? If not, the lift mechanism might need repair.

10. Damp paper can cause paper jams, creases, and wrinkles. Is the paper in the printer dry? Paper that is too thin can also crease or wrinkle in the printer.

11. For an inkjet printer, check if nozzles are clogged. Sometimes, leaving the printer on for a while will heat up the ink nozzles and unclog them.

12. If the print head of an impact printer moves back and forth but nothing prints, check the ribbon. Is it installed correctly between the plate and print head? Is it jammed? If the ribbon is dried out, it needs to be replaced.

13. Is there an error with the printer finisher? Some printers have a printer finisher, which staples or hole-punches papers at the end of a print job. If the stapler is malfunctioning, try resetting the finisher by power cycling the printer while the cable to the finisher is disconnected. Next, reseat or replace the staple cartridge, and remove any jammed staples. If the hole puncher is malfunctioning, dispose of the punch scraps, make sure all the paper sizes are the same for the hole-punch job, and make sure the paper type is appropriate for hole punching. Finally, check to make sure an administrator hasn't disabled one or both of the finishing features.

14. Check the service documentation and printer page count to find out if routine maintenance is due or if the printer has a history of similar problems. Check the user guide for the printer and the printer manufacturer's website for other troubleshooting suggestions.

If you still cannot get a printer to work, you might need to take the printer to a certified repair shop. Before you do, though, try contacting the manufacturer. You might also be able to open a chat session on the printer manufacturer's website.

Problems with Connectivity for a Network Printer or Shared Printer

If the printer's self-test page prints correctly (the printer is working) but you cannot ping the printer from the computer where the print job was issued, the next step is to suspect no connectivity between the printer and computer. We call this computer the client computer in the following steps for a network printer:

1. Consider that the entire network might be down or the client computer is offline. Can the client computer communicate with other devices or computers on the network? Can another computer on the network communicate with the printer?

2. Consider that the IP address of the printer might have changed, which can happen if the printer is receiving a dynamic IP address. Using Windows, delete the printer, and then install the printer again. If this solves the problem, assign a static IP address to the printer to keep the problem from reoccurring.

3. Can you print to another network printer? If so, there might be a problem with the first printer's configuration. Try uninstalling and installing the printer at the client computer.

4. Check the network port on the printer and the switch or router to which the printer connects. Do the network status indicator lights indicate connectivity and network activity? If not, try replacing the network cable to the printer.

5. Use the printer's browser-based utility, and check for status reports and error messages. Run diagnostic software that might be available on the utility menu. Try flashing the printer's firmware if updates are recommended by the manufacturer.

6. Is the printer installed directly on the client computer or on another host computer that is acting as a print server?

Even though you are using a network printer, it might have been installed as a printer that is shared on the network by the host computer. Let's look at an example of this situation. Figure 10-42 shows a Devices and Printers window with several installed printers. Notice the two installations of the EPSON XP-330 Series printer. The first installation was done by using a printer that was shared by another computer on the network. The second installation was done by installing the Epson printer as a network printer addressed by its IP address. When you print using the second installation of the Epson printer, you print directly over the network to the printer. When you print to the first installation of the Epson printer, you print by way of the other computer on the network. If this computer is offline, the print jobs back up in the print queue until the computer is available.

Figure 10-42 A network printer installed using two methods

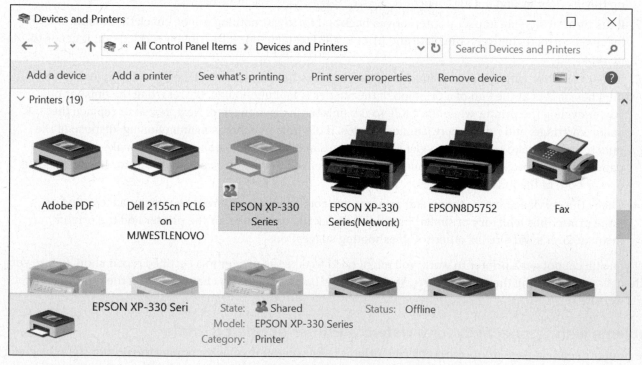

When a computer has shared a local or network printer with others on the network, follow these steps to solve problems with the shared printer:

1. Is enough hard drive space available on the client or host computer?
2. Did you get an "Access denied" message when you tried to print from the client computer? If so, you might not have access to the host computer. On the client computer, go to Explorer and attempt to drill down into resources on the printer's computer. Perhaps you have not entered a correct user account and password to access this computer; if that is the case, you will not be able to use the computer's resources. Make sure you have a matching Windows user account and password on each computer.
3. On the host computer, open the printer's Properties dialog box, and click the **Security** tab. Select **Everyone** and make sure Permissions for Everyone includes permission to print (refer back to Figure 10-18).
4. Using Windows on the client computer, delete the printer, and then install the printer again. For best results, install the printer directly over the network and not through another computer. Watch for and address any error messages that might appear.

Poor Print Quality

Core 1 Objectives 3.7, 5.6

Poor print quality can be caused by the printer drivers, the application, Windows, or the printer. Let's start by looking at what can cause poor print quality with laser printers and then move on to other problems that affect printouts.

Exam Tip

The A+ Core 1 exam might give you a scenario that requires you to resolve problems with faded prints, echoes, vertical lines or garbled characters on a page, wrong paper size, print appearing sideways on a page, and wrong print colors. All these problems are covered in this part of the module.

Poor Print Quality for Laser Printers

For laser printers, poor print quality can include printing blank pages or faded, smeared, wavy, speckled, or streaked printouts with vertical lines down the page. These problems often indicate that the toner is low. All major mechanical printer components that normally create problems are conveniently contained within the replaceable toner cartridge. In most cases, the solution to poor-quality printing is to replace this cartridge.

Follow these general guidelines to fix poor print quality with laser printers:

1. If you suspect the printer is overheated, unplug it and allow it to cool for 30 minutes.
2. The toner cartridge might be low on toner, or it might not be installed correctly. Remove the toner cartridge, and gently rock it from side to side to redistribute the toner. Replace the cartridge. To avoid flying toner, don't shake the cartridge too hard.
3. If this doesn't solve the problem, try replacing the toner cartridge immediately.
4. Econo Mode (a mode that uses less toner) might be on; turn it off.
5. The paper quality might not be good enough. Try a different brand of paper. Only use paper recommended for a laser printer. Also, be aware that some types of paper can receive print only on one side.
6. The printer might need cleaning. Clean the inside of the printer with a dry, lint-free cloth. Don't touch the transfer roller, which is the soft, spongy black roller.
7. If the transfer roller is dirty, the problem will probably correct itself after several sheets print. If not, take the printer to an authorized service center.

10

8. Does the printer require routine maintenance? Check the website of the printer's manufacturer to see how often to perform maintenance and to purchase the required printer maintenance kit.

> **Note 13**
>
> Extreme humidity can cause the toner to clump in the cartridge and give a Toner Low message. If this is a consistent problem in your location, you might want to invest in a dehumidifier for the room where your printer is located.

9. Streaking is usually caused by a dirty developer unit or corona wire. The developer unit is contained in the toner cartridge. Replace the cartridge or check the printer documentation for directions on how to remove and clean the developer unit. Allow the corona wire to cool, and clean it with a lint-free swab.

10. Speckled printouts can be caused by the laser drum. If cleaning the printer and replacing the toner cartridge don't solve the problem, replace the laser drum.

> **Note 14**
>
> If loose toner comes out with your printout, the fuser is not reaching the proper temperature, and toner is not being fused to the paper. Professional service is required.

11. Distorted images can be caused by foreign material inside the printer that might be interfering with the mechanical components. Check for debris that might be interfering with the printer operation.

12. If the page has a gray background or gray print, the image drum is worn out and needs to be replaced.

13. If an echo or ghost image appears as a double a few inches below the actual darker image on the page, the problem is usually with the image drum or toner cartridge. The drum is not fully cleaned in the cleaning stage, and toner left on it causes the ghost image. If the printer utility installed with the printer offers the option to clean the drum, try that first. The next solution is to replace the toner cartridge. If the problem is still not solved, replace the image drum.

Poor Print Quality for Inkjet Printers

To troubleshoot blank pages or poor print quality for an inkjet printer, check the following:

1. Is the correct paper for inkjet printers being used? The quality of paper determines the final print quality, especially with inkjet printers. In general, the better the quality of the paper you use with an inkjet printer, the better the print quality. Don't use less than 20-pound paper in any type of printer unless the printer documentation specifically states that a lower weight is satisfactory.

2. Is the ink supply low, or is there a partially clogged nozzle?

3. Remove and reinstall the cartridge(s).

4. Follow the printer's documentation to clean each nozzle. Is the print head too close to or too far from the paper?

5. In some printers, there is a little sponge near the carriage rest that can become clogged with ink. It should be removed and cleaned.

6. If you are printing transparencies, try changing the fill pattern in your application.

7. Missing lines or dots on the printed page can be caused by the ink nozzles drying out, especially when the printer sits unused for a long time. Follow the directions given earlier in the module for cleaning inkjet nozzles.

8. Streaks or lines down the page can be caused by dust or dirt in the print head assemblage. Follow the manufacturer's directions to clean the inkjet nozzles.

Garbled Characters on Paper

If scrambled or garbled characters print on all or part of a page, the problem may be caused by the document being printed, the application, connectivity between the computer and the printer, or the printer. Follow these steps to zero in on the problem:

1. First, cancel all print jobs in the print queue. Then try printing a different document from the same application. If the second document prints correctly, the problem is with the original document.

2. Try printing using a different application. If the problem is resolved, try repairing or reinstalling the application.

3. For a USB printer, the problem might be with a USB hub, port, or cable. Is the USB cable securely connected at both ends? If you are using a USB hub, remove the hub, connecting the printer directly to the computer. Try a different USB cable or USB port.

4. Recycle the printer by powering it down and back up or by pressing a Reset button.

5. Update the printer drivers. Go to the website of the printer manufacturer to find the latest drivers and follow the directions to install them.

6. If the problem is still not solved, the printer might need servicing. Does the printer need maintenance? Search the printer manufacturer's website for other solutions.

Paper Size Mismatch Errors

A printer gives a paper size error or paper mismatch error when the size of the paper, envelope, or other media in the paper tray or feeder doesn't match the paper size chosen in the printer's settings for the current print job. This error message prevents wasting toner or ink. To resolve the paper size mismatch error, do the following:

1. Check the paper size setting in the printer Properties or Printing Preferences dialog box, as shown in Figure 10-43. Make sure the size selected is the same size as the paper or envelope loaded in the tray or feeder.

Figure 10-43   Select the paper source in the printer Properties dialog box

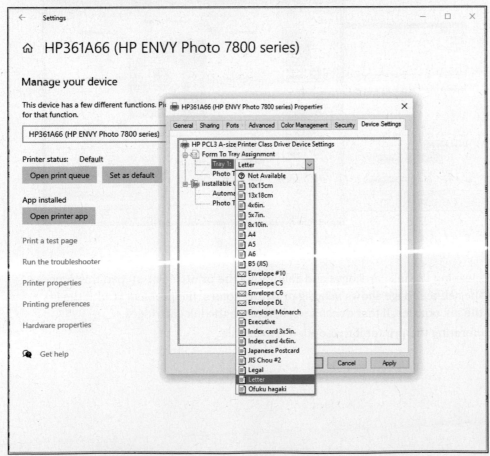

10

2. Remove and reload the paper in the tray or feeder. When reseating the paper, adjust the paper width guides to gently touch the sides of the paper. Confirm the tray setting indicates the correct tray.

3. Reset the printer to clear any errors. Unplug the printer, wait at least a minute, and then reconnect the power cord. Turn on the printer and wait for it to fully power on.

Print Comes out Sideways

Some printers try to fill the page with the print by automatically rotating from portrait mode to landscape mode or vice versa. If the print comes out rotated but doesn't fill the page, then use the printer's Property dialog box to change the setting to the opposite orientation. Another problem could be that the margins are set too small for the printer capabilities, causing it to automatically rotate to try fit the content on the page. Adjust the margins to what the printer can handle or use a different printer.

Wrong Print Colors

For a printer that is printing the wrong colors, sometimes called the chroma display, do the following:

1. Check to see if the paper you are using is designed to print on only one side. You might need to flip the paper in the printer.

2. Try adjusting the print quality. These adjustments vary by printer. For one color laser printer, open the **Printing Preferences** dialog box, and click the **Quality** tab (see the left side of Figure 10-44). You can try different selections on this tab. To manually adjust the color, check **Manual Color Settings**, and then click **Color Settings**. The Color Settings dialog box appears, as shown on the right side of Figure 10-44.

Figure 10-44   Adjust printing quality and color

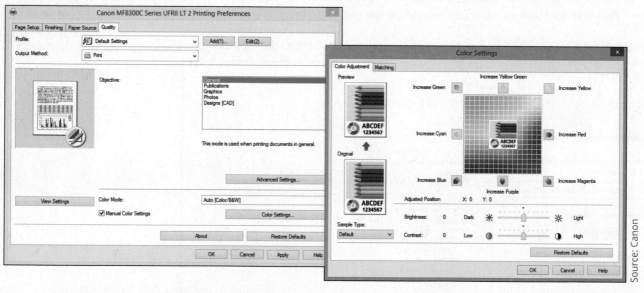

Source: Canon

3. For an inkjet printer, try cleaning the ink cartridges and calibrating the printer. One step in this process prints a self-test page. If the self-test page shows missing or wrong colors, the problem is with the ink cartridges. Try cleaning the ink nozzles. If that doesn't work, replace the ink cartridges.

4. For a laser printer, try calibrating the printer if that option is available.

Applying Concepts

Solving Problems with Printer Installations

Est. Time: 30 minutes
Core 1 Objectives: 3.7, 5.6

Here are some steps you can take if the printer installation fails or installs with errors:

1. If you have problems, consider that Windows might be using the wrong or corrupted printer drivers. Try removing the printer and then installing it again. To remove a printer in the Windows 10 Settings app, select a printer, and click **Remove device**. (In Windows 11, click **Remove**.) To use Control Panel, right-click the printer in the Devices and Printers window, and click **Remove device**. Try to install the printer again.

2. If the problem is still not solved, completely remove the printer drivers by using the printui command. The Printer User Interface command, **printui**, is used by administrators to manage printers and printer drivers on remote computers. You can also use it to delete drivers on the local computer. Follow these steps:

   a. If the printer is listed in the Settings app or the Devices and Printers window, remove it. (Sometimes Windows automatically puts a printer there when it finds printer drivers are installed.)

   b. Before you can delete printer drivers, you must stop the print spooler service. Open the **Services** console, and use it to stop the Print Spooler (refer to Figure 10-45). To delete any print jobs left in the queue, open **Explorer** and delete all files in the C:\Windows\System32\spool\PRINTERS folder.

Figure 10-45   **Use the printui command to delete printer drivers and possibly delete the driver package (driver store)**

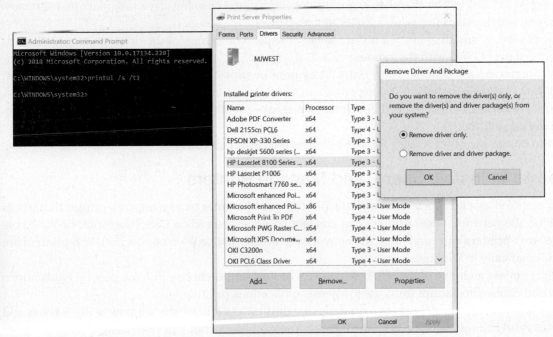

   c. You can now start the print spooler back up. Because the printer is no longer listed in the Settings app or the Devices and Printers window, starting the spooler will not tie up these drivers.

   d. Open an **elevated command prompt window**, which is a window used to enter commands that have administrator privileges. To open this window, type **cmd** in the Windows 10/11 search box, and then click **Run as administrator**. Respond to the UAC box.

   e. At the command prompt (see the left side of Figure 10-45), enter the command `printui /s /t2`. In the command line, the /s causes the Print Server Properties dialog box to open, and the /t2 causes the Drivers tab to be the selected tab.

(continues)

10

f. The Print Server Properties dialog box opens, as shown in the middle of Figure 10-45. Select the printer and click **Remove**. In the Remove Driver And Package dialog box (see the right side of Figure 10-45), select **Remove driver only**, and click **OK**. It is not necessary to remove the driver package. (This driver package, also called the driver store, can be installed on this computer or a remote computer; it holds a backup of the printer drivers.)

g. When a warning box appears, click **Yes**. Close all windows.

3. Try to install the printer again. Start the installation from the CD that came bundled with the printer or by using the printer setup program downloaded from the printer manufacturer's website.

Module Summary

Printer Types and Features

- The two most popular types of printers are laser and inkjet. Other types of printers are impact printers (dot matrix), thermal printers, and 3D printers. Laser printers produce the highest quality, followed by inkjet printers. Dot matrix printers have the advantage of being able to print multicopy documents. 3D printers use a plastic filament or a resin to build a 3D model of a digital image.
- The seven steps that a laser printer performs to print are processing, charging, exposing, developing, transferring, fusing, and cleaning. The charging, exposing, developing, and cleaning steps take place inside removable cartridges, which makes the printer easier to maintain.
- Inkjet printers print by shooting ionized ink at a sheet of paper. The quality of the printout largely depends on the quality of paper used with the printer.
- Dot matrix printers are a type of impact printer. They print by projecting pins from the print head against an inked ribbon that deposits ink on the paper.
- Direct thermal printers use heat to burn dots into special paper, and thermal transfer printers melt the ribbon or foil during printing.
- If you want to design your own images for three-dimensional printing, you'll need a 3D modeling program.

Using Windows to Install, Share, and Manage Printers

- A printer is installed as a local printer connected directly to a computer or as a network printer that works as a device on the network. Local printers can connect to a computer via a USB, Bluetooth, or Wi-Fi connection. Network printers can connect to the network via an Ethernet or Wi-Fi connection. USB printers are installed automatically in Windows.
- When a printer offers a choice of drivers between PCL or Postscript, choose PCL for general applications and speed, and choose Postscript for graphic-intense applications printing.
- Windows installs, manages, and removes a printer using the Printers & scanners window in the Settings app or the Devices and Printers window in Control Panel. You can also install a printer using a setup program provided by the printer manufacturer. Always print a test page after installing a printer.
- A print server can be a computer on the network, firmware embedded in a network printer, or other network hardware such as a router or firewall.
- A printer can be shared in Windows so others on the network can use it. To use a shared printer, the printer drivers must be installed on the remote computer.
- Network printers are identified on the network by their IP address.
- The Windows print queue is managed from the Printers & scanners window or from the Devices and Printers window.
- Secure a shared printer with user authentication, secured printing, audit logs, and badging.

- Network scan services include scan-to-email, scan-to-SMB, and scan-to-cloud.
- Printer features—such as duplexing, collating, and page orientation—are managed in a printer Properties dialog box.

Printer Maintenance

- An inkjet or laser printer can be calibrated to align the color on the page. The nozzles of an inkjet printer tend to clog or dry out, especially when the printer remains unused. The nozzles can be cleaned automatically by means of printer software or buttons on the front panel of the printer.
- Check the page count of the printer to know when service is due and you need to order a printer maintenance kit. The page count can be reported on the printer panel or through a web-based utility in the printer firmware.

Troubleshooting Printers

- When troubleshooting printers, first isolate the problem. Narrow the source to the printer, connectivity between the computer and its local printer, the network, Windows, printer drivers, the application using the printer, or the printer installation. Test pages printed directly to the printer or within Windows can help narrow the source of the problem.
- Poor print quality can be caused by the printer drivers, the application, Windows, or the printer. For a laser printer, consider that low toner can be the problem. For an inkjet printer, consider that the ink cartridges need cleaning or replacing. The quality of paper can also be a problem.

Key Terms

For explanations of key terms, see the Glossary for this text.

3D printer	extension magnet brush	network printer	resin
ADF (automatic document feeder) scanner	filament	page description language (PDL)	secured printing
	flatbed scanner		separate pad
	fuser assembly	pickup roller	separation pad
ad hoc mode	imaging drum	Postscript (PS)	thermal paper
calibration	impact paper	print bed	thermal printer
charging	impact printer	print head	thermal transfer printer
default printer	infrastructure mode	Printer Control Language (PCL)	toner vacuum
direct thermal printer	ink cartridge		tractor feed
duplex printer	inkjet printer	printer maintenance kit	transfer belt
duplexing assembly	integrated print server	printer self-test page	transfer roller
elevated command prompt window	laser printer	printui	
	local printer	remote printing	

Thinking Critically

These questions are designed to prepare you for the critical thinking required for the A+ exams and may use information from other modules and the web.

1. You're responding to a troubleshooting ticket about a laser printer in HR that isn't working. According to the ticket, the printer runs the print job and successfully sends the paper through with the text printed correctly. However, the toner smudges easily and sticks to other papers, equipment, and clothes. Which part in the printer probably needs replacing?

   a. Fuser assembly
   b. Imaging drum
   c. Transfer roller
   d. Toner cartridge

2. You are not able to print a Word document on a Windows computer to a printer on the network. The network printer is connected directly to the network, but when you look at the Devices and Printers window, you see the name of the printer as \\BRYANT\HP LaserJet Pro MFP. In the following list, select the possible sources of the problem. (Choose all that apply.)

   a. The BRYANT computer is not turned on.
   b. The HP LaserJet printer is not online.
   c. The BRYANT computer does not have file and printer sharing enabled.
   d. The Windows computer has a stalled print spool.

3. You are not able to print a test page from your Windows computer to your local, USB-connected Canon Pixma printer. Which of the following are possible causes of the problem? (Choose all that apply.)

   a. The network is down.
   b. The printer cable is not connected properly.
   c. The Windows print spool is stalled.
   d. File and printer sharing is not enabled.

4. What should you do if an inkjet printer prints with missing dots or lines on the page?

   a. Change the toner cartridge.
   b. Clean the heating element.
   c. Replace the image drum.
   d. Clean the inkjet nozzles.

5. Why might you assign a static IP address to a printer?

6. You left a receipt on a desk. You decide to eat lunch at your desk, and you set your hot plate on top of the receipt. When you pick up your plate, you notice that the receipt has turned black. What likely happened to the receipt?

7. Why does a 3D resin printer print objects upside down?

8. You've been certified through badging to use a 3D printer at your university. You design your first object to print. What file type do you bring with you to the 3D printer to print your object?

9. When unboxing a new printer, why is it important to remove all protective tapes or films from the printer?

10. You work at a print shop that produces marketing materials, and your manager asks you to install a new printer. The printer comes with two options for drivers. One uses PCL, and the other uses Postscript. Which driver is the best option and why?

11. An accounting agency needs a recommendation for a new printer. What feature included with a printer would provide an extra level of confidentiality to protect client financial information?

12. You have some documents that you need to scan and make available to different device platforms on different networks. Which network scan service is the best solution?

13. When you are working with a laser printer, toner spills and gets on your hands, clothes, and floor. What is the best way to clean up?

14. A laser printer is printing images with ghost images. What part(s) of the laser printer are the most likely source of the problem?

15. You created a flyer for an event to post around campus. You changed the margins so they are as narrow as possible to create more space for the contents of the flyer. When you go to print the flyer, however, it comes out sideways. What likely caused the flyer to print sideways?

Hands-On Projects

Hands-On Project 10-1

Researching Printer Support

Est. Time: 30 minutes
Core 1 Objectives: 3.7, 5.6

Your company plans to purchase a new printer, and you want to evaluate the printer manufacturers' websites to determine which site offers the best support. Research three websites listed in Table 10-1, and answer these questions, supporting your answers with pages that you have saved or printed from the websites:

1. Which website made it easiest for you to select a new printer, based on your criteria for its use?
2. Which website made it easiest for you to find help for troubleshooting printer problems?
3. Which website gave you the best information about routine maintenance for its printers?
4. Which website gave you the best information about how to clean its printers?

Hands-On Project 10-2

Selecting a Color Printer for a Small Business

Est. Time: 30 minutes
Core 1 Objectives: 3.6, 3.7

Jack owns a small real estate firm and has come to you asking for help with his printing needs. Currently, he has a color inkjet printer that he is using to print flyers, business cards, brochures, and other marketing materials. However, he is not satisfied with the print quality and wants to invest in a printer that produces more professional-looking materials. He expects to print no more than 8000 sheets per month and needs the ability to print envelopes, letter-size and legal-size pages, and business cards. He wants to be able to automatically print on both sides of a legal-size page to produce a three-column brochure. Research printer solutions, and do the following:

1. Save or print webpages to present to Jack showing three printers that satisfy his needs. Include at least one laser printer and at least one printer technology other than laser in your selections.
2. Save or print webpages showing the routine maintenance requirements of these printers.
3. Save or print webpages showing all the consumable products (other than paper) that Jack should expect to have to purchase in the first year of use.
4. Calculate the initial cost of the equipment and the total cost of consumables for one year (other than paper) for each printer solution.
5. Prepare a list of advantages and disadvantages for each solution.
6. Based on your research, which of the three solutions do you recommend? Why?

10

Hands-On Project 10-3

Printing in the Cloud

Est. Time: 45 minutes
Core 1 Objective: 3.6

To practice cloud printing using PaperCut Mobility Print, you'll need a computer with an installed printer and another computer somewhere on the Internet or on the same network.

On the computer with an installed printer, do the following to register your printer as a cloud printer:

1. If you don't already have PaperCut Mobility Print, go to *papercut.com/products/free-software/mobility-print*, download the software, and install it. During set up, create a local account.

2. After creating an account, the utility page to configure PaperCut Mobility Print opens. Click **Select printers**. The list of installed printers appears. Turn on publishing for only the printers you want to use for cloud printing. Close the Published printers menu.

3. To enable cloud printing from beyond the local network, click **Enable Cloud Print**. Click **Enable**. Next, you'll need to configure an invitation link to share with anyone you want to be able to print on your selected printer. PaperCut Mobility Print suggests setting an expiration date for the invitation.

4. Send the link to another computer anywhere on the Internet or on the local network.

On a computer anywhere on the Internet or on the local network, do the following:

1. Open the link received from PaperCut Mobility Print. Click **Open**. The link opens the Set up webpage for client printing.

2. Click **Download and run Mobility Print**. Open and run the installer package. Follow the on-screen instructions to install PaperCut Mobility Print Client.

3. Return to the Set up website for client printing. Click **Connect and get my printers**. Click **Open**. This automatically retrieves the printers that were shared in the invitation link.

4. Navigate to a webpage you want to print. In the browser menu, select **Print**.

5. On the Print page, select the shared printer. The printer name includes an IP address and the label Mobility. The page prints over the web to your printer. Did your print job print correctly? Describe any problems with the print job.

Real Problems, Real Solutions

Real Problem 10-1

3D Printer Badging

Est. Time: 30 minutes
Core 1 Objective: 3.6

3D printer badging is an interesting process. If you've never had access to a 3D printer before, consider taking a class to explore using a 3D printer. Completing such a class could be useful for you if you ever need to support a 3D printer. Research class options at your local library or university, and find out if they have a 3D printer available for community use. If you don't have a class available locally, you can find an online class available for free, such as the one offered by Pikes Peak Library District in Colorado. Go to their website (*research.ppld.org/3dprinting/badging*), and complete steps 1 and 2, which are to watch the video and take the assessment quiz. What was your score on the quiz?

Real Problem 10-2

Practicing Troubleshooting Printers

Est. Time: 1 hour
Core 1 Objective: 3.7

To practice troubleshooting printers, gather in a group or work individually on a printer available to you. On small pieces of paper, write down 10–15 printer problems that you have learned how to fix in this module. Fold up the pieces of paper, and put them in a pile. Take turns drawing a paper with a printer problem. Write down the problem you need to solve as well as possible causes. Then, on the printer, perform the steps you would take to resolve that issue. If you don't have a printer to practice with, then write down the steps you would take, and compare answers with your classmates. Possible problems you could use include the following:

- Lines down the printed pages
- Garbled print on the page
- Toner not fusing to the paper
- Paper jams
- Faded print
- Incorrect paper size
- Multipage misfeed
- Multiple prints pending in the queue
- Speckling on printed pages
- Ghost images
- Incorrect colors printing
- Grinding noise
- Finisher malfunctions
- Incorrect page orientation

10

Part

2

CompTIA A+
Core 2
(220-1102)

Module
11

The Complex World of IT Professionals

Module Objectives

1 Support customers with professionalism and respect, in addition to your technical skills

2 Describe support systems and documentation that address issues of asset management, network topology, ticketing systems, standard operating procedures, and change management

3 Grasp the complexity of diverse software environments, and prepare to work in these environments

Core 2 Certification Objectives

1.1 Identify basic features of Microsoft Windows editions.

1.8 Explain common OS types and their purposes.

1.9 Given a scenario, perform OS installations and upgrades in a diverse OS environment.

4.1 Given a scenario, implement best practices associated with documentation and support systems information management.

4.2 Explain basic change-management best practices.

4.7 Given a scenario, use proper communication techniques and professionalism.

Introduction

This module is the first of 11 modules that cover the CompTIA A+ Certification Exam Core 2 objectives. In this module, you first learn about interpersonal skills (people skills, sometimes called soft skills) needed by an IT support technician. Next, you learn what your employer might expect of you when using a ticketing system and dealing with issues of change management and standard operating procedures. Finally, you learn about several operating systems you might be called on to support, including their purposes, overarching differences, and issues surrounding how they talk with each other.

> **Exam Tip**
>
> The A+ Core 2 exam covers workstation and laptop operating systems, including Windows, Linux, macOS, and Chrome OS. It also covers cell phone and tablet OSs, including iPadOS, iOS, and Android.

What Customers Want: Beyond Technical Know-How

> **Core 2 Objective** 4.7

Probably the most significant indication that an IT technician is doing a good job is that customers are consistently satisfied. In your career as an IT support technician, commit to providing excellent service and to treating customers as you would want to be treated in a similar situation. One of the most important ways to achieve customer satisfaction is to do your best by being prepared, both technically and personally. Being prepared includes knowing what customers want, what they don't like, and what they expect from an IT technician.

Equally important to being prepared technically is knowing how to work effectively with people in a technical world, which is one of the most sought-after skills in today's service-oriented work environments. An employer once told me, "It's not hard to find technically proficient people these days. But it's next to impossible to find people who know how to get along with others and can be counted on when managers are not looking over their shoulders." I could sense his frustration, but I also felt encouraged to know that good social skills and good work ethics can take you far in today's world. My advice to you is to take this part of the module seriously. It's important to be technically proficient, but the skills learned in this part of the module just might be the ones that make you stand out above the crowd to land that new job or promotion.

> **Note**
>
> People respond reciprocally to the position of your facial muscles. Try smiling when you greet someone and see what happens.

Become a Competent and Helpful Support Technician

> **Core 2 Objective** 4.7

The following traits distinguish a competent and helpful technician from a technician who is incompetent or unhelpful in the eyes of the customer:

- **Be dependable and reliable.** Customers appreciate and respect those who keep their word. If you promise to be back at 10:00 the next morning, be there on time. If you cannot keep your appointment, never ignore your promise. Call, apologize, explain what happened, and reschedule your appointment. Also, do your best to return phone calls the same day and return email within two days.

Note 2

Quote from R.C., an employer: "When I choose a person to work for me, in a lot of cases, I choose based on their past dependability or attendance. I am less concerned about a person's ability because I can train anyone to do a specific job. I cannot, however, train anyone to do anything if they are not present for me to train. Being dependable and reliable has a profound impact on customer relationships as well."

- **Keep a positive and helpful attitude.** This helps establish good customer relationships. You communicate your attitude in your tone of voice, the words you choose, how you use eye contact, your facial expressions, how you dress, and in many other subjective and subtle ways. Generally, your attitudes toward your customers stem from how you see people, how you see yourself, and how you see your job. Your attitude is a heart issue, not a head issue. To improve your attitude, you must do it from your heart. That's pretty subjective and cannot be defined with a set of rules, but it always begins with a decision to change. As you work with customers or users, make it a habit not to patronize or talk down to them. Don't make customers or users feel inferior. People appreciate it when they feel your respect for them, even when they have made a mistake or are not knowledgeable about the issue you are trying to resolve. If a problem is simple to solve, don't make other people feel they have wasted your time. Your customer or user should always be made to feel that the problem is important to you.

Applying Concepts

Customer Service

Est. Time: 15 minutes
Core 2 Objective: 4.7

Josie walked into a computer parts store and wandered over to the cleaning supplies looking for Ace monitor wipes. She saw another brand of wipes, but not the ones she wanted. Looking around for help, she noticed Mary stocking software on the shelves in the next aisle. She walked over to Mary and asked for help finding Ace monitor wipes. Mary put down her box, walked over to the cleaning supply aisle without speaking, picked up a can of wipes, and handed them to Josie, still without speaking a word. Josie explained she was looking for Ace wipes. Mary yelled over three aisles to a coworker in the back room, "Hey, Billy! This lady says she wants Ace monitor wipes. We got any?" Billy came from the back room and said, "No, we only carry those," pointing to the wipes in Mary's hand, and returned to the back room. Mary turned to Josie and said, "We only carry these," and then put the wipes back on the shelf. She turned to walk back to her aisle when Josie said to Mary, "Well, those Ace wipes are great wipes. You might want to consider carrying them." Mary said, "I'm only responsible for software." Josie left the store.

Discuss this situation in a small group of students and answer the following questions:

1. If you were Josie, how would you feel about the service in this store?
2. What would you have expected to happen that did not happen?
3. If you were Mary, how could you have provided better service?
4. If you were Billy, is there anything more you could have done to help?
5. If you were the store manager, what principles of good customer service would you want Billy and Mary to know that would have helped them in this situation?

- **Listen without interrupting your customer.** When you're working with or talking to a customer, focus on them. Don't assume you know what your customer is about to say. Let them say it, listen carefully, and don't interrupt (see Figure 11-1). Make it your job to satisfy this person, not just your organization, your boss, your bank account, or the customer's boss.

Figure 11-1   Learn to listen before you decide what a user needs or wants

iStock.com/Sportstock

- **Use proper and polite language.** Speak politely and use language that won't confuse your customer. Avoid using slang or jargon, which is technical language that only technical people understand. Avoid acronyms (initial letters that stand for words). For example, don't say to a nontechnical customer, "I need to ditch your PCIe 16 card," when you could explain yourself better by saying, "I need to replace the circuit board inside your computer that controls video."
- **Show sensitivity to cultural differences.** Cultural differences between people from different countries and communities can result in different sets of expectations when it comes to customer service. For example, culture can affect our degree of tolerance for uncertainty. Some cultures are willing to embrace uncertainty, and others strive to avoid it. Those who tend to avoid uncertainty can easily get upset when the unexpected happens. For these people, you need to make special efforts to communicate early and often when things are not going as expected.
- **Express patience and honor to those with physical disabilities.** For the physically disabled, especially the hearing- or sight-impaired, communication can be more difficult. It's your responsibility in these situations to do whatever is necessary to find a way to communicate. It's especially important to have an attitude that expresses honor and patience, which you will unconsciously express in your tone of voice, your choice of words, and your actions.

Note 3

Employers look for technicians with good social skills and work ethics because they realize that technicians with these skills are good for business.

- **Take ownership of the problem.** Taking ownership of the customer's problem means accepting the problem as your own. Doing that builds trust and loyalty because the customer knows you can be counted on. Taking ownership of a problem also increases your value in the eyes of your coworkers and manager. People who don't take ownership of the problem at hand are likely to be viewed as lazy, uncommitted, and uncaring. One way to take ownership of a problem is not to engage your manager in unproductive discussions about a situation they expect you to handle on your own.
- **Portray credibility.** Convey confidence to your customers. Don't allow yourself to appear confused, afraid, or befuddled. Troubleshoot the problem in a systematic way that portrays confidence and credibility. Get the job done, and do it with excellence. Credible technicians also know when the job is beyond their expertise and when to ask for help.
- **Work with integrity and honesty.** Don't try to hide your mistakes from your customer or your manager. Everyone makes mistakes, but don't compound them by a lack of integrity. Accept responsibility and do what you can to correct the error.
- **Know the law with respect to your work.** For instance, observe the laws concerning the use of software. Don't use or install pirated software.
- **Behave professionally.** A professional at work knows not to allow his emotions to interfere with business relationships. If a customer is angry, allow the customer to vent, keeping your own professional distance. (You do, however, have the right to expect a customer not to talk to you in an abusive way.)

Applying Concepts

Self-Control

Est. Time: 15 minutes
Core 2 Objective: 4.7

Jack had a bad day on the phones at the networking help desk in Atlanta. An electrical outage coupled with a generator failure had caused servers in San Francisco to be down most of the day. The entire help desk team had been fielding calls all day explaining to customers why they did not have service and giving expected recovery times. The servers were finally online, but it was taking hours to get everything reset and functioning. No one had taken a break all afternoon, but the call queue was still running about 20 minutes behind. JinHee, the help desk manager, had asked the team to work late until the queue was empty. It was Jack's son's birthday, and Jack's family was expecting him home on time. Jack moaned as he realized he might be late for Tyler's party. Everyone pushed hard to empty the queue. As Jack watched the last call leave the queue, he logged off, stood up, and reached for his coat.

And then another call comes in. Jack is tempted to ignore it, but decides he needs to answer it. It's Lacy, the executive assistant to the CEO (the chief executive officer over the entire company). When Lacy calls, all other priorities yield to her, and Lacy knows it. The CEO is having problems printing to the laser printer in his office. Would Jack please walk down to his office and fix the problem? Jack asks Lacy to check the simple things: "Is the printer turned on? Is it plugged in?" Lacy gets huffy and says, "Of course, I've checked that. Now come right now. I need to go." Jack walks down to the CEO's office, takes one look at the printer, and turns it on.

He turns to Lacy and says, "I suppose the on/off button was just too technical for you." Lacy glares at him in disbelief. Jack says, "I'll be leaving now." As he walks out, he begins to form a plan as to how he'll defend himself to his manager in the morning, knowing the inevitable call to JinHee's office will come.

In a group of two or four students, one student should play the role of Jack and another the role of JinHee. Discuss these questions:

1. JinHee is informed the next morning of Jack's behavior, and calls Jack into her office. She likes Jack and wants him to be successful in the company. Jack is resistant and feels justified in what he did. As JinHee, what do you think is important that Jack understand? How can you explain this to Jack so he can accept it? What would you advise Jack to do?

2. Switch roles or switch team members and replay the roles.

3. What are three principles of relating to people that would be helpful for Jack to keep in mind?

- **Dress professionally.** Dress appropriately for the environment. Take a shower each day, and brush your teeth after each meal. Use mouthwash. Iron your shirt. If you're not in good health, try as best you can to take care of the problem. Your appearance matters. Match your attire to the requirements of your environment:
  - **Business casual.** For men, **business casual** is neutral-colored dress slacks, khakis, polo shirt, tailored shirt, sweater, dark socks, dress shoes, and/or optional sports coat and tie. For women, business casual is a blouse, tasteful sweater, simple dress or skirt, slacks, closed-toe shoe, and tasteful jewelry. For both men and women, T-shirts, jeans, and shorts are usually not included. In a typical IT workplace, assume business casual until your boss says otherwise.
  - **Business formal.** To shine at a job interview, always dress business formal. Business formal might also be appropriate at work when you attend an upper-level management meeting or event. For men, **business formal** includes matching jacket and slacks, shirt, and tie with dark socks and dress shoes. For women, business formal is a dress pant or skirt with matching jacket. Skirt lengths should be at or just above the knee. Make sure your blouse is not so short it shows your stomach and not so long it covers the hem of your skirt. Wear closed-toe shoes and tasteful jewelry.

Note 4

Your customers might never remember what you said or did, but they will always remember how you made them feel.

- **Control your words.** Don't gossip. Coworkers might listen attentively to your negative gossip about others, but they will now probably suspect that you'll gossip about them when their backs are turned. Your credibility and trustworthiness suffer when you gossip. And finally, don't use rough language; it is <u>never</u> appropriate.

Plan for Good Service

Core 2 Objective 4.7

Your customers can be internal, meaning you work for the same company and might consider the customers colleagues, or they can be external (they come to you or your company for service). Customers can be highly technical or technically naive, represent a large company or simply own a home computer, be prompt or slow at paying their bills, want only the best (and be willing to pay for it) or be searching for bargain service, be friendly and easy to work with or demanding and condescending. In each situation, the keys to success are always the same: Don't allow circumstances or personalities to affect your commitment to excellence, and treat the customer as you would want to be treated.

Exam Tip ✔

The A+ Core 2 exam expects you to know that when serving a customer, you should be on time, dress appropriately, avoid distractions, set and meet expectations and timelines, communicate the status of the solution with the customer, and deal appropriately with customers' confidential materials.

First impressions are often lasting, so let's start there.

Initial Contact With a Customer

Your initial contact with a customer might be when the customer comes to you (such as in a retail setting), when you go to the customer's site, when the customer calls you on the phone, when the customer reaches you by chat or email, or when you are assigned a **ticket** (sometimes called an incident) already created when another person made initial contact and entered the request in a tracking system of customer calls. In each situation, always follow the specific guidelines of your employer. Let's look at some general guidelines for handling first contact with customers.

When you answer the phone, identify yourself and your organization. (Follow your employer's guidelines on what to say.) Follow company policies to obtain specific information when answering an initial call, such as name (get the right spelling), phone number, and business name. For example, your company might require that you obtain a licensing or warranty number to determine whether the customer is entitled to receive your support. After you have obtained the information you need and confirmed you are authorized to help the customer, open up the conversation for the caller to describe the problem.

Prepare for on-site visits by reviewing information given to you by the person who took the call. Know the problem you are going to address, the urgency of the situation, and what computer, software, and hardware need servicing. Arrive with a complete set of equipment appropriate to the visit. That might include a toolkit, flashlight, multimeter, ESD strap and mat, and bootable media.

When you arrive at the customer's site, greet the customer in a friendly manner, and shake hands (see Figure 11-2). Use terms such as Mr. or Ms. and Sir or Ma'am when addressing the customer unless you are certain the customer expects you to use their first name. If the site is a residence, you should <u>not</u> remain there when only a minor is present. If a minor child answers the door, ask to speak with an adult, and don't allow the adult to leave the house with only you and the child present.

Figure 11-2   If a customer permits it, begin each new relationship
with a handshake

iStock.com/killerb10

After initial greetings, the first thing you should do is listen and ask questions. As you listen, it's fine to take notes, but don't start the visit by filling out your paperwork. Save the paperwork for later, or have the essentials already filled out before you reach the site.

Interview the Customer

Troubleshooting begins by interviewing the user. Take notes as you ask the user questions, and keep asking questions until you thoroughly understand the problem. Have the customer reproduce the problem, and carefully note each step taken and its results. This process gives you clues about the problem and the customer's technical proficiency, which helps you know how to communicate with the customer.

Use diplomacy and good manners when you work with a user to solve a problem. For example, if you suspect that the user dropped the computer, don't ask, "Did you drop the laptop?" Put the question in a less accusatory manner: "Could the laptop have been dropped?"

Set and Meet Customer Expectations

Professional technicians know that it is their responsibility to set and meet expectations with a customer. It's important to create an expectation of certainty with customers so they are not left hanging without knowing what will happen next.

Part of setting expectations is to establish a timeline with your customer for the completion of a project. If you cannot solve the problem immediately, explain to the customer what needs to happen, and outline the likely timeline for a solution. Then keep the customer informed about the progress of the solution. For example, you can say to a customer, "I need to return to the office and research the cost of parts that need replacing. I'll call you tomorrow before 10 a.m. with an estimate." If you later find out you need more time, call the customer before 10 a.m., explain your problem, and give him a new time to expect your call. This kind of service is very much appreciated by customers, and if you are consistent, you will quickly gain their confidence.

Figure 11-3   Advise and then allow a customer to make repair or purchasing decisions

iStock.com/Dean Mitchell

Another way to set expectations is to give customers an opportunity to make decisions about repairs to their equipment. When explaining to the customer what needs to be done to fix a problem, offer repair or replacement options if they apply (see Figure 11-3). Don't make decisions for your customer. Explain the problem and what you must do to fix it, giving as many details as the customer wants. When a customer must make a choice, state the options in a way that does not unfairly favor the most lucrative solution for you as the technician or for your company. For example, if you must replace a motherboard (a costly repair in parts and labor), explain the total cost of repairs, and then help the customer decide if it's better to purchase a new system or repair the existing one.

Work With a Customer on Site

As you work with a customer on site, avoid distractions. Don't accept personal calls or texts on your cell phone, and definitely don't check social media sites when you're on the job. Most organizations require that you answer calls from work while on site, but keep them to a minimum. Be aware that the customer might be listening, so be careful not to discuss problems with coworkers, your manager, or other situations that might put the company, its employees, or products in a bad light with the customer. If you absolutely must excuse yourself from the on-site visit for personal reasons, explain the situation to the customer, and return as soon as possible.

When working at a user's desk, follow these general guidelines:

1. As you work, be as unobtrusive as possible. Consider yourself a guest in the customer's office or residence. Don't make a big mess. Keep your tools and papers out of the customer's way. Don't pile your belongings and tools on top of the user's papers, books, and so forth.

2. Protect the customer's confidential and private materials. For example, if you are working on the printer and discover a budget report in the out tray, quickly turn it over so you can't read it, and hand it to the customer. If you notice a financial spreadsheet is displayed on the customer's computer screen, step away and ask the user if they want to first close the spreadsheet before you work with the computer. If sensitive documents are on the customer's desk, you might let them know and ask if they would like to put them out of your view or in a safe place.

3. Don't take over the mouse or keyboard from the user without permission.

4. Ask permission again before you use the printer or other equipment.

5. Don't use the phone without permission.

6. Accept personal inconvenience to accommodate the user's urgent business needs. For example, if the user gets an important call while you are working, don't allow your work to interfere. You might need to stop work and perhaps leave the room.

7. Also, if the user is present, ask permission before you make a software or hardware change, even if the user has just given you permission to interact with the computer.

8. Don't disclose information about a customer on social media sites, and don't use those public outlets to complain about difficulties with a customer.

In some IT support situations, it is appropriate to consider yourself a support to the user as well as to the computer. Your goals can include educating the user as well as repairing the computer. If you want users to learn something from a problem they caused, explain how to fix the problem, and walk them through the process if necessary. Don't fix the problem yourself unless they ask you to do so. It takes a little longer to train a user, but it

Figure 11-4 Teaching a user how to fix a problem can prevent it from reoccurring

iStock.com/Sportstock

Figure 11-5 Learn to be patient and friendly when helping users

iStock.com/Artstock Productions

is more productive in the end because the user learns more and is less likely to repeat the mistake (see Figure 11-4).

Work With a Customer on the Phone

Phone support requires more interaction with customers than any other type of IT support. To understand customers' problems and give clear instructions, you must be able to visualize what customers see at their computer. Patience is required if the customer must be told each key to press or command button to click.

Help desk support requires excellent communication skills, good phone manners, and lots of patience (see Figure 11-5). As your help desk skills improve, you will learn to think through the process as though you were sitting in front of the computer yourself. Drawing diagrams and taking notes as you talk can be very helpful. In some cases, help desk support personnel might use software, such as Freshdesk by Freshworks (*freshdesk.com*), that enables the remote control of customers' computers. Always communicate clearly with customers when using this type of software so they understand what type of access they are allowing you to have on their computers.

If your call is accidentally disconnected, call back immediately. Don't eat or drink while on the phone. If you must put callers on hold, tell them how long it will be before you get back to them. Speak clearly and don't talk too fast. Don't complain about your job, your boss, coworkers, your company, or other companies or products to your customers. A little small talk is okay and is sometimes beneficial in easing a tense situation, but keep it upbeat and positive.

Deal With Difficult Customers

Most customers are polite and appreciate your help. If you make it a habit to treat others as you want to be treated, you'll find that most of your customers will tend to treat you well, too. However, you occasionally will have to deal with a difficult customer. In this section of the module, you learn how to work with customers who are not knowledgeable, who are overly confident, and who complain.

When the Customer Is Not Knowledgeable When on site, you can put a computer in good repair without depending on a customer to help you. But when you are trying to solve a problem over the phone, with a customer as your only eyes, ears, and hands, a computer-illiterate user can present a challenge. Here are some tips for handling this situation:

- Be specific with your instructions. For example, instead of saying, "Open Explorer," say, "Using your mouse, right-click the Start button, and click File Explorer from the menu."
- Don't ask the customer to do something that might destroy settings or files without first having the customer back them up carefully. If you think the customer can't handle your request, ask for some on-site help.
- Frequently ask the customer what is displayed on the screen to help you track the keystrokes and action.
- Follow along at your own computer. It's easier to direct the customer keystroke by keystroke if you are doing the same things.
- Give the customer plenty of opportunity to ask questions.

- Genuinely compliment the customer whenever you can to help the customer gain confidence.
- If you determine that the customer cannot help you solve the problem without a lot of coaching, you might need to tactfully request that the caller have someone with more experience call you. The customer will most likely breathe a sigh of relief and have someone take over the problem.

Note 5

When solving computer problems in an organization other than your own, check with technical support within that organization instead of working only with the user. User might not be aware of policies that have been set on their computers to prevent changes to the OS, hardware, or applications.

When the Customer Is Overly Confident   Sometimes customers might want to give advice, take charge of a call, withhold information they think you don't need to know, or execute commands at the computer without letting you know so that you don't have enough information to follow along. A situation like this must be handled with tact and respect for the customer. Here are a few tips:

- When you can, compliment the customer's knowledge, experience, or insight.
- Slow the conversation down. You can say, "Please slow down. You're moving too fast for me to follow. Help me catch up."
- Don't back off from using problem-solving skills. You must still have the customer check the simple things, but direct the conversation with tact. For example, you can say, "I know you've probably gone over these simple things already, but could we just do them again together?"
- Be careful not to accuse the customer of making a mistake.
- Even though the customer might be using technical jargon, keep to your policy of not using jargon back to the customer unless you're convinced they truly understand you.

Exam Tip ✔

The A+ Core 2 exam expects you to know that it is important not to minimize a customer's problem and not to be judgmental toward a customer.

When the Customer Complains   When you are on site or on the phone, a customer might complain to you about your organization, products, or service or the product and service of another company. Consider the complaint to be helpful feedback that can lead to a better product or service and better customer relationships. Here are a few suggestions that can help you handle complaints and defuse customer anger:

- Be an active listener, and let customers know they are not being ignored. Look for the underlying problem. Don't take complaints or anger personally.
- Give the customer a little time to vent, and apologize when you can. Then start the conversation by asking questions, taking notes, and solving problems. Unless you must have the information for problem-solving, don't spend a lot of time finding out exactly who the customer dealt with and what happened to upset the customer.
- Don't be defensive. It's better to leave the customer with the impression that you and your company are listening and willing to admit mistakes. No matter how much anger is expressed, resist the temptation to argue or become defensive.
- Know how your employer wants you to handle a situation where you are verbally abused. For example, you might say something like this in a calm voice: "I'm sorry, but my employer does not require me to accept this kind of talk."

Figure 11-6   When a customer is upset, try to find a place of agreement

Elnur/Shutterstock.com

- If the customer is complaining about a product or service that is not from your company, don't start by saying, "That's not our problem." Instead, listen to the customer complain. Don't appear as though you don't care.
- If the complaint is against you or your product, identify the underlying problem if you can. Ask questions and take notes. Then pass these notes on to people in your organization who need to know.
- Sometimes simply making progress or reducing the problem to a manageable state reduces the customer's anxiety. As you are talking to a customer, summarize what you have both agreed on or observed so far in the conversation (see Figure 11-6).
- Point out ways that you think communication could be improved. For example, you might say, "I'm sorry, but I'm having trouble understanding what you want. Could you please slow down, and let's take this one step at a time?"

Applying Concepts

Culture of Honor

Est. Time: 15 minutes
Core 2 Objective: 4.7

Gawin is one of the most intelligent and knowledgeable support technicians in his group at CloudPool, Inc. He is about to be promoted to software engineer, and today is his last day on the help desk. Simone, a potential customer with little computer experience, calls asking for help in accessing the company website. Gawin says, "The URL is www dot cloud pool dot com." Simone responds, "What's a URL?" Gawin's patience grows thin. He's thinking to himself, "Oh, help! Just two more hours and I'm off these phones for good." In a tone of voice that makes it clear Gawin thinks she's an idiot, he says to Simone, "You know, lady! That address box at the top of your browser. Now enter www dot cloud pool dot com!" Simone gets flustered and intimidated and doesn't know what to say next. She really wants to know what a browser is, but instead she says, "Wait. I'll just ask someone in the office to help me," and hangs up the phone.

Discuss the situation with others in a small group and answer these questions:

1. If you were Gawin's manager and overheard this call, how would you handle the situation?
2. What principles of working with customers does Gawin need to keep in mind?

Two students sit back to back, one playing the role of Gawin and the other playing the role of Simone. Play out the entire conversation. Others in the group can offer suggestions and constructive criticism.

The Customer Decides When the Work Is Done

When you think you've solved the problem, allow the customer to decide if the service is finished to their satisfaction. For remote support, the customer generally ends the call or chat session, not the technician. If you end the call too soon and the problem is not completely resolved, the customer can be frustrated, especially if it is difficult to contact you again.

For on-site work, after you have solved the problem, complete these tasks before you close the call:

1. If you changed anything on the computer after you booted it, reboot one more time to make sure you have not caused a problem with the boot.

2. Allow the customer enough time to be fully satisfied that all is working. Does the printer work? Print a test page. Does the network connection work? Can the customer sign in to the network and access data on it?

3. If you backed up data before working on the problem and then restored the data from backups, ask the user to verify that the data is fully restored.

4. Review the service call with the customer. Summarize the instructions and explanations you have given during the call. This is an appropriate time to fill out your paperwork and explain to the customer what you have written. Then ask if they have any questions.

5. Explain preventive maintenance to the customer, such as deleting temporary files from the hard drive or cleaning the mouse. Most customers don't have preventive maintenance contracts for their computers and appreciate the time you take to show them how to take better care of their equipment. One technician keeps a pack of monitor wipes in his toolkit and ends each call by cleaning the customer's monitor screen.

> **Exam Tip** ✔
>
> The A+ Core 2 exam expects you to know to follow up with the customer at a later date to verify their satisfaction.

To demonstrate a sincere concern for your customer's business and that you have owned the problem, it's extremely important to follow up later with the customer. Ask if they are still satisfied with your work, and ask if they have any more questions. For example, you can say to the customer, "I'll call you on Monday to make sure everything is working and you're still satisfied with the work." On Monday, make that call. As you do, you're building customer loyalty.

Sometimes You Must Escalate a Problem

You are not going to solve every computer problem you encounter. Knowing how to **escalate** a problem properly so it is assigned to people higher in the support chain is one of the first things you should learn on a new job. Know your company's policy for escalation. What documents or entries in the ticketing system software do you use? Who do you contact? How do you pass the problem on—do you use email, a phone call, or an online entry in a database? Do you remain the responsible "support" party, or does the person now addressing the problem become the new contact? Are you expected to keep in touch with the customer and the problem, or are you totally out of the picture?

When you escalate, let the customer know. Tell the customer you are passing the problem on to someone who is more experienced or has access to more extensive resources. If you check back with the customer only to find out that the other support person has not called or followed through to the customer's satisfaction, don't lay blame or point fingers. Just do whatever you can to help within your company guidelines. Your call to the customer will go a long way toward helping the situation.

Working With Coworkers

Learn to be a professional when working with coworkers. A professional at work is someone who puts business matters above personal matters (see Figure 11-7). **In big bold letters, I can say the key to being professional is to learn not to be personally offended when someone lets you down or does not please you**. Remember, most people do the best they can considering the business and personal constraints they are up against. Getting offended leads to becoming bitter about others and about your job. Learn to keep negative opinions to yourself, and to expect the best of others. When a coworker starts to gossip, try to politely change the subject.

Figure 11-7   Coworkers who act professionally are fun to work with

Know your limitations, and be willing to admit when you can't do something. For example, Larry's manager stops by his desk and asks him to accept one more project. Larry already is working many hours overtime just to keep up. He needs to politely say to his boss, "I can accept this new project only if you relieve me of some of these tasks."

Applying Concepts

Active Learning

Est. Time: 15 minutes
Core 2 Objective: 4.7

Ray was a new member of a corporate help desk team that supported hospitals across the nation. He had only had a couple of weeks of training before he was turned loose on the phones. He was a little nervous the first day he took calls without a mentor sitting beside him. His first call came from Fernanda, a radiology technician who was trying to sign in to the network to start the day. When Fernanda entered her network ID and passcode, an error message stated her user account was not valid. She told Ray she had tried signing in several times on two different computers. Ray checked his database and found her account, which appeared to be in good order. He asked her to try again. She did and got the same results. In his two weeks of training, this problem had never occurred. He told her, "I'm sorry, I don't know how to solve this problem." She said, "Okay, well, thank you anyway," and hung up. She immediately called the help desk number back and the call was answered by Jackie, who sits across the room from Ray. Fernanda said, "The other guy couldn't fix my problem. Can you help me?"

"What other guy?" Jackie asked.

"I think his name was Ray."

"Oh, him! He's new and he doesn't know much. Besides that, he should have asked for help. Tell me the problem." Jackie reset the account and the problem was solved.

In a group of three or more students, discuss and answer the following questions:

1. What mistake did Ray make? What should he have done or said?
2. What mistake did Jackie make? What should she have done or said?
3. What three principles of relating to customers and coworkers would be helpful for Ray and Jackie to keep in mind?

Documentation and Support Systems

Core 2 Objectives 4.1, 4.2

Well-run IT departments rely on good documentation and support systems to keep up with all the information surrounding IT operations in the entire organization. In this part of the module, you learn about the types of documentation and support systems you might encounter in your IT career and what is generally expected of you as an IT technician to follow these best practices and policies.

Types of Documents and Support Systems

Core 2 Objective 4.1

Some examples of documents and systems an IT technician might encounter in an organization are:

- **Knowledge base.** A **knowledge base** is a collection of articles containing text, images, or video that give information about a network, product, or service. Here are two examples of how a knowledge base might be used:
  - **Customer service.** To better support customers, a company might publish a knowledge base about its products or services on its website. Technical support specialists usually have access to a knowledge base to aid in helping customers during support calls; the knowledge base might be integrated into a ticketing system.

Figure 11-8 The print on this tag is embedded under a protective surface so it can't be easily damaged

Source: MyAssetTag.com

- **IT training and troubleshooting.** As IT personnel install, configure, and troubleshoot devices and software, the information they learn can be documented in the IT department's knowledge base so it's readily available for future troubleshooting and for training new IT personnel.
- **Asset management. Asset management** tracks physical and digital assets, including end-user devices, network devices, IP addresses, software licenses, and related licenses. These inventory lists are typically maintained by software such as IT Asset Management by Alloy Software (*alloysoftware.com*). The application might track equipment by using an **asset tag** with an ID and a theft-prevention plate, such as the one shown in Figure 11-8. These tags and plates contain **barcodes** that are easily read by a laser scanner. Asset tracking software can scan the barcodes to report on existing inventory, track equipment, report needed maintenance, and help with identifying and returning stolen property.

The software and hardware inventory lists might be maintained in a database system that includes information used to manage the assets, such as the following:

- The **asset ID** used to identify hardware equipment tracked in the system.
- **Procurement life cycle** data needed to replace an aged asset. The procurement life cycle data might include information on suppliers for the asset, contract terms for preferred suppliers, purchase orders, invoices, payment processing, and delivery data.
- Warranty and licensing information, such as terms of warranty for a hardware device or licensing terms for an application or other software.
- Users who are authorized to use an asset. For example, when a laptop is checked out to an employee, the employee's name and information is recorded in the asset management system.
- Auditing trails. Asset management might be audited, and the system should be able to provide trails for noncurrent activity such as who has had the laptop checked out to them since it was purchased.

- **Password policy.** In the module "Securing and Sharing Windows Resources," you learn what is required to create a strong password and best practices for passwords (for example, allowing one to expire so that the user must occasionally change it). These requirements are sometimes documented as a password policy.
- **Network topology diagrams.** Network documentation should contain a map of a network's topology, which is called a **network topology diagram**. In networking, **topology** refers to the pattern in which devices on a network are connected with each other. For example, devices connected in a line are using a bus topology, and devices connected to a single, centralized device are using a star topology. As described in the module "Networking Fundamentals," most Ethernet networks today use a design called a star bus topology, which means that nodes are connected to one or more centralized devices that are connected to each other (see Figure 11-9).

A network topology diagram might show how nodes on a network are physically connected, such as the one in Figure 11-9, or it might show the logical network topology. For example, Figure 11-10 shows the logical connection among clients and servers to indicate how data flows among them.

Figure 11-9   A star bus network formed by nodes connected to multiple switches

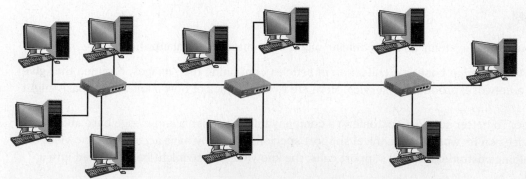

Figure 11-10   A logical network topology showing how data flows among computers

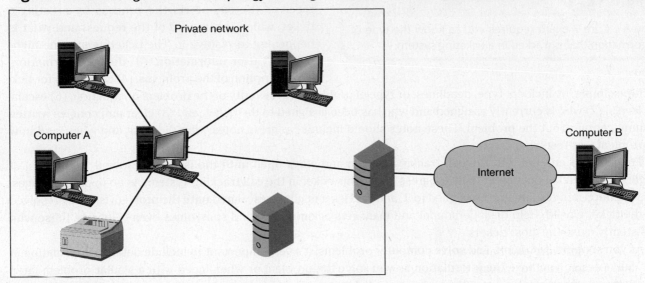

On small networks, a network topology diagram can be hand drawn, but for larger networks, inventory data is usually compiled automatically through network scans. For example, Spiceworks (*spiceworks.com*) offers a free network inventory product that probes devices on the network and presents a list of detected devices along with any available information, such as IP addresses, installed operating systems, and shared folders.

- **Ticketing systems.** One of the first systems you'll learn to use in an IT organization is its **ticketing system** used to track support calls and give technicians a place to keep their call notes. Figure 11-11 shows a window in a popular ticketing-system application called everything HelpDesk.

Figure 11-11   Ticketing system software allows you to create, edit, and close tickets used by technicians

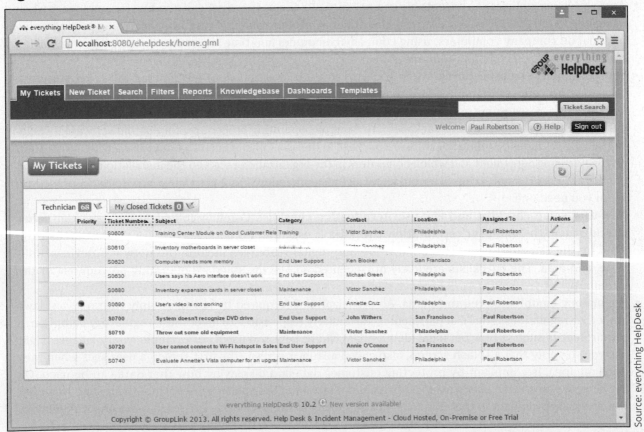

Source: everything HelpDesk

11

When someone initiates a call for help, whoever receives the call starts the process by creating a ticket, which is a record of the request and what is happening to resolve it. The ticketing system might track (1) user information, (2) device information, (3) description of the problems, (4) categories for tickets (for example, by incident type, deadlines, or type of problem), (5) severity of the problem or situation, (6) escalation levels, (7) who is currently assigned and who has been assigned to the ticket, and (8) clear and concise written communication about the problem. These notes should include progress notes, who did what and when, and how the problem was resolved.

The ticket is entered into the call tracking system and stays open until the issue is resolved. Support staff assigned to the ticket document their progress under this ticket in the call tracking system. As an open ticket ages, more attention and resources are assigned to it, and the ticket might be escalated until the problem is finally resolved and the ticket closed. Help desk personnel and managers acknowledge and sometimes even celebrate those who consistently close the most tickets!

As you support customers and solve computer problems, it's very important to include detailed information in your call notes so you have the information as you solve the problem or when faced with a similar problem later. Sometimes another person must pick up your open ticket, and they should not have to waste time finding out information you already knew. Also, tracking-system notes are sometimes audited.

- **Acceptable use policies.** An **acceptable use policy (AUP)** documents a code of conduct for employees when using corporate resources. For example, the AUP may prohibit an employee from accessing pornographic material on company computers, using company computers and time for personal shopping, or installing pirated software on company computers.
- **Standard operating procedures.** When you start in a new position, your job training will cover **standard operating procedures** that detail how to function in the organization, including how to perform basic procedures such as recording your overtime hours as well as more advanced procedures such as performing custom installations of software packages. For example, operating procedures for custom software installations might include recording the software package in the asset management system along with information on the licensing agreement and which computers in the organization received the installation. As with many employee tasks, it's not so important to know all these procedures as it is to know how to find a procedure when you need one.
- **New-user setup checklist and end-user termination checklist.** Carefully following the **new-user setup checklist** and the **end-user termination checklist** is essential for good security of the resources managed by the IT department. These hardware and digital resources include the network, devices, software, and data. The checklists are likely documented among the standard operating procedures for the IT department.
- **Regulatory compliance requirements.** An organization is required by law to comply with relevant laws and other regulations. The IT department is particularly responsible to meet these **regulatory compliance requirements** such as how personal identity data can be kept and used. For example, your manager might ask you to verify that a **splash screen**, also called a launch screen (the first screen a user sees when they open an app), is compliant by protecting customer data and displaying how that data can be used. On the screen, you see the user's email address and realize that the splash screen is not compliant. However, the screen is compliant in that it details what happens to the user data. You learn more about regulatory compliance in the module "Security Strategies."

One more type of documentation covered in this module is that used in change management best practices, which is discussed next.

Change Management

Core 2 Objective 4.2

As an IT support technician, you will undoubtedly be involved in new projects, such as installing hardware or software, upgrading networks, moving IT operations from on-site services to cloud-based services, rolling out virtualized desktops across the organization, implementing a VoIP communication platform, and much more. A project is temporary—it has a beginning, an end, and a singular, well-defined goal. A successful project depends on expert project management to direct a project team through specific tasks and deliver results on time, within the agreed-to budget, and with complete customer satisfaction.

Exam Tip ✔

The A+ Core 2 exam will give you a scenario and expect you to apply the basic principles of change management, including documenting business processes, purpose of change, scope of change, risk analysis, end-user acceptance, change boards, rollback plans, and the need to document change.

Figure 11-12   The general flow of change management

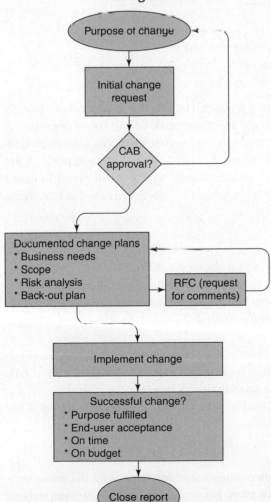

When a project is implemented, change happens. Change managed well means that people affected by the change can make a smooth transition from their current state to the project goal or end result. In most situations, **change management** is closely integrated with project management and often involves the same teams. For example, a project manager works with a team to plan, develop, test, and implement new software. A change manager might work with the same team to define how the software will affect people and manage all communication, scheduling, training, and support required so the affected people accept and embrace the end result.

A high-level change process is diagrammed in Figure 11-12. Know, however, that change processes vary widely. Next, we'll look at the basic elements of change management and how they might relate to you as an IT support technician.

Documented Business Processes

A business is complex, and leaders of well-run organizations know they must understand and document their core business goals and processes. **Documented business processes** are related activities that lead to a desired business goal, such as an efficient and cost-effective service, excellent customer satisfaction, or a superior product. For example, if customer satisfaction is a defined business goal, IT operational processes might describe how customers are taken care of, support tickets are documented, and customer satisfaction is measured.

As change happens, be aware of how this change affects documented business processes. For example, suppose help desk software is changed so the customer's electronic signature is required when a ticket is closed. If you forget the electronic signature, your company may not be able to collect payment or follow up with the customer for a satisfaction survey.

Purpose of Change

The starting point for every proposed change is a clear and concise purpose for the change. What will change? What is the current situation and expected outcome? Why is the change needed? What happens if the organization does not initiate this change? How will the success of the change be measured?

Note 6

IT technicians often communicate with people impacted by change. Therefore, it's important that you have a firm understanding of the purpose for the change so you can maintain a positive, helpful attitude.

A proposed change is formally submitted using a change request process. A change **request form** states what needs to be updated or changed but does not indicate how the change will be executed. A simple change request might require only preapproval from a manager. Complex changes, with higher impact and risks, are submitted to a change advisory board. The **change advisory board (CAB)** meets on a regular basis to assess, prioritize, authorize, and schedule changes. The change manager and other representatives approve changes based on the recommendations of the change advisory board.

Change Plan and Scope

The change plan defines the **scope of change**, which may outline the following:

- The purpose of the change, including key components of the change and how they will be addressed
- Skill sets, tasks, and activities required to carry out the change
- Staff member responsible for the managing the change
- Individuals or departments that will participate in the change
- Systems that will be affected by the change and the impact on those systems
- The date and possibly even the time the change will be implemented
- How the success of change is measured and when the change is completed

The scope of change defines your responsibilities in the change plan. It's important that you understand exactly your assignment for planning, implementing, and supporting the change and then work within these boundaries, which is called working "in scope." The scope of change might evolve through the feedback process of change management, but until the scope changes, it's important to work in scope. Although it might be tempting to perform yet one more step while implementing a change, don't make out-of-scope modifications, which might result in major disruption. Also, a project's purpose might expand as the project progresses, which is sometimes called scope creep. Too much scope creep can jeopardize the success of the entire change.

Risk Analysis

Change almost always involves risk, which refers to a problem (event, situation, or condition) that may or may not occur as a result of the change. Possible risks include the possibility the budget is inadequate, alienating customers, not finishing on time, not delivering the intended results, the number of employees affected, and downtime for the network or other systems. **Risk analysis** is the process of identifying potential risks and deciding if the risks are worth the change.

Sometimes a numeric value or **risk level** from 5 (highest risk) to 1 (lowest risk) is assigned to each risk. To determine these values, each administrator affected by the potential risk may be asked to assign a risk level to that risk. Change management software might receive all this input to calculate an overall risk level for the change.

As an IT technician, you need to be aware of the risks involved and how to execute the response plan if the problem actually happens.

Rollback Plan

What if a change goes bad—really bad? Suppose all users lose network connectivity for hours or all database servers that log all online sales orders spontaneously crash. The **rollback plan**, also called the back-out plan, defines the activities needed to recover to the original state in the event of an aborted or failed change implementation.

The rollback plan is created and sometimes tested even before the change starts, and it includes detailed steps to restore service to users. Obviously, you need to be aware of the rollback plan prior to implementing a change.

End-User Acceptance

Recall that change management is responsible for ensuring that people impacted by change are able to make a smooth transition during the change. End-user acceptance to change often fails because the focus of the change is on the technical side rather than the people side. To gain end-user acceptance, users must know

1. The purpose of the change, especially the business reasons for the change
2. That the leadership of the company agrees with the change
3. How the change will affect them and their job
4. How to get their individual concerns and questions answered and how their voices will be heard
5. That they will receive end-user training for the changes that impact them. For software changes, training often allows users to practice using the new software in a **sandbox**, which is an environment in which users can practice with data and processes that don't affect the real data and where mistakes have little consequence. (Technicians also use sandboxes to test software to make sure it works as designed.)

Before a change begins, an organization might request user feedback to the change in a **request for comments (RFC)**. Technical users often have valuable input in the RFC process that may affect the entire change process. IT technicians often play a major role in end-user acceptance. Users who struggle with change will appreciate your empathetic and positive outlook. When a proposed change has been clearly communicated and users understand "what's in it for them," you have made a significant contribution to a successful change.

Document Changes

No part of change management should rely on spoken communication. Everything related to changes must be documented, including how the change management process itself works. Change plans are documented and updated throughout the entire change management process. Many larger organizations use change management software, such as ChangeGear by SunView (*sunviewsoftware.com*), to manage all stages of change management from the change request form to the final close report. Smaller organizations may manually document change using Microsoft Word or Excel documents or database software. Regardless of the size of the organization, you will be expected to maintain proper documentation for all stages of a change in which you participate.

Working in Diverse Software Environments

Core 2 Objectives 1.8, 1.9

In the diverse world of IT, an IT support technician encounters a wide variety of hardware platforms, operating systems, and applications. In this section, we focus on what all operating systems have in common as well as the diversity you might encounter among operating systems.

What All Operating Systems Do

Core 2 Objective 1.8

An **operating system (OS)** is software that controls a computer, and all operating systems have common functions. In general, you can think of an operating system as the middleman between applications and hardware, between the user and hardware, and between the user and applications, as shown in Figure 11-13. (Individual components of an OS also shown in the figure are discussed later in this module.)

Figure 11-13 Users and applications depend on the OS to relate to all applications and hardware components

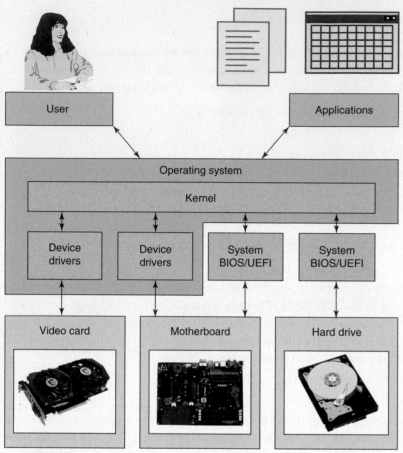

Several applications might be installed on a computer to meet various user needs, but a computer really needs only one operating system. Although there are important differences among them, all operating systems share the following four main functions:

- **Function 1:** Provide a user interface
  - Performing storage and housekeeping procedures requested by the user, such as reorganizing a hard drive and changing display settings
  - Providing a way for the user to manage the desktop, hardware, applications, and data
- **Function 2:** Manage files
  - Managing files on hard drives, DVD drives, CD drives, USB flash drives, and other drives
  - Creating, storing, retrieving, deleting, and moving files
- **Function 3:** Manage hardware
  - Interface with the BIOS/UEFI, which are programs permanently stored on hardware devices
  - Managing memory, which is a temporary place to store data and instructions as they are being processed
  - Diagnosing problems with software and hardware
  - Interfacing between hardware and software (that is, interpreting application software needs to the hardware and vice versa)
- **Function 4:** Manage applications
  - Installing and uninstalling applications
  - Running applications and managing the interface to the hardware on behalf of an application

Every OS offers a command-driven interface for the user, and almost every OS also offers one or more **graphical user interface (GUI**; pronounced "GOO-ee"). Workstation OSs always provide a graphical interface. Because server computers normally have little direct human interaction, their OSs, such as Linux Ubuntu Server, don't always require a graphical interface. IT technicians must be comfortable using both interfaces and also supporting users learning to use a graphical interface. The Windows graphical interface, called the desktop, is shown in Figure 11-14. Figure 11-15 shows a command-driven interface in a Linux server.

Figure 11-14   The Windows 10 desktop with browser, Control Panel, and File Explorer open

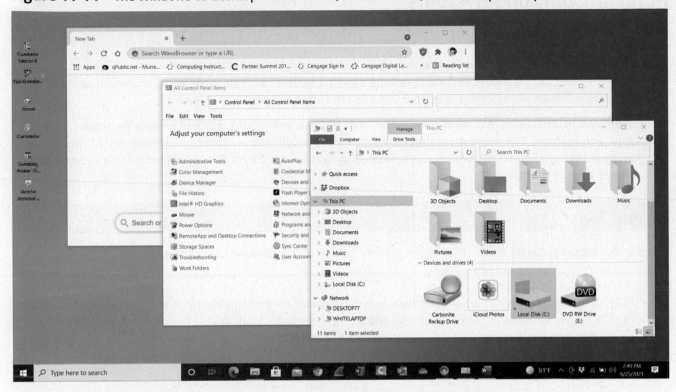

Figure 11-15   The command-driven interface for Ubuntu Server

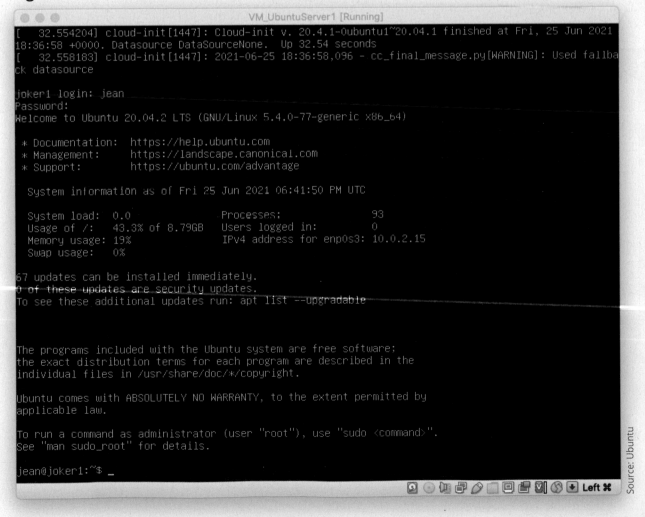

Popular Operating Systems

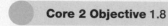

Core 2 Objective 1.8

As an IT technician, you might be called on to help a customer decide which type of OS to use in a given situation. Organizations often have a mix of several operating systems in use. The four most popular operating systems for workstations are Windows, macOS, Linux, and Chrome OS. Here's an overview of each OS:

- **Windows** by Microsoft (*Microsoft.com*) is the most popular workstation OS and installs on almost all desktops and laptops. The current version is Windows 11, which was an upgrade to Windows 10, which was an upgrade to Windows 8.1, which was preceded by Windows 7. Every IT support technician needs to be a power user of Windows.

Exam Tip ✔

The A+ Core 2 exam covers Windows 10 as the primary version of the Windows operating system.

- **macOS** by Apple (*apple.com*) is extremely easy to use, and its desktop interface is intuitive and beautiful. macOS comes installed on Apple desktops and laptops. Because Apple is able to control the hardware used by macOS, the OS is stable and reliable. Windows and macOS are the most popular OSs for workstations, and people tend to have strong opinions about which they prefer. It often boils down to user preference when deciding between the two OSs. Figure 11-16 shows the macOS desktop.

Figure 11-16   The macOS desktop with the Finder and System Preferences windows open

- **Linux** is a secure and extremely stable OS that doesn't take up much space on the hard drive. In fact, it takes up so little space that you install it on a USB drive and run the OS from the drive. The main advantage of Linux is that most distributions are free. Some disadvantages to Linux are that it requires more technical knowledge to use and support it, it doesn't have as many applications made for it as does Windows or macOS, and it doesn't support as many hardware peripherals. Linux comes in many distributions, also known as distros or flavors, such as Ubuntu, Linux Mint, Debian, Fedora, Red Hat, CentOS, and Puppy Linux. Figure 11-17 shows the desktop for Ubuntu Desktop.

Figure 11-17   The desktop for Ubuntu Desktop with the Files app open and software updates running

Source: Ubuntu

- **Chrome OS** by Google (*google.com*) is a relatively simple OS that works on personal devices including tablets and laptops, called Chromebooks (see Figure 11-18), and desktops, called Chromeboxes (see Figure 11-19).

Figure 11-18   Chromebooks are laptop computers that use the Chrome OS

Source: Google LLC

Figure 11-19   A Chromebox desktop is an inexpensive and light desktop solution

Source: Amazon.com, Inc.

Google calls its Chromebook a Google Pixelbook. Chrome OS apps are available from the Chrome Web Store. Chrome OS can also run Android apps, available from Google Play. Full applications, such as Microsoft Word, are not available for the Chrome OS. Chrome OS and its devices are relatively inexpensive compared to other personal devices, and they have traditionally been marketed to the education market as a more affordable solution when heftier computing capabilities are not required.

How an OS Manages Hardware

Core 2 Objectives 1.8, 1.9

Looking back at Figure 11-13, notice that the OS **kernel** is the part of the OS that is responsible for relating to hardware by way of device drivers and/or firmware on the hardware. In this section, we see how both methods work.

Device Drivers

Device drivers are small programs stored on the hard drive that tell the OS how to communicate with a specific hardware device such as a printer, network card, or scanner. These drivers are installed on the hard drive when the OS is first installed or when new hardware is added to the system. A device driver is written to work for a specific OS, such as Windows, macOS, or Linux.

In addition to the device drivers that are installed at the time the OS is installed, other drivers are provided by the manufacturer of each hardware device. When you purchase a printer, video card, digital camera, scanner, or other hardware device, a CD or DVD that contains the device drivers is usually bundled with the device along with a user manual (see Figure 11-20). You can also download the drivers for a device from the manufacturer's website. Before you install a new OS, be sure you have the correct device drivers for all your critical devices, such as your network card or motherboard.

Figure 11-20   A device such as this video card comes packaged with its device drivers stored on a CD

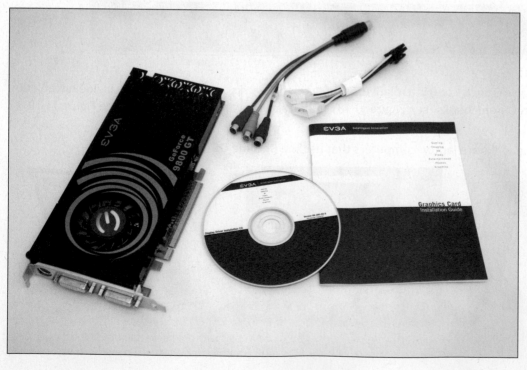

Older CPUs processed only 32 bits at a time, but all modern CPUs process 64 bits and can handle 32-bit processing for backward compatibility with older operating systems. An operating system is also designed to process 32 or 64 bits. When selecting device drivers, make sure you choose 32-bit drivers for a 32-bit OS (a really old OS) and 64-bit drivers for a 64-bit OS (most likely situation).

Firmware on the Motherboard

The most important hardware component in a computer is the motherboard, and every motherboard has firmware that controls it and interfaces with the OS. This firmware is stored on microchips on the board (see Figure 11-21). When a computer is first turned on, firmware on the motherboard starts up the computer, verifies essential hardware devices (such as memory and a CPU) are present, and then starts the process of searching for and loading an operating system.

Figure 11-21 Chips on a motherboard contain firmware used to start the computer, hold motherboard settings, and run essential devices; the chips retain power from a nearby coin battery when the computer is turned off

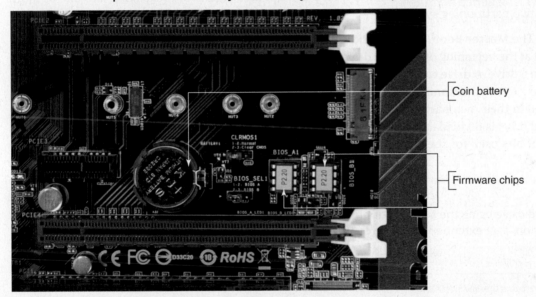

Coin battery

Firmware chips

All modern motherboards use firmware called **UEFI (Unified Extensible Firmware Interface)**. UEFI is a much-improved replacement for **BIOS (basic input/output system)** and offers legacy support for BIOS compatibility. BIOS stores its setup information on the motherboard, while UEFI stores its setup information, along with some drivers, on the motherboard and the hard drive. The motherboard BIOS/UEFI provides three main functions:

- The **system BIOS/UEFI** contains instructions for running essential hardware devices before an operating system is started. After the OS is started, it might continue to use system BIOS/UEFI or use device drivers to communicate with these devices.
- The **startup BIOS/UEFI** starts the computer and finds a boot device that contains an operating system. Boot devices that a system might support include an internal or external hard drive, a CD or DVD drive, a bootable USB flash drive, and the network. After it finds a boot device, the firmware turns the startup process over to the OS.

Note 7

When choosing a boot device, consider that solid-state drives are faster than magnetic hard drives because they have no moving parts. USB flash drives are also solid-state devices. Some hard drives might be hot-swappable, which means they are inserted into an easily accessible hot-swap bay and can be exchanged without powering down the system.

- The **setup BIOS/UEFI** is used to change motherboard settings. You can use it to enable or disable a device on the motherboard (for example, the network port, video port, or USB ports), change the date and time that is later passed to the OS, and select the order of boot devices for startup BIOS/UEFI to search when looking for an operating system to load. This order of boot devices is called the **boot priority order**.

Before you learn how the boot priority order is determined, you need to know a little about how the OS manages hard drives where the OS, applications, and data are normally stored.

How an OS Manages a Hard Drive

Core 2 Objectives 1.8, 1.9

Total capacities for today's hard drives are measured in GB (gigabytes, roughly one million bytes) or TB (terabytes, roughly one trillion bytes). Before a hard drive leaves the factory, a process called **low-level formatting** organizes all bits into a long series of logical blocks; this is called logical block addressing (LBA). Groups of bits are referred to as LBA 1, LBA 2, and so forth. Before an OS can use a hard drive, it first organizes these LBAs into one or more partitions using one of two partitioning systems:

- **MBR partitions.** The **Master Boot Record (MBR)** partitioning system keeps a map of partitions in a **partition table** stored at the beginning of the hard drive called the MBR. The MBR partition table can track up to four partitions on a drive. A drive can have one, two, or three **primary partitions**, also called volumes. The fourth partition is called an **extended partition** and can hold one or more volumes called **logical drives**, which are tracked in their own partition table separately from the primary partitions. Figure 11-22 shows how an MBR hard drive is divided into three primary partitions and one extended partition. Because of the limited number of bits used for the MBR, this partitioning system can handle only four partitions and up to 2.2 TB drives.

Figure 11-22   A hard drive using the MBR partitioning system, with four partitions; the fourth partition is an extended partition containing two logical drives

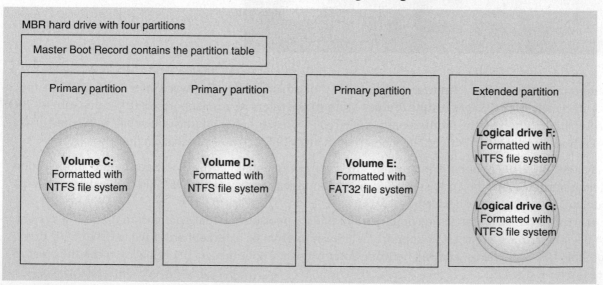

Exam Tip ✔

The A+ Core 2 exam expects you to know the difference between a primary and extended partition and between a volume and logical drive on an MBR hard drive.

- **GPT partitions.** The newer **Globally Unique Identifier Partition Table (GUID or GPT)** partitioning system can support up to 128 partitions and is required for drives larger than 2.2 TB. GPT requires a 64-bit operating system and UEFI firmware, and it is needed to use Secure boot, a feature of UEFI and the OS that adds security to the boot process. Most new computers sold today use the GPT system and UEFI firmware.

The first sector of a hard drive in a GPT system contains the protective MBR, which provides information to legacy software that doesn't recognize GPT systems so the legacy software will not attempt to repair or install an MBR system on the drive. GPT tracks all partitions in a single partition table, which it stores in the GPT header immediately following the protective MBR. GPT systems also back up the partition table at the end of the disk (see Figure 11-23).

Figure 11-23   A hard drive using GPT partitioning with six partitions

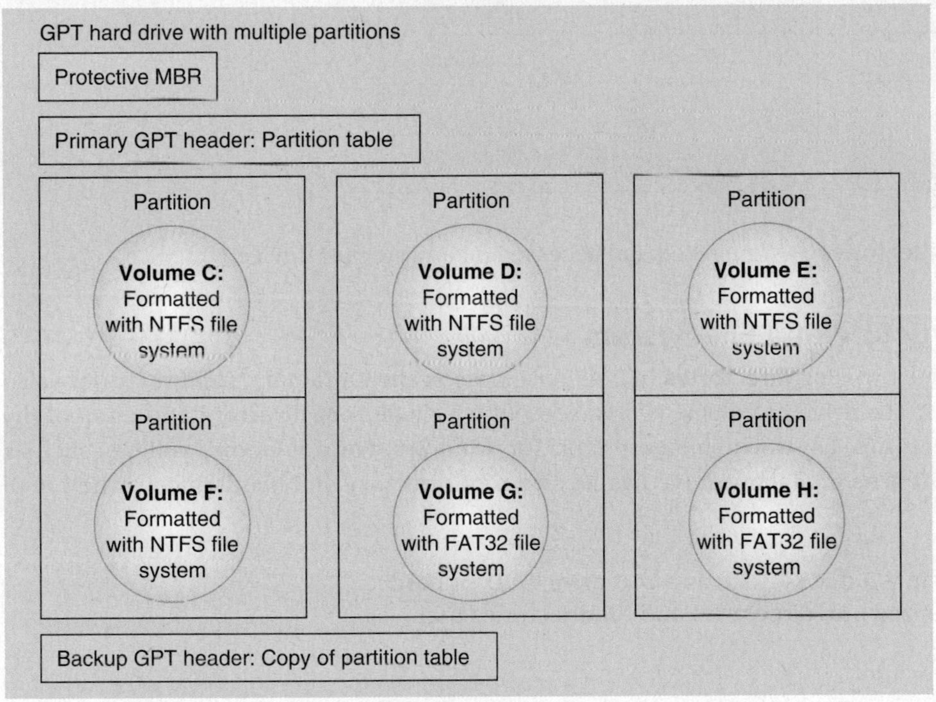

How File Systems Work

Core 2 Objective 1.8

Before a partition can be accessed, it must have a file system installed. The file system is the overall structure an OS uses to name, store, and organize files and folders on any storage device, including hard drives. For Windows, a hard drive partition or other storage device is assigned a drive letter (such as C: or D:) and is then called a **volume**. For a hard drive with multiple partitions, each partition is a volume that must be formatted with its own file system. See Figure 11-24. Installing a file system on a volume is called **formatting** the drive or **high-level formatting**. This **drive format** can happen during the OS installation or after the OS is installed. All USB flash drives, DVDs, smart cards, partitions on a hard drive, and other storage devices are formatted with a file system before they can be used.

Figure 11-24 A hard drive can be divided into one or more partitions; each becomes a volume and receives its own file system

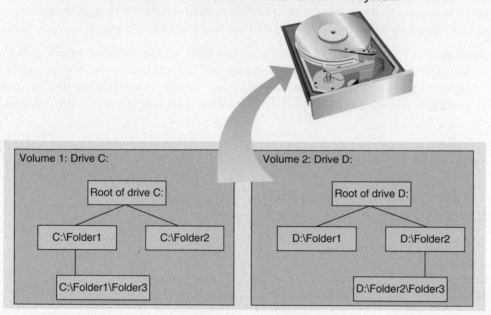

Next, let's see how files and directories are organized and accessed on any storage device.

Directory Hierarchical Structure of a File System

Every OS manages a storage device by using **directories** (a directory is also called a **folder**), **subdirectories** (also called **child directories**), and files. The drive or volume is organized with a single **root directory** at the top of the hierarchical structure of subdirectories, as shown in Figure 11-25 for Windows. For a Windows volume, such as drive C:, the root directory is written as C:. Each volume has its own root directory and hierarchical structure of subdirectories.

Figure 11-25 Storage devices in Windows—such as a USB drive, DVD, or hard drive—are organized into directories and subdirectories that contain files

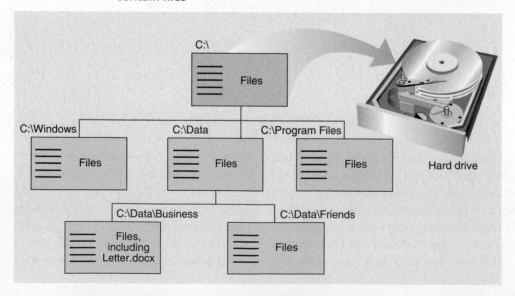

Any directory can have files and other subdirectories listed in it; for example, Figure 11-25 shows that one file on drive C: is C:\Data\Business\Letter.docx. In this path to the file, the C: identifies the volume and is called the drive letter. Drive letters used for a hard drive, CD, USB drive, or DVD are C:, D:, E:, and so forth.

Note 8

In Windows, the backslash is used in directory paths to separate items in the path: C:\Data\Business\Letter.docx. However, in macOS, Linux, and Chrome OS, the slash is used for the same purpose: /home/user2/Business/Letter.odt.

The drive and directories that point to the location of a file are called the **path** to the file. See Figure 11-26 for Windows. The first part of the name before the period is called the **file name** (Letter), and the part after the period is called the file extension (.docx). A **file extension** indicates how the file is organized or formatted, the type of content in the file, and what program uses the file. For example, the .docx file extension identifies the file type as a Microsoft Word document file.

Linux-based OSs, including macOS, Chrome OS, and all Linux distributions, such as Ubuntu, organize their file systems differently than does Windows. A Linux-based OS uses a single root directory indicated by a slash (/) for all hard drives, partitions, and other storage media. Think of this root directory as the highest level in the hierarchy for all storage media connected to the system. See Figure 11-27. The root contains directories—such as /home and /etc in the figure—that hold the Linux installation and other storage on the hard drive. The root also contains the /media directory that is the access point to the volumes on other storage devices, such as the USB flash drive

Figure 11-26   In Windows, the complete path to a file includes the volume letter, directories, file name, and file extension; the colon, backslashes, and period are required to separate items in the path

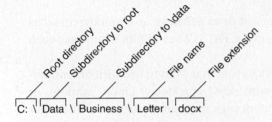

in the figure. In Linux terms, a subdirectory in the /media directory is called the **mount point** for the flash drive, and the flash drive is mounted to the system. Before a device can be mounted, it must be formatted with a file system; therefore, in effect, the file system on the device is mounted to the system.

Figure 11-27   In Linux-based OSs, storage media other than the media on which the OS is installed are mounted to a directory under the root

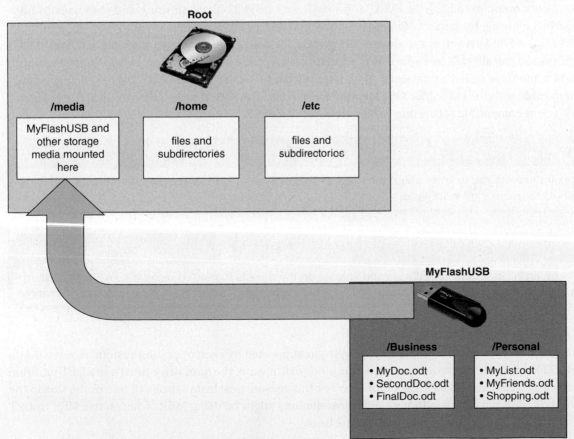

In Figure 11-27, you see a USB flash drive named MyFlashUSB that has a directory named /Business, which contains a LibreOffice Writer document file MyDoc with an .odt file extension. The path to this document file is

`/media/MyFlashUSB/Business/MyDoc.odt`

To find any media (USB flash drive, second hard drive, DVD, and so forth), look in the /media directory to find a subdirectory for the given media. This subdirectory (MyFlashUSB in our example) contains the contents of the storage device.

These same hierarchical directory structures for organizing directories and files are used by all file systems. Here is a list of file systems you are expected to know about for the A+ Core 2 exam:

- **NTFS.** For most editions of Windows, **NTFS (New Technology File System)** is required for the volume on which Windows is installed. NTFS was designed to replace the older FAT32 file system; it is more reliable, efficient, and secure than FAT32. NTFS supports encryption, disk quotas (limiting the hard drive space available to a user), and file and folder compression. If you boot the system from another boot medium such as a DVD, you can access a volume using a FAT file system. If the volume uses NTFS, an administrator password is required to gain access.
- **FAT32.** Use **FAT32** for small hard drives or USB flash drives because it does not have as much overhead as NTFS, and it is supported by macOS, Linux, Chrome OS, and other OSs. FAT32 uses 32 bits to address each unit of data on the volume.
- **exFAT.** Choose the **exFAT** file system for large external storage devices that you want to use with other operating systems. For example, you can use a smart card formatted with exFAT in a Mac or Linux computer or in a digital camcorder, camera, or smartphone. The exFAT file system uses the same structure as the older FAT32, but with a 64-bit-wide file allocation table (FAT). exFAT does not use as much overhead as the NTFS file system and is designed to handle very large files, such as those used for multimedia storage.
- **ext3.** The file system **ext3 (third extended file system)** was invented by Linux developers and was the first to support journaling, which is a technique that tracks and stores changes to the hard drive and helps prevent file system corruption.
- **ext4.** The current Linux file system is **ext4 (fourth extended file system)**, which is used by default when the OS is installed and another file system is not in place. It improved on ext3 with better performance and support for larger volumes. Similar to FAT32 and exFAT, ext3 used 32-bit addressing and ext4 uses 64-bit addressing, thus allowing for larger volumes.
- **APFS.** **APFS (Apple File System)** is the default file system for macOS. APFS allows multiple volumes on a single partition and can allocate free space as needed for each volume in the partition. In Apple terminology, a partition is sometimes called a container. APFS requires the GPT (also called GUID) partitioning system. APFS is compatible with the older Mac OS Extended file system, also called HFS+ (Hierarchical File System Plus), but it is not compatible with some earlier versions of macOS.

Exam Tip ✔

The A+ Core 2 exam expects you to know about the NTFS, FAT32, ext3, ext4, APFS, and exFAT file systems, including which is appropriate to use in a given scenario.

Note 9

Windows installs on an NTFS volume, but if a second volume on the drive is formatted using the FAT32 file system, you can convert that volume to NTFS. For large drives, NTFS is more efficient, and converting might improve performance.

Compatibility between Operating Systems

Table 11-1 summarizes the types of partitioning and file systems supported by each operating system. Modern motherboards support UEFI firmware; to take advantage of this modern firmware, the hard drive must use a GPT partition to hold the operating system used to boot the computer. For this reason, new installations of one of the OSs in the table will not install on MBR partitions, although older installations might be using MBR. You can use MBR or GPT on any partition or storage device that is not used for the boot.

Table 11-1   Operating systems, partitioning systems, and file systems

Operating System	Partitioning System		File System					
	MBR	GPT	NTFS	FAT32	ext3	ext4	APFS	exFAT
Windows	Yes	**Yes, required for boot**	**Yes, required for boot**	Yes	Read only with third party	Read only with third party	Read/write with third party	Yes
macOS	Yes	**Yes, required for boot**	Read only	Yes	Read/write with third party	Read/write with third party	**Yes, required for boot**	Yes
Linux	Yes	**Yes, preferred**	Yes	Yes	Yes	**Yes, preferred**	Read/write with third party	Yes
Chrome OS	Yes	**Yes, preferred**	Yes	Yes	No	No	No	Yes

You can also use **third-party drivers** to allow an OS that does not support a particular file system to read data on a computer using that file system. For example, Paragon Software (*paragon-software.com*) offers APFS for Windows, which installs in Windows to read/write to APFS partitions on macOS computers on the network.

Table 11-2 summarizes the tools and commands each OS uses to manage hard drives. Because macOS and Chrome OS are both built on a Linux foundation, they have some commands in common, as you will see in later modules when we cover several tools and commands.

Table 11-2   OS primary tools and commands to manage hard drives

	Graphics Tools	Commands
Windows	Disk Management	diskpart, format
macOS	Disk Utility	diskutil
Linux	GNOME Disks	parted, fdisk, fstype
Chrome OS	Partitioner, Format Device	NA

Types of OS Installations and Upgrades

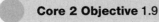

Core 2 Objective 1.9

An IT technician is often involved in installing, upgrading, and repairing an operating system. When it's time to install or upgrade any OS you support, you'll need to understand what type of installation you are performing, how the installation begins, and where the OS installation files are stored. All these topics are covered next.

Clean Install, Upgrade, or Repair

If you are installing an OS on a new hard drive, you must perform a clean install. If an OS is already installed on the hard drive, you have three choices:

- **Clean install.** You can perform a **clean install**, overwriting the existing operating system and applications. For Windows, the setup program calls a clean install a **custom installation**. The main advantage of a clean install is that problems with the old OS are not carried forward, and you get a fresh start. During the installation, you will have the option to reformat the hard drive, erasing everything on it. If you don't format the drive, data will still be on it. After the OS is installed, you will need to install third-party drivers and applications.

Note 10

For a Windows clean install, the previous Windows settings and user profiles are collectively stored in the **Windows. old folder** that setup creates on the hard drive. After you're sure the new installation is working as expected, you can delete the Windows.old folder to save space on the drive. Windows automatically deletes most of the content of this folder 10 days after the installation.

- **Upgrade.** If the upgrade path allows it and the OS is healthy enough, you can perform an upgrade installation. An upgrade is always started from within the existing operating system. Launch the OS and then launch the upgrade process. The upgrade carries forward user settings and installed applications from the old OS to the new one. An upgrade is faster than a clean install and is appropriate if the system is generally healthy and does not have problems. Before you start an upgrade, be sure to back up data stored on the hard drive. Here's the breakdown of how to start an upgrade for each OS:

  - **Windows upgrade.** Windows calls an upgrade an **in-place upgrade** because the old OS is already in place. To perform an in-place upgrade, Microsoft requires that certain editions and versions of Windows are already installed and running the latest version of either Windows 8.1 or Windows 7 with Service Pack 1 installed. These qualifying OSs are called **upgrade paths**. Table 11-3 outlines the acceptable upgrade paths for Windows 10 compatibility. To upgrade from an earlier edition of Windows to Windows 10, you'll need to purchase the product key from the Microsoft Store and download the installation files. To start a Windows in-place upgrade, launch Windows and follow the procedures you learn about in the module "Installing Windows" to perform the upgrade.

Table 11-3   In-place upgrade paths to Windows 10

Windows 8		Windows 7	
From OS	To OS	From OS	To OS
Windows 8.1	Windows 10 Home	Windows 7 Starter	Windows 10 Home or Windows 10 Pro
		Windows 7 Home Basic	
		Windows 7 Home Premium	
Windows 8.1 Pro	Windows 10 Pro	Windows 7 Professional	Windows 10 Pro or Windows 10 Enterprise
Windows 8.1 Pro for Students		Windows 7 Ultimate	

Note 11

A 64-bit version of Windows can only be upgraded to a 64-bit OS. A 32-bit OS can only be upgraded to a 32-bit OS. If you want to install a 64-bit version of Windows on a computer that already has a 32-bit OS installed, you must perform a clean install.

  - **macOS upgrade.** The latest edition of macOS is macOS Monterey. You can download and install a free upgrade if your Apple computer hardware qualifies for the OS. If you're currently running macOS Mojave or later, you can start the upgrade from System Preferences. If you're running an older version of macOS, use the App Store to start the upgrade. To know which OS is installed, click the apple, click **About This Mac**, and then select the **Overview** tab. You can also upgrade from this window. See Figure 11-28. A macOS upgrade takes a long time, and the system reboots several times, but you don't need to interact with the installation.

Figure 11-28   Use the About This Mac windows to find out which edition of macOS is installed, and upgrade to the latest macOS

- **Linux upgrade.** When you first log on to Linux, a list of available updates displays. To apply these updates, you use the apt-get and do-release-upgrade commands. How to use these commands is covered in the module "Linux and Scripting." Linux updates are free.
- **Chrome OS upgrade.** To upgrade to the latest Chrome OS, in the **Settings** app, open **About Chrome OS**, and click **Check for updates**. See Figure 11-29. If updates are available, they start to download automatically.

Figure 11-29   Use the Chrome OS Settings to update the OS

- **Repair.** Each OS has various tools and commands you can use to repair a corrupted installation, which you learn about in later modules. For laptop computers and brand name desktops, sometimes the hard drive contains a **recovery partition** that can be used to restore the computer back to its state when first purchased. How to use this partition is covered in the module "Troubleshooting Windows Startup."

11

Boot Methods

To perform a clean install, upgrade, or some OS repairs, you'll need the installation files provided by the OS manufacturer. In most cases, you download these files from the manufacturer website and store them on a device such as a USB solid-state flash drive or solid-state external hard drive, optical media (DVD), the network, and external or internal hot-swappable hard drive, or a second partition on the main internal hard drive. Sometimes you can perform the installation without downloading all files first, as the setup program can access files stored online.

For a new or corrupted hard drive, the storage device holding the installation files must be bootable, which means it can be accessed by BIOS/UEFI to launch an operating system. After the OS is running, it then launches the setup program to install the new OS. In later modules, you learn how to make this installation media bootable for each OS.

Applying Concepts

Selecting the Boot Priority Order

Est. Time: 15 minutes
Core 2 Objective: 1.8

To boot from a media other than the hard drive, you can use BIOS/UEFI setup to change the boot priority order. See the motherboard documentation to find out how to access and use BIOS/UEFI setup. Here are steps for one system:

1. Insert your bootable media, such as the DVD in the optical drive or a USB flash drive in a USB port.

2. To access BIOS/UEFI setup, press a key such as **Del** or **F2** early in the boot process before the OS starts to load. When the BIOS/UEFI setup screen appears, look for a screen to manage the boot. For example, the Boot screen for one motherboard's firmware is shown in Figure 11-30.

Figure 11-30   The Boot screen for BIOS/UEFI setup

Source: American Megatrends, Inc.

3. Normally, BIOS/UEFI is set to boot first from the internal hard drive. To boot from another device, look for a Boot screen or menu. For the system shown in Figure 11-31, boot options are the DVD drive, hard drive, and network port. Also, know that sometimes the DVD drive is labeled CD-ROM in BIOS/UEFI setup.

Figure 11-31   Set the boot priority order in BIOS/UEFI setup

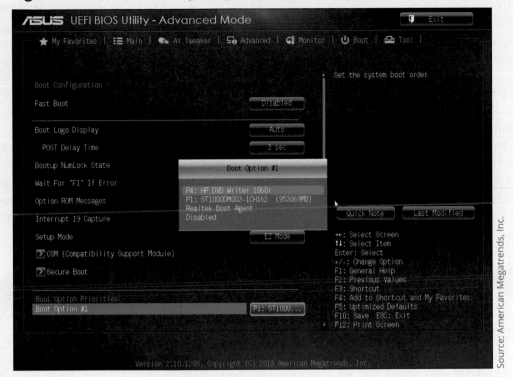

Source: American Megatrends, Inc.

4. Make your change and then use the Exit menu to save your changes and restart the system. The system should restart and look to your bootable media to launch an OS. Then the setup program on your bootable media should launch.

In a corporate or enterprise environment, automated methods might be in place to install a fresh copy of the OS on a workstation from deployment servers on the network. To use this method, you configure BIOS/UEFI setup to boot from the network and locate a deployment server to install the OS. How to do that is covered in the next module.

> **Note 12**
>
> In most situations, you use the GPT partitioning system for the hard drive. If you must use the MBR system, in BIOS/UEFI setup, change the mode to CSM (Compatibility Support Mode), which supports MBR.

Vendor End-of-Life Limitation and Product Life Cycle

Core 2 Objective 1.8

In practice, computers and their operating systems might stay in service long after manufacturer support for the OS has ended. However, it's important that you know when an OS will no longer be supported by its manufacturer and what to expect during the life cycle of the product. Here is the rundown:

- **Windows.** In the past, Microsoft released a new version of Windows about every three years, but with Windows 10, it seems to be extending the life of a Windows version by providing incremental **feature updates** to the OS, called Windows as a Service (WaaS). Windows 10 has been the current Windows version since 2015, and Windows 11 is scheduled to be released near the beginning of 2022. Feature updates, which are incremental releases of new versions of Windows 10, happen about every six months, and minor security and nonsecurity updates happen weekly. Windows 7 and Windows 8.1 are no longer supported or updated by Microsoft. It is expected that Windows 10 will be supported long after Windows 11 is released.

- **macOS.** Over the past 20 years, Apple has released versions of Mac OS X about once a year; it was renamed macOS in 2016. The OS version a Mac can support depends on the age of the Mac. For example, a MacPro made in 2013 or later should support Big Sur, a current macOS release, and a MacBook Air made in 2015 or later should support Monterey, the latest macOS release. Apple releases updates to the current OSs about every two to three months. Each version of macOS is supported with security updates for about three years after its release.

- **Linux.** How long a Linux distribution is supported depends on the developer. For example, Canonical (*canonical.com*), which makes Ubuntu Desktop and Ubuntu Server, releases a new distribution of Ubuntu about every two years and provides support of that release for about five years.

- **Chrome OS.** Google releases a complete Chrome OS update about every six weeks. Minor updates are released about every two or three weeks. Because Chrome OS is a relatively new OS, the updates are less regular than more mature OSs, and sometimes the updates have significant bugs. For best results, keep automatic updates turned on.

Applying Concepts

Get to Know the Chrome OS

Est. Time: 15 minutes
Core 2 Objective: 1.8

Figure 11-32 A Chromebook can be a lightweight laptop, a tablet, or a hybrid laptop-tablet

Source: Amazon.com, Inc.

We end this module with a quick look at the Chrome OS. In later modules, you learn about Windows, macOS, Linux, and also iOS and Android, the two most popular mobile operating systems.

Chrome OS is deeply integrated with Google's Chrome browser: Most of Chrome OS's native apps open directly in the Chrome browser and rely heavily on having an active Internet connection. While there are some apps that will function offline—such as Gmail, Docs, and Calendar—functionality is limited to data that is temporarily stored on the Chromebook until it can again be synced with the user's online account. Chrome OS functions exclusively on Chromebooks and Chomeboxes, although many manufacturers build and sell these laptops, tablets, and desktops. See Figure 11-32.

First Look at a Chromebook

Chromebooks and Chromeboxes come with a variety of external ports, depending on the manufacturer and model. Many feature USB and USB-C ports as well as HDMI. Some include SD card slots for adding extra storage space. The keyboard on a Chromebook (see Figure 11-33) looks similar to the typical laptop keyboard, with a few notable differences. The unique keys mostly run along the top of the keyboard and include these keys: search, previous and next pages, refresh, immersive mode (hides tabs and launcher), and overview mode (shows all open apps). Keyboard shortcuts, a popular feature with Chromebooks, use combinations of key presses to accomplish tasks such as opening a new Chrome window (**ctrl+n**) or tab (**ctrl+t**), taking a screenshot (**ctrl+overview**), locking the screen (**search+L**), and showing all keyboard shortcuts (**ctrl+alt+/**).

Figure 11-33   A Chromebook keyboard

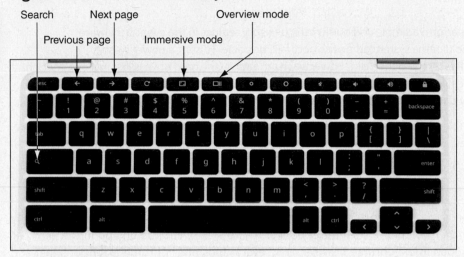

You sign in to Chrome OS using a Google Gmail email address and password. Google Drive, Gmail, and other Google apps are deeply integrated into the Chrome OS experience. Figure 11-34 shows the Chrome OS desktop with the Settings app, Chrome browser, and Notification Tray open. Also notice the shelf on the bottom and the status tray on the bottom right of the screen. The app launcher is in the shelf. To open the Settings app, click anywhere in the status tray, which opens the Notification tray, and then click the **Settings app** gear icon, which is labeled in Figure 11-34. Alternatively, you can click the App launcher and then click Settings.

Figure 11-34   The Chrome OS desktop

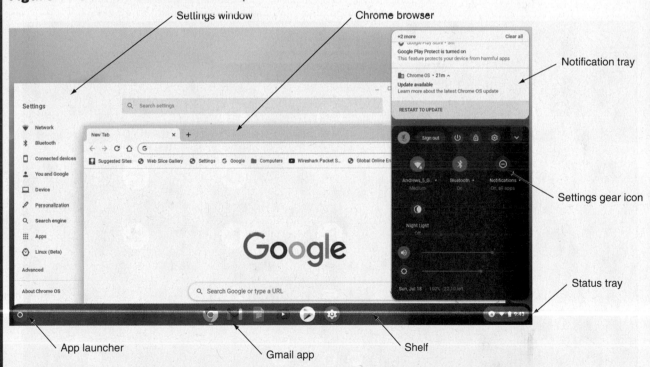

Chrome OS includes some significant security measures to protect the computer from malware, including built-in virus protection. Google took a four-pronged approach to security with Chrome OS:

Sandboxing. To help secure the system, each tab in the Chrome browser is isolated from the underlying OS and from processes in other tabs.

Verified boot. Similar to the Windows Secure boot, it protects the OS from changes being made to its underlying system files, automatically entering recovery mode if modifications are detected.

(continues)

Applying Concepts Continued

Power washing. The user can perform a simple and quick reset to factory settings in the event a malware infection does manage to take hold or the system otherwise becomes unstable. To start a power wash, press **Ctrl+Alt+Shift+r**, select **Restart**, and then click **Powerwash**. All data on the hard drive is lost in a power wash. **Quick updates.** The OS updates itself in the background without user intervention about every six weeks. If an update is needed for a security patch, it can happen within 48 hours.

The end effect is a very stable and secure OS that even security professionals rely on when traveling to techie, hacker, or security conferences, where the persistent threat of hacking attacks is an integral part of the overall experience.

Chrome OS Apps

The Chrome OS shelf contains icons for important apps; tap an icon to open the app. To view and open any installed app, tap the app launcher icon in the shelf (refer back to Figure 11-34), and tap an app in the launcher (see Figure 11-35). Most apps open in the Chrome browser, and several apps offer Chrome extensions that add functionality to the Chrome browser even when the app is not open. Users can get more apps through the Chrome Web Store app, or they can download Android apps through the Google Play Store app.

Figure 11-35   App launcher shows two apps used to download other apps

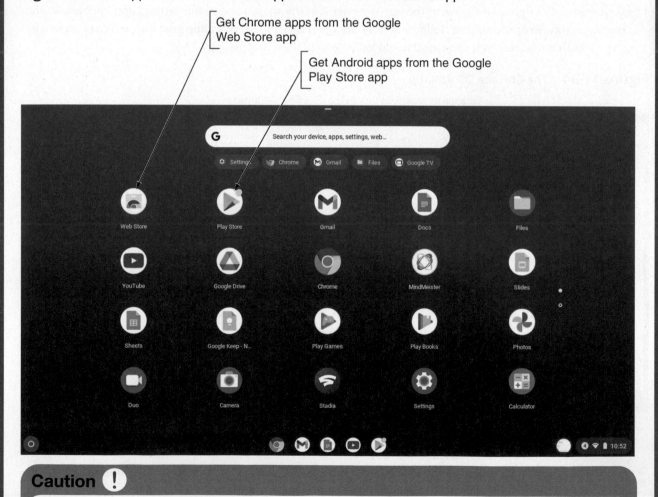

Get Chrome apps from the Google Web Store app

Get Android apps from the Google Play Store app

Caution (!)

Know that if you download Android apps to the Chromebook and then turn off the Play Store app, you'll lose all the Android apps' data and settings from the Chromebook.

Module Summary

What Customers Want: Beyond Technical Know-How

- Customers want more than just technical know-how. They want a positive and helpful attitude, respect, good communication, sensitivity to their needs, ownership of their problem, dependability, credibility, integrity, honesty, and professionalism.
- Customers expect their first contact with you to be professional and friendly, and they expect that your first priority will be listening to their problem or request.
- Know how to ask penetrating questions when interviewing a customer about a problem or request.
- Set and meet customer expectations by using good communication about what you are doing or intending to do and by allowing the customer to make decisions where appropriate.
- Dress professionally and match your attire to the requirements of your environment.
- Deal confidently and gracefully with customers who are difficult, including those who are not knowledgeable, are overly confident, or complain.
- When you first start a new job, find out how to escalate a problem you cannot solve.

Documentation and Support Systems

- Expect to find documentation in an IT environment about knowledge bases, asset management, password policies, network topology diagrams, ticketing systems, acceptable use policy, standard operating procedures, new-user and end-user termination checklists, regulatory compliance requirements, and the documentation needed for change management.
- Change management includes identifying the purpose and scope of change, developing a change plan, performing risk analysis, creating a rollback plan, getting approval from a change board, acquiring end-user acceptance, and documenting the entire change process.

Working in Diverse Software Environments

- An operating system manages hardware, runs applications, provides an interface for users, and stores, retrieves, and manipulates files.
- Popular operating systems for workstations are Windows, macOS, Linux, and Chrome OS.
- An OS interfaces with hardware via device drivers and firmware on the device.
- Motherboard firmware includes BIOS and UEFI, which together control the startup process and interface with components on the motherboard.
- A hard drive contains one or more partitions or volumes and can use the MBR or GPT partitioning system. Using GPT requires UEFI firmware and a 64-bit OS. Drives larger than 2.2 TB must use GPT.
- A file system is installed on storage devices to name, store, and organize files and folders on the device.
- File systems include NTFS, FAT32, exFAT, ext3, ext4, and APFS. Windows installs on the NTFS file system; MacOS installs on APFS, and Linux and Chrome OS install on ext4. FAT32 file system can be used by all these OSs to read and write data.
- An operating system can be installed as a clean installation or an in-place upgrade; sometimes an OS can be repaired without being reinstalled.
- An OS can be installed from the installation files stored on a USB solid-state flash drive or solid-state external hard drive, optical media (DVD), the network, and external or internal hot-swappable hard drive, or a second partition on the main internal hard drive.
- To boot the system from a media other than the primary hard drive, you can use BIOS/UEFI setup to change the boot priority order.
- When supporting an OS, you need to understand the product life cycle and the vendor's end-of-life limitation for the product.

11

- Chrome OS is designed solely for use on a Chromebook—which is a tablet, lightweight laptop, or convertible laptop-tablet—or a Chromebox, a desktop computer that uses the Chrome OS. Many manufacturers make Chromebooks and Chromeboxes.
- Chrome OS relies heavily on the Chrome browser and an active Internet connection. Chrome OS apps are distributed through the Chrome Web Store, and apps for the newer Chromebooks are distributed from the Google Play Store.

Key Terms

For explanations of key terms, see the Glossary for this text.

acceptable use policy (AUP)	drive format	kernel	request form
APFS (Apple File System)	end-user termination checklist	knowledge base	risk analysis
asset ID	escalate	Linux	risk level
asset management	exFAT	logical drive	rollback plan
asset tag	ext3 (third extended file system)	low-level formatting	root directory
barcode	ext4 (fourth extended file system)	macOS	sandbox
BIOS (basic input/output system)	extended partition	Master Boot Record (MBR)	scope of change
boot priority order	FAT32	mount point	setup BIOS/UEFI
business casual	feature update	network topology diagram	splash screen
business formal	file extension	new-user setup checklist	standard operating procedures
change advisory board (CAB)	file name	NTFS (New Technology File System)	startup BIOS/UEFI
change management	file system	operating system (OS)	subdirectory
child directory	folder	partition table	system BIOS/UEFI
Chrome OS	formatting	path	third-party driver
clean install	Globally Unique Identifier Partition Table (GUID or GPT)	primary partition	ticket
custom installation	graphical user interface (GUI)	procurement life cycle	ticketing system
device driver	high-level formatting	recovery partition	topology
directory	in-place upgrade	regulatory compliance requirements	UEFI (Unified Extensible Firmware Interface)
documented business processes		request for comments (RFC)	upgrade path
			volume
			Windows.old folder
			Windows

Thinking Critically

These questions are designed to prepare you for the critical thinking required for the A+ exams and may use information from other modules and the web.

1. Suppose you are a customer who wants to have a computer repaired. List five main characteristics that you would want to see in your computer repair person.

2. When you receive a phone call requesting on-site support, what is one thing you should do before you make an appointment?

3. You make an appointment to do an on-site repair, but you are detained and find out that you will be late. What is the best thing to do?

4. When making an on-site service call, what should you do before making any changes to software or before taking the case cover off a computer?

5. What should you do after finishing your computer repair?

6. What is a good strategy to follow if a conflict arises between you and your customer?

7. You have exhausted your knowledge of a problem, and it still is not solved. Before you escalate it, what else can you do?

8. If you need to make a phone call while on a customer's site and your cell phone is not working, what do you do?

9. What is one thing you can do to help a caller who needs phone support and is not a competent computer user?

10. Describe what you should do when a customer complains to you about a product or service that your company provides.

11. While working in a call center, you receive a call from Latisha, who says she can no longer access the online reporting application for her weekly reports through her web browser. You ask your manager, and she tells you that the server team changed the application's URL during an upgrade over the weekend. She asks you to make sure all the other technicians are aware of this change. What is the best way to share this information?

    a. Print a flyer with the new URL, and post it on the wall in the call center.
    b. Send out a mass email with the new URL to all the technicians.
    c. Update the knowledge base article that contains the application's URL in the ticketing system application.
    d. Yell the new URL to all technicians sitting in the call center.

12. Your manager asks you to work through the weekend to install new software on the applications server that serves up applications to 20 users. The following Monday, all users report they cannot open their data files. After speaking with technical support for the new application, you discover it is not compatible with the old data files. Which type of documentation should you refer to first to address this problem?

    a. Risk analysis documents
    b. Rollback plan documents
    c. Change management documents
    d. Scope of change documents

13. Your manager asks you to set up an environment for user training on the payroll system. What is included in this environment? (Choose all that apply.)

    a. A sandbox
    b. Live data
    c. Dummy data
    d. Access to the company payroll database

14. Which OS is most appropriate to support a web server on the Internet?

    a. Windows 10 Pro
    b. Ubuntu Server
    c. Chrome OS
    d. macOS

15. Which statements are false about the GPT partitioning system? (Choose all that apply.)

    a. It supports up to 128 partitions.
    b. It contains the legacy MBR system for backward compatibility.
    c. It can only be installed on drives that are larger than 2 TB.
    d. It keeps a backup copy of the GPT table.

16. Your organization has several Mac and Windows laptops that all access data on a file server on the local network. Which file system on the Linux file server is best suited to this situation, and how do you best set it up?

    a. ext4; on the same partition that holds the Linux installation
    b. APFS; on a different partition than the one that holds the Linux installation
    c. FAT32; on a different partition than the one that holds the Linux installation
    d. NTFS; on the same partition that holds the Linux installation

11

17. Which of the following statements is false?

    a. In Ubuntu Server, the mount point for an external hard drive is in the /media directory.

    b. In Windows, before you can use a smart card, it must have a drive letter assigned.

    c. In macOS, the mount point for removable media is the /Volumes directory.

    d. In Ubuntu Desktop, a USB flash drive must have a drive letter assigned before you can access it.

18. Which Chromebook security feature ensures that malware can't change the OS's system files?

    a. Quick updates

    b. Power washing

    c. Sandboxing

    d. Verified boot

Hands-On Projects

Hands-On Project 11-1

Using the System Information Utility

Est. Time: 10 minutes
Core 2 Objective: 1.3

A technician needs to know how to sit down at any computer and quickly get basic information about the system. For Windows, the best tool for this job is System Information. Do the following:

    1. In the Windows search box, enter the `msinfo32.exe` command to launch the System Information window.

    2. Browse through the different levels of information in this window, and answer the following questions:

        a. What OS and OS version are you using?

        b. What is your CPU speed?

        c. What is your BIOS manufacturer and version?

        d. How much video RAM is available to your video adapter card? Explain how you got this information.

        e. What is the name of the device driver file that manages your network adapter? Your optical drive?

Hands-On Project 11-2

Researching Third-Party Drivers

Est. Time: 20 minutes
Core 2 Objective: 1.9

A small office has asked for your help getting a Mac computer and a Windows computer to share data with each other. Research the web and answer these questions:

    1. You examine the Windows computer and see that the entire hard drive is using the NTFS file system. Which third-party driver software would you recommend the company install on the Mac so it can read and write data on the Windows computer? (Be sure the software gets good reviews.) Why are third-party drivers needed?

    2. Which third-party driver software would you recommend the company install on the Windows computer so it can read and write to data folders on the Mac computer? What type of reviews does the software get?

Real Problems, Real Solutions

Real Problem 11-1

Using Windows Help and Support

Est. Time: 20 minutes
Core 2 Objective: 1.8

The best IT support technicians are the ones who continually teach themselves new skills. You can teach yourself to use and support Windows by using the web and a couple of apps in Windows 10 called Get Help and Tips. To start the apps in Windows 10, type **get help** in the search box or type **tips** in the search box. If you are connected to the Internet, clicking links in either of these two apps will take you to the Microsoft website, where you can find information and watch videos about Windows.

Do the following to research a topic to help you become an independent learner about Windows:

1. The Windows 10 Snipping Tool can help you take screenshots of the Windows desktop. These screenshots are useful when documenting computer problems and solutions. Use Get Help or Windows Help and Support to find out how to use the Snipping Tool, and then use it to take a screenshot of your Windows desktop. Save the screenshot into a file on a USB flash drive or on the hard drive. Print the file contents.

2. Access the *support.microsoft.com* website for Windows support. Save or print one article from the Knowledge Base that addresses a problem when installing Windows 10.

3. Search the web to learn the purpose of the pagefile.sys file. What website did you use to find your answer? Why is the Microsoft website considered the best source for information about the pagefile.sys file?

Real Problem 11-2

Learning to Use Sway

Est. Time: 30 minutes
Core 2 Objective: 1.8

Sometimes you may be asked to help a user answer questions about an app you are not familiar with. In that case, you can search for the information you need in the application's Help system.

Follow these steps to teach yourself to use Sway to create a web document:

1. Go to *sway.office.com* and sign in with a Microsoft account. (If you don't have an account, create one. It's free, and you'll need it later in the text.)

2. Create a new Sway story.

3. Choose a design and layout.

4. Add a title, photographs, and text.

5. Add focus points on photographs.

6. Share the URL to your Sway story with other people and have them watch what you created using a web browser.

Real Problem 11-3

Installing and Using the Mouse Without Borders App

Est. Time: 30 minutes
Core 2 Objective: 1.8

This Real Problem requires two computers on the same network, both with Internet access. Install the free Microsoft app Mouse Without Borders on both computers. This app allows one computer's mouse and keyboard to control up to four computers. The app is very useful when you frequently switch between two different Windows computers. Complete the following tasks:

1. On the web, go to the Microsoft Download Center, and find the Mouse Without Borders app. Make sure your system meets the minimum system requirements.

2. Download and install the app.

3. Use Mouse Without Borders to connect two computers on the same network.

4. On the first computer, use the mouse and keyboard to control the second computer by opening an app on it without touching its mouse or keyboard.

Real Problem 11-4

Documenting How to Use an App

Est. Time: 45 minutes
Core 2 Objective: 4.1

A technician is often called on to create content for a corporate knowledge base. This problem requires a microphone, and a webcam would also be useful. Make a screen recording with a voice-over to teach end users how to use Sway or Mouse Without Borders. Do the following:

1. Screencast-O-Matic offers free software to make a screen recording with voice and video. Go to *screencast-o-matic.com* and launch the online video recording software. You might be required to download and install the software.

2. Use the Screencast-O-Matic software to make a screen recording that explains how to use Sway or Mouse Without Borders. The recording should be no longer than three minutes. Explain the steps as you go. The software records your screen movements, your voice if a microphone is detected, and your image if a webcam is detected.

3. View the video. If you see a problem, record it again. When you're satisfied with your video, save it as an MP4 file.

Module
12

Installing Windows

Module Objectives

1 Evaluate a system to determine whether it qualifies for Windows 10 or Windows 11

2 Understand how Windows supports networking and resources on the network

3 Plan for a Windows installation

4 Install Windows

5 Configure Windows settings, hardware, users, and applications after the installation

6 Describe special concerns when installing Windows in a large enterprise

Core 2 Certification Objectives

1.1 Identify basic features of Microsoft Windows editions.

1.3 Given a scenario, use features and tools of the Microsoft Windows 10 operating system (OS).

1.4 Given a scenario, use the appropriate Microsoft Windows 10 Control Panel utility.

1.5 Given a scenario, use the appropriate Windows settings.

1.6 Given a scenario, configure Microsoft Windows networking features on a client/desktop.

1.7 Given a scenario, apply application installation and configuration concepts.

1.9 Given a scenario, perform OS installations and upgrades in a diverse OS environment.

2.5 Given a scenario, manage and configure basic security settings in the Microsoft Windows OS.

Introduction

In this module, you learn how to evaluate a computer and its network so you can plan and perform a Windows installation in various scenarios. You also learn what to do after the OS is installed and what to expect when installing Windows on computers in a large enterprise.

> **Exam Tip** ✔
>
> Windows 10 is the primary Windows version covered on the A+ Core 2 exam. The exam has light coverage of Windows 11. When a Windows objective does not specify Windows 10, Windows 10 and 11 are assumed. In this and later modules, we focus on Windows 10 and also give light coverage of Windows 11. Previous versions of Windows, including Windows 8.1 and Windows 7 are no longer supported by Microsoft and are not covered in this text.

Evaluating a System for Windows 10 or Windows 11

 **Core 2 Objectives** 1.1, 1.3, 1.7

As an IT support technician, you can expect to be called on to install Windows in a variety of situations. You might need to install Windows on a new hard drive, after an existing Windows installation has become corrupted, or to upgrade from one OS to another. One decision you might be called on to make is which edition and version of Windows is needed; this partly depends on how the computer accesses resources on the network. You also need to verify that the computer hardware and applications qualify for Windows 10 or Windows 11. These concerns are all covered next, first for Windows 10 and then for Windows 11.

Choose a Windows 10 Edition

Core 2 Objective 1.1

Microsoft offers several editions of Windows 10. For all editions, the desktop styles and user interface work much the same way. The differences involve the additional features supported by each edition:

- **Windows 10 Home** edition is intended for laptops and desktop computers in a home or small office. This edition is less expensive than others because it does not include the features required for a corporate or enterprise environment.
- **Windows 10 Pro** edition adds to Windows 10 Home edition several features designed for work in a corporate setting. The most important features are as follows:
  - **Domain access.** In a home or small office setting, each computer on the network connects in a workgroup. If the computer connects to a corporate or educational network to access network resources, it requires access to a Windows domain, which manages resources on the network. More differences between a workgroup and a domain are covered later in this module.
  - **BitLocker.** BitLocker encrypts an entire volume on a drive to protect the data and can provide full hard drive encryption. This level of security is often required by corporations to secure a computer, its data, and its settings before the computer is allowed to connect to and access resources on a corporate network.
  - **Encryption File System (EFS).** EFS encrypts files and folders to protect the data. Although not as secure as full drive encryption, EFS is sometimes required by individuals and corporations to protect the data on a computer's hard drive.
  - **Remote Desktop Protocol (RDP).** RDP is a networking protocol used by two applications embedded in Windows Pro: Remote Desktop and Remote Assistance. You learn how to use both in a later module.
  - **Support for additional memory.** Windows Home supports up to 128 GB of memory (also called random access memory or RAM). Windows Pro supports up to 2 TB of RAM.

- **Local Group Policy. Group Policy** (command name is gpedit.msc) is used by Windows Server in a Windows domain to control what users and computers can do on the network. The Windows Pro Local Group Policy is an administrator tool that can be used to control the local user and workstation activities. You learn how to use Group Policy in the module "Securing and Sharing Windows Resources."
  - **Hyper-V. Hyper-V** is a Windows hypervisor that allows you to create and use virtual machines in Windows Pro. You learn to use Hyper-V later in this module.
- **Windows 10 Pro for Workstations** edition adds to the Windows 10 Pro edition these features to improve performance:
  - The **Resilient File System (ReFS)** improves on the NTFS file system with enhanced performance and improved fault tolerance to better protect data from corruption. It also works better with virtualization and RAID systems.
  - **SMB Direct**, which is also used by Windows Server, improves performance when sharing files on the network. SMB (Server Message Block) is a protocol used to share files on a network.
  - **Persistent Memory (PMem)** is a memory technology that retains its contents even when power is turned off and is faster than normal memory when interfacing with solid-state storage devices.
  - Windows 10 Pro for Workstations supports up to 6 TB of RAM and up to four CPUs.
- **Windows 10 Enterprise** edition allows for volume licensing and additional security features, including the following:

  - Windows Defender Credential Guard better secures credentialing information, such as encryption secrets used with passwords.
  - Endpoint detection and response can collect up to six months of information about suspicious activities to help technicians better understand past, active, and potential security threats.
  - Unified Write Filter (UWF) intercepts and redirects to a temporary location any suspicious writes to storage devices.

> **Exam Tip** ✔
>
> The A+ Core 2 exam expects you to be able to compare and contrast versions and editions of Windows and determine which is best in a given scenario in personal, small business, and enterprise environments.

12

Choose a Windows 11 Edition

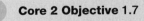
Core 2 Objective 1.1

Just as with Windows 10, Windows 11 comes in Windows 11 Home, Pro, Pro for Workstations, and Enterprise editions. Here are the significant differences between Windows 11 Home and Pro:

- **Windows 11 Pro features.** Like Windows 10 Pro, Windows 11 Pro offers features not included in Windows 11 Home, including BitLocker, Hyper-V, Microsoft Remote Desktop, MDM, Group Policy, capacity for more RAM, and support for joining Active Directory and Azure AD.
- **Windows 11 Home limitations.** Windows 11 Home requires an Internet connection, and a Microsoft account is required for installation. (After the installation, however, you can remove the Microsoft account from Windows 11 Home.) Windows 11 Pro, just as with Windows 10, can be installed with a local account and without Internet access.

32-Bit versus 64-Bit Version

Core 2 Objective 1.7

Recall that an operating system can process 32 bits or 64 bits at a time. A 64-bit installation of Windows 10/11 generally performs better than a 32-bit installation if you have enough RAM. Table 12-1 shows how much RAM is supported by popular editions of Windows. Also, 64-bit installations of Windows can support 64-bit applications,

Table 12-1 Maximum memory supported by Windows 10/11 editions and versions

Operating System	32-Bit Architecture	64-Bit Architecture
Windows Home	4 GB	128 GB
Windows Pro	4 GB	2 TB
Windows Pro for Workstations	4 GB	6 TB
Windows Enterprise	4 GB	6 TB

which run faster than 32-bit apps. Even though you can install 32-bit applications in a 64-bit OS, always choose 64-bit applications for best performance. Keep in mind that 64-bit installations of Windows require 64-bit device drivers.

Also note that a 64-bit version of Windows can only be upgraded to a 64-bit OS. A 32-bit OS can only be upgraded to a 32-bit OS. If you want to install a 64-bit version of Windows on a computer that already has a 32-bit OS installed, you must perform a clean install.

Note 1

All processors (CPUs) used in personal computers today are hybrid processors and can handle a 32-bit or 64-bit OS. However, the Intel Itanium and Xeon processors used in high-end workstations and servers are true 64-bit processors and require a 64-bit OS.

Note 2

The amount of memory or RAM you can install in a computer depends not only on the OS installed but also on how much memory the motherboard can hold. To know how much RAM a motherboard can support, see the motherboard documentation.

Verify That Your System Qualifies for Windows 10

Core 2 Objectives 1.1, 1.3

Before you purchase Windows 10, verify that all the applications installed on the system will work with Windows 10. Windows 10 is backward compatible with most applications written for Windows 8/7. You also need to make sure the computer meets the minimum hardware requirements:

- Processor (CPU): 1 GHz or faster
- RAM: 1 GB for a 32-bit OS or 2 GB for a 64-bit OS
- Free space on hard drive: 16 GB for a 32-bit OS or 20 GB for a 64-bit OS
- Graphics card: DirectX 9 or later with a WDDM 1.0 driver
- Display: 800 × 600 resolution

Exam Tip

The A+ Core 2 exam may give you a scenario and ask you to demonstrate hardware compatibility requirements for a Windows installation.

Recall that hardware devices require device drivers to interface with Windows. Look at all the hardware components and peripherals (graphics cards, printers, and even the motherboard) to verify Windows 10 device drivers are available. Download important ones, such as the drivers for the network card, before you install Windows. It's very important to have a Windows 10 driver for your network port without having to depend on the network or the Internet to get one after Windows 10 is installed. Also know that many Windows 8/7 drivers work with Windows 10.

For a laptop or brand-name computer, check with the computer manufacturer to make sure the specific computer model you are working with supports Windows 10.

Note 3

In general, it's best not to upgrade an OS on a laptop unless you want to use some feature the new OS offers. For laptops, follow the general rule, "If it ain't broke, don't fix it." Many hardware components in a laptop are proprietary, and the laptop manufacturer is the only source for those drivers. If you are considering upgrading a laptop to Windows 10, check the laptop manufacturer's website for advice and to download Windows 10 drivers, which are called third-party drivers because they are not included in BIOS/UEFI or Windows.

System Information Window

Core 2 Objective 1.3

To get useful details about what hardware and OS is currently installed in your system, open the **System Information** window (msinfo32.exe). To run System Information in Windows, enter `msinfo32` in the search box. The System Information window for one computer is shown in Figure 12-1. To drill down to more information in the window, click items in the left pane.

Figure 12-1   Use the System Information utility to examine details about a system

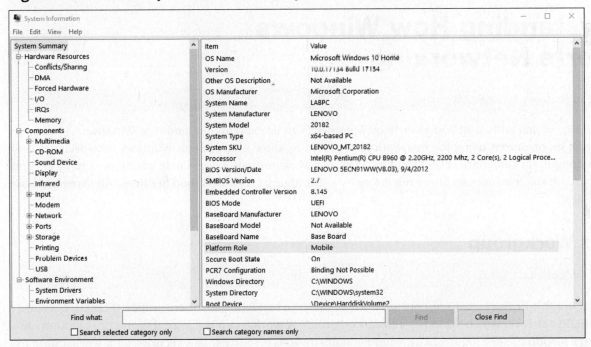

System Requirements for Windows 11

Core 2 Objectives 1.1, 1.3

As announced by Microsoft, the hardware requirements for Windows 11 are designed to limit computers that qualify for Windows 11 to those that are less than four years old. The requirements for a computer to qualify for Windows 11 are the same for Home and Pro editions:

- **Processor.** The processor must have two cores and a minimum speed of 1 GHz. In addition, Microsoft recommends specific Intel, AMD, and Qualcomm processors that are less than four years old. For Intel, that includes 8th generation processors released in 2017 or later.

- **Memory.** At least 4 GB RAM.

- **Storage.** At least 64 GB.

- **Security.** UEFI firmware with secure boot enabled, and a version 2.0 TPM chip on the motherboard.

- **Upgrade paths.** Currently, you can upgrade from Windows 10 to Windows 11 for free. You can also upgrade for free from Windows 7/8 to Windows 11, although apps and settings might not make it through the upgrade. For Windows 7/8 systems, you might want to first upgrade to Windows 10 and then upgrade Windows 10 to Windows 11. However, know that computers that are old enough to have Windows 7/8 installed as the original OS are most likely not going to qualify for Windows 11.

> **Caution** (!)
>
> If a processor is not on the Microsoft recommended list, but still has two cores and a minimum speed of 1 GHz speed, and the TPM chip is version 1.3 or later, the computer might still install Windows 11, but Microsoft has announced it will not guarantee such a system will receive Windows 11 updates, including security updates. If you do install Windows 11 on a system that does not qualify for it, don't trust it with important or sensitive data, because it might be vulnerable to attack without all the security updates.

Understanding How Windows Supports Networking

Core 2 Objectives 1.1, 1.6, 2.5

To help you decide which edition of Windows 10 or Windows 11 to use and understand how Windows will connect to a network and its resources using the installation, you need to know a little about Windows networking. Recall that Windows computers can connect to a local network in a workgroup or a domain. In addition, computers connected anywhere on the Internet can share resources by using Microsoft Azure Cloud Services. All three methods are described next.

Windows Workgroup

Core 2 Objectives 1.1, 1.6

A network that doesn't have centralized control, such as one in a small office or home office (SOHO), is called a **peer-to-peer (P2P)** network, which Windows calls a workgroup. A **workgroup** is a logical group of computers and users that share resources (see Figure 12-2), where administration, resources, and security on a workstation are controlled by that workstation.

> **Note** 4
>
> Recall from the module "The Complex World of IT Professionals" that the diagrams in Figure 12-2 and later in Figure 12-3 describe the logical connections between computers, which is called logical network topology, as opposed to the physical topology.

Figure 12-2 A Windows workgroup is a type of peer-to-peer network in which no single computer controls the network and each computer controls its own resources

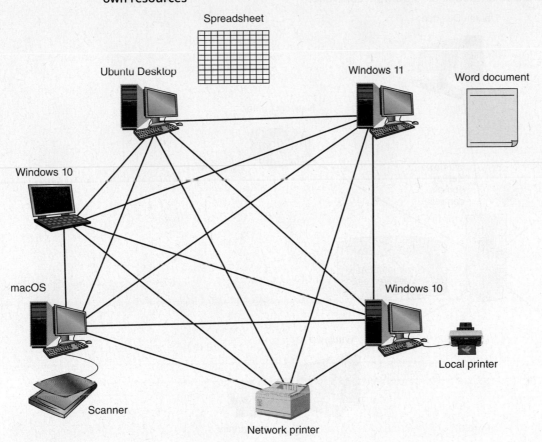

In a Windows workgroup, each computer maintains a list of users and their rights on that particular computer. The computer can share its resources with others on the network by creating share permissions for its files, folders, and connected devices, such as a printer.

Exam Tip ✔

The A+ Core 2 exam expects you to be able to contrast a workgroup and domain and know which to use in a given scenario.

Windows Domain

Core 2 Objectives 1.1, 1.6

A Windows **domain** is implemented on a larger, private network, such as a corporate or college network. The domain forms a logical group of networked computers that share a centralized directory database of user account information and security (see Figure 12-3). A Windows domain is a type of **client/server** network, which is a network where resources are managed by centralized computers. A computer making a request from another is called the client,

Figure 12-3   A Windows domain is a type of client/server network in which security on each computer or other device is controlled by a centralized database on a domain controller

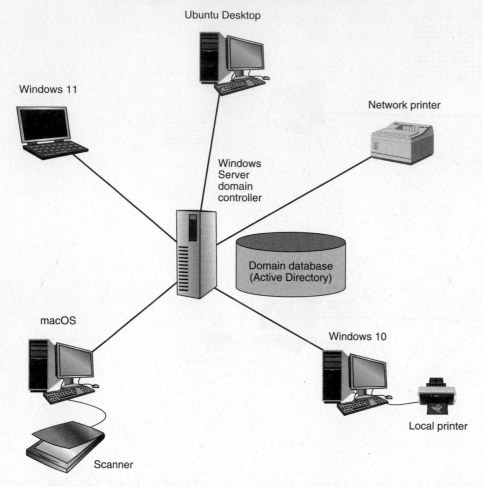

Ubuntu Desktop

Windows 11

Network printer

Windows Server domain controller

Domain database (Active Directory)

macOS

Windows 10

Local printer

Scanner

and the computer answering the request is called the server. Using the client/server model, the directory database is controlled by a network operating system (NOS). Examples of network operating systems are Windows Server and various forms of Linux such as Ubuntu Server and Red Hat Enterprise Linux (RHEL).

> **Note** 5
>
> Windows Home does not support joining a domain. If you plan to join a domain on your network, install Windows 10/11 Pro or Enterprise editions. Chrome OS, Linux, and macOS can all join a domain.

Active Directory

Windows Server controls a network using the directory database called **Active Directory (AD)**. All users on the network must have their own domain-level account, the most common of which is called a **domain user account** or **network ID**. These accounts are kept in AD and assigned by the network or system administrator. If you are connecting a computer to a domain, the administrator will tell you the network ID and password to the domain that you can use to sign in to the network. AD normally manages a domain for users on company premises. Remote users can join the domain using a VPN or DirectAccess connection. A **virtual private network (VPN)** is a security technique that encrypts data transmitted between a private network and a computer somewhere on the Internet. Windows DirectAccess was designed to eliminate the need for a VPN.

Connecting a Computer to a Windows Domain

If a Windows computer is already connected to a physical network, you have signed in to Windows with a local user account, and you want to access resources controlled by a Windows domain on the network, you'll need to change the way Windows connects to the network. To make the change, you'll need the network ID and password to the domain provided by the network administrator. Do the following:

1. Open the **Settings** app. Open the **Accounts** group, and then click **Access work or school**.
2. Under *Access work or school*, click **Connect**. See Figure 12-4 for Windows 10; Windows 11 works the same way.

Figure 12-4   Authenticate to the Local Active Directory or to Azure Active Directory

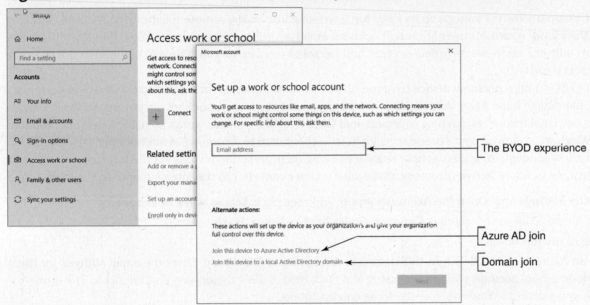

3. Click **Join this device to a local Active Directory domain**. Enter the domain name and click **Next**. Follow the on-screen directions. The next time you sign in to Windows, use your network ID on the domain.

> **Note 6**
>
> If your computer is part of a domain, press Ctrl+Alt+Del when Windows starts to display a sign-in screen, and then enter your network ID and password.

Chrome OS, Linux, and macOS can also connect to a Windows domain. You learn to do that in later modules.

Azure Active Directory

Core 2 Objective 1.6

Azure Active Directory (Azure AD or AAD) manages users in the cloud and creates a virtual network of users connected through the Internet. Whereas AD is managed by Windows Server installed on private computers on company premises, Azure AD runs in the cloud from more than 200 Microsoft data centers around the world that offer Azure AD as a public service. See Figure 12-5. This method is primarily intended as a way for work-owned devices to access cloud resources, such as Office 365, from anywhere on the Internet. For example, a company

12

Figure 12-5 Active Directory runs on private computers on company premises while Azure AD runs in the cloud

Active Directory

Azure AD in the Cloud

might provide company-owned laptops so its sales force working from many remote locations can access company resources in the cloud. Azure AD uses Microsoft account email addresses as account names. Windows 10/11 Pro and Enterprise editions allow work-owned devices and personal devices to join Azure AD. Windows 10/11 Home does not support Azure AD.

Microsoft calls joining a personal device to Azure AD the **BYOD experience (bring your own device experience)**. When a personal device joins Azure AD, you can access corporate resources, such as corporate databases, while still accessing personal resources, such as your personal OneDrive. The process works by using a personal account to sign in to Windows, followed by a secondary sign-in to authenticate to Azure AD. A school might use the BYOD experience to allow students to access school resources using their personal devices via the Internet.

To authenticate to Azure Active Directory, make sure you're connected to the Internet, and do the following:

1. Open the **Settings** app. Open the **Accounts** group, and then click **Access work or school**.
2. Under *Access work or school*, click **Connect**. (Refer back to Figure 12-4.)
3. Do one of the following:

   - For an Azure AD join, click **Join this device to Azure Active Directory**. Enter the email address for the work or school account you are accessing and click **Next**. Follow the on-screen directions. The next time you sign in to Windows, use the same email address.
   - For the BYOD experience, enter your Azure AD email address and click **Next**. Follow the on-screen directions. You will then have access to organizational resources using SSO (single sign-on) as well as access to your personal resources, such as your personal OneDrive. The next time you sign in to Windows, use your personal account. You will automatically be signed in to Azure AD.

Note 7

A Microsoft account is an example of a **single sign-on (SSO) account**, which accesses multiple, independent resources, systems, or applications after you sign in one time to one account.

Types of User Accounts

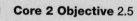
Core 2 Objective 2.5

To help keep it all straight, let's pause and summarize the three types of user accounts and how each is used:

- **Local account.** A **local account** is created on the local computer and is recognized only on the local computer. A local account is authenticated on the local computer.
- **Network ID.** Professional and enterprise editions of Windows allow a user to sign in to Windows with a network ID and password that are created and maintained on a Windows domain in Active Directory on the local network.

- **Microsoft account.** A **Microsoft account** is an email address initially set up at the Microsoft website (*live. com*). It gives you access to the Microsoft OneDrive cloud and several types of online accounts, including Facebook, LinkedIn, Twitter, Skype, and Outlook.com. In addition, if you have an account in Azure Active Directory given to you by your school or other organization, you use your Microsoft account to authenticate to these domain services in the cloud. As you learn later in the module, Microsoft makes every effort to encourage you to use a Microsoft account in Windows. In fact, Windows 11 Home requires you to have a Microsoft account to install the OS.

Table 12-2 summarizes the various ways to sign in to Windows, access Microsoft resources in the cloud, and join a domain. (Note that it is possible for a network administrator to configure Windows Server to associate a Microsoft account to a network ID so sign-in to the domain can be done with a Microsoft account.)

Table 12-2   Types of accounts and types of authentications

Type of Account	Local Computer	Microsoft Cloud	Windows Domain	Azure Domain Services	BYOD Experience
Local account	Yes	No	No	No	No
Network ID	Yes	No	Yes	No	No
Microsoft account	Yes	Yes	In most cases	Yes	Yes

Besides authenticating to the local computer, a network, or a cloud, any one of the three types of Windows accounts can be assigned a privilege level that apply to what the account is allowed to do on the local computer:

- A **standard account** has fewer privileges and is used for normal productivity work on a computer.
- An **administrator account** has more privileges than a standard account and is used by people responsible for maintaining and securing the system.

Next, let's look at the different ways that Windows handles public and private network connections.

Public and Private Networks

Core 2 Objective 1.6

When you connect a Windows computer to a network the first time, Windows asks how you want to secure the network connection. When connecting to a public network, such as when you connect your laptop to a public wireless network at a local airport, you always want to ensure that your computer is protected from outside hackers and malware. Windows 10/11 offers three ways to secure a network connection:

- **Public network.** When using Public network security, Windows configures strong firewall settings, the computer is hidden from other devices on the network, and you can't share files or printers. This option is the most secure.
- **Private network.** When using Private network security, the computer is discoverable and you can share files and printers. Windows 10/11 computers can join a workgroup.
- **Domain network.** When the computer is set up to join a Windows domain, it yields control for authenticating users and sharing files, folders, and printers to settings in Active Directory.

If you want to change the setting that controls how Windows secures a network connection, open the **Network and Sharing Center**, and click **Change advanced sharing settings**. In the Advanced sharing settings window (see Figure 12-6), you can change the public, private, home, or work status of a network connection, and you can turn network discovery and file and printer sharing on or off. You learn how to manage all these settings in the module "Network Security and Troubleshooting."

Figure 12-6 Change the security setting for a Windows network connection

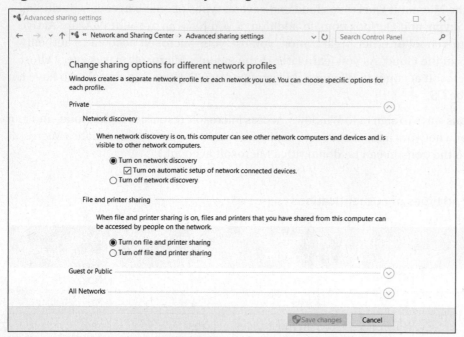

Final Checklist Before Beginning the Installation

 Core 2 Objectives 1.6, 1.9

Before you begin the installation, complete the final checklist shown in Table 12-3 to verify that you are ready.

Table 12-3 Checklist to complete before installing Windows

Questions to Answer	Further Information
Does the computer meet the minimum or recommended hardware requirement?	CPU: RAM: Hard drive partition size: Free space on the partition:
Do you have the Windows device drivers for your hardware devices and application setup files?	List hardware and software that need to be upgraded:
Do you have the product key available? (It might not be required if you are reinstalling Windows 10/11.)	Product key:
How will users be recognized on the network?	Domain name: Computer name: Network ID: Network password:
How will the computer be recognized on the network?	Static or dynamic IP addressing: IP address (for static addressing):
Will you do an upgrade or a clean install?	Current operating system: Does the old OS qualify for an upgrade?

(Continued)

Table 12-3   Checklist to complete before installing Windows (*Continued*)

Questions to Answer	Further Information
For a clean install, will you set up a dual boot?	List reasons for a dual boot: Size of the second partition: Free space on the second partition:
Have you backed up important data on your hard drive?	Location of backup:

Before getting into the step-by-step instructions for installing an OS, here are some general tips for installing Windows:

- Verify that you have all application software CDs or DVDs available and all third-party device drivers.
- Back up all important data on the drive. How to perform backups is covered in the module "Maintaining Windows." It's especially important to back up user data and preferences.
- For upgrade installations and clean installs in which you do not plan to reformat the hard drive, run antivirus/anti-malware software to make sure the drive is free of malware. After you have scanned for malware, if you still suspect malware is present, perform a clean installation of Windows.
- If Windows is giving errors or refuses to start, perform a clean installation.
- If you want to begin the installation by booting from the Windows USB flash drive or DVD, use BIOS/UEFI setup to verify that the boot sequence is first USB or the optical drive, and then the hard drive.
- In BIOS/UEFI setup, disable any virus protection setting that prevents the boot area of the hard drive from being altered.
- Set BIOS/UEFI to use UEFI mode (which uses GPT and possibly Secure boot) or UEFI CSM mode (which uses MBR partitions on the hard drive). Know that Windows 10 will install on a GPT drive only when CSM mode is disabled and will install on an MBR drive only when CSM mode is enabled. As you learn later in the module, Windows 11 installs only when Secure boot is enabled.
- For a laptop computer, connect the AC adapter and use that power source for the complete OS installation, updates, and installation of hardware and applications. You don't want the battery to fail in the middle of the installation.

The Size of the Windows Partition

Core 2 Objective 1.9

For a clean install, during the installation, you can decide not to use all the available space on the drive for the Windows partition. Here are reasons not to use all the available space:

- **You plan to install more than one OS on the hard drive, creating a dual-boot system.** For example, you might want to install Windows 10 on one partition and leave room for another partition where you intend to install Windows 11, so you can test software under both operating systems. (When setting up a dual boot, always install the older OS first.)
- **Some people prefer to use more than one partition or volume to organize data on their hard drives.** For example, you might want to install Windows and all your applications on one partition and your data on another. Having your data on a separate partition makes backing up easier. In another situation, you might want to set up a volume on the drive that is used exclusively to hold data backups on another computer on the network. When deciding on the size of the partition that will hold Windows, don't forget to allow plenty of room to install its applications as well as at least 15% of free space, which Windows needs to work.

Caution !

It's convenient to back up one volume to another volume on a different hard drive. However, don't back up one volume to another volume on the same hard drive; if the drive fails, all volumes on the drive might be damaged, and you could lose both your data and your backup.

12

In the module "Maintaining Windows," you learn to use the Disk Management utility after Windows is installed to create partitions from unallocated space and to resize, delete, and split existing partitions.

Verify That You Have the Windows Product Key

 Core 2 Objective 1.9

Typically, you'll purchase Windows 10/11 online, with the product key emailed to the Microsoft account used to make the purchase. If you purchased Windows 10/11 on a USB flash drive or DVD, look for the product key printed on the cover of the case, on a card inside the case, or affixed to the back of the Windows documentation booklet.

However, keep in mind that the product key might not be required to reinstall Windows. After Windows is activated the first time with a valid product key, Windows assigns a **digital license** to the machine and stores it along with information about the computer's physical hardware (called the **hardware signature**) on Microsoft activation servers. If Windows is installed later, it can retrieve this information from Microsoft servers rather than requesting that you reenter the product key.

In addition, for a laptop, all-in-one, or other brand-name computer, the computer manufacturer might have stored the Windows product key on motherboard firmware. When reinstalling Windows, setup can retrieve this product key from the firmware. Either way, the new Windows installation is assigned a digital license, and you don't have to enter the product key during the installation.

Note 8

To determine if Windows 10 was activated using a product key or digital license, open the **Settings** app, click **Update & Security**, and click **Activation** (see Figure 12-7). For Windows 11, open the **Settings** app, click **System**, and click **Activation**.

Figure 12-7 This installation of Windows was activated using a retail digital license associated with a Microsoft account

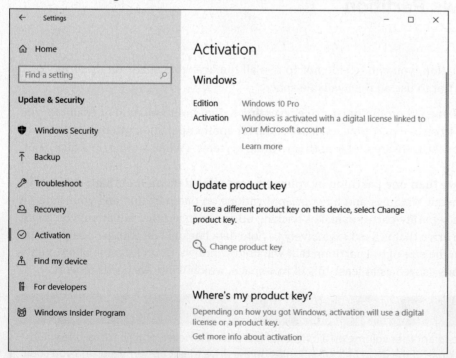

Applying Concepts

Using the Media Creation Tool to Create a Bootable Windows 10 Setup DVD or Flash Drive

Est. Time: 15 minutes excluding download time
Core 2 Objective: 1.9

When you download the Windows 10 setup files from Microsoft, you start by downloading the **Media Creation Tool**. After you install and launch the tool, you use it to download Windows setup files; you also have the option to create a bootable DVD or USB flash drive. You learn how to use the Media Creation Tool later in this module.

> **Note 9**
>
> The Media Creation Tool and Windows setup files can be downloaded for free from Microsoft. Therefore, when you purchase Windows 10, you are really only purchasing a product key, which is required to activate a license to use Windows 10. The product key is emailed to your Microsoft account email address.

To create the installation media, you'll need a blank DVD or an 8 GB or larger USB flash drive. You'll also need at least 8 GB of free space on your hard drive. Use a blank flash drive because any data on it will be lost. To use the Media Creation Tool to download Windows setup files and create a bootable DVD or USB flash drive, follow these steps:

1. To download and install the Media Creation Tool, use a working computer, go to the website microsoft.*com/ en-us/software-download/windows10*, and click **Download tool now**. Execute the file that downloaded.

2. Accept the license terms. In the next window, shown in Figure 12-8, select **Create installation media (USB flash drive, DVD, or ISO file) for another PC**, and click **Next**.

Figure 12-8   The Media Creation Tool can be used to upgrade a computer or to create installation media

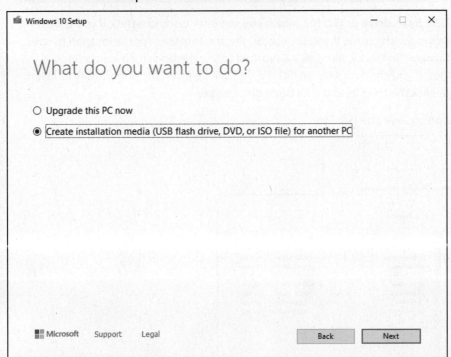

3. Select a language and architecture (64-bit, 32-bit, or both), as shown in Figure 12-9. (Windows 10 is the only edition available to select.) Alternatively, if you're creating installation media as a troubleshooting tool for the computer you're using, check **Use the recommended options for this PC**. Click **Next**.

(continues)

Applying Concepts Continued

Figure 12-9   The installation medium is bit specific: Choose 32-bit for a 32-bit computer or 64-bit for a 64-bit computer

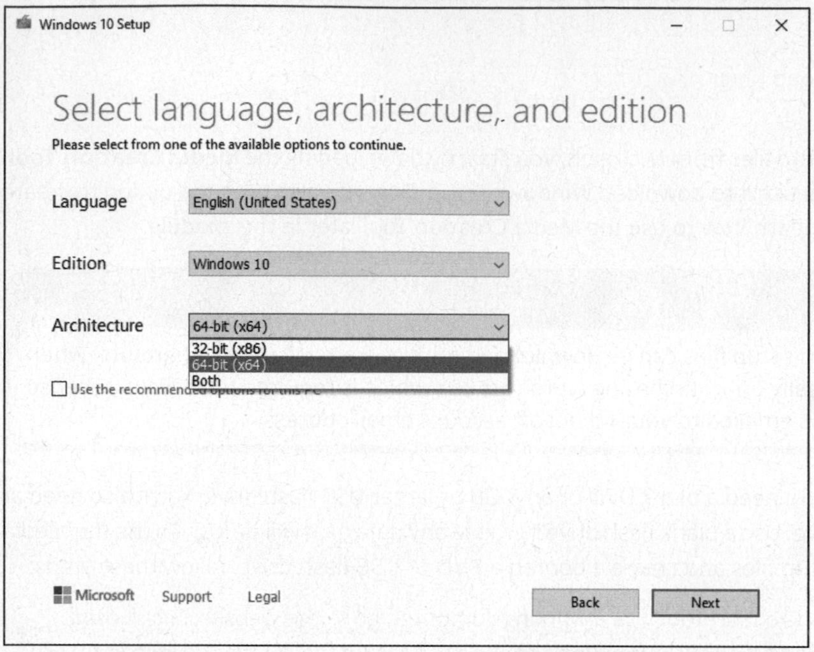

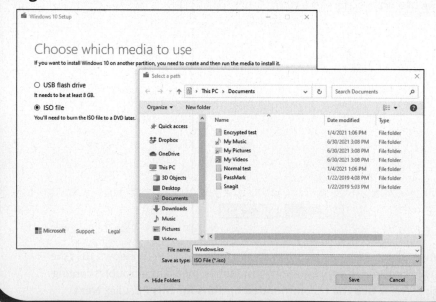

Windows 10 Setup   — ☐ ✕

Select language, architecture, and edition
Please select from one of the available options to continue.

Language   English (United States)   ⌄

Edition   Windows 10   ⌄

Architecture   64-bit (x64)   ⌄
                  32-bit (x86)
                  64-bit (x64)
                  Both

☐ Use the recommended options for this PC

■ Microsoft   Support   Legal   [Back]   [Next]

> ## Note 10
>
> The best practice is to save the Windows setup files to a USB flash drive or ISO image. You never know when you'll need the files later to repair a corrupted Windows installation.

4. On the next screen, select **USB flash drive** or **ISO file**, which you can later burn to a DVD. If you choose *USB flash drive*, the tool searches for the drive. If you choose *ISO file*, the tool asks for the location to save the file (see Figure 12-10). Navigate to the location, click **Save**, and follow the on-screen instructions. After the download completes, if you chose to save an ISO file, you will be given the opportunity to insert a DVD in the disk drive, right-click the ISO file, and click **Burn disc image**.

Figure 12-10   Select a location to save the ISO file

Windows 10 Setup   — ☐ ✕

Choose which media to use
If you want to install Windows 10 on another partition, you need to create and then run the media to install it.

○ USB flash drive
It needs to be at least 8 GB.

◉ ISO file
You'll need to burn the ISO file to a DVD later.

Select a path   ✕

← → ↑ 📁 › This PC › Documents   ⌄ ↻   Search Documents   🔍

Organize ▾   New folder   ▦ ▾ ❓

★ Quick access   Name   Date modified   Type
📦 Dropbox   📁 Encrypted test   1/4/2021 1:06 PM   File folder
                      🎵 My Music   6/30/2021 3:08 PM   File folder
☁ OneDrive   🖼 My Pictures   6/30/2021 3:08 PM   File folder
                      🎬 My Videos   6/30/2021 3:08 PM   File folder
💻 This PC   📁 Normal test   1/4/2021 1:06 PM   File folder
📦 3D Objects   📁 PassMark   1/22/2019 4:08 PM   File folder
🖥 Desktop   📁 Snagit   1/22/2019 5:03 PM   File folder
📄 Documents
⬇ Downloads
🎵 Music
🖼 Pictures
🎬 Videos

File name: Windows.iso   ⌄
Save as type: ISO File (*.iso)   ⌄

■ Microsoft   Support   Legal

∧ Hide Folders   [Save]   [Cancel]

Here's some useful information about an ISO file:

- An **ISO file**, also called an **ISO image** or disc image, is an image of an optical disc, including its file system and all its files and folders. An ISO (International Organization for Standardization) file has an .iso file extension.
- To see the contents of an ISO file, open **Explorer**, right-click the file, and click **Mount**. The ISO file is assigned a drive letter, and you can drill down into its contents.
- If you have an optical drive that can write to DVDs and you want to burn a DVD from an ISO file, insert a blank DVD in your optical drive, and double-click the ISO file. Follow the on-screen directions; Windows does the rest.
- You can mount an ISO file to a virtual DVD drive in a virtual machine and use it to install Windows in the VM, as you would with a physical DVD installed in a physical computer.

Prepare for a Windows 11 Upgrade or New Installation

 Core 2 Objectives 1.1, 1.3

When Windows 10 checks for updates and finds Windows 11 available and the system qualifies for Windows 11, the Windows Update window in the Settings app gives you the opportunity to download and install Windows 11. See Figure 12-11. Follow instructions on screen to perform the update.

Figure 12-11   Windows 10 update offers a free upgrade to Windows 11

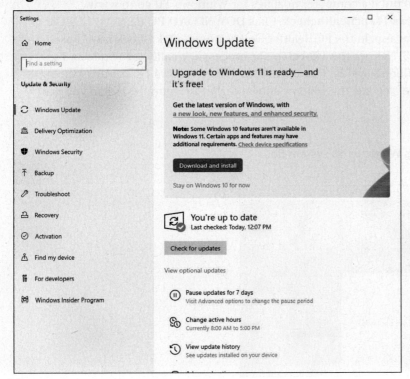

For a Windows system that does not automatically report the option to install Windows 11, you can follow these steps to find out if the system qualifies for Windows 11:

1. To verify that Secure Boot is enabled, enter **msinfo32.exe** in the search box to open the System Information window. Look for Secure Boot State, which appears as On or Off. Refer back to Figure 12-1.
2. To determine if the TPM chip is a high enough version and is enabled, enter **tpm.msc** in the search box. The Trusted Platform Module (TPM) window appears and reports the status of the TPM. See Figure 12-12. Notice TPM is enabled, but the version is version 1.2, which does not qualify for Windows 11. This Windows 10 computer is more than ten years old.)

Figure 12-12   For Windows 11, TPM version 2.0 or higher must be ready for use

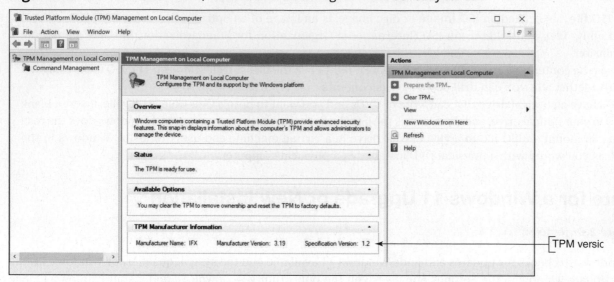

3. If you need to enable Secure Boot or the TPM chip, see the module "All About Motherboards."
4. To use the PC Health Check app to find out if a computer qualifies for Windows 11, go to **www. microsoft.com/en-us/windows/windows-11#pchealthcheck**. Click **DOWNLOAD PC HEALTH CHECK APP**, and download, install, and run the app. In the PC Health Check window, click **Check now**. Results for one system is shown in Figure 12-13. Neither the TPM chip nor processor qualify for Windows 11. Figure 12-14 shows the results for a different system that does qualify for Windows 11. For this system, when you click **Open Windows Update**, you see the window shown earlier in Figure 12-11 and you can proceed with the installation.

Figure 12-13   PC Health Check reports this Windows 10 system does not qualify for Windows 11

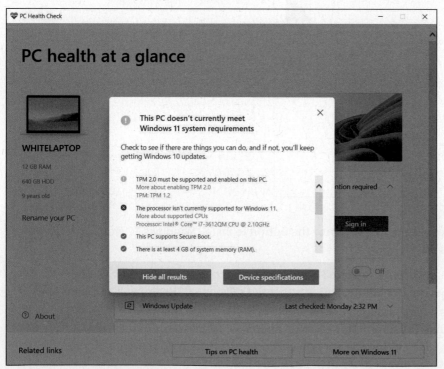

Figure 12-14   PC Health Check reports this Windows 10 system qualifies for Windows 11

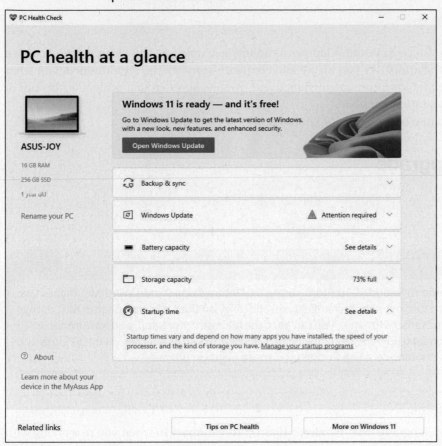

To manually force an upgrade to Windows 11 or perform a clean installation of Windows 11, follow these steps:

1. To get the Windows 11 installation files, go to **www.microsoft.com/software-download/windows11**. You have three options:

   - To upgrade the current Windows 10 system to Windows 11, download and run the **Windows 11 Installation Assistant**, which steps you through the process of verifying the hardware qualifies for Windows 11 and upgrading to Windows 11.

   - To perform an upgrade or clean install on another computer, click **Create Windows 11 Installation Media** and follow the directions to create a bootable USB drive or DVD. (The USB drive or blank dual-layer DVD must be at least 8 GB.) You can also use this option to download an ISO file.

   - To download an ISO file that contains multiple editions of Windows 11, click **Download Windows 11 Disk Image (ISO)** and follow the directions on screen.

Installing Windows 10 or Windows 11

 Core 2 Objective 1.9

In this part of the module, you learn the steps to install Windows as an in-place upgrade and clean install. You also learn how to handle problems with installations. As you install and configure software, be sure to document what you do. This documentation will be helpful for future maintenance and troubleshooting. In a project at the end of this module, you will develop a documentation template.

Let's begin with how to perform an in-place upgrade of Windows 10.

Windows 10 In-Place Upgrade

 Core 2 Objective 1.9

> **Note 11**
>
> You can upgrade from Windows 10 Home to Windows 10 Pro by using the Settings app within Windows. If you have already purchased a Windows 10 Pro product key, simply change the product key on the Activation page in the Settings app, and then follow the on-screen instructions. Alternately, you can go to the Microsoft Store app, purchase Windows 10 Pro, then follow the on-screen instructions. An upgrade from one edition of Windows 10 to another via the Settings app or the Microsoft Store is easy and does not require going through the entire upgrade process.

Here are the steps to perform an in-place upgrade from Windows 10/8.1/7 to Windows 10 when you're working with a Windows 10 setup DVD or USB flash drive:

1. Sign in to Windows using an administrator account, which is a user account that has the right to install system software.

2. As with any upgrade installation, do the following before you start the upgrade:

   - Scan the system for malware using an updated version of anti-malware software. When you're done, be sure to close the anti-malware application so it's not running in the background.

   - Uninstall any applications or device drivers you don't intend to use in the new installation.

   - Make sure your backups of important data are up to date, and then close any backup software running in the background.

3. Insert the Windows 10 setup DVD or flash drive or mount the setup ISO file. Recall that to mount an ISO file, you right-click it and click **Mount**. Windows assigns a drive letter to the file, and you can access its contents.

4. Open **File Explorer** and double-click the **setup.exe** program in the root of the device or mounted ISO file. (For a DVD, the setup program might start automatically.) When the User Account Control dialog box appears, click **Yes**. The setup program loads files, examines the system, and reports any problems it finds. If it finds the system meets requirements, the *Install Windows 10* window appears, telling you it will download current updates next. See Figure 12-15. To allow updates to download (recommended), click **Next**. If you don't want to download updates (such as when you have an unstable Internet connection), click **Change how Windows Setup downloads updates**, and then click **Not right now**.

Figure 12-15   Click Next to allow Setup to download current updates

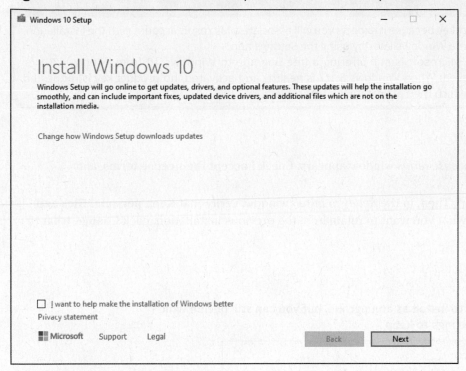

5. If setup recognizes it needs a product key to activate Windows, the *Activate Windows* screen appears (see Figure 12-16). You have two options:

- Enter the product key; Windows verifies that the key is valid. If the computer is connected to the Internet, setup will automatically activate Windows during the installation. Click **Next**.

- If you think Windows should activate without the product key, click **I don't have a product key**. On the next screen, select the Windows product you are installing, and click **Next**.

Figure 12-16   Enter a product key, which causes Windows to activate during the installation

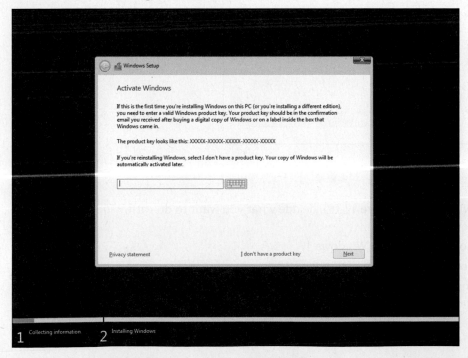

12

Note 12

Windows might not require a product key because it expects you will associate a Microsoft account with the installation. Setup lets you know you must activate Windows later by using the Settings app.

In addition, as of this writing, Microsoft is still offering a free upgrade to Windows 10 from Windows 8.1 or Windows 7 with Service Pack 2 applied. When Windows 8.1/7 is healthy and activated, no product key is requested when you upgrade to Windows 10, which then activates with no problem.

6. The *Applicable notices and license terms* window appears. Check **I accept the license terms**, and click **Next**.

7. Wait for updates to download. Then, in the *Ready to install* window, verify that **Keep personal files and apps** is selected. To specify what you want to retain from the previous installation, click **Change what to keep** (see Figure 12-17).

Figure 12-17   Windows is ready to install as an upgrade, but you can still decide which files, apps, and settings to keep

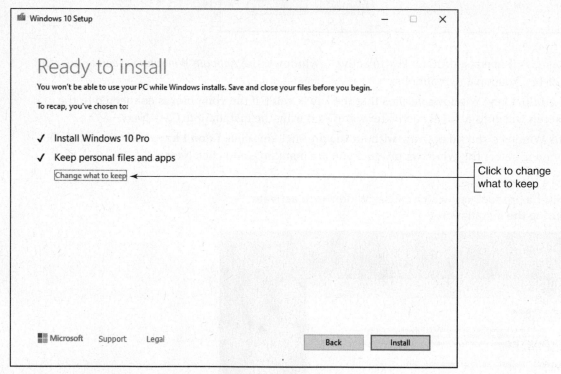

8. In the *Choose what to keep* window (see Figure 12-18), decide what you want to do with Windows settings, personal files, and apps:
   - The first two options perform upgrades to Windows 10.
   - The Nothing option performs a clean install of Windows 10.

   In this example, you are doing an in-place upgrade installation, so select **Keep personal files and apps**, and then click **Next**. The *Ready to install* window appears again.

Figure 12-18   Decide what to keep of the old installation

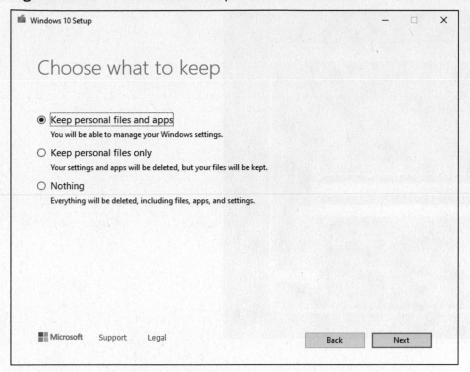

9. On the *Ready to install* window, verify the choices listed, and click **Install** to begin the installation.

10. During the installation, setup might restart the system several times. After you make your choices on the privacy settings screen, the Windows 10 desktop appears.

Windows 10 Clean Install

Core 2 Objective 1.9

Recall that a clean install is the best option to use if the current installation is sluggish or causing problems, the currently installed OS does not allow for an in-place upgrade, or you're installing Windows 10 on a new hard drive or new desktop computer you're building.

If you have a Windows 8.1/7 installation that qualifies for a Windows 10 upgrade and you need to do a clean install, follow these steps:

1. Begin by starting the installation from the Windows desktop as you would for an upgrade.

2. Follow the previous steps for an in-place upgrade. When you get to the *Ready to install* window (refer back to Figure 12-17), click **Change what to keep**.

3. On the *Choose what to keep* window (refer back to Figure 12-18), click **Nothing** and click **Next**. Then continue with the installation. The contents of the volume holding the previous version of Windows are deleted. If the hard drive has other volumes, they are left unchanged.

Use the following steps to perform a clean install on a newly installed hard drive, on a new computer you're building, or on a computer that has a corrupted Windows installation that refuses to start:

1. Boot from the Windows setup DVD or USB flash drive. Recall that you first might need to change the boot priority order in BIOS/UEFI. In the *Windows Setup* screen (see Figure 12-19), select the language and regional preferences, and click **Next**. On the next screen, click **Install now**.

Figure 12-19   Decide on language and keyboard preferences

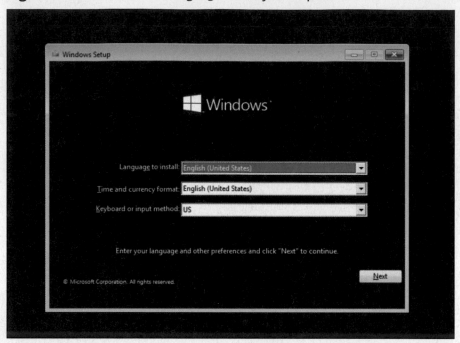

2. Continue the installation as you would for an upgrade. When you get to the *Which type of installation do you want?* screen (see Figure 12-20), click **Custom: Install Windows only (advanced)**.

Figure 12-20   Decide between an upgrade and a clean installation

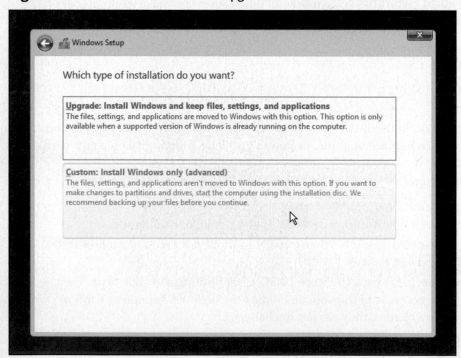

3. The *Where do you want to install Windows?* screen appears (see Figure 12-21). Select the drive and volume where you want to install Windows. By default, setup will use the entire unallocated space for the WindTows volume. If you want to use only a portion of the space, click **New** and enter the size of the

Figure 12-21   Select an existing partition to receive the Windows installation or create a new
partition

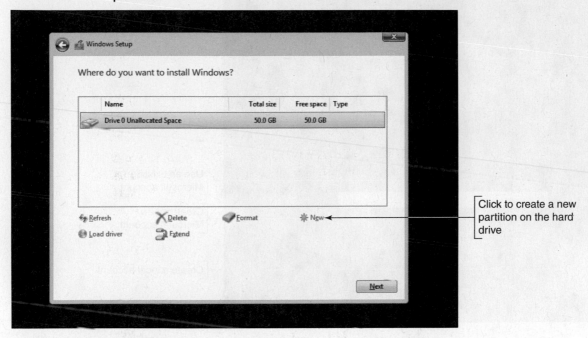

Click to create a new
partition on the hard
drive

volume. (Setup will also create a small system partition that it later uses for system files and the startup
process.) Click **Next** to continue.

4. The installation begins. Note that the system might restart several times. When the next screens appear,
choose your region and keyboard layout.

5. On the *How would you like to set up?* screen, you can choose *Set up for personal use*, which sets up a
local account intended for a peer-to-peer network or a Microsoft account. If you choose *Set up for an
organization*, you are prompted to enter a Microsoft account managed by an Azure domain or to join a
domain via a network ID. Select **Set up for personal use** and click **Next**.

Note 13

If you do not have a network connection set up, Windows
has you use an offline, local account by default.

6. On the *Let's add your account* screen, you
can choose to use an existing Microsoft
account, create a new Microsoft
account, or
create an offline account (see Figure 12-22).
To create a local, offline account, click **Offline
account**.

7. On the *Sign in to enjoy the full range of Microsoft apps and services* screen, Microsoft again nudges you to
use a Microsoft account. To continue creating an offline account, click **Limited experience**. (Microsoft
really pushes hard.)

8. On the following screens, enter the name for the user of the local account, a password twice, and
answers to three security questions. Then choose the privacy settings for the device, and decide how
you want to handle Cortana.

9. The installation continues, settings are applied, and the Windows desktop appears. A panel appears
asking how you want to connect to a network. Unless you're connected to a public network, click **Yes**.
You're now ready to use Windows 10.

Figure 12-22   Choose the type of account to set up

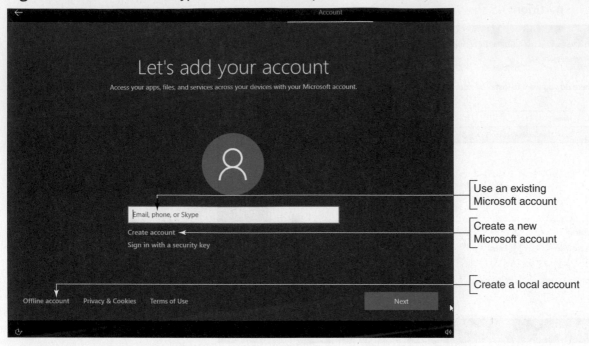

Clean Install in a Dual-Boot Configuration

If you want to install two OSs on the same computer in a dual-boot configuration, you might need to shrink a partition to make room for a second partition to hold the next OS. For Windows, use Disk Management to shrink a partition, create a new partition, or format a partition. How to use Disk Management is covered in the module "Maintaining Windows." After you have created a second partition to hold the second OS, start the installation. When you get to the *Where do you want to install Windows?* screen (see Figure 12-23), select the partition or unallocated space for the new OS, and continue with the clean install.

Figure 12-23   Select unallocated space or a partition other than the one
used by the first OS installation

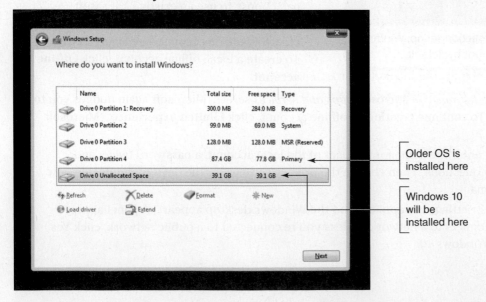

To create a dual-boot environment, always install Windows operating systems in order from older to newer. Also know you cannot boot more than one OS at a time. When you boot with a dual boot, the **boot loader menu** shown in Figure 12-24 appears for you to select the OS to boot.

When using a dual boot, you can execute an application while one OS is loaded even if the application is installed under the other OS, as long as each OS is using the same architecture (32-bit or 64-bit). If the application is not listed on the Windows 10 Start menu or the Windows 8.1 Start screen, locate the program file in Explorer. Double-click the application to run it.

Upgrade or Clean Install for Windows 11

Core 2 Objectives 1.1, 1.9

If you created a bootable Windows 11 USB flash drive or DVD or downloaded an ISO file, begin the Windows 11 upgrade or clean install using the media or ISO file. Upgrading to Windows 11 or performing a clean install works the same as it does for Windows 10.

Installations in a Virtual Machine

Core 2 Objective 1.9

Figure 12-24 Use the boot loader menu in a dual-boot environment

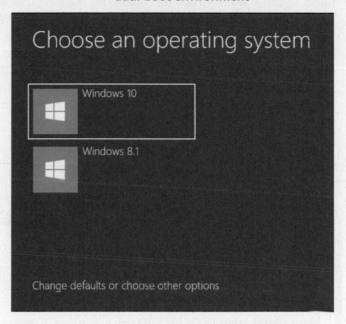

Another type of Windows installation is when you install Windows in a virtual computer. A virtual computer or **virtual machine (VM)** is software that simulates the hardware of a physical computer. Using this software, you can install and run multiple operating systems at the same time on a single computer, which is called the host machine. These multiple instances of operating systems can be used to train users, run legacy software, and support multiple operating systems. For example, help desk technicians can run a virtual machine for each OS they support on a single computer and quickly switch from one OS to another by clicking a window. Another reason to use a virtual machine is that you can capture screenshots of the boot process in a virtual machine, which is how some screenshots were made for this text.

Software used to create and manage VMs is called a **hypervisor**. Some popular hypervisors for Windows are Client Hyper-V by Microsoft (*microsoft.com*), VirtualBox by Oracle (*virtualbox.org*), and VMware Workstation Player by VMware, Inc. (*vmware.com*). Be aware that hypervisor software and VMs require a lot of memory and might slow down your system. Figure 12-25 shows two virtual machines running under VirtualBox.

Figure 12-25 Two virtual machines running under VirtualBox

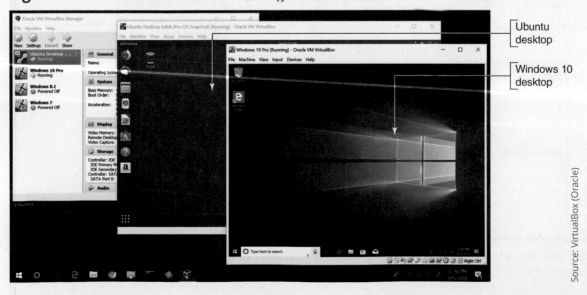

Source: VirtualBox (Oracle)

Install Windows in a Client Hyper-V VM

Client Hyper-V is the virtual machine (VM) manager that is part of 64-bit Windows 10/11 Pro. If your processor and motherboard support hardware-assisted virtualization (HAV), you can use Client Hyper-V to install and manage virtual machines on the desktop. Generation 1 VMs allow either a 32-bit or 64-bit installation of an OS in a VM. Generation 2 VMs require a 64-bit guest operating system. Hyper-V can connect a VM to the local network. Client Hyper-V supports dynamically expanding virtual hard drives and dynamically allocated memory. When using dynamically expanding virtual hard drives, the VM ties up only the portion of the host's hard drive that the VM's hard drive is actually using. When using dynamic memory, the VM ties up only the portion of allocated memory that it is actually using.

Applying Concepts

Setting Up a VM

Est. Time: 45 minutes excluding download time
Core 2 Objective: 1.9

Here are the steps to set up a VM using Windows 10 Pro:

1. Go into BIOS/UEFI setup on your computer, and make sure virtualization is enabled.

2. Hyper-V is disabled in Windows 10 Pro by default. To turn it on, open the **Settings** app, select the **Apps** group, select **Apps and features**, and click **Programs and Features**. In the Programs and Features window, click **Turn Windows features on or off**. Place a check mark by **Hyper-V** and click **OK**. You'll need to restart the system for the change to take effect.

3. To launch the Hyper-V Manager, open the search box, type **Hyper-V**, and then click **Hyper-V Manager**. The Hyper-V Manager window appears on the desktop. In the Hyper-V Manager pane on the left, select the host computer (see Figure 12-26).

Figure 12-26 Select the host computer for managing Hyper-V virtual machines

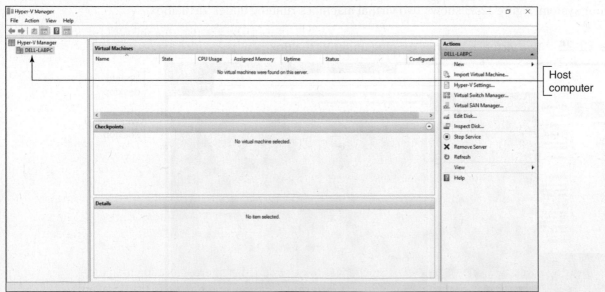

4. To give your VMs access to the network or the Internet, you first need to install a virtual switch. To create a virtual switch, click **Virtual Switch Manager** in the Actions pane on the right side of the Hyper-V Manager window.

5. The Virtual Switch Manager window appears (see Figure 12-27). In the left pane, make sure **New virtual network switch** is selected. To bind the virtual switch to the physical network adapter so the VMs can access the physical network, click **External** in the right pane. Click **Create Virtual Switch**.

Figure 12-27   Create a virtual switch

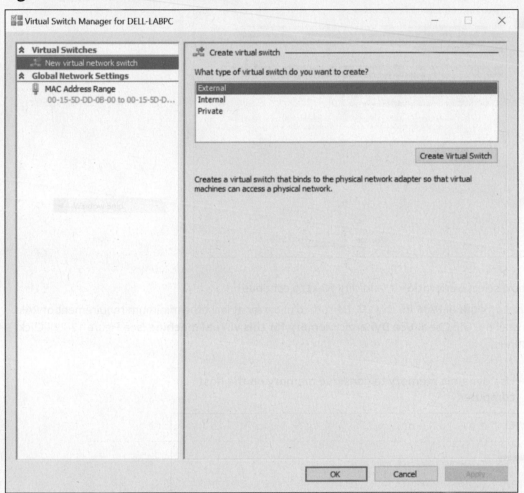

6. The Virtual Switch Properties dialog box appears; the new switch is shown in the right pane. In this pane, you can name the virtual switch or leave the default name. You can also select the network adapter to use for the switch. For most situations, that would be the wired Ethernet adapter. Make sure **Allow management operating system to share this network adapter** is checked, and then click **Apply**. Click **Yes** to create the virtual switch. Click **OK** to close the window.

7. You're now ready to create a VM. In the Actions pane, click **New**, and then click **Virtual Machine**. This opens the New Virtual Machine Wizard, where you can set the name and location of the VM files and configure memory and the virtual hard drive. Click **Next**. (Notice you can click **Finish** to accept default settings for the VM.)

8. Assign a name to the VM. If you want the VM files to be stored in a different location than the default, check **Store the virtual machine in a different location**, and browse to that location (see Figure 12-28). After you've selected the location, click **Next**.

Applying Concepts Continued

Figure 12-28   Name the VM and decide where the VM files will be
stored

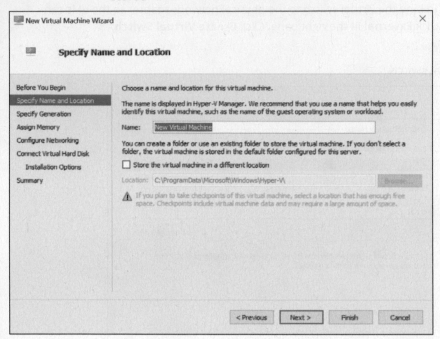

9. In the next box, select **Generation 1**, and click **Next** to continue.

10. Set the desired amount of RAM for the VM. Be sure to allow for at least the minimum requirement of RAM
    needed to install the OS. Check **Use Dynamic Memory for this virtual machine** (see Figure 12-29). Click
    Next to continue.

Figure 12-29   Use dynamic memory to conserve memory on the host
computer

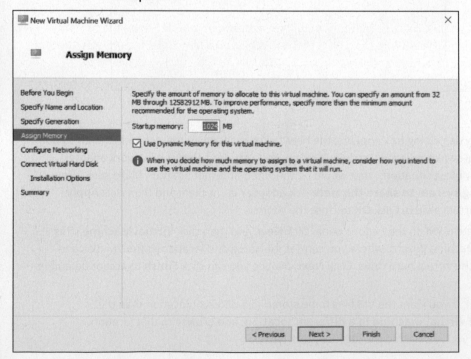

11. In the Configure Networking dialog box, select the virtual switch you created earlier, and click **Next**.

12. In the Connect Virtual Hard Disk dialog box, select **Create a virtual hard disk** and click **Next**.

13. The Installation Options dialog box appears (see Figure 12-30). To install Windows from the ISO file you downloaded earlier using the Media Creation Tool, select **Install an operating system from a bootable CD/DVD-ROM**. Select **Image file (.iso)**. Click **Browse** and select the ISO file for the Windows installation. Click **Next** to continue. The last dialog box in the New Virtual Machine Wizard shows a summary of your selections. Click **Finish** to create the VM. The new VM is listed in the Virtual Machines pane in the Hyper-V Manager window.

Figure 12-30 Decide how an OS will be installed in the VM

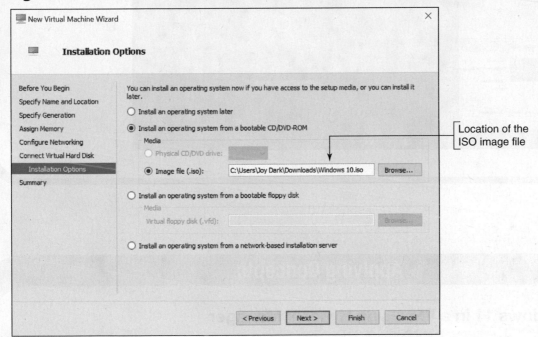

14. To manage the VM's virtual hardware, select the VM in Hyper-V Manager, and click **Settings** near the bottom of the Actions pane. The Settings dialog box for the VM appears. Select the hardware in the left pane, and apply your settings in the right pane.

15. To install Windows, you need to boot from the virtual DVD drive. Click **BIOS** in the left pane, and select **Boot from CD** in the right pane.

16. Close the **Settings** dialog box. To start the VM, select it and click **Start** in the Actions pane. The VM boots up and Windows setup starts. A thumbnail of the VM appears in the bottom-middle pane of the Hyper-V Manager window. To see the VM in a separate window, double-click the thumbnail. Figure 12-31 shows the VM window at the beginning of the OS installation. Notice in the figure that several VMs have been created, and three of them are currently running.

Note 14

If you are trying to install an OS in a new VM and you get an error after the Product Key screen, try shutting down and restarting the VM. Then start the install again.

(continues)

Applying Concepts Continued

Figure 12-31   Windows 10 is running in the VM

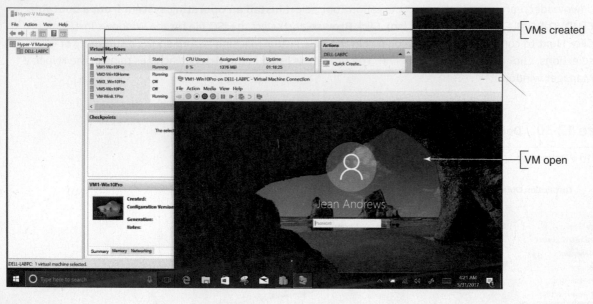

VMs created

VM open

Applying Concepts

Install Windows 11 in a VM Using Hyper-V Manager

Est. Time: 1 hour
Core 2 Objective: 1.9

Follow these steps to create a VM that meets requirements for Windows 11 and start the Windows 11 installation:

1. If you have not already done so, using the Microsoft link provided earlier, download the Windows 11 ISO file needed to install Windows 11.

2. In Hyper-V Manager, in the Action pane, click **New, Virtual Machine**. In the New Virtual Machine Wizard, click **Next**, name the VM, and select where you want to store it. Click **Next**.

3. Under Specify Generation, select Generation 2, which is needed to meet the UEFI-based firmware requirements and Secure Boot for Windows 11. See Figure 12-32.

4. For Startup memory, enter a minimum of **4096** and select **Dynamic Memory** for the VM. Connect the VM to a virtual switch to allow for Internet access, which is needed for a Windows 11 installation. Click **Next**.

5. Create a virtual hard drive for the VM, at least 64 GB capacity. Click **Next**.

6. Point to the Windows 11 ISO file you downloaded earlier, and click **Next**. Click **Finish**. The VM is created.

7. Select the VM and click **Settings**. Notice the VM is Secure Boot enabled. Select **Security** and check **Enable Trusted Platform Module**. See Figure 12-33. Click Apply.

Figure 12-32   A Generation 2 VM meets UEFI firmware requirements for Windows 11

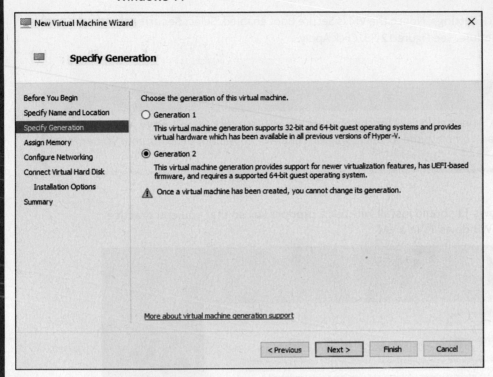

Figure 12-33   Secure Boot and TPM must both be enabled in the VM to support Windows 11

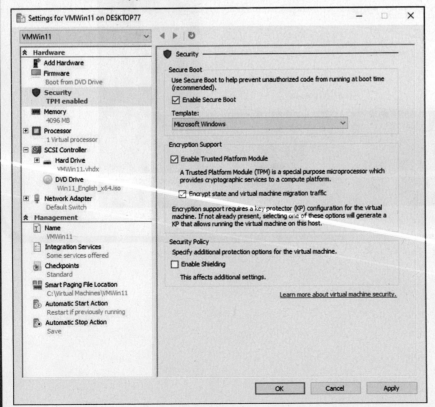

12

(continues)

Applying Concepts Continued

8. Select the VM and click **Settings**. Notice the VM is Secure Boot enabled. Select **Security** and check **Enable Trusted Platform Module**. See Figure 12-33. Click Apply.

Note 15

Just as with Windows 10, when setup asks for the product key, you can click **I don't have a product key**. See Figure 12-34. You can complete the installation, but Windows 11 will not activate until you enter a product key.

Figure 12-34   Windows 11 should install without a product key so that you can practice using Windows 11 in a VM

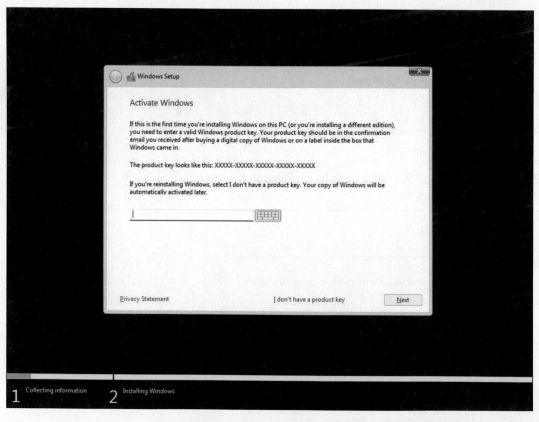

Solve Problems With Installations

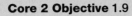

Core 2 Objective 1.9

In this part of the module, we look at a few special situations you might encounter when installing Windows and what to do about them, including how to install Windows on a new hard drive when you don't know its product key, and problems that require preparing a hard drive before the installation.

Verifying Windows Is Activated

When you enter a product key while installing Windows, Windows should already be activated. To view the activation status in Windows 10, open the **Settings** app (click **Start** and click the Settings cog icon), select the **Update & Security** group, and then select **Activation**. See Figure 12-35. For Windows 11, in the **Settings** app, click **System** and click **Activation**. If the system is not activated, click **Change product key** and enter the key.

Figure 12-35   View the activation status using the Settings app

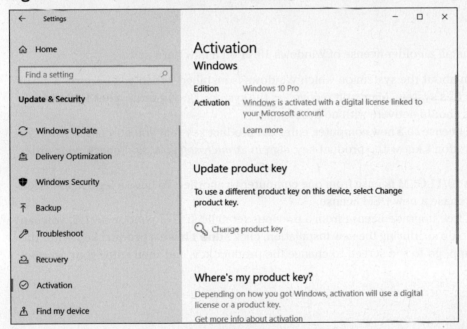

Dealing With Old and Unknown Product Keys

Suppose a hard drive that has Windows installed fails and you must install Windows 10/11 on the replacement hard drive, or you want to move your Windows installation from one computer to another. You need to be aware of how you deal with the product key associated with your license of Windows. Three ways you can purchase or acquire Windows are the following:

- An **Original Equipment Manufacturer (OEM) license** of Windows, which is less expensive than a retail license, can be purchased from third-party vendors such as Amazon (*amazon.com*) or Newegg (*newegg.com*).

12

The OEM license is associated with the motherboard on which it is first installed and, therefore, cannot be transferred to a new motherboard. It can, however, work with a new hard drive.

- A **retail license** for Windows can be purchased at the Microsoft online store (*microsoftstore.com*). The product key is sent to the Microsoft email address used to make the purchase. The retail license follows the Microsoft email account from one PC to another.
- Microsoft still offers a free upgrade to Windows 10/11 from Windows 8.1 or 7. The free upgrade does not have a Windows product key associated with it; instead, it is assigned a digital license.

Note 16

If you don't know the email address that was used to purchase a retail license, you can find the product key by opening an Administrator Command Prompt window and entering the command:

```
wmic path softwarelicensingservice get oa3xoriginalproductkey
```

The product key displays. If you are using a digital license, nothing displays. How to use a command prompt window is covered in the module "Maintaining Windows."

Here is what to do when you install an older license of Windows 10/11 on a new hard drive:

- Microsoft retains information about the system on which Windows is installed. When you perform a clean install on a new hard drive in this system, Microsoft recognizes the system. During setup, click **I don't have a product key**, and Windows should activate with no problem.
- If you move a Windows retail license to a new computer, enter the product key that you purchased from the Microsoft online store. If you don't know the product key, sign in at *microsoft.com*, and check your order history.
- You cannot move a Windows 10/11 OEM license from one computer to another. To have a legal installation of Windows, you need to purchase a new OEM license.
- If you have a Windows 10/11 free upgrade license from a previous retail license of Windows 8.1/7, you can move it to a new computer. To do so, during the new installation, click **I don't have a product key**. After the installation, in the **Settings** app, go to the screen to change the product key, and then enter your product key for Windows 8.1/7.

Note 17

Suppose Windows 10 Pro is activated on a system and then gets corrupted. You perform a clean install to fix the problem, but setup automatically installs and activates Windows 10 Home without asking for a product key. You can fix the problem by going to the Activation window and changing the product key to the **default product key** for Pro: VK7JG-NPHTM-C97JM-9MPGT-3V66T. The system should reactivate with Windows 10 Pro.

Applying Concepts

Converting an MBR Drive to GPT

Est. Time: 30 minutes
Core 2 Objective: 1.9

Suppose you want to use a 64-bit version of Windows and UEFI firmware mode for added security, thus requiring you to use the GPT partitioning system. However, your hard drive has already been partitioned with the MBR system. The error won't show up until you get to the step in the installation where you select the partition or unallocated space on the hard drive to hold the Windows installation (see Figure 12-36).

Figure 12-36   An error appears when Windows requires the GPT
                   partitioning system

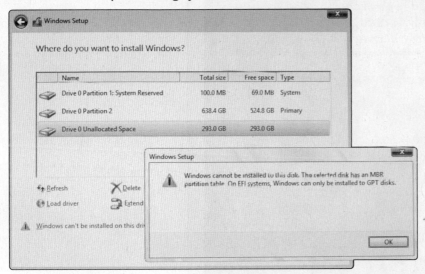

Follow these steps to use the **diskpart** command to wipe the partition system off the hard drive. All data on the drive will be destroyed, and then you can convert the drive to GPT:

1. Restart the computer from the Windows setup DVD or flash drive, and select your language and regional preferences. Click **Next**. On the next screen, select **Repair your computer** (see Figure 12-37).

Figure 12-37   Use the Windows setup DVD to launch a command prompt

(continues)

Applying Concepts Continued

2. On the next screen, click **Troubleshoot**. On the Advanced options screen, click **Command Prompt**. A command prompt window appears. Type **diskpart** and press **Enter**. The DISKPART> prompt appears, as shown in Figure 12-38.

Figure 12-38   The command prompt window with diskpart running

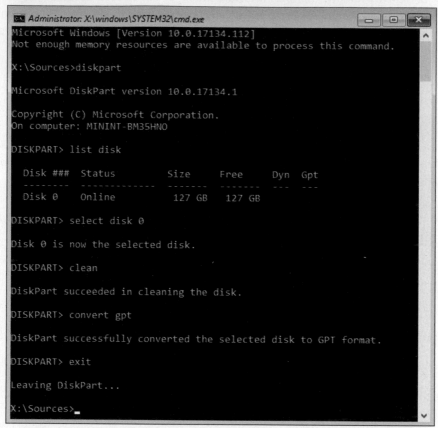

3. At the DISKPART> prompt, use the commands shown in Table 12-4 and Figure 12-38 to select the hard drive, clean it, and convert it to a GPT drive.

Table 12-4   Diskpart commands to convert an MBR drive to GPT

Command	Description
list disk	List the hard drives installed. If you have more than one hard drive, use the size of the drive to determine which one you want to clean. Most likely, you will have one hard drive identified as Disk 0.
select disk 0	Make Disk 0 the selected hard drive.
clean	Clean the partition table and all partitions from the drive.
convert gpt	Convert the partitioning system to GPT.
exit	Exit the diskpart utility.

4. Enter one more **exit** command to close the command prompt window. On the setup screen that appears, click **Turn off your PC**.

5. You can now restart the system and install Windows in UEFI mode, which uses the GPT partitioning system.

What to Do After a Windows Installation

Core 2 Objectives 1.4, 1.5, 1.6, 1.7, 2.5

After you have installed Windows 10/11, you need to do the following:

1. Verify that you have network access.
2. Install updates for Windows and verify update settings.
3. Verify anti-malware settings.
4. Install hardware.
5. Set up user accounts, and transfer or restore user data and preferences from backups to the new system.
6. Install applications.

Caution ❶

To protect your computer from malware, don't surf the web for drivers or applications until you have updated Windows and verified that anti-malware software is providing real-time protection from malware.

Verify Network Access

Core 2 Objective 1.6

Do the following to verify network and Internet access:

1. To make a wired connection to a network when using Windows, simply plug in the network cable and let Windows do the rest. To create a wireless connection, click the network icon in the taskbar and select the wireless network. You might need to enter a password to the Wi-Fi network.
2. To verify access to the local network, open **Explorer** and verify that you can see other computers on the network (see Figure 12-39). Try to drill down to see shared resources on these computers.

Figure 12-39   Use File Explorer to access resources on your network

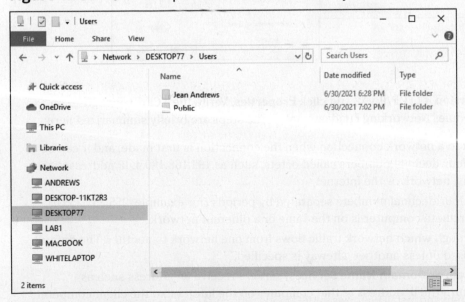

3. To verify Internet access, open the browser and try to navigate to a couple of websites.

If a problem arises, the problem might be that you need to install the drivers for the motherboard, including the drivers for the onboard network port. Also, the DNS, IP address, subnet mask, and gateway settings might be wrong.

Core to Core ⬌

The A+ Core 1 exam covers the Internet Protocol (IP) addressing scheme and how TCP/IP settings are configured. You can review this content in the modules "Networking Fundamentals" and "Network Infrastructure and Cloud Computing."

Do the following to verify TCP/IP settings:

1. In Control Panel, open the **Network and Sharing Center** and click **Change adapter settings**. The *Network Connections* window opens. Right-click the connection and select **Properties**. See Figure 12-40.

Figure 12-40   Verify TCP/IP settings for the current network connection

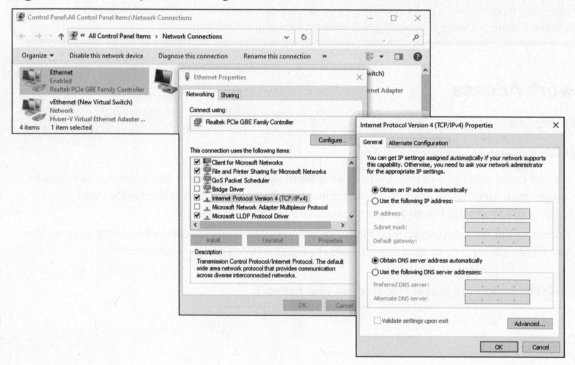

2. Select **Internet Protocol Version 4** (TCP/IPv4), and click **Properties**. Verify the TCP/IP configuration as you learned to do in the module "Networking Fundamentals." The steps are briefly summarized here:

   • An **IP address** is assigned to a network connection when the connection is first made, and it can be a 32-bit string written as four decimal numbers called octets, such as 192.168.100.4. IP addresses are used to locate devices on a network or the Internet.

   • A **subnet mask**, which is four decimal numbers separated by periods (for example, 255.255.255.0), tells Windows whether a remote computer is on the same or a different network.

   • A **gateway** is a device through which network traffic flows from one network to another. The **default gateway** is the gateway used unless another gateway is specified.

   • **DNS (Domain Name System or Domain Name Services) servers** receive an address such as *www.cengage.com* and return the IP address of that computer on the Internet so the client computer can use the IP address to locate the *www.cengage.com* computer.

- An IP address can be assigned as a **dynamic IP address** by a server each time the workstation connects to the network or as a **static IP address**, which is permanently assigned to the computer. If the network is using static IP addressing, verify the IP address, subnet mask, and default gateway are correct.
- When dynamic IP addressing is used, DNS server addresses are also most likely received automatically. However, if DNS server addresses are given, verify these DNS servers are working. A simple way to do that is to use the ping and nslookup commands. You learn to use both commands in the module "Network Security and Troubleshooting."

> **Exam Tip** ✔
>
> The A+ Core 2 exam expects you to know how to configure a wired or wireless network connection to include DNS settings, subnet mask, gateway address, and static or dynamic IP addressing.

Install Windows Updates

Core 2 Objective 1.5

To protect the system from malware, be sure to install Windows updates before you attempt to install applications or hardware. By default, Windows updates automatically on a regular basis. To apply any pending Windows 10 updates, open the **Settings** app, and click the **Update & Security** group. (For Windows 11, in the **Settings** app, click **Windows Update**.) In the Windows Update window (see Figure 12-41), you can view the update status and install any available updates. Depending on the situation, you might click **Restart now** to finish installing updates, click **Download and install** or click **Install now** to install available updates, or click **Check for updates** if no updates are available. Keep installing important updates and checking for more updates until no more are available. You might need to restart the system after certain updates are installed.

Figure 12-41   View and manage Windows 10 updates

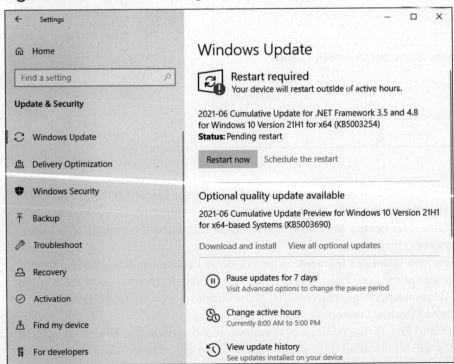

Note 18

If you see available updates that refuse to install on an older system, you can perform an in-place upgrade of Windows 10. The upgrade process should apply all available updates.

You can uninstall an update and/or manage update settings. Here's what you can do from the Settings app:

- **View or uninstall an update.** In the Settings app, click **Update & Security**, and then click **Windows Update** in the left pane. Click **View update history** to review recent updates and to uninstall updates that are available for uninstallation (see Figure 12-42). (For Windows 11, on the Windows Update window, click **Update history**.)

Figure 12-42 Use the Settings app to manage Windows 10 updates

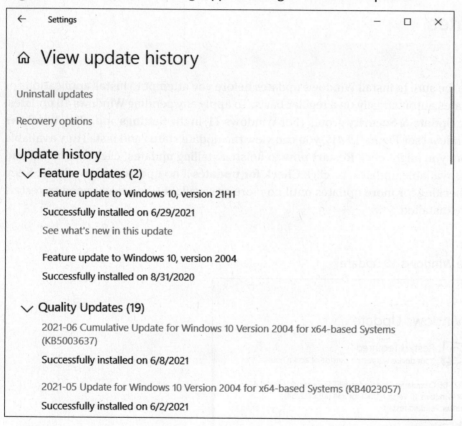

- **Schedule restarts and active hours.** In the Windows Update window, use the Update settings section to schedule a pending restart or to set **active hours**, during which time the computer will avoid automatic restarts. Note that if a scheduled restart occurs outside of active hours but when the computer is in use, you will have an opportunity to delay the restart.
- **Update other Microsoft products and Windows features.** In the Windows Update window, click **Advanced options**. In the Advanced options window (see Figure 12-43), you can choose to receive updates to other Microsoft products along with Windows updates. You can also allow Windows to automatically sign you in and finish installing updates after a Windows restart.
- **Defer or pause updates.** For Pro and Enterprise editions of Windows, you can open the Advanced options window to choose when updates will be installed or to pause updates. Notice in Figure 12-43 that updates can be deferred for up to 35 days. You cannot defer or pause security updates in this window.

Figure 12-43   Control how updates to Windows and Microsoft apps are installed

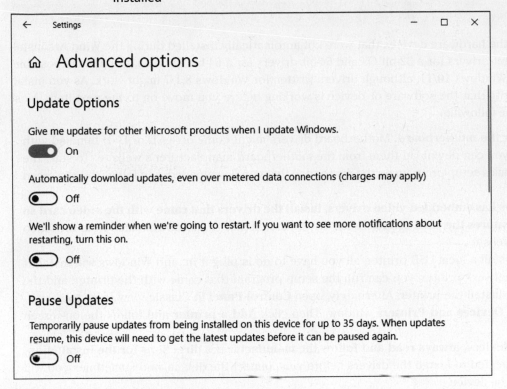

Malware Protection

> **Core 2 Objective** 2.5

Windows includes its own preinstalled anti-malware software called **Windows Defender** in Windows 10. To verify the utility settings, open the **Update & Security** app in Settings and click **Windows Security**. Look for *No actions needed* under *Virus & threat protection*. For more information, click **Open Windows Security**, and drill down in each section (see Figure 12-44). In Windows 11, the anti-malware software is called Microsoft Defender Antivirus. To manage it, click **Privacy & security** in the Settings app.

Figure 12-44   Verify Windows Defender is running

Install Hardware

 **Core 2 Objective** 1.3

You're now ready to install the hardware devices that were not automatically installed during the Windows installation. Be sure to install 32-bit drivers for a 32-bit OS and 64-bit drivers for a 64-bit OS. Also, as much as possible, install drivers designed for Windows 10/11, although drivers written for Windows 8.1/7 might work. As you install each device, reboot and verify that the software or device is working before you move on to the next item. Most likely, you will need to do the following:

- **Install the drivers for the motherboard.** Motherboard drivers might come on a CD or DVD bundled with the motherboard, or you can download them from the motherboard manufacturer's website. To start the installation, double-click a setup program on the disc or one that you downloaded, and follow the on-screen directions.
- **Even though Windows has embedded video drivers, install the drivers that came with the video card so you can use all the features the card offers.** These drivers are on disc or are downloaded from the video card manufacturer's website.
- **Install printers.** To install a local USB printer, all you have to do is plug it in, and Windows will install it automatically. For a network printer, you can run the setup program that came with the printer, and the program will find and install the printer. Alternately, open **Control Panel** in Classic view (how to is coming up) and open the **Devices and Printers** window. Then click **Add a printer** and follow the on-screen directions.
- **For other hardware devices, always read and follow the manufacturer's directions for the installation.** Sometimes you are directed to install the drivers before you connect the device, and sometimes you will first need to connect the device.

If a problem arises, turn to Device Manager, which you find in Control Panel.

Using Control Panel

Control Panel is a window containing several small utility programs called applets that are used to manage hardware, software, users, and the system. (In general, a utility program is used to maintain a system or fix a computer problem.) To access Control Panel in Windows 10/11, type **Control Panel** in the search box on the taskbar.

By default, Control Panel appears in **Category view**, with utilities grouped by category. To switch to **Classic view**, click **Category** and select either Large icons or Small icons. Figure 12-45 shows the Windows 10 Control Panel in Small icons view. Windows 11 Control Panel looks and works the same way. Use the search box in the title bar to help find information and utilities in Control Panel.

Figure 12-45   Many technicians prefer to use Control Panel in Classic view to more easily access utilities

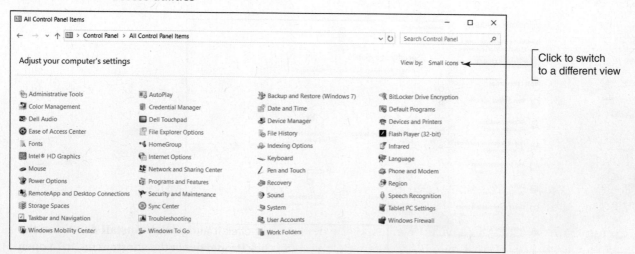

Exam Tip ✔

The A+ Core 2 exam expects you to be able to use Control Panel utilities in a given scenario. Utilities covered in this module include Devices and Printers, Programs and Features, Network and Sharing Center, System, User Accounts, Device Manager, and Ease of Access. Other utilities are covered in later modules.

Using Device Manager

Device Manager in Control Panel is your primary Windows tool for managing hardware. (Its program file is named devmgmt.msc.) It lists all installed hardware devices and the drivers they use. Using Device Manager, you can disable or enable a device, update its drivers, uninstall a device, and undo a driver update (called a **driver rollback**).

Exam Tip ✔

The A+ Core 2 exam expects you to know which scenarios are appropriate for using Device Manager. You also need to know how to use the utility and how to evaluate its results.

To access Device Manager, use one of these methods:

- Open **Control Panel** in Classic view, and click **Device Manager**.
- Right-click **Start** and select **Device Manager**.
- Enter the **devmgmt.msc** command in the Windows search box.

A Device Manager window is shown in Figure 12-46.

Figure 12-46   Use Device Manager to uninstall, disable, or enable a device

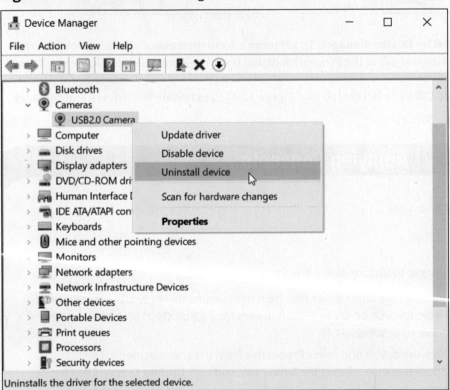

Click an arrow to expand the view of an item or to collapse the view. Here are ways to use Device Manager to solve problems with a device:

- **Uninstall and reinstall the device.** To uninstall the device, right-click it and click **Uninstall device** on the shortcut menu, as shown in Figure 12-46. (Alternately, you can click **Properties** in the shortcut menu to open the Properties dialog box and then click **Uninstall Device** on the Driver tab, as shown in Figure 12-47A.) Then reboot the system. Windows will recognize that the device is not installed and attempt to install the appropriate driver. Look for issues during the installation that point to the source of the problem. Sometimes, though, reinstalling a device is all you need to do. Notice in Figure 12-47B that the selected Device type is Cameras and that the camera is connected through a USB interface. Sometimes USB devices are listed in Device Manager, and sometimes they are not.

Figure 12-47 (A) Use the device's Properties dialog box to uninstall a device, and (B) solve problems with device drivers

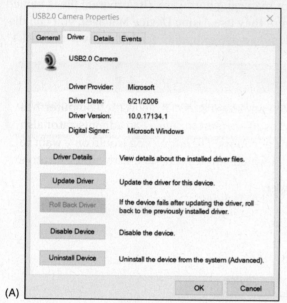

(A)

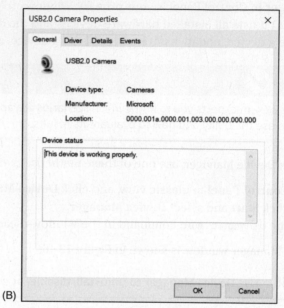

(B)

- **Look for error messages offered by Device Manager.** To get more information about a device, look for error messages that show up on the General tab of the Properties dialog box (see Figure 12-47B). Some messages might suggest a solution.
- **Update or roll back the drivers.** Click the **Driver** tab (see Figure 12-47A) to update the drivers and roll back (undo) a driver update.

Applying Concepts

Updating Device Drivers

Est. Time: 15 minutes
Core 2 Objective: 1.3

Follow these steps to use Device Manager to update device drivers:

1. For best results, locate and download the latest driver files from the manufacturer's website to your hard drive. Be sure to use 64-bit drivers for a 64-bit OS and 32-bit drivers for a 32-bit OS. If possible, use drivers specifically designed for Windows 10 or Windows 11.

2. Using Device Manager, right-click the device and select **Properties** from the shortcut menu. The Properties dialog box for that device appears. Select the **Driver** tab, and click **Update Driver**. The Update Driver Software dialog box opens.

3. To search the Internet for drivers, click **Search automatically for updated driver software**. If you have already downloaded drivers to your computer, click **Browse my computer for driver software**, and point to the downloaded files. Note that Windows is looking for an .inf file to identify the drivers. Continue to follow the on-screen directions to complete the installation.

**Note **

By default, Device Manager hides legacy devices that are not Plug and Play. To view installed legacy devices, click the **View** menu of Device Manager, and check **Show hidden devices**.

Manage User Accounts in Windows

Core 2 Objective 2.5

You might want to associate your local account with your Microsoft account so you can get easy access to Microsoft resources in the cloud, such as OneDrive. Keep these points in mind:

- **Administrator access to your online accounts.** Anyone with administrator rights on the computer has access to all the user data on the computer. When using a Microsoft account to sign in, an administrator also has access to your Microsoft private settings, apps, and online accounts. Therefore, you would only want to set up your Microsoft account on a computer in a situation in which you trust people with administrative access to the computer.
- **Switch to a Microsoft account.** To connect an existing local account or network ID to a Microsoft account, open the **Settings** app, click **Accounts**, and then click **Sign in with a Microsoft account instead**. See Figure 12-48. Follow the on-screen directions, which include entering your current Windows password.

Figure 12-48   Associate a local account with a Microsoft account

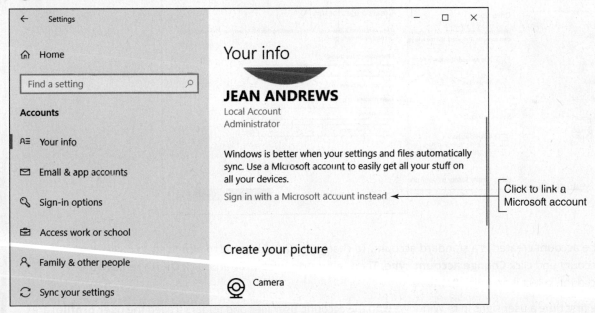

Note 20

To connect a network ID on a domain to a Microsoft account, the Group Policies controlling the Windows domain must allow it. Check with the network administrator for approval.

- **Switch back to a local account.** If you want to switch the user account back to the local account, go back to your account settings, click **Your info**, and click **Sign in with a local account instead**.

Applying Concepts

Creating a Local Account

Est. Time: 15 minutes
Core 2 Objective: 2.5

To create a new account, you can use the Windows 10/11 Settings app or the Computer Management console. In addition, you can manage user account by opening the User Accounts applet in Control Panel. You have more control over creating and setting up an account when you use the Computer Management console, as you learn in the module "Securing and Sharing Windows Resources." For now, let's use the Settings app to create a local account:

1. Sign in to Windows with an administrator account.

2. Open the **Settings** app. Click **Accounts**. Click **Family & other users**, and, for Windows 10, click **Add someone else to this PC** (for Windows 11, click **Add account**). See Figure 12-49. Click **I don't have this person's sign-in information**, and click **Add a user without a Microsoft account** (see the right side of Figure 12-49). Enter a user name, enter the password twice, and click **Next**.

Figure 12-49   Bypass the Microsoft account and create a local account

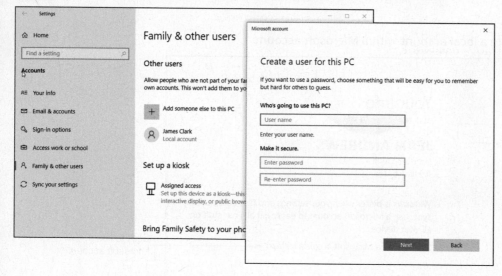

3. The account created is a standard account. To change the account type to administrator, click the account and click **Change account type**. Then select **Administrator** and click **OK**. To remove the account, select it and click **Remove**.

   The first time a user signs in to Windows with the account, user files and folders (called the **user profile**) are created in the C:\Users folder.

   If users want to use the **ease of access** features of Windows, show them how to go to Control Panel and open the Ease of Access Center the first time they sign in. When a setting is selected here (for example, the magnifier, narrator, or high contrast), it is automatically launched each time the user signs in.

After you have created user accounts in a new installation of Windows, you might want to copy user data files from the C:\Users folder or other folders on the hard drive of the old computer to the new computer. How to copy files and folders on a network is covered in the module "Maintaining Windows."

> **Note 21**
>
> After moving user data from one computer to another, the best practice is to leave the user data on the original computer untouched for at least two months. This practice gives the user plenty of time to make sure everything has been moved over.

User Account Control Dialog Box

At some point while you are working with a computer to maintain or troubleshoot it, the **User Account Control (UAC) dialog box** will pop up (see Figure 12-50). If the UAC dialog box appears and you are signed in as an administrator, all you have to do is click Yes to close the dialog box and move on, as shown in Figure 12-50A. If the user account does not have administrative privileges, you'll have to enter the password of an administrative account to continue, as shown in Figure 12-50B.

Figure 12-50   (A) The User Account Control dialog box of an administrator does not require an administrative password; (B) the UAC dialog box of a standard user requires an administrative password

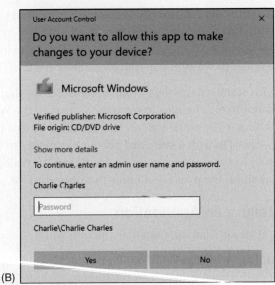
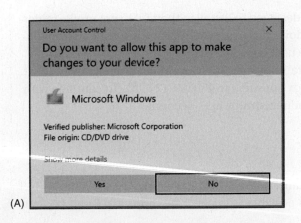

(A)   (B)

The purposes of the UAC dialog box are (1) to prevent malicious background tasks from gaining administrative privileges when the administrator is signed in and (2) to make it easier for an administrator to sign in using a less powerful user account for normal desktop activities but still be able to perform administrative tasks while signed in as a regular user. The UAC dialog box stands as a gatekeeper to malware installing behind your back, because someone has to click the UAC dialog box before the installation can proceed.

You can control how the UAC dialog box works. In Control Panel, click **User Accounts** and click **Change User Account Control settings**. The User Account Control Settings window appears (see Figure 12-51). In the figure, the recommended setting is selected.

12

Figure 12-51   Windows provides options to control the UAC dialog box

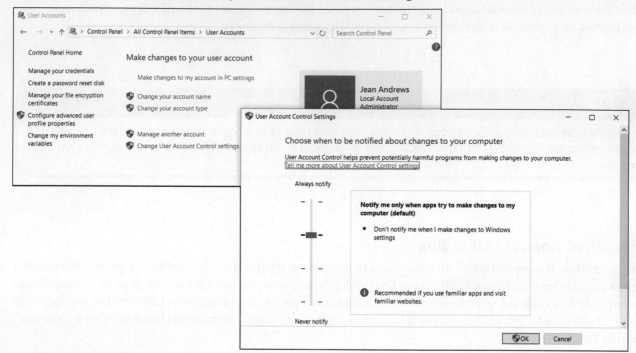

Install Applications

Core 2 Objective 1.7

A user account with administrator privileges has permission to install software for all users; this software is normally installed in the C:\Program Files folder for 64-bit software or the C:\Program Files (x86) folder for 32-bit software. Both folders require administrator permissions to edit the folder's contents. For these installations, expect a UAC dialog box to appear to verify the installation (refer back to Figure 12-50A). Here are two exceptions:

- A user with standard privileges can install software that is designed to install in their C:\Users profile folder if it does not make changes to protected areas of the Windows registry. (The registry is a database of Windows settings.) The software can only be used by this one user account.
- If a user signed in with a standard account attempts to install software, such as anti-malware software, that is designed to run under all user accounts, a UAC dialog box appears (see Figure 12-50B). To continue with the installation, the user must enter the password for an administrator user account.

Before Installing an Application

Before installing an application, consider the following:

- **Compatibility with the OS.** If at all possible, install applications designed for Windows 10 or Windows 11. For best performance, install 64-bit apps in a 64-bit OS. It's possible to install 32-bit apps in a 64-bit OS, but you cannot install 64-bit apps in a 32-bit OS.
- **Hardware requirements.** How much RAM will the app use when running? Does the CPU meet the minimum required? Is there enough free space on the hard drive for the app and its data? Does the app require significant Video RAM (VRAM)? Some graphics-intensive apps, such as video games, recommend a dedicated graphics card with embedded VRAM rather than the standard video components embedded on the motherboard (called integrated video).
- **Specialized hardware.** Some apps that require high security use a **hardware token** to help authenticate a user to the app. An external hardware token might require an input device such as a USB port required by the token shown in Figure 12-52. The token must be configured in the app according to IT department instructions.

Figure 12-52   This hardware token acts like a password to
authenticate the user account in an app

Source: University of Oxford

- **Impact to network performance.** Before installing software, research how much network activity the software produces. You might want to set its priority as high or low on the network to control its performance or to keep it from hogging network resources. Prioritizing applications on a network, which is called **Quality of Service (QoS)**, is done by using Device Manager to configure the network adapter on each computer on the network, configuring the router that gives access to the network, and, for a Windows domain, changing QoS settings in Group Policy.
- **Impact to device.** For an application that uses the Internet, consider if it will make the computer vulnerable to attack. Read manufacturer documentation and reviews about how to secure the application and the system, such as making changes to Windows Firewall or installing each app in its own secured virtual machine on the host computer.
- **Impact to operations.** Read online reviews about the software, and, if possible, talk with other IT professionals who have supported the software. Has it been reported that the software has security issues, bogs down the network, or is generally difficult to support? Are users satisfied with the software? Is it difficult to train users on the software? Consider how existing data will import into the software. Examine online documentation for the software. How difficult is it to install the software and import existing data into it? Are security patches and updates easy to attain and implement? In general, does it do what it claims to do with relatively little IT support?
- **Impact to business.** A business application—such as asset management, accounting, or payroll—should relieve the work of humans to make it possible for humans to focus on the core business of an organization. An application can do just the opposite if it does not work as expected, has bugs, is difficult to use, or constantly needs maintenance. Can you count on IT support from the software developer in the event of a software failure or errors? If the software is mission critical to the success of your organization, it's especially important to do your research about how much support you'll get when problems arise.

Installing and Uninstalling Apps

Applications can be installed from physical media (DVD, CD, or USB flash drive), from a downloaded application file, directly from the web, from the Windows Store, from an ISO file downloaded and mounted in Windows, or from a folder shared by another computer on the network.

To install applications from an ISO file, disc, USB flash drive, or software downloaded from the Internet, open Explorer, locate and double-click the setup program file, and follow the on-screen directions to launch the installation routine. After an application is installed, you might also need to install any updates available for the application on the manufacturer's website.

12

Exam Tip ✔

The A+ Core 2 exam expects you to know how to evaluate an application before you install it, how the software might be distributed, and how to install, update, and uninstall it.

If you need to uninstall an application, do the following:

1. In Settings, click **Apps**. The *Apps & features* window opens. Alternately, you can open **Control Panel** in Classic view and click **Programs and Features** to open the Uninstall or change a program window. See Figure 12-53.

Figure 12-53   Select a program from the list to view your options to manage the software

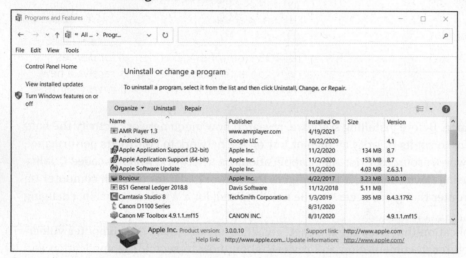

2. Select an app and click **Uninstall**. When you select an app in the Programs and Features window, the buttons at the top of the list will change based on the software. For example, in Figure 12-53, the Bonjour software offers the options to Uninstall and Repair the software. (Bonjour by Apple allows Windows to find resources on a network offered by Apple devices.)

Note 22

The Windows Store apps can be uninstalled only in the Apps & features window and not in the Programs and Features window.

Special Concerns When Working in a Large Enterprise

Core 2 Objective 1.9

Working as an IT support technician in a large corporate environment is different from working as an IT support technician for a small company or with individuals. In this section of the module, you learn how Windows is installed on computers in an enterprise.

Earlier in the module, you learned how to install Windows using a setup DVD, USB flash drive, or files downloaded from the Microsoft website, and you had to respond to each question asked during setup. These types of installations are called attended installations.

If, however, you were responsible for installing Windows on several hundred computers in a large corporation, you might need a less time-consuming method. These methods are called deployment strategies. As an IT support technician in a large corporation, you most likely would not be involved in choosing or setting up the deployment strategy. However, you need to be aware of the different strategies so you have a general idea of what will be expected when you are asked to provide desk-side or help desk support as Windows is being deployed in your organization or a desktop OS that has failed needs to be refreshed.

Beginning with Windows 10, Microsoft expanded the methods it offers to deploy Windows in an enterprise. These methods are listed in Table 12-5. Some methods were designed to work with on-premises domains controlled by Active Directory (AD), and others work with Azure Active Directory (AAD) in the cloud.

Table 12-5 Deployment strategies for Windows 10/11

Category	Method	Description
Modern deployments: Use these methods with AD or AAD domains.		
	Windows Autopilot	Streamlines the OOBE (out-of-box experience) for devices preregistered with the enterprise. When users receive a new device, turn it on, connect to the Internet, and enter their user account and password, the device is automatically joined to AAD and configured with settings and content specific for the organization without further user input.
	In-place upgrade	Automates an in-place upgrade from Windows 10/8/7 to Windows 10/11 using a setup created by a system administrator with tools in the **Microsoft Deployment Toolkit (MDT)**.
Dynamic deployments: Use these methods with AAD domains.		
	Subscription activation	Used to upgrade Windows Pro to Windows Enterprise. When a user signs in to AAD, the Windows upgrade happens automatically without user input or a restart. Product keys and Windows licensing information are kept in AAD, not on the local computer. This method creates a Windows subscription.
	Azure Active Directory join with MDM	MDM (mobile device management) is software that forces devices to comply with corporate policies when they join an AAD domain.
	Provisioning packages	When a device joins AAD and MDM is not implemented, a **provisioning package** containing settings, apps, and data specific for the enterprise is downloaded to the device and applied with minimal input from the user. This package is easier to set up than an image, which is used in traditional deployments.
Traditional image deployments: Use these methods for on-premises AD domains when older deployment strategies are already established in the enterprise.		
	Bare metal	Also called wipe-and-load deployment, a **standard image** is created that contains the OS, drivers, applications, settings, and data specific for the enterprise. The image can be deployed on a new, empty hard drive, or the drive can first be wiped clean.
	Refresh	Also called wipe-and-load deployment, user settings and data are saved, and the hard drive is wiped clean before the standard image is applied. Then the image is applied, and the user state is reinstalled.
	Replace	Used to replace an old device with a new one. After the standard image is applied to the new computer, the user state is copied from the old computer and applied to the new one.

12

Methods to Deploy a Standard Image

 Core 2 Objective 1.9

A standard image contains the entire Windows volume in a single Windows Imaging (WIM) file, which has a .wim file extension. Installing Windows on a computer via a standard image is called a **deployment image**. Here are a few details about image deployments:

- A standard image is hardware independent, meaning it can be installed on any computer. (In the module "Maintaining Windows," you learn to create other types of images that can only be used on the computer that created them.)
- A standard image is created in a process called **drive imaging**. Microsoft provides several tools you can use to image a drive; many are included in the MDT.
- Deploying a standard image always results in a clean install rather than an upgrade.

Image deployment can be started using one of these methods:

- **Local installation.** Your company might provide you with a bootable flash drive or DVD that contains the image. When you boot from the device, **Windows Preinstallation Environment (Windows PE)** is launched; this is a minimum operating system used to start the installation. Follow the on-screen instructions.
- **Network installation.** To boot to the network and deploy the image from a server, first go to BIOS/UEFI setup and configure it to boot from a network device. You might need to search the motherboard documentation for help; in general, you'll need to change the following or similar settings, which are likely to be on an Advanced screen or Boot screen:
  - Enable the Network Stack (see Figure 12-54). For the LAN controller, enable the PXE option. The **Preboot eXecution Environment or Pre-Execution Environment (PXE)** is programming contained in BIOS/UEFI that can start up the computer and search for a server on the network that can provide a bootable operating system (Windows PE on the deployment server).

Figure 12-54 Configure BIOS/UEFI setup to boot to the network

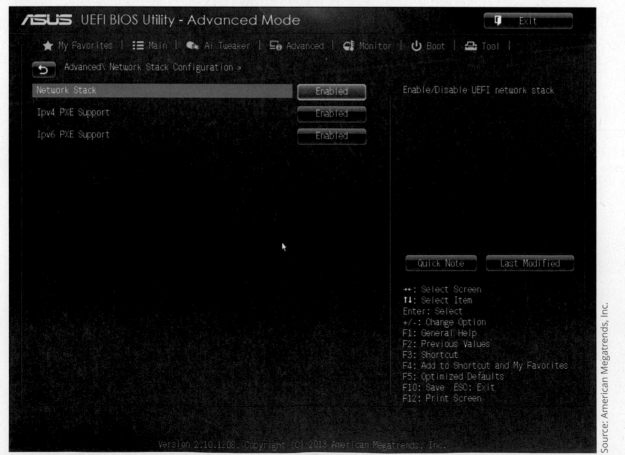

Source: American Megatrends, Inc.

- Disable Secure boot, Fast boot, and Quiet mode.
- Enable CSM support. In the CSM group, enable Boot from network devices.
- Change the boot priority so that an IPv4 Network boot is listed first. If you don't see it as an option, reboot after making the changes in the previous three bullets. The Network boot option should then be available.
- Select the Network boot option to have the computer launch PXE. The identification for the Network boot option might include IPv4 and the name of the network adapter, as shown in Figure 12-55. When you restart the computer, PXE searches for a server on the network, and Windows PE on the deployment server is launched.

Figure 12-55   When you click IPV4 Realtek PCIe GBE Family Controller, this system reboots to the network

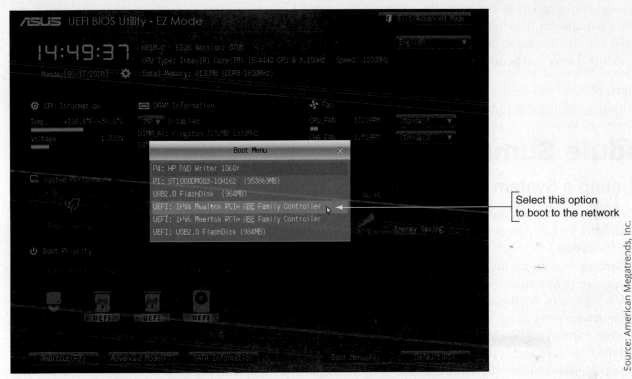

Source: American Megatrends, Inc.

- **Push automation.** A technician does not start the image deployment; rather, the installation uses **push automation** when a user is not likely to be sitting at the computer. The entire **remote network installation** is automated, and no user intervention is required. The process can turn on a computer that is turned off and even works when no OS is installed on the computer or the current OS is corrupted.

Depending on how the system administrator has set up the deployment, you might be required to respond to questions as the installation progresses. An **unattended installation** does not require any responses, such as the administrator password or domain name, because these responses are stored in an **answer file**. After the installation completes, the User State Migration Tool might be used to transfer user settings, user data files, and application settings to the new installation.

The degree of work required by a technician to deploy an image is called high-touch, lite-touch, or zero-touch. The less involved the technician or user is, the more work is required by the system administrator to set up the deployment. For this reason, lite-touch or zero-touch deployments are only used in very large organizations.

Note 23

IT support technicians find that large enterprises appreciate quick and easy solutions to desktop or laptop computer problems. Technicians quickly learn that their marching orders are almost always "replace or reimage." Little time is spent trying to solve the underlying problem when hardware can quickly be replaced or a Windows installation can quickly be reimaged.

Use USMT Software

 Core 2 Objective 1.9

The **User State Migration Tool (USMT)** can be used when deploying Windows in a Windows domain to copy user files and settings from one computer to another. Let's look briefly at what to expect when using the following three commands, which are part of the USMT software:

- **scanstate** copies user settings and files from the source computer to a safe location.
- **loadstate** applies these settings and files to the destination computer.
- **usmtutils** provides encryption options and hard drive management.

The scanstate, loadstate, and usmtutils command lines can be lengthy and include references to .xml files along with other parameters. The details of these command lines are not covered in this text. Most likely, the commands are stored in script file, sometimes called a batch file, provided by the system administrator. You learn to use scripts in the module "Linux and Scripting."

Module Summary

Evaluating a System for Windows 10 or Windows 11

- Windows 10 editions include Windows 10 Home, Windows 10 Pro, Windows 10 Pro for Workstations, and Windows 10 Enterprise. Each successive edition in the list costs more and offers more features than the previous one.
- Windows 11 editions include Windows 11 Home, Windows 11 Pro, Windows 11 Pro for Workstations, and Windows 11 Enterprise.
- Each edition of Windows 10/11 is available in either a 32- or a 64-bit version. A 32-bit OS cannot address as much memory as a 64-bit OS. A 64-bit OS performs better and requires more memory than a 32-bit OS.
- Before purchasing Windows, make sure your system meets the minimum hardware requirements and that all the hardware and applications will work under the OS. A 64-bit OS requires 64-bit drivers.
- Use the System Information (msinfo32.exe) window to gather information about Windows and the computer.

Understanding How Windows Supports Networking

- Windows computers can be configured on a network as a workgroup, which is a peer-to-peer (P2P) topology, or in a Windows domain, which is a client/server configuration created by Active Directory.
- Azure Active Directory (AAD) manages a virtual network of Windows computers in the cloud.
- A Windows account can be a local account, a network ID (to connect to a Windows domain), or a Microsoft account (to access Microsoft online resources and/or join an Azure AD domain).
- A Windows account can be a standard account or an administrator account with more privileges in the system.

Final Checklist Before Beginning the Installation

- Before you begin installing Windows, verify you have backed up all user data and preferences and that you have the Windows product key.
- Use the Media Creation Tool to create bootable media with the setup files for Windows 10/11.

Installing Windows 10 or Windows 11

- Windows can be installed as an in-place upgrade or a clean installation.
- Windows can be installed from the setup DVD, a USB flash drive, or from an ISO file, all created via the Media Creation Tool.

- An in-place upgrade begins from the Windows desktop of the old Windows installation.
- A clean install is the best option to use if the current installation is sluggish or giving problems, or if you're installing Windows on a new desktop computer that you're building.
- Windows 10/11 Pro and Enterprise include Client Hyper-V, which is a hypervisor used to create and manage virtual machines.

What to Do After a Windows Installation

- After a Windows installation, verify network access, install any Windows updates, verify anti-malware settings, install hardware, create user accounts, and install applications.

Special Concerns When Working in a Large Enterprise

- Three types of deployments for installing Windows in a large enterprise are modern deployments, dynamic deployments, and traditional image deployments. Modern deployments are done using Active Directory (AD) or Azure Active Directory (AAD), dynamic deployments use AAD, and traditional deployments use AD.
- Zero-touch deployments require the most time to set up but do not require a technician to be at the computer when the installation happens.

Key Terms

For explanations of key terms, see the Glossary for this text.

Active Directory (AD)	domain user account	peer-to-peer (P2P)	unattended installation
active hours	drive imaging	Persistent Memory	User Account Control
administrator account	driver rollback	(PMem)	(UAC) dialog box
answer file	dynamic IP address	Preboot eXecution	user profile
Azure Active Directory	ease of access	Environment or	User State Migration
(Azure AD or AAD)	gateway	Pre-Execution	Tool (USMT)
BitLocker	Group Policy	Environment (PXE)	usmtutils
boot loader menu	hardware signature	provisioning package	virtual machine (VM)
BYOD experience (bring	hardware token	push automation	virtual private network
your own device	Hyper-V	Quality of Service (QoS)	(VPN)
experience)	hypervisor	remote network	Windows 10 Enterprise
client/server	IP address	installation	Windows 10 Home
Control Panel	ISO file	Resilient File System	Windows 10 Pro for
default gateway	ISO image	(ReFS)	Workstations
default product key	loadstate	retail license	Windows 10 Pro
deployment image	local account	scanstate	Windows Defender
Device Manager	Media Creation Tool	single sign-on (SSO)	Windows Preinstallation
digital license	Microsoft account	account	Environment
diskpart	Microsoft Deployment	SMB Direct	(Windows PE)
DNS (Domain Name	Toolkit (MDT)	standard account	workgroup
System or Domain	network ID	standard image	
Name Services)	Original Equipment	static IP address	
servers	Manufacturer (OEM)	subnet mask	
domain	license	System Information	

12

Thinking Critically

These questions are designed to prepare you for the critical thinking required for the A+ exams and may use information from other modules and the web.

1. You are planning an upgrade from Windows 8.1 to Windows 10. Your system uses a network card that you don't find on the Microsoft Windows 10 list of compatible devices. What do you do next?

    a. Abandon the upgrade and continue to use Windows 8.1.
    b. Check the website of the network card manufacturer for a Windows 10 driver.
    c. Buy a new network card.
    d. Install a dual boot for Windows 8.1 and Windows 10, and only use the network when you have Windows 8.1 loaded.

2. You have just installed Windows 10 and now want to install your favorite game that worked fine under Windows 8.1. When you attempt the installation, you get an error. What is your best next step?

    a. Purchase a new version of your game—one that is compatible with Windows 10.
    b. Download any updates to Windows 10.
    c. Reinstall Windows 8.1.
    d. Install a VM running Windows 8.1.

3. You have 32-bit Windows 8.1 installed on your computer, and you purchase a license for Windows 10 Pro. You want to install Windows 10 using the 64-bit architecture. In which way(s) can you install Windows 10?

    a. You can perform an upgrade but not a clean install.
    b. You can perform an upgrade or a clean install.
    c. You can perform a clean install but not an upgrade.
    d. None of the answers are correct.

4. A laptop reports that it has made a wireless network connection but cannot access the network or the Internet. Arrange the following steps in the best order to troubleshoot the problem:

    a. Use Device Manager to uninstall the wireless adapter and install it again.
    b. Disable and enable the wireless network adapter.
    c. Disconnect the connection and connect again to the wireless network.
    d. Use Device Manager to update the wireless adapter drivers.

5. Which installation of Windows 10 requires you to enter a product key during the install process?

    a. You are replacing a failed hard drive that already had Windows 10 installed.
    b. You are replacing a failed motherboard on a system with Windows 10 installed and a Microsoft account was not used to sign in to Windows.
    c. You are replacing a failed motherboard on a system with Windows 10 installed and a Microsoft account had been used to sign in to Windows.
    d. Windows 10 has become corrupted, and you decide to perform a clean install to recover the OS.

6. Which of the following methods can you use to install Windows 10 in a VM? (Choose all that apply.)

    a. Clean install from an ISO image
    b. Clean install from a USB flash drive
    c. Upgrade from Windows 8.1 using an ISO image
    d. Clean install from a setup DVD

7. What is an advantage of using a dynamic hard drive in a VM?

8. Which command would you use to find out how much RAM is installed in a computer?

    a. msinfo32.exe
    b. gpedit.msc
    c. devmgmt.msc
    d. msconfig.exe

9. Suppose you want to boot a VM from its virtual DVD drive, but it boots to the VM's hard drive. Which of the following could be the source of this problem? (Choose all that apply.)

   a. There is no DVD or ISO file mounted to the virtual DVD drive.
   b. The virtual DVD drive is not enabled.
   c. The boot sequence is not correct in the VM's BIOS/UEFI settings.
   d. The hard drive does not have an OS installed.

10. You are setting up a Windows 10 desktop computer that requires 3 TB of storage. Which options work? (Choose all that apply.) Which option is the recommended best practice?

    a. Install one 3 TB hard drive with the MBR partitioning system and 64-bit Windows 10.
    b. Install two 1.5 TB hard drives with the GPT partitioning systems and 32-bit Windows 10.
    c. Install two 1.5 TB hard drives with the MBR partitioning systems and 64-bit Windows 10.
    d. Install two 1.5 TB hard drives with the GPT partitioning systems and 64-bit Windows 10.

11. If you suspect a computer is infected with a virus and you are ready to upgrade from Windows 8.1 to Windows 10, what is your best practice?

    a. Perform a clean install of Windows 10 rather than an upgrade.
    b. Scan the system for malware before you perform the Windows 10 upgrade.
    c. Install Windows 8.1 as an in-place upgrade to remediate the system, and then upgrade to Windows 10.
    d. Completely erase the hard drive with a full format, and then install Windows 10.

12. After setting up a dual-boot installation with Windows 8.1 and Windows 10, how do you boot the system into Windows 8.1?

    a. Start the system as normal; the oldest OS automatically loads.
    b. Start the system as normal; the newest OS automatically loads.
    c. Start the system and select the OS in the boot loader menu.
    d. Go into BIOS/UEFI setup and set the boot priority order to start with Windows 8.1.

13. After a Windows installation, what is the easiest way to determine that you have Internet access?

    a. Open the Network and Sharing Center, and verify that Wi-Fi is turned on and shows no errors.
    b. Open a browser and navigate to a website.
    c. Open Device Manager and check the network adapter for errors.
    d. Verify that the local router has lights blinking to indicate connectivity.

14. When Kristy recently started a photography business, she downloaded Photoshop to her computer to edit her photos. She notices her computer freezes when she is using Photoshop, so she asks you to help her fix the problem. Your research discovers that Photoshop requires a lot of RAM to run smoothly, and you need to know how much RAM Kristy's computer has to see if that is the problem. Which Windows tools from the following list can you use to know how much RAM is installed on a system? (Choose all that apply.)

    a. About window in Settings
    b. Power Options applet
    c. System Information window
    d. Network and Sharing Center

15. John is traveling for work and is spending a week at a new branch. He needs to print an email, but he isn't able to add the network printer to his computer. He is using a Windows 10 Pro laptop, is connected to the network, and can access the Internet. What is a likely and easy fix to John's problem?

    a. The computer is not set to find resources shared on the network; use the Settings app to fix the problem.
    b. The computer is not set to find resources shared on the network; use the Network and Sharing Center to fix the problem.
    c. John did not correctly authenticate to the Windows domain; use the Settings app to fix the problem.
    d. The drivers for the network printer need to be updated; use Device Manager to fix the problem.

12

16. Asha wants her 32-bit installation of Windows 10 Home to run faster. She has 4 GB of memory installed on the motherboard. She decides more memory will help. She installs an additional 2 GB of memory for a total of 6 GB but does not see any performance improvement. What is the problem, and what should you tell Asha?

    a. She should use Control Panel to install the memory in Windows. After it is installed, performance should improve. Tell Asha how to open Control Panel.
    b. A 32-bit OS cannot use more than 4 GB of memory. Tell Asha she has wasted her money.
    c. A 32-bit OS cannot use more than 4 GB of memory. Tell Asha to upgrade her system to the 64-bit version of Windows 10 Home.
    d. A 32-bit OS cannot use more than 4 GB of memory. Explain the problem to Asha, and discuss the possible solutions with her.

17. A technician needs to be prepared to launch programs even when utility windows or the Windows desktop cannot load. What is the program name for the System Information utility? What is the program name for the Remote Desktop utility?

18. After installing the device drivers for a video adapter, you still are not able to use the special features of the adapter. What is your next step?

    a. Open Device Manager and check for errors.
    b. Uninstall the adapter and try the installation again.
    c. Update Windows.
    d. Check the website of the video adapter's manufacturer for guidance.

19. The PXE programming code is used to boot a computer when it is searching for an OS on the network. Where is this code stored?

    a. On the deployment server
    b. On the motherboard
    c. On the Windows volume of the local hard drive
    d. In the cloud in Azure Active Directory

20. Ming is building an inexpensive computer to use for her online classes, and she needs to purchase Windows. What is the most cost-effective way Ming can purchase and activate a selected version of Windows?

Hands-On Projects

Hands-On Project 12-1

Using the Media Creation Tool

Est. Time: 30 minutes excluding download time
Core 2 Objective: 1.9

Use the Media Creation Tool to download Windows 10 setup files, and then create a Windows bootable DVD or USB flash drive ready to install Windows. Also save the setup files in an ISO file, which is handy to use for upgrades and to install Windows in a virtual machine. How large is the ISO file you created?

Hands-On Project 12-2

Installing 64-Bit Windows 10 Pro

Est. Time: 1-2 hours
Core 2 Objective: 1.9

Install 64-bit Windows 10 Pro on your lab computer. If you need help with the installation, see the directions in the module. Set up Windows to use a local account to sign in to Windows. Write down each decision you have to make as you perform the installation. If you get any error messages during the installation, write them down and list the steps you took to recover from them. How long did the installation take?

Hands-On Project 12-3

Using the Internet for Problem-Solving

Est. Time: 1-2 hours
Core 2 Objective: 1.9

Access the *support.microsoft.com* website for Windows 10 support. Print one article from the Knowledge Base that addresses a problem when installing Windows 10. In your own words, write a paragraph describing the problem and a paragraph explaining the solution. If you don't understand the problem or the solution from this article, do a search online for additional information so that you can give a well-rounded description of both the problem and the solution.

12

Hands-On Project 12-4

Installing Windows 10 in a VM

Est. Time: 1 hour
Core 2 Objective: 1.9

Virtual machines are useful for practicing OS installations and troubleshooting problems with OSs. Do the following:

1. Create a VM with one hard drive. In the VM, mount the Windows 10 ISO file you created. In the Settings app for the VM, verify the firmware settings to boot from the virtual DVD.

2. Start the VM and install Windows 10.

3. Verify that you can use your browser in the VM to surf the web.

Save the VM because you'll use it in a project at the end of the module "Maintaining Windows."

Hands-On Project 12-5

Recommended Updates

Est. Time: 15 minutes
Core 2 Objective: 1.9

On a Windows 10 system connected to the Internet, open the **Settings** app and click the **Update & Security** group. Under *Looking for info on the latest updates?*, click **Learn more**. Windows Update opens the Microsoft website and recommends Windows updates. Print the webpage showing a list of recommended updates. For a lab computer, don't perform the updates unless you have your instructor's permission.

Hands-On Project 12-6

Creating a Documentation Form

Est. Time: 30 minutes
Core 2 Objectives: 1.4, 1.9, 2.5

Support technicians are expected to maintain documentation for each computer for which they are responsible. Create a document that a technician can use when installing Windows and performing all the chores mentioned in the module that are needed before and after the installation. The document needs a checklist of what to do before the installation and a checklist of what to do after the installation. It also needs a place to record decisions made during the installation, the applications and hardware devices installed, user accounts created, and any other important information that might be useful for future maintenance or troubleshooting. Don't forget to include a way to identify the computer, the name of the technician doing the work, and when the work was done.

Hands-On Project 12-7

Researching Free Software

Est. Time: 15 minutes
Core 2 Objective: 1.9

Microsoft recommends PCmover Express by Laplink (*laplink.com*) to move user files, settings, and user profiles from an old installation of Windows to a new computer. Although the software was once free, you must now pay for it. Check out the Laplink website to find out how the software works. Can you find a free application that works as well as PCmover to easily move user data from one computer to another? Be sure the software gets good reviews.

Real Problems, Real Solutions

Real Problem 12-1

Recovering Data from a Corrupted Windows Installation

Est. Time: 15 minutes
Core 2 Objective: 1.7

As an IT support technician for a small organization, it's your job to support the computers, the small network, and the users. One of your coworkers, Jason, comes to you in a panic. His Windows 10 system won't boot, and he has important data files in several locations on the drive. He has no idea which folders hold the files. Besides the application data he's currently working on, he's especially concerned about losing email addresses, email, and his Microsoft Edge Favorites links.

After trying everything you know about recovering Windows 10, you conclude the OS is corrupted beyond repair. You decide there might be a way to remove the hard drive from Jason's computer and connect it to another computer so you can recover the data. Search the Internet and find a device that you can use to connect Jason's hard drive to another computer through one of its USB ports. The hard drive uses a SATA hard drive interface. Print the webpage showing the device and its price.

Real Problem 12-2

Troubleshooting an Upgrade

Est. Time: 15 minutes
Core 2 Objective: 1.9

Your friend, Chen, has upgraded his Windows 8.1 desktop to Windows 10. After the installation, he discovers his media card reader does not work. He calls you and asks you what to do. Do the following to plan your troubleshooting approach:

1. List the questions you should ask Chen to help diagnose the problem.
2. List the steps you would take if you were sitting at the computer solving the problem.
3. What do you think is the source of the problem? Explain your answer.

12

Module
13

Maintaining
Windows

Module Objectives

1. Set up and perform scheduled preventive maintenance tasks to keep Windows healthy and prepare for disaster

2. Use Windows tools, including Disk Management, to manage hard drives

3. Use commands to manage files, folders, and hard drives

Core 2 Certification Objectives

1.2 Given a scenario, use the appropriate Microsoft command-line tool.

1.3 Given a scenario, use features and tools of the Microsoft 10 operating system (OS).

1.4 Given a scenario, use the appropriate Microsoft 10 Control Panel utility.

1.8 Explain common OS types and their purpose.

4.3 Given a scenario, implement workstation backup and recovery methods.

Introduction

Earlier in the text, you learned how to install Windows. This module takes you to the next step in learning how to support a Windows operating system: maintaining the OS after it is installed. Most Windows problems stem from poor maintenance. If you are an IT support technician responsible for the ongoing support of several computers, you can make your work easier and your users happier by setting up and executing a good maintenance plan for each computer you support. A well-maintained computer gives fewer problems and performs better than one that is not maintained. In this module, you learn how to schedule regular maintenance tasks, prepare for disaster by setting up backup routines for user data and system files, and use Windows tools and commands to manage files, folders, and hard drives. As you read, you might consider practicing the steps in the module on a Windows 10/11 computer or VM.

Critical Windows Settings and Backup Procedures

 Core 2 Objectives 1.4, 4.3

Regular preventive maintenance includes verifying critical Windows settings and backing up data and system files. If you notice the system is slow as you perform these routine chores, you need to dig deeper to improve Windows performance, which is covered in the module "Troubleshooting Windows After Startup."

Users sometimes change Windows settings without realizing their importance. If you find settings that are incorrect, take time to explain to the computer's primary user how important they are.

Note 1

When you're responsible for a computer, be sure to keep good records of all that you do to maintain, upgrade, or fix it. When performing preventive maintenance, take notes and include them in your documentation. The Computer Inventory and Maintenance document available at *cengage.com* can help you organize your notes.

Here are the critical Windows settings you need to verify and what you can do to keep the system performing well. The first four settings are the most important:

- **Windows updates.** Install any important Windows updates that are waiting to be installed, and verify that Windows Update is configured to automatically allow updating. These updates may include updates to Windows, applications, device drivers, and firmware. You learned how to configure Windows Update in the module "Installing Windows."
- **Antivirus/anti-malware software.** Verify that anti-malware software is configured to scan the system regularly and that it is up to date. If you discover it is not scanning regularly, take the time to do a thorough scan for viruses. To verify this, follow the directions in the module "Installing Windows."
- **Network security setting.** Use the Network and Sharing Center to check that the network security type is set correctly for the optimum firewall settings. The network types are public and private. How to verify the network type was covered in the module "Installing Windows." The module "Network Security and Troubleshooting" goes deeper into configuring network security.
- **Backups of user data, the Windows volume, and system files.** Following directions given later in this module, verify that backup routines are running as expected to protect data and software from loss or corruption.
- **Uninstall software you no longer need.** This helps overall performance by reducing the number of startup processes running in the background and freeing up hard drive space. To uninstall software, use the Windows Apps & Features window or the Programs and Features window.

- **Clean up the hard drive.** A hard drive needs at least 15 percent free space on drive C:, where Windows is installed. Later in the module, you learn how to use Disk Cleanup to erase unnecessary files on drive C:. You can also move data on the drive to the cloud, other media, or other volumes on the same hard drive.
- **For laptops, verify power options.** Set power options to conserve power and increase the time before a battery pack needs recharging.

Note 2

Don't forget that what you learn about maintaining Windows also applies to Windows in a VM. All the skills you learn in this module apply to physical computers and VMs.

Before we get into maintenance chores, let take a quick look at some useful Windows settings.

Useful Settings and Control Panel Applets

Core 2 Objectives 1.4, 1.5

Here is a handy list of settings in the **Settings app** you can use to access numerous Windows 10/11 settings and a couple of applets in Control Panel. The A+ Core 2 exam expects you to know how to use all these in a given scenario:

- **Accounts.** Find your Windows account information here or link your account to a Microsoft account. The Accounts group also includes email and app accounts, sign-in options, Microsoft account sync settings, options to sign in to work or school networks, and options to add new user accounts to the computer.
- **Apps.** Use this group to uninstall applications, set default applications, and check other application settings. For example, to make Outlook the default app for email, click **Apps**, click **Default apps**, and then change the setting from Mail to Outlook.
- **Devices (Bluetooth & devices in Windows 11).** Find settings here for printers and scanners, connected devices, Bluetooth, mouse and touch pad devices, typing, AutoPlay, and USB.
- **Gaming.** This group contains settings for the Xbox Game bar, Game DVR, broadcasting, and Game Mode. When you turn on Game Mode, Windows improves the gaming experience by prioritizing system resources for the game being played on the computer.
- **Network & Internet.** This group provides network status, data usage information, and settings for different connections, including Wi-Fi, Ethernet, dial-up, VPN, and mobile hotspots. Go here to set up new connections. Airplane mode and proxy settings are also available for mobile devices. The link to the Network and Sharing Center takes you to more advanced connection settings.
- **Personalization.** Find settings here for the background, colors, lock screen, themes, Start menu, and taskbar.
- **Privacy (Privacy & security in Windows 11).** Find the settings here to restrict or allow Windows or apps access to your information and resources, including your location, camera, microphone, notifications, speech, inking, typing, account information, contacts, calendar, call history, email, messaging, radios, and file system. The Privacy group is also where you adjust settings for feedback, diagnostic, and usage data that is sent to Microsoft. You can also choose which apps are allowed to run in the background.
- **System.** Look here for catchall information and settings that affect functions of your computer, such as those for adjusting display, notifications, power, sleep, storage, and tablet-mode settings. Important information about the Windows system can be seen on the About window in the System group. See Figure 13-1.

Note 3

The About window in the System group gives information similar to what you find in the System Information window, including processor, RAM, Windows edition, architecture, and version. You can also get to several troubleshooting tools from this window. The About window can also be accessed by clicking **System** in Control Panel.

Figure 13-1 Use the About window to find out important information about hardware and the Windows installation

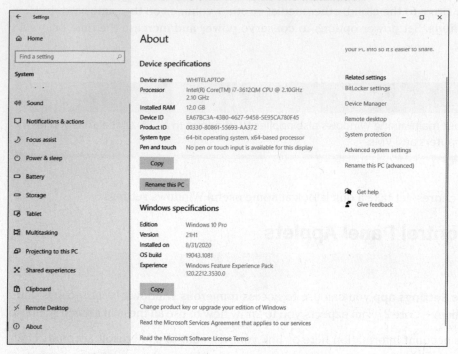

- **Time & Language.** The Time & Language group provides settings for date and time, region and language, and speech.
- **Update & Security.** Tools and settings found here include Windows updates, backups, recovery, activation, links to Find My Device, and settings for power users, such as device discovery, Remote Desktop, and PowerShell.

Note 4

Some items in the Settings app may be unavailable if you are logged in with a standard account. Use an account with administrative privileges to view all available settings.

Here are two applets in Control Panel that users find handy:

- The **Sound applet** is used to select a default speaker and microphone and to adjust how Windows handles sounds. To control volume, you can use the volume icon in the taskbar.
- Use the **Mail applet** in Control Panel to set up Outlook email. You can also configure Outlook from within the Outlook app.

Now let's turn our attention to maintenance chores. We begin with power options for laptops.

Power Options

Core 2 Objective 1.4

One maintenance chore for laptops is to verify that power options are set to conserve power and increase the amount of time before a battery pack on a laptop needs recharging. Power is managed by putting the computer into varying degrees of suspend or sleep modes. Use the **Power Options applet** of Control Panel to change these settings.

Exam Tip ✔

The A+ Core 2 exam might give you a scenario and expect you to know which power options to change to solve a problem, including using power plans and sleep (suspend), hibernate, and standby modes.

Here are the different power-saving states:

- **Sleep mode.** Using Windows, you can put the computer into **sleep mode**, also called **standby mode** or **suspend mode**, to save power when you're not using the computer. If applications are open or other work is in progress, Windows first saves the current state, including open files, to memory and saves some of the work to the hard drive. Then everything is shut down except memory and enough of the system to respond to a wake-up. In sleep mode, the power light on the laptop might blink from time to time. (A laptop generally uses about 1% to 2% of battery power for each hour in sleep mode.) To wake up the computer, press the power button; for some computers, you press a key or touch the touch pad. Windows wakes up in about two seconds. When Windows is in sleep mode, it can still perform Windows updates and scheduled tasks. Windows can be configured to go to sleep after a period of inactivity, or you can manually put it to sleep. To put the system to sleep manually, click **Start**, then click the power icon and select **Sleep**. See Figure 13-2. A laptop might also be configured to go to sleep when you close the lid.
- **Hibernation.** **Hibernation** saves all work to the hard drive and powers down the system. When you press the power button, Windows reloads its state, including all open applications and documents. When Windows is in sleep mode on a laptop and senses the battery is critically low, it will put the system into hibernation.

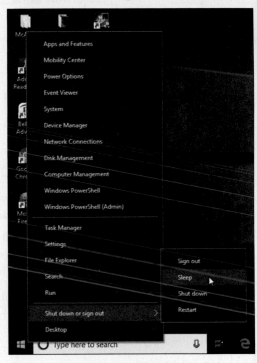

Figure 13-2 Put Windows to sleep using the Start menu

Note 5

Recall that hard drives are permanent or nonvolatile storage, and memory is temporary or volatile storage. A hard drive does not require power to hold its contents. Memory, on the other hand, is volatile and loses its contents when it has no power. In hibernation, the computer has no power; therefore, everything must be stored on the hard drive.

Applying Concepts

Configuring Windows Power Plans

Est. Time: 15 minutes
Core 2 Objective: 1.4

Follow these steps to configure power plans in Windows 10:

1. Open **Control Panel** in Classic view, and click **Power Options**. The Power Options window opens. Figure 13-3 shows the window for one laptop. The plans might be different for other laptops.

(continues)

Applying Concepts Continued

Figure 13-3   Power plans in Windows 10

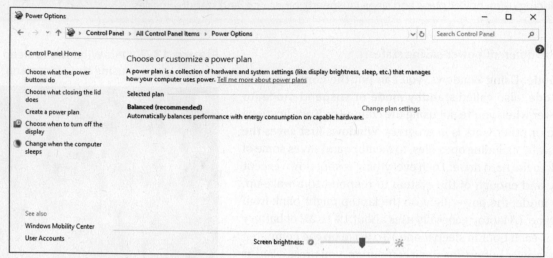

2. Use links in the left pane to choose what happens when you click a power button and close the lid. When you click **Choose what closing the lid does**, you can turn on fast startup to improve performance.

3. You can create and customize a power plan. For example, under Balanced (recommended), click **Change plan settings**. The Edit Plan Settings window appears (see the left side of Figure 13-4). Notice in the figure the various times of inactivity required before the computer goes into sleep mode; these are called **sleep timers**.

Figure 13-4   Customize a power plan

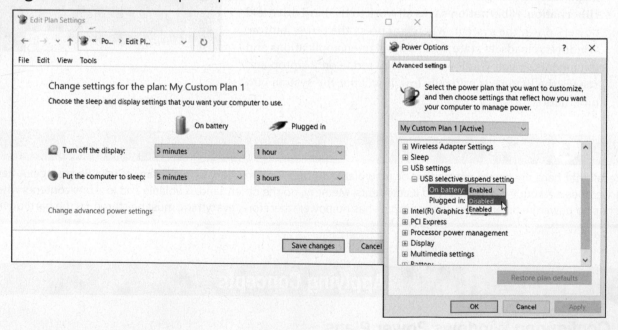

4. To see several other changes you can make, click **Change advanced power settings**. The Power Options dialog box opens. Check out the **USB selective suspend setting** shown on the right side of Figure 13-4. By default, Windows puts USB ports in a very low power state when they are not in use. If USB ports are not behaving reliably, one thing you can try is to disable selective suspend, as shown in the figure. Make your changes and click **OK** to close the box.

5. If you made changes, click **Save changes** in the Edit Plan Settings window. Close the Power Options window.

Exam Tip ✔

The A+ Core 2 exam expects you to know how to use Power Options in Control Panel to create a power plan, including choosing what to do when closing the lid, turning on fast startup, and disabling USB selective suspend.

Plan for Disaster Recovery

Core 2 Objective 4.3

In this part of the module, you learn how to make a disaster recovery plan and then learn how to use Windows to back up user data, entire volumes, and critical Windows system files.

Applying Concepts

Backups Pay Off

Est. Time: 5 minutes
Core 2 Objective: 4.3

Dave was well on his way to building a successful career as an IT support technician. His IT tech support shop was doing well, and he was excited about his future. But one bad decision changed everything. He was called to repair a server at a small accounting firm. The call was on the weekend when he was normally off, so he was in a hurry to get the job done. He arrived at the accounting firm and saw that the problem was an easy one to fix, so he decided not to do a backup before working on the system. During his repairs, the hard drive crashed, and all data on the drive was lost—four million dollars' worth! The firm sued, Dave's business license was stripped, and he was ordered to pay the money the company lost. A little extra time to back up the system would have saved his whole future. True story!

Note 6

With data and software, here's a good rule of thumb: If you can't get along without it, back it up.

The time to prepare for disaster is before it occurs. If you have not prepared, the damage from a disaster will most likely be greater than if you had made and followed disaster recovery plans. Suppose the hard drive on your computer or a particular USB flash drive stopped working and you lost all its data. What would be the impact? Are you prepared for this to happen? The following sections discuss some of the decisions you need to make for your backup and recovery plans.

Where to Keep Data and Backups

An overview of six options as to where to keep data and backups is shown in Figure 13-5. Here are the options if you keep your data on your local computer, as shown on the left side of Figure 13-5:

- **Option A: Use no backup.** When you have no backups and your hard drive fails, you have no other choice than to reenter your data.
- **Option B: Create and maintain your own backups.** Windows File History and Windows Backup and Restore are two Windows utilities designed to work in this type of scenario. An advantage of this option is that you have complete control over the data and the backups. The primary disadvantage is you're responsible for all backup and recovery operations. If you use this option, consider what would happen if a catastrophic event, such as a fire or flood, destroys the building where your original data and backups are all located. For this reason, always keep some backups at an off-site location.
- **Option C: Back up to the cloud.** Cloud services such as Carbonite (*carbonite.com*) and iDrive (*idrive.com*) are designed for this solution. They automatically copy your data to the cloud when you're connected to the Internet and in real time.

13

Figure 13-5   Where to keep data and backups

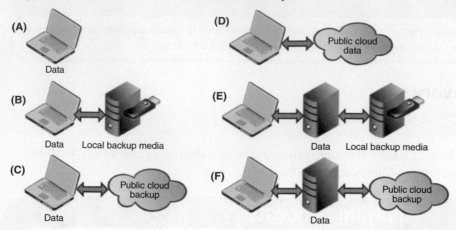

If you don't want to keep data on your local computer, you have these options, shown on the right side of Figure 13-5.

- **Option D: Keep your data in the public cloud.** Examples of cloud services designed to hold your original data and work with your applications are Microsoft OneDrive (*onedrive.live.com*), which works well with Microsoft Office, and Google Drive (*drive.google.com*), which integrates well with Google Docs. Using this method, you are trusting the cloud service with the only copy of your data unless you download files.
- **Option E: Data is kept on a local file server and backed up to private media.** Keeping data on a file server rather than the local computer gives more control of the data to the network administrator and makes it easier to share the data among users. The disadvantage of this method is that the user must be on the local network to access the data, which makes it more complicated to access data when traveling or working from home. With this option, the organization is responsible for maintaining backups.
- **Option F: Data is kept on a local file server and backed up to the cloud.** The main advantage of keeping the backups of an organization's data in a public cloud is the cloud service is responsible for all backup routines and supporting recovery operations when your data is lost.

Note 7

Even though it's easy to do, don't make the mistake of backing up your data to another volume or folder on the same hard drive. When a hard drive crashes, all volumes most likely will go down together, and you will lose your data and your backup. Back up to another device, and for extra safety, store it at an off-site location.

Many organizations trust all their data to a public cloud so the organization is not responsible for maintaining backup software and routines and testing the backups. However, experienced IT technicians agree that you should maintain two backups, one of which is kept off site. These operations standards follow the **3-2-1 backup rule**:

- **Three** copies of your data (the original data and two backups)
- **Two** media (for example, an external hard drive and in the cloud)
- **One** copy off site (for example, in the cloud)

Note 8

This author keeps two backups of data, both in the cloud. I use Carbonite for real-time backups to the cloud, and I back up data on my computer to Dropbox daily.

Many organizations maintain one or more backup routines, and you need to understand how backups and data recovery work and what you are expected to do when maintaining backups for your organization.

Backup Types

Generally, you should back up data for about every 4 to 6 hours of data entry. When you think about it, that's a lot of storage and procedures used for backups. To make backing up the most efficient, three types of backups are used:

- A **full backup** backs up all data designated for backup.
- An **incremental backup** backs up only files that have changed or been created since the last backup, whether that backup is itself an incremental or a full backup.
- A **differential backup** backs up files that have changed or been created since the last full backup. A differential backup does not consider if other differential backups have been performed.

A backup routine always begins with a full backup and then uses either an incremental or differential backup several times, with an additional full backup made occasionally. When a file, folder, or volume is recovered, the recovery process must reconstruct the lost or corrupted items from the latest full backup and then apply any changes reflected in all the incremental backups since the last full backup—or in the latest differential backup—to create the **synthetic** (reconstructed) file, folder, or volume.

Rotating Backup Media

Backup routines might use the **grandfather-father-son (GFS)** plan for rotating and reusing backup media. The plan is explained in Table 13-1. A **backup operator** would be responsible for putting the plan in writing and keeping a log of backups performed.

Table 13-1   The grandfather-father-son backup rotation plan

Name of Backup	How Often Performed	Storage Location	Description
Son backup	Daily	On site	Make six backups each week, rotated (reused) each week. A Friday backup is not made. Label the media Saturday, Sunday, Monday, and so forth. When you rotate the backup media each week, the backup for a given day is overwritten each week.
Father backup	Weekly	Off site	On Friday, perform a weekly full backup, and rotate or reuse the media each month. Label the media Friday1, Friday2, Friday3, and Friday4. Store the media off site.
Grandfather backup	Monthly	Off site, in a fireproof vault	Perform the monthly full backup on the last Friday of the month. Keep 12 media, one for each month, and label them January, February, March, and so forth. Store the media in a vault off site.

The plan shown in the table allows you to rotate media daily, weekly, and monthly. However, if an organization is required to retain data for a longer period, rotations happen less often.

Testing Your Backup Plan

After you have a backup plan working, test the recovery plan. Operations standards should state the frequency that the backup plan is tested to make sure all is still working as you expect and you know how to recover data. Do the following:

- **Test the recovery process.** Erase a file on the hard drive, and use the recovery procedures to verify that you can recreate the file from the backup. This test verifies that the backup media works, that the recovery software is effective, and that you know how to use it. After you are convinced that the recovery procedure works, document how to perform it. Write the documentation so others can follow it in the event you are not present when it's needed.
- **Keep backups in a safe place and routinely test them.** Don't leave a backup DVD, external hard drive, flash drive, or other media lying around for someone to steal. Backups of important and sensitive data should be kept under lock and key at an off-site location. Keep enough backups off-site so that you can recover data even if the entire building is destroyed.

Now let's see how to use Windows tools to back up user data, the entire Windows volume, and important Windows system files. How to back up in macOS and Linux is covered in later modules.

Back Up User Data and the System Image

 Core 2 Objective 4.3

Windows 10 offers File History and Backup and Restore to back up user data and create a system image. A **system image** is a backup of the entire Windows volume, including the Windows installation, applications, user settings, and data. The best time to create the image is right after you've installed Windows, hardware, applications, and user accounts and customized Windows settings. The image is stored in a single file with a .wim file extension. The WIM file uses the Windows Imaging File (WIM) format and is a compressed file that contains many related files.

> ## Note 9
>
> Windows uses only one backup tool at a time, either File History or Backup and Restore. One must be turned off to use the other. In addition, both tools allow only one backup routine. Therefore, if you want to use two backup routines (such as when you want to keep one backup on a local device and a second backup in the cloud), you must use third-party backup software that allows for multiple backup routines.

Windows File History

Windows **File History** is a simple backup utility that is easy for users but gives you limited control over backups. When the backup is enabled, it first makes a full backup to another medium. By default, it scans for file and folder changes every hour and keeps as many generations of backups as free space allows on the storage device.

To use File History, first connect your backup device. In the Settings app, click **Update & Security**, then click **Backup**. See the left side of Figure 13-6. You have two options for the backup location:

- To back up to OneDrive in the Microsoft cloud, click **Sign in to OneDrive** and follow directions to back up the Desktop, Documents, and/or Pictures to OneDrive. See the right side of Figure 13-6. Later, if you want to see or recover a file from your backups, open your OneDrive folder in Explorer.
- To back up to a local peripheral device or drive on the network, click **Add a drive** and select the location. By default, File History backs up all data folders in your user profile. To view and change what is backed up, click **More options** in the Backup window.

Figure 13-6   Select what to back up to OneDrive

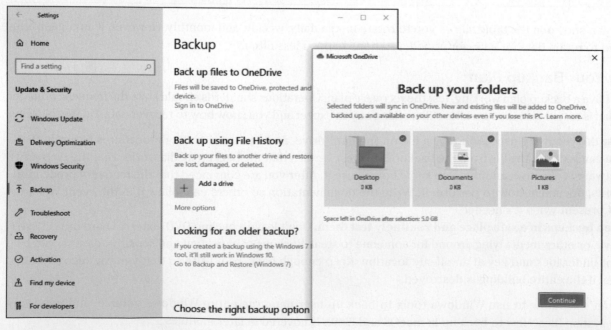

Exam Tip ✔

The A+ Core 2 exam might give you a scenario that expects you to create, use, and test backups.

File History can also be accessed through Control Panel, where you can turn File History on or off, change File History settings, and restore files from backup. Using the File History window in Control Panel, you can click System Image Backup (see Figure 13-7) to start the process of creating a system image.

Figure 13-7 Manage File History settings, create a system image, and restore files from backup

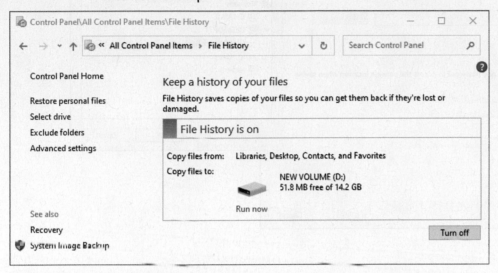

Windows Backup and Restore

Windows 10 offers **Backup and Restore** to back up any folder on the hard drive and create a system image. While File History is designed to be an easy tool for users to manage their own backups, Backup and Restore is designed for technicians who prefer more granular control of backups.

When you first turn on Backup and Restore, it does a full backup, followed by incremental backups and occasional full backups. If you've established a backup schedule in File History on a Windows 10 machine, those settings will appear in the Backup and Restore window.

Follow these steps to save a full backup and set up an ongoing backup schedule using Backup and Restore in Windows 10:

1. Open **Control Panel** in Classic view, and click **Backup and Restore**. If no backup has ever been scheduled on the system, the window will look like the one shown in Figure 13-8. Click **Set up backup**.

2. Select the device or location to hold the backup. All Windows 10 professional and enterprise editions allow you to save the backup to a network location. To do so, click **Save on a network**, click **Browse**, and point to the folder. See Figure 13-9. Also enter the user name and password on the remote computer that the backup utility will use to authenticate to that computer when it makes the backup. You cannot save to a network location when using Windows Home editions.

Figure 13-8   Use the Backup and Restore window to schedule backups

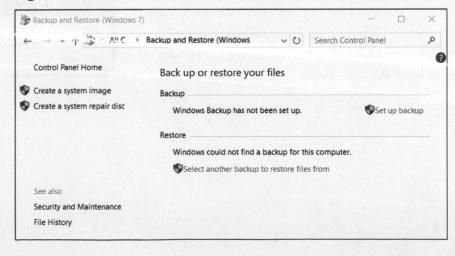

13

Figure 13-9   Point to a shared folder on the network to hold the backups

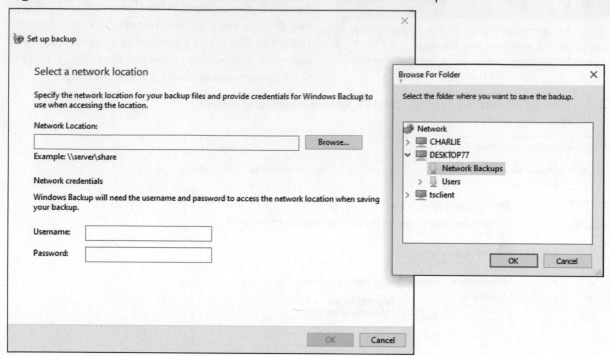

3. In the next box, you can allow Windows to decide what to back up or choose for yourself. Select **Let me choose** so you can select the folders to back up. Click **Next**.

4. In the next box, make your selections. If the backup medium can hold the system image, the option to include the image is selected by default. If you don't want to include the image, uncheck the option. Click **Next** to continue. Here are folders that might contain important user data:
   - Application data is usually found in C:\Users*username*\AppData.
   - Better still, back up the entire user profile at C:\Users*username*.
   - Even better, back up all user profiles at C:\Users.

5. In the next box, you can verify that the correct items are selected. To change the default schedule, click **Change schedule**. In the next box, you can choose to run the backup daily, weekly, or monthly and select the time of day. Make your selections and click **OK**.

6. Review your backup settings, and click **Save settings and run backup**. The backup proceeds. A shadow copy is made of any open files so they are included in the backup.

Later, you can return to the Backup and Restore window to change the backup settings or to turn off the backup.

> **Note 10**
>
> One limitation of Windows File History and Backup and Restore is that you can have only one scheduled backup routine.

Note 11

After Windows does a full backup, it only backs up files that have changed since the last full backup. Occasionally, it does another full backup. Each full backup is called a backup period. Windows keeps as many backup periods as it has space on the backup device. As free space fills, it deletes the oldest backup periods. To see how space is used on your backup media, click **Manage space** in the Backup and Restore window. In the Manage Windows Backup disk space, you can click **View backups** to delete a backup period, but be sure to keep the most recent backup periods.

Restoring Files and Folders

To restore backed-up items in File History, open **File History** in Control Panel, and click **Restore personal files**. To restore items in Backup and Restore, open the **Backup and Restore** window, and click **Restore my files**. Another way to restore a file or folder from backup is to use Explorer. Follow these steps:

1. When you restore a file or folder to a previous version, the current file or folder can be overwritten by the previous version. To keep the original, first copy—not move—the folder or file to a new location so you can revert to the copy if necessary.

2. Right-click the file or folder, and select **Restore previous versions** from the shortcut menu. The Properties dialog box for the file or folder appears with the Previous Versions tab selected. Windows displays a list of all previous versions of the file or folder it has kept (see Figure 13-10); these versions were created by File History or Backup and Restore.

Figure 13-10   Restore a file or folder from a previous version

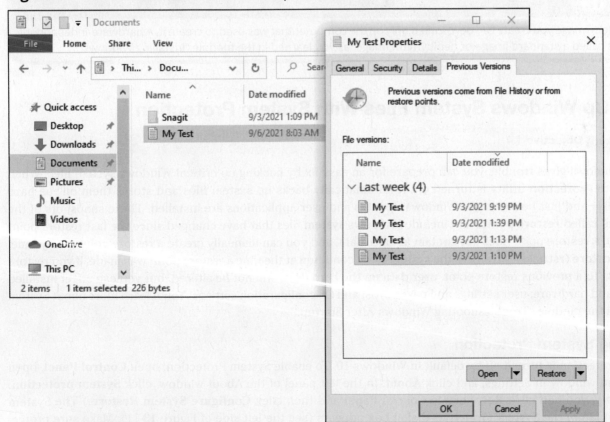

3. Select the version you want, and click **Restore**. A message box asks if you are sure you want to continue. Click **Restore** and then click **OK**.

4. Open the restored file or folder, and verify that it is the version you want. If you decide you need another version, delete the file or folder, and copy the file or folder you saved in Step 1 back into the original location. Then return to Step 2 and try again, this time selecting a different previous version.

Tips About the System Image

As you've already learned, the backup of a Windows volume is called a system image. Here are points to keep in mind when creating a system image and using it to recover a failed Windows volume:

- **Creating a system image takes some time.** Before creating a system image on a laptop, plug the laptop into an AC outlet so that a failed battery will not interrupt the process.
- **A system image includes the entire drive C: or other drive on which Windows is installed.** When you restore a hard drive using the system image, everything on the volume is deleted and replaced with the system image.
- **Don't depend just on the system image as your backup.** You should back up individual folders that contain user data separately from the system image. If only individual data files or folders need to be recovered, you would not want to use the system image for the recovery because it would totally replace the entire Windows volume.
- **You can create a system image any time after Windows is installed, and then you can use this image to recover from a failed hard drive.** Using the system image to recover a failed hard drive is called reimaging the drive. The details of how to reimage a drive are covered in the module "Troubleshooting Windows Startup."

Note 12

The system image you create can be installed only on the computer that was used to create it. A hardware-independent image is called a standard image or deployment image, as you learned in the module "Installing Windows."

Back Up Windows System Files With System Protection

 Core 2 Objective 1.4

Before Windows gives trouble, you can prepare for an easy fix by backing up critical Windows system files. When the **System Protection** utility is turned on, it automatically backs up system files and stores them on the hard drive weekly and just before major Windows updates and user applications are installed. These snapshots of the system are called **restore points** and include Windows system files that have changed since the last restore point was made. A restore point does not contain all user data, and you can manually create a restore point at any time. **System Restore** (rstrui.exe) restores the system to its condition at the time a restore point was made. If you restore the system to a previous restore point, user data on the hard drive will not be altered, but you can affect installed software and hardware, user settings and passwords, and OS configuration settings. You'll learn more about System Restore in the module "Troubleshooting Windows After Startup."

Enabling System Protection

System Protection is turned off by default in Windows 10. To enable System Protection, open **Control Panel**, open the **System** window in Settings, and click **About**. In the left panel of the About window, click **System protection**. (Alternately, you can click **Recovery** in Control Panel and then click **Configure System Restore**.) The System Protection tab of the System Properties dialog box appears (see the left side of Figure 13-11). Make sure protection is turned on for the drive containing Windows, which indicates that restore points are created automatically. In Figure 13-11, protection for drive C: is on, and other drives are not being protected. To make a change, click **Configure**. The System Protection dialog box appears, as shown on the right side of the figure. If you make a change to this box, click **Apply** and then click **OK**.

Figure 13-11   Make sure System Protection is turned on for the volume on which Windows is installed

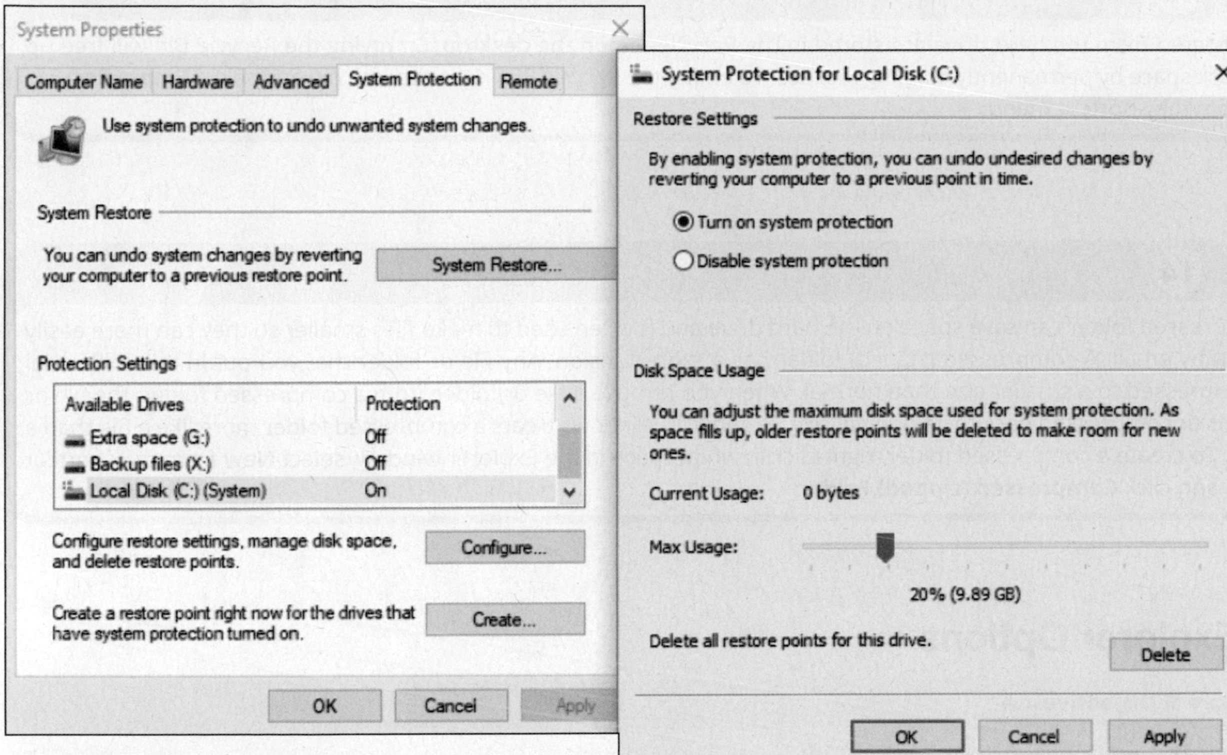

Restore points are normally kept in a hidden folder named C:\System Volume Information, which is not accessible to the user. Restore points are taken at least weekly, and they can use up to 10 GB or 5% of disk space. If overall disk space gets very low, restore points are no longer made, which is one more good reason to keep at least 15% or more of the hard drive free. Also notice in Figure 13-11 that you can limit how much of the disk can be used for restore points, and you can click **Delete** to delete all restore points.

Manually Creating a Restore Point

Before you make major changes to the system, you can manually create a restore point so you can back out of your changes if necessary. To create a restore point, use the System Protection tab of the System Properties box, as shown on the left side of Figure 13-11. Click **Create**. In the System Protection box, enter a name for the restore point, such as "Before I tested APP3 software," and click **Create**. The restore point is created.

Maintaining Hard Drives

Core 2 Objectives 1.3, 1.4, 1.5

For best performance, Windows needs at least 15% free space on the hard drive that it uses as working space, so it's important to uninstall software you no longer need and occasionally delete unneeded files. In addition, you can optimize a hard drive and control indexing to improve performance. You also need to know how to set up a new hard drive installed in a system. All these tasks are covered in this section of the module. Let's start with changing settings in File Explorer Options.

13

> **Note 13**
>
> Files deleted from the hard drive are stored in the Recycle Bin on the desktop. Emptying the Recycle Bin will free up your disk space by permanently deleting the files. To empty the Recycle Bin, right-click the bin and select **Empty Recycle Bin** from the shortcut menu.

> **Note 14**
>
> A compressed folder can save space on the hard drive and is often used to make files smaller so they can more easily be sent by email. A compressed (zipped) folder has a .zip extension. Any file or folder that you put in this folder will be compressed to a smaller size than normal. When you remove a file or folder from a compressed folder, the file or folder is uncompressed back to its original size. In general, Windows treats a compressed folder more like a file than a folder. To create a compressed folder, right-click in white space in the Explorer window, select **New** from the shortcut menu, and click **Compressed (zipped) Folder**.

File Explorer Options

Core 2 Objective 1.4

The Windows **File Explorer Options applet** in Control Panel is used to control how users view files and folders in Explorer and what they can do with these files. Windows has an annoying habit of hiding file extensions if it knows which application is associated with a file extension. For example, just after installation, it hides .exe, .com, .sys, and .txt file extensions, but does not hide .docx, .pptx, or .xlsx file extensions until the software to open these files has been installed. Also, Windows really doesn't want you to see its own system files, and it hides these files from view until you force it to show them.

> **Note 15**
>
> The Windows desktop is itself a folder on the hard drive and is located at C:\Users*username*\Desktop. For example, if the user, Anne, creates a folder named MyFiles on her desktop, the folder path is C:\Users\Anne\Desktop\MyFiles.

Applying Concepts

Changing File Explorer Options

Est. Time: 15 minutes
Core 2 Objective: 1.4

A technician is responsible for solving problems with system files (files that belong to the Windows operating system) and file extensions. To fix problems with these files and extensions, you need to see them first. To change File Explorer options so you can view system files and file extensions, do the following:

1. Open **Control Panel** in Classic view and click **File Explorer Options**. The File Explorer Options dialog box appears. On the General tab (see Figure 13-12A), you can change settings for how Explorer navigates folders and handles the navigation pane.

Figure 13-12   Use File Explorer Options to control how Explorer works and displays files and folders

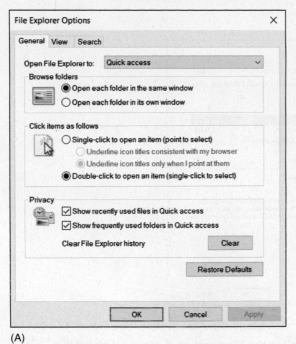

(A)

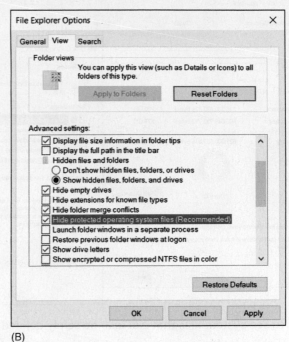

(B)

2. Click the **View** tab. Scroll down in the Advanced settings group, and make these selections to show hidden information about files, folders, and drives, as shown in Figure 13-12B:

   • Select **Show hidden files, folders, and drives**.

   • Uncheck **Hide extensions for known file types**.

   • Uncheck **Hide protected operating system files (Recommended)**, and respond to the Warning box.

3. To save your changes and close the File Explorer Options box, click **OK**.

13

Exam Tip

The A+ Core 2 exam expects you to know how to view hidden files and file extensions in Explorer.

Clean the Hard Drive

Core 2 Objective 1.3

The Windows **Disk Cleanup** (cleanmgr.exe) utility deletes temporary files on the drive. To delete unneeded files on a drive, do the following when starting the utilities from Explorer:

1. To delete unneeded files, open **Explorer**, right-click drive **C:**, and click **Properties**. On the General tab of the drive Properties box, click **Disk Cleanup** to calculate how much space can be cleaned up. See Figure 13-13.

Figure 13-13 Delete unneeded files on a hard drive to free up space

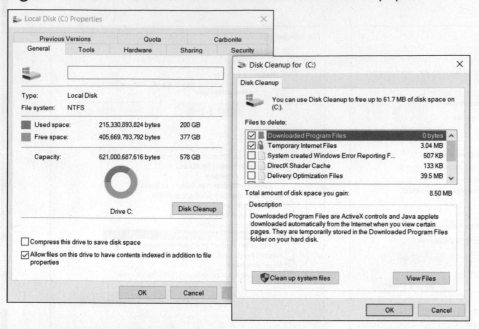

2. To see system files that can also be safely deleted, click **Clean up system files**. See Figure 13-14A. Highlight a file type to see a description about it. Select the file types to delete and click **OK**.

3. Click the **More Options** tab (see Figure 13-14B). When you click **Clean up** in the System Restore and Shadow Copies area, all but the most recent restore point are deleted, which can clean up even more disk space.

Figure 13-14 (A) Deleted unneeded files, including system files, and (B) delete all but the most recent restore point

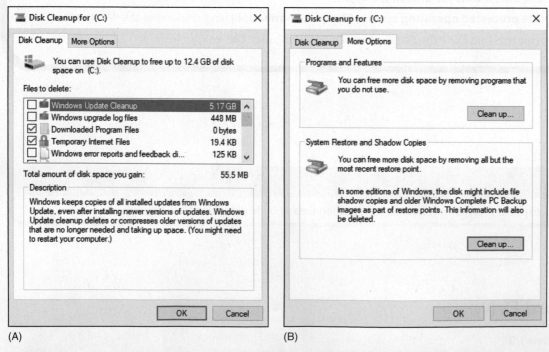

(A)   (B)

Note 16

When Windows installs, it stores the old installation in the Windows.old folder. Windows 10 deletes the folder 10 days after the installation. If you see the Windows.old folder left over from a Windows 8/7 systems, include it in the list to be deleted to free up disk space.

Optimize the Hard Drive

Core 2 Objective 1.3

Two types of hard drives are magnetic hard disk drives (HDDs), which contain spinning platters, and solid-state drives (SSDs), which contain flash memory. Windows uses the **Defragment and Optimize Drives** (dfrgui.exe) utility to automatically defragment a magnetic drive and to trim an SSD once a week. Let's look at what each of these operations accomplishes:

- **Magnetic hard drives.** To **defragment** (or defrag) is to rearrange fragments or parts of files on the drive so each file is stored on the drive in contiguous clusters. Each platter on a magnetic hard drive is divided into tracks, which are divided into sectors (see Figure 13-15). In a file system, a **cluster**, also called a **file allocation unit**, is a group of whole sectors. The number of sectors in a cluster is fixed and is determined when the file system is first installed. A file is stored in whole clusters, and the unused space at the end of the last cluster,

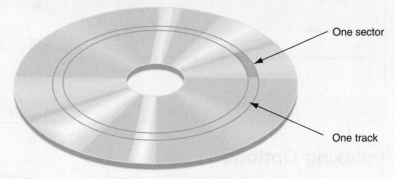

Figure 13-15   A magnetic hard drive is divided into concentric circles called tracks, and tracks are divided into sectors

One sector

One track

called **slack**, is wasted free space. As files are written and deleted from an HDD, clusters are used, released, and used again. New files written on the drive can be put in available clusters spread over the drive. Over time, drive performance is affected when the moving read/write arm of a magnetic drive must move over many areas of the drive to collect all the fragments of a file. Defragmenting a drive rewrites files in contiguous clusters and improves drive performance.

- **Solid-state drives.** The life span of an SSD is largely determined by the number of read/writes to the drive. Therefore, defragmenting an SSD can reduce the life of the drive and is not recommended—Windows disables defragmenting for solid-state drives. However, performance of an SSD can benefit from trimming. To **trim** an SSD is to erase a block on the drive that is filled with unused data. An SSD is organized in blocks, and each block contains many pages. A file can spread over several pages in various blocks. Each time a new page is written to the drive, the entire block to which it belongs must be read into a buffer, erased, and then rewritten with the new page included. When a file is deleted, information about the file is deleted, but the actual data in the file is not erased. This can slow down SSD performance and reduce the life of the drive because the unused data must still be read and rewritten in its block. Windows sends the trim command to an SSD drive to erase a block that no longer contains useful data so a write operation does not have to manage the data.

Follow these steps to optimize the hard drive:

1. Using Explorer, open the **Properties** dialog box for Drive C:, and select the **Tools** tab. Click **Optimize**. The Optimize Drives dialog box appears (see the left side of Figure 13-16). This system has two hard drives installed. Drive C: is an SSD, and drive E: is a magnetic HDD. Drive D: is a removable USB flash drive.

2. Here are tasks you can do:
   - For a magnetic drive, click **Analyze** for Windows to tell you if a drive needs defragmenting. To defrag the drive, click **Optimize**. The process can take a few minutes to several hours. If errors occur while the drive is defragmenting, check the hard drive for errors and try to defragment again.
   - For a solid-state drive, click **Optimize** to trim the SSD.
   - Near the bottom of Figure 13-16, you can see scheduled optimization is turned off. To turn it on, click **Turn on**. In the dialog box that appears (see the right side of Figure 13-16), check **Run on a schedule (recommended)**, and select **Weekly** for the Frequency. Click **OK**.

13

Figure 13-16 Windows is set to automatically defragment a magnetic hard drive once a week

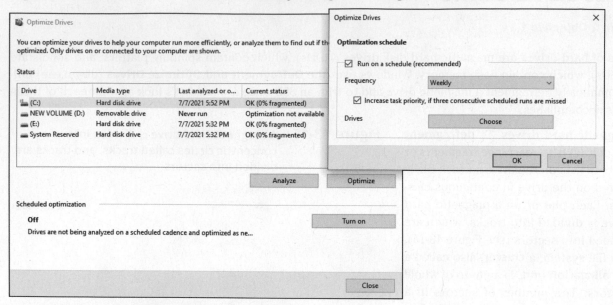

Indexing Options

Core 2 Objective 1.4

File Explorer and the Windows taskbar offer a search box that can be used to search the hard drive. The **Indexing Options applet** in Control Panel is used to control how Windows manages an index of content on the drive to help make searches go faster. See Figure 13-17.

Figure 13-17 Use Indexing Options to manage what Windows indexes to speed up searches

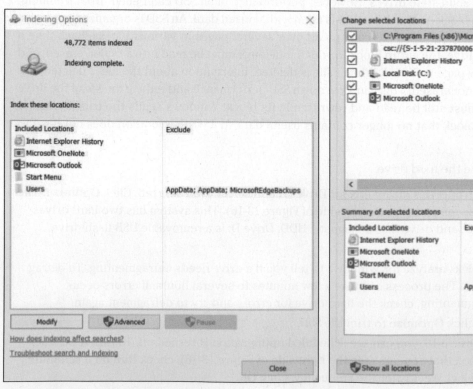

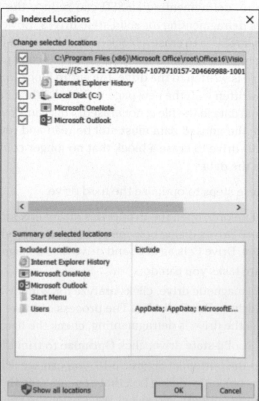

Do the following to explore how indexing can be managed:

1. Open **Control Panel** in Classic view and then open the **Indexing Options** applet. The Indexing Options dialog box on the left side of Figure 13-17 shows what is currently indexed.

2. To modify this list, click **Modify**. In the Indexed Locations dialog box (see the right side of Figure 13-17), select what you want to index and click **OK**.

3. Click **Advanced**. In the Advanced Options dialog box (see Figure 13-18), notice you can rebuild the index. This can fix a problem if searches are giving errors. Also notice the File Types tab in this box. Use this tab to select what file types (listed by their file associations) are indexed.

For best performance, select for indexing only those items that the user searches often. For example, at the top of Figure 13-17, you can see more than 48,000 items are being indexed. By selecting only a few types of files for indexing, such as OneNote and Outlook files, fewer system resources are required to maintain the index. If a user does not search often, turning off indexing can improve system performance. In addition, indexing is constantly writing to the hard drive, and if the drive is an SSD, the life span of the drive is decreased. Indexing is turned off by disabling the Windows Search background process, which you learn how to do in the module "Troubleshooting Windows After Startup." Searches still work; they are just slower.

Figure 13-18 Use Advanced Options to rebuild an index and decide what file types are indexed

Use Disk Management to Manage Hard Drives

> **Core 2 Objective 1.3**

13

In the module "Installing Windows," you learned how to install Windows on a new hard drive. This installation process initializes, partitions, and formats the drive. After Windows is installed, you can use **Disk Management** (diskmgmt.msc) to install and manage drives. In this part of the module, you learn to use Disk Management to manage partitions on a drive, prepare a new drive for first use, mount a drive, use Windows dynamic disks, and troubleshoot problems with the hard drive.

> **Caution** !
>
> Before you use Disk Management to make changes to a drive, be sure to back it up first.

Applying Concepts

Examining Hard Drives Using Disk Management

Est. Time: 15 minutes
Core 2 Objective: 1.3

Let's use Disk Management to view the hard drives in two systems:

1. To open the **Disk Management** window, use one of these methods:

   - Right-click **Start** and click **Disk Management**.
   - Enter **diskmgmt.msc** in the Windows search box in the taskbar.

(continues)

Applying Concepts Continued

In Figure 13-19, you can see an example of the Disk Management window showing three MBR hard drives in a system. In this computer, Windows is installed on Disk 0; Disk 1 is an unformatted drive, and Disk 2 is formatted using the NTFS file system. On Disk 0, the first partition is the System Reserved partition, which is designated the active partition and the Windows system partition. The boot partition is drive C:, where Windows is stored.

Figure 13-19   Three MBR disks with Windows 10 installed on Disk 0

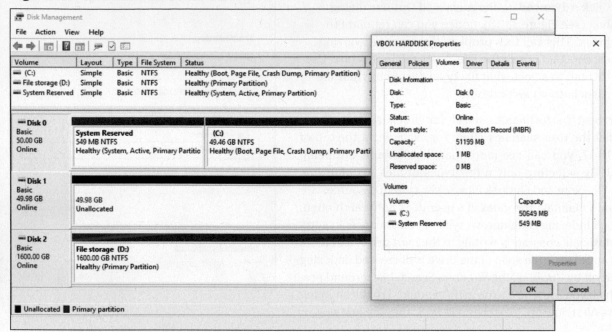

2. To see the Disk 0 Properties box, right-click **Disk 0** on the left side of the Disk Management window and click **Properties**. The Properties dialog box appears, as shown in Figure 13-19. Select the **Volumes** tab to find out the partitioning system for the disk.

Figure 13-20 shows another computer that has a single GPT hard drive installed. Among other partitions, it contains an OEM recovery partition, the EFI System Partition, and drive C:, which is designated the boot partition and holds the Windows 10 installation.

Figure 13-20   A GPT disk with Windows 10 installed

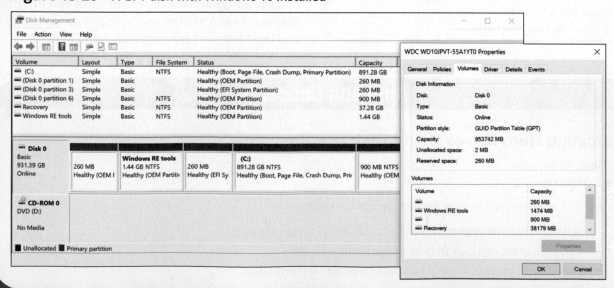

Resize, Create, and Delete Partitions

Suppose you have installed Windows 10 on a hard drive and used all available space on the drive for the one partition. Now you want to split the partition into two partitions so you can use the second one to hold the backups for another computer on the network. You can use Disk Management to shrink the original partition, which frees up some space for a new partition for Ubuntu on the network to use for backups. Let's see how it's done:

1. Open the **Disk Management** window (see Figure 13-21).

Figure 13-21   Shrink a volume to make room for a new partition

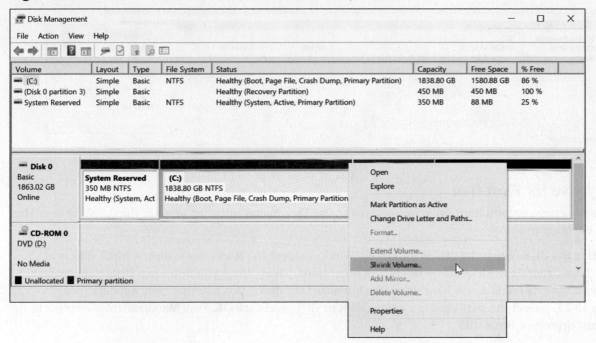

2. To shrink the existing partition, right-click in the partition space and select **Shrink Volume** from the shortcut menu (see Figure 13-21). The Shrink dialog box appears and shows the amount of free space on the partition. Enter the amount in MB to shrink the partition; this amount cannot be more than the available amount of free space so no data on the partition will be lost. (For best performance, be sure to leave at least 20% free space on the existing partition.) Click **Shrink**. The disk now shows unallocated space.

3. To create a new partition in the unallocated space, right-click in that space and select **New Simple Volume** from the shortcut menu (see Figure 13-22). The New Simple Volume Wizard opens.

4. Follow the on-screen directions to enter the size of the volume in MB, select a drive letter for the volume, and select a file system. Leave the Allocation unit size at Default. You can also enter a Volume label and decide to do a quick format. (A **quick format** does not check the volume for bad sectors.) The partition is then created and formatted with the file system you chose. When you open Explorer, you should see the new volume listed.

Notice in Figure 13-21 the options on the shortcut menu for this MBR system, where you can make the partition the active partition (the one BIOS/UEFI looks to for an OS), change the drive letter for a volume, format the volume (which erases all data on it), extend the volume (increase its size), and shrink or delete the volume. Any option not available for the particular volume and situation is grayed out.

Exam Tip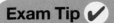

The A+ Core 2 exam expects you to know how to use Disk Management to extend, split, and shrink partitions and configure a new hard drive in a system.

Figure 13-22 Use unallocated space to create a new partition

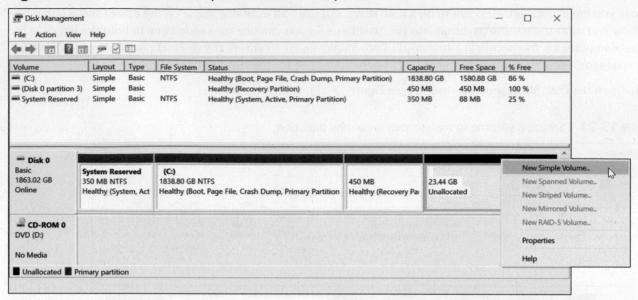

Prepare a Drive for First Use

When you install a new, second hard drive in a computer, use Disk Management to prepare the drive for use. This happens in a two-step process:

1. **Initialize the disk.** When the disk is initialized, Windows identifies it as a basic disk. A **basic disk** is a single hard drive that works independently of other hard drives. When you first open Disk Management after you have installed a new hard drive, the Initialize Disk dialog box automatically appears (see Figure 13-23). Select the partitioning system (MBR or GPT) and click **OK**. Disk Management now reports the hard drive as a Basic disk.

Figure 13-23 Use the Initialize Disk box to set up a partitioning system on new hard drives

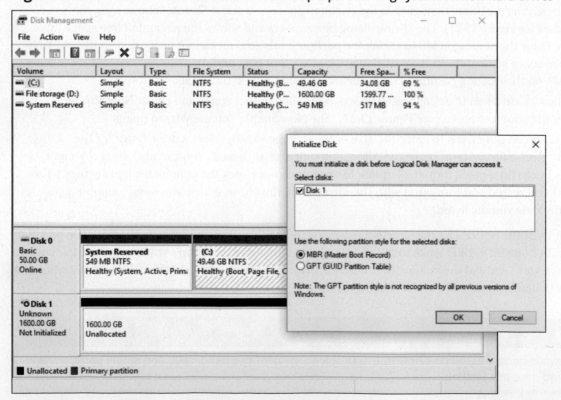

Note 17

After installing a new hard drive, if you don't see the Initialize Disk dialog box when you first open Disk Management, right-click in the Disk area and select Initialize Disk from the shortcut menu. The Initialize Disk dialog box will appear.

2. **Create a volume and format it with a file system.** As you learned to do earlier, you can now create a New Simple Volume in unallocated space on the disk.

How to Mount a Drive

A **mounted drive** is a volume that can be accessed by way of a folder on another volume so the folder has more available space. A mounted drive is useful when a folder is on a volume that is too small to hold all the data you want in the folder. In Figure 13-24, drive C: is 90 GB, and the mounted drive is 20 GB. The mounted drive gives the C:\Projects folder a capacity of 20 GB, which increases the effective space available for drive C: to 110 GB. Similar to how the ext4 file system works in Linux, the C:\Projects folder is called the mount point for the mounted drive.

Follow these steps to mount a drive:

1. Make sure the volume (drive C: in our example) that will host the mounted drive uses the NTFS file system. The folder on this volume, called the mount point, must be empty. You can also create the folder during the mount process. In this example, we are mounting a drive to the C:\Projects folder.

2. Using Disk Management, right-click in the unallocated space of a disk. Select **New Simple Volume** from the shortcut menu. The New Simple Volume Wizard launches. Using the wizard, specify the amount of unallocated space you want to devote to the volume. Our example uses 20 GB, although the resulting size of the C:\Projects folder will only show about 19 GB because of overhead.

Figure 13-24   The C:\Projects folder is the mount point for the mounted drive

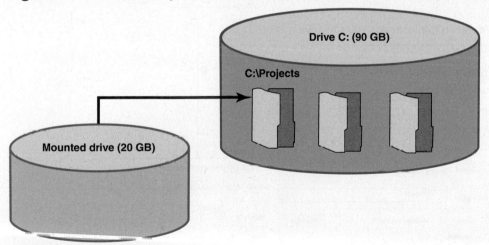

3. As you follow the wizard, the dialog box shown on the left side of Figure 13-25 appears. Select **Mount in the following empty NTFS folder**, and then click **Browse**. In the Browse for Drive Path dialog box that appears (see the right side of Figure 13-25), you can drill down to an existing folder or click **New Folder** to create a new folder on drive C:.

13

Figure 13-25   Select the folder that will be the mount point for the new volume

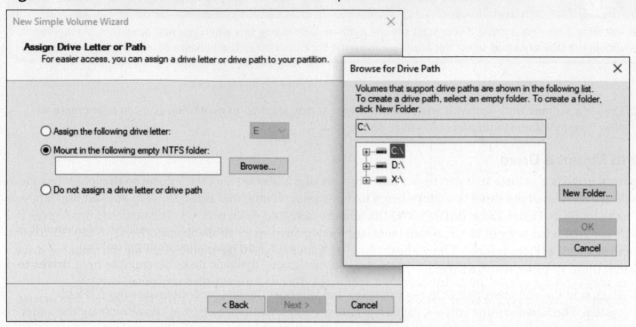

4.   Complete the wizard by selecting a file system for the new volume; you can also name the volume. The volume is created and formatted.

5.   To verify that the drive is mounted, open **Explorer** and then open the **Properties** dialog box for the folder. In our example, the Properties dialog box for the C:\Projects folder is shown in the middle of Figure 13-26. Notice the Properties dialog box reports the folder type as a Mounted Volume. When you click **Properties** in the Properties dialog box, the volume Properties box appears (see the right side of Figure 13-26). In this box, you can see the size of the mounted volume minus overhead.

Figure 13-26   The mounted drive in Explorer appears as a very large folder

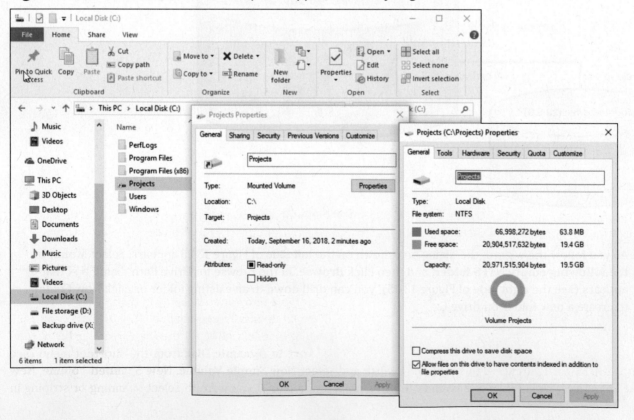

You can think of a mount point, such as C:\Projects, as a shortcut to a volume on a second hard drive. If you look closely at the left window in Figure 13-26, you can see the shortcut icon beside the Projects folder.

Windows Dynamic Disks

A basic disk works independently of other hard drives, but a **dynamic disk** can work with other hard drives to hold data. Volumes stored on dynamic disks are called **dynamic volumes**. Several dynamic disks can work together to collectively present a single dynamic volume to the system.

When dynamic disks work together, data to configure each hard drive is stored in a disk management database that resides in the last 1 MB of storage space on each hard drive. Note that Home editions of Windows do not support dynamic disks.

Here are three uses of dynamic disks:

- **Improve reliability.** For better reliability, you can configure a hard drive as a dynamic disk and allocate the space as a simple volume. This is the best reason to use dynamic disks and is a recommended best practice. Because of the way a dynamic disk works, the simple volume is considered more reliable than when it is stored on a basic disk. A volume that is stored on only one hard drive is called a **simple volume**.
- **Extend a volume across multiple drives.** You can implement dynamic disks on multiple hard drives to extend a volume across these drives (called spanning). This volume is called a spanned volume.
- **Improve performance and/or provide fault tolerance.** Dynamic disks can be used to piece data across multiple hard drives to improve performance and/or provide fault tolerance (protecting data against loss). The technology to configure two or more hard drives to work together as an array of drives is called **RAID (redundant array of inexpensive disks or redundant array of independent disks)**.
  - Joining hard drives together to improve performance is called **striping** or **RAID 0**. The volume is called a striped volume (see Figure 13-27). RAID 0 can improve performance because the work is shared between two hard drives. However, RAID 0 does not provide fault tolerance (if one drive fails, the data is lost).
  - Copying one hard drive to another as a backup is called **mirroring** or **RAID 1**. The volume is called a mirrored volume (see Figure 13-27). RAID 1 improves fault tolerance because if one drive fails, you have another copy of the data. RAID 1 can reduce performance because the drives operate at the speed of the slowest drive and all data must be written twice.

Figure 13-27   A simple volume is stored on a single disk, but a striped volume or a mirrored volume is stored on an array of dynamic disks

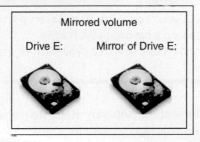

Simple volume

Drive C:

Striped volume

Drive D:

Mirrored volume

Drive E: Mirror of Drive E:

When RAID is implemented in this way using Disk Management, it is called **software RAID**. A more reliable way of configuring RAID is to use BIOS/UEFI setup on a motherboard that supports RAID, which is called **hardware RAID**.

Exam Tip ✔

The A+ Core 2 exam expects you to select which RAID type is appropriate to use in a given scenario.

You can use Disk Management to convert two or more basic disks to dynamic disks. Then you can use unallocated space on these disks to create a simple volume or a Windows **array** of disks using a spanned, striped, or mirrored volume. To convert a basic disk to dynamic, right-click the Disk area and select **Convert to Dynamic Disk** from the shortcut menu (see Figure 13-28). Then right-click free space on the disk and select **New Simple Volume**, **New Spanned Volume**, **New Striped Volume**, or **New Mirrored Volume** from the shortcut menu. If you were to select spanning or striping in

13

Figure 13-28   Convert a basic disk to a dynamic disk

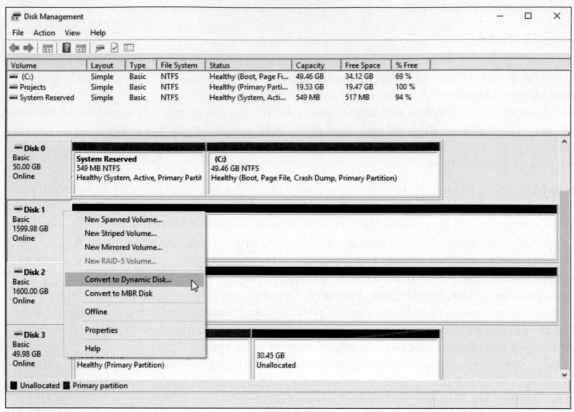

Figure 13-28, you could make Disk 1 and Disk 2 dynamic disks that hold a single volume. The size of the volume would be the sum of the space on both hard drives. If you were instead using mirroring in Figure 13-28, you could make Disk 2 mirror the volume on Disk 1 as a backup copy. The size of the volume would be the amount of space both hard drives have in common—which means it would be the size of the smaller of the two disks.

> **Note 18**
>
> When Windows implements RAID, you cannot install an OS on a spanned or striped volume that uses software RAID. You can, however, install Windows on a hardware RAID drive.
>
>   Also, after you have converted a basic disk to a dynamic disk, you cannot revert it to a basic disk without losing all data on the drive.

Now for some serious cautions about software RAID where you use Windows for spanning, striping, and mirroring: Microsoft warns that when Windows is used for software RAID, the risk of catastrophic failure increases and can lead to data loss. Microsoft suggests you only use Windows spanning, striping, or mirroring when you have no other option. In other words, spanning, striping, and mirroring in Windows aren't very safe. Instead, use a mounted drive or use hardware RAID to expand the size of a volume or to copy a volume to another drive.

Use Disk Management to Troubleshoot Hard Drive Problems

Notice in Figure 13-28 that the system has four hard drives (Disk 0, Disk 1, Disk 2, and Disk 3), and information about the disks and volumes is shown in the Disk Management window. When you are having a problem with a hard drive, it helps to know what the information in the window means. Here are the disk and volume statuses you might see in this window:

- **Healthy.** The healthy volume status shown in Figure 13-28 indicates that the volume is formatted with a file system and that the file system is working without errors.

- **Unknown.** The boot sector most likely is corrupted, which may have been caused by malware.
- **Unreadable.** The file system database cannot be read. Try a reboot.
- **Failed.** The hard drive is damaged, or the file system is corrupt. Replace the data cable to the drive, and make sure it's getting power. Data on a failed volume is likely to be lost.
- **Active.** One volume on an MBR system will be marked as Active. This is the volume that startup BIOS/UEFI looks to for an OS boot manager to load.
- **EFI System Partition.** In GPT systems, one volume will be marked as the EFI System Partition. BIOS/UEFI looks to this volume to find an OS boot manager to load an OS.
- **Unallocated.** Space on the disk is marked as unallocated if it has not yet been partitioned.
- **Formatting.** This volume status appears while a volume is being formatted.
- **Basic.** When a hard drive is first sensed by Windows, it is assigned the Basic disk status. A basic disk can be partitioned and formatted as a stand-alone hard drive.
- **Dynamic.** The following status indicators apply only to dynamic disks:
  - **Online.** An online disk status indicates the disk has been sensed by Windows and can be accessed by either reading or writing to the disk.
  - **Online (Errors).** A region of the disk is giving errors. Try returning the disk to online status. If the volume status does not return to healthy, back up all data and replace the drive.
  - **Offline or Missing.** An offline or missing disk status indicates a dynamic disk has become corrupted or is unavailable. The problem can be caused by a corrupted file system, a loose or bad drive cable, a failed hard drive, or another hardware problem. If you believe the problem is corrected, right-click the disk and select **Reactivate Disk** from the shortcut menu to bring the disk back online.
  - **Foreign drive.** If you move a hard drive that has been configured as a dynamic disk on one computer to another computer, it will report the disk as a foreign drive. To fix the problem, you need to import the foreign drive. Right-click the disk and select **Import Foreign Disks** from the shortcut menu. You should then be able to see the volumes on the disk.
  - **Data Incomplete.** Some but not all of the drives in the volume have been moved. Move and import the remaining disks.
  - **Healthy (At Risk).** The disk can be accessed, but I/O errors have occurred. Try returning the disk to online status. If the volume status does not return to healthy, back up all data and replace the drive.

If you are still having problems with a hard drive, volume, or mounted drive, check Event Viewer for events about the drive that might have been recorded there. These events might help you understand the nature of the problem and what to do about it. How to use Event Viewer is covered in the module "Troubleshooting Windows After Startup."

Throughout this module, you've learned a lot about Windows tools that use a graphical interface. The next part of this module discusses ways to perform many related tasks from a command-line interface.

Using a Command-Line Interface (CLI)

Core 2 Objective 1.2

IT support technicians find it much faster to manipulate files and folders and perform other tasks by using commands in a command prompt window than by using Explorer and other graphical tools. In some troubleshooting situations, you have no other option but to use a command prompt window.

Windows has two levels of command prompt windows: a standard window and an elevated window. In a standard window, the default directory is the currently signed-in user's folder and commands have the same permissions as that user. Commands issued in an **elevated command prompt window** have administrative privileges, and the default directory is C:\Windows\System32.

To open a standard command prompt window (see Figure 13-29), enter **command** or **cmd** in the Windows search box.

Figure 13-29 A command prompt window with two commands

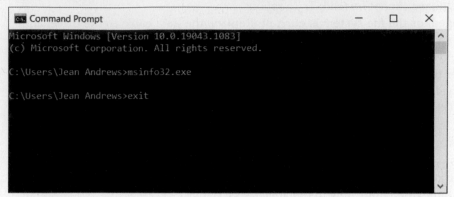

To open an elevated command prompt window, type **cmd** or **command** in the Windows search box, right-click **Command Prompt**, and click **Run as administrator**. Then respond to the UAC box. The Administrator: Command Prompt window is shown in Figure 13-30. Notice the word "Administrator" in the title bar, which indicates the elevated window, and the default directory, which is the C:\WINDOWS\system32 folder.

Figure 13-30 An elevated command prompt window with administrative privileges and two commands

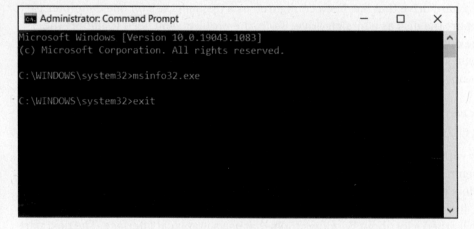

Here are some tips for working in a command prompt window:

- Type **cls** and press **Enter** to clear the window.
- To retrieve the last command you entered, press the up arrow. To retrieve the last command line one character at a time, press the right arrow.
- To terminate a command before it is finished, press **Ctrl+C**, **Ctrl+Break**, or **Ctrl+Pause**.
- To access settings for the command prompt window, right-click the title bar and click **Properties**. You can change the background color, font, font color, and font size so you can better read the text in the window, adjust opacity so you can see what's behind the window as you work, and access Ctrl key shortcuts.
- To close the window, type **exit** (see Figure 13-30) and press **Enter**.

Note 19

Many of the commands you learn about in this section can also be used in the Windows Recovery Environment (Windows RE), which can be loaded from within Windows during troubleshooting. When Windows fails to start, you can load Windows RE from Windows setup media or a USB or DVD recovery drive. How to use the Recovery Environment is covered in the module "Troubleshooting Windows Startup."

Note 20

Windows commands are not case sensitive. You can type help, Help, or HELP and you'll get the same result.

Help or <Command Name> /?

Use the **help** command to get help information about any command. You can enter help followed by the command name or enter the command name followed by /?. Table 13-2 lists some sample applications of this command.

Table 13-2   Sample help commands

Command	Result
help xcopy xcopy /?	Gets help information about the xcopy command
help	Lists all commands
help xcopy | more	Lists information about the xcopy command one screen at a time; press the spacebar to see the next screen, or press Enter to advance one line at a time

Winver

The **winver** command displays the About Windows box (see Figure 13-31), which gives information about the Windows edition, latest update installed, and registered owner of the computer.

Figure 13-31   Display information about the current Windows installation

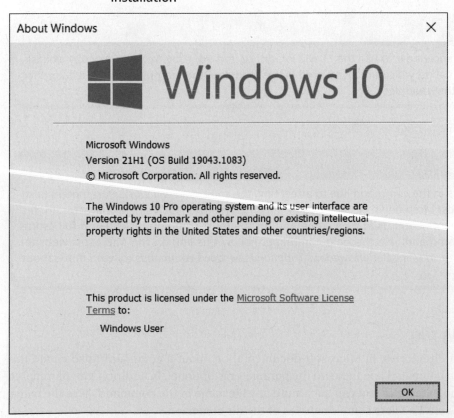

About Windows   ✕

Windows 10

Microsoft Windows
Version 21H1 (OS Build 19043.1083)
© Microsoft Corporation. All rights reserved.

The Windows 10 Pro operating system and its user interface are protected by trademark and other pending or existing intellectual property rights in the United States and other countries/regions.

This product is licensed under the Microsoft Software License Terms to:

Windows User

OK

Commands to Manage Files and Folders

If the command you are using applies to files or folders, the path to these files or folders is assumed to be the default drive and directory. The default drive and directory, also called the current drive and directory, shows in the command prompt. For example, in Figure 13-29, the default drive is C: and the default path is C:\Users\Jean Andrews. If you use a different path in the command line, the path you use overrides the default path. Also know that Windows makes no distinction between uppercase and lowercase in command lines (however, Linux does).

Now let's look at the file-naming conventions you will need to follow when creating files, wildcard characters you can use in command lines, and several commands useful for managing files and folders.

File-Naming Conventions

When using the command prompt window to create a file, keep in mind that file name and file extension characters can be the letters *a* through *z*, the numbers *0* through *9*, and the following characters:

    _ ^ $ ~ ! # % & - { } ( ) @ ' `

In a command prompt window, if a path or file name has spaces in it, it is sometimes necessary to enclose the path or file name in double quotation marks.

Wildcard Characters in Command Lines

As you work at the command prompt, you can use **wildcard** characters in a file name to apply the command to a group of files or to abbreviate a file name if you do not know the entire name. The question mark (?) is a wildcard for one character, and the asterisk (*) is a wildcard for one or more characters. For example, if you want to find all file names in a directory that start with *A* and have a three-letter file extension, you would enter the **dir a*.???** command.

> **Exam Tip** ✔
>
> The A+ Core 2 exam expects you to know how to use the /?, winver, dir, cd, md, rd, copy, xcopy, robocopy, chkdsk, format, diskpart, and shutdown commands, which are all covered in this module. Other commands also required for the A+ Core 2 exam are covered in other modules.

> **Note 21**
>
> Many commands can use parameters in the command line to affect how the command will work. Parameters (also called options, arguments, or switches) often begin with a slash or a hyphen followed by a single character. In this module, you learn about the basic parameters used by a command for the most common tasks. For a full listing of the parameters available for a command, use the help command. Follow this link on the Microsoft website: *docs.microsoft.com/en-us/windows-server/administration/windows-commands/windows-commands* to learn more about commands.

Dir [<*Filename*>] [/P] [/S] [/W] [/A]

Use the **dir** command to list files and directories. In Microsoft documentation about a command (also called the command syntax), the brackets [ ] in a command line indicate the parameter is optional. In addition, the parameter included in < >, such as *<filename>*, indicates that you can substitute any file name in the command. This file name can include a path or file extension. Table 13-3 lists some examples of the dir command.

Table 13-3 Sample dir commands

Command	Result
dir /p	Lists one screen at a time
dir /w	Presents information using wide format, where details are omitted, and files and folders are listed in columns on the screen
dir *.txt	Lists all files with a .txt file extension in the default path
dir d:\data*.txt	Lists all files with a .txt file extension in the D:\data\ folder
dir myfile.txt	Checks that a single file, such as myfile.txt, is present
dir /s	Includes subdirectory entries
dir /a	List all files, including hidden files and system files

CD [<Drive>:\[<Path>]] or CD..

The **cd (change directory)** command changes the current default directory. You enter **cd** followed by the drive (a volume letter, such as C:) and the entire path that you want to be current, like so:

```
C:\> cd C:\game\chess
```

The command prompt now looks like this:

```
C:\game\chess>
```

To move up from a child directory to its parent directory, enter the **..** (dot, dot) variation of the command:

```
C:\game\chess> cd..
```

The command prompt now looks like this:

```
C:\game>
```

Remember that .. (dot, dot) always indicates the parent directory. You can move from a parent directory to one of its child directories simply by stating the name of the child directory:

```
C:\game> cd chess
```

The command prompt now looks like this:

```
C:\game\chess>
```

Remember not to put a backslash in front of the child directory name; doing so tells the OS to go to a directory named chess that is directly under the root directory.

Drive Navigation

Whereas the cd command moves from one directory to another on the same drive, to move from one drive to another, type the drive letter followed by a colon. For example, to go from the D: drive to the C: drive:

```
D:\> c:
```

The command prompt now looks like this:

```
C:\>
```

Know that Windows is usually installed on drive C:.

Note 22

In the Windows Recovery Environment, the main drive is X:, but this drive is not always the same as the drive holding the Windows installation.

13

MD [<Drive>:]<Path>

The **md** or **mkdir** command creates a directory. If no drive is given, the directory is created on the current drive, and if no path is given, the directory is created in the current directory. For example, to create a subdirectory under the C:\game directory:

```
C:\game> md checkers
```

To create a game directory on the D: drive:

```
C:\game> md d:\game
```

Del [<Drive>:] [<Path>][<Filename>]

The **del** command deletes files. You can use the wildcard characters to delete multiple files. For example, to delete all files with a .txt file extension in the C:\game\chess directory, use this command:

```
C:\> del \game\chess\*.txt
```

Attrib [+ OR − S] [+ OR − H] [<Drive>:]<Path>

The del command does not delete a file that is a system file or a hidden file. To change the system and hidden attributes for a file(s), use the **attrib** command. For example, to remove the hidden and system attributes assigned to all files in the C:\game\chess directory, use this command:

```
C:\> attrib -h -s c:\game\chess\*.*
```

The del and attrib commands can be used together to delete Windows system files, making these commands scary powerful. Use them with caution!

RMDIR [<Drive>:]<Path> [/S]

The **rmdir** or rd command removes or deletes a directory. Before you can use the rmdir command, know the following:

- Unless you use the /s switch, the directory must be empty; it cannot contain files or subdirectories.
- The directory must not be the current directory.

For the C:\game\chess example given earlier, to remove the \game directory, you must first remove the chess directory:

```
C:\> rmdir c:\game\chess
C:\> rmdir c:\game
```

Use the /s switch to remove a directory that is not empty. The directory and all its subdirectories and files will be removed. With this switch, the rmdir command is very powerful—use it with caution!

Copy [/V] [/Y] <Source> [<Destination>]

The **copy** command copies a single file or group of files. The original files are not altered. To copy a file from one drive to another, use a command similar to this one:

```
E:\> copy C:\Data\Myfile.txt E:\mydata\Newfile.txt
```

The drive, path, and file name of the source file follow the copy command. The drive, path, and file name of the destination file follow the source file name. If you don't specify the file name of the destination file, the OS assigns the file's original name to this copy. If you omit the drive or path of the source or the destination, then the OS uses the current default drive and path.

To copy the file myfile.txt from the root directory of drive C: to drive E:, use the following command:

```
C:\> copy myfile.txt E:
```

Because the command does not include a drive or path before the file name myfile.txt, the OS assumes that the file is in the default drive and path. Also, because there is no destination file name specified, the file written to drive E: will be named myfile.txt.

To copy all files in the C:\Docs directory to the USB flash drive designated drive E:, use the following command:

```
C:\> copy c:\docs\*.* E:
```

To make a backup file named system.bak of the SYSTEM registry hive file in the \Windows\System32\config directory of the hard drive, use the following command:

```
C:\Windows\system32\config> copy system system.bak
```

If you use the copy command to duplicate multiple files, the files are assigned the names of the original files. When you duplicate multiple files, the destination portion of the command line cannot include a file name.

Here are two parameters that are useful with the copy command:

- **/v.** When the /v switch is used, the size of each new file is compared with the size of the original file. This slows down the copying but verifies that the copy is done without errors.
- **/y.** When the /y switch is used, a confirmation message does not ask you to confirm before overwriting a file.

Note 23

When trying to recover a corrupted file, you can sometimes use the copy command to copy the file to new media, such as from the hard drive to a USB drive. If the copy command reports a bad or missing sector during the copying process, choose the option to ignore that sector. The copying process then continues to the next sector. The corrupted sector will be lost, but others can likely be recovered. The recover command can be used to accomplish the same thing.

XCOPY *<Source>* [*<Destination>*] [/S] [/E] [/C] [/Y] [/D:[*Date*]]

The **xcopy** command is more powerful than the copy command. It follows the same general command-source-destination format as the copy command, but it offers several more options. Table 13-4 shows some of these options.

Table 13-4   Sample xcopy commands

Command	Result
xcopy C:\docs*.* E: /s	Uses the /s parameter to include subdirectories in the copy; this sample command copies all files in the directory C:\docs, as well as all subdirectories under \docs and their files, to drive E:, unless the subdirectory is empty
xcopy C:\docs*.* E: /e	Works the same as /s but empty subdirectories are included in the copy
xcopy C:\docs*.* E: /d :03-14-2022	Uses the /d switch to examine the date; this sample command copies all files from the directory C:\docs created or modified on or after March 14, 2022
xcopy C:\docs*.* E: /y	Uses the /y switch to overwrite existing files without prompting
xcopy C:\docs*.* E: /c	Uses the /c switch to keep copying even when an error occurs

Robocopy *<Source>* *<Destination>* [/S] [/E] [/Log:*<Logfile>*] [/Log+:*<Logfile>*] [/Move] [/Purge]

The **robocopy (robust file copy)** command is similar to the xcopy command. It offers more options than xcopy and is intended to replace xcopy. A few options for robocopy are listed in Table 13-5.

13

Table 13-5 Sample robocopy commands

Command	Result
robocopy C:\docs*.* E: /s	Uses the /s switch to include subdirectories in the copy but does not include empty directories
robocopy C:\docs*.* E: /e	Uses the /e switch to include subdirectories, even the empty ones
robocopy C:\docs*.* E: /log:Mylog.txt	Records activity to a log file and overwrites the current log file
robocopy C:\docs*.* E: /log+:Mylog.txt	Appends a record of all activity to an existing log file
robocopy C:\docs*.* E: /move	Moves files and directories, deleting them from the source
robocopy C:\docs*.* E: /purge	Deletes files and directories at the destination that no longer exist at the source

Exam Tip ✔

The A+ Core 2 exam expects you to know how to structure every command (and its parameters) covered in this and other modules.

Commands to Manage Hard Drives

Core 2 Objective 1.2

Several commands can be used to manage hard drives when setting up a new hard drive, refreshing a hard drive, or troubleshooting. Sometimes these commands are easier than digging through menus for a needed utility. If you're restricted to the Windows Recovery Environment during troubleshooting, these commands might be your only means of accessing some of these tools.

CHKDSK [<*Volume*>:] [/F] [/R]

The **chkdsk (check disk)** command fixes file system errors and recovers data from bad sectors. Recall that a file is stored on the hard drive as a group of clusters. The FAT32 and exFAT file systems use a **FAT (file allocation table)** to keep a record of each cluster that belongs to a file. In Figure 13-32, you can see that each cell in the FAT represents one cluster and contains a pointer to the next cluster in a file. The NTFS file system uses a database called the **master file table (MFT)** to hold similar information.

Figure 13-32 Lost and cross-linked clusters

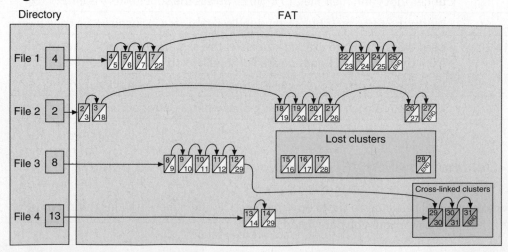

Used with the /f parameter, chkdsk searches for and fixes two types of file system errors made by the FAT or MFT:

- **Lost clusters (also called lost allocation units).** Lost clusters are clusters that are marked as used in the FAT or MFT, but they do not belong to any file. In effect, the data in these clusters is lost.
- **Cross-linked clusters.** Cross-linked clusters are marked in the FAT or MFT as belonging to more than one file.

Used with the /r parameter, chkdsk checks for lost clusters, cross-linked clusters, and bad sectors on the drive. The FAT and MFT keep a table of bad sectors that they normally do not use. However, over time, a sector might become unreliable. If chkdsk determines that a sector is unreliable, it attempts to recover the data from the sector and marks the sector as bad so the FAT or MFT will not use it again.

Used without any parameters, the chkdsk command only reports information about a drive and does not make any repairs.

An elevated command prompt is required to use the chkdsk command. In the following sample commands, the command prompt is not shown because the default drive and directory are not important. To check the hard drive for file system errors and repair them, use this command:

```
chkdsk C:/f
```

To redirect a report of the findings of the chkdsk command to a file that you can later print, use this command:

```
chkdsk C: >Myfile.txt
```

Use the /r parameter of the chkdsk command to fix file system errors and examine each sector of the drive for bad sectors, like so:

```
chkdsk C: /r
```

Note 24

Use either the /f or /r parameter, but not both, with chkdsk. Using both parameters is redundant. For the most thorough check of a drive, use /r.

Note 25

The chkdsk command is also available from the Windows Recovery Environment.

If chkdsk finds data that it can recover, it asks you for permission to do so. If you give permission, it saves the recovered data in files that it stores in the root directory of the drive.

The chkdsk command will not fix anything unless the drive is locked, which means the drive has no open files. If you attempt to use chkdsk with the /f or /r parameter when files are open, chkdsk alerts you to the problem and asks permission to schedule the run the next time Windows is restarted. Know that the process will take plenty of time.

Format <*Volume:*>[/Q] [FS:<*Filesystem*>]

You can format a hard drive or other storage device using Disk Management. In addition, you can use the **format** command from a command prompt window and from the Windows Recovery Environment. This high-level format installs a file system on the device and <u>erases all data on the volume</u>. Table 13-6 lists various sample uses of the format command.

Table 13-6   Sample format commands

Command	Result
format D:	Performs a full format of volume D: using the default file system for the volume type
format D: /q	Performs a quick format of volume D: by recreating an empty root directory; use it to quickly format a previously formatted disk that is in good condition; /q does not read or write to any other part of the disk
format D: /fs:NTFS	Formats volume D: using the NTFS file system
format D: /fs:FAT32	Formats volume D: using the FAT32 file system
format D: /fs:EXFAT	Formats volume D: using the extended FAT file system

Diskpart

Use the diskpart command interpreter to manage partitions on a hard drive. The command requires an elevated command prompt and is often used in the Windows Recovery Environment. Enter the diskpart command at the command prompt to see the diskpart prompt. Then list objects and select one of the objects to give it focus. Commands that follow apply to the object selected.

Applying Concepts

Prepare a Corrupted Hard Drive for a Clean Windows Installation

Est. Time: 15 minutes
Core 2 Objective: 1.2

Windows setup is not always able to overwrite or repair a corrupted partition table on a hard drive. To practice using the diskpart command to prepare a corrupted hard drive for a clean installation of Windows, do the following:

1. Using a VM you have already created in this course, add a second hard drive to the VM. Start the VM and open an elevated command prompt window.

2. Enter the **diskpart** command. At the diskpart prompt, enter the commands shown in Table 13-7 to clean all partitions off the drive, create a new partition, and format it using the NTFS file system. Then open **Explorer** in your VM, and verify that the second hard drive is present and available for use.

Table 13-7   Diskpart commands to partition and format a GPT hard drive

Diskpart Command	Result
`list disk`	Lists the hard drives installed; select the one to clean based on the size of the drive
`select disk=1`	Makes Disk 1 the selected hard drive
`clean`	Cleans the partition table and all partitions from the drive
`convert gpt`	Installs the GPT partitioning system
`create partition primary`	Creates the primary partition
`list partition`	Lists the partitions; note the number of the primary partition
`select partition=2`	Selects the primary partition
`format fs=ntfs quick`	Formats the drive using the NTFS file system
`assign letter=W`	Assigns a drive letter to the volume
`detail partition`	Displays partition details
`detail volume`	Displays volume details
`exit`	Exits diskpart

Note 26

For a complete list of diskpart commands, go to the Microsoft support site (*docs.microsoft.com*), and search on "Diskpart Commands."

Shutdown [/I] [/R] [/S] [/M \\<*Computername*>] [/T XX]

Use the **shutdown** command to shut down the local computer or a remote computer. You must be signed in with an administrator account to use this command. By default, the command gives users a 30-second warning before shutdown. To shut down a remote computer on the network, you must have an administrator account on that computer and be signed on the local computer with that same account and password. Table 13-8 lists some shutdown commands.

Table 13-8   Sample shutdown commands

Command	Result
shutdown /r	Restarts the local computer
shutdown /s /m \\bluelight	Shuts down the remote computer named \\bluelight
shutdown /s /m \\bluelight /t 60	Shuts down the \\bluelight computer after a 60-second delay
shutdown /i	Displays the Remote Shutdown dialog box so you can choose computers on the network to shut down

Module Summary

Critical Windows Settings and Backup Procedures

- Regular preventive maintenance includes verifying Windows Update, anti-malware, and network security settings, as well as backup routines. In addition, uninstall software you no longer need, and clean up and optimize the hard drive.
- Use the Power Options app in Control Panel to control power settings in a laptop.
- You need a plan for disaster recovery in the event the hard drive fails. This plan needs to include routine backups of data files and possibly the entire Windows volume, critical applications, and system files.
- Three types of backups are full, incremental, and differential backups.
- You can back up to local storage or to the cloud. Best practice is to maintain two backups and keep one backup off site. This is known as the 3-2-1 backup rule (three copies, two backup media, and one kept off site).
- Regularly test your backup plan to make sure you can recover files if needed.
- Windows File History and Backup and Restore can be used to schedule routine backups of user data files on a workstation. Both tools can back up a system image. Neither tool can maintain more than one backup routine.
- The best time to create a system image is right after you've installed Windows, hardware, applications, and user accounts and customized Windows settings.
- System Protection creates restore points, which include Windows system files that have changed since the last restore point was made.

Maintaining Hard Drives

- Use File Explorer Options to unhide files and file extensions that are hidden by default in Explorer.
- To improve hard drive performance, use the Disk Cleanup tool and the Defragment and Optimize Drives tool to clean and optimize the drive.
- Use Indexing Options to control which file types are indexed, which can speed up searches but potentially slow down overall system performance.
- Use Disk Management to manage hard drives and partitions. Use it to create, delete, and resize partitions, mount a drive, manage dynamic disks, and solve problems with hard drives.

Using a Command-Line Interface (CLI)

- Commands can use wildcard characters ? and * to apply the command to a group of files or to abbreviate a file name.
- Commands used to manage files, folders, and storage media include help, dir, cd, md, del, attrib, rmdir, copy, xcopy, and robocopy, The winver command displays the About Windows box.
- Commands to manage hard drives include chkdsk, format, and diskpart. The shutdown command shuts down the system.

Key Terms

For explanations of key terms, see the Glossary for this text.

3-2-1 backup rule	dynamic volume	master file table (MFT)	simple volume
array	elevated command	md	slack
attrib	prompt window	mirroring	sleep mode
Backup and Restore	FAT (file allocation	mkdir	sleep timer
backup operator	table)	mounted drive	software RAID
basic disk	file allocation unit	Power Options applet	Sound applet
cd (change directory)	File Explorer Options	quick format	standby mode
chkdsk (check disk)	applet	RAID (redundant array	striping
cluster	File History	of inexpensive disks	suspend mode
copy	format	or redundant array of	synthetic
defragment	full backup	independent disks)	system image
Defragment and	grandfather-father-son	RAID 0	System Protection
Optimize Drives	(GFS)	RAID 1	System Restore
del	hardware RAID	restore point	trim
differential backup	help	rmdir	USB selective suspend
dir	hibernation	robocopy (robust file	setting
Disk Cleanup	incremental backup	copy)	wildcard
Disk Management	Indexing Options applet	Settings app	winver
dynamic disk	Mail applet	shutdown	xcopy

Thinking Critically

These questions are designed to prepare you for the critical thinking required for the A+ exams and may use information from other modules and the web.

1. Jack needs to email two documents to a friend, but the files are so large his email server bounced them back as undeliverable. What is your advice?

   a. Tell Jack to open the documents, break each of them into two documents, and then email the four documents separately.

   b. Tell Jack to put the two documents in a compressed folder and email the folder.

   c. Tell Jack to put each document in a different compressed folder and email each folder separately.

   d. Tell Jack to put the documents on a USB drive and snail mail the drive to his friend.

2. Order the following routine maintenance tasks from most to least important when securing a computer.

   a. Verify anti-malware settings.

   b. Verify Windows Update settings.

   c. Verify the Recycle Bin is emptied weekly.

   d. Verify that hard drives are being optimized weekly.

3. While verifying Windows settings, you discover defragmenting is turned off for the hard drive. What do you do next?

   a. Immediately defrag the drive.

   b. Turn on defragmenting.

   c. Analyze the drive for errors.

   d. Check the type of hard drive installed.

4. Jawana has been working on a paper for her anatomy class for weeks. One day, her little brother was using her computer and accidentally deleted her paper from the Documents folder. How can Jawana recover her deleted paper?

5. What are reasons to uninstall software you no longer use? (Choose all that apply.)

   a. To prevent Windows errors

   b. To speed up Windows performance

   c. To free up hard drive space

   d. To clean the system of malware

6. What type of storage media can be used to create a Windows system image? (Choose all that apply.)

   a. DVDs

   b. Internal hard drive

   c. External hard drive

   d. Network drive

7. Which Windows utilities are used to create previous versions of files that can be recovered from the file properties dialog box? (Choose all that apply.)

   a. Windows File History

   b. Windows Backup and Restore

   c. Disk Management

   d. Windows Folder Options

8. Samolley is setting up Backup and Restore and wants to create a system image. She has discovered that drive E: in the system has plenty of free space for the image. What is the next thing she should do before she creates the image?

   a. Verify that the Windows volume has enough free space to perform the procedure.

   b. Decide if there is a drive on the network she can use. Network drive images are faster to create.

   c. Determine if drive E: is on the same hard drive as drive C:.

   d. Ask the user which folders on drive C: are the most important and need backing up.

9. You suspect malware might have infected restore points saved on the computer, and you want to delete them all. What is your next step?

   a. Turn off System Protection.

   b. Run anti-malware software to scan the system for malware.

   c. Harden the Windows Firewall, closing all open ports.

   d. Update Windows.

10. You suspect the hard drive is corrupted. Which window do you open to repair the drive?

   a. Command prompt window to use chkdsk

   b. Elevated command prompt window to use chkdsk

   c. Disk Management

   d. Explorer

13

11. You are planning to install Windows 10 on a computer in a dual-boot configuration. The computer already has Windows 8 installed. You open Disk Management and discover there is one hard drive with an EFI System Partition, a primary partition with plenty of free space, and no unallocated space. In Disk Management, how can you prepare the drive to hold the Windows 10 installation?

    a. There's nothing more to do in Disk Management. Close the windows and begin the installation.
    b. Shrink the EFI System Partition and create a new partition for Windows 10.
    c. Shrink the primary partition and create a simple volume for Windows 10.
    d. Shrink the primary partition and create a new basic disk for Windows 10.

12. Your friend is setting up a computer and plans to use Windows RAID striping. They ask you how many hard drives they should install in the system. What do you tell them?

    a. Install at least three drives: one to hold the Windows installation and two for the array.
    b. Install at least two drives. The striped array can install on two drives, and it can also hold the Windows installation.
    c. Only one drive is necessary. They can create extra partitions on the drive; the first can hold Windows and the other two can hold the array.
    d. Suggest to your friend that they use hardware RAID, which is more stable.

13. A family member calls and wants to copy the Notepad text editor to a folder they just created in the root of drive C:. They ask you to help construct the command line. Which is the correct command?

    a. Copy C:\notepad.exe C:\Windows
    b. Copy C:\Windows\Notepad.exe C:\
    c. Copy C:\Windows\System32\Notepad.exe C:\
    d. Copy notepad.exe C:\

14. Without changing the default folder, what is the command to list all files in the C:\Linda\test2 folder that have file extensions of only two characters?

    a. Dir C:\Linda\test2*.??
    b. Dir *.*
    c. Dir C:\Linda\test2********.**
    d. Dir C:*.*

15. You are trying to clean up a slow Windows 10 system that was recently upgraded from Windows 8, and you discover that the 75 GB hard drive has only 5 GB of free space. The entire hard drive is taken up by the Windows volume. What is the best way to free up some space?

    a. Compress the entire hard drive.
    b. Move the /Program Files folder to an external hard drive.
    c. Delete the Windows.old folder.
    d. Uninstall several applications.

16. A technician needs to be prepared to launch programs even when utility windows or the Windows desktop cannot load, and the A+ Core 2 exam expects you to know the commands to launch several Windows utilities. What is the command to launch Disk Management? Device Manager? Disk Cleanup? Disk Defragment?

17. Which is the best first step to protect important data on your hard drive?

    a. Use dynamic disks to set up a striped volume so the data has redundancy.
    b. Back up the data to another device.
    c. Compress the folder that holds the data.
    d. Put password protection on the data folder.

18. Which of the following tools can be used to improve Windows performance? (Choose all that apply.)

    a. System Protection
    b. Indexing Options
    c. System Restore
    d. Power Options
    e. File History

Hands-On Projects

Hands-On Project 13-1

Performing Routine Maintenance

Est. Time: 30 minutes
Core 2 Objective: 4.3

Sign in to a Windows system using a standard user account. Step through the process described in the module to do the following routine maintenance. As you work, note which chores you cannot perform unless you know the password to an administrator account. Do the following:

1. Verify critical Windows settings in Windows Update, anti-malware software, and the Network and Sharing Center.
2. Open **Explorer** and view the Properties dialog box of drive C:. What percentage of the volume is free space? Click **Disk Cleanup**. Is the Windows.old folder available for deletion? How much space will Disk Cleanup free?
3. Click **Clean up system files**. How much space will Disk Cleanup free when system files are included in the cleanup? To understand what types of files are selected for deletion, highlight an item and read its description. Don't include files in the cleanup that you think you might need later (for example, previously installed device drivers).
4. Unhide Windows system files and file extensions in Explorer. Verify in Explorer that you can view these files.
5. Clean the drive. After cleanup, what percentage of the volume is free space?
6. Find out the brand and model of the hard drive that holds Windows. What is the brand and model? Is the drive a magnetic or solid-state drive? How do you know?
7. Check hard drive optimization settings and change them as necessary. Analyze the hard drive and determine if it needs defragmenting or optimizing. If so, optimize the drive.
8. Check the hard drive for errors.

13

Hands-On Project 13-2

Using System Restore

Est. Time: 30 minutes
Core 2 Objective: 1.4

Do the following to find out how System Restore works and how it can affect a system:

1. Create a restore point.
2. Make a change to the display settings.
3. Change the desktop background.
4. Create a new text file in your Documents folder.
5. Restore the system using System Restore.

Is the text file still in your Documents folder? Are the other changes still in effect? Why or why not?

Hands-On Project 13-3

Using Disk Management on a Virtual Machine

Est. Time: 30 minutes
Core 2 Objective: 1.3

In a project in the module "Installing Windows," you used Client Hyper-V software to install Windows in a virtual machine. Use this VM to practice using Disk Management. Do the following:

1. Open **Hyper-V Manager**, but do not open the virtual machine.

2. With the virtual machine selected, click **Settings**. Use the Settings dialog box to add a new hard drive to the VM: Click **IDE Controller 0** in the left pane, click **Hard Drive** in the right pane, and then click **Add**. The Settings dialog box to add a hard drive appears (see Figure 13-33). With **Virtual hard disk** selected, click **New**.

Figure 13-33   Add a new virtual hard drive to IDE Controller 0

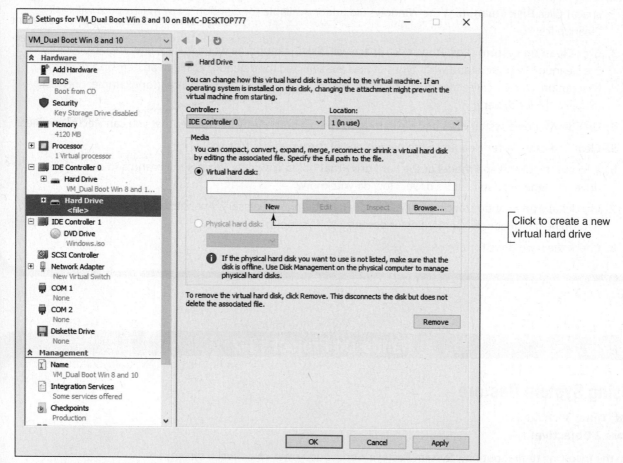

3. The New Virtual Hard Disk Wizard starts. Step through the wizard using these values:
   a. For the format type, select **VHDX**.
   b. For the type of virtual hard drive, select **Dynamically expanding**.
   c. Name the virtual hard drive: **HDD2**.
   d. To specify the location of the virtual hard drive, click **Browse** and point to the same folder where the VM is stored.
   e. Leave all other settings at their default values.

4. Click **Finish** to create the virtual hard drive. The wizard closes.

5. In the Settings box, click **Apply** to save your changes. Close the Settings box.

6. Start up the VM, sign in to Windows 10, and open **Disk Management**.

7. Use Disk Management to initialize the new disk and partition it. Create two partitions on the disk: one formatted using the NTFS file system and one using the FAT32 file system.

8. View the new volumes using Explorer.

9. Create and save a snip of your screen showing the virtual machine with the new volumes created. Email the snip to your instructor.

Hands-On Project 13-4

Researching Backup Software

Est. Time: 15 minutes
Core 2 Objective: 4.3

File History and Backup and Restore are limited in that they support only a single backup routine. Suppose you want to create two backups of data on your hard drive: one backup will be stored on an external hard drive, and the second backup will be stored in the cloud. Both backups should happen automatically. Research the web and propose the backup software solution to accomplish these tasks. Compare your work with another student and discuss who has the best solution.

Hands-On Project 13-5

Using a Batch File

Est. Time: 45 minutes
Core 2 Objective: 1.2

A file with a .bat file extension is called a batch file. You can use a batch file to execute a group of commands, sometimes called a script, from a command prompt. Do the following to learn to use a batch file:

1. Make sure you have at least two files in your Documents folder, not including subfolders. What are the names of the two files?

2. Using a command prompt window, copy the two files in your Documents folder to a folder named \Save on a USB flash drive. Don't include subfolders in the copy. Create a new subfolder named \Save\Myfiles on the flash drive. Copy (don't move) the two files in your \Save folder to the \Save\Myfiles folder.

3. Using Notepad, create a batch file named MyBatch.bat on the USB flash drive that contains the commands to do the following:
   a. Clear the Command Prompt window.
   b. Create the C:\Data folder on your hard drive.
   c. Use xcopy to copy the contents of the \Save folder and subfolder to your C:\Data folder.
   d. List the contents of the C:\Data\Myfiles folder.
   e. Create a new folder named \Save\Newfolder on your flash drive.
   f. Use the robocopy command to copy the contents of the \Save folder and both subfolders to the C:\Data folder, creating a log file of the command results on your flash drive. Name the log file Mylog.txt.

4. Using a command prompt window, execute the MyBatch.bat file, and fix any problems you see. What happens when you execute the batch file and the C:\Data folder already exists?

13

Hands-On Project 13-6

Verifying TCP/IP Settings

Est. Time: 15 minutes
Core 2 Objective: 1.2

To solve problems with failed network connections, the ipconfig, ping, and nslookup commands can help. Follow these steps to learn the basics of using these commands. You learn more about these commands in the module "Network Security and Troubleshooting."

1. Open a command prompt window, and enter the `ipconfig` command to verify TCP/IP settings for the network connection. What is the IP address of your connection? What is the IP address of the default gateway (a gateway is a computer on your network that allows access to the Internet)?

2. Enter the `ping cengage.com` command to verify you can reach that website.

3. To verify DNS is working, enter the `nslookup cengage.com` command. The results should show the IP address for *cengage.com*. What is the IP address?

Real Problems, Real Solutions

Real Problem 13-1

Researching the WinSxS Folder

Est. Time: 45 minutes
Core 2 Objective: 4.1

While cleaning up a hard drive, you begin to look for folders that are excessively large and discover the C:\Windows\ WinSxS folder is more than 7 GB. That's almost half the size of the entire C:\Windows folder on this drive. Use the web to research the purpose of the WinSxS folder. What goes in this folder and how does it get there? How can the size of the folder be reduced without causing major trouble with the OS? Write a one-page paper about this folder, and cite at least three articles about it that you find on the web.

Real Problem 13-2

Cleaning Up a Sluggish Windows System

Est. Time: 30 minutes
Core 2 Objective: 1.3

Do you have a Windows system that is slow and needs optimizing? If not, talk with family and friends, and try to find a slow system that could use your help. Using all the tools and techniques presented in this module, clean up this sluggish Windows system. Take detailed notes as you go, listing what you checked before you started to solve the problems, describing what you did to solve the problems, and describing the results of your efforts. What questions did you have along the way? Bring these questions to class for discussion.

Real Problem 13-3

Creating a Virtual Hard Drive

Est. Time: 15 minutes
Core 2 Objective: 1.3

You can use the Disk Management tool or the diskpart command to create a virtual hard drive (VHD) on a physical computer. The VHD is a file that takes up some free space on the physical hard drive, but to the Windows interface, it appears as a second hard drive. You can store data in folders and files on the VHD and even install Windows in the VHD. Follow these steps to create a VHD:

1. In Disk Management, click **Action** in the menu bar and click **Create VHD**. Follow the on-screen directions to create the VHD, specifying its location on the hard drive and its size. You can make the size dynamically expanding. The VHD is listed as a Disk in the Disk Management window.

2. Right-click the new disk and click **Initialize Disk**. Use the GPT partitioning system for the disk.

3. To format the disk, right-click the unallocated space on the disk, and click **New Simple Volume**. The VHD is now ready for use.

4. Open **Explorer** and verify you can access the new volume.

Discuss in your class and research online how a VHD might be useful. What are two uses of a VHD in which it offers advantages over using a physical hard drive?

13

Module
14

Troubleshooting Windows After Startup

Module Objectives

1 Describe how Windows works, how it is structured, and where it holds data for users and the system

2 Identify Windows tools used to solve problems with Windows, applications, and hardware

3 Apply recommended best practices to troubleshoot Windows-related problems

Core 2 Certification Objectives

1.2 Given a scenario, use the appropriate Microsoft command-line tool.

1.3 Given a scenario, use features and tools of the Microsoft Windows 10 operating system (OS).

3.1 Given a scenario, troubleshoot common Windows OS problems.

Introduction

In previous modules, you learned about the tools and strategies to install and maintain Windows and about the importance of keeping good backups. This module takes you one step further as an IT support technician so you can use Windows tools and methods to solve problems with Windows, applications, and hardware. This module is about problems that occur after startup. Troubleshooting Windows startup is covered in the module "Troubleshooting Windows Startup." We begin the module by learning about the Windows concepts and tools you'll need to optimize and troubleshoot Windows. Then we turn our attention to general steps you can follow when solving Windows, applications, and hardware problems. Finally, we move on to specific problems you might encounter and how to solve them. As you read the module, you might consider following along using a Windows 10 system.

Note

Windows installed in a virtual machine is an excellent environment to use when practicing the skills in this module.

Windows Under the Hood

 Core 2 Objective 1.3

Knowledge is power when it comes to supporting Windows. In this part of the module, you learn more about how Windows works and how it is structured. We also survey several Windows tools that are useful when solving a problem with Windows, applications, Windows users, and hardware. In later parts of the module, you learn to use these tools to solve typical problems you might encounter as an IT technician supporting Windows.

What Are the Shell and the Kernel?

Core 2 Objective 1.3

It might sound like we're talking about a grain of wheat, but Windows has a shell and a kernel, and you need to understand what they are and how they work so you can solve problems with each. A **shell** is the portion of an OS that relates to the user and to applications. The kernel is responsible for interacting with hardware. Figure 14-1 shows how the shell and kernel relate to users, applications, and hardware. In addition, the figure shows a third component of an OS, the configuration data. For Windows, this data is primarily contained in the registry.

The Windows Shell

The shell provides tools such as File Explorer and the Windows desktop as a way for the user to do such things as play music or launch an application. For applications, the shell provides commands and procedures that applications can call on to do such things as print a document, read from a storage device, or display a photo on the screen.

The shell is made up of several subsystems that all operate in **user mode**, which means these subsystems have only limited access to system information and can access hardware only through other OS services. One of these subsystems, the Win32 security subsystem, provides sign-in to the system as well as other security functions, including privileges for file access. All applications relate to Windows by way of the Win32 subsystem.

The Windows Kernel

The kernel, or core, of the OS is responsible for interacting with hardware. Because the kernel operates in **kernel mode**, it has more power to communicate with hardware devices than the shell has. Applications operating under

Figure 14-1   Inside an operating system, different components perform various functions

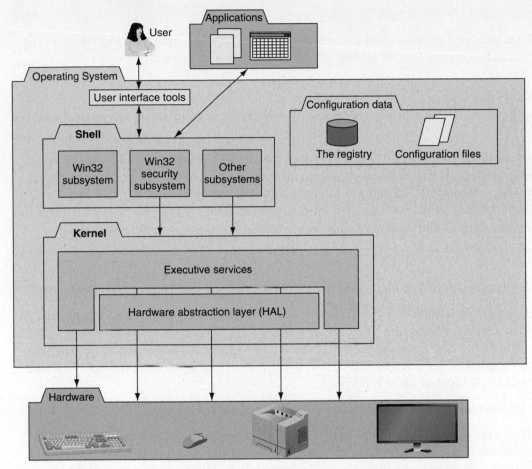

the OS cannot get to hardware devices without the shell passing those requests to the kernel. This separation of tasks provides for a more stable system and helps to prevent a wayward application from destabilizing the system.

The kernel has two main components: (1) the **HAL (hardware abstraction layer)**, which is the layer closest to the hardware, and (2) the **executive services** interface, which is a group of services that operate in kernel mode between the user mode subsystems and the HAL. Executive services contained in the ntoskrnl.exe program file manage memory, I/O devices, file systems, some security, and other key components directly or by way of device drivers.

Note 2

In Task Manager, the Windows processes group on the Processes tab shows that the Windows kernel process ntoskrnl.exe appears as System.

When Windows is first installed, it builds the HAL based on the type of CPU installed. The HAL cannot be moved from one computer to another, which is one reason you cannot copy a Windows installation from one computer to another.

Directory Structures

 Core 2 Objective 1.3

Folder or directory locations you need to be aware of include those for user files, program files, and Windows data. In the folder locations given in this discussion, we assume Windows is installed on drive C:.

User Profile Namespace

When a user first signs in to Windows, a user profile is created. This collection of user data and settings consists of two general items:

- **A user folder together with its subfolders.** These items are created under the C:\Users folder—for example, C:\Users\Jean Andrews. This folder contains a group of subfolders collectively called the **user profile namespace**. (In general, a namespace is a container to hold data—for example, a folder.)
- **NTUSER.DAT.** NTUSER.DAT is a hidden file stored in the C:\Users*username* folder that contains user settings. Each time the user signs in, the contents of this file are copied to a location in the registry.

Program Files

Here is where Windows stores program files unless you select a different location when a program is installed:

- Program files are stored in C:\Program Files for 32-bit versions of Windows. Only 32-bit applications can be installed in a 32-bit installation of Windows.
- In 64-bit versions of Windows, 64-bit programs are stored in the C:\Program Files folder, and 32-bit programs are stored in the C:\Program Files (x86) folder. (For best performance, when you have the option, install 64-bit applications in a 64-bit installation of Windows.)

Here are folders that applications and some utilities use to launch programs at startup:

- A program file or shortcut to a program file stored in the C:\Users*username*\AppData\Roaming\Microsoft\Windows\Start Menu\Programs\Startup folder launches at startup for an individual user.
- A program file or shortcut to a program file stored in the C:\ProgramData\Microsoft\Windows\Start Menu\Programs\Startup folder launches at startup for all users.

Folders for Windows Data

An operating system needs a place to keep hardware and software configuration information, user preferences, and application settings. This information is used when the OS is first loaded and when needed by hardware, applications, and users. Windows uses a database called the **registry** for most of this information. In addition, Windows keeps some data in text files called **initialization files**, which often have an .ini or .inf file extension.

Here are some important folder locations used for the registry and other Windows data:

- **Registry location.** The Windows registry is stored in the C:\Windows\System32\config folder.
- **Backup of the registry.** A backup of the registry is stored in the C:\Windows\System32\config\RegBack folder.
- **Fonts.** Fonts are stored in the C:\Windows\Fonts folder.
- **Temporary files.** These files, which are used by Windows when it is installing software and performing other maintenance tasks, are stored in the C:\Windows\Temp folder.

Note 3

Most often, Windows is installed on drive C:. If the drive letter of the Windows volume is not known, it is written in Microsoft documentation as *%SystemDrive%*. For example, the location of the Program Files folder is written as *%SystemDrive%*\Program Files.

How Windows Manages Applications

Core 2 Objective 1.3

When an application is first installed, its program files are normally stored on the hard drive. When the application is launched, the program is copied from the hard drive into memory, and there it is called a process. A **process** is a program that is running under the authority of the shell, together with the system resources assigned to it. System resources might include other programs the process has started and memory addresses to hold its data. When the process makes a request for resources, this request is made to the Win32 subsystem and is called a thread. A **thread** is a single task, such as the task of printing a file that the process requests from the kernel. Figure 14-2 shows two threads in action, which is possible because the process and Windows support multithreading. Sometimes a process is called an instance, such as when you say to a user, "Open two instances of Microsoft Edge." Technically, you are saying to open two Microsoft Edge processes.

Figure 14-2   A process with more than one thread is called multithreading

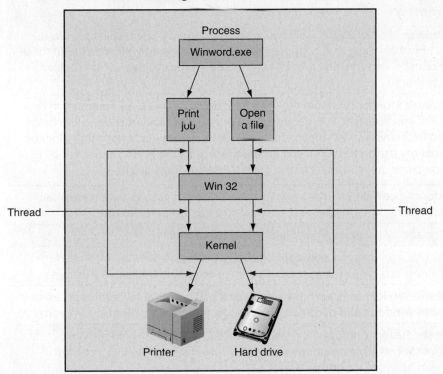

Survey of Windows Tools and Techniques for Troubleshooting

Core 2 Objectives 1.3, 1.4

With an understanding of how Windows is structured, let's turn our attention to useful tools and techniques for managing and troubleshooting Windows, applications, users, hardware, and networks. Table 14-1 lists many of these tools. As you read through the list, try to form a context for how you might use a tool to help you solve a Windows-related problem. To get started, launch each tool and take a look at how its window is organized, the basic functions available, and what is on each tab in a window. Later in the module, you learn how to apply each tool as you address many typical Windows problems.

14

Table 14-1 Tools and techniques to solve Windows-related problems

Tool	Description
Use these tools to conveniently access and manage other Windows tools:	
Control Panel	Control Panel is a collection of small programs, called applets, that are used to manage many Windows settings. You learned to use Control Panel in the module "Installing Windows."
Administrative Tools or Windows Tools	This applet in Control Panel contains several tools used by IT technicians. You need to be signed in to Windows with administrator privileges to use many of these tools. The applet is called Administrative Tools in Windows 10 and Windows Tools in Windows 11.
Computer Management (compmgmt.msc)	This console contains several administrative tools, including those that manage users and user groups.
Microsoft Management Console (MMC, mmc.exe)	Use this console to build your own customized console window where you can add Windows tools you use often for handy access.
Use these tools to observe Windows, Windows user, network, application, and hardware activities as tracked and logged by Windows:	
Event Viewer (eventvwr.msc)	Just about anything that happens in Windows is logged by Windows, and these logs can be viewed using Event Viewer in the Administrative Tools/Windows Tools group.
Resource Monitor (resmon.exe)	Resource Monitor monitors the CPU, hard drive, network, and memory in real time. If you suspect CPU, memory, hard drive, or network resources are being used excessively by an application or malware, you can use Resource Monitor to identify the process. You can access the tool on the Performance tab of Task Manager or in the Administrative Tools/Windows Tools group.
Performance Monitor (perfmon.msc)	Performance Monitor in the Administrative Tools/Windows Tools group can track activity by hardware and software to measure performance.
Solve Windows, application, networking, and Windows user problems with these tools:	
Task Manager (taskmgr.exe)	Task Manager lets you view applications, processes, and network and user activities. You can use it to end a process or to enable or disable a process.
Services console (services.msc)	Use the Services console in the Administrative Tools/Windows Tools group to control Windows and third-party services installed on a system.
System Configuration (msconfig.exe)	Use the System Configuration utility (commonly called "M-S-config") to temporarily disable programs from launching at startup and to perform a clean boot or Safe boot.
Registry Editor (regedit.exe)	Use the Registry Editor to back up and edit the Windows registry.
Solve Windows problems using these tools and techniques:	
System File Checker (sfc.exe)	Use System File Checker (SFC) to verify and replace Windows system files. It keeps a cache of current system files in case it needs to refresh a damaged file.
Windows Updates	Use Windows Updates in the Settings app to download and apply the latest Windows updates to solve problems with Windows, applications, and hardware.
System Restore (rstrui.exe)	Use System Restore to revert the system back to a previously saved restore point before a problem started.
Solve application errors or crashes with these tools and techniques:	
Programs and Features (appwiz.cpl)	Use the Programs and Features tool in Control Panel to repair and uninstall applications and enable and disable Windows features.

(continues)

Table 14-1 Tools and techniques to solve Windows-related problems (Continued)

Tool	Description
Secondary logon	Use a secondary logon using administrator privileges to run an application that refused to run under the authority of a standard user. Use the Properties dialog box of the application program file to perform a secondary logon.
Digital signature	A digital signature verifies that the application is not a rogue application and that it is certified as Windows-compatible by Microsoft. Verify a digital signature using the Properties dialog box of the application program file.
Task Scheduler (taskschd.msc)	Use Task Scheduler in the Administrative Tools/Windows Tools group to schedule a program to run at a future time, including at startup.
Manage and solve problems with hardware using these tools:	
Device Manager (devmgmt.msc)	Device Manager in Control Panel is the go-to tool to make sure Windows has correctly installed a hardware device and to solve problems with a device.
chkdsk	The chkdsk command checks the hard drive for a corrupted file system and bad sectors on the drive. Use the chkdsk c: /r command to check drive C: and recover data.

Exam Tip ✔

The A+ Core 2 exam gives you a scenario with possible alternatives toward a solution. It expects you to know which Windows tool to use and how to use it to resolve a problem. These Windows tools covered in this module include Event Viewer, MMC, Performance Monitor, the Registry Editor, Resource Monitor, the Services console, System Configuration, System File Checker, System Restore, Task Manager, and Task Scheduler.

Exam Tip ✔

In performance-based questions on the A+ Core 2 exam, you are expected to know how to access a Windows tool using more than one method. It's a good idea to know the command that launches a given tool.

Note 4

If you have not already used a tool listed in Table 14-1, open the tool, and take a good look at its features and menus before you continue with the module. If you can, open each tool using more than one method. Try to remember at least one way to open it. Don't worry if you don't know how to use the tool—that's coming up.

Exam Tip ✔

If an often-used Windows utility can be launched from a command prompt, the A+ Core 2 exam expects you to know the program name of that utility.

Now let's learn to use a few of these tools. You'll learn to use other Windows tools later in this and other modules.

Applying Concepts

Using Windows Tools to Manage Tools

Est. Time: 15 minutes
Core 2 Objective: 1.3

Windows offers several windows and consoles to help access and organize Windows tools. Take a quick look at each to get familiar with how a window or console works and the tools each one contains:

1. **Administrative Tools/Windows Tools.** In Classic view of Control Panel, click **Administrative Tools** in Windows 10 or **Windows Tools** in Windows 11 to see a group of tools used by technicians and developers to support Windows. Figure 14-3 shows the Administrative Tools window for Windows 10 Pro. The Home editions of Windows don't include several of these tools, including Hyper-V Manager, Local Security Policy, and Print Management.

Figure 14-3   Administrative tools available in Windows 10 Pro

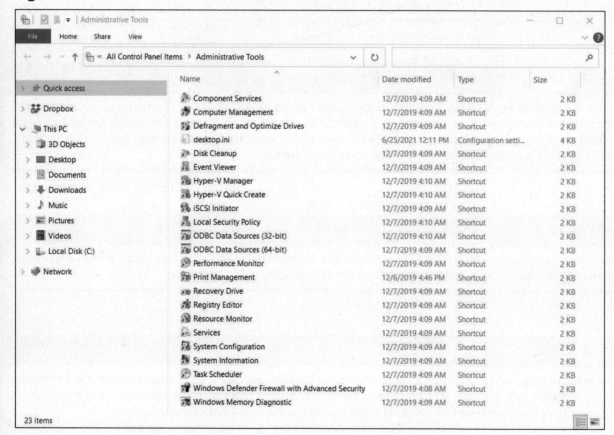

2. **Computer Management.** One of the items in Administrative Tools/Windows Tools is **Computer Management** (compmgmt.msc), which itself contains several tools to manage the local computer or other computers on the network. The window is called a **console** because it consolidates several Windows administrative tools. To use most of these tools, you must be signed in as an administrator, although you can view certain settings in Computer Management if you are signed in with lesser privileges. The Windows 10 Computer Management window is shown in Figure 14-4.

Figure 14-4 Windows Computer Management combines several administrative tools into a single, easy-to-access window

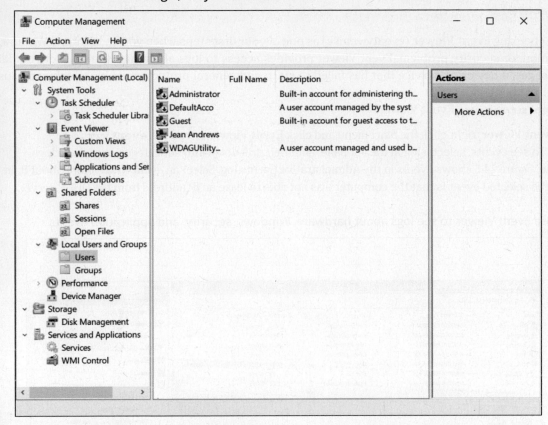

3. **Microsoft Management Console (MMC).** You can build your own console to hold the tools you use often, and you can copy this console to any computer you support. To build a console, first sign in to Windows using an account with administrator privileges, and then open the **Microsoft Management Console** (**MMC**; the program file is mmc.exe). A new empty console is created, as shown in Figure 14-5. Tools you add to your console are called **snap-ins**, and the console is saved in a file with an .msc file extension. You learn to create your own console in a project at the end of this module.

Figure 14-5 An empty console

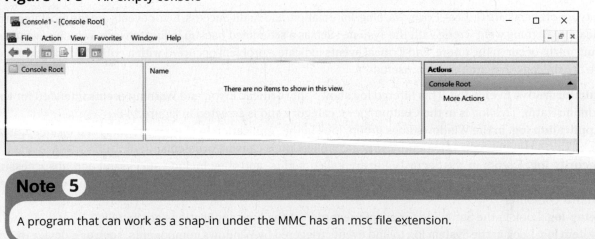

> **Note 5**
>
> A program that can work as a snap-in under the MMC has an .msc file extension.

Let's turn our attention to three tools you can use to examine the system: Event Viewer, Resource Monitor, and Performance Monitor.

Use Event Viewer to Look for Clues

 Core 2 Objective 1.3

Get in the habit of checking **Event Viewer** (eventvwr.msc) as one of your first steps when you encounter a Windows, hardware, application, or security problem. Event Viewer provides access to logs about hardware or network failure, OS error messages, a device or service that has failed to start, and general protection faults, which can cause Windows to lock up or hang.

Here are general steps to use Event Viewer:

1. To Open **Event Viewer**, right-click the **Start** menu and click **Event Viewer** or run the `eventvwr.msc` command. To see events, select a log in the left pane, and then drill down into subcategories of these logs. For example, Figure 14-6 shows events in the Administrative Events log. Select an event to see more about it. In the figure, the selected event is that the computer was not able to lease an IP address from the DHCP server.

Figure 14-6   Use Event Viewer to see logs about hardware, Windows, security, and application events

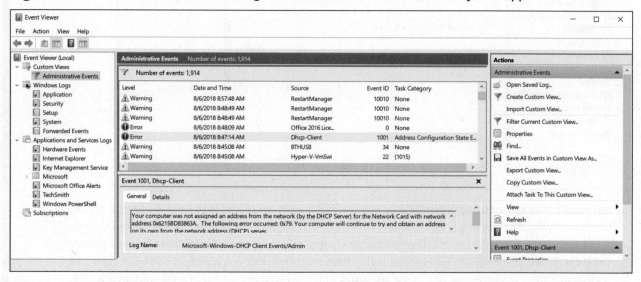

2. To sort a list of events, click a column heading in the middle pane. After you have selected an event, click the **Details** tab to show more information about the event.

The types of events are Critical, Error, Warning, Information, and Audit Success. Error events are the most important and indicate something went wrong with the system, such as a scheduled backup failing to work. Warning events indicate failure might occur in the future, and Critical events indicate a problem occurred with a critical Windows process. Here are the logs that are the most useful:

- **Administrative Events log.** This filtered log shows only Critical, Error, and Warning events intended for the administrator. This log is in the Custom Views category and is selected in Figure 14-6.
- **Application log.** In the Windows Logs group, look in the Application log for events recorded by an application. This log might help you identify why an application is causing problems.
- **Security log.** Events in the Security log are called audits, and they include successful and unsuccessful sign-ins to a user account and attempts from another computer on the network to access shared resources on this computer.
- **Setup log.** Look in the Setup log for events recorded at the time applications are installed.
- **System log.** Look in the System log to find events triggered by Windows components, such as a device driver failing to load or a problem with hardware.
- **Forwarded Events log.** This log receives events that were recorded on other computers and sent to this computer.

To save time, first check the Administrative Events log because it filters out all events except Critical, Error, and Warning events.

Resource Monitor Can Identify a Resource-Hungry Process

Core 2 Objective 1.3

Do you suspect a sluggish system is caused by a process hogging system resources? For a quick look, in the Administrative Tools/Windows Tools window, open **Resource Monitor** to view in real time how the CPU, hard drive, network, and memory are being used (see Figure 14-7). If you suspect CPU, memory, disk, or network resources are being used excessively by a process, you can use Resource Monitor to identify the process. Click individual tabs in this window to drill down for more detail. Check for such a process if you suspect malware might be at work in a denial-of-service (DoS) attack.

Figure 14-7   View how computer resources are being allocated and used

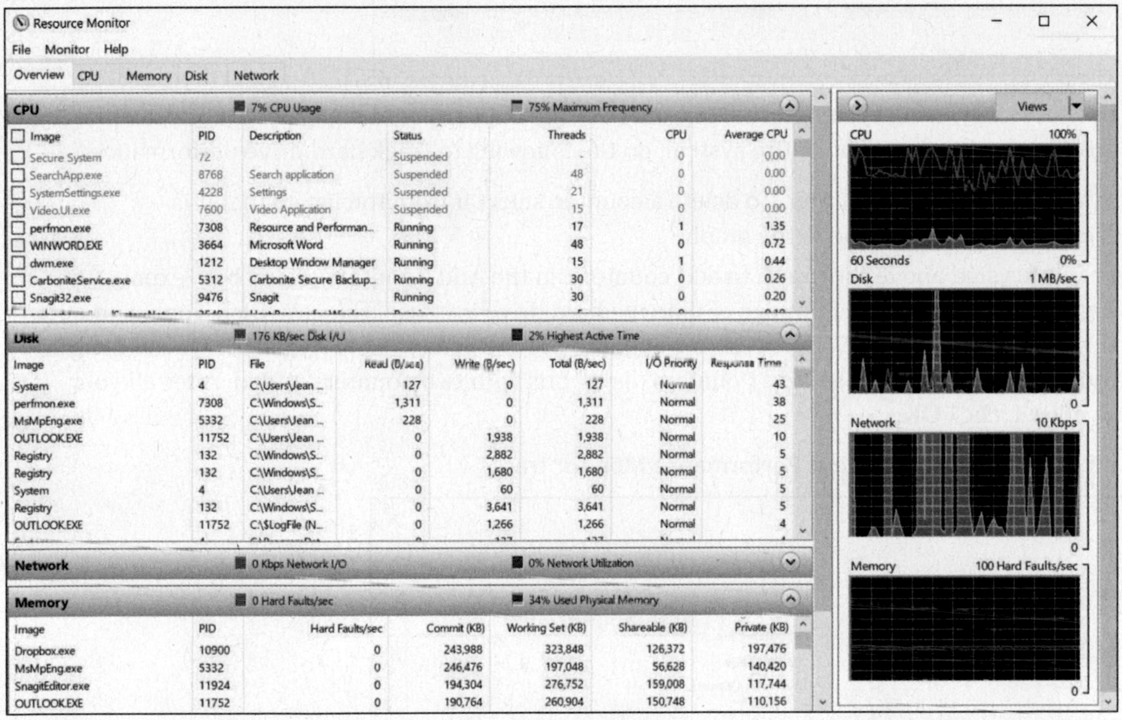

Performance Monitor Tracks Resource Use Over Time

Core 2 Objective 1.3

Performance Monitor (perfmon.msc) also tracks how resources are used in real time, and it can save collected data in logs for future use. Software developers might use this tool to evaluate how well their software is performing and to identify software and hardware bottlenecks.

To open Performance Monitor, click it in the Administrative Tools/Windows Tools group or enter the `perfmon.msc` command. Performance Monitor offers hundreds of counters used to examine many aspects of the system related to performance. The Windows default setting is to show the % Processor Time counter the first time you open the window (see Figure 14-8). This counter appears as a red line in the graph and tracks activity of the processor.

14

Figure 14-8   Performance Monitor uses counters to monitor various activities of hardware and software

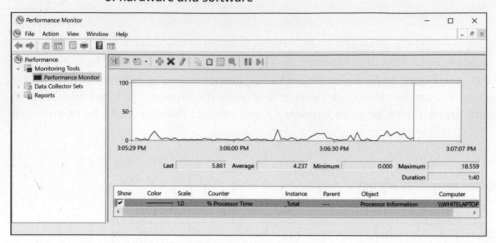

To keep from unnecessarily using system resources, only use the counters you really need. For example, if you suspect the hard drive is slowing down the entire system, do the following to track hard drive performance:

1. Remove the **% Processor Time** counter. To delete a counter, select it from the list so that it is highlighted, and click the red **X** above the graph.

2. Click the **green plus** sign above the graph to add counters. In the Add Counters dialog box, expand the **LogicalDisk** group. To track the percentage of time the hard drive is in use, select **% Disk Time**, and click **Add**. To track the average number of processes waiting to use the drive, select **Avg. Disk Queue Length**, and click **Add**. Figure 14-9 shows the Add Counters dialog box with two counters added. After all your counters are added, click **OK**.

Figure 14-9   Add counters to set up what Performance Monitor tracks

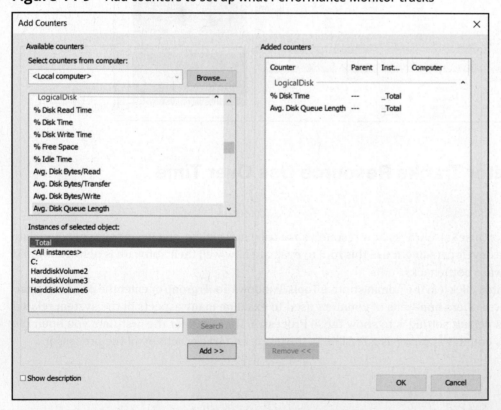

Allow Performance Monitor to keep running while the system is in use, and then check the counters. The results for one system are shown in Figure 14-10. Select each counter and note the average, minimum, and maximum values for the counter.

Figure 14-10   Two counters can measure hard drive performance

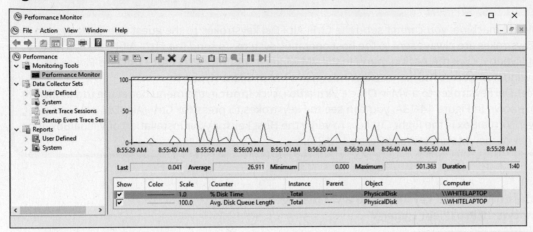

If the % Disk Time is more than 80% and the Avg. Disk Queue Length is more than two, you can conclude that the hard drive is working excessively hard and processes are slowed down waiting on the drive. Any time a process must wait to access the hard drive, you are likely to see degradation in overall system performance.

Note 6

To find out which counters to use to measure specific performances, search the Microsoft website or perform a general web search.

Task Manager Shows You What's Happening Now

Core 2 Objective 1.3

Task Manager lets you view activities of applications, processes, the CPU, memory, hard drives, networks, and users. Use Task Manager to end a process causing trouble and to enable or disable programs that launch at Windows startup. It's a powerful tool that technicians rely on to view and control what's happening now in Windows.

Here are two ways to open Task Manager:

- Press **Ctrl+Alt+Del**. Depending on your system, the security screen (see Figure 14-11) or Task Manager appears. If the security screen appears, click **Task Manager**. This method works well when the system has a problem and is frozen.
- Right-click the Start menu and click **Task Manager**.

Figure 14-11   Use the security screen to launch Task Manager

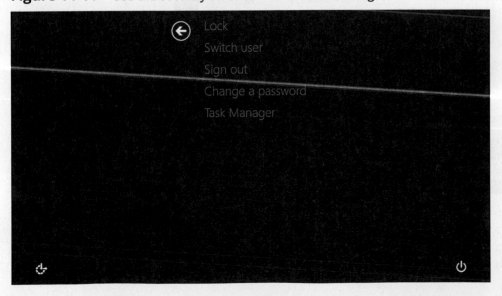

Note 7

When working with a virtual machine, you cannot send the Ctrl+Alt+Del keystrokes to the guest operating system in the VM because these keystrokes are always sent to the host operating system. To send the Ctrl+Alt+Del keystrokes to a VM in Windows Client Hyper-V, click the **Action** menu in the VM window, and click **Ctrl+Alt+Del** (see Figure 14-12). The module "Installing Windows" covers how to install Windows in a VM in Client Hyper-V.

To send the Ctrl+Alt+Del keystrokes to a VM in Oracle VirtualBox, click **Input** in the menu bar at the top of the VM window. For the system shown in Figure 14-13A, you can see the keystrokes to press for Ctrl+Alt+Del are Host+Del. By default, the Host key in VirtualBox is the Right Ctrl key. To verify the Host key for your installation of VirtualBox, look in the bottom-right corner of the VM window (see Figure 14-13B).

Figure 14-12   Send the Ctrl+Alt+Del keystrokes to a VM managed by Windows 10 Pro Client Hyper-V

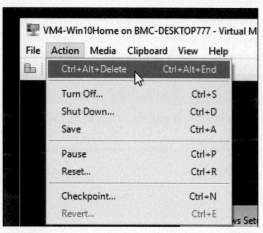

Figure 14-13   For Oracle VirtualBox, (A) send the Ctrl+Alt+Del keystrokes to a VM, and (B) verify the Host key for the VM

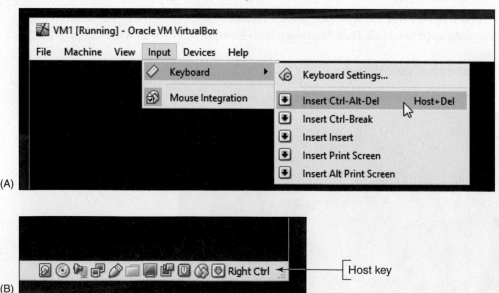

If you see very limited information in the Task Manager window, click **More details** to see the details on the Processes tab shown in Figure 14-14.

Figure 14-14   The Windows 10 Task Manager window with the Processes tab selected

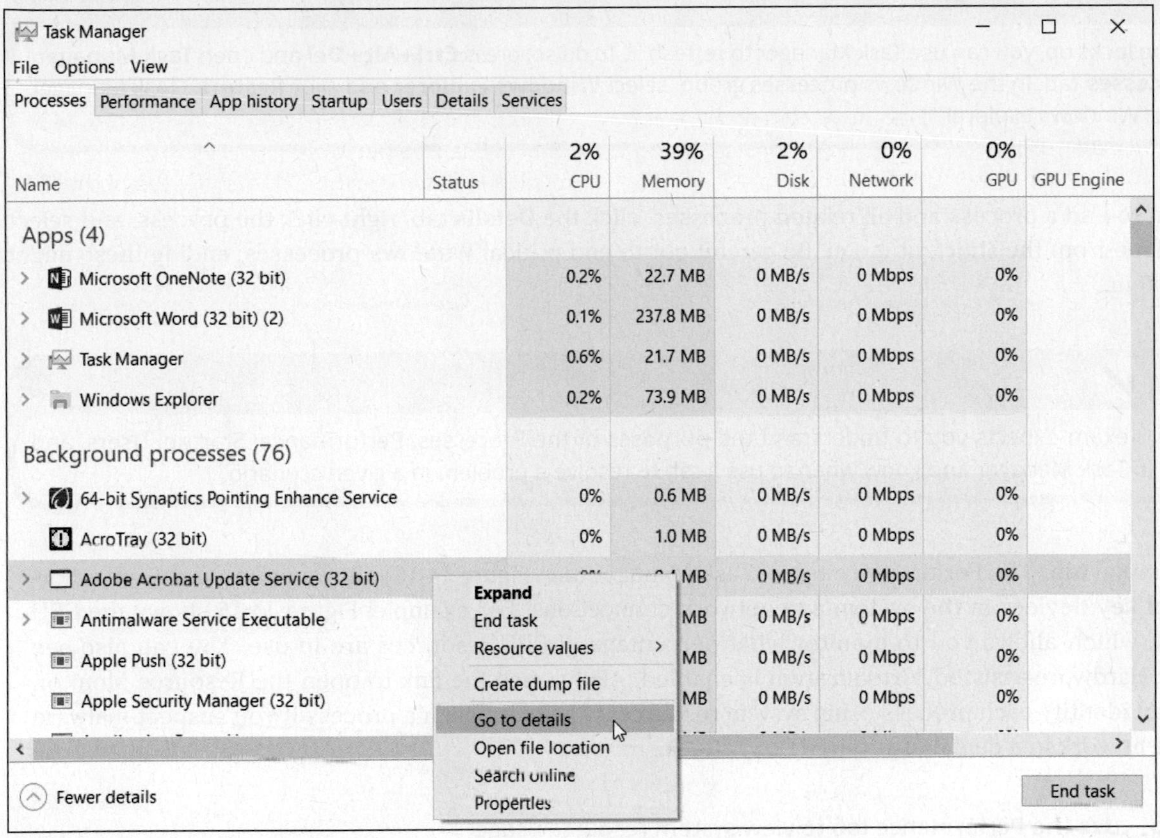

Name	Status	2% CPU	39% Memory	2% Disk	0% Network	0% GPU	GPU Engine
Apps (4)							
› ▥ Microsoft OneNote (32 bit)		0.2%	22.7 MB	0 MB/s	0 Mbps	0%	
› ▥ Microsoft Word (32 bit) (2)		0.1%	237.8 MB	0 MB/s	0 Mbps	0%	
› ▥ Task Manager		0.6%	21.7 MB	0 MB/s	0 Mbps	0%	
› ▥ Windows Explorer		0.2%	73.9 MB	0 MB/s	0 Mbps	0%	
Background processes (76)							
› ▥ 64-bit Synaptics Pointing Enhance Service		0%	0.6 MB	0 MB/s	0 Mbps	0%	
▥ AcroTray (32 bit)		0%	1.0 MB	0 MB/s	0 Mbps	0%	
› ▥ Adobe Acrobat Update Service (32 bit)		0%	... MB	0 MB/s	0 Mbps	0%	
› ▥ Antimalware Service Executable			MB	0 MB/s	0 Mbps	0%	
▥ Apple Push (32 bit)			MB	0 MB/s	0 Mbps	0%	
▥ Apple Security Manager (32 bit)			MB	0 MB/s	0 Mbps	0%	

Task Manager — File   Options   View — Processes   Performance   App history   Startup   Users   Details   Services

Context menu:
Expand
End task
Resource values ›
Create dump file
Go to details
Open file location
Search online
Properties

⌃ Fewer details   **End task**

Here are important details about each tab in Task Manager:

- **Processes tab and Details tab.** The Processes tab shows running processes organized by Apps, Background processes, and Windows processes. Right-click a process and click **Go to details** (see Figure 14-14) to jump to the Details tab (see Figure 14-15), where you see the name of the program file and other details about the running program. On the Details tab, a hung process is reported as Not Responding. To end the task, select it and click **End task**. The application will attempt a normal shutdown; if data has not been saved, you are given the opportunity to save it.

Figure 14-15   Use the Details tab to end a task that is not responding

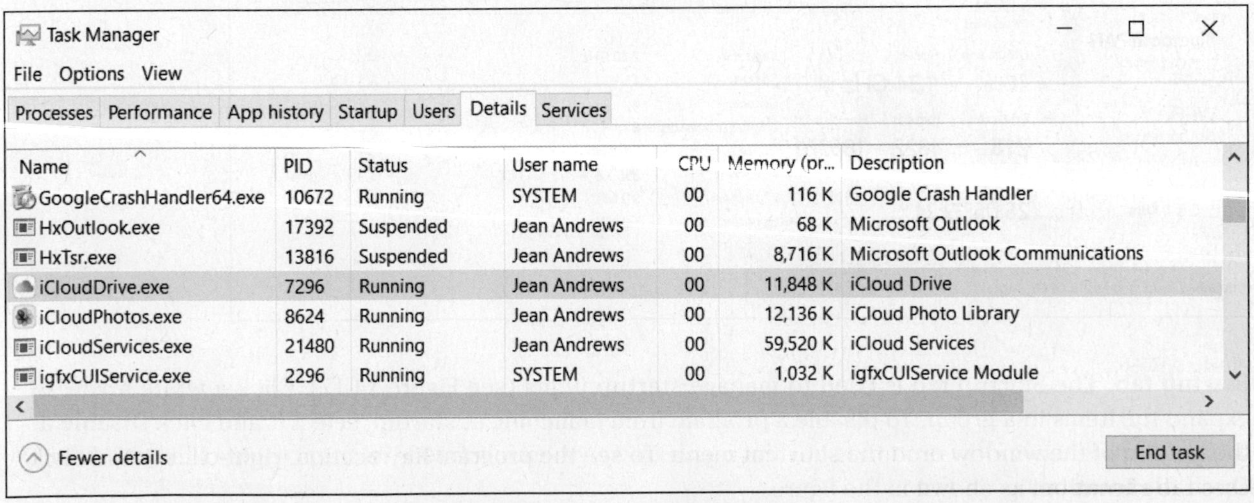

Task Manager — File   Options   View — Processes   Performance   App history   Startup   Users   Details   Services

Name	PID	Status	User name	CPU	Memory (pr...	Description
▦ GoogleCrashHandler64.exe	10672	Running	SYSTEM	00	116 K	Google Crash Handler
▥ HxOutlook.exe	17392	Suspended	Jean Andrews	00	68 K	Microsoft Outlook
▥ HxTsr.exe	13816	Suspended	Jean Andrews	00	8,716 K	Microsoft Outlook Communications
☁ iCloudDrive.exe	7296	Running	Jean Andrews	00	11,848 K	iCloud Drive
❋ iCloudPhotos.exe	8624	Running	Jean Andrews	00	12,136 K	iCloud Photo Library
▥ iCloudServices.exe	21480	Running	Jean Andrews	00	59,520 K	iCloud Services
▥ igfxCUIService.exe	2296	Running	SYSTEM	00	1,032 K	igfxCUIService Module

⌃ Fewer details   **End task**

14

Note 8

If your desktop locks up, you can use Task Manager to refresh it. To do so, press **Ctrl+Alt+Del** and open **Task Manager**. Click the **Processes** tab. In the Windows processes group, select **Windows Explorer** and click **Restart**. (Task Manager calls Explorer "Windows Explorer.")

If you want to end a process and all related processes, click the **Details** tab, right-click the process, and select **End Process Tree** from the shortcut menu. Be careful not to end critical Windows processes; ending these might crash your system.

Exam Tip ✔

The A+ Core 2 exam expects you to understand the purposes of the Processes, Performance, Startup, Users, and Services tabs in Task Manager and know when to use a tab to resolve a problem in a given scenario.

- **Performance tab.** The Performance tab of Task Manager (see Figure 14-16) allows you to monitor performance of key devices in the system and network connections. For example, Figure 14-16 shows the CPU selected, which allows you to monitor what percentage of CPU resources are in use. You can also see whether Hardware-assisted Virtualization is enabled. Also notice the link to open the Resource Monitor, which can identify each process using system resources. Check for such a process if you suspect malware might be at work in a denial-of-service (DoS) attack.

Figure 14-16   Use the Performance tab to view system resource usage

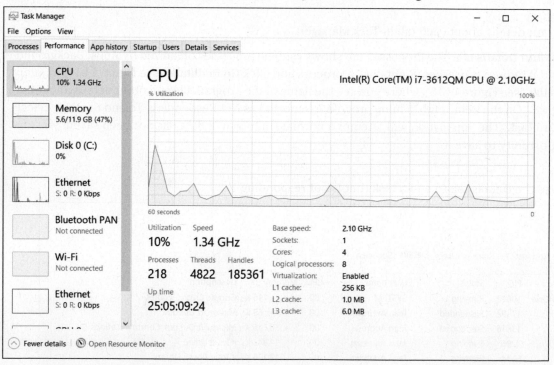

- **Startup tab.** The Startup tab is used to manage startup items (see Figure 14-17). Click a white arrow to expand the items in a group. To disable a program from launching at startup, select it and click **Disable** at the bottom of the window or in the shortcut menu. To see the program file location, right-click it and click **Open file location**, as shown in the figure.

Figure 14-17   Startup processes are managed on the Startup tab of Task Manager

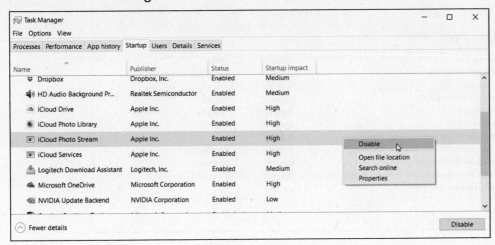

- **Users tab.** The Users tab (see Figure 14-18) lists currently signed-in users. Expand the list for a user to show processes started by the user that might be affecting overall system performance. Notice that the statuses of some programs on this tab are listed as Suspended. If certain apps remain idle for a short time, they're suspended so they don't require the attention of the CPU. When the app is used again, it automatically comes out of suspension, and the CPU once again begins servicing it. To disconnect a remote user or sign out a local user from the system, select the user and click **Disconnect** or **Sign out** at the bottom of the screen.

Figure 14-18   The Users tab shows system resources used by each signed-in user

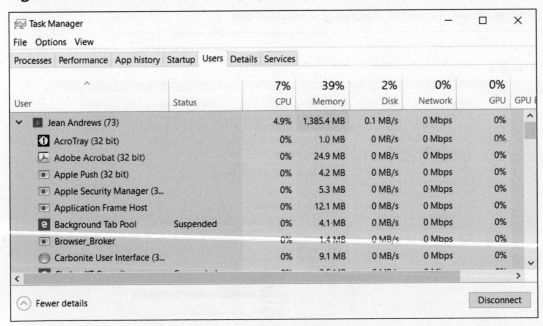

- **Services tab.** The Services tab (see Figure 14-19) lists the services currently installed along with the status of each service. You can stop, start, or restart a service by right-clicking it and selecting the action in the shortcut menu. Services can also be managed from the Services console.

Figure 14-19   The Services tab of Task Manager gives the current status of all installed services

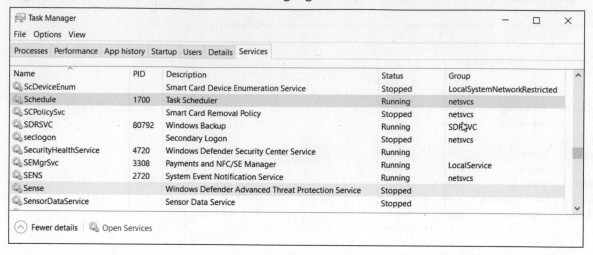

Services Console Manages Services

Core 2 Objective 1.3

Although you can temporarily solve a problem with a service using Task Manager, use the **Services console** (services.msc) to permanently adjust when services run in the background to support Windows and applications. To open the console, enter the `services.msc` command in the Windows search box. If the Extended tab at the bottom of the window is not selected, click it (see Figure 14-20). This tab gives a description of a selected service.

Figure 14-20   The Services console is used to manage Windows services

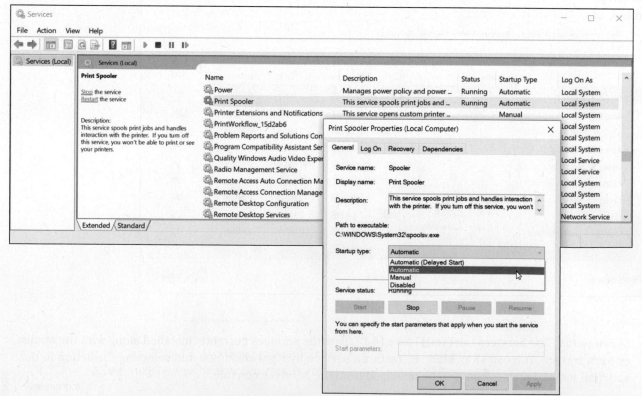

When you click a service to select it and the description is missing, it's most likely a third-party service put there by an installed application; in fact, it might be malware. To get more information about a service or to stop or start a service, right-click its name and select **Properties** from the shortcut menu. In the Properties box (see Figure 14-20), the startup types for a service are as follows:

- **Automatic (Delayed Start).** Starts shortly after startup and after the user signs in, so as not to slow down the startup process
- **Automatic.** Starts when Windows loads
- **Manual.** Starts as needed
- **Disabled.** Cannot be started

Use the Services console to make sure the service an application requires has started. If the service has failed to start, make sure it has an Automatic or Manual setting. If problems with the service or application persist, you might need to reinstall the service or the application that uses the service.

Other problems with a service can sometimes be resolved by stopping and restarting the service. For example, stopping and restarting the Spooler service might solve a problem with print jobs not moving on to the printer. To stop or restart, right-click the service and use the shortcut menu.

Applying Concepts

Task Scheduler Manages Startup Programs

Est. Time: 15 minutes
Core 2 Objective: 1.3

Task Scheduler (taskschd.msc) in the Administrative Tools/Windows Tools group of Control Panel is used to schedule a program to run at startup or some other time in the future. Application installations, including malware, can put an item in Task Scheduler. When solving a problem with a sluggish Windows system, always check Task Scheduler to remove unnecessarily scheduled tasks from Windows startup. Do the following to learn about this tool:

1. Task Scheduler stores tasks in files and subfolders in the C:\Windows\System32\Tasks folder. Open **Explorer** and drill down into this folder to see the list of scheduled task files. One example is shown in Figure 14-21.

Figure 14-21   The Tasks folder contains tasks managed by Task Scheduler

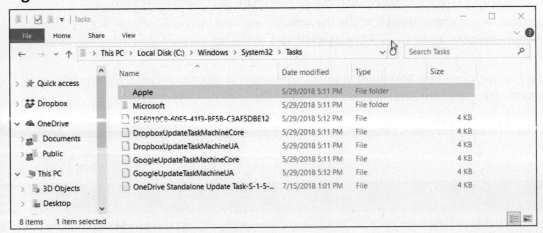

2. To open Task Scheduler, enter the `taskschd.msc` command or double-click **Task Scheduler** in the Administrative Tools/Windows Tools group. The Task Scheduler window is shown in Figure 14-22.

(continues)

14

Applying Concepts Continued

Figure 14-22   View and manage tasks from the Task Scheduler window

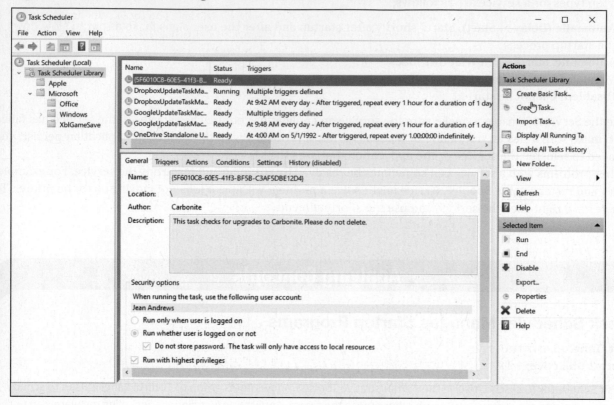

3. To explore tasks, drill down into groups and subgroups in the left pane. Notice in the left pane of Figure 14-22 that the groups and subgroups match up with the folder structure in the Tasks folder of Explorer. Tasks in a group are listed in the middle pane.

4. To see details about a task, including what triggers it, what actions it performs, the conditions and settings related to the task, and the history of past actions, select the task and then click the tabs in the lower-middle pane. For example, on the General tab shown in Figure 14-22, you can see that the Carbonite program task runs under the Jean Andrews account even when the user is not logged on.

5. To delete, disable, or run a task, select it, and in the Actions pane, click Delete, Disable, or Run. You can also create your own tasks. To do so, click **Create Basic Task** in the Actions pane, and follow the wizard to create the task.

6. When you're finished, close **Task Scheduler**. If you made changes in Task Scheduler, don't forget to restart the system to make sure all is well before you move on.

Note 9

Tasks can be hidden in the Task Scheduler window. To be certain you're viewing all scheduled tasks, unhide them. In the menu bar, click **View** and make sure **Show Hidden Tasks** is checked.

System File Checker

Core 2 Objective 1.2

Use the **System File Checker (SFC)** command to repair the Windows 10/11 system. The tool scans for and replaces corrupted or missing Windows system files, which include device drivers for many hardware devices. It cannot harm Windows, and it sometimes can solve problems with an unstable Windows system or essential hardware devices. To run SFC, close all applications, open an elevated command prompt window, and enter the `sfc /scannow` command (see Figure 14-23). If corrupted system files are found, the tool attempts to retrieve copies from its cache or download them through Windows Update.

Figure 14-23   Use System File Checker to verify Windows system files

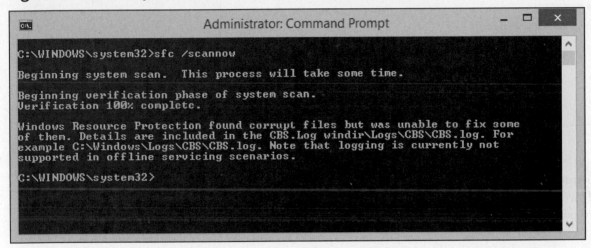

If you have problems running the SFC utility, use System Configuration to boot the computer into Safe boot, and run the `sfc /scannow` command again in Safe Mode. If you still have problems, the DISM command might help. You learn to use DISM in a project at the end of this module.

Note 10

Recall from the module "Maintaining Windows" that to get an elevated command prompt window, type **cmd** in the search box, right-click **Command Prompt**, and click **Run as administrator**.

System Configuration Offers Clean Boot and Safe Mode

Core 2 Objective 1.3

Use **System Configuration** (msconfig.exe) in the Administrative Tools/Windows Tools group to control Windows startup, including temporarily disabling programs from launching at startup. Doing so can help troubleshoot a startup problem or solve a problem with a sluggish Windows system. Do the following to learn more:

1. To open System Configuration, enter the `msconfig.exe` command. The System Configuration box is shown in Figure 14-24 with the General tab selected. Notice that Selective startup is selected, which means some items that would normally be launched at startup have been disabled. If you want a normal startup that loads all drivers and services, select **Normal startup**.

14

Figure 14-24   Use the General tab to control how Windows starts

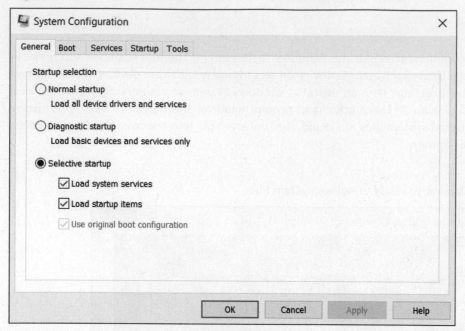

2. Click the **Services** tab, where you can disable any service from launching at startup.

3. Check **Hide all Microsoft services**. The list now shows only services put there by third-party software (see Figure 14-25). To perform what Microsoft calls a **clean boot**, you would click Disable all to disable all third-party software that would normally launch during the boot.

Figure 14-25   Use the Services tab of System Configuration to view and control services launched at startup

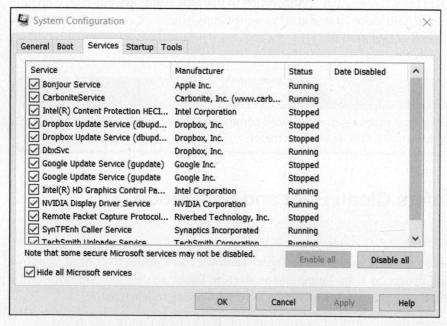

4. Click the **Boot** tab to see how you can further control the boot. Notice in Figure 14-26 that this system has a dual-boot configuration. When you select the Windows 7 installation on drive E:, you can click **Delete** to remove it from the boot menu, causing the computer to automatically boot to Windows 10. (You would also need to delete the Windows 7 installation files on drive E:.)

Figure 14-26   The Boot tab controls which installed OS launches

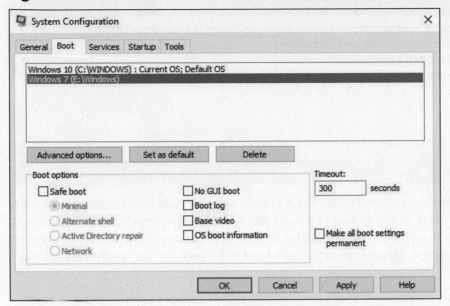

Safe Mode, also called Safe boot, goes beyond a clean boot by eliminating third-party software and also reducing startup to only the Windows minimum configuration necessary to start the OS. It can create a stable environment when the Windows system or device drivers become corrupted. There are several ways to start Safe Mode, which you learn about in the module "Troubleshooting Windows Startup." One way is to open System Configuration, click the **Boot** tab, and check **Safe boot** (see Figure 14-26). If the application in question needs the Internet to work, select **Network**. Click **OK** and restart the system.

If the application works in Safe Mode, you can assume the problem is not with the application but with the operating system or device drivers.

5. Click the **Tools** tab to get quick access to other Windows tools you might need during a troubleshooting session (see Figure 14-27).

Figure 14-27   The Tools tab makes it easy to find troubleshooting tools

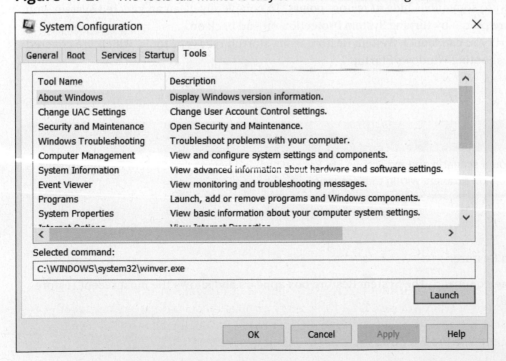

System Restore

Core 2 Objective 3.1

If you know the approximate date a Windows or application error started and that date is in the recent past, you can use System Restore (rstrui.exe) to restore the system to a point just before the problem started. Reverting to a restore point can solve problems with corrupted registry entries used by applications, device driver updates, or other Windows problems. However, System Restore can cause problems of its own, so use it with caution. Keep these points in mind:

- System Restore might make many changes to a system. If you know which change caused a problem, try to undo that particular change first. The idea is to use the least invasive solution first. For example, if updating a driver has caused a problem, first use Device Manager to perform a driver rollback and undo that change.
- System Restore won't help you if you don't have restore points to use. System Protection must be turned on so that restore points are automatically created.
- Restore points replace certain keys in the registry but cannot completely rebuild a totally corrupted registry. Therefore, System Restore can recover from errors only if the registry is somewhat intact.
- The restore process cannot remove a virus or worm infection. However, it might help you start a system that is infected with a virus that launches at startup. After Windows has started, you can then use anti-malware software to remove the infection.
- System Restore might create a new problem. Often when using a restore point, anti-malware software gets out of whack and sometimes even needs reinstalling. Therefore, use restore points sparingly.
- Restore points are kept in a hidden folder on the hard drive. If that area of the drive is corrupted, the restore points are lost. Also, if a user turns System Protection off, all restore points are lost.
- Viruses and other malware sometimes hide in restore points. To completely clean an infected system, you need to delete all restore points by turning System Protection off and back on.
- If Windows will not start, you can launch System Restore using startup recovery tools, which are covered in the module "Troubleshooting Windows Startup."

Exam Tip ✔

The A+ Core 2 exam gives you a scenario and expects you to know when and how to use System Restore to solve a Windows, hardware, or application problem within that scenario.

Here's how to use System Restore:

1. Enter the **rstrui.exe** command. The System Restore box appears and shows the most recent restore point (see Figure 14-28).

2. Do one of the following:

- For most situations, select the most recent restore point to make the least possible changes to your system, and then click **Next**.

- To see other restore points, select **Show more restore points**. Select a restore point. To see a list of programs that applying this restore point might affect, click **Scan for affected program**, write down the list of apps you might need to repair or install again, and then click **Close** to close the list.

3. Click **Next** and then click **Finish**. The system restarts and the restore point is applied.

Figure 14-28   Select the latest restore point

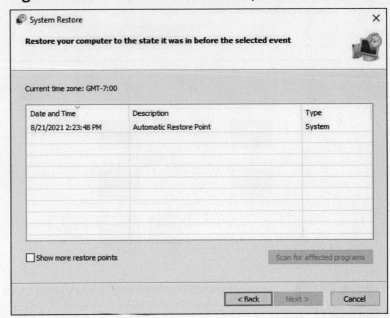

Registry Editor

Core 2 Objective 1.3

The **Registry Editor** (regedit.exe) is used to manually change the Windows registry. As an IT technician, you might be called on to edit the registry for a variety of purposes—if, for example, the Microsoft Edge browser gives an error and the Microsoft website tells you the problem can be solved by changing a particular value in a registry key.

Items in the registry are called keys, which are assigned values. A technician might need to remove a key or change its value. Let's learn how to manually edit the registry by first looking at how the registry is organized.

How the Registry Is Organized

The registry is the most important Windows component that holds information for Windows. The registry is a database designed with a treelike structure (called a hierarchical database) that contains configuration information for Windows, users, software applications, and installed hardware devices. During startup, Windows builds the registry in memory and keeps it there until Windows shuts down. During startup, after the registry is built, Windows reads from it to obtain information to complete the startup process. After Windows is loaded, it continually reads from many of the subkeys in the registry.

Windows builds the registry from the current hardware configuration and from information it takes from the following files:

- Five files stored in the C:\Windows\System32\config folder; these files are called hives, and they are named the SAM (Security Accounts Manager), SECURITY, SOFTWARE, SYSTEM, and DEFAULT hives.
- C:\Users*username*\Ntuser.dat file, which holds the preferences and settings of the currently signed-in user.

After the registry is built in memory, it is organized into five high-level keys (see Figure 14-29). Each key can have subkeys, and subkeys can have more subkeys and can be assigned one or more values. The way data is organized in the hive files is different from the way it is organized in registry keys. Figure 14-30 shows the relationship between registry keys and hives. For example, notice that the HKEY_CLASSES_ ROOT key contains data that comes from the SOFTWARE and DEFAULT hives, and some of this data is also stored in the larger HKEY_LOCAL_MACHINE key.

14

Figure 14-29 The Windows registry is logically organized in five keys with subkeys

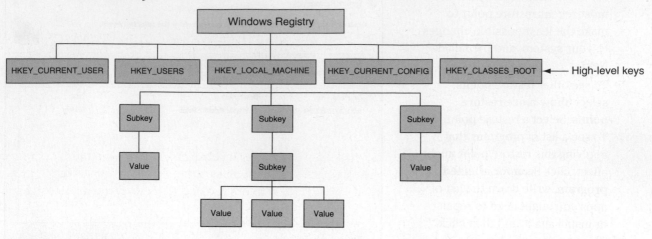

Figure 14-30 The relationship between registry keys and hives

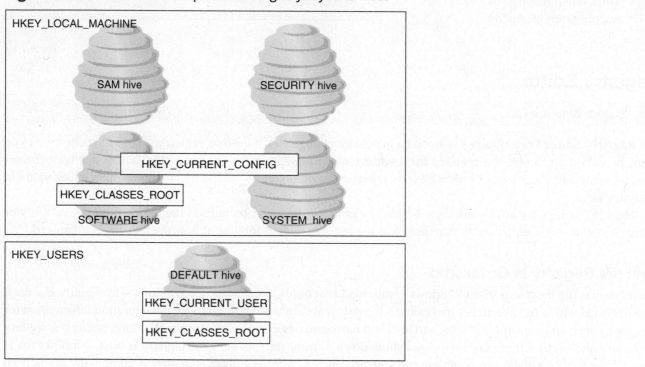

Here are the five keys, including where they get their data and their purposes:

- **HKEY_LOCAL_MACHINE (HKLM)** is the most important key and contains hardware, software, and security data. The data is taken from four hives: the SAM hive, the SECURITY hive, the SOFTWARE hive, and the SYSTEM hive. In addition, the HARDWARE subkey of HKLM is built when the registry is first loaded, based on data collected about the current hardware configuration.
- **HKEY_CURRENT_CONFIG (HKCC)** contains information that identifies each hardware device installed on the computer. Some of the data is gathered from the current hardware configuration when the registry is first loaded into memory. Other data is taken from the HKLM key, which got its data primarily from the SYSTEM hive.
- **HKEY_CLASSES_ROOT (HKCR)** stores information that determines which application to open when the user double-clicks a file. This file association relies on the file's extension. Data for this key is gathered from the HKLM key and the HKCU key.

- **HKEY_USERS (HKU)** contains data about all users and is taken from the DEFAULT hive.
- **HKEY_CURRENT_USER (HKCU)** contains data about the current user. The key is built when a user signs in using data kept in the HKEY_USERS key and in the Ntuser.dat file of the current user.

> **Note 12**
>
> Device Manager reads data from the HKLM\HARDWARE key to build the information it displays about hardware configurations. You can consider Device Manager to be an easy-to-view presentation of this HARDWARE key data.

Before You Edit the Registry, Back It Up!

When you think you need to edit the registry, if possible, first try to make the change from the Windows tool that is responsible for the key—for example, by using the Programs and Features applet in Control Panel. If that doesn't work and you must edit the registry, always back it up first. Changes made to the registry are implemented immediately.

> **Caution !**
>
> There is no undo feature in the Registry Editor, and no opportunity to change your mind once the edit is made. Errors made when editing the registry can do unexpected damage to the system. Be sure to back it up before you edit!

Here are the ways to back up the registry:

- **Use System Protection to create a restore point.** A restore point keeps information about the registry. You can restore the system to a restore point to undo registry changes as long as the registry is basically intact and not too corrupted.
- **Back up a single registry key just before you edit the key.** This method, called exporting a key, should always be used before you edit the registry. How to export a key is explained in the steps in the following section.
- **Make an extra copy of the C:\Windows\System32\config folder.** This is what I call the old-fashioned shotgun approach to backing up the registry. This backup will help if the registry gets totally trashed. You can boot from Windows setup media and use the Windows Recovery Environment to get a command prompt window that you can use to restore the folder from your extra copy. This method is drastic and not recommended except in severe cases. Still, just to be on the safe side, you can make an extra copy of this folder just before you start any serious digging into the registry.

In some situations, such as when you're going to make drastic changes to the registry, you'll want to play it safe and use more than one backup method. Extra registry backups are always a good thing! Now let's look at how to back up an individual key in the registry, and then you'll learn how to edit the registry.

Back Up, Edit, and Restore Individual Keys

A less time-consuming method of backing up the registry is to back up a particular key that you plan to edit. However, know that if the registry gets corrupted, having a backup of only a particular key most likely will not help you much when trying a recovery. Also, although you could use this technique to back up the entire registry or an entire tree within the registry, it is not recommended.

To back up a registry key along with its subkeys, follow these steps:

1. To open the Registry Editor, enter the **regedit** command and respond to the UAC box. Figure 14-31 shows the Registry Editor with the five main keys and several subkeys listed. Click the triangles on the left to see subkeys. When you select a subkey, such as KeyboardClass in the figure, the names of the values in that subkey are displayed in the right pane along with the data assigned to each value.

Figure 14-31 The Registry Editor showing the five main keys, subkeys, values, and data

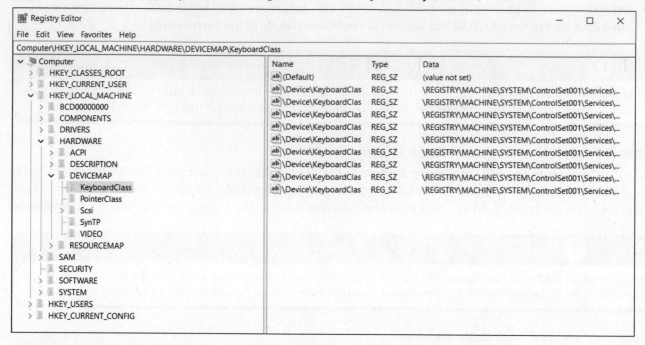

Note 13

The full path to a selected key is displayed in the bar at the top of the Registry Editor window. If the bar is missing, click View in the menu bar, and make sure Address Bar is checked.

2. Suppose we want to back up the registry key that contains a list of installed software, which is HKLM\SOFTWARE\Microsoft\Windows\CurrentVersion\Uninstall. (HKLM stands for HKEY_LOCAL_ MACHINE.) First click the appropriate triangles to navigate to the key. Next, right-click the key and select **Export** from the shortcut menu, as shown in Figure 14-32. The Export Registry File dialog box appears.

Figure 14-32 Using the Registry Editor, you can back up a key and its subkeys with the Export command

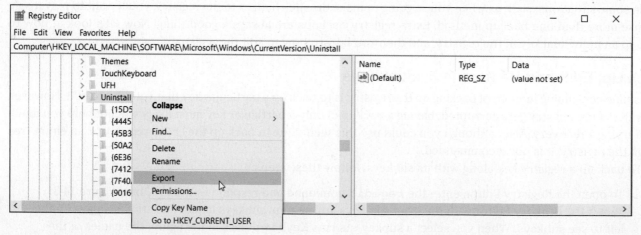

3. Select the location to save the export file, and name the file. The desktop is a convenient place to store an export file while you edit the registry. Click **Save** when done. The saved file will have a .reg file extension.

4. You can now edit a key you have exported or one of its subkeys. To search the registry for keys, values, and data, click **Edit** in the menu bar, and then click **Find**. Locate and select the key in the left pane of the editor. The values stored in the key display in the right pane.

5. To edit, rename, or delete a value, right-click it and select the appropriate option from the shortcut menu. Changes are immediately applied to the registry, and there is no undo feature. (However, Windows or applications might need to read the changed value before it affects their operations.)

6. Later, if you need to undo your changes, exit the Registry Editor, and double-click the saved export file. The key and its subkeys saved in the export file will be restored. After you're done with an export file, delete it so no one accidentally double-clicks it and reverts the registry to an earlier setting.

> **Caution** (!)
>
> Changes made to the registry take effect immediately. Therefore, take extra care when editing the registry. If you make a mistake and don't know how to correct a problem you create, double-click the exported key to recover. When you double-click an exported key, the registry is updated with the values stored in the key.

With a few tools in hand, let's tackle some common Windows problems. As we go, you'll pick up a few more tools and techniques.

Troubleshooting Windows Problems

Core 2 Objective 3.1

In this part of the module, we begin by listing in Table 14-2 some common problems you might encounter after Windows 10/11 has started up, along with the tools that might help you find a solution. Then we drill down into the details of solving these problems. Problems that occur during startup and their solutions are covered in the module "Troubleshooting Windows Startup."

Table 14-2   Common Windows problems and solutions after startup

Problems	Helpful Tools and Techniques
Services not starting	Use Task Manager and the Services console, uninstall and reinstall an app or service, and do a final reboot.
USB controller resource warnings	Use Device Manager, adjust settings in Power Options, and update the chipset drivers on the motherboard.
Time drift	On a Windows domain, use the Windows Time Service (W32Time) or third-party software for time accuracy.
Low memory warning	Use Task Manager, eliminate or repair an app with a memory leak, update the chipset drivers on the motherboard, and upgrade memory.
Sluggish performance	Use Task Manager, Resource Monitor, and Windows updates. Uninstall or disable unneeded apps, startup programs, and scheduled tasks. Try a clean boot. Upgrade hardware.
System instability	Use Event Viewer and Windows Update, repair or reinstall an app or service, and use Windows Memory Diagnostic, chkdsk, System File Checker, and Device Manager. Try a clean boot, Safe Mode, and System Restore. Repair Windows with a Windows 10/11 upgrade.
Application errors and crashes	Use Task Manager, taskkill, and uninstall and reinstall the app. Try a secondary logon and verify the app's digital signature. To eliminate conflicts with other apps, perform a clean boot, and then run the app.

14

Exam Tip

The common symptoms and problems listed in Table 14-2 are all on the A+ Core 2 exam. You need to know how to recognize the symptom, use Windows tools and other methods to observe the problem, and then fix the problem.

Steps to Solve Any Computer Problem

Core 2 Objective 3.1

You learned about the six steps to solve any computer problem in the Core 1 module "Power Supplies and Troubleshooting Computer Problems." Here is a summary of those steps:

- **Step 1. Identify the problem.** Begin by interviewing the user. Find out if the user has recently changed anything, and ask what happened around the time the problem started, such as recent thunderstorms and changes on the network. <u>Also ask if valuable data is on the system, and back it up if necessary.</u>

Core to Core ↔

You need to know A+ Core 1 content about best practices when solving any computer problem in the module "Power Supplies and Troubleshooting Computer Problems" to do well on the A+ Core 2 exam.

- **Step 2. Establish your theory of probable cause.** Ask the user to reproduce the problem while you watch. Many problems with applications are caused by user error. Watch carefully as the user shows you the problem. If you see them making a mistake, be tactful as you explain the problem and its solution.

Note 14

A problem might be caused by an underlying intermittent conflict or other issue. If the user is unable to reproduce the problem, don't dismiss the user's ability to help you understand the nature of the problem. Continue asking the user questions as you investigate the problem.

Try these things to discover the cause of the problem:

1. **Reboot the system.** Reboots solve a lot of application problems, and one might be a shortcut to your solution. (Before you restart the system, be sure to ask the user if they need to save their work.) Look for error messages that appear during Windows startup.
2. **Use Event Viewer, Task Manager, and Resource Monitor.** These tools can show you such things as error messages and events, services that have failed to start, and apps and devices hogging resources.
3. **Search the web and ask coworkers.** For Windows problems, search for the error message or description of the problem on the web. When you perform a Google search, add *site:microsoft.com* to the end of the search text to target your search to Microsoft websites. For problems with hardware and applications, try searching the website of the manufacturer for support and help. Also, search the web on the error message, application, or description of the problem. Look for forums where others have posted the same problem with the same app or device. Someone else has likely posted a solution. However, be careful and don't take the advice unless you trust the website. After you've made a reasonable effort to find help on your own, ask for help from coworkers who are more experienced.

Note 15

Working while a customer looks over your shoulder can be awkward. A customer needs the IT support technician to appear confident and in charge. To maintain your customer's confidence in your technical abilities, you might want to find privacy when searching the web or talking with coworkers.

- **Steps 3 and 4. Test your theory and fix the problem.** The rest of this module focuses on how to do that.
- **Steps 5 and 6. Verify, prevent, and document.** As you learned in the module "Power Supplies and Trouble-shooting Computer Problems," do one final reboot, and then verify with the user that all is working to their satisfaction. Implement preventive measures as appropriate, and don't forget to document your findings, actions, and outcomes.

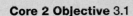

Note 16

> If you are troubleshooting a problem and make a change to the system, restart Windows and check to see if the problem is resolved before you move on to the next fix.

Now let's tackle each problem listed in Table 14-2.

Services Not Starting

Core 2 Objective 3.1

An error results when an application expects a background service to be running but it failed to start. Application documentation should tell you whether the app relies on a service to work. For example, suppose a user tells you that an app is not working; you verify that important data is backed up, and you research the web to discover that this app is dependent on a service running in the background. You now have a theory of probable cause. Here are the reasonable next steps to take:

- **Step 1. Task Manager.** Open **Task Manager** to find out what's currently running. On the **Processes** tab, you see the app is running, but the background process it requires is not running. You check the **Services** tab and see that the status of this service is Stopped. To start the service, right-click it and click **Start**.
- **Step 2. Services console.** Now you need to figure out why the service was not running in the first place. Open the **Services** console to make sure that the service is configured to start each time Windows starts.
- **Step 3. Final reboot.** Reboot the system to verify that the service and app are working as they should.

If problems persist, you might need to uninstall and reinstall the service or the application. Sometimes using the Programs and Features window to repair the application will take care of the problem.

USB Controller Resource Warnings

Core 2 Objective 3.1

USB ports might fail or become unreliable because their drivers are corrupted or because Power Options are not configured correctly. Do the following:

- **Step 1. Device Manager.** Check Device Manager for errors. Sometimes disabling or uninstalling a device and then enabling or reinstalling it can fix a problem. You can also try updating the USB drivers from Device Manager; however, a better option is to go to the motherboard manufacturer website and download and install the latest chipset drivers on the motherboard, following directions on the website.
- **Step 2. Power Options.** Open Power Options in Control Panel, and disable USB selective suspend, as you learned to do in the module "Maintaining Windows." Sometimes lowering the power state of inactive USB ports can make them unreliable.

Exam Tip

> The A+ Core 2 exam expects you to know how to configure Power Options to solve a problem with USB controller resource warnings.

14

Time Drift

Core 2 Objective 3.1

Time drift, also called **clock drift**, happens when a Windows system does not report accurate time to time-sensitive applications that require accuracy in milliseconds. When the CPU is operating consistently at high capacity (for example, in real-time stock trading applications), it might recognize a potential time drift and then request the time from the hardware clock on the motherboard. This clock, also known as the Real Time Clock (RTC) or the CMOS Clock, is not always accurate.

To prevent time drift, other methods must be used to synchronize the Windows clock. When Windows 10/11 is on a Windows domain, it can request the time via the **Windows Time Service (W32Time)**. Microsoft claims W32Time provides accuracy within 1 millisecond under reasonable operating conditions and does so by using the **Network Time Protocol (NTP)**. Using NTP, the primary time server, which is said to be working at Stratum 1 on the Windows domain, receives its time from an external time source working at Stratum 0 (see Figure 14-33). This time source can be a GPS or atomic device or a carrier service provided over the Internet. Computers that receive their time from the Stratum 1 server are at Stratum 2; computers at Stratum 3 receive their time from Stratum 2 servers. NTP requires there be no more than 15 Stratum layers. The higher the Stratum layer, the less accurate the time. Microsoft recommends the workstation be no further than Stratum 5 from the time source.

To set up a Windows workstation to use the W32Time service, do the following:

1. Use the **Services** console to set the W32Time service Startup type to Automatic. See Figure 14-34.
2. Edit the registry to set values given you by the network administrator, such as time intervals to poll the time server and the number of clock ticks to adjust for network latency (the time it takes on the network for the time server to send the time to the workstation).

Figure 14-33   NTP implements a time service providing time originating from a time device at Stratum 0

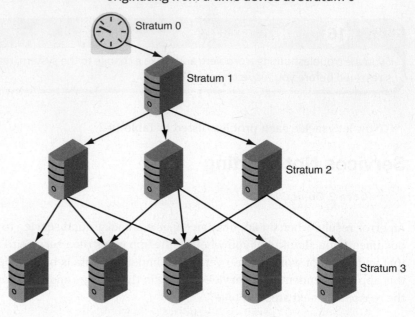

Figure 14-34   Set the W32Time service Startup type to Automatic

3. Stop and start the time service so the registry changes take effect.

4. To see the Stratum level assigned to a workstation, enter this command:

```
w32tm /query /status
```

If the Windows Time Service does not give accurate enough time, third-party applications can be used—some claim accuracy within 0.01 millisecond.

Low Memory Warning

 Core 2 Objective 3.1

You may get the Windows error message "Your computer is low on memory" because you do not have enough memory to run the applications you are using, malware or another program is sucking up system resources, the hard drive does not have enough free space to hold virtual memory, or you have too many apps and background processes running. A good computer troubleshooter checks the simple things first. Do the following:

- **Step 1. Task Manager.** Open **Task Manager** and check the Processes tab to find out which programs are using the most memory. Click the Memory column to sort by memory. Are there any memory-hungry apps you can close? Are there background services you don't need and can disable? Use Resource Monitor if you need more details as to how memory is used.

- **Step 2. Research the web.** If you see a suspicious process, search the web on the process name. Is it malware? How to scan for malware is covered in the module "Security Strategies." Does the web report that a process hogs memory or has a memory leak (does not release its unused memory back to the system)? Uninstall the program if you can do without it.

- **Step 3. Low on resources.** Windows uses both physical memory installed on the motherboard and **virtual memory** stored in pagefile.sys on the hard drive. The problem might be not enough physical memory or not enough virtual memory.

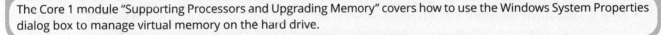

Core to Core

The Core 1 module "Supporting Processors and Upgrading Memory" covers how to use the Windows System Properties dialog box to manage virtual memory on the hard drive.

- **Step 4. System Information.** Use System Information to find out how much physical memory is installed. If you need to keep several apps open at the same time, you might need to add resources by upgrading memory or adding a second hard drive to hold virtual memory.

- **Step 5. Update chipset drivers.** If this is a new installation of Windows, updating the motherboard chipset drivers might help. It might be that the older drivers are not working well with Windows 10/11. Go to the motherboard manufacturer website to download and install the drivers.

Sluggish Performance

Core 2 Objective 3.1

Sluggish Windows performance can be caused by a variety of issues including malware, low system resources, too many programs and services running, and even a corrupted Windows installation. After you have interviewed the user and backed up data, follow these steps:

- **Step 1. Observe the system.** Too many programs running can slow down a system. Use Task Manager and Resource Monitor to help you identify programs that can be disabled or uninstalled, including programs that are no longer needed, those that are hogging resources, and rogue programs that might be malware.

14

- **Step 2. Verify Windows updates and antivirus settings.** Install the latest Windows updates, and verify the system is scanning for malware. Updates might solve known problems with applications, while a system scan can tell you if malware is at work.
- **Step 3. Uninstall applications you no longer need, and optimize the hard drive.** Uninstalling applications you no longer need should free up some space on the hard drive. Verify you have at least 15%–20% free space on the drive and that the drive is automatically optimized as you learned to do in the module "Maintaining Windows."
- **Step 4. Verify requirements for the OS and applications.** The system might be slow because the OS does not have the hardware resources it needs. Use System Information (msinfo32.exe) to find the model and speed of the installed processor and hard drive as well as the amount of memory installed. Compare all these values with the minimum and recommended requirements for Windows listed in the module "Installing Windows" and for each frequently used application. If you suspect that the processor, hard drive, or memory is a bottleneck, you can use Performance Monitor to get more information. If the bottleneck appears to be graphics, the problem might be solved by updating the graphics drivers or video adapter. If you find that the system is slow because of a hardware component, discuss the situation with the user.
- **Step 5. Search for unnecessary startup programs you can eliminate.** Open the **Startup** tab in Task Manager. In the list of startup items, look for a specific startup program you don't want. If you're not sure of the purpose of a program, right-click it, and click **Search online** in the shortcut menu. Then search the web for information on this program. Be careful to use only reliable sites for credible information.

Caution

A word of caution is important here: Many websites will tell you a legitimate process is malicious so you will download and use their software to get rid of the process. However, their software is likely to be adware or spyware that you don't want. Make sure you can trust a site before you download from it or follow its advice.

- **Step 6. Disable or uninstall startup items.** If you want to find out whether disabling a startup entry gives problems or improves performance, temporarily disable it using Task Manager. To permanently disable a startup item, it's best to uninstall the software or remove the entry from a startup folder. See the appendix "Entry Points for Windows Startup Processes" for a list of startup folders.

Note 17

The startup folder for all users is hidden by default. In the module "Maintaining Windows," you learned how to "unhide" folders that are hidden.

- **Step 7. Search for unwanted scheduled tasks.** Open **Task Scheduler** and search through tasks to find those you think are unnecessary or causing trouble. Research the software the task works with, and then decide if you want to uninstall the software or disable the task. The best way to uninstall a scheduled task is to uninstall the software that is responsible for the task.

For extremely slow systems that need a more drastic fix, set Windows for a clean boot. Then restart the system, enable the programs you really need, and watch for errors. Enable just the services and programs you need.

Regardless of the method you use, be sure to restart the system after each change and note what happens. Do you get an error message? Does a device or application no longer work? If so, you have probably disabled a service or program you need.

Has performance improved? If performance does not improve by disabling services or startup programs, go back and enable them again. If a non-Microsoft service or startup program didn't cause the problem, turn your attention to Microsoft services or startup programs. Start disabling them one at a time.

> **Caution** ⚠️
>
> You might be tempted to disable all Microsoft services. If you do, however, you will disable Networking, Event Logging, Error Reporting, Windows Firewall, Windows Installer, Windows Backup, Print Spooler, Windows Update, System Protection, and other important services. These services should be disabled only when testing for performance problems and then immediately enabled when the test is finished. Also, know that if you disable the Volume Shadow Copy service, all restore points kept on the system will be lost. If you intend to use System Restore to fix a problem with the system, don't disable this service. If you are not sure what a service does, read its description in the Services console before you change its status.

Remember that you don't want to permanently leave System Configuration or Task Manager in control of startup. After you have used these tools to identify the problem, use other tools to permanently remove the problem service or program from startup. Use the Services console to disable a service, use the Programs and Features window to uninstall software, and remove program files from startup folders. After the problem is fixed, return System Configuration and/or Task Manager to a normal startup.

Don't forget to restart the computer after making a change to verify that all is well.

System Instability

> **Core 2 Objective** 3.1

When a Windows system is unstable, it can hang or give errors at any time or even shut down unexpectedly. The problem can be caused by a virus, by corrupted data files, Windows system files, application software or device drivers, or by failing essential hardware devices. This part of the module covers what you can do to observe the system and solve the problem after you have interviewed the user and backed up data. A great place to begin to form your theory of probable cause is Event Viewer. And, as always, when you think the problem is solved, don't forget to do one last reboot to verify all is well and also complete your documentation.

Applying Concepts

Event Viewer Solves a Mystery

Est. Time: 15 minutes
Core 2 Objective: 1.3

Event Viewer can be useful in solving intermittent hardware problems. For example, I once worked in an office where several people updated Microsoft Word documents stored on a file server. For weeks, people complained about these Word documents getting corrupted. We downloaded the latest patches for Windows and Microsoft Office and scanned for viruses, thinking that the problem might be with Windows or the application. Then we suspected that a template file used to build the Word documents was corrupted. But nothing we did solved our problem of corrupted Word documents. Finally one day someone thought to check Event Viewer on the file server. Event Viewer had faithfully been recording errors when writing to the hard drive. What we had suspected to be a software problem was in fact a failing hard drive, which was full of bad sectors. We replaced the drive, and the problem went away. That day I learned the value of checking Event Viewer very early in the troubleshooting process.

14

Here are the general steps you can follow to observe the system and solve a problem with system instability (we'll discuss each step in more detail next):

- **Step 1.** Use Event Viewer to look for errors and warnings.
- **Step 2.** Update Windows and verify anti-malware settings.
- **Step 3.** Suspect a corrupted application or supporting service.
- **Step 4.** Suspect faulty memory.
- **Step 5.** Suspect a corrupted hard drive.
- **Step 6.** Suspect corrupted Windows system files.
- **Step 7.** Suspect corrupted device drivers.
- **Step 8.** Suspect corrupted third-party services or apps running in the background.
- **Step 9.** Suspect the Windows installation is corrupted.

Now let's look at the details of each of these nine steps:

- **Step 1. Use Event Viewer to look for errors and warnings.** Recall that the Administrative Events log in Event Viewer collects errors and warnings to help with problem solving. Investigate warning and error events that might point to the source of the problem. A web search on the message can help.
- **Step 2. Update Windows and verify anti-malware settings.** Make sure Windows is updated, and other Microsoft products are included in Windows updates. Eliminate malware by checking that anti-malware settings are correct. If you find real-time protection is not on, do a full scan for malware.
- **Step 3. Suspect a corrupted application or supporting service.** If you observe that instability happens when a particular application is running, try to repair the application. If that doesn't work, uninstall and reinstall the app.
- **Step 4. Suspect faulty memory.** Errors with memory are often difficult to diagnose because they can appear intermittently and might be mistaken for application errors, user errors, or other hardware component errors. With memory errors, the system may hang, a BSOD (blue screen of death) error might occur, or the system may continue to function, with applications giving errors or data being corrupted. You can quickly identify a problem with memory or eliminate memory as the source of a problem by using the Windows Memory Diagnostics (mdsched.exe) tool.

Applying Concepts

Is Memory Failing?

Est. Time: 30 minutes
Core 2 Objective: 3.1

The **Memory Diagnostics** (mdsched.exe) tool works before Windows is loaded to test memory for errors and can be used on computers that don't have Windows installed. Use one of these two methods to start the utility:

- **Use the mdsched.exe command.** After Windows has started, enter the **mdsched.exe** command. A dialog box appears and asks if you want the tool to immediately restart the system and run the test, or wait until the next restart.
- **Boot from Windows setup media.** If Windows is not the installed operating system or you cannot boot from the hard drive, boot the computer from the Windows setup USB drive or DVD to test memory for errors. Follow these steps:

1. If necessary, change the boot priority order in BIOS/UEFI setup to boot first from the optical drive or USB drive. Boot from the Windows setup DVD or USB drive.

2. On the opening screen, select your language and click **Next**. On the next screen (see Figure 14-35), click **Repair your computer**. Next choose **Troubleshoot**.

Figure 14-35   The opening menu when you boot from
                     Windows 10 setup media

3. On the Advanced options screen (see Figure 14-36), choose **Command Prompt**. In the command prompt window, enter the **mdsched.exe** command.

Figure 14-36   The Windows 10 Advanced options screen launched from
                     Windows 10 setup media

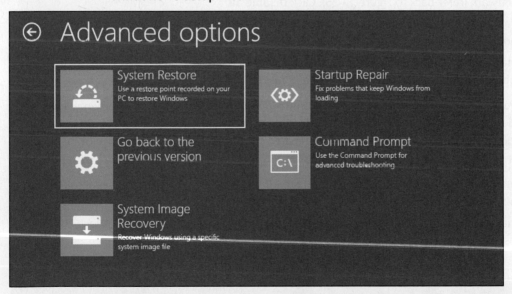

If the tool reports memory errors, replace all memory modules installed on the motherboard.

- **Step 5. Suspect a corrupted hard drive.** To eliminate the hard drive as the source of an unstable system, run the `chkdsk c: /r` command to check the drive. The error-checking utility searches for bad sectors on a volume and recovers the data from them if possible. It then marks the sector as bad so it will not be reused. Also check Event Viewer for warnings or errors regarding the hard drive.

- **Step 6. Suspect corrupted Windows system files.** Use the System File Checker (SFC) to scan for corrupted or missing system files, and replace them with a fresh copy. Enter the `sfc /scannow` command in an elevated command prompt window. If you still have problems, use System Configuration to perform a Safe boot. In Safe Mode, enter the `sfc /scannow` command. If that doesn't solve the problem, try System Restore.

- **Step 7. Suspect corrupted device drivers.** Check Device Manager for errors. If a device shows a problem that has recently been updated, roll back driver updates. Try updating drivers. Try uninstalling and reinstalling the device.

- **Step 8. Suspect corrupted third-party services or apps running in the background.** Follow the steps given next to perform a clean boot.

Applying Concepts

Perform a Clean Boot

Est. Time: 30 minutes
Core 2 Objective: 3.1

Here's how to perform a clean boot to disable all third-party software during Windows startup:

1. To open System Configuration, enter the `msconfig.exe` command. The System Configuration box is shown earlier in Figure 14-24 with the General tab selected.

2. Click the **Services** tab and check **Hide all Microsoft services**. The list now shows only services put there by third-party software (refer back to Figure 14-25). Click **Disable all**.

3. Click the **General** tab and notice that Selective startup is now selected. Click **Apply** and close the System Configuration box.

4. Open **Task Manager** and select the **Startup** tab (refer back to Figure 14-17). For each startup item, select it and click **Disable**. Close the Task Manager window and restart Windows.

Verify that the problem is solved in a clean boot environment. If the problem is solved, keep enabling several startup programs and rebooting until you zero in on the offending startup service or app.

After you have uninstalled the problem program or eliminated startup programs as the source of the problem, be sure to do the following to return to a normal Windows startup:

1. Open the **System Configuration** box. On the General tab, click **Normal startup**. On the Services tab, uncheck **Hide all Microsoft services**. Verify that all services are now checked.

2. Open **Task Manager**. In the Task Manager window, select each startup item and enable it. Close all windows and restart the system.

> **Caution** ⊙
>
> Don't depend on System Configuration or Task Manager to be a permanent fix to disable a startup program or service. Once you've decided you want to make the change permanent, use other methods to permanently remove that process from Windows startup. For example, you might uninstall a program, remove it from a startup folder, or use the Services console to disable a service.

- **Step 9. Suspect the Windows installation is corrupted.** By now in the troubleshooting process, you have eliminated memory, the hard drive, Windows system files, malware, and third-party services and programs as the likely source of system instability. It's time to consider the entire Windows installation might be corrupted. Recall from the module "Installing Windows" that you can repair Windows 10/11 by performing an in-place upgrade. Follow directions given in that module to download and upgrade the Windows 10/11 installation. If the problem is still not solved, consider whether the CPU or motherboard is failing.

Core to Core

How to troubleshoot a failing motherboard or CPU is covered in the Core 1 module "Power Supplies and Troubleshooting Computer Problems" and is content on the A+ Core 1 exam.

Application Errors and Crashes

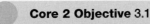
Core 2 Objective 3.1

For application errors and crashes—as you do for any computer problem—begin by interviewing the user, backing up important data, examining the system, investigating the problem, and establishing a theory of probable cause. For application crashes, consider and do these things:

- **Step 1. End a hung application.** If an application refuses to close, recall you can use Task Manager to end the application. If the app still refuses to close, do the following:

  1. On the **Details** tab of Task Manager, note the process identifier (PID) of the process—for example, 7132.
  2. In a command prompt window, enter the command `taskkill /f /pid:7132`, substituting the PID you noted in Step 1. The /f parameter forcefully kills the process. Be careful when using this command; it is so powerful that you can end critical system processes that will cause the system to shut down.

- **Step 2. Search the web on error messages and symptoms.** Suppose the error message in Figure 14-37 appears when a user clicks a link in an Outlook email message. A quick web search shows the problem is that the Microsoft browser is not the Windows default browser. Changing the default browser quickly solves the problem.

Figure 14-37 Search the web on an error message or symptom to find an explanation and solution

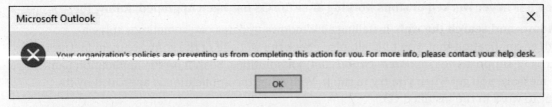

- **Step 3. Consider data corruption.** For applications such as Microsoft 365 that use data files, it might appear that the application, Windows, or hardware has a problem when the problem is really a corrupted data file. Try creating an entirely new data file. If that works, then suspect that previous errors might be caused by corrupted data.

> **Note 18**
>
> You might be able to recover part of a corrupted file by changing its file extension to .txt and importing it into the application as a text file.

- **Step 4. Check application settings and logs for errors.** Maybe a user has made one too many changes to the application settings, which can cause a problem with missing toolbars and other functions. Write down each setting the user has changed, and then restore all settings back to their default values. If the problem is solved, restore each setting to the way the user had it until you find the one causing the problem. The process will take some time, but users can get upset if you change their application settings without justification.
- **Step 5. Repair or update the application.** The application setup might have the option to repair the installation. Look for it in the Programs and Features window or on the manufacturer's website. If Windows update settings allow it, Microsoft apps are updated along with Windows updates.

> **Caution** !
>
> When researching a problem on the web, you might discover that Microsoft or a manufacturer offers a fix or patch you can download and apply. To get the right patch, recall you need to make sure you get a 32-bit patch for a 32-bit installation of Windows, a device driver, or an application. For a 64-bit installation of Windows, make sure you get a 64-bit device driver. An application installed in a 64-bit OS might be a 32-bit application or a 64-bit application.

- **Step 6. Uninstall and reinstall the application.** Do so with caution because you might lose any customized settings, macros, or scripts. Also know this still might not solve a problem with a corrupted application because registry entries might not be properly reset during the uninstall process.

Here are other errors that might occur with applications and what to do about them:

- **If a data file fails to open, change the default program for the file type.** Windows depends on the file extension to associate a data file with an application used to open it; this is called the **file association**. An application associated with a file extension is called its **default program**. To change a file association, right-click the file in Explorer and click **Open with**, click **Choose another app**, check **Always use this app to open files**, and then find and select the new application.
- **If an application has never worked or stops working after the OS has been upgraded, follow these steps:**
  1. **Update Windows and search the web.** Installing all Windows updates can sometimes solve a problem with an application that won't install. Also check the website of the software manufacturer and the Microsoft support site (*support.microsoft.com*) for solutions. Search on the application name or the error message you get when you try to run it. Verify that the application is approved by its manufacturer to work in the installed OS.
  2. **Run the installation program or application as an administrator.** The program might require that the user have privileges not assigned to the current user account. Try running the application with administrator privileges, which Windows calls a **secondary logon**. Use Explorer to locate the executable program file in a subfolder of the Program Files or Program Files (x86) folder. Right-click the file and select **Run as administrator** from the shortcut menu (see Figure 14-38).

Figure 14-38   Execute a program using administrative privileges

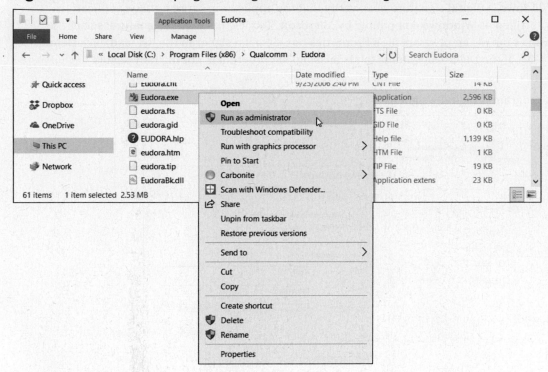

Note 19

To run a program from a user account other than administrator, hold down the Shift key and right-click the program file. Then select **Run as different user** from the shortcut menu. You must then enter the user name and password of another user account in the Windows Security box.

If the program works when you run it with administrative privileges, you can make that setting permanent. To do so, right-click the program and select **Properties** from the shortcut menu. Then click the **Compatibility** tab and check **Run this program as an administrator** (see Figure 14-39). Click **Apply** and then close the Properties box. If the Compatibility tab is missing in the Properties dialog box, you can enable it using the Group Policy Editor. You learn to use this editor in the module "Securing and Sharing Windows Resources."

Figure 14-39   Permanently change the privilege level of an application

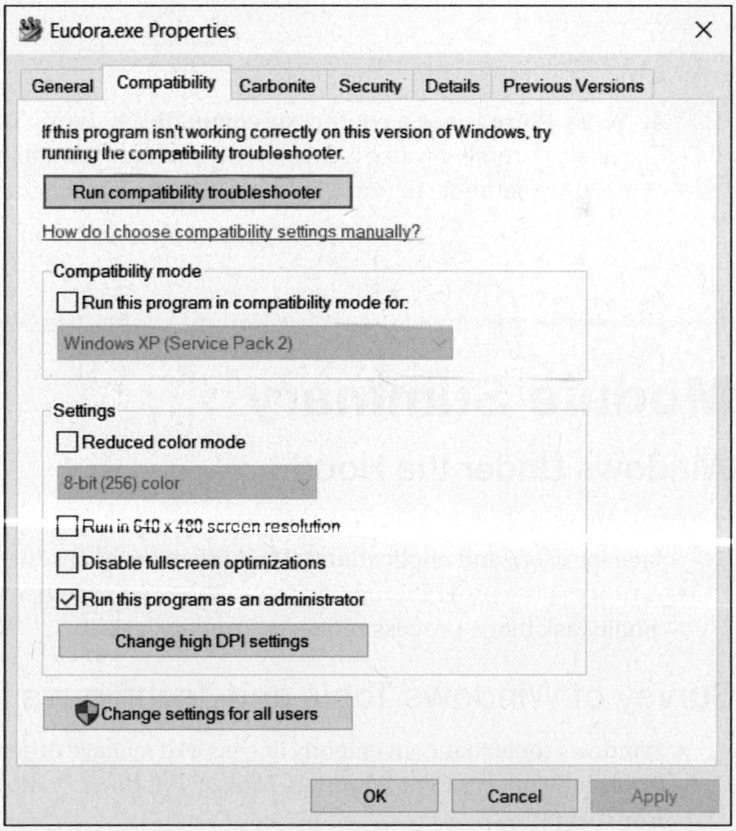

Eudora.exe Properties   ✕

General   **Compatibility**   Carbonite   Security   Details   Previous Versions

If this program isn't working correctly on this version of Windows, try running the compatibility troubleshooter.

[Run compatibility troubleshooter]

How do I choose compatibility settings manually?

Compatibility mode
☐ Run this program in compatibility mode for:

Windows XP (Service Pack 2)

Settings
☐ Reduced color mode

8-bit (256) color

☐ Run in 640 x 480 screen resolution

☐ Disable fullscreen optimizations

☑ Run this program as an administrator

[Change high DPI settings]

🛡 Change settings for all users

OK   Cancel   Apply

14

3. **Verify that the application is digitally signed.** Although applications that are not digitally signed can still run on Windows, a digital signature does verify that the application is not a rogue application and that it is certified as Windows-compatible by Microsoft. To view the digital signature, select the **Digital Signatures** tab of the program file's Properties box. Select a signer in the list, and click **Details** (see Figure 14-40). If the Digital Signatures tab is missing, the program is not digitally signed.

Figure 14-40   This program is digitally signed

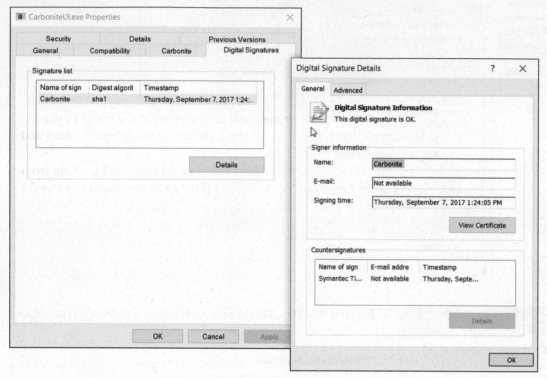

4. **Verify there is not a conflict or compatibility issue.** To eliminate these conflicts, run the application causing problems after a clean boot. If a clean boot allows the application to run without errors, you need to methodically zero in on the third-party program until you discover the one in conflict.

Module Summary

Windows Under the Hood

- The Windows OS is made up of two main components: the shell and the kernel. The shell provides an interface for users and applications. The kernel is responsible for interacting with hardware.
- A process is a program running under the shell, together with all the resources assigned to it. A thread is a single task that a process requests from the kernel.

Survey of Windows Tools and Techniques for Troubleshooting

- Windows tools that conveniently access and manage other Windows tools are Control Panel, Administrative Tools in Windows 10 or Windows Tools in Windows 11, Computer Management, and Microsoft Management Console (MMC).

- Tools to observe, track, and log Windows, user, network, application, and hardware activities are Event Viewer, Resource Monitor, and Performance Monitor.
- Tools for solving Windows, application, networking, and Windows user problems are Task Manager, the Services console, System Configuration, and the Registry Editor.
- Tools for solving Windows corruption are System File Checker, Windows Updates, and System Restore.
- Tools and techniques for solving application and hardware problems are Programs and Features, secondary logon, digital signature verification, Task Scheduler, Device Manager, and chkdsk.

Troubleshooting Windows Problems

- Problems related to Windows and its applications include services not starting, USB controller resource warnings, time drift, low memory warnings, sluggish performance, system instability, and applications crashing.
- For all computer problems, follow a six-step solution: (1) identify the problem by asking the user to explain what happened and show you the problem; (2) establish your theory of probable cause; (3) test your theory; (4) fix the problem; (5) verify the solution and, if possible, prevent the problem from happening again; and (6) document your findings, actions, and outcomes.
- When solving Windows-related problems, be sure to interview the user, back up data, and get help from error messages, the web, coworkers, and event logs. Also, consider that the data or the application might be corrupted; consider outside interference such as malware, faulty memory, a corrupted hard drive, low system resources, and incompatible applications or third-party services; and consider that Windows might be corrupted.
- Tasks that might be involved when troubleshooting Windows problems include rebooting; restarting a service; uninstalling, reinstalling, and updating an application; adding resources; verifying requirements; performing a system file check; and repairing Windows.
- A clean boot or booting into Safe Mode can help eliminate applications, services, and device drivers that might contribute to Windows problems.
- On a Windows domain, a time server can be accessed using NTP and the Windows Time Service (W32Time).
- In Explorer, use the shortcut menu for a data file to create a file association so Windows knows which application is associated with the given data file. This can solve the problem of a file that fails to open.

Key Terms

For explanations of key terms, see the Glossary for this text.

Administrative Tools	HKEY_CURRENT_ CONFIG (HKCC)	process	thread
clean boot		registry	time drift
clock drift	HKEY_CURRENT_USER (HKCU)	Registry Editor	user mode
Computer Management		Resource Monitor	user profile namespace
console	HKEY_LOCAL_MACHINE (HKLM)	Safe Mode	virtual memory
default program		secondary logon	Windows Time Service (W32Time)
Event Viewer	HKEY_USERS (HKU)	Services console	
executive services	kernel mode	shell	Windows Tools
file association	Memory Diagnostics	snap-in	
HAL (hardware abstraction layer)	Microsoft Management Console (MMC)	System Configuration	
		System File Checker (SFC)	
HKEY_CLASSES_ROOT (HKCR)	Network Time Protocol (NTP)	Task Manager	
	Performance Monitor	Task Scheduler	

14

Thinking Critically

These questions are designed to prepare you for the critical thinking required for the A+ exams and may use information from other modules and the web.

1. A user complains that their computer is performing slowly. They tell you the problem started about a week ago when new database software was installed. The software runs in the background to update a database synced between the user's workstation and the database server. Which is the best tool or method to use to determine if the new software is hogging computer resources?

   a. Uninstall the database software and see if performance improves.
   b. Use Performance Monitor and Process counters to observe performance.
   c. Use the Performance tab of Task Manager to observe database software activity.
   d. Install more memory to improve system resources to handle the new software.

2. You have exhausted your knowledge of a problem, and it still is not solved. Before you escalate it, what else can you do?

   a. Go back through the problem one more time, looking for what you overlooked.
   b. Explain to the user that you cannot solve the problem, but you will find someone who can.
   c. Ask a knowledgeable coworker for help.
   d. Interview the user one more time to make sure you correctly understand the problem.

3. You are having difficulty uninstalling freeware a user accidentally installed while surfing the web. You look online and see the software is designed to work in an x86-based version of Windows. In which folder should you expect to find the program files for the software?

   a. C:\Windows
   b. C:\Program Files (x86)
   c. C:\Program Files
   d. It depends on the version of Windows installed.

4. You are troubleshooting an application problem and want to eliminate faulty memory as a source of the problem. Which command do you use?

   a. mdsched.exe
   b. taskmgr.exe
   c. msconfig.exe
   d. sfc/scannow

5. When a user, Belinda Lim, signs in to Windows, she cannot see her Documents folder in Explorer, and some of her Windows user settings are lost. You suspect her user profile is corrupted. Which tool or method should you use first to investigate and/or solve the problem? Second?

   a. Check the C:\User\Belinda Lim\Documents folder.
   b. Check the C:\Users\Belinda Lim\Documents folder.
   c. Use the chkdsk command.
   d. Use the sfc command.

6. An application is frozen, and you cannot close its application window. What is the first thing you should do to end the process? Second?

   a. Use the tasklist command.
   b. Use Task Manager.
   c. Reboot the system.
   d. Use the taskkill command.

7. How can you eliminate the possibility that an application error is caused by another application or service running in the background?

8. How does Windows know which application to use to open a file when you double-click the file in Explorer?

9. When Windows first starts and the user signs in, a message about a missing DLL appears. Which tool or method should you use first to solve the problem? Second?

   a. Use Task Manager to identify the startup process.
   b. Use the Services console to stop the process that needed the DLL.
   c. Search the web on the error message to better understand the problem.
   d. Use Component Services to register the DLL.

10. If an application works after a clean boot but does not work when Windows is loaded normally, what can you assume?

11. A user tells you that Microsoft Word gives errors when saving a file. What should you do first? Second?

   a. Install Windows updates that also include patches for Microsoft Word.
   b. Ask the user when the problem first started.
   c. Do all you can to help the user save their work.
   d. Ask the user to save the error message as a screenshot the next time the error occurs and email it to you.
   e. Use Task Manager to end the Microsoft Word program.

12. When trying to improve performance of a slow system, you notice in Task Manager that the superfetch service is using a high percentage of CPU time. What is your best next step?

   a. Disable superfetch to improve performance.
   b. Update Windows to improve superfetch performance.
   c. Superfetch is an essential Windows process and should not be disabled. Move on to other solutions to improve performance.
   d. Ask the user if they use the superfetch service. If they don't, uninstall it.

13. You need to install a customized console on 10 Windows 10 computers. What is the best way to do that?

   a. When installing the console on the first computer, write down each step to make it easier to do the same chore on the other nine.
   b. Create the console on one computer, and copy the .mmc file to the other nine.
   c. Create the console on one computer, and copy the .msc file to the other nine.
   d. Make sure all computers are using Windows 10 Pro because Windows Home does not support MMC. Then create a console on each Windows 10 Pro computer.

14. What is the name of the program file that you can enter in the Windows search box to execute Event Viewer? What process is running when Event Viewer is displayed on the screen? Why do you think the running process is different from the program file name?

15. When cleaning up the startup process, which of these should you do first?

   a. Use the Registry Editor to look for keys that hold startup processes.
   b. Run System Configuration to see what processes are started.
   c. After you have launched several applications, use Task Manager to view a list of running tasks.
   d. Run the Defrag utility to optimize the hard drive.

16. Using the Internet, investigate each of the following startup processes. Identify the process and write a one-sentence description.

   a. Acrotray.exe
   b. CDASrv.exe

17. Using Task Manager, you discover an unwanted program that is launched at startup. Of the items listed, which ones might lead you to a permanent solution to the problem? Which ones would not be an appropriate solution to the problem? Explain why they are not appropriate.

   a. Look at the registry key that launched the program to help determine where in Windows the program was initiated.
   b. Use Task Manager to disable the program.
   c. Search Task Scheduler for the source of the program being launched.
   d. Use System Configuration to disable the program.
   e. Search the startup folders for the source of the program.

18. List the program file name and path for the following utilities. (Hint: You can use Explorer or a Windows search to locate files.)

   a. Task Manager
   b. System Configuration
   c. Services Console
   d. Microsoft Management Console
   e. Registry Editor

19. You suspect that Windows 10 has become corrupted. What is the least invasive solution to fix the problem?

   a. Use System Restore.
   b. Perform an in-place upgrade of Windows 10.
   c. Use the System File Checker.
   d. Perform a clean boot.

20. Which Event Viewer log do you search to find errors and warning? To find whether a particular user has entered multiple bad passwords trying to sign in to Windows?

   a. Administrative Events log
   b. Security log
   c. Setup log
   d. System log

21. When troubleshooting an unstable Windows installation, you discover the problem still persists when you perform a clean boot, but it does not present when you boot into Safe Mode. What does this tell you about the problem?

   a. Third-party services or apps are in conflict or corrupted
   b. User profiles are corrupted
   c. The Windows installation is corrupted
   d. Malware has infected the system

Hands-On Projects

Hands-On Project 14-1

Using the Microsoft Management Console

Est. Time: 30 minutes
Core 2 Objective: 1.3

Using the Microsoft Management Console, create a customized console. Put two snap-ins in the console: Device Manager and Event Viewer. Store your console on the Windows desktop. Copy the console to another computer, and install it on the Windows desktop.

Hands-On Project 14-2

Using Event Viewer

Est. Time: 15 minutes
Core 2 Objective: 1.3

Event Viewer can be intimidating to use, but it is really nothing more than a bunch of logs you can search and manipulate. If you have Microsoft 365 installed, open a Word document, make some changes in it, and close it without saving your changes. Now open **Event Viewer** and look in **Applications and Services Logs** and **Microsoft Office Alerts**. What event is recorded about your actions?

Hands-On Project 14-3

Launching Programs at Startup

Est. Time: 30 minutes
Core 2 Objective: 3.1

Do the following to practice launching programs at startup, listing the steps you took for each activity:

1. Configure Scheduled Tasks to launch Notepad each time the computer starts and any user signs in. List the steps you took.
2. Put a shortcut in a startup folder so any user launches a command prompt window at startup. See the appendix "Entry Points for Windows Startup Processes" for a list of startup folders.
3. Restart the system and verify that both programs are launched. Did you receive any errors?
4. Remove the two programs from the startup process.

Hands-On Project 14-4

Editing and Restoring the Registry

Est. Time: 30 minutes
Core 2 Objective: 1.3

When you install Windows on a new computer, Windows setup gives you the opportunity to enter the computer's registered owner and registered organization. Practice editing and restoring the registry by doing the following to change the registered owner name:

1. Enter the command `winver.exe`, which displays the About Windows box. Who is the registered owner and registered organization of the computer? If asked to do so by your instructor, take a screenshot of the About Windows box showing the registered owner.
2. Using the Registry Editor, export the registry key HKEY_LOCAL_MACHINE\SOFTWARE\Microsoft\Windows NT\CurrentVersion to an export file stored on the desktop.

(continues)

14

Hands-On Project Continued

3. With the HKEY_LOCAL_MACHINE\SOFTWARE\Microsoft\Windows NT\CurrentVersion key selected in the left pane, double-click the **RegisteredOwner** value in the right pane. The Edit String box appears (see Figure 14-41). Change the Value data, which is highlighted in the box, and click **OK**.

Figure 14-41   Change the name of the registered owner of Windows

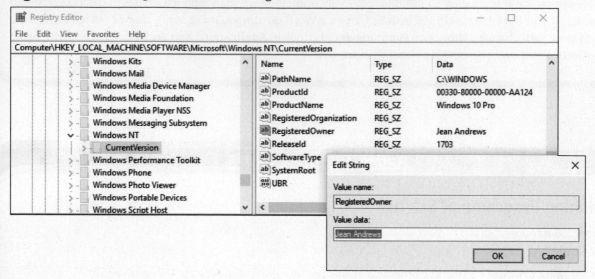

4. Enter the `winver` command again to display the About Windows box. Did the new name appear as the registered owner? Your instructor might require you to take a screenshot of the About Windows box showing the registered owner. Close the box.

5. Close the Registry Editor window. To restore the Value data to its original name, double-click the exported key on your desktop. Once again, run the `winver` command to display the About Windows box and verify that the original name is restored. Close the box.

6. Delete the exported registry key stored on the desktop.

Real Problems, Real Solutions

Real Problem 14-1

Performing a Clean Boot

Est. Time: 30 minutes
Core 2 Objective: 3.1

Look on the Startup tab in Task Manager, and research the purpose of each startup process in the list. Are any of these programs essential to Windows? Following directions in the module, perform a clean boot. Check the Startup tab in Task Manager again. Do you see any programs enabled? What effect did the clean boot have on your computer? Do you see a performance improvement?

Real Problem 14-2

Cleaning Up Startup

Est. Time: 45 minutes
Core 2 Objective: 3.1

Using a computer that has a problem with a sluggish startup, apply the tools and procedures you learned in this module to clean up the startup process. Take detailed notes of each step you take and its results. (If you are having a problem finding a computer with a sluggish startup, consider offering your help to a friend, a family member, or a nonprofit organization.)

Real Problem 14-3

Using DISM to Repair Windows

Est. Time: 45 minutes excluding download time
Core 2 Objective: 3.1

The DISM (Deployment Image Servicing and Management) commands are used to create, manage, and deploy standard system images. When SFC cannot fix a problem with a corrupted Windows 10/11 installation, you can use DISM commands to repair system files.

You'll need a standard image. If you don't have one, you can extract one from the Windows setup files:

1. If you don't have a copy of the Windows setup ISO file from the Microsoft website, follow directions in the module "Installing Windows" to download the ISO file.
2. In Explorer, right-click the ISO file, and click **Mount**. The ISO file is mounted and assigned a drive letter. You can now drill down into the file.
3. Copy the **install.esd** file in the \sources folder of the ISO drive to the root of drive C:.
4. Run this command to examine the install.esd file and to see the images in it:

```
dism /get-wiminfo /wimfile:C:\install.esd
```

What is the index number for Windows 10/11 Pro? In our example in Figure 14-42, the number for Windows 10 Pro is 6.

(continues)

14

Real Problem Continued

Figure 14-42   Examine the install.esd file for image indexes

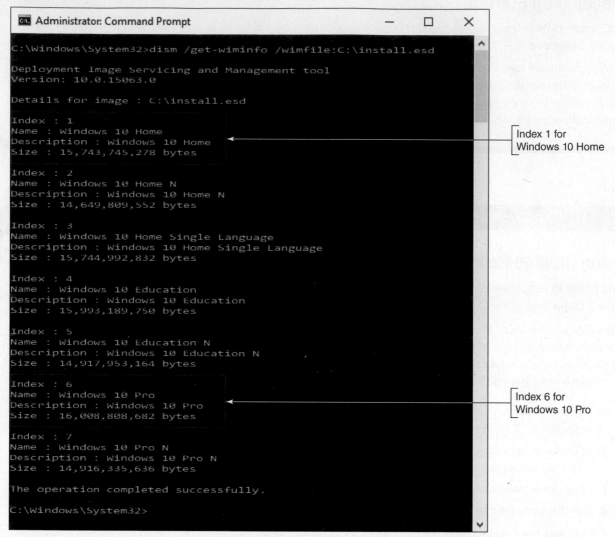

5. Recall that a standard image has a .wim file extension. Extract the install.wim file from install.esd for Windows 10/11 Pro. The install.wim file will be stored in the C:\Windows\System32 folder. Use the index number from Step 4 in this command:

```
dism /export-image /sourceimagefile:C:\install.esd /sourceindex:6
/ destinationimagefile:install.wim /compress:max /checkintegrity
```

6. Run this command to repair Windows system files using the files from the install.wim image you just extracted:

```
dism /online /cleanup-image /restorehealth /source:install.wim
/ limitaccess
```

7. To save space on your hard drive, you can delete the C:\install.esd file. However, you might want to leave install.wim in the C:\Windows\System32 folder in case you need it to later repair the Windows installation.

Module
15

Troubleshooting Windows Startup

Module Objectives

1 Describe the boot process from the time you press the power button until the Windows desktop loads

2 Create bootable media and backups to prepare for Windows startup problems

3 Implement appropriate Windows tools to solve Windows startup problems

4 Implement appropriate Windows tools to reinstall or reimage Windows

5 Troubleshoot Windows startup problems

Core 2 Certification Objectives

1.9 Given a scenario, perform OS installations and upgrades in a diverse OS environment.

3.1 Given a scenario, troubleshoot common Windows OS problems.

Introduction

You've already learned how to deal with application and hardware problems, and Windows problems after the OS has started. In this module, you take your troubleshooting skills one step further by learning to deal with startup problems caused by Windows. When Windows fails to start, it can be stressful if important data has not been backed up or the user has pressing work to do with the computer. What helps more than anything else is to have a good understanding of Windows startup and a good plan for approaching startup problems.

We begin the module with a discussion of what happens when you first turn on a computer and Windows starts. The more you understand about startup, the better your chances of fixing startup problems. Then you learn about Windows tools specifically designed to handle startup problems. Finally, you learn about strategies for solving startup problems. As you work, note that the troubleshooting tools and skills for Windows 10 work the same way as for Windows 11, with only a few minor changes in menu options.

Understanding the Boot Process

 Core 2 Objective 3.1

Knowledge is power. The better you understand what happens when you first turn on a computer until Windows is loaded and the Windows desktop appears, the more likely you will be able to solve a problem when Windows cannot start. Let's begin by noting the differences between a hard boot and a soft boot.

> **Note 1**
>
> Most techies use the terms "boot" and "startup" interchangeably. However, in general, the term "boot" refers to the hardware phase of starting up a computer. Microsoft consistently uses the term "startup" to refer to how its operating systems are booted—I mean, started.

Different Ways to Boot

 Core 2 Objective 3.1

The term **booting** comes from the phrase "lifting yourself up by your bootstraps" and refers to the computer bringing itself up to a working state without the user having to do anything but press the On button. There are two fundamental ways to boot a computer:

- A **hard boot**, or **cold boot**, involves turning on the power with the on/off switch.
- A **soft boot**, or **warm boot**, involves using the operating system to reboot. In Windows, a soft boot is called a restart.

A hard boot takes more time than a soft boot because a hard boot requires the initial steps performed by BIOS/UEFI. Most desktop cases have three power buttons; an example of these buttons on one system is shown in Figure 15-1.

Here's how the buttons work:

- The power button in front can be configured as a "soft" power button, causing a Windows restart.
- The reset button initializes the CPU so it restarts at the beginning of the BIOS/UEFI startup program. The computer behaves as though the power were turned off and back on and then goes through the entire boot process.
- The switch on the rear of the case simply turns off the power abruptly and is a "hard" power button. If you use this switch, wait 30 seconds before you press the power button on the front of the case to boot the system. This method gives you the greatest assurance that memory will clear. However, if Windows is abruptly stopped, it might give an error message when you reboot.

Figure 15-1   This computer case has two power buttons on the front and one power switch on the rear

How the front two buttons work can be controlled in BIOS/UEFI setup. Know, however, that different cases offer different options.

When Windows hangs, first try a restart. If that doesn't work, try a shutdown and then power the system back up. A Windows shutdown closes all open applications, user sessions, services, devices, and system processes and then powers down the computer. If a shutdown does not work, press the reset button on the front of the case. If that doesn't work, turn off the power switch on the rear of the case, wait 30 seconds, turn it back on, and then press the power button on the front of the case.

Steps to Boot the Computer and Start Windows

Core 2 Objective 3.1

Recall that BIOS/UEFI is responsible for getting a system up and going and finding an OS to load. Table 15-1 lists the components and files stored on the hard drive that are necessary to start Windows. The table can serve as a guide as you study the steps to see what happens from the time power is turned on until Windows is started. In these steps, we assume the OS is loaded from the hard drive.

Table 15-1   Software components and files needed to start Windows

Component or File	Partition and Path*	Description
BIOS systems using MBR partitioning		
MBR	The first sector of the hard drive is called the Master Boot Record (MBR)	BIOS looks to the partition table in the MBR to locate the active partition.
System partition	Also called the active partition or System Reserved partition	The system partition holds the Boot Manager, Boot Configuration Data (BCD) store, and other files and folders needed to begin Windows startup. For Windows, these files are stored in the root and \Boot directory of the hidden system partition.
Boot Manager	In the root of the system partition	Windows Boot Manager, bootmgr (with no file extension), accesses the BCD store and locates the Windows Boot Loader.

(continues)

15

Table 15-1 Software components and files needed to start Windows (Continued)

Component or File	Partition and Path*	Description
BCD store	\Boot directory on the system partition	The **Boot Configuration Data (BCD) store** is a database file named BCD (no file extension), and it is organized the same as a registry hive. It contains boot settings that control the Boot Manager and can be viewed and edited with the bcdedit command.
UEFI systems using GPT partitioning		
GPT partition table	At the beginning of the hard drive, with a backup copy at the end of the drive	UEFI looks to the GPT partition table to locate the EFI System Partition.
System partition	The EFI System Partition (ESP) is normally 100 MB to 200 MB in size.	The system partition holds the Windows Boot Manager, BCD, and other supporting files. For Windows, the Boot Manager is Bootmgfw.efi and is stored in \EFI\Microsoft\Boot. A backup copy of Bootmgfw.efi is at \EFI\Boot\bootx64.efi.
Boot Manager	For Windows, \EFI\Microsoft\ Boot on the ESP	Bootmgfw.efi loads EFI applications based on variables stored in onboard RAM and reads the BCD store to find out other boot parameters (such as a dual boot).
BCD store	\EFI\Microsoft\Boot on the ESP	Entries in the BCD store point the Windows Boot Manager to the location of the Windows Boot Loader program.
All Windows BIOS and UEFI systems		
Windows Boot Loader	C:\Windows\System32*	Windows Boot Manager turns control over to the **Windows Boot Loader**, which loads and starts essential Windows processes. Two versions of the program file are Winload.exe (BIOS) and Winload.efi (UEFI).
Resume from hibernation	C:\Windows\System32	Windows Boot Loader runs when Windows resumes from hibernation. Two versions of the program are Winresume.exe for BIOS and Winresume.efi for UEFI.
Ntoskrnl.exe	C:\Windows\System32	Windows kernel
Hal.dll	C:\Windows\System32	Dynamic Link Library handles low-level hardware details.
Smss.exe	C:\Windows\System32	Sessions Manager program responsible for starting user sessions
Csrss.exe	C:\Windows\System32	Win32 subsystem manages graphical components and threads
Winlogon.exe	C:\Windows\System32	Logon process
Services.exe	C:\Windows\System32	Service Control Manager starts and stops services
Lsass.exe	C:\Windows\System32	Authenticates users
System registry hive	C:\Windows\System32\ Config	Holds data for the HKEY_LOCAL_MACHINE key of the registry
Device drivers	C:\Windows\System32\ Drivers	Drivers for required hardware

*It is assumed that Windows is installed in C:\Windows.

A successful boot depends on essential hardware devices, BIOS/UEFI, and the operating system all performing without errors. Let's look at the steps to start a Windows computer. Several of these steps are diagrammed in Figures 15-2 and 15-3 to help you visually understand how the steps work.

Figure 15-2   Steps to booting the computer and loading Windows

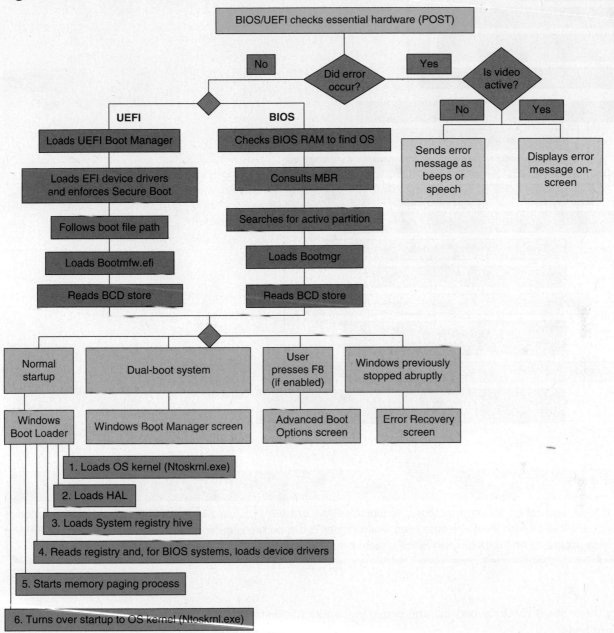

Figure 15-3   Steps to complete loading Windows

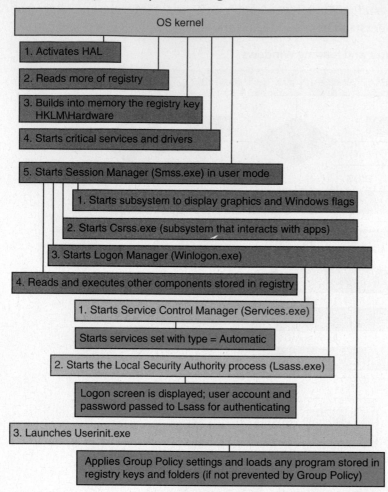

Note 2

Onboard RAM, also called onboard memory, nonvolatile RAM, or NVRAM, is used by BIOS/UEFI to hold configuration data. Onboard RAM, which keeps its data even when power is turned off, is different from system memory or RAM, which holds programs and data only while the system is turned on.

Study these steps carefully because the better you understand startup, the more likely you'll be able to solve startup problems:

1. Startup BIOS/UEFI is responsible for the early steps in the boot process. Onboard RAM accessible to BIOS/UEFI holds an inventory of hardware devices, hardware settings, security passwords, date and time, and startup settings. Startup BIOS/UEFI reads this information and then surveys the hardware devices it finds present, comparing it with the list kept in its RAM.

2. Startup BIOS/UEFI runs **POST (power-on self-test)**, which is a series of tests to find out if the firmware can communicate correctly with essential hardware components required for a successful boot. Any errors are indicated as a series of beeps, recorded speech, or error messages on the screen (after video is checked). If the key is pressed to request BIOS/UEFI setup, the BIOS/UEFI setup program runs.

3. Based on information kept in onboard RAM, startup UEFI loads the UEFI boot manager and device drivers. BIOS/UEFI then turns to the hard drive or other boot device to locate and launch the Windows Boot Manager. If BIOS/UEFI cannot find a Windows Boot Manager or cannot turn over operation to it, one of these error messages appears:

```
Missing operating system
No OS found
Error loading operating system
Windows failed to load
Invalid partition table
```

4. The Windows Boot Manager does the following:

   a. It reads the settings in the BCD.

   b. The next step depends on entries in the BCD and these other factors:

   - **Option 1.** For normal startups that are not dual booting, no menu appears, and Boot Manager finds and launches the Windows Boot Loader program.
   - **Option 2.** If the computer is set up for a dual-boot environment, Boot Manager displays the message, *Choose an operating system* screen, as shown in Figure 15-4.

Figure 15-4   In a dual-boot setup, Windows Boot Manager provides a choice of operating systems

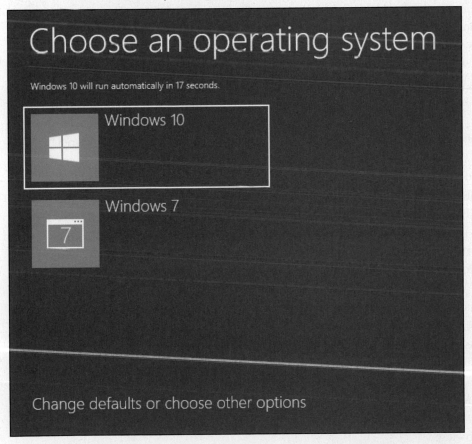

- **Option 3.** If Windows was previously stopped abruptly or another error occurs, the Windows Startup Menu appears (see Figure 15-5) to give you the option to troubleshoot the problem.

Figure 15-5   The Windows Startup Menu offers the opportunity
to troubleshoot a problem with startup

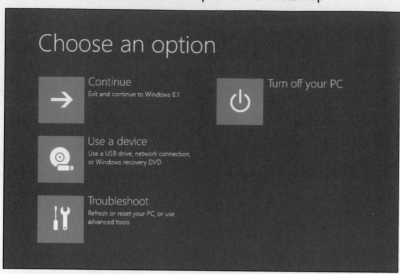

5. Windows Boot Loader (Winload.exe or Winload.efi) is responsible for loading Windows components. It does the following:

   a. For normal startups, Boot Loader loads into system memory the OS kernel, Ntoskrnl.exe, but does not yet start it. Boot Loader also loads into memory the hardware abstraction layer (Hal.dll), which will later be used by the kernel.

   b. Boot Loader loads into memory the system registry hive (C:\Windows\System32\Config\System).

   c. Boot Loader then reads the registry key just created, HKEY_LOCAL_ MACHINE\SYSTEM\Services, looking for and loading into memory the device drivers that must be launched at startup. The drivers are not yet started.

   d. Boot Loader starts up the memory paging process and then turns over startup to the OS kernel (Ntoskrnl.exe).

6. The kernel (Ntoskrnl.exe) does the following:

   a. It activates the HAL, reads more information from the registry, and builds into memory the registry key HKEY_LOCAL_ MACHINE\HARDWARE, using information about the hardware that has been collected.

   b. The kernel then starts critical services and drivers that are configured to be started by the kernel during the boot. Recall that drivers interact directly with hardware and run in kernel mode, whereas services interact with drivers. Most services and drivers are stored in C:\Windows\System32 or C:\Windows\System32\Drivers and have an .exe, .dll, or .sys file extension.

   After the kernel starts all services and drivers configured to load during the boot, it starts the Session Manager (Smss.exe), which runs in user mode.

7. The Session Manager (Smss.exe) loads the graphical interface and starts the client/server run-time subsystem (Csrss.exe), which also runs in user mode. Csrss.exe is the Win32 subsystem component that interacts with applications.

8. Smss.exe starts the Logon Manager (Winlogon.exe) and reads and executes other commands stored in the registry, such as a command to replace system files placed there by Windows Update.

9. Winlogon.exe does the following:

   a. It starts the Service Control Manager (Services.exe), which starts all services listed with the startup type of Automatic in the Services console.

   b. Winlogon.exe starts the Local Security Authority process (Lsass.exe). The sign-in screen appears (see Figure 15-6), and the user account and password are passed to the Lsass.exe process for authenticating.

   c. Winlogon.exe launches Userinit.exe. The Windows desktop is launched.

Figure 15-6   The Windows sign-in screen

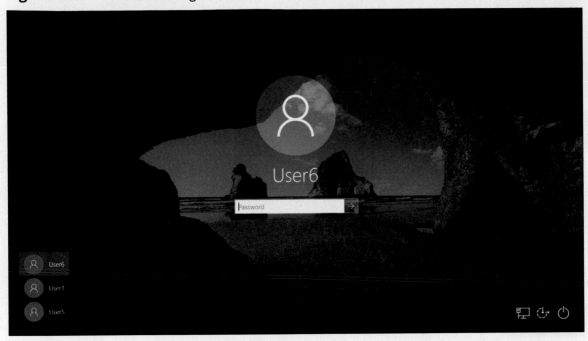

10. Userinit.exe applies Group Policy settings and any programs not trumped by Group Policy that are stored in startup folders and startup registry keys. See the appendix "Entry Points for Windows Startup Processes" for a list of these folders and registry keys.

The Windows startup is officially completed when the Windows desktop appears and the pinwheel wait icon disappears.

With this basic knowledge of the boot in hand, let's turn our attention to what you can do to prepare for problems when Windows refuses to load.

What to Do before a Problem Occurs

 Core 2 Objective 3.1

When troubleshooting startup, it helps to have a road map, which is the purpose of the diagram in Figure 15-7. It can help you organize in your mind the various ways to boot the system and the menus and procedures available to you depending on how the boot happens.

Figure 15-7 Methods to boot the system, menus that appear, and tools available on menus used to troubleshoot startup problems

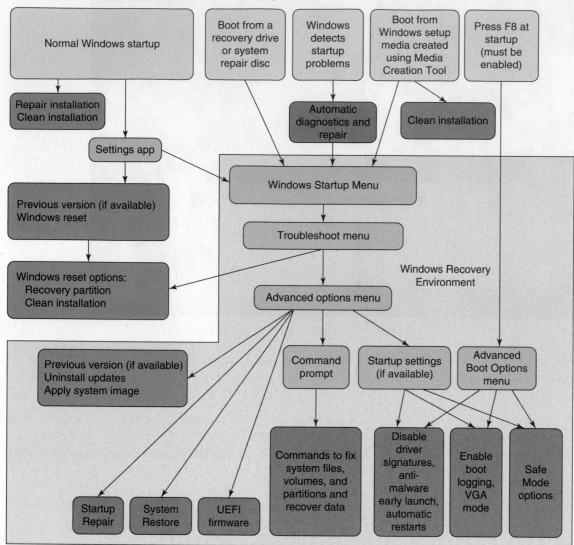

As you learn to use each tool, keep in mind that you want to use the tool that makes as few changes to the system as possible to fix the problem. Good preparation will make troubleshooting startup problems much simpler and more successful. When you are responsible for a computer and while the computer is still healthy, be sure to complete the following tasks:

- **Keep good backups.** The module "Maintaining Windows" covers methods to back up data, applications, and user settings.
- **Turn on System Restore.** Recall from the module "Maintaining Windows" that by default System Restore is turned off. Use the System Properties dialog box to turn it on.
- **Create a system image.** Recall from the module "Maintaining Windows" that a system image can be created right after you've installed Windows, hardware, applications, and user accounts and customized Windows settings. The image can be updated periodically.
- **Configure Windows to use the F8 key at startup.** The F8 key gives you access to the Advanced Boot Options menu in Windows, which you'll learn about later in this module. Windows 10/11 has the feature disabled by default. To enable the F8 key at startup, open an elevated command prompt window, and enter this command:

```
bcdedit /set {default} bootmenupolicy legacy
```

Figure 15-8 shows the Advanced Boot Options screen that appears when you press F8 during Windows 11 startup.

Figure 15-8   Use the Advanced Boot Options menu to troubleshoot difficult startup problems

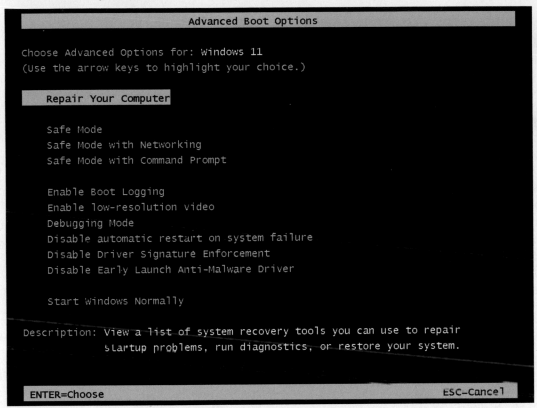

```
                        Advanced Boot Options

Choose Advanced Options for: Windows 11
(Use the arrow keys to highlight your choice.)

  Repair Your Computer

    Safe Mode
    Safe Mode with Networking
    Safe Mode with Command Prompt

    Enable Boot Logging
    Enable low-resolution video
    Debugging Mode
    Disable automatic restart on system failure
    Disable Driver Signature Enforcement
    Disable Early Launch Anti-Malware Driver

    Start Windows Normally

Description: View a list of system recovery tools you can use to repair
            startup problems, run diagnostics, or restore your system.


ENTER=Choose                                            ESC=Cancel
```

Later, if you want to disable the use of F8 at startup, open an elevated command prompt window, and enter this command:

```
bcdedit /set {default} bootmenupolicy standard
```

> **Caution !**
>
> As you learn to troubleshoot Windows startup, don't depend on the F8 key to work during the boot, because you never know when you'll work on a computer that has it disabled. All the tools available on the Advanced Boot Options screen are also available on the Windows 10 Startup Settings screen, which you can access without using F8. You learn about the Startup Settings screen later in this module. For Windows 11, you also learn how to access the Advanced Boot Options screen without using F8.

15

- **Create recovery boot media.** If Windows can't boot from the hard drive, you may be able to repair the Windows installation using tools available in the **Windows Recovery Environment (Windows RE or WinRE)**. Windows RE is normally stored on a hidden partition on the hard drive and is a lean operating system that can be launched to solve Windows startup problems. It provides both a graphical and command-line interface. The diagram shown earlier in Figure 15-7 shows Windows RE as a gray background. In that figure, menus in Windows RE are in green, tools are in blue and orange, and ways to launch Windows RE are in yellow boxes. Notice in Figure 15-7 that you can launch Windows RE after a normal Windows startup. However, if Windows won't start, you'll need other recovery boot media to launch it. Although it's possible to use recovery media created on a different computer than the one you are troubleshooting, the process is simplified if you already have these tools on hand. Figure 15-7 shows the three types of recovery boot media:
  - Windows 10/11 DVD system repair disc
  - Windows 10/11 USB recovery drive
  - Windows 10/11 setup media, which was created earlier by the Media Creation Tool

The key to using a system repair disc or recovery drive is to create the disc or drive before it is needed. Let's look at each of the three recovery boot media.

Note 3

All boot media are bit-specific. Use 32-bit media to repair a 32-bit Windows installation and 64-bit media to repair a 64-bit installation.

Windows 10/11 System Repair Disc

Core 2 Objective 3.1

A **system repair disc** is a bootable DVD with Windows repair tools that can start the system and fix problems. Using the DVD requires an optical drive. Open **Control Panel** and go to the **Backup and Restore (Windows 7)** window (see Figure 15-9). Click **Create a system repair disc**. A 32-bit Windows installation will create a 32-bit version of the repair disc, and a 64-bit Windows installation will create a 64-bit version of the repair disc. To use a system repair disc, boot the system from the disc, and select your keyboard layout. Then Windows RE is launched.

Figure 15-9 Create a system image or a system repair disc from Control Panel

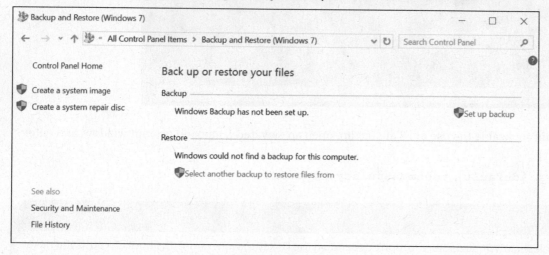

Windows 10/11 Recovery Drive

Core 2 Objective 3.1

Suppose the hard drive in a laptop completely fails. You can purchase a new hard drive for the system, but a problem might arise when you install Windows on the new drive. Most laptops, all-in-one, and other brand-name computers include an OEM recovery partition on the hard drive that contains a copy of the OS build, device drivers, diagnostics programs, and preinstalled applications needed to restore the system to its factory state. Before a problem occurs, you can back up this OEM recovery partition to a Windows recovery drive. A **recovery drive** is a bootable USB flash drive that can access Windows repair tools; in addition to holding an OEM recovery partition, it is handy when you need to repair a computer that doesn't have an optical drive.

Note 4

A recovery drive is bit-specific: Use a 32-bit recovery drive to repair a 32-bit Windows installation and a 64-bit recovery drive to repair a 64-bit installation.

If you include the system files on the recovery drive, you have the option of reinstalling Windows from the recovery drive. As you can see in Figure 15-7, a recovery drive can be used to perform a Windows 10/11 reset, which you learn about later in the module. You can use a recovery drive to repair a computer other than the one on which it was created. However, system files included on a recovery drive may not be compatible with all computers.

Do the following to create a recovery drive:

1. Open **Control Panel** in Classic view, and click **Recovery**. Click **Create a recovery drive**, and respond to the UAC dialog box.

2. Choose whether to include system files (see Figure 15-10), which will copy the OEM recovery partition to the recovery drive. If the computer doesn't have an OEM recovery partition, the check box on this dialog box is gray and not available. Click **Next** to continue.

Figure 15-10   Back up system files to the recovery drive so you can reinstall Windows later

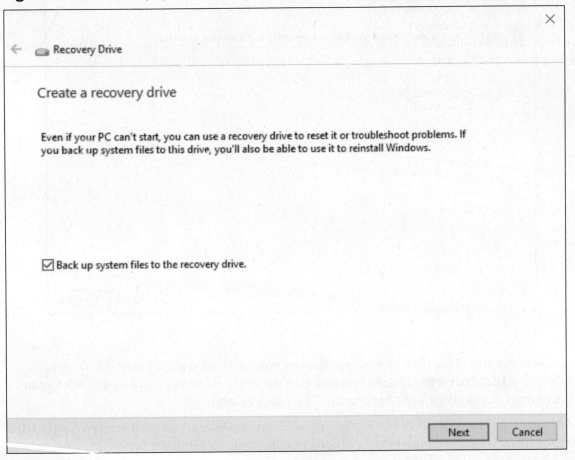

3. Windows reports the size of the USB flash drive needed (see Figure 15-11). Plug in a USB flash drive that is large enough. Know that the entire USB flash drive will be formatted, and everything on the drive will be lost.

Figure 15-11 Windows reports the size of the USB flash drive needed to hold the recovery drive

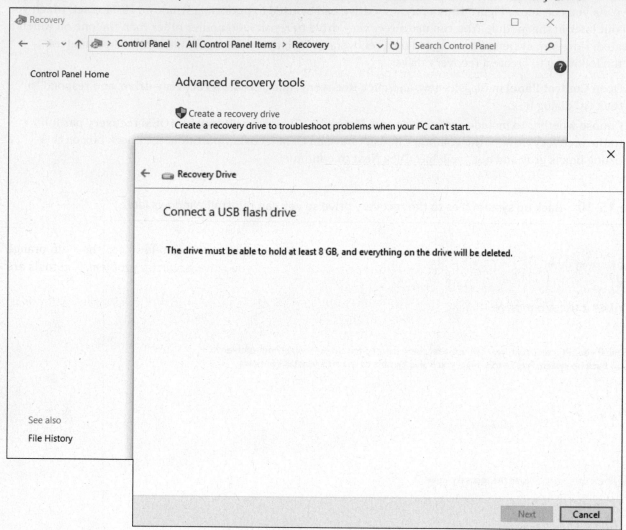

4. Windows inspects the size of the drive; if it is large enough, you see it listed among available devices. Be careful to select the USB flash drive because everything on the drive will be lost. Click **Next**. Click **Create** to begin the process. It will take a while to complete. Then click **Finish**.

Be sure to label the flash drive well, and put it in a safe place. For example, you can put it in an envelope, label it "Recovery drive for John Hawkins 64-bit Windows 10 Sony laptop," and store it in the computer's documentation file.

Note 5

If you copied the OEM recovery partition to the USB flash drive and are short on hard drive space on the computer, you can use Disk Management to delete the recovery partition and free up some space, and then expand the Windows volume.

Windows 10/11 Media Creation Tool

Core 2 Objective 3.1

You can launch Windows RE from a Windows setup DVD or flash drive. For Windows 10/11, recall you can use the Media Creation Tool on a working computer to create a bootable Windows setup ISO file, DVD, or flash drive. You learned how to use the Media Creation Tool in the module "Installing Windows."

Tools for Solving Windows Startup Problems

Core 2 Objective 3.1

Looking back at the diagram in Figure 15-7, note that tools to diagnose and repair Windows are shown in orange boxes. In this part of the module, we discuss how these tools can help you solve a startup problem. The tools are covered beginning with the least-invasive ones.

If Windows works well enough to get to the Windows desktop, you can use one of the following methods to launch Windows RE:

- **Windows 10/11 Settings app.** Open the **Settings** app and, for Windows 10, click **Update & Security**. For Windows 11, click **System**. In the left pane, click **Recovery**. Under Advanced startup, click **Restart now**. See Figure 15-12.

Figure 15-12   The Windows 10 Recovery page in the Settings app

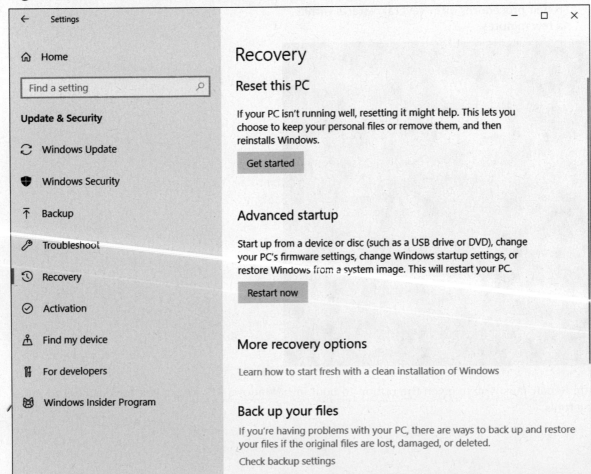

15

Note

The Advanced startup option is not available on the Recovery window when you are using a remote connection to the computer or when Windows 10/11 is installed in a VM. To force a VM into the recovery environment, in a command prompt window, run the command **reagentc /boottore**, and then restart the VM.

- **Shift+Restart.** From the Windows Start menu, click the **Power** icon. Press and hold the **Shift** key, and click **Restart**.
- **Command prompt.** In a command prompt window, enter `shutdown /r /o`. The /r parameter instructs the computer to restart, and the /o parameter opens Windows RE after the restart.

Note 7

You can also use the shutdown command to remotely shut down computers over the network.

Here are the methods to launch Windows RE when Windows cannot start normally:

- **Windows detects startup problems and launches automatic diagnostics and repairs.** If you restart the computer several times within a few minutes or if Windows detects errors during startup, it automatically launches diagnostics (see Figure 15-13) and takes you through steps to attempt to repair the system. The process, called Automatic Repair or Startup Repair, includes running both Check Disk and System File Checker.

Figure 15-13   Windows automatically launches diagnostic and repair procedures after several restarts within a few minutes

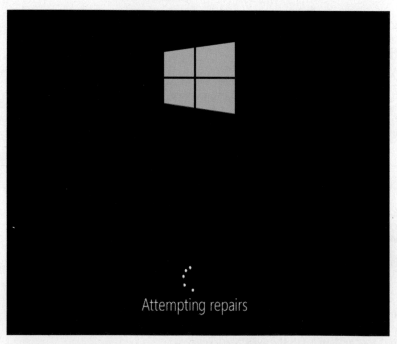

If Automatic Repair fails, you're given the option to boot into Windows RE, where you have access to other troubleshooting tools.

Note 8

When you are trying to restart a computer while troubleshooting it yourself, you might find that Automatic Repair slows down or interferes with your efforts. In this case, you can disable Automatic Repair as follows: Open an elevated command prompt window, enter `bcdedit /set recoveryenabled no`, and then perform your own repair steps. You can re-enable Automatic Repair later with the `command bcdedit /set recoveryenabled yes`.

- **From the sign-in screen.** If you can get to the sign-in screen, press and hold the **Shift** key as you click **Power** and then **Restart**. Windows RE launches. (This method also works in most VMs.)
- **Reboot Windows several times.** Each time you see the Windows screen appear, turn off power to the computer, wait 10 seconds, and press the power button to turn on the computer. After you do this several times, turn on the computer, and Automatic Repair should launch followed by Windows RE.
- **Boot from a USB recovery drive, DVD system repair disc, or Windows setup DVD or USB drive.** These boot recovery media give you the option to launch Windows RE. You might have to adjust BIOS/UEFI settings to boot from these alternate media. To launch Windows RE from a Windows setup DVD or flash drive, click **Repair your computer** when you see the Windows Setup screen.
- **Press F8 during startup.** Earlier in the module, you learned how to configure Windows to enable F8 at startup. If it is enabled, press **F8** during startup to launch the Advanced Boot Options menu (refer back to Figure 15-8), which is part of Windows RE.

Applying Concepts

Exploring Windows RE Menus and Options

Est. Time: 15 minutes
Core 2 Objective: 3.1

Let's explore the menu screens in Windows RE, which are shown in green boxes in Figure 15-7. Follow these steps to explore Windows RE menus:

1. Start Windows and use one of the methods listed earlier to launch Windows RE. The first screen you see after Windows RE launches is the Windows Startup Menu or the *Choose an option* screen (see Figure 15-14) for Windows 11. The Use a device option on the menu is new to Windows 11 and is used to recover a system from a network deployment server or other media.

Figure 15-14   The Windows Startup Menu is the first screen you see after launching Windows RE

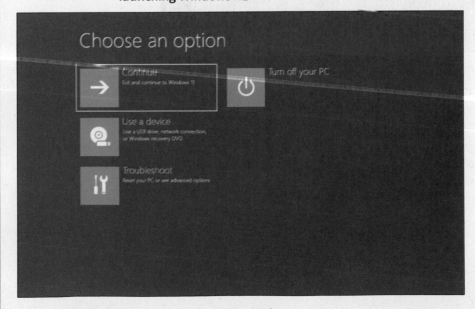

15

(continues)

Applying Concepts Continued

2. Click **Troubleshoot** to see the Troubleshoot menu screen (see Figure 15-15).

Note 9

Depending on the situation, you might see a seventh option on the Advanced options screen, which is UEFI Firmware Settings. Use this option to change settings in a computer's UEFI firmware.

Figure 15-15   Use the Troubleshoot menu to perform a Windows 10/11 reset

3. Click **Advanced options** to see the Advanced options screen in Figure 15-16. Some options on this screen or standard, and a few vary depending on the current state of the system.

Figure 15-16   The option to uninstall updates is available because this computer recently received a major Windows update

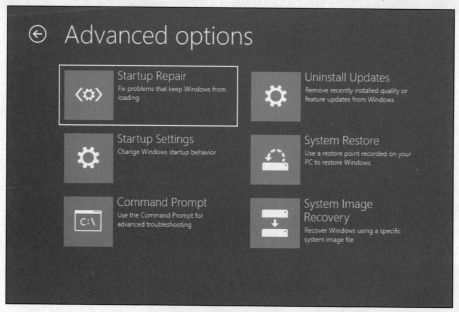

4. To get a command prompt, click **Command Prompt**. Here you can enter various commands to troubleshoot and solve problems. To exit the command prompt, enter the `exit` command. You are returned to the Advanced options screen.

5. The Startup Settings option is available on the Advanced options screen shown in Figure 15-16 because Windows RE was launched after a normal Windows startup. Click **Startup Settings** to see the startup options shown in Figure 15-17.

Figure 15-17   The Startup Settings menu gives options for how Windows starts up

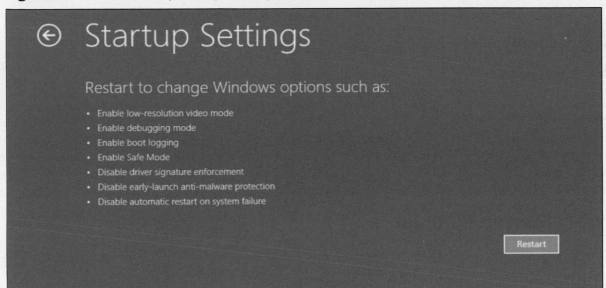

6. Click **Restart**. After the restart for Windows 10, another Startup Settings screen appears (see Figure 15-18), which has more options than the first one. Press numbers or function keys F1 through F9 to launch the tools on this screen. For Windows 11, after the restart, the Advanced Boot Options screen appears (refer back to Figure 15-8). Note the tools listed on either screen are the same tools, and you can also reach the Advanced Boot Options screen by pressing F8 at startup, assuming F8 has been enabled.

7. To return to the Windows Startup Menu shown earlier in Figure 15-14, press **F10**. On the *Choose an option* screen, click **Continue** to reload Windows 10/11.

Figure 15-18   Press a function key or number to restart the system in a given mode

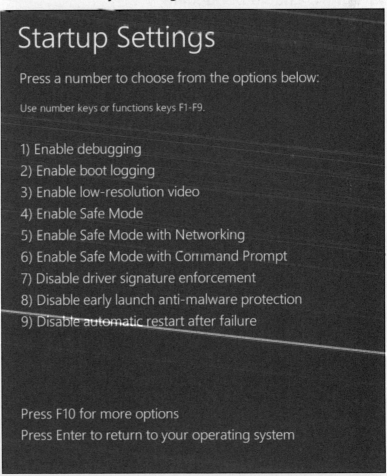

Next, we discuss some tools to repair Windows, including Startup Repair, Startup Settings, System Restore, uninstalling updates, and commands entered in a command prompt window.

Startup Repair

 Core 2 Objective 3.1

When addressing startup problems, the first tool to try is **Startup Repair**, which is a built-in diagnostic and repair tool. It can fix Windows system files without changing Windows settings, user data, or applications. You can't cause additional problems with the tool, and it's easy to use.

To run Startup Repair in Windows RE, drill down to the Advanced options screen (refer back to Figure 15-16) and click **Startup Repair**. Windows RE examines the system, fixes problems, reports what it did, and might offer suggestions for further fixes. A log file of the process can be found at C:\Windows\System32\LogFiles\SRT\SRTTrail.txt.

Changing Startup Settings

 Core 2 Objective 3.1

The Startup Settings option on the Advanced options screen shown in Figure 15-16 is available only when Windows RE is launched from the hard drive rather than other media. Following directions given earlier, launch Windows RE and drill down to the Windows 10 Startup Settings screen shown earlier, in Figure 15-18 or the Windows 11 Advanced Boot Options screen shown earlier in Figure 15-8. Here's a quick rundown of what these tools can do.

Press 1 or F1: Enable Debugging

This tool moves system boot logs from the failing computer to another computer for evaluation. The computers must be connected by way of a serial port. For Windows 11, the option is Debugging Mode.

Press 2 or F2: Enable Boot Logging

Windows loads normally and all files used during the load process are recorded in a log file, C:\Windows\ntbtlog.txt (see Figure 15-19). Use this option to see what did and did not load during the boot. For instance, if you have a problem getting a device to work, check Ntbtlog.txt to see what driver files loaded. Boot logging is much more effective if you have a copy of Ntbtlog.txt that was made when everything worked as it should. Then you can compare the good load with the bad load, looking for differences.

Figure 15-19   A sample C:\Windows\ntbtlog.txt log file

```
ntbtlog.txt - Notepad                                    —    □    ×
File  Edit  Format  View  Help
Microsoft (R) Windows (R) Versi 8  4 2015 09:14:41.352
BOOTLOG_LOADED \SystemRoot\system32\ntoskrnl.exe
BOOTLOG_LOADED \SystemRoot\system32\hal.dll
BOOTLOG_LOADED \SystemRoot\system32\kd.dll
BOOTLOG_LOADED \SystemRoot\system32\mcupdate_GenuineIntel.dll
BOOTLOG_LOADED \SystemRoot\System32\drivers\werkernel.sys
BOOTLOG_LOADED \SystemRoot\System32\drivers\CLFS.SYS
BOOTLOG_LOADED \SystemRoot\System32\drivers\tm.sys
BOOTLOG_LOADED \SystemRoot\system32\PSHED.dll
BOOTLOG_LOADED \SystemRoot\system32\BOOTVID.dll
BOOTLOG_LOADED \SystemRoot\system32\CI.dll
BOOTLOG_LOADED \SystemRoot\System32\drivers\msrpc.sys
BOOTLOG_LOADED \SystemRoot\system32\drivers\Wdf01000.sys
```

Note 10

The Ntbtlog.txt file is also generated when you boot into Safe Mode.

> ## Note 11
>
> If Windows hangs during the boot, try booting using the Enable Boot Logging option. Then look at the last entry in the Ntbtlog.txt file. This entry might be the name of a device driver causing the system to hang.

Press 3 or F3: Enable Low-Resolution Video (640 × 480)

Use this option when the video settings don't allow you to see the screen well enough to fix a bad setting (for example, black fonts on a black background or a corrupted video driver). Booting in this mode gives you a very plain, standard video in VGA mode. You can then go to **Display settings**, correct the problem, and reboot normally. For problems with video drivers, open **Device Manager**, and update, roll back, or uninstall and reinstall the video drivers.

Press 4 or F4: Enable Safe Mode

With this option, the Safe Mode desktop appears (see Figure 15-20) after the system restarts and you sign in to Windows. Launching Safe Mode and then restarting the system again can sometimes solve a startup problem.

Figure 15-20   The Windows 10 Safe Mode desktop

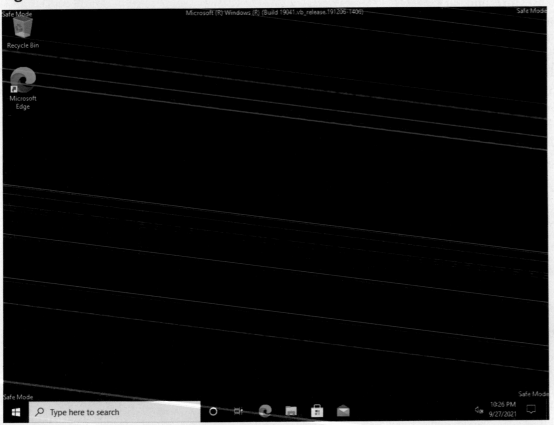

Other tasks you can try in Safe Mode include the following:

- Update Windows.
- Launch anti-malware software to scan the system for malware.
- Open Event Viewer to find events that are helpful in troubleshooting the system.
- Run the System File Checker command (sfc /scannow) to restore system files.
- Use Device Manager to roll back a driver.
- Use Memory Diagnostics (mdsched.exe) to verify memory.
- Use the chkdsk /r command to check for file system errors.
- Configure Windows for a clean boot on the next restart.

Recall from the module "Troubleshooting Windows After Startup" that you can also launch Safe Mode from the Boot tab on the System Configuration window, where Safe Mode is called Safe boot.

15

Exam Tip ✔

The A+ Core 2 exam gives you a scenario and expects you to know when and how to use Safe Mode to help resolve a Windows startup problem.

Press 5 or F5: Enable Safe Mode With Networking

Use this option when you need access to the network to solve the problem. For example, you might need to download updates to your anti-malware software. Also use this mode when the Windows installation files are available on the network, rather than Windows setup media, and you need to access those files.

Press 6 or F6: Enable Safe Mode With Command Prompt

If Safe Mode can't start, try Safe Mode with Command Prompt, which doesn't attempt to load the graphical interface. At the command prompt, use the sfc /scannow command to verify system files (see Figure 15-21). If the problem is still not solved, you can use the rstrui command to launch System Restore and then follow the on-screen directions to select a restore point. However, as Figure 15-22 shows, if restore points have not been previously made, System Restore cannot help. As you learn later in the module, you can also use this command prompt to restore a corrupted Windows registry from backups.

Figure 15-21 SFC finds and successfully repairs corrupted system files

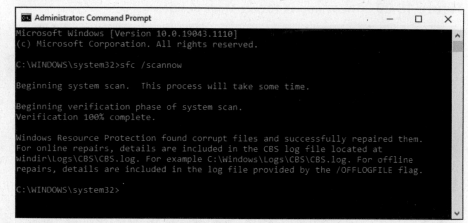

Figure 15-22 Use System Restore after booting to Safe Mode with Command Prompt

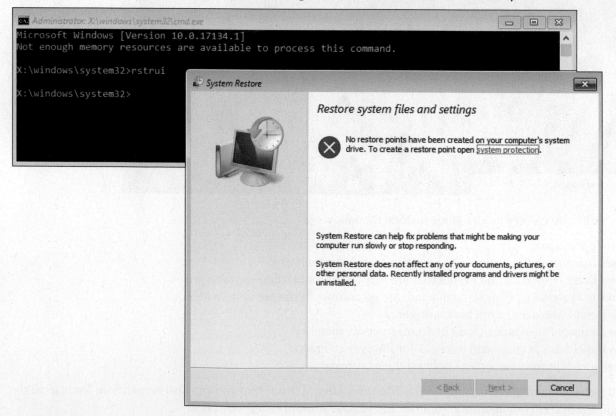

Press 7 or F7: Disable Driver Signature Enforcement

All 64-bit editions of Windows require that kernel-mode drivers be digitally signed. Developers use this option to disable driver signature enforcement when they test kernel-mode device drivers that are not yet digitally signed. Use this option for troubleshooting with caution because doing so might allow malware drivers to load.

> **Note 12**
>
> Suppose a recent Windows update that includes device driver updates has caused the system to hang. When you try to fix the problem by applying a restore point, the system hangs again. The problem is caused by device drivers in conflict. To fix the problem, you can disable driver signature enforcement, undo system restore, and apply the restore point again. This time, it should work.

Press 8 or F8: Disable Early Launch Anti-Malware Protection

Windows allows anti-malware software to launch a driver before any third-party drivers are launched so it can scan these drivers for malware. Unless you're sure a driver is the problem, don't disable this security feature.

Press 9 or F9: Disable Automatic Restart after Failure

By default, Windows automatically restarts immediately after a blue screen of death (BSOD) stop error, which is described in more detail later in this module. The error can cause the system to continually reboot rather than shut down. Press **F9** to disable automatic restarts and stop the rebooting.

> **Note 13**
>
> To permanently disable automatic restarts, right-click **Start**, click **System**, and in the About window, click **Advanced system settings**. In the Startup and Recovery group of the System Properties dialog box, click **Settings**. In the Startup and Recovery dialog box, uncheck **Automatically restart** (see Figure 15-23). Click **OK** twice and close the About window.

Figure 15-23   Permanently disable automatic restarts

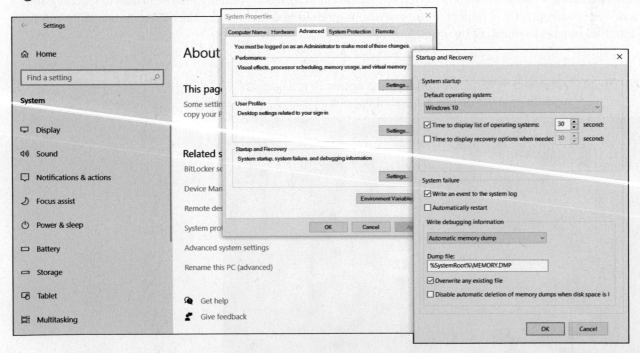

15

Press F10: Return to the Startup Settings Screen

Press F10 to return to the Windows 10 Startup Menu screen shown previously in Figure 15-14. For Windows 11, select **Start Windows Normally** to restart Windows.

> **Note**
>
> As you use these startup settings tools, be sure to reboot after each attempt to fix the problem to make sure it has not been resolved before you try another tool. To exit Windows RE and relaunch Windows, press Enter on the Startup Settings screen.

System Restore

Core 2 Objective 3.1

Windows gives you several opportunities during the startup troubleshooting process to use System Restore to restore the system to an earlier point in time when a restore point was made. You can select System Restore from the Windows RE Advanced options screen (refer back to Figure 15-16). You can also perform System Restore in Safe Mode or from a command prompt with the rstrui command.

System Restore can cause problems of its own because Windows updates and updates to anti-malware software can be lost, and hardware devices and applications might need to be reinstalled. System Restore won't help if the file system is corrupted or the registry is trashed. In these situations, the command prompt might help.

Uninstall Updates

Core 2 Objective 1.9

If you suspect a recent Windows update is preventing Windows from starting, you can uninstall or **roll back updates**. To uninstall a Windows update, you would normally use the Update & Security window in the Settings app or the Programs and Features window in Control Panel. But if Windows refuses to start, use the Advanced options screen in Windows RE. If there are recent updates, the screen shows the option to Uninstall Updates (see Figure 15-24). Click **Uninstall Updates** and follow directions on-screen. This method works well when the system fails to start because a critical driver is corrupted. In a project at the end of this module, you learn to use the DISM commands to roll back an update that refuses to uninstall by normal means.

Figure 15-24   After recent Windows updates, the option to roll back an update appears on the Advanced options screen

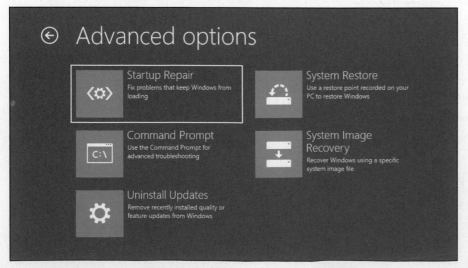

The Command Prompt Window in Windows RE

Core 2 Objective 3.1

Use the command prompt window in Windows RE when the graphical interface is missing or corrupted or when you want to use a specific command to fix a problem when Windows refuses to start. To access the Windows RE command prompt, click **Command Prompt** on the Windows Advanced options screen (refer back to Figure 15-16). After you have signed in with an account with administrative privileges, you have full read and write access to all files on all drives. The command prompt you first see in the window (see Figure 15-25) is X:\windows\system32> because Windows RE assigns drive X: to the drive containing the Windows installation. Many commands you learned about in module "Maintaining Windows" can be used at this command prompt.

Figure 15-25   The command prompt window in Windows RE

Next are some examples of how to use the Windows RE command prompt to repair a system. After you try each fix, reboot the system to see if the problem is solved before you try the next fix:

- **Manage data files and system files.** As you learned in the module "Troubleshooting Windows After Startup," you can use the SFC or DISM commands to restore critical Windows system files. The cd, copy, rename, and delete commands can be used to manage data files and system files.
- **Repair the hard drive file system.** A corrupted file system can cause a failure to boot. To repair the file system, try the chkdsk /r command.
- **Wipe the hard drive clean to prepare for a new Windows installation.** If you decide the hard drive is so corrupted you must start over with a fresh installation of Windows, you can use the diskpart command to totally wipe the hard drive clean of everything, including the partitioning system, before you install Windows again using Windows setup media. You learned to do this in module "Installing Windows."
- **Enable networking.** Networking is not normally available from the Windows RE command prompt. Use the wpeinit command to enable networking. The **wpeinit** command initializes Windows PE. Recall from the module "Installing Windows" that Windows PE is the preinstallation-environment operating system that is launched prior to installing Windows in a clean install and includes networking components.
- **Repair the BCD and boot sectors.** A failure to boot can be caused by a corrupted BCD. Startup Repair should fix the problem. But on some legacy systems, you will need to manually repair the BCD. Use the **bootrec** command to repair the BCD and boot sectors. Use the **bcdedit** command to manually edit the BCD. (Be sure to make a copy of the BCD before you edit it.) Use the **bootsect** command to repair a dual-boot system. To get helpful information about these commands, enter the command followed by /?, such as bcdedit /?. Some examples of the bootrec and bcdedit commands are listed in Table 15-2.

Table 15-2   Bootrec and bcdedit commands to repair system files and the file system

Command Line	Description
bootrec /scanOS	Scans the hard drive for Windows installations not stored in the BCD
bootrec /rebuildBCD	Scans for Windows installations and rebuilds the BCD
bootrec /fixboot	Repairs the boot sector of the system partition
bootrec /fixmbr	Repairs the MBR for hard drives using the MBR partitioning system
bcdedit /enum	Displays the contents of the BCD

15

Although a Startup Repair should solve the problem when you get an error message at startup that "Bootmgr is missing," rebuilding the BCD store should also be able to resolve the same problem on a legacy BIOS and MBR system.

Tools to Reinstall Windows

Core 2 Objectives 1.9, 3.1

After you have made reasonable efforts to repair a Windows installation, your next option is to reinstall Windows. The tools discussed in this section of the module affect the entire Windows installation on a computer rather than a few files or settings. Look back at Figure 15-7 and notice that these tools to reinstall Windows are shown in blue boxes; you can also see how to reach each tool. Some of these options allow you to keep personal data, and other options remove that data; the tools are listed here, starting with the least intrusive solutions:

1. **Go back to the previous version of Windows.** After you have upgraded to Windows 10/11 and the system is giving problems, you can go back to the previous version of Windows. This option is available on the Advanced options screen after upgrading to Windows 10/11 if the upgrade is not too old and the Windows.old folder is present. See Figure 15-26. In addition, you'll find the option in the Settings app: go to **Update & Security** and click **Recovery**.

Figure 15-26   The option to go back to a previous version is available because this computer was recently upgraded to Windows 10

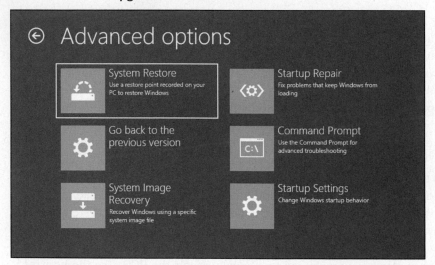

2. **Windows 10/11 repair installation.** Install Windows 10/11 as an upgrade over the existing installation, keeping personal data, apps, Windows settings, and device drivers.
3. **Reimage Windows 10/11.** Use a system image or deployment image to replace everything on the Windows volume. Current user data, Windows settings, apps, and device drives are lost.
4. **Install Windows 10/11 from the OEM recovery partition.** Laptops, all-in-ones, and brand-name computers may have an OEM recovery partition on the hard drive that can be used to restore the system to factory state. Some manufacturer procedures allow user data to be kept.
5. **Windows 10/11 reset.** Do a clean Windows 10/11 installation from the Microsoft cloud, recovery media, or the recovery partition on the hard drive. User data and preinstalled apps in a recovery partition can be restored.
6. **Windows 10/11 clean install from setup media.** This method, which is covered in module "Installing Windows," may allow you to keep user data on the hard drive.

Let's see how the Windows repair installation, reimage, OEM recovery partition, and reset work.

Windows 10/11 Repair Installation

Core 2 Objective 1.9

If you're having problems with Windows updates or basic Windows functionality but you can still boot into Windows, you might consider performing a repair installation, also known as a repair upgrade or in-place upgrade. A **repair installation** is a nondestructive installation of Windows 10/11 over an existing Windows installation. This is not the same as a full reinstall because the Windows volume will not be reformatted. Just as with an upgrade from Windows 8 to Windows 10, you can keep personal files, apps, and Windows settings. Essentially, you trick the machine into thinking it's being upgraded while potentially repairing the Windows installation.

Keep these points in mind when doing a repair installation:

- Create Windows setup media, on either DVD or USB, or save an ISO file on the local hard drive.
- Make sure that you can fully boot into Windows 10/11. If you can't, you'll have to use a different troubleshooting tool.
- Even though all data, apps, and settings should be protected in a repair installation, make a backup just in case.
- Gather all product keys for all installed apps to make reinstallation of these apps easier should it become necessary.

Note 15

Belarc Advisor (*belarc.com*) is a free tool that is quick and easy to use. It will produce a list of all installed devices and apps along with their product keys if that information is available. Print a copy of the report, and keep it in a safe place.

Applying Concepts

Performing a Repair Installation

Est. Time: 30 minutes
Core 2 Objective: 3.1

The easiest way to perform a repair installation is to start with an ISO file created by the Media Creation Tool, as described in the module "Installing Windows." Complete the following steps:

1. Sign in to Windows using an administrator account. Back up all personal data using one of the methods you learned about in the module "Maintaining Windows."
2. Following steps in the module "Installing Windows," download the correct ISO file for the Windows installation you're currently using on the computer to be repaired.
3. In Explorer, double-click the ISO file that you created with the Media Creation Tool. This mounts the image and shows the included files.
4. Double-click **setup.exe**, as shown in Figure 15-27. Click **Yes** in response to the UAC dialog box, and follow the directions on-screen.

15

(continues)

Applying Concepts Continued

Figure 15-27   To begin the repair installation, double-click setup.exe on the virtual DVD in Explorer

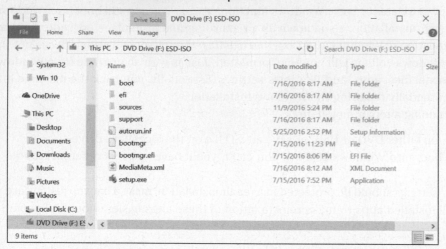

5. When you get to the *Choose what to keep* window, decide whether to keep personal files and apps, personal files only, or nothing. Sometimes setup makes these decisions for you and skips directly to the *Ready to install* window.

6. On the *Ready to install* window, make sure **Keep personal files and apps** appears and is checked, as shown in Figure 15-28. If it does not, click **Change what to keep** and select **Keep personal files and apps**, and then click **Next** to return to the *Ready to install* window. Click **Install** to begin the installation process, which will take a while and require several restarts. Enjoy a cup of tea or coffee while you wait.

Figure 15-28   You can keep user data and settings and third-party apps during a repair installation

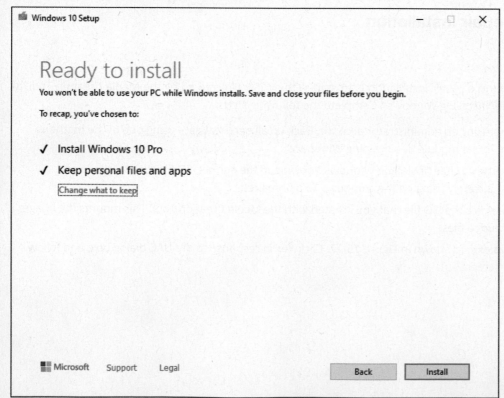

7. When the sign-in screen appears, sign in to Windows. Once you see the desktop, all your files, apps, and settings should still be in place.

Applying a Windows System Image

Core 2 Objectives 1.9, 3.1

You learned how to create a system image in the module "Maintaining Windows." System image recovery, sometimes called a **reimage**, tends to be an all-or-nothing recovery option with which you replace the entire contents of a hard drive with whatever operating system state and personal data are saved in the system image. It recovers all personal files, system files, and installed apps that were in place at the time the system image was most recently created or updated. If your system image is updated regularly, this option could work very well for you when repairing or replacing hardware, such as a failed hard drive. However, if a software-related problem has been building for a while, a recently updated system image won't necessarily fix the root of the problem.

To reimage Windows using a system image file stored locally (for example, on a flash drive or on the local network,) reboot the computer into Windows RE, drill down to the **Advanced options** screen (refer back to Figure 15-16), and select **System Image Recovery**.

Recall from the module "Installing Windows" that in an enterprise environment, you can install Windows from a deployment image on the network. Go into BIOS/UEFI setup and look for an advanced setup screen to enable PXE Support. Then reboot the computer to the network where it finds and loads Windows PE on the deployment server. The computer then boots to the Preboot eXecution Environment (PXE), and PXE then searches for a server on the network to provide the deployment image.

Exam Tip ✔

The A+ Core 2 exam expects you to know how to use a preinstallation environment and a recovery image to reimage Windows.

OEM Factory Recovery Partition

Core 2 Objectives 1.3, 1.9

Laptops, all-in-one computers, and brand-name desktops come with the OS preinstalled at the factory. This OEM (original equipment manufacturer) build of the OS is likely to be customized, and for laptops, the drivers might be specific to proprietary devices installed in the laptops.

Recall that a laptop or brand-name computer is likely to have a recovery partition on the hard drive used to restore the system to its factory state. This partition might or might not be hidden. For example, Figure 15-29 shows the Disk Management information for a hard drive on one laptop that has a 16.38 GB recovery partition.

15

Figure 15-29   This laptop hard drive has a 16.38 GB recovery partition that can be used to recover the system

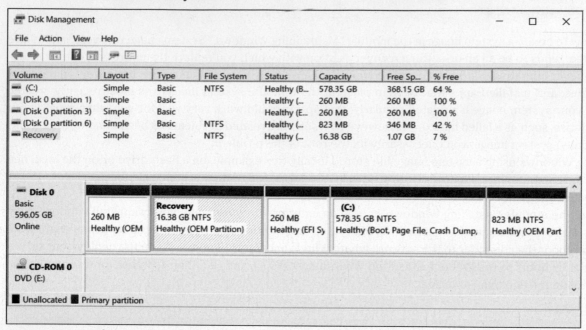

To know how to access the recovery tools stored on a recovery partition, see the manufacturer's website or look for a message at the beginning of the boot, such as "Press ESC for diagnostics" or "Press F12 to recover the system." For one Sony laptop, you press the red **ASSIST** button during the boot (see Figure 15-30). When you press the key or button, a menu appears with options to diagnose the problem, to repair the current OS installation, or to completely rebuild the entire hard drive to its factory state.

Figure 15-30   For this laptop, press the ASSIST button during the boot to launch programs on the recovery partition

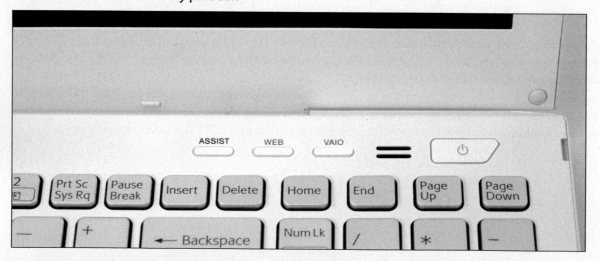

If the laptop doesn't have a recovery partition or if the partition is corrupted, look for the option to download recovery media from the manufacturer's website, and use it to create a bootable USB flash drive or DVD. You can then use the media to install Windows to its factory state.

Note 16

When you first become responsible for a laptop, use a USB flash drive to make a Windows recovery drive that includes the OEM recovery partition in case you must replace the laptop's hard drive. Know that if the laptop is more than three years old, the manufacturer might no longer provide the recovery media. You learned how to create a recovery drive earlier in the module. It is also important to save a copy of the power-on password in a safe place.

> **Caution** ⚠
>
> Before upgrading a laptop to Windows 10/11, make sure the laptop manufacturer provides Windows 10 or Windows 11 drivers for laptop components.

Windows 10/11 Reset

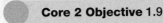
Core 2 Objective 1.9

A Windows 10/11 reset performs a clean installation of Windows with three options, as shown in Table 15-3.

Table 15-3   Windows 10/11 reset options

	Keep My Files	Remove Everything	Reinstall Preinstalled Apps
Option 1: My files and no bloatware	Yes	No	No
Option 2: My files with factory state	Yes	No	Yes
Option 3: Factory state	No	Yes	Yes

All options remove apps and drivers installed by the user and all changes made to settings. After the reset, a list of apps deleted from the system is stored on the Windows desktop. You'll then need to reinstall the apps you want to keep. Here are the ways in which the options differ:

- Option 1 keeps all personal files. All apps and settings are lost, and you get a clean installation of Windows.
- Option 2 keeps all personal files. If the computer came from a manufacturer with Windows 10/11 preinstalled, you can decide to restore the preinstalled apps (sometimes called bloatware) from the manufacturer. The apps, drivers, and diagnostics programs are reinstalled using the recovery partition on the hard drive or a recovery drive you created earlier.
- Option 3 removes everything on the drive, and you can also choose to clean the drive. Then Windows is reinstalled. If a recovery partition or recovery drive is present, the system is restored to factory state. This is an excellent choice if you are planning to sell, donate, or recycle your computer.

Applying Concepts

Resetting a Windows 10/11 Computer

Est. Time: 15 minutes
Core 2 Objective: 3.1

If you are not able to start Windows, you can use Windows 10/11 setup media or a recovery drive to launch Windows RE. Do the following:

1. Drill down to the Troubleshoot screen (refer back to Figure 15-15), and click **Reset this PC** to start the reset.
2. On the next screen (see Figure 15-31), you can choose to keep personal files or remove everything.

(continues)

15

Applying Concepts Continued

Figure 15-31   Windows reset can keep personal files or remove everything on your computer and reinstall Windows

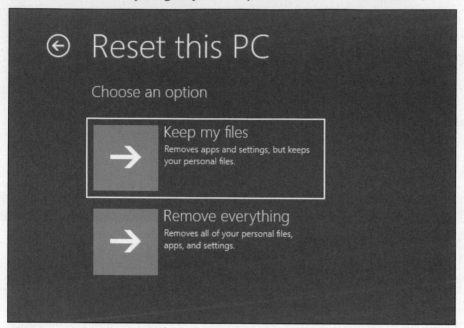

3. On the next screen (see Figure 15-32), you decide where installation files come from. If a recovery partition or recovery drive that has Windows 10/11 on it is present, you are next asked whether you want to restore preinstalled apps. Finally, click **Reset** to start the process.

Figure 15-32   Choose where to get files to reinstall Windows

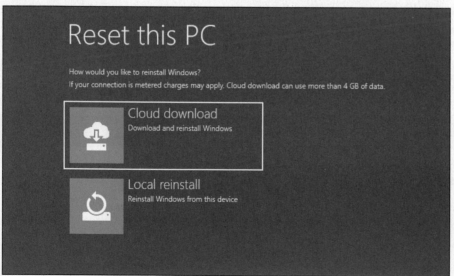

4. If Windows can start, you can use the Settings app to reset Windows. In the Windows 10 Settings app, open the **Update & Security** window, and click **Recovery**, as shown earlier, in Figure 15-12. Under *Reset this PC*, click **Get started** and follow the directions on-screen. For Windows 11, in the Settings app, open the **System** window, click **Recovery**, click **Reset PC** , and follow directions on-screen.

Troubleshooting Windows Startup

Core 2 Objective 3.1

And now the fun begins! With your understanding of the boot process and Windows tools for troubleshooting startup in hand, let's work through a bunch of errors and problems that can affect Windows startup and see what can be done about them. As with any computer problem, follow the troubleshooting steps you've learned in previous modules: (1) To identify the problem, interview the user, back up important data or verify that you have current backups, research and identify any error messages, and determine what has just changed that might be the source of the problem. (2) Establish your theory of probable cause. Be sure to search the web on error messages and symptoms. You're then ready to (3) test your theory and (4) resolve the problem. After you think the problem is solved, and (5) verify all is working as it should, implement preventive measures. Don't forget to (6) document your findings, actions, and outcomes.

When you know the source of the problem, decide which tool will be the least invasive to use yet still fix the problem. If that doesn't work, move on to the next tool. Remember that the tools are described earlier in the module in order from least to most invasive.

Important Data on the Hard Drive

Core 2 Objective 3.1

Working on a computer problem should always start with the most important question: Is there important data on the hard drive that's not backed up? Even if data is lost or corrupted, you might be able to recover it using Windows tools, third-party file recovery software, or commercial data recovery services. One good product is GetDataBack by Runtime Software (*runtime.org*), which can recover data and program files even when Windows cannot recognize the drive.

For less than $30, you can purchase a SATA-to-USB converter kit (see Figure 15-33) that includes a data cable and power adapter. You can use one of these kits to temporarily connect a desktop or laptop hard drive to a USB port on a working computer. Set the drive beside your computer and plug one end of the data cable into the drive and the other into the USB port. The AC adapter supplies power to the drive. While power is getting to the drive, be careful not to touch the circuit board on the drive.

Figure 15-33   Use a SATA-to-USB converter to recover data from a drive using a SATA connector

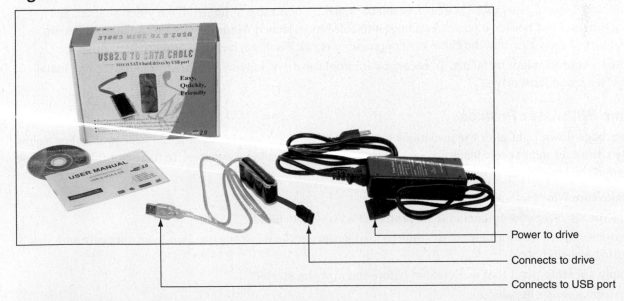

- Power to drive
- Connects to drive
- Connects to USB port

Using Explorer, you can browse the drive and copy data to other media. After you have saved the data, you can use diagnostic software from the hard drive manufacturer to examine the drive and possibly repair it or return the drive to its own computer and start troubleshooting there.

Error Messages and Problems

 Core 2 Objective 3.1

Problems that prevent Windows from booting can be caused by hardware, device drivers, services, applications, or Windows. This section covers what to do when error messages appear on a black or blue screen or when Windows gets corrupted.

Startup Error Messages on a Black Screen

Generally, problems that present as white text on a black screen are caused by hardware. Here are some possible error messages:

- No OS found
- A disk read error occurred
- Invalid boot disk
- Hard drive not found
- Disk boot failure
- No boot device found

Here is what's happening and what to do about it:

1. Start with the error message. Research the text shown on the screen so you understand the problem and get solutions from trusted websites.
2. If you see spinning white dots on a black screen, Windows may be installing updates before it launches. Wait. It may take some time for the update installations to complete. If the system hangs indefinitely, the updates might be causing a problem. If a reboot doesn't solve the problem, boot into Windows RE, and roll back updates or return to a previous version of Windows. Next try System Restore.
3. Consider that startup BIOS/UEFI might not be able to communicate with the hard drive. Check BIOS/UEFI setup for the boot sequence. Update the boot order so you can try booting from another device.
4. Try going into BIOS/UEFI setup and disabling any quick boot features. This causes BIOS/UEFI to do a more thorough job of POST and reports more information on the screen as it performs POST.
5. Windows might halt and show a black screen when it encounters a video problem at startup. Try restarting the system in Safe Mode, as you learned to do earlier in the module. Then check Event Viewer for clues, update Windows, use Device Manager to roll back drivers or disable or uninstall the video adapter, and use System File Checker. If you cannot boot into Safe Mode, launch Windows RE, and use Startup Repair, Memory Diagnostics, and the chkdsk /r command to check Windows, memory, and the hard drive.
6. The hard drive might be failing. To recover data from the drive, move it to another computer, and install it as a second hard drive.

Problems With User Profiles

If Windows bogs down right after the user signs in, the problem might be with loading the user profile. For a slow profile load, the user might see a black screen with spinning dots for several minutes. To fix the problem, try these tasks listed in the least invasive order:

1. Make sure Windows updates are applied.
2. Use the sfc /scannow command to fix problems with system files.
3. Reduce startup items. Compare the time to load a user profile when starting Windows normally and during a clean boot.
4. Apply a restore point that was created before the problem started.
5. Perform a repair installation.
6. Create a new user profile. You can copy user data files from the old profile into the new user profile namespace. (Locations of these files are given in the module "Troubleshooting Windows After Startup.")

If the user profile gets corrupted, it might not load at all, and you might see the error message, "The User Profile Service failed the logon." To rebuild the user profiles, do the following to repair Windows system files that affect the corrupted profiles:

- Do as many of the previous steps as you can do when a single user profile is slow to load.
- Following directions given in the module "Troubleshooting Windows After Startup," use the DISM commands to repair corrupted Windows system files.
- Perform a Windows reset. Be sure to back up data before you do a reset.

Sometimes you can recover a user account by deleting it without deleting its files and then creating a new one with the same name.

To delete the account and keep its files, open **Control Panel**, click **User Accounts**, select the account, and click **Delete the account**. In the Delete Account window (see Figure 15-34), click **Keep Files** and then click **Delete Account**. The files are stored in a folder on your desktop, and the account and its settings are deleted. Create a new account with the same name. Then you can copy the files saved to your desktop folder to the new user profile namespace.

Figure 15-34   Delete a user account and its settings, and keep the files in the user profile

If this doesn't work, you can edit the registry to delete an old profile or repair a corrupted one:

1. Launch the **Registry Editor** and back up this registry key:
   HKEY_LOCAL_MACHINE\SOFTWARE\Microsoft\Windows NT\CurrentVersion\ProfileList

2. Drill down into each S-1-5 folder in the key in Step 1 until you find the correct user profile in the ProfileImagePath subkey (see Figure 15-35). If the profile has a State subkey, set it to **0**, as shown in the figure. If the profile has a RefCount subkey, set it to **0**.

3. Close the Registry Editor, and restart the computer.

Figure 15-35   Set the State subkey value to 0

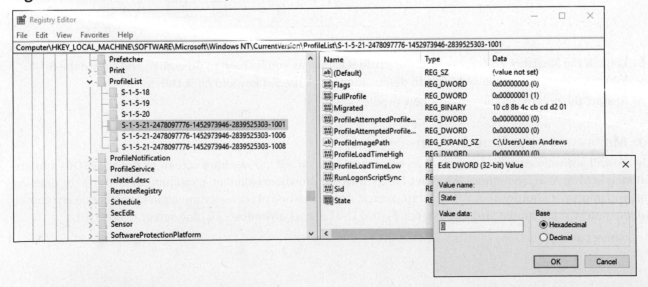

> **Note 17**
>
> If you're searching for the correct S-1-5 folder and it has .bak in the name, remove .bak from the folder name. To rename a folder, right-click it and click Rename.
>
> If you see two S-1-5 folders with the same name, except one has .bak at the end, you must switch the names: First rename the folder that does not contain .bak to .hold. Then remove the .bak from the other folder name. Next, rename the .hold folder to .bak. Then edit the S-1-5 folder that does not have .bak in the name.

If you still have problems with a user profile, you can follow these steps to delete the profile:

1. Manually copy any important data files in the user profile namespace to a new location. Recall that you can find these files in the C:\Users*username* subfolders.

2. Go to **Control Panel** and open the **System** window. Click **Advanced system settings**. In the System Properties dialog box, select the **Advanced** tab, and click **Settings** under User Profiles. See Figure 15-36. In the list of user profiles, select the profile and click **Delete**.

Figure 15-36   Delete the user profile

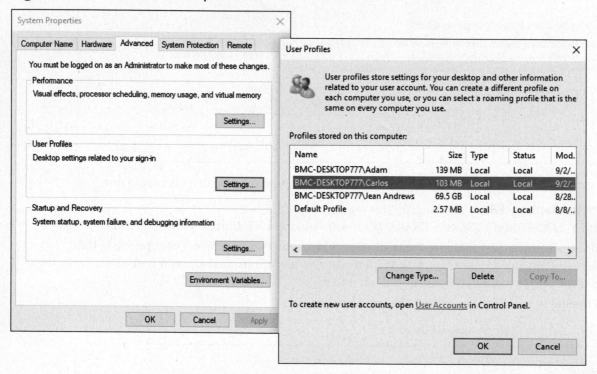

3. Launch the **Registry Editor**, back up the **ProfileList** key as you learned to do earlier, and locate the **S-1-5** folder for the user profile you want to delete. Right-click the **Sid** key and click **Delete**.

4. Restart the computer and create a new profile.

Error Messages on a Blue Screen

Hardware and software errors can present as error messages on a Windows **blue screen of death (BSOD)** and are called stop errors. Also, sometimes Windows hangs with the pinwheel spinning, continuously restarts, or does an abrupt and improper shutdown. A BSOD, or stop error, happens when processes running in kernel mode encounter a problem and Windows must stop the system. Figure 15-37 shows a Windows 10 blue screen stop error.

Figure 15-37   A Windows 10 stop error screen

A stop error can be caused by a corrupted Windows update, a corrupted registry, a system file that is missing or damaged, a device driver that is missing or damaged, bad memory, or a corrupted or failing hard drive. Stop errors can occur during or after startup. Here's what to do when you get a stop error:

1. As for the tools that are useful in solving stop errors, put the web at the top of your list! (But don't forget that some sites are unreliable, and others mean you harm.) Search the Microsoft websites on the text labeled in Figure 15-37, or use your smartphone to scan the QR code, which takes you directly to the BSOD webpages by Microsoft.

2. Disconnect any peripheral devices that might be causing trouble, such as a docking station, USB device, projector, or extra monitor.

3. Reboot the system. Immediately after a reboot following a stop error, Windows displays an error message box or bubble with useful information. Follow the links in the box.

4. If possible, restart the system and enable boot logging. Check the C:\Windows\ntbtlog.txt file to see if the correct driver files loaded.

5. Restart the computer a couple of times. Sometimes that's all you need to do to solve a problem. If Windows encounters errors, it will launch an automatic repair. If that doesn't fix the problem, you can launch Windows RE and restart Windows in **Safe Mode with Networking**. In Safe Mode, examine the log file created by Automatic Repair at C:\Windows\System32\LogFiles\Srt\SrtTrail.txt. See Figure 15-38. Also, recall that Safe Mode creates its own log file at C:\Windows\ntbtlog.txt.

Note 18

If the stop error prevents Windows from loading the desktop and F8 has not yet been enabled at startup, you can force automatic repair by turning off the computer a couple of times as Windows launches.

15

Figure 15-38   Examine the log file left by Automatic Repair

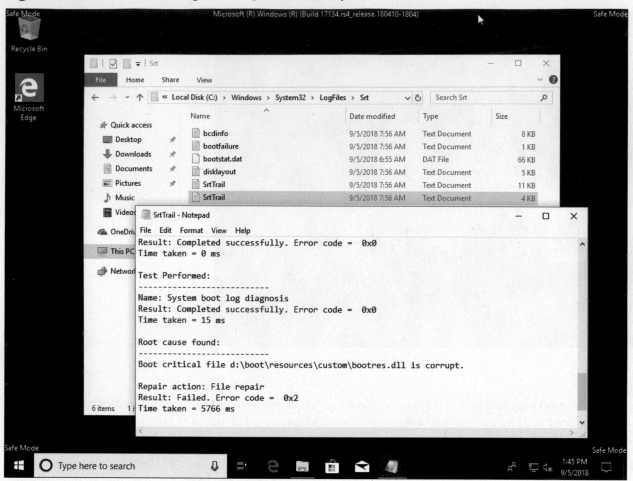

Errors With Hardware and Device Drivers

If the blue screen names a device or device driver that caused the problem, do the following:

1. A Windows update might fix the problem. Open the **Settings** app, and update Windows.
2. If the driver has been recently updated and the Safe Mode desktop is loaded, open **Device Manager** and roll back the driver.
3. Consider that the device driver might have been updated along with a Windows update. For recent Windows updates, try to roll back the updates or return to a previous version of Windows.
4. Use Device Manager to uninstall the device. When given the option, select **Delete the driver software for this device**. Then reboot the system.
5. If the stop error does not identify the device but names a program file, open **Explorer** on a working computer to locate the program file. Driver files are stored in the C:\Windows\System32\drivers folder. Right-click the file and select **Properties** from the shortcut menu. The Details tab of the Properties dialog box tells you the purpose of the file (see Figure 15-39). You can then reinstall the device or program that caused the problem.

Figure 15-39   Use the Details tab of a driver's Properties dialog box to identify the purpose of the driver

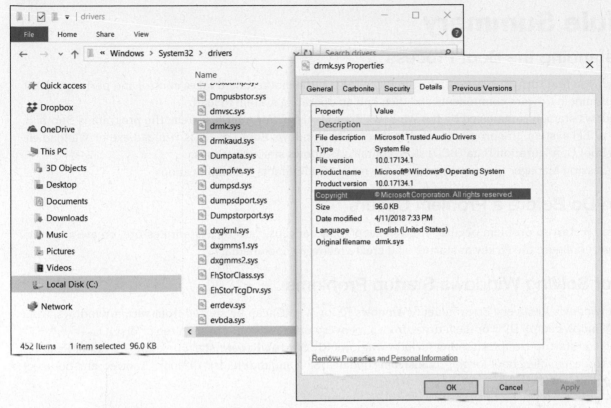

6. If you cannot start Windows in Safe Mode, use Windows RE to open a command prompt window. Then back up the registry, and open the Registry Editor using the regedit command. Drill down to the service or device key. The key that loads services and drivers can be found in this location:

HKEY_LOCAL_MACHINE\System\CurrentControlSet\Services

Disable the service or driver by changing the Start value to 0x4. Close the Registry Editor and reboot. If the problem goes away, use the copy command to replace the service or driver program file, and restart the service or driver.

> **Caution** (!)
>
> Consider that the device might be physically damaged. If you feel excessive heat coming from the computer case or a peripheral device, immediately unplug the device or power down the system. Don't turn the device or system back on until the problem is solved; you don't want to start a fire! Other symptoms that indicate potential danger are strong electrical odors, unusual noises, no noise (such as when the fan is not working to keep the system cool), liquid spills on a device, and visible damage such as a frayed cable, melted plastic, or smoke. In these situations, turn off the equipment immediately.

Improper or Frequent Shutdowns

Problems with improper or frequent shutdowns can be caused by overheating, a hardware problem, or the Windows kernel. After a restart, check Event Viewer for clues, apply Windows updates, verify memory with Memory Diagnostics, and use Check Disk (chkdsk /r) to check the hard drive for errors.

Next, consider that Windows might be corrupted. First try the least invasive solutions to repair Windows, including updating Windows, System File Checker, Startup Repair, running the system in Safe Mode, and System Restore.

If you decide the Windows installation is beyond repair, it's time to reimage or reinstall Windows. As you learned in this module, the tools to use in the least intrusive order are roll back Windows updates, Windows previous version (if available), Windows 10/11 repair installation, reimage Windows, reinstall Windows from the OEM recovery partition, and Windows 10/11 reset. After you have Windows up and running again, you can restore the user data from backups.

15

Module Summary

Understanding the Boot Process

- When you first turn on a system, startup BIOS/UEFI on the motherboard takes control and performs POST to examine hardware components and then find an operating system to load.
- Windows startup is managed by the Windows Boot Manager. For a BIOS system, the program is Bootmgr. For a UEFI system, the program is Bootmgfw.efi. The Windows Boot Loader is Winload.exe or Winload.efi. The Boot Configuration Data (BCD) store contains Windows startup settings.
- The Session Manager (Smss.exe) runs in user mode and interacts with applications.

What to Do Before a Problem Occurs

- Before a startup problem occurs, you can keep good backups, turn on System Restore, create a system image, configure the F8 key at startup, and create recovery boot media.

Tools for Solving Windows Startup Problems

- The Windows Recovery Environment (Windows RE or WinRE) can be started from within Windows, from the Windows setup DVD or flash drive, from a recovery drive, or from a system repair disc.
- Tools for startup troubleshooting include Windows RE; Startup Repair; startup settings; System Restore; Safe Mode; enabling boot logging; uninstalling updates; SFC; and the chkdsk, diskpart, bootrec, and bootsect commands.

Tools to Reinstall Windows

- Tools that can be used to reinstall Windows are Windows 10/11 previous version, repair installation, reimaging Windows, recovery partition, and reset. Some manufacturers offer a recovery partition on the hard drive to restore a computer to factory state. You can also reinstall Windows from Windows setup media.

Troubleshooting Windows Startup

- If a hard drive contains valuable data but will not boot, you might be able to recover the data by installing the drive in another system as the second, nonbooting hard drive.
- Use the web to research stop errors by the QR code, error title, and error number listed on a black or blue screen.
- Slow profile loads can be solved by updating Windows, System File Checker, reducing startup items, System Restore, repair installation, and new user profiles.
- When a device or service causes the system to hang during a normal boot, boot into Safe Mode or perform a clean boot and uninstall and install the device or service. System Restore can return the system to a previously saved restore point before the problem occurred.
- Improper and frequent shutdowns are most likely hardware related. Event Viewer might record failures. Use Memory Diagnostics and chkdsk to check memory and the hard drive. Consider overheating or a corrupted Windows installation as a source of the problem.

Key Terms

For explanations of key terms, see the Glossary for this text.

bcdedit	Boot Configuration	bootrec	hard boot
blue screen of	Data (BCD) store	bootsect	POST (power-on
death (BSOD)	booting	cold boot	self-test)

recovery drive   soft boot   Windows Boot Loader   wpeinit
reimage   Startup Repair   Windows Recovery
repair installation   system repair disc   Environment (Windows
roll back updates   warm boot   RE or WinRE)

Thinking Critically

These questions are designed to prepare you for the critical thinking required for the A+ exams and may use information from other modules and the web.

1. As a computer starts up, you see an error message about the HAL. At what point in startup does this error occur?

   a. When BIOS/UEFI is searching for an OS using devices listed in the boot priority order
   b. When Windows attempts to load the user profile
   c. When Windows attempts to launch critical device drivers
   d. When Windows attempts to launch the Windows kernel

2. Which Windows program must be running before a user can sign in to Windows?

   a. Kernel.exe
   b. Userinit.exe
   c. Explorer.exe
   d. Lsass.exe
   e. All of the answers are correct.

3. As a computer starts up, you see an error message about a missing operating system. At what point in startup does this error occur?

   a. When BIOS/UEFI is searching for an OS using devices listed in the boot priority order
   b. When Windows attempts to load the user profile
   c. When Windows attempts to launch critical device drivers
   d. When Windows attempts to launch the Windows kernel

4. Your friend sees an error message about a corrupted bootmgr file during Windows startup. They have another computer with a matching configuration and decide to copy the bootmgr file from the working computer to the computer with the problem. Where is the bootmgr file stored?

   a. C:\Boot\bootmgr
   b. System Reserved\Boot\bootmgr
   c. System Reserved\bootmgr
   d. All of the answers are correct.

5. Your friend mentioned in question 4 is having problems finding the bootmgr file and asks for your help. What is your best response?

   a. Use diskpart commands to "unhide" and locate the file.
   b. Use the File Explorer options applet to unhide the hidden bootmgr file.
   c. Explain to your friend that performing a Startup Repair is a better option.
   d. Explain to your friend that they can use the bootrec command to fix the bootmgr file without having to copy another file to the computer.

6. You see multiple errors about device drivers failing to launch at startup. Of the following, which is the best option to try first? Second?

   a. Apply a restore point.
   b. Perform a clean installation of Windows from setup media.
   c. Perform a Startup Repair.
   d. Perform a Windows reset.

15

7. A stop error halts the Windows 10 system while it is booting, and the booting starts over in an endless loop of restarts. How can you solve this problem?

   a. Use the Windows Startup Settings screen to disable automatic restarts.
   b. Press F8 at startup, and then disable automatic restarts.
   c. Launch Windows 10 from setup media, and perform a Windows 10 reset.
   d. Press F9 at startup, and then disable automatic restarts.

8. If you are having a problem with a driver, which of the following should you try first? Second?

   a. Update the driver.
   b. Use System Restore to apply a restore point.
   c. Update Windows.
   d. Perform a clean boot.

9. When error messages indicate that the Windows registry is corrupted and you cannot boot from the hard drive, what tool or method is the first best option to fix the problem? The second-best option?

   a. Use bootable media to launch Windows RE, and use System Restore to apply a restore point.
   b. Use bootable media to launch Windows RE and perform a Startup Repair.
   c. Use bootable media to launch Windows RE, and then use commands to recover the registry from backup.
   d. Reimage Windows using a system image.

10. Your Windows system boots to a blue screen stop error and no desktop. What do you do first?

    a. Reinstall Windows.
    b. Use the web to research the stop error messages and numbers.
    c. Attempt to boot into Windows RE using the Windows setup DVD or a recovery drive.
    d. Verify that the system is getting power.

11. You have important data on your hard drive that is not backed up, and your Windows installation is so corrupted you know that you must reinstall Windows. What do you do first?

    a. Use System Restore to apply a restore point.
    b. Make every attempt to recover the data.
    c. Perform a repair installation of Windows.
    d. Reformat the hard drive and reinstall Windows.

12. Your computer displays the error message, "A disk read error occurred." You try to boot from the Windows setup DVD, and you get the same error. What is most likely the problem?

    a. The Windows setup DVD is scratched or damaged in some way.
    b. The hard drive is so damaged the system cannot read from the DVD.
    c. Both the optical drive and the hard drive have failed.
    d. The boot device order is set to boot from the hard drive before the optical drive.

13. When a driver is giving problems in Windows 10, which tool offers the least intrusive solution?

    a. Device Manager
    b. Windows Update
    c. System Restore
    d. Registry Editor

14. An error message is displayed during Windows startup about a service that has failed to start, and then the system locks up. You try to boot into Safe Mode, but you get the same error message. What should you try next?

    a. Use the command prompt to edit the registry.
    b. Boot to Windows RE, and enable boot logging.
    c. Perform a repair installation of Windows.
    d. Boot to Windows RE, and perform a Startup Repair.

15. Stop errors happen when which types of processes encounter an error?

    a. Processes created by applications
    b. Processes created by Windows components running in user mode
    c. Processes created by Windows components running in kernel mode
    d. Processes created by anti-malware software

16. What is the command to use the System File Checker to immediately verify and repair system files?

17. What is the path and name of the log file created when you enable boot logging on the Windows 10 Startup Settings menu?

18. What information is contained in the C:\Windows\System32\LogFiles\Srt\SrtTrail.txt file?

19. Which tool is the least invasive solution to repair Windows?

    a. System Restore
    b. Startup Repair
    c. Windows reset
    d. Uninstall updates

20. On a computer with Windows 11 installed, you have used Disk Management to verify that a laptop has a recovery partition, but when you do a Windows reset, you don't see the option to restore preinstalled apps. What is the most likely problem?

    a. Windows reset is not working properly.
    b. Windows 11 Home is installed, and it does not offer the option to restore preinstalled apps.
    c. The laptop factory state uses an OS other than Windows 11.
    d. The recovery partition is corrupted.

21. A customer reports their recently purchased computer does not consistently run their old applications. Application errors occur intermittently, and data files get corrupted. They have tried uninstalling and reinstalling the apps, and the problems persist. As you troubleshoot the problem, you reboot the system and get a BSOD error. The customer tells you the BSOD has occasionally appeared. Which subsystem is most likely causing the problem, and what is the next best step?

    a. Windows is corrupted; reinstall Windows.
    b. Windows Update is not working; use System Restore.
    c. Memory is faulty; run Memory Diagnostics.
    d. Applications are faulty; uninstall and reinstall the applications causing errors.

Hands-On Projects

Hands-On Project 15-1

Using Boot Logs and System Information to Research Startup

Est. Time: 30 minutes
Core 2 Objective: 3.1

Boot logs can be used to generate a list of drivers that were loaded during a normal startup and during a Safe Mode startup. Do the following to use boot logs to research startup:

1. Boot to the normal Windows desktop with boot logging enabled. Save the boot log just created to a different name or location so it will not be overwritten on the next boot.

2. Reboot the system in Safe Mode, which also creates a boot log. Compare the two logs, identifying differences in drivers loaded during the two boots. You can print both files and lay them side by side for comparison. An easier method is to compare the files using the Compare tool in Microsoft Word.

(continues)

Hands-On Project Continued

3. Use the System Information utility or other methods to identify the hardware devices loaded during normal startup but not loaded in Safe Mode. Which devices on your system did not load in Safe Mode?

As you identify the drivers not loaded during Safe Mode, these registry keys might help with your research:

- Lists drivers and services loaded during Safe Mode:
  HKLM\System\CurrentControlSet\Control\SafeBoot\Minimal

- Lists drivers and services loaded during Safe Mode with Networking:
  HKLM\System\CurrentControlSet\Control\SafeBoot\Network

Hands-On Project 15-2

Taking Ownership and Replacing a Windows System File

Est. Time: 15 minutes
Core 2 Objective: 1.9

In the module "Troubleshooting Windows After Startup," you learned to use SFC and DISM commands to find and replace corrupted Windows system files. SFC keeps a log of its actions at C:\Windows\Logs\CBS\CBS.log, and DISM keeps a log at C:\Windows\Logs\DISM\dism.log. Sometimes these logs or BSOD error screens reveal the name and location of corrupted system or device driver files that Windows tools cannot replace. In this situation, you can manually replace the file. To do so, you can use the takeown command to take ownership of a file and the icacls command to get full access to the file. The Microsoft Knowledge Base Article 929833 at *support.microsoft.com* explains how to use these two commands.

Do the following to practice manually replacing a system file:

1. Boot the computer into Safe Mode with Command Prompt.

2. Take ownership and gain full access to the C:\Windows\System32\jscript.dll file. What commands did you use?

3. Rename the Jscript.dll file to Jscript.dll.hold. Run the **sfc /scannow** command. Did SFC restore the Jscript.dll file? What is the path and file name of the log file that lists repairs?

4. SFC restores a file using files accessed from Windows Update or stored on the Windows setup DVD or other folders on the hard drive. If SFC cannot restore a file, you might find a fresh copy in the C:\Windows\winsxs folder or its subfolders. Search these folders. Did you find a version of Jscript.dll that is the same file size as the one in C:\Windows\System32? Other than the C:\Windows\winsxs folder, where else can you find a known good copy of a corrupted system file or device driver file?

Note 19

To use a command prompt window to search for a file in a folder and its subfolders, use the dir /s command.

Hands-On Project 15-3

Viewing the BCD Store

Est. Time: 15 minutes
Core 2 Objective: 1.9

On two or more computers, open an elevated command prompt window, and use the bcdedit /enum command to view the BCD store. One BCD store is shown in Figure 15-40.

Answer the following questions:

1. Can you view the BCD store and determine if the system is using the MBR or GPT partitioning system? Why or why not?

2. Explain how you can look at the BCD store and tell if the system is a single boot or multiboot system.

Figure 15-40   A BCD store on a computer that uses the GPT partitioning system

```
Administrator: Command Prompt                              —    □    ×

Microsoft Windows [Version 10.0.15063]
(c) 2017 Microsoft Corporation. All rights reserved.

C:\WINDOWS\system32>bcdedit /enum

Windows Boot Manager
--------------------
identifier              {bootmgr}
device                  partition=G:
description             Windows Boot Manager
locale                  en-US
inherit                 {globalsettings}
default                 {current}
resumeobject            {358ebcf5-39df-11e7-a591-e188b1e0f934}
displayorder            {current}
                        {99744a22-9a96-11e3-b541-e3d79568548f}
toolsdisplayorder       {memdiag}
timeout                 300

Windows Boot Loader
-------------------
identifier              {current}
device                  partition=C:
path                    \WINDOWS\system32\winload.exe
description             Windows 10
locale                  en-US
inherit                 {bootloadersettings}
recoverysequence        {72f318ad-39df-11e7-a591-e188b1e0f934}
displaymessageoverride  startupRepair
recoveryenabled         Yes
allowedinmemorysettings 0x15000075
osdevice                partition=C:
systemroot              \WINDOWS
resumeobject            {358ebcf5-39df-11e7-a591-e188b1e0f934}
nx                      OptIn
bootmenupolicy          Standard
hypervisorlaunchtype    Auto
```

Hands-On Project 15-4

Researching Laptop Online Resources

Est. Time: 15 minutes
Core 2 Objective: 1.9

Suppose the hard drive in a laptop has failed, and you must replace the hard drive with a new one and then install Windows on the new drive. What online resources can help you? Do the following to find a service manual and recovery files for a laptop to which you have access, such as one you or a friend owns:

1. What are the brand, model, and serial number of the laptop?

2. What is the website of the laptop manufacturer? Save or print a webpage on that site that shows you what recovery files you can download to install Windows on a new hard drive for the laptop.

3. If the website provides a service manual, download the manual and print the pages that show how to replace the hard drive.

4. Based on what you have learned about online support for this laptop, what backups or recovery media do you think need to be created now, before a hard drive crash occurs?

Hands-On Project 15-5

Practicing Using System Recovery Options

Est. Time: 30 minutes
Core 2 Objective: 1.9

Launch Windows RE and do the following:

1. Execute the Startup Repair process. What were the results?

2. Launch **System Restore**. What is the most recent restore point? (Do not apply the restore point.)

3. Using the command prompt window, open the **Registry Editor**. What command did you use? Close the editor.

4. Using the command prompt window, copy a file from your Documents folder to a flash drive. Were you able to copy the file successfully? If not, what error message(s) did you receive?

Hands-On Project 15-6

Using Startup Repair

Est. Time: 15 minutes
Core 2 Objective: 3.1

When Startup Repair attempts to fix a system, it creates a log file with information about the steps taken during the repair process. If Startup Repair doesn't fix the system, you can use the log file to investigate the problem and perhaps manually fix it. Do the following to practice using Startup Repair and examine its log file:

1. Use the **Settings** app in Windows to launch Windows RE. From the initial Windows Startup Menu, click **Troubleshoot**, **Advanced options**, and then **Startup Repair**.

2. Diagnostics of the system are made, and the location of the log file appears. Note the path and name of the file. The default location of the log file is C:\Windows\System32\LogFiles\Srt\SrtTrail.txt. Click **Advanced options**. You are returned to the Windows Startup Menu.

3. To view the log file from the Windows RE command prompt, click **Troubleshoot** and click **Command Prompt**.

4. In the command prompt window, enter the command **c:** to access the hard drive. (You might need to use a different drive depending on the log file location reported in Step 2.)

5. Enter the following command to go to the directory where the log file is located:

```
cd \Windows\System32\LogFiles\SRT
```

6. To use Notepad to view the file contents, enter the following command:

```
notepad.exe SRTTrail.txt
```

7. In the log file, look for information about a failed test.

Hands-On Project 15-7

Using the DISM Commands

Est. Time: 15 minutes
Core 2 Objective: 3.1

Sometimes a Windows update crashes the system, and uninstalling the update doesn't work in the Settings app and in Windows RE. Another way to roll back the update is with the DISM commands. Do the following:

1. Launch the Windows RE command prompt window.

2. Enter this command to get a list of installed updates: **dism /online /get-packages**

3. Search through the list, and find the most recent one. Find the Package Identity. It's a long string that you will need to copy by selecting it and pressing **Ctrl+C**.

4. Don't uninstall the update. But if you intended to uninstall the update, you would use this command:
   dism /online /remove-package /PackageName:*[Insert the copied Package Identity here]*

5. DISM keeps a log at C:\Windows\Logs\DISM\dism.log. Open the log file in Notepad. Can you find the Package Identify string you copied in step 3? Where do you think DISM got its information about installed updates?

15

Real Problems, Real Solutions

Real Problem 15-1

Sabotaging a Windows System

Est. Time: 30 minutes
Core 2 Objective: 3.1

In a lab environment, follow these steps to find out if you can corrupt a Windows system so that it will not boot, and then repair the system. (This problem can be done using a Windows installation in a virtual machine.) Don't forget about the powerful takeown and icacls commands discussed in this module.

1. Rename or move one of the program files listed in Table 15-1. Which program file did you select? In what folder did you find it?

2. Restart your system. Did an error occur? Check in Explorer. Is the file restored? What Windows feature repaired the problem?

3. Try other methods of sabotaging the Windows system, but carefully record exactly what you did to sabotage the boot. Can you make the boot fail?

4. Now recover the Windows system. List the steps you took to get the system back to good working order.

Real Problem 15-2

Recovering Data from a Hard Drive

Est. Time: 30 minutes
Core 2 Objective: 3.1

To practice recovering data from a hard drive that won't boot, create a folder on a Windows 10 or Windows 11 VM. Put data files in the folder. What is the name of your folder? Move the hard drive to another working VM, and install it as a second hard drive in the system. Copy the data folder to the primary hard drive in this second VM. Now return the hard drive to the original VM, and verify that the VM starts with no errors. List the steps you used in this project.

Module
16

Security Strategies

Module Objectives

1 Explain how to secure resources on a network via physical and logical access control, user authentication, and user education

2 Detect, remove, and prevent malicious software on personal computers

3 Describe policies that address issues of software licensing, digital rights, regulated data, compliance policies, data destruction and disposal, and incident response

Core 2 Certification Objectives

1.3 Given a scenario, use features and tools of the Microsoft Windows 10 operating system (OS).

2.1 Summarize various security measures and their purposes.

2.2 Compare and contrast wireless security protocols and authentication methods.

2.3 Given a scenario, detect, remove, and prevent malware using the appropriate tools and methods.

2.4 Explain common social-engineering attacks, threats, and vulnerabilities.

2.5 Given a scenario, manage and configure basic security settings in the Microsoft Windows OS.

2.6 Given a scenario, configure a workstation to meet best practices for security.

2.8 Given a scenario, use common data destruction and disposal methods.

3.2 Given a scenario, troubleshoot common personal computer (PC) security issues.

(continues)

3.3 Given a scenario, use best practice procedures for malware removal.

4.1 Given a scenario, implement best practices associated with documentation and support systems information management.

4.6 Explain the importance of prohibited content/activity and privacy, licensing, and policy concepts.

Introduction

This module is the first of four modules focused on security. In this module, you learn about physical and logical tools and techniques used to secure buildings and the resources inside these buildings stored on personal computers and servers and accessible from the local network. You also learn how to recognize that a personal computer is infected with malware and how to clean an infected system and keep it clean. Finally, you learn what your employer might expect of you when dealing with issues of software licensing, regulated data, compliance policies, data destruction and disposal, and incidence response.

In later modules focused on security, you learn the concepts and principles of securing Windows resources on workstations and networks, securing mobile devices, and securing networks. Later in your career as a support technician, you can build on the skills learned in these modules to implement even more security measures, such as controlling how Windows stores its passwords.

However, keep in mind that even the best security will eventually fail. As a thief once said, "Locks are for honest people," and a thief will eventually find a way to break through. Security experts tell us that security measures basically make it more difficult and time consuming for a thief to break through so they get discouraged and move on to easier targets.

Physical and Logical Security

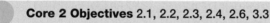

Core 2 Objectives 2.1, 2.2, 2.3, 2.4, 2.6, 3.3

In this section of the module, you learn about both physical and logical methods of protecting computer resources, including how to control staff access to these resources.

Physical Security and Access Controls

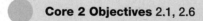

Core 2 Objectives 2.1, 2.6

Physically protecting access to a computer's resources is often seen by security experts as the most important—and most overlooked—form of security. Here are some best practices for physical security used to protect buildings, parking lots, corporate campuses, or other locations:

- **Use security fences and bollards to protect the building.** Your first line of defense to protect valuable data and property is to secure the building through the use of physical barriers such as a **security fence**. A high wire-mesh security fence installed in concrete footings with a secure gate eliminates any possible hiding places and is difficult for someone to climb over or get under, around, or through it. **Bollards**, which are strong metal posts positioned to prevent vehicles from accidentally or intentionally ramming into a protected space, can be used to help protect equipment and the entrance to a building, or to direct traffic. See Figure 16-1.

Figure 16-1   Bollards in front and security fences in the back protect this parcel locker at a London underground station

iStock.com/Peter Fleming

- **Use an access control vestibule and security guard.** The ultimate in physical security is an **access control vestibule**, also called a **mantrap**, which consists of two doors on either end of a small entryway where the first door must close and/or lock before the second door can open. A separate form of identification might be required for each door, such as a wired or wireless **badge reader** to scan staff badges for the first door (see Figure 16-2) and a fingerprint scanner for the second door. A security guard might also maintain an **entry control roster**, which is a list of people allowed into the restricted area and a log of any approved visitors.

Figure 16-2   A badge reader authenticates a staff badge to allow entry into a secured building

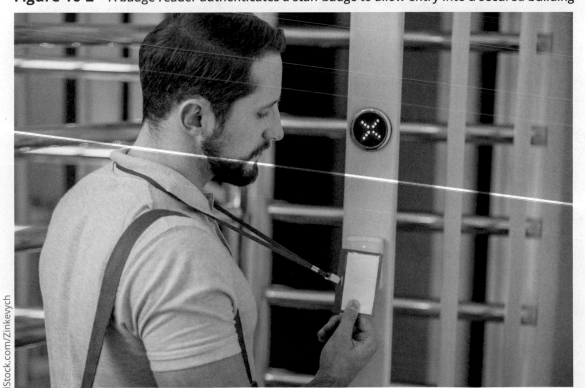

iStock.com/Zinkevych

16

- **Video surveillance.** A **video surveillance** system includes cameras installed in strategic locations by a government, organization, or school that are monitored for improper activity. A surveillance camera, sometimes called an IP camera, has an IP address to connect it to the local network and is considered a part of the **Internet of Things (IoT)**. It can transmit output to video surveillance software anywhere on the Internet via a wired or wireless connection. Cameras, such as those shown in Figure 16-3, may be fixed or may be able to pan, tilt, or zoom and may have night vision or require proper lighting to work well. A surveillance camera may have a **motion sensor** that can alert security personnel when activity is happening in the vicinity of the camera and turn on recording.

Figure 16-3   Video surveillance cameras

Pixinoo/Shutterstock.com

    The system typically requires large-capacity storage to keep recordings for several days, weeks, or months. Some systems allow real-time monitoring only at one security location or over the Internet, and other systems don't allow real-time monitoring at all; recordings must be viewed after they happen. Important security considerations for a video surveillance system include who in the organization is authorized to view the video and in what capacity the video recordings can be used.

- **Alarm systems.** **Alarm systems** generally use a low-voltage electrical system installed on doors and windows, motion sensors, and perhaps even smoke and carbon monoxide detectors. When alarm sensors detect an interruption in electrical flow or motion, they set off sirens or strobe lights to scare off intruders and wake up sleeping residents, or they may send alerts via text message or phone call to notify security personnel responsible for monitoring the system. An alarm system needs a control panel or other method to stop the alerts when authorized activity is happening.

- **Metal detectors.** A metal detector (see Figure 16-4) uses a **magnetometer**, which detects electromagnetic fields to detect metal objects, such as handguns. Metal detectors are often placed at the front entrance to buildings supervised by security personnel.

Note 1

Good security involves multiple layers of defense, which are collectively called **defense in depth**.

Figure 16-4   Metal detectors at entrances to buildings use a magnetometer to detect electromagnetic fields

Andrey Burstein/Shutterstock.com

Next, we look at physical security focused on protecting data and computers:

- **If the data or equipment is really private, keep it behind a locked door or under lock and key.** You can use all kinds of security methods to encrypt, password-protect, and hide data, but if it really is that important, one obvious thing you can do is to keep the computer behind a locked door. It sounds simple, but it works. You can also store the data on a removable storage device such as an external hard drive, and when you're not using the data, put the drive in a fireproof safe. (And, of course, keep two copies stored in different locations.) Don't forget that printouts of sensitive documents should be kept under lock and key, as well as any passwords you have written down. Door locks and safes come in several types, including keyed locks and combination locks.

- **Equipment locks.** Some computer cases allow you to add a lock so you can physically prevent others from opening the case (see Figure 16-5A). These equipment locks, called **server locks**, might be used on computers that hold corporate data. You can also use a **cable lock**, or **Kensington lock**, to secure a laptop or other computer to a table so someone can't walk away with it (see Figure 16-5B). Most laptops have a security slot on the case to connect the cable lock; this slot is called a **Kensington Security Slot** or K-Slot. Many thefts occur in private offices or hotel rooms, so even if you're not sitting in a public area with your laptop, consider keeping it locked to a nearby table or post. Be sure to choose a cable lock that resists tampering with pliers or cable cutters. Never leave a device out of your sight in a public place.

16

Figure 16-5   To physically secure a computer, (A) use a computer case lock and key for a desktop to prevent intrusion, or (B) use a cable lock system for a laptop to prevent theft

(A)

(B)

- **Secure ports with port locks.** Any exposed port on a device, such as an RJ-45 port or a USB port, can be used to access the device and compromise its security. USB ports in particular are security risks due to the ease of uploading malware or downloading sensitive data using a small flash drive carried in someone's pocket. If you can't restrict access to the device itself, you might install a **port lock** to restrict physical access to the exposed ports. The **USB lock** by PadJack, Inc., consists of three pieces, as shown in Figure 16-6. The smaller two pieces are inserted into the USB port, sealed into place with the wire loop, and cannot be removed without damaging the port or destroying the lock. Other port lock designs can lock a cable into the port so it can't be easily removed.

Figure 16-6   These port locks are reusable, but the wire loop seal can be used only once

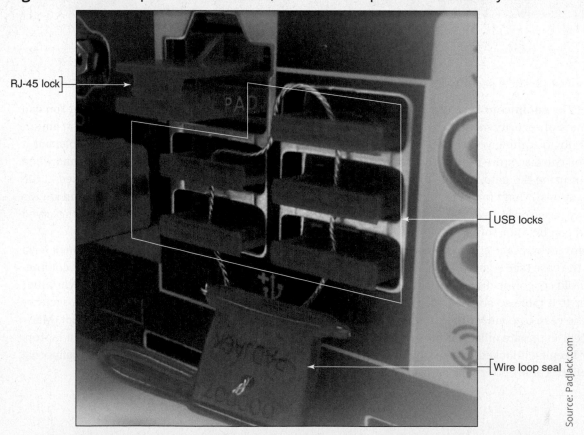

RJ-45 lock

USB locks

Wire loop seal

Source: Padjack.com

- **Use privacy screens.** To keep other people from **shoulder surfing** (secretly peeking at your monitor screen as you work), you can install a **privacy screen**, also called a **privacy filter**, that fits over the screen to prevent it from being read from a wide angle. This is especially useful in tight quarters, such as on an airplane, bus, or subway, or in other exposed locations such as a receptionist's desk.

- **Install a theft-prevention plate.** As an added precaution, physically mark a computer case or laptop so it can be identified if it is later stolen. You can embed a **theft-prevention plate** into the case and engrave or tattoo your ID information into it. See Figure 16-7. To further help you identify stolen equipment, record serial numbers and model numbers in a safe place separate from the equipment. This information can also be included in an asset management system.

Figure 16-7   The security plate and the tattoo beneath it serve as an asset-management tag and theft-prevention plate

Source: Computer Security

Using AAA for Control Access

Core 2 Objectives 2.1, 2.2

When controlling access by staff, vendors, contractors, customers, and other people to secured areas of a building and to protected resources available on the network or Internet, three types of security measures are used: To control access to a resource, a person is first authenticated, and they are also authorized to do only certain things with these resources. In addition, what a person attempts to do or actually does—and the time it takes to do it—can be tracked or logged for future auditing. These three security measures are generally known as **AAA (authenticating, authorizing, and accounting)** or **triple A**. You need to be aware of the following two principles of AAA:

- **A person is authenticated only if they are on the list.** In networking, an **access control list (ACL)** includes which users, devices, or programs have access to a particular resource—such as a printer, folder, or file on a corporate network or computer. Most security measures enforce **multifactor authentication (MFA)**, which requires more than one factor or action to authenticate someone. **Two-factor authentication (2FA)** is most often used, and the two factors normally involve what the user
  - Knows (such as a Windows or Facebook password)
  - Possesses (a token such as a key, smart card, or key fob)
  - Does (such as voice or speech recognition)
  - Is (through the use of biometric data, such as a fingerprint)
- **A person is authorized to do only what their job requires.** Using the **principle of least privilege**, a user is classified to determine the privileges they need to do their jobs. For example, some users need the privilege

to sign in to a system remotely, and others do not. Generally, when a new employee begins work, that employee's job description, with exceptions approved by their supervisor, determine what privileges the employee needs to perform their job. You, as the support technician, would be responsible to make sure the user account assigned to the employee has these privileges and no more.

Hard and Soft Tokens

Tokens used to restrict who can access a secured physical location, such as entrance into a building or to a network, might be a **hard token** (a physical device you possess) or a **soft token** (data you can retrieve):

- **Key.** It may sound old-fashioned, but a simple key is a hard token that can open a locked door. In the security world, it's important to know who has been assigned a given key and which locks the key can open.
- **Smart card.** A **smart card** used as a hard token has an embedded microprocessor usually installed on the card under a small gold plate. For example, most current credit cards have a gold plate and microprocessor and are smart cards, as opposed to earlier credit cards that used only a magnetic strip with no internal processor. The microprocessor contains information that is read by a **smart card reader** or badge reader when the device is inserted into the reader or transmitted wirelessly. Refer back to Figure 16-2.

    A smart card that is able to authenticate the reader is called a command access card (CAC). This **mutual authentication** occurs when authentication goes in both directions at the same time and both entities confirm the identity of the other. A CAC used by the Department of Defense can include personal data such as the user's name, digital signature, fingerprints, photo, department, date of birth, and even medical records. See Figure 16-8.

    Because a smart card contains a microprocessor and data, it's considered both a hard token and a soft token.

Figure 16-8   A webpage by the DoD shows the smart cards used for mutual authentication and transfer of data

Welcome to the DoD ID Card Reference Center

Do you have questions about your Common Access Card (CAC) or your Uniformed Services ID Card? This site guides you through the process of obtaining, using, and maintaining both types of cards.

Common Access Card (CAC)

"Smart" ID card for active-duty military personnel, Selected Reserve, DoD civilian employees, and eligible contractor personnel.

- CAC Types & Eligibility
- Getting Your CAC
- Managing Your CAC

Next Generation Uniformed Services ID (USID) Card

ID Card for military family members and military retirees to access service benefits and privileges. Beginning July 31, 2020, the Next Generation USID Card will be issued to eligible individuals at select DoD ID card facilities.

- ID Card Types & Eligibility
- Getting Your ID Card
- Managing Your ID Card

- **Key fob.** A **key fob** is a token that fits conveniently on a keychain, such as the one shown in Figure 16-9. When a user signs in to the network, they must enter the number on the key fob, which changes every 60 seconds and is synchronized with the network authentication service. Entering the number proves that the user has the key fob in hand. Because the device doesn't actually make physical contact with the system, it is called a contactless token or disconnected token.

- **Biometrics. Biometric locks** require special input called **biometric data** to identify a person via a retina scanner, fingerprint scanner, or palm print scanner. Figure 16-10 shows a fingerprint scanner. Many mobile devices, such as iPads and some laptops, have fingerprint scanners built in.

- **Digital certificates.** Think of a **digital certificate** as a digital signature that proves a person or entity, such as a web server, is who they say they are. It's a small file that holds information about the identity of the person or entity. In addition, a public encryption key is used to prove the certificate is legitimate; it's similar to a notary verifying that a signature is legitimate. The digital certificate and public encryption key are assigned by a **Certificate Authority (CA)** that has confirmed your identity in a separate process. VeriSign (*verisign.com*), GlobalSign (*globalsign.com*), and Let's Encrypt (*letsencrypt.org*) are three well-known CAs. You purchase a digital certificate from a CA and then install it on your desktop, laptop, or other computing device; in some cases, you can install it on a smart card or flash drive that you can use on any computer.

  Digital certificates are used to authenticate individuals (such as to digitally sign and encrypt email or to connect to a corporate network via a VPN), software (Windows can require that device drivers be digitally signed), or server applications (many web servers are digitally signed). For example, to see a web server's digital certificate, navigate to the webpage in your browser, click the lock icon, and then click Certificate. Figure 16-11 shows information about the **.google.com* certificate.

Figure 16-9 A security token such as this key fob is used to authenticate a user gaining access to a secured network

Source: iStock.com/David Clark

Figure 16-10 This access control device accepts typed code, fingerprint, or smart card input

Source: iStock.com/Viiwwee

16

Figure 16-11 The *google.com* website certificate includes the IP address of the web server

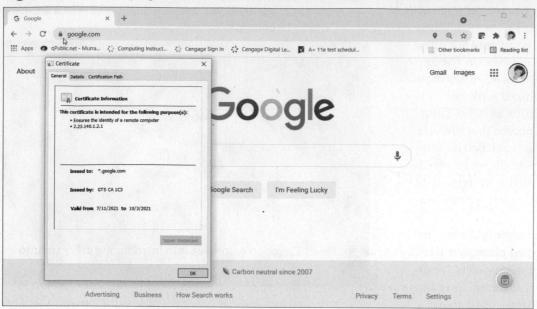

Figure 16-12 When you sign in to your account, Facebook requests the token generated by the 2FA app

Source: Twilio, Inc.

- **Authenticator apps.** An **authenticator app**, sometimes called a software token app, is installed on your smartphone or other computing device to provide a counter or number generator similar to that provided by a key fob for one factor in multifactor authentication. The app is synchronized with the same calculations on the server so the app and the server expect the same number at the same time. Software token providers for 2FA include Google Authenticator (*google.com*), Twilio Authy (*authy. com*), and LastPass Authenticator (*lastpass.com/auth*). Many online accounts—such as banking accounts, Facebook, Google, and Amazon—can be set to use 2FA and software tokens. For example, the Authy app by Twilio can be used to require 2FA to sign in to Facebook (see Figure 16-12).

In general, to set up 2FA with an online account, you would do the following:

1. Sign up for and configure the 2FA service with a 2FA provider such as Twilio. You'll need to download and install its authenticator app to your phone or computer.
2. Enable 2FA with a Facebook, Google, banking, or other account you want to secure.
3. Configure the account to use the 2FA service.
4. Now, each time you sign in to the account, you must provide your password and the number generated by the authenticator app.

Note 2

A common use of multifactor authentication (MFA) is sending a confirmation code by text to your smartphone using a phone number the server already has on file. The problem with this method is that text messages are sent to a phone using the **short message service (SMS)** protocol, which is not encrypted and can be hacked. The same goes for voice calls used for MFA, which can also be hacked because voice is not encrypted. Rather than text or voice MFA, for better security, use an authenticator app.

Email Filtering

One more security feature that controls what someone is authorized to do on the job is email filtering. Most email providers offer **email filtering** to filter out suspicious messages based on databases of known scams, spammers, and malware. Corporations might route incoming and outgoing email through a proxy server for filtering with the following goals in mind:

- Incoming email is inspected for scams or spam that might trick an employee into introducing malware into the corporate network.
- Outgoing email from employees might be filtered for inappropriate content. This lawful interception is intended to verify that an employee is complying with privacy laws (for example, laws that protect confidential medical records) and is not accidentally or intentionally leaking corporate data and secrets. Email filtering software used in this way is an example of **data loss prevention (DLP)** software, which helps protect against leaking corporate data.

Social Engineering and User Education

Core 2 Objectives 2.3, 2.4, 2.6, 3.3

Generally speaking, people are the weakest link in setting up security in a computer environment. That's because people can often be tricked into giving out private information and allowing access to secure systems. Even with all the news and hype about identity theft and criminal websites, it's amazing how well they still work. Many users naively download a funny screen saver, open an email attachment, or enter credit card information on a website without regard to security. In the IT arena, **social engineering** is the practice of tricking people into giving out private information or allowing unsafe programs into a network or computer.

A good support technician is aware of the criminal practices used and is able to teach users how to recognize and avoid this mischief. Many organizations routinely offer **security awareness training**, also known as **anti-phishing training**, to its employees to help them recognize common threats and social engineering situations. In this part of the module, you learn about several of these need-to-know practices.

Protect Passwords

It's important for users to understand they need to protect their passwords, personally identifiable information (PII), and other sensitive data. Train users to not send this type of data over email or carelessly leave it in sight on a desk or printer. Always shred documents containing sensitive data before putting them in the trash. Sanitize a device before disposing of it (you learn about ways to sanitize devices later in this module). Other ways to protect passwords include the following:

- Never give out your passwords to anyone, not even a supervisor or tech support person who calls and asks for it.
- Don't store your passwords on a computer unless you use company-approved password vault software (for example, KeePass or LastPass). Some organizations even forbid employees from writing down their passwords.
- Don't use the same password on more than one computer, network, application, or website.

16

You learn more about protecting passwords in later modules.

Prevent Tailgating

Users need to be on the alert for **tailgating**, which is when an unauthorized person follows an employee through a secured entrance to a room or building or continues a Windows session after the authorized user has stepped away. To help prevent tailgating a Windows session, a user needs to do the following:

- **Sign out of or lock the workstation.** Make it a habit to sign out of or lock the workstation when not in use. To do that in Windows, click **Start**, click the account icon, and click either **Sign out** or **Lock**. To use the keyboard shortcut to lock the workstation, press **Windows+L**. See Figure 16-13. The difference between the two is that when you sign out, all your apps are closed and your Windows session ends. When you lock the workstation, your session stays open, and your apps continue to run until you enter your password to continue your session.

- **Screensaver lock.** After a period of inactivity, a computer normally displays a screensaver and goes into sleep mode until a key is pressed to wake it up. A **screensaver lock** locks the computer before it goes to sleep and requires a password to unlock it before restoring the user session. To configure a screensaver lock in Windows, in the Settings app, select **Accounts** and then **Sign-in options**. See Figure 16-14. Verify **When PC wakes up from sleep** is selected.

Figure 16-13 Sign out or lock Windows when the workstation is not in use

Figure 16-14 Require signing in each time your computer wakes from sleep mode

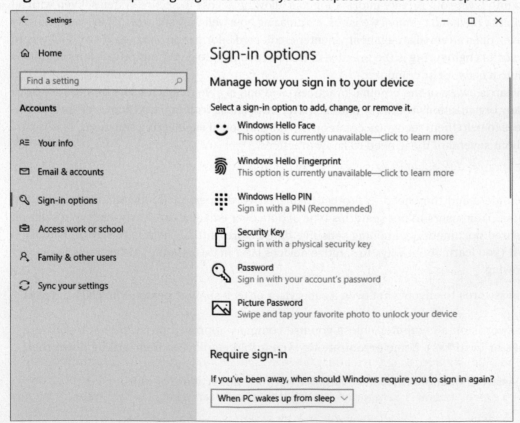

Common Social Engineering Techniques

Users need to be aware of these social engineering techniques and understand how to resist hackers trying to gain access to networks, computers, and sensitive data:

- **Dumpster diving and impersonation. Dumpster diving** is looking for useful information in someone's trash to help create a convincing **impersonation** of an individual or company to aid in a malicious attack. Even something that might appear harmless, such as an organizational chart, can help a thief create a convincing email hoax message. For best security, shred all papers and printouts before recycling, and educate users about the importance of shredding.
- **Phishing, whaling, and vishing. Phishing** (pronounced "fishing") is a type of identity theft in which the sender of an **email hoax** scams you into responding with personal data about yourself. A phishing attack that targets a high-profile employee, such as the CEO or CFO, is called **whaling**. **Vishing** is phishing with voice and is a phone call scam that tries to lure you into giving out personal information.
- **Spear phishing and spoofing.** Even more plausible than phishing is **spear phishing**, where an email appears to come from companies you already do business with. The scam artist baits you by asking you to verify personal data on your bank account, ISP account, credit card account, or something of that nature. Often a convincing impersonation of an individual or company tricks you into responding to the email or clicking a link in the email message, which takes you to an official-looking site complete with corporate or bank logos, where you are asked to enter your user ID and password to enter the site. This tactic is called **spoofing**, which means the scammer makes both the email and website look like the real thing. An email message might contain a link that leads to a malicious script. If you think an email is legitimate, be on the safe side and don't click the link. To keep a script from running, type the website's home page into your browser address bar and navigate to the relevant page on the website.

Good sites to help you debunk a virus hoax or email hoax are the following:

- *snopes.com* by Snopes Media Group Inc.
- *breakthechain.org* by John R. Ratliff
- *securelist.com* by Kaspersky Lab

Don't forward an email hoax. If you get a hoax from a person you know, do us all a favor and send that person some of the preceding links!

> **Exam Tip** ✔
>
> The A+ Core 2 exam expects you to recognize and distinguish among examples of social engineering situations that might compromise security, such as shoulder surfing, tailgating, dumpster diving, impersonations, phishing, whaling, vishing, spoofing, and insider threats.

Next, we turn our attention to dealing with malware. As an IT support technician, you will most certainly be called on to handle it.

16

Dealing with Malicious Software on Personal Computers

> **Core 2 Objectives** 1.3, 2.3, 2.4, 2.5, 3.2, 3.3

Malicious software, also called **malware**, is any unwanted program that is intended to harm and is transmitted to your computer without your knowledge. **Grayware** is any annoying and unwanted program that might or might not intend harm—for example, adware that produces all those unwanted pop-up ads. In this section of the module, you learn about the different types of malware and grayware, what to do to clean up an infected system, and how to protect a system from infection.

What Are We Up Against?

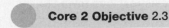 Core 2 Objective 2.3

You need to know your enemy! According to metadata from anti-malware developers, more than 560,000 new malware programs are detected daily. Different categories of malware and scamming techniques are listed next:

- **Viruses.** A **virus** is a program that replicates by attaching itself to other programs. The infected program must be executed for a virus to run. The program might be an application, a macro in a document, a Windows system file, or a boot loader program.
- **Spyware.** **Spyware** spies on you to collect personal information that it transmits over the Internet to web-hosting sites. An example of spyware is a **keylogger** that tracks all your keystrokes and can be used to steal your identity, credit card numbers, Social Security number, bank information, passwords, email addresses, and so forth.
- **Worms.** A **worm** is a program that copies itself throughout a network or the Internet without a host program. A worm creates problems by overloading the network as it replicates and can even hijack or install a server program such as a web server.
- **Trojans.** A **Trojan** does not need a host program to work; rather, it substitutes itself for a legitimate program. In most cases, a user launches it thinking they are launching a legitimate program. A Trojan is often embedded in the files of legitimate software that is downloaded from an untrustworthy website, or a user is tricked into opening an email attachment (see Figure 16-15).

Figure 16-15   By opening this email attachment, a user is likely to introduce a Trojan into the system

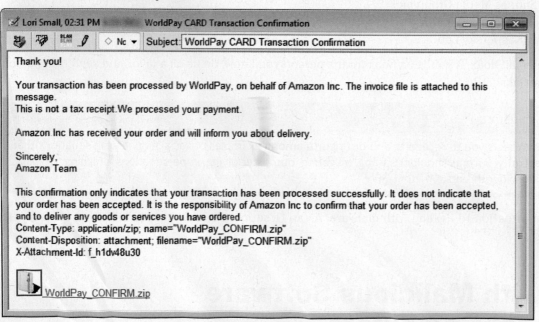

- **Rootkits.** A **rootkit** loads itself before the OS boot is complete. It can hide in boot managers, boot loader programs, or kernel mode device drivers. UEFI secure boot is especially designed to catch rootkits that launch during the boot. Because a rootkit is already loaded when most anti-malware software loads, it is sometimes overlooked by the software. A rootkit can hide folders that contain software it has installed, cause Windows Task Manager to display a different name for its process, hide registry keys, and can operate in user mode or kernel mode. This last trick helps it remain undetected (see Figure 16-16).

Figure 16-16   A rootkit can run in user mode or kernel mode

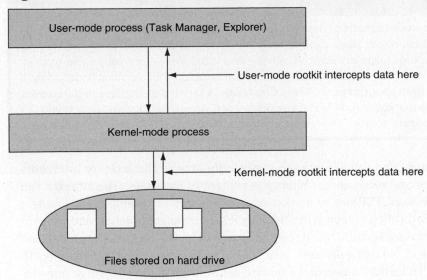

A rootkit running in user mode intercepts the API calls between the time the API retrieves the data and when it is displayed in a window. A rootkit running in kernel mode actually interferes with the Windows kernel and substitutes its own information in place of the raw data read by the Windows kernel. Because most anti-malware software to one degree or another relies on operating system tools and components to work, the rootkit is not detected or cannot be deleted if the OS tools themselves are infected.

Caution (!)

If anti-malware software reports that a rootkit is present but cannot delete it, the best solution is to immediately disconnect the computer from the network (if you have not already done so), back up your important data, format your hard drive, and reinstall the OS.

- **Boot sector virus.** A **boot sector virus** infects the first sector on a MBR (Master Boot Record) hard drive and can infect the partition table in that sector. The virus works by replacing the program in the first sector, which is used to boot the system. The infection usually happens when you boot a computer with bootable media, such as a USB flash drive, that is infected. To remove a boot sector virus, you'll need antivirus software that runs in a preinstallation environment before the OS launches. Boot sector viruses are not as common as they once were because hard drives use the newer GPT partitioning system rather than the more vulnerable MBR system and also because modern BIOS/UEFI is designed to detect and stop these viruses.

Note 3

Although malicious software is designed to do varying degrees of damage to data and software, it does not damage computer hardware. However, when partition table information is destroyed on a hard drive, the drive can appear to be physically damaged.

- **Ransomware.** **Ransomware** holds your computer system hostage until you pay money. For example, the infamous CryptoLocker Trojan program was embedded in email attachments and was known to work on Windows, Android, and even some iOS systems. When the user clicked the attachment, the program encrypted the computer's personal files. If the user didn't pay within a 24-hour period, all the files were lost. Many users who did not have backups of their data chose to pay the ransom. A computer infected with ransomware can infect all computers on the network and even cloud servers to which the computer connects.

16

> **Caution** ❗
>
> The best defense against ransomware is to keep backups of data file versions in a location that is not accessible from Windows File Explorer or macOS Finder. A ransomware attack can infect any storage device connected or mapped to your computer, and a single layer of data file backups might be replaced with the encrypted files before you're able to clean your computer and restore the backed-up data. Use a backup method that retains multiple file versions (indefinitely, if possible) and that is not directly accessible from your computer. Many cloud backup services meet these requirements, such as Carbonite (*carbonite.com*), Backblaze (*backblaze.com*), and IDrive (*idrive.com*). After a ransomware attack, you can wipe the computer, reinstall software from original sources, and restore unaffected file versions from your online backups.

- **On-path attack.** In an **on-path attack**, also called a **man-in-the-middle attack**, the attacker intercepts communication between two parties and reads and/or alters the content of messages. The attacker can impersonate a legitimate website, network, FTP site, or person in a chat session. For example, a user might connect to a fraudulent Wi-Fi hotspot, called an **evil twin**, thinking it's a legitimate hotspot, and attempt to start a chat session with a business associate. The attacker pretends to be the business associate and continues the chat with the intention of obtaining private information. The best protection against on-path attacks is to use digital certificates to identify a person or service before transmitting sensitive information. Sometimes an evil twin hotspot exists only to steal passwords. When connecting to a public hotspot, especially one that requires signing in, be sure the hotspot is legitimate.

- **Zero-day attack.** A **zero-day attack** can happen in two ways: A hacker discovers a security hole in software that is unknown to the developer of the software, or a hacker takes advantage of a recently reported gap in software security before users apply patches released by the developer. The race is on for the vendor to provide a patch to the software and for users to apply those patches before hackers have even one day to use the hole to infect systems and steal user data. Microsoft normally publishes security patches on the second Tuesday of each month (known as patch Tuesday), but sometimes releases patches off schedule so hackers have less time to attack customers.

- **Denial of service.** A **denial-of-service (DoS)** attack overwhelms a computer or network with requests or traffic until new connections can no longer be accepted. A **distributed denial-of-service (DDoS)** attack happens when multiple computers are involved in the attack. As shown in Figure 16-17, DDoS attacks are sometimes performed by zombies and botnets, which are described next.

Figure 16-17   A DDoS attack might use a network of zombies called a botnet

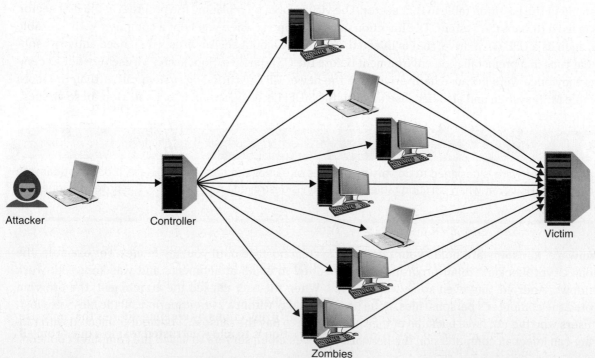

- **Zombies and botnets.** A **zombie** is a computer that has been hacked, and the hacker is using the computer to run repetitive software in the background without the knowledge of its user. For example, the zombie might be email spamming or performing DDoS attacks. A hacker might build an entire network of zombies, which is called a **botnet** (a network of robots). The CryptoLocker Trojan program was distributed by a botnet and ultimately isolated when the botnet was taken down. **Cryptojacking** is a type of zombie attack that installs crypto mining software to run mining operations. **Crypto miner** software validates cryptocurrency transactions, and these transactions are linked to the ongoing chains of transactions called blockchains.
- **Dictionary attack.** A **dictionary attack** can be used to crack a password by trying words in a dictionary. Password cracker software might combine a **brute force attack** (systematically trying every possible combination of letters, numbers, and symbols) with a dictionary attack to guess the password. A dictionary attack is usually more efficient than using brute force.
- **Rainbow tables.** A **rainbow table** contains a long list of plaintext passwords, just as users would enter, and the password hash list (after it is encrypted). Organizations store only hashed passwords and not plaintext passwords. When hackers obtain a stolen list of hashed passwords, they can compare this list with those in their rainbow tables to find a match. When two hashed passwords match, they can use the plaintext password in the rainbow table to sign in to the system, impersonating the user.

  Rainbow tables make cracking passwords faster than dictionary cracking or brute force cracking. The best defenses against rainbow table attacks are for an organization to use the very best hashing techniques to encrypt their passwords and to add extra characters to the password hash (called salting the passwords).

Exam Tip ✔

The A+ Core 2 exam might give you a scenario that requires you to identify, detect, remove, or prevent viruses, Trojans, spyware, keyloggers, ransomware, rootkits, boot sector viruses, on-path attacks, zero-day attacks, DoS/DDoS attacks, crypto mining software, and dictionary attacks.

What Makes Us the Most Vulnerable?

Core 2 Objective 2.4

Listed next are some reasons systems are the most vulnerable to attacks:

- **Noncompliant systems.** A system administrator needs techniques in place to routinely scan BYOD and corporate-owned smartphones, tablets, laptops, desktops, and servers for **noncompliant systems** that violate security best practices, such as an OS that is not kept updated or anti-malware software that is not up to date or not even installed. One software suite of products designed to manage user devices in an organization is Microsoft Endpoint Manager. One component of this suite is Configuration Manager, which can scan devices for noncompliance. BYODs are particularly susceptible to noncompliance because a corporation generally has less control over a user-owned device than one owned by the corporation and assigned to the user.
- **Unprotected and unpatched systems.** Personal devices that are not managed by a corporation are especially vulnerable when the OS is not kept up to date with all available patches and anti-malware is not running in real time or kept up to date. For a workstation or laptop system, it's also important that firewalls are set for maximum protection, especially when the computer is connected to a public network.
- **End-of-life OS.** If the OS has reached the end of its life cycle, the developer no longer provides security patches, making the OS vulnerable to attack. It's time to upgrade the OS to a current edition.
- **Structured Query Language (SQL) injections.** **Structured Query Language (SQL)** is a popular scripting and programming language designed primarily to query databases. SQL programmers can carelessly create vulnerabilities in their software, making it possible for hackers to inject their own code in a query to the database and retrieve data they are not authorized to access. An **SQL injection** happens when part of a user's typed text is used to construct a query, and a hacker familiar with SQL uses text that actually changes the query (see Figure 16-18). The programmer can prevent SQL injections by creating queries that only use prepared text rather than untrusted user text. Another solution is to allow untrusted text in a query only if the text can be found in a whitelist of approved text.

16

Figure 16-18 An SQL injection alters an SQL query to change the output from the query

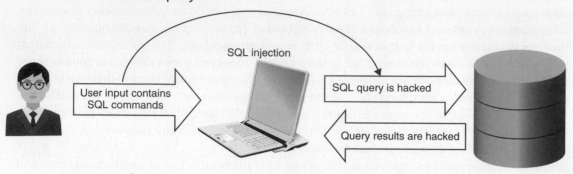

- **Cross-site scripting (XSS).** **Cross-site scripting (XSS)** happens when an attacker sends a malicious script to an online application, and the application unknowingly sends the script to an unsuspecting user's browser, which executes the script under the user's credentials. See Figure 16-19. This script might instruct the online app to send sensitive data to the hacker or even give the hacker control of the app. An online app is vulnerable to this type of injection attack if the app's developer does not carefully test each data entry point in the app to ensure that scripts cannot be accepted as user input.

Figure 16-19 A cross-site scripting (XSS) attack

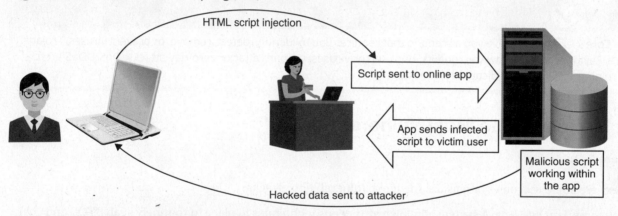

Note 4

SQL and HTML scripts are vulnerable to injection attacks because the scripts can be a combination of text and commands, and text can be interpreted as commands by simply inserting a few key characters in the right place. You learn more about scripting in the module, "Linux and Scripting."

- **Insider threats.** Employees and others who have legitimate access to the network and data can be a threat if they are careless or negligent and accidentally leak data or fall victim to a social engineering attack. In addition, malicious insiders might intentionally steal data or do other damage.
- **Lack of user education.** Cybint (*cybintsolutions.com*) reports that 95% of online attacks are caused by human error. Lack of user education about how to avoid attacks makes systems especially vulnerable.

Step-By-Step Attack Plan

Core 2 Objective 3.3

This section provides a step-by-step attack plan to clean up an infected system. We use **anti-malware software**, also called **antivirus software**, to remove all types of general malware, including viruses, spyware, worms, and rootkits. Then we'll use some Windows tools to check out the system, making sure all remnants of malware have been removed and the system is in tip-top order.

Caution ❗

If a system is highly infected and will later hold sensitive data, a fresh start might be in order. In fact, Microsoft recommends reinstalling Windows as the safest way to deal with highly infected systems. If you have recent backups of data, format the hard drive, reinstall or reimage Windows, and restore data from backups.

If you don't have recent backups for a Windows 10/11 system, you can try a repair installation or a Windows reset without losing user data. In the module, "Troubleshooting Windows Startup," you learned about all of these options to reinstall Windows.

As you work your way through the steps described next to remediate an infected system, at any point in the process, you might realize the system is highly infected and the best course of action is to stop remediating the system and to simply reinstall the OS.

Step 1: Identifying and Researching Malware Symptoms

Core 2 Objectives 1.3, 3.2, 3.3

An IT support technician needs to know how to recognize that a system is infected. Here are some warnings that suggest malicious software is at work:

- **Pop-up ads, browser redirection, and desktop alerts.** Basically, a user is losing control of their system. Pop-up ads (see Figure 16-20) are randomly appearing and the browser home page has changed. A browser might also have an uninvited toolbar. The user enters the URL for one website and another site appears in the browser window. Security alerts—real or spoofed—regularly appear on the desktop to interrupt the user's activity.

Figure 16-20 Random and frequent pop-up ads indicate malware

Source: Forbes

- **Unable to access the network or the Internet, application crashes, and OS update failures.** These types of problems seem to plague the system with no reasonable explanation that is specific to the network, application, or Windows update.
- **Rogue antivirus software and false alerts.** You see false alerts from software that claims to be antivirus software protecting your system. When the user tries to run Microsoft Defender Antivirus (anti-malware software embedded in Windows 10/11), it refuses to run. In the Windows Security window, you find that Defender Antivirus has been disabled because other antivirus software the user did not install is running.

16

Note 5

Windows allows only one anti-malware product to run at a time. You can use Task Manager to stop the rogue antivirus software and then start Microsoft Defender Antivirus.

- **Strange notifications and slow performance.** Generally, the system works much slower than before. Programs take longer than normal to load. Strange or bizarre error messages appear. Programs that once worked now give errors. Task Manager shows unfamiliar processes running. The computer's operating system might lock up.
- **Problems with files.** Personal files now have weird names or their file sizes seem excessively large. Executable files have changed size or file extensions change without reason. Files mysteriously disappear or appear. Windows system files are renamed. Files constantly become corrupted. Files you could once access now give access-denied messages, and file permissions change.
- **Problems updating your anti-malware software.** Even though you can browse to other websites, you cannot access anti-malware software sites such as *symantec.com* or *mcafee.com*, and you cannot update your anti-malware software.
- **Certificate warnings.** An OS is responsible for validating certificates used to secure communication. For Windows, Microsoft maintains a database of trusted root certificates issued by Certificate Authorities (CAs). A **root certificate** is the original certificate issued by the CA. When a Windows system opens a secure email or visits a secure website and encounters a new digital certificate, it requests Microsoft's trusted root certificate, which is downloaded to the computer. The download happens seamlessly without the user's knowledge unless there's a problem. If Windows cannot obtain the root certificate to validate the email or website, it displays an error (see Figure 16-21). Don't trust websites or email whose certificates have expired or have been revoked.

Figure 16-21   Windows reports a problem with a digital certificate

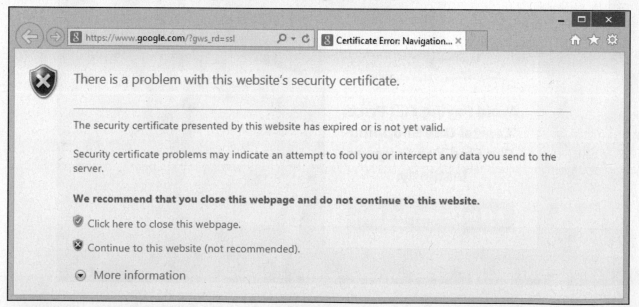

Note 6

If a computer gives certificate warnings, check that the Windows date is correct. A wrong Windows date before the certificate was issued can cause the problem.

You can use the **Certificate Manager** (certmgr.msc) in the Microsoft Management Console (MMC) to view and delete root certificates, as shown in Figure 16-22. For example, the Superfish virus injects a rogue root certificate into the Microsoft store of trusted certificates on the local computer so it can perform an in-path attack to display adware on secure websites a user visits. If you see a Superfish certificate listed among trusted root certificates, be sure to delete it.

Figure 16-22   Windows Certificate Manager can be used to view and delete root certificates kept in the store of trusted certificates

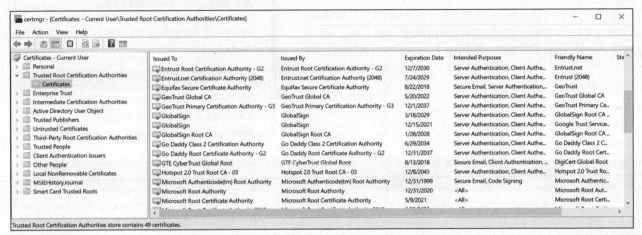

 Exam Tip ✔

The A+ Core 2 exam might give you a scenario that requires you to recognize the common symptoms of malware listed previously and to know how to quarantine and remediate an infected system.

Step 2: Quarantining an Infected System

Core 2 Objective 3.3

If an infected computer is connected to a wired or wireless network, immediately disconnect the network cable or turn off the wireless adapter. You don't want to spread a virus or worm to other computers on your network. A **quarantined computer** is not allowed to use the regular network that other computers use. If you need to use the Internet to download anti-malware software or its updates, take some precautions first. Consider your options. Can you disconnect other computers from the network while the infected computer is connected? Can you isolate the computer from your local network and connect it directly to the ISP or a special quarantined network? If neither option is possible, try downloading the anti-malware software updates while the computer is booted into Safe Mode with Networking or after a clean boot. (Safe Mode doesn't always allow downloads.) Malware might still be running in Safe Mode or after a clean boot, but it's less likely to do so than when the system is started normally.

Always keep in mind that data on the hard drive might not be backed up. Before you begin cleaning up the system, back up data to another media.

Step 3: Disabling System Protection

Core 2 Objective 3.3

In Windows, some malware hides its program files in restore points stored in the System Volume Information folder that's maintained by System Protection. If System Protection is on, anti-malware software can't clean this

16

protected folder. To get rid of the malware, turn off System Protection so anti-malware software can clean the System Volume Information folder (see Figure 16-23). Realize that when you turn off System Protection, all your restore points are lost, so first consider whether you might need those restore points to troubleshoot the malware infection before you disable System Protection. Also consider that a restore point might be infected and, when applied, might reintroduce the malware back into the system.

To turn off System Protection, right-click **Start**, click **System**, and in the About window, click **System protection**. Later, when you are sure the system is clean, turn System Protection back on, and create a new restore point that you can use in the future if problems arise.

Figure 16-23   Malware found in a restore point

Source: McAfee Inc.

> **Caution**
>
> Some highly infected systems will not allow anti-malware software to run. In this situation, you can boot the computer into Safe Mode and use System Restore to apply a restore point that was taken before the infection. Applying a restore point cannot be counted on to completely remove an infection, but it might remove startup entries the malware is using, making it possible to run the anti-malware software from the normal Windows desktop or to run the software in Safe Mode. Consider that you might need to apply a restore point before you disable System Protection, which deletes all your restore points.

Step 4: Remediating the Infected System

Core 2 Objectives 2.5, 3.3

Microsoft Defender Antivirus software is embedded in Windows 10/11 and activated by default. Table 16-1 lists other popular anti-malware software for personal computers and their websites, which also provide information about malware. Before selecting a product, be sure to read some reviews about it and check out some reliable websites that rate anti-malware software. Don't make the mistake of using an infected computer to purchase and download anti-malware software because keyloggers might be spying and collecting credit card information.

Table 16-1   Anti-Malware Software and Websites

Anti-Malware Software	Website
Malwarebytes Premium	malwarebytes.com
Norton AntiVirus Plus	norton.com
Bitdefender Antivirus Plus	bitdefender.com
Kaspersky Anti-Virus	kaspersky.com
McAfee AntiVirus Plus	mcafee.com

To find out what anti-malware software is installed and turned on, in the Windows 10 Settings app, open **Update & Security**, click **Windows Security**, and then click **Virus & threat protection** (see Figure 16-24). If third-party software is running, Defender Antivirus is deactivated by default. For Windows 11, in the Settings app, click **Privacy & security**, **Windows Security**, and **Virus & threat protection**.

Figure 16-24   McAfee VirusScan is protecting the system rather than Microsoft Defender Antivirus, the default Windows solution

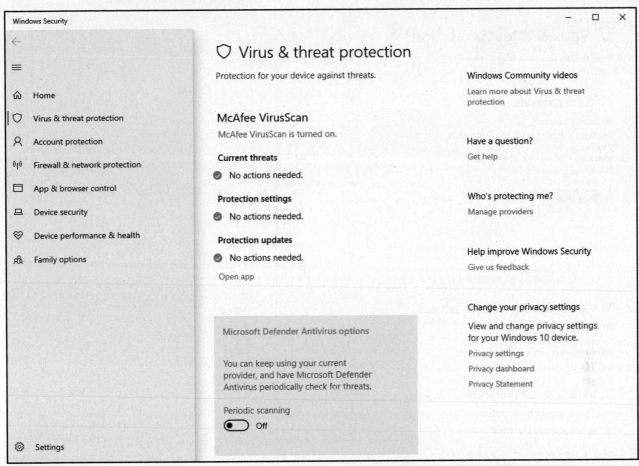

Caution (!)

Beware of websites that appear as sponsored links at the top of search results for anti-malware software. These sites might appear to be the home site for the software, but they are really trying to lure you into downloading adware or spyware.

Now let's look at different situations you might encounter when attempting to run anti-malware software.

Update and Run Anti-Malware Software

Anti-malware software can't find what it doesn't know to look for. As new malware gets into the wild (becomes available on the Internet), anti-malware software needs to be updated with these latest **malware definitions**, also called **malware signatures**. Do the following to update and run the software:

1. Verify the anti-malware software is up to date. Microsoft Defender Antivirus normally gets its updates in Windows security updates. To manually check for updates for Windows 10 Defender Antivirus, in Settings, open **Update & Security**, click **Windows Security**, and click **Virus & threat protection**. In the Virus & threat protection window (see Figure 16-25), click **Check for updates**. For Windows 11, in Settings, click **Privacy & security, Windows Security, Virus & threat protection, Protection updates**, and **Check for updates**. If you are using third-party anti-malware, open the app and look for the update feature in the app's window.

16

Figure 16-25   Manually update Microsoft Defender Antivirus

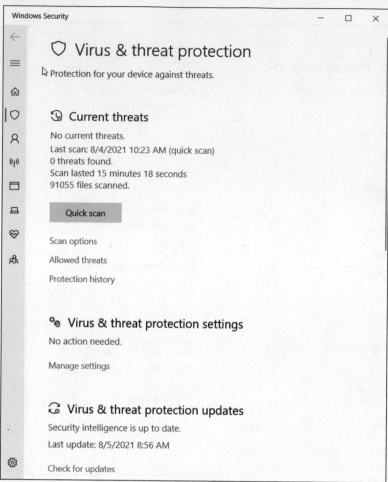

2. Use the anti-malware software to perform a full scan of the system. For example, for Defender Antivirus, in the *Virus & threat protection* window (see Figure 16-25), click **Scan options**. In the Scan options window (see Figure 16-26), select **Full scan** and click **Scan now**. As it scans, the software might ask you what to do with an infected program (see Figure 16-27), or it might log the event in an event viewer or history log it keeps. In most situations, you would delete an infected program.

Figure 16-26   A full scan can take some time and is preferred
when a virus is suspected

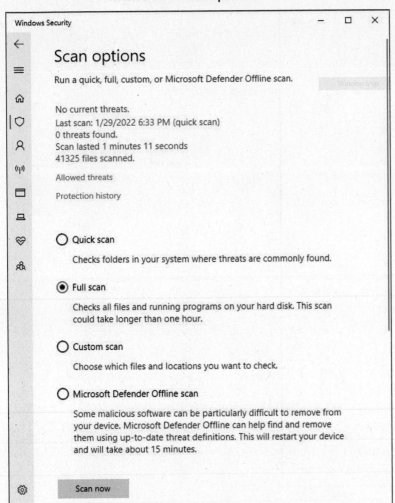

3. After the scan is complete and you have decided what to do with each suspicious file, reboot the system, allow the software to update itself again, and then scan the system again. Most likely, some new malware will be discovered. Keep rebooting and rescanning until a scan comes up clean.

Note 7

If you ever encounter a virus that your updated anti-malware software did not find, be sure to let the manufacturer of the software know so they can research the problem.

16

When Anti-Malware Software Gives Errors

If Defender Antivirus detects malware it cannot remove, it asks permission to run Microsoft Defender Offline. When you agree, the system reboots and runs a scan in the recovery environment (preinstallation environment). Defender Offline can detect and remove rootkits, boot sector viruses, and other persistent malware that cannot be dealt with

Figure 16-27   It is better to remove a threat rather than quarantine or allow it

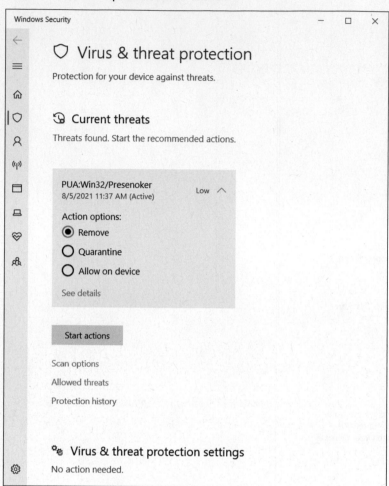

after Windows starts. If Defender Antivirus or third-party anti-malware software refuses to run or runs with errors, follow these steps:

1. **Perform a Microsoft Defender Offline scan.** Sign in to Windows using an administrator account. In the Scan options window (refer back to Figure 16-26), select **Microsoft Defender Offline scan**, and click **Scan now**. Respond to the UAC dialog box. The computer reboots in the preinstallation environment and scans the system.

2. **Boot into Safe Mode and scan the system.** Some malware prevents anti-malware software from running. In this situation, try booting the system in Safe Mode or performing a clean boot and then running the anti-malware software. Recall that to launch Windows in Safe Mode, also called Safe boot, enter the `msconfig` command in the Windows search box. In the System Configuration dialog box, click the **Boot** tab and check **Safe boot** (see Figure 16-28). To launch Safe Mode with Networking so you can update your anti-malware software, select **Network** in the list of options. Then restart the system.

Figure 16-28   Use the Safe boot option to boot the system in Safe Mode
and prevent malware from launching at startup

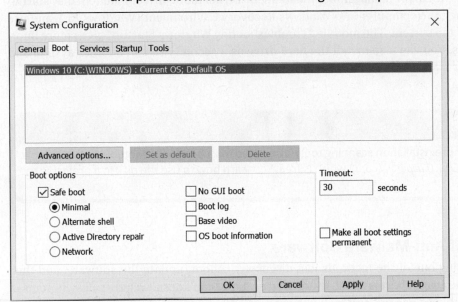

Note 8

If viruses are launched even after you boot in Safe Mode and you cannot get the anti-malware software to work, try searching for suspicious entries in the Windows registry subkeys under HKLM\System\CurrentControlSet\Control\SafeBoot. Subkeys under this key control what is launched when you boot into Safe Mode. How to edit the registry is covered in the module "Troubleshooting Windows After Startup."

3. **Scan the system using a healthy networked computer.** Follow these steps:

   a. On the infected computer, share drive C: so you can reach it from another computer.

   b. Make sure the remote computer has its software firewall set for maximum protection and its installed anti-malware software is up to date and running.

   c. Network the two computers. (Don't connect the infected computer to the entire network. If necessary, you can connect the two computers using a crossover cable or using a small switch and network cables.)

   d. To make your work easier, you can map a network drive from the remote computer to drive C: on the infected computer.

   e. Perform an anti-malware scan on the remote computer, pointing the scan to drive C: on the infected computer. For Defender Antivirus, open the **Scan options** window (refer back to Figure 16-26), select **Custom scan**, click **Scan now**, and point to the infected computer under Network.

Note 9

How to network two computers with a switch and cables is covered in the Core 1 module, "Networking Fundamentals." How to share a drive or folder and how to mount a network drive are covered in the module, "Securing and Sharing Windows Resources."

16

When an Infected Computer Will Not Boot

If an infected computer will not boot, the boot manager, boot loaders, or kernel mode drivers launched at startup might be infected or damaged. Launch the computer into Windows Recovery Environment (Windows RE), and use the Startup Repair process to repair the system. The module "Troubleshooting Windows Startup" gives more information about solving boot problems. You can also install the hard drive as a second drive in another system and use that system to scan the drive for malware.

Note 10

Some anti-malware companies offer preinstallation scanning tools, also called rescue disks or bootable antivirus tools. One example is Kaspersky's Rescue Disk (*kaspersky.com*), which is free. You learn how to use the disk in a project at the end of this module.

Run More Than One Scan of Anti-Malware Software

After you've scanned the system using one of the methods just discussed, reboot, update the software, and then keep scanning and rebooting until the scan report is clean. If a second or third scan doesn't remove all symptoms of malware, consider installing and running a second anti-malware program. What one anti-malware program cannot detect or remove, another one might. For example, Defender Antivirus on one system removed malware it detected, but did not detect or remove the downloader *dnsatlantic.exe*, which hijacked a browser and is still running in the background (see Figure 16-29).

Figure 16-29   The malware downloader *dnsatlantic.exe* is still running after multiple scans of anti-malware software

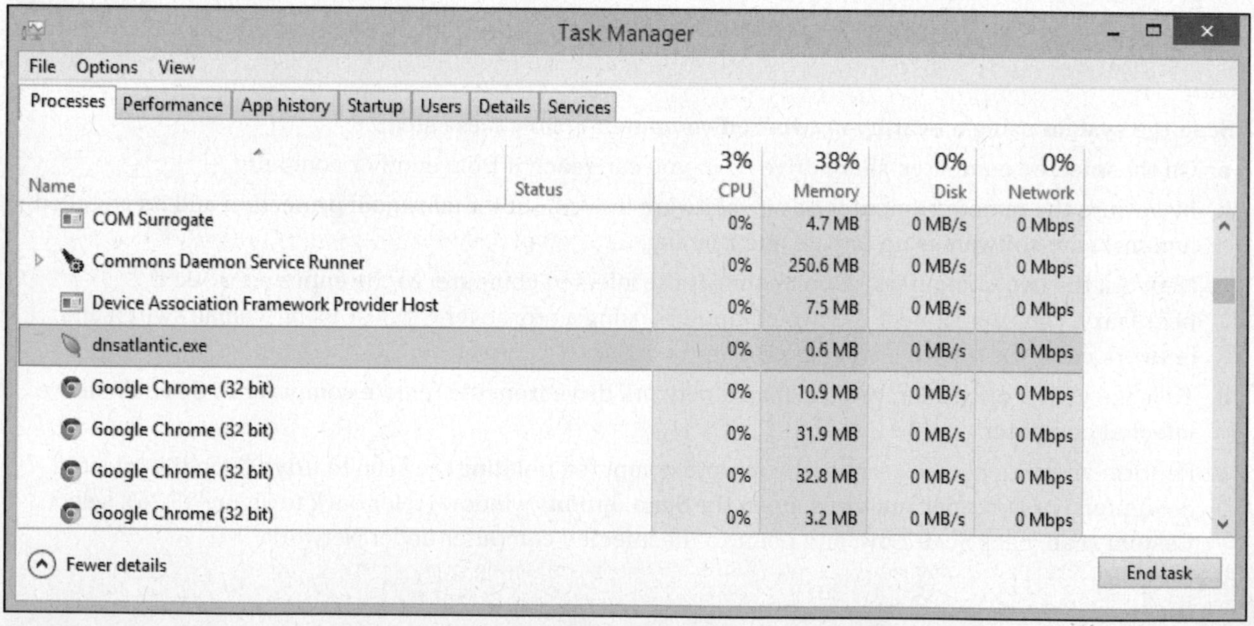

In this situation, try another anti-malware program. For example, Microsoft Safety Scanner (*docs.microsoft.com/en-us/windows/security/threat-protection/intelligence/safety-scanner-download*) is not designed for ongoing malware prevention but can sometimes remove malware that Defender Antivirus did not find. Download and run the latest version of the software.

Clean Up What's Left Over

Next, you'll need to clean up anything the anti-malware software left behind. Sometimes anti-malware software tells you it is not able to delete a file, or it deletes an infected file but leaves behind an orphaned entry in the registry or startup folders. If the anti-malware software tells you it was not able to delete or clean a file, first check the anti-malware software website for any instructions you might find to manually clean things up. Here are some general actions you can take to clean up what the software left behind:

1. **Respond to any startup errors.** On the first boot after anti-malware software has declared a system clean, you might still find some startup errors caused by incomplete removal of the malware. Use Task Manager to find out how a startup program is launched. If the program is launched from the registry, you can back up and delete the registry key. If the program is launched from a startup folder, you can move or delete the shortcut or program in the folder. See the appendix "Entry Points for Windows Startup Processes" for a list of startup folders and startup registry keys.

2. **Research malware types and program files.** Your anti-malware software might alert you to a suspicious program file that it quarantines and then ask you to decide if you want to delete it. The web is your best tool to use when making your decision about a program. Some websites that offer **malware encyclopedias** that are reliable and give you symptoms and solutions for malware include the following:

   - Process Library by ProcessLibrary at *processlibrary.com*
   - DLL Library by Uniblue Systems Limited at *liutilities.com*
   - All the anti-malware software sites listed earlier in Table 16-1

   Beware of using other sites! Much information on the web is written by people who are just guessing, and some of the information is put there to purposefully deceive. Check things out carefully, and learn which sites you can rely on.

3. **Delete files.** For each program file the anti-malware software told you it could not delete, delete the program file yourself by following these steps:

   a. First try Explorer to locate a file and delete it. For peace of mind, don't forget to empty the Recycle Bin when you're done.

   b. If the file is hidden or access is denied, open an elevated command prompt window and use the commands listed in Table 16-2 to take control of a file so you can delete it. If the commands don't work using an elevated command prompt window, use the commands in a command prompt window in Windows RE.

   c. To get rid of other malware files, use the Disk Cleanup process in the Drive C: properties dialog box, or delete the browsing history using the Internet Options dialog box.

   d. Delete all subfolders and files in the C:\Windows\Temp folder, which Trojan downloaders are likely to use.

Table 16-2   Commands used to take control of a malware file so you can delete it

Command	Description
attrib –r –s *filename.ext*	Remove the read-only and system attributes to a file.
tasklist | more taskkill /f /pid:*9999*	To stop a running process, first use the tasklist command to find out the process ID for the process. Then use the taskkill command to forcefully kill the process with the given process ID.
takeown /f *filename.ext*	Take ownership of a file.
icacls *filename.ext* /grant administrators:f	Take full access of a file.

16

4. **Clean up your browsers and uninstall unwanted programs.** Adware and spyware might install add-ons to a browser (including toolbars you didn't ask for), install cookie trackers, and change your browser security settings. Anti-malware software might have found all these items, but as a good defense, take a few minutes to find out for yourself. The module "Network Security and Troubleshooting" covers how to use the Internet Options dialog box to search for unwanted add-ons and delete ActiveX controls. You can uninstall unwanted toolbars, plug-ins, and other software using the Programs and Features window.

Step 5: Protecting the System with Scheduled Scans and Updates

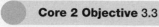
Core 2 Objective 3.3

Once your system is clean, you'll certainly want to keep it that way. The following are three best practices to protect a system against malware:

- **Use anti-malware software.** Microsoft Defender Antivirus is enabled and automatically updated by default. If you decide to use other anti-malware software, configure the software so it (1) runs in the background in real time to alert users of malware that attempts to run or install, (2) automatically scans incoming email attachments, and (3) performs scheduled scans of the system and automatically downloads updates to the software.
- **Always use a software firewall.** Never, ever connect your computer to an unprotected network without using a firewall. Windows Defender Firewall is turned on by default. Recall that you can configure Windows Defender Firewall to allow no uninvited communication or to allow the exceptions that you specify. Details about Windows Defender Firewall are covered in the module "Network Security and Troubleshooting."
- **Keep Windows updates current.** Microsoft continually releases updates to plug vulnerable entrances in Windows where malware might attack and updates to Defender Antivirus. Recall that you can verify Windows Update settings in the Settings app.

Step 6: Enabling System Protection and Creating a Restore Point

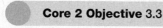
Core 2 Objective 3.3

Now that the system is clean, you can turn System Protection back on if necessary and create a restore point. You learned how to do this in the module "Maintaining Windows."

Step 7: Educating the End User

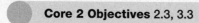
Core 2 Objectives 2.3, 3.3

Now would be a good time to sit down with the user and go over the tips presented earlier in this module to keep the system free from malware. Sometimes the most overlooked step in preventing malware infections is to educate the user. Even with all your security measures in place, a user can still download and execute a Trojan, which can install more malware in the system.

Exam Tip ✔

The A+ Core 2 exam might give you a scenario that requires you to perform one or more of the seven steps to remove malware. Memorize these seven steps and know how to use them in the correct order.

Now we turn our attention to other ways an IT technician might be called on to protect data and other resources, including enforcing licensing and security policies and protecting regulated data.

Licensing, Regulated Data, and Security Policies

Core 2 Objectives 2.6, 2.8, 4.1, 4.6

An IT technician is expected to follow company security policies for software licensing and regulated data. You also need to know what to do if you discover that these policies have been violated.

Software Licensing and Digital Rights

Core 2 Objective 4.6

As an IT support technician, you need to be especially aware of the issues surrounding software licensing. When someone purchases software from a software developer, that person or organization has only purchased a **license** for the software, which is the right to use it. The buyer does not legally own the software and therefore does not have the right to distribute it. Important facts about software licensing include the following:

- **The copyright.** The right to copy the work, called a **copyright**, belongs to the creator of the work or others to whom the creator transfers this right. Copyrights are intended to legally protect the intellectual property rights of organizations or individuals to creative works, which include books, images, and software.
- **The EULA.** Your rights to use or copy software are clearly stated in the **End User License Agreement (EULA)** that you agree to when you install the software (see Figure 16-30). The EULA is a legally binding contract between the user and software owner. If the user violates the agreement, the software license is no longer valid. A non-expiring software license does not require renewing, or the license might be valid only for a period of time.
- **Software piracy.** Making unauthorized copies of original software violates the Federal Copyright Act of 1976 and is called **software piracy** or, more officially, software copyright infringement. (This act allows for one backup copy of software to be made.) Making a copy of software and then selling it or giving it away is a violation of the law. Normally, only the employee who violates the copyright law is liable for infringement; however, in some cases, an employer or supervisor is also held responsible, even when the copies were made without the employer's knowledge.

Figure 16-30 Agreeing to the EULA is required before software installs

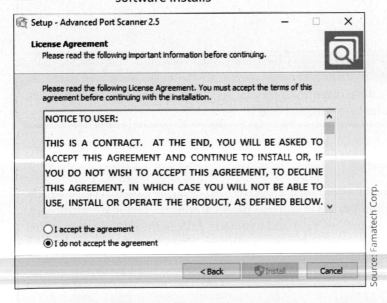

Source: Famatech Corp.

Note 11

When an individual or organization purchases the right to install one instance of software, the license is called a **personal use license**. By purchasing a **site license**, also called a **commercial use license**, a company can obtain the right to multiple installations of software.

- **Digital rights management.** Many software companies, including Microsoft, have implemented measures to control the use of their software, a practice called **digital rights management (DRM)**. For example, recall that the retail release of Windows 10/11 requires a valid product key or a digital license for activation, and Microsoft carefully verifies and monitors that this product key is used only in one installation.
- **Open-source license.** As you have learned, **open-source software** (such as Linux OS and Apache web server) is developed in a public, collaborative way and can be used for any purpose. **Closed-source software** (such as Windows or PhotoShop) is owned by the creator (developer). When you download open-source software, you must agree to a EULA that describes how you can use the software and receive an **open-source license**. Two popular types of open-source licenses are
    - **Copyleft.** A copyleft open-source license allows you to use the software for free, but you cannot sell it or sell modified versions of it to others.
    - **Permissive.** With a permissive open-source license, anything goes. You can use it for free, modify it, and sell it.

Regulated Data and Compliance Policies

 Core 2 Objectives 2.6, 4.6

Certain types of data are protected by special governmental regulations and are called **regulated data**; this data must be provided to the regulatory agency on demand. In addition, each industry must comply with a variety of regulations, policies, and laws, which are collectively called **regulatory and compliance policies**. For example, in the healthcare industry, patient data is highly regulated, and most hospitals employ one or more regulatory and compliance officers to ensure that the hospital is compliant. Other areas of regulation include copyright laws regulated by the U.S. Copyright Office, workplace safety regulated by the Occupational Safety and Health Administration (OSHA), and consumer protection regulated by the Federal Trade Commission (FTC). Many of these policies directly affect IT operations. When you're first hired by a company, you should receive training on how these issues affect your work and what is expected of you.

Note 12

An IT technician needs to know their organization's **data retention** policy for regulated data, which can include the number of years regulated data must be retained after a termination date.

Let's look at some specific types of regulated data:

- **Personal identity. PII (personally identifiable information)** is a legal term to describe data that can uniquely identify a person, including a Social Security number, email address, physical address, birthdate, birthplace, mother's maiden name, marital status, phone numbers, race, and biometric data. Some PII is more sensitive than other information and should be protected more vigilantly.

- **Healthcare data.** **PHI (protected health information)** includes any data about a person's health status or health care. This data is protected by regulations defined by HIPAA (the Health Insurance Portability and Accountability Act), passed in 1996. HIPAA gives patients the rights to monitor and restrict the sharing of their medical information. Hospitals, medical personnel, and other entities covered by HIPAA regulations risk steep penalties for privacy breaches.
- **Credit card data.** The **Payment Card Industry (PCI)** standards were defined to help prevent credit card fraud and are backed by all the major credit card brands (Visa, MasterCard, and others). PCI standards apply to how credit card data is protected in transit (such as when receiving payments) and at rest (when stored, such as when keeping records for recurring billing) by vendors, retailers, and financial institutions.
- **Personal government-issued information.** Documents—including a birth certificate, Social Security card, state-issued driver's license, military ID card, or passport—and biometric data—such as fingerprints—that a government creates or collects to identify a person is regulated in how it can be collected, stored, and shared and how individuals must be noticed if their data is hacked. You also need to know that the GDPR (General Data Protection Regulation) is a group of regulations implemented in 2018 in the European Union (EU) to protect personal data of EU citizens.

> **Note 13**
>
> Organizations and individuals who have access to regulated data are at risk legally and financially if they do not comply with the legal requirements regarding the security of this data. When you work in an organization that handles regulated data, ensure your own protection by making certain you understand and comply with all laws regarding this data.

Data Destruction and Disposal

Core 2 Objective 2.8

As an IT technician, you might be asked to properly dispose of storage media. In addition to the risks posed by dumpster diving, consider its potential impact. Before you throw out a hard drive, flash drive, CD, DVD, tape, or other media that might have regulated or corporate data on it, completely destroy the data on the device. Trying to wipe a drive clean by deleting files or even formatting the drive does not completely destroy the data. Here are some ways to destroy printed documents and sanitize storage devices:

- **Overwrite data on the drive.** A drive needs to be wiped clean before you recycle or repurpose it. Today's devices receive a **low-level format** at the factory, which writes sector marks on a drive. (This is different from a **standard format** in Windows that configures a file system on the drive.) Today's hard drives cannot be low-level formatted by users. However, users can erase or wipe clean a drive using a **zero-fill utility** that overwrites all data on the drive with zeroes; sometimes this is inaccurately called a low-level format. You can download a zero-fill utility or so-called low-level format utility from many hard drive manufacturers' websites. This method works for most low-security situations, but professional thieves know how to break through it. If you use one of these utilities, run it multiple times to write zeroes on top of zeroes. Data recovery has been known to reach 14 levels of overwrites because each bit is slightly offset from the one under it.

16

> **Note 14**
>
> An app called a file shredder can permanently delete an individual file or folder by overwriting it multiple times. Check the reviews before downloading and using one of these apps.

Figure 16-31 Use a degausser to sanitize a magnetic hard drive or tape drive

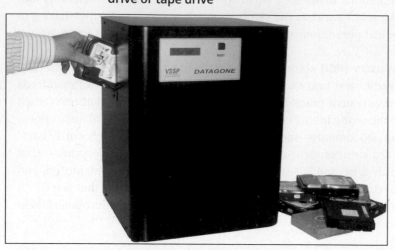

- **For solid-state devices, use a Secure Erase utility.** As required by government regulations for personal data privacy, the American National Standards Institute (ANSI) developed the **ATA Secure Erase** standards to wipe clean a solid-state device such as a USB flash drive or SSD. You can download a Secure Erase utility from the manufacturer of the device and run it to sanitize the drive, or you can securely erase all data on the device and then reuse or dispose of it.

- **Physically destroy the storage media.** Use a drill to drill many holes all the way through the drive housing. Break CDs and DVDs in half, and do similar physical damage with a hammer to flash drives or tapes, even to the point of setting them on fire to incinerate them. Again, expert thieves can still recover some of the data.

Figure 16-32 This drive shredder pulverizes small storage devices such as hard drives, flash drives, and smartphones

- **For magnetic devices, use a degausser.** A **degausser** exposes a storage device to a strong electromagnetic field to completely erase the data on a magnetic hard drive or tape drive (see Figure 16-31). A degaussed drive can't be recycled, but for the best destruction, use the degausser and physically destroy the drive. Degaussing does not erase data on a solid-state hard drive or other flash media because these devices don't use magnetic surfaces to hold data.

- **Use a shredder.** You can use a paper **shredder** to destroy all documents that contain sensitive data. The best paper shredders apply multiple passes to cross-cut the paper instead of strip-cutting; this cuts the paper into smaller pieces that can't be easily reassembled. Many paper shredders can handle credit cards or thin cardboard. **Multimedia shredders** can also destroy optical discs. **Disk drive shredders**, such as the one from Whitaker Brothers (*whitakerbrothers.com*) shown in Figure 16-32, can destroy magnetic hard

Source: Whitaker Brothers

drives, solid-state drives, flash drives, optical discs, and even mobile devices such as smartphones or small tablets.

- **Use a secure third-party data-destruction vendor.** For the very best data destruction, consider a secure data-destruction service. To find a vendor providing the service, search the web for "secure data destruction." However, don't use a service unless you have thoroughly checked its references and guarantees of legal compliance that your organization is required to meet. The service should provide you with a digital **certificate of destruction**, which verifies that the data has been destroyed beyond recovery. Paper certificates can be forged, but digital certificates produced by the software that performs the destruction will provide auditable results of the destruction process.

Exam Tip ✔

The A+ Core 2 exam might give you a scenario that requires you to implement data-destruction techniques, including using a shredder, degausser, incineration, drill, hammer, and recycling or repurposing techniques (low-level formats, overwriting, and drive wipes).

Incident Response for Prohibited Content and Activities

Core 2 Objectives 4.1, 4.6

As you know, employees in an organization are often asked to agree to an acceptable use policy (AUP) that documents a code of conduct when using corporate resources. For example, the AUP may prohibit an employee from accessing pornographic material on company computers, using company computers and time for personal shopping, or installing pirated software on these computers.

An **incident** is when an employee or other person has negatively affected safety or corporate resources, violated the code of conduct for the organization, or committed a crime. When you start a new job, ask your employer what procedures you follow for an **incident response**. If you're the first person to discover an incident, such as the intentional misuse of regulated data or other activities, you're responsible to perform certain **first response** duties. One of these tasks is to document what happened in an **incident report**. This report is important to prevent future incidents and crucial to a criminal investigation. Here are some things you need to know:

- **Identify and go through proper channels.** When you identify what you believe to be an infringement of the law or the company's code of conduct, where do you turn to report the issue? To management and/or to law enforcement? Make sure you go only through proper channels; don't spread rumors or accusations.
- **Preserve data and devices.** What data or device should you immediately preserve as evidence for what you believe has happened? For example, if you believe you have witnessed a customer or employee using a company computer for a crime, should you remove and secure the hard drive from the computer, or should you remove and secure the entire computer? Are you expected to make a copy of the data or image the hard drive before you turn the device over to others?
- **Incident documentation. Incident documentation**, also called an **incident report**, surrounding the evidence of an incident is important to prevent future incidents and crucial to a criminal investigation. What documentation are you expected to submit and to whom is it submitted? This documentation might track the **chain of custody (CoC)** for the evidence, which includes exactly what, when, and from whom it was collected, the condition of this evidence, and how the evidence was secured while it was in your possession. Each device or item includes a paper trail of each person to whom the evidence has been passed on and when. For example, suppose you suspect that a criminal act has happened and you hold a flash drive that you believe contains evidence of this crime. You need to carefully document exactly when and how you received the flash drive. Also, don't pass it on to someone else in your organization unless you have the

16

person's signature on a chain-of-custody document so you can later prove you handled the evidence appropriately. You don't want the evidence to be disallowed in a court of law because you have been accused of misconduct or tampering with the evidence. Also know that more information than a signature, such as a copy of a driver's license, might be required to identify people in the chain of custody.

Exam Tip ✔

The A+ Core 2 exam expects you to be able to explain the process of an incident response, which includes reporting prohibited content or activity through the proper channels and to law enforcement as necessary, copying and preserving relevant data and evidence, and tracking evidence through an appropriate chain-of-custody document.

Module Summary

Physical and Logical Security

- Physical security can include security fences, bollards, access control vestibules, guards, video surveillance, alarm systems, magnetometers (metal detectors), locks and keys, port locks, privacy screens, and theft-prevention plates.
- Staff access to resources is controlled by AAA (authenticating, authorizing, and accounting) measures, including an access control list, multifactor authentication, the principle of least privilege, hard and soft tokens, smart cards, key fobs, biometric locks, digital certificates, authenticator apps, and email filtering.
- Users should be trained to detect and resist social engineering, including shoulder surfing, tailgating, dumpster diving, impersonation, phishing, email hoaxes, whaling, vishing, spear phishing, and spoofing.

Dealing with Malicious Software on Personal Computers

- Malware includes viruses, spyware, keyloggers, worms, Trojans, rootkits, boot sector viruses, ransomware, on-path attacks, zero-day attacks, DoS (denial-of-service) attacks, DDoS (distributed denial-of-service) attacks, zombies, botnets, and crypto miners. Attacks on passwords include dictionary, brute force, and rainbow table attacks.
- Vulnerability to attack is increased by noncompliant systems, unpatched systems, an OS working past its end of life, careless programming that allows for SQL injections and cross-site scripting, insider threats, and lack of user education.
- Symptoms that indicate malware is present include pop-up ads, browser redirection, desktop alerts, application crashes, failed OS updates, antivirus false alerts, slow performance, error messages and logs, file errors, email problems, and invalid digital certificates.
- Some systems become so highly infected that the only solution is to format the hard drive, reinstall Windows, and restore data from backups.
- To clean up an infected system, (1) know how to identify common malware symptoms, (2) quarantine the infected system, (3) disable System Protection, (4) remediate the system, (5) protect the system with scheduled scans and updates, (6) enable System Protection and create a restore point, and (7) educate the end user.

Licensing, Regulated Data, and Security Policies

- The owner of a copyright for software has the right to allow the software to be copied and used and assign a license to do so, after the user agrees to a EULA (End User License Agreement).
- Two types of licenses for copyrighted software are a personal use license and a commercial use license. Two types of open-source licenses are a copyleft and permissive license.
- Regulatory and compliance policies help protect regulated data, which can include PII (personally identifiable information), PHI (protected health information), PCI (Payment Card Industry) data, and government-issued personal information that is regulated by governmental agencies.
- Data can be partly or completely destroyed using a low-level format, zero-fill utility, Secure Erase utility, drill, hammer, incinerator, degausser, paper shredder, or multimedia shredder.
- Professional data-destruction vendors may provide a certificate of destruction for legal purposes.
- A chain-of-custody document is part of incident documentation and provides a paper trail of the evidence in response to an incident that is suspected to be criminal.

Key Terms

For explanations of key terms, see the Glossary for this text.

AAA (authenticating, authorizing, and accounting)
access control list (ACL)
access control vestibule
alarm system
anti-malware software
anti-phishing training
antivirus software
ATA Secure Erase
authenticator app
badge reader
biometric data
biometric lock
bollards
boot sector virus
botnet
brute force attack
cable lock
Certificate Authority (CA)
Certificate Manager
certificate of destruction
chain of custody (CoC)
closed-source software
commercial use license
copyright

cross-site scripting (XSS)
crypto miner
cryptojacking
data loss prevention (DLP)
data retention
defense in depth
degausser
denial-of-service (DoS)
dictionary attack
digital certificate
digital rights management (DRM)
disk drive shredder
distributed denial-of-service (DDoS)
dumpster diving
email filtering
email hoax
End User License Agreement (EULA)
entry control roster
evil twin
first response
grayware
hard token
impersonation

incident
incident documentation
incident report
incident response
Internet of Things (IoT)
Kensington lock
Kensington Security Slot
key fob
keylogger
license
low-level format
magnetometer
malicious software
malware
malware definition
malware encyclopedia
malware signature
man-in-the-middle attack
mantrap
Microsoft Defender Antivirus
motion sensor
multifactor authentication (MFA)
multimedia shredder
mutual authentication
noncompliant system

on-path attack
open-source license
open-source software
Payment Card Industry (PCI)
personal use license
PHI (protected health information)
phishing
PII (personally identifiable information)
port lock
principle of least privilege
privacy filter
privacy screen
quarantined computer
rainbow table
ransomware
regulated data
regulatory and compliance policies
root certificate
rootkit
screensaver lock
security awareness training

16

security fence
server lock
short message
   service (SMS)
shoulder surfing
shredder
site license
smart card
smart card reader

social engineering
soft token
software piracy
spear phishing
spoofing
spyware
SQL injection
standard format

Structured Query
   Language (SQL)
tailgating
theft-prevention
   plate
triple A
Trojan
two-factor
   authentication (2FA)

USB lock
video surveillance
virus
vishing
whaling
worm
zero-day attack
zero-fill utility
zombie

Thinking Critically

These questions are designed to prepare you for the critical thinking required for the A+ exams and may use information from other modules and the web.

1. An employee uses a key fob to access corporate resources from their home office. What type of authentication are they using?

   a. Mutual authentication
   b. Soft token
   c. Authenticator app
   d. SMS messaging

2. What tool is best to use when destroying data on an SSD?

   a. Zero-fill utility
   b. Low-level format
   c. Degausser
   d. ATA Secure Erase

3. What is one difference between a video surveillance camera and a webcam? Select all that apply.

   a. One camera is a part of the IoT, and the other is not.
   b. One camera is accessible from the Internet, and the other is not.
   c. One camera has an IP address, and the other does not.
   d. One camera has a lens, and the other does not.

4. What device can be installed on a laptop to prevent shoulder surfing?

   a. USB port
   b. Smart card reader
   c. Fingerprint reader
   d. Privacy filter

5. Which definition describes a virus? A Trojan?

   a. A program that can replicate by attaching itself to another program
   b. A program that can spread copies of itself throughout a network without a host program
   c. A program that does not need a host program to work; it substitutes itself for, and pretends to be, a legitimate program
   d. A program that displays ads in a web browser

6. What is the best way to determine if an email message warning about a virus is a hoax?

   a. Check websites that track virus hoaxes.
   b. Scan the message for misspelled words or grammar errors.
   c. Open the message and see what happens.
   d. Scan your email inbox for malware.

7. What is the first thing you should do when you discover a computer is infected with malware? The second thing?

    a. Turn off system protection.
    b. Update installed anti-malware software.
    c. Format the hard drive.
    d. Quarantine the computer.

8. What does anti-malware software look for to determine that a program or a process is a virus?

9. What registry key keeps information about services that run when a computer is booted into Safe Mode?

10. What folder is used by Windows to hold restore points?

11. What must you do in Windows to allow anti-malware software to scan and delete malware it might find in the data storage area where restore points are kept?

12. A virus has attacked your hard drive. Instead of seeing the Windows Start screen when you start up Windows, the system freezes, and you see a blue screen of death. You have important document files on the drive that are not backed up. What do you do first? Explain why this is your first choice.

    a. Try a data-recovery service even though it is expensive.
    b. Remove the hard drive from the computer case, and install it in another computer.
    c. Try GetDataBack by Runtime Software (*runtime.org*) to recover the data.
    d. Use Windows utilities to attempt to fix the Windows boot problem.
    e. Run antivirus software to remove the virus.

13. You sign in to your personal computer with your Microsoft account, and you want to set up your computer as a trusted device to make changes to the account settings. Microsoft sends a code to your cell phone in a text message. You enter the code on a Windows screen. This type of authentication is called _____.

    a. multifactor authentication
    b. mutual authentication
    c. biometric authentication
    d. None of the answers are correct.

14. At a restaurant, you overhear people discussing an interesting case they treated while working in a dental office that day. Which type of regulated data policies are most likely to have been violated?

    a. PII
    b. PHI
    c. PCI
    d. GDPR

15. Among the following, which is the best protection against ransomware?

    a. Windows File History
    b. Carbonite
    c. Keylogger software
    d. Authy by Twilio

16. When you started your new job, your training included reading through the company intranet website AUP pages. This morning you see a coworker violating a policy. You ask whether they are aware that they are violating the policy, and they respond that they are aware. What is your next step?

    a. Ignore the incident and wait to see whether it happens again.
    b. Tell your manager about the situation.
    c. Tell another coworker and ask them what you should do.
    d. Ask a coworker how to fill out an incident report.

16

17. You sign in to your banking website on a new computer and get a request that the bank needs to send you a text code to your cell phone to authenticate the sign in. Why is this method of authentication not secure?

   a. Biometric data is not being used.
   b. The digital certificate for the bank's website may be outdated.
   c. Multifactor authentication does not authenticate the user.
   d. SMS text is not encrypted.

18. You suspect a boot sector virus has infected your computer. How can you remove the virus?

   a. Perform a full scan using Microsoft Defender Antivirus.
   b. Replace the hard drive.
   c. Perform a Microsoft Defender Offline scan.
   d. Boot the system in Safe Mode with Networking, and run Microsoft Defender Antivirus.

19. You work in the IT department of a large hospital, and your manager has asked you to dispose of several old laptops previously used by the medical staff. How do you proceed?

   a. Delete all user accounts on the laptops, and donate them to a nonprofit organization.
   b. Remove the hard drives from all the laptops, replace them with new hard drives, and then donate them to a nonprofit organization.
   c. Physically destroy all the hard drives, and then donate the laptops to the computer repair labs at the local community college.
   d. Sell the laptops on eBay.com, and donate the money to a charity of your choice.

Hands-On Projects

Hands-On Project 16-1

Using the Web to Learn About Malware

Est. Time: 15 minutes
Core 2 Objective: 2.3

One source of information about malware on the web is F-Secure Corporation. Go to the website *f-secure.com* or another anti-malware site, and find information about the latest malware threats. Answer the following questions:

1. Which site did you use to research the latest malware?
2. Name and describe a recent Trojan downloader. How does the Trojan install, and what is its payload (the harm it does)?
3. Name and describe a recent rootkit. How does the rootkit install, and what is its payload?
4. Name a recent worm. How does it get into the network, and what is its payload?

Hands-On Project 16-2

Researching CoC and Incidence Response Documents

Est. Time: 15 minutes
Core 2 Objective: 4.6

Your manager has been asked to create the documentation necessary for your new data-destruction company to be compliant when handling regulated data. They have asked you to recommend some sample documentation for chain-of-custody (CoC) and incident-response documents. Find three examples of each document. For the CoC documents, which components do each sample have in common? For the incident-response documents, which components do each sample have in common? Which CoC document would you recommend? Which incident-response document would you recommend?

Hands-On Project 16-3

Researching HIPAA Rules and Compliance

Est. Time: 15 minutes
Core 2 Objective: 4.6

You have just landed your perfect next job working in the IT department of your local hospital as a systems analyst on the security team. Your new manager tells you that your first task on the job is to learn as much as you can about HIPAA. To get started, research the following topics, write a brief overview of each topic, and don't forget to cite an authoritative source (a source that is the final authority on a matter) to support your findings:

1. Two rules that generally govern HIPAA regulations are the HIPAA privacy rule and the HIPAA security rule. Briefly describe each rule.
2. List three methods that are included in the guidance for compliance for each HIPAA rule.
3. Which organization is responsible for adopting, communicating, and enforcing the national standards for the two HIPAA rules?
4. Which entities or individuals are responsible for abiding by these HIPAA rules?

Hands-On Project 16-4

Researching Disposal Rules

Est. Time: 15 minutes
Core 2 Objective: 4.5
Research the laws and regulations in your community concerning the disposal of batteries and old computer parts. Answer these questions:

1. How do you properly dispose of a monitor in your community?
2. How do you properly dispose of a battery pack used by a notebook computer?
3. How do you properly dispose of a large box of assorted computer parts, including hard drives, optical drives, computer cases, and circuit boards?

16

Real Problems, Real Solutions

Real Problem 16-1

Downloading and Using Anti-Malware Software

Est. Time: 30 minutes
Core 2 Objective: 2.3

A free trial of AVG Protection software is available on the AVG site at *avg.com*. Do the following to download, install, and run the software:

1. Download the free trial version of AVG Protection software from *avg.com* and install the software.
2. Update the software with the latest malware signatures.
3. Perform a complete scan of the system. Were any suspicious programs found?
4. Verify the software is set to scan for rootkits.
5. Verify the software is set to scan incoming and outgoing email and their attachments.

Real Problem 16-2

Creating and Using an Anti-Malware Software Rescue Disk

Est. Time: 45 minutes including file download time
Core 2 Objective: 3.3

When an infected computer refuses to boot, one method to clean the infection is to create and use an anti-malware rescue disk. For example, the rescue disk currently offered by Kaspersky is Kaspersky Rescue Disk 18. Do the following to create a bootable USB flash drive, CD, or DVD; use it to scan a computer; and answer the following questions:

1. Go to *support.kaspersky.com/krd18* and get familiar with the directions to create and use the rescue disk. Download the rescue disk software. What are the name and size of the download file for the rescue disk?
2. Create a bootable USB flash drive, CD, or DVD, and then write the Kaspersky image to the boot media.
   a. Which boot media did you use?
   b. Which program did you use to make the media bootable?
3. Boot from the rescue disk. On the opening menu, highlight **English** and press **Enter**. What are the options on the next menu screen?
4. Continue the boot using the rescue disk graphic mode. Accept the EULA. Using the default parameters, is the software set to scan the Windows volume? Boot sectors? BIOS firmware?
5. Label the disk or flash drive, and save it in case you need it to remediate an infected computer.

Module

17

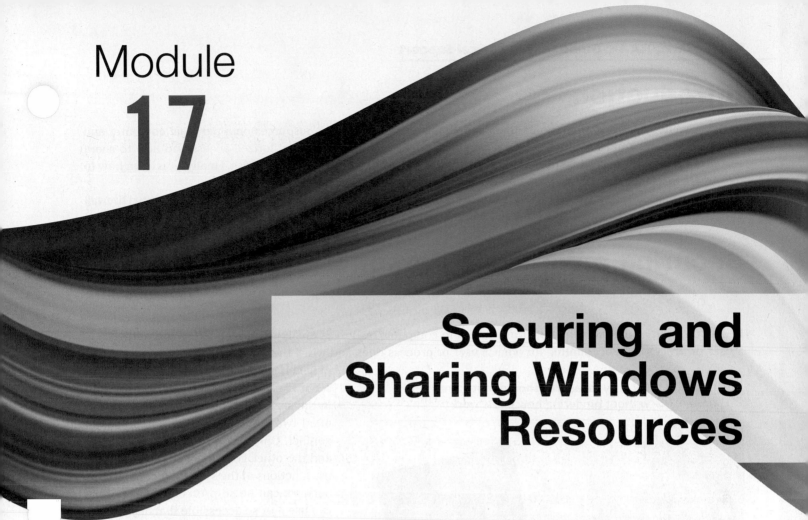

Securing and Sharing Windows Resources

Module Objectives

1 Secure a Windows personal computer using Windows tools on the local computer

2 Share and secure folders, files, and printers on a network

3 Support network resources using Active Directory

Core 2 Certification Objectives

1.2 Given a scenario, use the appropriate Microsoft command-line tool.

1.3 Given a scenario, use features and tools of the Microsoft Windows 10 operating system (OS).

1.4 Given a scenario, use the appropriate Microsoft Windows 10 Control Panel utility.

1.6 Given a scenario, configure Microsoft Windows networking features on a client/desktop.

2.1 Summarize various security measures and their purposes.

2.5 Given a scenario, manage and configure basic security settings in the Microsoft Windows OS.

2.6 Given a scenario, configure a workstation to meet best practices for security.

Introduction

In this module, you learn about some tools and techniques to secure the resources on a personal computer and Windows domain. You learn how to lock down a personal computer from unauthorized access and how to share resources on the network while protecting them from people who should not have access. Finally, you learn how to use Active Directory to manage users and resources on a network.

In later modules, you learn more about securing resources on a network, such as configuring a personal firewall and securing browsers, mobile devices, and wireless networks.

Securing a Windows Personal Computer

 Core 2 Objectives 1.2, 1.3, 2.5, 2.6

Recall from earlier modules that securing access to computer resources involves authenticating and authorizing a user or process and accounting for what a user or process does and when the resources were being used—all of which is collectively referred to as AAA security measures. When you have a choice in the security measures you use, keep in mind two goals, which are sometimes in conflict. One goal is to protect resources, and the other goal is not to interfere with the functions of the system. A computer or network can be so protected that no one can use it or so accessible that anyone can do whatever they want with it. The trick is to find the right balance between security and user convenience (see Figure 17-1).

Figure 17-1 Security measures should protect resources without hindering how users work

Prostockstudio/Dreamstime.com

Also, too much security can sometimes force workers to find insecure alternatives. For example, requiring users to change their passwords weekly might result in more of them writing their passwords down to help remember them.

Note 1

The best protection against attacks is layered protection. If one security method fails, the next might stop an attacker. When securing a workstation, use as many layers of protection as you reasonably can that are justified by the value of the resources you are protecting. These layers of defense are collectively called defense in depth.

BIOS/UEFI Passwords

 Core 2 Objective 2.6

One example of defense in depth is requiring a power-on password as well as a Windows password to access a Windows workstation. BIOS/UEFI firmware on the motherboard offers power-on passwords, which include an administrator or supervisor password (required to change BIOS/UEFI setup) and a user password (required to use the system or view BIOS/UEFI setup). Some firmware may also offer a drive lock password, which is required to access the hard drive. The drive lock password is stored on the hard drive so that it will still control access if the drive is removed from the computer and installed on another system. Figure 17-2 shows a BIOS/UEFI setup Security screen where you can set the Administrator and User passwords.

Figure 17-2   BIOS/UEFI passwords can control access to BIOS/UEFI setup and to boot the system

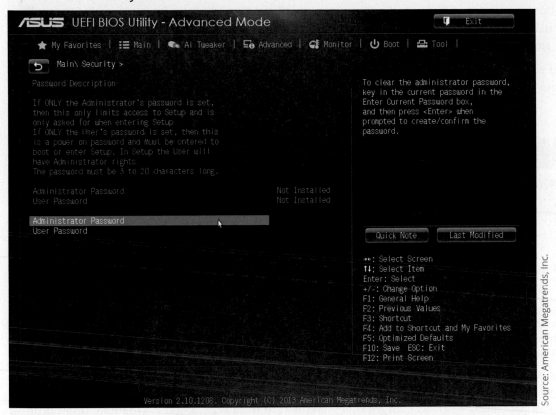

Source: American Megatrends, Inc.

Securing Windows User Accounts

Core 2 Objectives 1.2, 1.3, 2.5, 2.6

When a computer is on a Windows domain, Active Directory (AD) is responsible for AAA services. For a peer-to-peer network, authentication, authorization, and accounting must happen at the local computer. As an administrator, when you first create a Windows account, be sure to assign it a password. It's best to give the user the ability to change the password at any time. In this section of the module, you learn how to use Local Group Policy, Local Security Policy, and other Windows 10/11 tools to secure Windows user accounts.

Create Strong Passwords

Normally, Windows authenticates a user with a Windows password. A password needs to be a **strong password**, which means it should not be easy to guess either by people or by computer programs using various methods, including a simple brute force attack, which is guessing with every single combination of characters until it discovers your password.

A strong password, such as *y*3Q1693pEWJaTz1!*, meets all of the following criteria:

- Use 16 or more characters; a long password is your best protection against a password attack because the longer the password, the more guesses it takes to discover it. After a few thousand guesses, a hacker is likely to move on.
- Combine uppercase and lowercase letters, numbers, and symbols. Use at least one symbol in your password.
- Don't use consecutive letters or numbers, such as "abcdefg" or "12345."

17

- Don't use adjacent keys on your keyboard, such as "qwerty."
- Don't use your sign-in name in the password.
- It's best to not use words in any language. Don't even use numbers or symbols for letters (as in "p@ssw0rd") because programs can easily guess those as well.
- Don't use the same password for more than one system.

Although it's not recommended you write your password down, if you do write it down, keep it in as safe a place as you would the data you are protecting. Don't send your passwords over email or chat.

Note ②

How secure is a password? Go to *howsecureismypassword.net* and find out how long it will take a computer to crack the password.

Rather than writing down passwords, consider storing your passwords with a password manager app such as Dashlane (*dashlane.com*), Sticky Password (*stickypassword.com*), or LastPass (*lastpass.com*). These apps can keep your passwords in the cloud or on your own device, and the passwords they create are longer and stronger than those you would be able to memorize.

Don't type your passwords on a public computer. For example, computers in hotel lobbies or Internet cafés should only be used for web browsing—not for signing in to your email account or online banking account. These computers might be running keystroke-logging software put there by criminals to record each keystroke. Several years ago, while on vacation in a foreign country, I entered credit card information on a computer in a hotel lobby. Months later, I was still protesting $2 or $3 charges to my credit card from that country. Trust me. Don't do it—I speak from experience.

In some situations, a blank Windows password might be more secure than an easy-to-guess password such as "1234." That's because you cannot authenticate to a Windows computer from a remote computer unless the user account has a password. A criminal might be able to guess an easy password and authenticate remotely. For this reason, if a computer is always in a protected room such as a home office and the user doesn't intend to access it remotely, they might choose not to use a password. However, if the user travels with a laptop, always recommend that the user create a strong password.

Fingerprints, Facial Recognition, and PINs

Windows account security can be further improved by configuring Windows Hello, a Windows feature that allows a user to sign in to Windows using their face, iris, fingerprint, or PIN. Captured biometric data, which is digitized, encrypted, and stored locally on the one Windows device, applies only to that one device and is never transmitted to a server. Because your Microsoft account can be used for single sign-on (SSO), when someone steals your password, they can access your Microsoft resources from any Windows device; however, your PIN works only on the one device.

To set up Windows Hello, open the **Settings** app, and select **Accounts** and **Sign-in options** (see Figure 17-3). When you select Windows Hello Face or Windows Hello Fingerprint in this window, you are also required to set up a PIN, which can be used if signing in using your face or fingerprint is not an option, such as if you are injured or the face sensor or fingerprint sensor is not working. Face, fingerprint, and PIN sign-in don't replace the Windows password, but they are used in place of the password for this one device. If you have multiple Windows devices, you would need to set up Windows Hello on each device.

Figure 17-3   Use face recognition, fingerprint or PIN for Windows sign-in

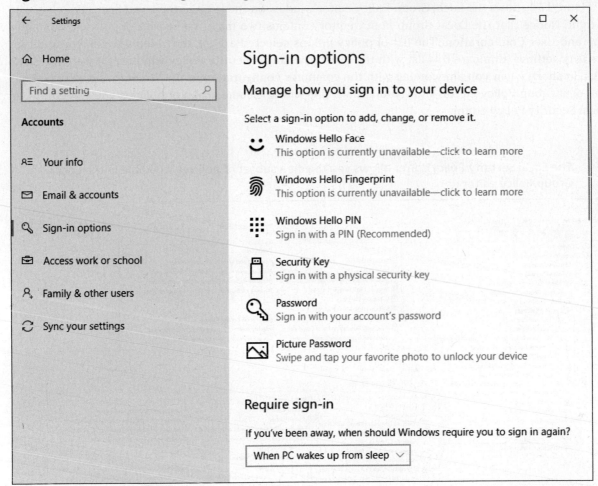

Exam Tip ✔

The A+ Core 2 exam expects you to know about OS login options, including passwords, PINs, fingerprints, facial recognition, and SSO.

Next, let's see how Local Group Policy and Local Security Policy consoles can be used to enforce security best practices on a workstation.

Local Group Policy Editor

You need to be aware of three tools for managing policies that control what users and computers can do with a system or network:

- Group Policy (gpedit.msc) works in Active Directory on a Windows domain to control the privileges of computers and users on the domain. You learn more about Group Policy and Active Directory later in this module.
- **Local Group Policy** (gpedit.msc) contains a subset of policies in Group Policy; this subset applies only to the local Windows 10/11 computer or local user.
- **Local Security Policy** (secpol.msc) contains a subset of policies in Local Group Policy, which apply only to the local computer's Windows security settings. Local Security Policy is a Windows 10 Administrative Tools or Windows 11 Windows Tools snap-in in Control Panel.

17

The Local Group Policy and Local Security Policy editors are available with business and professional editions of Windows. Figure 17-4 shows the Local Group Policy Editor window on the left and the Local Security Policy window on the right. Notice that the Local Group Policy editor contains two major categories of policies: Computer Configuration and User Configuration. The list of policy groups selected are for the computer configuration for Windows security settings. Compare this list with the one in the Local Security Policy window; they are the same list of policies. In short, when you are working with the computer configuration in the Windows security settings group of the Local Group Policy editor, know you are working with the same group of policies you can edit when using the Local Security Policy editor.

Figure 17-4   The Local Security Policy editor allows you to edit a subset of policies available in the Local Group Policy editor

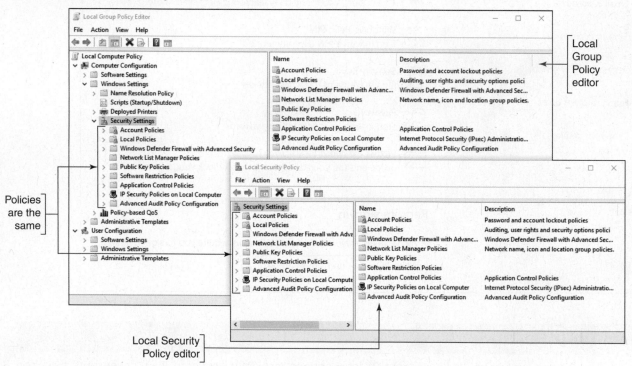

Now let's see how you can use the Local Group Policy editor to secure a workstation. For example, you can set policies to require all users to have passwords. Once you have enabled a policy, a standard user of the workstation would be required to comply and would not be able to change the policy.

Applying Concepts

Applying Local Security Policies

Est. Time: 45 minutes
Core 2 Objective: 2.6

Follow these steps to set a few important policies to secure a workstation:

1. Sign in to Windows using an administrator account on a system that uses Windows 10/11 Pro or Enterprise.

2. To start Local Group Policy, enter the `gpedit.msc` command in the Windows search box. The Local Group Policy Editor console opens.

3. To change a policy, first use the left pane to drill down into the appropriate policy group, and then use the right pane to view and edit a policy. Here are important policies you can use to secure a workstation:

- **Require user passwords and password expiration and complexity.** To require that all user accounts have passwords, drill down to the **Computer Configuration**, **Windows Settings**, **Security Settings**, **Account Policies**, **Password Policy** group (see the left side of Figure 17-5). Use the **Minimum password length** policy, and set the minimum length to at least eight characters (see the right side of Figure 17-5).

Figure 17-5   Require that each user account have a password by setting the minimum password length policy

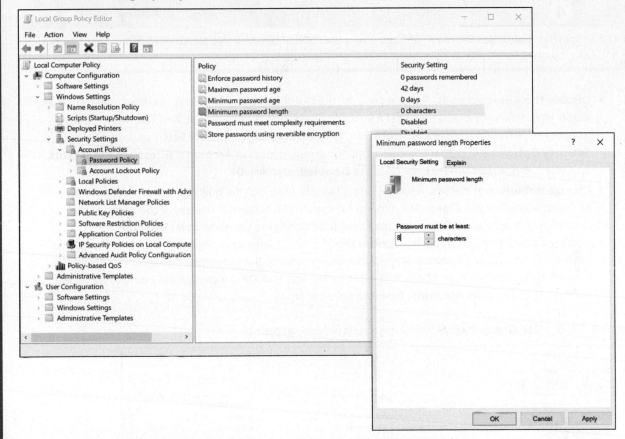

- **Require password complexity.** To require that passwords contain uppercase and lowercase letters, numbers, and symbols—and do not contain the user name—open the **Password must meet complexity requirements** and enable this policy.
- **Password expiration.** To require users to change their passwords frequently, open the **Maximum password age** policy, and set the age to up to 999 days. You can also set the *Minimum password age* policy so a user cannot cycle back to a favorite password immediately after they have changed it.

Note 3

For years, the security community has advised changing passwords often, but now security experts advise creating a very strong password and sticking to it unless you think the password has been compromised.

- **Screen lock timeout.** Windows can monitor for inactivity and run the screen saver after a set amount of time, locking the session. This prevents another person from continuing a Windows session after the user has stepped away from the computer, which is called tailgating. Drill down to the **Computer Configuration**, **Windows Settings**, **Security Settings**, **Local Policies**, **Security Options** group. Use the **Interactive logon: Machine inactivity limit** policy to set the number of seconds of inactivity before the screen saver runs and locks the workstation until a user signs in.

(continues)

17

Applying Concepts Continued

- **Set a threshold for failed logon attempts.** Windows can be configured to lock a user account if too many incorrect logons are attempted. Drill down to the **Computer Configuration**, **Windows Settings**, **Security Settings**, **Account Policies**, **Account Lockout Policy** group. Use the **Account lockout threshold** policy to set the number of invalid logon attempts. When the number is exceeded, the account will be locked.

> **Note 4**
>
> The Properties dialog box for many policies offers the Explain tab. Use this tab to read more about a policy and how it works.

- **Disable the Guest account.** For best security, the Guest account should stay disabled; you don't want a user to accidentally enable it. To set a policy to disable the Guest account, first use the left pane to navigate to the **Computer Configuration**, **Windows Settings**, **Security Settings**, **Local Policies**, **Security Options** group. In the Security Options group, right-click **Accounts: Guest account status**, and select **Properties**. Change the status to **Disabled**, and click **OK**.
- **Change default user names.** A hacker is less likely to hack into the built-in Administrator account or Guest account if you change the names of these default accounts. To change the name of the Administrator account, drill down to the **Computer Configuration**, **Windows Settings**, **Security Settings**, **Local Policies, Security Options** group (see the left side of Figure 17-6). In the right pane, double-click **Accounts: Rename administrator account**. In the Properties dialog box for this policy (see the right side of Figure 17-6), change the name, and click **OK**. To change the name of the Guest account, use the policy **Accounts: Rename guest account**.

Figure 17-6 Use Group Policy to rename a default user account

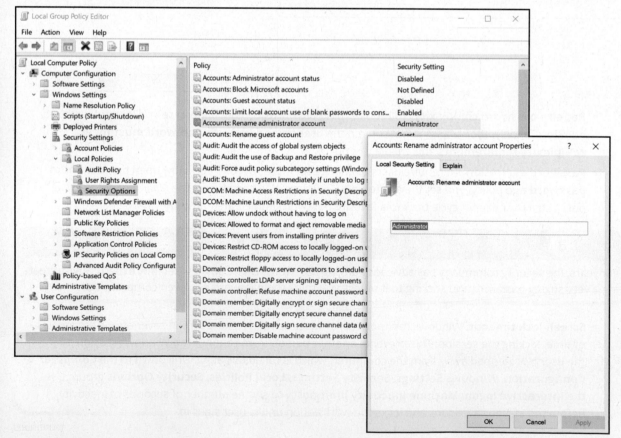

Note 5

The Administrator account is a built-in account that you might need in an emergency when other user accounts fail. Be sure to create a password for this account. One way to do that is to open an elevated command prompt window and enter the following commands to activate the account and set its password:

```
net user Administrator /active:yes
net user Administrator <password>
```

Because this account and password are extremely valuable and not used very often, don't trust your memory—keep the user account name and password in a protected and secure place.

- **Audit logon failures.** Group Policy offers several auditing policies that monitor and log security events. You can then review these Security logs using Event Viewer. For example, to set an audit policy to monitor a failed logon event, drill down to the **Computer Configuration**, **Windows Settings**, **Security Settings**, **Local Policies**, **Audit Policy** group. Use the **Audit logon events** policy. You can audit logon successes and failures. To keep the log from getting too big, you can select **Failure** to log only these events.

Note 6

When a computer is on a Windows domain managed by Active Directory, you can block a user from signing in to Windows locally, using a local account. To do that, go to the **Computer Configuration**, **Windows Settings**, **Security Settings**, **Local Policies**, **User Rights Assignments**, and **Allow log on locally** policy. Remove the **Users** group from those allowed to log on locally. It's best to still allow the Administrators group to log on locally in case that logon is needed to troubleshoot the system.

All the previous policies are also found in the Local Security Policy console. The following policies are available only in Local Group Policy:

- **Logon time restrictions.** In some situations, users should only be allowed access to a workstation during specific hours, such as during office hours. The schedule for a user's or group's logon hours is set through Active Directory on the domain. When logon hours set by Active Directory have expired, individual workstations can be configured to disconnect, lock, or log off the user, or to allow the user to continue the current session. To configure what happens when a user's logon hours have expired, drill down to the **User Configuration**, **Administrative Templates**, **Windows Components**, **Windows Logon Options** group. Double-click **Set action to take when logon hours expire**. Select **Enabled**, and then choose **Lock**, **Disconnect**, or **Logoff**. If the policy is not enabled, the user's session will continue, but the user will not be able to log on outside of the assigned logon hours once the current session has been terminated.

- **Disable Microsoft account resources.** Recall that a Microsoft account is a single sign-on (SSO) account, which means it provides authentication to multiple services and resources. When a user signs in to a Windows 10/11 computer with a Microsoft account, they have access to online resources such as OneDrive and OneNote and can sync settings on the computer with other computers that use the same Microsoft account. Settings include Start tiles, desktop personalization, installed apps and app settings, web browser favorites, and passwords to apps, websites, and networks.

Note 7

To see and edit the sync settings available for a Microsoft account, open the Windows 10/11 **Settings** app, click the **Accounts** group, and select **Sync your settings** in the left pane.

17

(continues)

Applying Concepts Continued

Depending on your company's policy, you might need to restrict access to online resources and sync settings that are linked to a user's Microsoft account. To disable OneDrive, for example, drill down to the **Computer Configuration**, **Administrative Templates**, **Windows Components**, **OneDrive** group. Enable the **Prevent the usage of OneDrive for file storage** policy to prevent users and programs from accessing OneDrive. Additionally, in the **Windows Components** submenu, click the **Sync your settings** group, and use these policies to disable syncing apps, app settings, passwords, and other Windows settings (see Figure 17-7). You can also block using Microsoft accounts altogether by setting the **Block Microsoft accounts** policy in the **Computer Configuration**, **Windows Settings**, **Security Settings**, **Local Policies**, **Security Options** group.

Figure 17-7   Restrict SSO authentication to online resources associated with a Microsoft account

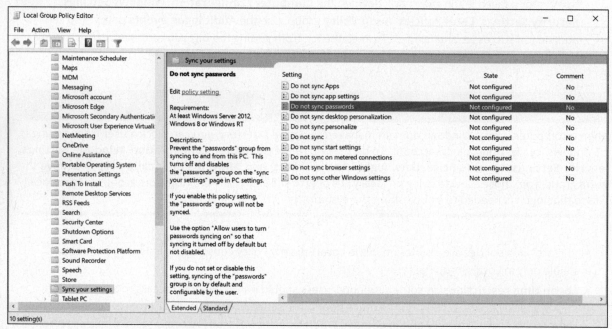

- **Disable AutoRun and AutoPlay.** When you attach a USB flash drive or external hard drive or insert a disc in the optical drive, Windows automatically accesses the storage media and then requests instructions for what to do next. Media files can be played automatically, which is called AutoPlay. Executable files can be run automatically, which is called AutoRun. You can disable both of these features to add yet another layer of security protection. To disable AutoPlay, drill down to the **Computer Configuration**, **Administrative Templates**, **Windows Components**, **AutoPlay Policies** group. Enable the **Turn off Autoplay** policy. To disable AutoRun, enable **Set the default behavior for AutoRun** and use the **Disabled** option.

4. When you finish setting your local security policies, close the Local Group Policy Editor console. To put your changes into effect, restart the system or open a command prompt window, and enter the command **gpupdate /force**. The command might request that you restart the computer for all policies to take effect. The **gpupdate** command refreshes local group policies as well as group policies set in Active Directory on a Windows domain.

Exam Tip ✔

The A+ Core 2 exam expects you to know how to secure a workstation in a given scenario, including managing user accounts. You need to know how to configure password length, characters, complexity, and expiration and how to restrict user permissions, configure login times, disable the guest account, set failed login attempts before lockout, set timeout screen locks, change the default administrator user account name and set its password, and disable AutoRun and AutoPlay. All these settings are done by using the Local Group Policy editor to edit these policies.

Now let's turn our attention to using encryption to secure workstation resources.

File and Folder Encryption

Core 2 Objective 2.5

Data needs to be protected when at rest (while stored on a hard drive, flash drive, or other storage device) and in motion (while being transmitted over a network or the Internet). Encryption is an effective way to protect data, but the encryption techniques and protocols used are different depending on whether the data is at rest or in motion. In Windows, **data-at-rest encryption** can be accomplished using the Windows **Encrypting File System (EFS)**. EFS encrypts files and folders stored on drives using the NTFS file system and business and professional editions of Windows. If a folder is marked for encryption, every file created in the folder or copied to the folder will be encrypted. An encrypted file remains encrypted if you move it from an encrypted folder to an unencrypted folder on the same or another NTFS volume.

To encrypt a folder or file, right-click it and open its **Properties** dialog box (see Figure 17-8). On the General tab, click **Advanced**. In the Advanced Attributes dialog box, check **Encrypt contents to secure data**, and click **OK**. In Explorer, encrypted file and folder names are displayed in green by default.

Note 8

In the module "Network Security and Troubleshooting," you learn how to encrypt data in motion on a network or the Internet.

Figure 17-8   Encrypt a folder and all its contents

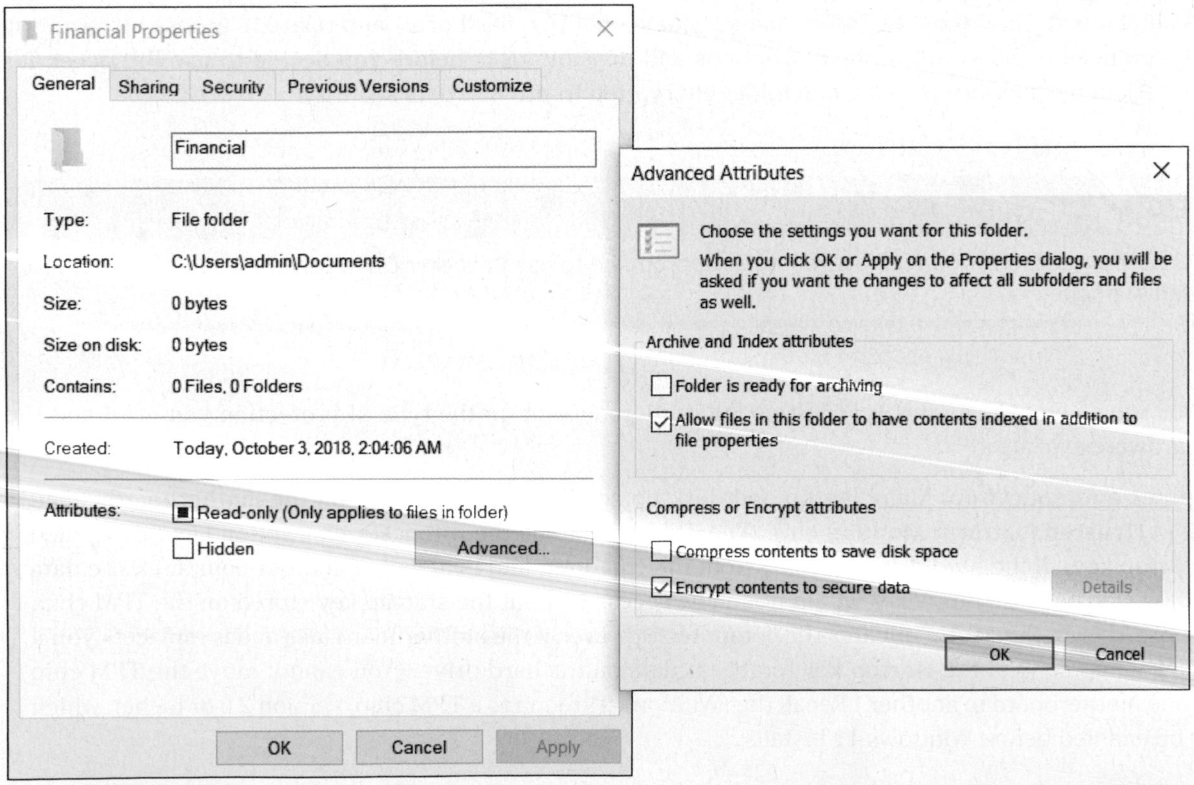

Note 9

If the folder or file doesn't display in a green font in Explorer, you can change the setting by opening **Control Panel** and clicking **File Explorer Options**. On the View tab, check **Show encrypted or compressed NTFS files in color**. Click **OK**.

Caution ❗

If a user forgets a password, an administrator can reset the forgotten password. However, know that if an administrator resets a user password, the user will lose all their EFS encrypted folders and files, personal digital certificates, and passwords stored on the computer. To reset a user password, you can use the Network Places Wizard tool (netplwiz.exe), as shown in Figure 17-9. Select the user and click **Reset Password**. Later in the module, you learn to reset a password using the Local Users and Groups console.

Figure 17-9   Use the Network Places Wizard to reset a user password

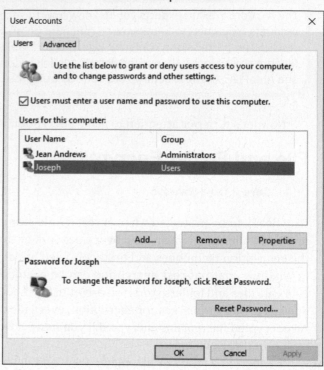

Bitlocker Encryption

> **Core 2 Objective** 2.5

BitLocker Drive Encryption in Windows professional and business editions locks down a hard drive by encrypting the entire Windows volume and any other volume on the drive and restricts access by requiring one or two encryption keys. A similar feature, **BitLocker To Go**, encrypts data on a USB flash drive and restricts access by requiring a password. You need to be aware of the restrictions and possible risks before you decide to use BitLocker. It's intended to work in partnership with file and folder encryption to provide data security.

Exam Tip ✔

The A+ Core 2 exam expects you to know when it is appropriate to use BitLocker Drive Encryption and BitLocker To Go in a given scenario.

The three ways you can use BitLocker Drive Encryption depend on the type of protection you need and the computer hardware available:

- **Computer authentication.** Many laptop and desktop computers have a chip on the motherboard called the **TPM (Trusted Platform Module)** chip. The TPM chip holds the BitLocker encryption key (also called the startup key). If the hard drive is stolen from the computer and installed in another computer, the data would be safe because BitLocker would not allow access without the startup key stored on the TPM chip. Therefore, this method authenticates the computer. However, if the motherboard fails and is replaced, you'll need a backup copy of the startup key to access data on the hard drive. (You cannot move the TPM chip from one motherboard to another.) Recall that Windows 11 requires a TPM chip, version 2.0 or higher, which must be enabled before Windows 11 installs.

- **User authentication.** For Windows 10 computers that don't have TPM, the startup key can be stored on a USB flash drive (or other storage device the computer reads before the OS is loaded). The user installs the flash drive or enters a personal identification number (PIN) to unlock Windows startup. This method authenticates the user. For this method to be the most secure, the user must never leave the flash drive stored with the computer. (Instead, the user might keep the USB startup key on their key ring or a lanyard.)
- **Computer and user authentication.** For best security, two-factor authentication is used: the TPM chip to authenticate the computer and the flash drive or PIN to authenticate the user.

Note 10

Most computers manufactured within the last five years implement TPM 2.0, which is required to run Windows 11.

BitLocker Drive Encryption provides great security, but security comes with a price. For instance, you risk the chance your TPM will fail or you will lose all copies of the startup key. In these events, recovering the data can be messy. Therefore, use BitLocker only if the risks of using it do not outweigh the risks of stolen data. If you decide to use BitLocker, make extra copies of the startup keys and/or PIN, and keep them in a safe location.

Caution !

In the module "Security Strategies," you learned that some data, such as healthcare data, is regulated by the government, and organizations that are negligent in protecting it can be held legally responsible for data breaches. For this type of data, encryption and other security measures may be mandated by law.

To start the process of using BitLocker Drive Encryption, first go into BIOS/UEFI setup and enable the TPM chip. Then open the **BitLocker Drive Encryption** applet in Control Panel (see Figure 17-10). Using this window, you can click **TPM Administration** to manage the TPM chip and turn on BitLocker or BitLocker To Go.

Figure 17-10 Manage BitLocker Drive Encryption, the TPM chip, and BitLocker To Go

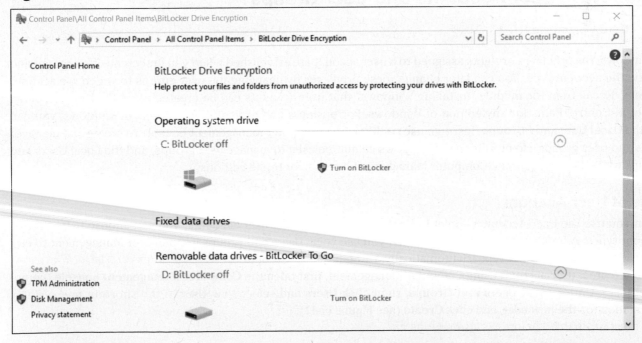

17

Note 11

For detailed instructions on how to set up BitLocker Drive Encryption, see the Microsoft article "BitLocker" at *docs.microsoft.com/en-us/windows/security/information-protection/bitlocker/bitlocker-overview*.

Controlling Access to Folders, Files, and Printers

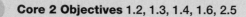

Core 2 Objectives 1.2, 1.3, 1.4, 1.6, 2.5

Responsibility for a peer-to-peer network or domain can include controlling access to folders and files for users of a local computer and for remote users accessing shared resources over the network. Managing shared resources is accomplished by (1) assigning privileges to user accounts and (2) assigning permissions to folders, files, and printers.

Note 12

In Windows, the terms "privileges" and "permissions" have different meanings. Privileges (also called rights) refer to the tasks an account is allowed to do in the system, such as installing software or changing the system date and time. Permissions refer to which user accounts or user groups are allowed access to data files and folders. Privileges are assigned to an account, and permissions are assigned to data files and folders.

Let's first look at the strategies used for controlling privileges for user accounts and controlling permissions for folders and files. Then you learn the procedures in Windows for assigning these privileges and permissions.

Classifying User Accounts and User Groups

Core Objectives 1.3, 2.5

In Windows, the privileges or rights assigned to a user account are established when you first create the account and decide the account type. You can later change these privileges by changing the user groups to which the account belongs. Recall from the module "Installing Windows" that user accounts can be created using the User Accounts applet in Control Panel for any edition of Windows. For business and professional editions of Windows, you can use the **Local Users and Groups** (lusrmgr.msc) utility in the Computer Management console to create and manager users and user groups. Home editions of Windows cannot be used to manage user groups, and the Local Users and Groups utility is missing in the Computer Management console for Home editions.

Type of User Account

When you use the User Accounts applet in Control Panel to manage user accounts, you can choose between two account types: Administrator or Standard. When you use Local Users and Groups in Computer Management to create an account, the account type is automatically a standard user account.

To create a user account using Computer Management, first open the **Computer Management** console (compmgmt.msc). Under **Local Users and Groups**, right-click **Users** and select **New User** in the shortcut menu. Enter information for the new user, and click **Create** (see Figure 17-11).

Figure 17-11   Create a new user

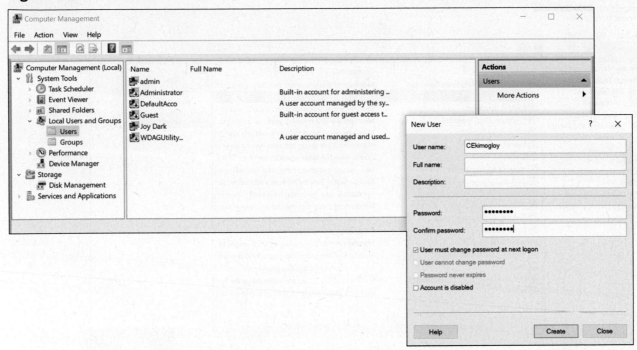

Exam Tip ✔

The A+ Core 2 exam expects you to be able to compare privileges assigned to the administrator, standard user, power user, and guest user groups.

Built-In User Groups

A user account can belong to one or more user groups. Windows offers several built-in user groups, and you can create your own. Here are important built-in user groups:

- **Administrators and Users groups.** By default, administrator accounts belong to the **Administrators** group, and standard user accounts belong to the **Users group**. If you want to give administrator privileges to a standard user account, use the Computer Management console to add the account to the Administrators group.
- **Guests group.** The **Guests group** has limited privileges on the system and is given a temporary profile that is deleted when the user signs out. Windows automatically creates one account in the Guests group named the Guest account, which is disabled by default.
- **Power Users group.** Older editions of Windows have a **Power Users group** that can read from and write to parts of the system other than its own user profile folders, install applications, and perform limited administrative tasks. Windows 10/11 offers a Power Users group only for backward compatibility with legacy applications.

To view user groups installed on a system, open the **Computer Management** console. Under Local Users and Groups, click **Groups** (see Figure 17-12).

17

Figure 17-12   User groups installed on a system

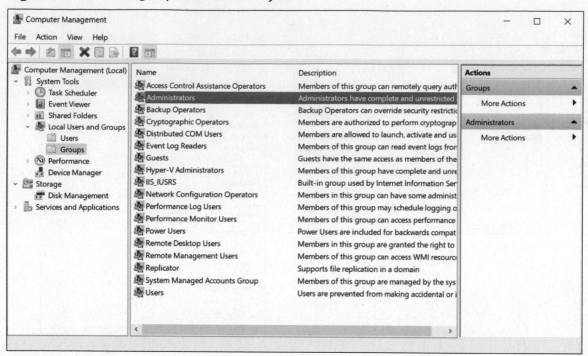

To change the groups a user account is in, click **Users** under Local Users and Groups. The list of user accounts appears in the right pane of the console window (see the left side of Figure 17-13). Right-click the user account, and select **Properties** in the shortcut menu. In the user account Properties dialog box, click the **Member Of** tab (see the middle of Figure 17-13). Click **Add** and enter the user group name. You must type the user group name exactly as it appears in the list of user groups that you saw earlier (refer back to Figure 17-12). To verify that the group name is correct, click **Check Names**. A verified name is underlined. (Alternately, you can click **Advanced**, click **Find Now**, and select the group name from the list of groups that appears.) Click **OK** twice to close both dialog boxes.

Figure 17-13   Add a user account to a user group

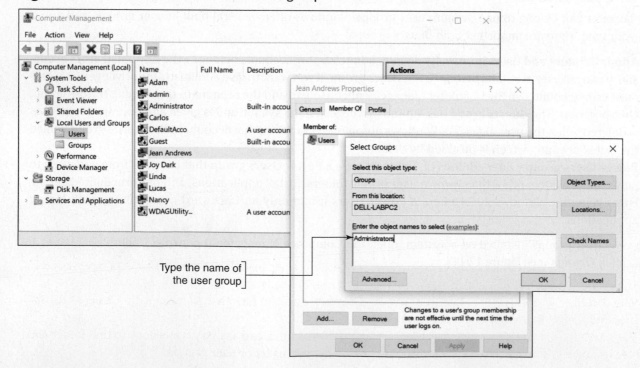

In addition to the groups you can assign to an account, Windows might automatically assign one of these built-in user groups to an account when it is determining permissions assigned to a file or folder:

- The **Authenticated Users group** includes all user accounts that can access the system except the Guest account. These accounts include domain accounts (used to sign in to the domain) and local accounts (used to sign in to the local computer). The accounts might or might not require a password. When you create a folder or file that is not part of your user profile, Windows gives access to all Authenticated Users by default.
- The **Everyone group** includes the Authenticated Users group as well as the Guest account. When you share a file or folder on the network, Windows gives access to the Everyone group by default.
- **Anonymous users** are users who have not been authenticated on a remote computer. If you sign in to a computer using a local account and then attempt to access a remote computer, you must be authenticated on the remote computer. You will be authenticated if your user account and password match on both computers. If you signed in to your local computer with an account and password that do not match an account and password on the remote computer, you are considered an anonymous user on the remote computer. As an anonymous user, you might be allowed to use Explorer to view shared folders and files on the remote computer, but you cannot access them.

Customized User Groups

Recall from the module "Security Strategies" that the principle of least privilege says that a person in an organization is assigned the privileges necessary to do their job and no more. One convenient way to comply with this principle is to assign privileges to user groups rather than individual users. First, create a user group based on a job description and then assign permissions to this user group. Any user account that you put in this group then acquires or inherits the same permissions. For example, you can set up an Accounting group and a Medical Records group for a small office. Users in the accounting department and users in the medical records department go into their respective user groups. Then you only need to manage the permissions for two groups rather than multiple user accounts. You learn how to set all this up later in the module.

Methods to Assign Permissions to Folders and Files

Core 2 Objective 1.6

There are two general strategies for managing shared files and folders (also called directories) in Windows:

- **Workgroup sharing.** With workgroup sharing, all privileges and permissions are set up on each local computer so that each computer manages access to its files, folders, and printers shared on the peer-to-peer network. The local user decides which users on the network have access to which shared folder and the type of access they have.
- **Domain controlling.** If a Windows computer belongs to a domain instead of a workgroup, all security should be managed by the network administrator for the entire network. Although individual users on workstations can share files and folders with other users in the domain, this is not considered a security best practice.

On a Windows peer-to-peer network, each workstation shares its files and folders with others in the workgroup, or files and folders on a file server are shared. Here are some tips about which folders to use to hold shared data on a file server or personal computer:

- Private data for an individual user is best kept in the C:\Users folder for that user. User accounts with limited or standard privileges cannot normally access these folders because they belong to another user account. However, accounts with administrative privileges do have access.
- The C:\Users\Public folder is intended to be used for folders and files that all users share. It is not recommended that you use this folder for controlled access to data.
- For best security, create a folder that's not in the C:\Users folder, and assign permissions to that folder and its subfolders. You can allow all users access or only certain users or user groups.

17

Note 13

Some applications can be shared with others on the network. If you share a folder that has a program file in it, a user on another computer can double-click the program file and execute it remotely on their desktop. This is a handy way for several users to share an application that is installed on a single computer. However, know that not all applications are designed to work this way.

Share Permissions and NTFS Permissions

Regardless of whether you are sharing to a workgroup or domain, Windows offers two methods to share a folder over the network:

- **Share permissions. Share permissions** grant permissions only to network users, and these permissions do not apply to local users of a computer. Share permissions work on NTFS, FAT32, and exFAT volumes and are configured using the Sharing tab in a folder's Properties dialog box. Share permissions apply to a folder and its contents, but not to individual files.
- **NTFS permissions. NTFS permissions** apply to local users and network users and to both folders and individual files. NTFS permissions work on NTFS volumes only and are configured using the Security tab in a file or folder's Properties dialog box. (The Security tab is missing on the Properties dialog box of a folder or file on a FAT volume.)

Here are some tips when implementing share permissions and NTFS permissions:

- If you use both share permissions and NTFS permissions on a folder, the more restrictive permission applies. For NTFS volumes, use only NTFS permissions because they can be customized better. For FAT volumes, your only option is share permissions.
- If NTFS permissions are conflicting—for example, when a user account has been given one permission and the user group to which this user belongs has been given a different permission—the more liberal permission applies.

Inherited Permissions and Explicit Permissions

- **Inherited permissions** are permissions that are attained from a parent folder. Passing permissions from a parent object to a child is called permission propagation. When you create, copy, or move an object (file or folder) that has inherited permissions enabled into a parent folder, the new object takes on the permissions of the parent folder.
- **Explicit permissions** apply to an object (folder or file) that has inherited permissions disabled. When an object with explicit permissions is moved from one parent folder to another on the same volume, the object retains its original permissions. When an object with explicit permissions is copied from one folder to another—or moved from one volume to another—it inherits the new parent object permissions because when copied, a new object is created in the new location.

Exam Tip ✔

The A+ Core 2 exam expects you to compare NTFS and share permissions, including how allow and deny conflicts are resolved with each and what happens to permissions when you move or copy a file or folder. A project at the end of this module will help you practice this skill.

How to Share Folders and Files

Core 2 Objectives 1.6, 2.5

Now that you know about the concepts and strategies for managing users and user groups and sharing folders and files, let's look at the details of how to use Windows to set up users and user groups and assign file and folder permissions to these groups.

Applying Concepts

Creating User Groups and Folder Shares

Est. Time: 45 minutes
Core 2 Objective: 1.6

Makani is responsible for a peer-to-peer network at a medical doctor's office. Four computers are connected to the small company network; one of these computers acts as the file server for the network. Makani has created two classifications of data, Financial and Medical. Two workers (Nancy and Adam) require access to the Medical data, and two workers (Linda and Carlos) require access to the Financial folder. In addition, the doctor, Lucas, requires access to both categories of data. Makani must do the following to set up the users and data:

1. Create folders named Financial and Medical on the file server. Create five user accounts, one each for Lucas, Nancy, Adam, Linda, and Carlos. All the accounts belong to the Windows standard user group. Create two user groups, Financial and Medical.

2. Using NTFS permissions, set the permissions for the Financial and Medical folders on the file server so only the members of the appropriate group can access each folder.

3. Test access to both folders using test data, and then copy all real data into the two folders and subfolders. Set up a backup plan for the two folders (as you learned to do in the module "Maintaining Windows").

Let's look at how each of these three steps is done.

Step 1: Create Folders, User Accounts, and User Groups

Follow these steps to create the folders, user accounts, and user groups on the file server computer that is using Windows 10/11 Pro:

1. Sign in to the system as an administrator.

2. Using an NTFS volume, create these two folders: **C:\Medical** and **C:\Financial**.

3. Open the **Local Users and Groups** console, and create user accounts for **Lucas**, **Nancy**, **Adam**, **Linda**, and **Carlos**. The account types are automatically standard user accounts.

4. To create the Medical user group, right-click **Groups** under Local Users and Groups, and select **New Group** in the shortcut menu. The New Group dialog box appears. Enter the name of the group (**Medical**) and its description (**Users have access to the Medical folder**), as shown in Figure 17-14.

Figure 17-14   Setting up a new user group

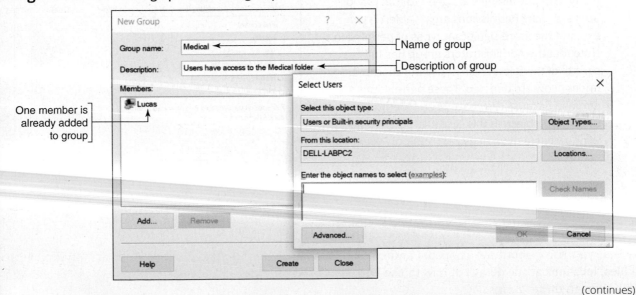

(continues)

Applying Concepts Continued

5. Add all the users who need access to medical data (Lucas, Adam, and Nancy). To add members to the Medical group, click **Add**. The Select Users dialog box opens, as shown on the right side of Figure 17-14. Under *Enter the object names to select*, enter the name of a user. Click **Check Names** to verify the user. Click **OK**. As each user is added, their name appears under Members in the New Group dialog box, as shown in Figure 17-14. To create the group, click **Create** in the New Group dialog box.

6. In the same way, create the Financial group, and add Lucas, Linda, and Carlos to the group. Later, you can use the Local Users and Groups console to add or remove users from either group.

7. Close the Local Users and Groups console.

> **Exam Tip** ✔
>
> The A+ Core 2 exam expects you to be able to set up a user account or group and know how to add and remove users from a group.

Step 2: Set NTFS Folder Permissions For User Groups

Follow these steps to set the NTFS permissions for the two folders:

1. Open **Explorer**, right-click the **Medical** folder, and select **Properties** in the shortcut menu. The Properties dialog box for the folder appears.

2. Click the **Security** tab (see Figure 17-15). Notice in the dialog box that Authenticated Users, SYSTEM, Administrators, and Users all have access to the C:\Medical folder. When you select a user group, the type of permissions assigned to that group appears in the Permissions area. Table 17-1 explains the more significant types of permission. Note that the Administrators group has full control of the folder. Also notice the checks under Allow are dimmed. These permissions are dimmed because they have been inherited from the parent object. In this case, the parent object is Windows default settings.

Figure 17-15   Permissions assigned to the Medical folder

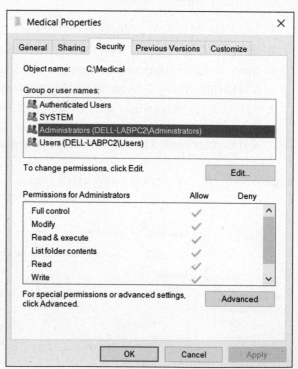

Table 17-1   Permission levels for files and folders

Permission Level	Description
Full control	Can read, change, delete, and create files and subfolders, read file and folder attributes, read and change permissions, and take ownership of a file or folder.
Modify	Can read, change, and create files and subfolders. Can delete the folder or file but cannot delete subfolders and their files. Can read and change attributes. Can view permissions but not change them. Cannot take ownership.
Read & execute	Can read folders and contents and run programs in a folder. (Applies to both files and folders.)
List folder contents	Can read folders and contents and run programs in a folder. (Applies only to folders.)
Read	Can read folders and contents.
Write	Can create a folder or file and change attributes but cannot read data. This permission is used for a drop folder, where users can drop confidential files that can only be read by a manager. For example, an instructor can receive student homework in a drop folder.

3. To remove the inherited status from these permissions so you can change them, click **Advanced**. The Advanced Security Settings dialog box appears (see the left side of Figure 17-16). Click **Change permissions** and **Disable inheritance**. The Block Inheritance dialog box appears (see the right side of Figure 17-16). To keep the current permissions but remove the inherited status placed on them, click **Convert inherited permissions into explicit permissions on this object**. Click **Apply**.

Figure 17-16   Remove the inherited status from the current permissions

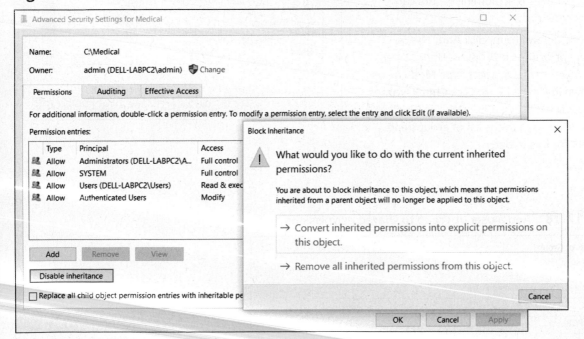

17

(continues)

Applying Concepts Continued

Note 14

Now that the Medical folder is using explicit permissions rather than inherited permissions, if you were to move (not copy) the folder to a new folder on the same NTFS volume, it would retain its original permissions in the new location.

4. Close the Advanced Security Settings dialog box.

5. In the Medical Properties dialog box, notice the permissions are now checked in black, indicating they are no longer inherited but rather explicit permissions and can be changed. Click **Edit** to change these permissions.

6. The Permissions dialog box opens (see Figure 17-17). Select the **Authenticated Users** group, and click **Remove**. Also remove the **Users** group. Don't remove the SYSTEM group, which gives Windows the access it needs. Also, don't remove the Administrators group. You need to leave that group as is so administrators can access the data.

7. To add a new group, click **Add**. The Select Users or Groups box opens. Under *Enter the object names to select*, type **Medical**, as shown in Figure 17-18. Click **Check Names** to verify the group. Click **OK**. The Medical group is added to the list of groups and users for this folder.

Figure 17-17   Change the permissions to a folder

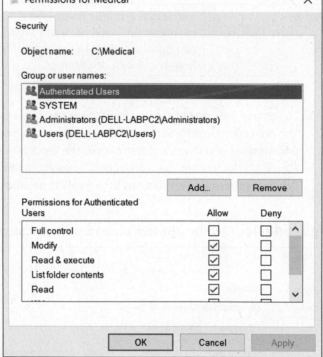

Figure 17-18   Add a user or group to shared permissions

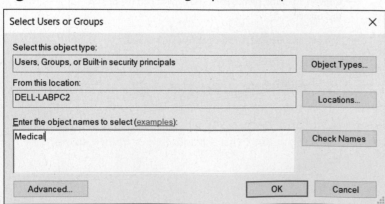

8. In the Permissions dialog box, make sure the **Medical** group is selected. Under *Permissions for Medical*, check **Allow** under *Full control* to give that permission to this user group. Click **OK** twice to close the Properties dialog box.

9. In a similar way, change the permissions of the C:\Financial folder so Authenticated Users and Users are not allowed access and the Financial group is allowed full control.

Step 3: Test, Set Share Permissions, and Go Live

It's now time to test your security measures. <u>Never be tempted to skip testing every aspect of a new security measure. A security measure that does what you didn't intend it to do can allow in hackers or lock out wanted users.</u> Do the following to test the NTFS permissions and implement your shared folders:

1. Test a user account in each user group to make sure the user can read, write, and delete in the folder they need but cannot access the other folder. Put some test data in each folder. Then sign in to the system using an account you want to test and try to access each folder. Figure 17-19 shows the dialog box that appears when an unauthorized user attempts to access a local folder. When you click **Continue**, entering an administrator password in the resulting UAC dialog box gives you access.

Figure 17-19   Access to a folder is controlled

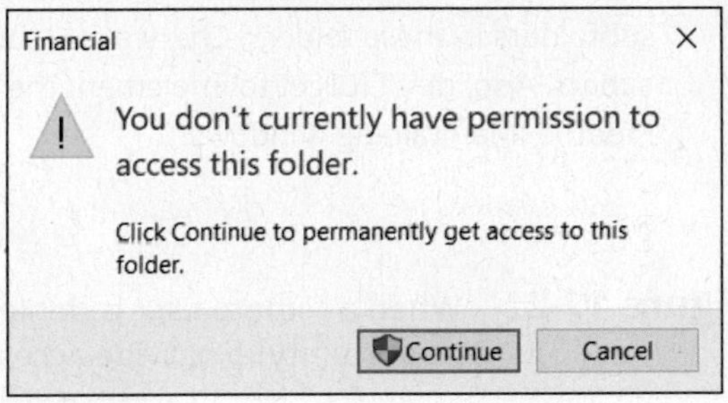

2. Now that NTFS permissions are set correctly for each local and network user, you are ready to allow access over the network. To do that, both NTFS and share permissions must allow network access. (Share permissions apply only to network access, not local access.) The best practice is to allow full access using share permissions and restrictive access using NTFS permissions. Remember that the most restrictive permissions apply. To allow full access using share permissions, click the **Sharing** tab of each folder's Properties dialog box, and click **Advanced Sharing**.

Exam Tip ✔

The A+ Core 2 exam expects you to know that NTFS permissions can be customized better than share permissions.

3. In the Advanced Sharing dialog box, check **Share this folder** if it is not already checked. Then click **Permissions**. To add a new group, click **Add**. The Select Users or Groups dialog box opens. Under *Enter the object names to select*, type **Everyone** and click **OK**. The Everyone group is added to the list of groups and users for this folder.

4. With **Everyone** selected, check **Allow** under *Full control* to give that permission to the Everyone user group. Click **OK** twice, and then close the Properties dialog box.

5. Now that you have the security settings in place for one computer, go to each computer on the network, and create the user accounts that will be using this computer. Then test the security and make sure each user can or cannot access the \Financial and \Medical folders, as you intend. To access shared folders, you can drill down into the Network group in Explorer. Another method is to type the IP address (for example, **\\192.168.1.112**) or computer name (for example, **\\DELL-LABPC2**) in the address bar of the Explorer window, as shown in Figure 17-20.

17

(continues)

Applying Concepts Continued

Figure 17-20   Use the computer name to access shared folders on that computer

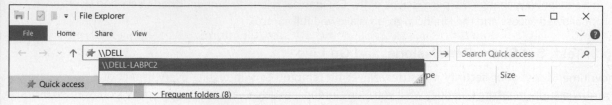

6. Figure 17-21 shows the error message that appears when an unauthorized user attempts to access a network share. After you are convinced the security works as you want it to, copy all the company data to subfolders in these folders. Check a few subfolders and files to verify that each has the permissions you expect. Also, don't forget to implement the backup procedures on the file server, as you learned in the module "Maintaining Windows."

Figure 17-21   When a remote user is denied access to a network resource, there is no opportunity to provide access from this screen

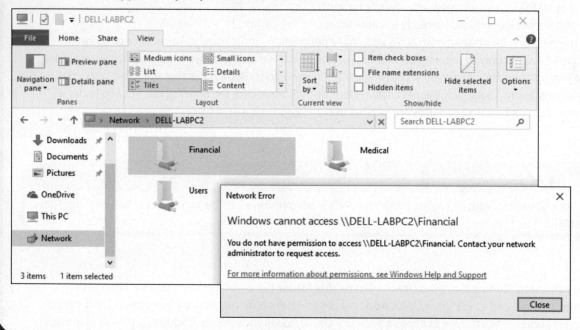

User and Group Information with the gpresult Command

You can pull a list of all the groups a user belongs to with the **gpresult** command. This information can be helpful when troubleshooting user group issues or Group Policy problems; the command displays user groups a user belongs to and all the currently applied policies set by Group Policy. To retrieve information about a user other than the one signed in, open an elevated command prompt window and enter the command:

```
gpresult /scope user /user username /r
```

Figure 17-22 shows output for the user Adam; you can verify that he belongs to the Medical group. You learn more about the gpresult command later in this module.

Figure 17-22 The /r parameter requests a summary of the gpresult information instead of more verbose (/v) output

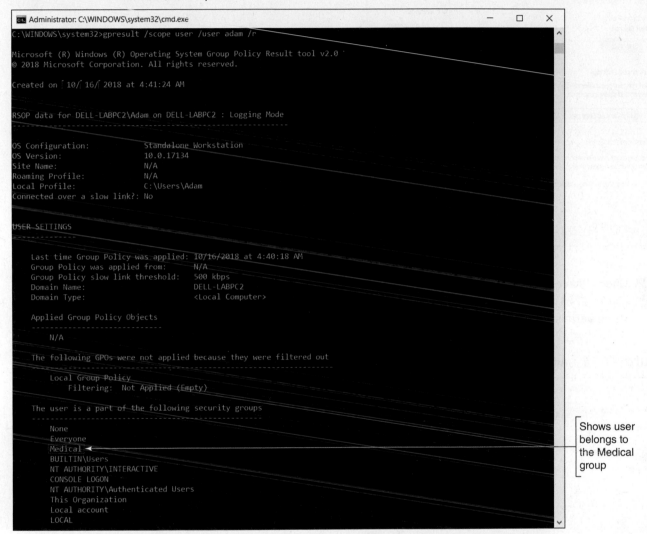

Shows user belongs to the Medical group

How to Use Share Permissions

Although you can mix NTFS permissions and share permissions on the same system, life is simpler if you use one or the other. For NTFS volumes, NTFS permissions are the way to go because they can be customized better than share permissions. However, you must use share permissions on FAT volumes. To do so, follow these steps:

1. Open the **Properties** dialog box for the folder (*Personnel* in this case). Notice in Figure 17-23 that the Security tab is missing because the folder is on a FAT volume. Select the **Sharing** tab and click **Advanced Sharing**. The Advanced Sharing dialog box opens (see the right side of Figure 17-23).

17

Figure 17-23 Use the Sharing tab of a folder Properties dialog box to set up share permissions on a FAT volume

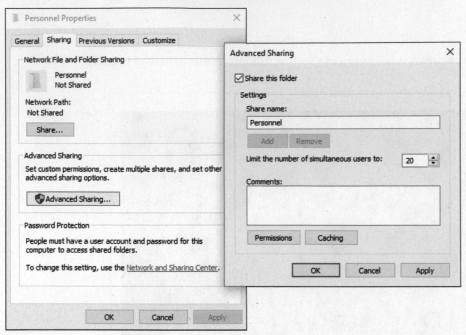

2. Check **Share this folder**. Then click **Permissions**. The Permissions dialog box opens (see the left side of Figure 17-24). Initially, the folder is shared with Everyone. Also notice that share permissions offer only three permission levels: Full Control, Change, and Read.

Figure 17-24 Add a user or user group to assign share permissions

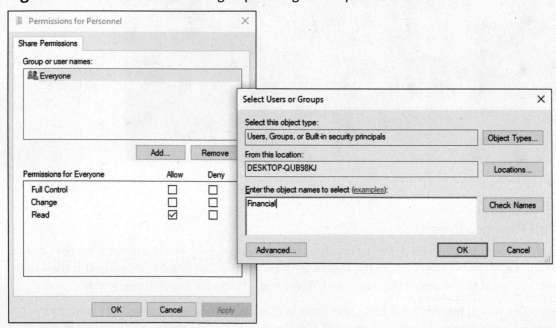

3. Click **Add**. The Select Users or Groups dialog box appears (see the right side of Figure 17-24). Enter a user account or user group and click **OK**.

4. To delete the Everyone group, select it in the Permissions dialog box, and click **Remove**. Click **OK** to close each open dialog box in turn.

Support and Troubleshoot Shared Folders and Files

You have just seen how to set up user groups and folder permissions assigned to these groups. If you have problems accessing a shared resource, follow these steps:

1. Windows might be able to solve the problem for you. In Control Panel, click **Troubleshooting**. In the Troubleshooting window, click **Access shared files and folders on other computers**, and walk through the Shared Folders troubleshooter.

2. Open the **Network and Sharing Center**. Make sure your network location is set to Private.

3. In the left pane, click **Change advanced sharing settings**. The Advanced sharing settings window opens. See Figure 17-25.

Figure 17-25   Configure the security level for network connections

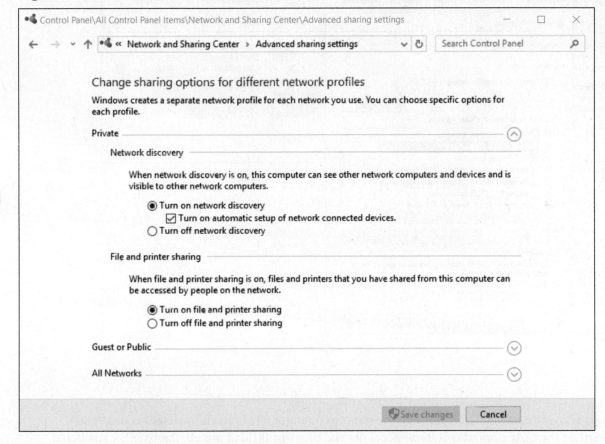

4. Verify that the settings here are the default settings for a Private network profile:

- Select **Turn on network discovery**, and make sure **Turn on automatic setup of network connected devices** is checked.

- Select **Turn on file and printer sharing**.

- If you want to share the Public folder to the network, go to the Public folder sharing section under All Networks, and select **Turn on sharing so anyone with network access can read and write files in the Public folders**.

- If you want the added protection of requiring that all users on the network must have a valid user account and password on this computer, select **Turn on password protected sharing**.

17

5. After you have made your changes, click **Save changes** at the bottom of the window.

6. In the Network and Sharing Center, click **Change adapter settings**. The Network Connections window appears. Right-click the network connection icon, and select **Properties** in the shortcut menu. In the Properties dialog box, verify that **File and Printer Sharing for Microsoft Networks** is checked (see Figure 17-26).

Figure 17-26 Verify that the properties for the network connection are set for sharing resources over the connection

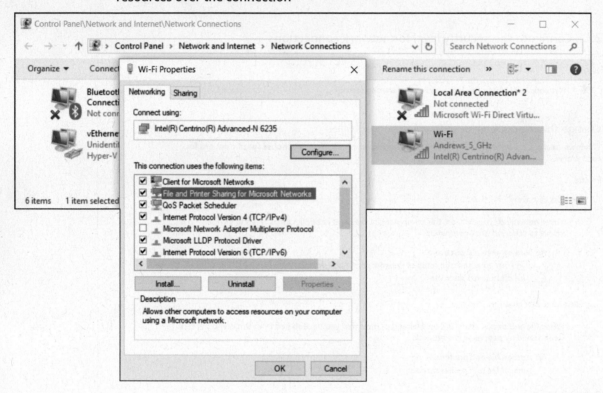

7. The user account name and password on the remote computer must match the user account and password on the host computer. If these accounts and passwords don't match, the user is considered an anonymous user and is denied access to resources shared on the remote computer. To verify that account names and passwords match, open the **Local Users and Groups** console, where you can view user account names, create new accounts, and set or reset passwords.

Here are a few additional tips about managing shared folders and files:

- **Use advanced permissions settings.** If you need further control of the permissions assigned to a user or group, click **Advanced** on the Security tab of a folder's Properties dialog box. The Advanced Security Settings dialog box appears (see Figure 17-27A). You can see that the Medical user group was given full control. To change these permission details, double-click the user group. In this example, the Medical group is being edited. The Permission Entry dialog box opens. Click **Show advanced permissions** to see these advanced permissions, as shown in Figure 17-27B.

Figure 17-27   Advanced permissions settings

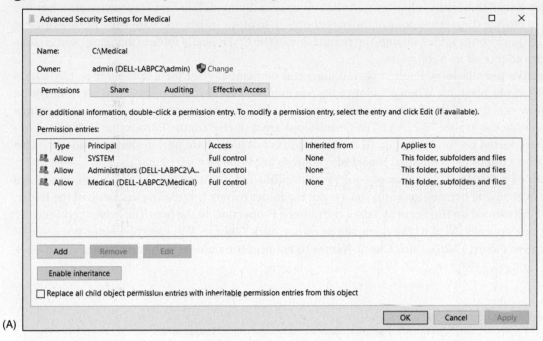

(A)

(B)

Detailed permissions can now be changed. For example, to prevent users in the Medical group from deleting the Medical folder, its subfolders, and its files, uncheck **Delete subfolders and files** and uncheck **Delete**. Click **OK** to close each dialog box. The resulting change means that users of the Medical group cannot delete or move a file or folder. (They can, however, copy the file or folder.)

Exam Tip ✔

The A+ Core 2 exam expects you to be able to implement permissions so that a user can copy but not move a file or folder and to understand how to apply Allow and Deny permissions.

17

- **Manage permissions using the parent folder.** When a subfolder is created, it is assigned the permissions of the parent folder. Recall that these inherited permissions appear dimmed. The best way to change inherited permissions is to change the permissions of the parent object. In other words, to change the permissions of the C:\Financial\QuickBooks folder, change the permission of the C:\Financial folder. Changing permissions of a parent folder affects all its subfolders.
- **Check the effective permissions.** Explicit permissions can be manually set for a subfolder or file, which overrides inherited permissions. When a folder or file has inherited and explicit permission set, it might be confusing to know exactly which permissions are in effect. To find out, see the **Advanced Security Settings** dialog box. (Refer back at Figure 17-27A.) NTFS permissions are reported on the Permissions tab and share permissions are reported on the Share tab. (If the Share tab is missing, share permissions are not set.) Use the Effective Access tab to get a detailed report of resources available to a particular user.
- **Take ownership of a folder.** The owner of a folder always has full permissions for the folder. If you are having a problem changing permissions and you are not the folder owner, try taking ownership of the folder. To do that, click **Advanced** on the Security tab of the folder's Properties dialog box. The Advanced Security Settings dialog box appears. Next to the name of the owner, click **Change**. You can then enter the name of the new owner (see Figure 17-28). Click **Check Names** to confirm the name is entered correctly, and click **OK** twice.

Figure 17-28   Change the owner of a folder

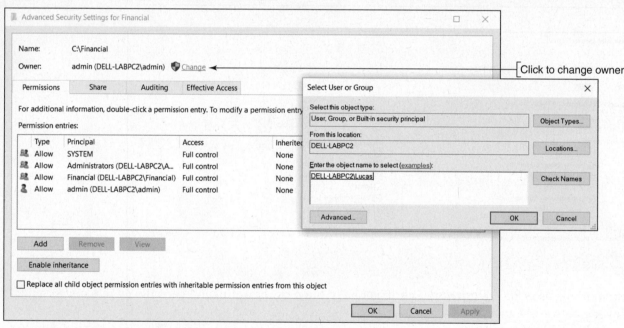

- **Use only one workgroup.** On a peer-to-peer network, it's not necessary that all computers belong to the same workgroup in order to share resources. However, performance improves when they are all in the same workgroup.
- **Require passwords for all user accounts.** Don't forget that for best security, each user account needs a password. In a workgroup, the policy to require that all accounts have passwords is set using Local Group Policy. On a domain, Group Policy is used.
- **Use the network path to access a shared folder.** To access shared folders on the network in the Explorer navigation bar or in a command prompt window, type the **network path** to the share as two backslashes, the computer name, one backslash, and the folder name, as shown in Figure 17-29 for Explorer and in a command line in Figure 17-30.
- **Use a mapped network drive.** For the convenience of remote users, map network drives for shared folders that are heavily used. How to do that is coming up next.

Figure 17-29   Network path to a shared folder using the Explorer navigation bar

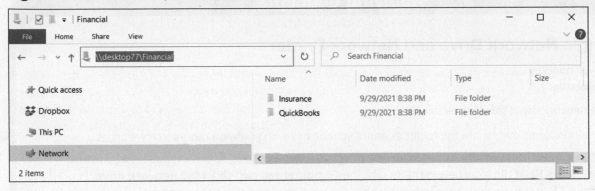

Figure 17-30   Network path to a shared folder using a command line

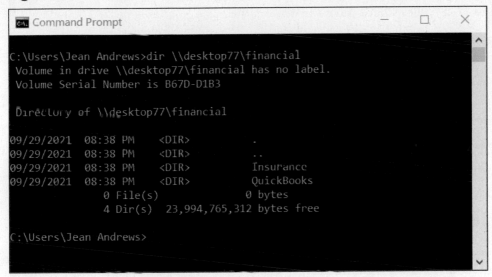

How to Map a Network Drive or Network Printer

Core 2 Objective 1.6

A **mapped drive**, also called a **network share**, is one of the most powerful and versatile methods of communicating over a network. A mapped drive makes one computer (the client) appear to have a new hard drive, such as drive E:, that is really hard drive space on another host computer (the server). The client computer creates and saves a shortcut associated with a drive letter that points to the host computer's shared folder or drive. This is called **mapping** the drive. In addition to mapping a network drive, you can also map a network printer to a computer.

17

Note 15

By default, this client/server arrangement is managed by the Windows Server Message Block (SMB) protocol, which you first learned about in the Core 1 module "Networking Fundamentals." Alternately, Windows can use the Network File System (NFS) protocol, which is compatible with Linux and UNIX file sharing on the network. Linux and UNIX also support Windows SMB via the Samba application. You learn more about Samba in the module "Linux and Scripting." Regardless of which protocol is used, host computers using different OSs—such as Windows, macOS, or Linux—can still share network resources.

Applying Concepts

Mapping a Network Drive and Network Printer

Est. Time: 30 minutes
Core 2 Objective: 1.6

To set up a network drive, follow these steps:

1. On the host computer, share the folder or entire volume to which you want others to have access.

2. On the remote computer that will use the network drive, open **Explorer**. In the left pane, click **This PC**. For Windows 10, at the top of the window, click the **Computer** tab, and click **Map network drive**. For Windows 11, at the top of the window, click the ... *See more* icon, and select **Map network drive**.)

3. The Map Network Drive dialog box opens, as shown on the left side of Figure 17-31. Select a drive letter from the drop-down list.

Figure 17-31 Mapping a network drive to a host computer

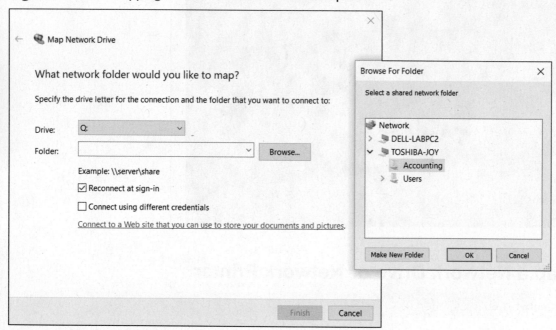

4. Click the **Browse** button, and locate the shared folder or drive on the host computer (see the right side of Figure 17-31). Click **OK** to close the Browse For Folder dialog box, and click **Finish** to map the drive. The folder on the host computer now appears as one more drive in Explorer on your computer.

Note 16

When mapping a network drive, you can type the network path to the host computer rather than clicking the Browse button to navigate to the host. To enter the path, open the **Map Network Drive** dialog box and type the network path—for example, **\\FILESERVER\Projects**—and then click **Finish**.

If a network drive does not work, go to the Network and Sharing Center, and verify that the network connection is good. You can also use the net use command to solve problems with mapped network drives. You learn about the net use command in the module "Network Security and Troubleshooting."

Core to Core ⇄

A host computer might be in sleep mode or powered down when a remote computer attempts to make a mapped drive connection at startup. To solve this problem, configure the host computer for Wake-on-LAN, as you learned in the Core 1 module "Networking Fundamentals."

Note 17

A network-attached storage (NAS) device provides hard drive storage for computers on a network. Computers on the network can access this storage using a mapped network drive.

To install a network printer, follow these steps:

1. In Control Panel in classic view, open the **Devices and Printers** applet, and click **Add a printer**. Windows searches for available printers. If the printer is not found, click **The printer that I want isn't listed**. See the left side of Figure 17-32.

Figure 17-32   Select a network printer identified by its IP address or host name

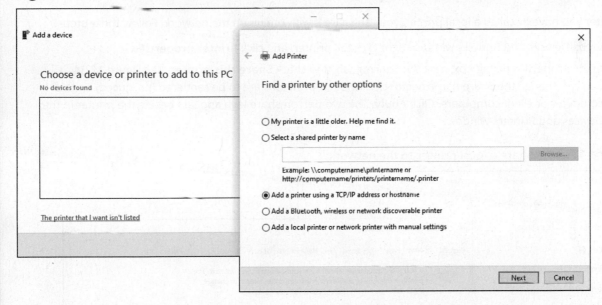

2. In the Add Printer dialog box (see the right side of Figure 17-32), select **Add a printer using a TCP/IP address or hostname**, and click **Next**.

3. Enter the printer's IP address or hostname, and click **Next**. Windows searches the network for the printer. If it finds the printer, the installation proceeds, and you can select the printer manufacturer and model and then name the printer (for example, CanonInHallway). Alternately, you can provide printer drivers that you can download to your computer. After the printer is installed, be sure to print a test page.

If you have problems installing a network printer, do the following:

- To verify the printer is online and you know its IP address, open a command prompt window and use the ping command, as shown in Figure 17-33.
- Download the printer drivers from the website of the printer manufacturer, and follow the manufacturer's directions to install the printer.

17

(continues)

Applying Concepts Continued

Figure 17-33 Ping a printer to verify it is online and the IP address is correct

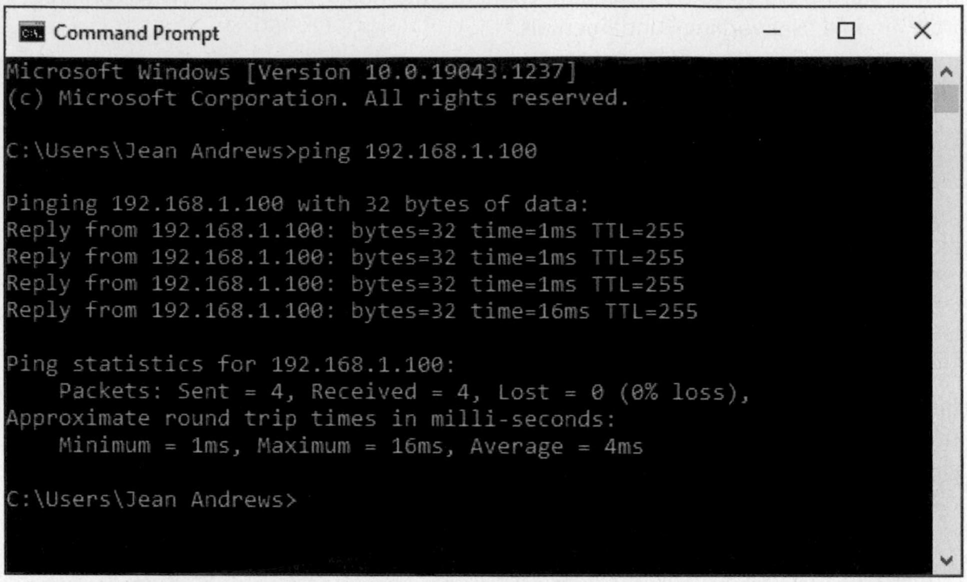

Command Prompt
Microsoft Windows [Version 10.0.19043.1237]
(c) Microsoft Corporation. All rights reserved.
C:\Users\Jean Andrews>ping 192.168.1.100
Pinging 192.168.1.100 with 32 bytes of data:
Reply from 192.168.1.100: bytes=32 time=1ms TTL=255
Reply from 192.168.1.100: bytes=32 time=1ms TTL=255
Reply from 192.168.1.100: bytes=32 time=1ms TTL=255
Reply from 192.168.1.100: bytes=32 time=16ms TTL=255
Ping statistics for 192.168.1.100:
Packets: Sent = 4, Received = 4, Lost = 0 (0% loss),
Approximate round trip times in milli-seconds:
Minimum = 1ms, Maximum = 16ms, Average = 4ms
C:\Users\Jean Andrews>

After you have installed a local printer, you can share it with others on the network. Follow these steps:

1. In the Devices and Printers window, right-click the printer, and click **Printer properties**.
2. In the Properties dialog box, click the **Sharing** tab, and check **Share this printer**. See Figure 17-34. You can change the Share name and decide whether print jobs are to be rendered (produced) on this computer or client computers. Click **Apply**. The two-person share icon appears beside the printer in the Devices and Printers window.

Figure 17-34 Share a local printer to the network

Control Panel\All Control Panel Items\Devices and Printers
« All ... › Devic...
Add a device
Add a printer
Devices (4)
Multimedia Devices (3)
Printers (6)
Fax
Microsoft Print to PDF
Snagit 2018
CanonInHallway
13 items
CanonInHallway Properties
General
Sharing
Ports
Advanced
Color Management
Security
Device Settings
Profile
If you share this printer, any user on your network can print to it. The printer will not be available when the computer sleeps. To change these settings, use the Network and Sharing Center.
Share this printer
Share name:
CanonInHallway
Render print jobs on client computers
Drivers
If this printer is shared with users running different versions of Windows, you may want to install additional drivers, so that the users do not have to find the print driver when they connect to the shared printer.
Additional Drivers...
OK
Cancel
Apply
Help

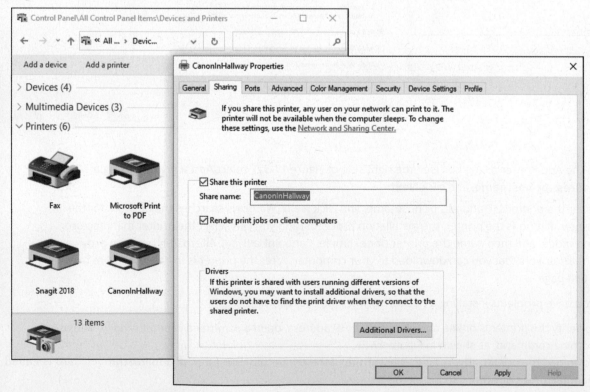

Core to Core ⬌

More information about managing shared printers is covered in the Core 1 module "Supporting Printers."

Other computers on the network can now see the printer in their Explorer window when they drill down into resources shared by the computer. To install the printer on a client computer, right-click the printer and click **Connect**.

Exam Tip ✔

The A+ Core 2 exam expects you to know the difference between a shared printer and a network printer. A printer installed locally on a computer can be shared with other computers. This is different from a network printer, which is accessed by each networked computer directly through the network.

Hidden Network Resources and Administrative Shares

Core 2 Objective 1.6

Sometimes you may need to securely share a file or folder on the network or ensure that a folder or file is not visible or accessible from the network or by other users. When you need to protect confidential data from users on the network, you can do the following:

- **Disable File and Printer Sharing.** If no resources on the computer are shared, use the Network and Sharing Center to disable File and Printer Sharing for Microsoft Networks.
- **Hide a shared folder.** If you want to share a folder but don't want others to see the shared folder in Explorer, add a $ to the end of the share name in the Advanced Sharing dialog box, as shown in Figure 17-35. This shared and hidden folder is called a **hidden share**. Others on the network can access the folder only when they know its network path. For example, to access a shared folder named Personnel$ on the computer named Desktop77, a user must enter ***Desktop77\Personnel$** in the Explorer navigation bar.

Figure 17-35 A $ at the end of the share name hides the share unless the exact name is used in a network path to locate it

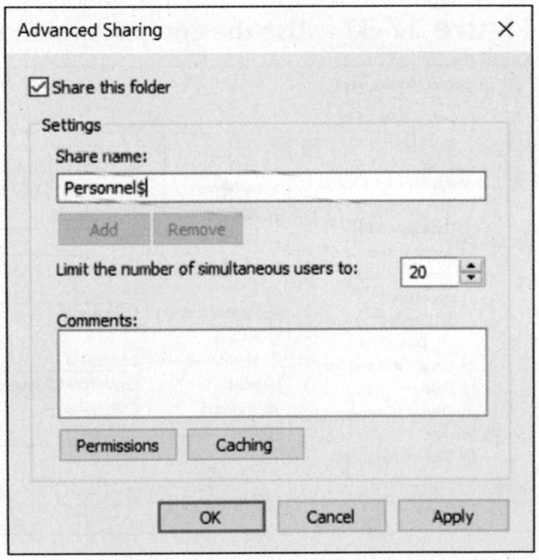

So far in this module, you have learned about folders and files on a computer that are shared with other users on the network; these shares are called **local shares**. For computers that belong to a domain, you need to be aware of another way folders are shared, called administrative shares. **Administrative shares** are folders shared by default that administrator accounts at the domain level can access. You don't need to manually share these folders because Windows automatically does so by default. The following are two types of administrative shares:

- **The %systemroot% folder.** Enter the path ***computername\admin$** to access the *%systemroot%* folder (most likely the C:\Windows folder) on a remote computer in order to work with that computer's system folders and files. For example, to connect to the ws14 workstation shown in Figure 17-36, the entry in the Explorer navigation bar is \\**ws14\\*admin$**. The authenticate dialog box appears; enter **Administrator** as the user name and the password to the Administrator account. The admin$ administrative share is called the **Remote Admin share**.

17

Figure 17-36   Access an administrative share on a domain

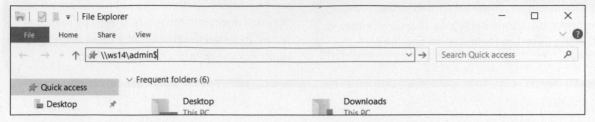

- **Any volume or drive**. To access the root level of any volume or drive on the network, enter the computer name and drive letter followed by a $—for example, **\\ws14\C$**.

Figure 17-37   Use the Computer Management console to view all shares

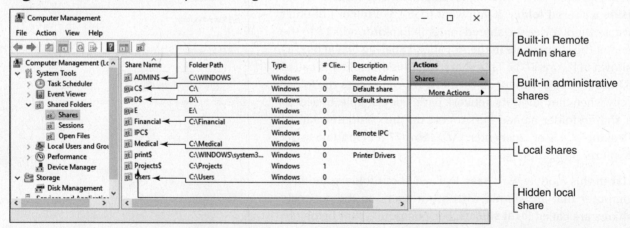

Now let's turn our attention to securing resources on a Windows domain.

Using Active Directory Domain Services

Core 2 Objective 2.1

Recall that Active Directory (AD) is a suite of services and databases provided by Windows Server that is used to manage Windows domains, including access to the domain and what users and computers can do in the domain. AD incorporates five groups of services:

- **Active Directory Domain Services (AD DS)** authenticates accounts and authorizes what these accounts can do.
- AD Certificate Services (AD CS) secures identities of services, computers, and users.
- AD Federation Services (AD FS) secures trust relationships with outside organizations.
- AD Rights Management Services (AD RMS) secures data.
- AD Lightweight Directory Services (AD LDS) secures applications.

Active Directory organizes resources in a top-down hierarchical structure, as shown in Figure 17-38. Users and resources of a company or school managed by AD are organized into a **forest** (the entire enterprise), which contains a domain (for example, *mycompany.com*). For a few very large enterprises, domains can contain subdomains (for example, *mycompany.com* and *mycompany-dev.com*), but in most situations, a forest contains only a single domain. Domains can contain sites (for example, a New York branch office and a San Francisco branch). Domains and sites are also organized into various organizational units.

Figure 17-38   The Active Directory organizational structure

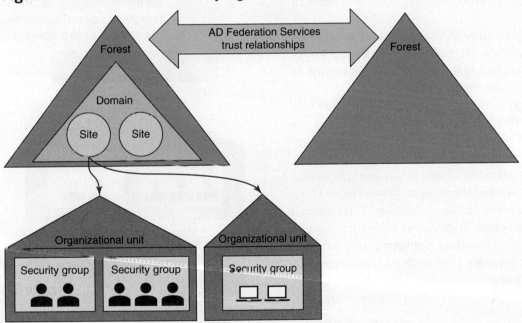

Organizational units (OU) are created to make it easier for technicians to assign privileges to users and computers that are assigned to an OU. In general, an administrator creates an OU tree to follow the job descriptions within an organization. For example, Figure 17-39 shows the Domain Users OU includes everyone in the company. Other OUs are created based on job responsibilities. Although it is possible to put users and computers in the same OU, it is not recommended because generally their privileges are very different.

17

Figure 17-39 Organizational units structured to follow the organization of a company

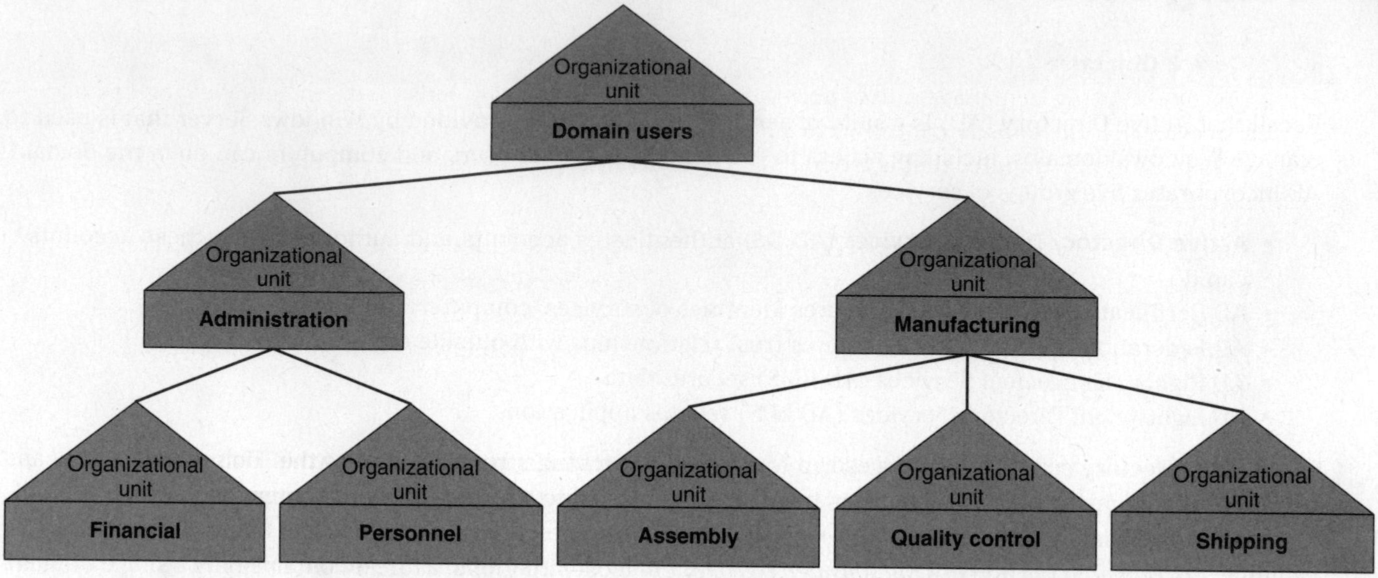

Organizational
unit
Domain users

Organizational
unit
Administration

Organizational
unit
Manufacturing

Organizational
unit
Financial

Organizational
unit
Personnel

Organizational
unit
Assembly

Organizational
unit
Quality control

Organizational
unit
Shipping

An OU can contain groups of users or computers called **security groups**, which are similar to user groups in a Windows workgroup except a security group can include a computer or a user.

Privileges are assigned to OUs using policies created by Group Policy. These policies are contained in **Group Policy Objects (GPOs)** that are applied to the OU and, by inheritance, to each security group, user, and computer in the OU.

Permissions assigned to folders work much the same way as they do in Windows 10/11. NTFS and share permissions are assigned to a folder on a server in the domain by assigning permissions to an OU or security group, and the users in this OU or group inherit these assigned permissions. In summary, managing resources in AD revolves around the tools shown in Figure 17-40.

In this module, we focus on the skills an IT technician needs to manage user accounts with Active Directory Domain Services—including creating, resetting, unlocking, enabling, and disabling user accounts; resetting user account passwords; and managing login scripts. You also learn how Group Policy can be used to assign privileges to an OU and the security groups and users in the OU.

Figure 17-40 Group policies apply to OUs, and NTFS and share permissions apply to folders to control access to the resources in a domain

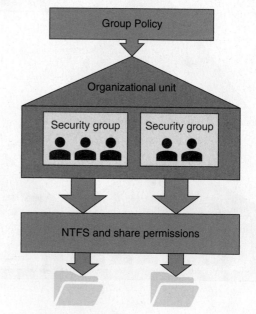

Creating and Managing User Accounts in AD

Core 2 Objective 2.1

Before we discuss how to manage a user account on a Windows domain, let's pause to see how you can access Domain Services on the domain controller to get to the tools you need. You'll need a local administrator account for a Windows Server computer that is a domain controller. Then you can use one of these methods to access the domain controller:

- **Sitting at the computer.** While physically seated at the Windows Server computer, sign in to Windows Server with an administrator account. Then click **Start** and click **Server Manager** in the Start menu. The Server Manager console is shown in Figure 17-41 with the Tools menu open. The **Server Manager** console contains the tools used to manage Active Directory and is included in Windows Server. It can also be installed in Windows 10/11.

Figure 17-41 The Windows Server desktop with the Server Manager console showing the Tools menu

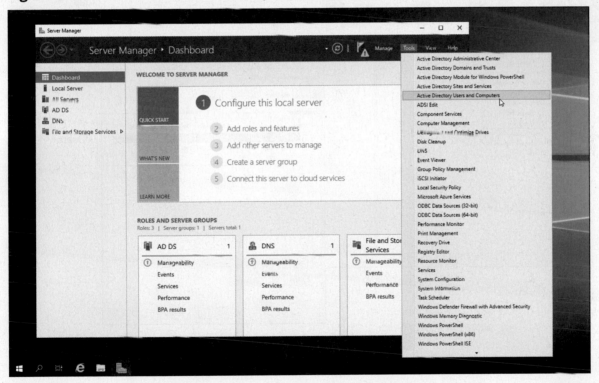

- **Remote access via Remote Desktop.** You can use Remote Desktop from anywhere on the Internet to connect to a Windows Server computer, sign in, and open Server Manager. Details about Remote Desktop are covered in the module "Network Security and Troubleshooting," and you get a first look at it in a project at the end of this module. Remote Desktop is included in Windows 10/11 Pro and Enterprise editions.
- **Remote access via Windows Admin Center.** Windows Admin Center is a console you download and install for free in Windows 10/11. It works inside a browser and contains various tools for remotely managing Windows Server.

Note 19

If you don't have access to Active Directory and a Windows domain to practice the skills in this part of the module, you can follow the steps in Real Problem 17-2 at the end of this module to set up your own Windows domain in Windows Server using the free Google Cloud Platform at *cloud.google.com*.

17

Use Server Manager and Create a New User

Let's get started learning to use Server Manager. In Server Manager, follow these steps to view the OU structure and create a new user:

1. Sign in to Windows Server with an administrator account, and open **Server Manager**.
2. Click **Tools** (refer back to Figure 17-41), and click **Active Directory Users and Computers**. (The utility is also available in Control Panel under Administrative Tools.) The Active Directory Users and Computers window displays. Figure 17-42 shows the sample domain *homerun.com*, which belongs to our fictitious company, Homerun Sports Medicine, Inc.

Figure 17-42   Users, computers, and OUs in the domain

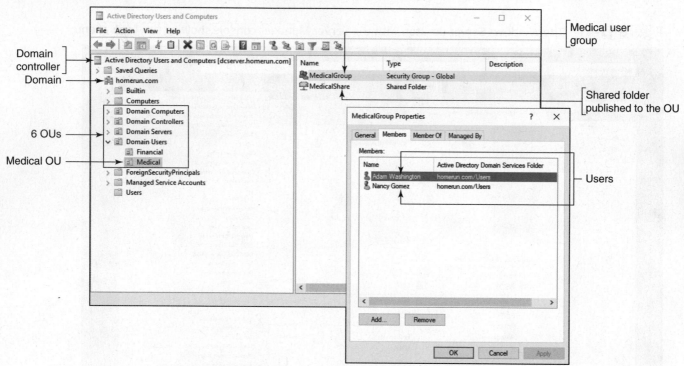

There are six OUs currently in the domain:

- Domain Controllers is a default OU created when the domain was created. It contains all the domain controllers managing Active Directory. Our controller is named dcserver.
- Domain Computers and Domain Servers OUs were created by the system administrator directly under the *homerun.com* domain so appropriate policies can more easily be applied to the computers assigned to these OUs.
- Domain Users OU was created directly under the *homerun.com* domain, and all users will be assigned to this OU. Domain Users contains two OUs: Financial and Medical. Each of these OUs contains a security group, and every new user will be assigned to one of these two security groups.
- In Figure 17-42, note the Medical OU is selected, and it contains the MedicalGroup security group and one shared folder. (You can give an OU and a security group the same name, but to avoid confusion, use different names.)

3. Double-click the **MedicalGroup** to view its Properties dialog box. Click the **Members** tab to see that Nancy Gomez and Adam Washington are members of the group, as shown in Figure 17-42.

4. To add a new user, you can create the account inside an OU. (Right-click the OU, point to **New**, and click **User**.) Alternately, you can add the new user to the User folder. Right-click **User**, point to **New**, and click **User**, as shown in Figure 17-43.

Figure 17-43   Right-click the User group or an OU to create a new user

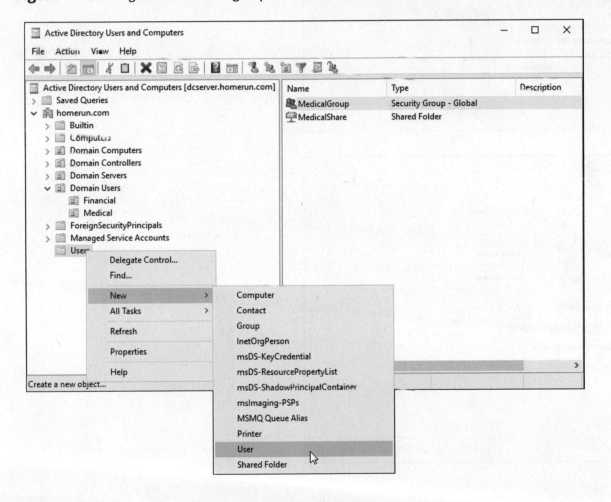

5. Enter the user's first name, last name, and user name (see Figure 17-44A). Click **Next**. On the next screen, decide how to handle the password (see Figure 17-44B).

17

Figure 17-44 To create a new user, (A) enter a name and logon name, and (B) decide how to handle the password

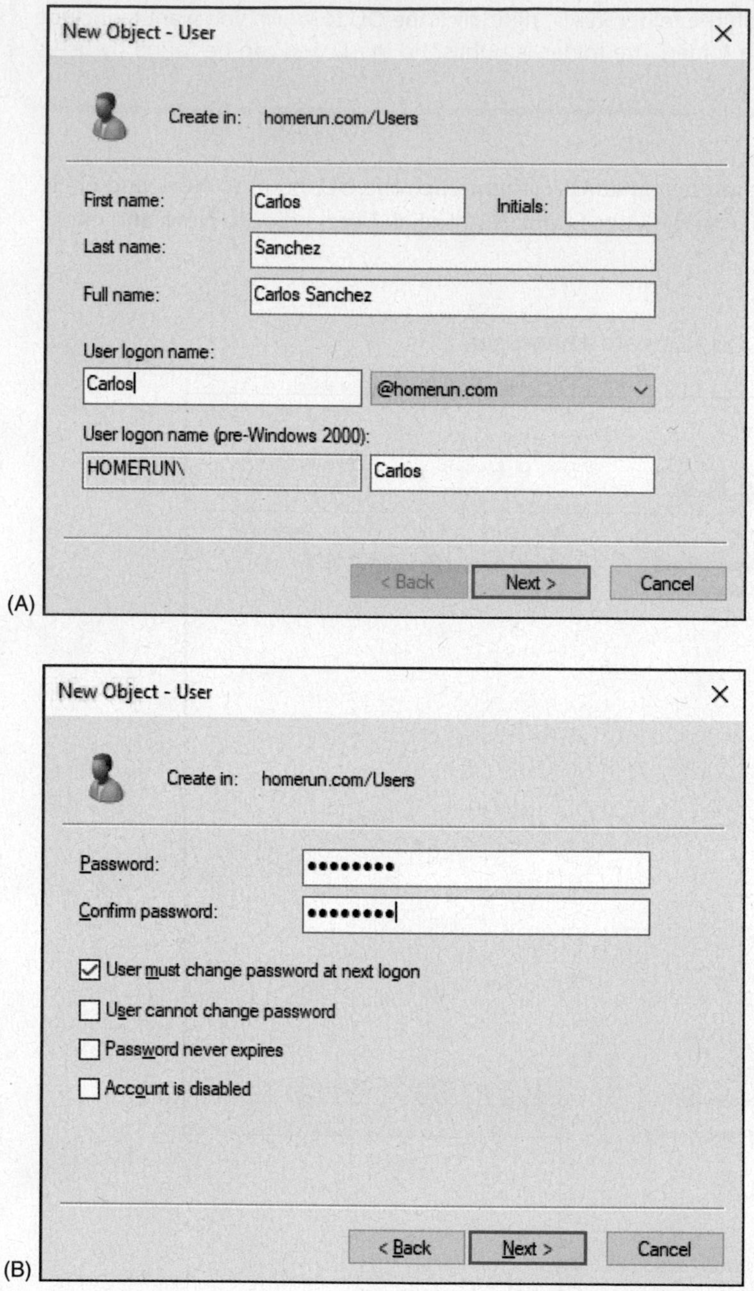

(A)

(B)

Here are the best practices for these password options:

- Always require a password.
- By default, the password you enter must meet AD's complexity requirements: It must have at least eight lowercase and uppercase letters, numbers, and symbols, and it cannot contain any three consecutive letters in the user name or display name.
- The best practice is to require the user to change the password at next logon.
- Notice you can select *Account is disabled*. This might be appropriate when you are setting up an account well in advance of the account actually being used.

6. Click **Next** and click **Finish**. The account is created.

7. After the account is created, you can add it to an existing security group. Right-click the user account and click **Add to a group** (see Figure 17-45).

Figure 17-45 Add the user account to an existing user group

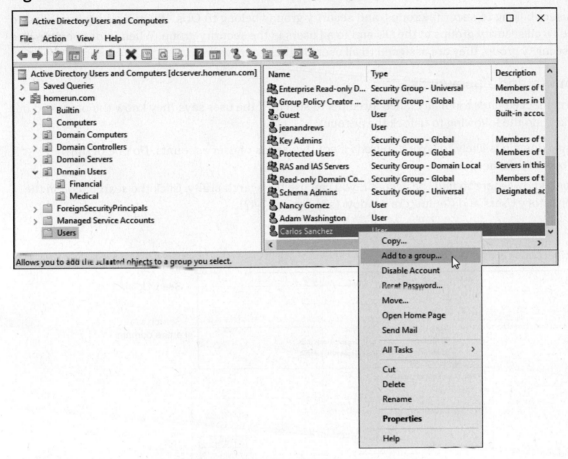

8. Type the group name, and click **Check Names**. Windows verifies the name of the group and confirms it by underlining the name. Click **OK** (see Figure 17-46).

Figure 17-46 Type the user group name and click Check Names

Select Groups	×
Select this object type:	
Groups or Built-in security principals	Object Types...
From this location:	
homerun.com	Locations...
Enter the object names to select (examples):	
FinancialGroup	Check Names
Advanced...	OK Cancel

17

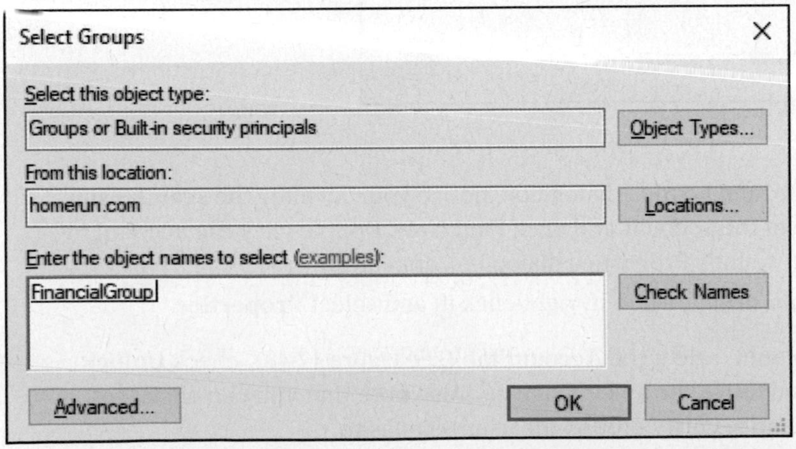

Note 22

To create a new security group, right-click the OU where you want to add the group, click **New**, and click **Group**. You can then name the group.

In summary, users belong to security groups, and security groups belong to OUs. When a policy is applied to an OU, it is applied to all security groups in the OU and to all users in the security group. When folder permissions are assigned to a security group, they are assigned to all users in the security group.

Manage Accounts and Passwords

An account might get locked after too many failed attempts to sign in. If the user says they know the password but the account is locked, do the following to unlock the account:

1. An enterprise domain is likely to have hundreds if not thousands of user accounts. Do one of the following to locate the account:

   - If you don't know where to find the account, you can use the search utility. Click the search icon in the Active Directory Users and Computers window (see Figure 17-47).

Figure 17-47   Search for a user account

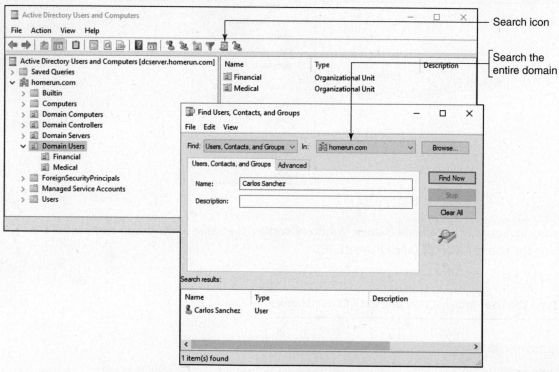

Near the top of the Find Users, Contacts, and Groups dialog box, notice you can filter the search using the drop-down menus. Enter the name of the account and click **Find Now**. Double-click the account in the list of matches that appears. The account's Properties dialog box appears.

   - If you know where to find the account, drill down to it, right-click it, and select **Properties**.

2. In the Properties dialog box for the account, select the **Account** tab (see Figure 17-48), check **Unlock account**, and click **Apply**. The user should then be able to sign in. (Also note that you can click the **Member Of** tab to find out which OUs and security groups the user belongs to.)

Figure 17-48 Unlock a locked account

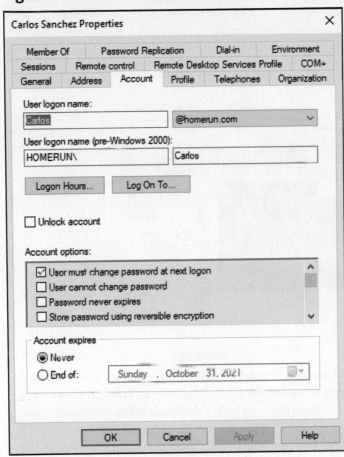

Follow these steps to reset a forgotten password and disable, enable, or delete an account:

1. Locate the account and right-click it. In the shortcut menu, click **Reset Password** (refer back to Figure 17-45). In the Reset Password dialog box (see Figure 17-49), enter a new password twice. It's a good idea to leave the *User must change password at next logon* box checked. If the account has been locked, check **Unlock the user's account**. Click **OK**.

Figure 17-49 Reset the user password

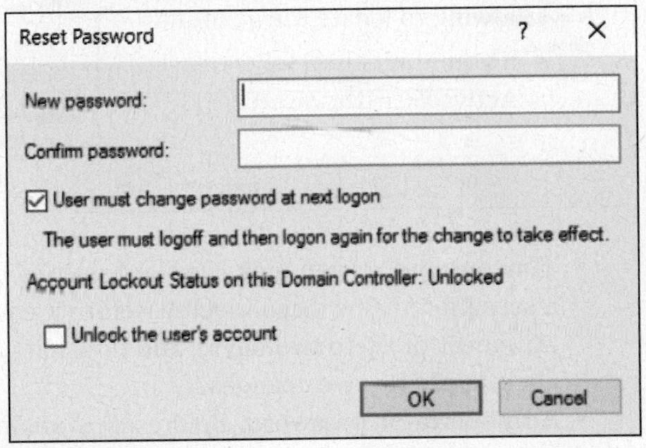

2. In the account's shortcut menu shown earlier in Figure 17-45, note the options to disable and delete an account. When you click **Disable Account**, the user cannot sign in, but the account's user profile still exists, and you can later enable the account using the same shortcut menu. Click **Delete** to delete the account, which deletes the user profile. You can also disable and enable an account and designate when an account will expire using options on the Account tab of the user's Properties dialog box.

Note 23

The user account is considered an object in Active Directory. When you delete an AD object, it goes to the Active Directory Recycle Bin, where it can be recovered until the Recycle Bin is emptied.

17

Here are a few other tips to help you manage accounts in Active Directory:

- **Disable the Guest account.** In Active Directory, the Guest account is disabled by default. For best security, leave the account disabled. If you find the Guest account enabled, right-click it and select **Disable Account**.
- **Logon time restrictions.** By default, a user can sign in to AD at any time. Suppose, however, that midnight to 8:00 a.m. every Sunday is restricted for routine maintenance. To set logon time restrictions, open the user's **Properties** dialog box, select the **Account** tab, and click **Logon Hours** (see Figure 17-50). Click an hour, and then click **Logon Denied**. Notice that in Figure 17-50, midnight to 8:00 a.m. on Sunday is denied.

Figure 17-50 Logon time restrictions

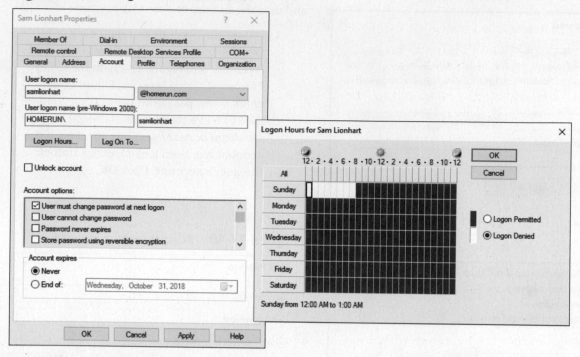

- **Timeout and screen lock.** On the Sessions tab of the user's Properties dialog box, you can limit how long a session remains disconnected before it ends (never or up to two days), how long an active session stays up (never or up to two days), and how long an idle session stays up. After you have made your selections, click **Apply** to save changes.

- **Administrator password.** Before AD Domain Services can be configured to be a domain controller on the network, the Administrator account on its computer must have a strong password (including lowercase and uppercase letters, numbers, and symbols). To manage the properties of the Administrator account, open **Users** in the **Active Directory Users and Computers** window, right-click **Administrator**, and click **Properties**. See Figure 17-51. To change the password of the Administrator account, you can run the following command in an elevated command prompt window in Windows Server:

```
net user Administrator <password>
```

Figure 17-51 Manage the properties of the Administrator account

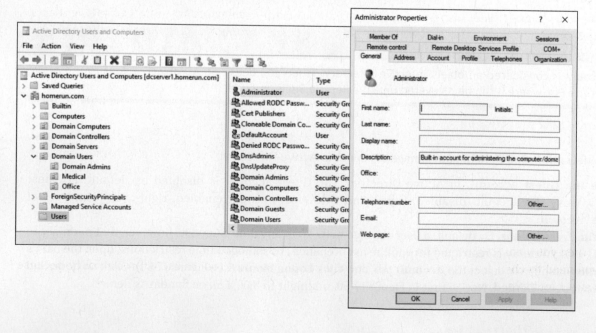

- **Home folder.** The **Home folder** is the default folder that is presented to the user whenever they are ready to save a file. On a peer-to-peer network, the Home folder in Windows is normally the Documents folder in the user profile at C:\Users*username*\Documents. Active Directory is able to change this Home folder location to a share on the network, which is called **folder redirection**. Here are two reasons to apply folder redirection to the Home folder:
  - On a domain, a user might sign in to different computers. When their Home folder is stored on the network, it's always available and does not need to be copied to each computer they use.
  - It's easier for backups to be maintained when all Home folders are on a network server rather than on individual workstations. In an organization, individual workstations are generally not backed up regularly, but servers on the network are backed up at least every night.
  - To see if a user's Home folder is on their local computer or on the network, select the **Profile** tab of the user's Properties dialog box (see Figure 17-52). For this user, the Home folder is in a network share.

Figure 17-52   This user's Home folder is contained in a network share

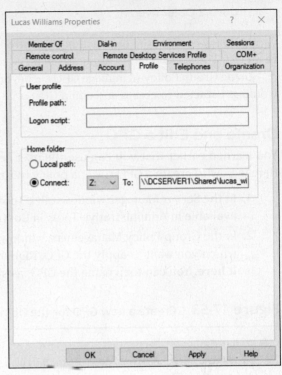

> ### Note 24
> Many corporations are beginning to use cloud services rather than managing data on their premises. One way to do this is to set up OneDrive in the Microsoft cloud for each user in the Windows domain. Users are then encouraged to use their OneDrive for personal files rather than their Home folders stored on a network share.

- **Logon scripts.** A **logon script**, also called a login script, is a list of commands stored in a script file that is performed each time a user signs in to Windows. In Active Directory, logon scripts are normally stored on the domain controllers in a network share named Netlogon. Types of logon scripts supported by Active Directory include Windows batch files (.bat file extension), VBScript files (.vbs file extension), and Power-Shell scripts (.ps2 file extension). After the script file is stored in the Netlogon share, to assign the script to a single user, select the **Profile** tab in the user's Properties dialog box. See Figure 17-52. Under Logon script, enter the name of the script file along with its file extension.
- **Multifactor authentication.** Some organizations require multifactor authentication (MFA) to sign in a domain to protect the credentials of certain privileged users. Azure Active Directory in the Microsoft cloud can implement the optional Microsoft Identity Manager (MIM) system that requires MFA along with other security measures to protect these privileged accounts. In addition, Windows Server Active Directory on premises can provide Privileged Access Management (PAM) that works with MIM to enforce MFA as well as other security measures. How these systems are implemented is beyond the scope of this text.

Normally, when you want to change a setting for a single user, you use the user's Properties dialog box, as just explained. If you need to change settings for all the users in an OU, the best tool to use is Group Policy because these policies affect multiple users.

17

Group Policy Objects

 Core 2 Objective 2.1

Group Policy can be used on the domain controller to create Group Policy Objects, which contain policies that apply to an OU. These OU policies apply to users, computers, shared folders, and printers in the OU.

Using Group Policy to manage GPOs is beyond the scope of this text. However, let's take a quick look at how you would get started to create and edit a GPO.

Create and Edit a GPO

You learned earlier that you can use the user account Properties dialog box to set a logon script for a single user. Here is how to create a GPO to set a policy to run a logon or logoff script for all users in the domain or an OU:

1. In the Server Manager window, click **Tools** and click **Group Policy Management**. (The tool is also available in Administrative Tools in Control Panel.)

2. In the Group Policy Management window (see Figure 17-53), drill down into the OUs to find the one to which you want to apply the GPO. Right-click the OU, and click **Create a GPO in this domain**, **and Link it here**. You can then name the GPO, as shown in the figure, and click **OK**.

Figure 17-53 Create a new GPO for the Domain Users OU

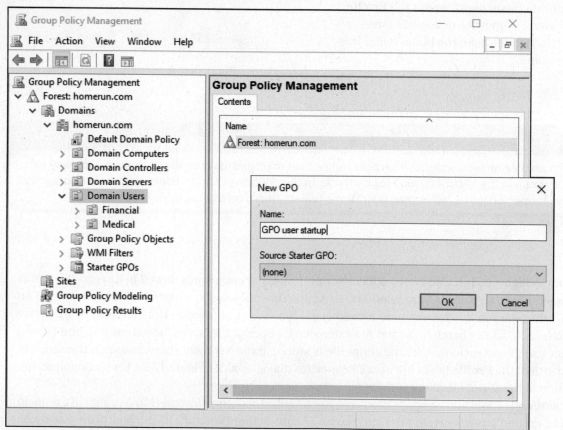

3. The new GPO appears in the list under the OU and in the Group Policy Objects list. To display details about the GPO, click it and click **OK**. The GPO details display in the right pane with the Scope tab selected.

4. To edit a GPO, right-click it in the left pane, and click **Edit**. The Group Policy Management Editor window opens so you can edit the GPO. You can see the GPO name at the top of the left pane of the editor (see Figure 17-54).

Figure 17-54   Drill down into the policies to find the ones you need

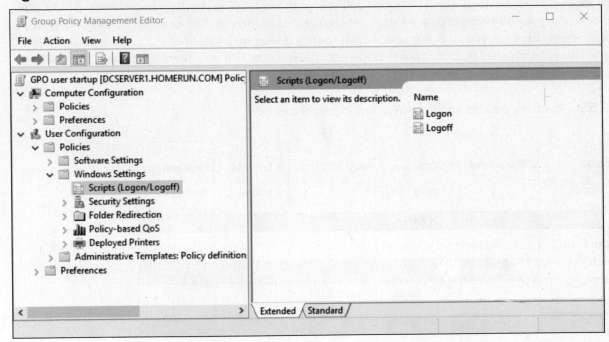

5. Just as with Local Group Policy, policies apply to either the computer or the user. You can drill down into the Computer Configuration or User Configuration policies and find and set the ones you want. For example, to add a logon script for all users in the OU to which the GPO belongs, drill down in the **User Configuration**, **Policies**, **Windows Settings**, **Scripts (Logon/Logoff)** group, as shown in Figure 17-54.

6. When you're done setting policies, close the GPO editor to return to the Group Policy Management window.

7. GPO updates are automatically pushed down to clients on the domain in the same site in just a few minutes. On a client computer, just as with Local Group Policy, you can run the **gpupdate /force** command to apply new policies to the client.

Which Policy Wins?

Sometimes policies overlap or conflict. Here is the order in which policies are applied; the last policy to be applied wins:

1. **Local.** All local policies are applied first. As you learned earlier, Local Group Policy on the local computer can create policies that apply to the local computer or users.

2. **Site.** Policies for sites are applied next.

3. **Domain.** Policies for a domain are applied next.

4. **OU.** Policies for an OU are applied next, followed by policies for sub-OUs.

5. **Enforced.** Policies that are tagged as Enforced policies are applied last and always win over other policies.

Note 25

To tag a GPO as Enforced, right-click the GPO in the Group Policy Management window, and click **Enforced**.

Where there is a conflict of policies, the last policy applied wins. It's important to remember the order in which policies are applied, and the acronym LSDOE (usually pronounced "LS-doe") can help: Local, Site, Domain, OU, and Enforced.

17

Figure 17-55 shows what can happen when there are conflicting policies. In the figure, you see that policies A, B, C, and D are applied. To understand which policy is applied at each level, follow the diagram from left to right. First, notice that local policy A wins because policy A does not exist at the site, domain, OU, or enforced level. For policy B, domain policy B wins over site policy B. For policy C, site policy C wins over local policy C. Although OU policy D would have won over local policy D, the OU policy D was not applied because it was overridden by enforced policy D. Therefore, the resultant policies are local policy A, domain policy B, site policy C, and enforced policy D.

Figure 17-55   Resulting policies applied when conflicting policies exist

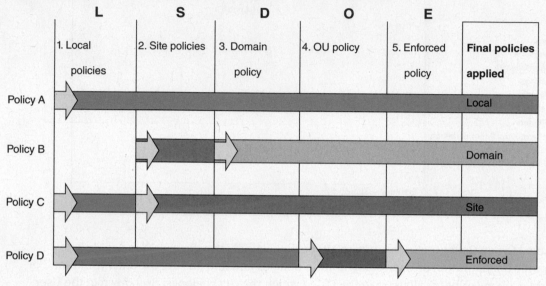

To find out the resulting policies for the computer or user, do one of the following:

- In a command prompt window, enter the **rsop.msc** command. The **Resultant Set of Policy (RSoP)** window opens, where you can drill down to see the policies set for the computer or user. For example, Figure 17-56 shows the RSoP for the Password Policy.

Figure 17-56   The Resultant Set of Policy for the Password Policy

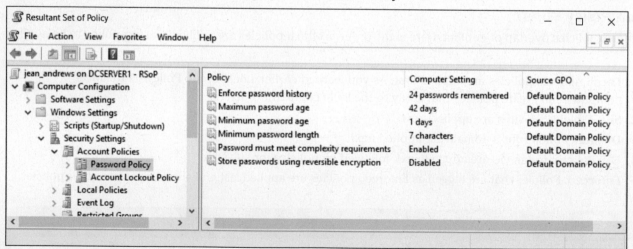

- In a command prompt window, enter the **gpresult /v** command, which displays the policies currently applied to the computer and user. The report is very long; you can save it to an HTML file so you can later search it. For example, use this command: **gpresult /h C:\myfile.html**. To view the file, double-click it in Explorer. The HTML file opens in your default browser window. Figure 17-57 shows a snip of the file that includes the Password Policy.

Figure 17-57   The gpresult output displayed as an HTML file in a browser

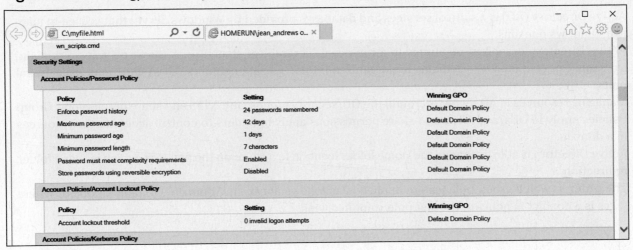

Module Summary

Securing a Windows Personal Computer

- Power-on passwords are managed by BIOS/UEFI firmware on the motherboard and work before Windows is launched.
- A long password is a strong password.
- Windows allows fingerprints, facial recognition, and PINs to be used to authenticate to Windows. This authentication data is kept on the local machine and applies only to the one device.
- Use Local Group Policies (gpedit.msc) and Local Security Policies (secpol.msc) to control what users and computers can do on the computer or network.
- Encrypting File System (EFS) encrypts files and folders on an NTFS file system. BitLocker Drive Encryption encrypts an entire volume on a hard drive. Both are available on business and professional editions of Windows and make use of a TPM chip on the motherboard.

Controlling Access to Folders, Files, and Printers

- Access to folders and files on a network is controlled by assigning privileges to user accounts and assigning permissions to folders and files.
- Apply the principle of least privilege when assigning privileges to users. You can change the privileges of an account by adding it to or removing it from a user group.
- You can create customized user groups to make it easier to manage privileges to multiple user accounts.
- Two ways to share files and folders on the network are to use workgroup sharing in a peer-to-peer network and Active Directory to control a domain. You can use share permissions and NTFS permissions.
- A mapped network drive makes it easier for users to access drives and folders on the network.
- A Windows domain supports administrative shares. You can also hide network resources so that a user must know the name of the resource to access it.

17

Using Active Directory Domain Services

- Active Directory (AD) is a suite of services and databases provided by Windows Server that is used to manage Windows domains.
- Active Directory organizes resources in a top-down hierarchical structure. A forest contains a domain. Domains can contain sites. Domains are organized into organizational units (OUs) and suborganizational units.
- Managing resources in AD revolves around the OU, security groups, and NTFS and share permissions. Group Policies apply to OUs, and NTFS and share permissions apply to folders to control access to the resources in a domain.
- Active Directory is able to change the Home folder location to a share on the network, which is called folder redirection.
- The order in which group policies are applied is as follows: local, site, domain, OU, and enforced. Where there is a conflict in policies, the last policy applied wins.

Key Terms

For explanations of key terms, see the Glossary for this text.

Active Directory Domain Services (AD DS)
administrative shares
Administrators group
anonymous user
Authenticated Users group
BitLocker To Go
data-at-rest encryption
Encrypting File System (EFS)
Everyone group
explicit permissions
folder redirection
forest
gpresult
gpupdate
Group Policy Object (GPO)
Guests group
hidden share
Home folder
inherited permissions
Local Group Policy
Local Security Policy
local share
Local Users and Groups
logon script
mapped drive
mapping
network path
network share
NTFS permissions
organizational unit (OU)
Power Users group
Remote Admin share
Resultant Set of Policy (RSoP)
security group
Server Manager
share permissions
strong password
TPM (Trusted Platform Module)
Users group

Thinking Critically

These questions are designed to prepare you for the critical thinking required for the A+ exams and may use information from other modules and the web.

1. Your organization has set up three levels of classification for data accessed by users on a small network:
   - Low security: Data in the C:\Public folder
   - Medium security: Data in a shared folder that some, but not all, user groups can access
   - High security: Data in a shared and encrypted folder that requires a password to access. The folder is shared only to one user group.

   Classify each of the following sets of data:
   a. Directions to the company's Fourth of July party
   b. Details of an invention made by the company president that has not yet been patented
   c. Resumes presented by several people applying for a job with the company
   d. Payroll spreadsheets
   e. Job openings at the company

2. You work in the accounting department and have been using a network drive to post Excel workbook files to your file server as you complete them. When you attempt to save a workbook file to the drive, you see the error message: "You do not have access to the folder 'J:\'. See your administrator for access to this folder." What should you do first? Second? Explain the reasoning behind your choices.

   a. Ask your network administrator to give you permission to access the folder.
   b. Check Explorer to verify that you can connect to the network.
   c. Save the workbook file to your hard drive.
   d. Using Explorer, remap the network drive.
   e. Reboot your PC.

3. What is the command to launch each of the following tools?

   a. Local Group Policy
   b. Local Security Policy
   c. Computer Management console
   d. Local Users and Groups console
   e. Resultant Set of Policy (RSoP)

4. What hardware component is needed to set up BitLocker Encryption so you can authenticate the computer?

5. Where in Group Policy can you locate the policy that requires a smart card to be used to authenticate a user to Windows?

   a. Computer Configuration, Windows Settings, Security Settings, Local Policies, Biometrics
   b. Computer Configuration, Administrative Templates, System, Logon
   c. Computer Configuration, Windows Settings, Security Settings, Local Policies, Security Options
   d. User Configuration, Administrative Templates, System, Logon

6. You open a folder Properties dialog box to encrypt the folder, click Advanced, and discover that *Encrypt contents to secure data* is dimmed. What is the most likely problem?

   a. Encryption has not been enabled. Use the Computer Management console to enable it.
   b. You are not using an edition of Windows that supports encryption.
   c. Most likely a virus has attacked the system and is disabling encryption.
   d. Encryption applies only to files, not folders.

7. You have shared a folder, C:\DenverCO, with your team. The folder contains information about your company branch in Denver, Colorado. Your company decides to reorganize into zones, so you move the folder as a subfolder in the folder G:\Zone3. When your team members try to access G:\Zone3\DenverCO, they get an error message saying they have been denied access. What happened to the permissions when you moved the folder to its new location?

8. What command do you enter in the Explorer search box to access the Remote Admin share on the computer named Fin?

9. In your organization, each department has a folder on a shared drive. Your manager frequently copies the folder to their local computer to run reports. You have noticed that the folder for your department keeps disappearing from the shared drive. You discover that the folder isn't being deleted and often gets moved into a random nearby folder. You suspect that coworkers in other departments are being careless with their mouse clicks while accessing their own folders on the shared drive and are dragging and dropping your department folder into other folders without noticing. How can you prevent this folder from being moved but still allow it to be copied? What steps do you take?

10. If you are having a problem changing the permissions of a folder that was created by another user, what can you do to help solve the problem?

17

11. When setting up OUs in a new domain, why might it be useful to put all computers in one OU and all users in another?

    a. It will be easier to inventory computers in the domain.
    b. It will help organize users into user groups.
    c. An OU must contain either users or computers but not both.
    d. Policies generally apply to either computers or users.

12. You have set up a user group named Accounting and have put all employees in the accounting department in this group, which has been given permission to use the Financial folder on a file server. You are now asked to create a subfolder under Financial named Payroll. Megan, the payroll officer, is the only employee in the accounting department allowed to access this folder. What is the best way to configure the new share?

    a. Assign Megan read/write permissions to the Payroll folder, and explain to your manager that it is not a best practice to give only one employee access to an important folder.
    b. Assign Megan read/write permissions to the Payroll folder.
    c. Create a new user group named Payroll, put Megan in the group, and assign the group read/write permissions to the Payroll folder.
    d. Ask your manager to allow you to put the folder outside of the Financial folder so you can assign a new user group read/write permissions to this folder that will not conflict with the Accounting user group.

13. Which of the following is true about NTFS permissions and share permissions? (Choose all that apply.)

    a. Share permissions do not work on an NTFS volume.
    b. NTFS permissions work only on an NTFS volume.
    c. If share permissions and NTFS permissions are in conflict, NTFS permissions win.
    d. If you set NTFS permissions but do not set share permissions, NTFS permissions apply on the network.

14. Which security features are available on Windows 10 Home? (Choose all that apply.)

    a. Local Group Policy
    b. NTFS permissions
    c. Active Directory
    d. Share permissions

15. When NTFS and share permissions are used on the local file server, can a user signed in on a Windows 10 Home computer access these shares? Why or why not?

    a. No, because Windows 10 Home does not have the Local Users and Groups console
    b. No, because Windows 10 Home does not support NTFS permissions
    c. Yes, because Windows 10 Home can join a Windows domain
    d. Yes, because the user is authenticated on the file server to access its shares

16. Which Windows tool is used to reset the password for a user's Windows account?

    a. Network Places Wizard (netplwiz.exe)
    b. Local Group Policy Editor (gpedit.msc)
    c. Accounts page in the Settings app
    d. Disk Management

17. As the new network administrator managing Active Directory in your organization, you decide to set up a backup system for all folders in the domain authorized for users to store their data. Which tasks should you do first before you configure the backup routine? (Choose all that apply.)

    a. Have a company-wide gathering to explain the idea to all users.
    b. Evaluate backup software and storage requirements.
    c. Apply all available updates to Windows Server.
    d. Apply folder redirection to the Home folder for each user.

Hands-On Projects

Hands-On Project 17-1

Exploring Password Management Software

Est. Time: 30 minutes
Core 2 Objective: 2.5

Password management software, also called password vault software—such as KeePass (*keepass.info*), LastPass (*lastpass.com*), and Dashlane (*dashlane.com*)—can hold your passwords safely so you don't forget them or have to write them down. Choose one of these programs and a second of your own selection that interests you, then answer the following questions about each one:

1. Which platforms are supported?
2. Which web browsers are supported?
3. From how many competitors can the program import passwords?
4. What types of authentication are supported (e.g., master password, fingerprint, etc.)?
5. Where are the passwords stored? Are they synced across devices? How is the information protected?
6. What are some of the differences between the free edition of each program and the paid versions?
7. What happens to the user's account if the user dies or is incapacitated?

Hands-On Project 17-2

Using Group Policy to Secure a Workstation

Est. Time: 30 minutes
Core 2 Objective: 2.5

Using Windows 10/11 Professional or Enterprise, set local security policies to require a password for each account, to audit failed logon events, and to create a logon script that displays the message, "The Golden Pineapple Was Here!" when anyone signs in to the system. Test your policies by verifying that a password is required, your script executes when you sign in, and a failed sign-in event using an invalid password is logged and can be viewed in Event Viewer. Answer the following questions:

1. Which policies did you set, and what setting was applied to each policy?
2. What software did you use to create your script? What is the exact path and file name (including the file extension) to your script?
3. Which log in Event Viewer shows the logon failure event?
4. List three more policies you find in Group Policy that can make a workstation more secure but are not discussed in this module.

17

Hands-On Project 17-3

Researching a Laptop with a TPM Chip

Est. Time: 15 minutes
Core 2 Objective: 2.5

Many laptops sold today have a TPM chip, and some have encryption-enabled hard drives that don't require encryption software such as BitLocker. Research the web for a laptop that offers a TPM chip and answer these questions:

1. What is the brand and model of laptop that has the TPM chip? Save or print the webpage that lists the laptop specifications for the chip.

2. Is the chip optional? If so, what is the cost of including the chip?

3. Does the laptop have an encryption-enabled hard drive?

4. Does the laptop come bundled with encryption software? If so, what is the name of the software?

5. Does the laptop offer a drive lock password?

6. What is the cost of the laptop, including the TPM chip?

Hands-On Project 17-4

Sharing and Securing a Folder

Est. Time: 30 minutes
Core 2 Objective: 2.5

Using two computers networked together, do the following to practice sharing and securing folders using Windows:

1. Create a user account named **User1** on Computer 1. In the Documents folder for that account, create a folder named **Folder1**. Create a text file named **File1** in the folder. Edit the file and add the text **Golden Egg**.

2. On Computer 2, create a user account named **User2**. Try to read the Golden Egg text in File1 on Computer 1. What is the result?

3. Configure the computers so that User1 signed in to Computer 2 can open File1 and edit the text "Golden Egg," but User2 cannot view or access the contents of Folder1. List the steps you took to share and secure the folder and to test this scenario to make sure it works.

4. Now make the folder private so that it cannot be seen from Computer 2 in Explorer but can be accessed if User1 knows the folder name. Describe how you did that.

Real Problems, Real Solutions

Real Problem 17-1

Demonstrating Inherited and Explicit Permissions

Est. Time: 30 minutes
Core 2 Objective: 2.5

In this activity, you set up situations to demonstrate how inherited and explicit permissions work. Do the following:

1. Sign in to Windows with an administrative account. Create two folders C:\Folder1 and C:\Folder2 on your hard drive.

2. Create the following text files. Be sure to put some text in each file:
   - C:\Folder1\File1.txt
   - C:\Folder2\File2inherited.txt
   - C:\Folder2\File3explicit.txt

3. Create a user account named User1.

4. Set the following permission:
   - User1 has full permission for access to Folder1.
   - User1 cannot access Folder2.
   - Change the permissions for C:\Folder2\File3explicit.txt from inherited permissions to explicit permissions.

5. Sign in to Windows with the User1 account, and verify that User1 can view and modify File1.txt in Folder1 but cannot access the contents of Folder2.

6. Sign in to Windows with your own administrative account.

7. With inherited permissions set, you would expect that File2inherited.txt will inherit the permissions of Folder1 when the file is copied or moved to Folder1. With explicit permissions set for File3explicit.txt, you would expect that File3explicit.txt retains its permissions when it is moved from Folder2 to Folder1. To verify this theory, move (don't copy) both files to Folder1. Open the **Security** tab for each file, and verify one file inherited the permissions of Folder1 and the other file retained its original permissions.

8. Sign in to Windows with the User1 account.

9. Verify that User1 can access the contents of C:\Folder1\File2inherited.txt but cannot access the contents of C:\Folder1\File3explicit.txt.

10. Sign in to Windows with your own administrative account. You have demonstrated that a file with explicit permissions retains its permissions when moved to a new parent folder. What happens when you copy the file? To find out, move File3explicit.txt back to Folder2, and then copy (don't move) it to Folder1. Check the file's Security tab, and note that File3explicit.txt inherited the permissions of Folder1 when copied to the folder. This occurred because, when you copy a file, a new file is actually created in the new location and therefore inherits the permissions of the new parent folder.

11. It's interesting to note that when you move or copy a file from one NTFS volume to another NTFS volume, the file always inherits the permissions of the parent object. This is because, when a file is moved or copied to a new volume, a new file is always created on the new volume, and, therefore, inherits permissions of its parent object. If you have access to two NTFS volumes on the same computer, you can set up this scenario and verify these actions.

17

Real Problem 17-2

Setting Up a Windows Domain in Google Cloud

Est. Time: 45 minutes
Core 2 Objective: 2.1

In the Core 1 module "Network Infrastructure and Cloud Computing" you used Google Cloud Platform to create a VM with Windows Server installed. To use that VM or a new VM to create a Windows domain, do the following:

1. Go to **cloud.google.com**. If you have not already set up a free trial, click **Get started for free**. You will need to sign in using a Google account. If you don't have an account, you can create one with any valid email address. When you first set up an account, you must enter payment information, which Google promises not to use during your free trial period. Create an individual account type, enter your information, and click **START MY FREE TRIAL**. Google automatically sets up your first project, aptly named My First Project.

2. In the left pane of the Google Cloud Platform page, click **Compute Engine**. (If you don't see the left pane, click the three-bar icon in the top-left corner.) If you don't already have a VM created with Windows Server, do the following:

   a. Click **CREATE INSTANCE** in the VM instances menu to create a VM.
   b. Use the default settings, except:
      - Change the name of the VM to **dcserver**.
      - Change the Boot disk to **Windows Server 2019 Datacenter**.
   c. Click **Select**, click **Create**, and then wait for Google to create the instance.

3. In the VM instances list, click the **dcserver** instance, which takes you to the VM instance details page. Click **Set Windows password** and assign a user name to your VM instance. Note the user name and click **SET**. Google Cloud assigns a password, which displays on the screen. Copy the password, save it somewhere safe, then click **CLOSE**.

4. A domain controller needs a static IP address on the domain. To set the Primary internal IP address to a static address, follow these steps:

   a. On the VM instance details page, in the *Network interfaces* group under *Network*, click **default**. The VPC network details page appears.
   b. Click **STATIC INTERNAL IP ADDRESSES**. Then click **RESERVE STATIC ADDRESS**.
   c. Under Name, enter **dcserver**. Click **RESERVE**.

5. To return to the list of VM instances, click the three-bar icon in the top-left corner, and then click **Compute Engine**. Click **VM instances**. Your list of VMs appears.

6. For the dcserver VM instance, write down the Internal IP and External IP addresses.

Note 26

Remote Desktop is a Windows utility that allows you to remotely control another computer. In this project, you use Remote Desktop from your workstation to remotely control your Windows Server in Google Cloud. You learn more about Remote Desktop in the module "Network Security and Troubleshooting."

7. You are now ready to use Remote Desktop with screen and file sharing to access your VM. Follow these steps:

   a. Enter **mstsc** in the Windows 10/11 search box. In the Remote Desktop Connection dialog box, enter the External IP address of your VM, which is its public IP address available on the Internet. Click **Connect**.
   b. In the *Enter your credentials* box, enter your Windows user name and password to dcserver. Click **OK** to connect.

8. The Windows Server desktop appears in the Remote Desktop window with the Server Manager window open. In the Networks pane on the right, click **Yes** to turn on network discovery.

9. You are now ready to set up your Windows domain. Follow these steps:

   a. In the Server Manager window, under *Configure this local server*, click **Add roles and features**. The Add Roles and Features Wizard opens. Click **Next**.

   b. On the *Select installation type* page, accept the default values, and click **Next**.

   c. On the *Select destination server* page, accept the default values, and click **Next**.

   d. Under *Select server roles*, check **Active Directory Domain Services**, and click **Add Features**.

   e. Under *Select server roles*, check **DNS Server** and click **Add Features**. A warning message appears. Click **Continue**. (The message was caused by Google Cloud handling tasks that the domain controller would normally handle.)

   f. Click **Next** four times to step through pages in the wizard, accepting default values. When the *Confirm installation selections* page appears, check **Restart the destination server automatically if required**, and click **Yes** to confirm. Then click **Install**. Wait while the installation happens. You can click the flag in the upper-right corner of the Server Manager window to view the progress. See Figure 17-58. When the process finishes, click **Close** to close the Add Roles and Features Wizard.

Figure 17-58   The notification flag reports installation progress

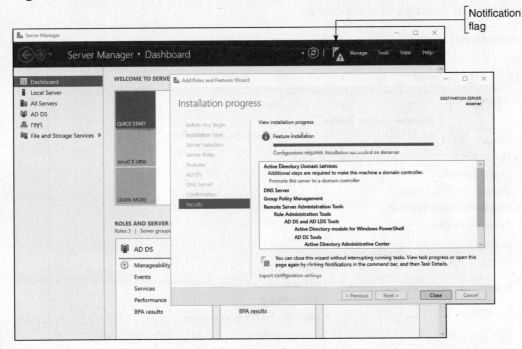

10. Although AD Domain Services is now installed, you cannot promote the server to a domain controller until you first set a password for the all-powerful Administrator account. (Recall that this account is different from your user name account, which has Administrative privileges.) To set the password, do the following:

    a. To open an elevated command prompt window, enter **cmd** in the Windows search box, right-click **Command Prompt**, and click **Run as administrator**. Respond to the UAC dialog box.

    b. Use a password that satisfies AD complexity requirements. For example, in the command prompt window, enter this command:

    ```
    net user Administrator Passw0rd /passwordreq:yes
    ```

    c. Close the command prompt window.

11. Click the notification flag in the Server Manager window, and then click **Promote this server to a domain controller**. The *Deployment Configuration* window appears. Select **Add a new forest**. Enter your root domain name. You can use **homerun.com** or another domain name. Click **Next**.

12. In the Domain Controller Options window, enter the DSRM password twice, and click **Next**. Ignore any warning messages and click **Next** several times to step through the wizard. Finally, click **Install**.

(continues)

17

Real Problem Continued

13. After the system reboots, you will need to connect again through Remote Desktop. At this point, you have a working domain controller and can practice the skills you learned in this module to manage Active Directory. Here is how to get started:

    a. Each time you use Remote Desktop to connect to the server, check the VM instances page to verify the external IP address that you use with Remote Desktop has not changed. Use the current external IP address.

    b. On the Windows Server desktop, if Server Manager is not already open, click **Start** and click **Server Manager**.

    c. In the Server Manager window, to manage OUs, user groups, and users, click **Tools** and then click **Active Directory Users and Computers**. (Refer back to Figure 17-42.)

    d. By default, your domain has one OU: Domain Controllers. To create another OU directly under the domain, right-click the domain name, point to **New**, and click **Organizational Unit** (see Figure 17-59). You can then name the OU.

Figure 17-59   Create an OU directly under the domain

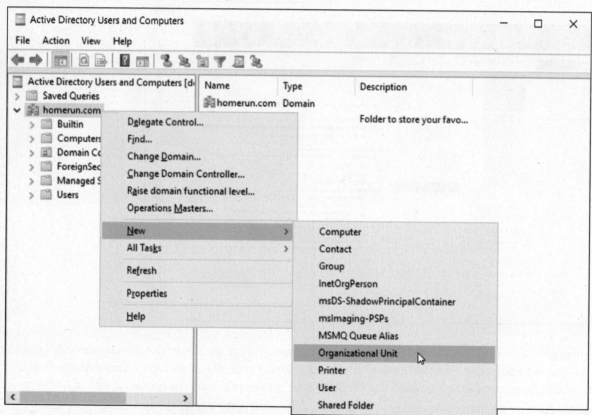

14. Have fun poking around and learning to use Active Directory! Every great IT technician needs to have a working knowledge of AD, and you have started to develop that in this module. When you're finished working with AD, avoid accumulating any charges against your free quota by shutting down the server VM in the Remote Desktop Connection dialog box.

Note 27

You will use the Google Cloud Platform service for another project in the module "Linux and Scripting." Do not disable your Google Cloud Platform account until after you have completed that project.

Module

18

Mobile Device Security

Module Objectives

1 Back up mobile devices using a variety of techniques and restore a device from backup

2 Secure mobile devices using operating system tools, anti-malware, firewalls, locator apps, remote wipes, device access controls, and best practices for managing a device

3 Troubleshoot mobile devices using a variety of troubleshooting techniques to address common problems with the OS and apps

Core 2 Certification Objectives

1.8 Explain common OS types and their purposes.

2.1 Summarize various security measures and their purposes.

2.7 Explain common methods for securing mobile and embedded devices.

3.4 Given a scenario, troubleshoot common mobile OS and application issues.

3.5 Given a scenario, troubleshoot common mobile OS and application security issues.

Introduction

Many employees expect to be able to use their mobile devices to access, synchronize, and edit data on the corporate network. To protect this data, corporations require that employee mobile devices be secured and that data, settings, and apps be synchronized to other storage locations. In this module, you learn how to secure mobile devices. You also learn about tools and resources available for troubleshooting mobile operating systems and apps.

Exam Tip

There is quite a bit of overlap between the CompTIA A+ Core 1 (220-1101) exam objectives and the A+ Core 2 (220-1102) exam objectives regarding mobile devices. For this reason, this Core 2 module relies heavily on the content already presented in the Core 1 module "Supporting Mobile Devices." If you have not already studied that module, it would be helpful to read it before you turn your attention to this module.

Backing Up Mobile Devices

Core 2 Objectives 1.8, 2.7

Methods of backing up mobile devices rely heavily on the OS they use. Currently, the most popular mobile OSs are Android by Google (*google.com*) and iOS and iPadOS by Apple (*apple.com*). Here is a summary of the tools and techniques covered in more detail in the Core 1 module "Supporting Mobile Devices":

- **Navigating Android and iOS.** The OS provides a home screen; navigation interface; and ways to download, install, uninstall, open, and close apps.
- **Settings.** The Settings app is used to manage most OS and app settings, although some app settings can be managed within the app.
- **Quick access settings.** Each OS has a quick-access settings screen that is easily accessed from the home screen. Android uses the notification area, and iOS uses the Control Center.
- **OS updates.** Updates to the OS are managed in the Settings app and are normally set to automatically download and update.
- **Wireless connections.** Wireless connections on a mobile device can include cellular voice and data, Wi-Fi, GPS, Bluetooth, NFC (near-field communication), and AirDrop (Apple only). These connections are managed in the Settings app.
- **Purpose of MDM.** Large corporations use **mobile device management (MDM)** software on both the server and mobile device to enforce MDM policies designed to secure corporate data and apps (for example, email) for both corporate-owned and personal devices. For personal devices, these policies are known as **BYOD (bring your own device)** policies.
- **Data syncing.** Google and Apple both provide methods for syncing data via the cloud among mobile devices that use the same Google or Apple account. This data includes email, contacts, calendars, photos, document files, and other content. Sync settings are managed in the Settings app or in individual apps that manage content (for example, the Photos or email app). Synced data is available in the cloud at *google.com* for Goggle and *iCloud.com* for Apple.
- **Troubleshooting.** When troubleshooting a mobile device, useful techniques include updating the OS and restarting and rebooting the device. A technician might be called on to solve problems related to malware infections, display and touch screen issues, connectivity issues, damaged ports and liquid damage, and battery, overheating, and charging issues.

Core to Core

In this module, we dig deeper into several of the skills listed earlier. If you are not familiar with each of these skills—including how to navigate, update, and manage each OS and troubleshoot a mobile device—now would be the time to review this content in the Core 1 module "Supporting Mobile Devices."

In this section of the module, you learn about updating and backing up mobile devices.

Update the OS

Core 2 Objective 2.7

Updates to the Android OS are automatically pushed to the device from the manufacturer. Because each manufacturer maintains its own versions of Android, these updates might not come at the same time Google announces a major update, which limits availability of updates for some devices. Also, vendors don't continue to make these modifications indefinitely—eventually, a device ages out of the vendor's updates in what's called an **end-of-life (EOL)** limitation. When the device does receive notice of an update, it might display a message asking permission to install the update. With some devices, you can also manually check for updates at any time, but not all devices provide this option.

To see if manual updates can be performed on an Android device, go to the **Settings** app and tap **System**, **Advanced**, and **System update** (see Figure 18-1). Tap **Check for update**. The device turns to the manufacturer's website for information and reports any available updates.

To check for and install updates on an iOS device, you must first be signed in to your device with an Apple ID, which requires an associated credit card number. Then open the **Settings** app, and tap **General** and **Software Update**. Any available updates will be reported here and can be installed (see Figure 18-2A). Tap the right arrow next to "Automatic Updates" to view and change update settings (see Figure 18-2B).

Figure 18-1 Use the Android Settings app to see the latest OS update and manually check for new updates

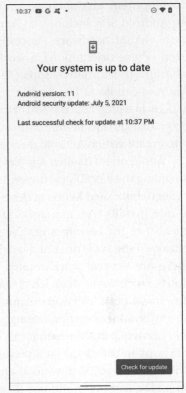

Figure 18-2 iOS has an available update to install

(A)

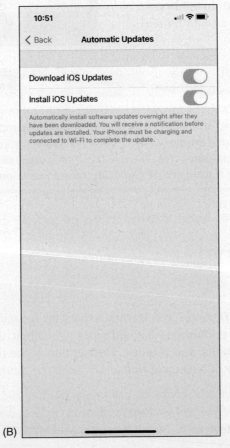

(B)

18

Mobile Apps Development

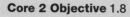

Both Android and iOS offer tools for mobile app development that you can use to learn more about supporting and securing mobile devices. To write and test Android apps, an app developer uses a group of tools in an **SDK (software development kit)**, such as Android Studio (*developer.android.com*) or Visual Studio (*visualstudio.microsoft.com*). An Android SDK includes an Android **emulator**, which is software that creates a virtual Android device complete with virtual hardware (buttons, camera, and even device orientation), a working installation of Android, and native apps (see Figure 18-3A). Android Studio is free and is released as open source. In a project at the end of this module, you'll download and install Android Studio, and then use it to create virtual Android devices or emulators.

Figure 18-3   (A) Android emulator with the app drawer open; (B) iPhone 11 Pro emulator with home screen

(A)   (B)

Apple offers its own app-development tools, including the iOS SDK (software development kit), collectively called Xcode at *developer.apple.com*. Xcode installs free in macOS along with Apple emulators for testing apps (see Figure 18-3B). Although the tools are not available in Windows, there are several workarounds, such as React Native (*reactnative.dev*), which can install in Windows and build iOS apps using JavaScript, and MacInCloud (*macincloud.com*), which provides macOS virtual machines that can be used to build iOS apps in the cloud. In a project at the end of this module, you'll download and install Xcode on a Mac computer and use it to run an iPhone emulator.

> **Note 1**
>
> You can follow along with the steps in the following sections using a real smartphone or tablet (Android or iOS), or you can use an Android, iPhone, or iPad emulator. Projects at the end of this module give you step-by-step instructions to install and configure the free Android Studio (which includes several Android emulators) on a Windows computer and the Xcode simulators on a Mac computer. You can use these emulators with real features that work like those on a physical device, including a power button, rotate capability, camera function, and much more.

The first step to secure a mobile device is to maintain good backups. How to back up a device is discussed next.

Backup and Recovery

Core 2 Objective 2.7

In the module "Supporting Mobile Devices," you learned to back up app data, which is an important skill. If, however, your mobile device is lost, stolen, or damaged beyond repair, you might need to recover not only app data but also mobile device settings, configurations, and profiles. This section of the module covers how to back up the entire device. Let's start with a summary of backup options:

- **File-level backup.** Syncing emails, contacts, calendars, photos, and other data through online accounts or to your computer is called a **file-level backup** because each file is backed up individually. File-level backups, however, don't include your OS settings, such as your Wi-Fi passwords, account profile, or device and app configuration.

- **Partial image-level backup.** A true image-level backup includes everything on the device and can completely restore the device to its previous state. A mobile device OS, however, offers only a partial image-level backup that includes settings, native app data, Wi-Fi passwords, the account profile, and device and app configuration. Third-party app configurations and their data are not included in the OS backup.
- **Combination of file-level and partial image-level backups.** To prepare for catastrophic failure or loss, you need to use both backup methods: Sync app data to your computer or the cloud, and use the OS backup for other types of data and settings. Make sure that syncing and backups include critical apps, their configuration, and data. In reality, though, backups for mobile devices will miss some configurations, such as app installations or third-party app configurations. For this reason, you might also need third-party software, such as Dr.Fone (*drfone.wondershare.net*), to make a full device backup that includes third-party apps and app data.

Generally, you can back up to the cloud or to your computer. Let's look next at how Android backs up to Google Drive.

Google Drive Backup

To enable Android's backup feature, open the **Settings** app, and tap **System** and then **Backup**. Make sure that **Back up to Google Drive** is turned on, and change the backup account if needed. You can also fine-tune what content is included in the backup and back up now. Your backup data is stored on Google servers and is associated with your Google account. When you first turn on a new Android device, you are given the chance to enter your Google account information and restore an existing Google backup to the new device.

> **Caution** ❗
>
> You cannot restore a backup to a new device if the new device uses a version of Android that is lower than the Android version of the old device.

Back Up Android Data to a Computer

You can use a USB cable to transfer files between an Android device and a computer. Connect the cable and then open the **Settings** app. Tap **Connected devices** and then **USB**, and select **File Transfer**. Content can then be accessed in Explorer on a Windows computer (see Figure 18-4) or in Finder on a Mac.

Figure 18-4   Transfer files between a Windows computer and an Android device

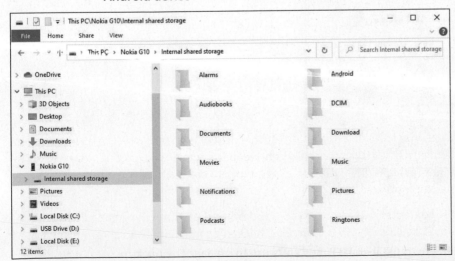

To create a detailed backup of an Android device—including the device configuration as well as the content—to a computer, you need a third-party app or a manufacturer's app. First check with the device manufacturer for its backup app. To use the app, you'll need to first set up a user account with the manufacturer. Also know that an Android device manufacturer is likely to provide cloud storage to keep remote backups of your device.

iCloud Backup

An iPhone or iPad can back up to a computer or to the cloud using iCloud. The best practice is to use both methods. To set up iCloud backups, go to **Settings**, tap the user name, and then tap **iCloud**. Scroll down and tap **iCloud Backup**. See Figure 18-5. When you turn on iCloud Backup, it backs up daily whenever the device is plugged into a power source and connected to Wi-Fi, the screen is locked, and there's enough unused iCloud storage to hold the backup. However, you can also create a new backup at any time by clicking **Back Up Now**, as shown in Figure 18-5. iCloud backs up app data, call history, device settings, text, photos, and videos unless these items are already included in iCloud syncing.

Back Up iOS to a Computer

An iPhone or iPad can back up to a Mac computer without any extra software. On a Mac, connect the iPhone or iPad to the Mac using a cable (for example, a Lightning to USB cable). Unlock the device, and open the **Finder** window. (The Finder window is similar to Explorer in Windows.) Select the device in the left pane (see Figure 18-6). In the right pane, select **General** and **Back up all of the data on your iPhone to this Mac**, as shown in the figure. Notice you also have the option to encrypt the backup. Click **Back Up Now**.

Figure 18-5   iCloud Backup is on, and you can back up now

Figure 18-6   Back up an iPhone to a Mac computer

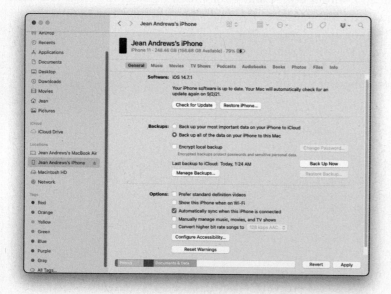

To back up to a Windows computer, you must install iTunes software to manage the backup.

Applying Concepts

Back Up an iPhone or iPad to a Windows Computer

Est. Time: 30 minutes
Core 2 Objective: 2.7

On a Windows computer, do the following to back up an iPhone or iPad:

1. Go to the Microsoft Store, and search for **iTunes**. Download and install **iTunes** by Apple Inc. iTunes is used to manage digital entertainment media, and its secondary purpose is to back up Apple devices on a Windows computer.

2. Open **iTunes**, connect your iPhone or iPad to the computer with a USB cable, and unlock the device.

3. You'll need to enter your passcode to the device or respond to a message on the device asking whether you trust the computer. Enter your response.

4. A message in iTunes asks if you want to allow the computer to access the device. Click **Continue**.

5. In the iTunes window, click the device icon near the top of the screen (see Figure 18-7).

Figure 18-7   Click the device icon in the menu bar to view options for the connected device

6. Under *Automatically Back Up*, select **This Computer**. See Figure 18-8. Notice you can also select the option to encrypt the backup. Click **Back Up Now** to start the backup.

(continues)

18

Applying Concepts Continued

Figure 18-8   Use iTunes to back up an iPad to this Windows computer

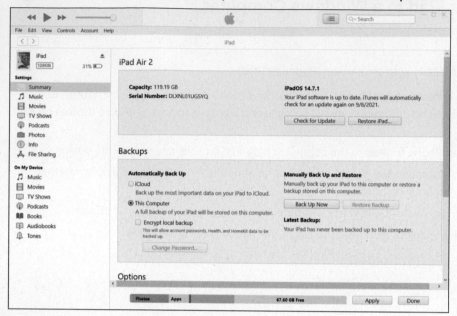

Later, if you need to recover from the backup, connect your device to the computer, and in the Finder window on a Mac or iTunes window on a Windows computer, select your device. Then click **Restore Backup** (refer back to Figure 18-6). You can then select a backup based on the date of each backup.

Whatever backup method you use, it's important to occasionally test the backup recovery process to verify that you know how to use it, the recovery works, and you know exactly what's being recovered. After you test the recovery process, you might realize you need additional backup methods in place to make sure everything is covered.

Note 2

If you're about to buy a new phone or tablet, be sure to back up your old device before you switch your carrier service or your Google or Apple account to the new device. If possible, also back up your phone or tablet before taking it in for repair at a service center.

Recover from the Backup

Here are two situations when you might want to use a backup to recover a device:

- **To the original mobile device.** If you have reset the device while troubleshooting a problem and have a backup in the cloud, sign in to the device using your Google or Apple account. You will then be given the option to recover from backup or set up the device as a new device. You'll learn more about resetting a device later in this module. For iOS, if you have a backup on your computer and connect the device to your computer, macOS or iTunes in Windows gives you the option to restore from backup.

- **To a new device.** The same recovery options are offered when you first sign in to a new mobile device using your Google or Apple account—or, for iOS, when you connect a new device to your Mac computer or Windows computer with the iTunes app. When you're setting up a new device, the setup process asks if you want to restore content from a previous backup and also asks which backup to use.

Securing Mobile Devices

Core 2 Objectives 2.1, 2.7, 3.5

Because smartphones and tablets are so mobile, they get stolen more often than other types of computers. Therefore, protecting data on a mobile device is especially important. Consider what might be revealed about your life if someone stole your smartphone or tablet and the data on it.

- Your apps and personal data could expose email, calendars, call history, voice mail, text messages, Google Pay, Apple Pay, PayPal, banking apps, Dropbox, iCloud Drive, Google Maps, Gmail, QuickMemo, YouTube, Amazon, Facebook, videos, photos, notes, contacts, and bookmarks and browsing history in web browsers.
- Videos and photos might reveal private information and might be tagged with date and time stamps and GPS locations.
- Network connection settings include Wi-Fi security keys, email configuration settings, user names, and email addresses.
- Purchasing patterns and history as well as credit card information might be stored—or at least accessible for use—in mobile payment apps, in apps developed by retailers, through membership card databases, or through email records.

To keep your data safe, consider what apps you can use to protect your data, how to control access to your device, and which BYOD (bring your own device) policies might be used in an enterprise environment to secure corporate data stored on a device.

Most of the methods discussed here require the user to understand the importance of a security measure and how to use it:

- **OS updates and patches.** Apply OS updates and patches to plug up security holes. Recall that Android automatically pushes updates to many of its devices, but iOS devices require manual updates.
- **Antivirus/anti-malware.** Because Apple closely protects iOS and its apps, it's unlikely an Apple device will need anti-malware software. The Android OS and apps are not as closely guarded, so Android anti-malware apps are recommended. Before installing one, be sure to read reviews about it. Most of the major anti-malware software companies provide Android anti-malware apps.
- **Firewalls.** As with Windows computers, a firewall on a mobile device helps control which apps or services can use network connections. When you install an app, you're required to agree to the permissions it requests in order to get the app. A firewall gives you more control over an app's network access. For example, a firewall can prevent the Facebook app from sending SMS messages.

  Most firewall apps for Android devices mimic a VPN connection, which forces all network communication to be routed through the firewall. Figure 18-9 shows an example of one firewall app, NetGuard (*netguard.me*), on an Android smartphone; the app allows you to decide which other apps can use the networks.

Figure 18-9 Use NetGuard VPN connection in Android to control which apps can access the Internet

18

- **Android locator application and remote wipe.** You can use Find My Device (*google.com/android/find*), Android's built-in **locator application**, to locate your phone on a map, force it to ring at its highest volume, lock the device, display a message on the screen, or remotely erase all data from the device to protect your privacy, which is called a **remote wipe**. See Figure 18-10. To use the locator app to locate your device or perform a remote wipe, Find My Device must already be turned on using the **Security** screen in the Settings app. Third-party locator applications are also available in the Play Store.

Figure 18-10   Locate a lost Android device using any web-enabled computer or mobile device and your Google account

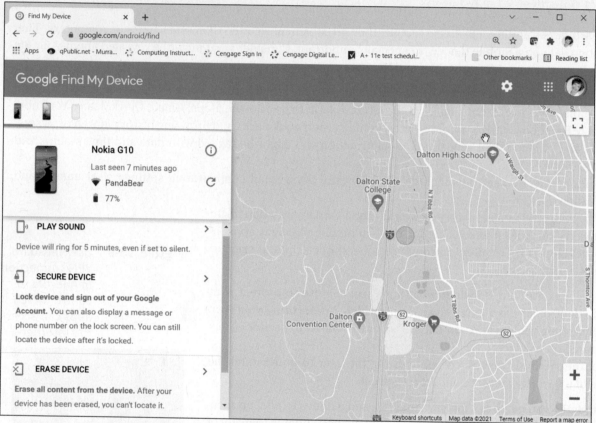

- **iOS locator application and remote wipe.** Similar to Android's Find My Device, iCloud offers the ability to locate a lost iOS device if the feature is already enabled on the device before it's lost. On an iPad or iPhone, open the **Settings** app, tap the *user name*, and turn on **Find My iPad** or **Find My iPhone**. To find the device, using any browser, go to **icloud.com/find** and sign in with your Apple ID. Besides using a browser on a computer to find your device, you can also download Find My iPhone or Find My iPad to another Apple device and use it to locate your lost device. Both apps are free. If your device was stolen or you have given up on finding your device, you can use iCloud to perform a remote wipe.

Device Access Controls

Core 2 Objective 2.7

To control access to the device, consider the following lock methods:

- **Lock the screen.** A screen lock requires the correct input to unlock the device. Mobile devices provide a variety of options for unlocking the screen. As the complexity of a lock code increases, so does the security of the device:
  - **Swipe lock.** Swipe your finger across the screen to unlock the device. (This is not very secure, but it prevents a pocket dial.)

- **PIN code lock.** Enter a numeric code with numbers.
- **Password lock.** Enter an alphanumeric code with letters and/or numbers.
- **Pattern lock.** Draw a pattern across a display of dots on the screen.
- **Fingerprint lock.** Use a specialized scanner that collects an optical, electrical, or ultrasonic reading of a person's fingerprint and then compares this information to stored data. The fingerprint reader might be on the front or side of the device (see Figure 18-11).
- **Facial recognition lock.** Use the device's camera to perform facial recognition. A facial lock requires a backup method, such as those shown in Figure 18-12A, because facial recognition is not that secure—your device can be unlocked when you look at it even if you didn't intend to unlock it; someone who looks like you can unlock the device; or someone can hold up the device in front of you to unlock it if your eyes are open.

Figure 18-11   Access the device via a fingerprint scan

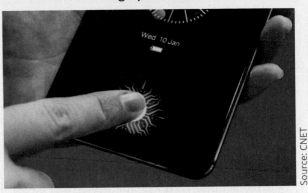

Source: CNET

Figure 18-12   (A) Screen lock options on an Android smartphone; (B) Smart Lock exceptions to keep the screen unlocked

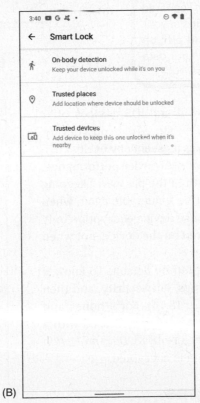

(A)

(B)

Figure 18-12A shows screen lock options on an Android smartphone, including a pattern, fingerprint, and face lock. Android also allows the user to set exceptions to the screen lock, as shown in Figure 18-12B. Using these options, the smartphone might stay unlocked when it detects it's being carried, when it detects its location, such as the user's home or office, or when another trusted device is nearby. Android calls this feature Smart Lock.

18

Note 3

Fingerprint and facial recognition are both forms of bio-metric authentication. Biometric authentication collects biological data about a person's fingerprints, handprints, face, voice, retina, iris, and handwritten signatures to confirm the person's identity. In some states, you cannot legally be forced to give your phone's password to investigators, but you can be required to give your fingerprint.

- **Restrict failed login attempts.** With Android devices, login attempt restriction options vary by manufacturer. With iOS, the device can be set to erase all data after 10 failed passcode attempts. See Figure 18-13. With each attempt, you must wait for a longer time before you can try again. If the device permanently locks and you've created a backup on a Mac or in iTunes in Windows, you can sync to the backup to access the phone. Otherwise, you'll have to use recovery mode, which erases the device.

Caution !

If you set your device to erase data after repeated failed login attempts, be sure to keep backups of your data and other content. A small child could pick up your smartphone and accidentally erase all your data with just a few finger taps.

- **Full device encryption.** Both Android and iOS devices offer **device encryption**, which encrypts all the stored data on a device. Encrypting a device's stored data makes it essentially useless to a thief. However, encryption might slow down device performance, and data is only as safe as the strength of the password keeping the data encrypted. Also, data might be vulnerable again when it's being viewed or transmitted because device encryption only encrypts data while it's at rest or stored on the device, not when it's in motion or being transmitted.

    Most Android devices are encrypted by default. To know if the device is encrypted, look in **Settings**, tap **Security**, and then **Encryption & credentials** (see Figure 18-14). For iPhones and iPads, data is encrypted whenever the device is secured with a passcode. Notice, near the bottom of Figure 18-13, *Data protection is enabled*, which indicates that all data is encrypted.

Use Trusted Sources for Apps

Core 2 Objective 2.7

iOS devices are limited to installing apps only from Apple's App Store. Android devices can download and install apps from other sources, only some of which are trustworthy. **Trusted sources** generally include Google Play Store (*play.google.com*) and other well-known app stores, such as Amazon

Figure 18-13 Set iOS to erase all data after 10 failed attempts at sign-on

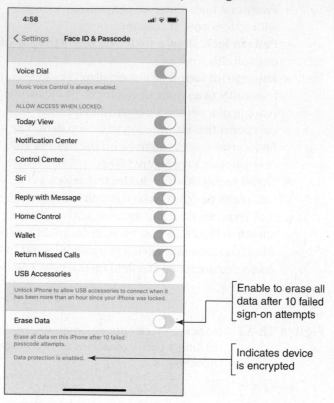

Enable to erase all data after 10 failed sign-on attempts

Indicates device is encrypted

Figure 18-14 This Android device is encrypted

Appstore for Android (*amazon.com/appstore*), SlideME (*slideme.org*), your bank's website, your employer, or your school. Before downloading an app, look for lots of reviewer feedback as one measure of safety.

To reduce the threat of apps from untrusted sources, Android requires you to first proactively allow apps from untrusted sources before you can download and install them. To do that, go to **Settings**, **Apps & notifications**, **Advanced**, **Special app access**, and **Install unknown apps** (see Figure 18-15). Select an app, and choose **Allow from this source**. If you decide to use third-party app sources, be sure you already have a good anti-malware program and a firewall running on your device.

One reason you might want to install an app from an unknown source is when you're developing and testing an app not yet ready for distribution. An Android app developed using Android Studio is compiled into a collection of software files called an **Android package (APK)**, sometimes called an Android package kit, and the APK file has an .apk file extension. When you download an app from Google Play, you download an .apk file, and then Android installs the app on your device. In addition, you can download and install .apk files from any source when your device is set to allow this, a process called side-loading the app.

Security Threats in Developer Mode

You can use Developer mode on your Android device to test and debug apps you are building. Android hides Developer mode by default. To enable it, go to **Settings**, **About phone**, and tap **Build number** seven times. To see the Developer screen, in **Settings**, go to **System**, **Advanced**, and **Developer options**. Notice on the Developer options screen (see Figure 18-16) you can turn Developer options on or off and set many functions in Android designed to test and debug apps.

Users sometimes turn on Developer mode so they can use an option, such as Force 4x MSAA to improve image quality in a game or enable USB Debugging so a backup app or other type of app on their computer can interface with the Android device over a USB connection. This last option might pose a security threat if an app on the computer is malicious.

Security Threats from Root Access, Jailbreaking, and Bootlegged Apps

To get more control over what can be done with an Android or iOS device, including downloading and installing **bootlegged apps** (illegal apps), some users have discovered they can get root or administrative privileges to the OS and the entire file system (all files and folders), and complete access to all commands and features. For Android, the process is called **rooting**, and for iOS, the process is called **jailbreaking**. After jailbreaking, an iOS phone can get apps from any source, but Apple has the right to void the warranty or refuse to provide support. Rooting and jailbreaking might also violate BYOD policies in an enterprise environment. In addition, rooting or jailbreaking makes a device more susceptible to malicious apps and hackers using a technique called **application spoofing** to present to a user an app pretending to be a legitimate app the user wants when, in fact, it is malicious.

Figure 18-15   Choose which apps can install apps from unknown sources

Figure 18-16   Developer options used to test and debug Android apps

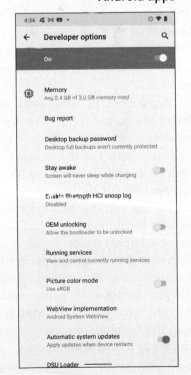

18

Applying Concepts

Rooting and Jailbreaking

Est. Time: 15 minutes
Core 2 Objective: 3.5

Here is how you can tell if a device is rooted or jailbroken:

- **Rooted Android device.** Use one of these methods to find out if an Android device has been rooted:
  - Download and run a root checker app from Google Play; this will tell you if the device is rooted.
  - Download and run a terminal window app from Google Play. (A terminal window in Linux is similar to a command prompt window in Windows.) When you open the app, look at the command prompt. If the prompt is a #, the device is rooted. If the prompt is a $, the device is likely not rooted. With the $ prompt showing, enter the `sudo su root` command, which in Linux allows you root access. If the prompt changes to #, the device is rooted.
- **Jailbroken iOS device.** To find out if an iOS device has been jailbroken, look for an unusual app on the home screen—for example, the Electra, Meridian, Cydia, or Sileo app. If any of these apps is present, the device has been jailbroken. If you have any app icon on your home screen that is not available in the App Store, the app is most likely a jailbreak app or other malware. When you update iOS or perform a factory reset, the jailbreak will be removed. How to do that is covered later in the module.

> **Note 4**
>
> In Linux, the # command prompt displays when a user has root access, and the $ command prompt displays when a user does not.

Mobile Security in Corporate Environments

Core 2 Objectives 2.1, 2.7

Recall from the Core 1 module "Supporting Mobile Devices" that corporations and schools might provide corporate-owned devices, which are secured and managed by corporate policies and procedures, or the organization might have BYOD policies and procedures that allow an employee or student to connect their own device to the corporate network.

Regardless of who owns the device, mobile device management (MDM) software downloads and enforces a security profile to the device before allowing it to connect to the network. A **security profile**, sometimes called a work profile, is a set of policies and procedures to restrict how a user can access, create, and edit the organization's resources. Profile security requirements can include full device encryption, backups, remote wipes, location apps, access control, authenticator apps, multifactor authentication, firewalls, anti-malware measures, and use of VPN connections. All requirements must be clearly outlined with assurance that devices continue to meet the baseline requirements, and users must be educated on how to use them.

> **Note 5**
>
> To find out if an Android device has a corporate security profile installed, open **Settings**, go to **Accounts**, and look for a Work section. A passcode is required to access the section. If you don't see a Work section, the device does not have a security profile installed. When the device has a security profile, you must enter a passcode to access the profile or enter one to access corporate apps on the device. A corporate app has a briefcase icon.
>
> After an iOS device receives the download from the MDM server, apps on the device that belong to the corporation, called managed apps, are accessed via a passcode.

Although Google and Apple offer free or inexpensive backup services for their OSs, security profiles might require installing a **remote backup application**, which remotely backs up the device's data to the company's secured cloud storage. These apps might also sync files both directions and provide support for larger files. For example, Acronis Cyper Backup (*acronis.com*) provides enterprise-level backups for Windows, macOS, iOS, and Android devices.

Troubleshooting Mobile Devices

Core 2 Objectives 3.4, 3.5

When learning to troubleshoot any OS or device, remember the web is a great source of information. Depend on the *support.google.com/googleplay* and *support.apple.com* websites to give you troubleshooting tips and procedures for their respective mobile devices. In this section, we'll first explore troubleshooting tools for mobile device OSs, and then we'll consider several common symptoms and problems and what to do about them.

Troubleshooting Techniques

Core 2 Objectives 3.4, 3.5

In the Core 1 module "Supporting Mobile Devices," you learned several techniques for troubleshooting mobile devices. In this module, we review these techniques and add some more. The following steps are ordered to solve a problem while making the fewest changes to the system (i.e., try the least invasive solution first). Try the first step; if it does not solve the problem, move on to the next step. With each step, first make sure the device is plugged in or already has sufficient charge to complete the step. After you try one step, check to see if the problem is solved before you move on to the next step. Here are the general steps we're following, although some might not be possible, depending on the situation:

Figure 18-17   Restart or power-off an Android device

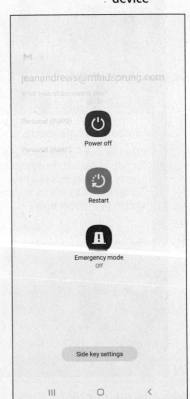

1. **Close, uninstall, and reinstall an app.** If you suspect an app is causing a problem, uninstall it and use the app store to reinstall it.
2. **Restart the device (also called a soft boot).** Recall to restart an Android device, press and hold the power button, and select **Restart**. See Figure 18-17. To restart an Apple device, press and hold the side or top button, and slide the power-off message to the right.
3. **Reboot the device (also called a hard boot).** For most Android devices, hold down the power button to see the menu shown in Figure 18-17, and tap **Power off** twice. If that doesn't work, try holding down the power button and the volume-down button at the same time. (Check Android device manufacturers for details.) To reboot an iPhone or iPad, hold down the side or top button and the volume-down button at the same time until the Apple logo appears. (For older iPhones and iPads, press and hold the side or top button and the Home button.)
4. Update, repair, or reinstall the OS, or recover the system from the last backup.
5. Start over by resetting the device to its factory state (all data and settings are lost).

Let's look at the last two steps in a little more detail. For more specific instructions, search the website of the device manufacturer.

Note 6

If the device has a removable battery and it refuses to hard boot, you can open the back of the device and then remove and reinstall the battery as a last resort (unless the device is under warranty).

Update, Repair, or Restore the System

As you progress through troubleshooting steps, try these options to update, repair, or restore a device:

1. **Back up content and settings.** Before you try any of the techniques in this section, first try to back up data and settings using one or more of the methods discussed earlier in the module.

2. **Update the OS.** Try installing any updates, if available.

For Android devices, you can try these options to repair and restore your system:

1. **Boot into Android Safe Mode.** Similar to Windows computers, Android offers a Safe Mode for troubleshooting. In Safe Mode, only the original software installed on the phone will run so that you can eliminate third-party software as the source of the problem. However, be aware that booting to Safe Mode might result in the loss of some settings, such as synched accounts. The combination of buttons to access Safe Mode varies by device, so see the manufacturer's website for specific instructions. For Google's Pixel smartphone, you access Safe Mode by holding down the power button until the power menu appears. Tap and hold the **Power Off** option until the pop-up shown in Figure 18-18A appears. Tap **OK** to restart the phone in Safe Mode, as shown in Figure 18-18B. Notice the *Safe mode* flag at the bottom of the screen. In Safe Mode, only apps native to the Android installation can run, and troubleshooting tools can be accessed through the Settings app to back up data, test configuration issues, or reset the device. To exit Safe Mode, restart the phone normally.

Figure 18-18   (A) Restart in Safe Mode; (B) in Safe Mode, third-party apps don't load

(A)

(B)

2. **Restore from backup.** If you have used Google Drive or a third-party app to back up the Android OS, its data or settings, now is the time to restore the system from this backup.

Several troubleshooting apps have been developed to help resolve Android problems. Most of these apps work only if they have already been installed before the problem occurs. If you have not already installed a troubleshooting app, your best resource at this point is to do a Google search on the problem and depend as much as possible on the device manufacturer's website.

For iOS devices, you have several options for repairing and restoring your system, which are listed beginning with the least invasive:

1. **Reset all iOS settings.** To erase settings, open the **Settings** app and tap **General** and then **Reset**. On the Reset screen (see Figure 18-19), tap **Reset All Settings**.

2. **Restore from backup.** Use one of these methods to restore from backup:

   • **Restore the device from iCloud.** If you have an iCloud backup, open the **Settings** app and tap **General**, **Reset**, and **Erase All Content and Settings** (see Figure 18-19). Then tap **Restore** and **iCloud backup**. You'll need to sign in to iCloud.

   • **Restore the device from a Mac or from iTunes in Windows.** If you have used a Mac or iTunes in Windows to back up the device, connect the device to your computer, start Finder on the Mac or iTunes in Windows, and click **Restore iPhone**. Refer back to Figure 18-6.

3. **Reinstall iOS.** If an iOS device won't turn on or start up, first consider that the battery might be dead. Try to charge it for at least an hour. If you still can't turn it on, you can use a Mac or iTunes in Windows to try to reinstall iOS without losing your data. (You can use any Mac or iTunes on any Windows computer, even if you have not previously used it to back up your device.)

   a. If necessary, download and install iTunes. Make sure iTunes is updated, and then close it.

   b. Connect the iPhone or iPad to the computer and start the Mac Finder or iTunes in Windows. Check the Apple website (*support.apple.com*) for the correct keys to press to put the device in Recovery Mode. For iPhone 8 or later, press and release the volume-up button followed by the volume-down button, and then press and hold the Slide button until you see the Recovery Mode screen (see Figure 18-20A). For newer iPads, press and hold the top button and volume down button at the same time. For older iPhones or iPads, press and hold the power button and volume down button at the same time. Follow the directions until you see the screen shown in Figure 18-20B, and then click **Update**. The latest version of iOS that works on your device should install, keeping your existing data.

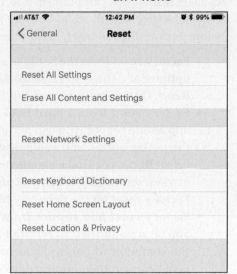

Figure 18-19   The reset screen on an iPhone

Figure 18-20   Use Recovery Mode on a Mac or with iTunes in Windows to reinstall iOS on an iOS device that will not start

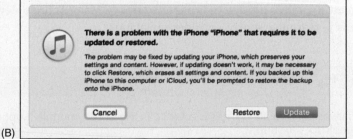

(A)   (B)

18

Start Over with a Factory Reset

As a last resort, you can perform a factory reset. The reset erases all data and settings and resets the device to its original factory default state. You can then apply a backup if you have one, so try to back up all data and settings before performing the reset, if possible. Here are your options:

- **Factory reset from the Settings app.** In Android, open the **Settings** app, tap **System**, tap **Advanced**, tap **Reset options**, and then tap **Erase all data (factory reset)**. In iOS, open the **Settings** app, and then tap **General** and **Reset**. On the Reset screen, tap **Erase All Content and Settings**.

- **Factory reset from a hard boot (Android only).** If you cannot start Android or cannot get to the Settings app after a reboot, you can perform a factory reset from a hard boot. For most Android devices, hold down the power button and volume-down button at the same time until you see the Android bootloader menu. Select **Recovery Mode**, and then check the device manufacturer's website for other options on the Recovery Mode screen that you can try before a full factory reset. If you decide that you have no other options, select **Factory reset** on the Recovery Mode screen.

- **Factory reset and restore from a Mac or iTunes backup (iOS only).** If an iOS device won't turn on and you've already tried to reinstall iOS using a Mac or iTunes in Windows, as discussed earlier, you can use the computer to perform a factory reset. Connect the device to a Mac or Windows computer with iTunes installed, and then put the device in Recovery Mode, as you learned to do earlier. Then click **Restore** (see Figure 18-20B). All data and settings on the device are erased, and iOS is reinstalled. If you have previously used this computer to back up your device, the device is restored from the backup. If you have an iCloud backup, you will be given the opportunity to restore from iCloud the first time you sign on to the device with your Apple ID.

Note 7

If you have backed up to iCloud and you sign into iOS for the first time with your Apple ID on a new or factory reset device, you are given the chance to restore the device from the iCloud backup.

If you've tried the previous steps and your device is still not working properly, search for more troubleshooting tips online, review the list of common problems in the next section, or take the device to the place of purchase for repair.

Common Problems and Solutions

Core 2 Objective 3.4

Several common problems with mobile devices can be addressed with a little understanding of what has gone wrong behind the scenes. Here's a description of how to handle some common problems:

- **Short battery life or power drain.** Too many apps or malware running in the background will drain the battery quickly, as will Wi-Fi, Bluetooth, or other wireless technologies. Disable wireless connections and close apps when you're not using them to save battery juice. Consider that malware might be at work. If the battery charge still lasts an extremely short time, try exchanging the charger cable. If that doesn't work, exchange the battery unless the device is under warranty. Many Android devices have replaceable batteries, so if a battery is performing poorly, consider replacing it.

Core to Core

How to deal with malware on mobile devices is covered in the Core 1 module "Supporting Mobile Devices."

- **Screen does not autorotate.** Try these things:
  - In the Android Settings app, check the Display screen to verify auto-rotate is turned on (see Figure 18-21A).
  - For Apple devices, swipe from the upper-right corner to open the Control Center (see Figure 18-21B), and check the auto-rotate button.
  - Don't touch the screen when you're rotating it.
  - Update the OS, and restart the device.
  - If you recently installed a third-party app when the touch screen became unresponsive, try uninstalling that app. Sometimes third-party apps can cause a touch screen to freeze.

Figure 18-21   Verify auto-rotate is turned on with (A) an Android phone and (B) an iPhone

Auto-rotate button in Control Center

(A)   (B)

- **OS fails to update.** Try these things:
  - The OS might fail to update if there's not enough free space on the device to download and install the update. The Settings app on an Android device displays how much storage space is available (see Figure 18-22A) and what content can be removed (see Figure 18-22B). If free space is needed, try uninstalling some unneeded apps or moving some data to the cloud.

18

Figure 18-22   (A) Android reports how storage is used and (B) makes suggestions to free up some storage space

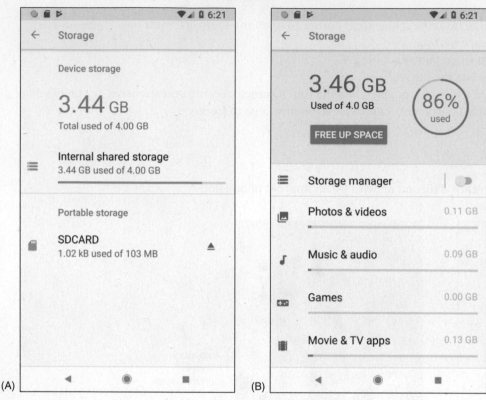

(A)   (B)

- Make sure the battery is charged and the network connection is good.
- Try a different network. Restart the device, and try again.
- For iOS, you can try removing a failed update and updating the OS again. To remove an update, go to **Settings**, **General**, and **iPhone Storage**; tap the update; and tap **Delete Update**. Then try the update again. To use iTunes to update the OS, plug in the Apple device to your computer, open **iTunes** in Windows or Finder on a Mac, locate your device, and click **Check for Updates**. Refer back to Figure 18-6.
- **Apps fail to launch or are slow to respond.** Check and try these things:
  - When apps are slow to respond, slow to launch, or won't launch at all, a hot or failing battery might be the problem. Having too many apps open at once will use up memory, which can also slow down overall performance. Close apps you're not using, clean cached data, and disable live wallpapers.
  - Try to update the app, or uninstall it and install it again.
  - The device might be short on storage space; uninstall unused apps and delete files that are no longer needed.
  - Consider downloading an app to clean up storage space or monitor how apps are using memory.
  - Consider performing a factory reset, and start over by installing only the apps you actually use.
- **Apps crash, fail to close, or fail to update.** Apps might crash or fail to close or update when an app is corrupted, storage is low, or the Wi-Fi network or cellular signal is slow or unstable. Try these things:
  - Free up some storage, and try a different network.
  - Make sure the OS is up to date.
  - For Android apps failing to update, try clearing the Google cache: In Settings, go to **Apps & notifications**, **Google**, and **Storage & cache**, and tap **CLEAR CACHE**. See Figure 18-23. If the problem persists, force stop the Google app.

- **Random reboots.** Random reboots are usually caused by bad apps, overheating, corrupted OS, or defective hardware. First try uninstalling any suspected apps and updating the OS. For Android, go to the Play Store, and update all apps: Tap your profile icon, tap **Manage apps & device** and **Update all**. For iOS, in Settings, tap **App Store** and turn on **App Updates**.

Core to Core ⬌

How to deal with overheating is covered in the Core 1 module "Supporting Mobile Devices."

- **Signal drop/weak signal.** Sometimes updating the device's firmware can solve problems with dropped calls or network connections due to a weak signal because the update might apply to the radio firmware, which manages the cellular, Wi-Fi, and Bluetooth radios. This is sometimes referred to as a **baseband update**. For most of today's mobile devices, firmware updates are pushed out by the manufacturer at the same time as OS updates. If your device allows for managing firmware updates separately, that option will usually be available in the Settings app (see Figure 18-24) in the same place as the OS update option. You might also be able to download firmware updates directly from the device manufacturer (for example, for LG devices, go to *lg.com/us/support/software-firmware-drivers*). Be careful when applying a firmware update because a failed update can "brick" the device, which means to make it useless.
- **System lockout.** If a device is locked because of too many failed attempts to sign in (such as when a child has attempted to unlock your device or you have forgotten the passcode), wait until the timer on the device counts down, and try to sign in again. With Android devices, you might also be able to sign in using your Google account and the password associated with the device. After you have entered the account and password, you must reset your passcode or screen swipe pattern. If you still can't unlock the device, know that Google offers many solutions to this problem. Go to *accounts.google.com*, and search for additional methods and tools to unlock your device.

Figure 18-23 Clearing the Google cache might solve the problem of apps failing to update

Figure 18-24 This LG phone lists several options for applying updates

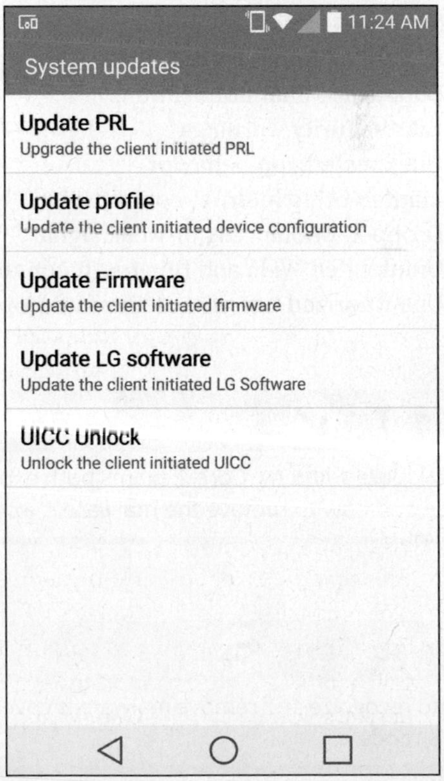

If you have forgotten the passcode for an iOS device, Apple advises that your only solution is to reset the device, which erases all data and settings, and then restore the device from a backup. You can restore from a backup stored on your computer or from iCloud.

Connectivity Issues

Connectivity issues might arise with Bluetooth, Wi-Fi, and NFC on both Android and Apple devices. You might also face issues with Apple AirDrop connections.

Exam Tip ✔

The A+ Core 1 and A+ Core 2 exams both expect you to know how to troubleshoot mobile device connectivity problems with Bluetooth, Wi-Fi, NFC, and AirDrop connections.

Core to Core ↔

Connectivity issues with mobile devices are covered in the Core 1 module "Supporting Mobile Devices" and are not repeated in this module.

Security Concerns

Common symptoms that malware is at work on a device, indicating that the security features in place have been breached, include the following:

- Excessive power drain
- Sluggish response time
- Slow data speeds and high network traffic
- Unauthorized account access or leaked personal data or other data
- Strange text messages or phone calls
- High number of ads
- Data-usage limit notifications
- Fake security warnings
- Unexpected app behavior
- Limited or no Internet connectivity
- Dropped phone calls or weak signal
- Unintended Wi-Fi and Bluetooth connections
- Unauthorized use of camera or microphone

Exam Tip ✔

The A+ Core 1 and A+ Core 2 exams both expect you to know how to recognize malware might be at work on a mobile device and how to remove the malware.

Core to Core ↔

How to recognize and remove malware is covered in the Core 1 module "Supporting Mobile Devices" and is not repeated in this module.

Module Summary

Backing Up Mobile Devices

- Currently, the most popular operating systems used on mobile devices are Android by Google and iOS and iPadOS by Apple.
- A mobile OS can be updated until it ages out of manufacturer updates based on end-of-life (EOL) limitations.
- Mobile apps are usually developed using development tools provided by Google and Apple in a software development kit (SDK).
- Backups for mobile data include file-level backups and full and partial image-level backups, which can be made to a local computer or to the cloud.

Securing Mobile Devices

- Secure mobile device data and resources by regularly updating and patching the OS, using an anti-malware app with the Android OS, implementing a firewall, configuring a locator app and the ability to remote wipe the device, and getting apps only from trusted sources.
- Control access to a mobile device by restricting failed login attempts, encrypting the device, and configuring a screen lock, such as a swipe lock, PIN lock, passcode lock, pattern lock, fingerprint lock, or face lock.
- Allowing root access to an Android device or jailbreaking an Apple device can expose the device to bootlegged apps, spoofing apps, or apps from untrustworthy sources.
- In corporate environments, a security profile might require the use of full device encryption, remote backups, remote wipes, access control to the device, authenticator apps, multifactor authentication, firewalls, anti-malware measures, and VPN connections to protect company resources on the mobile device.

Troubleshooting Mobile Devices

- To troubleshoot a mobile device using tools in the OS, you can close running apps, uninstall and reinstall an app, restart or reboot the device, update the OS, reset all settings (iOS only), use Safe Mode (Android only), use Recovery Mode and restore from backup, or perform a factory reset.
- To address specific, common symptoms on a mobile device, you might need to replace the battery if it's not under warranty, adjust device settings, update the OS, uninstall or update problem apps, free up space on the device, clear the Google cache, update firmware, reset the device, or consult with tech support for the device manufacturer or app.
- Symptoms of malware on mobile devices include excessive power drain, slow performance, slow data speeds, high network traffic, leaked personal files or data, data transmission over limits, strange text messages or phone calls, signal drops, weak signal, unintended Wi-Fi connections, unintended Bluetooth pairing, unauthorized account access, unauthorized location tracking, and unauthorized camera or microphone activation.

Key Terms

For explanations of key terms, see the Glossary for this text.

Android package (APK)	device encryption	locator application	rooting
application spoofing	emulator	mobile device	SDK (software
baseband update	end-of-life (EOL)	management (MDM)	development kit)
bootlegged app	file-level backup	remote backup	security profile
BYOD (bring your own	image-level backup	application	trusted source
device)	jailbreaking	remote wipe	

18

Thinking Critically

These questions are designed to prepare you for the critical thinking required for the A+ exams and may use information from other modules and the web.

1. Which of the following is the best reason to replace a mobile device with a new one in a corporate environment?

   a. The device has only a single camera, and MDM requires a minimum of two cameras for two-factor authentication.
   b. The device does not have an SD card slot required for MDM management tools.
   c. The latest version of Android the device can support has reached its EOL limitation.
   d. The device will not update to the latest version of Android.

2. An app that cost you $4.99 is missing from your Android. What is the best way to restore the missing app?

   a. Go to backup storage and perform a restore to recover the lost app.
   b. Purchase the app again.
   c. Go to the Play Store where you bought the app and install it again.
   d. Go to the Settings app and perform an application restore.

3. Suppose you and your friend want to exchange lecture notes taken during class. Your friend has an iPhone, and you have an iPad. What is the easiest way to make the exchange?

   a. Copy the files to an SD card, and move the SD card to each device.
   b. Drop the files in OneDrive, and share notebooks with each other.
   c. Send a text to each other with the files attached.
   d. Transfer the files through an AirDrop connection.

4. You have set up your Android phone using one Google account and your Android tablet using a second Google account. Now you would like to download the apps you purchased on your phone to your tablet. What is the best way to do this?

   a. On your tablet, set up the Google account that you used to buy apps on your phone, and then download the apps.
   b. Buy the apps a second time from your tablet.
   c. Back up the apps on your phone to your SD card, and then move the SD card to your tablet and transfer the apps.
   d. Call Google support and ask them to merge the two Google accounts into one.

5. What is one effective way to implement a VPN connection on your Android device?

   a. Enable Android Firewall in the Settings app on your device.
   b. Install a firewall app that includes a VPN connection in its services.
   c. Subscribe to a website service that provides mobile device firewalls.
   d. VPN connections are not important to secure the device because all Wi-Fi and cellular transmissions are encrypted in Android.

6. Before allowing apps from untrusted sources to be installed on your Android device, what should you do? (Choose all that apply.)

   a. Install a firewall app.
   b. Install an anti-malware app.
   c. Use Android settings to allow apps from untrusted source.
   d. All of the answers are correct.

7. Android apps are contained in an Android package kit, which has what file extension?

   a. .apx
   b. .apk
   c. .and
   d. .exe

8. What is a potential security risk when enabling Developer mode in Android?

    a. Android updates can install without your knowledge.

    b. Malicious software might reach your device when it is connected to a computer via a USB cable.

    c. A video game might contain malware that can reach the Android root level of your mobile device.

    d. Malicious software can easily download and install from the web without your knowledge.

9. How can you configure an iPhone so it can download and install any app from any website on the Internet?

    a. Use an app to jailbreak the iPhone.

    b. Use Finder on a Mac computer to reset the iPhone.

    c. Go to Settings, General, and then set the iPhone to allow apps from untrusted sources.

    d. Go to the Apps Store, and download and install the AllApps app.

10. When is it appropriate to use iTunes to restore an iPad from backup?

    a. When the backup has been created on a Windows computer

    b. When the backup has been created on a Mac computer

    c. When the backup has been created in iCloud

    d. All of the answers are correct.

11. Where is the biometric data for an Android facial recognition lock or fingerprint lock kept?

    a. On the Android device and in the cloud

    b. Only on the Android device

    c. On the Android device and with any backups of data

    d. Only in the Google cloud

12. Which of the following are true about Android Safe Mode? (Choose all that apply.)

    a. Only apps native to the Android installation can run in Android Safe Mode.

    b. A Safe Mode flag displays somewhere on the screen.

    c. Safe Mode helps you eliminate third-party apps as the source of a problem.

    d. To exit Safe Mode, restart the device normally.

13. Your friend has an iPhone that refused to start, and you helped them use a Mac computer to perform a factory reset. They had previously backed up the phone to iCloud. How do you instruct your friend to restore the phone from the iCloud backup?

    a. Reconnect the phone to the Mac computer, and use the Finder window to restore the phone from the iCloud backup.

    b. Turn the phone on, and set it up without the backup. After the phone is operational, use the Settings app to restore from backup.

    c. Turn on the phone, enter their Apple ID, and step through the questions to restore the phone from the iCloud backup.

    d. Take the phone to an Apple service center, and ask them to help restore the phone from the iCloud backup.

14. What is the most effective thing you can do to prevent a mobile device battery from draining too quickly?

    a. Turn off Wi-Fi when Wi-Fi is not available.

    b. Close the browser app.

    c. Enable airplane mode.

    d. Turn off your mobile hotspot.

15. A friend is having problems with their iPhone randomly rebooting. When you examine the phone, you notice the Cydia app installed. What do you recommend your friend try first to fix the problem?

    a. Update the OS to eliminate the jailbreak.

    b. Restore the iPhone to factory state to remove the malware.

    c. Restore the iPhone to factory state to eliminate the jailbreak.

    d. Update the Cydia app to eliminate the random reboots.

Hands-On Projects

Hands-On Project 18-1

Researching Apps for Mobile Payment Services

Est. Time: 30 minutes
Core 2 Objective: 2.7

iPhone and Android phones both offer a mobile payment service, which allows you to use your smartphone to pay for merchandise or services at a retail checkout counter. iPhone has Apple Pay, and Android uses Google Pay. Mobile payment services rely on NFC (near-field communication) technology to exchange financial information between your phone and the reader at the checkout counter. You might want to pay with a credit card stored on your phone or get discounts with a store rewards account reported by your phone as you check out. But how secure is your sensitive financial information?

Research the following topics, and answer the following questions:

1. Research how mobile payment systems use NFC technology. How can you activate NFC on an Android phone for making a payment with Google Pay? On an iPhone for making a payment with Apple Pay?

2. Find and read some articles online or watch videos that describe the details of storing financial information for mobile payment systems, accessing the information when needed, and transmitting the information securely. What security measures are in place? Where is the data actually stored? What information is actually transmitted at the point of transaction?

3. List three third-party mobile payment apps available either in Apple's App Store or in Google's Play Store. On which mobile OS versions will the apps work? What are advantages and disadvantages of each app? How much do the apps cost? What security measures do the apps use?

4. If you were to purchase one of these apps, which one would it be? Why?

Hands-On Project 18-2

Practicing Locating Your iOS or Android Device

Est. Time: 15 minutes
Core 2 Objective: 2.7

Whether you have an Android device or an iOS device, knowing how to locate it when it gets lost or stolen and knowing how to perform a remote wipe can be crucial skills in an emergency. Using your own device or a friend's, complete the following steps to find out how these tasks work:

1. If you have an iOS device, go to *iCloud.com/find*. If you have an Android device, go to *google.com/android/find*.

2. Sign in, and make sure the correct device is selected. Was the website able to locate your device? If not, check your device settings and make any adjustments necessary until the website successfully locates the device.

3. Explore the site to see how to make the device ring, how to lock the device, and how to erase the device. What did you learn about your device?

One potential snag in finding or remotely wiping your device would be relying on passwords stored in your device to access your Google or iCloud account. Be sure to store your sign-in information for these accounts in password vault software or memorize the information.

Hands-On Project 18-3

Using Xcode to Launch a Virtual iPhone

Est. Time: 15 minutes
Core 2 Objective: 2.7

Complete the following steps to download and install Xcode on a Mac computer, and use it to run an iPhone emulator on the Mac. For more information about using a Mac, see the module "Supporting macOS."

1. Verify that you have at least 40 GB of free space on the hard drive. Xcode will not install without this much free space. To find out how much free space is on your Mac, open the **Finder** window, right-click the hard drive, and click **Manage Storage**.

2. Open the **App Store** app, and locate and install **Xcode**. (The download is about 12.5 GB, and the installation takes some time.)

3. Launch **Xcode**. With the Xcode window active, on the menu bar, click **Xcode**, **Open Developer Tool**, and **Simulator**. The simulator program for the latest iPhone launches.

4. To start the simulator, click its power button on the right side. Figure 18-25 shows the simulator running. Try some of the features of the iPhone to verify how the simulator works.

Figure 18-25   The default simulator represents the latest model iPhone

5. To see what other simulators are available, with the simulator selected, in the Simulator menu bar, click **File**, **New Simulator**. Notice that Xcode offers simulators for iPhones, iPods, iPads, Apple TVs, and Apple Watches.

6. To uninstall Xcode when you are finished with it, go to Launchpad, and drag and drop the Xcode icon into the Trash.

18

Hands-On Project 18-4

Backing Up Your iPhone to a Computer

Est. Time: 15 minutes
Core 2 Objective: 2.7

If you have an iPhone, follow the directions given in the module to back it up to a Mac or Windows computer. If you are using a Windows computer, you first must download and install iTunes. Connect your iPhone to the computer, and use either Finder on a Mac or iTunes in Windows to back up the device. How much space on your hard drive did the backup take? If you don't want to keep the backup, you can delete it. In the Finder or iTunes window, click **Manage Backups**, and select and delete the backup.

Real Problems, Real Solutions

Real Problem 18-1

Using Android Studio to Run an Android Emulator

Est. Time: 45 minutes
Core 2 Objective: 2.7

For this project, you might want to work with a partner so you will have someone with whom to discuss the project in case the installation requires some troubleshooting. Make sure you're using a computer that meets the minimum requirements. Although Android Studio also works on macOS and Linux platforms, these instructions apply specifically to Windows 10. Here are the Windows system requirements:

- Microsoft Windows 10 64-bit
- 8 GB RAM minimum recommended
- 8 GB of available storage space minimum
- 1280 × 800 minimum screen resolution

Complete the following steps:

1. Make sure that your computer does not have Hyper-V enabled. To check this, open **Control Panel**, click **Programs and Features**, and click **Turn Windows features on or off**. Make sure that **Hyper-V** is not checked. If it is, uncheck it. Click **OK**. If you had to disable Hyper-V, restart your computer.

2. Make sure that hardware virtualization is enabled in your motherboard's BIOS/UEFI. The name and steps to access this feature vary by motherboard. If necessary, check your motherboard's documentation to determine how to enable this feature.

3. Download Android Studio at *developer.android.com/studio*. Run the .exe file that you downloaded.

4. Follow the setup wizard, and accept all default settings, installing any SDK packages that it recommends. When you reach the Choose Components window, be sure **Android Virtual Device** is selected.

5. When the installation is complete, launch **Android Studio**, accepting all default settings. The user interface is shown in Figure 18-26. In the dropdown menu under *More Actions*, click **AVD Manager**, as shown in the figure.

Figure 18-26   Android Studio is designed to enable app developers
to build and test their products

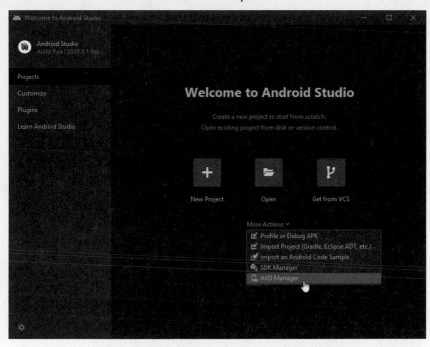

6. In the following window, click **Create Virtual Device**.

7. In the Select Hardware window, in the Phone group, select a model phone, and then click **Next**. In the next window, select a system image, and click **Next**. You might have to download the system image from the Play Store. Click **Finish**.

8. Your new virtual device is created. Click the play button to start the emulator, which is shown in Figure 18-27.

Figure 18-27   List of installed emulators and one running emulator

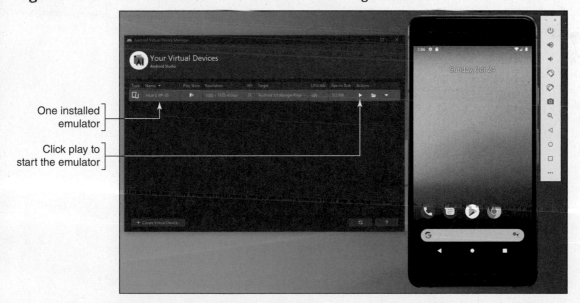

One installed emulator

Click play to start the emulator

9. Play around with the UI to see how well it emulates a real smartphone. Open the **Settings** app, and try some of the features discussed in this module.

18

Module
19

Network Security and Troubleshooting

Module Objectives

1 Secure a workstation on a network—including managing a browser, VPN, WWAN connection, metered connection, and Windows Defender Firewall—and secure IoT devices

2 Secure a multifunctional router for a SOHO network

3 Use remote access technologies and know how to secure these products

4 Troubleshoot network connections using a variety of Windows networking commands

Core 2 Certification Objectives

1.2 Given a scenario, use the appropriate Microsoft command-line tool.

1.4 Given a scenario, use the appropriate Microsoft Windows 10 Control Panel utility.

1.6 Given a scenario, configure Microsoft Windows networking features on a client/desktop.

2.2 Compare and contrast wireless security protocols and authentication methods.

2.5 Given a scenario, manage and configure basic security settings in the Microsoft Windows OS.

2.7 Explain common methods for securing mobile and embedded devices.

2.9 Given a scenario, configure appropriate security settings on small office/home office (SOHO) wireless and wired networks.

2.10 Given a scenario, install and configure browsers and relevant security settings.

4.9 Given a scenario, use remote access technologies.

Introduction

In previous modules, you have learned much about networking, including concepts related to TCP/IP networking, managing network cabling and hardware, setting up a local network, network connections to the Internet, managing and securing resources on a network, virtual networks, and cloud computing. This module takes you one step closer to being able to provide comprehensive support for networks and their administration. In this module, you learn how to secure a workstation on a network, how to use a SOHO router to secure a LAN—including how to use wireless security protocols and authentication methods to secure a wired or wireless network—how to use and secure remote access technologies, and how to troubleshoot when networks don't work as expected. By the time you complete this module and its related lab activities, it is our hope that you will feel confident that you are ready to begin your IT career as an apprentice to a network administrator.

Securing Workstations and IoT Devices on a Network

 Core 2 Objectives 1.4, 1.6, 2.5, 2.7, 2.10, 4.9

In this section of the module, we focus on securing a workstation that is connected to a local network. You learn how to secure Windows Microsoft Edge and other browsers, how to set up a VPN connection so a computer can securely connect to resources on a remote network, and how to configure a personal firewall for optimum security. You also learn about securing IoT devices connected to the Internet.

Secure a Browser

 Core 2 Objectives 1.4, 2.10

In the discussion about securing browsers that follows, we show examples of either Google Chrome, currently the most popular browser, or Microsoft Edge, the default browser in Windows 10/11. However, know that each browser supports all the functions listed, as do most popular browsers. Do the following to secure Chrome or Edge browsers:

- **Sign in to a browser and sync data across devices.** Browser syncing is a service offered by Google, Microsoft, and other browser developers to sync browser settings and data across each installation of the browser on multiple devices. For Google Chrome, in the Chrome browser, click the profile icon in the upper-right corner (see Figure 19-1). When you click **Turn on sync**, you will be prompted to sign in to your Google account.

Figure 19-1 To turn on browser syncing, you must sign in to your Google account

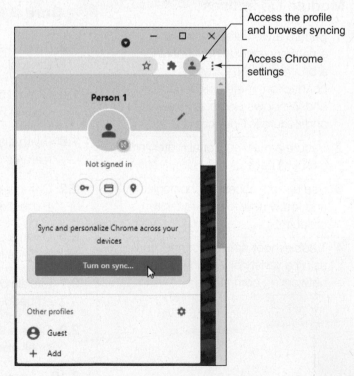

For Edge syncing, go to Edge settings by clicking the settings clog in the left panel of the Edge window (see Figure 19-2). Select **Profiles**, and sign in to the browser. Edge will ask if you want to sync across all your signed-in devices.

Figure 19-2   Use Microsoft Edge settings to manage Edge profile settings, including passwords

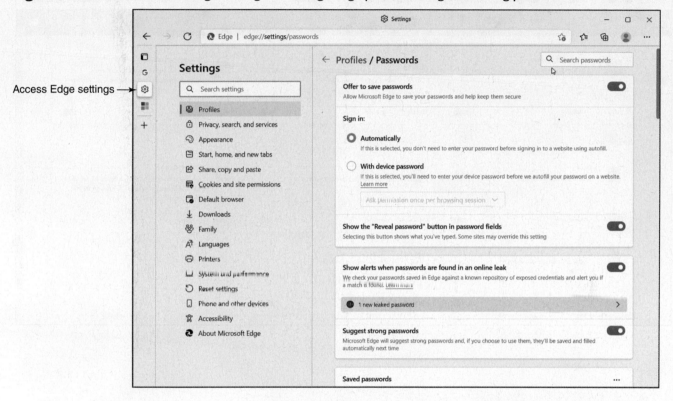

> **Note 1**
>
> Although browser syncing is a convenience and might be appropriate in some situations, best practice for security is to not sign in to a browser and not turn on browser syncing.

- **Manage extensions and plug-ins.** Browser **plug-ins** and **extensions** are small programs that install in a browser to change the way the browser functions or to enhance the features of a single website, such as the Cisco Webex Extension shown in Figure 19-3. A user might unintentionally install an extension or plug-in into their browser. For example, the Easy 2 Convert 4 Me plug-in shown in Figure 19-3 was accidentally installed in Google Chrome and works to display pop-up ads and redirect webpages. To remove the extension, go to Chrome settings by clicking the three-dot menu icon in the upper-right corner of the Chrome window (as shown in Figure 19-1). In settings, click **Extensions** in the left pane. A list of extensions appears, as shown in Figure 19-3. Click **Remove** in the extensions box to delete it.

19

Figure 19-3   Manage extensions installed in Google Chrome

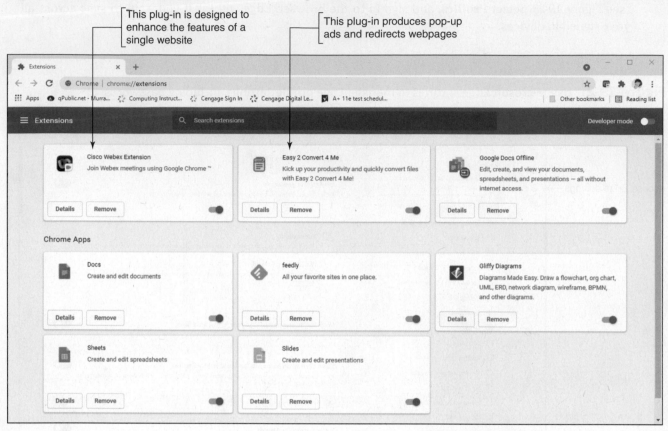

Before installing an extension or plug-in, verify it comes from a trusted source. Read reviews about it, and install it only from the trusted source website, not from other untrusted sources on the web that might have altered the original software or embedded malware in the download.

- **Password manager.** To control how Edge manages passwords, in Edge settings, select **Profiles** and **Passwords**. (Refer back to Figure 19-2.) In the Passwords pane you can turn on or off saving passwords, decide how passwords are managed, and copy, edit, or delete passwords saved by Edge.
- **Pop-up blocker and ad blockers.** In Edge settings, select **Cookies and site permissions** and then **Ads** or **Pop-ups and redirects** to turn on or off pop-ups, redirects, and intrusive or misleading ads.
- **Clear the cache and all browsing data.** In Edge settings, select **Privacy, search, and services**. Use the Tracking prevention area on this page to manage trackers used by Microsoft and other websites that collect and use information about your browsing habits. In the *Clear browsing data area* of the page, you can choose to clear your browsing data at any time. Select **Choose what to clear every time you close the browser** to see the page shown in Figure 19-4, where you can decide to clear cached images and files and all other browser data each time you close the browser. Clearing all data about you each time you close the browser is a suggested best practice to secure a browser.

Figure 19-4 Configure Edge to clear all browsing data each time you close the Edge browser

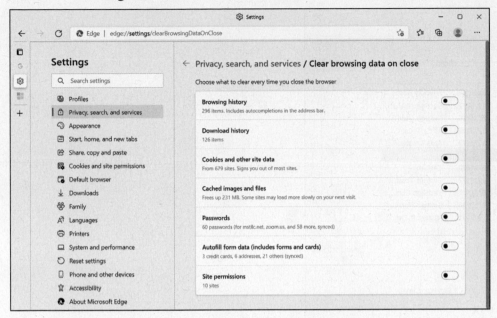

- **Privacy browsing.** In Edge settings, select **Privacy, search, and services** and use options in the Privacy area (see Figure 19-5) to send "Do Not Track" requests to websites you visit. Microsoft and Google say that even though you might send this request to a website, it does not guarantee that the website will honor the request.

Figure 19-5 Send "Do Not Track" requests to websites you visit

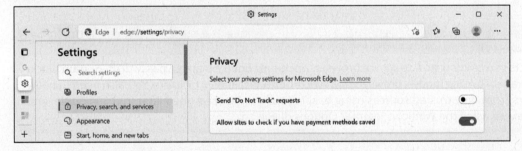

- **Secure connections and sites and valid certificates.** When browsers use HTTPS and SSL encryption protocols to communicate with secured websites, they validate a website's digital certificate. To view and manage these certificates, in Chrome settings, select **Privacy and security**, and click **Manage certificates**. In Edge settings, click **Privacy, search, and services** and then click **Manage certificates**. In both cases, the Windows Certificate dialog box appears where you can view, remove, import, and export certificates. See Figure 19-6.

Figure 19-6   View and manage certificates validated by
Windows

• **Update or repair Edge.** If you have a problem with Microsoft Edge, to update it, in Edge settings, click **About Microsoft Edge**. The update begins immediately. To repair Edge, use the **Apps & features** page in the Windows Settings app.

Exam Tip ✔

The A+ Core 2 exam expects you to know how to secure browsers, including how to manage passwords, pop-up blockers, clearing the cache, private-browsing modes, browser data synchronization, and ad blockers. You also need to know how to download browsers from only trusted sources using hashing techniques (described later in this module) and how to configure proxy servers using the Windows Internet Options dialog box.

Internet Options and Proxy Settings

Windows 10 offers two browsers: the newer Edge and the older Internet Explorer browsers. Windows 11 offers only the Edge browser, but for legacy websites that require Internet Explorer, you can enable IE Mode in Edge. Internet Explorer in Windows 10 is configured via the **Internet Options** applet in Control Panel. For both Windows 10 and Windows 11, a few settings in Internet Options also affect Edge and other browsers installed in the system, including proxy settings.

Many large corporations and ISPs use proxy servers to speed up Internet access. A web browser does not have to be aware that a proxy server is in use. However, one reason you might need to configure Internet Options and use a proxy server is when you are on a corporate network and are having a problem connecting to a secured website (one using HTTP over SSL or another encryption protocol). The problem might be caused by Windows trying to connect using the wrong proxy server on the network. Check with your network administrator to find out if a specific proxy server should be used to manage secure website connections.

Exam Tip ✔

The A+ Core 2 exam expects you to know how to configure proxy settings on a client desktop. For Windows 10/11, this is done with Internet Options.

If you need to configure Internet Options to use a specific proxy server, open **Control Panel** in classic view, and then open **Internet Options**. On the **Connections** tab, click **LAN settings**. In the settings dialog box, check **Use a proxy server for your LAN**, and enter the IP address of the proxy server (see Figure 19-7). If your organization uses more than one proxy server, click **Advanced**, and enter IP addresses for each type of proxy server on your network (see the right side of Figure 19-7). You can also enter a port address for each server, if necessary. If you are trying to solve a problem of connecting to a server using HTTP over SSL or another secured protocol, use the Secure field to enter the IP address of the proxy server that is used to manage secure connections.

Figure 19-7   Configure Microsoft Edge and other installed browsers to use one or more proxy servers

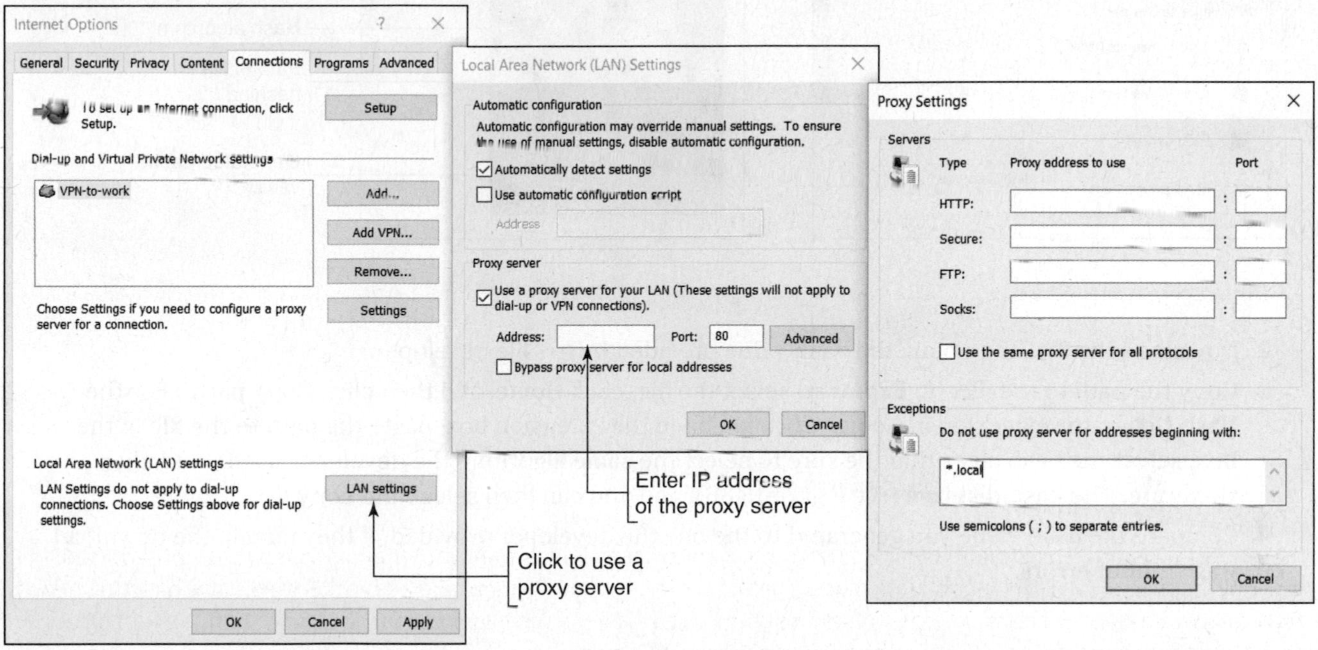

When you configure a proxy server in Internet Options, the setting applies to the entire Windows system, including Edge, Chrome, and other browsers and apps that can use a proxy server. If you want to use a proxy server just for a particular browser, know that Chrome, Edge, and Windows 10 Internet Explorer don't support customizing a proxy setting, but the Firefox browser (*mozilla.org*) can use either proxy servers set up in Internet Options for the entire system or a customized proxy configured in Firefox.

Downloading Browsers Securely

When you download a new browser, such as Firefox or Chrome, be sure to download only from a trusted source. To verify the download is genuine, the software to install it that downloads with the browser file might be digitally signed. In addition, you can verify the download is error-free by comparing hashes. A **hash**, sometimes called a checksum, is a value generated by applying a specific algorithm to a file or text string. If the browser developer provides a hash value for the file before it is downloaded, you can compare the two values. If the two hash values match, you know the download happened without errors.

19

Types of hashing algorithms are MD5, which is mostly used for small files and produces a 128-bit hash value, and SHA-1 and SHA-2, used for larger files. SHA-2 hashing produces a 224-, 256-, 384-, or 512-bit hash value. Here are the general steps to use hashing to verify that a file downloads with no errors:

1. You need a hash generator program, which can install as an extension in your browser. For example, for Google Chrome, go to the Chrome Web Store (*chrome.google.com/webstore*), and search for a hash generator. Select your generator, and add it as a Chrome extension. It creates a tab in the browser menu bar, as shown in Figure 19-8A.

Figure 19-8   (A) Hash Generator installed as a Chrome extension, and (B) Hashing a file using the SHA-256 hash algorithm

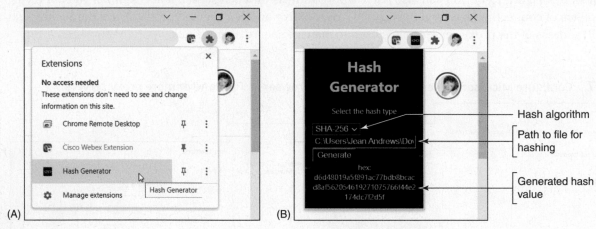

(A)   (B)

2. Download the file, and obtain the hash value provided by the file developer.
3. Copy the path to the file. (In **Explorer**, select the file, click **Home**, and then click **Copy path**.) For the Hash Generator extension in Google Chrome, open the extension box, paste the path to the file in the box, select the hash algorithm (be sure to select the same algorithm the developer used), and click **Generate**. The hash displays (see Figure 19-8B), and you can then select and copy it.
4. Compare the hash value you generated to the one the developer provided. If they match, the download was without errors.

Exam Tip ✔

The A+ Core 2 exam expects you to be able to use hashing when verifying that a browser download was successful. However, in practice, very few browser developers provide hash values for their browser installation files. Other types of software developers do routinely provide hash values to verify their downloaded files, and you can use hashing to verify these downloads. When a developer provides a hash value for a file, you might see the value displayed beside the download link on the download page. See Figure 19-9.

Figure 19-9   Developer provides a hash value for its download using the SHA-1 hash algorithm

| Download (3.3 GB) | Sha 1 hash — 0xD76AD96773615E8C504F63564AF749469CFCCD57 |
| Download (2.5 GB) | Sha 1 hash — 0x8BED436F0959E7120A44BF7C29FF0AA962BDEFC9 |

Source: 7 Labs

Create a VPN Connection

Core 2 Objectives 1.6, 4.9

A virtual private network (VPN) is often used by telecommuting employees to connect to the corporate network by way of the Internet. A VPN protects data by encrypting it from the time it leaves the remote computer until it reaches a server on the corporate network, and vice versa. The encryption technique is called a tunnel or **tunneling** (see Figure 19-10). Encryption protocols used with a VPN include SSL, TLS, OpenVPN, IKEv2/IPsec, L2TP/IPsec, SSTP, and WireGuard. Managed switches, which you learned about in the Core 1 module "Network Infrastructure and Cloud Computing," sometimes provide VPN servers embedded in their firmware so they can support VPN connections for remote users of the private network to which they belong.

Figure 19-10   A VPN connection secures all traffic between the VPN client and the VPN server on the private network

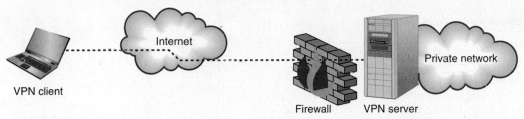

VPN client

Internet

Firewall   VPN server

Private network

A VPN can be managed by operating systems, routers, or third-party software such as OpenVPN (*openvpn.net*) or NordVPN (*nordvpn.com*). A VPN connection is a virtual connection, which means you are setting up the tunnel over an existing connection to the Internet. When creating a VPN connection on a personal computer, always follow directions given by the network administrator who hosts the VPN. The company website might provide VPN client software to download and install on your computer. For example, NordVPN provides an app to install on the client computer. Then you might be expected to double-click a configuration file to complete the VPN connection. OpenVPN uses an .ovpn file for this purpose.

Here are the general steps using Windows 10/11 to connect to a VPN:

1. You can set up a VPN connection beginning from the Internet Options dialog box or from the Network and Sharing Center. To open the Network and Sharing Center, open **Control Panel** in classic view and then click **Network and Sharing Center** (see Figure 19-11).

Figure 19-11   Network and Sharing Center

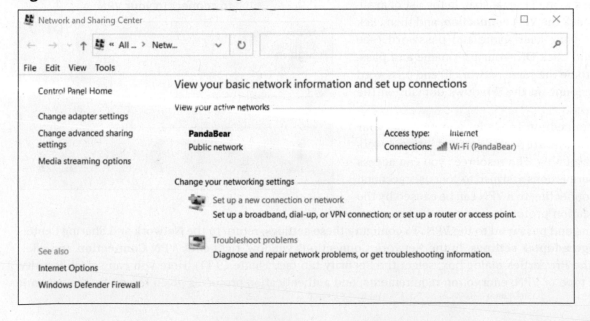

2. Click **Set up a new connection or network**. Then select **Connect to a workplace** and click **Next**.

3. In the Connect to a Workplace dialog box, click **Use my Internet connection (VPN)**. In the next dialog box, enter the IP address or domain name of the network (see Figure 19-12). Your network administrator can provide this information. Name the VPN connection, and click **Create**.

Figure 19-12   Enter connection information to the VPN

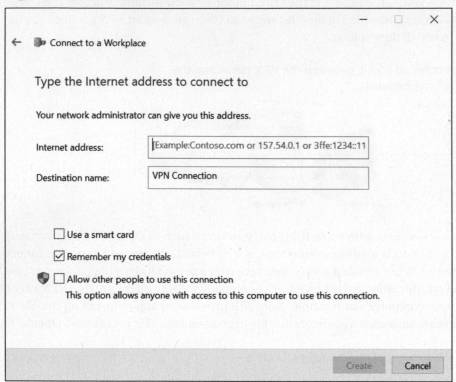

Whenever you want to use the VPN connection, click the **Network** icon in the taskbar. In the list of available networks, click the **VPN connection**, and then click **Connect**. Enter your user name and password (see Figure 19-13), and click **OK**. Your user name and password are likely to be the same network ID and password to your user account on the Windows domain on the corporate network.

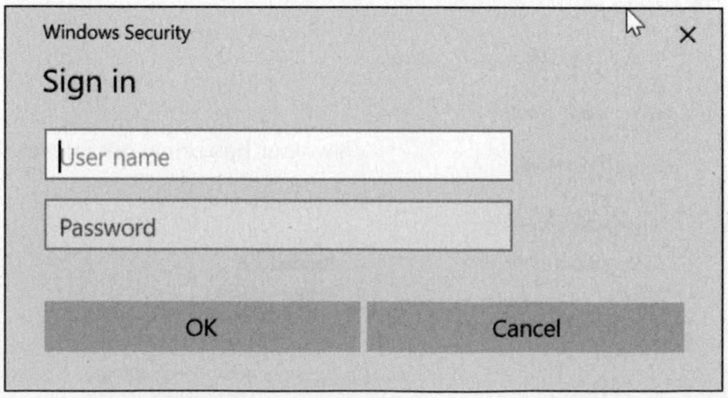

After the connection is made, you can use your browser to access the corporate secured intranet websites or other resources. The resources you can access depend on the permissions assigned to your user account.

Problems connecting to a VPN can be caused by the wrong authentication protocols being used when passing the user name and password to the VPN. To configure these settings, return to the Network and Sharing Center, and click **Change adapter settings**. In the Network Connections window, right-click **VPN Connection** and click **Properties**. In the Properties dialog box, select the **Security** tab (see Figure 19-14). Here you can select security settings for the type of VPN, encryption requirements, and authentication protocols given to you by the network administrator.

Figure 19-13   Enter your user name and password to connect to your VPN

Figure 19-14   Configure the VPN's security settings

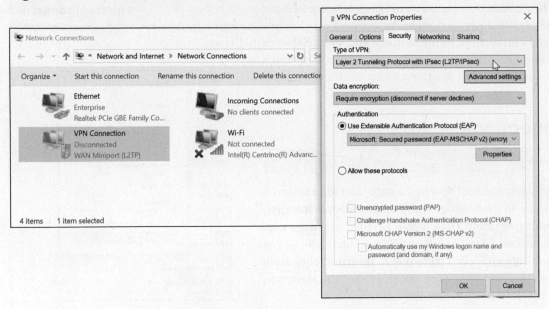

Create a WWAN Connection

Core 2 Objective 1.6

A WWAN (Wireless Wide Area Network) connection requires a contract with a cellular carrier and a USB broadband device (see Figure 19-15) or a SIM slot on a laptop. Install the SIM card in the slot on the laptop,

> **Exam Tip** ✔
>
> The A+ Core 2 exam expects you to know how to create VPN and WWAN connections and how to configure an alert when you have neared a data usage limit on a metered connection.

or install the card in the USB device and then insert the device in the USB slot. When the device installs, it automatically launches a program for you to connect to the carrier with a user name and password. Alternately, for a laptop

Figure 19-15   A USB broadband modem by Sierra Wireless

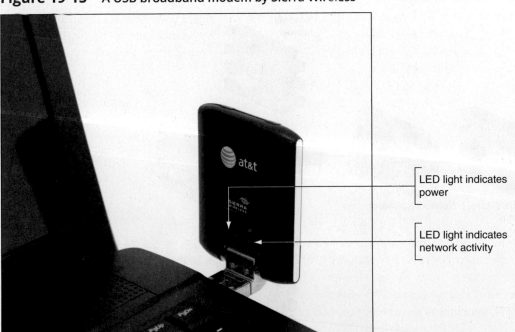

LED light indicates power

LED light indicates network activity

19

with a SIM slot, you can use the utility provided by the laptop manufacturer, such as the HP Connection Manager, to connect to the cellular network, or you can allow Windows to manage the connection. To allow Windows to manage the connection, in the Settings app, click **Network & Internet**, **Cellular**, and **Let Windows manage this connection**. You'll need the user name and password for the mobile account with the cellular carrier.

Metered Connections

 Core 2 Objective 1.6

To set an alert when you have almost reached a data limit for a metered connection in Windows 10, in the **Settings** app, click **Network & Internet**, and **Status**. On the Status page, click **Data usage**. On the Data usage window, click **Enter limit**, and set a limit in MB or GB (see Figure 19-16). For Windows 11, in the **Settings** app, click **Network & internet**, click **Data usage**, click **Enter limit**, and set your limit. After you set the alert, you will be warned when the data usage nears the limit.

Figure 19-16   Set a data limit for a metered connection

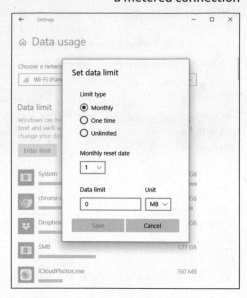

Windows Defender Firewall

 Core 2 Objectives 1.4, 1.6, 2.5

Recall from the Core 1 module "Networking Fundamentals" that a SOHO router can serve as a hardware firewall to protect its network from attack over the Internet, and the best protection from attack is layered protection (see Figure 19-17). In addition to a network hardware firewall, a large corporation might use a software firewall, also called a corporate firewall, installed on a computer that stands between the Internet and the network to protect the network. This computer has two network cards installed, and the installed software firewall filters the traffic between the two cards.

Figure 19-17   Three types of firewalls used to protect a network and individual computers on the network

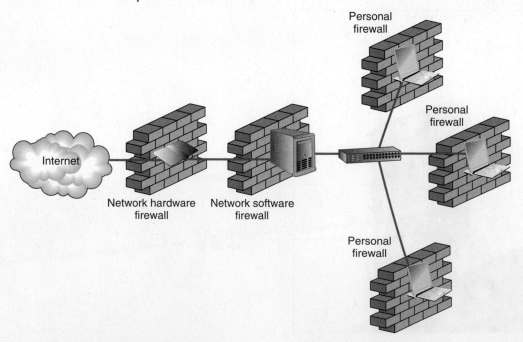

A personal firewall, also called a host firewall or application firewall, is software installed on a personal computer to protect it. A personal firewall provides redundant protection from attacks over the Internet, filters inbound traffic to protect a computer from attack from other computers on the same network, and filters outbound traffic to prevent attacks on other computers on the same network. When setting up a SOHO network or a personal computer, configure a personal firewall on each computer.

Windows Defender Firewall is a personal firewall that protects a computer from intrusion and from attacking other computers; it is automatically configured when you set up your security level for a new network connection. To set the security for a network connection, open the **Network and Sharing Center** in Control Panel, and click **Change advanced sharing settings**. In the Windows 10/11 Advanced sharing settings window (see Figure 19-18), you can choose private or public security levels and set other security options for the network connection. All these settings affect settings in Windows Defender Firewall.

Figure 19-18   Configure the security level for network connections

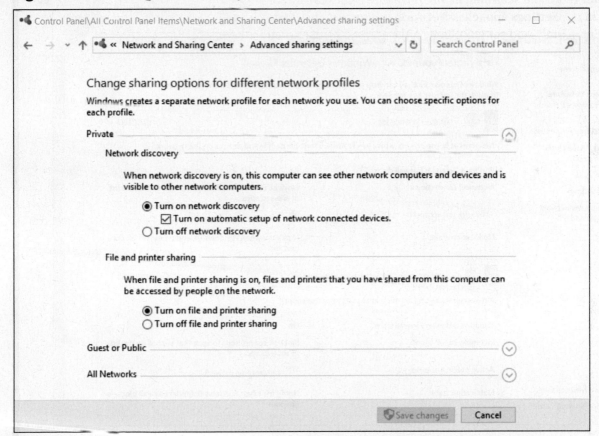

Applying Concepts

Configuring Windows Defender Firewall

Est. Time: 15 minutes
Core 2 Objective: 1.4

You can use the Windows Defender Firewall window in Windows 10/11 to configure even more firewall settings. As you work, be careful that you don't accidentally change a setting that leaves your computer open to attack. Follow these steps to find out more:

1. Open **Control Panel** in classic view, and click **Windows Defender Firewall**. See Figure 19-19.

Figure 19-19   Windows Defender Firewall shows the firewall is turned on to protect private and public network connections

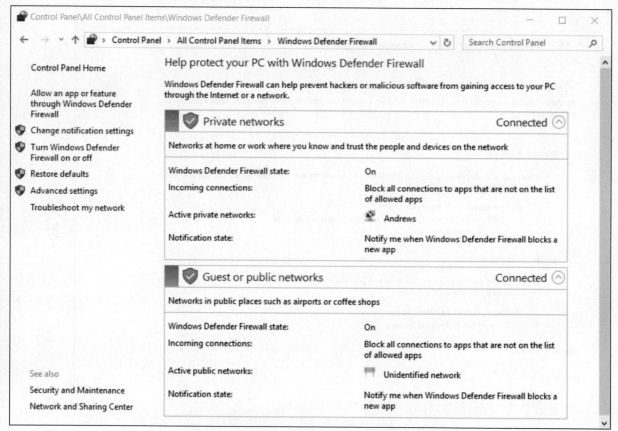

2. In general, Windows Defender Firewall works by allowing or denying network traffic on incoming or outgoing ports. Recall that a port is a number an application on the computer uses to connect to another application on the network or Internet. Here are some basic settings you can configure in Windows Defender Firewall:

    a. Use the left pane to turn Windows Defender Firewall on or off. When the firewall is disabled (not a good idea), all traffic is allowed to pass, and your computer is unprotected.

    b. When the firewall is enabled, all traffic is stopped unless you have specified an exception. To allow or deny a specific app access to the computer, click **Allow an app or feature through Windows Defender Firewall**. You can then select the app from a list of apps and decide how it can use the network connection.

c. To allow or deny all other types of traffic, not just those related to apps, click **Advanced settings**. On the Advanced Security window (see Figure 19-20), you can click Inbound Rules or Outbound Rules to create or edit an inbound or outbound rule and control traffic. A rule can specify how port numbers, TCP/IP protocols, programs, services, computers, and remote users can use the network connection. A rule can apply to public, private, and domain networks.

Figure 19-20   Customize an inbound or outbound rule to control exactly what incoming or outgoing traffic is allowed through the firewall

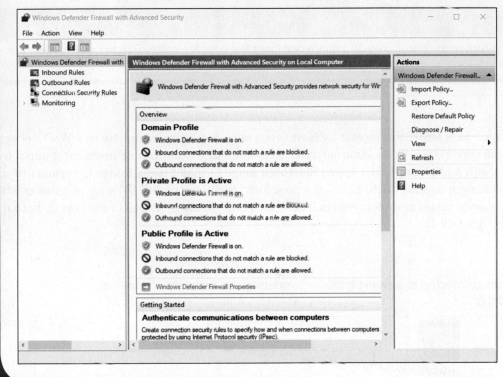

Now let's turn our attention to securing other devices, including the Internet of Things devices.

Secure Internet of Things Devices

 Core 2 Objective 2.7

For a device, such as a refrigerator or doorbell, to be considered part of the Internet of Things (IoT), the device or its controller or bridge must have an IP address. After all, a node can't connect to the Internet without an IP address. In most cases, IoT devices are monitored and controlled by wireless connections. Besides Wi-Fi and Bluetooth, Z-Wave and Zigbee are two other wireless communication protocols commonly used by smart locks, smart light bulbs, and other IoT devices. Here are the primary facts about Z-Wave and Zigbee:

- **Z-Wave** transmits around the 900 MHz band and requires less power than Wi-Fi. It has a larger range than Bluetooth, reaching a range of up to 100 meters in open air (although significantly less inside buildings).
- **Zigbee** operates in either the 2.4 GHz band or the 900 MHz band, requires less power than Wi-Fi, and generally reaches a range of about 20 meters inside, but it can reach much farther.

19

- Z-Wave and Zigbee are not compatible. Zigbee is faster than Z-Wave. Z-Wave and Zigbee both use encryption and are considered safe from hackers.
- Both Z-Wave and Zigbee devices can connect in a mesh network, which means that devices can "hop" through other devices to reach the destination device. Z-Wave and Zigbee devices are not normally assigned IP addresses unless another protocol, such as Z/IP or Zigbee IP, is working to manage TCP/IP networking.
- Typically, Zigbee and Z-Wave compete about equally for the wireless standard of choice for IoT devices in the residential market. Zigbee is the choice for large-scale commercial or industrial use because it is more robust.

Note 2

When worker honeybees return to their nest, they do a dance that looks like a zig-zag pattern. Zigbee was named after this phenomenon: *zig bee*.

Some smart devices, such as a smart thermostat by Nest (*nest.com*), can connect directly to a Wi-Fi network via an embedded Wi-Fi radio (see Figure 19-21). Alternately, devices such as a door lock or thermostat might use Bluetooth to communicate with a phone or tablet within Bluetooth range or might use a bridge to connect to the Wi-Fi network. Other devices, such as smart light bulbs or a door lock, might use Zigbee, Z-Wave, or another wireless technology that the phone or tablet does not use. Such devices require a bridge device to connect them to the Wi-Fi network, as shown in Figure 19-21.

Figure 19-21   IoT devices connected to a smart home network may use a variety of wireless technologies

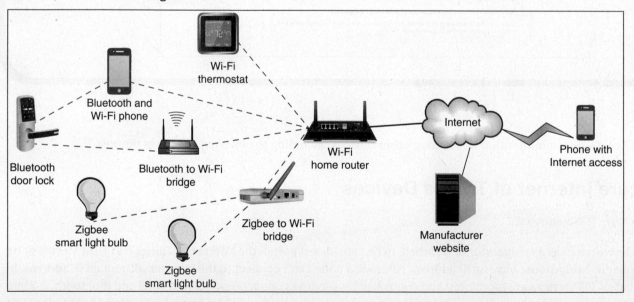

For smart devices to truly be IoT devices, you must be able to control them over the Internet. For that to happen, they must connect directly or through a bridge to a home or business Wi-Fi network that has Internet access. Notice in Figure 19-21 that the manufacturer's website is involved when managing many IoT devices. For example, Figure 19-22 shows the webpage where two exterior webcams, three interior webcams, and two thermostats by Nest (*nest.com*) can be monitored and managed from anywhere on the web.

Figure 19-22   IoT device manufacturers provide websites to manage their devices

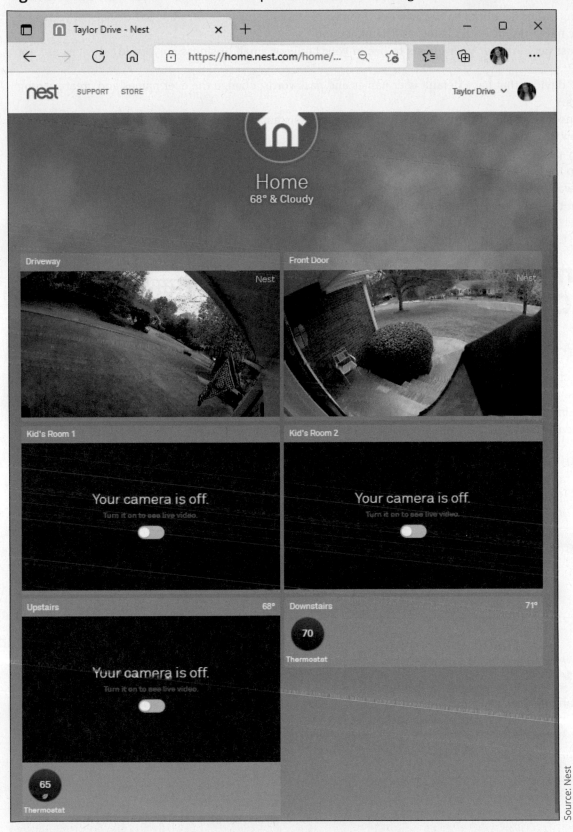

Here are some tips to secure IoT devices:

- Avoid using public networks on the Internet when you're monitoring or controlling IoT devices. If you must use public networks, consider using a VPN connection.
- Set up guest networks for your guests to use in your home or small business so your IoT devices are not exposed.
- For all IoT devices that have default user names and passwords, change the user names and create strong passwords.
- Don't connect locks and security cameras to your voice assistant. You don't want an intruder to yell through the window, "Alexa, open the front door!"
- Frequently purge the data kept by Amazon for Alexa and by Google for Google Assistant. You can use your phone app to delete.
- Keep software and firmware up to date to make sure security patches are current.
- Implement the wireless security methods for your wireless router covered next.

Securing a Multifunction Router for a SOHO Network

Core 2 Objectives 2.2, 2.5, 2.9

An IT support technician is likely to be called on to set up a small office or home office (SOHO) network. As part of setting up a small network, you need to know how to set up and secure a multipurpose router to stand between the network and the Internet. A **router** (see Figure 19-23) is a device that manages traffic between two or more networks and can help find the best path for traffic to get from one network to another.

Figure 19-23   Cisco Catalyst 8200 Series Edge Platform router is suited for small and medium-sized enterprise branch offices

Source: Cisco

Exam Tip

The A+ Core 1 and A+ Core 2 exams both require you to be able to install and configure a SOHO wired and wireless router. The A+ Core 2 exam expects you to be able to secure the router and SOHO network.

Core to Core

In the Core 1 module "Networking Fundamentals," you learned to install and set up a SOHO router. This module takes you one step further to learn how to secure the router and the local network it supports. If you have not yet read the module "Networking Fundamentals," now would be a good time to work your way through it and then turn back to this module.

A SOHO router stands between the Internet and a small local network (LAN) to connect the LAN to a network that belongs to an ISP, which connects to the Internet. See Figure 19-24.

Figure 19-24   A SOHO router stands between the local network and the IPS's network, which connects to the Internet

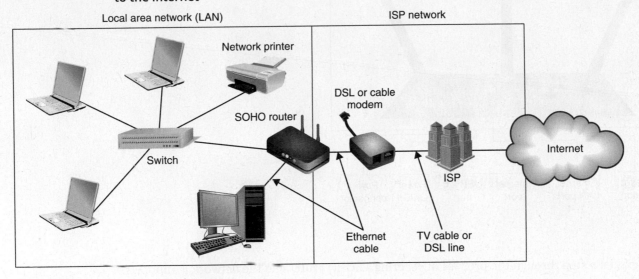

Here is a brief review of the functions of a SOHO router you learned about in the module "Networking Fundamentals":

- As a router, it stands between two networks—the ISP network and the local network—and routes traffic between the two networks.
- As a **switch**, it manages several network ports that can be connected to wired devices on the local network.
- As a DHCP server, it can provide IP addresses to computers and other devices on the local network.
- As a **wireless access point (WAP)**, it enables wireless devices to connect to the network. These wireless connections can be secured using wireless security features.
- As a firewall, it blocks unwanted traffic from the Internet and can restrict Internet access for local devices behind the firewall.
- If an external storage device, such as a USB flash drive or external hard drive, connects to the router via the USB port, the router can be used as a file server for network users.

An example of a multifunction router is the Nighthawk AC1900 by NETGEAR, shown in Figures 19-25 and 19-26. It has one Internet port (also called the WAN or wide-area-network port) to connect to the ISP by way of a modem or ONT and four ports for devices on the network. The USB port can be used to plug in a USB external hard drive for file sharing on the network. The router is also a wireless access point with multiple antennas to increase speed and range.

Figure 19-25   The NETGEAR Nighthawk AC1900 dual-band Wi-Fi Gigabit router

Source: Amazon.com, Inc.

19

Figure 19-26   Connections and ports on the back of
the NETGEAR router

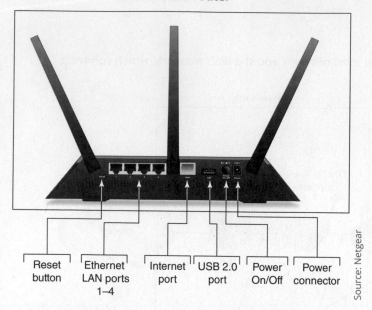

Reset
button

Ethernet
LAN ports
1–4

Internet
port

USB 2.0
port

Power
On/Off

Power
connector

Source: Netgear

Next, let's step through the process of securing a SOHO router and the network it supports.

Router Placement for Best Security

Core 2 Objective 2.9

When securing a router, consider its physical security. If the router will be used as a wireless access point, make sure it is centrally located to create the best Wi-Fi hotspot for users. For physical security in a small business, don't place the router in a public location, such as the lobby. For best security, place the router behind a locked door accessible only to authorized personnel in a location with access to network cabling. The indoor range for a Wi-Fi hotspot is up to 70 meters; this range is affected by many factors, including interference from walls, furniture, electrical equipment, and other nearby hotspots. For the best Wi-Fi strength, position your router or a stand-alone wireless access point in the center of where you want your hotspot, and know that a higher position (near the ceiling) works better than a lower position (on the floor).

For routers that have external antennas, raise the antennas to vertical positions. Plug in the router and connect network cables to devices on the local network. Connect the network cable from the ISP modem or other device to the uplink port on the router.

Basic Security Features of a Router

Core 2 Objectives 2.5, 2.9

To configure a router for the first time or change its configuration, always follow the directions of the manufacturer. You can use any computer on the network that uses a wired connection (it doesn't matter which computer) to configure the firmware on the router. You'll need the IP address of the router and the default user name and password to the router setup. To find this information, look in the router documentation or search online for your model and brand of router.

Here are the general steps for one router, the ASUS RT-AX55. The setup screens for your router may be different:

1. **Sign in to router.** Open your browser, and enter the IP address of the router in the address box. In our example, the address is 192.168.1.1. Enter the user name and password to the router firmware. The router firmware main menu screen appears.

2. **Change the default password.** One important security setting is to change the default password to the router firmware. For the ASUS router, click **Administration** in the left pane, and then click the **System** tab to change the router name and password. See Figure 19-27.

Figure 19-27 Change the password to the router firmware configuration

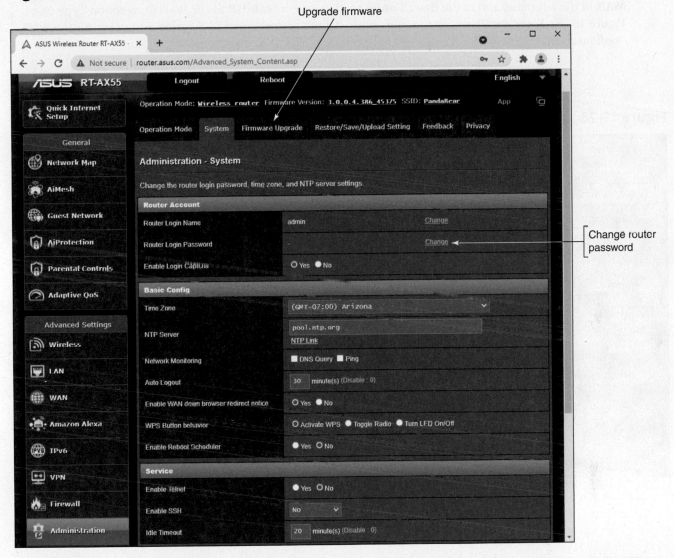

Caution

Changing the router password is especially important if the router is a wireless router. Unless you have disabled or secured the wireless access point, anyone within its range—even outside your building—can use your wireless network. If they guess the default password to the router, they can change the password to hijack your router. Also, your wireless network could be used for criminal activity.

19

3. **Update firmware.** Also notice in Figure 19-27 the Firmware Upgrade tab in the Administration group. On this tab, you can check online for a firmware update and then download and install the update. If the update fails while it is installing, you can manually download and install the ASUS Firmware Restoration utility to undo the update.

4. **Static wide-area network (WAN) IP address.** Normally, the ISP serves up a dynamic IP address, subnet mask, default gateway, and DNS server addresses to the router for its connection to the ISP network. However, if your local network publishes a website, email service, or other service on the Internet, the router will need a static IP address configuration on the WAN so computers on the Internet can find your network. For this purpose, you can lease a public IP address from the ISP or other source and configure the router to use this static IP address. To configure this connection, for the ASUS router, click **WAN** in the left pane, and in the **Basic Config** section, select **Static IP** as the WAN Connection Type (see Figure 19-28). Enter the IP address, subnet mask, default gateway, and DNS server addresses for the WAN configuration.

Figure 19-28 Configure static IP addressing for the WAN connection

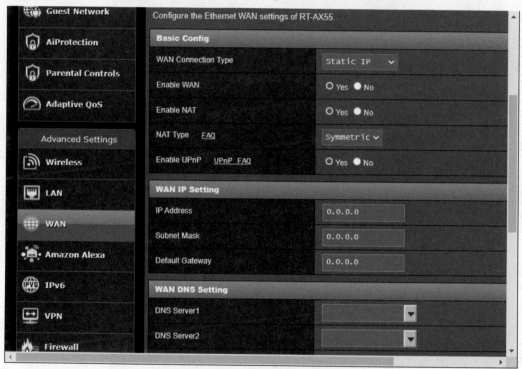

Caution !

After you make a change to the router firmware, be sure to click **Apply** at the bottom of the screen to save your changes before you move on to another firmware screen.

5. **DHCP reservations.** Recall from the module "Networking Fundamentals" that you can set the local IP address for the router, the subnet mask, and the range of IP addresses that the router's DHCP server can serve up to local hosts on the network. See Figure 19-29. In addition, you can reserve an IP address for a host on the network, such as a printer, that requires a static IP address so other hosts on the network can find it. In Figure 19-29, notice the Canon printer is assigned the static IP address 192.168.1.100. The printer was initially identified by its MAC address, also shown in the figure.

Figure 19-29   Configure the DHCP server and reserve a static IP address for a host

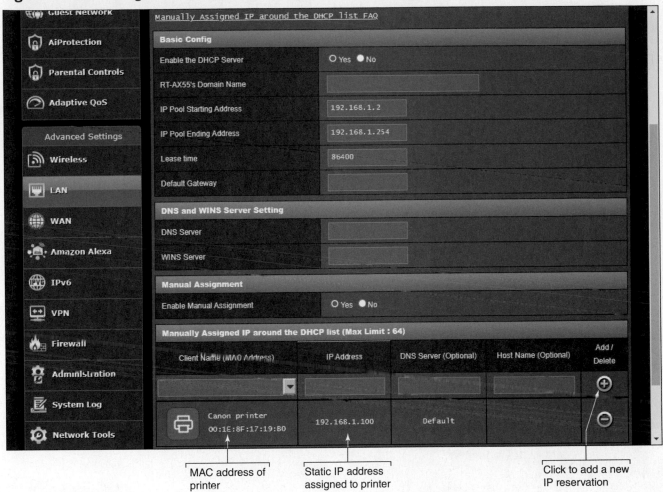

MAC address of printer

Static IP address assigned to printer

Click to add a new IP reservation

Exam Tip ✔

The A+ Core 1 and A+ Core 2 exams both require you to know about DHCP servers and how to reserve an IP address for a host that requires a static IP address on the network.

6. **Universal Plug and Play (UPnP).** Some devices—such as printers, mobile devices, and some smart home IoT appliances—might be enabled for **Universal Plug and Play (UPnP)**, which allows them to discover and communicate with each other on the network. Enable UPnP if devices on your network are having a problem establishing communication. Basically, a device can then use the router to advertise its service and automatically communicate with other devices on the network. UPnP is considered a security risk because shields between devices are dropped, which hackers might exploit. Also, UPnP increases chatter on the network and can affect performance. Therefore, use UPnP with caution. For our sample router, UPnP is enabled in the WAN group, in the Basic Config section (refer back to Figure 19-28).

7. **QoS for an application.** As you use your network and notice that one application, such as VoIP, gaming, or media streaming, is not getting the best service, you can improve its network performance using the Quality of Service (QoS) feature discussed in earlier modules. For our sample router, click **Adaptive QoS** in the left pane and the **QoS** tab in the right pane. Then turn on **Enable QoS**. See Figure 19-30. You can then use the buttons near the bottom of this window to promote a type of application or click **Customize** to further fine-tune which apps get priority with network bandwidth.

19

Figure 19-30   Configure QoS to manage which apps get priority service on the network

Now let's look at the concepts and steps to put up a firewall to control traffic to and from your network and the Internet. Then we'll look at how to set up a wireless network.

Firewall Settings

 Core 2 Objectives 2.5, 2.9

To protect resources on the network, a router's firewall can examine each message coming from the Internet and decide if the message is allowed onto the local network. When a message arrives at the router, it is directed to a particular computer (identified by its IP address) and to a particular application running on that computer (identified by a port number, also called a port or **port address**.)

Recall that most applications used on the Internet or a local network are client/server applications. Client applications—such as Microsoft Edge, Google Chrome, or Outlook—communicate with server applications such as a web server or email server. Each client and server application installed on a computer listens at a predetermined port that uniquely identifies the application on the computer.

Suppose a computer with an IP address of 138.60.30.5 is running an email server listening at port 25 and a web server application listening at port 80. If a client computer sends a request to 138.60.30.5:25 (IP address and port 25), the email server listening at that port responds. On the other hand, if a request is sent to 138.60.30.5:80 (IP address and port 80), the web server listening at port 80 responds (see Figure 19-31).

Figure 19-31   Each server application running on a computer is addressed by
a unique port number

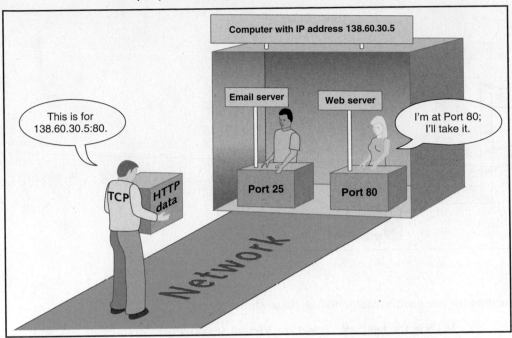

Core to Core ⬌

For a refresher on how client/server applications use port addresses and the common ports they use, see the Core 1
module "Networking Fundamentals."

Firewalls on routers offer the option to disable (close) all ports, which means that no activity initiated from
the Internet can get in. For some routers, you must explicitly disable all ports. For the ASUS router in our example,
all ports are disabled (closed) by default. You must specify exceptions to this firewall rule in order to allow unsolicited traffic from the Internet. Exceptions are allowed using port forwarding or a DMZ (described later in this
module). In addition to managing ports, you can also limit Internet traffic by filtering content. All these techniques
are discussed next.

Port Forwarding

Suppose you're hosting an Internet game or website or you want to use Remote Desktop to access your home computer from the Internet. In these situations, you need to enable (open) certain ports to certain computers so that
activity initiated from the Internet can get past your firewall. This technique, called **port forwarding** or port mapping,
means that when the firewall receives a request for communication from the Internet to the specific computer and
port, the request will be allowed and forwarded to that computer on the network. The computer is defined to the
router by its static IP address. For example, in Figure 19-32, port 80 is open and requests to port 80 are forwarded to
the web server listening at that port. This one computer on the network is the only one allowed to receive requests
at port 80.

19

Figure 19-32   Port forwarding allows a port to receive incoming
traffic to a specific host on the network

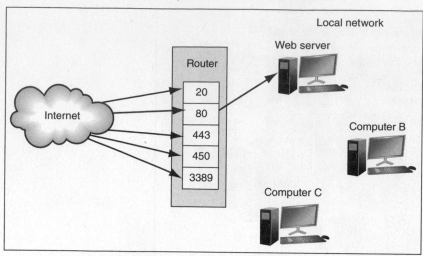

To configure port forwarding for our sample router, follow these steps:

1. In the router firmware, click **WAN** in the left pane, select the **Virtual Server/Port Forwarding** tab, and turn on **Enable Port Forwarding** (see Figure 19-33).

Figure 19-33   Enable port forwarding to allow unsolicited Internet traffic through your firewall

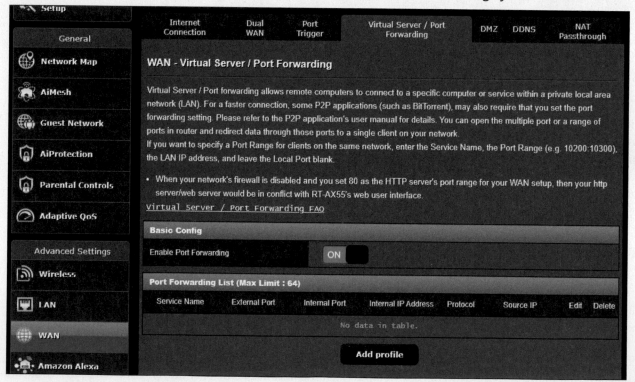

2. To add a port forwarding rule, click **Add profile**. For a web server, in the box that appears, select **HTTP (80)** as shown in Figure 19-34. The TCP protocol is selected automatically.

Figure 19-34   Select the service that is to receive traffic from the Internet

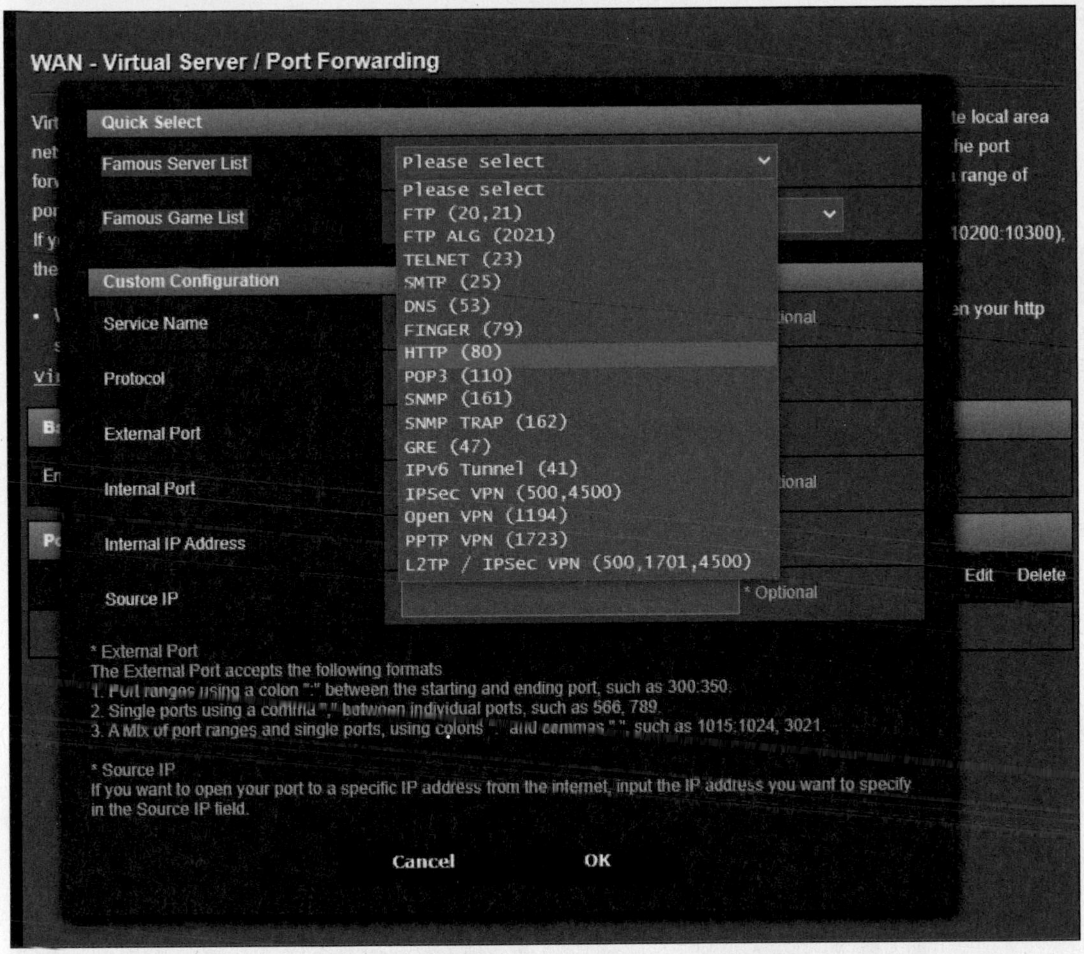

3. In the dropdown list of internal IP addresses, select the IP address of the web server. Click **OK**.

4. Be sure to test your port forwarding rule by using a device connected to the Internet but not connected to your LAN or router. Can the device reach your website?

Note 3

If you want to use a domain name rather than an IP address to access a computer on your network from the Internet, you'll need to purchase the domain name and register it in the Internet namespace to associate it with your public static IP address. Assign this public IP address to your router, which forwards requests to the web server behind the firewall. Several websites on the Internet let you lease domain names and public IP addresses; one such site is by Network Solutions (*networksolutions.com*).

Here are some tips to keep in mind when using port forwarding:

- You must have a static IP address for the WAN side of your router so people on the Internet can find you. Most ISPs will provide you a static IP address for an additional monthly fee, or you can lease one from another source and inform your ISP about it.
- For port forwarding to work, the computer on your network must have a static IP address so the router knows where to send the communication.
- Using port forwarding, your computer and network are more vulnerable because you are allowing external users directly into your private network. For better security, turn on port forwarding only when you know it's being used and be sure to disable any unused ports you don't need open.

DMZ and Screened Subnet

A **DMZ (demilitarized zone)** in networking is a computer or network that is not protected by a firewall or has limited protection. You can drop all your shields protecting a computer by putting it in a DMZ, and the firewall will no longer protect it. If you are having problems getting port forwarding to work, putting a computer in a DMZ can free it to receive any communication from the Internet. All unsolicited traffic from the Internet that the router would normally drop is forwarded to the computer designated as the DMZ server.

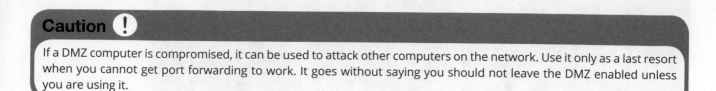

> **Caution** (!)
>
> If a DMZ computer is compromised, it can be used to attack other computers on the network. Use it only as a last resort when you cannot get port forwarding to work. It goes without saying you should not leave the DMZ enabled unless you are using it.

To set up a DMZ server for our sample router, click **WAN** in the left pane, click the **DMZ** tab, and enable the DMZ. You can then enter the static IP address of the one computer you want to put in the DMZ. See Figure 19-35.

Figure 19-35   Configure an unprotected DMZ computer exposed to the Internet

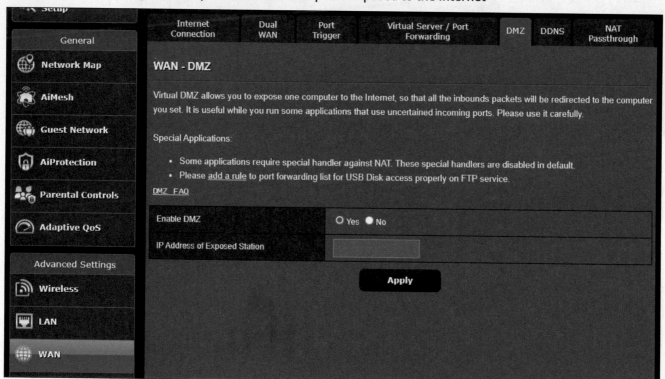

A **screened subnet** is a variation of a DMZ, and the two terms are often used interchangeably. As in the previous example, the computer labeled as computer A in Figure 19-36 is in the DMZ and is exposed to all Internet traffic. Computer B is in the screened subnet and is partially protected by a firewall provided by the exterior router, sometimes called an access router. A second router, the interior router, protects another subnet containing computer C, which is the most protected of all. In an organization, web servers and other servers that are exposed to unsolicited Internet traffic are put in the screened subnet, which offers some protection, and all other computers are put in the highly protected LAN. To reach these computers, traffic must make its way through two firewalls.

Figure 19-36   A screened subnet offers some protection for computers behind the first firewall

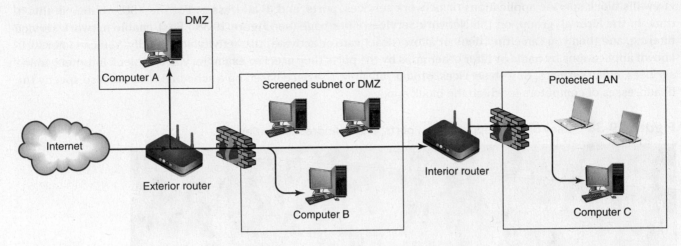

Content Filtering

Routers normally provide a way for employers or parents to limit the content that computers on the local network can access on the Internet. Filtering can apply to specific computers, users, websites, categories of websites, keywords, services, time of day, and day of the week. Criteria for filtering can draw from **blacklists** (lists of what cannot be accessed) or **whitelists** (lists of what can be accessed).

For our sample ASUS router, to manage content filtering, click **Firewall** in the left pane and the **Keyword Filter** tab. In this window, you can enable keyword filtering, and then enter a list of key words. Unsecured webpages that contain these key words will be blocked. Webpages that use HTTPS will not be filtered. See Figure 19-37.

Figure 19-37   Content filtering blocks unsecured web pages that contain specified key words

General	URL Filter	Keyword Filter	Network Services Filter

Firewall - Keyword Filter

Keyword Filter allows you to block the clients' access to webpages containing the specified keywords.

Limitations of the filtering function :

   1. Compressed webpages that use HTTP compression technology cannot be filtered. See here for more details.

   2. Https webpages cannot be filtered.

Basic Config

Enable Keyword Filter	● Enabled ○ Disabled

Keyword Filter List (Max Limit : 64)

Keyword Filter List	Add / Delete
	⊕
No data in table.	

Apply

Application and Port Security and IP Filtering

Firewalls block specific applications or network services, ports, and IP addresses. For the ASUS router, all this is done in the Firewall group, on the Network Services Filter page (see Figure 19-38.) First enable network service filtering, and then you can either deny or allow (deactivate or activate) the activity you specify. You can filter well-known applications by name or filter other apps by the ports they use. For example, you can block Internet gaming services, email services, or web services, or you can allow a service based on a schedule. You can also specify the IP addresses of computers to which the block applies.

Figure 19-38   Deny or allow applications, ports, and IP address activities

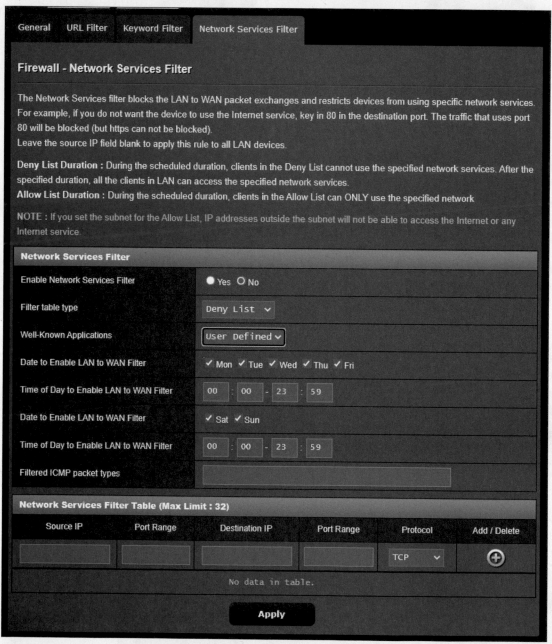

Now let's turn our attention to configuring a wireless access point provided by a router.

Securing a Wireless Network

Core 2 Objectives 2.2, 2.9

A wireless network is created by a wireless access point using the Wi-Fi standards. These Wi-Fi standards are technically the IEEE 802.11 standards—collectively known as the 802.11 a/b/g/n/ac/ax standards—and have evolved over the years. Table 19-1 lists older and current standards.

Table 19-1   Wi-Fi technologies

Standard	Maximum Speed	Description
802.11a	Up to 54 Mbps	No longer used. Used 5 GHz frequency with a range up to 50 meters.
802.11b	Up to 11 Mbps	Experiences interference from cordless phones and microwaves. Used 2.4 GHz frequency and a range up to 100 meters.
802.11g	Up to 54 Mbps	Compatible with and has replaced 802.11b. Uses 2.4 GHz frequency and range up to 100 meters.
802.11n (Wi-Fi 4)	Up to 600 Mbps	An access point can have up to four antennas to improve performance. Uses both 2.4 and 5 GHz frequencies, with an indoor range up to 70 meters and outdoor range up to 250 meters.
802.11ac (Wi-Fi 5)	Theoretically up to 7 Gbps, but currently limited to 1.3 Gbps	Supports up to eight antennas and beamforming to increase signal strength toward connected devices. Uses 5 GHz frequency only and has the same ranges as 802.11n.
802.11ax (Wi-Fi 6)	Up to 10 Gbps	This throughput is possible when using the 160 MHz channel spacing and eight antennas. (Each antenna provides one spatial stream.) Uses both 2.4 and 5 GHz frequencies and has a range a bit better than 802.11n/ac.

Wireless computers and other devices on the wireless LAN (WLAN) must support the latest wireless standard for that standard to be used. If they do not, the connection uses the latest standard supported by both the WAP and the client. Figure 19-39 shows a wireless adapter that has two antennas and supports the 802.11ax standard. Most new adapters, wireless computers, and mobile devices support 802.11ax and are backward compatible with older standards.

Now let's look at the various features and settings of a wireless access point needed to secure the wireless network.

Figure 19-39   A wireless network adapter with two antennas supports 802.11a/b/g/n/ac/ax Wi-Fi standards

Source: Amazon.com, Inc.

Note 4

When configuring your wireless access point, it's important you are connected to the router using a wired connection. If you change a wireless setting and you are connected wirelessly, your wireless connection will be dropped immediately, and you will not be able to continue configuring the router until you connect again.

19

Require a Security Key

The most common and effective method of securing a wireless network is to require a security key before a client can connect to the network. By default, a network that uses a security key encrypts data traversing the network. Use the router firmware to set the security key. For best security, enter a security key that is different from the password for the router's firmware utility.

Note 5

When it comes to making secure passwords and passphrases, longer is better and randomness is crucial. To make the strongest passphrase or security key, use a random group of numbers, uppercase and lowercase letters and, if allowed, at least one symbol. At the bare minimum, use at least eight characters in the passphrase.

For our sample router, to set the security keys, click **Wireless** in the left pane. On the **General** tab, notice the key must be set for each Wi-Fi band, 2.4 GHz and 5 GHz (see Figure 19-40). Here, the security key is called the WPA Pre-Shared Key. Click **Apply** to save your changes.

Figure 19-40   Configure the router's wireless access point

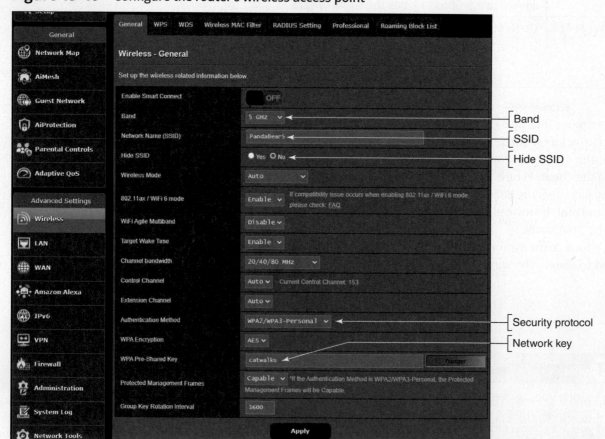

Change the Default SSID and Disable SSID Broadcasting

The **Service Set Identifier (SSID)** is the name of a wireless network. Referring back to Figure 19-40, you can see that each frequency band has its own SSID, and you can change that name. Each band is its own wireless network, which is connected by the access point (router) to the local wired network. When you assign an SSID that includes 2.4 or 5 in the name (PandaBear5 in Figure 19-40), a user can more easily select the network using the 5 GHz band in order to get the faster speeds.

Also notice in Figure 19-40 the option to Hide SSID, which disables SSID broadcasting. Doing so causes the wireless network to appear as Unnamed or Unknown Network on an end user's device. When a user selects this network, they are given the opportunity to enter the SSID. If they don't enter the name correctly, they will not be able to connect. This security method is not considered strong because software can be used to discover an SSID that is not being broadcast.

Select Channels for the WLAN

A **channel** is a specific radio frequency within a broader frequency. For example, two channels in the 2.4 GHz band are 2.412 GHz and 2.437 GHz. In the United States, eleven channels are available for wireless communication in the 2.4 GHz band. In order to avoid channel overlap, however, devices in the 2.4 GHz band select channels 1, 6, or 11, resulting in three nonoverlapping channels available for use. The 5 GHz band offers up to 24 nonoverlapping channels in the United States, but some of those channels are restricted in certain areas, such as near an airport. For most networks, you can allow auto channel selection so the device scans for the least busy channel. However, if you are trying to solve a problem with interference from a nearby wireless network, you can manually set each network to a different channel and make the channels far apart to reduce interference. For example, in the 2.4 GHz band, set the network on one WAP to channel 1 and set a nearby WAP's network to channel 11. For our sample router, the drop-down menu for channel selection in the 2.4 GHz band is shown in Figure 19-41. To allow the router to automatically select the least busy channel, select **Auto**.

Figure 19-41   Select Auto or a specific channel in the
2.4 GHz range

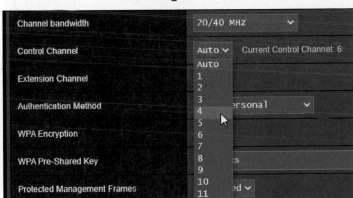

Disable Guest Access

A SOHO router is likely to offer the option to set up guest networks. A guest network provides access to the Internet but does not allow access to the local network. For our sample router, click **Guest Network** in the left pane to see the setup shown in Figure 19-42. Using this window, you can configure up to three 2.4 GHz and three 5 GHz guest networks. Best security practices recommend you not allow guest access and disable these guest networks.

19

Figure 19-42 Configure up to six guest networks to allow Internet access but not access to the LAN

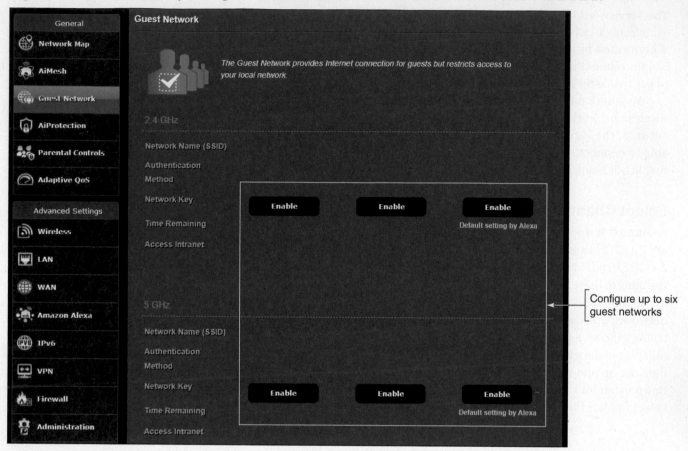

Set Encryption

When you set a security key, routers by default encrypt wireless transmissions. You can change the encryption protocols used or disable encryption. (Encrypting transmissions increases security but slows down the network; disabling encryption can improve performance and might be appropriate when you are not concerned about transmissions being hacked.) The three main security standards for 802.11 wireless networks are as follows:

- **WPA. WPA (Wi-Fi Protected Access)** is an older encryption standard and typically uses **TKIP (Temporal Key Integrity Protocol**, pronounced "tee-kip") for encryption. TKIP generates a different key for every transmission; however, the encryption algorithm used for its calculations is no longer considered secure.
- **WPA2. WPA2 (Wi-Fi Protected Access 2)** typically uses **AES (Advanced Encryption Standard)** for encryption, which provides faster and more secure encryption than TKIP. All wireless devices sold today support the WPA2 standard.
- **WPA3. WPA3 (Wi-Fi Protected Access 3)** offers better encryption and additional features over WPA2. For example, you can securely configure a nearby wireless device, such as a wireless webcam or motion sensor, over the wireless network, eliminating the need to connect the device with a wired connection to configure it. Another feature is Individual Data Encryption, which allows a secure connection for your laptop or other wireless device over a public, unsecured Wi-Fi network.

To configure Wi-Fi encryption for our sample router, first know that each band (2.4 GHz and 5 GHz) is assigned its own encryption type. For the most flexibility, set both bands to the highest encryption standards the router and wireless devices support. By selecting WPA2/WPA3-Personal (see Figure 19-43), a wireless connection will use WPA3 unless an older device does not support it, in which case the connection reverts to WPA2 encryption. Click **Apply** to save your changes.

Figure 19-43 Select the highest encryption
standards the network supports

Note 6

Looking back at Figure 19-40, you can see that WPA2/WPA3-Personal is selected as the authentication method. A Personal method relies on a passphrase shared with all network users, which could be compromised. An Enterprise method relies on an authentication server to manage authenticating all users to the network. Very few SOHO networks, however, have the resources to set up and host an authentication server. In most cases, when setting up a SOHO network, your most secure option is Personal.

Exam Tip ✔

The A+ Core 2 exam may give you a scenario that requires you to install and configure a wireless network—including Wi-Fi 802.11standards, frequencies, channels (1–11)—and encryption protocols including WPA2, WPA3, TKIP encryption, and AES encryption.

Authentication Services in an Enterprise

If you are called on to configure a SOHO router in an enterprise environment, you might need to configure the security protocol with an Enterprise standard, for example, WPA3-Enterprise. In this situation, authentication to the wireless network is done using an authentication server in cooperation with Active Directory on a Windows domain. Three well-known security protocols to provide authentication services for large networks are RADIUS, TACACS+, and Kerberos:

- **RADIUS (Remote Access Dial-In User Service)** protocol was originally designed just for authentication, but it has evolved to include authentication, authorization, and accounting (AAA) services. It works with dial-up, wired and wireless networking, and VPNs. RADIUS uses the UDP protocol and port 1812 for authentication and authorization and port 1813 for accounting.
- **TACACS+ (Terminal Access Controller Access Control System Plus)** is a proprietary Cisco protocol for AAA services, specifically designed for network administrators and technicians to remotely connect to a network to configure and manage Cisco network devices, such as routers, switches, and firewalls. TACACS+ uses TCP protocol and port 49.
- **Kerberos** is strictly an authentication protocol and is used when a Windows computer authenticates a user to Active Directory in a Windows domain. It uses AES encryption, UDP protocol, and port 88. Kerberos supports two-factor authentication, whereas RADIUS and TACACS+ do not.

19

RADIUS, TACACS+, and Kerberos can each authenticate a user to resources on a network using an authentication server, and that server will most likely turn to Active Directory to authenticate user credentials. The key differences among the three protocols are when and where they are used:

- RADIUS and TACACS+ extend authentication out to non-Windows devices—such as a switch, router, or WAP—to connect a device to the network.
- For a wireless network, RADIUS or TACACS+ is used to authenticate via an authentication server rather than using a network security key.
- TACACS+ is used on Cisco switches, routers, and other networking devices. RADIUS is used on non-Cisco devices, such as an ASUS wireless router.
- Kerberos is used on Windows computers already connected to the network to authenticate to a Windows domain.

Notice in Figure 19-44 that either the WAP using RADIUS or the switch using TACACS+ acts as the client, which is responsible for querying the authentication server before allowing the device on the network. The authentication server interfaces with Active Directory as part of the authentication process. (Cisco calls its TACACS+ server the Identify Service Engine server or ISE server.)

Figure 19-44   Authentication services provided by (A) RADIUS, (B) TACACS+, and (C) Kerberos

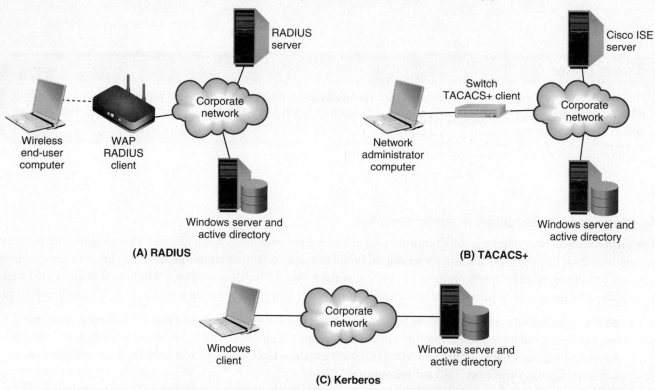

To configure RADIUS for wireless authentication using our sample ASUS router, click **Wireless** in the left pane, and click the **RADIUS Setting** tab. See Figure 19-45. Select the wireless band, and enter the IP address of the RADIUS authentication server and the Connection Secret, which is used to generate encrypted messages to the server. Notice in the figure the RADIUS port on the server is 1812, which is the default RADIUS port.

Figure 19-45   Configure RADIUS for network authentication in an enterprise

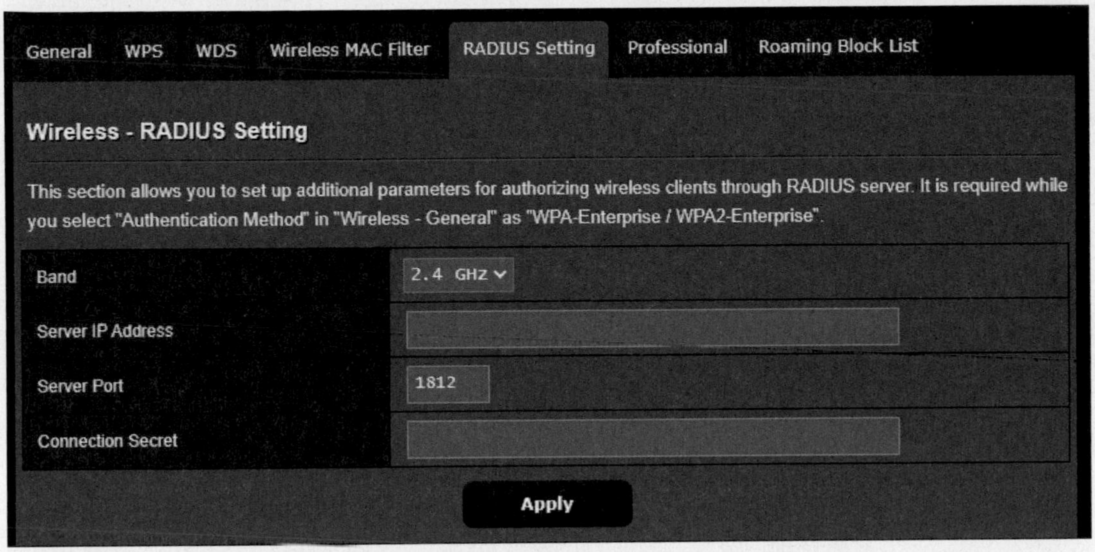

General	WPS	WDS	Wireless MAC Filter	RADIUS Setting	Professional	Roaming Block List

Wireless - RADIUS Setting

This section allows you to set up additional parameters for authorizing wireless clients through RADIUS server. It is required while you select "Authentication Method" in "Wireless - General" as "WPA-Enterprise / WPA2-Enterprise".

Band	2.4 GHZ ⌄
Server IP Address	
Server Port	1812
Connection Secret	

Apply

Note 7

Often, a basic WAP isn't smart enough to act as the RADIUS or TACACS+ client. In an enterprise environment, many WAPs are connected to a wireless controller device in the data closet, which in turn does the work of managing client requests to the RADIUS or ISE server.

Exam Tip ✔

The A+ Core 2 exam expects you to be able to compare and contrast RADIUS, TACACS+, and Kerberos, including identifying which authentication protocol supports multifactor authentication.

Using Remote Access Technologies

Core 2 Objective 4.9

An IT technician often finds it necessary to remotely access systems they support and use. You might need to remotely transfer files, access your Windows desktop or a corporate server, access monitoring and management software that you are using to oversee critical systems, assist users by accessing their systems with screen sharing, or support corporate video conferencing.

Several methods and tools to help with these tasks have already been covered in previous modules. In this section of this module, we summarize tools already covered, look at some new ones, and consider security issues when using these tools. Let's begin with file transfers.

File Transfers over the Internet

Core 2 Objective 4.9

In previous modules, you learned about FTP, the tried-and-true tool to transfer files over a network or the Internet. FTP software is free and easy to install, but it has some limitations. Services on the web that have slowly replaced FTP as the file transfer tool of choice include OneDrive (*onedrive.live.com*), Dropbox (*dropbox.com*), Box (*box.com*), Google Drive (*drive.google.com*), and other web-based solutions. Figure 19-46 shows OneDrive and Dropbox embedded in Explorer in Windows 10.

Figure 19-46   The author team keeps files for this text in Dropbox

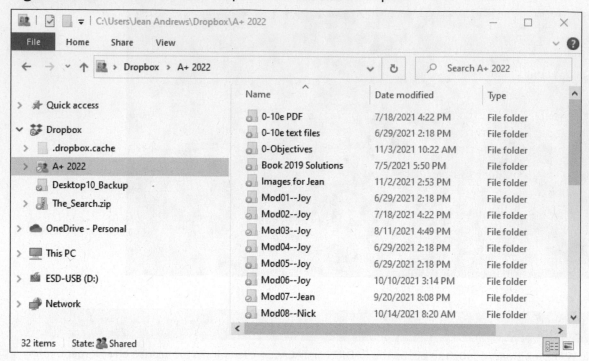

Comparing Dropbox to FTP, Dropbox is faster, more secure, and easier to use. FTP uses the FTP protocol and incoming and outgoing ports 20 and 21. With FTP, several commands pass back and forth before a file can be transferred, causing a slower transfer process. Dropbox uses a single HTTPS connection for both uploads and downloads, and it can compress files before transferring. In addition, Dropbox is able to upload only the parts of a file (call the diff or difference) that have changed since the last upload, and it can upload a file in segments to multiple IP addresses, further speeding up the process.

Windows 10/11 Remote Control Tools

Core 2 Objective 4.9

Windows 10/11 offers two solutions to remotely access a computer: Remote Desktop Connection and Microsoft Remote Assistance. Both tools use the RDP protocol and port 3389 and require a little setup to use. Let's see how each works.

Remote Desktop Connection (RDC)

Remote Desktop Connection (RDC), commonly called Remote Desktop, gives a user access to a Windows desktop from anywhere on the Internet. As a software developer, I find Remote Desktop extremely useful when I work from a remote location (my home office) and need to access a corporate network to support software on that network. Using the Internet, I can access a file server on these secured networks to make my software changes. Remote Desktop is easy to use and relatively safe for the corporate network. To use Remote Desktop, the computer you want to remotely access (the server) must be running business or professional editions of Windows 10/11, but the computer you're using to access it (the client) can be running any version of Windows.

Exam Tip ✔

The A+ Core 2 exam expects you to know how to use Remote Desktop and Remote Assistance and to know which port and protocol they use and which tool is appropriate in a given scenario.

Applying Concepts

Configuring Remote Desktop on Two Computers

Est. Time: 30 minutes
Core 2 Objective: 4.9

The host or server computer is the computer that serves up Remote Desktop to client computers that can "remote in to" (remotely access) the server. To prepare your host computer, you need to configure it for static IP addressing and then configure the Remote Desktop service. Here are the steps needed:

1. Configure the computer for static IP addressing.

Core to Core

How to assign a static IP address is covered in the Core 1 module "Networking Fundamentals."

Figure 19-47   Configure a computer to run the Remote Desktop service

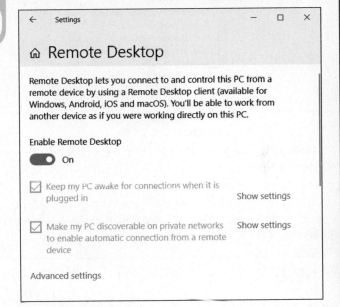

2. If your computer is behind a firewall, configure the router for port forwarding and allow incoming traffic on port 3389. Forward that traffic to the IP address of your desktop computer.

3. To turn on the Remote Desktop service, right-click **Start** and click **System**. In the About window, click **Remote desktop**. In the Remote Desktop window (see Figure 19-47), enable Remote Desktop. You can also control other Remote Desktop settings from this window.

Note 8

Server applications such as Remote Desktop listen for network activity from clients. If you want these server applications to be available at all times, you can set your network adapter properties to Wake-on-LAN, which you learned about in the Core 1 module "Networking Fundamentals."

4. To verify that Windows Defender Firewall is set to allow Remote Desktop activity on this computer, open **Control Panel** in classic view, and click **Windows Defender Firewall**. In the Windows Defender Firewall window, click **Allow an app or feature through Windows Defender Firewall**.

5. The Allowed apps window appears. Scroll down to Remote Desktop, and adjust the settings as needed (see Figure 19-48). Click **OK** to apply any changes. You are now ready to test Remote Desktop.

(continues)

19

Applying Concepts Continued

Figure 19-48   Allow Remote Desktop communication through Windows Defender Firewall on your local computer

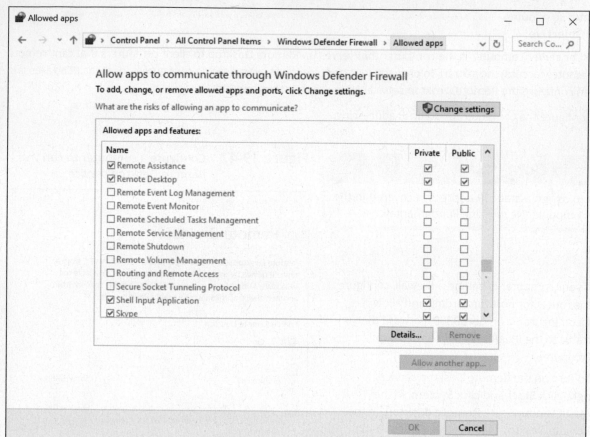

Try to use Remote Desktop from another computer somewhere on your local network, and make sure it works before testing the Remote Desktop connection from the Internet. On the client computer, you can start Remote Desktop to remote in to your host computer by using **Microsoft Terminal Services Client (mstsc.exe)**.

Follow these steps to use Remote Desktop:

1. Sign in to Windows with an administrator account. Enter **mstsc** in the Windows 10/11 search box. The Remote Desktop Connection box opens (see Figure 19-49).

2. Enter the IP address or the host name of the computer to which you want to connect. If you decide to use a host name, begin the name with two backslashes, as in *CompanyFileServer*.

Figure 19-49   The IP address of the remote computer can be used to connect to it

Note 9

If you have trouble using the host name to make a Remote Desktop connection on a local network, try entering the host name and IP address of the remote computer in the hosts file in the C:\Windows\System32\drivers\etc folder of the client computer.

3. If you plan to transfer files from one computer to the other, click **Show Options**, and then click the **Local Resources** tab, as shown on the left side of Figure 19-50. Click **More** to see the dialog box on the right side of the figure. Check **Drives** and click **OK**. Click **Connect** to make the connection. If a warning box appears, click **Connect** again. If another warning box appears, click **Yes**.

Figure 19-50   Allow drives and other devices to be shared using the Remote Desktop Connection

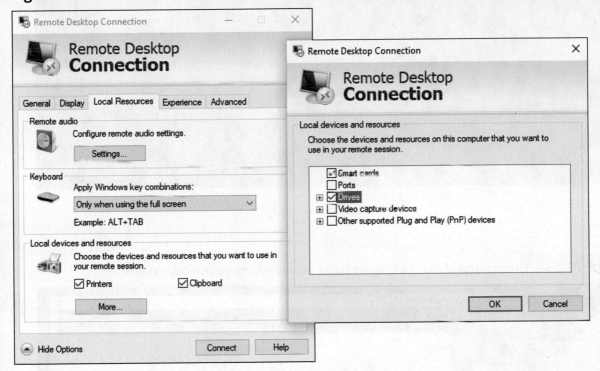

4. A Windows Security dialog box is displayed by the remote computer (see Figure 19-51). Sign in with an administrator user name and password for the remote computer. If a warning box reports that the remote computer might not be secure, click **Yes** to continue the connection.

5. The desktop of the remote computer appears with a toolbar at the top of the screen, as shown in Figure 19-52. Click **Restore Down** to show both the remote desktop and the local desktop on the same screen, as shown in Figure 19-53.

Figure 19-51   Enter your user name and password on the remote computer

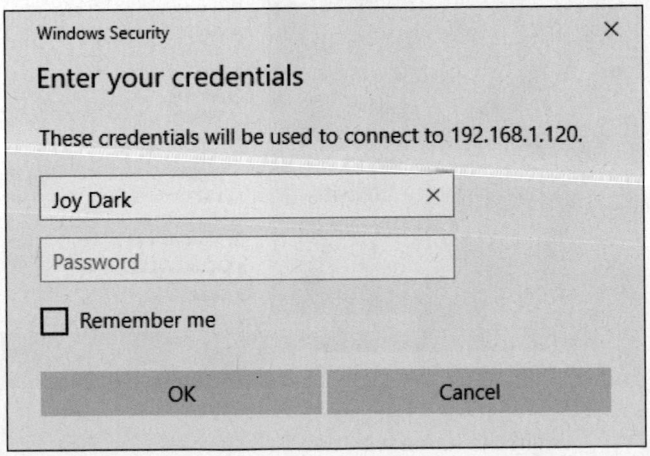

19

(continues)

Applying Concepts Continued

Figure 19-52   The RDC connection toolbar is pinned to the top of the window showing the remote computer's screen

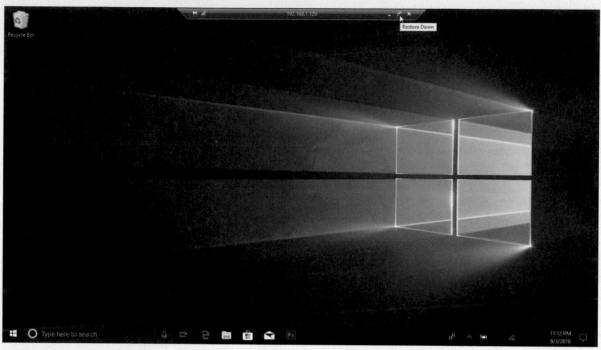

Figure 19-53   The desktop of the remote computer is available on your local computer

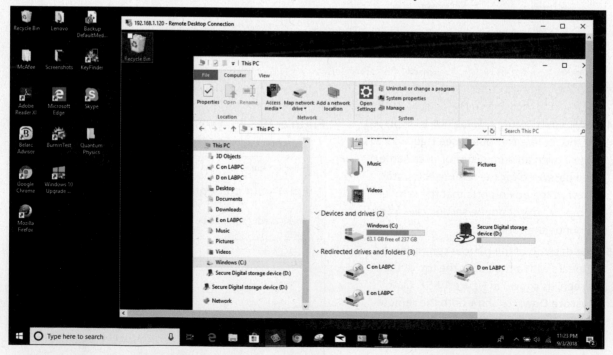

> ### Note 10
>
> When a remote desktop connection is made, the user sitting at the remote computer will see it return to the Windows sign-on screen.

6. When you click in the remote desktop's window, you can work with the remote computer just as if you were sitting in front of it, except response time is slower. To move files back and forth between computers, use Explorer on the remote computer. Files on your local computer and on the remote computer will appear in the Explorer window on the remote computer. For example, you can see drive C: on each computer labeled in Figure 19-53. To close the connection to the remote computer, sign out from the remote computer or close the desktop window.

> ### Note 11
>
> Even though Windows normally allows more than one user to be signed in at the same time, this is not the case with Remote Desktop. When a Remote Desktop session is open, all local users on the remote computer must sign out after receiving a warning.

Is your host computer as safe as it was before you set it to serve up Remote Desktop and enabled port forwarding to it? Actually, no, because a port has been opened, so take this into account when you decide to use Remote Desktop.

Microsoft Remote Assistance (MSRA)

Core 2 Objective 4.9

Microsoft Remote Assistance (MSRA) differs from Remote Desktop in that a user on the server computer can remain signed in during the remote session, retains control of the session, and can see the screen. This is helpful when troubleshooting problems on a computer. The user who needs your help sends you an invitation by email or chat to connect to their computer using Remote Assistance. When you respond to the invitation, you can see the user's desktop just as they see it; if the user gives you permission, you can take control of their computer to change settings or do whatever else is needed to fix their problem or show them how to perform a task. Think of Remote Assistance as a way to provide virtual desk-side support.

There are several ways to initiate a Remote Assistance session. The first method listed is the most reliable:

- The user saves an invitation file and then sends that file to the technician. The file can be sent by any method, including email, chat, or posting to a shared folder on the network.
- The user can send an automated email through the Remote Assistance app. This option only works if the system is configured with a compatible email program.
- The user can use Easy Connect, which is the easiest method to start a Remote Assistance connection, but it only works if both computers used for the connection are using Windows. Also know that some routers don't support the Peer Name Resolution Protocol (PNRP), which is the protocol Easy Connect uses to establish a Remote Assistance connection.
- The technician can initiate a session. This method is the most difficult to use; it requires that Group Policies be applied on the technician's computer.

Note 12

Easy Connect is the easiest method for the user when initiating a Remote Assistance connection, but it can be the most difficult for the technician to set up. If Easy Connect is grayed out when starting a session, chances are that the PNRP service might be down. To start the service, enter the `services.msc` command to open the Services console (see Figure 19-54). Select **Peer Name Resolution Protocol**, and click **Start**.

Figure 19-54   Use the Services console to start a service

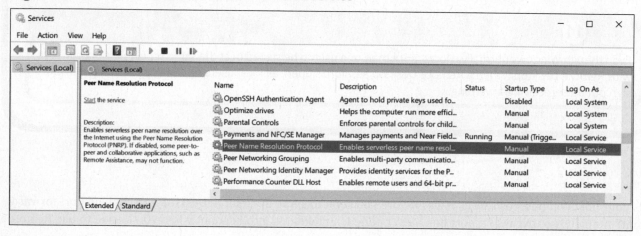

To initiate a Remote Assistance connection when the user sends an invitation to the technician, follow these steps:

1. To allow Remote Assistance sessions on the user's computer, called the host computer, right-click **Start**, and click **System**. In the About window, click **System protection**. In the System Properties dialog box, click the **Remote** tab. See Figure 19-55.

2. In the Remote Assistance area, check **Allow Remote Assistance connections to this computer**, and then click **OK**.

3. In the search box, type **remote assistance**, and then click **Invite someone to connect to your PC and help you, or offer to help someone else**. The Windows Remote Assistance box appears, as shown in Figure 19-56.

Figure 19-55   Configure a computer to allow Remote Assistance connections

System Properties

Computer Name | Hardware | Advanced | System Protection | Remote

Remote Assistance

☑ Allow Remote Assistance connections to this computer

What happens when I enable Remote Assistance?

Advanced...

Remote Desktop

Choose an option, and then specify who can connect.

○ Don't allow remote connections to this computer

● Allow remote connections to this computer

☑ Allow connections only from computers running Remote Desktop with Network Level Authentication (recommended)

Help me choose   Select Users...

OK   Cancel   Apply

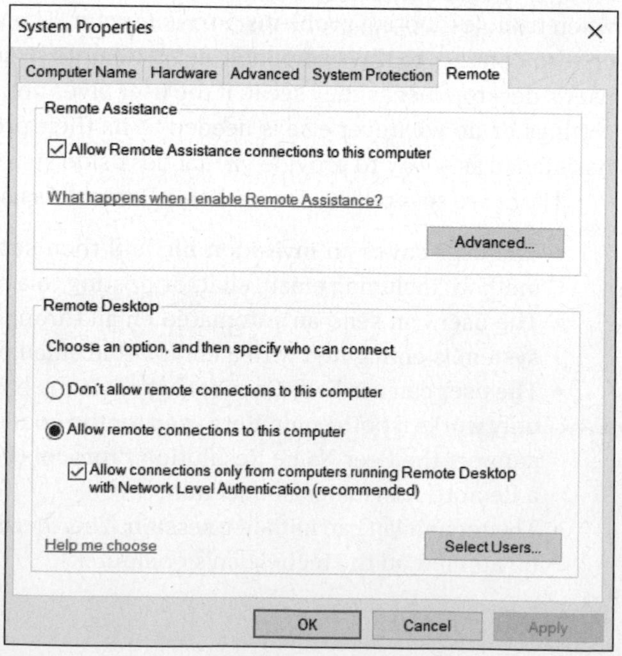

Figure 19-56   Create or respond to an invitation to connect

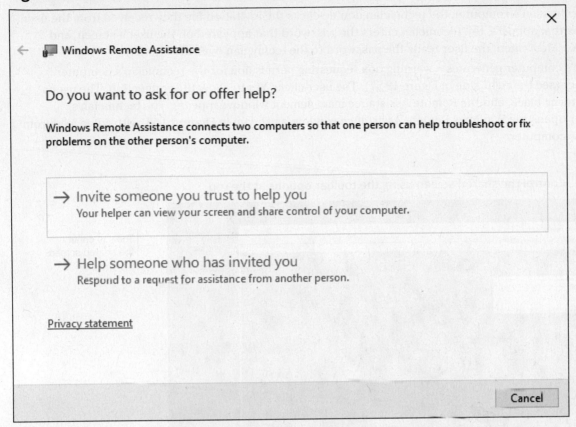

4. Click **Invite someone you trust to help you**, and then click **Save this invitation as a file**. Point to a location to save the file, and click **Save**. Remote Assistance provides a password for the user to give the technician in order to create the connection (see the left side of Figure 19-57). The user can send the invitation file to the technician as an email attachment or by other means.

Figure 19-57   The user's computer shows a password the technician must
enter to connect Remote Assistance

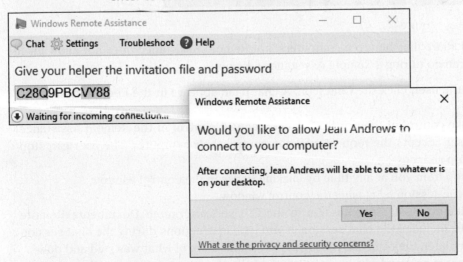

The technician can respond to the invitation into Remote Assistance as follows:

1. On the technician's computer, the technician double-clicks the invitation file they received from the user. In the box that appears, the technician enters the password that appeared on the user's screen, and clicks **OK**. (Most often, the user reads the password to the technician over the phone.)

2. The user's computer generates a warning box requesting permission for the technician's computer to connect (see the right side of Figure 19-57). The user clicks **Yes** to allow the connection. The user's desktop turns black, and the Remote Assistance management window appears. The technician's computer opens the Windows Remote Assistance window, as shown in Figure 19-58, with a live feed from the user's computer.

Figure 19-58   Control the shared screen using the toolbar options at the top

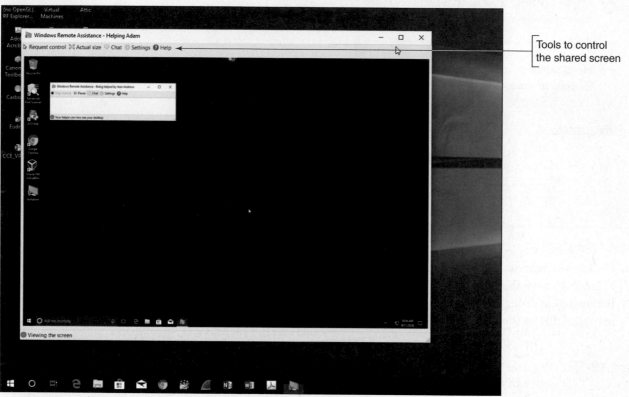

Tools to control the shared screen

With Remote Desktop, you can share files between computers, but Remote Assistance does not allow for file sharing. Here are some things you can do during a Remote Assistance session:

- To open a chat session with the user, click the **Chat** icon. A chat pane appears in the Remote Assistance window on both desktops.
- To ask the user if you can take control of their desktop, click **Request control** in the Remote Assistance control window. When the user accepts the request, you can control their computer. The user can stop sharing control by clicking **Stop sharing**.
- The user can hide their desktop from you at any time by clicking **Pause** in the control window.
- Either of you can disconnect the session by closing the control window.
- A log file is kept of every Remote Assistance session in the C:\Users*username*\Documents\Remote Assistance Logs folder. The file includes the chat session. If you type instructions during the chat session that will be helpful for the user later, they can use the log file to remind them of what was said and done.
- If an invitation created by a user is not used within six hours, the invitation expires. This time frame can be changed by clicking **Advanced** in the Remote Assistance section on the Remote tab of the System Properties dialog box.

If you have problems making the connection, consider the following:

1. Windows Defender Firewall on the user's computer might be blocking Remote Assistance. Verify that Remote Assistance is checked as an exception to blocked apps in the Windows Defender Firewall window.
2. If you are outside the user's local network, the hardware firewall protecting their network might be blocking Remote Assistance. Verify that port forwarding on that hardware firewall is enabled for Remote Assistance. Remote Assistance uses port 3389, the same RDP port used by Remote Desktop.

Note 13

Because Remote Assistance can be difficult to set up, Windows 10/11 offers Quick Assist, which is more universally compatible with existing network hardware configurations. For Quick Assist to work, both computers must be running Windows 10 or Windows 11, the technician providing assistance must have a Microsoft account, and the person receiving the connection must agree to it by entering a code generated by the technician's client computer.

Virtual Network Computing (VNC)

Core 2 Objective 4.9

Virtual Network Computing (VNC) is client/server software used to remotely control a computer, file transfers, and screen sharing. VNC Connect (*realvnc.com*) by RealVNC is one example of this type of software. See Figure 19-59. It can be used for virtual desktop support and unattended access to a remote computer. When used for virtual

Figure 19-59 A Mac computer uses a VNC viewer to remotely control a Windows 10 computer acting as the VNC server

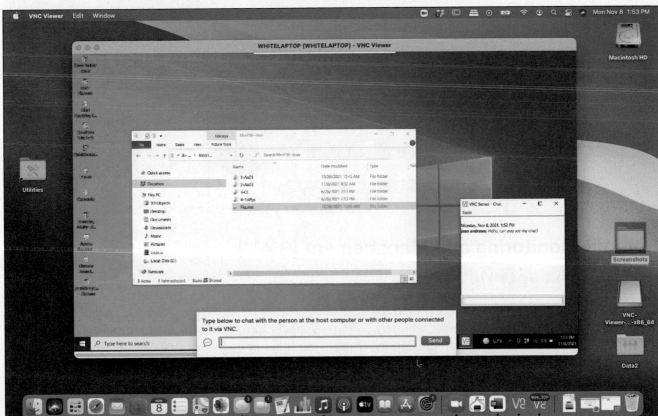

19

desktop support, the person being helped can watch what the technician does with their computer and interact as needed. VNC uses port 5901 and the Remote Framebuffer Protocol, which provides a simple way of communicating where images of the desktop and keystrokes are passed between client and server. The server side of VNC—the computer being controlled—can be installed in Windows, Linux, and macOS. The client side of VNC, called the viewer, controls the other computer and can be installed in Windows, UNIX, Linux, macOS, Android, and iOS.

Weaknesses of VNC include the large volume of screen data transferred during a session and poor encryption that can be hacked. To secure a VNC session, you can use a VPN connection, which encrypts the session end to end. Alternately, for Linux systems, you can use an SSH tunnel to encrypt the connection. In a project at the end of this module, you practice using a VNC session to remotely control a Windows computer.

Secure Shell (SSH)

Core 2 Objective 4.9

Secure Shell, also called the **SSH protocol**, is open-source software to remotely sign in to and control another computer. It was designed to replace Telnet and FTP on Linux systems. Recall from the Core 1 module "Networking Fundamentals" that Telnet can remotely control another computer, and FTP is used for file transfers; neither of these programs encrypts transmissions. Secure Shell encrypts the entire session, including the authentication of credentials used to sign in. The server end of Secure Shell is preinstalled in most UNIX and Linux systems. A well-known client program for Secure Shell is PuTTY (*putty.org*), a file transfer program available in Linux and Windows. You can establish a secure session between a client computer and Linux server using Secure Shell and then run another program, such as a VNC program, over the Secure Shell connection using tunneling.

Secure Shell uses port 22 and creates an encrypted session using a method called public key encryption with two SSH keys. See Figure 19-60. The SSH client starts the process by contacting the server and requesting its public SSH key. The server sends the public key and starts negotiating the parameters of the secure channel. The client uses the public key to authenticate the server and uses its own private key to encrypt the user's credentials, which are sent to the server for the server to authenticate the user to the server OS. In a project at the end of this module, you learn to use SSH and PuTTY.

Figure 19-60   Public key encryption is used to secure an SSH session

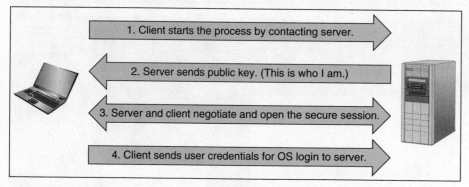

1. Client starts the process by contacting server.

2. Server sends public key. (This is who I am.)

3. Server and client negotiate and open the secure session.

4. Client sends user credentials for OS login to server.

Remote Monitoring and Management (RMM)

Core 2 Objective 4.9

Remote Monitoring and Management (RMM) software, such as RMM by Atera (*atera.com*), is installed on systems to monitor and manage these systems remotely so IT personnel can more easily support these systems. RMM software can be used in-house to help the internal IT department better do its job, or it can be used by a managed services provider (MSP), which is an IT organization that a company contracts with to support its IT needs. RMM software features include the ability to monitor systems in real time, send alerts to management and IT personnel when potential problems arise, automatically run scripts (for example, backup scripts and scripts to install security patches), and analyze and report system performance and reliability.

Security Benefits of Third-Party Tools

> **Core 2 Objective** 4.9

You've just learned about several screen-sharing, video-conferencing, file transfer, desktop management, and RMM software suites. When evaluating the security risks of one of these types of programs, consider whether the program requires you to open a port to your network. For example, Remote Desktop and Remote Assistance both require you to open port 3389, which is a security risk. Third-party remote access software executed from a browser window is more secure because the browser initiates communication outside the protected network, and opening listening ports is not required. Examples of this type of software, some of which are free, are TeamViewer (*teamviewer.com*), GoToMyPC by Citrix (*gotomypc.com*), LogMeIn (*logmein.com*), and Zoom (*zoom.us*). When evaluating third-party remote access applications, consider the following:

- Where is software installed—on the host, on the client, or on both computers?
- How secure is the connection? Are you required to open incoming ports?
- How are live screens shared? For example, is a live screen shared only by the host computer, or can it be shifted to another computer in the same screen-sharing session?
- Can files be shared in one or both directions during the same screen-sharing session?

Troubleshooting Network Connections

> **Core 2 Objective** 1.2

Windows 10/11 includes several utilities you can use to troubleshoot networking problems. In this section of the module, you learn to use ping, hostname, ipconfig, nslookup, tracert, pathping, two net commands, and netstat. Most of these program files are found in the \Windows\System32 folder.

> **Exam Tip** ✔
>
> The A+ Core 2 exam expects you, when given a scenario, to know when and how to use these network utilities: ping, hostname ipconfig, nslookup, ifconfig, tracert, pathping, net use, net user, and netstat. You should know when and how to use each utility and how to interpret results. In addition, these commands form the foundation you'll need when studying more advanced networking.

Now let's see how to use each utility.

ping [–a] [–t] [targetname]

> **Core 2 Objective** 1.2

The **ping** command tests connectivity by sending an echo request to a remote computer. If the remote computer is online, detects the signal, and is configured to respond to a ping, it responds. (Responding to a ping is the default Windows setting, although some companies disable responding to ping, especially on computers that can be reached from the Internet.) Use ping to test for connectivity or to verify that DNS is working. Ping cannot verify other network services on the computer are working. If a ping does not work, after reasonable investigation into the source of the problem, check with a security administrator to determine if the network might be under attack.

> **Note 14**
>
> If a ping to a host using its IP address works, but a ping to the same host using its domain name does not work, DNS is down. Try different DNS servers, such as 8.8.8.8 and 8.8.4.4, the Google public DNS servers.

A few examples of ping are discussed in Table 19-2. Two examples are shown in Figure 19-61.

Table 19-2   Examples of the ping command

Ping Command	Description
ping 69.32.208.75	Ping tests for connectivity using an IP address. If the remote computer responds, the round-trip times are displayed.
ping –a 69.32.208.75	The –a parameter tests for name resolution. Use it to display the host name and verify that DNS is working.
ping –t 69.32.208.75	The –t parameter causes pinging to continue until interrupted. To display statistics, press Ctrl+Break. To stop pinging, press Ctrl+C.
ping 127.0.0.1	This is called a loopback address test. The IP address 127.0.0.1 always refers to the local computer. If the local computer does not respond, you can assume there is a problem with the network connection's configuration.
ping cengage.com	Use a host name to find out the IP address of a remote computer. If the computer does not respond, suspect there is a problem with DNS. On the other hand, some computers are not configured to respond to pings.

Figure 19-61   Use ping to test for connectivity and name resolution

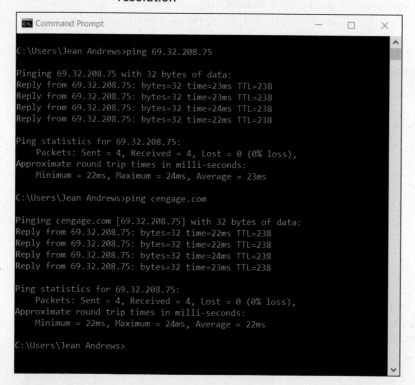

hostname

Core 2 Objective 1.2

The **hostname** command displays the hostname of the computer. The command has no parameters.

ipconfig [/all] [/release] [/renew] [/displaydns] [/flushdns]

Core 2 Objective 1.2

The **ipconfig (IP configuration)** command can display network configuration information and refresh the TCP/IP assignments for a connection, including its IP address. Some examples of the command are listed in Table 19-3.

Table 19-3   Examples of the ipconfig command

Ipconfig Command	Description
ipconfig /all	Displays a network connection's configuration information, including the MAC address.
ipconfig /release	Releases the IP address and other TCP/IP assignments when dynamic IP addressing is being used.
ipconfig /release6	Releases an IPv6 address and other TCP/IP assignments.
ipconfig /renew	Leases a new IP address from a DHCP server. Make sure you release the IP address before you renew it.
ipconfig /renew6	Leases a new IPv6 address from a DHCP IPv6 server. Make sure you release the IPv6 address before you renew it.
ipconfig /displaydns	Displays information about name resolutions that Windows currently holds in the DNS resolver cache.
ipconfig /flushdns	Flushes the name resolver cache, which might solve a problem when the browser cannot find a host on the Internet.

Note 15

Only the more commonly used parameters or switches for each command are discussed in this module. For several of these commands, you can use the /? or /help parameter to get more information. For even more information about each command, search the *docs.microsoft.com* site.

nslookup [computername]

Core 2 Objective 1.2

The **nslookup (namespace lookup or name server lookup)** command is used to test name-resolution problems with DNS servers by allowing you to request information from a DNS server's zone data, which is the portion of the DNS namespace that the server knows about. For example, to find out what your DNS server knows about the domain name *microsoft.com*, enter this command:

```
nslookup microsoft.com
```

Figure 19-62   The nslookup command reports information about the Internet namespace

Figure 19-62 shows the results. Notice in the figure that the DNS server reports five different IPv4 addresses assigned to *microsoft.com*. It also reports that this information is nonauthoritative, meaning that it is not the authoritative, or final, name server for the *microsoft.com* domain name.

A **reverse lookup** is when you run the nslookup command to find the host name when you know a computer's IP address, such as:

`nslookup 69.32.208.75`

To find out the default DNS server for a network, use the nslookup command with no parameters.

Note 16

The Linux dig command gives information similar to the Windows nslookup command. You learn to use dig in the module "Linux and Scripting."

---

tracert [targetname]

Core 2 Objective 1.2

The **tracert (trace route)** command can be useful when you're trying to resolve a problem reaching a destination host such as an FTP site or website. The command sends a series of requests to the destination computer and displays each hop to the destination. (A hop happens when a message moves from one router to another.) For example, to trace the route to the *cengage.com* web server, enter this command in a command prompt window:

`tracert cengage.com`

The results of this command for one location are shown in Figure 19-63; your results will be different. A message is assigned a Time to Live (TTL), which is the number of hops it can make before a router drops the message and sends an error message back to the host that sent the original message (see Figure 19-64). The tracert command creates its report from these messages. If a router doesn't respond, the *Request timed out* message appears.

Figure 19-63　　The tracert command traces a path to a destination computer

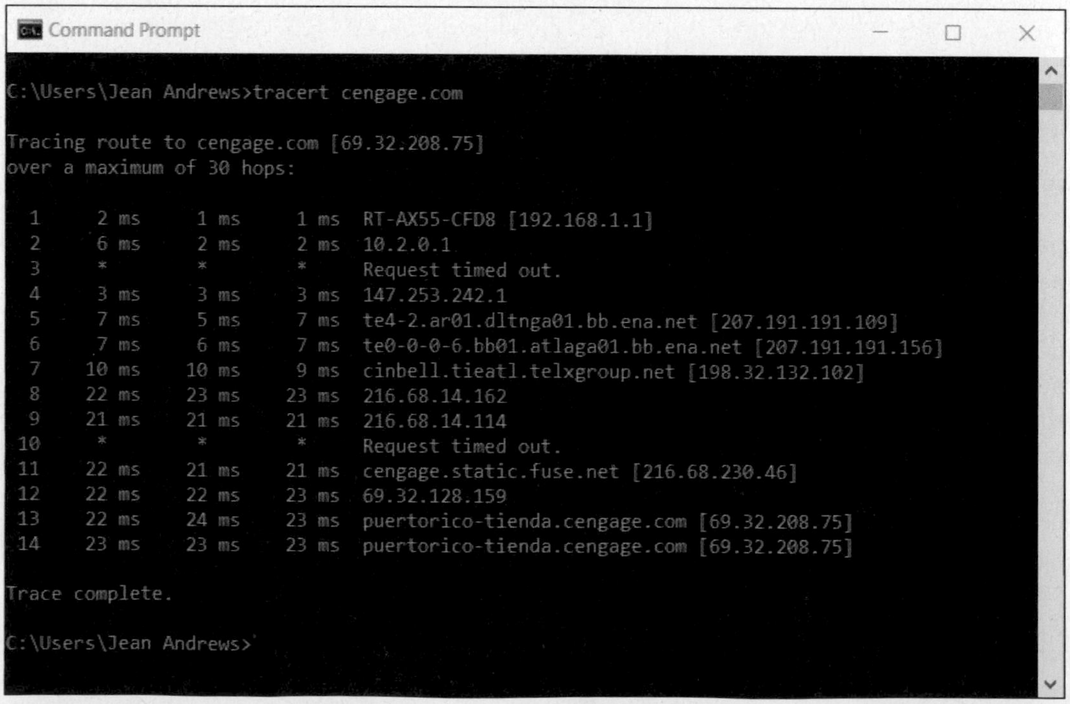

```
Command Prompt                                        —    □    ×

C:\Users\Jean Andrews>tracert cengage.com

Tracing route to cengage.com [69.32.208.75]
over a maximum of 30 hops:

  1     2 ms     1 ms     1 ms  RT-AX55-CFD8 [192.168.1.1]
  2     6 ms     2 ms     2 ms  10.2.0.1
  3      *        *        *     Request timed out.
  4     3 ms     3 ms     3 ms  147.253.242.1
  5     7 ms     5 ms     7 ms  te4-2.ar01.dltnga01.bb.ena.net [207.191.191.109]
  6     7 ms     6 ms     7 ms  te0-0-0-6.bb01.atlaga01.bb.ena.net [207.191.191.156]
  7    10 ms    10 ms     9 ms  cinbell.tieatl.telxgroup.net [198.32.132.102]
  8    22 ms    23 ms    23 ms  216.68.14.162
  9    21 ms    21 ms    21 ms  216.68.14.114
 10      *        *        *     Request timed out.
 11    22 ms    21 ms    21 ms  cengage.static.fuse.net [216.68.230.46]
 12    22 ms    22 ms    23 ms  69.32.128.159
 13    22 ms    24 ms    23 ms  puertorico-tienda.cengage.com [69.32.208.75]
 14    23 ms    23 ms    23 ms  puertorico-tienda.cengage.com [69.32.208.75]

Trace complete.

C:\Users\Jean Andrews>
```

Figure 19-64   A router eliminates a message that has exceeded its TTL

pathping

 Core 2 Objective 1.2

The **pathping** command combines the ping and tracert commands into a single command to help identify where on the network path the network might be slow or giving problems. For example, to show problems along the way to the *cengage.com* site, enter this command:

```
pathping cengage.com
```

The net Commands

 Core 2 Objective 1.2

The net command is several commands in one, and most of the net commands require an elevated command prompt window, which allows commands that require administrator privileges in Windows. In this section, you learn about the net use and net user commands. The **net use** command connects or disconnects a computer from a shared resource, or it can display information about connections.

Enter the following commands to pass a user name and password to the \\bluelight remote computer, and then map a network drive to the \Medical folder on that computer:

```
net use \\bluelight\Medical /user:"Jean Andrews" mypassword
net use z: \\bluelight\Medical
```

The double quotation marks are needed in the first command because the user name has a space in it.

A persistent network connection is one that happens at each logon. To make the two commands persistent, add the /persistent parameter like this:

```
net use \\bluelight\Medical /user:"Jean Andrews" mypassword /persistent:yes
net use z: \\bluelight\Medical /persistent:yes
```

To disconnect a network drive, enter this command:

```
net use z: /delete
```

The **net user** command manages user accounts. For example, the built-in administrator account is disabled by default. To activate the account, enter this net user command:

```
net user administrator /active:yes
```

19

> **Note 17**
>
> One way to get an elevated command prompt window is to open **Task Manager**, click **File**, click **Run new task**, type `cmd`, check **Create this task with administrative privileges**, and then click **OK**. See Figure 19-65. The command prompt window that opens has Administrator in the title bar.

Figure 19-65   Open an elevated command prompt window

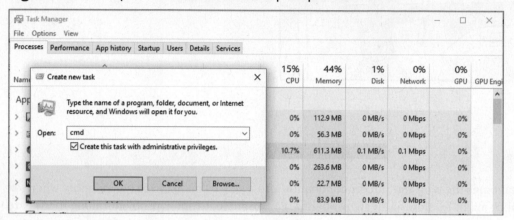

netstat [–a] [–b] [–o]

Core 2 Objective 1.2

The **netstat (network statistics)** command gives statistics about network activity, and it includes several parameters. Table 19-4 lists a few netstat commands.

Table 19-4   netstat commands

netstat Command	Description
netstat	Lists statistics about the network connection, including the IP addresses of active connections.
netstat >>netlog.txt	Directs output to a text file.
netstat –b	Lists programs that are using the connection (see Figure 19-66) and is useful for finding malware that might be using the network. The –b switch requires an elevated command prompt.
netstat –b –o	Includes the process ID of each program listed. When you know the process ID, you can use the taskkill command to end the process.
netstat –a	Lists statistics about all active connections and the ports the computer is listening on.
netstat –na	List all open ports.

Figure 19-66 netstat –b lists programs that are using a network connection

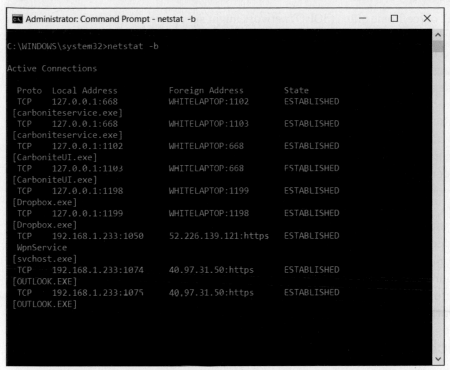

```
Administrator: Command Prompt - netstat -b                          —     □     ×

C:\WINDOWS\system32>netstat -b

Active Connections

  Proto  Local Address          Foreign Address        State
  TCP    127.0.0.1:668          WHITELAPTOP:1102       ESTABLISHED
 [carboniteservice.exe]
  TCP    127.0.0.1:668          WHITELAPTOP:1103       ESTABLISHED
 [carboniteservice.exe]
  TCP    127.0.0.1:1102         WHITELAPTOP:668        ESTABLISHED
 [CarboniteUI.exe]
  TCP    127.0.0.1:1103         WHITELAPTOP:668        ESTABLISHED
 [CarboniteUI.exe]
  TCP    127.0.0.1:1198         WHITELAPTOP:1199       ESTABLISHED
 [Dropbox.exe]
  TCP    127.0.0.1:1199         WHITELAPTOP:1198       ESTABLISHED
 [Dropbox.exe]
  TCP    192.168.1.233:1050     52.226.139.121:https   ESTABLISHED
  WpnService
 [svchost.exe]
  TCP    192.168.1.233:1074     40.97.31.50:https      ESTABLISHED
 [OUTLOOK.EXE]
  TCP    192.168.1.233:1075     40.97.31.50:https      ESTABLISHED
 [OUTLOOK.EXE]
```

Note 18

Other important net commands are net localgroup, net accounts, net config, net print, net share, and net view. Consider doing a Google search on these commands to find out how they work.

Module Summary

Securing Workstations and IoT Devices on a Network

- Most browsers allow you to sign in and sync data across devices and to the cloud; manage extensions, plug-ins, and passwords to websites; block pop-ups and ads; clear the browsing cache; and control privacy settings.
- Browsers use digital certificates to validate the identity of websites.
- Internet Options in Control Panel can be used to manage proxy server settings for the Windows system and all installed browsers.
- To download a new browser securely, verify the download and installation routine is digitally signed and compare hashes for the downloaded file.
- Use a VPN connection to encrypt communication with a remote network across the Internet.
- A computer can use a USB or embedded broadband device with a SIM card to make a WWAN connection to the Internet via a cellular carrier.
- Windows can monitor a metered connection to send an alert when data usage has reached a threshold.
- Windows Defender Firewall in Windows 10/11 provides personal firewall services on a laptop or workstation to protect the computer from attack over the Internet.
- Z-Wave and Zigbee are wireless communication protocols used by IoT devices on a network. Both protocols use encryption. Neither supports TCP/IP without an additional protocol layer such as Z/IP or Zigbee IP. Zigbee is more robust than Z-Wave and is generally the choice for large-scale industrial use.

19

Securing a Multifunction Router for a SOHO Network

- A multifunction router for a small office/home office (SOHO) network might serve several functions, including router, switch, DHCP server, wireless access point (WAP), firewall, and file server.
- Place a router in a secure location, and it if is being used as a WAP, make sure it is centrally located for users.
- It's extremely important to change the administrative password on a router as soon as you install it, especially if the router also serves as a wireless access point.
- To configure a router to secure and serve the local network, you can update firmware, assign a static WAN IP address, reserve IP addresses for the DHCP server, configure UPnP, and configure QoS for priority applications.
- To allow certain network traffic initiated from the Internet past your firewall, you can use port forwarding, a DMZ, screened subnets, and content filtering with whitelists or blacklists.
- Access to the network can be controlled by allowing or denying certain applications and ports and by IP filtering.
- To secure a wireless access point, you can require a security key, change the default SSID, select specific Wi-Fi channels, disable guest access, and enable encryption (WPA, WPA2, or WPA3).
- An enterprise might use RADIUS, TACACS+, and/or Kerberos software to help with authentication to the network and/or enterprise resources. On a wireless network, RADIUS or TACACS+ is used rather than a network security key to authenticate to the wireless network. TACACS+ is used specifically with Cisco devices. Kerberos is used within a network for a Windows client to authenticate to a Windows domain.

Using Remote Access Technologies

- File transfer technologies include FTP and HTTP-based technologies such as Dropbox and Google Drive.
- Windows 10/11 offers Remote Desktop Connection (RDC) and Microsoft Remote Assistance (MSRA) to remotely manage a Windows 10/11 desktop. Remote Desktop gives you access to your Windows desktop and file sharing from anywhere on the Internet. Remote Assistance lets you provide remote support to users but does not allow file sharing.
- Virtual Network Computing (VNC) is used for remote desktop management, screen sharing, and file transfers. Software must be installed on both the client and the server.
- Secure Shell (SSH) is open-source software that is preinstalled in most Linux and UNIX systems and provides an encrypted connection for a client computer to remotely control a Linux or UNIX host.
- Remote Monitoring and Management (RMM) software remotely monitors and manages systems to support IT personnel responsible for these systems either in-house or in a managed services provider (MSP) role.
- When evaluating third-party remote access applications, consider the security of the connection and how screens and files are shared.

Troubleshooting Network Connections

- Useful Windows command-line utilities for network troubleshooting are ping, hostname, ipconfig, nslookup, tracert, pathping, net use, net user, and netstat.

Key Terms

For explanations of key terms, see the Glossary for this text.

802.11a	AES (Advanced	extension	Kerberos
802.11ac (Wi-Fi 5)	Encryption Standard)	hash	Microsoft Remote
802.11ax (Wi-Fi 6)	blacklist	hostname	Assistance (MSRA)
802.11b	channel	Internet Options	Microsoft Terminal
802.11g	DMZ (demilitarized	ipconfig (IP	Services Client (mstsc.
802.11n (Wi-Fi 4)	zone)	configuration)	exe)

net use

net user

netstat
  (network
  statistics)

nslookup (namespace
  lookup or
  name server
  lookup)

pathping

ping

plug-in

port address

port forwarding

RADIUS (Remote
  Access Dial-In User
  Service)

Remote Desktop
  Connection (RDC)

Remote Monitoring and
  Management (RMM)

reverse lookup

router

screened subnet

Secure Shell

Service Set Identifier
  (SSID)

SSH protocol

switch

TACACS+ (Terminal
  Access Controller
  Access Control System
  Plus)

TKIP (Temporal Key
  Integrity Protocol)

tracert (trace route)

tunneling

Universal Plug and Play
  (UPnP)

Virtual Network
  Computing (VNC)

whitelist

Windows Defender
  Firewall

wireless access point
  (WAP)

WPA (Wi-Fi Protected
  Access)

WPA2 (Wi-Fi Protected
  Access 2)

WPA3 (Wi-Fi Protected
  Access 3)

Z-Wave

Zigbee

Thinking Critically

These questions are designed to prepare you for the critical thinking required for the A+ exams and may use information from other modules and the web.

1. As an IT technician, you arrive at a customer's home office to troubleshoot problems they are experiencing with their printer. While questioning the customer to get an understanding of their network, you find they have a new Wi-Fi router that connects wirelessly to a new desktop and two new laptops, in addition to multiple smartphones, tablets, and the network printer. They also have several smart home devices, including security cameras, light switches, door locks, and a thermostat supported by an IoT controller hub. To work on the printer, which type of network will you be interacting with?

   a. PAN
   b. WAN
   c. WMN
   d. LAN

2. While you work on the customer's printer, they continue chatting about their network and the problems they've been experiencing. One complaint is that the Internet service slows down considerably in the evening. You suspect you know the cause of this problem: Their neighbors arrive home in the evening and bog down the ISP's local infrastructure. To be sure, you take a quick look at the back of their modem. What type of cable connected to the WAN port would confirm your suspicions and why?

3. Your customer then asks you if it would be worth the investment for them to have Ethernet cabling installed to reach each of their workstations instead of connecting them by Wi-Fi to the network. Specifically, they want to know if that would speed up communications for the workstations. You examine their router and find that it's using 802.11ac Wi-Fi. Would you advise them to upgrade to Ethernet? Why or why not?

   a. Yes, because Ethernet is faster than 802.11ac.
   b. Yes, because wired connections are always faster than wireless connections.
   c. No, because installing Ethernet cabling is more expensive than the increased speed is worth.
   d. No, because 802.11ac speeds are faster than Ethernet.

4. You run the ipconfig command on your computer, and it reports an IP address of 169.254.75.10 on the Ethernet interface. Which device assigned this IP address to the interface?

   a. The ISP's DNS server
   b. The local network's DHCP server on the SOHO router
   c. The cable modem
   d. The local computer

19

5. You've just received a call from human resources asking for assistance with a problem. One of your company's employees, Ahmed, has recently undergone extensive surgery and will be homebound for three to five months. He plans on working from home and needs a solution to enable frequent and extended access to the company network's resources. Which WAN technology will you need to configure for Ahmed, and which tool will you use to configure it?

   a. WWAN using the Network Connections window
   b. Wi-Fi using the Network and Sharing Center
   c. Ethernet using the Network Connections window
   d. VPN using the Network and Sharing Center

6. Your manager has asked you to configure a DHCP reservation on the network for a Windows computer that is used to configure other devices on a network. To do this, you need the computer's MAC address. What command can you enter at the command line to access this information?

7. You're setting up a Minecraft gaming server so you and several of your friends can share a realm during your gameplay. To do this, your friends will need to access your server over the Internet, which means you must configure your router to send this traffic to your game server. Which router feature will you use, and which port must you open for TCP traffic?

8. While troubleshooting an Internet connection problem for your network, you restarted the modem and then the router. The router is now communicating with the Internet, which you can confirm by observing the blinking light on the router's WAN indicator. However, now your laptop is not communicating with the router. Order the following commands to confirm there is no connectivity, apply a fix to the problem, and confirm connectivity.

   a. ping
   b. ipconfig /renew
   c. nslookup microsoft.com
   d. ipconfig /release

9. You need a VPN to connect to a private, remote network in order to access some files. You click the network icon in your taskbar to establish the connection, and you realize there is no VPN option available on the menu. What tool do you need to use to fix this problem?

   a. net command
   b. netstat command
   c. Network and Sharing Center
   d. Network Connections window

10. To prepare to remotely work on a Linux server at work while you are at home, you install VNC Server for Linux by RealVNC (*realvnc.com*) on the system at work. When you get home, you install the VNC Viewer for Windows on your Windows 10 laptop. When you try to make the connection, you get an error about a refused connection. Which could be a cause of the error? (Choose all that apply.)

   a. VNC Viewer for Windows will not work with a Linux server. Use Remote Desktop instead.
   b. Port 5901 is not set for port forwarding on the corporate router. Configure the router next time you're in the office.
   c. VNC Server for Linux must be configured to tunnel through SSH. Set up the SSH tunnel next time you're in the office.
   d. A VNC solution will not work with Linux. Configure Remote Desktop on the Linux server, and use it with the Remote Desktop client on your home computer.

11. You're troubleshooting a network connection for a client at their home office. After pinging the network's default gateway, you discover that the cable connecting the desktop to the router had been damaged by foot traffic and is no longer providing a reliable signal. You replace the cable, this time running the cable along the wall, so it won't be stepped on. What do you do next?

   a. Apply port forwarding on the router.
   b. Use the ping command.
   c. Use the hostname command.
   d. Reboot the router.

12. Which type of server can function as a firewall?

   a. Mail server
   b. Proxy server
   c. Print server
   d. FTP server

13. Your company has recently been hired to install a smart security system for a large office building. The system will include security cameras, voice-controlled lights, smart locks, and smart thermostats. Some of the security cameras will be installed outdoors throughout the parking lot. Which wireless IoT protocol should your company use for the installation?

   a. Wi-Fi, because it is always encrypted
   b. Zigbee, because it is always encrypted
   c. Z-Wave, because it is the fastest wireless standard
   d. Bluetooth, because it is easiest to configure

14. Of the 10 devices shown earlier in Figure 19-21, how many are assigned IP addresses?

   a. Four: two phones, a web server, and a router
   b. Three: two phones and a web server
   c. Seven: a thermostat, a router, two phones, two bridges, and a web server
   d. All 10

15. As a bank employee, you often work from home and remotely access a file server on the bank's network to correct errors in financial data. Which of the following services is most likely the one you are using to authenticate to the network and track what you do on the network?

   a. RADIUS
   b. Secure DNS
   c. Active Directory
   d. TACACS+

16. Mia works from home occasionally and needs to set up her Windows 10 computer at work so she can remote in from her home office. Which tools should she use?

   a. Zoom
   b. Remote Assistance
   c. Secure Shell
   d. Remote Desktop

17. Daunte frequently calls your help desk asking for instructions on how to use Windows 10. What is the best way to help Daunte?

   a. Open a chat session with Daunte over Facebook and talk with him about Windows 10.
   b. Use Remote Assistance to show Daunte how to use Windows 10, and point him to the log file created.
   c. Explain to Daunte that a help desk is not the place to go to learn to use new software and that he needs to look elsewhere for help.
   d. Email Daunte some links to online video tutorials about Windows 10.

19

18. Remote Desktop and Remote Assistance require a technician to change port settings and firewall settings, but third-party apps such as GoToMyPC do not. Why is this?

    a. Microsoft makes its apps more secure than third-party apps.
    b. GoToMyPC and other third-party apps use ports already left open for web browsing and don't require additional incoming connections.
    c. Remote Desktop and Remote Assistance allow incoming connections at the same port 80 that is already left open for web browsing.
    d. GoToMyPC and other third-party apps are not concerned about security because they depend on Windows to secure a network connection.

19. Manuel works on a help desk and is assigned a ticket that was automatically generated by a server because of an error. The error message states that the server has run out of storage space because logs were not set to delete at a certain size. Rather than going to the data center to physically access that server on the rack, what Windows tool might Manuel use to troubleshoot the server?

20. While investigating the settings on your SOHO router, you find two IP addresses reported on the device's routing table, which is used to determine where to send incoming data. The two IP addresses are 192.168.2.1 and 71.9.200.235. Which of these IP addresses would you expect to see listed as the default gateway on the devices in your local network? How do you know?

21. The documentation for your router says that it can provide content filtering to filter out keywords except for pages that use the HTTPS protocol. Why is that?

    a. Privacy laws make it illegal to filter content in HTTPS pages.
    b. HTTPS pages are encrypted, and the router cannot decrypt them to read the content.
    c. The router must use its public key to transmit HTTPS pages.
    d. The software to filter content in HTTPS pages is not installed on this particular router.

22. Your manager asks you to transmit a small file that includes sensitive personnel data to a Linux server on the network. The server is running a Telnet server and an SSH server. Why is it not a good idea to use Telnet to reach the remote computer?

    a. Telnet transmissions are not encrypted.
    b. Telnet is not reliable, and the file might arrive corrupted.
    c. SSH is faster than Telnet.
    d. SSH running on the same computer as Telnet causes Telnet not to work.

23. While troubleshooting an IPv4 network connection problem, you start to wonder if the local computer's NIC is configured correctly for TCP/IP settings. What command should you enter at the command prompt to test your theory?

24. Your SOHO router has failed, and you have installed a new router. The old router's static IP address on the network is 192.168.0.1. The new router has a static IP address of 10.0.0.1. You go to a computer to configure the new router, and you enter 10.0.0.1 in the browser address box. The router does not respond. You open a command prompt window and try to ping the router, which does not work. Next, you verify that the router has connectivity, and you see that its local connection light is blinking, indicating connectivity. What is the most likely problem and its best solution?

    a. The computer you are using to configure the router has a corrupted TCP/IP configuration. Restart the computer.
    b. The router is defective. Return it for a full refund.
    c. The computer and the router are not in the same subnet. Release and renew the IP address of the computer.
    d. The computer and the router are not in the same subnet. Change the subnet mask assigned to the computer.

25. While troubleshooting a network connection problem, you run the command ipconfig /all in a command prompt window and get the following output:

```
Ethernet adapter Ethernet:
   Connection-specific DNS Suffix.:
   Description.....................: Realtek PCIe GBE Family Controller
   Physical Address...............: 54-53-ED-BB-AB-A3
   DHCP Enabled...................: Yes
   Autoconfiguration Enabled......: Yes
   Link local IPv6 Address........: fe80::64d2:bd2e:fa62:b911%10 (Preferred)
   IPv4 Address...................: 192.168.2.166(Preferred)
   Subnet Mask....................: 255.255.255.0
   Lease Obtained.................: Sunday, August 19, 2022 10:56:41 AM
   Lease Expires..................: Sunday, August 19, 2022 1:56:41 PM
   Default Gateway................: 192.168.2.1
   DHCP Server....................: 192.168.2.1
   DHCPv6 IAID....................: 257184749
   DHCPv6 Client DUID.............: 00-01-00-01-18-81-16-9A-54-53-ED-BB-AB-A3
   DNS Servers....................: 8.8.8.8      8.8.4.4
   NetBIOS over Tcpip.............: Enabled
```

Is the computer using a wired or wireless network connection? What is the local computer's MAC address? What is the IP address of the router on the local network?

26. Which two of the following hosts on a corporate intranet are on the same subnet?

    a. 192.168.2.143/8

    b. 172.54.98.3/16

    c. 192.168.5.57/8

    d. 172.54.72.89/16

Hands-On Projects

Hands-On Project 19-1

Researching a Wireless LAN

Est. Time: 15 minutes
Core 2 Objective: 1.6

Suppose you have a DSL connection to the Internet in your home, and you want to connect two laptops and a desktop computer in a wireless network with access to the Internet. You need to purchase a multifunction wireless router like the ones you learned to configure in this module. You also need a wireless adapter for the desktop computer. (The two laptops have built-in wireless networking.) Use the web to research the equipment needed to create the wireless LAN, and answer the following questions:

    1. Save or print two webpages showing two different multifunctional wireless routers. What is the brand, model, and price of each router?

    2. Save or print two webpages showing two different wireless adapters a desktop computer could use to connect to the wireless network. Include one external device that uses a USB port and one internal device. What is the brand, model, and price of each device?

    3. Which router and wireless adapter would you select for your home network? What is the total cost of both devices?

19

Hands-On Project 19-2

Using Google Chrome

Est. Time: 15 minutes
Core 2 Objective: 2.10

Microsoft Edge is not the only browser available, and many users prefer others such as Mozilla Firefox (*mozilla.org*) or Google Chrome (*google.com*). Go to the Google website, and download and install Google Chrome. Use it to browse the web. How does it compare with Microsoft Edge? What do you like better about it? What do you not like as well? In what situations might you recommend that someone use Chrome rather than Microsoft Edge? What security features does Google Chrome offer? What are the steps to import your favorites list from Edge into Chrome?

Hands-On Project 19-3

Practicing Using a VNC Product

Est. Time: 30 minutes
Core 2 Objective: 4.9

In the module, in Figure 19-59, you saw RealVNC installed as a viewer on a Mac computer, controlling the desktop of a Windows 10 computer. Do the following to practice setting up your own VNC desktop management scenario. You might want to work with a partner, with each of you using your own computer for this project. Although each person can have their own RealVNC account to do this project, to keep things simple, the partners will share the same RealVNC account to make the connection:

1. Go to RealVNC at **realvnc.com**, and sign up for RealVNC. You will need an email address to sign up for the free trial. Download and install the RealVNC server on one computer. Sign in to RealVNC server on your computer.

2. On a different computer, install the RealVNC viewer. Sign in to RealVNC in the viewer software using the same email account you used in step 1.

3. Use the viewer on the second computer to control the desktop on the first computer. Can you use the viewer to open and use a chat window that works on the server host?

4. When you are finished with this project, sign out of the software, and perhaps uninstall it.

Hands-On Project 19-4

Setting Up a Persistent Network Drive

Est. Time: 15 minutes
Core 2 Objective: 1.2

Using two networked computers, do the following to set up and test a persistent network drive:

1. On the computer that will host the network drive:
   a. Create a folder under the root of drive C: named MyShare, and create one file in the folder.
   b. Share the folder on the network, giving users read/write permissions to the folder.
   c. Run the `hostname` command to find out the computer name.

2. On the second computer:

   a. Run the **net** commands to map a persistent network drive onto the MyShare folder on the first computer.

   b. Test the folder to make sure you can copy the file in the folder to your computer and write a new file to the shared folder.

   c. Restart your computer. Is the network drive persistent?

   d. Run the **net** command to delete the mapped drive.

Hands-On Project 19-5

Scanning a Network for Connected Devices

Est. Time: 15 minutes
Core 2 Objective: 1.2

To help document devices connected to your network, you can use Advanced IP Scanner. Do the following to install and use the software:

1. Go to **advanced-ip-scanner.com**, and then download and install Advanced IP Scanner by Famatech Corp. Install and run the software.

2. Make sure the range of IP addresses includes all the IP addresses on your network. Click **Scan**. Figure 19-67 shows the results of one scan. Notice the software reports nodes on the network, their IP addresses, services they are running, and shared folders.

Figure 19-67   Scan for nodes on a local network and information about each host

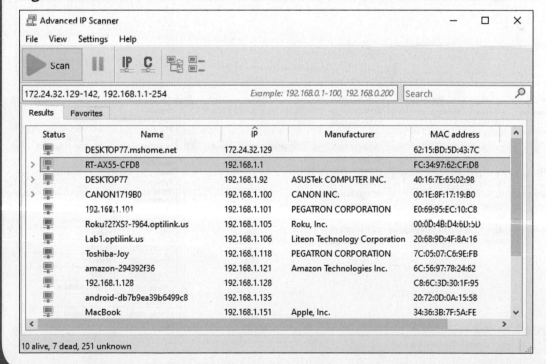

Status	Name	IP	Manufacturer	MAC address
🖥	DESKTOP77.mshome.net	172.24.32.129		62:15:BD:5D:43:7C
🖥	RT-AX55-CFD8	192.168.1.1		FC:34:97:62:CF:D8
🖥	DESKTOP77	192.168.1.92	ASUSTek COMPUTER INC.	40:16:7E:65:02:98
🖥	CANON1719B0	192.168.1.100	CANON INC.	00:1E:8F:17:19:B0
🖥	192.168.1.101	192.168.1.101	PEGATRON CORPORATION	E0:69:95:EC:10:C8
🖥	Roku?2?XS?-?964.optilink.us	192.168.1.105	Roku, Inc.	00:0D:4B:D4:6D:5D
🖥	Lab1.optilink.us	192.168.1.106	Liteon Technology Corporation	20:68:9D:4F:8A:16
🖥	Toshiba-Joy	192.168.1.118	PEGATRON CORPORATION	7C:05:07:C6:9E:FB
🖥	amazon-294392f36	192.168.1.121	Amazon Technologies Inc.	6C:56:97:78:24:62
🖥	192.168.1.128	192.168.1.128		C8:6C:3D:30:1F:95
🖥	android-db7b9ea39b6499c8	192.168.1.135		20:72:0D:0A:15:58
🖥	MacBook	192.168.1.151	Apple, Inc.	34:36:3B:7F:5A:FE

10 alive, 7 dead, 251 unknown

19

Real Problems, Real Solutions

Real Problem 19-1

Using a Port Scanner

Est. Time: 30 minutes
Core 2 Objective: 1.2

Port-scanning software can be used to find out how vulnerable a computer is with open ports. This project requires the use of two computers on the same network to practice using port-scanning software. Complete the following steps:

1. On computer 1, download and install Advanced Port Scanner by Famatech at **advanced-port-scanner.com**. Install and run the software.

2. Open the **Network and Sharing Center**, click **Change advanced sharing settings**, and turn off network discovery and file and printer sharing.

3. In the Advanced Port Scanner window, make sure that the range of IP addresses includes the IP address of computer 2. Change the default port list to TCP ports 0 through 6000. Then click **Scan**.

4. Browse the list, and find computer 2. List the number and purpose of all open ports found on computer 2.

5. On computer 2, turn on network discovery and file and printer sharing. Open the **System** window, click **Remote settings**, and allow Remote Assistance connections to this computer. Close all windows.

6. On computer 1, rescan and list the number and purpose of each port now open on computer 2. Figure 19-68 shows the results for one computer, but yours might be different.

Figure 19-68 Advanced Port Scanner shows open ports on networked computers

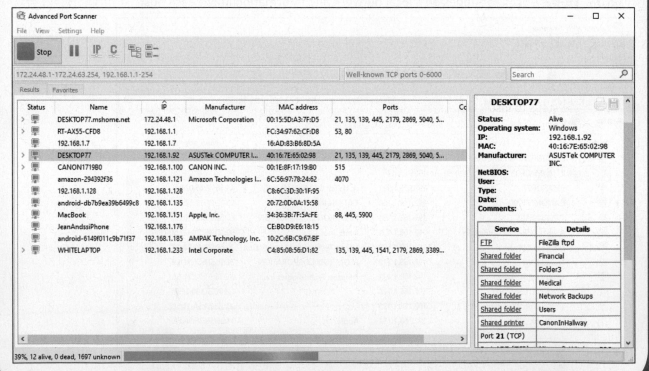

Real Problem 19-2

Implementing More Security for Remote Desktop

Est. Time: 30 minutes
Core 2 Objective: 4.9

When Hakim travels on company business, he finds it's a great help to be able to access his office computer from anywhere on the road using Remote Desktop. However, he wants to make sure his office computer and the corporate network are as safe as possible. One way you can help Hakim add more security is to change the listening port that Remote Desktop uses. Knowledgeable hackers know that Remote Desktop uses port 3389, but if you change this port to a secret port, hackers are less likely to find the open port. Search the Microsoft Knowledge Base articles (*support.microsoft.com* and *docs.microsoft.com*) for a way to change the listening port that Remote Desktop uses. Practice implementing this change by doing the following:

1. Set up Remote Desktop on a computer using a business or professional edition of Windows. This computer is your host computer. Use another computer (the client computer) to create a Remote Desktop session to the host computer. Verify that the session works by transferring files in both directions.

2. Next, change the port that Remote Desktop uses on the host computer to a secret port. Save or print a screenshot showing how you made the change. Use the client computer to create a Remote Desktop session to the host computer using the secret port. Print a screenshot showing how you made the connection using the secret port. Verify that the session works by transferring files in both directions.

3. What secret port did you use? What link on the Microsoft websites gave you the information you needed?

Real Problem 19-3

Using SSH and PuTTY

Est. Time: 30 minutes
Core 2 Objective: 4.9

Follow these steps to install Linux in a VM, and use the PuTTY program for remote access to the Linux host via an SSH connection:

1. To download Ubuntu Server, go to **releases.ubuntu.com**, and download the latest release of Ubuntu Server install image, which is an ISO file.

2. In Windows 10/11 Pro, open **Hyper-V Manager**, and use it to create a new VM. Use the downloaded ISO file to install Ubuntu Server in the VM. What is the server name, your user name, and your password? Accept all default settings. When you get to the screen that gives you the option to install the OpenSSH server, choose to install the server. Notice that Ubuntu allows you to import your SSH keys from GitHub or Launchpad. It is not necessary to import SSH keys at this time.

3. Remove the ISO file from the VM's virtual DVD drive, and reboot the server.

4. Sign in to Ubuntu Server, and enter this command to install some networking tools, including the ifconfig command:

```
sudo apt install net-tools
```

5. Enter the **ifconfig** command to find out the IP address of the server. What is its IP address?

(continues)

19

Real Problem Continued

6. Go to **putty.org** and download and install the PuTTY program on your Windows 10/11 computer. Launch **PuTTY**.

7. Enter the IP address of your server in the PuTTY window, and make sure PuTTY is set to use SSH. What port does SSH use? Connect your Windows 10/11 computer to the Ubuntu Server in an SSH session. When asked if you trust the host key the server presented, click **Accept**.

8. Remotely log in to the server with your Ubuntu Server user name and password. Try the hostname command in the PuTTY window. Did the command return the name of the Ubuntu Server?

9. Use this command in the PuTTY window to shut down the server:

   ```
   sudo shutdown now
   ```

10. You can now close all windows.

Be sure to save your Ubuntu Server VM because you'll need it again for the module "Linux and Scripting," where you learn much more about Ubuntu Server.

Module
20

Supporting macOS

Module Objectives

1 Use the macOS desktop

2 Maintain and support macOS

3 Update macOS and drivers

4 Troubleshoot macOS startup

Core 2 Certification Objectives

1.8 Explain common OS types and their purposes.

1.10 Identify common features and tools of the macOS/ desktop OS.

Introduction

In this module, you learn about another operating system for desktops and laptops other than Windows: macOS. As you will see, understanding Windows gives you a solid foundation to approach learning and supporting other operating systems, including macOS. IT technicians are expected to be familiar with a variety of operating systems and operating environments. This module and the module "Linux and Scripting" equip you with the skills you will need to work in those environments.

Getting to Know the macOS Desktop

Core 2 Objective 1.10

macOS, previously called Mac OS X, is a proprietary operating system that is only available for Macintosh computers by Apple Inc. (*apple.com*). Like Linux, macOS is built on a UNIX foundation and has been evolving and improving since its original release in 1984. (UNIX is a popular OS used to control networks and to support server applications available on the Internet.) At the time of this writing, macOS Monterey was just released, and some users are converting to it from the last release, macOS Big Sur.

The Mac keyboard has some special keys. See Figure 20-1. However, don't depend on these special keys because a customer might have a regular keyboard connected via a USB port. The touch pad on a Mac laptop is called the trackpad, and it is a touch pad on steroids; you can use multiple fingers and actions called **gestures**, which you learn about as you read through this section of the module. Some newer MacBooks have Touch ID as a biometric scanner for fingerprints included on the keyboard as seen in Figure 20-1.

Figure 20-1   Special keys on a Mac keyboard

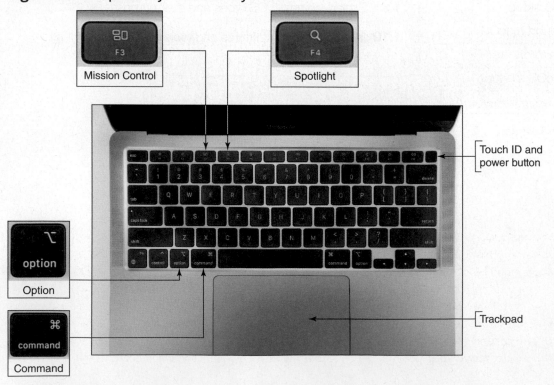

Now let's get to know the macOS interface, including the desktop with its dock and Apple menu, Finder, Launchpad, System Preferences, Spotlight, Mission Control, multiple desktops, iCloud Drive, Keychain, Screen Sharing, Remote Disc, and Terminal.

The macOS desktop, with its major components labeled, is shown in Figure 20-2. The **Finder** application, which can help you find applications and data files, is open and active. Because Finder is the currently active application, the menu bar for the Finder window is displayed at the top of the screen. The Finder menu bar provides drop-down menus that contain options for working with applications, files, and the interface.

Figure 20-2 The macOS desktop with a Finder window showing the Applications pane

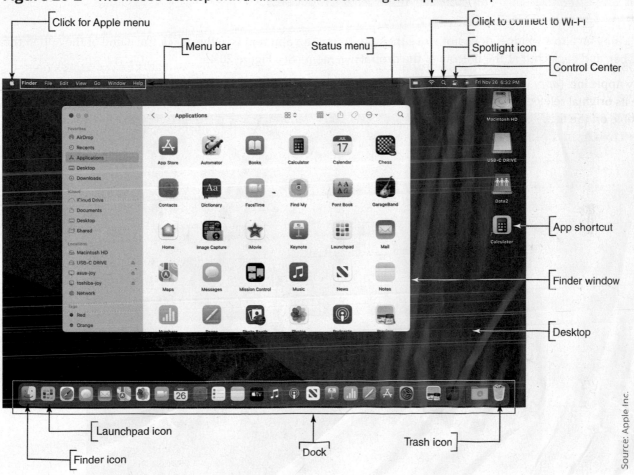

By default, the **dock** appears at the bottom of the desktop. It contains shortcut icons to access frequently used applications. To open an application from its icon in the dock, click it once. The icons in the dock that represent open applications have a small black or white dot underneath them. The macOS desktop can also include shortcuts that provide quick access to files, folders, and applications.

When a window is open, three circles in the upper-left corner (see Figure 20-3A) provide options for manipulating the window. The red circle closes the window, the yellow circle minimizes the window to the dock in the lower-right corner of the screen (see Figure 20-3B), and the green circle maximizes the window to full-screen size. To exit full-screen mode, move your pointer to the top of the screen. When the circle icons appear, click the green circle.

20

Figure 20-3   (A) Close, minimize, or expand a window; (B) this Finder window has been minimized, but the app is still running and its window is easily accessible in the dock

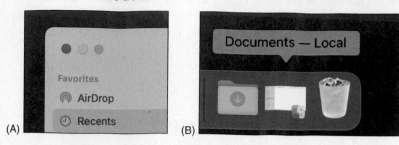

(A)   (B)

Closing an app's window does not close the app. To quit an app that is active, click the name of the app in the menu bar, and click **Quit** at the bottom of the drop-down menu. See Figure 20-4.

Figure 20-4   To close an app, select Quit in the app's menu

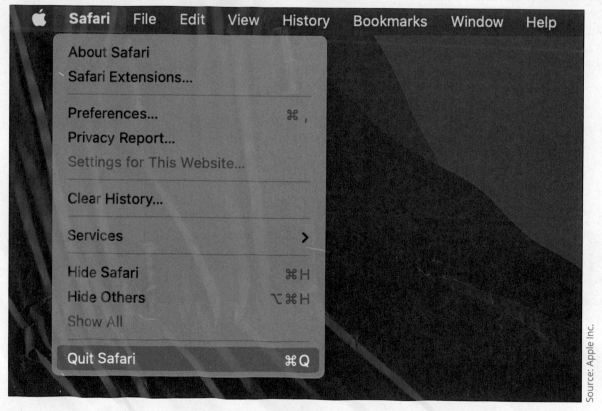

Finder

 **Core 2 Objective** 1.10

The Finder window, shown earlier in Figure 20-2 and again in Figure 20-5, functions something like File Explorer in Windows; use it to find and access files, applications, and macOS utility programs. To open the Finder window, click it in the dock. Note that the Finder is always running; you can close the Finder window, but you can't end the Finder utility. Here are useful things you can do with Finder:

- **Files and folders.** To open files and folders, click **Documents** or some other storage location, such as iCloud Drive or Downloads. Double-click a folder to drill down into it, and double-click a document file to open it. You can drag and drop a file or folder into and out of a folder or location window.

Figure 20-5   The Finder window showing the Documents folder contents

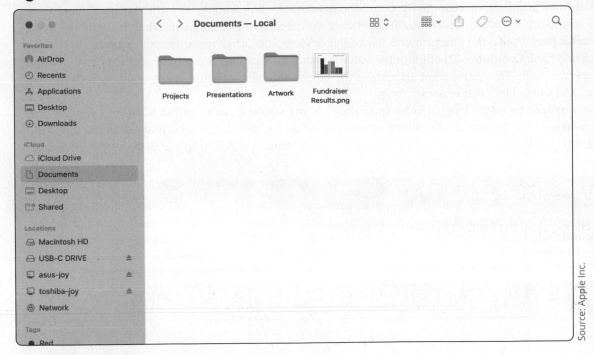

- **Applications.** To open an app, click **Applications** in the sidebar, scroll to the app, and click it. You can also open apps from Launchpad.
- **macOS utilities.** macOS offers several utility programs that are accessed from the Finder window. Click **Applications**, scroll down to the **Utilities** folder, and click it. See Figure 20-6. You learn to use several of these utilities later in this module.

Figure 20-6   Utilities to support a Mac are in the Utilities folder under Applications in the Finder window

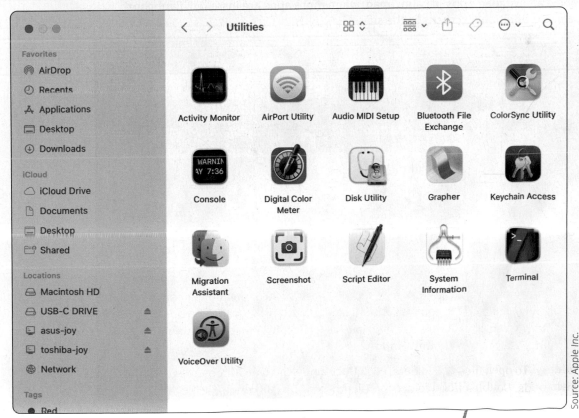

Source: Apple Inc.

20

- **Locations.** As shown on the left side of Figure 20-6, available locations are the Mac, the internal hard drive (Macintosh HD), a USB drive, Remote Disc, and the network. Drill down into any of these locations to see available resources. When you drill down into Network, you see network devices and their shared resources.
- **Finder menu bar.** To use the Finder menu bar to list devices and other resources, click **Go** in the Finder menu bar, and click **Computer**. The Computer window shows all locations and storage devices, and you can drill down into them. To control what appears in the Finder sidebar or on the desktop, click **Finder** in the menu bar, and then click **Preferences**.
- **Tags.** Tags are used to assign a tag or color to a file or folder to make it easier to find later. For example, you can secondary-click a file, and use the shortcut menu to assign it a blue tag. (A **secondary-click** is a tap of the trackpad with two fingers.) Later, click the blue tag in the left column of Finder to see all items with blue tags.

Note 1

If you use an app, such as GarageBand, frequently, you can add it to the dock or desktop. In Finder, click **Applications**, and then click and drag the app's icon to the dock or desktop. To remove an icon from the dock or desktop, click and drag the icon to the Trash icon.

Launchpad

Core 2 Objective 1.10

Launchpad (see Figure 20-7), which is somewhat similar to a combination of the Windows Start menu and Programs and Features window, shows all apps installed on the computer. Use one of these methods to open Launchpad:

- **Use the dock.** Click the Launchpad icon in the dock.
- **Use a gesture.** Pinch with three fingers and your thumb on the trackpad.
- **Use a key.** Press the Launchpad key at the top of the Mac keyboard.

Figure 20-7   View all installed apps in Launchpad; when more apps are installed, Launchpad creates additional screens to the side

Source: Apple Inc.

In the Launchpad window shown in Figure 20-7, notice the two dots above the dock, which indicate that Launchpad requires two screens to show all installed apps. Swipe left or right with two fingers to move through the screens.

Here are some tips on how to use Launchpad:

- Click an app to open it, which also closes Launchpad.
- To uninstall an app, press and hold the **Option (⌥)** key, which causes the app icons to jiggle. Click an **X** on an icon to uninstall its app. You can also rearrange jiggling icons, similar to the way you can work with icons on an iPad and iPhone. Release the Option key when you're done.
- To close Launchpad and return to the desktop, use a pinch gesture with three fingers and your thumb spread apart.

Apple Menu

Core 2 Objective 1.10

The menu at the top of the macOS screen changes with each application that is active—except for the Apple icon, which is always shown at the far left of the menu bar. The **Apple menu** (see Figure 20-8) opens when you click the Apple icon. Use the Apple menu to put the computer to sleep, log out, restart, or shut down the system.

Figure 20-8   The Apple menu is always available no matter which application is active

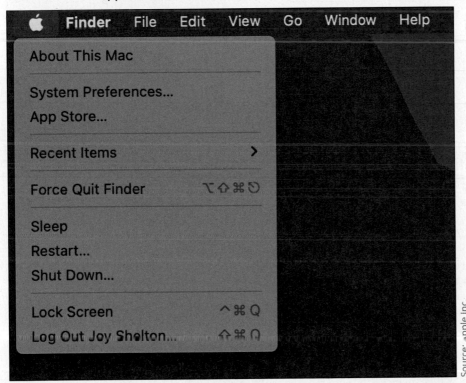

Source: Apple Inc.

The Apple menu also provides access to system information, system preferences, the App Store, recent items, and the Force Quit option. Similar to ending a task from Task Manager in Windows, you can **force quit** an app by clicking **Force Quit**. In the Force Quit Applications window (see Figure 20-9), select the app, and click **Force Quit**. The application closes. You can also access the Force Quit Applications window by pressing **Command (⌘)+Option+Esc**.

Figure 20-9   Force Quit can be used to close an app that is not responding

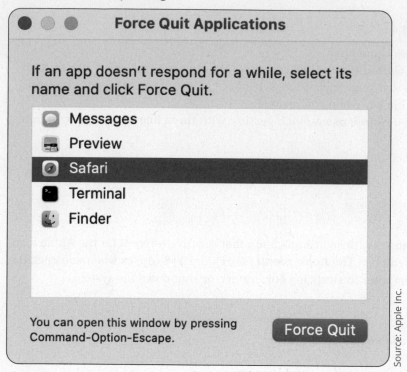

Source: Apple Inc.

System Preferences

Core 2 Objective 1.10

The **System Preferences** window is used to change and customize macOS settings and is similar to the Settings app in Windows. It can be opened from the Apple menu (refer back to Figure 20-8) or from the System Preferences icon in the dock (see Figure 20-10). The System Preferences window is shown in Figure 20-11.

Figure 20-10   The System Preferences icon in the dock shows the app is open

Source: Apple Inc.

Figure 20-11   The System Preferences window is used to customize the macOS interface

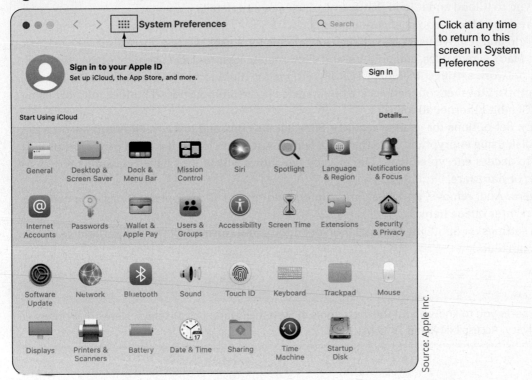

Click at any time to return to this screen in System Preferences

Source: Apple Inc.

Click an icon in System Preferences to change settings for that tool, feature, or app. Here are a few important tools in System Preferences you might use as an IT technician:

- **Trackpad.** Click Trackpad to adjust trackpad gestures.
- **Displays.** Set resolution, brightness, and color profile.
- **Accessibility.** Configure customizations to adapt to individual needs, as seen in Figure 20-12.

Figure 20-12   Accessibility features available in macOS can be customized in System Preferences

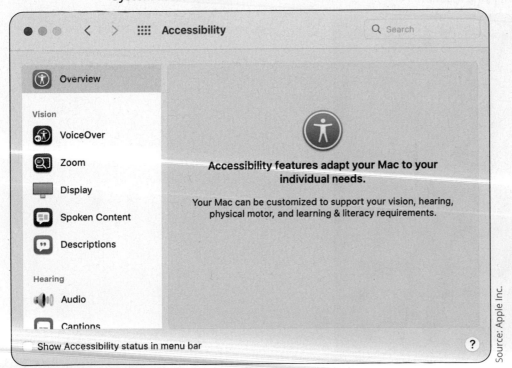

Source: Apple Inc.

- **iCloud.** Click **Apple ID**, and select **iCloud** in the left pane. Set up an iCloud account on this computer, choose what content to sync to iCloud and iCloud Drive, and adjust account details.
- **Time Machine.** Use Time Machine to configure backups.
- **Users & Groups.** Add and remove users and change login items for a user.
- **Sharing.** Share the Mac's screen, files, and printers, and allow remote login and management of the computer.
- **Network.** Change network settings, including TCP/IP settings for Bluetooth, Wi-Fi, and Ethernet connections. (For Mac laptops, Ethernet connections are often made via the multipurpose Thunderbolt port using a Thunderbolt to Gigabit Ethernet adapter.)
- **Security & Privacy.** Set options for general security, FileVault, firewall, and privacy. **FileVault** secures the data on the hard disk using encryption. Note that data will be lost if you forget the login password or lose the recovery key to access encrypted data. The privacy tab shows which apps have requested access to certain apps, data, or hardware.
- **Printers & Scanners.** Add, remove, and configure printers and printer-sharing preferences. You can also view and edit the printer queue here.
- **Spotlight.** Change settings for Spotlight, the macOS search utility. You can control where Spotlight searches and its keyboard shortcuts.

> **Exam Tip** ✔
>
> The A+ Core 2 exam expects you to know about the these tools in System Preferences: Displays, Network, Printers & Scanners, Security & Privacy, Accessibility, and Time Machine.

Control Center

Core 2 Objective 1.10

Introduced with Big Sur, the control center is shown in Figure 20-13. The control center offers a convenient location for accessing commonly used settings, such as Wi-Fi, Bluetooth, AirDrop, Focus, keyboard brightness, screen mirroring, display brightness, sound volume, and music track control.

Figure 20-13   The Control Center gathers frequently accessed settings into one location

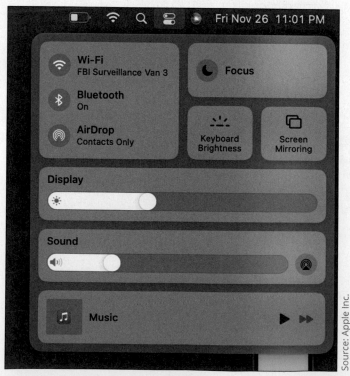

Source: Apple Inc.

Spotlight

Core 2 Objective 1.10

If you're having a problem locating a file or folder, **Spotlight** can search for it. To open Spotlight, click the search icon on the right side of the menu bar or press **Command** (⌘)**+spacebar**. In the Spotlight Search box (see Figure 20-14), type the name of the file, folder, or text you want to find. For example, if you type **Projects**, Spotlight lists a folder named Projects as the Top Hit (see Figure 20-15).

Figure 20-14   Spotlight searches the local computer and online resources

Source: Apple Inc.

Figure 20-15   Use Spotlight to search for files and folders

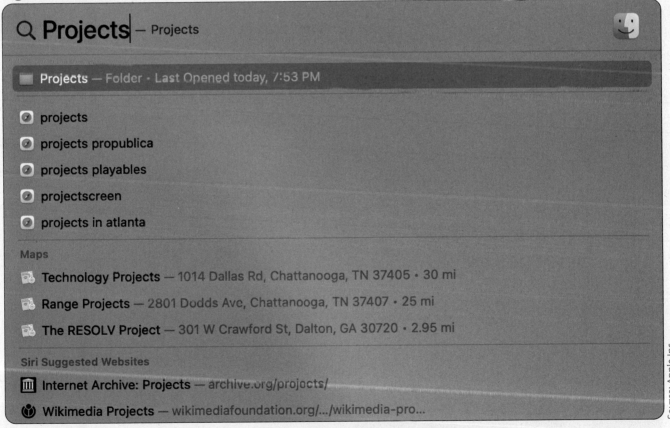

Source: Apple Inc.

Note ②

When you no longer need a file or folder, drag its icon to the Trash icon until the Trash is highlighted, and release the icon. When an item is in the Trash, you can recover it: Click **Trash** to open it and drag an item in the Trash to another location. To empty the trash, click **Finder** in the menu bar, and click **Empty Trash**.

20

Mission Control and Multiple Desktops

 Core 2 Objective 1.10

Mission Control gives you a quick view of all open windows and desktops and lets you switch among them. The macOS includes a feature called **multiple desktops**—which, as its name indicates, is several desktop screens, each with its own collection of open windows. Suppose you're working with several windows for a school project, and you have a few more windows open for a project at work. You can place the school project windows on one desktop, called a **Space**, and place the work project windows on a separate desktop or Space.

To accomplish this, first open Mission Control using one of these methods:

- Press the **Mission Control (F3)** key.
- Click **Mission Control** in the Launchpad window.
- Swipe up with three or four fingers on your trackpad.
- Press **Control+up arrow**.

A Mission Control window is shown in Figure 20-16. Three desktops have been created on the system, as you can see in the Spaces bar at the top of the window. Also, when an app is in full-screen mode, it acts as a separate Space and shows up in the Spaces bar along with desktops. To create a new desktop, drag an open window into the Spaces bar or click + on the right side of the Spaces bar. To delete a desktop, hover over it in the Spaces bar and click the X. Desktop configurations apply to each user and remain in place even when the computer is rebooted.

Figure 20-16 Mission Control allows you to create multiple desktops to contain windows

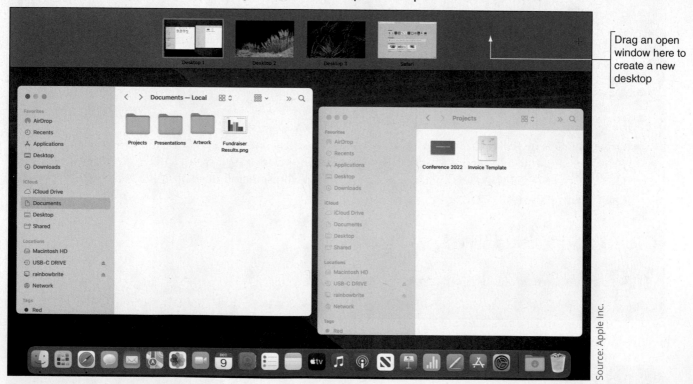

Source: Apple Inc.

Here are a few more tips about multiple desktops:

- **Move among desktops.** To move among desktops already created as you work, swipe left or right with three fingers or press **Control+left arrow** or **Control+right arrow**.
- **Organize desktops.** To help keep your desktops organized, it helps to customize each desktop with a different wallpaper. Go to a desktop and secondary-click. In the menu that appears on the desktop background, click **Change Desktop Background** (see Figure 20-17A). The Desktop & Screen Saver window opens. (This window is one of the tools in System Preferences.) Select your wallpaper and close the window. Wallpaper settings in other existing desktops won't be affected.

Figure 20-17   (A) Set a different background for each desktop, and (B) assign different apps in the dock of each desktop

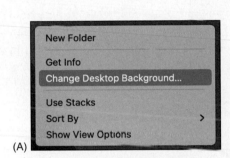
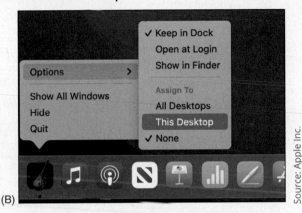

Source: Apple Inc.

(A)   (B)

Note 3

If the desktop background you choose isn't available on your computer yet, click the Cloud Download icon to make that background available.

- **Organize apps in desktops.** To help keep your apps organized, you can assign an app to a specific desktop. Go to that desktop, and secondary-click the app's icon in the dock (see Figure 20-17B). Select **Options**, and then click **This Desktop**. Later, when you open the app, the selected desktop will appear with the app's open window.

iCloud and iCloud Drive

Core 2 Objective 1.10

Looking back at the Finder window shown earlier in Figure 20-5, notice that iCloud Drive is listed in the sidebar along with other storage locations such as Desktop, Documents, and Downloads. When a user signs in to macOS for the first time, they are given the opportunity to set up iCloud with their Apple ID, or the setup can be done later in System Preferences. In System Preferences, you can also control which apps store their data in iCloud (see Figure 20-18).

Figure 20-18 Choose what content to sync with iCloud

Source: Apple Inc.

To open iCloud Drive, click it in the Finder window. Drag and drop files in and out of the iCloud Drive window. The contents are synced with any iPhone, iPad, or Windows desktop that has the iCloud Drive app installed, or with another device that is set up with your Apple ID. (On iPhone and iPad, recall that you can manage iCloud Drive using the Files app.) You can also access your iCloud content, including iCloud Drive, from any device with a browser by going to *icloud.com* and signing in with your Apple ID.

Keychain

Core 2 Objective 1.10

Keychain is the macOS built-in password manager. To open Keychain, go to the Finder window, drill down into the **Applications** list, and then click **Utilities** (refer back to Figure 20-6). Double-click **Keychain Access** app. From the Keychain Access window (see the left side of Figure 20-19), you can view, edit, and remove accounts for applications, websites, and servers. You can also manage personal accounts that you've added, such as credit card and bank accounts.

Figure 20-19   The data stored in Keychain is encrypted

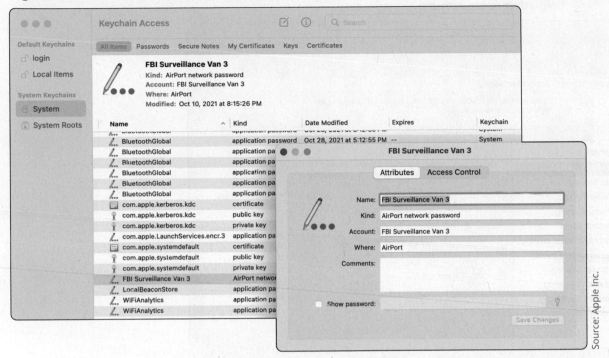

If you have problems with Keychain, you can delete all saved passwords and restore from backup. In the **Keychain Access** menu, click **Preferences**. In the Preferences dialog box, click **Reset My Default Keychains**. Login and Local Items keychains are created, and they are empty. If you have Time Machine backups, try to restore the keychains from backup to recover lost passwords.

Screen Sharing

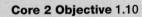

In System Preferences, click **Sharing** to open the Sharing window, where you can set up file and folder sharing on the network, printer sharing, remote access, and screen sharing. **Screen Sharing** works like Remote Desktop in Windows. In the Sharing window (see Figure 20-20), turn on Screen Sharing, and set it up to allow all users or only certain users that you add.

20

Figure 20-20   Screen Sharing makes it easier to collaborate on projects or to help other users with their computers

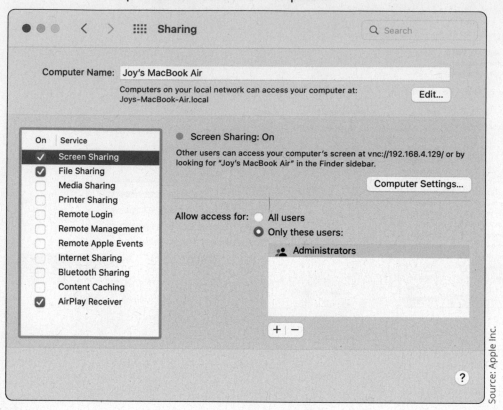

Source: Apple Inc.

To use screen sharing, a user of another Mac on the network should be able to see your shared Mac in their Finder window in the Locations group. They can click your computer, and then click **Share Screen**. They then have the opportunity to sign in to your computer with a user name and password recognized by your computer. Using screen sharing, they can move files and folders between the two computers.

Note 4

Screen Sharing uses incoming port 5900. To access a Mac from the Internet, set up port forwarding on your router to allow incoming traffic on port 5900.

How secure is macOS screen sharing? Some of the content moved between computers is encrypted and some is not, and you must open an incoming port on your router. Therefore, macOS screen sharing is not as secure as other types of remote access software. Also, as you'll recall from the module "Network Security and Troubleshooting," third-party remote access apps that use a browser are considered more secure than OS tools that open ports for incoming traffic initiated from the Internet. Two examples of apps that use browsers and provide encrypted communication are join.me (*join.me*) and Zoom (*zoom.us*).

Remote Disc

> **Core 2 Objective** 1.10

For Macs that have macOS Mojave 10.14 or earlier, Remote Disc is an option for accessing an optical drive on another computer. If your Mac has an optical drive, the Sharing window includes the option DVD or CD Sharing. This feature, called **Remote Disc**, gives other Mac computers on the network access to the computer's optical drive. After you turn on DVD or CD Sharing on a Mac that has an optical drive, go to the Mac that doesn't have an optical drive and open **Finder**. In Finder, click **Remote Disc** in the sidebar under Locations (see Figure 20-21). Apple has retired this feature and no longer supports Remote Disc on macOS Catalina 10.15 and newer.

Figure 20-21 In older macOS systems, access shared optical drives in the Locations area of Finder

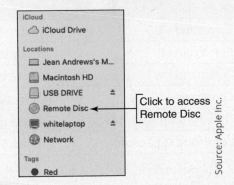

Source: Apple Inc.

Note 5

You can enable remote disc sharing on a Windows computer to be used with an older Mac. To share a Windows computer's optical drive with Macs on your network, download and install **DVD or CD Sharing Update 1.0 for Windows**, which is available at *support.apple.com/kb/DL112?locale=en_US*.

Terminal

> **Core 2 Objective** 1.10

Terminal in macOS is similar to a command prompt window in Windows, except Terminal uses UNIX commands because macOS is based on UNIX. To open Terminal, open **Finder**, click **Applications**, double-click the **Utilities** folder, and double-click **Terminal**. The Terminal window opens, as shown in Figure 20-22. Many of the Linux commands you learn about in the module "Linux and Scripting" work in the macOS Terminal.

Figure 20-22 Terminal in macOS uses most of the same commands as Linux

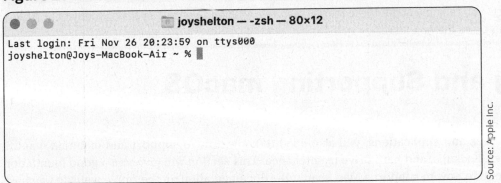

Source: Apple Inc.

Summary of Gestures and Keystrokes

> **Core 2 Objective** 1.10

We finish up this section of the module with Table 20-1, which lists shortcuts and gestures you might find helpful when supporting a Mac. You've already learned to use several of these.

20

Table 20-1 Useful keystrokes, substitute keys, and gestures

Keystrokes, Substitute Keys, and Gestures	Description
Keystrokes	
Command+X	Cut the selected item.
Command+C	Copy the selected item.
Command+V	Paste the selected item.
Command+A	Select all items.
Option+Command+Esc	Force quit an app.
Command+spacebar	Open Spotlight.
Shift+Command+5	Take a screenshot of the entire screen or part of the screen. By default, screenshots are saved to the desktop.
Substitute keys when using a regular keyboard instead of a Mac keyboard	
Command key	The Windows logo key or Control key is the substitute.
Option key	The Alt key is the substitute.
Gestures (gesture actions can be changed in the trackpad app's System Preferences)	
Secondary-click	Tap the trackpad with two fingers.
Swipe	Swipe left or right with three fingers to move among desktops. On a keyboard, press Control+right arrow and Control+left arrow.
Scroll	Swipe up or down with two fingers.
Zoom	Pinch in or out with two fingers.
Pinch	Pinch in with three fingers and thumb to show Launchpad. Do a spread-apart pinch with three fingers and thumb to return to the desktop. If you are already on the desktop, a spread-apart pinch pushes all open windows to the edges to clear the desktop.

Exam Tip ✔

The A+ Core 2 exam expects you to know about these macOS features: Mission Control, Keychain, Spotlight, iCloud, Finder, Remote Disk, FileVault, and the App Store.

Maintaining and Supporting macOS

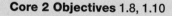 **Core 2 Objectives** 1.8, 1.10

In addition to working with files and applications, you also need to know how to support and maintain macOS, including performing updates, backups, and hard drive maintenance. This section will give you a good foundation for these skills. To dig deeper into how to support a Mac, search the documentation on the Apple website (*support. apple.com*).

Caution ❗

Many Apple computers are covered by an Apple Care warranty, which provides excellent coverage for Macs. Always be absolutely certain that a Mac is not covered by Apple Care before opening the case or doing anything else that might void the warranty.

macOS Directory Structures

Core 2 Objectives 1.8, 1.10

First let's learn some of the basics of macOS directory structures. Here are the file systems macOS supports:

- APFS (Apple File System) is the default file system for SSDs and can also be used for magnetic hard drives. APFS allocates free space as needed for each volume on the drive. APFS uses the GUID (also called GPT) partitioning system.
- The FAT32 and exFAT file systems are supported for compatibility with Windows and Linux.

Note 6

Windows cannot read from storage devices that are using the APFS file system unless third-party drivers are installed in Windows.

You need to be familiar with the directory structure in macOS. Here are some tips:

- To see the directory structure, click **Go** on the Finder menu bar, and then click **Computer**. In the Finder window, click the hard drive, which is labeled Macintosh HD in most systems. In Figure 20-23, you can see the four folders at the root level. (Other folders in the root are hidden.) User data is in the Users folder.

Figure 20-23   Folders visible in the root of the hard drive

Name	Date Modified	Size	Kind
> Applications	Nov 23, 2021 at 5:57 PM	--	Folder
> Library	Oct 28, 2021 at 5:12 PM	--	Folder
> System	Oct 17, 2021 at 11:30 PM	--	Folder
v Users	Oct 17, 2021 at 11:30 PM	--	Folder
v joyshelton	Today at 8:25 PM	--	Folder
> Downloads	Today at 8:14 PM	--	Folder
> iCloud Drive (Archive)	Today at 2:36 PM	--	Folder
> iCloud Drive (Archive) - 1	Today at 7:11 PM	--	Folder
> Movies	Nov 22, 2021 at 2:20 PM	--	Folder
> Music	Today at 8:01 PM	--	Folder
> Pictures	Today at 7:10 PM	--	Folder
> Public	Today at 8:28 PM	--	Folder
> Shared	Nov 5, 2021 at 12:19 AM	--	Folder

Favorites: AirDrop, Recents, Applications, Downloads
iCloud: iCloud Drive, Documents, Desktop, Shared
Locations: Macintosh HD, USB-C DRIVE, asus-joy, toshiba-joy, Network

Macintosh HD

Four root folders

Source: Apple Inc.

- You can also browse the directory structure using the Terminal and Linux commands. In **Finder**, open **Applications**, open **Utilities**, and double-click **Terminal**. All commands, as well as file and directory names, are case sensitive. Use the cd command to move through the directory structure and the ls command to list files and directories. For example, Figure 20-24 shows the root directory of the Macintosh HD. Compare Figure 20-23 with Figure 20-24, and notice that some folders that appear in the Terminal window are hidden in the Finder window. You learn more about these directories later in this module.

20

Figure 20-24   Contents of the root directory on a Mac hard drive

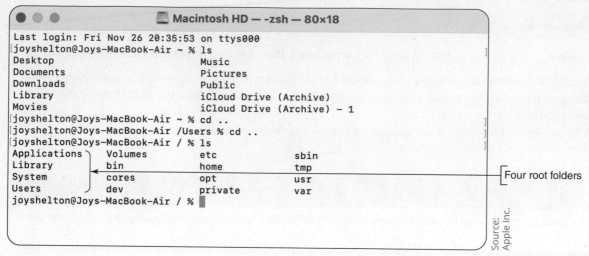

File Types

Three common file types you might encounter while supporting macOS are the following:

- **DMG.** A **DMG file** (.dmg) is a disk image file, similar to an ISO file used in Windows. DMG files can be used for delivering software. DMG files appear as a virtual disk drive on macOS. When you double-click a DMG file, the virtual disk is mounted to macOS, and you can then access the files inside it.
- **PKG.** A **PKG file** (.pkg) is a package file, similar to a setup.exe file used in Windows. A PKG file contains installer files used for software installations. A PKG file is often compressed like a ZIP file, which is used in Windows. After an installation is complete, the PKG file can be deleted.
- **APP.** An **APP file** (.app) is an application file, similar to a .exe file used in Windows to run an application.

Exam Tip ✔

The A+ Core 2 exam expects you to be able to identify .dmg, .pkg, and .app files. Remember that file names are case sensitive in macOS.

Installing Apps

 Core 2 Objective 1.10

Recall from the module "Mobile Device Security" that Apple streamlines installing apps in Apple devices through its App Store. The **App Store** is a central location where you can find, install, support, and update apps. macOS allows for apps to be installed from trusted sources, such as a developer's website, but the most reliable method to install a new app is through the App Store. If you must download an app from a trusted website, always make sure you're choosing the file that is made for macOS and not Windows or Linux.

Applying Concepts

Install and Uninstall Apps in macOS

Est. Time: 30 minutes
Core 2 Objective: 1.10

Follow these steps to install an app from the App Store:

1. Open the **App Store**.
2. Browse or search for the app you want to install. As an example, search for **Adobe Lightroom**, an app used to manage and edit photos. Click the app name to view the app's ratings, description, and reviews.

3. Click **Get**, then **Install**. If required, provide your Apple ID and password to continue with the installation.

4. When the installation is complete, in the App Store click **Open** to open Adobe Lightroom.

Uninstalling an app is just as easy. Follow these steps to uninstall an app that was installed by the App Store:

1. Open **Launchpad**, and find the icon for the app you want to uninstall. In this case, let's uninstall Adobe Lightroom, which we just installed.

2. Press and hold the **Option** key or the app icon until the apps jiggle.

3. Click the **Delete** key, or the **X** in the corner of the app icon. Then click **Delete**. The app is uninstalled.

To install an app from a trusted website, do the following steps:

Browse to the trusted website to download the file. For example, go to *papercut.com/products/free-software/mobility-print/#downloadSection*, and download the PaperCut Mobility Print app for macOS, seen in Figure 20-25.

Figure 20-25   Select the macOS download from trusted sources

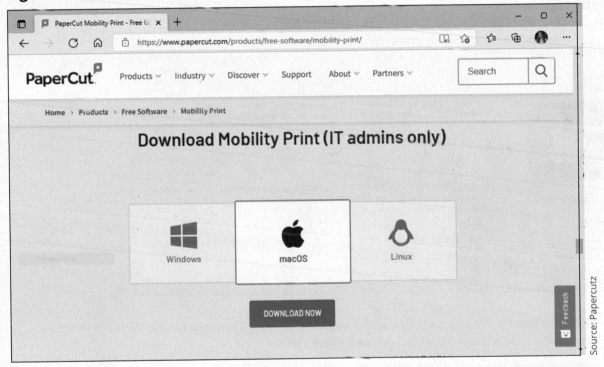

Source: Papercutz

4. Open the **DMG file** in the Downloads folder in Finder.

5. Double-click the **PKG file** to start the installation, and click **Install**. Follow the on-screen instructions to complete the installation.

If an app was installed without using the App Store, you must use Finder to uninstall it. Follow these steps to uninstall an app:

1. Open **Finder** and click **Applications** in the left pane.

2. Find the app you want to uninstall—for example, **PaperCut Mobility Print**. Drag and drop the app icon to **Trash** in the dock.

3. Provide your credentials to allow the uninstallation.

4. Empty **Trash**.

20

Managed Apple IDs

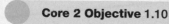 **Core 2 Objective** 1.10

Recall from the module "Installing Windows" that you can sign in to Windows using a local account, a Microsoft account (possibly for Azure), or an AD network ID. Remember that an AD network ID or a Microsoft account can be used to join a domain. The same applies to macOS. You can sign in to a Mac using a local account, an Apple ID, a Managed Apple ID, or an AD network ID. A Managed Apple ID and an AD network ID are used to join a domain. For personal accounts, use a local account or an Apple ID. The Apple ID creates continuity among Apple devices—as a Microsoft account does across Windows devices.

If a user has already connected their iCloud account, then they have signed in with their Apple ID. If they have not, then they can set up their Apple ID in System Preferences. Follow these steps with an sign in with an Apple ID:

1. Open **System Preferences**. Click **Sign In**.
2. As shown Figure 20-26, you can sign in with your Apple ID if you already have one, or you can create an Apple ID if necessary. If you don't remember your password, click **Forgot Apple ID or password?** to look up your Apple ID or reset your password.

Figure 20-26   Sign in with Apple ID to access your data stored in iCloud

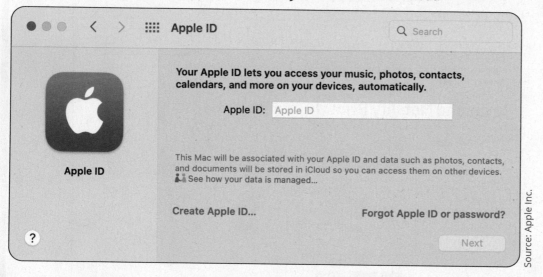

Source: Apple Inc.

3. When you sign in, you may be prompted to enter the password for your local account or to verify a passcode sent to a trusted device, such as a mobile phone.

To sign in using a Managed Apple ID, which must be an email address, simply use the Managed Apple ID credentials provided by your administrator. Upon signing in the first time, you will be prompted to change the password. The administrator of the Managed Apple IDs through Apple Business Manager is able to put restrictions on the Apple devices by assigning role privileges. Apple Business Manager is accessed through an Apple website (*business.apple.com*).

Note 7

To review the role privileges that can be set in Apple Business Manager, visit the Apple support website: *support.apple.com/guide/apple-business-manager/role-privileges-axm97dd59159*.

Apple Business Manager must be connected to a verified domain service, such as Azure AD, which can offer more control on restrictions based on the capabilities of the domain service you are using. When using Azure AD, the Azure AD credentials can be used as Managed Apple ID credentials.

Update macOS and Drivers

Core 2 Objective 1.10

Just like Windows, macOS needs regular updates. Updates often address zero-day vulnerabilities, which makes these updates important to maintaining a healthy system. However, sometimes the updates themselves introduce bugs, which is why many Mac experts advise against setting macOS updates to install automatically. Instead, wait a few days after a macOS update is released before manually installing the update; this gives you a chance to see if the update introduces any significant issues. These updates also include any firmware updates available.

You can access macOS updates in System Preferences. To manually update macOS, open **System Preferences**, then click **Software Update** in the left pane. Figure 20-27 shows a recently updated app. Any available OS updates will be shown near the top of the screen.

Figure 20-27   The Updates window shows recently installed updates and needed updates when available

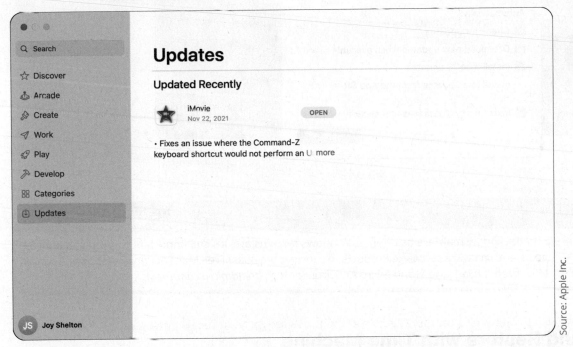

Source: Apple Inc.

Updates for apps are found in the App Store. To manually update apps, click the **App Store** icon in the dock, and then click **Updates** in the left pane. Any apps that need updates are listed in the Updates window.

Note 8

Printer, scanner, and graphics driver updates are usually included in macOS updates. Other devices that require drivers, if not included in macOS, can be downloaded from the manufacturer's website and installed. These drivers will not be updated through macOS updates. If any problems are encountered with these devices, you'll need to check the manufacturer's website for updates.

20

To change the settings for automatic updates, open **System Preferences**, and click **Software Update**. The OS checks for and reports available updates. For automatic updates, check **Automatically keep my Mac up to date**. To change detailed update settings, click **Advanced** (see Figure 20-28). Here is an explanation of each option:

- **Check for updates.** Automatically check for updates.
- **Download new updates when available.** Download available updates without installing them.
- **Install macOS updates.** Install all updates to the operating system without first requiring user approval.
- **Install app updates from the App Store.** Install all updates to App Store applications without first requiring user approval.
- **Install system data files and security updates.** Install critical system patches that address known vulnerabilities.

Figure 20-28 Manage how automatic updates are handled

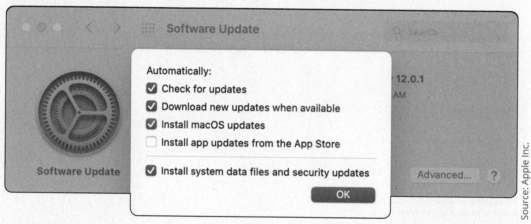

Source: Apple Inc.

Note

Although Macs are not attacked by malware as often as Windows systems are, it's still important to protect a Mac by installing and maintaining anti-malware software. Products to consider are Avast Free Mac Security (*avast.com*), Sophos Home Premium for Mac (*sophos.com*), and Trend Micro Antivirus for Mac (*trendmicro.com/mac*).

Back Up and Restore with Time Machine

Core 2 Objective 1.10

Like iOS mobile devices, Mac computers can use iCloud Drive to store files and folders in the cloud and sync this content across all of your devices. Unlike the mobile devices you learned about in the module "Supporting Mobile Devices," Mac computers cannot be fully backed up using iCloud. For this purpose, macOS includes **Time Machine**, which is a built-in backup utility that automatically backs up user-created data, applications, and the entire macOS system. You can back up to the following:

- A USB or Thunderbolt external hard drive or a USB flash drive
- Another Mac on the local network
- Network-attached storage (NAS) devices that support Time Machine

After Time Machine is set up, backups are updated in the background. Depending on the space available on the backup drive, Time Machine keeps hourly backups for 24 hours, daily backups for a month, and weekly backups until the disk is full. The oldest backups are deleted to make space for new backups. You can also set up multiple backup schedules for more than one backup device.

To set up Time Machine in macOS, open **System Preferences**, and click **Time Machine**. The Time Machine window appears, as shown in Figure 20-29.

Figure 20-29   Configure Time Machine backups

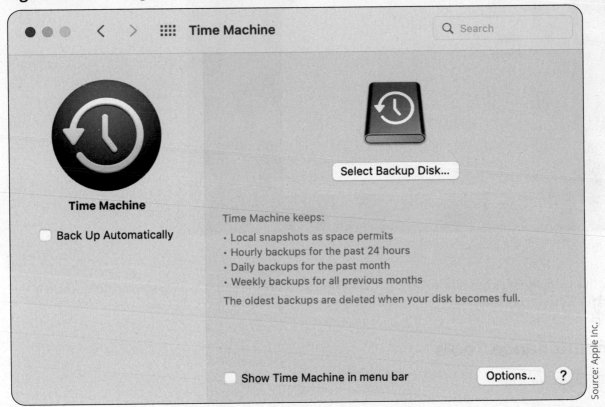

Source: Apple Inc.

Follow the on-screen directions to select a backup disk and configure backup options. Note that everything already on the disk will be erased. The original backup will be at least 20 GB, includes the entire macOS volume, and takes some time to complete.

Note 10

When your Mac is not connected to the backup disk, Time Machine stores backup copies, called local **snapshots**, of created, modified, or deleted files on the hard drive. When you reconnect the computer to the backup disk, the local snapshots are copied to the backup disk. Local snapshots stay on the hard drive as long as they don't take up too much space, and they can be restored from the hard drive if needed. Time Machine saves one snapshot each day and one weekly snapshot for each week the backup disk is disconnected.

You can use the backups to recover files, folders, or the entire macOS volume. To recover a file or folder from Time Machine, open **Finder**. In the **Applications** group, double-click **Time Machine**. The timeline and available backups in Finder appear (see Figure 20-30). Use the Finder window to locate the file or folder. Then go back through time to find the version of the file or folder you want to restore. To move through time, you can use the timeline on the right, the arrow buttons, or click a Finder window in the stack of available windows. Select the item, and click **Restore**.

20

Figure 20-30 Locate an item, and then go back through time to find the version to restore

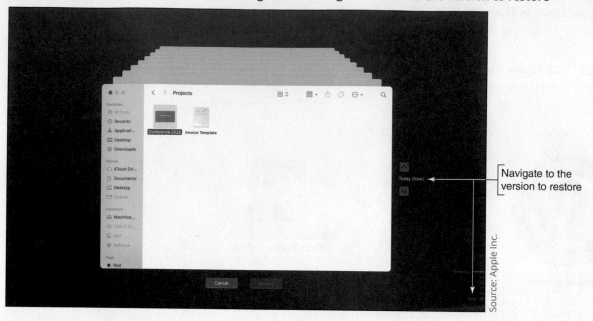

Source: Apple Inc.

Navigate to the version to restore

Later in this module, you learn how to use Time Machine to restore the entire macOS **startup disk**, which is the volume on which macOS is installed.

Drive Maintenance Tools

Core 2 Objective 1.10

Hard drives in Mac computers require very little maintenance. However, performing a few simple tasks on a regular basis can help keep things running smoothly:

- **Empty the trash.** To empty the Trash, click the **Trash** icon in the dock. Trash contents appear in a Finder window (see Figure 20-31). Click **Empty**, and then click **Empty Trash** in the warning box. Items are permanently deleted.

Figure 20-31 Check the contents of the Trash Can before emptying it

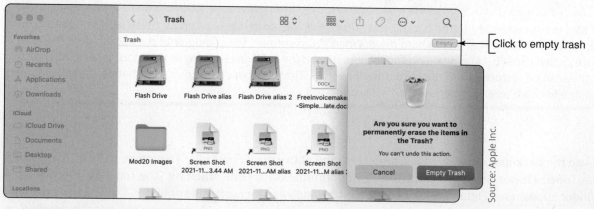

Click to empty trash

Source: Apple Inc.

- **Free up space.** Maintain at least 15%–20% free space on the hard drive for optimal performance. To see how much free space is available on the drive, open the Apple menu, click **About This Mac**, and then click the **Storage** tab, as shown in Figure 20-32.

Figure 20-32 Maintain at least 15% free space on the hard drive

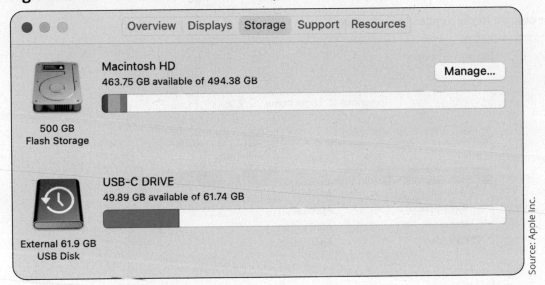

Source: Apple Inc.

- **Install updates.** Regularly check for and install macOS and app updates, which you learned to do earlier in this module.
- **Verify no startup items.** Programs that automatically launch at startup are called **startup items**, and programs that automatically launch after a user logs in are called **login items**. Apple discourages the use of startup items because they slow down the startup process, and items in the startup folder might be malware. You can verify that the system doesn't have startup items by looking in two directories that can contain them: /Library/StartupItems and /System/Library/StartupItems (see Figure 20-33).

Figure 20-33 For best performance, the StartupItems folder should remain empty

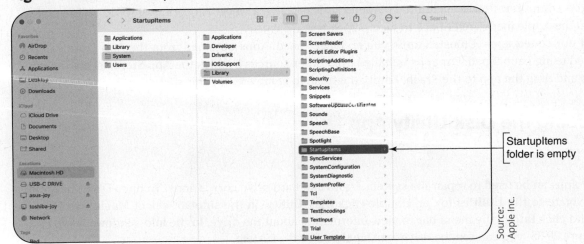

Source: Apple Inc.

- **Remove login items.** Launching too many programs at login slows down the boot process and uses up valuable RAM. To adjust login items, open **System Preferences**, and click **Users & Groups**. Select a user account in the sidebar, and then click the **Login Items** tab (see Figure 20-34). Use the + and − buttons at the bottom of the items list to add or remove login items.

Figure 20-34   A list of login items applies to each user

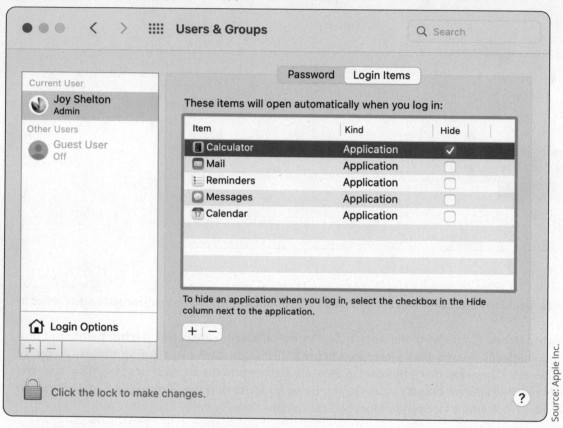

Source: Apple Inc.

- **Restart the computer.** Power-cycle the computer at least once a week. A quick way to do so is to click **Restart** in the Apple menu (refer back to Figure 20-8).
- **Uninstall unneeded apps.** Uninstall apps you no longer need. Apps obtained from the App Store can be uninstalled using Launchpad. For apps installed from other sources besides the App Store, locate the app in Finder, and drag the app to the Trash. Empty the trash to complete the uninstall.

Repairs Using the Disk Utility App

 Core 2 Objective 1.10

The Disk Utility app can be used to repair file system errors and hard drive corruptions. To open Disk Utility, open **Finder**, and navigate to the **Utilities** folder. Double-click **Disk Utility**. In the sidebar, select **Macintosh HD** (see Figure 20-35), and click **Info** in the menu bar to view information about the drive. In the Info window shown on the right side of Figure 20-35, you can see the drive is using the APFS file system.

Figure 20-35   Manage drives from the Disk Utility app

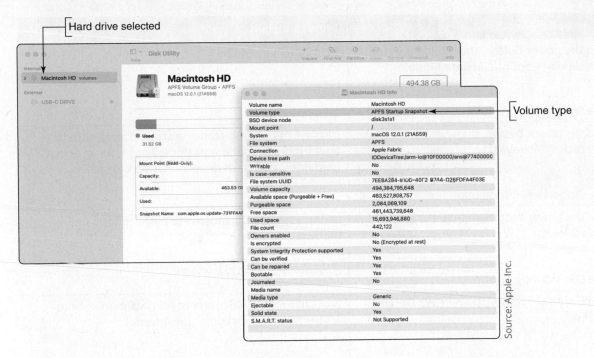

You can use **First Aid** in Disk Utility to scan the hard drive for file system errors and repair them. In Disk Utility, select the drive in the sidebar, click **First Aid**, and click **Run** in the dialog box that appears. A warning box reports that apps will not respond while the drive is repaired. Click **Continue**. The process can take some time. Click **Done** when it completes.

Note 11

If you plug in an external hard drive and macOS does not recognize the drive, you can use Disk Utility to fix the problem. In the Disk Utility window, select the drive, and click **Mount**. If the mount does not work, click **First Aid** and then try to mount the drive again. When you mount a drive, it can be viewed by the OS, the drive is listed in the sidebar of the Finder window, and its icon appears on the desktop.

Exam Tip ✔

The A+ Core 2 exam expects you to know how to repair a hard drive using the Disk Utility.

Troubleshooting macOS Startup

Core 2 Objective 1.10

When you have problems with macOS startup, use the options discussed in this section of the module to diagnose and fix the problems. These options are summarized in Table 20-2. Turn on the Mac and press certain keys at startup to launch tools or boot from other media. Release the keys as soon as you see the Apple logo.

Table 20-2   Keys to press to access Mac startup options

Keys to Press as a Mac Boots	Tools Launched
Press and hold the power button, then hold down the **Shift** key while clicking **Continue in Safe Mode**. or Hold down the **Shift** key during boot.	Boots into Safe Mode
Press and hold the power button, then hold down the **Shift** key while clicking **Always Use**. or Hold down the **Option** key during boot.	Displays the Startup Manager so you can choose to boot from different media (for example, the external hard drive, USB flash drive, or network locations)
Press and hold the power button, then press and hold the **Command+D** keys. or Hold down the **D** key during boot.	Launches Apple Diagnostics to perform tests on hardware
Press and hold the power button, then select **Options**, and click **Continue**. or Hold down the **Command+R** keys during boot.	Launches macOS Recovery to reinstall macOS from a Time Machine backup or the Internet

Note 12

To review more startup options, visit the Apple website (*support.apple.com/en-us/HT201255*).

Note 13

Many of these same steps can also help when troubleshooting kernel panics. A **kernel panic** is similar to a BSOD in Windows. It might be caused by something simple, such as a crashed app or a network communication issue, or it might result from a corrupted macOS installation. macOS restarts automatically when experiencing a kernel panic. If the kernel panic continues to prompt restarts, macOS will stop trying and shut down the computer after five attempts.

Safe Mode

 Core 2 Objective 1.10

Starting the computer in Safe Mode can solve problems when the computer won't start due to file system errors or corrupted startup or login items. Safe Mode in macOS loads essential kernel components, prevents startup items and login items from launching, and loads a minimum of user processes. It also verifies the startup disk and repairs any file system errors it finds.

To boot into Safe Mode, press and hold the power button, and then hold down the **Shift** key while clicking **Continue in Safe Mode**. Or if your Mac uses an Intel processor, hold down the **Shift** key as a Mac starts up. To verify that the computer booted into Safe Mode, open **System Report** under About This Mac. In the Software group, look for Boot Mode, which should report Safe (see Figure 20-36).

Figure 20-36   Boot Mode indicates the computer is booted into Safe Mode

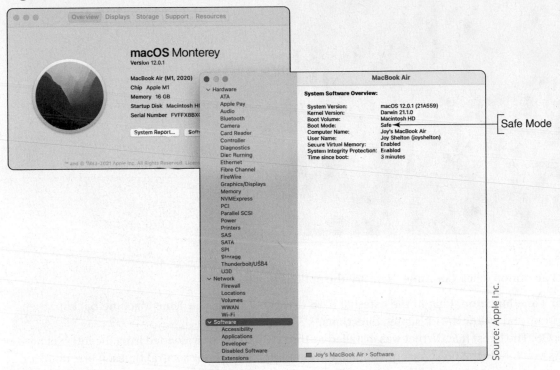

Source: Apple Inc.

Do these things in Safe Mode:

- When Safe Mode starts, it automatically attempts to fix many problems. Restart the computer normally, and see whether the problem is solved.
- Delete startup and login items that you suspect are causing a problem.

macOS Recovery

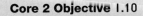 **Core 2 Objective** 1.10

Using the macOS Recovery tools, you can reinstall macOS from a Time Machine backup or from the Internet. You can also erase the hard drive before you perform the image recovery. Press and hold the power button, then select **Options**, and click **Continue**, or turn on the Mac and press and hold **Command+R** until you see the Apple logo. macOS Recovery launches and you see the macOS Utilities menu (see Figure 20-37).

Figure 20-37 Boot into macOS Recovery to reinstall macOS

Restore from Time Machine
If you have backup of your system that you want to restore.

Reinstall macOS Monterey
Install a new copy of macOS Monterey onto your Mac.

Safari
Browse Apple Support to get help with your Mac.

Disk Utility
Repair or erase a disk using Disk Utility.

Continue

Source: Apple Inc.

After you select an option, click **Continue**. Here are the options you'll see:

- **Restore from Time Machine.** Plug in the external hard drive that holds the Time Machine backup, then select this option, and follow the on-screen directions.
- **Reinstall macOS.** The latest macOS that was installed on the computer is downloaded from the Internet and reinstalled. As you follow the on-screen directions, the computer will reboot several times. If errors occur during the process, try erasing the hard drive and reinstalling again. After the new installation of macOS boots up, any data backed up with Time Machine can be restored.
- **Disk Utility.** If you need to erase the hard drive (for example, before you give away a Mac), select **Disk Utility**, and follow the on-screen directions.

Note 14

Suppose you are attempting to reinstall macOS from the Internet and you are not able to get an Internet connection through Wi-Fi or Ethernet. In this situation, you can use another Mac to create a bootable installation device and use it to reinstall macOS. This bootable device is created using commands in the Terminal window and is not covered in this text. The commands and process can be found at *support.apple.com/en-us/HT201372*.

Module Summary

Getting to Know the macOS Desktop

- macOS is used only for Macintosh computers by Apple Inc. Like Linux, macOS is built on a UNIX foundation.
- The dock appears at the bottom of the desktop on a Mac. The icons in the dock that represent open applications have a small black circle underneath them.

- Important macOS tools used to manage and support a Mac include Finder, Launchpad, the Apple menu, System Preferences, Control Center, Spotlight, Mission Control, Keychain, Screen Sharing, Terminal, and gestures on a trackpad.
- For IT technicians, the most important tools in System Preferences are accessed through Time Machine, Users & Groups, and Sharing. Screen Sharing, one of the Sharing tools, works like Remote Desktop in Windows.

Maintaining and Supporting macOS

- Common file types used for installing and using apps include DMG, PKG, and APP.
- Install and uninstall most apps using the App Store. Trusted websites can be used to download apps, too.
- Use a Managed Apple ID to restrict permissions for use with organizations.

Update macOS and Drivers

- macOS updates often address zero-day vulnerabilities, which makes these updates important for maintaining a healthy system.
- Time Machine is a built-in backup utility that automatically backs up user-created data, applications, and system files to an external hard drive that's attached either directly to the computer or through the local network.
- First Aid in Disk Utility can scan and repair file system errors on a hard drive.

Troubleshooting macOS Startup

- Tools to fix macOS startup problems include Safe Mode and macOS Recovery.

Key Terms

For explanations of key terms, see the Glossary for this text.

APP file	First Aid	Mission Control	Space
App Store	force quit	multiple desktops	Spotlight
Apple menu	gesture	PKG file	startup disk
DMG file	kernel panic	Remote Disc	startup item
dock	Keychain	Screen Sharing	System Preferences
FileVault	Launchpad	secondary-click	Terminal
Finder	login item	snapshot	Time Machine

Thinking Critically

These questions are designed to prepare you for the critical thinking required for the A+ exams and may use information from other modules and the web.

1. Why is the scrollbar typically hidden from view in macOS?
2. Which app manages multiple desktop screens in macOS?
3. Which app provides tools for customizing the macOS interface?
4. A scanner connected to your Mac is giving you problems, and you suspect corrupted device drivers. What should you do first? Second?
   a. Download and install drivers from the scanner manufacturer.
   b. Back up the macOS startup disk using Time Machine.
   c. Update macOS.
   d. Uninstall the scanner and install it again.

20

5. How often does Time Machine create new backups, and how long are these backups kept?

6. Your macOS installation is corrupted, and you want to boot from an external Thunderbolt hard drive to repair the installation. Which key(s) do you hold down at startup to boot from the external hard drive if you have an Intel-based Mac?

   a. D key
   b. Command+R keys
   c. Shift key
   d. Option key

7. What Apple file type is similar to an ISO file used in Windows?

8. You work on a help desk, and you receive a call from a user who needs help on their MacBook. What feature does macOS include that allows you to assist the user without having to travel to their location?

9. What solution does Apple offer to assign permissions to user accounts in an organization?

10. What file system does macOS support in order to be compatible with Windows?

Hands-On Projects

Hands-On Project 20-1

Practicing Using the macOS Desktop

Est. Time: 30 minutes
Core 2 Objective: 1.10

If you're not used to a Mac, the macOS desktop might feel strange compared with Windows, but with a little practice, you'll find all of the essential functions right at your fingertips. Complete the following steps to explore the macOS desktop:

1. **Confirm that you have a Wi-Fi connection.** Look for the Wi-Fi icon in the upper-right corner of the screen. If there is no connection, the icon will have a slash through it (see Figure 20-38). Click the Wi-Fi icon, turn on Wi-Fi if it's not on already, and connect to the network.

Figure 20-38 Click the switch button to turn on Wi-Fi, or click Open Network Preferences to set other options

Source: Apple Inc.

2. **Install an app from the App Store.** Click the App Store icon in the dock; sign in if necessary. Select a free app and install it. A good one to try is Evernote. After installation is complete, leave the App Store window open. Use Finder to open the app.

3. **See all open windows with Mission Control.** On a laptop, swipe up with three fingers to open Mission Control. On a desktop, open **Mission Control** by pressing **Control+up arrow** or the **Mission Control** key. Click a window to go to that window on the desktop.

4. **Uninstall the app you installed.** Close all open windows on the desktop. If you installed the Evernote app, you might need to use the Evernote menu on the menu bar to close it. Next, open Launchpad. On a laptop, use a trackpad gesture; on a desktop, click **Launchpad** in the dock. In Launchpad, locate the icon for the app you installed. Press and hold the icon. All the icons jiggle. Some apps, such as Mission Control, are embedded in macOS and cannot be uninstalled; apps that can be uninstalled have an X on the upper-left corner of the icon (see Figure 20-39). Click the **X** on the app you want to uninstall, and then click **Delete** in the message bubble that appears, as shown in the figure. Click an open space on the screen to make the icons stop jiggling. Click the open space again to return to the desktop.

Figure 20-39   Use Launchpad to uninstall an app

Source: Apple Inc.

Hands-On Project 20-2

Practicing macOS Commands

Est. Time: 30 minutes
Core 2 Objective: 1.10

Practice using the commands listed in Table 20-3 in Terminal.

Table 20-3   Practice using commands in Terminal

Task	Command	Description
1	`ls -l`	Lists files and directories in the current directory; in macOS, a directory is treated more like a file than it is in a Windows directory
2	`pwd`	Displays the full path to the current directory; when you first log in to a system, that directory is /home/*username*
3	`mkdir mydir`	Creates a directory named mydir; the directory is created in the current directory
4	`cd mydir`	Goes to the directory you just created in the /home/*username* directory
5	`touch myfile`	Creates a blank file named myfile in the current directory
6	`ls`	Lists the current directory's contents
7	`cd ..`	Moves up one level in the directory tree
8	`cd /etc`	Changes the directory to the /etc directory, where text files are kept for configuring installed programs
9	`ls`	Lists the contents of the /etc directory
10	`cd /home`	Changes the directory to the /home directory
11	`ping 127.0.0.1`	Pings the loopback address; pinging continues until you stop it by pressing Control+C
12	`ifconfig`	Displays TCP/IP configuration data
13	`man ifconfig`	Displays the page from the System Manager's Manual about the ifconfig command; press Q to exit
14	`df`	Displays free space on the hard drive and the file system used

Do research online, and answer the following questions about closing the macOS Terminal window:

1. What does the exit command do in the macOS Terminal window?
2. How can you adjust Terminal settings so that the exit command closes the Terminal window if the shell exited cleanly?
3. What keyboard shortcut can you use instead to close the Terminal window?

Note 15

Even if you don't have a Mac computer to use, you can still research the answers to the preceding questions. The information is readily available online.

Hands-On Project 20-3

Killing a Process in macOS

Est. Time: 30 minutes
Core 2 Objective: 1.10

macOS Terminal is a powerful tool and can be used to kill a hung process or to kill a process you suspect to be malware. First, try to use Force Quit to end the process. If that doesn't work, use Terminal to end the process. Follow these general directions to practice this skill:

1. Once again, install the Evernote app, but don't launch it.
2. Open **Terminal**. Run the following command to list all running processes (the x option displays all processes, even those not started in this shell or user interface): `ps x`
3. Leave Terminal open. Launch the **Evernote** app. Return to the Terminal window, and list all running processes again. What are the Evernote app process IDs? Of the two process IDs, which one represents the application itself, and which one represents a login item?
4. The pgrep command combines the functionality of ps and grep. The grep command searches for text within a file. Do research online to find the Apple "man page," or manual page, for pgrep. What do the –f and –l options do?
5. Confirm the Evernote app's process IDs with the command `pgrep -f -l Evernote`. (Be sure to capitalize the E in Evernote.) Do the process IDs match the information you found earlier?
6. Use Terminal to kill the Evernote app (not the login item).
7. Return to the macOS desktop and uninstall Evernote.

Real Problems, Real Solutions

Real Problem 20-1

Sharing a Folder to the Network from a Mac Computer and Mapping the Drive on a Windows Computer

Est. Time: 30 minutes
Core 2 Objective: 1.10

In the module "Securing and Sharing Windows Resources," you shared a folder on the network and mapped a network drive. These tasks can also be done in macOS, which makes it easier to share files between computers of various operating systems. Complete the following steps to set up a network share from a Mac computer:

1. **Create a folder to share.** Use Finder to create a subfolder in the Documents folder, and name the new folder **Meeting Minutes**.
2. **Set sharing options.** Open **System Preferences** and click **Sharing**. Select **File Sharing** in the sidebar, and make sure it's turned on. Click the **Options** button, and make sure that *Share files and folders using SMB* is checked. Under Windows File Sharing, check the box to turn on file sharing for your macOS user account with Windows computers. Enter your macOS user account password if necessary, and click **OK**. Click **Done**.

(continues)

20

Real Problem Continued

3. **Share the folder.** Under Shared Folders, click the + button below the Shared Folders list, and then navigate to **Documents**. Double-click the **Meeting Minutes** folder, which should then be added to the Shared Folders list. Click **Meeting Minutes** to select it. Under Users, make sure the **Everyone** group is set to **Read Only**. Return to the System Preferences main window.

4. **Enable shared folders for the guest account.** Click **Users & Groups**. Click the lock icon in the lower-left corner of the window so you can make changes to user settings, and sign in. Click the **Guest User** account in the sidebar. Check **Allow guest users to connect to shared folders**, and return to the main System Preferences window. Also check **Allow guests to log into this computer**.

5. **Set a static IP address.** In System Preferences, click **Network** and then click **Advanced**. Click the **TCP/IP** tab. Configure the IPv4 address with a manual address as directed by your instructor. Click **OK**.

6. **Map the network share on a Windows computer.** On your Windows 10 computer, open **File Explorer**, right-click **This PC**, and click **Map network drive** on the Computer ribbon. (For Windows 11, at the top of the Explorer window, click the ... *See more* icon, and select **Map network drive**.) In the **Map Network Drive** dialog box, enter the Mac's IP address and the name of the shared folder, as shown in Figure 20-40, adjusting the specific details to your situation. Check *Connect using different credentials*, and then click **Finish**. When asked for a user name and password, enter **Guest** for the user name, and leave the password blank. Explorer should open a new window that shows the mapped drive.

Figure 20-40   Folder information includes the IP address of the remote computer and the folder name

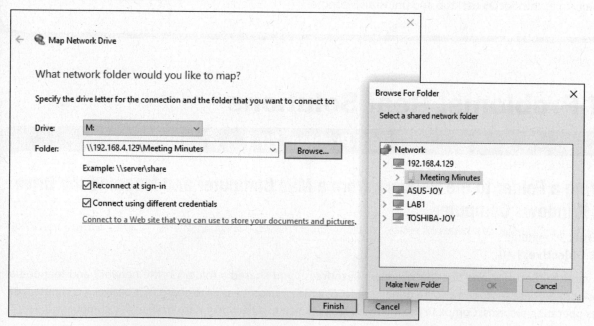

7. **Check the network share.** Create a file on the Mac computer, and save it to the shared folder. Does it appear in the mapped network drive on the Windows computer? If not, troubleshoot and fix the problem. Create a file on the Windows computer and save it to the shared folder. What message did you get when you tried to create a new file?

Real Problem 20-2

Exploring Accessibility Features

Est. Time: 30 minutes
Core 2 Objective: 1.10

Your company has hired a new employee who needs assistance while using their Mac. The employee has requested Voice Control to be enabled on their Mac. You've not yet taken the time to explore these features, so you decide you need to invest the time so you can fully support the technical needs of the new employee. Do the following to explore Voice Control.

1. In **System Preferences**, go to **Accessibility**, and enable **Voice Control**. This may take a moment.

2. Once Voice Control is enabled, speak the following commands:
   a. Show commands
   b. Open Safari
   c. Go to *www.google.com*
   d. Search now
   e. Dictation mode
   f. Mac voice commands
   g. Command mode
   h. Search now
   i. Quit Safari
   j. Open Pages
   k. Click New document
   l. Show grid
   m. [Say the number where you want to click.]
   n. Click Create
   o. Dictation mode
   p. Voice command is helpful
   q. Command mode
   r. Quit Pages
   s. Click Delete
   t. Go to sleep

Were you able to comfortably navigate the Mac? How did this experience help you better support others with all abilities or disabilities?

Module
21

Linux and Scripting

Module Objectives

1 Use and support Linux client and server distributions

2 Identify common scripting languages and software

3 Summarize common uses of scripts

Core 2 Certification Objectives

1.8 Explain common OS types and their purposes.

1.11 Identify common features and tools of the Linux client/desktop OS.

4.8 Identify the basics of scripting.

4.9 Given a scenario, use remote access technologies.

Introduction

In this module, you learn about the Linux operating system and scripting. Linux is commonly used in data centers, and, increasingly, it is being used in cloud infrastructures around the world. Being familiar with the interface and basic administrative functions of Linux is important for an IT technician. This module also covers the fundamentals of scripting used in many scripting languages and environments and presents examples of scripts that can be used to automate repetitive tasks.

Linux Operating System

 Core 2 Objectives 1.8, 1.11, 4.9

A variation of UNIX is Linux (pronounced "Lih-nucks"), an OS created by Linus Torvalds when he was a student at the University of Helsinki in Finland. Basic versions of this OS are open source, and all the underlying programming instructions (called source code) are freely distributed. Linux is popular because it's inexpensive and very stable (it seldom crashes). Linux is used as an OS for desktops, servers, mobile devices, and even IoT devices. It's the most popular OS for server applications such as web servers and email servers. In addition, Android and Chrome OS for mobile devices are based on Linux, and bootable CDs and flash drives that contain utility software often use Linux. Versions of Linux are called distributions or flavors; the more popular ones for desktops and servers are listed in Table 21-1. Hardware requirements for Linux vary widely by distribution.

Table 21-1 Popular Linux distributions for desktops and servers

Name	Comments	Website
Arch Linux	Arch Linux must be manually configured. It has excellent online documentation and community support, and Linux professionals appreciate its simplicity.	archlinux.org
Fedora	Fedora has been around for a long time and is backed by a stable company. When updates are released, they tend to work well without errors. It's a great distribution for just about any OS purpose.	getfedora.org
Linux Mint	Linux Mint is based on Ubuntu with several features added. Mint is great for users who are familiar with the Windows desktop environment, as its appearance is similar.	linuxmint.com
openSUSE	openSUSE is made for servers, desktops, and mobile devices. Applications install without a hassle; go to software.opensuse.org, select an app, and perform a Direct Install.	openSUSE.org
Red Hat Enterprise Linux	Designed for enterprise use on servers and workstations, this commercial distribution is stable and comes with long-term support.	redhat.com
Ubuntu	Ubuntu is one of the most popular distributions of Linux for desktops and servers, and it comes with tons of online tutorials and help.	ubuntu.com

> **Note 1**
>
> For more information on Linux, see *linux.org* as well as the websites of the different Linux distributors.

Linux itself is not a complete operating system; it is only the kernel for the OS. You also need a shell for user and application interfaces, and Linux shells vary widely by distributions. Many distributions of Linux include a GUI shell or desktop, which is called a windows manager. For example, Figure 21-1 shows the desktop or windows manager for Ubuntu Desktop. Some distributions of Linux designed for server applications don't have a windows manager. For example, Ubuntu Server installs with only a command-line interface. In this module, we use Ubuntu Desktop and Ubuntu Server as our sample Linux distributions.

Figure 21-1   Ubuntu Desktop with the Mozilla Firefox browser window open

You can install Ubuntu Desktop or Ubuntu Server in a VM or on a hard drive, CD, or USB flash drive. When you install Ubuntu on a CD or USB flash drive, it is called a **Live CD** or **Live USB**. A Live CD or USB can boot up a live version of Linux, complete with Internet access and all the tools you normally have available in a hard drive installation of Linux, but without installing the OS on the hard drive.

Let's first install and explore Ubuntu Desktop with its graphical interface, and then you'll learn to install and use Ubuntu Server with its command-line interface.

Applying Concepts

Installing Ubuntu Desktop in a VM

Est. Time: 1 hour
Core 2 Objectives: 1.8, 1.11

Follow these steps to install Ubuntu Desktop in a VM:

1. Recall that you learned how to install a hypervisor and create a VM in the module "Installing Windows." If you don't already have a hypervisor installed, install one that you can use to manage VMs. For example, in 64-bit Windows 10/11 Pro, you can use the Programs and Features window to enable Client Hyper-V, which comes embedded in the OS. Alternately, you can download and install one of these free hypervisors:

   - Oracle VirtualBox at *virtualbox.org/wiki/Downloads*
   - VMware Workstation Player at *https://customerconnect.vmware.com/en/downloads/info/slug/ desktop_end_user_computing/vmware_workstation_player/16_0*

2. Go to **ubuntu.com/download/desktop** and download the free Ubuntu Desktop OS to your hard drive. The file that downloads is an ISO file.

Note 2

Ubuntu Desktop is only available as a 64-bit OS. To install a 64-bit guest OS in a VM, the host OS must also be 64 bit. As of this publication, the LTS (long-term support) Ubuntu version is 20.04.3.

3. Open your hypervisor software, and create a new VM with at least 4 GB of RAM and at least a 25 GB virtual hard drive capacity. Mount the ISO file that contains the Ubuntu Desktop download to a virtual DVD in your VM.

4. Start up the VM, and install Ubuntu Desktop in the VM, accepting all default settings. Be sure to write down the name of the VM and your Ubuntu host name, Ubuntu user name, and password. When given the option, decline to install any extra software bundled with the OS. If needed, the software can be installed later.

Note 3

If you need help learning to use your hypervisor of choice, try searching for some tutorial videos at *youtube.com* or on the hypervisor manufacturer's website.

5. When asked to restart the VM, first dismount (remove) the ISO file from the optical drive so the VM boots to the hard drive. After Ubuntu Desktop launches, log in with your user name and password. Figure 21-2 shows the desktop with the Settings window active and the Network setting selected. To open this window, click the **Apps** button, and then click **Settings**. When a window is active, its menu appears at the top of the screen. Also notice the System menu is displayed. To open the System menu, click the **system icons** area in the upper-right corner of the screen.

6. Take a few minutes to poke around the desktop. You'll see how it resembles macOS in many ways. For example, to open a terminal window where you can enter Linux commands, click **Activities**, and type **terminal** in the search box. Click **Terminal** in the list that appears. Using the terminal, you can enter Linux commands to manage and support the OS.

Figure 21-2   Ubuntu Desktop with the Settings window open

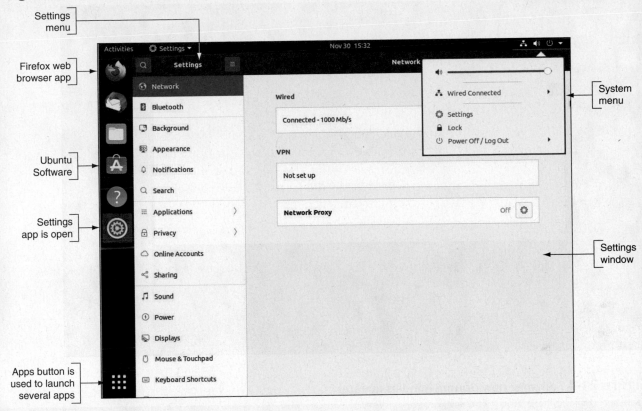

Settings menu

Firefox web browser app

Ubuntu Software

Settings app is open

Apps button is used to launch several apps

System menu

Settings window

7. To shut down Ubuntu Desktop, click the system icons area in the upper-right corner of the screen. The System menu opens. Click **Power Off/Log Out**, and then click **Power Off**.

The Ubuntu Desktop Guide at *help.ubuntu.com/stable/ubuntu-help* is an excellent resource if you want to learn more about using Ubuntu Desktop.

Linux Installs, Updates, and Backups

Core 2 Objective 1.11

When supporting a Linux system, an IT technician needs to know how to install software, update the OS and apps, and create and maintain scheduled backups. Here are a few details to get you started:

- **Install software.** To install software, click the **Ubuntu Software** icon. Ubuntu Desktop software opens. Click an item and then click **Install** to start its installation. You can also install an app by clicking a setup file you have downloaded from the web.
- **Update Ubuntu and apps.** To update, click **Updates** in the Ubuntu Software window. Updates for Ubuntu are listed first, followed by app updates. Click **Install** beside the updates you want to install. Figure 21-3 shows that no updates are available.
- **Change update settings.** To change update settings, open the **Apps** menu, and click **Software & Updates** in the drop-down list. Then click the **Updates** tab in the Software & Updates window (see Figure 21-4).

Figure 21-3   Ubuntu Desktop is up to date

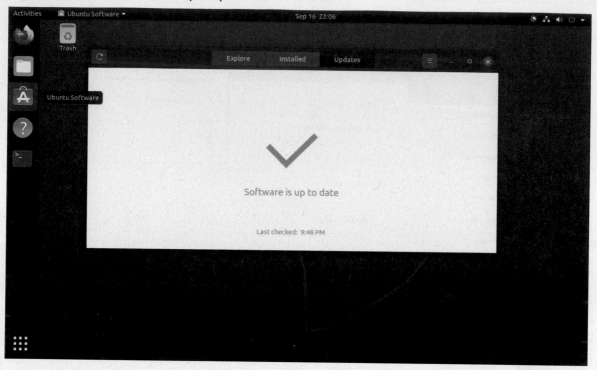

Figure 21-4   Change how Ubuntu handles updates

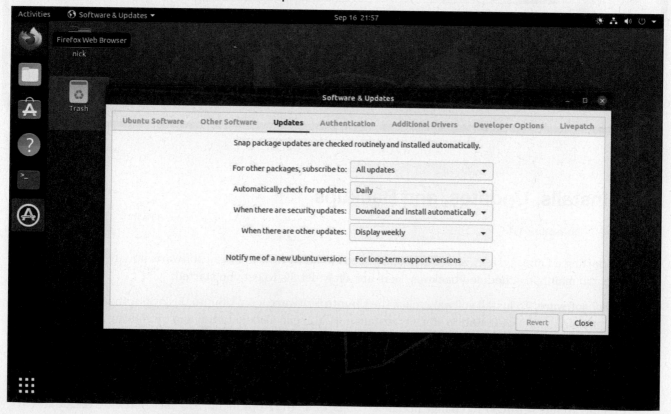

- **Configure backups.** Click the **Apps** button. In the list of apps, scroll down and click **Utilities** (see Figure 21-5). Click the **Backups** utility. Using the Backups window (see Figure 21-6), you can schedule backups, decide where the backups are stored, and select which items are included in the backup.

Figure 21-5   Ubuntu Desktop utilities

Figure 21-6   Schedule an Ubuntu Desktop backup

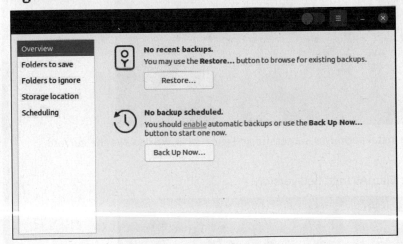

- **Antivirus and anti-malware solutions.** As with every computing environment, you should protect your Linux system with an antivirus or anti-malware solution. Examples of solutions that have been developed specifically for Linux include the ClamAV, Comodo, and Sophos applications. An antivirus solution should be updated regularly to ensure system protection is maintained. Some vendors provide updates multiple times a week or even daily. Externally connected media and downloaded files should be scanned to minimize the threat of malware infecting your system.

Applying Concepts

Installing ClamAV

Est. Time: 15 minutes
Core 2 Objective: 1.11

To use ClamAV to protect your previously installed VM installation of Ubuntu against malware, follow these steps:

1. Launch your VM, and log in using your root credentials.

2. Open a terminal window, and update your system by running the following command:

   ```
   sudo apt-get update
   ```

3. After your system is updated, run the following command to install ClamAV:

   ```
   sudo apt-get install clamav clamav-daemon
   ```

4. Press **Enter** when prompted to continue. (Because the Y is uppercase, as shown in Figure 21-7, the default answer to the prompt is Yes.) After the installation finishes, enter the following command to confirm that ClamAV was installed correctly:

   ```
   clamscan --version
   ```

Figure 21-7   Installing ClamAV on Ubuntu

```
nick@nick-ubuntu1: ~

nick@nick-ubuntu1:~$ sudo apt-get install clamav clamav-daemon
Reading package lists... Done
Building dependency tree
Reading state information... Done
The following additional packages will be installed:
  clamav-base clamav-freshclam clamdscan libclamav9 libcurl4 libmspack0 libtfm1
Suggested packages:
  libclamunrar clamav-docs daemon libclamunrar9
The following NEW packages will be installed:
  clamav clamav-base clamav-daemon clamav-freshclam clamdscan libclamav9 libcurl4 libmspack0
  libtfm1
0 upgraded, 9 newly installed, 0 to remove and 0 not upgraded.
Need to get 0 B/1,691 kB of archives.
After this operation, 6,175 kB of additional disk space will be used.
Do you want to continue? [Y/n]
```

If a version shows for ClamAV, then the installation was successful. In Figure 21-8, we can see the current version of ClamAV is 0.103.2.

Figure 21-8   Terminal window showing ClamAV installed version

```
Processing triggers for man-db (2.9.1-1) ...
Processing triggers for libc-bin (2.31-0ubuntu9.2) ...
nick@nick-ubuntu1:~$ clamscan --version
ClamAV 0.103.2/26297/Thu Sep 16 09:59:37 2021
```

Now that you have learned some of the basics about Ubuntu Desktop and have installed an antivirus solution, let's turn our attention to Ubuntu Server.

Installing and Exploring Ubuntu Server

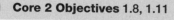

Core 2 Objectives 1.8, 1.11

Ubuntu Server does not include a windows manager but instead uses a command-line interface called the terminal. The default shell for the terminal is the **Bash shell**, which stands for "Bourne Again Shell" and takes the best features from two previous shells, the Bourne and Korn shells. In this module, we use Ubuntu Server and its default Bash shell. In Linux, a command prompt in the terminal is called a **shell prompt**.

Note 4

To find out what shell is the default shell for the Linux system, enter the `echo $SHELL` command. To find out which shell you are currently using, enter the `echo $0` command.

Applying Concepts

Installing Ubuntu Server in a VM

Est. Time: 15 minutes
Core 2 Objectives: 1.8, 1.11

To practice Linux skills covered in this module, you need an installation of Ubuntu Server. Before you continue with this module, follow these steps to install Ubuntu Server in a VM on a Windows computer:

1. Go to **ubuntu.com/download/server** and download the Ubuntu Server OS to your hard drive. The file that downloads is an ISO file.

2. Open your hypervisor software, and create a new VM. For Ubuntu Server, you'll need at least 4 GB of RAM and at least a 25 GB virtual hard drive. For this example, we selected a 50 GB virtual hard disk. Mount the ISO file that contains the Ubuntu Server download to a virtual DVD in your VM.

3. Start up the VM, and install Ubuntu Server, accepting all default settings until you get to the Guided storage configuration screen (see Figure 21-9). To improve Ubuntu performance, you can set up a **swap partition**, which is used to hold virtual memory. In Linux, a swap file or swap partition can hold virtual memory, but a swap partition yields better performance. Select **Custom storage layout**, as shown in the figure, so you can create three partitions on the hard drive.

Figure 21-9   Partition the hard drive to include a swap file

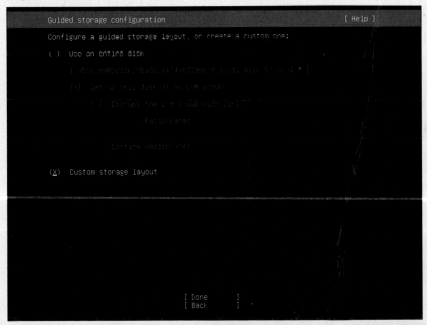

Note 5

When installing Ubuntu, use the arrow keys to navigate menus, and press **Enter** to select. The **Esc** key takes you back one level in a menu.

(continues)

Applying Concepts Continued

4. On the next screen, under AVAILABLE DEVICES, select the first device listed, and then press **Enter**. In the drop-down menu that appears, select **Add GPT Partition**, as shown in Figure 21-10.

Figure 21-10 Create a new partition on the drive

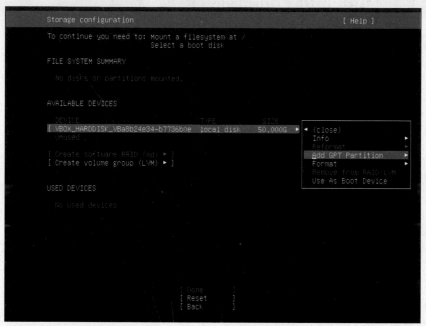

5. In the Adding partition box, enter the size of the boot partition (at least 25 GB), and select the file system type **ext4**, as shown in Figure 21-11.

Figure 21-11 Select ext4 for the file system of the new Ubuntu partition

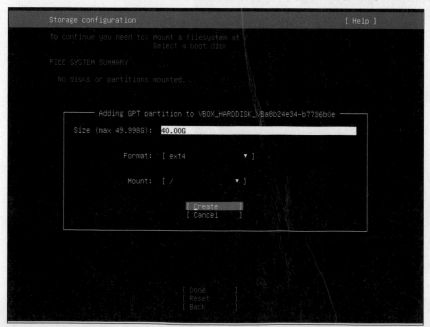

6. Add a second partition, and select **swap** as the file system type. Make the partition size a little larger than the amount of installed memory. Figure 21-12 shows the resulting Storage configuration screen with three partitions created. Notice that not all the hard drive is partitioned in our example:

Figure 21-12   Partitions are created to hold the Ubuntu installation

- **Partition 1.** The small BIOS grub spacer partition is automatically created and is used to boot the system in a dual-boot environment. **GRUB (GR and Unified Bootloader)** is a boot loader used to manage dual-boot systems.
- **Partition 2.** The 40 GB partition that will hold the OS uses the ext4 file system.
- **Partition 3.** The 5 GB swap partition is used to hold virtual memory. A swap partition does not have a file system installed.

7. Select **Done** to complete the installation, accepting all defaults. Be sure to write down the name of the VM and your Ubuntu host name, Ubuntu user name, and password. When given the option, decline to install any extra software bundled with the OS. Notice this software includes add-ons to be used when Ubuntu Server is installed in the cloud using Amazon Web Services or Google Cloud. If needed, the software can be installed later.

8. After the VM restarts, Ubuntu Server launches, and you should see the terminal shell in the VM. See Figure 21-13.

9. You might need to press **Enter** to see the shell prompt. Then enter your user name and password, and you're logged in to Ubuntu Server. In Figure 21-13, the server is named spock and the logged-in user is evan. Notice that Ubuntu reports that six packages can be updated. In Ubuntu, a **package** is the collection of files needed to install software.

10. When you are ready to shut down Ubuntu Server, run the **sudo shutdown now** command.

Typically, the shell prompt includes the user name, host name, and the current directory, followed by a $. For example, in Figure 21-13, the shell prompt shows the user name is evan, and the host name is spock. The ~ character indicates the user's home directory, which for the evan account is /home/evan. When you first log in to Linux, the current directory is always the home directory of the logged-in user. (In Linux, directories in a path are separated with forward slashes, in contrast to the backward slashes used by Windows.)

21

Applying Concepts Continued

Figure 21-13   When you log in to Ubuntu Server, available updates are listed

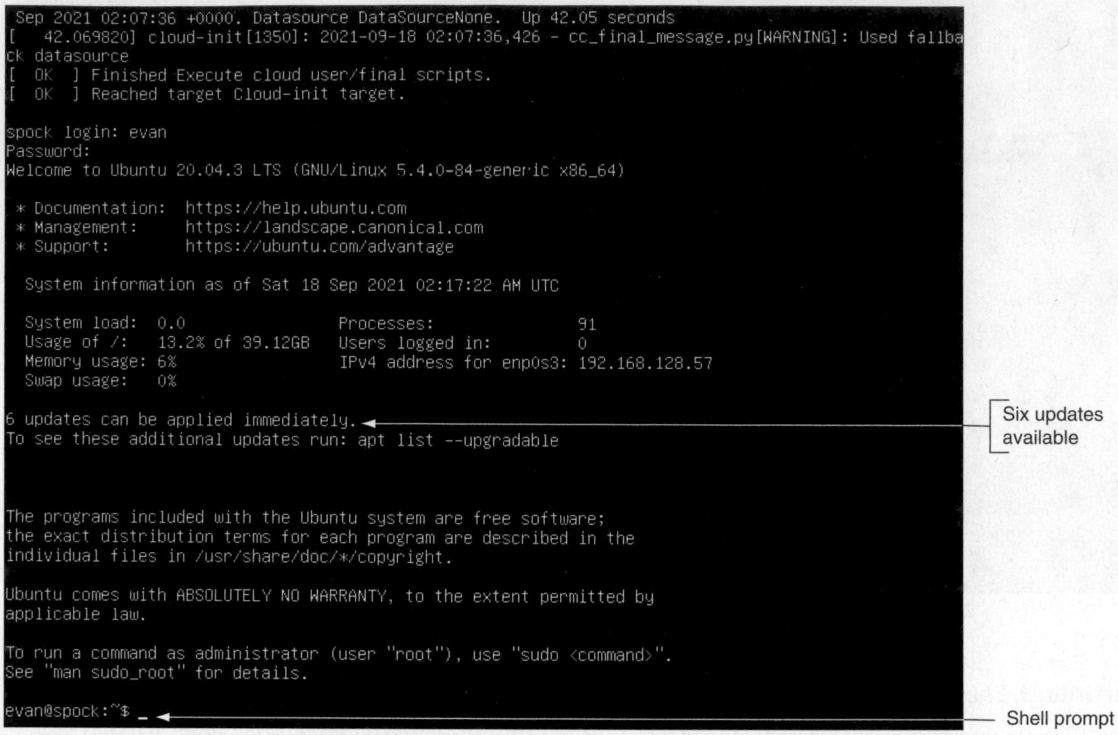

```
Sep 2021 02:07:36 +0000. Datasource DataSourceNone.  Up 42.05 seconds
[   42.069820] cloud-init[1350]: 2021-09-18 02:07:36,426 - cc_final_message.py[WARNING]: Used fallba
ck datasource
[  OK  ] Finished Execute cloud user/final scripts.
[  OK  ] Reached target Cloud-init target.

spock login: evan
Password:
Welcome to Ubuntu 20.04.3 LTS (GNU/Linux 5.4.0-84-generic x86_64)

 * Documentation:  https://help.ubuntu.com
 * Management:     https://landscape.canonical.com
 * Support:        https://ubuntu.com/advantage

  System information as of Sat 18 Sep 2021 02:17:22 AM UTC

  System load:  0.0                Processes:             91
  Usage of /:   13.2% of 39.12GB   Users logged in:       0
  Memory usage: 6%                 IPv4 address for enp0s3: 192.168.128.57
  Swap usage:   0%

6 updates can be applied immediately.                          ◄──── Six updates
To see these additional updates run: apt list --upgradable            available


The programs included with the Ubuntu system are free software;
the exact distribution terms for each program are described in the
individual files in /usr/share/doc/*/copyright.

Ubuntu comes with ABSOLUTELY NO WARRANTY, to the extent permitted by
applicable law.

To run a command as administrator (user "root"), use "sudo <command>".
See "man sudo_root" for details.

evan@spock:~$ _   ◄────────────────────────────── Shell prompt
```

It's easiest to install a swap partition when you install Ubuntu. If Ubuntu is installed on a single partition on the hard drive and you want to improve performance later, you can shrink the Ubuntu partition and create a swap partition in the free space. This text does not cover how to do that.

Note 6

As you learn to use Ubuntu, know that the help.ubuntu.com website contains a wealth of information about Ubuntu and links to even more help.

Exam Tip ✔

The A+ Core 2 exam expects you to know that a swap partition improves performance and that you can create one during or after the installation. You also need to know about the ext4 and ext3 file systems.

Recall from the module "The Complex World of IT Professionals" that each OS has file systems it can support. Linux file systems include:

- **ext4.** The current Linux file system is ext4 (fourth extended file system). This is why you selected ext4 when you installed Ubuntu Desktop and Server.
- **ext3.** The ext3 file system was the first to support journaling, which is a technique that tracks and stores changes to the hard drive and helps prevent file system corruption.
- **FAT32 and NTFS.** The FAT32 and NTFS file systems are supported for compatibility with Windows and macOS. Windows can use either FAT32 or NTFS, and macOS can use FAT32. Ubuntu should not be installed on a FAT32 or NTFS volume.

Note 7

On a local network or in a dual boot with Windows and Linux, you might want to access files in either volume from either OS. Know that Linux can access the NTFS file system on the Windows volume, but Windows cannot access the ext4 file system on the Linux volume. You can, however, install third-party software, such as Paragon ExtFS for Windows (*paragon-software.com*), to access the ext4 volume.

As you read along and learn about Linux commands, you can use your Ubuntu VMs to practice these commands.

Directory Structures

Table 21-2 lists some important directories that are created in the root during a typical Linux installation. (Some distributions of Linux modify the directory structure.) Not all directories in the root are listed in the table. You will need to be familiar with the directories list in Table 21-2 and understand their uses.

Table 21-2   Important directories in a typical Linux root directory

Directory	Description
/bin	Contains programs and commands necessary to boot the system and perform other system tasks not reserved for the administrator, such as shutdown and reboot.
/boot	Consists of components needed for the boot process, such as boot loaders.
/dev	Holds device names, which consist of the type of device and a number identifying the device; actual device drivers are located in the /lib/modules /[*kernel version*]/ directory.
/etc	Contains system configuration data, including configuration files and settings and their subdirectories; these files are used for tasks such as configuring a user account, changing system settings, and configuring a domain name resolution service. This directory should be backed up on a regular basis.
/home	Contains user data; every user of the system has a directory in the /home directory, such as /home/evan or /home/robyn, and when a user logs in, that directory becomes the current working directory. This directory should be backed up on a regular basis to protect user-saved documents and files.
/lib	Stores common libraries used by applications so more than one application can use the same library at one time; an example is the library of C programming code, without which only the kernel of the Linux system could run.
/lost+found	Stores data that is lost when files are truncated or when an attempt to fix system errors is unsuccessful.
/opt	Contains installations of third-party applications such as web browsers that do not come with the Linux OS distribution; this directory should be included in your regular backups.
/root	Serves as the home directory for the root user and contains only files specific to the root user; don't confuse this directory with the root, which contains all the directories listed in this table. This directory should also be backed up to ensure a copy of the root user account is saved.
/sbin	Stores commands required for system administration, with root-level privileges required.
/tmp	Stores temporary files, such as the ones that applications use during installation and operation.
/usr	Contains executable programs, libraries, and shared resources that are not critical to the Ubuntu system; this directory and two subdirectories should be backed up. Those subdirectories (/usr/local/bin and /usr/local/sbin) may include applications that have been installed and are not part of the /usr parent directory.
/var	Holds variable data such as logs, email, news, print spools, and administrative files; this directory should also be backed up on a regular basis.

21

Applying Concepts

Exploring Directories and Files

Est. Time: 15 minutes
Core 2 Objective: 1.11

Let's learn a few Linux commands that we can use to explore directories and files. As shown in Figure 21-14, enter these commands:

Figure 21-14   Directories in the root

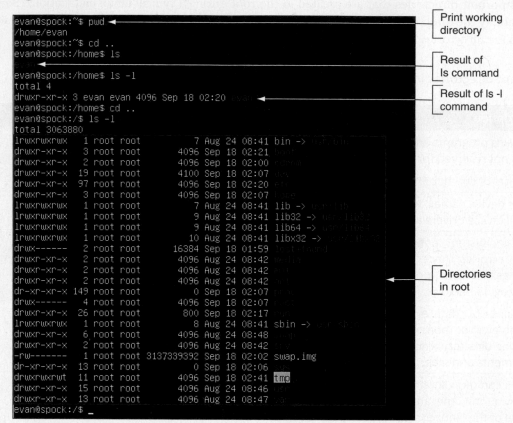

Print working
directory

Result of
ls command

Result of ls -l
command

Directories
in root

1. Open a new terminal window, or run the **clear** command to clear an existing window of all its clutter.

2. Enter the **pwd** command (print working directory) to display the full path to the current directory, which is /home/evan in the figure.

3. Run the **cd ..** command to move up one directory to /home. (Note the space after the d.)

4. Run the **ls** command to display the list of files and subdirectories in the /home directory. Notice in the figure that the one subdirectory in the /home directory is evan.

5. Enter the **ls -l** command to display the results using the long format. (Note the space after the s.) As you can see in the figure, the results are as follows:

```
drwxr-xr-x 3 evan evan 4096 Sep 18 02:20 evan
```

Here is an explanation of the types of information in the list:

- **Attributes.** The first 10 characters (drwxr-xr-x) define the file or directory attributes. The first character identifies the type of item: A "d" is a directory, "a –" is a regular file, and a "1" indicates the item is a link to another location. The other nine characters ("rwxr-xr-x") define the read, write, and execute permissions assigned to the file or directory; these permissions are explained in detail later in the module.

- **Links.** The second column lists the number of links the item has, which is three in our example. In Linux, a link is similar to a Windows shortcut to a file or directory.
- **Owners.** The third column lists the user owner, and the fourth column lists the group that owns the file or directory. In Figure 21-14, the owner is evan, and the owner group is also evan.
- **Size, date, and name.** The last columns list the size of the file or directory in bytes, the date the item was last modified, and the name of the file or directory. The name of directory, evan, is listed in blue.

6. Enter the `cd ..` command again to move up to the main directory in Linux, called the root directory, which is indicated with a forward slash. Run the `ls -l` command to list the files and subdirectories in the root.

Root Account and User Accounts

A Linux system administrator is responsible for installing updates to the OS (called patches), managing backups, installing software and hardware, setting up user accounts, resetting passwords, and generally supporting the OS and users. To accomplish this, they require root privileges or access to all the functions of the OS. Two ways Linux allows for root privileges are as follows:

- **Superuser.** The principal user account is called the **root account**. Notice in Figure 21-14 that all the directories and files in the root directory belong to the root account. When logged in to the root account, the user is called the **superuser**. Because the root account is so powerful, Ubuntu disables login to this account by default. The root account is similar to the Windows Administrator account.
- **Regular user account with root privileges.** Any user account can be assigned root privileges. If the user has root privileges, they can execute any command that requires root access by adding sudo to the beginning of the command line. An account with root privileges is similar to a Windows account that has been assigned administrative rights.

The command to switch users is su. To switch to the root account, use the command sudo su root, as shown in Figure 21-15.

Figure 21-15   The user account, host name, and current directory appear in the shell prompt, along with a # or $ to indicate the root account or other account

```
evan@spock:/$ sudo su root
[sudo] password for evan:
root@spock:/# su evan
evan@spock:/$
```

Notice in the figure that the shell prompt changes to root@spock:/#. The Linux command prompt for the root user is different from the command prompt for regular users. The root command prompt is #, and other users have the $ command prompt. To switch back to the evan account, use the command su evan. As a general practice, never log in to Linux as root unless you have no other option; you can do a lot of damage as root.

Linux Commands

Table 21-3 describes some basic Linux commands, together with simple examples of how some are used. As you read along, be aware that all commands entered in Linux are case sensitive, meaning that uppercase and lowercase matter. You can practice these commands in a Ubuntu VM, or you can practice the commands by booting a computer from the Live Ubuntu bootable USB drive you created in the Core 1 module "Hard Drives and Other Storage Devices."

Table 21-3 Some common Linux commands

Command	Description
adduser	Add a user to a system: adduser <*username*>
apt-get	Install and remove applications and other programs (called packages) in Linux. When you first install Linux, it installs with only a bare-bones set of commands and utilities, and it includes a library of packages that you can install as needed. For example, to install the SSH (Secure Shell) package so you can remotely connect to your Linux server: sudo apt-get install ssh The apt-get command requires root access, which means you must precede the command with sudo.
cat	View the contents of a file. Many Linux commands can use the redirection symbol > to redirect the output of the command. For example, use the redirection symbol with the cat command to copy a file: cat /etc/shells > newfile The content of the shells file is written to newfile.
cd	Change the directory. To change the directory to /etc: cd /etc To move up one level in the directory tree: cd .. To go to the root: cd /
chmod	Change modes (or permissions) for a file or directory. You'll see several examples of this command later in the module.
chown	Change the owner of a file or directory. To change the owner of /mystuff to root: chown root /mystuff
clear	Clear the screen. This command is useful when the screen has become cluttered with commands and data that you no longer need to view.
cp	Copy a file: cp <*source*> <*destination*>
df	Show the amount of disk free space available in Linux and to understand the file systems that are attached, or mounted, to the system. Use the df (disk file system) command with no parameters to report file system device names, free space, and mount points: df
dig	Query for DNS information. This is similar to the Windows command nslookup. To lookup the DNS information for *linux.org*: dig linux.org
echo	Display information on the screen. You can also save the information to a file. For example, to create a new file that contains text: echo "Hello World" > myfile
exit	Log out; the login shell prompt appears, and you can log in again.

Table 21-3   Some common Linux commands (Continued)

Command	Description
find	"Walk" through the file hierarchy to find files and directories. To find a file, the syntax of the command is as follows: find <*directoryname*> -name <*filename*>
grep	Search for a specific pattern in a file or in multiple files. This command is useful when searching through long log files: grep <*pattern*> <*file*>
ifconfig	Troubleshoot problems with TCP/IP network connections. This command can disable and enable network adapters and assign a static IP address to an adapter. For example, to show all configuration information: ifconfig –a To enable or disable an adapter, use the up or down parameter. For example, to enable eth0, the first Ethernet interface: sudo ifconfig eth0 up To assign a static IP address to the eth0 interface: ifconfig eth0 192.168.1.90
ip	Display IP addresses and property information of the various network interfaces on the system. This command can also be used to configure and modify routes, tunnel over IP, and modify the interface statuses. Many Linux distributions have moved to the ip command rather than using ifconfig. For example, to show the ip address information: ip a *or* ip addr To assign the 192.168.1.100 ip address and 255.255.255.0 subnet mask to the eth0 interface: ip a add 192.168.1.100/255.255.255.0 dev eth0
iwconfig	Display information about the wireless adapter's configuration or to change the configuration. This command works like ifconfig but applies only to wireless networks. To set the wireless NIC to Ad-Hoc mode so other devices within range can connect directly to it, use this command, where wlan0 identifies the wireless adapter: iwconfig wlan0 mode Ad-Hoc To force the NIC to use channel 3: iwconfig wlan0 channel 3
kill	Kill a process instead of waiting for it to terminate. Use the ps command to list process IDs. To end a process, use the kill command followed by the PID. For example, to kill the process with a PID of 984: kill 984 The command sends a signal to the process to end itself in an orderly way. If the process doesn't die peacefully, you can get the kernel involved to forcefully end the process (this is called a forced kill): kill -kill 984

(continues)

21

Table 21-3   Some common Linux commands (Continued)

Command	Description
ls	Display a list of directories and files (similar to the Windows dir command). For example, to list files in the /etc directory, use the long parameter for a complete listing: ls -l /etc To include hidden files in the list: ls -la /etc (Note that in Linux, hidden files begin with a period.)
man	Display the online help manual, called man pages. For example, to get information about the echo command: man echo The manual program displays information about the command. To exit the manual program, type q.
mkdir	Make a new directory: mkdir *<directory>*
mv	Move a file or rename it, if the source and destination are the same directory: mv <source> <destination> For example, to move myfile from the evan directory to the home directory: sudo mv /home/evan/myfile /home/myfile Note that because the /home directory is owned by the root account, the sudo command is required.
nano	Launch a full-screen editor that can be used to edit a file: nano <filename>
passwd	Change a password. When a user enters the command, they are asked for the old password and then can change it. The superuser can change the password for any account and does not need to enter the account's old password, making it possible to reset a forgotten password.
ping	Test network connections by sending a request packet to a host. If a connection is successful, the host will return a response packet. For example: ping 192.168.1.100 The ping results continue until you manually stop the process. Press Ctrl+C to break out of the process. To specify the number of pings: ping 192.168.1.100 -c 4
ps	Display the process table so you can identify process IDs for currently running processes. The command stands for "process status." (Once you know the process ID, you can use the kill command to terminate a process.) To list processes of the current user: ps To list processes owned by all users: ps aux
pwd	Show the name of the current or present working directory. The command stands for "print working directory." When you first log in to Linux, the directory is /home/*username*.
rm	Remove or delete the file or files that are specified: rm *<file>*

Table 21-3   Some common Linux commands (Continued)

Command	Description
rmdir	Remove or delete an empty directory: rmdir <directory>
shutdown	Automatically shut down the system. To shut down now: sudo shutdown now To warn users and then shut down: sudo shutdown -h +10 "Everyone log out now. The system will shut down in 10 minutes for maintenance." To reboot now: sudo shutdown -r now
su	Switch to a different user account. The command stands for "substitute user" or "switch user." When switching to superuser, add sudo to the command. To switch to the root account: sudo su root To switch back to the evan account: su evan
sudo	Run a command as the superuser. The command stands for "substitute user to do the command," and it is pronounced "sue-doe" or "sue-doo." When logged in as a normal user with an account that has the right to use root commands, you can start a command with sudo to run the command as the superuser. A user password may be required. For example: sudo shutdown now
top	Display the Linux processes. This command shows a dynamic, real-time view of the running processes and threads currently being managed by the Linux kernel.
yum	Get, install, delete, and manage software packages in RPM (Red Hat Package Manager). The yum (Yellowdog Update Manager) command is the primary tool for performing these functions in RPM. This command is similar to the apt-get update command used in this module to update distributions such as Ubuntu. For example, to download updates for all installed software: sudo yum update

Exam Tip ✔

The A+ Core 2 exam expects you to be familiar with these Linux commands: apt-get, cat, chmod, chown, cp, df, dig, find, grep, ip, ls, man, mv, nano, ps, pwd, rm, top, yum.

Here are a few tips when using commands at a shell prompt:

- **Retrieve previous commands.** Press the up arrow key to retrieve previously entered commands and then edit a command that appears.
- **Use wildcard characters.** Linux, similar to Windows, can use the * and ? wildcard characters in command lines. For example, use the ls *.??? command to list all files with a file extension of three characters. In addition, Linux provides a third wildcard: Brackets can give a choice of characters. For example, use the ls *.[abc]* command to list all files whose file extension begins with a, b, or c.

- **Redirect output.** Normally, output from a command displays on the screen. To redirect that output to a file, use the redirection symbol >. For example, to redirect the output of the ifconfig command to myfile, use the ifconfig > myfile command.
- **Page the output.** Append | more to the end of a command line to display the results of the command on the screen one page at a time. For example, to page the ls command: ls -l | more.
- **Use Ctrl+C.** To break out of a command or process, press **Ctrl+C**. Use it to recover after entering a wrong command or to stop a command that requires a manual halt.

The Nano Editor

The nano editor is a text editor that allows you to easily make changes to text-based files. In this section, you learn how to create a text file in the nano editor, edit text, and save your changes.

Let's create and work with a file called mymemo:

1. You can save a file to your home directory because you own that directory. If you are not already in your home directory, run the **cd** command to go there. For example:
   cd /home/evan

2. To open the nano editor and create the new file, enter the command **nano mymemo**. The nano editor screen appears, and the file name is shown at the top center of the screen.

3. When you first open the nano editor, you can immediately edit the file by typing in the window. Type the first sentence of step 2 as the text for your memo (see Figure 21-16).

Figure 21-16 The nano text editor with commands displayed at bottom of screen

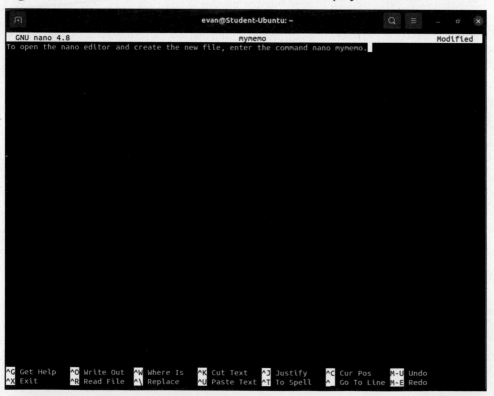

4. At the bottom of the screen are several commands. The carrot (^) symbol is used to represent the Control (Ctrl) key on your keyboard. To see all the commands available in nano, press **Ctrl+G**.

5. To save your changes, press **Ctrl+O**, and then press **Enter** to save the changes to the listed file name. To exit, press **Ctrl+X**. Alternatively, you can just use the Exit command, and nano will ask if you want to save any changes made to the file.

Applying Concepts

Installing FTP Server in Ubuntu

Est. Time: 15 minutes
Core 2 Objective: 1.11

In the following steps, you learn to use several Linux commands to install and configure software and examine a log file. Follow these steps to set up an FTP server in Ubuntu:

1. Log in to Ubuntu Server with your user name and password.
2. To create a short file to test the FTP server, you can use the echo command with redirection. Create mymemo2 in your /home/*username* directory by entering this command:

    ```
    echo "my typing" > /home/username/mymemo2
    ```

3. To install the FTP program named vsftpd, enter this command:

    ```
    sudo apt-get install vsftpd
    ```

4. Respond to the prompts, and then wait for the package to install.
5. Now you need to configure the FTP program by editing the /etc/vsftpd.conf text file. Before you edit the file, go to the /etc directory and make a backup copy of the file just in case you need it later. The sudo command is needed because files in the /etc directory belong to root:

    ```
    cd /etc
    sudo cp vsftpd.conf vsftpd.backup
    ```

6. Use the nano editor to edit the FTP configuration file:

    ```
    sudo nano vsftpd.conf
    ```

7. Verify and/or change three lines in the file to create the following settings:

    *   Disable anonymous logins: **anonymous_enable=NO**
    *   If necessary, remove the # to uncomment the line, and allow local users to log in:
        local_enable=YES
    *   If necessary, remove the # to uncomment the line, and allow users to write to a directory:
        write_enable=YES

    Part of the file, including these three lines, is shown in Figure 21-17.

(continues)

21

Applying Concepts Continued

Figure 21-17   Part of the vsftpd.conf text file

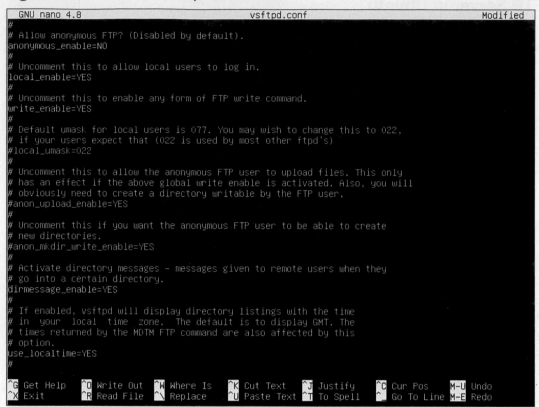

8. Exit the nano editor, saving your changes. Restart the FTP service by running this command:

```
service vsftpd restart
```

9. To find out the IP address of the server, type **ifconfig**. If net-tools are not installed, you will need to install them.

Note 8

If an error appears stating "Command 'ifconfig' not found, but can be installed with: apt install net-tools," you can run the command **apt install net-tools** to install the networking tools.

10. On your host Windows computer, open a command prompt window, and go to a directory on your Windows computer where you have a file stored. To test your FTP server, open an FTP session using the IP address of the server—for example: ftp 192.168.128.57 (your IP address may be different). Then enter your user name and password. The ftp> prompt appears. See Figure 21-18.

Figure 21-18   Use FTP to transfer files between a Windows and Ubuntu system

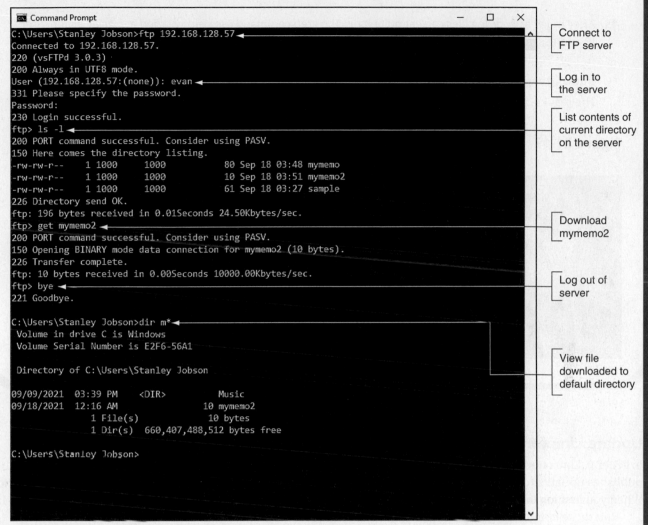

```
C:\Users\Stanley Jobson>ftp 192.168.128.57          ◄────── Connect to
Connected to 192.168.128.57.                                  FTP server
220 (vsFTPd 3.0.3)
200 Always in UTF8 mode.
User (192.168.128.57:(none)): evan              ◄────── Log in to
331 Please specify the password.                          the server
Password:
230 Login successful.
ftp> ls -l       ◄──────────────────────────── List contents of
200 PORT command successful. Consider using PASV.         current directory
150 Here comes the directory listing.                     on the server
-rw-rw-r--   1 1000     1000           80 Sep 18 03:48 mymemo
-rw-rw-r--   1 1000     1000           10 Sep 18 03:51 mymemo2
-rw-rw-r--   1 1000     1000           61 Sep 18 03:27 sample
226 Directory send OK.
ftp: 196 bytes received in 0.01Seconds 24.50Kbytes/sec.
ftp> get mymemo2    ◄──────────────────────── Download
200 PORT command successful. Consider using PASV.         mymemo2
150 Opening BINARY mode data connection for mymemo2 (10 bytes).
226 Transfer complete.
ftp: 10 bytes received in 0.00Seconds 10000.00Kbytes/sec.
ftp> bye    ◄──────────────────────────────── Log out of
221 Goodbye.                                              server

C:\Users\Stanley Jobson>dir m*    ◄────────── View file
 Volume in drive C is Windows                            downloaded to
 Volume Serial Number is E2F6-56A1                       default directory

 Directory of C:\Users\Stanley Jobson

09/09/2021  03:39 PM    <DIR>          Music
09/18/2021  12:16 AM               10 mymemo2
               1 File(s)            10 bytes
               1 Dir(s)  660,407,488,512 bytes free

C:\Users\Stanley Jobson>
```

11. Next, run the `ls -l` command to see a list of directories and files. You should see the file mymemo2 that you created in your /home/*username* directory earlier.

12. If you want to transfer files with FTP commands, use the get and put commands. To download the mymemo2 file, run the command **get mymemo2**. To transfer a file from your Windows computer to your Ubuntu server, run the **put** command.

13. Type **bye** to disconnect from the FTP server. At the Windows command prompt, run the **dir m*** command, as shown in Figure 21-18, to verify that the file was received on the Windows computer.

14. Return to Ubuntu Server and examine the FTP log file, /var/log/vsftpd.log. Because the file is short, you can run the cat command to display the entire log. The sudo command is required because /var files belong to root:

```
sudo cat /var/log/vsftpd.log
```

(continues)

21

Applying Concepts Continued

15. After much activity, log files can get quite long. The grep command can help you find a specific action, user, IP address, file name, or directory name. For example, to display lines in the log file that contain the text "LOGIN," enter this grep command:

```
sudo grep "LOGIN" /var/log/vsftpd.log
```

The results of the cat and grep commands are shown in Figure 21-19.

Figure 21-19   **The grep command can be used to search for specific text in log files**

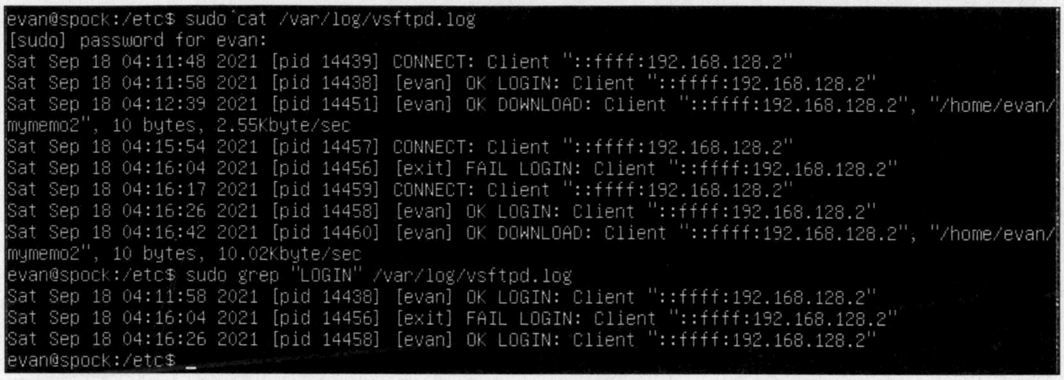

```
evan@spock:/etc$ sudo cat /var/log/vsftpd.log
[sudo] password for evan:
Sat Sep 18 04:11:48 2021 [pid 14439] CONNECT: Client "::ffff:192.168.128.2"
Sat Sep 18 04:11:58 2021 [pid 14438] [evan] OK LOGIN: Client "::ffff:192.168.128.2"
Sat Sep 18 04:12:39 2021 [pid 14451] [evan] OK DOWNLOAD: Client "::ffff:192.168.128.2", "/home/evan/
mymemo2", 10 bytes, 2.55Kbyte/sec
Sat Sep 18 04:15:54 2021 [pid 14457] CONNECT: Client "::ffff:192.168.128.2"
Sat Sep 18 04:16:04 2021 [pid 14456] [exit] FAIL LOGIN: Client "::ffff:192.168.128.2"
Sat Sep 18 04:16:17 2021 [pid 14459] CONNECT: Client "::ffff:192.168.128.2"
Sat Sep 18 04:16:26 2021 [pid 14458] [evan] OK LOGIN: Client "::ffff:192.168.128.2"
Sat Sep 18 04:16:42 2021 [pid 14460] [evan] OK DOWNLOAD: Client "::ffff:192.168.128.2", "/home/evan/
mymemo2", 10 bytes, 10.02kbyte/sec
evan@spock:/etc$ sudo grep "LOGIN" /var/log/vsftpd.log
Sat Sep 18 04:11:58 2021 [pid 14438] [evan] OK LOGIN: Client "::ffff:192.168.128.2"
Sat Sep 18 04:16:04 2021 [pid 14456] [exit] FAIL LOGIN: Client "::ffff:192.168.128.2"
Sat Sep 18 04:16:26 2021 [pid 14458] [evan] OK LOGIN: Client "::ffff:192.168.128.2"
evan@spock:/etc$ 
```

Update Linux from the Shell Prompt

In general, Linux updates don't come as often as Windows or macOS updates. The creator of your Linux distribution publishes updates to packages in the current release of a distribution and publishes new releases of a distribution. When you first log in to the system, Linux reports the package updates that are available (refer back to Figure 21-13).

Run these commands to update the packages previously installed in your system:

1. To refresh the list of all available updates:

```
sudo apt-get update
```

2. To update only the installed packages:

```
sudo apt-get upgrade
```

A new release of a distribution contains all updates since the last release. As a Linux administrator, you need to stay aware of the latest release of the distribution you are using and decide when or if it's appropriate to upgrade to that release. Before you upgrade to a new release, be sure you have backups of your data and a disk image (called a **clone**) of the entire Linux partition.

Here's how to upgrade to a new release for Ubuntu Server:

1. Follow the previous steps to update all packages installed in the system.

2. To make sure the latest update manager program is installed, enter the command:

```
sudo apt-get install update-manager-core
```

3. To install the latest release of Ubuntu Server, enter the command:

```
sudo do-release-upgrade
```

If a new release is available, the last command reports it, and you can follow directions to install it.

Note 9

Ubuntu Server does not have an easy-to-use backup service. Normally, the system administrator installs third-party software, such as Bacula, to perform backups. Another option is to write your own **shell scripts**, which are similar to batch files, that include tar commands to create an archive of many files and copy it to other media, such as a USB drive or network storage. Files recommended for your Linux backup processes are noted in the list of directories in Table 21-2, presented earlier in the module.

Assign Permissions and Ownership of Files or Directories

A file or directory can have read, write, and/or execute permissions assigned to it. Permissions can be assigned to (a) the owner, (b) other users in the same group as the owner, and (c) all users. The chmod command is used to manage permissions for files and directories. To see current permissions, examine the 10 characters in the left column that display when you use the ls -l command. For example, suppose the output for the ls -l command on the /home/evan directory is that shown in Figure 21-20.

Figure 21-20   Information about the evan directory displayed using the ls -l command

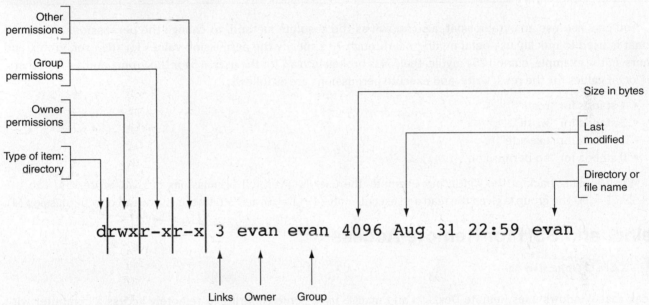

Here is the explanation of these characters:

- The first character identifies the type of item (d is a directory; - is a regular file).
- Characters 2–4 show the permissions assigned to the user or owner (for example, rwx means the user has read, write, and execute permissions).
- Characters 5–7 show the permissions assigned to the group (for example, r-x means the group has read and execute permissions, but not write permission).
- Characters 8–10 show the permissions for others (for example, r-x means other users have read and execute permissions, but not write permission. By contrast, — would mean others don't have read, write, or execute permission).

The chmod command changes these permissions. To change permissions on files and directories, you can use either the symbolic (characters) format or the absolute (octal numbers 0 through 7) format. Using the example in Figure 21-20, if the user evan wants to give read, write, and execute permissions to everyone (group and other), he can use this symbolic formatted command:

    chmod g=rwx,o=rwx /home/evan

The g assigns permission to the group, and the o assigns permissions to others. (The u can assign permissions to the owner.) For a folder, you must move out of the folder before you change its permissions. Also, the command has no space before or after a comma.

21

Let's look at an example of when you might need to change the ownership of a directory or file. Suppose you are setting up an FTP server so users who have accounts on the server can use FTP to upload files to their home directories. Table 21-4 lists commands that might be useful to set up the user directories.

Table 21-4 Commands to set up user directories with appropriate write permissions

Command	Description
sudo adduser hector	Creates the user account and its home directory
sudo mkdir /home/hector/files	Creates a subdirectory named files for hector to store their files when using FTP; the sudo command is required to create the directory in another user's account, and this new directory belongs to root
sudo chown hector:hector /home/hector/files	Changes the owner of the files directory. The user:group component of the command written as hector:hector says that the user owner is hector, and also the group owner is the hector group. Note there is no space before or after the colon.
sudo chmod u+w, g-w,o-w /home/hector/files	Gives write permissions to the user, and removes write permissions from the group and other

You can also use an octal format, also known as the absolute method, to change the permissions. The octal format is used to quickly use octal numbers 0 through 7 to specify the permission values for the user, group, and others. In the example, chmod 754 myfile, the 754 is broken into a 7 for the user, a 5 for the group, and a 4 for others. The octal values for the read, write, and execute permissions are as follows:

- 4 stands for "read"
- 2 stands for "write"
- 1 stands for "execute"
- 0 stands for "no permission"

When looking back at the 754 in our example, the user is given full permissions of read, write, and execute (4 + 2 + 1 = 7). The group is given the read and execute only (4 + 1 = 5), and others are given read only permission (4).

Telnet and SSH for Remote Access

Core 2 Objective 4.9

Recall that Windows uses Remote Desktop and macOS uses Screen Sharing to remotely access a computer with screen and file sharing. Windows also makes use of SSH for secure remote access, as you learned in the module "Network Security and Troubleshooting." In Linux, the primary utilities for remote access at a shell prompt are **Telnet** and SSH (Secure Shell). Telnet does not encrypt transmissions, but SSH encrypts all transmissions. Therefore, SSH is more secure than Telnet and is the most common method to remotely access a Linux system. Use the commands in Table 21-5 to install Telnet and SSH in Linux.

Table 21-5 Install and run Telnet and SSH in Linux

Command	Description
sudo apt-add-repository universe	Add the universe repository to the list of places Ubuntu can find apps. This is an official repository of apps, but it is not supported by Ubuntu. (Note that when you attempt to add the repository and it is already available, a message appears, saying the component is already enabled.)
sudo apt-get update	Download and update all apps available to Ubuntu, including the ones in the universe repository.
sudo apt-get install openssh-server	Install and run the SSH server in Linux.
sudo apt install telnet	Install and run the Telnet server.

In Windows, SSH is enabled by default, and Telnet Client can be turned on using the Windows Features window, which is available in the Programs and Features window. Here are the steps to remotely access a Linux system from a Windows or Linux computer:

1. For Telnet using Windows, turn on **Telnet Client** in the **Windows Features** window.
2. For Telnet, at a Windows command prompt or Linux shell prompt, run the following command to open a Telnet session, substituting the IP address for the Linux system you want to remote in to:

   `telnet 192.168.1.160`

3. The Linux login prompt appears. Enter your user name and password. To close the session, run the `logout` command.
4. To use SSH to remote in, enter the following command, substituting your user name and IP address for the remote Linux system:

   `ssh evan@192.168.1.160`

5. Enter your password to log in to Linux. To close the session, run the `logout` command.

Samba File Servers

 Core 2 Objective 1.11

A Linux **Samba** file server allows for file sharing across different operating systems within a network. The name Samba comes from the Windows protocol server message block (SMB). Whereas SMB is used solely in a Windows environment for file and printer sharing, Samba provides the ability for Linux-hosted files and printers to be accessed across the Windows network. Figure 21-21 shows the Samba service running on Ubuntu, and in the window open toward the bottom of Figure 21-21, you can see the Shoppinglist.txt file that is located on the Ubuntu hard drive.

Figure 21-21   Samba service running in background and Shoppinglist text file in the sambashare directory

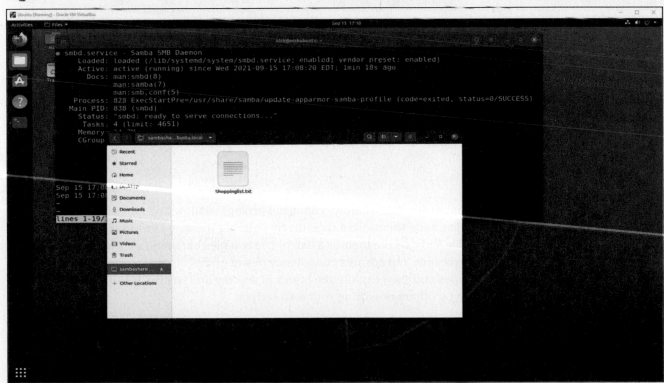

In Figure 21-22, you can see that same Shoppinglist file being accessed from a Windows operating system. This is because the file was shared by the Ubuntu system using the Samba service.

Figure 21-22   Shoppinglist text file shown in Windows

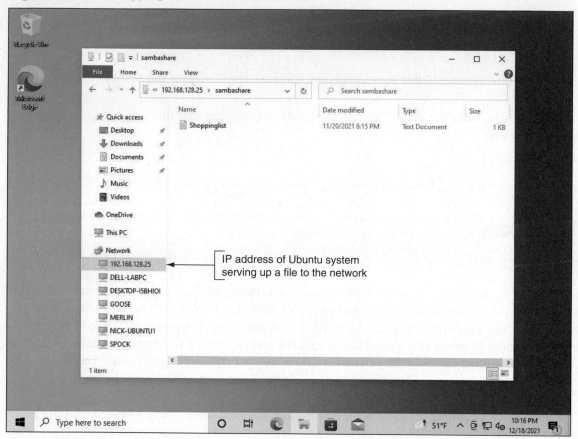

You learn how to install and use Samba later in this module with Real Problem 21-3. Now let's turn our attention to the last topic of the module, scripting.

Scripting Software and Techniques

Core 2 Objective 4.8

In this text, you've learned to use commands in a Windows command prompt window and Linux commands within the Linux terminal. When a technician finds themselves repetitively entering the same group of commands, they might decide to store them in a text file and execute them as a batch. The text file containing such a list of commands is called a **script**; using scripts can save time and ensures consistency (fewer errors). In this part of the module, you learn about the various script file types and then explore the basics of reading and writing scripts, which will help get you started using scripts written by others or writing your own scripts.

Script File Types

In the module "Maintaining Windows," you learned to create a batch file that contains Windows commands. This and other script file types are listed in Table 21-6 with a description of the software that can read and interpret each command in a script file and execute these commands in a **run-time environment**.

Table 21-6   Types of script files and scripting software

Script File Extension	Description
.bat	A **batch file** contains a list of Windows commands that can be executed in a command prompt window.
.ps1	A **PowerShell script** contains PowerShell commands, also known as **cmdlets**, that are executed in Windows PowerShell. The script is written using **dynamic type checking**, which means each cmdlet is checked by the PowerShell interpreter as it is typed to verify that the command can be executed as it is added to the script file. Many scripting and programming applications support dynamic type checking.
.vbs	A .vbs script is written with **VBScript**, which is modeled after the more complex Visual Basic, a full-fledged programming language.
.sh	A UNIX or Linux script, also called a shell script, contains Linux commands and is executed in a UNIX or Linux shell.
.py	A **Python script** is a group of Python commands interpreted by Python. Python can also compile the commands into an executable program.
.js	A .js script written in **JavaScript** is a text file that contains commands normally used with webpages. These scripts can be embedded in an HTML file, which is downloaded from a web server to a browser and used to build an interactive webpage in the browser. To ensure this works, JavaScript needs to be activated or turned on from the browser settings.

Note 10

With the release of Windows 11, Microsoft now includes the Windows Terminal application, in addition to PowerShell version 7.2. You can use Windows Terminal to run commands from Command Prompt and cmdlets from PowerShell. Scripts should still be created in the PowerShell ISE.

Scripts are simpler to write and use than programs. Differences between a script and a program include the following:

- **A script is interpreted.** A script is read, interpreted, and executed command by command directly from the script file by software called an interpreter. For example, a technician types the commands into a script file, and the commands are verified to work by PowerShell or VBScript. When a technician executes the script, PowerShell or VBScript reads, interprets, and executes each command in the file.
- **A program is compiled.** A program is first written using a programming language such as Visual Basic or Python, which interprets the code to verify that it can be executed. Then the coding file is compiled by the Visual Basic or Python complier into a binary executable file that has an .exe file extension. The executable file can then be run or executed by an operating system.

Basics of Scripting

Ready to learn a little scripting? Let's get started with some key terms:

An **environmental variable** (sometimes called a system variable) is information the OS makes available to a script. For example, the Windows and Linux PATH variable lists the paths (drives, directories, and subdirectories) the script can use. Another example is the TEMP variable, which tells a script where it can store its temporary files. To view and edit environmental variables in Windows, open the **System** window, and click **Advanced system settings**. On the Advanced tab of the System Properties dialog box, click **Environmental Variables**. See Figure 21-23.

Figure 21-23 View, create, edit, and delete environmental variables

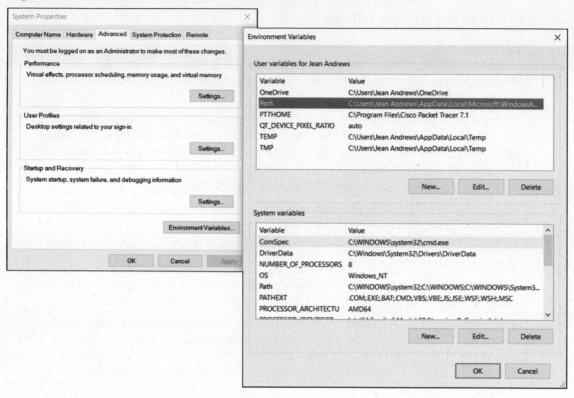

- Comments are text you put in a script to document the script. They can include your name, the date, the purpose of the script, and documentation that might help someone understand command lines in the script. **Comment syntax** refers to how you tag the text as a comment so it is not interpreted as a command. For example, in PowerShell, a line in the script file can hold a comment if you begin the line with a #.
- A **basic loop** executes the same commands multiple times until some condition is met.
- A **variable** is the name of an unknown data item and can be assigned a value, which is called initializing the variable. In PowerShell, a variable name is preceded by $. You can assign a value to a variable using the equal symbol (=).
- A data type determines what type of value a variable can be assigned. Two common data types are **integers** (whole numbers) and **strings** (text).

In the world of scripting and programming, it is common practice that the very first script or program a person learns how to write does nothing more than say "Hello World." Although it is a simple program, it proves you know how to create, save, and execute a script. Let's create one in a shell script:

1. At an Ubuntu shell prompt, make sure the current directory is your home directory. Then enter this command, saving the .sh file in your home directory:

```
echo "echo Hello World" > my-script.sh
```

2. To assign execute permission to the file, run this command:

```
chmod u=rwx my-script.sh
```

3. To execute a shell script, type ./ before the script file name. Enter this command (see Figure 21-24):

```
./my-script.sh
```

Figure 21-24   A simple shell script is created and executed

```
jean@spock:~$ echo "echo Hello World" > my-script.sh          ⎤ Create the
jean@spock:~$ ls -l                                           ⎦ script
total 12
drwxrwxr-x 2 jean jean 4096 Sep 27 21:09 Hold
-rw-rw-r-- 1 jean jean   17 Sep 27 21:17 my-script.sh
-rw------- 1 jean jean    4 Sep 12 19:57 MyTestFile.txt
jean@spock:~$ chmod u=rwx my-script.sh
jean@spock:~$ ls -l
total 12
drwxrwxr-x 2 jean jean 4096 Sep 27 21:09 Hold
-rwxrw-r-- 1 jean jean   17 Sep 27 21:17 my-script.sh
-rw------- 1 jean jean    4 Sep 12 19:57 MyTestFile.txt
jean@spock:~$ ./my-script.sh                                  ⎤ Execute
Hello World                                                   ⎦ the script
jean@spock:~$ _
                                                              ⎤ Script
                                                              ⎦ results
```

Now let's create a PowerShell script with a loop using Windows 10 **PowerShell ISE**, the PowerShell Integrated Scripting Environment, where scripts are created and tested:

1. In the Windows 10 search box, type **powershell** and then click **PowerShell ISE**. The PowerShell ISE window opens.

2. PowerShell ISE does dynamic type checking. As the command is interpreted, color coding is added to indicate the purpose of what you type. Type the following lines in the script pane (see Table 21-7):

Table 21-7   Commands to enter for a script with a basic loop

Command	Purpose
$i = 0	Defines an integer variable i that is assigned the value 0
While ($i -lt 3)	Continues looping as long as the variable is less than 3
{	Defines the beginning of the loop
Write-output "Hello World"	Displays "Hello World"
$i++	Adds one to the i variable
}	Defines the end of the loop

3. To execute the script, click the **Run Script** button, or click **File** and then click **Run**. The script is executed in the lower pane. See Figure 21-25.

Figure 21-25   A PowerShell script with a basic loop is executed

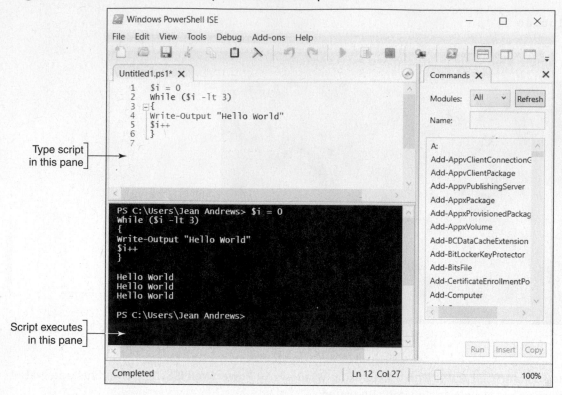

Type script in this pane

Script executes in this pane

4. To save your script, click **File**, click **Save**, and save the script to your desktop. Name the script **MyLoopScript**. By default, the .ps1 file extension is assigned to the file.

5. Close the **PowerShell ISE** window, and open a standard **PowerShell** window.

6. By default, running PowerShell scripts is disabled. To set the execution policy so scripts will run except those downloaded from the Internet without a valid digital signature, enter this cmdlet:

```
Set-ExecutionPolicy RemoteSigned
```

7. Run this alias cmdlet to go to your Windows desktop folder:

```
cd desktop
```

8. Run the `dir` alias cmdlet to list the contents of your desktop folder. You should see the script file listed.

9. To execute a PowerShell script, begin with ./. Enter this cmdlet to execute your script:

```
./MyLoopScript
```

Those are the basics of scripting. Now, let's discuss why IT personnel write scripts and examine various instances when you might want to use a script.

Uses for Scripting

Core 2 Objective 4.8

As you just learned, scripts can be used to write simple programs to perform tasks such as writing the "Hello World" statement. However, more complicated uses for scripts include the following:

- Restarting systems and services remotely
- Automating various administrative processes such as application installs, updates, and backups
- Remapping network file shares for users to access and save files across the network

- Installing and removing applications from systems
- Gathering information from network nodes, such as their IP address and MAC address information
- Initiating updates for various applications and the operating system itself

As you further explore scripting, you may want to start learning to script by writing one to rename files or collect information from computers on your network.

Applying Concepts

Using PowerShell to Assist in System Administration

Est. Time: 30 minutes
Core 2 Objective: 4.8

PowerShell can make Windows system administration easier through automation. In this activity, you will use the PowerShell ISE to script the following:

- Create a TestUser account without a password
- Create a MyTestDocuments directory in the My Documents folder of the TestUser
- Create four text documents named File1, File2, File3, and File4 in that newly created MyTestDocuments directory
- Check the status of DHCP Client service
- Restart the Explorer service
- Get a list of all your computer's information

1. In the Windows 10 search box, type **powershell** and then click **Run as administrator** under the PowerShell ISE. The PowerShell ISE window opens.

2. Run the command `Set-ExecutionPolicy RemoteSigned` in the bottom window. This allows you to run locally written and signed scripts you get from the Internet.

3. Enter the commands listed in Table 21-8 in the top pane of the PowerShell ISE. After all the commands have been entered, the screen should look like the one in Figure 21-26.

Table 21-8 PowerShell commands to enter for the script

Command	Purpose
`New-LocalUser -Name "TestUser" -NoPassword`	Creates a new local user named TestUser and sets the account to not have a password
`Add-LocalGroupMember -Group "Users" -Member "TestUser"`	Adds the TestUser account to the Users group in Windows 10
`Get-LocalUser`	Gets a list of users from your Windows 10 computer
`New-Item -Path "C:\Users\TestUser\ Documents" -Name "MyTestDocs" -ItemType "directory"`	Creates a new directory named MyTestDocs in the TestUser's Documents directory
`("File1.txt", "File2.txt", "File3.txt", "File4.txt" | foreach { New-Item -Path "C:\Users\TestUser\Documents\ MyTestDocs" -Name "$_"})`	Uses a foreach loop to create four new text files in the previously created MyTestDocs directory
`Get-Service -DisplayName 'DHCP Client'/`	Gets the status of the DHCP Client Service
`Stop-Process -ProcessName explorer`	Stops the explorer process (It will auto-restart.)
`Get-ComputerInfo	Out-File "C:\ Users\TestUser\Documents\MyTestDocs\ ComputerInfo.txt"`	Gets information about your local computer and redirects it to a file

(continues)

21

Applying Concepts Continued

Figure 21-26   The PowerShell script is shown in the PowerShell ISE

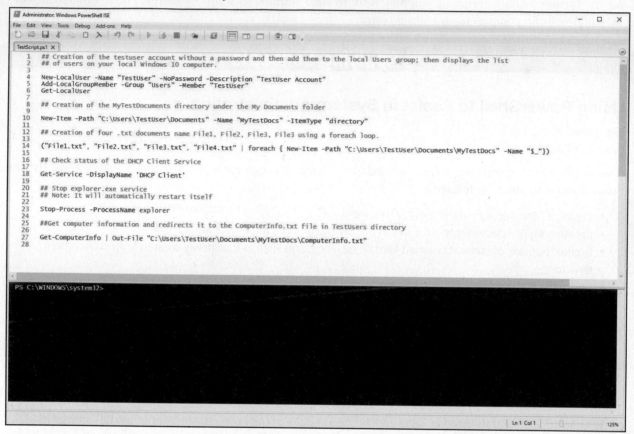

```
1   ## Creation of the testuser account without a password and then add them to the local Users group; then displays the list
2   ## of users on your local Windows 10 computer.
3
4   New-LocalUser -Name "TestUser" -NoPassword -Description "TestUser Account"
5   Add-LocalGroupMember -Group "Users" -Member "TestUser"
6   Get-LocalUser
7
8   ## Creation of the MyTestDocuments directory under the My Documents folder
9
10  New-Item -Path "C:\Users\TestUser\Documents" -Name "MyTestDocs" -ItemType "directory"
11
12  ## Creation of four .txt documents name File1, File2, File3, File3 using a foreach loop.
13
14  ("File1.txt", "File2.txt", "File3.txt", "File4.txt" | foreach { New-Item -Path "C:\Users\TestUser\Documents\MyTestDocs" -Name "$_"})
15
16  ## Check status of the DHCP Client Service
17
18  Get-Service -DisplayName 'DHCP Client'
19
20  ## Stop explorer.exe service
21  ## Note: It will automatically restart itself
22
23  Stop-Process -ProcessName explorer
24
25  ##Get computer information and redirects it to the ComputerInfo.txt file in TestUsers directory
26
27  Get-ComputerInfo | Out-File "C:\Users\TestUser\Documents\MyTestDocs\ComputerInfo.txt"
28
```

```
PS C:\WINDOWS\system32>
```

Note 11

In Figure 21-26, the green lines with double number signs indicate that a line is a comment. Comment lines are not read during the execution of a script and are only there for documentation within the script. Comments are often used to document what the command below the comment is doing. Using comments in this way is a best practice when writing scripts. Someone may have to edit your script later, and comments can help them understand what is happening at each step in the script.

4. Save the script to your Desktop as TestScript.ps1.

5. Click the green play button in the top toolbar. Alternatively, you can press the F5 key to run the script within the ISE.

6. The script executes. You can confirm the user was created along with the files by navigating in File Explorer to
C:\Users\TestUser\Documents\MyTestDocs.

The PowerShell ISE contains all the commands that can be run within your Windows environment. In enterprise networks, additional command modules can be added to support domain-wide administrative functions, including creating domain users and email accounts and deploying Windows installations to remote systems across the network.

Let's look at another PowerShell script, shown in Figure 21-27. Each line that begins with a # is a comment. In the image, you can see that the script is automating a variety of tasks.

Figure 21-27   An Advanced PowerShell script with comments

```
WindowsAutomation.ps1*  X
 1
 2   # This prompts the administrator to enter their credentials
 3   # This ensures that the admin account is used for mounting the network drive
 4   $cred = Get-Credential -Credential USERNAME
 5
 6   # Connects a network drive letter S to the Application Files folder on a system with
 7   # IP address 192.168.128.3 by using the above credentials
 8   New-PSDrive -Name "S" -PSProvider "FileSystem" -Root "\\192.168.128.3\Application Files" -Credential $cred
 9
10   # Executes the installation file for Adobe Reader from the newly mounted network drive
11   # The argument list is used as answers to the installation wizard and accepts the End
12   # User License Argreement(EULA)
13   Start-Process -FilePath "S:\Application Files\PDF_Application\PDFRdrDC1800920044_en_US.exe" `r
14   -ArgumentList "/sAll /rs /rps /msi /norestart /quiet EULA_ACCEPT=YES"
15
16   # Collect System Information including Computer Name, Operating System Info,
17   # Processor Info, and Installed Memory
18
19   echo "This computers name is $env:COMPUTERNAME" `n
20
21   echo "Operating System Information"
22   Get-ComputerInfo OsName, OsVersion, OsBuildNumber, WindowsVersion`
23
24   echo "Processor Information"
25   Get-CimInstance -ClassName Win32_Processor | Select-Object -ExcludeProperty "CIM*" `
26
27   echo "Installed Memory in GB"
28   (Get-CimInstance -ClassName Win32_PhysicalMemory | Measure-Object -Property capacity -Sum).sum /1gb
29
30   # Install the Windows Update Powershell Module and then run updates
31   Install-Module PSWindowsUpdate -Force
32   Get-WindowsUpdate -AcceptAll -Install
33
34   # Restart the Computer after 240 seconds
35   Restart-Computer -Wait  Timeout 240
```

Line 4 is asking for the administrator's log in credentials and then storing them. This is useful if there is a need for the credentials at any point in the script. Line 8 is connecting a remote network share folder to the local machine. The folder will show up as the drive letter S. This is sometimes called mounting a network share.

Lines 13 and 14 are installing an application using the .exe file that is located on the newly mounted network share. Lines 19–28 are collecting and displaying information about the computer. In this example, the computer's name, its operating system, its processor information, and the amount of installed memory will be displayed. Using a script can assist a technician in gathering information from the systems on a network to create an accurate inventory—making an administrator's life somewhat easier.

Lines 31 and 32 are installing the Windows Update module to the local system's PowerShell and using the Get-WindowsUpdate cmdlet to update the local system. In enterprise environments, this is extremely helpful to ensure all the network computers stay updated. Finally, in line 35, the script will restart the computer after a period of 240 seconds.

Exam Tip ✔

The A+ Core 2 exam expects you to be familiar with scripts used for basic automation, restarting machines, remapping network drives, installing applications, automating backups, gathering information, and initiating updates. You are not expected to know how to write these scripts or understand each command line in a script.

Now that we have explored PowerShell, let's turn our attention back to Linux and how scripts are written for that operating system.

Applying Concepts

Using Scripts to Assist in Backups of Linux Directories

Est. Time: 45 minutes

Core 2 Objective: 4.8

Scripts can also be used to simplify the process of backing up important directories in Linux. This script will create a backup of the directories identified in Table 21-2 earlier in this module.

1. Start your Ubuntu VM, and log in using your user name and password.
2. Open a terminal window by selecting the Terminal app from the Apps menu.
3. Type the commands in Table 21-9, pressing the **Enter** key after each line.

Table 21-9   Shell commands to enter for the script

Command	Purpose
`#!/bin/sh`	Loads the correct interpreter for your script
`DATE=$(date +%Y-%m-%d-%H%M%S)`	Uses the system's date and time and formats it so we can use it as the file name
	%Y is the year, %m is the month, %d is the day, %H is the hour, %M is minute, and %S is second.
	By using this command, we create a unique file name each time the script is run.
`BACKUP_DIR="/"`	Records the directory you want to save the backup to. In this example, we are saving the backup in the root directory.
`SOURCE="/etc /home / opt /root /var"`	Describes the files you want to back up
`tar -cvf $BACKUP_DIR/ backup-$DATE.tar.gz $SOURCE`	Creates the backup of our listed directories. The tar command stands for tape archive, and the -cvf options mean the following:
	-c: Creates the Archive
	-v: Displays Verbose information
	-f: Creates the archive with the given file name
`Echo "Backup completed"`	Displays the words "Backup completed" after the backup finishes

After it is complete, you should have something that looks like the script in the upper-left portion of Figure 21-28. The lower portion of Figure 21-28 shows the backup file that was created with the script. Your file name will be different because the date and time will be unique to your system and when you ran the script.

Figure 21-28   Shell script to create a backup of Linux directories

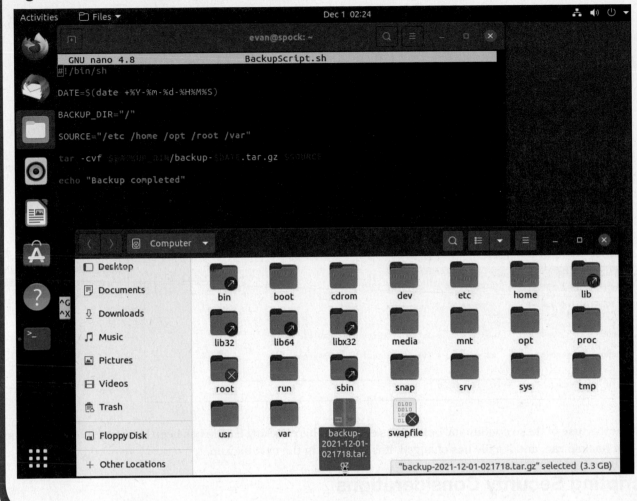

You can also make use of computer programming fundamentals to create a script in which a portion of the script only runs if a certain condition is met. An example of this would be a script that checks for the last time the computer checked for updates, and if the time since the last update check exceeds three days, it runs the update check. Other examples include checking for directories and files that have been modified or changed since a certain date and listing those files for the technician or only installing an application if it has not already been installed.

The script in Figure 21-29 is used to check the status of the ClamAV installed during this module. First, there is a check to see if a network connection to the Internet has been established. Then, there is a check of the installed signature file and a comparison to the version found on the ClamAV server. The comparison of the installed signature file and the version on the ClamAV server is only able to run if there is a network connection. The installed version on the local computer is then checked and compared with the version on the server.

Figure 21-29   Script file checking network connection and file comparison

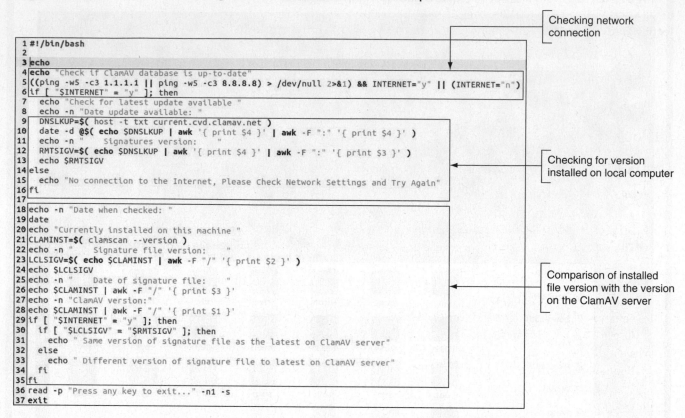

```
1 #!/bin/bash
2
3 echo
4 echo "Check if ClamAV database is up-to-date"
5 ((ping -w5 -c3 1.1.1.1 || ping -w5 -c3 8.8.8.8) > /dev/null 2>&1) && INTERNET="y" || (INTERNET="n")
6 if [ "$INTERNET" = "y" ]; then
7    echo "Check for latest update available "
8    echo -n "Date update available: "
9    DNSLKUP=$( host -t txt current.cvd.clamav.net )
10   date -d @$( echo $DNSLKUP | awk '{ print $4 }' | awk -F ":" '{ print $4 }' )
11   echo -n "    Signatures version:    "
12   RMTSIGV=$( echo $DNSLKUP | awk '{ print $4 }' | awk -F ":" '{ print $3 }' )
13   echo $RMTSIGV
14 else
15   echo "No connection to the Internet, Please Check Network Settings and Try Again"
16 fi
17
18 echo -n "Date when checked: "
19 date
20 echo "Currently installed on this machine "
21 CLAMINST=$( clamscan --version )
22 echo -n "    Signature file version:    "
23 LCLSIGV=$( echo $CLAMINST | awk -F "/" '{ print $2 }' )
24 echo $LCLSIGV
25 echo -n "    Date of signature file:    "
26 echo $CLAMINST | awk -F "/" '{ print $3 }'
27 echo -n "ClamAV version:"
28 echo $CLAMINST | awk -F "/" '{ print $1 }'
29 if [ "$INTERNET" = "y" ]; then
30   if [ "$LCLSIGV" = "$RMTSIGV" ]; then
31     echo " Same version of signature file as the latest on ClamAV server"
32   else
33     echo " Different version of signature file to latest on ClamAV server"
34   fi
35 fi
36 read -p "Press any key to exit..." -n1 -s
37 exit
```

Callouts: Checking network connection — Checking for version installed on local computer — Comparison of installed file version with the version on the ClamAV server

Another use of these conditional operations could involve checking if a file has been modified or changed since the last backup ran, and if a file has changed, it is included in the next backup.

Scripting Security Considerations

There is also the chance that scripts could be used for malicious reasons. They can be used to download malware to a system, maliciously change system settings, or even cause a system to crash due to overloaded use of system resources.

For instance, a Microsoft Excel file with embedded scripts, called macros, stored in the cells of the spreadsheet, could contain malware. When a user opens the Excel file, the macros can activate, downloading malware from a malware server on the Internet. The malware can then be used to create a backdoor into the user's system or gather information from the network to send off to a potential adversary.

Therefore, it is best to ensure that only authorized scripts are allowed on your network and that standard users, by default, do not have permission to run scripts. This can be controlled by using local and remote group policies within the operating system or from a server that manages domain policy. How to use Group Policy in a Windows domain is covered in the module "Securing and Sharing Windows Resources."

When using scripts, you should also be mindful of the changes that are made to the system settings by the script. For example, a script may be used to uninstall several applications; however, the script might also inadvertently remove a file during the uninstall process that is needed by another program on the computer. This can be caused by applications sharing files or a newer version of an application using an old version of a file. An administrator would have to then spend time reinstalling the missing file or recovering it from a backup. This can cause a delay in the technician's already busy day.

It is also wise to review how a script is accessing and using system resources such as memory or the computer processor. Overuse or misuse of system resources can lead to an application malfunction or even a total system crash. Legitimate scripts that are written in JavaScript are sometimes found on webpages and run within your web browser. Some malicious JavaScript scripts found within a webpage can also be used to steal user credentials from your computer or personal data from your browsing history. They can even cause the browser application to crash because it malfunctioned or ran out of allocated memory. Therefore, you should be cautious when running scripts that were downloaded from the Internet or from unknown sources.

As you can see, learning to script can be helpful in completing the day-to-day tasks of a computer technician. By using a script, you can save time by automating processes that repeat themselves, such as updating a computer, collecting important system information for inventory, or simply copying files and installing or uninstalling applications.

Module Summary

Linux Operating System

- Distributions of Linux provide a shell prompt in the Linux terminal and might also provide a desktop with a GUI. The default command-line shell for Linux is the Bash shell.
- Ubuntu Desktop with its windows manager offers Ubuntu software to install apps and update Ubuntu.
- The root account in Linux has access to all features of the OS. When logged in to the root account, the user is called the superuser.
- Important Linux commands include apt-get, cat, chmod, chown, cp, df, dig, find, grep, ip, ls, man, mv, nano, ps, pwd, rm, top, and yum.
- Telnet and SSH can be used to remotely access a Linux computer. Telnet transmissions are not secured. All SSH transmissions are encrypted, and SSH is the preferred method of remote access for Linux and Unix systems.
- Windows and macOS are popular OSs for desktops and laptops, and Linux is popular as an application server OS. For compatibility, the FAT32 file system can be used by Windows, macOS, and Linux.
- Samba can be used to share files and share printer resources between the operating systems.

Scripting Software and Techniques

- Scripts are executed in a run-time environment without first being compiled like programs are.
- Script file types include batch files, PowerShell scripts, VBScript, shell scripts (for Linux and UNIX), Python scripts, and JavaScript.

Uses for Scripting

- Scripts may be used to automate administrative processes, restart machines, map network storage drives, install and remove applications, perform system updates, back up files, and even gather information from your network devices.
- Careful testing, reviewing, and monitoring of scripts is necessary to protect the integrity of the operating system and hardware resources.

Key Terms

For explanations of key terms, see the Glossary for this text.

apt-get	cmdlet	grep	ls
Bash shell	comment syntax	GRUB (GR and Unified	man
basic loop	cp	Bootloader)	mv
batch file	df	integer	nano
cat	dig	ip	package
chmod	dynamic type checking	JavaScript	PowerShell ISE
chown	environmental variable	Live CD	PowerShell script
clone	find	Live USB	ps

pwd	Samba	su	top
Python script	script	sudo	variable
rm	shell prompt	superuser	VBScript
root account	shell script	swap partition	yum
run-time environment	string	Telnet	

Thinking Critically

These questions are designed to prepare you for the critical thinking required for the A+ exams and may use information from other modules and the web.

1. You are helping your friend troubleshoot a problem with their Linux server. You enter a common Linux command and discover it doesn't work exactly as you expected. What might be the problem, and what do you do next?

   a. The Linux installation is corrupted; restore the system from backup.

   b. The Linux shell is not the one you expected; use the echo $SHELL command.

   c. You probably don't know how to use the Linux command; search the web for information about the command.

   d. The Linux shell is not the one you expected; use the echo $0 command.

2. What is the full path to the home directory of the user account evan in Linux?

3. You are running a web server app in Ubuntu Server. Users complain that their browsers are loading webpages with errors. Where are you likely to find the log file where the web server reports its errors?

   a. /app/log

   b. /bin

   c. /var/log

   d. /root

4. In Linux, when logged in as a normal user with root privileges, which command must precede the apt-get command in the command line in order to install a program?

   a. sudo

   b. sudo user

   c. su

   d. root

5. Which file system does Linux currently use for the volume on which Linux is installed?

6. You have set up an FTP server in Ubuntu Server. Dominque, a user, calls to say she gets an error when trying to put a file in her /home/dominque/files directory. You look at the directory structure and see that you forgot to give the user ownership of the directory. Which command can fix the problem?

   a. chown dominque:dominque /home/dominque/files

   b. sudo chmod u=rwx /home/dominque/files

   c. sudo chown dominque:dominque /home/dominque/files

   d. chmod u-rwx /home/dominque/files/

7. What is the Linux nano editor command to save your changes and exit the editor?

8. You are managing an FTP server installed in Ubuntu Server. The server has created a very large log file, vsftpd.log. Which command is appropriate to search the log file for activity of the user nolan?

   a. sudo cat /var/log/vsftpd.log

   b. grep "nolan" /var/log/vsftpd.log

   c. sudo grep "nolan" /var/log/vsftpd.log

   d. cat /var/log/vsftpd.log

9. You work at an IT help desk and have been asked to set up 25 new user accounts in Active Directory. Your manager tells you to save time by using a PowerShell script that's available on a network share. You look at several script files named CreateNewUsers that are stored on the drive. Which one is likely to be the one you want?

   a. The file with a .js file extension
   b. The file with a .bat file extension
   c. The file that is the largest
   d. The file with a .ps1 file extension

10. A coworker is complaining that their connection to the Internet does not work. When you ask to examine the system, they show you a MacBook with Ubuntu Linux installed. Your initial assessment is that the Ethernet port does not have any lights flashing. You now want to check the configuration of the network card. Which of the following commands would allow you to view the necessary information?

    a. ipconfig /all
    b. ip route
    c. ip address
    d. traceroute

11. Backups of files can help restore files when something goes missing. Which of the following commands can be used to copy a file named ImportantInfo.txt from the desktop to a directory named Backups in the root directory?

    a. copy Desktop/ImportantInfo.txt ./Backups
    b. mv Desktop/ImportantInfo.txt ./Backups/ImportantInfo.txt
    c. cp Desktop/ImportantInfo.txt ./Backups/ImportantInfo.txt
    d. mkdir root/ImportantInfo

12. While browsing the Internet, your web browser is not displaying the webpage correctly. The images and multimedia content are not showing or playing, and you want to watch your favorite music video on YouTube. What is one possible explanation for this issue?

    a. The Internet is not working.
    b. The JavaScript add-on is not activated.
    c. Your wireless network card is suffering from interference.
    d. The display driver needs updating.

13. You want to restart your Windows computer at the end of a PowerShell script you have built to update the operating system. Which of the following commands could be used to perform the restart in your script?

    a. PowerOff Restart
    b. shutdown
    c. Reboot-Computer
    d. Restart-Computer

14. Cait is trying to execute a script file to update a Linux workstation. The script has been written and is saved. When Cait checks the permissions using ls -l, the following information is displayed in the terminal window:

    -r–r–r– 1 evan evan 1437 Sep 18 07:01 UpdateLinux.sh

    Cait needs to ensure that everyone can read and execute the file. Using the absolute mode format, which of the following commands would change the permissions on the UpdateLinux.sh file?

    a. chmod 555 UpdateLinux.sh
    b. chown 757 UpdateLinux.sh
    c. chmod u=rx,g=rx,o=rx UpdateLinux.sh
    d. chmod 535 UpdateLinux.sh

15. A new user is exploring the Linux terminal and wants to read an explanation of the dig command and see several examples. Which command would help them understand this command?

    a. dig man
    b. man dig
    c. help dig
    d. dig –help

Hands-On Projects

Hands-On Project 21-1

Practicing Linux Commands

Est. Time: 30 minutes
Core 2 Objective: 1.11

Practice the Linux commands listed in Table 21-10 using the Ubuntu Server VM you created earlier in this module. You could also use the Live Ubuntu on a USB you created in the Core 1 module "Hard Drives and Other Storage." As you complete the commands, you'll examine the directory structure, create a new directory, and put a blank file in it.

Table 21-10　Linux commands to practice

Task	Command	Description
1	ls -l	Lists files and directories in the current directory; in Linux, a directory is treated more like a file than it is in a Windows directory
2	pwd	Displays the full path to the current directory; when you first log in to a system, that directory is /home/*username*
3	mkdir mydir	Creates a directory named mydir; the directory is created in the current directory
4	cd mydir	Goes to the directory you just created in the /home/*username* directory
5	touch myfile	Creates a blank file named myfile in the current directory
6	ls	Lists the current directory's contents
7	cd ..	Moves up one level in the directory tree
8	cd /etc	Changes the directory to the /etc directory, where text files are kept for configuring installed programs
9	ls	Lists the contents of the /etc directory
10	cd /home	Changes the directory to the /home directory
11	ping 127.0.0.1	Pings the loopback address; pinging continues until you stop it by pressing Ctrl+C
12	ifconfig	Displays TCP/IP configuration data
13	man ifconfig	Displays the page from the Linux Manual about the ifconfig command; type q to exit
14	df -T	Displays free space on the hard drive and the file system used
15	exit	Logs out; the login shell prompt appears, where you can log in again

Hands-On Project 21-2

Changing Permissions for an Ubuntu Directory

Est. Time: 30 minutes
Core 2 Objective: 1.11

Follow these steps to change permissions for your home directory and then create a new user account to test these permissions:

1. Create a new user account named nadia. Log in to Ubuntu Server as nadia, and try to copy a file to your own home directory. For example, you can run this command to make a new copy of the mymemo file you created earlier in this module:

   ```
   cp mymemo mymemo.nadia
   ```

   When you do so, permission is denied.

2. Log back in to Ubuntu Server with your own account.

3. To install the chmod command, enter this command:

   ```
   sudo apt-get install coreutils
   ```

4. Run the **chmod** command to give full read, write, and execute permissions to everyone for your home directory.

5. Log out and log back in to the system as nadia, and verify that the user nadia can now copy a file to your home directory.

Hands-On Project 21-3

Using Telnet and SSH

Est. Time: 30 minutes
Core 2 Objective: 1.11

Following directions given earlier in the module, install Telnet and SSH in your Ubuntu Server VM. If you get an error, Ubuntu Server might need updating. Commands to update Ubuntu are also given in the module.

On your Windows host computer, turn on Telnet Client from the Programs and Features area of Control Panel. Open a command prompt window, and remote in to your Ubuntu Server VM using both Telnet and SSH. Alternatively, you can use the PuTTY program shown in the module "Securing and Sharing Windows Resources" to complete this.

21

Real Problems, Real Solutions

Real Problem 21-1

Using Google Cloud Platform to Create a Red Hat Enterprise Linux VM and Update the OS

Est. Time: 45 minutes

Core 2 Objective: 1.11

Recall from the Core 1 module "Network Infrastructure and Cloud Computing" that Google Cloud Platform offers a PaaS that you can use to experiment with other operating systems. To use the service to create a Red Hat Enterprise Linux VM, do the following:

1. Go to **cloud.google.com** and click **Get started for free**. You will need to sign in using a Google account. If you don't have an account, you can create one with any valid email address.

2. In the Developers Console, create a new project. Then drill down into **Compute, Compute Engine**, and **VM instances**. You will need to enable the API for the project. Create a VM instance with the latest RHEL version (RHEL 7 at the time of this writing) as the installed OS. Then wait several minutes for Google to create the instance.

3. Note the External IP assigned to the VM instance. Click **SSH**. In the drop-down menu that appears, click **Open in browser window**, and remote in to your VM using the SSH utility. The VM opens in a separate window where you can use Linux commands to navigate the directory structure (see Figure 21-30). Try updating the OS using the yum command by typing: `sudo yum update`.

Figure 21-30   Google Cloud VM configuration and SSH connection

SSH remote connection through browser window executed the df command

RHEL VM instance external IP address

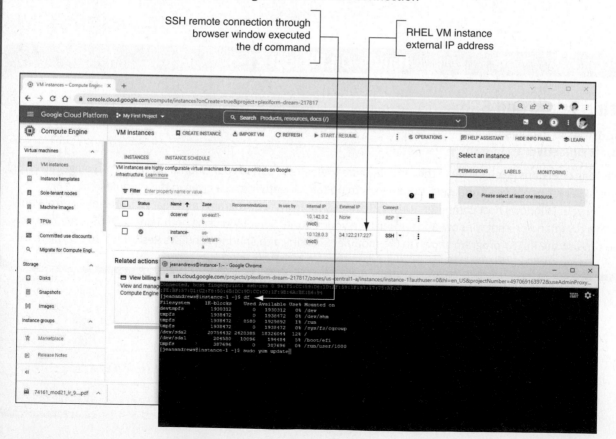

4. You can also try using other commands, such as df, to check the disk space and file systems on your VM or even try creating, editing, copying, and moving files. You can refer to Table 21-3 or use the manual pages to complete the following tasks:

   a. Create and edit a new file in the home directory named testfile.
   b. Create a directory in your home directory named data and copy the testfile from the home directory to the data directory.
   c. Delete the testfile from the home directory.
   d. Change permissions or ownership of the testfile that is in the data directory so the root account is the owner and has full permissions for the testfile.
   e. Search for a specific word in the testfile.
   f. View network interface configurations.

5. After you are finished, shut down the VM by running the **sudo shutdown** command.

Note 12

When you set up your Google Cloud account, your credit card information was required. If you're now done with your Google Cloud 90-day free trial, close your billing account so your credit card will not be charged at the end of your free trial period. Click the three-bar icon on the far-left side of the blue Google Cloud Platform menu bar, and click Billing. Then select Account management, and click CLOSE BILLING ACCOUNT at the top. Google normally will not automatically charge you after the trial period ends unless you upgrade your account to a full account, but it's better to be safe and close your billing account to prevent any unnecessary problems.

Real Problem 21-2

Configuring Network Adapters

Est. Time: 15 minutes
Core 2 Objective: 1.11

A user reports that their Ubuntu virtual machine cannot access the Internet. After taking control of the VM, you identify the following:

- The network card is enabled.
- The web browser is not loading *linux.org*.
- Other users are not reporting any issues browsing the Internet.

You suspect there is a problem with the network settings, and you will need to reconfigure the adapter to support full network connectivity. You decide that troubleshooting this error will be easily fixed through the terminal.

1. What command would you run to verify the current network card ip configuration?
2. You are shown that the inet address is 169.254.9.18. What does this information tell you? Describe how you might correct this problem using the terminal.
3. After performing the first two steps, you are shown a new ip address of 192.168.128.14. How can you verify connectivity to *linux.org*?

Real Problem 21-3

Installing and Using Samba

Est. Time: 30 minutes
Core 2 Objective: 1.11

Remember that Samba can be used to share files and printers between Linux and Windows systems. For this activity, you will need both your Windows 10 VM from the module "Installing Windows" and your Ubuntu VM from earlier in this module. Ensure both VMs are started and running, and then complete the following steps:

1. In the Ubuntu VM, open the terminal window, and run the following:

```
sudo apt update
sudo apt install samba
```

Enter your sudo password, and then press **Enter**. When asked if you want to continue, press **Enter**.

Figure 21-31 shows the installation of Samba in terminal.

Figure 21-31   Installation of the Samba service on Ubuntu

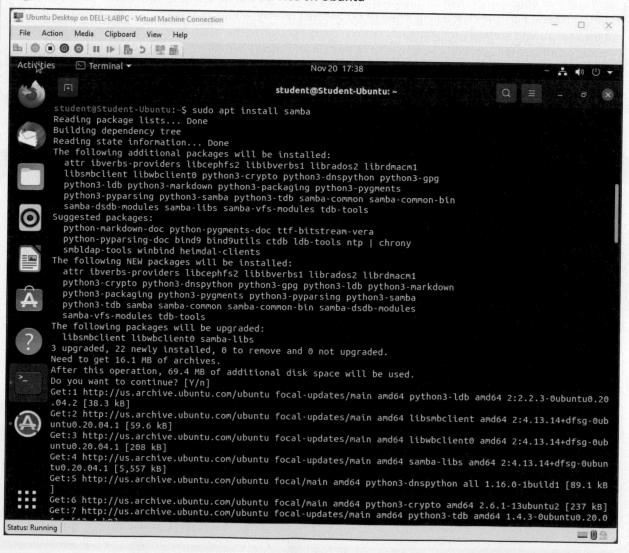

2. Now that Samba is installed, you need to create a directory for Samba to share with the network. Type the following command into the terminal window, substituting your user name where *<username>* is shown:

```
mkdir /home/<username>/sambashare/
```

3. Now that the directory you want to share is created, you need to ensure that the Samba configuration file includes it as a shared item for the network. Run the `sudo /nano /etc/<username>/sambashare` command in terminal, and then add the following lines to the end of the file:

```
[sambashare]
    comment = Samba on Ubuntu
    path = /home/<username>/sambashare
    read only = no
    browsable = yes
```

Then press **Ctrl+O** to save and **Ctrl+X** to exit the nano editor. Figure 21-32 shows the lines added to the end of the file. They are highlighted in white.

Figure 21-32   Editing the smb.conf file

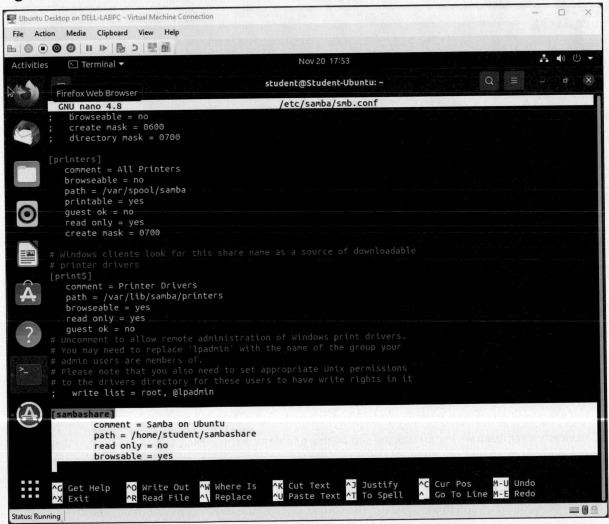

4. Restart the smbd service by running the `sudo service smbd restart` command. Then, allow Samba traffic through the Ubuntu firewall by running the `sudo ufw allow samba` command, as shown in Figure 21-33.

(continues)

Real Problem Continued

Figure 21-33   Restarting the Samba service and modifying the firewall rules to allow Samba
connections through

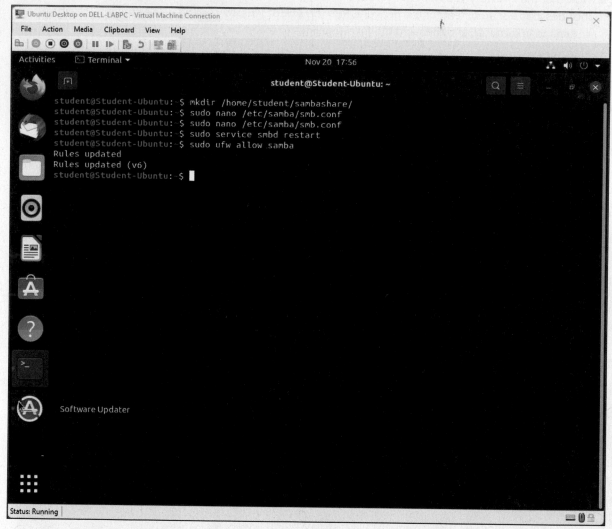

5. Next, you will set up a user for the Samba service by entering the following command (using your own
   Ubuntu user account name):

   ```
   sudo smbpasswd -a username
   ```

   Enter your desired password twice, and then close the terminal. Be sure to remember this password, as
   you will need it to connect from your Windows VM and access the shared directory.

6. To view the sambashare folder, click the **sambashare folder** icon on the left side of the Ubuntu desktop.
   The sambashare folder should be shown in the Home directory, as shown in Figure 21-34. Any documents
   or files that are placed in the sambashare directory can now be accessed across the network. Add a
   document or file to the sharefolder by first creating the document using LibreOffice writer or another
   software application and then saving it in the correct sambashare directory of your home directory. You can
   see an example Accounts.txt file is saved to the proper directory in Figure 21-35.

Figure 21-34   Sambashare directory (selected on the right) is displayed on the Ubuntu system

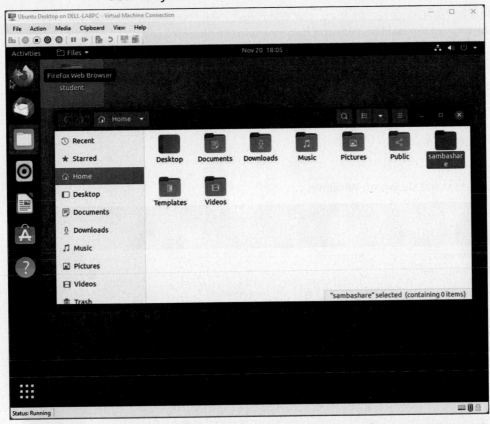

Figure 21-35   Accounts.txt file shown in the sambashare folder on Ubuntu

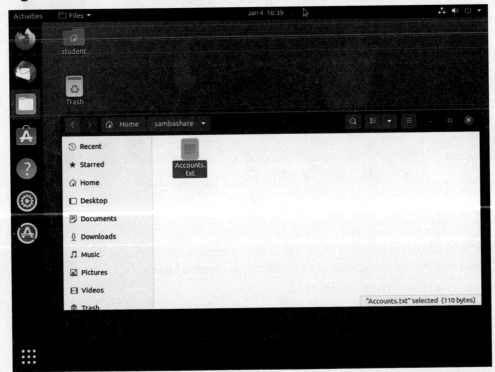

Real Problem Continued

7. To access the files that are shared via samba from your Windows 10 VM, first connect to your VM, and then open **File Explorer** from the taskbar. Type the following into the directory path: `\\ip-address\ sambashare`.

   Be sure to use the correct ip address of your Ubuntu VM in place of the word ip-address. This can be found by running the `ifconfig` command from the terminal window. You will be prompted to enter your Ubuntu user name and password.

8. You should now be able to see the file you saved in step 6 in File Explorer. See Figure 21-36, and note that the example Accounts.txt file is shown.

Figure 21-36 Accounts text file shown on Windows

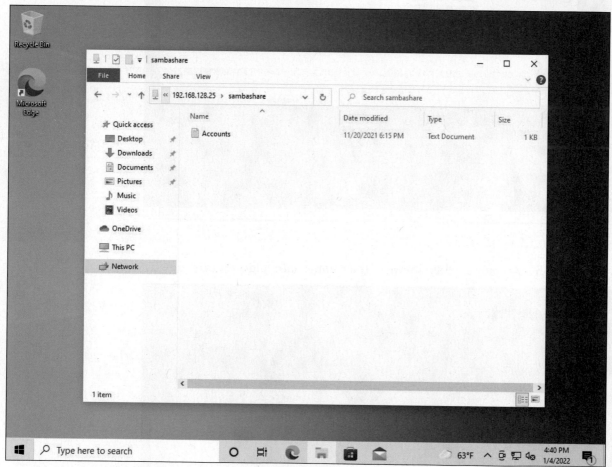

9. Alternatively, you could connect from your host machine to the sambashare directory. If you are using Windows as your host OS, follow step 7. If you are on a Mac, use the Finder menu, and select **Go > Connect**, and then enter the following: `smb://ip-address/sambashare`

   Again, be sure to change "ip-address" to the Ubuntu VM's.

10. If you have a printer attached to your host machine, try printing the document as well.

Real Problem 21-4

Preparing for the A+ Core 2 Exam

Est. Time: Unknown
Core 2 Objectives: 1.1–4.9

In this text, the modules "The Complex World of IT Professionals" through "Linux and Scripting" and the appendix "Safety Procedures and Environmental Concerns" prepare you for the A+ Core 2 exam. When you have completed these modules and appendix, you are ready to make your final review of the A+ Core 2 objectives and sit for the exam. Read through the objectives listed at the beginning of this text and make sure you understand each objective. If you don't understand an objective, reread that section in the text or do a general Google search. You may also want to form a study group as you prepare for the certification exam. Your instructor might also suggest other exam-prep tasks.

You can go to the CompTIA website at *comptia.org* to sign up for the exam or use another method suggested by your instructor. A+ Certification requires that you pass both the A+ Core 1 exam and the A+ Core 2 exam.

Appendix

A

Safety Procedures and Environmental Concerns

Module Objectives

1 Identify the properties and measurements of electricity

2 Describe how to stay safe as you work with computer hardware and networks

3 Describe how to protect equipment as you work with computer hardware and networks

4 Identify several ways to protect the environment when performing the duties of an IT support technician

Core 2 Certification objectives

4.4 Given a scenario, use common safety procedures.

4.5 Summarize environmental impacts and local environmental controls.

Introduction

In this appendix, we discuss electricity and how it is measured. Then we address the very important topics of how to protect yourself and equipment when working on computer hardware and networks from electricity and other potential hazards. Finally, we turn our attention to protecting the environment when performing your duties as an IT technician.

Measures and Properties of Electricity

 Core 2 Objectives 4.4, 4.5

In our modern world, we take electricity for granted, but we miss it terribly when it's cut off. Nearly everyone depends on it, but few really understand it. A successful hardware technician does not expect to encounter failed processors, fried motherboards, smoking monitors, or frizzed hair. To avoid these excitements, you need to understand how to measure electricity and how to protect computer equipment from its damaging power.

Let's start with the basics. To most people, volts, ohms, joules, watts, and amps are vague terms that simply mean electricity. All these terms can be used to measure some characteristic of electricity, as listed in Table A-1.

Table A-1 Measures of electricity

Unit	Definition	Computer Example
Volt (for example, 115 V)	Electrical force is measured in **volts**. The symbol for volts is V.	A power supply steps down the voltage from 115 V house current to levels of 3.3, 5, and 12 V that computer components can use.
Amp or ampere (for example, 1.5 A)	An **amp** is a measure of electrical current. The symbol for amps is A.	An LCD monitor requires about 5 A to operate. A small laser printer uses about 2 A. An optical drive uses about 1 A.
Ohm (for example, 20 Ω)	An **ohm** is a measure of resistance to electricity. The symbol for ohm is Ω.	Current can flow in typical computer cables and wires with a resistance of near zero Ω.
Joule (for example, 500 J)	A joule is a measure of work or energy. One **joule** (pronounced "jewel") is the work required to push an electrical current of 1 A through a resistance of 1 Ω. The symbol for joule is J.	A **surge suppressor** (see Figure A-1) is rated in joules—the higher the better. The rating determines how much work a device can expend before it can no longer protect the circuit from a power surge. To protect against lightning, use a suppressor rated at 2000 joules or higher.
Watt (for example, 20 W)	A watt is a measure of the total electrical power needed to operate a device. One **watt** is one joule per second. Watts can be calculated by multiplying volts by amps. The symbol for watts is W.	The power consumption of an LCD computer monitor is rated at about 14 W. A DVD burner uses about 25 W when burning a DVD.

Figure A-1   A surge suppressor protects electrical equipment from power surges and is rated in joules

Rating is
720 joules

Note ①

To learn more about how volts, amps, ohms, joules, and watts measure the properties of electricity, see "Electricity and Multimeters" in the student companion site that accompanies this text at *cengage.com*.

Now let's look at how electricity gets from one place to another and how it is used in house circuits and computers.

AC and DC

Core 2 Objectives 4.4, 4.5

Electricity can be either AC or DC. **Alternating current (AC)** goes back and forth, or oscillates, rather than traveling in only one direction. House current in the United States is AC and oscillates 60 times in one second (60 hertz). Voltage in the system is constantly alternating from positive to negative, which causes the electricity to flow first in one direction and then in the other. Voltage alternates from +115 V to –115 V. AC is the most economical way to transmit electricity to our homes and workplaces. By decreasing current and increasing voltage, we can force alternating current to travel great distances. When alternating current reaches its destination, it is made more suitable for driving our electrical devices by decreasing voltage and increasing current.

Direct current (DC) travels in only one direction and is the type of current that most electronic devices, including computers, require. A **rectifier** is a device that converts AC to DC, and an **inverter** is a device that converts DC to AC. A **transformer** is a device that changes the ratio of voltage to current. The power supply used in computers is both a rectifier and a transformer.

Large transformers reduce the high voltage on power lines coming to your neighborhood to a lower voltage before the current enters your home. The transformer does not change the amount of power in this closed system; if it decreases voltage, it increases current. The overall power stays constant, but the ratio of voltage to current changes, as illustrated in Figure A-2.

Figure A-2 A transformer keeps power constant but changes the ratio of current to voltage

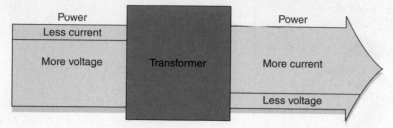

Again, direct current flows in only one direction. Think of electrical current like a current of water that flows from a state of high pressure to a state of low pressure or rest. Electrical current flows from a high-pressure state (called hot) to a state of rest (called ground or neutral). For a power supply, a power line may be either $+5$ or -5 volts in one circuit or $+12$ or -12 volts in another circuit. The positive or negative value is determined by how the circuit is oriented, either on one side of the power output or the other. Several circuits coming from the power supply accommodate different devices with different power requirements.

Hot, Neutral, and Ground

Core 2 Objectives 4.4, 4.5

AC travels on a hot line from a power station to a building and returns to the power station on a neutral line. When the two lines reach the building and enter an electrical device, such as a lamp, the device controls the flow of electricity between the hot and neutral lines. If an easier path (one with less resistance) is available, the electricity follows that path. This can cause a short, a sudden increase in flow that can also create a sudden increase in temperature—enough to start a fire and injure both people and equipment. Never put yourself in a position where you are the path of least resistance between the hot line and ground!

Caution ❗

It's very important that computer components be properly grounded. Never connect a computer to an outlet or use an extension cord that doesn't have the third ground plug. The third line can prevent a short from causing extreme damage. In addition, the bond between the neutral and ground helps eliminate electrical noise (stray electrical signals) within the computer that is sometimes caused by other nearby electrical equipment.

To prevent uncontrolled electricity in a short, the neutral line is grounded. Grounding a line means that the line is connected directly to the earth; in the event of a short, the electricity flows into the earth and not back to the power station. Grounding serves as an escape route for out-of-control electricity because the earth is always capable of accepting a flow of current. A surge suppressor can be used to protect a computer and its components against power surges.

Caution ❗

Beware of the different uses of black wire. In desktop computers and in DC circuits, black is used for ground, but in home wiring and in AC circuits, black is used for hot!

The neutral line to your house is grounded many times along its way (in fact, at each electrical pole) and is also grounded at the breaker box where the electricity enters your house. You can look at a three-prong plug and see the three lines: hot, neutral, and ground (see Figure A-3). When grounding the device is not important, either a polarized plug (hot and neutral are designated) or a non-polarized plug (hot and neutral depend on how the plug is inserted in the outlet) can be used.

Figure A-3 A polarized plug showing hot and neutral, and a three-prong plug showing hot, neutral, and ground

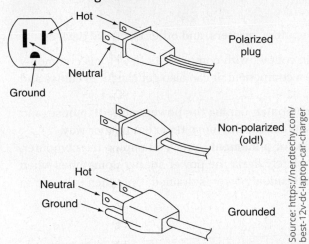

Source: https://nerdtechy.com/best-12v-dc-laptop-car-charger

Note 2

House AC voltage in the United States is about 110–120 V, but in other countries, this is not always the case. In many other countries, the standard is 220 V. Outlet styles also vary from one country to the next.

Now that you know about electricity, let's discuss how to protect yourself against the dangers of electricity and other factors that might harm you as you work around computers.

Protecting Yourself

Core 2 Objectives 4.4, 4.5

To protect yourself against electrical shock when working with any electrical device—including computers, printers, scanners, and network devices—disconnect the power if you notice a dangerous situation that might lead to electrical shock or fire. When you disconnect the power, do so by pulling on the plug at the AC outlet. To protect the power cord, don't pull on the cord itself. Also, don't just turn off the on/off switch on the device; you need to actually disconnect the power. Note that any of the following can indicate a potential danger:

- You notice smoke coming from the computer case, or the case feels unusually warm.
- The power cord is frayed or otherwise damaged in any way.
- Water or other liquid is on the floor around the device or was spilled on it.
- The device has been exposed to excess moisture.
- The device has been dropped, or you notice physical damage.
- You smell a strong electronics odor.
- The power supply or fans are making a whining noise.

Safely Working Inside Computers, Printers, and Other Electrical Devices

 Core 2 Objectives 4.4, 4.5

To stay safe, always do the following before working inside computers, printers, and other electrical devices:

- **Remove jewelry.** Remove any jewelry that might come in contact with components. Jewelry is commonly made of metal and might conduct electricity if it touches a component. It can also get caught in cables and cords inside computer cases.
- **Power down the system and unplug it.** For a desktop computer, unplug the power, monitor, mouse, and keyboard cables, unplug any other peripherals or cables attached, and move them out of your way.
- **For a computer, press and hold down the power button for a moment.** After you unplug the computer, press the power button for about three seconds to completely drain the power supply. Sometimes when you do so, you'll hear the fans quickly start and go off as residual power is drained. Only then is it safe to work inside the case.

Electrical Fire Safety

 Core 2 Objectives 4.4, 4.5

Never use water to put out a fire fueled by electricity because water is a conductor and you might get a severe electrical shock. A computer lab needs a fire extinguisher that is rated to put out electrical fires. Fire extinguishers are rated by the type of fires they put out:

- Class A extinguishers can use water to put out fires caused by wood, paper, and other combustibles.
- Class B extinguishers can put out fires caused by liquids such as gasoline, kerosene, and oil.
- **Class C fire extinguishers** use nonconductive chemicals to put out a fire caused by electricity (see Figure A-4).

Figure A-4   A Class C fire extinguisher is rated to put out electrical fires

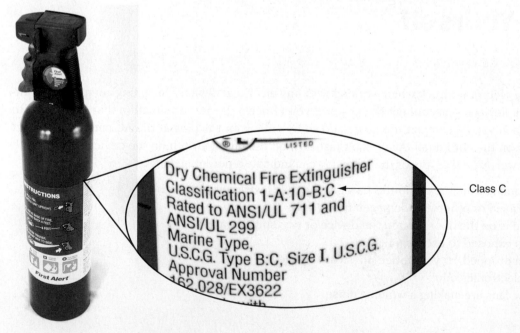

Proper Use of Cleaning Pads and Solutions

Core 2 Objectives 4.4, 4.5

As a support technician, you'll find yourself collecting different cleaning solutions and cleaning pads to clean a variety of devices, including the mouse and keyboard, CDs, DVDs, Blu-ray discs and their drives, and monitors. Figure A-5 shows a few of these products. For example, the contact cleaner in the figure is used to clean the contacts on the edge connectors of expansion cards; a good cleaning can solve a problem with a faulty connection.

Figure A-5   Cleaning solutions and pads

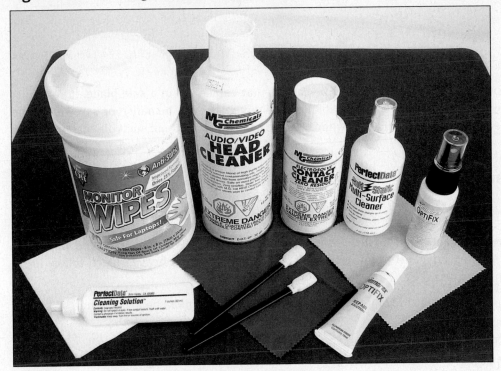

Most of these cleaning solutions contain flammable and poisonous materials. Take care when using them so they don't get on your skin or in your eyes. To find out what to do if you are accidentally exposed to a dangerous solution, look at the instructions printed on the can or check out the material safety data sheet (see Figure A-6). A **material safety data sheet (MSDS)** explains how to properly handle substances such as chemical solvents and how to dispose of them.

An MSDS includes information such as physical data, toxicity, health effects, first aid, storage, shipping, disposal, and spill procedures. The MSDS comes packaged with the chemical; you can also order one from the manufacturer or find one on the Internet (see *ilpi.com/msds*).

Figure A-6   Each chemical you use should have a material safety data sheet (MSDS) available

Exam Tip

The A+ Core 2 exam expects you to know how to use MSDS documentation to dispose of chemicals and help protect the environment. You also need to know that you must follow all local government regulations when disposing of chemicals and other materials dangerous to the environment.

If you have an accident with cleaning solutions or other dangerous products, your company or organization might require you to report the accident and/or fill out an incident report. Check with your organization to find out how to report these types of incidents.

Managing Cables

 Core 2 Objectives 4.4, 4.5

People can trip over cables or cords left on the floor, so be careful that cables are in a safe place. If you must run a cable across a path or where someone sits, use a cable or cord cover that can be nailed or screwed to the floor. Don't leave loose cables or cords in a traffic area where people can trip over them; such objects are called **trip hazards**.

Lifting Heavy Objects

Core 2 Objectives 4.4, 4.5

Back injury caused by lifting heavy objects is one of the most common work injuries. Whenever possible, put heavy objects, such as a large laser printer, on a cart to move them. If you do need to lift a heavy object, follow these guidelines to keep from injuring your back:

1. Look at the object and decide which side of it to face so the load will be the most balanced when you lift it.
2. Stand close to the object with your feet apart.
3. Keeping your back straight, bend your knees and grip the load.
4. Lift with your legs, arms, and shoulders, not with your back or stomach.
5. Keep the load close to your body, and avoid twisting your body while you're holding the load.
6. To put the object down, keep your back as straight as you can, and lower the object by bending your knees.

Don't try to lift an object that is too heavy for you. Because there are no exact guidelines for when heavy is too heavy, use your best judgment as to when to ask for help.

Safety Goggles and Air Filter Mask

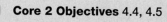 **Core 2 Objectives** 4.4, 4.5

If you work in a factory environment where flying fragments, chips, or other particles are about, your employer might require you to wear **safety goggles** to protect your eyes. In addition, if the air is filled with dust or other contaminants, your employer might require you to wear an air-purifying respirator, commonly called an **air filtration mask**, which filters out the dust and other contaminants. If safety goggles or a mask is required, your employer is responsible for providing one that is appropriate for your work environment.

Protecting the Equipment

 Core 2 Objectives 4.4, 4.5

As you learn to troubleshoot and solve computer problems, you gradually begin to realize that many of them could have been avoided by good computer maintenance, which includes protecting the computer against environmental factors such as humidity, dust, and out-of-control electricity.

Protect the Equipment Against Static Electricity or ESD

 Core 2 Objectives 4.4, 4.5

Suppose you come indoors on a cold day, pick up a comb, and touch your hair. Sparks fly! What happened? Static electricity caused the sparks. Electrostatic discharge (ESD), commonly known as **static electricity**, is an electrical charge at rest. When you came indoors, this charge built up on your hair and had no place to go. An ungrounded conductor (such as wire that is not touching another wire) or a nonconductive surface (such as your hair) holds a charge until it is released. When two objects with dissimilar electrical charges touch, electricity passes between them until the dissimilar charges become equal.

To see static charges equalizing, turn off the lights in a room, scuff your feet on the carpet, and touch another person. Occasionally, you can see and feel the charge in your fingers. If you can feel the charge, you discharged at least 1500 volts of static electricity. If you hear the discharge, you released at least 6000 volts. If you see the discharge, you released at least 8000 volts of ESD. A charge of only 10 volts can damage electronic components! You can touch a chip on an expansion card or motherboard, damage the chip with ESD, and never feel, hear, or see the electrical discharge.

ESD can cause two types of damage to an electronic component: catastrophic failure and upset failure. A catastrophic failure destroys the component beyond use. An upset failure damages the component so it does not perform well, even though it may still function to some degree. Upset failures are more difficult to detect because they are not consistent and not easily observed. Both types of failures permanently affect the device. Components are easily damaged by ESD, but because the damage might not show up for weeks or months, a technician may get careless and not realize the damage they are doing.

> **Caution** ❗
>
> Unless you are measuring power levels with a multimeter or power supply tester, never touch a component or cable inside a computer case while the power is on. The electrical voltage is not enough to seriously hurt you but is more than enough to permanently damage the component.

Before touching or handling a component (for example, a hard drive, motherboard, expansion card, processor, or memory modules), protect it against ESD by always grounding yourself first. You can ground yourself and the computer parts by using one or more of the following static control devices or methods:

- **ESD strap.** An ESD strap, also called a **ground bracelet, antistatic wrist strap**, or ESD bracelet, is a strap you wear around your wrist. The strap has a cord attached with an alligator clip on the end. Attach the clip to the computer case you're working on, as shown in Figure A-7. Any static electricity between you and the case will be discharged. Therefore, as you work inside the case, you will not damage the components with static electricity. The bracelet also contains a resistor that prevents electricity from harming you.

Figure A-7   A ground bracelet, which protects computer components from ESD, can clip to the side of the computer case and eliminate ESD between you and the case

> **Caution** ⚠
>
> When working on a laser printer, <u>don't</u> wear the ESD strap. You don't want to be the ground for these high-voltage devices.

- **Ground mats.** A ground mat, also called an ESD mat, dissipates ESD and is commonly used by bench technicians (also called depot technicians) who repair and assemble computers at their workbenches or in an assembly line. Ground mats have a connector in one corner that you can use to connect the mat to the ground (see Figure A-8). If you lift a component off the mat, it is no longer grounded and is susceptible to ESD, so it's important to use an ESD strap with a ground mat.

Figure A-8   An ESD mat dissipates ESD and should be connected to the ground

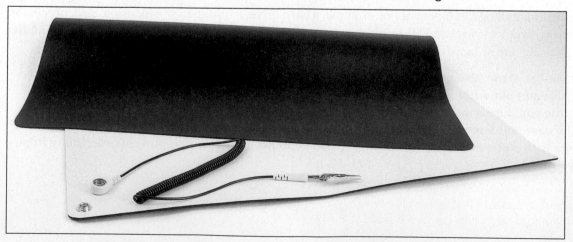

- **Static shielding bags.** New components come shipped in static shielding bags, also called antistatic bags. These bags are a type of Faraday cage (named after Michael Faraday, who built the first cage in 1836). A Faraday cage is any device that protects against an electromagnetic field. Save the bags to store other devices that belong in a computer but are not currently installed. As you work on a computer, know that a device is not protected from ESD if you place it on top of the bag; the protection is inside the bag (see Figure A-9).

Figure A-9   An antistatic bag helps protect components from ESD

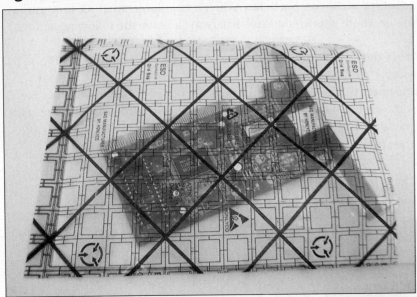

> **Caution** ❗
>
> An older CRT monitor can also damage components with ESD. Don't place or store expansion cards on top of or next to a CRT monitor, which can discharge as much as 29,000 volts onto the screen.

The best way to guard against ESD is to use an ESD strap together with a ground mat. Consider an ESD strap essential equipment when working on a computer. However, if you are in a situation in which you must work without one, touch the computer case or the power supply before you touch a component in the case, which is called **self-grounding**. Self-grounding dissipates any charge between you and whatever you touch. Here are some rules that can help protect computer parts against ESD:

- When passing a circuit board, memory module, or other sensitive component to another person, ground yourself and then touch the other person before you pass the component.
- Leave components inside their protective bags until you are ready to use them.
- Work on hard floors, not carpet, or use antistatic spray on the carpet.
- Don't work on a computer if you or the computer has just come in from the cold because there is more danger of ESD when the atmosphere is cold and dry.
- When unpacking hardware or software, remove the packing tape and cellophane from the work area as soon as possible because these materials attract ESD.
- Keep components away from your hair and clothing.

> **Exam Tip** ✔
>
> The A+ Core 2 exam emphasizes that you should know how to protect computer equipment as you work on it, including how to protect components against damage from ESD.

Physically Protect Your Equipment from the Environment

Core 2 Objectives 4.4, 4.5

When you protect equipment from ongoing problems with the environment, you are likely to have fewer problems later, and you will have less troubleshooting and repair to do. Here is how you can physically protect a computer:

- **Protect a computer against dust and other airborne particles.** When a computer must sit in a dusty environment, around those who smoke, or where pets might leave hair, you can take the following actions to protect it:
  - Use a plastic keyboard cover to protect the keyboard. When the computer is turned off, protect the entire system with a cover or enclosure.
  - Install air filters over the front or side vents of the case where air flows in. Put your hand over the case of a running computer to feel where the air flows in. For most systems, air flows in from the front vents, or it vents on the side of the case that is near the processor cooler. The air filter shown in Figure A-10 has magnets that hold the filter to the case when screw holes are not available.

Figure A-10   This air filter is designed to fit over a case fan, power supply fan, or panel vent on the case

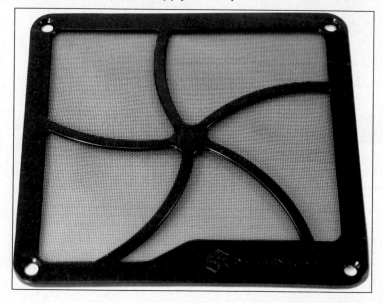

  - Use compressed air or an antistatic vacuum (see Figure A-11) to remove dust from inside the case, if you have the case cover open. Figure A-12 shows a case fan that jammed because of dust and caused a system to overheat. While you're cleaning up dust, don't forget to blow or vacuum out the keyboard.

Note 3

When working at a customer site, be sure to clean up any mess you created by blowing dust out of a computer case or keyboard.

Figure A-11   An antistatic vacuum is designed to work inside sensitive electronic equipment such as computers and printers

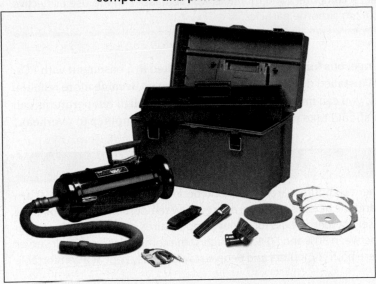

Figure A-12   This dust-jammed case fan caused a system to overheat

- **Allow for good ventilation inside and outside the system.** Proper air circulation is essential to keeping a system cool. Don't block air vents on the front and rear of the computer case or on the monitor. Inside the case, make sure cables are tied up and out of the way so as to allow for airflow and not obstruct fans from turning. Put covers on expansion slot openings at the rear of the case and put faceplates over empty bays on the front of the case. Don't set a tower case directly on thick carpet because the air vent on the bottom front of the case can be blocked. If you are concerned about overheating, monitor temperatures inside and outside the case.

Exam Tip ✔

The A+ Core 2 exam expects you to know how to keep computers and monitors well ventilated and to use protective enclosures and air filters to protect the equipment from airborne particles.

- **High temperatures and humidity can be dangerous for hard drives.** I once worked in a basement with PCs, and hard drives failed much too often. After I installed dehumidifiers, the hard drives became more reliable. If you suspect a problem with room humidity, you can monitor it using a hygrometer. High temperatures can also damage computer equipment, and you should take precautions not to allow a computer to overheat.

Note 4

The temperature and humidity in a server room where computers are located and people don't spend long hours are usually set to balance the needs of the equipment and the need to conserve energy. Low temperatures and moderate humidity are best for the equipment, although no set standards exist for either temperatures or humidity. Temperatures might be set from 65°F to 70°F and humidity between 30% and 50%, although some companies keep their server rooms at 80°F to conserve energy. A data center where both computers and people stay is usually kept at a comfortable temperature and humidity for humans.

- **Protect electrical equipment from power surges.** Lightning and other electrical power surges can destroy computers and other electrical equipment. If a house or office building does not have surge protection equipment installed at the breaker box, be sure to install a protective device at each computer. The least expensive device is a power strip that is also a surge suppressor, although you might want to use an uninterruptible power supply for added protection.

Lightning can also get to your equipment across network cabling coming in through an Internet connection. To protect against lightning, use a surge suppressor such as the one shown in Figure A-13 in line between the ISP device (for example, a DSL modem or cable modem) and the computer or home router to protect it from spikes across the network cables. Notice the cord on the surge suppressor, which connects it to ground.

Figure A-13   A surge protector by APC for Ethernet lines

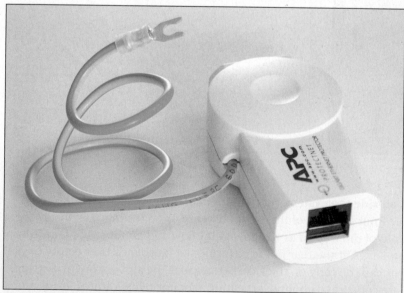

An **uninterruptible power supply (UPS)** is a device that raises the voltage when it drops during under-voltage events, called **brownouts** or **sags** (temporary voltage reductions). A UPS also does double duty as a surge suppressor to protect the system against power surges or spikes. In addition, a UPS can serve as a battery backup to provide enough power for a brief time during a total power failure, called a blackout, so you can save your work and shut down the system. A UPS is not as essential for a laptop computer as it is for a desktop because a laptop has a battery that can sustain it during a blackout. Also, consider using a UPS to protect power to a router, switch, or other essential network device.

A common UPS device is a rather heavy box that plugs into an AC outlet and provides one or more electrical outlets and perhaps Ethernet and USB ports (see Figure A-14). It has an on/off switch, requires no maintenance, and is very simple to install. Use it to provide uninterruptible power to your desktop computer, monitor, and essential network devices. It's best not to connect a UPS to nonessential devices such as a laser printer or scanner. The UPS shown in Figure A-14 has a USB port so a computer can monitor power management and network ports to block harmful voltage on the network.

Figure A-14   The front and rear of an uninterruptible power supply (UPS)

Source: dell.com

> **Note 5**
>
> If a power outage occurs and you don't have a reliable power conditioner installed at the breaker box in your house or building, unplug all power cords to the computers, printers, monitors, and peripherals. Sometimes when the power returns, sudden spikes are accompanied by another brief outage. You don't want to subject your equipment to these surges. When buying a surge suppressor, look for one that guarantees protection against damage from lightning and that reimburses for equipment destroyed while the surge suppressor is in use.

Protecting the Environment

Core 2 Objectives 4.4, 4.5

IT support technicians need to be aware that they can do damage to the environment if they dispose of used computer equipment improperly. As a support technician, one day you're sure to face an assortment of useless equipment and consumables (see Figure A-15). Before you decide to trash it all, take a moment and ask yourself if some of the equipment can be donated or at least recycled. Think about fixing up an old computer and donating it to an underprivileged middle school student. If you don't have the time for that, consider donating to the local computer repair class. The class can fix up such computers as a class project and donate them to young students.

Figure A-15   Keep, trash, recycle, or donate?

When disposing of any type of equipment or consumables, make sure to comply with local government environmental regulations. Table A-2 lists some items and how to dispose of them.

Table A-2   Computer parts and how to dispose of them

Parts	How to Dispose of Them
Alkaline batteries, including AAA, AA, A, C, D, and 9-volt	Dispose of these batteries in the regular trash. First check to see if there are recycling facilities in your area.
Button batteries used in digital cameras and other small equipment; battery packs used in notebook computers	These batteries can contain silver oxide, mercury, lithium, or cadmium and are considered toxic waste that require special toxic waste handling. Dispose of them by returning them to the original dealer or by taking them to a recycling center. To recycle, pack them separately from other items. If you don't have a recycling center nearby, contact your county for local disposal regulations.
Cell phones and tablets	Most cell phone carriers will buy back old cell phones to recycle or refurbish. If you can restore the device to factory state, donate it to charity. Before tossing it in the trash, check with local county or environmental officials for laws and regulations in your area that cover proper disposal of the item. E-waste recycling companies, such as Eco-Cell (*eco-cell.com*), receive cell phones for resale or recycling.
Laser printer toner cartridges	Return these to the manufacturer or dealer to be recycled.
Ink-jet printer cartridges, cell phones, tablets, computer cases, power supplies, other computer parts, monitors, chemical solvents, and their containers	Check with local county or environmental officials for laws and regulations in your area that cover proper disposal of these items. The county might have a recycling center that will receive the items. Discharge a CRT monitor before disposing of it. See the MSDS documents for chemicals to know how to dispose of them.
Storage media such as hard drives, CDs, DVDs, and BDs	As discussed in the module "Security Strategies," destroy the data on the media so it is not possible for sensitive data to be stolen. Then the device can be recycled or put in the trash. Your organization might have to meet legal requirements to destroy data. If so, make sure you understand these requirements and how to comply with them.

Exam Tip ✔

The A+ Core 2 exam expects you to know how to follow environmental guidelines to dispose of batteries, laser printer toner, cell phones, tablets, chemical solvents, and containers. If you're not certain how to dispose of a product, see its MSDS document.

Be sure a CRT monitor is discharged before you dispose of it. Most CRT monitors are designed to discharge after sitting unplugged for 60 minutes. They can be manually discharged by using a high-voltage probe with the monitor case opened. Ask a technician who's trained to service monitors to do this for you.

Appendix Summary

Measures and Properties of Electricity

- Ways to measure electricity include volts, amps, ohms, joules, and watts.

Protecting Yourself

- Disconnect power from any device that poses an electrical shock indicated by smoke, frayed or otherwise damaged power cord, water or other spill, excessive moisture, physical damage, strong electrical odor, or a loud whining noise coming from the device.
- Before working inside a computer, first power down and unplug the device.
- Consult an MSDS to know how to handle a chemical substance.

Protecting the Equipment

- An ESD bracelet, ground mat, and antistatic bags can help protect a computer against static electricity.

Protecting the Environment

- To protect the environment, follow governmental regulations for proper disposal of batteries, cell phones, toner cartridges, storage media, and other computer parts.

Key Terms

For explanations of key terms, see the Glossary for this text.

air filtration mask	ground bracelet	safety goggles	uninterruptible power
alternating current (AC)	inverter	sag	supply (UPS)
amp (A)	joule (J)	self-grounding	volt (V)
antistatic wrist strap	material safety data	static electricity	watt (W)
brownout	sheet (MSDS)	surge suppressor	
Class C fire extinguisher	ohm (Ω)	transformer	
direct current (DC)	rectifier	trip hazard	

Thinking Critically

These questions are designed to prepare you for the critical thinking required for the A+ exams and may use information from modules in the text and from the web.

1. Your friend tells you that they recently added more RAM to their desktop computer and now applications crash at odd times. What is one question you might ask your friend to understand the source of the problem?

   a. Did you void the warranty when you opened the computer case?
   b. Did you wear an ESD bracelet when you did the upgrade?
   c. Did you smell smoke when you first turned on the computer after the upgrade?
   d. Have you cleaned up the hard drive after the RAM upgrade?

2. You are setting up a small network for a home office and plan to purchase a surge suppressor to protect the equipment. Which type of measurement of electricity will you look for to rate the surge suppressor?

   a. Volts
   b. Joules
   c. Watts
   d. Ohms

3. You are building a computer from scratch and plan to use it to do your schoolwork. What range and electrical measurement might you expect is reasonable for the power supply in the system?

   a. 200–500 volts
   b. 100–1000 watts
   c. 200–500 watts
   d. 100–1000 volts

4. Which of the following statements is true? (Choose all that apply.)

   a. A rectifier converts AC to DC, and an inverter converts DC to AC.
   b. An inverter converts AC to DC, and a rectifier converts DC to AC.
   c. A transformer changes the ratio of DC to AC.
   d. A transformer changes the ratio of voltage to current.

5. Inside a desktop computer, which color wire is likely to be ground?

   a. Red
   b. Yellow
   c. White
   d. Black

6. Which device or tool is designed to protect a computer against ESD?

   a. Power supply
   b. Class C fire extinguisher
   c. Surge suppressor
   d. Ground bracelet

7. Which of the following is most likely to damage a hard drive installed and running inside a computer in a business environment?

   a. Humidity
   b. High temperature
   c. ESD
   d. Electrical fire

8. What is best practice for disposing of laser printer toner cartridges?

    a. Throw them in the trash.
    b. Return them to the manufacturer.
    c. Put them in a recycling bin.
    d. Mail them to the government recycling center.

9. Which type of fire extinguisher is rated for electrical fires?

    a. Class A
    b. Class B
    c. Class C
    d. All of these

Hands-On Projects

Hands-On Project A-1

Practicing Handling Computer Components

Est. Time: 15 minutes
Core 2 Objective: 4.4

Working with a partner, you'll need some computer parts and the antistatic tools you learned about in this appendix. Practice touching and picking up the parts and passing them between you. As you do so, follow the rules to protect the parts against ESD. Have a third person watch as you work, and point out any ways you might have exposed a part to ESD. As you work, be careful not to touch components on circuit boards or the gold "fingers" on the edge connector of an expansion card. When you are finished, store the parts in antistatic bags.

Hands-On Project A-2

Safely Cleaning Computer Equipment

Est. Time: 30 minutes
Core 2 Objective: 4.5

Practice some preventive maintenance tasks by following these steps to clean a computer:

1. Shut down the computer and unplug it. Press the power button to drain power.
2. Clean the keyboard, monitor, and mouse. For a wheel mouse, remove the ball and clean the wheels. Clean the outside of the computer case. Don't forget to clean the mouse pad.
3. Open the case and use a ground bracelet to clean the dust from the case. Make sure all fans move freely.
4. Verify that the cables are out of the way of airflow. Use cable ties as necessary.
5. Check that each expansion card and memory module is securely seated in its slot.
6. Power up the system and make sure everything is working.
7. Clean up around your work area. If you left dust on the floor as you blew it out of the computer case, be sure to clean it up.

Hands-On Project A-3

Researching Disposal Rules

Est. Time: 15 minutes
Core 2 Objective: 4.5

Research the laws and regulations in your community concerning the disposal of batteries and old computer parts. Answer these questions:

1. How do you properly dispose of a monitor in your community?
2. How do you properly dispose of a battery pack used by a notebook computer?
3. How do you properly dispose of a large box of assorted computer parts, including hard drives, optical drives, computer cases, and circuit boards?

Real Problems, Real Solutions

Real Problem A-1

Purchasing a Surge Suppressor

Est. Time: 15 minutes
Core 2 Objective: 4.5

When purchasing a surge suppressor, consider these factors:

- The number and types of outlets
- Rating in joules
- Types of equipment it is designed to protect
- Maximum spike voltage
- Warranty rated in dollar of connected equipment
- Price

Find three surge suppressors for sale online, and list the six ratings for each suppressor. Which suppressor would you purchase and why?

Appendix

B

Entry Points for Windows Startup Processes

This appendix contains a summary of the entry points that can affect Windows 10/11 startup. The entry points include startup folders, Group Policy folders, the Scheduled Tasks folder, and registry keys. To see all the subfolders listed in this appendix, use File Explorer Options in Control Panel to unhide folders that don't normally display in Explorer. Note that, for some installations of Windows 10/11, a startup folder or registry key might be missing.

Programs and shortcuts to programs are stored in these startup folders:

- C:\Users*username*\\AppData\\Roaming\\Microsoft\\Windows\\Start Menu\\Programs\\Startup
- C:\ProgramData\\Microsoft\\Windows\\Start Menu\\Programs\\Startup

Startup and shutdown scripts used by Group Policy are stored in these folders:

- C:\Windows\\System32\\GroupPolicy\\Machine\\Scripts\\Startup
- C:\Windows\\System32\\GroupPolicy\\Machine\\Scripts\\Shutdown
- C:\Windows\\System32\\GroupPolicy\\User\\Scripts\\Logon
- C:\Windows\\System32\\GroupPolicy\\User\\Scripts\\Logoff

Scheduled tasks are stored in this folder:

- C:\Windows\\System32\\Tasks

To see a list of scheduled tasks, enter the **schtasks** command in a command prompt window. These keys cause an entry to run once and only once at startup:

- HKLM\\Software\\Microsoft\\Windows\\CurrentVersion\\RunOnce
- HKLM\\Software\\Microsoft\\Windows\\CurrentVersion\\RunServiceOnce
- HKLM\\Software\\Microsoft\\Windows\\CurrentVersion\\RunServicesOnce
- HKCU\\Software\\Microsoft\\Windows\\CurrentVersion\\RunOnce

Group Policy places entries in the following keys to affect startup:

- HKCU\Software\Microsoft\Windows\CurrentVersion\Policies\Explorer\Run
- HKLM\Software\Microsoft\Windows\CurrentVersion\Policies\Explorer\Run

Windows loads many DLL programs from the following key, which is sometimes used by malicious software. Don't delete one unless you know it's causing a problem:

- HKLM\Software\Microsoft\Windows\CurrentVersion\ShellServiceObjectDelayLoad

Entries in the keys listed next apply to all users and hold legitimate startup entries. Don't delete an entry unless you suspect it to be bad:

- HKLM\Software\Microsoft\Windows\CurrentVersion\Run
- HKCU\Software\Microsoft\Windows NT\CurrentVersion\Windows
- HKCU\Software\Microsoft\Windows NT\CurrentVersion\Windows\Run
- HKCU\Software\Microsoft\Windows\CurrentVersion\Run

These keys and their subkeys contain entries pertaining to background services that are sometimes launched at startup:

- HKLM\Software\Microsoft\Windows\CurrentVersion\RunService
- HKLM\Software\Microsoft\Windows\CurrentVersion\RunServices

The following key contains a value named BootExecute, which is normally set to autochk. It causes the system to run a type of Chkdsk program to check for hard drive integrity if it was previously shut down improperly. Sometimes another program adds itself to this value, causing a problem. The Chkntfs utility can be used to exclude volumes from being checked by autochk. For more information about this situation, search for "CHKNTFS.EXE: What You Can Use It For" at *support.microsoft.com*.

- HKLM\System\CurrentControlSet\Control\Session Manager

Here is an assorted list of registry keys that have all been known to cause various problems at startup. Remember, before you delete a program entry from one of these keys, research the program file name so you don't accidentally delete something you want to keep:

- HKCU\Software\Microsoft\Command
- HKCU\Software\Microsoft\Command Processor\AutoRun
- HKCU\Software\Microsoft\Windows\CurrentVersion\RunOnce\Setup
- HKCU\Software\Microsoft\Windows NT\CurrentVersion\Windows\load
- HKLM\Software\Microsoft\Windows NT\CurrentVersion\Windows\AppInit_DLLs
- HKLM\Software\Microsoft\Windows NT\CurrentVersion\Winlogon\System
- HKLM\Software\Microsoft\Windows NT\CurrentVersion\Winlogon\Us
- HKCR\batfile\shell\open\command
- HKCR\comfile\shell\open\command
- HKCR\exefile\shell\open\command
- HKCR\htafile\shell\open\command
- HKCR\piffile\shell\open\command
- HKCR\scrfile\shell\open\command

Finally, check out the subkeys in the following key; they apply to 32-bit programs installed in a 64-bit version of Windows:

- HKLM\Software\Wow6432Node

Other ways in which processes can be launched at startup include the following:

- Services can be set to launch at startup. To manage services, use the Services console (services.msc).
- Device drivers are launched at startup. For a listing of installed devices, use Device Manager (devmgmt.msc) or the System Information utility (msinfo32.exe).

Appendix C

CompTIA Acronyms

CompTIA provides a list of acronyms that you need to know before you sit for the A+ exams. You can download the list from the CompTIA website at *comptia.org*. The list is included here for your convenience. However, CompTIA occasionally updates the list, so be sure to check the CompTIA website for the latest version.

Acronym	Spelled Out
AAA	Authentication, Authorization, and Accounting
AC	Alternating Current
ACL	Access Control List
ADF	Automatic Document Feeder
AES	Advanced Encryption Standard
AP	Access Point
APFS	Apple File System
APIPA	Automatic Private Internet Protocol Addressing
APK	Android Package
ARM	Advanced RISC [Reduced Instruction Set Computer] Machine
ARP	Address Resolution Protocol
ATA	Advanced Technology Attachment
ATM	Asynchronous Transfer Mode
ATX	Advanced Technology Extended

Acronym	Spelled Out
AUP	Acceptable Use Policy
BIOS	Basic Input/Output System
BSOD	Blue Screen of Death
BYOD	Bring Your Own Device
CAPTCHA	Completely Automated Public Turing Test to Tell Computers and Humans Apart
CD	Compact Disc
CDFS	Compact Disc File System
CDMA	Code-Division Multiple Access
CERT	Computer Emergency Response Team
CIFS	Common Internet File System
CMD	Command Prompt
CMOS	Complementary Metal-Oxide Semiconductor
CPU	Central Processing Unit
DC	Direct Current
DDoS	Distributed Denial of Service
DDR	Double Data Rate
DHCP	Dynamic Host Configuration Protocol
DIMM	Dual Inline Memory Module
DKIM	DomainKeys Identified Mail
DMA	Direct Memory Access
DMARC	Domain-Based Message Authentication, Reporting, and Conformance
DNS	Domain Name Service or Domain Name Server
DoS	Denial of Service
DRAM	Dynamic Random Access Memory
DRM	Digital Rights Management
DSL	Digital Subscriber Line
DVI	Digital Visual Interface
DVI-D	Digital Visual Interface–Digital
ECC	Error Correcting Code
EFS	Encrypting File System
EMI	Electromagnetic Interference
EOL	End-of-Life
eSATA	External Serial Advanced Technology Attachment
ESD	Electrostatic Discharge
EULA	End User License Agreement
exFAT	Extended File Allocation Table
ext	Extended File System
FAT	File Allocation Table

Acronym	Spelled Out
FAT12	12-bit File Allocation Table
FAT16	16-bit File Allocation Table
FAT32	32-bit File Allocation Table
FSB	Front-Side Bus
FTP	File Transfer Protocol
GFS	Grandfather-Father-Son
GPS	Global Positioning System
GPT	GUID [Globally Unique Identifier] Partition Table
GPU	Graphics Processing Unit
GSM	Global System for Mobile Communications
GUI	Graphical User Interface
GUID	Globally Unique Identifier
HAL	Hardware Abstraction Layer
HAV	Hardware Assisted Virtualization
HCL	Hardware Compatibility List
HDCP	High-Bandwidth Digital Content Protection
HDD	Hard Disk Drive
HDMI	High-Definition Media Interface
HSM	Hardware Security Module
HTML	Hypertext Markup Language
HTTP	Hypertext Transfer Protocol
HTTPS	Hypertext Transfer Protocol Secure
I/O	Input/Output
IaaS	Infrastructure as a Service
ICR	Intelligent Character Recognition
IDE	Integrated Drive Electronics
IDS	Intrusion Detection System
IEEE	Institute of Electrical and Electronics Engineers
IMAP	Internet Mail Access Protocol
IOPS	Input/Output Operations Per Second
IoT	Internet of Things
IP	Internet Protocol
IPS	Intrusion Prevention System
IPS	In-Plane Switching
IPSec	Internet Protocol Security
IR	Infrared
IrDA	Infrared Data Association
IRP	Incident Response Plan

Acronym	Spelled Out
ISP	Internet Service Provider
ITX	Information Technology eXtended
KB	Knowledge Base
KVM	Keyboard-Video-Mouse
LAN	Local Area Network
LC	Lucent Connector
LCD	Liquid Crystal Display
LDAP	Lightweight Directory Access Protocol
LED	Light-Emitting Diode
MAC	Media Access Control or Mandatory Access Control
MAM	Mobile Application Management
MAN	Metropolitan Area Network
MBR	Master Boot Record
MDM	Mobile Device Management
MFA	Multifactor Authentication
MFD	Multifunction Device
MFP	Multifunction Printer
MMC	Microsoft Management Console
MSDS	Material Safety Data Sheet
MSRA	Microsoft Remote Assistance
MX	Mail Exchange
NAC	Network Access Control
NAT	Network Address Translation
NetBIOS	Networked Basic Input/Output System
NetBT	NetBIOS over TCP/IP [Transmission Control Protocol/Internet Protocol]
NFC	Near Field Communication
NFS	Network File System
NIC	Network Interface Card
NTFS	New Technology File System
NVMe	Non-Volatile Memory Express
OCR	Optical Character Recognition
OLED	Organic Light-Emitting Diode
ONT	Optical Network Terminal
OS	Operating System
PaaS	Platform as a Service
PAN	Personal Area Network
PC	Personal Computer
PCIe	Peripheral Component Interconnect Express

Acronym	Spelled Out
PCL	Printer Control Language
PE	Preinstallation Environment
PII	Personally Identifiable Information
PIN	Personal Identification Number
PKI	Public Key Infrastructure
PoE	Power over Ethernet
POP3	Post Office Protocol 3
POST	Power-On Self-Test
PPP	Point-to-Point Protocol
PRL	Preferred Roaming List
PSU	Power Supply Unit
PXE	Preboot Execution Environment
RADIUS	Remote Authentication Dial-In User Service
RAID	Redundant Array of Independent (or Inexpensive) Disks
RAM	Random Access Memory
RDP	Remote Desktop Protocol
RF	Radio Frequency
RFI	Radio Frequency Interference
RFID	Radio Frequency Identification
RJ11	Registered Jack Function 11
RJ45	Registered Jack Function 45
RMM	Remote Monitoring and Management
RTO	Recovery Time Objective
SaaS	Software as a Service
SAN	Storage Area Network
SAS	Serial Attached SCSI [Small Computer System Interface]
SATA	Serial Advanced Technology Attachment
SC	Subscription Channel
SCADA	Supervisory Control and Data Acquisition
SCP	Secure Copy Protection
SCSI	Small Computer System Interface
SDN	Software-Defined Networking
SFTP	Secure File Transfer Protocol
SIM	Subscriber Identity Module
SIMM	Single In-Line Memory Module
S.M.A.R.T.	Self-Monitoring, Analysis, and Reporting Technology
SMB	Server Message Block
SMS	Short Message Service

Acronym	Spelled Out
SMTP	Simple Mail Transfer Protocol
SNMP	Simple Network Management Protocol
SODIMM	Small Outline Dual Inline Memory Module
SOHO	Small Office/Home Office
SP	Service Pack
SPF	Sender Policy Framework
SQL	Structured Query Language
SRAM	Static Random-Access Memory
SSD	Solid-State Drive
SSH	Secure Shell
SSID	Service Set Identifier
SSL	Secure Sockets Layer
SSO	Single Sign-On
ST	Straight Tip
STP	Shielded Twisted-Pair
TACACS	Terminal Access Controller Access-Control System
TCP	Transmission Control Protocol
TCP/IP	Transmission Control Protocol/Internet Protocol
TFTP	Trivial File Transfer Protocol
TKIP	Temporal Key Integrity Protocol
TLS	Transport Layer Security
TN	Twisted Nematic
TPM	Trusted Platform Module
UAC	User Account Control
UDP	User Datagram Protocol
UEFI	Unified Extensible Firmware Interface
UNC	Universal Naming Convention
UPnP	Universal Plug and Play
UPS	Uninterruptible Power Supply
USB	Universal Serial Bus
UTM	Unified Threat Management
UTP	Unshielded Twisted-Pair
VA	Vertical Alignment
VDI	Virtual Desktop Infrastructure
VGA	Video Graphics Array
VLAN	Virtual LAN [Local Area Network]
VM	Virtual Machine
VNC	Virtual Network Computer

Acronym	Spelled Out
VoIP	Voice over Internet Protocol
VPN	Virtual Private Network
VRAM	Video Random-Access Memory
WAN	Wide Area Network
WISP	Wireless Internet Service Provider
WLAN	Wireless Local Area Network
WMN	Wireless Mesh Network
WPA	Wireless Protected Access
WWAN	Wireless Wide Area Network
XSS	Cross-Site Scripting

Glossary

100BaseT An Ethernet standard that operates at 100 Mbps and uses twisted-pair cabling up to 100 meters (328 feet); variations of 100BaseT are 100BaseTX and 100BaseFX. *Also called* Fast Ethernet.

20-pin P1 connector A connector used by an older ATX power supply and motherboard; it provided +3.3 volts, +5 volts, +12 volts, −12 volts, and an optional and rarely used −5 volts.

24-pin P1 connector A connector used by an ATX Version 2.2 power supply and motherboard; it provides additional power for PCI Express slots.

2G A standard to transmit cellular data on a cellular network; first used by GSM to transmit secured voice, text, and limited data. CDMA used a later and faster version of 2G.

3-2-1 backup rule An IT best-practice operations standard for backups that includes keeping three copies of data (original and two backups) on two media, with one copy kept off site.

32-bit operating system A type of operating system that processes 32 bits at a time.

3D printer A printer that uses a plastic filament or resin to build a 3D model of a digital image.

3G A third-generation cellular wireless Internet connection standard used with CDMA or GSM mobile phone services that allows for transmitting data and video.

4G A fourth-generation cellular wireless Internet connection standard typically used with LTE (Long Term Evolution) technology; 4G transmits data and video up to 1 Gbps.

4G LTE A cellular wireless network standard that replaced CDMA and GSM for voice, text, and data transmissions; requires a SIM card to function.

4-pin 12 V connector An auxiliary motherboard connector used for an extra 12 volts of power to the processor.

5G A fifth-generation cellular wireless Internet connection standard that currently has an average speed of 150 Mpbs and is expected to peak at up to 10 Gbps.

64-bit operating system A type of operating system that processes 64 bits at a time.

802.11 a/b/g/n/ac/ax The collective name for the IEEE 802.11 standards for local wireless networking, which is the technical name for Wi-Fi.

802.11a An outdated Wi-Fi standard that transmitted up to 54 Mbps.

802.11ac (Wi-Fi 5) A Wi-Fi standard that supports up to 7 Gbps (actual speeds are currently about 1300 Mbps) and uses 5.0 GHz radio frequency and beamforming. *Also called* Wi-Fi 5.

802.11ax (Wi-Fi 6) A Wi-Fi standard that supports up to eight antennas and beamforming to increase signal strength; uses 5 GHz frequency only. *Also called* Wi-Fi 6.

802.11b An outdated Wi-Fi standard that transmitted up to 11 Mbps and experienced interference from cordless phones and microwaves.

802.11g An outdated Wi-Fi standard that was compatible with and replaced 802.11b.

802.11n (Wi-Fi 4) A Wi-Fi standard that supports up to 600 Mbps, uses 5.0 GHz or 2.4 GHz radio frequency, and supports MIMO. *Also called* Wi-Fi 4.

8-pin 12 V connector An auxiliary motherboard connector used for an extra 12 volts of power to the processor; it provides more power than the older 4-pin auxiliary connector.

A record (address record) A type of DNS record in the DNS namespace that points a host name to its IP address.

A+ Certification A certification awarded by CompTIA (Computer Technology Industry Association) that measures an IT technician's knowledge and skills.

AAA (authenticating, authorizing, and accounting) The three major methods used to secure a network and its resources. Authenticating controls access to the network, authorizing controls what a user or computer can do on the network, and accounting tracks what a user or computer has done on the network. *Also called* triple A.

AAAA record A type of DNS record in the DNS namespace for IPv6 addresses; points a host name to its IPv6 address.

AC adapter A device that converts AC to DC and can use regular house current to power a laptop computer.

accelerometer A type of gyroscope used in mobile devices to sense the physical position of the device.

acceptable use policy (AUP) A document that explains to users what they can and cannot do on the corporate network or with company data, and the penalties for violations.

access control list (ACL) A record or list of the resources (e.g., a printer, folder, or file) that a user, device, or program has access to on a corporate network, server, or workstation.

access control vestibule A method to physically secure a building. It consists of two doors on either end of a small entryway; the first door must close and/or lock before the second door can open. *Also called* a mantrap.

Action bar On an Android device, an area at the bottom of the screen that can contain up to five custom software buttons, called Home touch buttons. The three default buttons are back, home, and overview.

Active Directory (AD) A suite of services and databases provided by Windows Server to manage Windows domains; includes five groups of services: Domain Services, Certificate Services, Federation Services, Rights Management, and Lightweight Directory Services.

Active Directory Domain Services (AD DS) A component of Active Directory that is responsible for authenticating accounts and authorizing what these accounts can do.

active hours The range of time during the day when Windows avoids automatic restarts while applying updates.

active partition For MBR hard drives, the primary partition on the drive that boots the OS. Windows calls the active partition the system partition.

ActiveSync A technology used by Microsoft Exchange servers to comply with MDM policies to sync email, calendars, contacts, and other types of data between the server and a mobile device.

ActiveX control A small app or add-on that can be downloaded from a website along with a webpage and is executed by a browser to enhance the webpage.

ad hoc mode A peer-to-peer wireless network between computers where each wireless computer serves as its own wireless access point and is responsible for securing each connection.

adapter address *See* MAC (Media Access Control) address.

address reservation The act of a DHCP server assigning a static IP address to a DHCP client. For example, a network printer might require a static IP address so that computers on the network can find the printer.

ADF (automatic document feeder) scanner A component of a copier, scanner, or printer that can automatically pull individual items of paper, cards, or envelopes from a stack into a roller system for processing.

administrative shares The folders and volumes shared by default on a network that administrator accounts can access but are invisible to standard users. Use the fsmgmt.msc command to view a list of shared folders and volumes.

Administrative Tools A group of Windows 10 tools accessed through Control Panel and used to manage the local computer or other computers on the network. In Windows 11, the same group of tools is called Windows Tools.

administrator account In Windows, a user account that grants an administrator rights and privileges to all hardware and software resources; includes the right to add, delete, and change accounts and to change hardware configurations. *Compare with* standard account.

Administrators group A type of Windows user group. When a user account is assigned to this group, the account is granted rights that are assigned to an administrator account.

AES (Advanced Encryption Standard) An encryption standard used by WPA2; it is currently the strongest encryption standard used by Wi-Fi.

agent A small app installed on a client that communicates with a server. For example, MDM on-boarding might install an agent on a mobile device to verify that the device complies with security measures.

air filtration mask An air-purifying respirator to protect against dust or other contaminants in the air.

AirDrop A feature of iOS whereby iPhones and iPads can transfer files between nearby devices. The devices use Bluetooth to detect nearby devices and Wi-Fi to establish connectivity and transfer files.

airplane mode A setting within a mobile device that disables the cellular, Wi-Fi, and Bluetooth antennas so the device cannot transmit signals.

AirPrint A technology by Apple that allows Apple computers and mobile devices to print to an AirPrint-capable printer without first installing the printer.

alarm system A type of low-voltage security system with a control panel, installed on doors, windows, and other strategic locations; may include motion sensors and smoke and carbon monoxide detectors. The system can set off a siren or strobe light or alert security personnel who monitor the system.

alias A nickname or shortcut for a cmdlet in Windows PowerShell. For example, dir is an alias for the Get-ChildItem cmdlet.

all-in-one computer A computer that has the monitor and computer case built together and uses components that are common to both a notebook and a desktop computer.

alternate IP address When configuring TCP/IP in Windows, the static IP address that Windows uses if it cannot lease an IP address from a DHCP server.

alternating current (AC) Current that cycles back and forth rather than traveling in only one direction. In the United States, the AC voltage from a standard wall outlet is normally between 110 and 115 V. In Europe, the standard AC voltage from a wall outlet is 220 V.

AM3+ A type of pin grid array CPU socket used with AMD Piledriver and Bulldozer processors and the 9-series chipset.

AM4 A type of CPU socket used with AMD Ryzen and Athlon processors and the AM4 family of chipsets. AM4 is typically used in mainstream desktop systems. The socket has 1331 pins in a pin grid array.

A-Male connector A common type of USB connector that is flat and wide and connects an A-Male USB port on a computer or USB hub.

amp (A) A measure of electrical current.

analog A continuous signal with infinite variations which is a series of binary values—1s and 0s. *Compare with* digital.

Android An operating system for mobile devices that is based on the Linux OS and supported by Google.

Android package (APK) A file with an .apk file extension that contains an Android app ready for installation. *Also called* Android package kit.

anonymous users User accounts that have not been authenticated on a remote computer.

ANSI (American National Standards Institute) A nonprofit organization dedicated to creating trade and communications standards.

answer file A file of information that Windows requires in order to do an unattended installation.

anti-malware software Utility software that can prevent infection, scan a system, and detect and remove all types of general malware, including viruses, spyware, worms, and rootkits.

anti-phishing training *See* security awareness training.

antistatic bag A static shielding bag that new computer components are shipped in.

antistatic wrist strap *See* ESD strap.

antivirus software Utility software that can prevent infection, scan a system, and detect and remove viruses.

anycast address Using TCP/IP version 6, a type of IP address used by routers that identifies multiple destinations. Packets are delivered to the closest destination.

APFS (Apple File System) In macOS, the default file system for SSDs that uses the GUID partitioning system; can also be used for magnetic hard drives.

APIPA (automatic private IP address) *See* automatic private IP address (APIPA).

APK (Android package) *See* Android package (APK).

app drawer An app embedded in the Android OS that lists and manages all apps installed on the device.

APP file In macOS, an application file that is similar to an .exe file in Windows.

App Store The app on an Apple device (iPad, iPhone, iPod touch, or MacBook) that can be used to download content from the App Store website (*apple.com/app-store*).

Apple ID   A user account that uses a valid email address and password and is associated with a credit card number; allows you to download iOS and macOS updates and patches, apps, and multimedia content.

Apple menu   In macOS, the menu that appears when the user clicks the Apple icon in the upper-left corner of the screen.

application spoofing   A type of hacking in which a hacker presents a malicious app to a user pretending the app is legitimate; this technique is possible when a device has been rooted or jailbroken.

application virtualization   The practice of using virtualization to create a virtual environment in memory for an application to virtually install itself.

Apps Drawer   An Android app that lists and manages all apps installed on the device. By default, this app's icon is in the favorites tray on an Android screen.

apt-get   A Linux and macOS command to install and remove software packages and install OS updates.

array   A group of hard drives that work together to provide a single storage volume.

artifact   A horizontally torn image on a computer screen.

asset ID   A string of characters used to identify hardware in an inventory list that is used to manage assets in an IT operation.

asset management system   An IT system used to track physical and digital assets; it may include end-user devices, network devices, IP addresses, software licenses, and related licenses.

asset tag   A tag used by an asset-management system to track hardware that contains an asset ID and perhaps a theft-prevention plate.

ATA Secure Erase   Standards developed by the American National Standards Institute (ANSI) that dictate how to securely erase data from solid-state devices such as a USB flash drive or SSD in order to protect personal privacy.

attrib   A Windows command to view and change the attributes of a file, for example, to remove the hidden and system attributes assigned to a file so that you can view and delete the file.

ATX (Advanced Technology Extended)   The most common form factor for desktop computer cases, motherboards, and power supplies; it was originally introduced by Intel in 1995. ATX motherboards and cases make better use of space and resources than the earlier AT form factor.

ATX12V power supply   An ATX Version 2.1 power supply that provides an extra 12 V power cord with a 4-pin connector and is used with the auxiliary 4-pin power connector on motherboards to provide additional power for processors.

audio port   A port that can be used by microphone, audio in, audio out, and stereo audio out connections. *Also called* a sound port.

Authenticated Users group   In Windows, all user accounts, except the Guest account, that have been authenticated to access the system. *Compare with* anonymous users.

authentication, authorization, and accounting (AAA) server   Application software or a computer used to secure and control access to the network and its resources by authenticating users and computers to the network, authorizing what a user or computer can do after they have access, and accounting in logs for what a user or computer did with the resources and the time it took.

authentication server   A server responsible for authenticating users or computers to the network so they can access network resources.

authenticator app   An app installed on a smartphone to provide multifactor authentication—for example, Google Authenticator, Microsoft Authenticator, and Authy.

autodetection   A feature of BIOS/UEFI that detects a new drive and automatically selects the correct drive capacity and configuration, including the best possible standard supported by both the hard drive and the motherboard.

automatic private IP address (APIPA)   In TCP/IP version 4, an IP address in the address range 169.254.x.y; used by a computer when it cannot successfully lease an IP address from a DHCP server.

auto-switching   A function of a laptop computer's AC adapter that enables it to automatically switch between 110 V and 220 V AC power.

Azure Active Directory (Azure AD or AAD)   Microsoft domain services managed by Microsoft servers in the cloud. Windows 10/11 business and professional editions support joining an Azure domain.

back flash   To revert to an earlier version of BIOS/UEFI after flashing BIOS/UEFI.

backout plan   *See* rollback plan.

Backup and Restore   The Windows utility used to create and update scheduled backups of user data and the system image.

backup operator   An IT job role that is responsible for implementing backup routines.

Backup Operators group   A type of Windows user account group. When a user account belongs to this group, it can back up and restore any files on the system, regardless of whether it has access to those files.

badge reader   A device that can read the microchip or magnetic stripe on a card, such as a credit card, and transmit the information to a computer.

bandwidth   In relation to analog communication, the range of frequencies that a communications channel or cable can carry. In general use, the term refers to the volume of data that can be transmitted on a bus or over a cable; bandwidth is stated in bits per second (bps), kilobits per second (Kbps), megabits per second (Mbps), or gigabits per second (Gbps). *Also called* data throughput *or* line speed.

barcode   A pattern of numbers and variable-length lines that can be read by a machine; a barcode is often used to identify a manufacturer and product.

base station   A fixed transceiver and antenna used to create one cell within a cellular network.

baseband update   An update to radio firmware on a mobile device; radio firmware manages cellular, Wi-Fi, and Bluetooth radios; may be included in OS updates.

Bash shell   The default shell used by the terminal for many distributions of Linux.

basic disk   The term Windows uses to describe a hard drive when it is a stand-alone drive in the system. *Compare with* dynamic disk.

basic loop   A scripting or programming technique used to execute the same group of commands multiple times until a condition is met.

batch file   A script text file that has a .bat file extension and contains a series of Windows commands.

BCD (Boot Configuration Data)   A small Windows database that is structured the same as a registry file and that contains configuration information about how Windows is started. The file is stored in the \Boot directory of the hidden system partition.

bcdedit   A Windows command used to manually edit the BCD.

BD (Blu-ray disc)   An optical disc technology that uses the UDF version 2.5 file system and a blue laser beam, which is shorter than any red beam used by DVDs or CDs. The shorter blue laser beam allows Blu-ray discs to store more data than a DVD.

beamforming   A technique supported by the IEEE 802.11ac Wi-Fi standard; detects the location of connected devices and increases signal strength in that direction.

best-effort protocol   *See* connectionless protocol.

biometric authentication   The use of biometric data, such as a fingerprint or retinal data, to authenticate to a network, computer, or other computing device. Touch ID on an iPhone or face lock on an Android device can perform biometric authentication.

biometric data   Data that identifies a person by a fingerprint, handprint, face, retina, iris, voice, or handwritten signature.

biometric device   An input device that can identify biological data about a person's fingerprints, handprints, face, voice, eyes, and handwriting.

biometric lock   A lock that can be opened by input of biometric data.

BIOS (basic input/output system)   Firmware that can control much of a computer's input/output functions, such as communication with the keyboard and the monitor. *Compare with* UEFI.

BIOS setup   The program in system BIOS that can change the values in CMOS RAM. *Also called* CMOS setup.

BitLocker Drive Encryption   A utility in Windows that is used to lock down a hard drive by encrypting the entire Windows volume and any other volume on the drive. *Also called* BitLocker *or* BitLocker Encryption.

BitLocker To Go   A Windows utility that can encrypt data on a USB flash drive and restrict access by requiring a password.

bitmap   Rows and columns of bits that collectively represent an image.

blacklist   In filtering, a list of items that are not allowed—for example, a list of websites that computers on a local network are not allowed to access. *Compare with* whitelist.

blue screen of death (BSOD)   A Windows error that occurs in kernel mode, is displayed against a blue screen, and causes the system to halt. The error might be caused by problems with devices, device drivers, or a corrupted Windows installation. *Also called* a stop error.

Bluetooth   A short-range wireless technology used to connect two devices in a small personal network.

Bluetooth PIN code   A code that may be required to complete the Bluetooth connection in a pairing process.

Blu-ray disc (BD)   *See* BD.

B-Male connector   A USB connector that connects a USB 1.x or 2.0 device such as a printer.

BNC connector   An outdated network connector used with thin coaxial cable; some are T-shaped and are called T-connectors. One end of the T connects to the NIC, and the two other ends can connect to cables or end a bus formation with a terminator.

bollards   Strong metal posts positioned to prevent vehicles from accidentally or intentionally ramming into a protected space, or to direct traffic.

Boot Camp   A utility in macOS that allows you to install and run Windows on a Mac computer.

Boot Configuration Data (BCD) store   *See* BCD.

boot loader menu   A startup menu in a dual-boot system that gives the user the choice of which operating system to load, such as Windows 11 or Windows 10. Multiples OSs are installed on a dual-boot system.

boot partition   The hard drive partition where the Windows OS is stored. The system partition and the boot partition may be different partitions.

boot priority order   A list of devices stored in firmware on the motherboard that BIOS/UEFI startup uses in the order listed to search for and load an operating system.

boot sector virus   A virus that can infect the MBR program in the first sector on a MBR hard drive, which is used to boot the system.

booting   The process of starting up a computer and loading an operating system.

bootlegged app   An illegal app.

BootMgr   The file name of the boot manager program responsible for loading Windows on a BIOS system. The file has no file extension.

bootrec   A Windows command used to repair the BCD and boot sectors.

bootsect   A Windows command used to repair a dual-boot system.

botnet   A network of zombies or robots.

bridge   A networking device that stands between two segments of a network and manages traffic between them.

broadband   A transmission technique that carries more than one type of transmission on the same medium, such as voice and DSL on a regular telephone line.

broadcast message   A message sent over a TCP/IP version 4 local network to all devices on the network; the message does not contain recipient information.

brownout   A temporary reduction in voltage that can sometimes cause data loss. *Also called* sag.

brute force   Systematically trying every possible combination of letters, numbers, and symbols to crack a password.

brute force attack   A method to hack or discover a password by trying every single combination of characters.

BSOD (blue screen of death)   *See* blue screen of death (BSOD).

burn-in   When a static image stays on a monitor for many hours, leaving a permanent impression of the image on the monitor.

bus   The paths, or lines, on the motherboard on which data, instructions, and electrical power move from component to component.

business casual   For men, neutral-colored dress slacks, khakis, polo shirt, tailored shirt, sweater, dark socks, dress shoes, and optional sports coat and tie. For women, blouse, tasteful sweater, simple dress or skirt, slacks, closed-toe shoes, and tasteful jewelry. This attire is appropriate for a typical IT workplace unless your manager says otherwise.

business formal   For men, matching jacket and slacks, shirt, and tie with dark socks and dress shoes. For women, dress pants or a skirt with matching jacket, skirt lengths just above the knee, closed-toe shoes, and tasteful jewelry. This attire is appropriate for a job interview or upper-level management meeting or event.

BYOD (bring your own device)   A corporate policy that allows employees or students to connect their own devices to the corporate network.

BYOD Experience (bring your own device experience)   A Microsoft feature that allows a personal device to join an Azure domain and access corporate resources on the domain.

cable Internet   A broadband technology that uses cable TV lines and is always connected (always up).

cable lock   A cable with a lock used to physically secure a laptop or computer to a table or other stationary device. *Also called* a Kensington lock.

cable modem   A device that converts a computer's digital signal to analog before sending it over cable TV lines and that converts incoming analog data to digital.

cable stripper   A hand tool used to cut away the plastic jacket or coating around the wires of a network cable.

cable tester   A tool used to test a cable to find out if it is good or to identify a cable that is not labeled.

calibration   The process of checking and correcting the graduations of an instrument or device, such as an inkjet printer.

call tracking software   *See* ticketing system.

capture card   A peripheral device or an expansion card used to record and stream content from an external device, such as a gaming console or webcam.

CAS Latency   A method of measuring access timing to memory, which is the number of clock cycles required to write or read a column of data off a memory module. CAS stands for Column Access Strobe.

case fan   A fan inside a computer case; used to draw air out of or into the case.

cat   Short for concatenate; reads the data of a file and shows it on the screen.

CAT-5 (Category 5)   A rating used for UTP cables and rated for Fast Ethernet; seldom used today.

CAT-5e (Category 5e)   A popular rating used for UTP cables and rated for Fast Ethernet and Gigabit Ethernet.

CAT-6 (Category 6)   A rating used for twisted-pair cables that have less crosstalk than CAT-5e cables. CAT-6 cables might contain a plastic cord down the center that helps to prevent crosstalk, but they are less flexible and more difficult to install than CAT-5e.

CAT-6a (Category 6a)   A rating used for twisted-pair cables that are thicker and faster than CAT-6 and rated for 10GBase-T (10-Gigabit Ethernet).

CAT-6e (Category 6e)   An unofficial name for CAT-6a.

CAT-7 (Category 7)   A rating used for twisted-pair cables that have shielding to almost completely eliminate crosstalk and improve noise reduction.

Category view   The default view in Control Panel that presents utilities grouped by category.

cd (change directory)   The Windows command to change the current default directory.

CD (compact disc)   An optical disc technology that uses a red laser beam and can hold up to 700 MB of data.

CDFS (Compact Disc File System)   The 32-bit file system for CD discs and some CD-R and CD-RW discs. *Also see* Universal Disk Format (UDF).

CDMA (Code Division Multiple Access)   A protocol standard used by cellular WANs and cell phones for transmitting digital data over cellular networks.

cellular data   Voice, text, and other types of data that a telecommunications carrier can send from the carrier's network to the Internet for distribution.

cellular network   A network that can be used when a wireless network must cover a wide area. The network is made up of cells, each controlled by a base station. *Also called* a cellular WAN *or* wireless wide area network (WWAN).

central processing unit (CPU)   The component where almost all processing of data and instructions takes place; receives data input, processes information, and executes instructions. *Also called* a microprocessor *or* processor.

Centrino   A technology used by Intel whereby the processor, chipset, and wireless network adapter are all interconnected as a unit, which improves laptop performance.

Certificate Authority (CA)   An organization, such as VeriSign, that assigns digital certificates or digital signatures to individuals or organizations. *Also called* certification authority.

Certificate Manager   A Windows utility (certmgr.msc) in the Microsoft Management Console used to view and delete root certificates.

certificate of destruction   Digital or paper documentation that assures customers their data has been destroyed beyond recovery by a secure service.

CFexpress card   A flash memory device that allows for faster data transfer because they are designed using the PCIe 3.0 interface standard; CFexpress; comes in three form factors: A, B, and C.

chain of custody (CoC)   Documentation that tracks all evidence collected and used in an investigation, including when and from whom the evidence was collected, the condition of the evidence, and how the evidence was secured while in possession of a responsible party.

change advisory board (CAB)   The team in an organization charged with assessing, prioritizing, authorizing, and scheduling change.

change management   The processes for successfully bringing people forward to an end result or goal.

channel   A specific radio frequency within a broader frequency range or category.

charging   In laser printing, the process of placing a high electrical charge on the imaging drum to condition it before an image is exposed to the drum.

chassis   A case for any type of computer.

chassis air guide (CAG)   A round air duct that helps to pull and direct fresh air from outside a computer case to the cooler and processor.

child directory   *See* subdirectory.

chipset   A group of chips on the motherboard that controls the timing and flow of data and instructions to and from the CPU.

chkdsk (check disk)   A Windows command to verify that the hard drive does not have bad sectors that can corrupt the file system.

chmod   A Linux and macOS command to change modes (or permissions) for a file or directory.

chown   A Linux and macOS command to change the owner of a file or directory.

Chrome OS   An OS by Google that is built on the open-source Chromium OS and used on Google Chromebooks. The OS looks and works much like the Chrome browser and relies heavily on web-based apps and storage.

CIDR (Classless Interdomain Routing) notation   A shorthand notation (pronounced "cider notation") for expressing an IPv4 address and subnet mask; the IP address is followed by a slash (/) and the number of bits in the IP address that identifies the network—for example, 15.50.35.10/20.

CIFS (Common Internet File System)   A file access protocol and the cross-platform version of SMB used between Windows, Linux, macOS, and other operating systems; a spinoff of the SMB2 protocol.

Class C fire extinguisher   A fire extinguisher rated to put out electrical fires.

Classic view   A view in Control Panel that presents utilities as small or large icons that are not grouped.

clean boot   A process of starting Windows with a basic set of drivers and startup programs; a clean boot can be useful when software does not install properly.

clean install   A process used to install the OS on a new hard drive or overwrite the existing operating system and applications when installing the OS.

client/server   Two computers communicating using a local network or the Internet. One computer (the client) makes requests to the other computer (the server), which answers the request.

client/server application   An application where a client program installed on one computer requests information from a server program installed on another computer on the network or Internet.

client-hosted desktop virtualization   When a local computer is used to host a hypervisor and its virtual machines.

client-side virtualization   Using this virtualization, a personal computer provides multiple virtual environments for applications.

clock drift   *See* time drift.

clone   In Linux and macOS, an image of the entire partition on which the OS is installed.

closed-source software   Software owned by a vendor that requires a commercial license to install and use. *Also called* vendor-specific *or* commercial license software.

cloud-based network controller   A manager of network resources in the cloud through services that are also in the cloud. These network resources are managed through a browser and might include Wi-Fi access points, network servers, routers, switches, and firewalls. An example of a cloud-based network controller is CloudTrax (*cloudtrax.com*).

cloud computing   A service where server-side virtualization is delegated to a third-party service, and the Internet is used to connect server and client machines.

cloud file storage service   A way of storing files in the cloud. Examples are Google Drive, iCloud Drive, Dropbox, and OneDrive.

cluster   On a magnetic hard drive, one or more sectors that constitute the smallest unit of space on the drive for storing data (also referred to as a file allocation unit). Files are written to a drive as groups of whole clusters.

cmdlet   A prebuilt script (pronounced "command-let") written for Windows PowerShell, a command-line interface.

CMOS (complementary metal-oxide semiconductor)   The technology used to manufacture microchips. CMOS chips require less electricity, hold data longer after the electricity is turned off, and produce less heat than earlier technologies. The configuration or setup chip is a CMOS chip.

CMOS battery   The lithium coin-cell battery on the motherboard used to power the CMOS chip that holds BIOS setup data so that the data is retained when the computer is unplugged.

CMOS RAM   Memory contained on the CMOS configuration chip.

CNAME (Canonical Name) record   A type of DNS record in the DNS namespace that redirects from one host name to another.

coaxial (coax) cable   A cable that has a single copper wire down the middle and a braided shield around it.

cold boot   *See* hard boot.

color depth   The accuracy of color representation on a monitor screen; color depth is important for editing photographs and in graphic design.

comment syntax   The text in a script or program that tags a line as documentation so it is not interpreted as a command in the script or program.

commercial mail app   An email client application, such as Microsoft Outlook, that is paid for and generally offers more features than a mobile embedded mail app or free open-source mail apps.

commercial use license   *See* site license.

community cloud   Online resources and services that are shared between multiple organizations but are not available publicly.

CompactFlash (CF) card   A flash memory device that allows for sizes up to 137 GB, although current sizes range up to 512 GB.

compatibility mode   A group of settings that can be applied to older drivers or applications so that they might work using a newer version of Windows than the one they were designed to use.

Compatibility Support Module (CSM)   A feature of UEFI that allows it to be backward-compatible with legacy BIOS devices and drivers.

Component Services (COM+)   A Microsoft Management Console snap-in that can be used to register components used by installed applications.

compressed (zipped) folder   A folder with a .zip extension that contains compressed files. When files are put in the folder, they are compressed. When files are moved to a regular folder, they are decompressed.

Computer Management   A Windows console (compmgmt.msc) that contains several administrative tools used by support technicians to manage the local computer or other computers on the network.

computer name   *See* host name.

connection-oriented protocol   In networking, a TCP/IP protocol that confirms a good connection has been made before transmitting data to the other end, verifies that data was received, and resends data if it was not received; an example is TCP. *Compare with* connectionless protocol.

connectionless protocol   A TCP/IP protocol, such as UDP, that works at the Transport layer and does not guarantee delivery; it does not establish a connection or check whether data is received. *Also called* best-effort protocol. *Compare with* connection-oriented protocol.

console   A window that consolidates several Windows administrative tools.

contrast ratio   The contrast between true black and true white on a screen.

Control Panel   A window containing several small utility programs called applets that are used to manage hardware, software, users, and the system.

controller hub   A device that controls the smart devices in an IoT network to create an integrated smart home experience. *Also called* smart home hub.

cooler   A cooling system that sits on top of a processor and usually consists of a fan and a heat sink.

copy   The Windows command to copy a single file, a group of files, or a folder and its contents.

copyright   The right to copy a creative work; a copyright belongs to the creator(s) of the work or others to whom the creator transfers this right.

Cortana   A Windows 10/11 voice-enabled digital assistant and search feature.

cp   Copy command used to copy a file or directory to a new location.

CPU   *See* central processing unit (CPU).

crimper   A hand tool used to attach a terminator or connector to the end of a cable.

critical applications   Applications that are required to keep a business functioning and that require alternative solutions if they are not functioning.

cross-platform virtualization   Virtualization of different OSs on the same host platform.

cross-site scripting (XSS)   An attack in which a hacker sends a malicious script to an online app, and the app unknowingly sends the script to an unsuspecting user's browser, which executes the script via the user's credentials.

crossover cable   A cable used to connect two like devices such as a hub to a hub or a computer to a computer (to make the simplest network of all). The transmit connectors at one end of the cable are wired as the receiving connectors at the other end of the cable and vice versa.

crypto miner   Software that validates cryptocurrency transactions linked to the ongoing chains of transactions called block chains.

cryptojacking   A type of zombie attack that installs crypto mining software to run mining operations.

custom installation   In the Windows setup program, the option used to overwrite the existing operating system and applications, producing a clean installation of the OS. The main advantage of a custom installation is that problems with the old OS are not carried forward.

custom refresh image   In Windows 8, an image of the entire Windows volume, including the Windows installation. The image can be applied during a Windows 8 refresh operation.

data-at-rest encryption   A type of encryption—for example, the Windows Encrypting File System—used for stored data, as opposed to data in transit.

data loss prevention (DLP)   Methods that protect corporate data from being exposed or stolen; for example, software that filters employee email to verify that privacy laws are not accidentally or intentionally being violated.

data retention   Storing data after the data has been terminated (no longer required for normal operations) in order to satisfy regulated policies an organization is required to follow.

data source   A resource on a network that includes a database and the drivers required to interface between a remote computer and the data.

Data Sources   A connection between a local application and a remote database so that the application can manage the database. *Also called* ODBC (Open Database Connectivity) Data Sources.

data throughput   *See* bandwidth.

DB15 port   *See* VGA (Video Graphics Array) port.

DB9 port   *See* serial port.

dd   In Linux and macOS, the command to copy and convert files, directories, partitions, and entire DVDs or hard drives. You must be logged in as a superuser to use the command.

DDR   *See* Double Data Rate SDRAM.

DDR3   Memory that is faster and uses less power than DDR2; can support quad, triple, or dual channels or function as single DIMMs.

DDR3L   Memory that is faster and uses less power than regular DDR3; used in laptops.

DDR4   Memory that is faster and uses less power than DDR3; can support quad or dual channels or function as single DIMMs.

DDR5   Memory that is faster and uses less power than DDR4; can support quad or dual channels or function as single DIMMs.

DE15 port   *See* VGA (Video Graphics Array) port.

dead pixel   A pixel on an LCD monitor that is not working and can appear as a small white, black, or colored spot on the screen.

default gateway   The gateway a networked computer uses to access another network unless it knows to specifically use another gateway for quicker access.

default printer   The designated printer to which Windows prints unless another one is selected.

default product key   A product key that can be used to fix a problem created when Windows setup installs the wrong edition of the OS.

default program   A program associated with a file extension that is used to open the file.

defense in depth   Layered protection for a system or network so that, if one security method fails, the next might stop an attacker.

defrag   The Windows command that examines a magnetic hard drive for fragmented files and rewrites these files to the drive in contiguous clusters.

Defrag and Optimization tool (dfrgui.exe)   A Windows utility that defragments a magnetic hard drive and trims an SSD to improve performance. *Also called* Defragment and Optimize Drives utility.

defragment   A drive maintenance procedure that rearranges fragments or parts of files on a magnetic hard drive so each file is stored on the drive in contiguous clusters.

Defragment and Optimize Drives   *See* Defrag and Optimization tool.

defragmentation tool   A utility or command to rewrite a file to a disk in one contiguous chain of clusters, thus speeding up data retrieval.

degausser   A machine that exposes a storage device to a strong magnetic field to completely erase the data on a magnetic hard drive or tape drive.

del   The Windows command to delete a file or group of files. *Also called* the erase command.

denial-of-service (DoS)   An attack that overwhelms a computer or network with incoming traffic until new connections can no longer be accepted.

deployment image   A standard image used to install Windows; the installation can begin from local bootable media, by requesting the image from a network server, or by using push automation from a deployment server on the network.

deployment strategy A procedure to install Windows, device drivers, and applications on a computer; it can include the process to transfer user settings, application settings, and user data files from an old installation to the new installation.

desktop case A computer case that lies flat and sometimes serves double duty as a monitor stand. A tower case is sometimes called a desktop case.

destination network address translation (DNAT) When a firewall using NAT allows uninitiated communication to a computer behind the firewall through a port that is normally closed. *Also see* port forwarding.

device driver A small program stored on the hard drive and installed in Windows that tells Windows how to communicate with a specific hardware device such as a printer, network, port on the motherboard, or scanner.

device encryption An Android or iOS service that encrypts all the stored data on a device, making the device essentially useless to a thief.

Device Manager The primary Windows tool (devmgmt.msc) for managing hardware.

df Command used to display the amount of free disk space left on the system.

DHCP (Dynamic Host Configuration Protocol) server A computer or other device that provides an IP address from a pool of addresses to a client computer that requests an address.

DHCP (Dynamic Host Configuration Protocol) A protocol used by a server to assign a dynamic IP address to a computer when it first attempts to initiate a connection to the network and requests an IP address.

DHCP client A computer or other device (such as a network printer) that requests an IP address from a DHCP server.

DHCPv6 server A DHCP server that serves up IPv6 addresses.

dictionary attack A method to discover or crack a password by trying words in a dictionary.

differential backup A backup routine that backs up files that have changed or have been created since the last full backup.

dig Command in Linux and Unix operating systems to look up DNS information.

digital A signal consisting of a series of binary values—1s and 0s. *Compare with* analog.

digital assistant A service or app, such as Apple's Siri and Microsoft's Cortana, that responds to a user's voice commands with a personable, conversational interaction to perform tasks and retrieve information. *Also called* personal assistant *or* virtual assistant.

digital certificate Encrypted data that serves as an electronic signature to authenticate the source of a file or document or to identify and authenticate a person or organization sending data over a network. The data is assigned by a certificate authority such as VeriSign and includes a public key for encryption. *Also called* a digital ID *or* digital signature.

digital license A Windows 10/11 license assigned to a computer after Windows has been activated on the machine.

digital rights management (DRM) Software and hardware security limitations meant to protect digital content and prevent piracy.

digital signature *See* digital certificate.

digitizer *See* graphics tablet.

digitizing tablet *See* graphics tablet.

DIMM (dual inline memory module) A miniature circuit board installed on a motherboard to hold memory.

dir The Windows command to list files and directories.

direct burial A type of cable designed to be buried in the ground without any conduit.

direct current (DC) Current that travels in only one direction (the type of electricity provided by batteries). Computer power supplies transform AC to low DC.

direct thermal printer A type of thermal printer that burns dots onto special coated paper, as older fax machines did.

directory A container in a file system that can hold files and other subdirectories.

DirectX A Microsoft software development tool that developers can use to write multimedia applications such as games, video-editing software, and computer-aided design software.

disc image *See* ISO image.

discolored capacitor An indicator of a failing motherboard; such capacitors might have bulging heads or crusty corrosion at their base.

Disk Cleanup A Windows utility to delete temporary files and free up space on a drive.

disk cloning *See* drive imaging.

disk drive shredder A device that can destroy magnetic hard drives, SSDs, flash drives, optical discs, and mobile devices so that sensitive data on the device is also destroyed.

Disk Management   The Windows utility (diskmgmt.msc) used to install and manage drives.

diskpart   A Windows command to manage hard drives, partitions, and volumes.

DISM (Deployment Image Servicing and Management)   A set of commands to create, capture, and manage a Windows standard image. The commands can also be used to repair a corrupted Windows 10/11 installation.

DisplayPort   A port that transmits digital video and audio (not analog transmissions) and can be used in the place of VGA and DVI ports on personal computers.

distorted geometry   Images that are stretched inappropriately on a monitor.

distributed denial-of-service (DdoS)   A DoS attack performed by multiple computers and sometimes by botnets, even when users of the botnet computers are not aware of the attack.

distribution server   A file server holding Windows setup files that are used to install Windows on computers networked to the server.

distribution share   The collective files in an installation that include Windows, device drivers, and applications. The package of files is served up by a distribution server.

DKIM (DomainKeys Identified Mail) record   A TXT record in the DNS namespace used to authenticate that an email message came from a trusted source. A domain name identifier is attached to the record.

DMARC (Domain-based Message Authentication, Reporting, and Conformance) record   A TXT record in the DNS namespace that is used to tell a recipient's mail server what to do when it receives a fraudulent email message. DMARC is designed to work with DKIM and SPF TXT records in the DNS namespace.

DMG file   In macOS, a disk image file similar to WIM or ISO files in Windows.

DMZ (demilitarized zone)   A computer or network that has limited or no firewall protection within a larger organization of protected computers and networks.

DNS (Domain Name System or Domain Name Service)   A distributed pool of information (called the namespace) that keeps track of assigned host names and domain names and their corresponding IP addresses; also refers to the system that allows a host to locate information in the pool and the protocol the system uses.

DNS (Domain Name System or Domain Name Service) server   A Domain Name Service server that uses a DNS protocol to find an IP address for a computer when the fully qualified domain name is known. An Internet service provider is responsible for providing access to one or more DNS servers as part of the service it provides for Internet access.

DNS client   The service used when Windows queries the DNS server for name resolution, which means to find an IP address for a computer when the fully qualified domain name is known.

dock   (1) For the Android OS, the area at the bottom of the Android screen where up to four apps can be pinned. (2) For macOS, a bar that appears by default at the bottom of the screen and contains program icons and shortcuts to files and folders.

docking port   A connector on the bottom of the laptop that connects to a port replicator or docking station.

docking station   A device that receives a laptop computer and provides additional secondary storage and easy connection to peripheral devices.

documented business processes   Stated goals of a business, including how the business achieves those goals.

domain   In Windows, a logical group of networked computers, such as those on a college campus, that share a centralized directory database of user account information and security.

domain name   A name that identifies a network and appears before the period in a website address, such as *microsoft.com*. A fully qualified domain name is sometimes loosely called a domain name. *Also see* FQDN (fully qualified domain name).

domain user account   An account assigned to a user by Active Directory that identifies the user and defines user rights on the domain. *Also called* network ID.

Double Data Rate SDRAM (DDR SDRAM)   A type of memory technology used on DIMMs that runs at twice the speed of the system clock, has one notch, and uses 184 pins. *Also called* DDR SDRAM, SDRAM II, *and* DDR.

double-sided   A DIMM feature whereby memory chips are installed on both sides of a DIMM.

drive format   The process of installing a file system on a portion (volume) of a storage device, so that the volume can hold files and directories.

drive imaging   Making an exact image of a hard drive, including partition information, boot sectors, operating system installation, and application software, to replicate the hard drive on another system or recover from a hard drive crash. *Also called* disk cloning *or* disk imaging.

driver rollback   To undo a device driver update by returning to the previous version.

driver store   The location where Windows stores a copy of the driver software when first installing a device.

DSL (Digital Subscriber Line)   A telephone line that carries digital data from end to end and is used as a type of broadband Internet access.

DSL modem   A device that converts a computer's digital signal to analog before sending it over telephone lines and converts incoming analog data to digital.

dual boot   The ability to boot using either of two different OSs, such as Windows 11 and Windows 10. *Also called* multiboot.

dual channels   A motherboard feature that improves memory performance by providing two 64-bit channels between memory and the chipset. DDR, DDR2, DDR3, DDR4, and DDR5 DIMMs can use dual channels.

dual processors   Two processor sockets on a server motherboard. *Also see* multisocket.

dual rail   A power supply with a second +12 V circuit or rail used to ensure that the first circuit is not overloaded.

dual ranked   Double-sided DIMMs that provide two 64-bit banks. The memory controller accesses one bank and then the other. Dual-ranked DIMMs do not perform as well as single-ranked DIMMs.

dual-voltage selector switch   A switch on the back of the computer case where you can change the input voltage to the power supply to 115 V (in the United States) or 220 V (in other countries).

dumb terminal   *See* zero client.

dumpster diving   Looking for useful information in someone's trash to help create an impersonation of an individual or company to aid in a malicious attack.

duplex printer   A printer that is able to print on both sides of the paper.

duplexing assembly   In a duplex printer, an assembly of several rollers that enables printing on both sides of the paper.

DVD (digital versatile disc or digital video disc)   A technology for optical discs that uses a red laser beam and can hold up to 17 GB of data.

DVD-ROM   Stands for DVD read-only memory.

DVD-RW   Stands for DVD rewriteable memory.

DVD-RW DL   Stands for DVD rewriteable memory, dual layers. It doubles storage capacity.

DVI (Digital Video Interface) port   A port that transmits digital or analog video.

DVI-D   A DVI video port that works only with digital monitors.

DVI-I   A DVI video port that supports both analog and digital monitors.

DXDiag (DirectX Diagnostics Tool)   A Windows command (dxdiag.exe) used to display information about hardware and diagnose problems with DirectX. The command returns the version of DirectX installed.

dxdiag.exe   *See* DXDiag (DirectX Diagnostics Tool).

dynamic disk   A way to partition one or more hard drives so that they can work together to increase space for data storage or to provide fault tolerance or improved performance. *Also see* RAID. *Compare with* basic disk.

dynamic IP address   An IP address assigned by a DHCP server for the current session only and leased when the computer first connects to a network. When the session is terminated, the IP address is returned to the list of available addresses. *Compare with* static IP address.

dynamic RAM (DRAM)   The most common type of system memory; it requires refreshing every few milliseconds.

dynamic type checking   A technique in scripting and programming whereby each command line is checked by the command interpreter software to verify that the command can be executed.

dynamic volume   A volume type used with dynamic disks; allows you to create a single volume that uses space on multiple hard drives.

ease of access   Windows features available in the Ease of Access app in Control Panel that makes Windows easier to use, including a narrator, magnifier, and on-screen keyboard.

ECC (error-correcting code)   A chipset feature on a motherboard that checks the integrity of data stored on DIMMs or RIMMs and can correct single-bit errors in a byte. More advanced ECC schemas can detect, but not correct, double-bit errors in a byte.

EFI System Partition (ESP)   For a GPT hard drive, the bootable partition used to boot the OS; contains the boot manager program for the OS.

electrostatic discharge (ESD)   Another name for static electricity, which can damage chips and destroy motherboards, even though it might not be felt or seen with the naked eye.

elevated command prompt window A Windows command prompt window that allows commands requiring administrator privileges.

email filtering To search incoming or outgoing email messages for matches kept in databases to identify known scams and spammers and protect against social engineering.

email hoax An email message that tries to tempt you to give out personal information or tries to scam you.

embedded MMC (eMMC) Internal storage used instead of an SSD in mobile devices such as cell phones, tablets, and laptops.

emergency notifications Government alerts, such as AMBER alerts, that are sent to mobile devices in an emergency.

emulator A virtual machine that emulates hardware, such as the hardware buttons on a smartphone.

Encrypting File System (EFS) A way to use a key to encode a file or folder on an NTFS volume and protect sensitive data. Because it is an integrated system service, EFS is transparent to users and applications.

end-of-life (EOL) The point at which the manufacturer of software or hardware stops providing updates or patches for its product.

End User License Agreement (EULA) A digital or printed statement of your rights to use or copy software, which you agree to when the software is installed.

end-user termination checklist The list of tasks that must be performed by IT personnel when a user leaves the organization, necessary for good security of resources (hardware, software, data, and other digital resources) managed by the IT department.

endpoint device A computer, laptop, smartphone, printer, or other host on a network.

endpoint management server A server that monitors various endpoint devices on the network to ensure that endpoints are compliant with security requirements such as anti-malware and that OS updates are applied.

enterprise license A license to use software that allows an organization to install multiple instances of the software. *Also called* a site license.

entry control roster A list of people allowed into a restricted area and a log of approved visitors; used and maintained by security guards.

environmental variable Data the OS makes available to a script or program for use during its execution. *Also called* a system variable.

eSATA (external SATA) A standard and port used to connect external SATA drives to a computer; uses a special shielded SATA cable up to 2 meters long.

escalate To assign a problem to someone higher in the support chain of an organization. This action is normally recorded in call tracking software.

ESD mat A mat that dissipates ESD and is commonly used by technicians who repair and assemble computers at their workbenches or in an assembly line. *Also called* a ground mat.

ESD strap A strap worn around the wrist and attached to a computer case, ground mat, or another ground so that ESD is discharged from the body before touching sensitive components inside a computer. *Also called* an antistatic wrist strap *or* a ground bracelet.

Ethernet port *See* network port.

Event Viewer A Windows tool (Eventvwr.msc) useful for troubleshooting problems with Windows, applications, and hardware. It displays logs of significant events, such as a hardware or network failure, OS failure, OS error messages, a device or service that has failed to start, and General Protection Faults.

Everyone group In Windows, the Authenticated Users group as well as the Guest account. When you share a file or folder on the network, Windows gives access to the Everyone group by default.

evil twin An attack in which a fraudulent Wi-Fi hotspot or access point is used to impersonate a legitimate website, network, FTP site, or person in order to obtain private information.

Exchange Online An email service provided by Microsoft that is hosted on Microsoft servers.

executive services In Windows, a group of components running in kernel mode that interfaces between the subsystems in user mode and the HAL (hardware abstraction layer).

exFAT A file system suitable for large external storage devices and compatible with Windows, macOS, and Linux.

expand The Windows command that extracts files from compressed distribution files, which are often used to distribute files for software installation.

expansion card A circuit board inserted into a slot on the motherboard to enhance the capability of the computer. *Also called* an adapter card.

expert system Software that uses a database of known facts and rules to simulate a human expert's reasoning and decision-making processes.

explicit permissions Permissions in Windows that apply to a file or folder for which inherited permissions are disabled.

ext3 (third extended file system) The Linux file system that was the first to support journaling, which is a technique that tracks and stores changes to the hard drive and helps prevent file system corruption.

ext4 (fourth extended file system) The current Linux file system, which replaced the ext3 file system.

Extended ATX (E-ATX) A larger version of the ATX form factor.

extended partition On an MBR hard drive, the only partition that can contain more than one logical drive. In Windows, a hard drive can have only a single extended partition. *Compare with* primary partition.

extender A device that amplifies and retransmits a wireless signal to a wider coverage area and retains the original network name.

extension *See* plug-in.

extension magnet brush A long-handled brush made of nylon fibers that are charged with static electricity to pick up stray toner inside a laser printer.

external enclosure A housing designed to store hard drives outside the computer.

external SATA (eSATA) port A port for external drives based on SATA that uses a special, external shielded SATA cable up to 2 meters long.

F connector A connector used with an RG-6 coaxial cable for connections to a TV; it has a single copper wire.

F-Type A connector found on coaxial cable that is commonly used for cable TV and cable modems.

factory default The state of a mobile device or other computer at the time of purchase. When a device is reset to this state, the operating system is reinstalled and all user data and settings are lost.

Fast Ethernet *See* 100BaseT.

FAT (file allocation table) A table on a hard drive or other storage device used by the FAT file system to track the clusters used to contain a file.

FAT32 A file system suitable for low-capacity hard drives and other storage devices and supported by Windows, macOS, and Linux.

fat client *See* thick client.

fault tolerance The degree to which a system can tolerate failures. Adding redundant components, such as disk mirroring or disk duplexing, is a way to build in fault tolerance.

favorites tray On Android devices, the area above the Action bar that contains up to seven apps or groups of apps. These apps stay put as you move from home screen to home screen.

feature update In Windows, one of the incremental updates for the OS that happen about every six months.

ferrite clamp A clamp installed on a network cable to protect against electrical interference.

fiber optic As applied to Internet access technologies, a dedicated, leased line that uses fiber-optic cable from the ISP to a residence or place of business.

fiber-optic cable Cable that transmits signals as pulses of light over glass or plastic strands inside protected tubing.

field replaceable unit (FRU) A component in a computer or device that can be replaced with a new component without sending the computer or device back to the manufacturer. Examples include a power supply, DIMM, motherboard, and hard disk drive.

filament A thermoplastic strand used by a 3D printer to build three-dimensional objects.

file allocation unit *See* cluster.

file association The association between a data file and an application to open the file; this association is determined by the file extension.

file attributes The properties assigned to a file. Examples of file attributes are read-only and hidden status.

File Explorer The Windows 10/11 utility used to view and manage files and folders.

File Explorer Options applet The Windows 10/11 applet used to determine how files and folders are displayed in File Explorer.

file extension A portion of the file name that indicates how the file is organized or formatted, the type of content in the file, and what program uses the file. In command lines, the file extension follows the file name and is separated from it by a period—for example, in Msd.exe, exe is the file extension.

File History A Windows 10/11 utility that can schedule and maintain backups of data. It can also create a system image.

file-level backup A process that backs up and restores individual files.

file name The first part of the name assigned to a file, which does not include the file extension. In Windows, a file name can be up to 255 characters.

file server A computer dedicated to storing and serving up data files and folders.

file system   The overall structure that an OS uses to name, store, and organize files on a disk. Examples are NTFS and FAT32. Windows is always installed on a volume that uses the NTFS file system.

file vault   In macOS, a hard drive encryption feature.

find   Linux/Unix command used to find a file or directory within the file hierarchy

Finder   The macOS utility used to find and view applications, utilities, files, storage devices, and network resources available to macOS; similar to Windows File Explorer.

firewall   Hardware and/or software that blocks unwanted Internet traffic from a private network and can restrict Internet access for local computers.

firmware   Software that is permanently stored in a chip; BIOS or UEFI on a motherboard are examples.

First Aid   A macOS tool in the Disk Utility group of tools that scans a hard drive or other storage device for file system errors and repairs them.

first response   The duties of the person who first discovers an incident, which may include identifying and going through proper channels to report the incident, preserving data or devices, and documenting the incident.

flashing BIOS   *See* flashing BIOS/UEFI.

flashing BIOS/UEFI   The process of upgrading or refreshing the programming stored on a firmware chip of a motherboard.

flat-panel monitor   *See* LCD (liquid crystal display) monitor.

flatbed scanner   A scanner with a flat, glass surface that holds paper to be scanned. The scan head moves under the glass, and the scanner might have feeders to scan multiple copies.

folder   *See* subdirectory.

folder redirection   The technique in Active Directory of using a shared folder on the network instead of a user's Home folder on the local computer.

force quit   In macOS, to abruptly end an app without allowing the app to go through its close process.

forest   The entire enterprise of users and resources that is managed by Active Directory.

form factor   A set of specifications for the size, shape, and configuration of a computer hardware component such as a case, power supply, or motherboard.

format   The Windows command to prepare a hard drive volume, logical drive, or USB flash drive for use (e.g., format d:). This process erases all data on the device.

formatting   *See* format.

FPC (flexible printed circuit) connectors   Flat and flexible ZIF and non-ZIF connectors used for tight locations in electronic equipment.

FQDN (fully qualified domain name)   A host name and domain name that identifies a computer and the network to which it belongs, for example, *joesmith.mycompany.com* is an FQDN. An FQDN is sometimes loosely referred to as a domain name.

fragmented file   A file that has been written to different portions of the disk so that it is not in contiguous clusters.

Fresh Start   The Windows 10 process to perform a clean installation of the OS using the most recent version of Windows 10 available from Microsoft.

front panel connector   A group of wires running from the front or top of the computer case to the motherboard.

front panel header   A group of pins on a motherboard that connect to wires at the front panel of the computer case.

Front Side Bus (FSB)   *See* system bus.

FRU (field replaceable unit)   *See* field replaceable unit (FRU).

FTP (File Transfer Protocol)   A TCP/IP protocol and application that uses the Internet to transfer files between two computers.

FTP server   A server using the FTP or Secure FTP protocol to download or upload files to remote computers.

full backup   A backup routine that backs up all files designated for backup. *Compare to* differential backup *and* incremental backup.

full device encryption   *See* device encryption.

full duplex   Communication that happens in two directions at the same time.

fully qualified domain name (FQDN)   *See* FQDN (fully qualified domain name).

fuser assembly   A component in laser printing that uses heat and pressure to fuse the toner to paper.

gateway   Any device or computer that network traffic can use to leave one network and go to a different one.

GDPR (General Data Protection Regulation)   A group of regulations implemented by the European Union to protect the personal data of its citizens.

geotracking   A mobile device's routine reporting of its position to Apple, Google, or Microsoft at least twice a day, making it possible for these companies to track your device's whereabouts.

gesture   An action performed on the Mac trackpad using one or more fingers.

ghost cursor   A trail on the screen left behind when you move the mouse.

Gigabit Ethernet   A version of Ethernet that supports rates of data transfer up to 1 gigabit per second.

gigahertz (GHz)   One thousand MHz, or one billion cycles per second. *Also see* hertz *and* megahertz.

global account   An account used at the domain level, created by an administrator, and stored in the SAM (security accounts manager) database on a Windows domain controller. *Also called* a domain account *or* network ID. *Compare with* local account.

global address   *See* global unicast address.

global unicast address   In TCP/IP version 6, an IP address that can be routed on the Internet. *Also called* a global address.

Globally Unique Identifier Partition Table (GUID or GPT)   *See* GUID Partition Table (GPT).

Gmail   An email service provided by Google at *mail.google.com*.

Google account   A user account identified by a valid email address that is registered on the Google Play website (*play.google.com*) and used to download content to an Android device.

Google Play   The official source for Android apps (also called the Android marketplace), at *play.google.com*.

gpresult   The Windows command to find out which group policies are currently applied to a system for the computer or user.

GPS (Global Positioning System)   A receiver that uses the system of 24 or more satellites orbiting Earth. The receiver locates four or more of these satellites and uses their locations to calculate its own position in a process called triangulation.

gpupdate   The Windows command to refresh local group policies as well as group policies set in Active Directory on a Windows domain.

grandfather-father-son (GFS)   A plan for rotating backup media. For example, a son backup media is rotated daily, a father backup media is rotated weekly, and a grandfather backup media is rotated monthly.

graphical user interface (GUI)   An interface that uses graphics as opposed to a command-driven interface.

graphics processing unit (GPU)   A processor that manipulates graphic data to form the images on a monitor screen; can be embedded on a video card, on the motherboard, or integrated within the processor.

graphics tablet   An input device that can use a stylus to hand draw. It works like a pencil on the tablet and uses a USB port. *Also called* digitizing tablet *and* digitizer.

grayware   A program that is potentially harmful or potentially unwanted.

grep   A Linux and macOS command to search for and display a specific pattern of characters in a file or multiple files.

ground bracelet   *See* ESD strap.

ground mat   *See* ESD mat.

Group Policy   A console (gpedit.msc) available in Windows Server and Windows 10/11 professional and business editions that is used to control what users can do and how the local and network computers on the Windows domain can be used.

Group Policy Object (GPO)   A named set of policies that have been created by Group Policy and are applied to an organizational unit.

GRUB (GR and Unified Bootloader)   The current Linux boot loader, which can handle dual boots with another OS installed on the system.

GSM (Global System for Mobiles)   An open standard for cellular WANs and cell phones that uses digital communication of data and is accepted and used worldwide.

Guests group   A type of user group in Windows. User accounts that belong to this group have limited rights to the system and are given a temporary profile that is deleted after the user logs off.

GUID Partition Table (GPT)   A method for partitioning hard drives that allows for drives of any size. For Windows, a drive that uses this method can have up to 128 partitions. The GPT partitioning system is required to use a Secure Boot with UEFI firmware.

gyroscope   A device that contains a disc that can move and respond to gravity as the device is moved.

HAL (hardware abstraction layer)   The low-level part of Windows, written specifically for each CPU technology, so that only the HAL must change when platform components change.

half duplex   Communication between two devices whereby transmission takes place in only one direction at a time.

Handoff   A technique of Apple devices and computers that lets you start a task on one device, such as an iPad, and then pick up that task on another device, such as a Mac desktop or laptop.

hard boot   A restart of the computer by turning off the power or pressing the Reset button. *Also called* a cold boot.

hard disk drive (HDD)   *See* hard drive.

hard drive   The main secondary storage device of a computer. Two technologies are currently used by hard drives: magnetic and solid state. *Also called* a hard disk drive (HDD).

hard reset   (1) For Android devices, a factory reset, which erases all data and settings and restores the device to its original factory default state. (2) For iOS devices, a forced restart similar to a full shutdown, followed by a full clean boot of the device.

hard token   A physical device required to access a secured physical location, such as an entrance to a building or a network.

hardware address   *See* MAC (Media Access Control) address.

hardware RAID   One of two ways to implement RAID. Hardware RAID is more reliable and performs better than software RAID, and is implemented using BIOS/UEFI on the motherboard or a RAID controller card. *Compare with* software RAID.

hardware security module (HSM)   An expansion card or external device added to a system to provide encryption for the hard drive.

hardware signature   Information kept on Microsoft activation servers along with a digital license to identify a machine that has activated a Windows installation.

hardware token   A security feature whereby an app is not available until the user has been authenticated to it by use of a specialized hardware device, such as a USB flash drive token.

hash   A value generated by applying a specific algorithm to a file or string of text. When values are compared before and after the file or text is downloaded, the download is verified to be error free if the values match. *Also called* a checksum.

HD15 port   *See* VGA (Video Graphics Array) port.

HDMI (High-Definition Multimedia Interface) port   A digital audio and video interface standard currently used on desktop and laptop computers, televisions, and other home theater equipment. HDMI is often used to connect a computer to home theater equipment.

HDMI connector   A connector that transmits both digital video and audio and is used on most computers and televisions.

HDMI mini connector   A smaller type of HDMI connector used for connecting devices such as smartphones to a computer. *Also called* a mini-HDMI connector.

header   On a motherboard, a connector that consists of a group of pins that stick up on the board.

heat sink   A piece of metal with cooling fins that can be attached to or mounted on an integrated chip package (such as the CPU) to dissipate heat.

help   A Windows command that gives information about any Windows command.

hertz (Hz)   A unit of measurement for frequency calculated in terms of vibrations or cycles per second. For example, for 16-bit stereo sound, a frequency of 44,000 Hz is used. *Also see* megahertz *and* gigahertz.

hibernation   A power-saving state that saves all work to the hard drive and powers down the system.

hidden share   A folder whose name ends with a $ symbol. When you share the folder, it does not appear in the Explorer window of remote computers on the network.

high latency   A term that describes communications in which there is significant delay in the receipt of the data after transmission.

high-level formatting   A process performed by the Windows Format program (e.g., FORMAT C:/S), the Windows installation program, or the Disk Management utility. The process creates the boot record, file system, and root directory on a hard drive volume or other storage device. *Also called* formatting, OS formatting, *or* operating system formatting. *Compare with* low-level formatting.

high-touch using a standard image   A strategy to install Windows that uses a standard image for the installation. A technician must perform the installation on the local computer. *Also see* standard image.

high-touch with retail media   A strategy to install Windows where all the work is done by a technician sitting at the computer using Windows setup files. The technician also installs drivers and applications after the Windows installation is finished.

HKEY_CLASSES_ROOT (HKCR)   A Windows registry key that stores information to determine which application is opened when the user double-clicks a file.

HKEY_CURRENT_CONFIG (HKCC)   A Windows registry key that contains information about the hardware configuration that is used by the computer at startup.

HKEY_CURRENT_USER (HKCU)   A Windows registry key that contains data about the current user. The key is built when a user logs on using data kept in the HKEY_USERS key and data kept in the Ntuser.dat file of the current user.

HKEY_LOCAL_MACHINE (HKLM) An important Windows registry key that contains hardware, software, and security data. The key is built using data taken from the SAM hive, the Security hive, the Software hive, and the System hive and from data collected at startup about the hardware.

HKEY_USERS (HKU) A Windows registry key that contains data about all users and is taken from the Default hive.

Home button A hardware button on the bottom of Apple's iPhone or iPad.

Home folder The default Windows folder presented to a user when they are ready to save a file. On a peer-to-peer network, the Home folder is normally the Documents folder in the user profile.

host A device, such as a desktop computer, laptop, or printer, on a network that requests or serves up data or services to other devices.

host name A name that identifies a computer, printer, or other device on a network; can be used instead of the computer's IP address to address the computer on the network. The host name together with the domain name is called the fully qualified domain name. *Also called* computer name.

Hosts file A file in the C:\Windows\System32\drivers\etc folder that contains computer names and their associated IP addresses on the local network. The file has no file extension.

hot-plugging Plugging in a device while the computer is turned on. The computer will sense the device and configure it without rebooting. In addition, the device can be unplugged without an OS error. *Also called* hot-swapping.

hot-swappable The ability to plug in or unplug devices without first powering down the system. USB devices are hot-swappable.

hot-swapping *See* hot-plugging.

hotspot A small area that offers connectivity to a wireless network, such as a Wi-Fi network.

HTTP (Hypertext Transfer Protocol) The TCP/IP protocol used for the World Wide Web and used by web browsers and web servers to communicate.

HTTPS (HTTP secure) The HTTP protocol working with a security protocol such as Secure Sockets Layer (SSL) or Transport Layer Security (TLS) to create a secured socket that includes data encryption. TLS is better than SSL.

hub A network device or box that provides a central location to connect cables and distributes incoming data packets to all other devices connected to it. *Compare with* switch.

hybrid cloud A combination of public, private, and community clouds used by the same organization. For example, a company might store data in a private cloud but use a public cloud email service.

HyperThreading The Intel technology that allows each logical processor within the processor package to handle an individual thread in parallel; other threads are handled by other processors within the package.

HyperTransport The AMD technology that allows each logical processor within the processor package to handle an individual thread in parallel; other threads are handled by other processors within the package.

Hyper-V or Hyper-V Manager A utility available in Windows Pro that allows you to create and manage virtual machines.

hypervisor Software that creates and manages virtual machines on a server or on a local computer. *Also called* virtual machine manager (VMM).

IaaS (Infrastructure as a Service) A cloud computing service that provides only hardware, which can include servers, storage devices, and networks. Does not include an installed OS from the provider.

iCloud A website by Apple (*icloud.com*) used to sync content on Apple devices in order to provide a backup of the content.

iCloud Backup A feature of an iPhone, iPad, or iPod touch that backs up the device's content to the cloud at *icloud.com*.

iCloud Drive Storage space at *icloud.com* that can be synced with files stored on any Apple mobile device or any personal computer, including a macOS or Windows computer.

IDE (Integrated Drive Electronics or Integrated Device Electronics) A hard drive whose disk controller is integrated into the drive, eliminating the need for a controller cable and thus increasing speed as well as reducing price.

IDS (intrusion detection system) *See* intrusion detection system (IDS).

IEEE 802.11ac *See* 802.11ac (Wi-Fi 5).

IEEE 802.11ax *See* 802.11ax (Wi-Fi 6).

IEEE 802.11n *See* 802.11n (Wi-Fi 4).

ifconfig (interface configuration) A Linux and macOS command similar to ipconfig that displays details about network interfaces and can enable and disable an interface. Has been replaced by the ip command.

image deployment Installing a standard image on a computer.

image-level backup A process that backs up and restores everything on a device, such as a hard drive, smartphone, or tablet. The restore process restores the device to a previous state.

imaging drum An electrically charged rotating drum found in laser printers.

IMAP (Internet Message Access Protocol) A TCP/IP protocol used by an email server and client that allows the client to manage email stored on the server without downloading the email. *Compare with* POP3.

IMEI (International Mobile Equipment Identity) A unique number that identifies a mobile phone or tablet device worldwide. The number can usually be found imprinted on the device or reported in the About menu of the OS.

impact paper Paper used by impact printers that comes in a box of fanfold paper or in rolls (used with receipt printers).

impact printer A type of printer that creates a printed page by using a mechanism that touches or hits the paper.

impersonation Pretending to be another individual or company to aid in a malicious attack.

IMSI (International Mobile Subscriber Identity) A unique number that identifies a cellular subscription for a device or subscriber, along with its home country and mobile network. Some carriers store the number on a SIM card installed in the device.

incident When an employee or other person has negatively affected safety or corporate resources, violated the code of conduct for an organization, or committed a crime.

incident documentation Documentation, including chain-of-custody documents, surrounding the evidence of an incident that may be used to prevent future incidents and as evidence in a criminal investigation.

incident report A report that can be legally included in a criminal investigation; documents what happened when an incident occurred. *Also see* incident.

incident response Predefined corporate procedures that are to be followed when an incident occurs.

incremental backup A backup routine that backs up files that have changed or been created since the last backup, whether that backup is itself an incremental or a full backup.

Indexing Options applet A Windows applet in Control Panel used to control how Windows manages an index of content, which helps to make searches go faster.

Infrared (IR) *See* IR (infrared).

infrastructure mode A mode in which Wi-Fi devices connect to a Wi-Fi access point, such as a SOHO router, which is responsible for securing and managing the wireless network.

inherited permissions Permissions assigned by Windows that are obtained from a parent object.

initialization files Text files that keep hardware and software configuration information, user preferences, and application settings; used by the OS when first loaded and when needed by hardware, applications, and users.

ink cartridge A cartridge in inkjet printers that holds different colors of ink.

inkjet printer A type of ink dispersion printer that uses cartridges of ink. The ink is heated to a boiling point and then ejected onto the paper through tiny nozzles.

in-place upgrade *See* repair installation.

in-plane switching (IPS) A class of LCD monitor that offers truer color images and better viewing angles, although it is expensive and has slower response times.

integer In scripting and programming, a type of data that is a whole number.

integrated print server A printer feature that allows it to connect to a network, manage print jobs from multiple computers, monitor printer maintenance tasks, and perhaps send email alerts when a problem arises.

interface In TCP/IP version 6, a node's attachment to a link. The attachment can be a physical attachment (e.g., when using a network adapter) or a logical attachment (e.g., when using a tunneling protocol). Each interface is assigned an IP address.

interface ID In TCP/IP version 6, the last 64 bits or four blocks of an IP address that identify the interface.

internal components The main components installed in a computer case.

Internet of Things (IoT) The network of devices, such as cameras, refrigerators, and locks, that have an IP address and can connect to the local network and are accessible from the Internet.

Internet Options A Control Panel applet to manage settings for apps that use the network, such as identifying a proxy server available on the network.

Internet service provider (ISP) *See* ISP (Internet service provider).

intranet Any private network that uses TCP/IP protocols. A large enterprise might support an intranet that is made up of several local networks.

intrusion detection system (IDS) Software that monitors all network traffic and creates alerts when suspicious activity happens; can run on a UTM appliance, router, server, or workstation. *Compare with* intrusion prevention system (IPS).

intrusion prevention system (IPS) Software that monitors and logs suspicious activity on a network and can prevent the threatening traffic from burrowing into the system. *Compare with* intrusion detection system (IDS).

inventory management In an IT organization, the methods used to track end-user devices, network devices, IP addresses, software licenses, and other software and hardware equipment.

inverter An electrical device that converts DC to AC.

I/O shield A plate installed on the rear of a computer case that provides holes for I/O ports coming off the motherboard.

IOPS (input/output operations per second) A measurement of read or write operations performed in one second.

iOS The operating system owned and developed by Apple and used for their various mobile devices.

IoT *See* Internet of Things (IoT).

ip Unix/Linux command used to view the ip configuration of the system. Similar to ipconfig in Windows.

IP (Internet Protocol) The primary TCP/IP protocol, used by the Internet layer, that is responsible for getting a message to a destination host. In the OSI model, the Internet layer is called the Network layer.

IP address A 32-bit or 128-bit address used to uniquely identify a device or interface on a network that uses TCP/IP protocols. Generally, the first numbers identify the network; the last numbers identify a host. An example of a 32-bit IP address is 206.96.103.114. An example of a 128-bit IP address is 2001:0000:B80::D3:9C5A:CC.

iPad A handheld tablet developed by Apple.

iPadOS The Apple operating system used on Apple's iPad tablet devices.

ipconfig (IP configuration) A Windows command that displays TCP/IP configuration information and can refresh TCP/IP assignments to a connection, including its IP address.

iPhone A smartphone developed by Apple.

IPS (intrusion prevention system) *See* intrusion prevention system (IPS).

IPv4 (Internet Protocol version 4) Version 4 of the TCP/IP protocols and standards that define 32-bit IP addresses and how they are used.

Ipv6 (Internet Protocol version 6) Version 6 of the TCP/IP protocols and standards that define 128-bit IP addresses and how they are used.

IR (infrared) A wireless connection that requires an unobstructed line of sight between transmitter and receiver and uses light waves just below the visible red-light spectrum.

ISATAP In TCP/IP version 6, a tunneling protocol that has been developed for Ipv6 packets to travel over an Ipv4 network; stands for Intra-Site Automatic Tunnel Addressing Protocol.

ISDN (Integrated Services Digital Network) A broadband telephone line that can carry data at about five times the speed of regular telephone lines. Two channels (telephone numbers) share a single pair of wires. ISDN has been replaced by DSL.

ISO file *See* ISO image.

ISO image A file format that has an .iso file extension and holds an image of all the data that is stored on an optical disc, including the file system; stands for International Organization for Standardization.

ISP (Internet service provider) An organization, such as Spectrum, that provides individuals and organizations access to the Internet via a technology such as cable Internet, DSL, or cellular.

iTunes Software by Apple installed on a Mac or Windows computer to sync an iPhone or iPad to iOS updates downloaded from *itunes.com* and to troubleshoot problems with the Apple mobile device.

iTunes Store The Apple website at *itunes.com* and the Apple app on an Apple mobile device, where apps, music, TV shows, movies, books, podcasts, and iTunes U content can be purchased and downloaded to a device.

ITX *See* Mini-ITX.

iwconfig A Linux and macOS command similar to ifconfig that applies only to wireless networks. Use it to display information about a wireless interface and configure a wireless adapter.

jailbreaking A process to break through the restrictions that only allow apps for an iOS device to be downloaded from the App Store at *apple.com/app-store*; gives the user root or administrator privileges to the operating system and the entire file system and complete access to all commands and features.

JavaScript A scripting language normally used to create scripts for webpages; the scripts are embedded in an HTML file to build an interactive webpage in a browser.

joule (J) A measure of work or energy. One joule of energy produces 1 watt of power for one second.

jumper Two small posts or metal pins that stick up side by side on a motherboard or other device and are used to hold configuration information. The jumper is considered closed if a cover is over the wires and open if the cover is missing.

Kensington lock *See* cable lock.

Kensington Security Slot A security slot on a laptop case to connect a cable lock. *Also called* K-Slot.

Kerberos An authentication protocol used when a Windows computer authenticates a user to Active Directory on a Windows domain.

kernel The portion of an OS that is responsible for interacting with the hardware.

kernel mode A Windows "privileged" processing mode that has access to hardware components.

kernel panic A Linux or macOS error from which it cannot recover; similar to a blue screen of death in Windows.

Key-Exchange Key (KEK) A Secure Boot database that holds digital signatures provided by OS manufacturers.

key fob A device, such as a type of smart card, that can fit conveniently on a key chain.

Keychain In macOS, a built-in password manager utility.

keylogger A type of spyware that tracks your keystrokes, including passwords, chat room sessions, email messages, documents, online purchases, and anything else you type on your computer. Text is logged to a text file and transmitted over the Internet without your knowledge.

keystone RJ-45 jack A jack that is used in an RJ-45 wall jack.

kill A Linux and macOS command used to forcefully end or kill a process.

knowledge base A collection of articles containing text, images, or video that give information about a network, product, or service.

KVM (Keyboard, Video, and Mouse) switch A switch that allows you to use one keyboard, mouse, and monitor for multiple computers. Some KVM switches also include sound ports so that speakers and a microphone can be shared among multiple computers.

LAN (local area network) A network bound by routers or other gateway devices that usually covers only a small area, such as one building.

land grid array (LGA) A socket that has blunt protruding pins in uniform rows that connect with lands or pads on the bottom of the processor. *Compare with* pin grid array (PGA).

laptop A portable computer that is designed for travel and mobility. Laptops use the same technology as desktop computers, with modifications for conserving voltage, taking up less space, and operating while on the move. *Also called* a notebook computer.

laser printer A type of printer that uses a laser beam to control how toner is placed on the page and then uses heat to fuse the toner to the page.

latency Delays in network transmissions that result in slower network performance; measured by the round-trip time it takes for a data packet to travel from source to destination and back to the source.

launcher The Android graphical user interface (GUI) that includes multiple home screens and supports windows, panes, and 3D graphics.

Launchpad The macOS utility used to launch and uninstall applications.

LC (Lucent connector) A fiber-optic cable connector that can be used with either single-mode or multi-mode fiber-optic cables and is easily terminated; smaller than an SC connector.

LCD (liquid crystal display) monitor A monitor that uses LCD technology; produces an image using a liquid crystal material made of large, easily polarized molecules. *Also called* a flat-panel monitor.

LDAP (Lightweight Directory Access Protocol) A TCP/IP protocol used by client applications to query and receive data from a database; does not include encryption.

LED (light-emitting diode) A technology used in an LCD monitor that requires less mercury than earlier technologies.

legacy software Operating systems and applications that are no longer supported by the developer.

Level 1 cache (L1 cache) Memory on the processor die used as a cache to improve processor performance.

Level 2 cache (L2 cache) Memory in the processor package but not on the processor die. The memory is used as a cache or buffer to improve processor performance. *Also see* Level 1 (L1) cache.

Level 3 cache (L3 cache)   Cache memory that is further from the processor core than Level 2 cache but still in the processor package.

LGA1151   A CPU socket for Intel processors that uses a land grid array and 1151 pins. Two versions of the socket currently exist; the older version works with 6th and 7th generation chipsets and processors, and the newer version works with 8th and 9th generation chipsets and processors. The two sockets are not compatible because the pins are used differently on each version of the socket.

LGA1200   A CPU socket for Intel processors that uses a land grid array and 1200 pins. The socket works with the 10th and 11th generation chipsets and processors.

LGA1700   A CPU socket for Intel processors that uses a land grid array and 1700 pins. The socket works with the 12th generation chipsets and processors.

library   A collection of one or more folders that can be stored on different local drives or on the network.

license   In IT operations, the right to use software an individual or organization has purchased.

licensed frequency   A frequency that has been allocated for a specific purpose and is strictly regulated. *Compare to* unlicensed frequency.

Lightning port   The proprietary Apple connector used on Apple iPhones, iPods, and iPads for power and communication.

Lightweight Directory Access Protocol (LDAP)   *See* LDAP (Lightweight Directory Access Protocol).

line-of-sight wireless connectivity   A type of connection used by satellites that requires an unobstructed path—free of mountains, trees, and tall buildings—from the satellite dish to the satellite.

link   In TCP/IP version 6, a local area network or wide area network bounded by routers. *Also called* local link.

link local address   *See* link local unicast address.

link local unicast address   In TCP/IP version 6, an IP address used for communicating among nodes in the same link; this IP address is not allowed on the Internet. *Also called* local address *and* link local address.

Linux   An OS based on UNIX that was created by Linus Torvalds of Finland. Basic versions of this OS are open source, and all the underlying programming instructions are freely distributed.

lite-touch, high-volume deployment   A strategy that uses a deployment server on the network to serve up a Windows installation after a technician starts the process at the local computer.

lithium ion   Currently the most popular type of battery for notebook computers; it is more efficient than earlier types. Sometimes abbreviated as "Li-Ion" battery.

Live CD   In Linux, a CD, DVD, or flash drive that can boot up a live version of Linux, complete with Internet access and all the tools you normally have available in a hard drive installation of Linux; however, the OS is not installed on the hard drive.

live tiles   On the Windows 10 Start menu, tiles used by some apps to offer continuous real-time updates.

Live USB   In Linux, a live CD stored on a USB flash drive. *Also see* Live CD.

load balancer   A technology where requests for connection are spread across multiple physical or logical systems. Common in cloud computing to increase availability of systems and data under periods of high activity.

loadstate   A command used by the User State Migration Tool (USMT) to copy user settings and data temporarily stored at a safe location to a new computer. *Also see* scanstate.

local account   A Windows user account that applies only to the local computer and cannot be used to access resources from other computers on the network. *Compare with* global account.

local area network (LAN)   *See* LAN (local area network).

Local Group Policy   A console (gpedit.msc) available in Windows professional and business editions that applies only to local users and the local computer. *Also see* Group Policy.

local link   *See* link.

local printer   A printer connected to a computer by way of a port on the computer. *Compare with* network printer.

Local Security Policy   A Windows Administrative Tools snap-in in Control Panel that can manage the Security Settings group of policies. This same group can also be found in Group Policy in the Local Computer Policy/Computer Configuration/Windows Settings group.

local share   A folder on a computer that is shared with others on the network by using the folder's Properties box; used with a workgroup and not with a domain.

Local Users and Groups   For business and professional editions of Windows, a Windows utility console (lusrmgr.msc) that can be used to manage user accounts and user groups.

location data   Data that a device can routinely report to a website so that the device can be located on a map.

location independence A function of cloud computing whereby customers generally don't know the geographical locations of the physical devices providing cloud services.

locator application An app on a mobile device that can be used to locate the device on a map, force the device to ring, change its password, or remotely erase all data on the device.

logical drive On an MBR hard drive, a portion or all of a hard drive's extended partition that is treated by the operating system as though it were a physical drive or volume. Each logical drive is assigned a drive letter, such as drive F, and contains a file system. *Compare with* volume.

logical topology The logical way computers connect on a network.

login item In macOS, a program that automatically launches after a user logs in. Login items are managed in the Users & Groups utility in System Preferences.

logon script A group of commands stored in a script file that is performed each time a user signs in to Windows. *Also called* a login script.

LoJack A technology by Absolute Software that tracks the whereabouts of a laptop computer and, if the computer is stolen, locks down access to it or erases data on it. The technology is embedded in the BIOS/UEFI of many laptops.

long-range fixed wireless (LRFW) Wireless networking technology similar to the Wi-Fi connection in your home but utilizing high-powered antennas for long-distance coverage areas.

Long Term Evolution (LTE) *See* LTE (Long Term Evolution).

loopback address An IP address that indicates your own computer and is used to test its TCP/IP configuration.

loopback plug A device used to test a port in a computer or other device to make sure the port is working; might also test the throughput or speed of the port.

low-level format A type of formatting, usually done at the factory, where sector marks are added to the platters of a magnetic hard drive.

low-level formatting A process (usually performed at the factory) that electronically creates the hard drive tracks and sectors and tests for bad spots on the disk surface. *Compare with* high-level formatting.

LPT (Line Printer Terminal) Assignments of system resources that are made to a parallel port and used to manage a print job. Two possible LPT configurations are referred to as LPT1: and LPT2:.

ls List command used to list files and directories in Linux.

LTE (Long Term Evolution) In telecommunications, a set of wireless communication standards that define data and voice transmissions over cellular networks; expected to replace GSM and CDMA.

M.2 connector A motherboard or expansion card slot that connects to a mini add-on card. The slot uses a PCIe, USB, or SATA interface with the motherboard chipset, and several variations of the slot exist. *Also called* a Next Generation Form Factor (NGFF) connector.

MAC (Media Access Control) address A 48-bit (6-byte) hardware address unique to each NIC or onboard network controller; the address is assigned by the manufacturer at the factory and embedded on the device. The address is often printed on the adapter as hexadecimal numbers; an example is 00 00 0C 08 2F 35. *Also called* a physical address, an adapter address, *or* a hardware address.

MAC address filtering A technique used by a router or wireless access point that allows computers and devices to access a private network if their MAC addresses are on a list of approved addresses.

macOS The proprietary desktop operating system by Apple based on UNIX and used only on Apple computers; formerly called Mac OS X.

magnetic hard drive One of two technologies used by hard drives where data is stored as magnetic spots on disks that rotate at a high speed. *Compare with* solid-state drive (SSD).

magnetometer A device that can sense electromagnetic fields in order to detect metal objects, such as handguns; often placed at the front entrance to a building supervised by security personnel.

Mail applet The default Windows email client available in Control Panel that can be managed from the Apps and features window in the Settings app.

main board *See* motherboard.

malicious software Any unwanted program that is transmitted to a computer without the user's knowledge and that is designed to do varying degrees of damage to data and software. Types of infestations include viruses, Trojan horses, worms, adware, spyware, keyloggers, browser hijackers, dialers, and downloaders. *Also called* malware, infestation, *or* computer infestation.

malware *See* malicious software.

malware definition Information about malware that allows anti-malware software to detect and define malware. *Also called* malware signature.

malware encyclopedia   A list of malware, including symptoms and solutions, often maintained by manufacturers of anti-malware software and made available on their websites.

malware signature   *See* malware definition.

man   A Linux command used to display the user manual of any command within the Linux OS.

MAN (metropolitan area network)   A type of network that covers a large city or campus.

man-in-the-middle attack   *See* on-path attack.

managed switch   A switch that has firmware that can be configured to monitor, manage, and prioritize network traffic.

mantrap   A physical security technique of using two doors on either end of a small entryway where the first door must close before the second door can open. A separate form of identification might be required for each door, such as a badge for the first door and a fingerprint scan for the second door. In addition, a security guard might monitor people as they come and go.

mapped drive   *See* network share.

mapping   A process in which the client computer creates and saves a shortcut (called a network drive) to a folder or drive shared by a remote computer on the network. The network drive has an associated drive letter that points to the network share.

Master Boot Record (MBR)   A partitioning system used by hard drives with a capacity less than 2 TB. On an MBR hard drive, the first sector is called the MBR; it contains the partition table and a program motherboard that firmware uses to boot an OS from the drive.

master file table (MFT)   The database used by the NTFS file system to track the contents of a volume or logical drive.

material safety data sheet (MSDS)   A document that explains how to properly handle substances such as chemical solvents; it includes information such as physical data, toxicity, health effects, first aid, storage, disposal, and spill procedures.

mATX   *See* microATX.

MBR (Master Boot Record)   *See* Master Boot Record (MBR).

md (make directory)   The Windows command to create a directory.

MDM policies   Policies that establish compliance standards used by mobile device management (MDM) and may include various forms of security enforcement, such as data encryption requirements and remote wipes.

Media Creation Tool   Software downloaded from the Microsoft website and used to download Windows setup files, which in turn are used to create setup media or to install Windows.

megahertz (MHz)   One million Hz, or one million cycles per second. *Also see* hertz *and* gigahertz.

memory bank   The memory a processor addresses at one time. Today's desktop and laptop processors use a memory bank that is 64 bits wide.

Memory Diagnostic Tool   A Windows 10/11 utility (mdsched.exe) used to test memory.

Memory Diagnostics   *See* Memory Diagnostic Tool.

meter   Service calculations used to charge end customers for use of a service, system, or application.

micro USB   A smaller version of the regular USB connector.

Micro-A connector   A USB connector that has five pins and is smaller than the Mini-B connector. It is used on digital cameras, cell phones, and other small electronic devices.

microATX (mATX)   A smaller version of the ATX form factor; addresses some technologies that were developed after the original introduction of ATX.

Micro-B connector   A USB connector that has five pins and a smaller height than the Mini-B connector; used on digital cameras, cell phones, and other small electronic devices.

microprocessor   *See* central processing unit (CPU).

Microsoft 365   Previously called Office 365, a subscription-based productivity suite of apps by Microsoft, including Word, Excel, PowerPoint, Outlook, and Visio.

Microsoft account   For Windows 10/11, an email address registered with Microsoft that allows access to several types of online accounts, including Microsoft OneDrive, Facebook, LinkedIn, Twitter, Skype, and Outlook.

Microsoft Assessment and Planning (MAP) Toolkit   Software that can be used by a system administrator from a network location to query hundreds of computers in a single scan and determine if a computer qualifies for a Windows upgrade.

Microsoft Defender Antivirus   Antivirus software embedded in Windows 10/11 to detect, prevent, and remove malware.

Microsoft Deployment Toolkit (MDT)   A suite of Microsoft tools that can automate a Windows installation.

Microsoft Exchange   A popular server application used by large corporations for employee email, contacts, and calendars.

Microsoft Management Console (MMC)   A Windows utility to build customized consoles. These consoles can be saved to a file with an .msc file extension.

Microsoft Remote Assistance (MSRA)   A remote Windows application useful for virtual desktop support; allows a technician to provide help to a user on a remote computer. The user can remain signed in and retains control of the session while the technician gives help.

Microsoft Terminal Services Client (mstsc.exe)   *See* mstsc (Microsoft Terminal Services Client).

MIDI (musical instrument digital interface)   A set of standards that are used to represent music in digital form. A MIDI port is a 5-pin DIN port that looks like a keyboard port, only larger.

MIMO (multiple input/multiple output)   *See* multiple input/multiple output (MIMO).

Mini-B connector   A USB connector that has five pins and is often used to connect small electronic devices, such as a digital camera, to a computer.

Mini-DIN-6 connector   A 6-pin variation of the S-Video port that looks like a PS/2 connector; used by a keyboard or mouse.

Mini DisplayPort   A smaller version of DisplayPort that is used on laptops or other mobile devices.

mini-HDMI connector   *See* HDMI mini connector.

Mini-ITX   A smaller version of the microATX form factor. *Also called* ITX *and* mITX.

Mini PCI Express (Mini PCIe)   A standard used for a notebook's internal expansion slots that follows the PCI Express standards.

Mini PCIe   *See* Mini PCI Express (Mini PCIe).

mini USB   A smaller version of the regular USB connector; also smaller than microUSB.

mirrored volume   The term used by Windows for the RAID 1 level that duplicates data on one drive to another drive and is used for fault tolerance. *Also see* RAID 1.

mirroring   Copying one hard drive to another as a backup. *Also called* RAID 1.

Mission Control   In macOS, a utility and screen that gives an overview of all open windows and thumbnails of the Dashboard and desktops.

mITX   *See* Mini-ITX.

mkdir   *See* md.

mobile application management (MAM)   Applications that enhance MDM software designed to protect corporate apps and their data. MAM apps can be stand-alone or embedded in MDM applications.

mobile device management (MDM)   Software that includes tools for tracking mobile devices and managing the security of data on the devices according to established MDM policies.

mobile hotspot   A location created by a mobile device so that other devices or computers can connect by Wi-Fi to the device and to the Internet.

mobile payment service   An app that allows you to use your smartphone or other mobile device to pay for merchandise or services at a retail checkout counter.

modem port   A port used to connect dial-up phone lines to computers.

modular power supply   A power supply with cables, some or all of which can be detached for a cleaner space inside a computer for better airflow inside the computer case. *Also called* modular cable systems.

Molex connector   A 4-pin power connector used to provide power to a PATA hard drive, optical drive, or other internal component.

motherboard   The main board in the computer. The CPU, ROM chips, DIMMs, and interface cards are plugged into the motherboard. *Also called* the system board.

motion sensor   A surveillance camera that can detect motion to alert security personnel when activity is happening in the vicinity of the camera and turn on recording.

mount point   A folder that is used as a shortcut to space on another volume, which effectively increases the size of the folder to the size of the other volume. *Also see* mounted drive.

mounted drive   A volume that can be accessed by way of a folder on another volume so that the folder has more available space. *Also see* mount point.

msinfo32.exe   A Windows utility that gathers and displays information about the system.

mstsc (Microsoft Terminal Services Client)   A command (mstsc.exe) that allows you to remote in to a host computer using Remote Desktop Connection.

MT-RJ (mechanical transfer registered jack) connector   A type of connector that can be used with either single-mode or multimode fiber-optic cables and is more difficult to connect than the smaller LC connector.

multiboot *See* dual boot.

multicast address In TCP/IP version 6, an IP address used when packets are delivered to a group of nodes on a network.

multicasting In TCP/IP version 6, the transmission of messages from one host to multiple hosts, such as when the host transmits a videoconference over the Internet.

multicore processing A processor technology whereby the processor housing contains two or more processor cores that operate at the same frequency but independently of each other.

multifactor authentication (MFA) The use of more than one method to authenticate access to a computer, network, or other resource.

multimedia shredder A device that can destroy optical discs, flash drives, SSDs, and other devices so that sensitive data stored on the device is also destroyed.

multimeter A device used to measure the various attributes of an electrical circuit. The most common measurements are voltage, current, and resistance.

multiple desktops A feature of Mission Control in macOS, where several desktop screens, each with its own collection of open windows, are available to the user.

multiple input/multiple output (MIMO) A feature of the IEEE 802.11n/ac standards for wireless networking whereby two or more antennas are used at both ends of transmissions to improve performance.

multiple-monitor misalignment When the display is staggered across multiple monitors, making the display difficult to read. Fix the problem by adjusting the display in the Windows Screen Resolution window.

multiple-monitor orientation The aligned orientation of dual monitor screens. When the display does not accurately represent the relative positions of multiple monitors, use the Windows Screen Resolution window to move the display for each monitor so they are oriented correctly.

multiplier The factor by which the bus speed or frequency is multiplied to get the CPU clock speed.

multiprocessing Two processing units installed within a single processor; first used by the Pentium processor.

multiprocessor platform A system that contains more than one processor. The motherboard has more than one processor socket, and the processors must be rated to work in this multiprocessor environment.

multisocket A motherboard with two or more processor sockets. A multisocket motherboard is typically used in a server. *Also called* dual processors *or* multiprocessor platform.

mutual authentication To authenticate in both directions at the same time as both entities confirm the identity of the other.

mv Move command in Linux to move a file or directory to a new location. Does not copy the file; it moves the original file to a new location.

MX (Mail Exchanger) record A type of DNS record in the DNS namespace that points an email server domain name to an IP address.

name resolution The process of associating a character-based name with an IP address.

namespace The entire collection of DNS databases stored on DNS servers (also called name servers) around the globe.

NAND flash memory The type of memory used in SSDs. NAND stands for "Not AND" and refers to the logic used when storing a 1 or 0 in the grid of rows and columns on the memory chip.

nano Text-based editor application used to edit files on screen in Linux and Unix operating systems.

NAS (network-attached storage) A group of hard drives inside an enclosure that connects to a network via an Ethernet port and is used for storage on the network.

NAT (Network Address Translation) A technique that substitutes the public IP address of the router for the private IP address of a computer on a private network when the computer needs to communicate on the Internet.

native resolution The actual (and fixed) number of pixels built into an LCD monitor. For the clearest display, always set the resolution to the native resolution.

navigation pane In File Explorer, a pane on the left side of the window where devices, drives, and folders are listed. Double-click an item to drill down into it.

nbtstat (NetBIOS over TCP/IP Statistics) A Windows TCP/IP command that is used to display statistics about the NetBT protocol.

near-field communication (NFC) *See* NFC.

neighbors In TCP/IP version 6, two or more nodes on the same link.

net localgroup A Windows TCP/IP command that adds, displays, or modifies local user groups.

net use A Windows TCP/IP command that connects or disconnects a computer from a shared resource or can display information about connections.

net user A Windows TCP/IP command used to manage user accounts.

NetBIOS (Network Basic Input/Output System) A legacy suite of protocols used by Windows before TCP/IP.

netbook A low-end, inexpensive laptop with a 9- or 10-inch screen and no optical drive that is generally used for web browsing, email, and word processing by users on the go.

NetBoot A technology that allows a Mac to boot from the network and then install macOS on the machine from a clone DMG file stored on a deployment server.

NetBT (NetBIOS over TCP/IP) A feature of Server Message Block (SMB) protocols that allows legacy NetBIOS applications to communicate on a TCP/IP network.

netstat (network statistics) A Windows TCP/IP command that displays statistics about TCP/IP and network activity and includes several parameters.

network adapter *See* network interface card (NIC).

Network and Sharing Center The primary Windows utility used to manage network connections.

Network Attached Storage (NAS) A device that provides multiple bays for hard drives and an Ethernet port to connect to the network. The device is likely to support RAID.

network drive map Mounting a drive to a computer, such as drive E:, that is actually hard drive space on another host computer on the network. *Also see* mount point.

Network File System (NFS) *See* NFS (Network File System).

network ID The leftmost bits in an IP address. The rightmost bits of the IP address identify the host.

network interface card (NIC) An expansion card that plugs into a computer's motherboard and provides a port on the back of the card to connect a computer to a network. *Also called* a network adapter.

network jitter Measurement of the fluctuations in latency of packets on a network.

network path Typed in the Explorer navigation bar or a command line, the text that identifies a resource on the network; includes two backslashes, the computer name, one backslash, and the folder name.

network port A port used by a network cable to connect to the wired network. *Also called* an Ethernet port.

network printer A printer that any user on the network can access, either through the printer's own network card and connection to the network, through a connection to a stand-alone print server, or through a connection to a computer as a local printer that is shared on the network. *Compare with* local printer.

network share A networked computer (the client) that appears to have a hard drive, such as drive E:, which is actually hard drive space on another host computer (the server). *Also called* mapped drive.

network tap A test access point (TAP) used to monitor network traffic. Commonly used with an IDS/IPS or packet capture application.

Network Time Protocol (NTP) The protocol that requests and reports the time on a Windows domain; time is reported by the primary time server, which receives its time from an external time source, such as a GPS or atomic device.

network topology diagram A documented map of network devices that includes the patterns or design used to connect the devices, either physically or logically.

new-user setup checklist The list of tasks that must be performed by IT personnel when a user joins the organization; necessary for good security of resources (hardware, software, data, and other digital resources) managed by the IT department.

NFC (near-field communication) A wireless technology that establishes a communication link between two NFC devices (e.g., two smartphones or a smartphone and an NFC tag) that are within 4 inches (10 cm) of each other.

NFS (Network File System) A client/server distributed file system that supports file sharing over a network across platforms. For example, a Linux-hosted NFS server can serve up file shares to Windows workstations on the network. Windows 10/11 supports NFS client connections.

NIC (network interface card) *See* network interface card (NIC).

node Any device that connects to the network, such as a computer, printer, or router.

noncompliant system A system that violates security best practices, such as out-of-date anti-malware software or cases where it's not installed.

nonvolatile RAM (NVRAM) Flash memory on the motherboard that UEFI firmware uses to store device drivers and information about Secure Boot. Contents of NVRAM are not lost when the system is powered down.

North Bridge The portion of the chipset hub that connects faster I/O buses (e.g., video bus) to the system bus. *Compare with* South Bridge.

notebook *See* laptop.

Notepad A text-editing program.

notification area An area to the right of the taskbar that holds the icons for running services; these services include the volume control and network connectivity. *Also called* the system tray *or* systray.

notifications Alerts and related information about apps and social media sent to mobile devices and other computers.

nslookup (namespace lookup or name server lookup) A TCP/IP command that lets you read information from the Internet namespace by requesting information about domain name resolutions from the DNS server's zone data.

NTFS (New Technology file system) A file system that supports encryption, disk quotas, and file and folder compression; required for the volume that holds a Windows installation.

NTFS permissions A method to share a folder or file over a network; these permissions can be applied to local users and network users. The folder or file must be on an NTFS volume. *Compare with* share permissions.

NVMe (Non-Volatile Memory Express or NVM Express) An interface standard used to connect an SSD to the system and that uses the PCI Express ×4 interface to communicate with the processor; about five times faster than SATA Revision 3.x.

octet In TCP/IP version 4, each of the four numbers that are separated by periods and make up a 32-bit IP address. One octet is 8 bits.

off-boarding The established process used when a mobile device is removed from the MDM fleet of devices allowed to connect to a corporate network and its resources. *Compare with* on-boarding.

Offline Files A utility that allows users to work with files in a designated folder when the computer is not connected to the corporate network. When the computer is later connected, Windows syncs up the offline files and folders with those on the network.

ohm (Ω) The standard unit of measurement for electrical resistance. Resistors are rated in ohms.

OLED (organic light-emitting diode) monitor A type of monitor that uses a thin LED layer or film between two grids of electrodes and does not use backlighting.

onboard NIC A network port embedded on the motherboard.

onboard port A port that is directly on the motherboard, such as a built-in keyboard port or onboard network port.

on-boarding The established process used when a mobile device is added to the MDM fleet of devices allowed to connect to a corporate network and its resources. *Compare with* off-boarding.

on-demand A service that is available to users at any time. On-demand cloud computing means the service is always available.

on-path attack An attack in which communication between two parties is intercepted. The attacker pretends to be a legitimate website, network, FTP site, or person in a chat session in order to obtain private information. *Also called* a man-in-the-middle attack.

OneDrive A file-hosting service from Microsoft that offers free and purchased storage space in the cloud.

Open Database Connectivity (ODBC) A technology that allows a client computer to create a data source so that the client can interface with a database stored on a remote (host) computer on the network. *Also see* data source.

open-source license The terms of use in the EULA that you agree to when you download open-source software.

open-source software Source code for an operating system or other software that is available for free; anyone can modify and redistribute the source code.

operating system (OS) Software that controls a computer; controls how system resources are used and provides a user interface, a way of managing hardware and software, and ways to work with files.

optical connector A connector used with a fiber-optic cable.

optical network terminal (ONT) A fiber-optic connection that converts fiber optic to copper cabling for connection to customer equipment.

organizational unit (OU) An object that defines a collection of user groups and/or computers in Active Directory.

Original Equipment Manufacturer (OEM) license A Microsoft Windows license available for purchase only by manufacturers or builders of personal computers and intended to be installed only on a computer for sale.

OS X *See* macOS.

OSI (Open Systems Interconnection) model   A model for understanding and developing computer-to-computer communication that divides networking functions among seven layers: Physical, Data Link, Network, Transport, Session, Presentation, and Application.

overclocking   Running a processor at a higher frequency than that recommended by the manufacturer; can result in an unstable system, but is a popular practice when a computer is used for gaming.

overheat shutdown   When a device, such as a projector, overheats and automatically powers off. Allow it to cool down before powering it up again.

PaaS (Platform as a Service)   A cloud computing service that provides hardware and an operating system and is responsible for updating and maintaining both.

package   A collection of files needed to install software.

packet   A message sent over a network as a unit of data; the information at the beginning of the packet identifies the type of data, where it came from, and where it's going. *Also called* data packet *or* datagram.

page description language (PDL)   A language used by printers that describes the appearance of the printed page.

pagefile.sys   The Windows swap file used to hold virtual memory, which enhances physical memory installed in a system.

paired   When two Bluetooth devices have established connectivity and are able to communicate.

pairing   The process of two Bluetooth devices establishing connectivity.

PAN (personal area network)   A small network consisting of personal devices at close range; the devices can include smartphones, PDAs, and notebook computers.

parallel ATA (PATA)   An older IDE cabling method that uses a 40-pin flat or round data cable or an 80-conductor cable and a 40-pin IDE connector. *Also see* SATA.

parity   An older error-checking scheme used with SIMMs in which a ninth, or "parity," bit is added. The value of the parity bit is set to either 0 or 1 to provide an even number of 1s for even parity and an odd number of 1s for odd parity.

partition   A division of a hard drive that can hold a volume. MBR drives can support up to four partitions on one hard drive. In Windows, GPT drives can have up to 128 partitions.

partition table   A table that contains information about each partition on the drive. For MBR drives, the partition table is contained in the Master Boot Record. For GPT drives, the partition table is stored in the GPT header and a backup of the table is stored at the end of the drive.

passive CPU cooler   A CPU cooler that functions without using a fan or other moving parts.

passwd   A Linux and macOS command to change a password. A superuser can change the password for another user.

password policy   A set of rules that defines the minimum length of a password, complexity requirements, and how frequently the password must be reset.

patch   A minor update to software that corrects an error, adds a feature, or addresses security issues. *Also called* an update. *Compare with* service pack.

patch cable   *See* straight-through cable.

patch panel   A device that provides multiple network ports for cables that converge in one location such as an electrical closet or server room.

path   A drive and list of directories pointing to a file, such as C:\Windows\System32.

pathping   A TCP/IP Windows command that combines the ping and tracert commands into a single command to help identify where a network might be slow or giving problems.

Payment Card Industry (PCI)   Regulated credit card and debit card data and the standards that regulate how this data is transmitted and stored to help prevent fraud; applies to vendors, retailers, and financial institutions.

PCI (Peripheral Component Interconnect)   A bus common to personal computers that uses a 32-bit wide or 64-bit data path. Several variations of PCI exist. On desktop systems, one or more notches on a PCI slot keep the wrong PCI cards from being inserted in the slot.

PCI Express (PCIe)   An evolution of PCI that is not backward-compatible with earlier PCI slots and cards. PCIe slots come in several sizes, including PCIe ×1, PCIe ×4, PCIe ×8, and PCIe ×16.

PCIe 6/8-pin connector   A power cord connector used by high-end video cards with PCIe ×16 slots to provide extra voltage to the card; the connector can accommodate a six- or eight-hole port.

PCI-X   The second evolution of PCI, which is backward-compatible with conventional PCI slots and cards, except 5 V PCI cards. PCI-X is focused on the server market.

PCL (Printer Control Language) *See* Printer Control Language (PCL).

PDU (protocol data unit) A message on a TCP/IP network; might be called a packet or frame, depending on its complexity.

peer-to-peer (P2P) As applied to networking, a network of computers that are all equals, or peers. Each computer has the same amount of authority, and each can act as a server to the other computers.

Performance Monitor A Windows Microsoft Management Console snap-in that can track activity by hardware and software to measure performance.

permission propagation When Windows passes permissions from parent objects to child objects.

permissions Varying degrees of access assigned to a folder or file and given to a user account or user group. Access can include full control, write, delete, and read-only.

Persistent Memory (Pmem) A memory technology available in Windows 10/11 Pro for Workstations that retains its contents even when the computer is turned off and is faster than normal memory.

personal use license A license that gives a user the right to install and use one or two instances of software.

PHI (protected health information) Regulated data about a person's health status or health care as defined by HIPAA (the Health Insurance Portability and Accountability Act), which includes steep penalties and risks for noncompliance.

phishing Sending an email message with the intent of getting the user to reveal private information that can be used for identity theft. *Also see* spear phishing.

physical address *See* MAC (Media Access Control) address.

physical topology The physical arrangement of connections between computers.

pickup roller A part in a printer that pushes a sheet of paper forward from the paper tray.

PII (personally identifiable information) Regulated data that identifies a person, including a Social Security number, email address, physical address, birthdate, birthplace, mother's maiden name, marital status, phone numbers, race, and biometric data.

pin grid array (PGA) A socket that has holes aligned in uniform rows around it to receive the pins on the bottom of the processor. *Compare with* land grid array (LGA).

ping (Packet InterNet Groper) A TCP/IP command used to troubleshoot network connections; verifies that the host can communicate with another host on the network.

pinning Making a frequently used application more accessible by adding its icon to the taskbar on the desktop.

pixel A small spot on a fine horizontal scan line. Pixels are illuminated to create an image on the monitor.

pixel pitch The distance between adjacent pixels on the screen.

PKG file In macOS, a package file that is similar to a setup.exe file used in Windows to install an application.

plasma monitor A type of monitor that provides high contrast with better color than LCD monitors; works by discharging xenon and neon plasma on flat glass, and it doesn't contain mercury.

platform The hardware, operating system, runtime libraries, and modules on which an application runs.

Platform Key (PK) A digital signature that belongs to the motherboard or computer manufacturer; authorizes turning Secure Boot on or off and updating the KEK database.

plenum The area between floors of a building.

plug-in A small program that is installed in a browser to change the way the browser functions or to enhance a feature of a single website. *Also called* an extension.

PoE injector (Power over Ethernet) A device that adds power to an Ethernet cable so the cable can provide power to a device.

PoE-rated switch A switch capable of transmitting power to PoE-capable devices.

POP3 (Post Office Protocol, version 3) The TCP/IP protocol that an email server and client use when the client requests the downloading of email messages. The most recent version is POP version 3. *Compare with* IMAP.

port (1) As applied to services running on a computer, a number assigned to a process on a computer so that the process can be found by TCP/IP. *Also called* a port address *or* port number. (2) A physical connector, usually at the back of a computer, that allows a cable to be attached from a peripheral device, such as a printer, mouse, or modem.

port address *See* port.

port filtering   To open or close certain ports so they can or cannot be used. A firewall uses port filtering to protect a network from unwanted communication.

port flapping   A condition when an interface or a port on a switch is continually going up and down.

port forwarding   A technique that allows a computer on the Internet to reach a computer on a private network using a certain port when the private network is protected by NAT and a firewall that controls the use of ports. *Also called* port mapping.

port lock   A physical lock, such as a USB lock, that prevents use of a computer port.

port mapping   *See* port forwarding.

port number   *See* port.

port replicator   A nonproprietary device that typically connects to a laptop via a USB port and provides ports to allow the laptop to easily connect to peripheral devices, such as an external monitor, network, printer, keyboard, mouse, or speakers. *Also called* a universal docking station.

port security   Controlled access to ports on a managed switch; usually done through MAC address filtering for one or more ports.

port triggering   When a firewall opens a port because a computer behind the firewall initiates communication on another port.

POST (power-on self-test)   A self-diagnostic program used to perform a simple test of the CPU, RAM, and various I/O devices; performed by startup BIOS/UEFI when the computer is first turned on.

POST card   A test card installed in a slot on the motherboard or plugged in to a USB port that is used to discover and report computer errors and conflicts that occur when a computer is first turned on and before the operating system is launched.

POST diagnostic card   *See* POST card.

PostScript (PS)   A printer language developed by Adobe Systems that tells a printer how to print a page.

Power Options applet   A Windows applet accessed through Control Panel that manages power settings to conserve power.

Power over Ethernet (PoE)   A feature that might be available on high-end wired network adapters that allows 15.4 watts of power to be transmitted over Ethernet cable to remote devices. *Compare to* Power over Ethernet plus.

Power over Ethernet plus (PoE+)   A feature that might be available on high-end wired network adapters that allows 25.5 watts of power to be transmitted over Ethernet cable to remote devices. *Compare to* Power over Ethernet.

power supply   A box inside the computer case that receives power and converts it for use by the motherboard and other installed devices. Power supplies provide 3.3, 5, and 12 volts DC. *Also called* a power supply unit (PSU).

power supply tester   A device that can test the output of each power cord coming from a power supply.

power supply unit (PSU)   *See* power supply.

Power Users group   A type of Windows user account group. Accounts assigned to this group can read from and write to parts of the system other than their own user profile folders, install applications, and perform limited administrative tasks.

PowerShell   A Windows command-line interface (CLI) that processes objects called cmdlets, which are prebuilt programs built on the .NET Framework, rather than processing text in a command line.

PowerShell ISE   Software used to create, edit, and test PowerShell scripts. ISE stands for Integrated Scripting Environment.

PowerShell script   A text file of PowerShell commands that can be executed as a batch.

Preboot eXecution Environment (PXE)   Programming contained in the BIOS/UEFI code on the motherboard that is used to start up the computer and search for a server on the network to provide a bootable operating system. *Also called* Pre-Execution Environment (PXE).

Pre-Execution Environment (PXE)   *See* Preboot eXecution Environment (PXE).

Preferred Roaming List (PRL)   A database of preferred service providers or radio frequencies a telecommunications carrier wants a mobile device to use when it is outside the carrier's network. The device can download and update its PRL.

PRI (Product Release Instructions)   Instructions about an update to an OS or other software published by the product manufacturer to alert users about what to expect from the update.

primary partition   A hard disk partition that can be designated as the active partition. An MBR drive can have up to three primary partitions. In Windows, a GPT drive can have up to 128 primary partitions. *Compare with* extended partition.

principle of least privilege   An approach where computer users are classified and the rights assigned are the minimum rights required to do their job.

print bed   On a 3D printer, the platform where the filament is deposited.

print head   The part in an inkjet or impact printer that moves across the paper, creating one line of the image with each pass.

Print Management   A utility in the Administrative Tools group of Windows 10 or the Windows Tools group of Windows 11 professional and business editions that allows you to monitor and manage printer queues for all printers on the network.

print server   Hardware or software that manages the print jobs sent to one or more printers on a network.

print spooler   A queue for print jobs.

Printer Control Language (PCL)   A language used by printers that was developed by Hewlett-Packard. Used by a majority of manufacturers and supported by many different OSs.

printer maintenance kit   A kit purchased from a printer manufacturer that contains the parts, tools, and instructions needed to perform routine printer maintenance.

printer self-test page   A test page that prints by using controls at the printer. The page allows you to eliminate a printer as a problem during troubleshooting and usually includes test results, graphics, and information about the printer, such as its resolution and how much memory is installed.

printui   The Windows Printer User Interface command, which is used by administrators to manage printers on local and remote computers.

privacy filter   *See* privacy screen.

privacy screen   A device that fits over a monitor screen to prevent other people from viewing it from a wide angle. *Also called* privacy filter.

private cloud   Services on the Internet that an organization provides on its own servers or that are established virtually for a single organization's private use.

private IP address   In TCP/IP version 4, an IP address used on a private network that is isolated from the Internet.

privileges   The access to data files and folders given to user accounts and user groups. *Also called* rights.

PRL (Preferred Roaming List)   A list of preferred service providers or radio frequencies your carrier wants a mobile device to use; stored on a Removable User Identity Module (R-UIM) card installed in the device.

process   A program that is running under the authority of the shell, together with the system resources assigned to it.

processor   *See* central processing unit (CPU).

processor frequency   The speed at which the processor operates internally, usually expressed in GHz.

processor thermal trip error   A problem when the processor overheats and the system restarts.

procurement life cycle   Data required when replacing an aged asset in an IT asset management system; might include information on suppliers, contract terms, previous purchase orders, invoices, and payment processing.

product activation   The process that Microsoft uses to prevent software piracy. For example, once Windows 10 is activated for a particular computer, it cannot be legally installed on another computer.

product key   A series of letters and numbers assigned by Microsoft that is required to activate a license to use Windows.

Product Release Instructions (PRI)   Information published by the manufacturer of an operating system that describes what to expect from a published update to the OS.

profile security requirements   A set of policies and procedures that define how a student or employee's profile settings are configured for security purposes. For example, a policy might require encryption and backup software to be installed on the student or employee's personal devices that connect to the organization's network.

Programs and Features   A Windows Control Panel applet that lists the programs installed on a computer; you can use it to uninstall, change, or repair programs.

projector   A device used to shine a light that projects a transparent image onto a large screen; often used in classrooms or with other large groups.

protocol   A set of rules and standards that two entities use for communication. For example, TCP/IP is a suite or group of protocols that define many types of communication on a TCP/IP network.

protocol data unit (PDU)   A message sent over a network; the message might have a header or trailer, depending on which layer protocol sent the message.

provisioning package   A package of settings, apps, and data specific to an enterprise that is downloaded and installed on a device when it first joins Azure Active Directory.

proxy server   A computer that intercepts requests that a client (e.g., a browser) makes of a server (e.g., a web server); can serve up the request from a cache it maintains to improve performance, or it can filter requests to secure a large network.

ps A Linux command used to view processes and process IDs.

PS/2 port A round 6-pin port used by an older keyboard or mouse.

public cloud Cloud computing services provided over the Internet to the general public. Microsoft 365 and Amazon Web Service's EC2 and S3 service are examples.

pull automation An installation from a deployment server that requires the local user to start the process. *Compare with* push automation.

public IP address In TCP/IP version 4, an IP address available to the Internet.

punchdown block A physical connection device used to connect wiring to patch panels or an on-site telephone system. *Also called* a 110-block.

punchdown tool A hand tool used to punch individual wires from a network cable into their slots on a punchdown block to terminate the cable.

push automation An installation automatically pushed by a server to a computer when a user is not likely to be manning the computer. *Compare with* pull automation.

PVC (polyvinyl chloride) The product used to cover Ethernet cables; it is not safe to be used in a plenum because it gives off toxic fumes when burned.

pwd A Linux command used to display the Present Working Directory.

Python script A text file of Python commands that can be executed as a batch.

QoS (Quality of Service) *See* Quality of Service (QoS).

quad channels Technology used by a motherboard and DIMMs that allows the memory controller to access four DIMMS at the same time. DDR3, DDR4, and DDR5 DIMMs can use quad channels.

Quality of Service (QoS) A feature used by Windows and network hardware devices to improve network performance for an application. For example, VoIP requires a high QoS.

quarantined computer A computer that is suspected of infection and not allowed to use the network, is put on a different network dedicated to such computers, or is allowed to access only certain network resources.

quick format A format procedure for a hard drive volume or other drive that doesn't scan the volume or drive for bad sectors; use it only when a drive has been previously formatted and is in healthy condition. *Compare with* full format.

Quick Launch menu The menu that appears when the Windows Start button is right-clicked.

QuickPath Interconnect (QPI) The technology used first by the Intel X58 chipset for communication between the chipset and the processor; uses 16 serial lanes, similar to PCI Express. QPI replaced the 64-bit wide Front Side Bus used by previous chipsets.

radio frequency (RF) The frequency of waves generated by a radio signal, which are electromagnetic frequencies above audio and below light. For example, Wi-Fi 802.11n transmits using a radio frequency of 5 GHz and 2.4 GHz.

RADIUS (Remote Access Dial-in User Service) A standard to authenticate and authorize users to wired, wireless, and VPN network connections. Authentication is made to a user database such as Active Directory.

RAID (redundant array of inexpensive disks or redundant array of independent disks) Several methods of configuring multiple hard drives to store data to increase logical volume size and improve performance or to ensure that if one hard drive fails, the data is still available from another hard drive.

RAID 0 Using space from two or more physical disks to increase the disk space available for a single volume. Performance improves because data is written evenly across all disks. Windows calls RAID 0 a striped volume. *Also called* striping *or* striped volume.

RAID 1 A type of drive imaging that duplicates data on one drive to another drive and is used for fault tolerance. Windows calls RAID 1 a mirrored volume. *Also called* mirrored volume.

RAID 1+0 *See* RAID 10.

RAID 10 A combination of RAID 1 and RAID 0 that requires at least four disks to work as an array of drives and provides the best redundancy and performance.

RAID 5 A technique that stripes data across three or more drives and uses parity checking, so that if one drive fails, the other drives can re-create the data stored on the failed drive. RAID 5 drives increase performance and provide fault tolerance. Windows calls these drives RAID-5 volumes.

RAID 5 volume The term used by Windows for RAID 5. *See* RAID 5.

rainbow table A list of plaintext passwords and matching password hashes (encrypted passwords) used by hackers for reverse lookup. When the password hash is known, a hacker can find the plaintext password and use it to hack into a computer or network.

RAM (random access memory) Memory modules on the motherboard that contain microchips used to temporarily hold data and programs while the CPU processes both. Information in RAM is lost when the computer is turned off.

ransomware Malware that holds your computer system hostage with encryption techniques until you pay money or a time period expires and the encrypted content is destroyed.

rapid elasticity A cloud computing service that is capable of scaling up or down as a customer's need level changes.

raw data Data sent to a printer without any formatting or processing.

rd (remove directory) The Windows command to delete a directory (folder) or group of directories (folders).

RDP (Remote Desktop Protocol) *See* Remote Desktop Protocol (RDP).

read/write head A sealed, magnetic coil device that moves across the surface of a disk in a hard disk drive (HDD), either reading data from or writing data to the disk.

recover The Windows command that can recover a file when part of it is corrupted.

recovery drive A Windows 10/11 bootable USB flash drive that can be used to recover the system when startup fails; the drive can be created using the Recovery applet in Control Panel. The drive can hold an OEM recovery partition copied from the hard drive.

recovery partition A partition on a hard drive that contains a recovery utility and installation files to recover the OS back to its factory state.

Recovery System In macOS, a lean operating system that boots from a hidden volume on the macOS startup disk and is used to troubleshoot macOS when startup errors occur.

rectifier An electrical device that converts AC to DC. A computer power supply contains a rectifier.

redundant power supply (RPS) Two power supplies fully capable of supplying the full power requirements of a system. Only one of the power supplies is used at a time; in case of failure, a seamless transition happens to the other power supply to prevent any disruption of power.

refresh rate As applied to monitors, the number of times in one second the monitor can fill the screen with lines from top to bottom. *Also called* vertical scan rate.

registry A database that Windows uses to store hardware and software configuration information, user preferences, and setup information.

Registry Editor The Windows utility (Regedit.exe) used to edit the Windows registry.

Regsvr32 A utility for registering component services used by an installed application.

regulated data Data that is protected by special governmental laws or regulations; industry must comply with these regulations or face penalties.

regulatory and compliance policies The governmental policies or rules that an industry must follow to protect regulated data.

regulatory compliance requirements Requirements as determined by laws and regulations, such as how personal identity data can be kept and used, that an IT organization is often responsible to enforce.

reimage A recovery technique that replaces the entire contents of a hard drive with whatever operating system state and personal data are saved in the system image used for the recovery.

reliability history *See* Reliability Monitor.

Reliability Monitor A Windows utility that provides information about problems and errors that happen over time. *Also called* reliability history.

Remote Admin share A default share that gives the Administrator user account access to the Windows folder on a remote computer in a Windows domain.

Remote Assistance A Windows tool that allows a technician to remote in to a user's computer while the user remains signed in, retains control of the session, and can see the screen. This is helpful when a technician is troubleshooting problems on a computer.

remote backup application A cloud backup service on the Internet that backs up data to the cloud and is often used for laptops, tablets, and smartphones.

Remote Desktop Connection (RDC) A Windows tool that gives a user access to a Windows desktop from anywhere on the Internet.

Remote Desktop Protocol (RDP) The Windows protocol used by Remote Desktop and Remote Assistance utilities to connect to and control a remote computer.

Remote Disc A feature of older macOS that gives other computers on the network access to the Mac's optical drive.

Remote Monitoring and Management (RMM) An application or suite of apps that monitors and manages remote computers so IT personnel can more easily support these systems. RMM software can monitor a system in real time, send alerts when problems arise, run scripts, and analyze and report system performance and reliability.

remote network installation An automated installation for which no user intervention is required.

remote printing Printing from a computer or mobile device to a printer that is not connected directly to the computer or device.

remote wipe An operation that remotely erases all contacts, email, photos, and other data from a device to protect your privacy.

ren (rename) The Windows command to rename a file or group of files.

repair installation A nondestructive installation of Windows over an existing Windows installation in which personal files, apps, and Windows settings are kept; the process can repair the existing installation. *Also called* a repair upgrade *or* in-place upgrade.

repair upgrade *See* repair installation.

repeater A networking device that amplifies and retransmits a wireless signal to a wider coverage area and uses a new network name for the rebroadcast.

request for comments (RFC) Feedback to a proposed change that is requested by an organization of its customers or users.

request form The media used to request that an update or change be made to a system supported by the IT department.

resiliency In Windows Storage Spaces, the degree to which the configuration can resist or recover from drive failure.

Resilient File System (ReFS) A file system that offers excellent fault tolerance and compatibility with virtualization and data redundancy in a RAID system; included in Windows 10 Pro for Workstations and Windows 11 Pro for Workstations, although the versions of ReFS in each OS are not the same.

resin A liquid photopolymer used by a 3D printer to build three-dimensional objects.

resolution The number of pixels on a monitor screen that are addressable by software (e.g., 1024 × 768 pixels).

Resource Monitor A Windows tool that monitors the performance of the processor, memory, hard drive, and network.

resource pooling Cloud computing services to multiple customers that are hosted on shared physical resources and dynamically allocated to meet customer demand.

resource record (RR) An individual entry, such as one that associates a host name with a given IP address, in a DNS database that is part of the DNS namespace; collected into zone files.

restore point A snapshot of the Windows system, usually made before installation of new hardware or applications; created by the System Protection utility.

Resultant Set of Policy (RsoP) A Windows command and console (rsop.msc) that displays the policies set for a computer or user.

retail license For Microsoft Windows, a license that can be purchased at the Microsoft online store (*microsoftstore.com*) and sent to the Microsoft account email address. The license follows the email address from one computer to another.

retinal scanning As part of the authentication process, some systems acquire biometric data by scanning the blood vessels on the back of the eye; this method is considered the most reliable of all biometric data scanning.

reverse lookup A way to find the host name when you know a computer's IP address. The Windows and Linux nslookup command can perform a reverse lookup.

revoked signature database (dbx) A Secure Boot database that is a blacklist of signatures for software that has been revoked and is no longer trusted.

RFID (radio-frequency identification) A wireless technology used on small tags that contain a microchip and antenna; often used to track and identify car keys, clothing, animals, and inventory.

RFID badge A badge worn by an employee and used to gain entrance into a locked area of a building. An RFID token transmits authentication to the system when the token gets within range of a query device.

RG-59 coaxial cable An older and thinner coaxial cable once used for cable TV.

RG-6 coaxial cable A coaxial cable used for cable TV that replaced the older and thinner RG-59 coaxial cable.

riser card A card that plugs into a motherboard and allows for expansion cards to be mounted parallel to the motherboard. Expansion cards are plugged into slots on the riser card.

risk analysis The process of identifying potential problems that might arise as a change plan is implemented; this process is done before the change begins.

risk level A numeric value assigned to a risk to measure the risk to help decide if the change is worth the risk involved.

RJ-11 A phone line connection or port found on modems, telephones, and house phone outlets. *Also called* RJ-11 port.

RJ-45 A port that looks like a large phone jack and is used with twisted-pair cable to connect to a wired network adapter or other hardware device. RJ stands for registered jack. *Also called* RJ-45 port *or* Ethernet port.

rm Command used to remove a file or directory in Linux/Unix operating systems.

rmdir The Windows command that removes or deletes a directory; the directory must be empty and cannot be the current working directory.

robocopy (robust file copy) A Windows command that is similar to and more powerful than the xcopy command; used to copy files and folders.

roll back updates The process of uninstalling a recent Windows update.

rollback plan A record of the activities needed to recover to the original state in the event a change must be aborted or has failed. *Also called* backout plan.

root account In Linux and macOS, the account that gives the user access to all the functions of the OS; the principal user account.

root certificate The original digital certificate issued by a Certificate Authority.

root directory The main directory, at the top of the top-down hierarchical structure of subdirectories, created when a hard drive or disk is first formatted. In Linux, it's indicated by a forward slash. In Windows, it's indicated by a backward slash.

rooting The process of obtaining root or administrator privileges to an Android device, which then gives you complete access to the entire file system and all commands and features.

rootkit A type of malicious software that loads itself before the OS boot is complete and can hijack internal OS components so that it masks information the OS provides to user-mode utilities such as Windows Explorer or Task Manager.

router A device that manages traffic between two or more networks and can help find the best path for traffic to get from one network to another.

RS-232 A 9-pin serial connector used with rack server consoles and older mice, keyboards, dial-up modems, and other peripherals.

run-time environment The environment provided by the operating system in which commands contained in a script file are interpreted and executed.

S.M.A.R.T. (Self-Monitoring Analysis and Reporting Technology) A BIOS/UEFI and hard drive feature that monitors hard drive performance, disk spin-up time, temperature, distance between the head and the disk, and other mechanical activities of the drive in order to predict when it is likely to fail.

S1 state On the BIOS/UEFI power screen, one of the five S states used by ACPI power-saving mode to indicate different levels of power-saving functions. In this state, the hard drive and monitor are turned off and everything else runs normally.

S2 state On the BIOS/UEFI power screen, one of the five S states used by ACPI power-saving mode to indicate different levels of power-saving functions. In this state, the hard drive and monitor are turned off and everything else runs normally. In addition, the processor is also turned off.

S3 state On the BIOS/UEFI power screen, one of the five S states used by ACPI power-saving mode to indicate different levels of power-saving functions. In this state, everything is shut down except RAM and enough of the system to respond to a wake-up. S3 is sleep mode.

S4 state On the BIOS/UEFI power screen, one of the five S states used by ACPI power-saving mode to indicate different levels of power-saving functions. In this state, everything in RAM is copied to a file on the hard drive, and the system is shut down. When the system is turned on, the file is used to restore the system to its state before shutdown. S4 is hibernation mode.

S5 state On the BIOS/UEFI power screen, one of the five S states used by ACPI power-saving mode to indicate different levels of power-saving functions. S5 is the power-off state after a normal shutdown.

SaaS (Software as a Service) A cloud computing service that delivers software applications to subscribers through a web interface rather than installing on their local machine. Microsoft 365 is an example.

Safe Mode The technique of launching Windows with a minimum configuration, eliminating third-party software, and reducing Windows startup to only essential processes. The technique can sometimes launch Windows when a normal Windows startup is corrupted.

safety goggles Eye goggles worn while working in an unsafe environment such as a factory, where fragments, chips, or other particles might cause eye injuries.

sag *See* brownout.

Samba The file and printer-sharing service used in Linux/Unix operating systems. Provides sharing between both the Linux and Unix systems and also in Windows environments.

SAN (storage area network) Specialized network segment used for storage of data and information using a high-speed connection.

sandbox An environment in which users and developers can practice or test with data and processes that don't affect the real data or system where mistakes have little consequence.

SATA (Serial Advanced Technology Attachment or Serial ATA) An interface standard used mostly by hard drives, optical drives, and other storage devices. Current SATA standards include SATA3, SATA2, and eSATA.

SATA Express An interface standard that uses a unique SATA connector and combines PCIe and SATA to improve on the performance of SATA Revision 3.x; three times faster than SATA Revision 3.x but not as fast as NVMe.

SATA power connector A 15-pin flat power connector that provides power to SATA drives.

satellite A network connection that connects a ground station with a satellite located in space.

SC (subscriber connector) A type of snap-in connector that can be used with either single-mode or multimode fiber-optic cables; not used with the fastest fiber-optic networking.

SCADA *See* supervisory control and data acquisition (SCADA).

scanstate A command used by the User State Migration Tool (USMT) to copy user settings and data from an old computer to a safe location such as a server or removable media. *Also see* loadstate.

scope of change Part of a change plan that defines (1) the key components of change and how they will be addressed; (2) the people, skills, tasks, and activities required to carry out the change; (3) how the results of the change will be measured; and (4) when the change is complete.

screen orientation The layout or orientation of the screen, which is either portrait or landscape.

screen resolution The number of dots or pixels on the monitor screen, expressed as two numbers, such as 1680 × 1050.

Screen Sharing In macOS, a utility to remotely view and control a Mac; similar to Remote Desktop in Windows.

screened subnet A group of networked computers in the same subnet that stands between the Internet and a more protected area of the corporate network; the two groups are separated by an interior router. *Sometimes called* a DMZ.

screensaver lock The OS process of locking down a computer before it goes to sleep; requires a password to unlock it before restoring the user session.

script A text file that contains a list of commands that can be interpreted and executed by the OS.

SCSI (Small Computer System Interface) An interface between a host adapter and the CPU that can daisy-chain as many as 7 or 15 devices on a single bus.

SD (Secure Digital) card A group of standards and flash memory storage cards that come in a variety of physical sizes, capacities, and speeds.

SDK (software development kit) A group of tools that developers use to write apps. For example, Android Studio is a free SDK that is released as open source.

secondary-click An action in macOS applied to an item on the macOS screen, such as displaying a shortcut menu for a file; similar to a right-click in Windows. By default, the action is a tap with two fingers on the Mac trackpad.

secondary logon Using administrator privileges to perform an operation when you are not logged on with an account that has these privileges.

sector On a hard disk drive or SSD, the smallest unit of bytes addressable by the operating system and BIOS/UEFI. On hard disk drives, one sector usually equals 512 bytes; SSDs might use larger sectors.

Secure Boot A UEFI and OS feature that prevents a system from booting up with drivers or an OS that is not digitally signed and trusted by the motherboard or computer manufacturer.

Secure Digital (SD) card A type of memory card used in digital cameras, tablets, cell phones, MP3 players, digital camcorders, and other portable devices. The three standards used by SD cards are 1.x (regular SD), 2.x (SD High Capacity or SDHC), and 3.x (SD eXtended Capacity or SDXC).

Secure DNS A security service offered by providers such as Comodo to interrupt a phishing attack by monitoring a browser's requests for websites and redirecting the browser when it attempts to visit a known malicious site. To implement Secure DNS, use the provider's DNS server addresses for your DNS service.

Secure FTP (SFTP) A TCP/IP protocol used to transfer files from an FTP server to an FTP client using encryption.

Secure Shell (SSH) A protocol and application that encrypts communication between a client and server and is used to pass login information to a remote Linux computer and control that computer over a network.

secured printing A security feature that allows documents to print confidentially by using a passcode at the printer to complete a print job.

security awareness training Training to help employees recognize common threats and social engineering situations. *Also called* anti-phishing training.

security fence A high wire-mesh fence installed in concrete footings with a secure gate that is difficult for someone to climb over or get under, around, or through.

security group In Active Directory, a group of users and/or computers within an organizational unit (OU).

security profile A set of policies and procedures that restrict how a student or employee can access, create, and edit the organization's resources.

security token A smart card or other device that is one factor in multifactor authentication or can serve as a replacement for a password.

self-grounding A method to safeguard against ESD that involves touching the computer case or power supply before touching a component in the computer case.

separation pad A printer part that keeps more than one sheet of paper from moving forward.

serial ATA (SATA) *See* SATA (Serial Advanced Technology Attachment or Serial ATA).

Serial Attached SCSI (SAS) An interface used mostly by storage devices; the successor of SCSI; typically used in servers and workstations.

serial port A male 9-pin or 25-pin port on a computer system used by slower I/O devices such as a mouse or modem. Data travels serially, one bit at a time, through the port. Serial ports are sometimes configured as COM1, COM2, COM3, or COM4. *Also called* DB-9 *or* DB9 port.

server lock A physical lock that prevents someone from opening the computer case of a server.

Server Manager A Windows Server console, also available in Windows 10/11, that contains the tools used to manage Active Directory.

Server Message Block (SMB) A protocol used by Windows to share files and printers on a network.

server-side virtualization Using this virtualization, a server provides a virtual desktop or application for users on multiple client machines.

service A program that runs in the background to support or serve Windows or an application.

service pack A collection of several patches or updates that is installed as a single update to an OS or application.

Service Set Identifier (SSID) The name of a wireless access point and wireless network.

Services console A console used by Windows to stop, start, and manage background services used by Windows and applications.

Settings app In Windows 10/11, an app to view and change many Windows settings.

setup BIOS/UEFI Firmware used to change motherboard settings. For example, you can use it to enable or disable a device on the motherboard, change the date and time that is later passed to the OS, and select the order of boot devices for startup BIOS/UEFI to search when looking for an operating system to load.

shadow copy A copy of open files made so that they are included in a backup.

share permissions A method to share a folder (not individual files) to remote users on the network, including assigning varying degrees of access to specific user accounts and user groups. These permissions do not apply to local users of a computer; they can be used on an NTFS or FAT volume. *Compare with* NTFS permissions.

shell The portion of an OS that relates to the user and applications.

shell prompt In Linux and macOS, the command prompt in the terminal.

shell script A text file of Linux commands that can be executed as a batch.

shielded twisted-pair (STP) cable *See* STP (shielded twisted-pair) cable.

Short Message Service (SMS) A technology that allows users to send a test message using a cell phone.

shoulder surfing As you work, other people secretly peeking at your monitor screen to gain valuable information.

shredder A device, such as a paper shredder or multimedia shredder, that destroys sensitive data by destroying the paper or storage device that holds the data.

shutdown The Windows or Linux command to shut down the local computer or a remote computer.

Side button The physical button on the upper-right side of an iPhone or iPad.

signature database (db) A Secure Boot database that holds a list of digital signatures of approved operating systems, applications, and drivers that can be loaded by UEFI.

SIM (subscriber identity module) card A small flash memory card that contains all the information a device needs to connect to a GSM or LTE cellular network, including a password and other authentication information needed to access the network, encryption standards used, and the services that a subscription includes.

SIMM (single inline memory module) An outdated miniature circuit board used to hold RAM. SIMMs held 8, 16, 32, or 64 MB on a single module. SIMMs have been replaced by DIMMs.

Simple Network Management Protocol (SNMP) *See* SNMP (Simple Network Management Protocol).

simple volume A type of volume used on a single hard drive. *Compare with* dynamic volume.

single channel The memory controller on a motherboard that can access only one DIMM at a time. *Compare with* dual channel, triple channel, *and* quad channel.

single-core processing An older processor technology whereby the processor housing contains a single processor or core that can process two threads at the same time. *Compare with* multicore processing.

single-sided A DIMM that has memory chips installed on one side of the module.

single sign-on (SSO) account An account that accesses multiple independent resources, systems, or applications after signing in one time to one account. An example is a Microsoft account.

site license A license that allows a company to install multiple copies of software or allows multiple employees to execute the software from a file server.

slack Wasted space on a hard drive caused by not using all available space at the end of a cluster.

sleep mode A power-saving state for a computer when it is not in use. *Also called* standby mode *or* suspend mode. *Also see* S3 state.

sleep timer The number of minutes of inactivity before a computer goes into a power-saving state such as sleep mode.

small form factor (SFF) A motherboard used in low-end computers and home theater systems; often used with an Intel Atom processor and sometimes purchased as a motherboard-processor combo unit.

smart camera A digital camera that has embedded computing power to make decisions about the content of the photos or videos it records, including transmitting alerts over a wired or wireless network when it records certain content. *Also called* a vision sensor.

smart card Any small device that contains authentication information that can be keyed into a sign-in window or read by a reader to authenticate a user on a network.

smart card reader A device that can read a smart card to authenticate a person onto a network.

smart speaker A speaker that includes voice-activated digital assistant software and connects by Wi-Fi or other wireless technology to the Internet.

smart TV A television that has the ability to run apps, store data, and connect to the Internet.

smartphone A cell phone that can send text messages with photos, videos, and other multimedia content, surf the web, manage email, play games, take photos and videos, and download and use small apps.

SMB (Server Message Block) A file access protocol originally developed by IBM and used by Windows to share files and printers on a network. The current SMB protocol is SMB3.

SMB Direct A feature of Windows 10/11 Pro for Workstations used to improve performance of file sharing on the network; uses the SMB protocol.

SMB2 *See* CIFS (Common Internet File System).

S/MIME (Secure/Multipurpose Internet Mail Extensions) A protocol that encrypts an outgoing email message and includes a digital signature; more secure than SMTP, which does not use encryption.

SMTP (Simple Mail Transfer Protocol) A TCP/IP protocol used by email clients to send email messages to an email server and on to the recipient's email server. *Also see* IMAP *and* POP.

SMTP AUTH (SMTP Authentication) An improved version of SMTP used to authenticate a user to an email server when the email client first tries to connect to the email server to send email. The protocol is based on the Simple Authentication and Security Layer (SASL) protocol.

snap-in A Windows utility that can be installed in a console window by Microsoft Management Console.

snapshot In macOS, a backup created by Time Machine that is stored on the hard drive when the computer is not connected to backup media and copied to backup media when connectivity is restored.

SNMP (Simple Network Management Protocol) A versatile TCP/IP protocol used to monitor network traffic and manage network devices. The SNMP server works with SNMP agents installed on devices being monitored.

social engineering The practice of tricking people into giving out private information or allowing unsafe programs into the network or computer.

socket (1) In computer hardware, a rectangular connector with pins or pads and a mechanism to hold the CPU in place; it is used to connect a CPU to the motherboard. (2) In networking, an established connection between a client and a server, such as the connection between a browser and web server.

SO-DIMM (small outline DIMM) A type of memory module for laptop computers that uses DIMM technology. A DDR4 SO-DIMM has 260 pins, and a DDR3 SO-DIMM has 204 pins.

soft boot To restart a computer without turning off the power; for example, in Windows 10/11, press Win+X, point to Shut down or Sign out, and click Restart. *Also called* warm boot.

soft reset (1) For Android, to forcefully reboot the device (full shutdown and cold boot) by pressing and holding the power button. (2) For iOS, to put the device in hibernation and not clear memory by pressing the wake/sleep button.

soft token Data that authenticates a user to gain access to a secured physical location or network. A smart card or key fob can hold a soft token.

software-defined networking (SDN) A network management concept in which a network-wide software controller makes dynamic and efficient decisions about the configurations and routing of data rather than relying on the networking hardware to do so.

software piracy The act of making unauthorized copies of original software, which violates the Federal Copyright Act of 1976.

software RAID Using Windows to implement RAID. The setup is done using the Disk Management utility. *Compare with* hardware RAID.

software token An app or digital certificate that serves as authentication to a computer or network.

solid-state device (SSD) An electronic storage device with no moving parts that uses memory chips to store data instead of spinning disks (such as those used by magnetic hard drives and optical drives). Examples are jump drives (also known as key drives or thumb drives), flash memory cards, and solid-state disks used as hard drives in notebook computers designed for the most rugged uses. *Also called* solid-state disk (SSD) *or* solid-state drive (SSD). *Compare with* magnetic hard drive.

solid-state drive (SSD) *See* solid-state device (SSD).

Sound applet An applet accessed through Control Panel to select a default speaker and microphone and adjust how Windows handles sounds.

sound card An expansion card with sound ports.

South Bridge The portion of the chipset hub that connects slower I/O buses (e.g., a PCI bus) to the system bus. *Compare with* North Bridge.

Space In macOS, one desktop screen. Multiple desktops or Spaces can be open and available to users.

spacer *See* standoff.

spanning A configuration of two hard drives that hold a single Windows volume to increase the size of the volume. *Sometimes called* JBOD (just a bunch of disks).

SPDIF (Sony-Phillips Digital InterFace) sound port A port that connects to an external home theater audio system, providing digital audio output and the best signal quality.

spear phishing A form of phishing in which an email message appears to come from a company you already do business with.

SPF (Sender Policy Framework) record A TXT record in the DNS namespace used to combat email spoofing by informing a recipient's email server which email servers can send email from the given domain.

splash screen The first screen a user sees when opening an app. *Also called* a launch screen.

spoofing Tricking someone into thinking an imitation of a website or email message is legitimate. For example, a phishing technique tricks you into clicking a link in an email message, which takes you to an official-looking website where you are asked to enter your user ID and password to access the site.

spooling Placing print jobs in a queue so that an application can be released from the printing process before printing is completed. Spool is an acronym for simultaneous peripheral operations online.

Spotlight In macOS, the search app that can be configured to search the local computer, Wikipedia, iTunes, the Maps app, the web, and more.

spudger A metal or plastic flat-head wedge used to pry open casings without damaging plastic connectors and cases when disassembling a notebook, tablet, or mobile device.

spyware Malicious software that installs itself on your computer or mobile device to spy on you. It collects personal information about you and transmits it over the Internet to web-hosting sites that intend to use the information for harm.

SQL injection A hacking technique where part of a user's typed text is used to construct an SQL query to change the query in a malicious way.

SSD (solid-state drive or solid-state device) *See* solid-state device (SSD).

SSH (Secure Shell) protocol *See* Secure Shell (SSH).

SSID (Service Set Identifier) *See* Service Set Identifier (SSID).

SSO (single sign-on) *See* single sign-on (SSO).

ST (straight tip) connector A type of connector that can be used with either single-mode or multimode fiber-optic cables. The connector does not support full-duplex transmissions and is not used on the fastest fiber-optic systems.

standard account The Windows user account type that can use software and hardware and make some system changes but cannot make changes that affect the security of the system or other users. *Compare with* administrator account.

standard format *See* high-level formatting.

standard image An image that includes Windows, drivers, applications, and data, which are standard to all the computers that might use the image.

standard operating procedures Documented details of procedures regarding how to function in an organization.

standby mode *See* sleep mode.

standoff Round plastic or metal pegs that separate the motherboard from the case so that components on the back of the motherboard do not touch the case.

startup BIOS/UEFI Part of UEFI or BIOS firmware on the motherboard that is responsible for controlling the computer when it is first turned on; gives control to the OS once the OS is loaded.

startup disk In macOS, the entire volume on which macOS is installed.

startup items In macOS, programs that automatically launch at startup. Apple discourages the use of startup items, which are stored in two directories: /Library/StartupItems and /System/Library/StartupItems. Normally, both directories are empty.

Startup Repair A Windows 10/11 utility that restores many of the Windows files needed for a successful boot.

static electricity *See* electrostatic discharge (ESD).

static IP address A permanent IP address that is manually assigned to a computer or other device.

static RAM (SRAM) RAM chips that retain information without the need for refreshing, as long as the computer's power is on; more expensive than traditional DRAM.

storage area network *See* SAN (storage area network).

storage card An adapter card used to manage hardware RAID rather than using the firmware on the motherboard.

Storage Spaces A Windows utility that can create a storage pool using any number of internal or external backup drives.

STP (shielded twisted-pair) cable A cable that is made of one or more twisted pairs of wires and is surrounded by a metal shield. *Compare with* UTP (unshielded twisted-pair) cable.

straight-through cable An Ethernet cable used to connect a computer to a switch or other network device. *Also called* a patch cable.

string In scripting and programming, a type of data that can contain any character but cannot be used for calculations.

striped volume The term used by Windows for RAID 0, a type of dynamic volume used for two or more hard drives; writes to the disks evenly rather than filling up allotted space on one and then moving on to the next. *Compare with* spanned volume. *Also see* RAID 0.

striping *See* RAID 0.

strong password A password that is not easy to guess.

Structured Query Language (SQL) A popular scripting and programming language designed primarily to query a database.

sTRX4 socket A type of CPU socket used with AMD Threadripper processors and the TRX40 chipset, typically used in high-end systems. The socket has 4094 pins in a land grid array.

stylus   A device that is included with a graphics tablet and works like a pencil on the tablet.

su   A Linux and macOS command to open a new terminal shell for a different user account; stands for substitute user.

subdirectory   A directory or folder contained in another directory or folder. *Also called* a child directory *or* folder.

subnet   A group of local networks tied together in a subsystem of the larger intranet. In TCP/IP version 6, a subnet is one or more links that have the same 16 bits in the subnet ID of the IP address. *See* subnet ID.

subnet ID   In TCP/IP version 6, the last block (16 bits) in the 64-bit prefix of an IP address. The subnet is identified using some or all of these 16 bits.

subnet mask   In TCP/IP version 4, 32 bits that include a series of ones followed by zeroes—for example, 11111111.11111111.11110000.0000 0000, which can be written as 255.255.240.0. The 1s identify the network portion of an IP address, and the 0s identify the host portion of an IP address. The subnet mask tells Windows if a remote computer is on the same or different network.

subscription model   A method of licensing software with a paid annual subscription and the software is installed on your local computer. Microsoft 365 uses a subscription model.

sudo   A Linux and macOS command to execute another command as a superuser when logged in as a normal user with an account that has the right to use root commands; stands for substitute user to do the command.

superuser   A user who is logged in to the root account.

supervisory control and data acquisition (SCADA)   A control system used in industrial environments to control and supervise machines and processes for machinery plants.

surge protector   A device that protects against voltage spikes by blocking or grounding excessive voltage. *Also called* surge suppressor.

surge suppressor   *See* surge protector.

suspend mode   *See* sleep mode.

S-Video port   A 4-pin or 7-pin round video port that sends two signals over the cable, one for color and the other for brightness; used by some high-end TVs and video equipment.

swap partition   A partition on a Linux hard drive used to hold virtual memory.

swapfile   In macOS, the file used to hold virtual memory, similar to pagefile.sys in Windows.

switch   A device used to connect nodes on a network in a star network topology. When it receives a packet, it uses its table of MAC addresses to decide where to send the packet.

Sync Center   A Control Panel applet that allows two computers to sync the contents of a shared folder or volume.

synchronization app   An app on a mobile device or other computer to sync data and settings to cloud storage accounts such as Google Cloud and iCloud and between devices.

synchronous DRAM (SDRAM)   The first DIMM to run synchronized with the system clock; it has two notches and uses 168 pins.

synthetic   When recovering a file, folder, or volume from backups, the reconstructed backup that is created from the latest full backup and any incremental or differential backups that contain data more current than the full backup.

syslog   A protocol that collects event information about network devices, such as errors, failures, and users logging in or out, and sends the information to a syslog server.

syslog server   A server that receives and analyzes syslog data to monitor network devices and create alerts when problems arise that need attention.

system BIOS/UEFI   UEFI (Unified Extensible Firmware Interface) or BIOS (basic input/output system) firmware on the motherboard that is used to control essential devices before the OS is loaded.

system board   *See* motherboard.

system bus   The bus between the CPU and memory on the motherboard. The bus frequency in documentation is called the system speed, such as 400 MHz. *Also called* the memory bus, FrontSide Bus, local bus, *or* host bus.

system clock   A line on a bus that is dedicated to timing the activities of components connected to it; provides a continuous pulse that other devices use to time themselves.

System Configuration   A Windows utility (Msconfig.exe) that can identify what processes are launched at startup and can temporarily disable a process from loading.

System File Checker (SFC)   A Windows utility that verifies and, if necessary, refreshes a Windows system file, replacing it with one kept in a cache of current system files or downloaded from the Internet with the help of Windows Updates.

system image   The backup of the entire Windows volume; it can also include backups of other volumes. The system image works only on the computer that created it, and it is created using Windows File History or the Windows Backup and Restore utility.

System Information   A Windows tool (Msinfo32.exe) that provides details about a system, including installed hardware and software, the current system configuration, and currently running programs.

system partition   The active partition of the hard drive, which contains the boot loader or boot manager program and the specific files required to start the Windows launch.

System Preferences   In macOS, a utility to customize the macOS interface; it is available on the Apple menu.

System Protection   A utility that automatically backs up system files and stores them in restore points on the hard drive at regular intervals and just before you install software or hardware.

system repair disc   A disc you can create in Windows 10/11 to launch Windows RE.

System Restore   A Windows utility used to restore the system to a restore point.

system state data   In Windows, the files that are necessary for a successful load of the operating system.

system tray   *See* notification area.

systray   *See* notification area.

T568A   Standards for wiring twisted-pair network cabling and RJ-45 connectors; in T568A, the green pair of wires is connected to pins 1 and 2, and the orange pair is connected to pins 3 and 6.

T568B   Standards for wiring twisted-pair network cabling and RJ-45 connectors; in T568B, the orange pair of wires uses pins 1 and 2, and the green pair is connected to pins 3 and 6.

tablet   A computing device with a touch screen that is larger than a smartphone and with functions similar to a smartphone.

TACACS+ (Terminal Access Controller Access Control System Plus)   A Cisco AAA service specifically designed for network administrators to remotely connect to a network and configure and manage Cisco routers, switches, firewalls, and other network devices. The service authenticates, authorizes, and tracks activity on the network and can work with Active Directory.

tailgating   When an unauthorized person follows an employee through a secured entrance to a room or building.

tap pay device   A device in a point-of-sale system that uses an encrypted wireless NFC connection to read and send payment information from a customer's smartphone to a vendor's account.

Task Manager   A Windows utility (Taskmgr.exe) that lets you view the applications and processes running on your computer as well as information about process and memory performance, network activity, and user activity.

Task Scheduler   A Windows tool that can set a task or program to launch at a future time, including at startup.

Task View   A Windows 10/11 feature used to create and manage multiple desktops.

taskbar   A bar normally located at the bottom of the Windows desktop that displays information about open programs and provides quick access to others.

taskkill   A Windows command that uses the process identifier (PID), a number that identifies each running process, to kill a process.

tasklist   A Windows command that returns the process identifier (PID), which is a number that identifies each running process.

TCP (Transmission Control Protocol)   The protocol in the TCP/IP suite of protocols that works at the OSI Transport layer, establishes a session or connection between parties, and guarantees packet delivery.

TCP/IP (Transmission Control Protocol/Internet Protocol)   The group or suite of protocols used for almost all networks, including the Internet. Fundamentally, TCP is responsible for error-checking transmissions and IP is responsible for routing.

TCP/IP model   In networking theory, a simple model used to divide network communication into four layers; simpler than the OSI model, which uses seven layers.

technical documentation   Digital or printed technical reference manuals that are included with software packages and hardware to provide directions for installation, usage, and troubleshooting. The information extends beyond that given in user manuals.

Telnet   A TCP/IP protocol and application used to allow an administrator or other user to control a computer remotely.

Teredo   In TCP/IP version 6, a tunneling protocol to transmit TCP/IPv6 packets over a TCP/IPv4 network; named after the Teredo worm that bores holes in wood. Teredo IP addresses begin with 2001, and the prefix is written as 2001::/32.

terminal In Linux, macOS, and now Windows 11, the command-line interface. In macOS, the terminal is accessed through the Terminal utility in the Applications group of the Finder window.

test access point (TAP) *See* network tap.

test development Experimentation with software application, hardware system configurations, or other technology before implementation to production systems.

tether To connect a computer to a mobile device that has an Internet cellular connection so that the computer can access the Internet by way of the mobile device.

theft-prevention plate A plate embedded into a computer case or other valuable device, engraved with identifying information, and used to identity the owner of stolen equipment.

thermal compound *See* thermal paste.

thermal pad A thick pad that is used as an alternative to thermal paste; more easily applied but still allows for unwanted air gaps between the bottom of the cooler heat sink and the top of the processor.

thermal paper Special coated paper used by thermal printers.

thermal paste A creamlike substance that is placed between the bottom of the cooler heat sink and the top of the processor to eliminate air pockets and help draw heat off the processor. *Also called* thermal compound.

thermal printer A type of line printer that uses wax-based ink, which is heated by heat pins that melt the ink onto paper.

thermal transfer printer A type of thermal printer that uses a ribbon containing wax-based ink. The heating element melts the ribbon onto special thermal paper so that it stays glued to the paper as the feeder assembly moves the paper through the printer.

thick client A regular desktop computer or laptop that is sometimes used as a client by a virtualization server. *Also called* fat client. *Compare with* thin client.

thin client A computer that has an operating system but little computing power and might only need to support a browser used to communicate with a virtualization server. *Compare with* thick client.

third-party drivers Drivers that are not included in BIOS/UEFI or Windows and must come from the manufacturer.

thread Each process that the processor is aware of; a thread is a single task that is part of a larger task or request from a program.

throughput A measurement of the amount of data that flows through a point in the data path over one second's time. Usually measured in MB/sec.

Thunderbolt *See* Thunderbolt 3 port.

Thunderbolt 3 port A multipurpose standard and connector used for communication and power. Early versions were limited to Apple products and used a modified DisplayPort; can use modified USB-C ports on Apple and non-Apple devices.

Thunderbolt 4 A multipurpose standard and connector used for communication and power with speeds up to 40 Gbps and cables up to 2 meters in length. Requires a USB-C connector.

ticket An entry in a call tracking system made by the person who receives a call for help; used to track and document actions taken and stays open until the issue is resolved.

ticketing system In an IT organization, a system used to track support calls and in which technicians can keep their call notes.

time drift When a Windows system does not report accurate time to a time-sensitive application that requires accuracy in milliseconds.

Time Machine In macOS, a built-in backup utility that can be configured to automatically back up user-created data, applications, and system files to an external hard drive attached either directly to the computer or the local network.

TKIP (Temporal Key Integrity Protocol) A type of encryption protocol used by WPA to secure a wireless Wi-Fi network. *Also see* WPA (Wi-Fi Protected Access).

tone generator and probe A two-part kit used to find cables in the walls of a building. The toner connects to one end of the cable and puts out a pulsating tone that the probe can sense. *Also called* a toner probe *or* tone probe.

toner vacuum A vacuum cleaner designed to pick up toner used in laser printers; the toner is not allowed to touch any conductive surface.

top The command used to display Linux processes that are running on the system.

topology In networking, the physical or logical pattern or design used to connect devices on a network.

touch pad A common pointing device on a notebook computer.

tower case The largest type of personal computer case; stands vertically and can be up to two feet tall. Tower cases have more drive bays and are a good choice for computer users who anticipate making significant upgrades.

TPM (Trusted Platform Module) A chip on a motherboard that holds an encryption key required at startup to access encrypted data on the hard drive. Windows BitLocker Encryption can use the TPM chip.

TR4 (Threadripper 4) socket A land grid array socket for AMD Ryzen processors and X399 chipsets. The socket is used with high-end AMD processors.

trace A wire on a circuit board that connects two components or devices.

tracert (trace route) A TCP/IP command that enables you to resolve a connectivity problem when attempting to reach a destination host such as a website.

track One of many concentric circles on the surface of a hard disk drive.

tractor feed A continuous feed within an impact printer that feeds fanfold paper through the printer rather than individual sheets; this format is useful for logging ongoing events or data.

transfer belt A laser printer component that completes the transferring step in the printer.

transfer roller A soft, black roller in a laser printer that puts a positive charge on the paper. The charge pulls the toner from the drum onto the paper.

transformer An electrical device that changes the ratio of current to voltage. A computer power supply is basically a transformer and a rectifier.

trim To erase entire blocks of unused data on an SSD so that write operations do not have to manage the data.

trip hazard Loose cables or cords in a traffic area where people can trip over them.

triple A *See* AAA (authenticating, authorizing, and accounting).

triple channels When the memory controller accesses three DIMMs at the same time. DDR3 DIMMs support triple channeling.

Trivial FTP (TFTP) A small, simple application used to transfer files and often used to transfer BIOS updates to firmware.

Trojan A type of malware that tricks you into downloading and/or opening it by substituting itself for a legitimate program.

Troubleshooting applet A Control Panel applet used to automatically troubleshoot and fix many common Windows problems involving applications, hardware, sound, networking, Windows updates, and maintenance tasks.

trusted source A source for downloading software that is considered reliable, such as app stores provided by a mobile device manufacturer and websites of well-known software manufacturers.

tunneling A technique used by a VPN or other utility to move data from one network to another through a process called encapsulation; in the example of a VPN, the data is encrypted from end to end.

twisted nematic (TN) A class of LCD monitor that has fast response times to keep fast-moving images crisper. TN monitors are brighter, consume more power, and have limited viewing angles.

twisted-pair cabling Cabling, such as a network cable, that uses pairs of wires twisted together to reduce crosstalk.

two-factor authentication (2FA) When two tokens or actions are required to authenticate to a computer or network. Factors can include what a person knows (password), what they possess (a token such as a key fob or smart card), what they do (such as typing a certain way), or who they are (biometric data).

TXT (Text) record A type of DNS record in the DNS namespace that is a general-purpose record used to insert text into the DNS namespace.

Type 1 hypervisor Software to manage virtual machines that is installed before any operating system is installed.

Type 2 hypervisor Software to manage virtual machines that is installed as an application in an operating system.

UDF (Universal Disk Format) A file system for optical media used by all DVDs and some CD-Rs and CD-RWs.

UDP (User Datagram Protocol) A connectionless TCP/IP protocol that works at the OSI Transport layer and does not require a connection to send a packet or guarantee that the packet arrives at its destination. The protocol is commonly used for broadcasting to multiple nodes on a network or the Internet. *Compare with* TCP (Transmission Control Protocol).

UEFI (Unified Extensible Firmware Interface) *See* Unified Extensible Firmware Interface (UEFI).

unattended installation A Windows installation in which answers to installation questions are stored in a file that Windows calls so that they do not have to be typed in during the installation.

unicast address Using TCP/IP version 6, an IP address assigned to a single node on a network.

Unified Extensible Firmware Interface (UEFI) An interface between firmware on the motherboard and the operating system; improves on legacy BIOS processes for managing motherboard settings, booting, handing over the boot to the OS, loading device drivers and applications before the OS loads, and securing the boot to ensure that no rogue operating system hijacks the system.

unified threat management (UTM) A computer, security appliance, network appliance, or Internet appliance that stands between the Internet and a private network; a UTM device runs a firewall, anti-malware software, and other software to protect the network and is considered a next-generation firewall.

uninterruptible power supply (UPS) A device that raises the voltage when it drops during brownouts.

unique local address (ULA) In TCP/IP version 6, an address used to identify a specific site within a large organization. It can work on multiple links within the same organization. The address is a hybrid between a global unicast address that works on the Internet and a link local unicast address that works on only one link.

Universal Plug and Play (UPnP) *See* UPnP (Universal Plug and Play).

unlicensed frequency A frequency that is not assigned for a particular radio frequency application. Frequency is normally not governed or managed by any governing body.

unmanaged switch A switch that requires no setup or configuration. *Compare with* managed switch.

unshielded twisted-pair (UTP) cable *See* UTP (unshielded twisted-pair) cable.

upgrade path A qualifying OS required by Microsoft in order to perform an in-place upgrade.

UPnP (Universal Plug and Play) A feature of a SOHO router that enables computers on the local network to have unfiltered communication so they can automatically discover services provided by other computers on the network; considered a security risk because hackers might exploit the vulnerability created when computers advertise their services on the network.

USB (Universal Serial Bus) Multipurpose bus and connector standards used for internal and external ports for a variety of devices. Current USB standards are USB4 and USB versions 3.2, 3.1, 3.0, and 2.0.

USB 2.0 A version of USB that runs at 480 Mbps and uses cables up to 5 meters long. *Also called* Hi-Speed USB.

USB 3.0 A version of USB that runs at 5 Gbps and uses cables up to 3 meters long. *Also called* SuperSpeed USB.

USB 3.0 B-Male connector A USB connector used by SuperSpeed USB 3.0 devices such as printers or scanners.

USB 3.0 Micro-B connector A small USB connector used by SuperSpeed USB 3.0 devices. The connectors are not compatible with regular Micro-B connectors.

USB 3.1 A version of USB that runs at 10 Gbps and uses cables up to 3 meters long. *Also called* SuperSpeed+ USB.

USB 3.2 A version of USB that runs at 20 Gbps and uses cables up to 1 meter long. *Also called* SuperSpeed+ USB.

USB4 A version of USB that runs at 40 Gbps and uses cables up to 1 meter long with only USB-C connectors.

USB-C A USB connector that is flat with rounded sides used by smartphones and tablets. The connector is required for USB4 and USB 3.2 devices to attain maximum speeds.

USB lock A type of port lock used to control access to a USB port on a computer.

USB optical drive An external optical drive that connects to a computer via a USB port.

USB port A type of port designed to make installation and configuration of I/O devices easy; provides room for as many as 127 devices daisy-chained together.

USB power share A USB port feature that allows a USB device to charge even when the computer is turned off.

USB selective suspend setting A Windows power setting that controls the power state of USB ports when they are not in use; disabling this setting can sometimes solve problems with unreliable USB ports.

USB to Bluetooth adapter A device that plugs into a USB port on a computer to connect to Bluetooth devices.

USB to RJ-45 dongle An adapter that plugs into a USB port and provides an RJ-45 port for a network cable to connect to a wired network.

USB to Wi-Fi dongle An adapter that plugs into a USB port and provides wireless connectivity to a Wi-Fi network.

USB wake support A USB port feature that allows a USB device to wake a computer on action.

User Account Control (UAC) dialog box A Windows security feature that displays a dialog box when an event requiring administrative privileges is about to happen.

User Accounts A Windows utility (netplwiz.exe) that can be used to change the way Windows sign-in works and to manage user accounts, including changing passwords and changing the group membership of an account. *Also called* Network Places Wizard.

user mode In Windows, a mode that provides an interface between an application and the OS, and only has access to hardware resources through the code running in kernel mode.

user profile A collection of files and settings about a user account that enables the user's personal data, desktop settings, and other operating parameters to be retained from one session to another.

user profile namespace The group of folders and subfolders in the C:\Users folder that belong to a specific user account and contain the user profile.

User State Migration Tool (USMT) A Windows utility that helps you migrate user files and preferences between computers to help a user make a smooth transition from one computer to another. *Also see* usmtutils.

Users group A type of Windows user account group. An account in this group is a standard user account, which does not have as many rights as an administrator account.

usmtutils A command used by the User State Migration Tool (USMT) that provides encryption options and hard-link management.

UTM (unified threat management) *See* unified threat management (UTM).

UTP (unshielded twisted-pair) cable Twisted-pair networking cable commonly used on LANs that is less expensive than STP cable and does not contain shielding to prevent electromagnetic interference. *Compare with* STP (shielded twisted-pair) cable.

variable The name of one item of data used in a script or program.

VBScript A scripting language that creates scripts modeled after the more complex Visual Basic programming language. VBScripts have a .vbs file extension.

VDI (virtual desktop infrastructure) *See* virtual desktop infrastructure (VDI).

vertical alignment (VA) A class of LCD monitor that is a compromise between TN and IPS monitors; ideally used for general use and in TVs.

VGA (Video Graphics Adapter) port A 15-pin analog video port popular for many years. *Also called* DB-15, DB15 port, DE15 port, or HD15 port.

vi editor In Linux and macOS, a text editor that works in command mode (to enter commands) or in insert mode (to edit text).

video capture card An adapter card that captures video input and saves it to a file on the hard drive. *Also see* capture card.

video memory Memory used by the video controller. The memory might be contained on a video card or be part of system memory. When it is part of system memory, the memory is dedicated by Windows to video.

video surveillance A security system that includes cameras installed in strategic locations that monitor for improper activity.

virtual assistant *See* digital assistant.

virtual desktop When a hypervisor manages a virtual machine and presents the VM's desktop to a user. A remote user normally views and manages the virtual desktop via a browser on the local computer.

virtual desktop infrastructure (VDI) A presentation of a virtual desktop made to a client computer by a hypervisor on a server in the cloud.

virtual LAN (VLAN) A subnet of a larger network created to reduce network traffic. Managed switches are commonly used to set up VLANs.

virtual machine (VM) Software managed by a hypervisor that simulates the hardware of a physical computer, creating one or more logical machines within one physical machine.

virtual memory A method whereby the OS uses the hard drive as though it were RAM. *Also see* pagefile.sys.

Virtual Network Computing (VNC) A client/server application used to remotely control the server computer; includes file transfers and screen sharing, useful for virtual desktop support.

virtual NIC A network adapter created by a hypervisor that is used by a virtual machine and emulates a physical NIC.

virtual private network (VPN) A security technique that uses encrypted data packets between a private network and a computer somewhere on the Internet.

virtual RAM   *See* virtual memory.

virtualization   When one physical machine hosts multiple activities that are normally done on multiple machines.

virtualization server   A computer that serves up virtual machines to multiple client computers and provides a virtual desktop for users on these client machines.

virus   A program that often has an incubation period, is infectious, and is intended to cause damage, such as destroying data and programs.

vishing   Phishing with voice; a phone call scam trying to lure you into giving out personal information.

vision sensor   *See* smart camera.

VM (virtual machine)   *See* virtual machine (VM).

VoIP (Voice over Internet Protocol)   A TCP/IP protocol and an application that provides voice communication over a TCP/IP network. *Also called* Internet telephone.

volt (V)   A measure of potential difference or electrical force in an electrical circuit. A computer ATX power supply usually provides five separate voltages: +12 V, −12 V, +5 V, −5 V, and +3.3 V.

volume   A primary partition that has been assigned a drive letter and can be formatted with a file system such as NTFS. *Compare with* logical drive.

VPN (virtual private network)   *See* virtual private network (VPN).

wait state   A clock tick in which nothing happens; it is used to ensure that the microprocessor isn't getting ahead of slower components. A 0-wait state is preferable to a 1-wait state. Too many wait states can slow down a system.

wake-on-LAN   Configuring a computer so that it will respond to network activity when the computer is in a sleep state. *Also called* WoL.

WAN (wide area network)   A network or group of networks that span a large geographical area.

WAP (wireless access point)   *See* wireless access point (WAP).

warm boot   *See* soft boot.

watt (W)   The unit of electricity used to measure power. A typical computer may use a power supply that provides 500W.

wear leveling   A technique used on a solid-state drive that ensures the logical block addressing does not always address the same physical blocks; this technique distributes write operations more evenly across the device.

web server   A server application using HTTP protocols that sends webpages to a browser or other client application when the client requests the page.

WEP (Wired Equivalent Privacy)   An encryption protocol used to secure transmissions on a Wi-Fi wireless network; however, it is no longer considered secure because the key used for encryption is static (it doesn't change).

whaling   A phishing attack that targets a high-profile employee, such as the CEO or CFO.

whitelist   In filtering, a list of items that is allowed through the filter—for example, a list of websites that computers on a local network are allowed to access. *Compare with* blacklist.

Wi-Fi (Wireless Fidelity)   The common name for standards for a local wireless network, as defined by IEEE 802.11. *Also see* 802.11 a/b/g/n/ac/ax.

Wi-Fi 4   The new naming standard for 802.11n-compliant devices.

Wi-Fi 5   The new naming standard for 802.11ac-compliant devices.

Wi-Fi 6   The new naming standard for 802.11ax-compliant devices.

Wi-Fi analyzer   Hardware and/or software that monitors a Wi-Fi network to detect devices not authorized to use the network, identify attempts to hack transmissions, or detect performance and security vulnerabilities.

Wi-Fi Protected Setup (WPS)   A method to make it easier for users to connect their computers to a secured wireless network when a hard-to-remember SSID and security key are used; considered a security risk that should be used with caution.

wildcard   An * or ? character used in a command line that represents a character or group of characters in a file name or extension.

Windows   The most popular operating system for desktop and laptop computers, made by Microsoft.

Windows 10   Currently, the most popular Microsoft operating system for personal computers and tablets, although Windows 11 is the latest Microsoft operating system.

Windows 10 Enterprise   An edition of Windows 10 that allows for volume licensing and has additional security features over Windows Pro, including Windows Defender Credential Guard. Windows 11 Enterprise is similar to Windows 10 Enterprise.

Windows 10 Home An edition of Windows 10 intended for laptops and desktop computers used in a home or small office that don't require features needed in a corporate or enterprise environment. Windows 11 Home is similar to Windows 10 Home; one exception is a Microsoft account is required to install Windows 11 Home.

Windows 10 Pro An edition of Windows 10 that adds to Windows 10 Home features designed to work in corporate settings, including the ability to join a Windows domain. Windows 11 Pro is similar to Windows 10 Pro.

Windows 10 Pro for Workstations An edition of Windows 10 that adds to Windows 10 Pro features to improve performance. Windows 11 Pro for Workstations is similar to Windows 10 Pro for Workstations.

Windows Boot Loader One of two programs that manage the loading of Windows 10/11. The program file (winload.exe or winload.efi) is stored in C:\Windows\System32, and it loads and starts essential Windows processes.

Windows Boot Manager (BootMgr) The Windows program that manages the initial startup of Windows. For a BIOS system, the program is bootmgr; for a UEFI system, the program is bootmgfw.efi. The program file is stored in the root of the system partition.

Windows Defender Anti-malware software embedded in Windows 10 that can detect viruses, prevent them, and clean up a system infected with viruses and other malware. In Windows 11, a similar tool is called Microsoft Defender Antivirus.

Windows Defender Firewall A personal firewall in Windows that protects a computer from intrusion and is automatically configured when you set your network location in the Network and Sharing Center.

Windows Defender Offline (WDO) Scanning software available in Windows 10/11 or downloaded from the Microsoft website that launches before Windows to scan a system for malware; works in the WinPE environment.

Windows.old folder When using an unformatted hard drive for a clean installation, this folder is created to store the previous Windows operating system settings and user profiles.

Windows pinwheel A Windows graphic that indicates the system is waiting for a response from a program or device.

Windows Preinstallation Environment (Windows PE) A minimum operating system used to start a Windows installation. *Also called* WinPE.

Windows Recovery Environment (Windows RE) A lean operating system installed on the Windows 10/11 setup media and on the Windows volume that can be used to troubleshoot problems when Windows refuses to start.

Windows Time Service (W32Time) A Windows Server service on a Windows domain that uses the Network Time Protocol (NTP) to report the time accurate to within one millisecond when requested by a client computer.

Windows Tools A group of Windows 11 tools accessed through Control Panel and used to manage the local computer or other computers on the network. In Windows 10, the same group of tools is called Administrative Tools.

winver A Windows command that displays the About Windows box containing information about the Windows edition, latest update installed, and registered owner of the computer.

wire stripper A tool used when terminating a cable. The tool cuts away the plastic jacket or coating around the wires in a cable so that a connector can be installed on the end of the cable.

wireless access point (WAP) A wireless device that is used to create and manage a wireless network.

wireless Internet service provider (WISP) Internet service provider that connects customers to the Internet using high-powered wireless antennas.

wireless LAN *See* WLAN (wireless local area network).

WLAN (wireless local area network) A type of LAN that does not use wires or cables to create connections but instead transmits data over radio or infrared waves.

workgroup In Windows, a logical group of computers and users in which administration, resources, and security are distributed throughout the network without centralized management or security.

worm An infestation designed to copy itself repeatedly to memory, drive space, or a network until little memory, disk space, or network bandwidth remains.

WPA (Wi-Fi Protected Access) A data encryption method for wireless networks that uses the TKIP (Temporal Key Integrity Protocol) encryption method. The encryption keys are changed at set intervals while the wireless LAN is in use. WPA is stronger than WEP.

WPA2 (Wi-Fi Protected Access 2) A data encryption standard compliant with the IEEE802.11i standard that uses the AES (Advanced Encryption Standard) protocol.

WPA3 (Wi-Fi Protected Access 3) A standard that offers improved data encryption over WPA2 and allows for Individual Data Encryption, whereby a laptop or other wireless device can create a secure connection over a public, unsecured Wi-Fi network.

wpeinit The Windows command that initializes Windows PE and enables networking. *Also see* Windows Preinstallation Environment (Windows PE).

WPS (Wi-Fi Protected Setup) *See* Wi-Fi Protected Setup (WPS).

x86 processor An older processor that first used the number 86 in the model number; it processes 32 bits at a time.

x86-64 bit processor A hybrid processor that can process 32 bits or 64 bits.

XaaS (Anything as a Service or Everything as a Service) An open-ended cloud computing service that can provide any combination of functions depending on a customer's exact needs.

xcopy A Windows command more powerful than the copy command that is used to copy files and folders.

XPS Document Writer A Windows feature that creates a file with an .xps file extension. The file is similar to a PDF and can be viewed, edited, printed, faxed, emailed, or posted on websites.

XQD card A flash memory device used in high-end cameras. Successor to CF cards; succeeded by CFexpress cards.

yum The primary command used to retrieve, install, and delete applications and updates for Red Hat Enterprise Linux distributions.

zero insertion force (ZIF) connector A connector that uses a lever or latch to prevent force from being used on a sensitive connection; stands for zero insertion force.

zero insertion force (ZIF) socket A processor socket with one or two levers on the sides that are used to move the processor out of or into the socket so that equal force is applied over the entire socket housing.

zero-day attack An attack in which a hacker discovers and exploits a security hole in software before its developer can provide a protective patch to close the hole.

zero-fill utility A hard drive utility that fills every sector on the drive with zeroes.

ZIF (zero insertion force) connector *See* zero insertion force (ZIF) connector.

Zigbee A wireless standard used by smart devices that works in the 900-MHz or 2.4 GHz band, has a range up to 100 meters, and is considered more robust than Z-Wave, a competing standard. *Compare with* Z-Wave.

zombie A computer that has been hacked to run repetitive software in the background without the knowledge of its user. *Also see* botnet.

zone file A file that holds resource records for the DNS namespace; often holds all the records for a single domain, such as cengage.com.

Z-Wave A wireless standard used by smart devices; works in the 900-MHz band and has a range up to 20 meters. Z-Wave competes with Zigbee but is not considered as robust as Zigbee. *Compare with* Zigbee.

Index